# GREECE – 431
*at the start of the*
## PELOPONNESIAN WAR

D1378733

| Neutral Greek States | Sparta and Allies | Athens ana Allies |

## GRECIAN ARCHITECTURE

*richness ornamentation*

*slenderness grace*

### Corinthian
A modification of the Ionic, appearing in the 4th Century B.C.

*simplicity strength solidity*

### Ionic Order
First used in cities of Ionia, about 6th Century B.C.

### Doric Order
Oldest form.
Appeared in late 7th Century B.C.
Used by ancient Dorians.

BLACK SEA

THRACE

Epidamnus

ndisium

MACEDONIA

Pella

Thasos

Chalcidice

Sea of Marmara

PHRYGIA

PERSIAN

Thracian Sea

Lemnos

EPIRUS

THESSALY

AEGEAN

Corcyra

Dolopia

Scyrus

Lesbos

EMPIRE

IONIAN

Leucas

AETOLIA

Euboea

SEA

Chios

LYDIA

SEA

Cephalonia

Delphi

Locris

Boeotia

Eretria

Thebes

Zacynthus

Achaia

Attica

Samos

Elis

Corinth

Athens

Andros

Miletus

Olympia

Delos

Halicarnassus

Messenia

Sparta

Naxos

Cyclades

IONIA

Laconia

Rhodes

Cythera

CRETAN SEA

Carpathos

## Olympia
—site of Olympic Games

Cnossus

CRETE

| 0 | 100 | 200 |
miles

Kotscha

# The Heritage of the Past

*From the Earliest Times to the Close of the Middle Ages*

HOLT, RINEHART AND WINSTON

New York • Chicago • San Francisco

Toronto • London

**STEWART C. EASTON**

*The City College, College of the City of New York*

# The Heritage of the Past

FROM THE EARLIEST TIMES TO THE CLOSE OF THE MIDDLE AGES

CARTOGRAPHY: *Vincent Kotschar*
DESIGN: *Marilyn Marcus*

# Preface

This book is the result of many years' effort to deal effectively with the problems involved in the first part of a survey course in world history. The chief problem, as every instructor will recognize, is how to provide an interpretation of major past civilizations while at the same time giving enough facts to make the interpretation meaningful. The student needs both fact and interpretation; and in my view he needs both *before* he comes into class.

This text is not short of facts. In each of the strictly historical chapters there is a chart presenting chronologically the material studied within that chapter. Most of the charts follow the same outline as the chapters they accompany, and therefore should be studied at the same time. But the facts are subordinated to an overview of each civilization as a whole. Those facts are chosen for emphasis which bear a special relevance to the interpretative generalizations. I am convinced that what is needed above all in a course in the history of civilization is a concentration on the essential similarities and differences between civilizations, and that I have attempted to provide in this book.

It has been my experience that students gain much more from a course which appeals to their understanding rather than too exclusively to their capacity for memorizing. Most

college students have a real desire to comprehend, and too often their elementary college courses do not ask enough of them, but leave them at the end still seriously undernourished. This text asks rather a lot of the student. It is longer than most in the field, and assignments will necessarily be longer than is customary. I cannot deny that some chapters, such as that on the Roman Republic, are difficult. But the historical process is not simple. It is not possible to describe the institutions of the Roman Republic, a democracy in form but an oligarchy in its functioning, in a few well-chosen superficial sentences merely outlining its form and the events that brought about this particular form. It is no more possible for the institutions of the Roman Republic than it would be for the Constitution of the United States. Students in their first two years of college are cutting their mental teeth. I do not believe it is wise or necessary to give them pap especially prepared for easy digestion.

The general topical arrangement of the chapters serves to concentrate attention on essentials instead of diverting it to unessentials. Several of the chapters fall naturally into two or more sections, with sometimes a break in the topic, and sometimes a natural break in the chronology. In the Egyptian chapter, for example, the achievements of the Old Kingdom can be studied separately from those of the later period of decline; the history of the Greek peoples as a whole, together with Sparta, can be studied separately from the very important development of Athenian political institutions; the discussions of England and France in the concluding chapter form a natural division of the subject matter. Such divisions will help the instructor to make his assignments on the basis of time available in the course. If time is running short, some of the more easily understood sections can be assigned for private study with a minimum of class discussion. For example, even if time does not permit a full class discussion of medieval culture, the chapter on that subject has been made especially full and explanatory in order that the student may be spared the stereotype of the Middle Ages as a period of blind faith and unprogressive superstition.

A word should be said on the illustrations and maps. Almost every illustration has been chosen for the light it will throw on the text. The publisher has designed the book in such a way that, with rare exceptions, a picture will be found on the same page as the point illustrated. The illustrations, though they may incidentally be decorative, were not included for decorative purposes. They are an integral part of the text, which in some sections, as for instance that on medieval architecture, cannot be well understood without them. The maps have been specially designed to give important information supplementary to that in the text. They are all drawn to an exact scale. While in many cases serving to illustrate definite topics and movements—as, for instance, in the maps showing the penetration of Western Europe by the barbarians in the fifth century A.D., and the original map showing the territory held by Pope Innocent III in his capacity of feudal lord—the maps also mention important cities and natural geographical features by name. Every place mentioned in the text has been included in one map or another, and the index indicates on which map each such place is to be found. Like the text itself, the maps strive to hold a balance between useful

information and impressionism. In each case the student should be able to grasp the general picture at once, and then study later the details for the purpose of acquiring essential information.

I am greatly indebted to the cartographer, Mr. Vincent Kotschar, for his brilliant work in designing the maps to bring out the points that I felt needed to be made. In the selection of fitting illustrations I am indebted especially to Miss Mildred McGill of the Metropolitan Museum of Art, and to Miss Mary M. Kenway of the Pierpont Morgan Library, as well as to the many other persons and institutions by whose courtesy the illustrations have been permitted to appear.

I cannot praise too highly the enthusiastic cooperation of my publisher at every phase of the work. Several colleagues of the Department of History of the College of the City of New York read portions of the manuscript at different stages of the work and made useful comments and suggestions. Particular mention should be made of Mr. Vito Caporale, who read almost the whole of the manuscript and whose comment and encouragement were of the greatest help. I am also indebted to Madeline R. Robinton, Associate Professor of History, Brooklyn College, for suggestions pertaining to Chapter 22, and to Robert I. Crane, Assistant Professor of Modern History, The University of Chicago, for a number of useful suggestions for Chapter 6. I am particularly grateful to Marshall Dill, Jr., Assistant Professor of History, University of Pennsylvania, for a detailed critique of the entire manuscript. Mr. Irving Garbati, a candidate for the Ph.D. degree at Columbia University, prepared the index and made suggestions for improving the text.

It will be apparent to all those familiar with modern American Egyptology and the research being carried on at the Oriental Institute of the University of Chicago, how deeply I have drawn on the published writings of Henri Frankfort, John A. Wilson, and their colleagues, especially for the interpretations offered in the chapters on the ancient Near East. There are specific footnote references to the work of these scholars, but these references do not begin to cover the suggestions and ideas obtained from them. Though their work is a pioneer effort, it seems to me that explanations and interpretations of the kind they present are in the highest degree valuable, even though in detail these may not be accepted by posterity. Indeed, I must admit to having drawn further conclusions from their work that might not be considered acceptable even by themselves. I am sure, however, that nothing is further from their minds than any belief that their early interpretations should be considered definitive; and I am equally confident that the general outlines of their work will stand the test of time. So, for the first time in a textbook as far as I am aware, there is an explanation of Egyptian civilization as a whole which has appeared to make sense to several generations of students as well as to myself, and will now perhaps find a wider audience.

If the book is now readable and free from grievous error it is because of all these who have helped specifically, and of countless historians stretching back as far in time as Herodotus; what remains in error is entirely my own responsibility.

STEWART C. EASTON

*The College of the City of New York*
*January, 1955*

# Contents

# III Classical Civilization in the West

# IV  The Centuries of Transition

# V  Civilization of the Middle Ages in Europe

# Illustrations

# Maps

# I Before History

*The Black Bull, a prehistoric fresco from the Lascaux Caves, Dordogne, France. From L'art préhistorique; peintures, gravures, et sculptures rupestres, 1951.* (COURTESY LES ÉDITIONS BRAUN ET CIE, PARIS, NEW YORK)

# 1

# The Foundations of an Organized Society

*The economic, political, and cultural foundations of a society* • *The rise and fall of civilizations* • *Theories of history: Marx, Spengler, Toynbee* • *The necessity of objectivity and imagination in historical study*

---

▶ ## The economic, political, and cultural foundations of a society

THE ECONOMIC REQUIREMENTS OF A SOCIETY

Every human being as an individual has certain cultural and religious needs, as a member of a society he has to regulate his relations with other human beings, and as a producer and consumer he must take his part in economic affairs. These three necessities in his life have always been reflected in human societies. Our first task must therefore be to consider the cultural, political, and economic foundations upon which social institutions have rested.

While each society is in some degree unique, the difference between societies is most visible in the field of culture, in which the creativeness of the individual human being finds the greatest opportunity for expression. In culture, taken in its widest sense, the possibilities for creativeness are infinite; whereas the economic needs of human beings are ultimately limited by their far from infinite ability to consume material goods and in historical societies by the availability of adequate resources and techniques. It is essential for the historian to indicate

how each society organized to produce these material goods, and to show how far its failure to produce enough for all the needs of the human beings in it seriously limited their leisure to engage in cultural pursuits and affected its political organization in a crucial manner. But the economic activities in themselves have been so similar in all the societies considered in this book that it has not been thought necessary to go into much detail unless a particular society made important innovations. In a premachine society such as existed from the Neolithic period to the modern Industrial Revolution, the overwhelming majority of mankind was forced to labor for long hours under difficult conditions to make a bare subsistence. Only since the Industrial Revolution, when man was presented with the necessity of organizing the production and consumption of material goods on a scale hitherto unheard of, did the human efforts to do this become a subject worthy of detailed study in itself.

The basic economic requirements of human beings may be limited to three—food, shelter, and clothing. In the earliest societies known to us, their pursuit consumed such an enormous proportion of available human

3

energies that there was little left for other activities. Food could be obtained from animals and wild plants, which were hunted or harvested in accordance with the skills and techniques available to the society. Such an economy may be termed a natural one—man was dependent entirely upon what was provided for him by nature, especially if he clothed himself in animal skins and lived in caves. When nature failed him, he moved on to a more favorable location, where he continued to live in a natural economy.

At the next stage of development, called the Neolithic Revolution, man ceased to be totally dependent upon nature and began in some degree to control it. He learned to breed and tend animals, so that they were always available to him for food when he needed them, and he taught them to work for him and supplement the labor of his own hands. He also learned to plant crops and harvest them, laying down seeds in some spot cleared for the purpose and in which such plants did not grow by nature. He learned to build himself a home where none had been provided by nature, and he even discovered how to grow special crops such as flax from which he could make himself clothing.

Having thus learned in some degree to control and harness nature, man at last found himself both with leisure to produce luxuries which made life more pleasant and comfortable, and with a surplus of crops beyond the consuming needs of his society. These surpluses of manufactured luxuries, and of crops for human consumption, he was able to offer in exchange for goods produced by other men outside his immediate group. This *trade* was ultimately supplemented and fed by the products of *industry*. Industrial production is characterized by a more intensive division of labor under which some members of the society, freed from direct agricultural work, specialize in manufacturing a varied assortment of articles to be consumed at home or to be traded in exchange for foreign products. An economically advanced society is characterized by the diversity of products manufactured, and by effective or-

ganization of production to take advantage of specialized skills, and minimize the waste of human energies in unnecessary labor.

### THE POLITICAL REQUIREMENTS OF A SOCIETY

#### Protection through government and law

It used to be thought that man in a state of nature was forced to compete with all other human beings for his very subsistence, or, in the famous words of Thomas Hobbes, that his life was "solitary, poor, nasty, brutish, and short." We have no record of such a way of life, either in early times, or among present-day "primitive" men. And it no longer seems as probable to us as it did in the nineteenth century, under the influence of the biological ideas of Darwin, that human survival was a matter of success in the constant struggle for existence, if this struggle is conceived of as a struggle between human beings. It now seems more probable that survival has always been due to successful cooperation between human beings to resist the always dangerous forces of nature.

The first political necessity for men has always been, and remains still, protection—whether from animals, natural hazards, or hostile human beings; and protection must necessarily mean that some human beings band together under some kind of accepted political organization. The first requirement of any government is that it should possess power to enforce its will upon individuals, forcing them to behave in accordance with its dictates. This power may be either military or moral or both; but a government cannot survive without one kind or the other. It follows that a government must be acceptable either to a majority of the people or to a minority who possess enough moral or military power to coerce the majority. No government, whether by one man or by many, can survive without some support and acceptance.

A government, to ensure its acceptance by any of the people, cannot behave in an arbitrary and unpredictable manner. It must make clear what its policy is to be in matters of daily concern to the people. This need for certainty is satisfied by the establishment of law, which explains to the people what is expected of them, and decrees penalties for the behavior it defines as unacceptable. Law is essentially the regulation of the public behavior of human beings in an organized society, and it is enforced by the power of the government, as long as the government is able to maintain its authority.

From very early times men have considered that laws should be made in accordance with an abstraction called justice. But, as there has never been any agreed conception of justice at any time in history, individuals in each society have arrived at their own conceptions of justice by their own thought, and have tried to modify the law accordingly. Justice has remained a valuable ideal, but in fact it has been the enforceable law which has prevailed rather than the abstract and unenforceable ideal. Most lawgivers in early societies claimed that they received the law from the gods and that their laws were therefore in accordance with the ideal of justice; hence they decreed severe penalties for anyone who should attempt, from his feeble human thinking, to change them. In ancient Egypt there was no written law at all until a very late date. The Pharaoh was supposed to "know the hearts of men," and since he was in constant touch with divine powers, he could judge cases in the light of his intuitive and immediate perception of justice.

### Evolution of political institutions—From clans and tribes to the national state

In every society there has always been some form of government, since authority has always been necessary, however small the social unit. A natural social unit is the family; and it may be that in some far-off age the self-sufficient family may also have been the political unit, with one member exercising an authority recognized and accepted by the other members. This state of affairs, however, presupposes the self-sufficiency of the one family, and such self-sufficiency is unlikely at any time or in any place. The clan, or union of a small number of families, sometimes closely connected by blood relationship, with perhaps a recent common ancestor, is known as a historical unit, with the leaders of the component families exercising the functions of government. A larger unit is the tribe, composed of several clans. When tribes or clans are gathered together in one area, the government may be made up of the heads of families, or perhaps of a tribal chieftain, acceptable to the other heads by virtue of his birth into one leading family, or because of his own personal, military, or other qualities.

When these tribal units emerge into the light of history there is usually such a chieftain occupying the position of the head of the tribal government, advised by other minor chiefs or heads of families, and sometimes by the whole body of adults, who form an assembly whose advice is called for on special occasions, and whose consent is necessary for important decisions. Such a government is a Primitive Democracy, of the kind we shall find in Mesopotamia at an early date, and traces of which are found among other peoples, such as the primitive Greeks, Romans, and Germans of the West. In other societies we find at an early time the institution of kingship, with the ruler having already been granted the power to govern without the formality of consultation with his subjects. Larger units of government are city-states; empires, which sometimes rule over wide areas subdued by warfare; and, in our own times, national states. Common to all these forms of government are systems of law and officials who carry out the policies of the government under authority delegated by it. From the very primitive to the most advanced and modern forms of government the essential function is always the provision of protection to the governed; and though modern governments have undertaken multifarious subsidiary tasks, essentially they perform these tasks instead of the people themselves because the people have requested or allowed them to do so—tasks supposedly for their benefit which, in their view, can best be performed by common rather than private effort and under direction from above. The modern political and economic theory known as socialism emphasizes the importance of the role of the government in providing for the people what they are unable to provide for themselves.

### Historical forms of government— Monarchy, oligarchy, democracy

The essential requirement of government is, then, that it be effective, and that its authority should be accepted in the area entrusted to it. Many forms of government may fulfill these criteria, and many forms are known to history; human inventiveness may yet devise new combinations. But three main classifications are usually recognized—monarchy, or rule by one; oligarchy, or rule by a few; and democracy, or rule by the people. Each of these may exist in pure or mixed forms. Monarchy may consist of rule by a king or a single ruler under some other title and his chosen advisers, with the responsibility ultimately resting with the ruler, or it may be a rule limited by the legal or moral necessity for him to consult his advisers, by whom he may be overruled. The latter is a limited or constitutional monarchy, and within this classification there are many degrees of limitation, down to the point where the "advisers" rule, and the king is merely a respected figurehead and symbol of unity, as in England. An oligarchy may be elected, or it may be entitled to rule by hereditary right; and it may have to consult the people in certain matters and submit to being overruled on occasion. A democracy may be direct, as in Athens, or representative as in modern states, the representatives subject to re-election or recall. The form of government, then, is always subject to change and modification in accordance with the needs of the time and the wishes of the people governed; but, whatever the form, and whatever the label—some modern labels are devised purely with the aim of confusing—a government's functions are those described in the preceding section.

THE "CULTURE" OF A SOCIETY

### The common elements of all cultures—The accumulated heritage from the past

In every society it is the free activity of men—their thoughts, their feelings, and their actions—which molds its characteristic institutions, and gives it its characteristic way of looking at life. Together the social organization, political institutions, economic activities, law, science, art, religion, and thought are called the culture of a society. The cave paintings of the Old Stone Age and the mass-production economic technique of the twentieth century are equally an expression of the cultural creativeness of these particular societies. They are the work of men living in the society, making use of the physical environment provided for them by nature. Their creativeness is limited by the natural conditions, but not determined by them. The men of the Old Stone Age could hardly have progressed at a single leap to the mass-production technique of the twentieth century or to its representative political government, since the thoughts of men had first to traverse all the intermediate stages, and the institutions of their society had to be modified in accordance with these newer thoughts. Men had first to live in settled communities, and develop institutions fit for such communities; they had to make the necessary technical inventions, means of communication, transportation, and production, and again slowly develop social institutions which could release and take advantage of natural human inventiveness.

But it is not necessary for each society to start again from scratch, inventing its techniques from the beginning. It can take advantage of the achievements of its predecessors. Once the Neolithic Revolution had taken place and agriculture was seen to be an improvement over the ancient food gathering, this fundamental invention became a part of the permanent possession of mankind, and any new society could build on the foundations laid by Neolithic man. Cultural progress, therefore, is cumulative. The thoughts of mankind have been, as it were, built into the world—and the world has been changed by them, forever. Only if every literate human being were suddenly killed, and all knowledge of human deeds in the last seven thousand years were lost, would it be necessary for mankind to return to the conditions of the Old Stone Age and start again.

### The uniqueness of each culture

Yet, although each society does build on the foundations laid by its predecessors and exploits its cultural heritage, it is also, in a sense, unique. The men of ancient Egypt developed a political institution, the divine kingship, which they were unwilling to abandon, yet which was not copied by other societies; they developed an art which had little influence on subsequent art in other countries, and yet has been considered by many to be a perfect expression of the Egyptian attitude toward life. This attitude toward life seems to be the unique element in every society, which gives it its characteristic form. While the ancient Egyptians denied the fact of change, regarding it as illusory, and had therefore no interest in progress, we in the twentieth century not only recognize the fact of change, but try to take advantage of it and help it on by our own efforts. We set ourselves goals which we try to achieve; then, having achieved them, we set ourselves ever more distant goals and strive toward them. We make our ideas into ideals, into the achieving of which we put the whole strength of our wills.

But no society before ours had any such conception of progress. Many societies looked back to a Golden Age in the past which they longed to recapture, and even the Greeks, whose ideas in so many ways were similar to ours, lacked that sense of the importance of building for the future which is characteristic of modern Western civilization. It is necessary, therefore, in studying civilization as it was manifested in a particular society, to try to discover its own characteristic attitude toward life and to view its cultural achievements in the light of this attitude, while at the same time noting those cultural advances which it made and passed on to its successors as part of the total cultural heritage of mankind.

### The diffusion of culture

Cultural advances first made within a particular society may be taken up by other societies and spread throughout the entire world. But they must be able to find their proper place in the receiving society, they must find a fertile ground for reception and propagation. The divine kingship of Egypt would not have fitted into the existing contemporary society in Mesopotamia, and even if the Mesopotamian peoples had known of it, they would hardly have tried to graft it onto their existing native institutions. On the other hand, the Christian and other religions have been diffused through many countries where they supplied answers to the problems which the inhabitants of those countries had been trying to solve and where they fitted in with the psychological predisposition of those peoples. The system of representative government first developed in medieval England was gradually diffused throughout Europe and, especially since World War I, has spread into many countries of the world which desired to accept a form of government that had apparently proved itself to be effective in the war itself. But in other places it has so far failed to take root because of the tenacity of existing institutions.

Technical inventions do not, as a rule, meet with the same opposition as religious or political innovations, and can be passed from one society to another with less disturbance. There are thousands of examples of such diffusion of inventions from the earliest times to the present. Probably the idea of food growing and the domestication of animals spread throughout the world from some center in the Near East, though the possibility of the separate invention of such a fundamental idea cannot be ruled out. The invention of writing was almost certainly diffused from the ancient land of Sumer, though the earliest receivers, the Egyptians, modified and improved upon the Sumerian practice, using their own pictures and symbols, and developing new writing materials available to them but not to the Sumerians. It is not known by how many millenniums the use of language preceded the written symbols, but the languages of peoples in historic times have many resemblances to each other which can only be explained by diffusion from one people to another. Linguists have classified several families of languages, which they have called by such names as Semitic, Hamitic, and Indo-European, and by examining them have even tried to reveal laws under which the changes take place between one language and another after diffusion, in accordance with certain well-defined principles.[1] Other inventions such as printing, gunpowder, and the cultivation of the silkworm can be traced in some detail by the historian from their first use in one country to their full development in another.

Each society, then, receives by diffusion some of its cultural heritage, and it adds to what it has received the characteristic products of its own genius. It may even invent unnecessarily for itself things which have already been developed elsewhere, unknown to it, which it could have received by diffusion if it had had wider cultural contacts. On the other hand, not all knowledge available to any one people has been preserved

[1] At one time the different peoples who spoke one or another of these groups of languages were given the same classification. They were called Semitic, Hamitic, and Indo-European peoples, and certain physical characteristics were assigned to them. But recent discoveries have tended to show many similarities between the languages of these peoples, and other more ancient languages have been uncovered which seem to fit into none of these categories (as, for instance, the ancient Sumerian language itself). Informed opinion among linguists has therefore been modified, and at the present time there is a tendency to believe that there were earlier languages as yet unknown to us from which these families themselves sprang. The racial classifications have also been increasingly abandoned as equally unsatisfactory. Though we shall still use the words "Semitic," "Hamitic," and "Indo-European" in this book, the possibility is not ruled out that all these peoples in the not so very distant past came from some earlier root stock or stocks, in spite of a few markedly different physical characteristics which can be noted in historic times.

or transmitted to others. The ancient Sumerians knew all the basic forms of architecture, but the Egyptians and Greeks did not make use of them; medieval European technical knowledge—as, for instance, of the rotation of crops—was in many ways markedly inferior to that of several earlier peoples. The Renaissance Italians had to reinvent many commercial aids known to the Hellenistic world. Each civilization does not accept the entire cultural heritage of its predecessors and build on it; it accepts only what fits its own environment and its own way of living. Even our immense technical achievements, valuable as we may think them—and likely to bring great material benefits if adopted by the peoples we consider backward—may not be universally acceptable. History has yet to show to what extent Western technology will be accepted by a people like, say, the Hindus, who do not share our view of the relation between the material and the spiritual and the relative importance to be assigned to this world and the hereafter. To receive and use what we are willing to transmit to them, perhaps their whole scheme of values must be altered, and their civilization may fall into decay rather than adopt such an alien scheme of values as ours.

## ▶ The rise and fall of civilizations

THEORIES OF HISTORY—MARX, SPENGLER, TOYNBEE

In recent centuries the attention of the historian has been especially concentrated on the rise and fall of the many civilizations that have been known in the past. Why, he asks, has a civilization or a society known some sudden period of great creativeness, and why, then, does life seem to have gone from it, and the cultural leadership of mankind, which it held for a brief season, to have passed from it into other hands? Many have been the answers propounded, but none has gained universal assent. It may indeed be that no answer can ever be given in material terms and that no explanation will ever be satisfactory because in fact there *is* no explanation of universal validity. Karl

Marx tried to show that the economic conditions of an epoch determine the cultural achievements of a civilization, but he failed to give sufficient attention to the diversity of human institutions and achievements in spite of very similar economic conditions at many different stages of history. Hence the Marxist historians have always suffered from the temptation to make the facts fit the theory, tending to neglect those facts which are not in conformity with it. In Marxian theory, then, the fall of a civilization is determined by changes in economic conditions. Oswald Spengler tried to show that the life of a society followed certain laws of growth and decay analogous to those to be found in the plant world.

Arnold Toynbee has tried to explain the arresting of progress as a failure to respond creatively to a challenge presented by certain difficulties which had to be faced by the society. Toynbee, of course, thus assumed that a society ought to evolve, and make progress; and that if it failed to do so, it was in some way not fulfilling its proper tasks. It is doubtful if this is a fair assumption, as there is no inherent reason why a society should wish to progress, and should not be simply content with its present way of life, as apparently the ancient Egyptians were. The desire to progress is a typically modern and Western ideal, and should not be assumed as part of the make-up of earlier peoples; though perhaps when we look back upon the history of mankind from our vantage point we are not unjustified in observing that they *did not* make progress, even if there is no reason why they should have wished to do so. The value of Toynbee's approach is a moral one. He wishes to remind us that change is always with us, whether we will it or not, and as human beings we have to learn how to deal with it by being willing and ready to change ourselves and our outlook in order to cope with the ever new situations that confront us. A few further remarks on Toynbee's theory of history will appear in Chapter 3, with special reference to the ancient civilizations that preceded the Greek.

## THE NECESSITY FOR OBJECTIVITY AND IMAGINATION IN HISTORICAL STUDY

The moralist's approach to history, however, is not one to be wholeheartedly recommended. It obscures too much, and it tends to prevent a true appreciation of the past. The student of history should strive to see each society and civilization first of all in its own terms, and should try to appreciate its outlook and attitude toward life, carefully refraining from moral judgments based on experience in our own society—should see, for instance, whether to be a slave was the same thing in ancient Egypt, in fifth-century Athens or Sparta, and in the nineteenth-century southern states of America. The student of history might well conclude that it was a totally different thing to be the slave of an Egyptian Pharaoh in the days before individual freedom and self-realization had become an ideal. Our student should not, with the Marxists, overhastily transfer his knowledge of Western European class struggles into the ancient world, and assume, for example, that the breakdown of Egyptian government after the Old Kingdom was in any way the equivalent of the French or Russian Revolutions. He should try to avoid being taken in by the use of the same word to describe events which occurred in totally different cultural contexts.

Such a procedure requires the exercise of historical imagination, and this can only be acquired by study, life experience, and hard effort. But the effort is well worth while, for it enlarges the horizons and develops that perspective which can be of the utmost value in ordinary affairs.

Second, the student should also try to see the indebtedness of one civilization to another, trace the process of cultural assimilation and transmission, and see how each people has stood upon the shoulders of its predecessors. Such understanding may lead him to a sense of responsibility toward his own heritage from the past, and to the determination to pass this heritage on to posterity substantially unimpaired, and if possible increased.

The general form of this book has been designed to show the separate characteristics of each society and civilization considered, and also to reveal the cumulative heritage of mankind and how all the achievements of mankind in our society have their roots far back in the past; and how impossible it would have been for us to have reached our present heights if the slow tedious work of developing the intellectual and physical tools had not been done for us by those giants who went before us, who had so little to work with and such a long road to travel.

When we tend to neglect this debt and overestimate ourselves and our achievements, it is perhaps wise for us to stop for a moment, think, and remember once more that "we are the heirs of all the ages."

▶  ## Suggestions for further reading

The three most famous modern interpretations of history are those of Toynbee, Spengler, and Marx, referred to in the text. The full six-volume edition of Toynbee's great work, Arnold J. Toynbee, *A Study of History* (2nd ed.; London: Oxford University Press, 1935), should, in the opinion of this writer, be attempted, even by the beginning student, since the one-volume abridgment by D. C. Somervell, Arnold J. Toynbee, *A Study of History* (New York: Oxford University Press, 1947), necessarily appears to be dogmatic, and the conclusions are not invariably sustained by the condensed evidence.

Most of the material concerning the beginnings of history and the general statement of the challenge and response theory appear in Volume 1 of the six-volume work. Spengler's cyclical theory of history is contained in his monumental work *The Decline of the West* (tr. C. F. Atkinson, special one-volume edition; New York: Alfred A. Knopf, Inc., 1939), but this book is very difficult to read and is not recommended for beginning students. It is probably better to use an effective digest of his theories, such as H. S. Hughes, *Oswald Spengler; A Critical Estimate* (New York: Charles Scribner's Sons, 1952).

The theories of Karl Marx are to be found scattered through many of his works, but not in easy or convenient form. An extremely interesting criticism of the historical theories of Toynbee, Spengler, and Marx, as well as those of other philosophers of history, is presented in Karl R. Popper, *The Open Society and Its Enemies* (rev. ed.; Princeton, N.J.: Princeton University Press, 1950), and is well worth reading, though it is hardly less opinionated and dogmatic than the work of the men it criticizes.

Among other recent works on the meaning and purpose of history the following are highly recommended: H. J. Muller, *The Uses of the Past* (New York: Oxford University Press, 1952), and Herbert Butterfield, *History and Human Relations* (New York: The Macmillan Company, 1952). A stimulating little book on the way in which culture and ideas are diffused, with valuable and thought-provoking illustrations from all periods of history, is Gilbert Highet, *The Migration of Ideas* (New York: Oxford University Press, 1954).

# 2

# Prehistoric Man

*Difficulties of studying prehistory • The first beginnings of man • Paleoan-
thropic man • Lower Paleolithic period • Neanderthal man • Upper Paleolithic period • Neolithic Revolution • The beginnings of metallurgy*

---

▶ ## Difficulties of studying prehistory

It is now believed that a creature recognizable as man has walked the earth for more than half a million years. He has not always lived in the same areas of the earth, for at different times the movements of glaciers and changes of climate have made some regions uninhabitable. But at no time was the whole earth uninhabitable in the last half million years, and immense periods of time have separated the great glacial epochs from each other. Yet it is, at the most, ten thousand—probably not more than eight thousand—years ago that man first began to grow his own food and domesticate the useful animals.

This presents to us at once the great question—why so long? Could prehistoric man not have taken this supreme step earlier, and started on the road to civilization thousands, perhaps millions, of years before 8000 B.C.?

To this fundamental question it is impossible to give an answer. The truth is that we know very little indeed about prehistoric man, and the unremitting labors of archaeologists and anthropologists, fruitful though

these have been, have only scratched the surface of our almost total ignorance. Besides, no two experts are ever in agreement on all points in their interpretation of the meager data available.

It is necessary to stress this point because all that will be said in this chapter is still in the realm of opinion. It is possible that in two hundred years none of it will be acceptable to our less ignorant descendants. One of the most famous living anthropologists, A. L. Kroeber, brought out an edition in 1948 of a book he had first written in 1923.[1] The new edition was scarcely recognizable as the same book, so much had the information available changed during a short twenty-five years. No one should think that prehistory or even ancient history stands still. On the contrary, the older the history the more it can gain from archaeology, and from the discovery and reinterpretation of documents and inscriptions unknown or neglected before. Every discovery of a new fossil of early man is important, every discovery of a cave, or every excavation of an early camp site may alter in fundamental points some of our recon-

[1] A. L. Kroeber, *Anthropology* (New York: Harcourt Brace & Company, 1923, 1948).

structed history of early man, whereas even the discovery of a hitherto unknown manuscript or a painting of Leonardo da Vinci would not alter in any important respect our knowledge of the general history of the Italian Renaissance.

## ▶ The first beginnings of man

### THE EVOLUTION OF MAN AS A SPECIES

The evolutionary theory of the origin of man has been greatly modified since Darwin first propounded it in crude form in the middle of the nineteenth century. There are still many inconvenient facts, especially in the animal world, which seem very difficult to explain on the basis of natural selection. But, for the present, the total theory is still widely accepted in the Western world, outside of Russia, and it explains reasonably well what we know of early man. According to this theory those species of living organisms which were best fitted to survive in their environment did survive, and were gradually modified in form by the process of mutation, a process which can be observed in the laboratory in the case of certain animals. The ancestors of man were not those most specialized and suitable for a particular environment. On the contrary, they were more "generalized" and adaptable. From time to time new mutations appeared in the species, and those of them that could survive best in a changed environment did so, and propagated, while the older, less adaptable species died out. The huge animals became overspecialized and incapable of adaptation, perhaps in a modified environment, and so became extinct; while the smaller, unspecialized creatures, forced to adapt themselves or perish, developed mutations with survival value. Thus, it is hypothesized, the ancestors of man first came on to dry land from the ocean, lived for countless aeons in trees, and at last descended to the earth and began to walk upright, in the process increasing their brain capacity. And finally we had the first real men, the protoanthropi, of whom the oldest so far discovered is the so-called Java man, or *Pithecanthropus erectus*.

### THE NATURE OF THE EVIDENCE FOR THE ACTIVITIES OF EARLY MAN

Before we deal with the early men known to us from archaeology it should be stated clearly that it is not permissible to use evidence from people who are living today under primitive conditions and assume at once that they are living in the same way as our ancestors of the Old Stone Age. It is not impossible that these contemporary "primitive" men, though they now use tools recognizably similar to those discovered in ancient deposits, have lost certain knowledge their ancestors once possessed, and so their culture would then represent a decline from some higher stage. On the other hand, they may have made some slight progress in ten thousand years, though not as much as civilized man. We can only use our knowledge of these contemporaries of ours to create an imaginative picture of what Old Stone Age men were like, and of the life they lived. But it remains an imaginative picture, which may or may not be true to reality, and cannot be used as evidence in any way the equal of the inferences we may make from the actual remains discovered by archaeologists.

We have just said that the archaeologist has to make inferences. By this it is meant that he unearths objects, not written records; and the objects tell no clear story by themselves. We have before us, say, a dead body painted with ocher in a corner of a cave, and there are tools beside the body, and perhaps food. We infer some kind of primitive religion from the juxtaposition of these objects, but we cannot be certain of the existence of this religion. It has been suggested that such finds prove that a belief was held in a future life, in which the soul is supposed to return to earth to use the tools he used once in life and to eat the food left for him; or alternatively he needs these things for his use in a future life. But such an inference as this can never be proved true, and, as a result, archaeologists are frequently at odds with each other, and wide agreement is rare. Perhaps the tools

# ► chronological chart
## Ages of Prehistory

| Type of Man | Cultural Epoch | Geological Epoch | Approximate Date (B.C.) |
|---|---|---|---|
| Pithecanthropus (Java man) | Lower Paleolithic (Food gathering) | Pleistocene Age | 500,000 |
| Sinanthropus (Peking man) | Lower Paleolithic (Food gathering) | Pleistocene Age | 500,000 |
| Neanderthal | Lower Paleolithic (Food gathering) | Pleistocene Age | 150,000 |
| Neanderthaloid (Rhodesian and Palestinian) | Lower Paleolithic (Food gathering) | Pleistocene Age | 150,000 |
| Cro-Magnon Grimaldi | Upper Paleolithic (Cave paintings *ca.* 20,000 B.C.) | (Würm glaciation) | 50,000 |
| | Mesolithic (Domestication of dog) | Holocene (recent age) | 12,000 |
| | Neolithic Revolution (Food growing—Middle East and Europe) | Holocene (recent age) | 8000–5500 |
| | *Followed by:*  Copper Age | | *ca.* 4500 |
| | Bronze Age | | *ca.* 3500 |
| | Iron Age | | *ca.* 1800 |

All the above dates are in dispute, and no consensus is to be found among scholars. Only the authentically different and widely distributed early men have been included, as in the text.

were considered to be a part of the man's personality; perhaps they were believed to bring bad luck upon anyone who used them after he was dead. The food might be a simple remnant of a funeral feast partaken of by the survivors. The ocher may have been a primitive cosmetic, and the smearing of the corpse a ceremony of no more significance than the attentions lavished upon the American dead by "morticians" in the twentieth century. The objects alone tell us little beyond the fact that such or such objects were in use. All the rest is inference; and though we shall use it sparingly in this chapter we shall avoid drawing any analogies from present-day primitive men altogether, as likely to create possibly untrue impressions in the reader's mind, like the famous reconstructions of early men—Neanderthal looking like a not-too-distant cousin to the ape, Cro-Magnon man a handsome rugged type, and so on which were for many years very popular, especially as illustrations in textbooks. On this occasion the reader will be spared them by courtesy of author and publisher, and left to imagine them for himself.

THE PROTOANTHROPI, OR FIRST MEN,
*ca.* 500,000 B.C.

It is one of the hazards of the profession of paleontology (the study of fossils) that the description "erectus" should have been given prematurely to the first Java man discovered, on the basis of a skull and thighbone found in the same deposit and supposed to belong to the same creature. Later scientists with impressive and unusual unanimity have doubted that these fossils belonged together, since the thighbone seems too delicate ever to have been attached to such a massive skull. Three more pithecanthropi have since been discovered in the same area, but, alas, not a thighbone. Scientists continue to believe that the pithecanthropi were indeed men; but the evidence on which the supposition was based has been dissipated, and his erect stature, like so much information on prehistoric men, is now based only upon an act of faith.

These four protoanthropi are dated on the best authority as about 500,000 B.C. Almost contemporary is a considerable series of "men" found in hills and caves in China, near Peking (Sinanthropi, or Peking men). There are only superficial differences between the China and Java protoanthropi, and thighbones have fortunately been found for the Chinese variety. From these we know that these Peking men did stand erect, and there is further interesting, if not quite conclusive, evidence that they were cannibals. Peking man seems also to have possessed fire and primitive "chopping tools" of stone and bone. Both Java and Peking men had brain cavities about twice as large as those of gorillas, very thick skulls, enormous eyebrow ridges, and no chins.

It is just possible, however, that the thick skulls of these creatures helped to preserve their remains through so many centuries, and that other less thick-skulled fossils perished. This is a hazard which cannot be eliminated. If any primitive men happened to have bones and skulls that were unusually soft, if indeed a whole species failed to develop the degree of hardness present in the fossils discovered, we should know nothing of them unless we found their artifacts instead of their bones.

After these two species of early men there is a long break. For a good many years it was believed that an English fossil known as Piltdown man was almost as ancient as Java and Peking men. British enthusiasts named him *Eoanthropus Dawsoni* (the "dawn-man" of Dawson) after his discoverer. But German experts, led by the noted anthropologist Weidenreich (perhaps jealous, and anxious to establish their own Heidelberg man as the earliest European), never accepted the claim for Piltdown man, and indeed Weidenreich demanded many years ago that he be "erased from the list of human fossils." "Piltdown man" consisted of a comparatively modern skull, and the most primitive jawbone and teeth yet claimed to be human. He was discovered in a shallow deposit in southern England. On the other hand, Heidelberg man consisted of a lower jaw found at Heidelberg in solitary human isolation among extinct mammoths. He was once thought to be a real protoanthropus; but, though undoubtedly genuine, opinion now inclines to place him as a specially rugged type of Neanderthal, the species next to be considered.

The fate of Piltdown man was decided in 1953, when it was finally revealed through chemical analysis that he was simply a fake. The skull was indeed comparatively modern, discolored by artificial means to look older than it was; while the jawbone and teeth were those of an ape, also modern and artificially aged. Detective work is still in progress to try to discover whose misplaced ingenuity was responsible for this astonishing attempt to deceive the world of archaeology, so far without official results. But we do now know for certain that Piltdown man should indeed be "erased from the list of human fossils." The illustration of "Piltdown man" included in the text should be looked upon therefore as a melancholy example of the fallibility of experts in this highly speculative field of human inquiry. These reconstructed heads, so familiar to readers of textbooks, may be

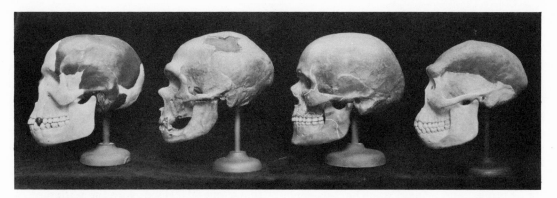

*Skulls of prehistoric men; from left to right, "Piltdown," Neanderthal, Cro-Magnon, Pithecanthropus. Restoration by J. H. McGregor. Unfortunately, Dr. McGregor made these restorations before it was proved that Piltdown man was a fake.* (COURTESY AMERICAN MUSEUM OF NATURAL HISTORY)

no more accurate resemblances to actual prehistoric men as they were known to their contemporaries than was "Piltdown man" himself.

▶ **Paleoanthropic man—Lower Paleolithic period—Neanderthal man (ca. 150,000 B.C.)**

Neanderthal is a paleoanthropus. He is not yet styled *Homo* as distinct from *Anthropus* because it is not believed that modern *Homo sapiens* (or thinking man) derives directly from him. He became extinct some time in the comparatively recent past after a long career dating from perhaps as long ago as 450,000 B.C. to about 70,000 B.C. The first Neanderthal fossil was found in a cave of the Neander Gorge near Düsseldorf in Germany in 1856, and thus received his name. But in the past century many specimens of his type have been found throughout Europe, and similar types, with only superficial differences, have been unearthed as far away as Rhodesia in South Africa. Very important finds have also been made in Palestine, together with blade tools of a kind superior to anything known to have been used by other Neanderthal men.[2] It would

seem, therefore, that Neanderthal man inhabited this planet for a far longer total period than any other type, and over the hundreds of thousands of years during which he was the chief representative of the human species he may well have wandered over the whole earth.

Physically, Neanderthal man was the owner of a brain already of a size not greatly inferior to our own. But at the same time he had a curvature of the thighbone even more marked than that of his predecessors, the protoanthropi. He used chipped bone, he flaked flint tools, and he used fire. A kind of all-purpose tool, something between a pick and an ax, and no doubt serving the purpose of both, was in use (called by the French a *coup de poing*, from the fact that it resembles a human fist). Many of the Neanderthal finds have been in caves, where these men lived for at least part of the year. Some of the skeletons seem to have been laid away with care, in the bottom of the caves, with food and implements beside them, suggesting formal burial practices, if not a belief in immortality.

The period when Neanderthal man roamed the earth is generally called the Lower Paleolithic Age—lower because in fossil deposits the lower remains are earlier, and Paleolithic (Old Stone) because all implements were made of either bone or stone. The classification by implements has become

[2] Rhodesian and Palestinian men of this period are usually classed as Neanderthaloid rather than Neanderthal men by scientists who feel the differences between the two are too great to be considered "superficial."

conventional, but it is not satisfactory unless one wishes to speak only of the tools used. The development in tools from the Paleolithic to the Neolithic (New Stone) Age was far less important than the epoch-making change from food gathering to food producing which characterized these periods.

The whole of the Lower Paleolithic period is placed within the geological age known as the Pleistocene. During this time most authorities recognize four glaciations for Europe and America. The glaciers stretched down as far south as France, making the climate bitterly cold within their range. When they receded, the climate was as warm as, or perhaps even warmer than, now. It is possible that even at the present time we are in an interglacial period, since it is only about 50,000 years since the last

glaciers (Würm glaciation) began to recede, not a long time for an interglacial period. They had perhaps not receded to their present position until almost the end of the Upper Paleolithic Age.

### ▶ Upper Paleolithic period

HOMO SAPIENS—CRO-MAGNON AND GRIMALDI *ca.* 50,000 B.C.

We date the Upper Paleolithic period from about 50,000 B.C., with the beginning of *Homo sapiens,* or modern man (neoanthropi, as distinct from paleoanthropi and protoanthropi). There are many remains dating from this period which can be fairly accurately dated, and successive phases of Upper Paleolithic culture have been agreed upon. The people of this age in Europe, apparently

*Tools of prehistoric men, showing various phases of development, and revealing why some of these tools were called "coups de poing" [blows of fist].* (COURTESY AMERICAN MUSEUM OF NATURAL HISTORY)

of Caucasian stock, are called Cro-Magnon. Contemporary with them are Grimaldi men found in Southern Europe, which had physical characteristics similar to those of present-day Negroes. Further south in North Africa are other remains of people with Caucasian features, as have the inhabitants of these areas today. It is considered unlikely that a full Negro race was present in Southern Europe in Upper Paleolithic times and then disappeared without a trace. Since naturally no hair or skin has survived, it is impossible to say whether Grimaldi man was actually a Negro.

Cro-Magnon man lacked the protruding eyebrow ridge of his predecessors, and, curiously enough, he had a larger brain than present-day man's. The average height of the specimens examined is five feet ten inches. It is, of course, again possible that only the finest specimens have survived. But the physical examination of Cro-Magnon man conclusively proves that the later advances of Neolithic man were not due to the evolution of a physically superior people. Nor can we say anything about the functioning of the brain from the mere measurement of the skull capacity. He would indeed be a hardy male who would dare to put forward such a hypothesis today when it is known that the average female skull capacity in our time is some 10 per cent smaller than the male's!

Cro-Magnon's experiments in improved living, however, are impressive by any standard. In toolmaking he began to make a more sophisticated use of bone. There were bone knives, pins, needles, fish hooks, and harpoons as well as sharp boneheads for spears. He made beads of bone for ornament, and later also used horn and ivory. The needles suggest that he (or his wife) sewed and stitched garments. But above all he used paints, not only for covering dead bodies, which are often smeared with red ocher, but for the first real art.

THE CAVE PAINTINGS OF CRO-MAGNON MAN

Cave paintings have been discovered in southern France and northern Spain which were undoubtedly made by men in Upper Paleolithic times. The paintings, in which several colors were used, are mostly of animals, though there are a few also of human beings. Controversy has raged fiercely about these paintings ever since they were discovered, and indeed there are many problems connected with them.

Paintings were sometimes superimposed upon one another; they are often on the walls near the roof of the caves. They obviously were not made to be admired by human beings. How did the artists obtain enough light to be able to make their paintings in such dim, almost inaccessible corners? No primitive torch could give our own artists enough light to duplicate them, even if they could manage, as these early artists manifestly could, to do without living models. There are paintings which are so far from the ground that elaborate scaffolding must have been erected, as the floor does not seem to have sunk since Paleolithic times.

The suggestion has been made that the paintings were superimposed one upon another and in an almost inaccessible position because the act of painting, rather than the contemplation of the finished work of art, was important. Since the animals are frequently shown transfixed with weapons, it has been suggested that the act of painting was an act of magic designed to ensure success in hunting expeditions above ground. Perhaps the paintings were made while the hunt was in progress. Other writers have insisted that the true artist paints for the joy the very act of painting gives him. It is possible that the paintings did not appeal to his sense of sight. But in drawing the movements of the animal—and these paintings all show animals in movement which is extremely vividly suggested—he himself experienced something of the life and movement of the animal he was picturing. At all events it seems necessary to assume that these early artists had a remarkable visual memory in that they could paint in this way without models. It also seems legitimate to suppose that their eyes were able, perhaps from long living in caves, to see in the dark,

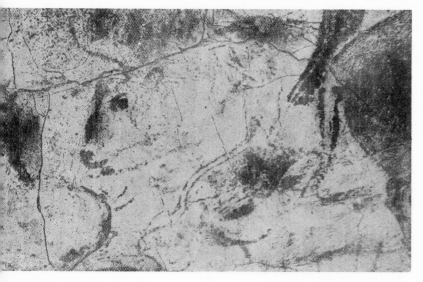

*This photograph shows one of the cave paintings at Altamira, Spain, as it actually appears. Notice that the same portion of the wall is occupied by several animals, and that it is difficult to distinguish between them. The neat pictures of individual animals sometimes shown are copies made by modern artists who have separated the animals from their surroundings. At Altamira the pictures are made in color.*

*Charcoal drawings, not colored, from Cave of Las Monedas (also Spanish). The vast majority of the known examples of cave art are either drawn in charcoal or scratched with sharp stone implements.*

or near dark. There seems little doubt that once the painting had been completed there was no need for anyone to look at it—it was not, therefore, for decoration. The magical explanation seems easier to believe, and it is in keeping with what we know of magical practices in present-day "primitive" tribes. But it is well to remember that we cannot know for certain. The strength, speed, and power of animals, so greatly revered in later times in Egypt, might well have been qualities envied by our cave men; and by drawing and painting these animals the artists may have been trying to identify themselves with, and absorb into themselves, some of these powerful qualities. The only conclusion that it is safe to draw is that the paintings were neither crudely utilitarian nor merely ornamental, but are indicative of some belief in what we should call "supernatural" powers. If they were only, as has been urged, the natural effort at self-expression by early artists and had no ulterior purpose whatsoever, it seems impossible to explain the inaccessible positions and the superimposition.

All Paleolithic men lived by hunting and

food gathering. They were dependent for their subsistence on their manual skills and their observation. Living in caves or crude huts, they necessarily moved from place to place as hunting grounds became exhausted or as the climate changed. They lived in the same world as the animals, but had not yet learned to make use of them except for food.

THE DOMESTICATION OF THE DOG (MESOLITHIC AGE), *ca.* 12,000 B.C.

The first great advance to be observed in the archaeological record is the domestication of the dog. This occurs in the period conventionally known as the Mesolithic (Middle Stone) Age, a period arbitrarily intervening between the Paleolithic and the Neolithic. Geologists speak of the Mesolithic Age as the beginning of the geologically recent or Holocene Age. The glaciers were receding, pine, birch, and willow were gradually creeping northward. The older tundra gradually became more thickly forested and the larger animals moved away or became extinct. Smaller game had to be hunted, requiring a greater expenditure of labor. Cave art died away, and it seems that tools became smaller. But the dog came to live with man, perhaps even then as an aid to hunting the smaller game. The bow and arrow also are first authenticated in the Mesolithic.

▶ **The Neolithic Revolution**

TRANSITION TO FOOD GROWING, *ca.* 8000–5500 B.C.

This age of comparative quiet shades over into the age when occurred what is certainly man's greatest advance to this day—the advance that has made all later civilization possible. The Neolithic Revolution, as it has been called, was characterized by the domestication of several animals, but above all by the first conscious breeding of plants.

In earlier studies, when a classification by implements was adopted, the New Stone Age shaded off into the Bronze Age and then into the Iron Age. As has been indicated, the change of implements is by no means fundamental. Neolithic man polished his tools, and

they were sharper than those of his predecessors, but it is not for his tools that he is remembered in history.

When man lived by food gathering and hunting, he was dependent upon his environment. His sole influence upon this environment consisted in his depredations. He could not repair any damage he did to it; his only remedy was to move away. In this respect his life was like that of the animals. If it were not for his art we should be tempted to say that he was still only one of the animals, less specialized and able to make use of tools beyond their capacity, but not yet fully able to use his superior mind to take control of his environment. This now became possible with the conscious growing of plants. It was a social and, as we shall show, an intellectual revolution rather than a technical one. Man could have continued, as certain tribes still existing today have continued, to make his living only by food gathering. But he did not. For hundreds of thousands of years he had lived in the same old way, never settling down permanently, building no cities, producing no surplus for a leisured population. Now all these activities became possible.

If we consider the matter, it is not obvious that a plant grows from a seed. It is possible that many of us would never notice the way in which plant life is propagated if we were not first shown. If we lived in a land where the only plants were perennials, or where the plants were naturally fertilized year by year by wind, birds, or bees, we should take these phenomena for granted. We should sow and reap, take what we needed each year; then when the soil from this constant self-seeding and monoculture became exhausted we should take this as a natural thing and pass on to new lands still unspoiled. It requires acute observation to see *how* a plant grows, to perceive the sequence of cause and effect between the seed and the plant. Then it requires experiment to take a seed, plant it in some other place, and predict that it will grow, and then at last to see the prediction fulfilled. This was the act of some great scientist. The observation and the experiment must have been made by someone, one of the greatest heroes in history. The Persians claim in their holy books and legends that a great prophet Zara-thustra was told by Ahura-Mazda, the sun-god, of the secrets of agriculture. We shall not quarrel with them. If it was not he, then it was someone else.

It is not yet certain when and where the revolution began, nor is it known whether it sprang from a single center and was diffused through other areas. Obviously such a fruit-ful idea, once it had been thought out, was capable of application by all other peoples in a similar stage of development. Planting sites have been uncovered in many different parts of the world, but opinion is divided on which had priority. Even the dates of the sites uncovered are in dispute, though it is hoped that the new technique of dating by measuring the radioactive carbon content of remains may be of service.[3] At the present time conservative opinion would place the date of the earliest known finds at about 5500 B.C., while other authorities would pre-fer a date as early as 8000 B.C. There are farms and villages in Egypt of a very early date, but there are others in Mesopotamia and the Near East for which priority is claimed (one of the earliest is certainly the site of Sialk in Persia).

It is, however, fairly certain that the revolution first occurred in the Near East or possibly in Egypt; it was many centuries before it spread to Europe. Independent dis-

covery of food growing in several Near East-ern centers is possible. It is difficult to ac-count for the American Indians' knowledge of agriculture by the theory that it was dif-fused from Europe or Asia, though it is pos-sible and cannot be disproved. Within the Near East itself, similar agricultural tools suggest diffusion—they are not in all cases the obvious and only tools suitable for their purpose—but, above all, the long period dur-ing which there was only food gathering suggests it. Wanderers from a food-growing center would quite certainly inform their new hosts of the possibilities, and the latter would be quick to adopt the practice. This does not mean that the actual plants would be ex-ported. Only the *idea* was necessary, and then local plants and animals would quickly be domesticated. Barley and wheat, olives, grapes, and flax were known in the Near East in the Neolithic period, while rice, cotton, and sugar cane derive from the Far East.

Domestication of farm animals and the cultivation of plants seem to have begun about the same time, and in the same coun-tries. It is clear that, especially in lands where permanent pasture is not possible, the ani-mals must be fed from the cultivated crops. However, domestication of animals and cul-tivation of plants need not necessarily have come into existence together, for Asiatic nomads, even in historical times, have grown no food, but merely moved their beasts to new pastures when necessary. The North American Indians, as a rule, even though they grew their own food, did not domesti-cate any animals except the dog. But there is no evidence to support the traditional belief, probably derived from the Bible, that all peoples passed through a stage of nomad life with domesticated animals, and then turned to agriculture when they desired to settle down and cease their wanderings.

The obvious possibilities in food grow-ing must have been realized early. All the excavations of Neolithic sites have been of villages or hamlets, small communities pre-sumably living in cooperation. We know nothing about the system of landholding, but

---

[3] Briefly stated, the method is as follows: All living organisms incorporate a very small amount of radioactive carbon 14, but cease to incorporate it when they die. This carbon has a half life of 5,568 years, and thereafter disintegrates according to a consistent and predictable time schedule. It is now possible to detect on a sensitive Geiger counter the amount of carbon 14 that still remains in a long-dead organism, and thus calculate the period during which it died. The older the organism the more difficult exact calculations become, and thus the less certain the dates. There is always a margin of error, some-times considerable, in all dating by this method; but, on the whole, results obtained from the use of the technique have checked fairly closely with dates known from historical records, giving scientists en-couragement to think that dates not to be checked by other means are reasonably accurate also. The most sensitive of Geiger counters at the present time are limited to about 25,000–30,000 years.

*Lake dwellings of Neolithic man (Switzerland)—a model constructed by the American Museum of Natural History. Refuse thrown to the ground from these houses constitutes an important source of information about the lives of Neolithic men in Europe.* (COURTESY AMERICAN MUSEUM OF NATURAL HISTORY)

certainly a more definite organization was necessary than there had been in the nomadic food-gathering times. In the periods of the year when the crops had been harvested or when they were in the ground, the family must nevertheless remain close to its fields. It could not leave for distant places, as in the past. Crops had to be stored and guarded, and the beasts had to be tended. So the result was that more permanent houses of wood and adobe were built. Man finally came up above ground, where he has lived ever since—even though occasionally he has had to go below ground for protection, and may be forced to again.

Actual grains have been found in Egypt, where the exceptionally dry climate has helped to preserve them, and even rather frail wooden objects have been kept intact in

specially favorable areas. One of the best-preserved sites is in Europe, considerably later than the Near Eastern developments, but still Neolithic, giving us a fair picture of Neolithic culture as it probably also existed elsewhere. More than a hundred sites have been examined of Swiss lake dwellers who built their houses on piles above water, lakes, and rivers, as well as occasionally in the same style above dry land. The refuse from these houses, dropped into the water and so preserved for future generations, is of the utmost interest. Many different species of plants, vegetables, and fruits were in use, and there were several different kinds of stone tools with wooden handles. These Neolithic peoples who had learned to spin, used cloth. But by this time the Bronze Age was already in full swing in the Near East, and the first large-scale settlements, the heralds of an urban civilization, had come into being, together with a host of superior inventions.

## POTTERY

During the Neolithic period pottery first came into wide use. Almost all known Neolithic communities used it. This was a real invention, probably spread by diffusion from the community that invented it. It had to be discovered that potter's clay can be made to hold its form indefinitely after it has been baked at a fairly high temperature (about 600°C). The ancient potter molded the clay to whatever shape he (or, as is generally believed, she) desired, then fired it, making this shape permanent. But before good vases or utensils could be made, the raw material had to be carefully selected, purged of impurities, and, in some cases, supplemented with sand or a similar substance. All these processes were rather complicated, and no doubt took many centuries to perfect. In Neolithic times there is no evidence of the use of the potter's wheel which in later historic times must have revolutionized the ceramic industry, making possible large-scale production. Crude wheeled vehicles were known as early as 3500 B.C. in Mesopotamia, and it is at about this time that the first pieces of wheel-turned pottery are also known to have appeared. But whether the wheel was invented for use in ceramics or for transport is not yet known.

## STONE MONUMENTS—MENHIRS, CROMLECHS, DOLMENS

One feature of the Late Neolithic Age in Europe has given rise to controversy at least since the twelfth century, A.D., though recent research with scientific techniques has given us new clues. Any visitor to Brittany, Wales, or Salisbury Plain in England is sure to have seen menhirs, large single pillars of stone, and the circles of such stones, which are called cromlechs. Stone slabs or blocks, with other slabs serving as a roof, making a kind of chamber of stones, are not uncommon; these are known as dolmens. The controversy has concerned the purpose of these monuments (which are collectively called megaliths, "large stones"), and most authorities agree that the stones are in some way connected with the very ancient and natural religion of sun worship.

One of the most impressive of these formations is in Brittany, at Carnac, which, curiously enough, is also the name of the burial place of kings in Egypt, a fact still awaiting explanation by linguists. At Carnac in Brittany there are long avenues of stones, often stretching for several hundred yards. Here it is supposed that the ancient priest stood at the head of the avenue to welcome the new day when the sun came up on the horizon. But it is also possible that what were so sacred to these ancient men were the shadows cast by these stones rather than

*Megaliths at Carnac (Brittany). Note the size of the stones in relation to the size of the man in the left foreground.* (COURTESY AMERICAN MUSEUM OF NATURAL HISTORY)

*Aerial view of Stonehenge (England). Note how this view emphasizes the fact that these megaliths make up a temple. Beneath the stones at the outer edge of the circle are remains of burials.* (COURTESY BRITISH INFORMATION SERVICES)

the stones themselves. This may account for the forms taken by some of the stone groups which throw shadows making complex geometrical figures. Burial remains have been found near some of the megaliths, but this need mean no more than that the stones were sacred and burial was naturally carried out near them as in our times in the churchyards of country churches.

Far the most impressive of all the Neolithic monuments is Stonehenge on Salisbury Plain in England. This is a circle of megaliths, and is clearly an ancient temple. Close to this temple are burial pits which probably antedate the stone circle itself. The bodies were cremated and the remains buried in these pits. These remains have been recently dated by the radioactive carbon method as about 1850 B.C. Many problems are connected with this famous circle, not all of which have yet been solved. Some of the smaller stones ("blue stones") used for the

outer circle of the monument are of a kind not found locally, and it seems that Neolithic man transported them more than three hundred miles, presumably, for the most part, by sea and river. Why was this particular stone believed to be so sacred? The lintels (crosspieces) are secured with very great care onto the uprights by tenons and sockets, and to one another by mortise joints. How did Neolithic man attain such precision with his crude stone tools? Though the huge stones had to be dragged a shorter distance than the smaller "blue stones," the distance was still upward of fifty miles and through soft, pathless, uncleared country. How did they accomplish such a feat? But if we do not have the answers to these technical questions, at least we do know that the axis of the circle points to the spot where the sun would have risen at the summer solstice about 1700 B.C., and this seems to prove conclusively that the stones and temple were

23

connected with sun worship. But the Druids, with whom the monument has been traditionally associated, almost certainly did not build it, though the Druids could have used the temple built by their predecessors when the former came on the scene at a later date.[4]

## SIGNIFICANCE OF THE NEOLITHIC REVOLUTION

It will by this time be clear that the Neolithic Revolution was perhaps the most important event in the history of man since he first began to live on dry land. The next great revolution of comparable importance took place only in the nineteenth century, when man first began to use extensively the power of machinery rather than the labor of his own hands and back. From Neolithic times to the Industrial Revolution a condition of universal plenty was never possible, even if men had been able to achieve the social organization required. Every human being can do only a limited amount of work himself in a day. He can produce only a limited surplus which cannot keep any very large number of people fed and clothed who are not themselves engaged in actual production. The leisured classes in such circumstances must always be strictly limited in number. Improvement in transportation and organization can distribute very widely the surplus of the many producers. But this total surplus can never be very great. This inconvenient fact has conditioned all civilizations between the Neolithic and Industrial revolutions. A small class of leisured people, with their needs and even luxuries provided for, have been the leaders in civilization. In our own times, with the machine harnessed to provide almost unlimited power, plenty for all has at last, and for the first time, become theoretically possible.

Before the Neolithic Revolution man was condemned to live from hand to mouth. He

[4] For an excellent account of recent research and findings on Stonehenge, see Jacquetta Hawkes, "Stonehenge," *Scientific American*, 188, No. 6 (June, 1953), 25–31.

had no means of preserving his food, which had to be killed and eaten as he needed it. He took whatever crops were provided for him by his environment. With the Neolithic Revolution it was possible for some favored people to be spared the manual labor of farming because each farmer could now produce a small surplus over and above his immediate needs. Moreover, it was possible even for the farmer himself to spend a part of his year without filling every hour of the day in manual labor. He could spend at least some of his time in thinking and in cultural activities not immediately connected with his bodily sustenance; and many producers could spare enough so that an occasional man need not work with his hands at all. All that was needed now was better organization of production, an improved social order, and the technological equipment and understanding for the production of a new range of materials and manufactures.

## ▶ The beginnings of metallurgy

### THE BRONZE AGE, *ca.* 3500 B.C.

The earliest development of towns and cities will be considered in the next chapter. With these, and the development of the first written records, we shall have passed out of prehistory into the light of history. But the period that, according to convention, follows the Neolithic Revolution still antedates the first known cities and is characterized by the development of the first use of metals.

Metalworking presupposes a higher degree of social organization than a wholly agricultural hamlet or small village. We shall probably never know either who first thought of the use of bronze, or how the invention was made. Bronze, of course, does not appear in nature. It is composed of copper and tin, which must both be smelted to produce bronze. Copper ore can be used in its natural state and can be roughly molded by beating and by other Stone Age methods. It can thereafter be used without treatment by heat. But copper is never found with tin in a natural state, and tin ore, in addition to being very rare, especially in the Near East where, as far as we know, it was first used, does not look as if it contained any metal at all. What kind of luck was necessary before the idea of bronze could be worked out is difficult to imagine. But the fact is undoubtedly there, awaiting explanation.

Copper tools were known before bronze, but not long before. Gold was known at the same time, but then, as now, it was primarily used for ornaments, and no doubt "placer-mined" out of river gravels. In some places, therefore, a Copper Age is recognized before the long-lived Bronze Age, which only slowly gave way to the Age of Iron. Tin ore must be treated with heat to produce the metal, copper must be treated with heat if it is to be made into efficient tools; impure copper ore must in any case be so treated if the copper is to be usable. This process must have been discovered at the end of the Neolithic period, ushering in the Age of Metals, it must be supposed, by accident. Then the early metallurgists, aware of the process, can only be supposed to have tried it out even on the most unpromising-looking rocks, and by accident happened upon tin ore. We can also only suppose that tin was discovered in some Near Eastern deposit where it is not known to exist in modern times. The chief sources for tin in the Bronze Age were Spain and Cornwall in England. But it has not yet been suggested that bronze was first produced in these countries, which were so far from the main stream of development. Once the process had been discovered, no doubt it also spread by diffusion, and new sources of supply were sought out.

Bronze was first known in the Near East before 3500 B.C. Daggers, swords, and certain high-grade tools and ornaments were made from it. No doubt the metal was much prized. We do know that exports from the Near East must have gone to Europe in fairly early times. It is almost certain that it was not discovered independently in Europe because the forms of European bronze implements are Oriental and not native, even when they were later manufactured in the West.

THE IRON AGE, *ca.* 1800 B.C.

It was at least 2,000 years after the Bronze Age that the Age of Iron began. By this time towns and cities and a considerable urban culture had existed for many hundreds of years. Iron in meteoric form had probably been occasionally molded and beaten into tools before this. Iron ornaments were known long before the first use of terrestrial iron, and their meteoric origin is to be recognized by the high component of nickel always found in this kind of iron. Although iron is so much more common than tin or copper, the process of making steel, the most usable form of the metal, is complex and was not discovered until wrought iron had been in use for many centuries. The processes of extracting tin and copper and bronze founding do not require the extremes of heat necessary for cast iron nor the long-continued hammering by the blacksmith necessary for wrought iron. There is no reason why a bronze caster should ever discover the use of iron, as his methods would not uncover it. Iron ore would seem quite useless to a bronze worker. Hence when iron ore was finally smelted and beaten into wrought iron by the muscular activity of the smith, the invention was probably made quite independently of the bronze workers, and made by a people who used or invented the bellows, without which the heat necessary for ironworking could not be produced. The Greeks later attributed the invention to a people called the Chalybes in the region now called Armenia, later incorporated into the Hittite Empire. The Hittite kings' monopoly of the product excited the cupidity and envy of their neighbors, and there are records of occasional gifts of iron made by them to friendly potentates.

Once iron had been invented, however, its progress was assured. It was readily available, and could be used not only by kings, heroes, and nobles, but by common men. It could be used on farms as well as in palaces.

Derided as it no doubt was, it was destined to replace bronze for all but decorative purposes until this day.

▶ **Suggestions for further reading**

One of the best short accounts of the present state of our knowledge of prehistoric man will be found in R. J. Braidwood, *Prehistoric Man* (2nd ed.; Chicago: Natural History Museum, 1951), a book which its publishers seem determined to keep up to date. A good popular work on the achievements of archaeologists is C. W. Ceram, *Gods, Graves and Scholars* (New York: Alfred A. Knopf, Inc., 1951), which is generally reliable. Two useful interpretations readily available are V. G. Childe, *Man Makes Himself* (New York: New American Library of World Literature, 1951), and V. G. Childe, *What Happened in History* (Harmondsworth, Middlesex: Penguin Books, 1946). *Man Makes Himself* was written as long ago as 1936 and is therefore seriously out of date in some respects. But it is still the most effective short treatment of the probable stages of development of prehistoric man, and of his transition to a settled life. Almost all writers on the subject owe a considerable debt to Childe, even though some of his theories are no longer acceptable. *What Happened in History* is a supplement to the earlier book and should be read in conjunction with it. Sir Leonard Woolley's little book, *Digging Up the Past* (Harmondsworth, Middlesex: Penguin Books, 1931), is a useful introduction to the work archaeologists actually do, by one of the leading pioneers in the field.

There is one outstanding book on cave art, which is unfortunately very expensive and not readily available except in good libraries. But it is well worth making the effort to find it and examine not only the interesting text but the hundreds of fine photographs taken in the caves themselves. This is H. Breuil, *Four Hundred Centuries of Cave Art* (tr. M. E. Boyle; Montignac, France: Centre d'études et de documentation préhistoriques, 1952).

Any standard book on anthropology will contain much supplementary information on all phases of the activity of prehistoric man. Specially recommended is A. L. Kroeber, *Anthropology* (rev. ed.; New York: Harcourt, Brace & Co., Inc., 1948), especially pages 1–13, 43–58, 78–123, 622–678, 689–732.

# II
## East of the Mediterranean—
## the Foundation of Civilization

*A modern photograph of the pyramids at Gizeh at the time of the inundation of the Nile. From this picture it can be seen why the ancient Egyptians were likely to choose the period of the inundation for transporting the building materials required for the pyramids.* (PHOTO BY FUZANI)

# 3

# Egyptian Civilization

*Reason for extended study* • *"River valley" civilizations: the meaning of the classification* • *Contrast between Egyptian and Mesopotamian river valleys: physiography, government, outlook on life* • *Prehistoric or predynastic Egypt* • *The Old Kingdom* • *First Intermediate Period* • *The Middle Kingdom* • *Second Intermediate Period* • *The New Kingdom: period of expansion* • *The New Kingdom: period of decline* • *General summary of Egyptian achievements*

---

## ▶ General considerations—Reason for extended study

Before coming to the history of ancient Egypt a few words of explanation should be given for the order in which this history is treated in this book and for the amount of space devoted to it. Egypt was probably not the "cradle of civilization"; that honor, as far as we know now, belongs to Mesopotamia. In a strictly chronological history of civilization, therefore, Mesopotamia ought to be studied first. Moreover, the Egyptians, of all great peoples, left fewest traces upon subsequent civilizations. The legacy of Egypt cannot, in our view, be in any way compared in depth or magnitude with the legacy of Mesopotamia and Israel. Why, then, should such a long chapter be devoted to Egypt?

This chapter has also followed a procedure different from that adopted in the rest of this book. Instead of treating the civilization as a whole and listing its contributions systematically under various topics,

an attempt has been made to show the close connection between the political and economic events and the very slight changes to be observed in the attitude toward life on the part of the Egyptian people as expressed in their religion and art. This procedure has necessitated the mention of some historical facts which in themselves would have been of little interest to twentieth-century students but are of importance in their Egyptian context. An effort has been made to introduce only those historical facts which have a bearing on the changes in the Egyptian attitude toward life, while others, doubtless of equal importance to a professional historian or student of Egyptian history, have been omitted.

Egyptian civilization seems to the author to be unique in history for several reasons. It was a very long-lived civilization, lasting more than 2,500 years. It changed very slowly indeed during this span of time; but it did change, as we shall see. All the great discoveries made by the Egyptians were the result of work done during the first few centuries of the existence of that civilization. Its forms and its art were evidently found satisfactory by the Egyptian people, who felt no need to change them. Thus it was a stable civilization, more stable than any other known to us, with the possible exception of China. This stability was reflected in Egyptian religion as well as in its art forms.

Western civilization has at no time been noted for its stability. It has at all times been a dynamic civilization, and in its latter centuries has been accompanied by an idea of eternal progress toward something new and better. This has meant constant disorder and constant wars. But it has also meant that the people, even while living in the midst of these uncertainties, have always had the hope that something better would come out of them—and indeed it cannot be said that we have been unsuccessful in our aims. We in America have produced for ourselves by our efforts a world in which we enjoy a far higher standard of material comfort than was known in, say, the Middle Ages in the early days of Western civilization.

But the Egyptians felt no urge toward progress. On the contrary, the constant rising and setting of the sun was the inspiration for their idea of human life. The sun rises and sets in almost the same quarter on the same day each year—it is no accident that the Egyptians did not discover the precession of the equinoxes. Change, to the Egyptians, was the same thing as disorder, and they did not enjoy it. Yet in spite of this, or more probably just because of this, the Egyptian civilization lasted longer than the civilization of the Greeks or the Romans, and longer than any Western civilization has lasted since. In this chapter, therefore, we shall make the effort to study this unique civilization as a whole, trying to show how everything in it contributed to the stability of the entire civilization, symbolized by the pyramids, which may well outlast any physical manifestation of our own era.

And yet, as we shall see, Egypt did change underneath. It was not possible to restore completely the old divinely ordained social order which the people believed was a reflection of the unchanging cosmic order. As the centuries passed it was increasingly difficult to deny the obvious *fact* of change, and it was found impossible really to restore the past. The last Pharaohs, diligently copying ancient inscriptions while barbarians threatened, and even at times ruled, their kingdom, are a pathetic reminder to us of the truth that there can be no standing still in history without falling back, and may serve to reconcile us to our world of disorder and progress. But the history of Egypt may also remind us that there was one great people which tried to hold back the clock, which developed and maintained a set of values altogether alien to ours, and yet survived for so long a time that we have difficulty in imagining it. If we count backward the time span of Egyptian civilization from the middle of the twentieth century A.D. we shall reach the dawn of Greek civilization. Solon had not yet been born, and Homer had not been long in his grave. How much of history and change have we encompassed in the 2,575 years since then, and how restricted a space do we give to the study of the history of Egypt from the First Dynasty to the last inglorious defeat by the Persians in 525 B.C.!

The Egyptian civilization is a working model of a truly homogeneous culture, affected very little indeed by other cultures. Yet, successful as it may have been from its own point of view, it bears almost no resemblance to ours, and its influence on the whole stream of civilization has been so slight that very little intensive study has been given to it except by specialists. The general student receives a vague impression of pyramids and tombs and otherworldliness; but it all seems so alien to him and so unworthy of serious attention in these modern days that he quickly passes on to Greece, whose people are recognizably like ourselves, and whose governments and philosophies have served as foundations for our own. Much of this misunderstanding, indeed, may be laid to the door of the Greeks themselves, who admired Egypt greatly because of its age and general impressiveness, but had little understanding of the Egyptian achievement, nor why the Egyptians had become as the Greek traveler and historian Herodotus described them.

Yet it is possible to gain some understanding of Egypt if the effort is made. And the effort, in the view of this writer, is eminently worth while because it may teach us that our own type of society and civilization is not the only possible one, that people can pass their lives satisfactorily without any idea of progress, without aggression upon their neighbors at least until the civilization was falling into decay, without those drives and urges which we have been led to consider as natural and inevitable for survival in a cruel and competitive world. It is not impossible that the human psyche has evolved since the days of the ancient Egyptian civilization; but, if so, it is surely worth while to consider at some length, before dealing with the main stream of civilization, the nature of man and his pysche as they were in those long-past days, if only to gain some perspective, and even some greater knowledge of ourselves by contrast with what we have evidently ceased to be.

In view of the fundamental differences between the Egyptian beliefs and way of life and our own, it is of the utmost importance for us to try to enter imaginatively into Egyptian beliefs and values, and not to contrast them with ours, except momentarily. It has therefore seemed to the author that it would be improper in this chapter to be content with listing Egyptian contributions to *our* civilization. Such a procedure would distort the facts and conceal their meaning. We should notice the period *when* any particular contribution was made, we should examine when a particular event took place and what its effect was upon the people. We are looking for real changes underneath an appearance of stability. The divine monarchy suffered a relapse at the end of the Old Kingdom, and it was restored during the Middle Kingdom; then again Egypt was ruled by foreigners during the so-called Second Intermediate Period, but the monarchy was restored for a new period of brilliance

during the New Kingdom. But was Egypt fundamentally changed, in spite of the façade?

Thus a chronological framework is essential to the understanding of the process of change. The Old, Middle, and New Kingdoms must be distinguished from one another, and the so-called religious revolution of Akhnaton, the period most familiar to modern students by reason of the popular novels written about it (e.g., Mika Waltari's *The Egyptian*) will be dealt with in some detail as an important symptom of this process of change. The last part of Egyptian history, on the other hand, when there were no changes of consequence, will require very little space in comparison. The gradual sinking into a cultural coma can safely be taken for granted when the end is known.

▶ **"River-valley" civilizations—The meaning of the classification**

Before proceeding to the history of Egyptian civilization proper it is necessary to say a few words about the conventional classification of ancient civilizations as "river-valley" or maritime or land-based. Three of the first civilizations known to us began in the valleys of great rivers where agriculture was comparatively easy, and a surplus of produce could be made available for those who did not themselves work on the land. By the Nile in Egypt, by the Tigris and Euphrates in Mesopotamia, and by the Indus in northwestern India, civilizations sprang up at an early date. There is still no agreement upon which of these was first, and it is quite possible that China, where archaeological investigation has lagged, holds a complete priority. Brief mention of the Indus civilization will be made in a later chapter; meanwhile the other river valleys will be discussed in some detail since their influence on Europe was more marked.

Slightly later than the river-valley civilizations are those which were from the first primarily dependent on the sea. These maritime civilizations lived by trade. The land available to them was limited, as in Phoenicia; nevertheless some agriculture was indispensable to provide a basis for subsistence. These maritime civilizations have throughout history been in a dangerous economic position. They have been forced to protect their lines of commerce, and for this purpose to build navies or arm their merchantmen. Their livelihood has depended upon their ability to trade successfully; they have always imported more food than they exported and they have paid for these imports by the products of industry and by their services as distributors.

It is at once clear that it is not possible to classify all civilizations, even the very early ones, as river-valley or maritime. Mere geographical proximity to the sea does not necessarily mean that the people live by maritime trade. The Hebrew people usually had a fairly long coast line under their control, but they remained primarily a pastoral people. Lower Egypt and Crete had enough land available to make their economies a mixture of agriculture and maritime commerce. But for purposes of convenience, and because it has become conventional, we shall in this book retain these two broad classifications, and the Hebrews will be discussed as if all the peoples who lived in Palestine and Syria used the sea as their means of livelihood, and they were not a great exception to the rule.

▶ **Contrast between Egyptian and Mesopotamian river valleys—Physiography, government, outlook on life**

Of all the river-valley civilizations, Egypt was the most clearly dependent upon its great river, the Nile. A glance at a conventionally colored map of Egypt will show the thin strip of green bordering the Nile Valley, with the uncultivable desert hemming it in on both sides. Egypt is an almost rainless land, and the annual inundations of the Nile provide it not only with all its usable moisture, but with great quantities of new fertile soil which are deposited in the fields.

If the flood were allowed to run its natural course without any human interference, the area of land fertilized by it would be small indeed. In ancient times the uncivilized peoples to the south of Egypt made no effort to control the floods, and the areas bordering the Nile remained, for the most part, uncultivated. They were the home of waterfowl and animals and lush semitropical water plants rather than of industrious peasants; and we can infer from this natural condition what would have been the fate of Egypt if it had not been for the efforts of man.

The birth of Egyptian civilization, then, was the result of the labor of those unnamed men and women who first cleared and drained the land and then learned to understand and control the floods, building dikes to hold the water for a longer time than it would have been held in the course of nature, leading it by canals and projects of irrigation beyond the natural boundaries of the flood into adjoining areas of what had previously been a desert, but could be made to bear fruits by human labor and ingenuity.

We know nothing of these early human efforts but we know that they must have been made. Early pictures exist showing the abundant life of the marshes, and the tangle of reeds and brush that called forth the efforts of generations of prehistoric men. Once completed, the work did not need to be done again; and the valley of the Nile from that day to this has remained one of the great fertile regions of the earth. But it did require eternal vigilance and endless toil to make the most of the gift of the great river; and above all it needed cooperation between the peoples inhabiting the valley. The flood was not uniform; it did not always arrive at a given place on the same day each year, and the flood might be high or low, depositing a greater or lesser amount of water and soil. If the Nile was low one year, it might be high the next. Sooner or later there has always been a return to normal. But there might be years when marginal fields could not be cultivated and the dry desert winds would blow away the topsoil.

# ▸ chronological chart

| | | |
|---|---|---|
| Neolithic Age | *ca.* | 6000–3000 |
| | | |
| Old Kingdom: Dynasties I–VI | *ca.* | 3000–2200 |
|    Unification of Upper and Lower Egypt | *ca.* | 3000 |
|    "Stepped" pyramid of Zoser | *ca.* | 2700 |
|    Great Pyramid of Khufu | *ca.* | 2600 |
|    Memphite Theology | *ca.* | 2600 |
|    Instructions of Ptah-hotep | *ca.* | 2600 |
|    Pyramid Texts | | 2350–2175 |
| | | |
| First Intermediate Period: Dynasties VII–XI | *ca.* | 2200–2000 |
|    Prophecies of Ipuwer | *ca.* | 2100 |
|    Tale of the Eloquent Peasant | *ca.* | 2100 |
|    Reconquest by Theban prince of north | | 2050–2000 |
| | | |
| Middle Kingdom: Dynasty XII | *ca.* | 2000–1792 |
|    Coffin Texts | | 2150–1700 |
| | | |
| Second Intermediate Period: Hyksos Invasion—Dynasties XIII–XVII | *ca.* | 1800–1550 |
|    Reconquest of Egypt by Theban princes | | 1580–1550 |
| | | |
| New Kingdom: Period of Empire—Dynasties XVIII–XX | | 1570–1090 |
|    Hatshepsut | | 1486–1468 |
|    Thutmose III (minor till death of Hatshepsut) | | 1490–1436 |
|    Battle of Megiddo—Conquest of Syria and part of Mesopotamia | | 1468 |
|    Book of the Dead (present form) | *ca.* | 1400 onward |
|    Religious revolution of Akhnaton | *ca.* | 1377–1360 |
|    Restoration by Tutankhamon | *ca.* | 1360 |
|    Horemhab | | 1349–1319 |
|    Rameses II (captivity and exodus of Israelites?) | | 1301–1234 |
|    Battle of Kadesh and treaty with Hittites | | 1297 |
|    Rameses III | | 1195–1164 |
|    Victory of Rameses over the "Sea Peoples" | | 1190 |
|    Tomb Robberies | | 1120 |
| | | |
| New Kingdom: Post-imperial period—Dynasties XXI–XXX | *ca.* | 1090–525 |
|    Conquest by Assyria | *ca.* | 670 |
|    Conquest by Persia | | 525 |
|    Conquest by Alexander the Great | | 332 |

All dates are before Christ.

*Sources:* G. E. Wright and F. V. Filson, eds., *Westminster Historical Atlas to the Bible* (Philadelphia: Westminster Press, 1945), and J. A. Wilson, *The Burden of Egypt* (Chicago: The University of Chicago Press, 1951), pp. vii–viii.

These would be years of famine such as those described in the Bible when Joseph advised the Pharaoh to build granaries and store supplies.

All these dangers could be overcome by good government and organization. The approach of the inundation could be signaled all the way from the Fourth Cataract beyond the boundaries of Egypt right to the Delta. The labor of the peasants could be coordinated, manpower quickly transferred to the areas where it was most needed. The height of the flood, when it was known in advance, could be communicated to workers nearer to the mouth, and preparations made accordingly. The prosperity of Egypt was bound up with the efficiency of its governmental organization to a degree hardly equaled anywhere else in the world, and this fact, as we shall see, was appreciated by the ancient Egyptians themselves. If it would be too much to say that the form of government of ancient Egypt was determined by the river and the necessities connected with it, it is not too much to say that the extraordinary worship given to the Pharaoh and the prestige of his government can best be explained by the intimate connection between its efficiency and the prosperity of the Egyptian people.

In the river valleys of Western Asia all this was different. The Tigris and Euphrates overflowed, but less predictably than the Nile; there were torrential rains (the Egyptians said they had a "Nile in the sky") and hurricanes. There were terrible sandstorms as well as uncontrollable floods. The peoples of Mesopotamia could not look upon their rivers as the source of all life when they were as destructive as they were beneficent. Though irrigation was practiced, as in Egypt, it necessarily took on a different character; a strong government was not required with such urgency as in Egypt. The contrasts between Mesopotamia and Egypt are almost as great as the similarities, as we shall see; the kind of river is as important in the study of these civilizations as the mere fact of the river and its valley. If we are only studying

the predominant manner of making a living, that is, by agriculture on irrigated land, then the classification is important and valid. If, however, we are studying the whole civilization and its accomplishments, then the contrasts must be equally examined. And at once the inadequacy of the geographical and environmental explanation becomes apparent.

It would be going too far in a work of this nature to try to produce a philosophy of history adequate to cover the vast material. Clearly no single factor or even complex of many factors *determines* history. The peoples of the upper Nile could have produced a civilization comparable to that of the Egyptians, but they did not; the Egyptians produced a certain kind of civilization because of their particular kind of river, but they need not have produced a civilization at all, and it could have taken different forms. It survived so long because the original ideas were found adequate for thousands of years, though, as we shall see, they were in important respects modified. The Mesopotamian peoples knew more different kinds of government than did the Egyptians, and none of them survived as long as the Egyptian. But what are we to say of the Hebrews? Could only a people such as this have given birth to monotheism and maintained it? Other peoples were in a similar position of insecurity, continually in danger of extinction from their neighbors, but they remained polytheists or "idol worshipers"; they did not conceive of themselves as specially chosen by God and protected by him.

These spiritual achievements were not determined by environment, though it may be true to say they were limited by it. If they had known a different environment the ideas might not have survived because they did not fit their experience. The Egyptian idea that the king, or Pharaoh, was a god manifest on earth, all-wise and all-powerful, could not survive the earthly experience that he was obviously not all-powerful because he was defeated by his enemies. This experience had to be explained away if the belief was to be retained, or, if it could not be explained, the religion must be modified accordingly. The Hebrews explained their own defeats in spite of their position as the chosen people of God in different ways at different times, as we shall see. God was trying their faith, God did not value earthly victories as man did, God punished man for his sins. Ultimately, when all other explanations had failed, they thought that God would redress the balance of this world in the next. The Egyptians might say that their Pharaoh was not the true one, that his power had grown weak and needed reviving by magical means; or they could abandon interest in this life in favor of the next. The Mesopotamian peoples could and did give up all attempt at explanation of their misfortunes, regarding themselves as incapable of understanding what the gods wanted of them. The gods were arbitrary, perhaps unjust, and certainly not behaving in a rational manner toward them in accordance with any such contract as the Hebrews believed they possessed with their God. For all these beliefs one can see some justification in the life experience and environment of these peoples. But can one say that the beliefs were *necessarily* such as they were, and that no other was possible?

Mention has already been made in Chapter 1 of Toynbee's theory of challenge and response. According to Toynbee, all peoples at all stages of their careers have certain challenges to meet. A people may meet such a challenge by accepting it and producing a response which will carry them one stage further in civilization, until another challenge is presented. If a people do not respond in a creative manner, then their civilization will decay; or they may respond in such a way as to use up all their creative energies without making further progress. In the latter case they respond continuously, but they cannot move onward. The study of history, in Toynbee's view, consists in trying to determine the nature of the challenges and of peoples' responses to them; and in trying to find lessons in history by discovering what are our own challenges, and whether we are responding or can respond in a creative manner.

There can be no question of the existence of these challenges and responses. At every moment in the life of a human being or a people there is some insistent problem that requires solution. This is so obviously true as to be hardly worth stating as a contribution to the understanding of history. But it has the supreme value of directing our attention to the human element in history as distinct from the environmental factors that shape it. History is the story of how human beings reacted to their environment and changed it; only human beings have history and only human beings make and record it. The story of the animal world, as of the earth itself, is an account of the external environment and its effects. But man has always had the choice of reacting creatively or being driven by forces beyond his control. For the thousands of years of prehistory dealt with in Chapter 2, man was like the animals insofar as he accepted his environment and lived as they did; he began to act like a human being when by thinking and planning and consciously willed action he changed that environment.

▶ **Prehistoric or predynastic Egypt**

The early Egyptians in the time called prehistoric or predynastic[1] had already laid the foundation for their later civilization under the Pharaohs. There is no evidence of planned irrigation before the union of Upper and Lower Egypt, but the inhabitants had cleared and drained the areas adjacent to the Nile, they lived in villages, and they had learned agriculture and the domestication of animals. There was already fine pot-

[1] A dynasty is the period of time during which one particular family held the throne of Egypt. Conventionally the First Dynasty of Egypt refers to the period immediately following the unification by Menes. The term "dynasty" or its equivalent, however, was unknown to the ancient Egyptians themselves, and the conventional division stems from the work of Manetho, a late Egyptian priest.

tery in predynastic times, though apparently without the use of the potter's wheel; this art, however, had reached a climax and deteriorated before the First Dynasty. The Neolithic settlements in Egypt show much the same characteristics as elsewhere. There were crude oval huts of mud followed by houses of shaped mud bricks with small windows. Since they knew the use of flax and cultivated it, the people wore clothes of linen. They had hoes made of wood and sickles with flint teeth. They were not cut off from the outside world, since there were already sailing ships on the Nile; indeed, Egyptian goods of the period have been found as far away as Persia. In the last centuries before the union of Upper and Lower Egypt and the great creative act of "Menes"[2] the unifier, metal began to be used in Egypt and the copper mines to be exploited. Ivory, myrrh, lapis lazuli, and other foreign products were known and used.

Predynastic Egypt has left no writings, and we cannot know for certain about much of the religion and government of the people. Various figurines and symbolic objects have been found in graves dating back to this period, and from the considerable numbers of warlike implements we can assume that warfare was not unknown. It is probable that, until very late predynastic times, the basic governmental unit was the tribe, and that this unit gradually increased in size, containing different peoples not related by blood, until rather suddenly it became possible for local rulers to extend their authority by agreement and conquest, thus laying the basis for the remarkable unification of all Egypt that marks the beginning of Egyptian history proper.

It was believed until very recently that

[2] It may perhaps be significant that there is much doubt as to whether any king of Egypt ever possessed the name "Menes" or "Mena," for kings of other names seem to have performed the deeds ascribed to him. If the linguistic connections could ever be established, the consonants M-N might be found to constitute the essential parts of the names of many mythical founders of kingdoms and civilizations, from Mannus of Germany mentioned by Tacitus to Minos of Crete and Manu of India.

*Predynastic Egyptian jar, decorated with gazelles and ostriches. Note the considerable skill of the artist at this very early stage of Egyptian history.* (COURTESY THE METROPOLITAN MUSEUM OF ART)

the Egyptians adopted a solar calendar and a year of 365 days as early as 4241 B.C. and therefore well within the predynastic period. This theory has now been abandoned and the adoption of this calendar placed within the period of the first three dynasties. But before it could be adopted there must have been many years of recorded observations. Probably these observations extended back into the predynastic times, though not necessarily very far into them. Writing appears also in a developed state early in the dynastic period, suggesting that its first elements were laid down before. Most modern opinion inclines to the view that in late predynastic Egypt there was quite extensive borrowing from Mesopotamian civilization, which in some respects was further developed at an earlier date. Monumental architecture, the cylinder seal, the potter's wheel, various artistic motifs, and, above all, writing, were known in Mesopotamia before there is any evidence for their use in Egypt. It is therefore probable that the last achievements of the predynastic age took place under foreign influence and provided the necessary stimulus for the great step forward which occurred as soon as the political conditions for further advance came into being.

It should be stated at once that the intensive study of Egyptian history is comparatively new. Until the early nineteenth century the Egyptian language was unknown to us. In 1798 the Rosetta Stone, bearing an inscription in Greek and two forms of Egyptian writing, was discovered by an officer in the army of Napoleon. Some thirty years afterward the French scholar Champollion had progressed so far in his comparison of the unknown language with the known Greek that he was able to produce an Egyptian grammar and dictionary. But great numbers of Egyptian texts are now known, and more are discovered every year. Even today it cannot be said that all the important ones have been read and analyzed. Moreover, in addition to the written texts, archaeologists have provided and are still providing us with an enormous mass of new material, all of which needs to be evaluated by modern criticism in the light of existing information. It is a far cry indeed now from the days when the information given by Greek tourists and historians, who themselves lived thousands of years after the Pyramid Age and obtained their information from priests often as ignorant as themselves, was regarded as accurate. Indeed it can be said definitely that we, with access to the contents of tombs unknown to the Greeks and with a knowledge of the Egyptian language not possessed by them, have a far greater and more accurate knowledge of ancient Egypt than they had, even though we are living more than two thousand years after the inquiries of Herodotus. And, to complete the paradox, we probably know more about the history of ancient Egypt than did the later Egyptians themselves, since they did not have access to the tombs, which have been entered and examined by modern archaeologists and evaluated by modern scholars with modern tools of research.

It was natural that histories of Egypt should be written in the nineteenth and early twentieth centuries on the basis of insufficient information, since the interest in ancient Egypt outstripped the research of early Egyptologists. It is not to be wondered at that much of what these pioneers wrote must be modified by later discoveries and more thorough criticism. Even the best translations made during the period prior to World War I must be used with great caution, so great has been the progress since that time in our understanding of the language. These older histories were the best available in their time, however, and served as a useful stimulus for further study. But, as in the field of anthropology discussed in the first chapter, even now there is little that can be taken for granted as unquestionably true, and the histories to be written a hundred years hence should be incomparably better than ours. There are still today very few competent Egyptologists, and the findings of each cannot be dissociated from his subjective prejudices. The most famous of American Egyptologists, the late Professor Breasted, with his Christian predilections, was too anxious to discover Hebrew thought in Egyptian documents to be completely objective; and, with our predominantly Christian and Jewish heritage, too many of us are inclined to use terms belonging to this heritage and apply them to ancient Egypt. Sin, evil, righteousness, and such terms all stem from this background, and a translator is hard put to it to discover neutral synonyms and often cannot do so. Perhaps, after all, there are some advantages in a picture language where the reader is free to clothe the symbols with whatever emotional content he pleases rather than try to extract the whole weight of his tradition from the finished words presented to him.

▶ The Old Kingdom

THE CREATIVE ACT OF "MENES"—UNIFICATION
OF UPPER AND LOWER EGYPT

Through the whole land of Egypt, as

has been said, flows the life-giving Nile. The fertile area is bounded on the east and the west by the desert, sparsely peopled by groups of nomads, who, for lack of numbers, are incapable at any time of conquering the settled groups in the valley. To the north is the sea, over which invaders could come, but were not likely to come in sufficient numbers to overpower a united people. To the northeast again is the desert of Sinai which could be crossed, but nevertheless constituted a formidable barrier to invasion. To the south are the six cataracts of the Nile, the first, at the usual boundaries of Egypt, easily navigated or by-passed in ancient times, while the remainder presented serious barriers to navigation, and thus to invasion by river. Potential enemies to the south, the Nubians and the Ethiopians, could be held in check by small frontier forces which needed only to patrol the narrow fertile area, since the desert was a sufficient protection on the flanks.

Egypt thus formed a compact and defensible unity against invaders from every direction. On the other hand, within itself it was not a unity. There was the sharpest distinction between the Delta, the mouth of the Nile in Lower Egypt, which faced the sea and maintained contact with foreigners, and Upper Egypt, which lived in natural isolation. In Lower Egypt also the fertile land of the Delta is many miles wide, while in Upper Egypt the desert hems the cultivable land within closely confined barriers. The whole life of Upper Egypt was the river and the small area watered by it.

Before the creative act of "Menes" the Upper and Lower areas were under separate jurisdiction, with the geographical advantages manifestly on the side of the north. But it was nevertheless a prince of Upper Egypt who united them, presumably by conquest, and established the capital of the new kingdom at Memphis in Lower Egypt. By the time of the Third Dynasty this kingship of the Two Lands was regarded as a peculiar gift of the gods to Egypt and the king himself (Pharaoh or Great House, as he was

later called) was the god manifest on earth, which he remained throughout the whole of Egyptian history. Though the capital changed several times during the course of this history, it was a fixed dogma of the religion that the Pharaoh was always "Ruler of the Two Lands," and he wore the double crown of Upper and Lower Egypt, even though there was no longer any geographical or administrative distinction. At the coronation of the king, all rituals and ceremonies were performed for each land, and separate offices for each were maintained for the king's use in spite of the fact that he performed no separate duties.

There is no mention in Egyptian documents of any armed conquest of Lower Egypt by "Menes." The unification is always stated as a divine act performed by him; the natural divine order was manifested on earth

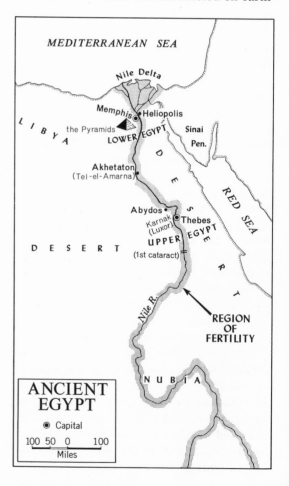

ANCIENT EGYPT

◉ Capital

100  50  0          100

Miles

by the deed of "Menes," though this essential unity had always existed even before it was made manifest. We are thus left in doubt as to the means employed; but in physical terms we are bound to assume that the unification did not take place without some struggle; indeed, the records give some signs of rebellion against the new rule. But it is certain that the consolidation was ultimately accepted by all, and endured essentially throughout all Egyptian history, in spite of the topographical differences between Upper and Lower Egypt. There can be no doubt that this union of Upper and Lower appealed to the Egyptian sense of symmetry so noticeable in both Egyptian art and religion—the conception of an underlying unity manifested in dual form. Egyptian gods always come in pairs, the right and left banks of the Nile balance each other, the eastern mountain range balances the western; so no doubt divine monarchy was a unity, but manifesting itself in rulership over the Two Lands.

THE DIVINE KINGSHIP

The conception of the divine king is not peculiar to Egypt, and indeed is still to be found among certain African tribes, possibly a decadent survival of the once-great Egyptian civilization of that continent. But the god who appears on earth, as distinct from the king who becomes a god at death (as under the Roman Empire) or the representative of the gods on earth (the Mesopotamian notion), was, as far as we know, unique in that age. Since it had the most profound consequences for Egypt, and was indeed her key institution, it needs a more detailed treatment than is usually given in textbooks.

In our culture we are accustomed to think in monotheistic terms of a transcendent God who is apart from the world, however much he may have been responsible for its existence, and however great the interest he takes in it. Such a conception would have been completely alien to Egyptian thinking and feeling, as it is to most Oriental peoples today. The polytheism of the Egyptians is

as natural a belief and even as intellectually respectable as monotheism, provided the conception is appraised not from our point of view but from theirs. At times the Egyptians thought of all their gods as manifestations of an underlying unity and thus approached closely to monotheism; at other times they laid more stress on the functions and powers of the gods, and then each function was represented by a personified god, or, in our terms, a natural force. The modern civilized man whose feelings are turned in awe toward the wonderful works of God thinks first of one divine power or attribute and then of another. He cannot encompass them all at the same moment. Where he thinks of the power of God as manifested in creation, the Egyptian might think of Hathor the cow-goddess; where he might think of death and resurrection the Egyptian would think of Osiris; where he might think of the first great creation by the divine mind the Egyptian would turn to Ptah, who created the world by giving utterance to the thought that was in his heart. An Egyptian would personify all these powers by the names of gods and goddesses; but these powers were experienced doubtless as powers in which the Egyptians saw the activities of the gods. It is a mistake to think of all polytheism as "idol worship" in the sense used by the Hebrews.

The ruler of Egypt was pre-eminently a Horus, the son of Osiris, who had been conceived by his mother Isis after the death of his father Osiris, who had been killed by his own brother Set, the power of darkness. The myth of the great struggle between Osiris and Set, the birth of Horus and his rise to manhood, and the drawn battle between him and his uncle in which Horus lost his eye—this fundamental myth is found in different forms at different periods in Egyptian history. But the basis remains the same. Osiris fought with Set and was killed; his sister-wife found him after a long search and either revived him sufficiently to enable her to bear Horus, or she conceived Horus after his resurrection. At all events, Osiris thereafter reigned as king in the world of the dead and Horus was his successor on earth. Thus each new king of Egypt was a Horus, but by the proper ritual burial he became an Osiris after death. When the old king became an Osiris through burial, then a Horus could be born again upon earth.

But the king was not only a Horus, son of Osiris; he was also the son of Re, the great sun-god, and at times this is the emphasis given to his divinity. The point to be understood is that these titles are not mutually exclusive. The fact that he was the son of Re or of Amon did not mean that he was not also the son of Osiris. To us a son has only one father and one mother, and this is of course true in a physical sense. But a king may be a son of many gods, for all have their share in him, and the worshiper or subject may emphasize now one aspect of his divinity and now another. By giving him more titles the worshiper enhances the god's dignity and his power, and enriches the conception of the king-god rather than detracts from it. The Egyptians had several different stories of creation and, to them, all were true; they were not alternative hypotheses only one of which could be true. The heavens were created by the action of a huge cow who stood up. The heavens were supported by four posts. Shu and Tefnut, air and moisture, gave birth to earth and sky and to Geb and Nut, the gods of earth and sky—and, as we have seen, all were created also by the mouth of Ptah. All of these conceptions were true, from their separate point of view, to the ancient Egyptian—not, as has sometimes been supposed, at different stages of Egyptian history, but at one and the same time. They were not hypotheses framed by the thinking mind to account for, to *explain* the how of creation, but an intuitive perception of the infinite depth and breadth of the creative process.

So the Pharaoh of Egypt partook of all the possible aspects of divinity; yet even he was not as great as the all-encompassing "total" deities; he had something of the nature of Osiris, something of Re, something of Atum and Amon and Ptah in him; but, being on earth, he was limited, and thus is usually spoken of as the son of Re or Amon rather than these great gods in their entirety. It was not until the limiting restrictions of the body had been cast off that he would become a true Osiris, and go around the heavens in the boat of the sun-god as himself now an aspect of the sun-god. But he was also not simply one of the gods, a minor god who was given charge over the land of Egypt, or a representative of God who had to make petition to higher gods. As a god he was possessed above all of three supreme powers, authoritative utterance or creative command (*hu*), perception or understanding (*sia*), and *Ma'at*, an untranslatable word which will be discussed more fully later. These powers enabled him to rule the land of Egypt with infallible judgment and unquestioned authority. His command was not limited to command over men. He was himself responsible by his divine powers for the inundation of the Nile. He made the Nile rise, and did not merely predict it; if the Nile overflow was insufficient or excessive, it was the Pharaoh who was responsible. When the king grew old and had been long on the throne, a special festival (the Sed festival) was celebrated for him, a kind of thirty-year jubilee for the renewal of his powers. Rameses II of the Nineteenth Dynasty celebrated the festival not only after thirty years of rule but at frequent intervals thereafter, perhaps because he felt his own life-forces to be in need of renewal.[3]

THE DIVINE GOVERNMENT ON EARTH—*Ma'at*

As a consequence of his position as a god, all Egypt was naturally subject to him, and all authority derived from him. His viziers and ministers only held office at his pleasure, and all spoke in his name. He owned all the land, though in most periods he did not exercise his right to ownership, and land was bought and sold as if it belonged to the "tenants." In theory he could, however, always resume his ownership, and in the New Kingdom there is evidence that

[3] Certain African tribes today perform a similar rite for their kings.

he did so, and had the land worked through nominees. In theory he even owned all that existed in foreign countries, so that an ordinary commercial transaction would have to be disguised as a "gift" or "tribute" even when the foreign country was in fact entirely independent and the goods were bought and paid for.[4]

It was of course possible for a Pharaoh to abuse his position. Such overwhelming power in our more self-conscious age would be an intolerable tyranny, however paternally the power was administered. It would be an affront to the dignity of the human individual. We could not conceivably allow any man, however wise and however saintly, to possess such power as of right, simply by what we would call the "accident of birth." The whole political history of recent centuries has been a struggle to take power away from the hereditary autocrat and divide it among the people. Such an idea would have been inconceivable at any stage of Egyptian history, simply because the Pharaoh was believed to be a god, with all the attributes that divinity entails. Our fear would be that the autocrat would use his power arbitrarily, consulting only his own whims and pleasures. The Egyptians did not have this fear because a god would not do this; hence they were secure, while we would be insecure, with a "divine" king.

The record of Egyptian monuments, from the beginning to the end of their history, never allows the idea to appear that the kings are fallible individuals. If there were arbitrary and unjust individuals among them, we do not know of them. We know of Akhnaton, who changed the religion of Egypt and tried to destroy the old one, but though the

[4] The system was that the Pharaoh's servants would send gifts to the foreigner on behalf of their master, and the equivalent "gifts" from the foreigners would then be left for the Egyptians to collect and record on their monuments as "tribute." In an informal account of an expedition to the stone quarries, on one occasion when a remarkable incident occurred which revealed the presence of a fine block of granite, the incident was recorded as having "happened to his majesty," although the Pharaoh was hundreds of miles away at the time.—H. Frankfort, *Ancient Egyptian Religion* (New York: Columbia University Press, 1948), p. 58.

priests opposed him they do not seem to have questioned his *right* to make the change. Even the records of victory are rarely fully individualized. They follow a certain type, and in some cases even the names of the conquered reappear in different inscriptions hundreds of years afterward. Pharaohs with but a few exceptions did not take pride in their personal exploits.

In all the sculptures of royal victories the contests to us appear unfair. The Pharaoh is depicted as of superhuman size, while his enemies are dwarfs cringing before him. And while it is true that the personal prowess of some Pharaohs is extolled by the sculptor, this is only because the latter wished to emphasize the Pharaoh's power and glory and the good fortune of Egypt that she had a powerful god to lead her to such smashing victories. Even Amenhotep II, who took such evident pride in his achievements as athlete and hunter, was clearly never in danger from man or beast; his prowess was only to be expected.

Such power carries truly awful responsibilities, and in all ages of Egyptian history we have no indication that they were not fully realized by the rulers. The king consulted his advisers but the decisions were all his. As a god he was expected to have the knowledge necessary to make them wisely. The records always speak merely of the offerings of opinion by the counselors, followed by the revelation of the king and the acclaim of the counselors. "The king took counsel in making disclosures," or "The king made his appearance [the same word is used as for the rising of the sun] with the double crown, and gave commands." The counselors answer, "Authoritative utterance is in thy mouth. Understanding follows thee . . . it is thy plans which come to pass."

The reason that the Pharaoh alone was able to make decisions, the reason that he "made disclosures" was that he alone knew the true nature of the universe. The order of the universe, the static perfected universe of the Egyptians, not subject to change and established from the beginnings of time, was called in the Egyptian language *Ma'at*. The

*The New Kingdom Pharaoh Thutmose III destroying his enemies. Note the gigantic size of the Pharaoh and the conventional puniness of his enemies.*

*Amenhotep II (New Kingdom) was evidently very proud of his skill as a lion hunter. Here the convention is observed of showing the Pharaoh as far larger and more powerful than his enemies, animal and human alike. Hence the lion is rather a puny beast and, as in all Egyptian conventional art depicting the fighting of a Pharaoh, the hunt is strictly "no contest."* (COURTESY THE METROPOLITAN MUSEUM OF ART)

Egyptians did not deny apparent change, the recognized recurrent change, the return to the starting point as of the eternal sequence of day and night. Such change was part of the established order. But no fundamental change was possible. The union of Upper and Lower Egypt had not taken place in time, but was a permanent fact. Only creation was a real change; but even at the time of creation divine monarchy had existed. *Ma'at,* then, in its original meaning was the divine order of creation, order created out of chaos. But this is only one kind of order. Falsehood is manifestly disorder; so is injustice. *Ma'at* can therefore mean also both truth and justice. When the Egyptians claimed that they lived by *Ma'at,* this only means that they were living in accordance with the divinely established order. A rebel against the Pharaoh would have ceased to live by *Ma'at,* as he wished to substitute chaos for order. When the Pharaoh made a decision, he made it by virtue of his knowledge of what the right order was—not for moral reasons, or because such an action was useful. Rather, because it was *harmonious.* As a god he also knew naturally what was just. It was not necessary for him to listen to evidence, and seek out where the truth lay; his decree was infallible for he was the source of justice. He could not of course decide upon every case throughout the land of Egypt, and thus his power devolved upon his representatives; but it was always clear that they only held their power, and indeed their knowledge, from him.

This conception of justice as known only by the Pharaoh effectively accounts for the complete absence in Egypt of any codified law.[5] No doubt it was customary law that was administered in practice, as it has always been. But precedents, even cited from the decisions of the Pharaoh, could never be officially quoted since the decision could

only naturally hold for the particular case, and, as far as we know, there was never any reference made to earlier cases or decisions rendered by earlier Pharaohs. As the sole possessor of *Ma'at,* the sole *knower* of what was just, orderly, and right, his word was law and against it there could be no appeal.

As god the Pharaoh was, of course, both head of the religion and the object of worship. But he was not high priest as has sometimes been stated. The high priest was theoretically subject to the Pharaoh and appointed by him, though in later times, at least, the office tended to remain semihereditary in certain families. In the later New Kingdom during the decline of the monarchy there is no doubt that the priesthood held tremendous power and was perhaps the real governing body of the country. Nevertheless it was possible for the autocrat Akhnaton to abolish the whole priesthood of the ruling god Amon for at least the duration of his reign without producing a rebellion. But in early times we hear little of the high priests and can only assume their effectively subordinate position.

Thus the king combined in himself enough functions to make him the most completely absolute monarch of any civilized people in history. He was the supreme ruler whose word was law beyond any questioning; he was the fount of all power in Egypt, natural and political; he owned all the land, appointed all officials, and was the source of justice. He acknowledged no authority whatsoever, not even that of the gods whose equal and partner he was. And in the Old Kingdom, as far as we can tell from the records, only he possessed certain immortality, and only he was able to ensure immortality for those of his subjects who served him to the end and were buried under his protection.

From all this it follows that the only danger for the people of Egypt was that the new king might not be a god as his predecessors were. He always did become a god at his coronation, when the old king was mummified and buried. But he had not been born as a god, and there was always a period

[5] It was once thought that forty scrolls of the law lay before the vizier when he tried a case on behalf of the Pharaoh. But these are now recognized as forty leather thongs, the symbol of his authority.— J. A. Wilson, *The Burden of Egypt* (Chicago: The University of Chicago Press, 1951), p. 172 and note references.

of uncertainty from the moment of the death of the old king to the coronation of the new. The new king came to the throne as the sun rose on the day following the death of the old. There was an impressive ceremony for this accession and a mystery play was performed. But at the accession of the new king, the dead king had not yet become an Osiris; consequently the new king was not yet a Horus. For the all-important coronation the appropriate season in nature had to be awaited, some decisive moment when there was a beginning in nature—either the beginning of the season of the inundation, or the beginning of what the Egyptians called the Season of Coming Forth when the crops were sown. Since the successful enthronement of the new king as a Horus depended on the successful transfiguration of the late king as an Osiris, tremendous importance was attached to the funerary rites of the old. In this understanding may lie the key to the great monuments of the Old Kingdom, the ever-impressive pyramids of this age.

### THE PYRAMIDS—SYMBOL OF EQUILIBRIUM AND STABILITY

Not all the pyramids were built during the Old Kingdom, but all the more impressive ones, including the so-called Great Pyramid of Khufu (Cheops in Greek) at Gizeh. Although they have almost all been fully excavated and examined and measured, there is still no general agreement either on how they were built or their real purpose. Though later Egyptians built some smaller pyramids and there was another whole age of pyramid

building far to the south by the Ethiopians who controlled Egypt during her last years, there have been few attempts to imitate them by other peoples. To our taste they are not particularly beautiful nor do they serve a useful function. With modern machines they could probably be built with only a tithe of the manpower used by the Egyptians, but we do not want to build them, although it is possible they will outlast any other buildings at present existing in our world. The Greeks, and even the Egyptians of the New Kingdom, visited them as tourists, and were given such information as the priests then possessed. But there is no reason to believe these priests knew even as much as we do about them, since they were without our scientific curiosity and, moreover, had no means of examining them as thoroughly as we have examined them. The descriptions of the Greek historian Herodotus are only valuable insofar as they give us the knowledge of what existed in his day and has disappeared since, and his explanations are only as valuable as the tradition from which they were taken. The Muslim Caliph Mamun in the ninth century A.D. authorized an expedition to examine the Great Pyramid in search of treasure. It was successfully broken open, but the treasure was missing if it had ever been there. There is no certain knowledge that there ever was enough to repay the labor of stealing it.

The kings of the First and Second Dynasties were buried in mastabas, a kind of better-built version of the contemporary house, and intended as the everlasting home of the in-

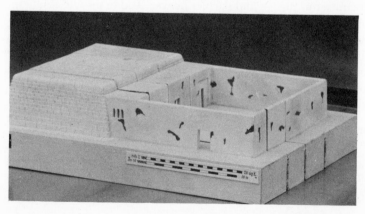

*Model of a mastaba constructed by The Metropolitan Museum of Art.* (COURTESY THE METROPOLITAN MUSEUM OF ART)

*The stepped pyramid of Zoser at Sakkarah (IIIrd Dynasty). This shows the earliest form of a pyramid.* (PHOTO BY LEKEGIAN)

*Model of the Great Pyramid complex, constructed by The Metropolitan Museum of Art. Note the impressive mortuary temples leading up to the pyramid itself.* (COURTESY THE METROPOLITAN MUSEUM OF ART)

cumbent. It was not until the Third Dynasty that the first pyramid was built, and this was built in steps or layers. It is not now generally believed that the pyramid developed from the mastaba, but rather that the pyramidal form represented some change in the solar religion and the beliefs in the afterworld, so that the pyramid became a suitable form for the body of the dead king to inhabit. None stood by itself in lonely grandeur as the pyramids appear today. Each was part of a complex, including a mortuary temple where rites for the dead king were celebrated. More simple tombs for the queens, nobles, and officials, and women of the household were erected in the same area, presumably in order that they might continue to serve the king in the hereafter.

After the stepped pyramid of Zoser in the Third Dynasty began the erection of the great pyramids of the Fourth. These were true pyramids, made of huge granite blocks, all encased in limestone, so that the surface of the whole pyramid was smooth and regular. This surface has now been removed or worn off, exposing the granite blocks, and giving an appearance of irregularity unknown in ancient times.

The Great Pyramid of Khufu stands on a square base facing exactly the four points of the compass with a tiny margin of error. Out of a total of 755.8 feet, the longest line of this square is only 7.9 inches longer than the shortest. The east side is 5'30" west of north, the greatest variation of the four sides. It is not known how this almost incredible jewelers' precision was attained with the instruments then known to the Egyptians, for it could not be achieved merely with the use of the North Star. The Egyptians, of course, did not have the magnetic compass. The height of the pyramid, when complete, rose to 481.4 feet and the area covered by its base was 13.1 acres. This, it has been estimated, would give room for the cathedrals of Milan, Florence, and St. Peter at Rome, as well as Westminster Abbey and St. Paul's Cathedral, and still leave some space to spare. There are more than two million separate blocks of granite in the structure, weighing two and a half tons each. Inside the pyramid, which is entered 55 feet above the ground, there is a great gallery leading upward to a spacious chamber called the King's Chamber by the Muslims, while there is another gallery leading downward to what is certainly erroneously known as the Queen's Chamber. There is no evidence whatsoever that a queen was buried there, but much evidence to the contrary.

The engineering and labor problems involved in the erection of these gigantic structures raise many questions, not all of which can be satisfactorily answered. Herodotus' statement of the hundred thousand men employed for three months for twenty years is only a nice round estimate given to tourists of his day by Egyptian priests and may not even represent the priestly tradition any more than do modern statements given to wide-eyed tourists by professional guides. We do know from quarry marks on stone transported to other pyramids that the laborers worked in gangs with popular names such as "Boat Gang," "Vigorous Gang," "Craftsmen Gang," and so on, and we know of the later use of ramps, along which the stones were propelled up a fairly gentle slope and then eased into position. The pulley principle was unknown in ancient Egypt. Presumably all the dressing for the stones was done by skilled craftsmen below. The stones were finished with incredible precision, fitting into position with but one hundredth of an inch out of alignment from the true square.

The quarrying of these quantities of granite must have presented problems almost as difficult as the problems of construction, though the river, which at full flood at Gizeh closely approached the base of the pyramids, could be used for transportation. The amount of labor expended was, of course, enormous, when the whole project is considered, though not necessarily as large as the estimate of Herodotus, since so much would depend upon intricate and careful planning and organization. That a state should have reached such an extraordinarily high degree of efficiency in organization still excites the admiration of our technical age.

There is no reason to suppose that the labor was provided by slaves. We are too often misled by the Biblical stories of the Children of Israel who, thousands of years later, labored for the Pharaoh. The monuments of the Ramessids of the Nineteenth Dynasty were far inferior to those of their great predecessors in the Pyramid Age. Little precision was used and most of these monuments rest on comparatively feeble foundations; on the other hand, everything connected with the Great Pyramid was carried out with the utmost honesty, clearly by true craftsmen who had a real feeling for the work they were doing, and strove to make it as perfect as possible. It is not only in the finish but in the unseen parts of the structure that this scrupulous honesty was observed. In the Old Kingdom of Egypt there were few foreign wars, and thus few opportunities to win slaves.

The building of the pyramids was done in the period of the year when work on the land was impossible. Probably, as in the case of the ancient Peruvian peasants working for the Incas, their king-gods, every Egyptian also had the obligation to spend part of each year in the service of his king-god, service which was given gladly or reluctantly according as he believed in the purpose of the work or did not.

There remains the question of the purpose of the monuments. Unfortunately inside the pyramids of the Fourth Dynasty there are no carved reliefs or texts of an explanatory nature. In those of the Fifth and Sixth Dynasties, however, there are numerous writings, mostly in the form of spells. There can be no doubt that some of them are very old and refer to conditions long before these later pyramids were built. So we are reasonably justified in regarding them as in some degree applicable to the pyramids of the Fourth Dynasty, those of Gizeh. It would seem from these spells, as also from the design of the pyramid, that a pyramid was regarded as a kind of ladder to the heavens, upon which the dead king might ascend to his final resting place. No more perfect symbol of equilibrium between heaven and earth has ever

been devised than a pyramid whose summit —and there is some evidence to show that the Egyptians sometimes finished theirs in gold—catches the rays of the sun before they reach the earth beneath.

Yet we also know that the Egyptians, both before and after the Great Pyramid, believed that the afterlife was spent in the tomb. The *ba* (perhaps the nearest Egyptian equivalent to the soul, or principle animating the body) is shown in some pictures as hovering over the body, and descending the tomb shaft to visit it, presumably attracted back to its earthly habitation, preserved by the piety of its descendants. The blessed afterlife was indeed in all periods ensured by proper burial rites and mummification. The presence of a mortuary temple right against some pyramids, with its sanctuary adjoining it and a false door leading from the pyramid, suggests also that the dead king, like his subjects, could return to his tomb. It is possible also that two shafts leading from the king's burial place in the pyramid to the outer air, the purpose of which is still unknown, might act as a passageway for the *ba*.

The foregoing considerations therefore suggest to the author that the pyramid had two functions to perform. One was to act as the means of ascent for the dead king so that he might join his colleagues and ancestors in the circumpolar stars, which was one of the greatest hopes of the Egyptian. This would account for the extreme precision used in the erection of the pyramid and its astronomical accuracy. But when he had ascended he had become an Osiris, superior to the rank he had attained on earth, and superior to the present incumbent of the throne. We know from other sources that it was hoped that the dead king would still be able to help his people after death. If, then, he had become as powerful as the pyramid spells tried to make him, then he might indeed be able to help them if he could be given some means of returning to earth. What above all did he need most, the one thing he had used in life but now no longer possessed in death? His body. If his *ba* could be attracted back into the pyramid to animate his mummy, and come into the sanctuary kept ready for him by his priests who were specially endowed for the purpose, what blessings would such a powerful being not be able to bestow upon the land of Egypt?

It must be admitted that there is no positive evidence in the texts that such a future was hoped for; indeed, the pyramid spells do not suggest it. On the other hand, the spells perhaps perform only one part of the process. Their purpose was to ensure the Pharaoh's power in the next world as an Osiris, a prerequisite for his assistance in this. If it were well known at the time that the pyramid would ensure the continued presence of the Pharaoh, there would be no need to stress it in the texts. If such a hypothesis is tenable, then all the other facts fit into place. The people of Egypt would not be building the pyramids to satisfy a megalomaniac desire on the part of their king to force his way into immortality by sheer physical force, as Breasted suggested, nor would it even be an act of gratitude on the part of the people for the lifetime deeds of a great king. On the contrary, it would be for their own benefit, to ensure that his power, immensely enhanced by his presence among the gods, would remain with them during the lives of his successors. Then the labor would be, as Moret suggests, an "act of faith" indeed, but also an act of faith that looked for a reward in the present life, with which the people of the Old Kingdom were so well satisfied. It would be comparable to the devotion of the medieval men who built the great French cathedrals by an enormous cooperative effort, and no more a reluctant and forced labor than theirs.[6]

### ASPECTS OF OLD KINGDOM CREATIVITY

#### Technical advances—Improvement in stoneworking, architecture, and sculpture

It has already been suggested that an extraordinary technical advance took place between the Third Dynasty pyramid of Zoser and the Great Pyramid of Khufu. This advance was not confined to technical accomplishment but found expression in all fields of Egyptian activity, and the people seem to have been aware of it. This period of less than a century seems to have been one of those rare, almost incredibly creative eras in the history of mankind comparable to fifth-century Athens. Unfortunately for Egypt, we do not possess the roster of great names, and few besides those of the Pharaohs are known to us. There is no accounting for these eras by noting the presence of certain determining factors; the historian can only suggest conditions favorable to them. The union of Upper and Lower Egypt was by now thoroughly accepted, the belief in the king-god protecting Egypt gave her people an unprecedented sense of security, foreign enemies gave them no trouble, and the frontiers could be maintained with a mimimum of effort, so that no standing armies were necessary; harvests were good, the bountiful land, aided by its beneficent river, gave three crops regularly every year—these no doubt were contributing factors. Responsible and creative leadership and patronage by the Pharaohs assured the artisan of a

[6] There are, of course, many other theories on the purpose of the pyramids, and the meaning of their symbolism. It is certain from the texts that the dead king did ascend from the pyramid to the sky, and there he was greeted by his divine colleagues. It is not known whether he returned to the pyramid after death, as other *ba*'s were believed to return in later times. It has been suggested that the pyramid is an enlarged version of the primeval hill on which the Creator-God stood when he made the world (H. Frankfort, *Kingship and the Gods* [Chicago: The University of Chicago Press, 1948], pp. 152–154), or that it was a simple copy of the solar symbol at Heliopolis (James H. Breasted, *Development of Religion and Thought in Ancient Egypt* [New York: Charles Scribner's Sons, 1912], p. 72). It used to be commonly held that the pyramid evolved naturally as a piece of funerary architecture from the earlier mastaba through the stepped pyramid to a true pyramid. For the whole problem see I. E. S. Edwards, *The Pyramids of Egypt* (Harmondsworth, Middlesex: Penguin Books, 1947), pp. 232–241. It may be added that Osiris at this period was also the god of the Nile and of vegetation. The ascent of the Pharaoh and his reception as an Osiris may therefore have been regarded by the Egyptians as a means of enlisting heavenly assistance for the inundation of the Nile and the growth of crops.

*Diorite statue of Khafre, with the Horus Falcon behind him. The statue depicts the Pharaoh with the majesty of a god and no sign of human failings. This statue should be contrasted with the statues of Middle Kingdom pharaohs which appear on the following pages.*

market for his output and his worship called forth the highest efforts of his skill.

But not even the combination of these things can account for the tremendous outburst of energy, discovery, and advance in all fields that characterizes this age. The engineering and technical advances have already been described. In Zoser's time the stepped pyramid was certainly built in stone, unlike the earlier mastabas of brick. But the stone was cut up into small blocks, which were laid as if they were bricks. The potentialities of stone itself as a material in its own right were not realized until this age. The sculptured figures of the earlier dynasties were cylindrical, giving place in the Pyramid Age to the cubic; sculpture in the round and relief sculpture came into their own. The familiar flat planes skillfully twisted, with head and shoulders in full frontal view while the rest of the body was in profile, belong to this period of experimentation. The art forms in the earlier dynasties were to a large degree conditioned by their material, and the Egyptians before the Fourth Dynasty

could not handle stone, though they were successful with ivory. Stone statues were merely massive. But the royal statues of Fourth Dynasty Khafre—whether in diorite or in softer stones—all alike give the desired impression of majesty as well as any in the whole period of Egyptian history. One statue, carved from diorite, a hard and difficult stone to work, was probably never equaled again for the monumental majesty it expresses and is the most reproduced of all Egyptian sculptures.

The relief carvings of this age show unbounded energy, life, and apparent optimism. The Egyptian is already preoccupied with death, but his death promises only, at this time, a fuller life. Harvest scenes, hunts, games, and festivals are abundant. The tomb scenes, so different from those of the New Kingdom, really show a denial of death and the future by projecting the present into the hereafter.[7] It may seem unfortunate to us that Egypt gained a high degree of artistic mastery so early in her history, since nearly all later Egyptian art consists of elaborations of these earlier art forms. To us, therefore, Egyptian art lacks variety. The early establishment of basic art forms is a phenomenon to be found elsewhere in the ancient world; for instance, some observers have

[7] One might be tempted to say that the Egyptian at no time ever *doubted* his immortality itself. He hoped it would be better than this life in the sense of being more abundant and full, but essentially unchanged. We should beware of reading into Egyptian thought the idea that immortality must be *won*. In the Old Kingdom nobles were buried with the Pharaoh so that they might continue to serve him afterward. But this was the established order of things and it was good. They could not be supposed to desire immortality as lonely individuals, not integrated into any social system, when they had never been individuals in this sense in life. Likewise the masses of the people, unable to conceive of life without their lords, could equally not conceive of death without them. The *kind* of immortality to be won became of the greatest importance in later Egypt when the old peaceful static order had disappeared and the kingship had decayed and belief in the god-king was shaking—when, as the Egyptian said, *Ma'at* was no longer in the land. Then personal immortality, without assistance from the king, and outside the disintegrating social order, naturally became more important, and mummification and proper burial rites were emphasized.

noted it in China. But it is nowhere so striking as in Egypt. There may be more exquisite workmanship in the Middle Kingdom, as there is certainly a more finished literature; but the same general standards and forms, once having been found and approved, persisted. They became, in Egyptian terms, part of "the right order of the world established from the beginning," and so not to be changed. Only the heretic Akhnaton set a new standard, but his reforms did not survive his dynasty.

It might be argued that in a static society presided over by a king-god, from whom all authority stemmed, there would be a social rigidity that would be hard to endure. But it does not seem that such a rigidity ever existed in the Old Kingdom. We possess several autobiographies of self-made men, some of them reading like modern success stories. Even a peasant could rise to high position if he showed ability. Where all were equal under the king, it was within his power to raise anyone by his favor, as Joseph in the Biblical story was raised out of prison to be the chief steward of the realm. We know of one Uni, keeper of a modest government storehouse, who rose to be Governor of Upper Egypt and ultimately—an even higher post—royal Tutor. An architect tells how the king's favor raised him from the position of a common builder to be Royal Constructor and Architect. Though giving due credit to the Pharaoh, he nevertheless implies that it was his own ability which was justly rewarded. Within the framework of this completely unquestioned Pharaonic government a man might strive for his own wealth and fortune and succeed. In the extant documents of this age, no gloomy fears and no doubts were voiced. There was, on the contrary, everywhere an air of bustle and achievement, as if the people knew they were living in a great age and gloried in it. The book of Instructions written by Ptah-hotep, a vizier in the Old Kingdom, gives clear advice to his son on how to get on in the world by striving for personal improvement—and explains the rules which must be kept. In his words "Ma'at is great and its appropriateness is lasting; it has not been disturbed since the time of him who made it, whereas there is punishment for him who passes over its law."[8] This was the eternal and unchanging social order within the framework of which a man should progress.[9]

### Religious speculation—The "Memphite Theology"

Another aspect of the special creativeness of the Pyramid Age is to be seen in the remarkable and original document commonly known as the Memphite Theology, which, though only known in a late copy, can be dated with certainty to the Old Kingdom. There is very little indeed in Egyptian religion that can be called speculative. As suggested earlier, the Egyptian was inclined to enrich his conceptions of the divine by the multiplication of symbols rather than by trying to understand the essential nature of divinity. He concentrated upon the multiplicity of divine manifestations rather than seeking to discover the underlying unity. But in the Memphite Theology the priestly writers really tried to come to grips with the problem of the nature of divinity as both cause and continuous effect. This account does not deny the other stories of creation, but goes much more deeply into the matter than do other extant Egyptian documents.

[8] J. B. Pritchard, ed., *Ancient Near Eastern Texts Relating to the Old Testament* (J. A. Wilson, tr.; Princeton, N. J.: Princeton University Press, 1950), p. 412. Extracts from this source are used by permission of Princeton University Press.

[9] Though all the teachings of Ptah-hotep and similar sages may be interpreted as simple advice on how to get on in the world, there can be little doubt that this interpretation does not exhaust their meaning. If this is all that they were, it would be hard to account for the great veneration in which they were held in later years. It would probably be more accurate to say that they were primarily useful as teachings concerning the established order, or *Ma'at*, and wherein it consisted. Hence their importance when *Ma'at* was no longer in the land, and it was the duty of teachers to try to restore it. On this point see, especially, Frankfort, *Ancient Egyptian Religion*, pp. 61–76.

Ptah, the Great One . . . gave birth to the gods. There came into being as the heart and there came into being as the tongue, something in the form of Atum. The mighty Great One is Ptah, who transmitted life to all gods. . . . Thus it happened that the heart and tongue gained control over every other member of the body, by teaching that he, Ptah (as heart and tongue), is in every body and in every mouth of all gods, all men, all cattle . . . by thinking and commanding everything that he wishes. . . .

Thus all the gods were formed . . . all the Divine Order really came into being through what the heart thought and the tongue commanded. . . . Thus were made all work and all crafts, the action of the arms, the movement of the legs, and the activity of every member, in conformance with this command which the heart thought, which came forth through the tongue, and which gives value to everything. . . . Thus it happened that it was said of Ptah: "He who made all and brought the gods into being."[10]

## Medicine and surgery

It is probable that the so-called Edwin Smith Surgical Papyrus, the finest Egyptian medical document, also describes medical knowledge from this period, although the document itself dates from the Middle Kingdom. In this papyrus there is a curious physiological parallel to the Memphite teaching about Ptah. Instead of the usual account of home remedies and herb lore which constitutes most Egyptian medical documents, this papyrus explains how the heart "speaks" in various parts of the body, and how the doctor may "measure for the heart" in these parts. Most of the treatise is concerned with how to set fractures, and which of them were curable. In the manner later used in the Greek Hippocratean corpus the writer denies demoniacal force, "the breath of some outside god," as the reason for partial paralysis as a result of some fractures. No later Egyptian medical document adopts such a scientific attitude.

10 Pritchard, *Ancient Near Eastern Texts*, p. 5.

## ► First Intermediate Period

DECLINE OF CENTRALIZED GOVERNMENT

It has already been remarked that the Fourth Dynasty pyramids are the largest, the most impressive, and the most solidly and accurately built of the pyramids. In the Fifth and Sixth Dynasties the pyramids are smaller, though the total pyramid complex reaches almost the same proportions, with more space devoted to the temple buildings than in the Fourth Dynasty. And the new pyramids possess the texts and spells which were presumably considered unnecessary by the Fourth Dynasty monarchs Khufu and Khefren. Was this already the beginning of a doubt? The realm was still prosperous, but it is usually suggested that its resources had been overtaxed by the immense labor expenditure and wastage of materials required for the pyramids, and even rich Egypt could not afford a pyramid for every king. At all events, during the long reign of Pepi II in the Sixth Dynasty, signs of decay began to appear, and suddenly after his death the Old Kingdom disintegrated.

The period that followed the collapse of the Old Kingdom used to be called the Feudal Age (Seventh to Eleventh Dynasties). It is now more usually given the name of the First Intermediate Period. There is no doubt that it possessed elements of feudalism in that the central government had broken down, and the nobles, for want of a better authority, usurped the local governments[11] and refused to recognize the weak kings of Memphis who exercised jurisdiction only over small areas. When the capital was transferred for two dynasties to the city in central Egypt called Heracleopolis by the Greeks, the kings of this city expanded their sway until it embraced more than half of Egypt. But the land as a whole was still disunited, and local nobles were still the

11 Traditionally Egypt had been divided into forty-two nomes or provinces.

effective rulers in most of the country. With the breakdown of the central government, foreigners from the north penetrated into Lower Egypt and the Delta lands, and settled there, although there is no indication of any armed invasions. The trouble was of internal origin, and seems to have been altogether due to the breakdown of the old way of life and the security that went with it.

The texts of this period are of special interest in that they reveal so clearly the characteristically Egyptian way of reacting to such troubles. In the first place there is no sign whatever of any revolutionary attempts by the common people to obtain any share in the government. It is true that all social values were overturned, that the poor man now lived where his master lived before. But he did not seem to like it. What he gained was nothing in comparison with the loss of his physical and psychological security, or, as he put it, the fact that "*ma'at* has disappeared from the land." The prophet Ipuwer said: "Why, really, the land spins round as does a potter's wheel . . . all maidservants make free with their tongues; when the mistresses speak it is burdensome to the servants . . . the children of nobles are dashed against the walls . . . noble ladies are gleaners, and nobles are in the workhouse. . . . He who never slept on a plank is now the owner of a bed. . . . Behold the owners of robes are now in rags . . . he who never wove for himself is now the owner of fine linen." A harpist sang: "The gods who lived formerly rested in their pyramids; the beatified dead also, buried in their pyramids, and they who built houses—their places are no more. Foreign trade has ceased." Ipuwer again said: "No one really sails north to Byblos today. What shall we do for cedar for our mummies . . . ? How important it now seems when the oasis people come carrying nuts and plants and birds." And it is all due to the absence of kingship. "Where is he today? Does he sleep perchance? Behold his might is not seen."[12]

[12] Pritchard, *Ancient Near Eastern Texts,* pp. 441–442, 467.

There was no voice of triumph arising from the people whose day might seem to have come. And though this conclusion may simply be due to our lack of records from this side, it does not seem likely. There was certainly no organized attempt on the part of the people to gain more rights, and there was certainly great rejoicing when Upper and Lower Egypt were once more united in the Middle Kingdom. But from what we know of the importance of order and stability to the Egyptian, from the way in which these values were re-established and endured after this period, and from the complete dependence upon this order in the Old Kingdom, it seems impossible to believe that this people, with its lack of individual self-reliance, could have relished the change.

For the nobles it was a different matter. The great change for them was that they now appropriated for themselves the rituals and ceremonies hitherto reserved only for the king. The pyramid texts are now to be found, substantially unchanged, within the coffins of the nobles. They used the same spells and looked forward to the same future. Commoners who had the wealth also sought similar privileges. From this time onward their own life in the afterworld was ensured by their own funerary ceremonies, and this age marked the beginning of that extraordinary preoccupation with death that we associate with Egypt, and that attained its fullest expression in the relatively late New Kingdom compilation of spells that constitutes the Book of the Dead, and the ascendancy of the priesthood that resulted from that preoccupation. Egypt would never be quite the same carefree land again. Anxiety had entered into Egyptian psychology for the first time.

### DAWN OF THE IDEA OF SOCIAL JUSTICE FOR ALL

But there is another side to this tale of the disintegration of old values. The loss of *Ma'at* is the responsibility of the Pharaoh, as it is his duty to restore it. Ipuwer, a commoner, stands up to the great Pharaoh himself and accuses him of misrule, and the

Pharaoh apologizes and excuses himself, almost humbly. "Authority, perception and *Ma'at* are with thee," Ipuwer tells him, "but it is confusion thou wouldst set throughout the land together with the noise of contention."[13] And the Pharaoh answers that he had tried to protect the people but failed for lack of resources. One Pharaoh confesses to his son: "Behold, a misfortune happened in my time; the Thinite regions were hacked up. It really happened through what I had done, and I knew of it only after it was done." The king is no longer infallible and conscious of his relationship with the gods.

From this period also comes the famous Tale of the Eloquent Peasant, in which the peasant, despoiled of his goods by trickery, makes appeal to the king's steward for restitution, reminding him that he is the custodian of *Ma'at,* and it is his duty to see that justice is done, even to a poor peasant. *Ma'at,* from being merely "right order," has now become justice, for the poor man as well as for the rich. Though, of course, the earlier conception of *Ma'at* had included justice of this kind, it is not until the Intermediate Period that it is emphasized and insisted on from the point of view of the poor man who needs it. Under the earlier administration the king-god "listened to it with his heart," and spoke it forth in infallible pronouncements, and we hear nothing of the *right* of anyone else to receive it.

FIRST IDEA OF A "LAST JUDGMENT"

Finally we have the first suggestion of a judgment after death. Re, the sun-god, will "count up character" and "weigh *Ma'at.*" He will see whether a man has lived in accordance with the right order of the universe. If so, that man will then be permitted to dwell in the Field of Rushes, or go round the earth in the boat of the sun-god or in some other way become integrated with the life of nature and the universe.

A word is necessary here on the difference between the Egyptian conception of wrongdoing and the Hebrew idea of sin, a

distinction also important in our study of Mesopotamia. Sin, as moral misdeed, is a distinctive Hebrew and late Oriental idea and is not to be found in Egypt, as far as we can tell from studying the texts as they are written. Translations which use the words "evil" and "sin" are as misleading when they deal with Egyptian thinking as they are in Greek thought. Evil to the Egyptian seems to have been a failure to integrate himself with the harmonious workings of the universe. Like the Greek, he could lack restraint and so bring misfortune upon himself; or he could lack understanding, and thus make foolish mistakes which would draw down upon him the anger of the gods. As Ptah-hotep says: "It is the heart that makes the owner into one that hears or one that hears not. His heart is a man's fortune. . . . As for a fool that hears not he can do nothing at all. He regards knowledge as ignorance and good as bad. He lives on that of which one dies; his food is untruth."[14]

So at all stages of Egyptian history it is disharmony that is the only evil; and to be out of harmony with the universe is a long way from the Hebrew or Christian conception of sin and moral evil.[15] But at least the relationship between a man's deeds on earth and a happy life in the next world is suggested at this period. This, to our way of thinking, is a distinct moral advance. The idea of a divine sanction for human misdeeds was, of course, to bear fruit in the later thinking of the Hebrews and Christians. When we bear in mind that the greatest hope of the Egyptian was to be permitted after death to join the stars or circle the earth with the sun-god, and when we think also that harmony with the divine order was the only true moral good for the Egyptian, then it is perceived that the Egyptian concep-

---

[13] *Ibid.,* p. 443.

[14] *Ibid.,* p. 414 (abbreviated).

[15] The Greek idea of *Hybris,* discussed in the Greek section below, is closer to Egyptian thought than it is to Hebrew or Christian. It was primarily an error of judgment, in that man, through his excessive prosperity, came to believe it was his own doing, thus misunderstanding and underestimating what he owed to the gods.

tion possesses an inner logic. An understanding of this point will help also to show why the famous Declaration of Innocence or Negative Confession, so often quoted as evidence of Egyptian moral thinking, should not be taken as seriously as it has been by writers permeated by the Hebrew and Christian tradition of sin and punishment.[16]

## ▶  The Middle Kingdom

RESTORATION OF THE DIVINE ORDER OF SOCIETY
(*Ma'at*)

The First Intermediate Period was brought to an end by the conquest of the whole of Egypt, presumably largely by force of arms, by princes of Thebes in the Eleventh Dynasty; hence Thebes, hitherto an unimportant provincial town, now became the capital of the Two Lands. War, however, was resumed after the death of Eleventh Dynasty Mentu-hotep, and the real founder of the Middle Kingdom was Amenemhet I, who had been a vizier under his predecessor.

THE COMING OF AGE OF EGYPTIAN CIVILIZATION

### Mature idea of social justice

In many ways the Middle Kingdom was the period of Egypt's maturity. The divine monarchy was re-established, but all the lessons of this Intermediate Period had not been lost. We now hear of the king as the good shepherd of the people. He himself is now aware of his responsibilities even more than before. Amenemhet claims: "I gave to the destitute and brought up the orphan. I caused him who was nothing to reach his goal, like him who was somebody." It has frequently been pointed out in what a marked manner the portrait statues of these Middle Kingdom monarchs differ from the serene majesty of those of the Old Kingdom. We learn from the records about much of the unceasing activity on behalf of the people, the renewal of foreign trade and the cultural rather than military imperialism, of these Pharaohs—

[16] See below, Chapter 5.

treaties made, records kept of the height of the Nile and its approach, even as high up the river as the Second Cataract. They adopted a strong frontier policy to the south against the penetration of the Nubians and erected fortresses. The conditions of the Old Kingdom seemed to have been restored. The documents of the time all show a renewed dependence upon the king-god. His favor was required for advancement and the people were happy and contented. For a while these Pharaohs even built pyramids again, though never of such size and magnificence as those of the Old Kingdom. Perhaps the Pharaohs themselves now thought of them as an anachronism; if they knew of the original purpose of the pyramids, this purpose had patently not been fulfilled during the period of anarchy. They and their successors quietly turned to elaborate funeral rites and tombs, more sumptuous and magnificent than those of nobles or commoners as befitted their rank, but still of the same kind, and not unique, like the great pyramids.

*Head of Amenemhet III (Middle Kingdom). Note the more humanized features as contrasted with the statue of Old Kingdom Khafre.* (COURTESY THE METROPOLITAN MUSEUM OF ART)

*Granite statue of Senusert III (Middle Kingdom), showing careworn features of the monarch.* (COURTESY THE METROPOLITAN MUSEUM OF ART)

The Middle Kingdom was a beneficent despotism. It re-established ownership of all the land by the king; but the people within this framework seem to have had their rights more fully maintained. Peasant cultivators did not need to fear eviction from their lands or other arbitrary acts. The way of the scribe was a way that offered advancement to anyone who cared to learn, for once a scribe he could become a government official. The highest officials in the Old Kingdom had usually been members of the royal family; in the Middle Kingdom they were bureaucrats who had reached their position through merit.

### "Democratization of the hereafter," equal rights in the next world

But, probably even more important for the Egyptian, his rights in the next world were equalized. All classes of society from Pharaohs to peasants are found in the great Middle Kingdom necropolis of Abydos, though, of course, the wealthy and the notables can afford more elaborate funerals. This naturally meant the increase of the influence of the priesthood, even though it never attained at this time, as far as we know, any power to dictate to the king, as it did in late New Kingdom days. Amon, originally the special god of Thebes, was eminently fitted to become the supreme god of Egypt. His name meant "the Hidden One"; he was formless and invisible, immanent everywhere. With such a scope it was possible to graft him onto all other gods. In his form of Amon-Re, king of the gods, he became later the great imperial god of the Empire. As breath and wind he was the source of all life in man or beast. "He is too mysterious for his glory to be revealed, too great for questions to be asked of him, too powerful to be known. . . . One hears his voice but he is not seen, while he lets all throats

*Model of a Middle Kingdom weaving shop. Such models are often found in graves of Egyptian manufacturers.* (COURTESY THE METROPOLITAN MUSEUM OF ART)

breathe." While there is doubtless a considerable element of political and religious imperialism in his rise to be god of all, and without the rise of Thebes he would never have received such a promotion, it is theologically sound that it should be he and no other, and perhaps helps to explain the continued allegiance of the people to him even under the heretical Pharaoh Akhnaton.

Since the Pharaoh had ceased to be the sole user of funerary equipment and his subjects now sought to fill their tombs with as much magnificence as they could afford, the market for such objects naturally increased. And it was not unnatural that the high standards set for such materials in the Old Kingdom could no longer be maintained. The craftsmen still produced exquisite objects especially for the kings and rich nobles and they were greatly assisted by the new use of bronze, but it was no longer possible to devote so much time to their work as had their predecessors in the Old Kingdom, and the temple reliefs are never superior to, and

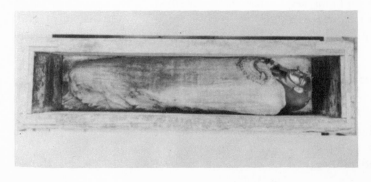

*Mummy of an Egyptian minister (Middle Kingdom).* (COURTESY THE METROPOLITAN MUSEUM OF ART)

were frequently less conscientiously executed than, those of earlier times. There was no experimentation with new forms except insofar as the temple replaced the pyramid. It seems that the Egyptians were living on their heritage rather than trying to make progress toward new forms and experimenting creatively as in the great age of Khufu and Khefren. As has already been suggested, change was never looked upon as natural or desirable, but as a departure from the harmony of the established universe. But in the Middle Kingdom this idea had not yet become a dogma. There was as yet no conscious archaism as in the declining years of the civilization.

## SECOND INTERMEDIATE PERIOD—CONQUEST BY THE HYKSOS

We know little of the last Pharaohs of the Middle Kingdom, but we can guess that the administration suffered from some complacency, as at most periods of prosperity. For it is clear from what happened that there must have been considerable laxity in the guarding of at least the northern frontiers. The Egyptians were always contemptuous of foreigners, and their dogma of the divine king bestowed only on Egypt supported their attitude. The "wretched Asiatic" was plagued with rain and storms, they said, unlike the favored land of Egypt, where everything was as it should be. It was all right to trade with barbarians, because Egypt could use their products; but it must always be remembered that Egypt was the one land protected by the gods, and all other peoples were naturally subject to it. Other countries, however, could not be expected to accept this viewpoint, and while Egypt was standing still the peoples to the north were making progress. They were no longer so small and disorganized as they had been in the old days. They had begun to use the horse and chariot, and had made other military improvements unknown to the Egyptians. And at the end of the long-lived Twelfth Dynasty there were signs that there were internal troubles in Egypt and disputed successions.

It has already been mentioned that even

*Necklace of drop beads of gold, carnelian, lapis lazuli, and green feldspar. This necklace belonged to an Egyptian princess of the Middle Kingdom.* (COURTESY THE METROPOLITAN MUSEUM OF ART)

before the Middle Kingdom foreigners had infiltrated into the Delta lands. But now it seems that there were more organized expeditions, and the Egyptians were at last forced to take notice of them. Various documents "cursing" foreign enemies are extant from the late Middle Kingdom. So when there was internal trouble in Egypt and the foreign people called the Hyksos pressed in on the land from the north, they apparently met less resistance, and were in sufficient numbers not to become absorbed easily and at once into the superior Egyptian culture.[17]

[17] No certain antecedents are known for the people called the Hyksos. Late tradition called them "Shepherd-Kings," but they were more probably sea peoples and not people of the desert. The Egyptians called them merely *"hikau khasut*—rulers of foreign countries," the corruption of which into "Hyksos" is evident.

The Hyksos, invading from the north with horse and chariot, first subdued Lower Egypt and built fortresses to keep it in subjection; then they gradually pushed south. Probably they never occupied the whole

*Obelisk of Thutmose III (New Kingdom) found at Heliopolis and transported to Central Park, New York, where it still stands.* (COURTESY THE METROPOLITAN MUSEUM OF ART)

of Upper and Lower Egypt, though they did establish their leaders as Pharaohs, and the Fourteenth to Seventeenth Dynasties are credited to them. The native Egyptians always regarded them with abhorrence as barbarians "ruling without Re," and their national pride was deeply wounded. But the remains from this period do not show them in quite the same light as their victims regarded them. At least they used the Egyptian language and adopted Egyptian names and customs. But the Egyptians never accepted them, and gradually beyond the reach of their power the more defiant among the Egyptians learned to use their weapons and military technique against them. Again a prince of Thebes, who had been permitted some degree of independence, led the war of liberation, and his successor Ahmose I drove their remnants out of Egypt and founded the great Eighteenth Dynasty.

## ▶ The New Kingdom—Period of expansion

IMPERIALISM

### The conquests

The first task of the new dynasty was the restoration of internal security. The expulsion of the Hyksos by princes of Thebes was a clear sign that Amon-Re was the chief of gods and these princes were his colleagues. So in the so-called New Kingdom the dogma of the king-god was reinforced more strongly than ever, though we suspect it needed centuries of success to make much impression on the people. All the old rituals were re-established. With the accession of imperial wealth from trading expeditions and conquests, these ceremonies could be and were more magnificent than ever. But this is also the age of the Book of the Dead, and of the great *fear* of the afterlife. Gone is the old security and isolationism, gone is the certainty of Egyptian superiority over all other peoples and cultures. Now Egypt's power rests at least as much on the sword as on divine right, and the king-god's position is dependent primarily upon his suc-

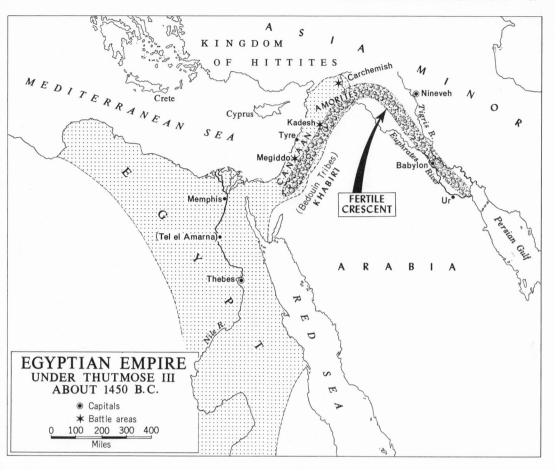

EGYPTIAN EMPIRE
UNDER THUTMOSE III
ABOUT 1450 B.C.

◉ Capitals
✶ Battle areas

0    100   200   300   400
Miles

cess. Not all the magnificent temples of Thutmose III and his successors nor the great tombs of their nobles can conceal the evidence of internal decay. And the kingship had a competitor, potentially as strong as itself, in the priesthood of Amon.

Thutmose III was certainly a successful imperialist. In a series of victorious campaigns he penetrated as far as the Euphrates, pacifying Syria and maintaining it as a tributary province under his own governor, and breaking up at Megiddo the coalition of Asiatic peoples which was the only serious threat to Egypt. After the initial conquests he thoroughly reorganized his army on a professional basis and established military posts throughout the empire. At the first sign of rebellion he would send a lightning raid against the rebels with unvarying success. His power of retaliation was so greatly feared that ridiculously small garrisons were suffi-

cient to keep prosperous cities in check and ensure the payment of the tribute, upon which the economy of Egypt was henceforth to be based. Thutmose III must indeed have seemed like an invincible god not only to his own people but to those far beyond the borders of Egypt.

## Consequences of the conquests

*Social cleavage between rich and poor— foreign slaves*—The results of these conquests were momentous for Egyptian society. There could be no returning to the old cultural isolationism. As in the later Roman Empire, the Egyptians, like the Romans, preferred to avoid the hardships of army life, and the less civilized Asiatic peoples took their place. Asiatics rose to high position not only in the army but in the state. Foreign cultures, though less advanced than the Egyptian, nevertheless

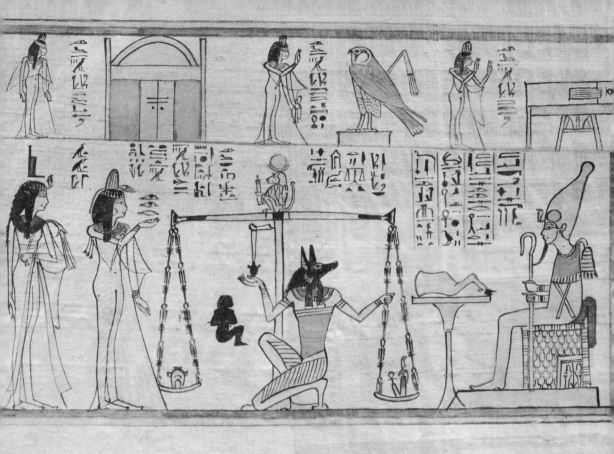

*Funerary papyrus of an Egyptian princess of the XXIst Dynasty. The heart of the deceased is shown being weighed in the scales before the god Osiris. On the opposite side of the scale are the symbols for truth and life. The god Anubis performs the weighing ceremony.* (COURTESY THE METROPOLITAN MUSEUM OF ART)

made their influence felt, especially in the vulgarization of the old austere tradition. Foreign slaves, prisoners of war, became an essential part of the economy, and many of these, as in Rome, held positions superior to those of poor native peasants. But the latter, unlike the Roman proletariat, had no political rights, and were dependent upon the divine justice of the Pharaoh, who became clothed in an even greater majesty than before. The enormous public buildings of the Eighteenth and Nineteenth Dynasties were now in fact, as Herodotus believed they always had been, built by forced slave labor, driven by overseers. And even native Egyptians lost their freedom for various reasons, and were forced to work on these projects. The conditions described in the Book of Exodus were those of the New Kingdom.

A great cleavage became noticeable be-tween rich and poor. Theoretically the Pharaohs continued to dispense impartial justice, and the country as a whole was wealthy. But this influx of wealth did not apparently penetrate down to the masses, who had lost their security but gained nothing comparable in return. Most of the land now in actuality as well as in theory belonged to the Pharaoh, who farmed it as his own estate, with the peasants as his serfs, or foreign slaves, working them. And again the result is to be seen in an increasing hope for a better future life, and its accompaniment—the fear of death and the unknown.

*Religions—Rise of religious imperialism and early monotheism—Influence of the priesthood—The Book of the Dead*—The priesthood gained from the empire in two directions. On the one hand the Pharaoh appears now less as an infallible and ever-successful god in his own right than as a nominee of the gods, supported by Amon-Re but definitely subordinate to him. Amon-Re gives him his victories, Amon-Re dictates to him when to go to war and "lends him his sword," and in return the rewards of empire also go to Amon-Re. Extensive lands and all other forms of wealth are given to the priesthood on behalf of Amon, thus laying the foundation for its extraordinary wealth which it retained long after the decline of the empire. And from the opposite side we see the people more and more dependent upon the priesthood for their one hope of a blessed hereafter, and enriching it by purchasing spells and funeral services. The next world is no longer a beautiful repetition of life on earth, for life on earth is no longer so delightful to them. In the Book of the Dead, the great collection of spells and information concerning the next world, which no doubt incorporates beliefs already thousands of years old, we are given the final Egyptian thought on the nature of the hereafter, and we can see all the gross superstition that had been allowed to grow up—the means of cheating Osiris, the god of the netherworld, the means for overcoming all the monsters set in the path of the dead man. The originally austere Osirian religion, now the one hope of the masses, has itself become vulgarized. The trials and dangers of the dead man lost all dignity in this atmosphere, calm and beautiful though some of the descriptions remain. One of these trials was the passing before the forty-two judges, and the Declaration of Innocence, the weighing of the heart against *Ma'at*, which by this time had become the regular symbol for truth. Other trials of perhaps equal importance in this journey of the dead man were the encounters with monsters armed with knives, and with bullying porters and ferrymen; and his fear that he might forget his name, or that he might have to walk upside down, or eat dirt, or be forced to work.[18] All such ene-

mies could be overcome by possessing the right spells written on a piece of papyrus, by having access to the right magic; and it was only the priests who could provide these.

## THE RELIGIOUS AND POLITICAL REVOLUTION OF AKHNATON

### The new "teaching"—Supremacy of Aton, the sun-disk—Artistic naturalism

So the ground was laid for the revolt of the Pharaoh Akhnaton, who preached a new and purified religion, who defeated the priesthood for the duration of his reign, but whose work, un-Egyptian as it was in many respects, and necessarily unpopular, could not endure. In the reign of his father, Amenhotep III, the civilization of the New Kingdom reached its height, and betrayed at the same time its innate weaknesses. The reign of Amen-hotep III was long, and the nobles and upper classes enjoyed many years of peace and prosperity. Like his predecessors, he built many imposing monuments, including the two great colossi which even in Roman days used to sound forth at the rising of the sun and attracted the curiosity and interest of Roman tourists. He gave costly gifts to foreigners, and he made an important marriage alliance with an Asiatic princess; he built immense temples at Karnak and Luxor. But toward the end of his reign he was faced with a rebellion in Syria, and Semitic nomads began to enter Palestine without hindrance. When he died all Palestine was in revolt, and appeals from the Egyptian governors had already begun to pour in upon the capital. But Akhnaton, when he succeeded to the throne, paid very little attention to his empire. His interests were concentrated elsewhere.

Egyptian culture and religion had already been greatly affected by the new imperial and international contacts. From the time of Thutmose III there had been a tendency to make Amon-Re no longer the exclusive god of Egypt but a god of the whole world. No doubt this was a form of religious

---

[18] On this point see especially Frankfort, *Ancient Egyptian Religion*, pp. 118–119.

imperialism on the part of the Pharaoh and his god Amon.[19] But there was also a tendency in the opposite direction to equate the native Egyptian gods with foreign gods found in the empire. Egyptian governors even erected temples to these under their foreign and Egyptian names. And for at least forty years before Akhnaton a hitherto unknown god, Aton, the disk of the sun, had been accorded worship. The Aton had fought on the side of Thutmose iv "to make the foreigners to be like the Egyptian people, in order to serve the Aton for ever." This Aton was now to become the center of a religious and political revolution unique in Egyptian history.

The new Pharaoh seems to have acted as co-regent during the last years of his father before coming to the throne as Amenhotep iv, and he had already built temples to the god Amon. Then suddenly he announced a new revelation, called himself Akhnaton—"He who is serviceable to the Aton"—and proposed to build himself a new capital, Akhetaton—"The place of the effec-

[19] In one document Amon is greeted with these words: "Jubilation to thee from every foreign country, to the heights of heaven, to the width of earth, to the depth of the great green sea."—Quoted by Wilson, *The Burden of Egypt,* p. 211.

tive glory of the Aton" (now known as Tel-el-Amarna). We do not know the immediate reasons for this break, but no doubt the political and religious were closely intermingled. As Pharaoh, Akhnaton was a divine king and was entitled to receive a revelation. This the priests of Amon, whatever they may have thought privately about the divinity of the king, could not publicly deny. He must have realized the political and economic strangle hold of the priesthood of Amon on the resources of Egypt, and at the same time the gross superstitions of the Osirian cult of the dead. At all events he tried with all his power to overthrow both these religions and substitute the far purer worship of the Aton, the sun-disk, usually represented in Egyptian art as holding outstretched hands over the land of Egypt. It is a measure of the extraordinary power that a Pharaoh still exercised that he was able to accomplish this revolution apparently without bloodshed or armed protest. He was able to retire to his new capital and supervise its building without hindrance for many years, even though his empire itself and its sources of income were disintegrating through his neglect.

There will always be something appealing about this piece of "modernism," and in

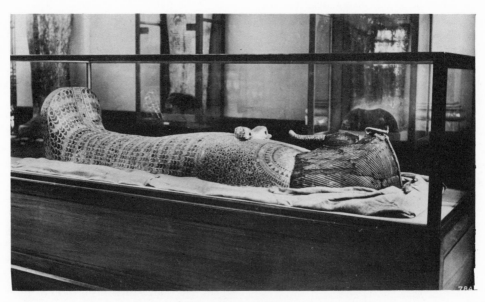

*Gold coffin of Akhnaton.*

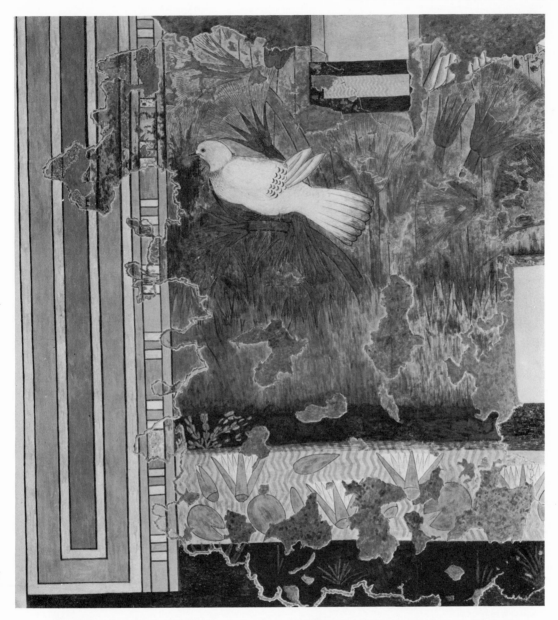

*Copy of an original painting from the time of Akhnaton. Note the fresh naturalism of the bird and plants typical of this period.* (COURTESY THE METROPOLITAN MUSEUM OF ART)

our day we may prefer the extreme naturalism and vivacity of the art forms of the new movement above the static splendor of traditional religious art. The hymns to the Aton, who never seems to have been anything beyond the solar disk in all its splendor and simplicity giving life, as it does, to all creatures on the earth, are usually considered by modern taste as the most beautiful poems in Egyptian literature. Yet what a supreme certainty Akhnaton must have had in his revelation and his belief in his chosen mission that he should have attempted to overthrow the faith of almost all his people, and substitute, not a truly monotheistic ethical religion, but a kind of intellectual nature

*The Pharaoh Akhnaton worshiping. Note how he himself offers worship to the sun god Aton, whose rays enfold him, while his family, at a lower eminence, appear to be worshiping the Pharaoh rather than Aton.* (COURTESY CAIRO MUSEUM)

worship. And the supremacy of the Aton by no means diminished his own position as god-king. On the contrary, the Aton was his own personal father, only to be worshiped by himself and his own immediate family. For all others the only approach to the Aton was through himself. His title always included the words "the good god." The scenes in the tombs of the new city all show him serving the living sun-disk, while his courtiers bow in adoration before their Pharaoh, to whom they pray in such words as these:

"May I continue in the service of the good god (Akhnaton) until he assigns to me the burial that he gives. Let him remain here until the swan turns black, until the raven turns white, until the mountains stand up to walk, until the sea runs up the river." Another courtier prays that he may "hear thy sweet voice in the sanctuary when thou performest that which pleases thy father, the living Aton." And in one hymn Akhnaton himself says to the Aton: "Thou art in my heart and there is no other knows thee except thy son (Akhnaton) whom thou hast initiated into thy plans and into thy power."[20]

All this, however, did not mean that the Pharaoh held himself in austere seclusion from his people. Though he made a vow that he would never leave his new city, and those who came to live there and built it were his own followers and owed their positions to his favor, he and his sister-wife showed themselves continuously to the workers, driving through the rising city in their chariot, with their daughters around them, showing their affection publicly—all in the highest possible degree repugnant to Egyptian tradition. His religion was naturalistic (in accordance with *truth*, if the *Ma'at* of Akhnaton can bear this meaning) as Amarna art is also naturalistic—both apparently foreign to Egyptian feeling and filling no great need in their lives. This is evidenced by the speed with which it was overthrown, and the failure in nearly another thousand years of history to revert to anything similar. The naturalistic art left its imprint upon later Egyptian art, it is true. But it was quietly absorbed as Egyptian artists returned to their old well-tried forms; later art was all

[20] Quoted by Wilson, *op. cit.*, pp. 223–224.

slightly changed, a little more naturalistic than it probably would have become without the inspiration of the new revelation and the new city.

### Persecution of the priesthood of Amon— Lack of popular support

But, however much we may sympathize with the reformer, it cannot be denied that the new religion offered to the Egyptian people even less than the religion of Amon and Osiris. If it were true, if Akhnaton had really received a new revelation of *Ma'at*, if the truth were as he declared it to be, then all the preparations they had made for the next world, all their hopes, were doomed; and everything they and their ancestors had spent was wasted. And, even theologically, it cannot be asserted categorically that the monotheism of Akhnaton was necessarily superior to contemporary polytheism. As suggested earlier, it depends on the way in which the many gods are accepted and viewed by the worshiper. And Amon was not just one imperial god among many; as Amon-Re he was immanent in all nature and the whole universe. The Aton could be incorporated into the pantheon of the Egyptian

*Relief sculpture of the period of Akhnaton. Note the naturalism of the horse, and the strained appearance of the workers—unlike the usual conventional pose depicted in most Egyptian reliefs.* (COURTESY THE METROPOLITAN MUSEUM OF ART)

gods where there was room for him, for the sun-disk undoubtedly represents one manifestation of Amon-Re. But Akhnaton denied all other gods but the Aton, and this meant the abandonment of the whole manner of worship of the Egyptians. It is not surprising, then, that only a few intellectuals and courtiers could be found to support the Pharaoh. Only if there had been a deep ethical content in this religion—and no such ethical content is discernible in any of the extant writings—could it have sufficed to take the place of the comfortable secure world of Egyptian polytheism—and the whole story of the Old Testament is a commentary on the difficulties facing the reformer who wishes to introduce an ethical monotheism into such a world. If Egyptian polytheism had not been so decadent under the New Kingdom, even such a single-minded autocrat as Akhnaton would hardly have felt the necessity of trying to destroy it.[21]

### Restoration of Amon—Strengthened hold of priesthood

Probably political reasons primarily caused the downfall of the new religion. Though the army under Horemhab was still favorable to the Pharaoh and antagonistic to his priestly enemies, the whole monarchy had lost prestige from its failure to support the army in Syria. But there is evidence to show that a younger brother of Akhnaton returned to Thebes before the end of his reign, and Queen Nefertiti seems to have fallen into disfavor. Perhaps the Pharaoh realized that the power of the priesthood of Amon was too strong to break. At all events we know that his successor Tutankhamon,

[21] It has sometimes been urged that Moses knew of the Akhnaton "monotheistic" worship. But not only had it died out as an official religion long before the earliest acceptable date for Moses' birth, but it is the ethical content of the Hebrew religion that is paramount and this could not have been gained from Akhnaton. The verbal similarity between some of the Psalms and the hymns of Akhnaton, which probably shows borrowing, reveals no connection with Akhnaton. The nature hymns were not exclusive to Aton and could well have remained part of Egyptian literature. For a fuller treatment of this problem, see Wilson, op. cit., pp. 224–228.

who had at first been a devotee of the new religion and had married a daughter of Akhnaton, made a full submission when he himself became Pharaoh. In restoring the worship of Amon he says: "The temples of the gods and goddesses . . . had gone to pieces. Their shrines had become desolate, and had become overgrown mounds . . . . The land was topsy-turvy and the gods had turned their backs upon this land. . . . If one prayed to a god to seek counsel from him, he would never come. If one made supplication to a goddess similarly she would never come at all. Their very hearts were hurt, so that they destroyed that which had been made." So Tutankhamon "expelled deceit throughout the Two Lands and Ma'at was set up, and lying was made an abomination as in its first time."[22]

The revolution was over. The Pharaoh had been exhibited as one who had no longer the right to receive revelations and to decree Ma'at. He had become only the interpreter of the will of the gods, the head of the state, but to be guided by the priests. He had become almost what the kings in Mesopotamia had always been. And although he remained in appearance king-god, and the same age-old ceremonies were carried on throughout the rest of Egyptian history as if he had been a god, he had become a prisoner of the priests, except insofar as his power rested in his command of the army like any other absolute ruler. It was no accident that the restorer of order after the revolution was the army general Horemhab, and that he was recognized by the priesthood as the first legitimate Pharaoh since Amen-hotep III.

### ▶ The New Kingdom—Period of decline

PARTIAL RESTORATION OF EMPIRE UNDER HOREMHAB AND EARLY RAMESES PHARAOHS

The rest of Egyptian history is soon told. Horemhab restored internal order in the country and all vestige of the revolution was destroyed. The Nineteenth Dynasty

[22] Quoted by Wilson, op. cit., p. 216.

*The immense temple of Amon at Karnak was built over many years by pharaohs from the XVIIIth Dynasty to almost the end of Egyptian independence. Sometimes parts of the structure were used as a reservoir of building materials for others. The imposing entrance (above), with its avenue of sphinxes, was built by Rameses II; the lower picture shows part of the temple court, with the statues of the gods, built by Rameses III. The whole temple complex is in the process of being restored by the Service des Antiquités and the Egyptian government.*

undertook to restore the empire and was partially successful. The smaller empire continued to pay enough taxes to Egypt to enable Rameses II to sustain the enormous building program, the results of which are so evident today to any visitor to Egypt.[23]

## HUGE BUILDINGS OF KARNAK AND LUXOR

His buildings at Karnak and Luxor are large and impressive, colossal in size, and still today overpowering to the visitor. But he built too quickly, and his craftsmen were no longer what they had been in the past. The foundations of the magnificent buildings were too often only rubble, suggesting the commercial contractor rather than the conscientious religious builder. He built a new capital at Tanis in the Delta which was renamed Rameses and no doubt inspired the Biblical tradition of the forced labor of the exiled Children of Israel. In the lifetime of Rameses II there was peace, but new and distant tribes of peoples were beginning

[23] A theory has recently been put forward by the late Alexandre Varille and others in France which is exciting great interest and some bitter controversy, especially in French archaeological circles. He has produced some evidence, and a closely knit theory based on observation and examination of the temples themselves, to the effect that the temples of Rameses and other late monumental structures have deliberately used materials from those of their predecessors for astronomical reasons. Into the temples had been built all the secret knowledge of the universe possessed by the Egyptian priests; they were not built casually to symbolize power and magnificence. As the heavens changed in the course of time, so new temples were required which would continue to be true pictures of the heavens in stone. Especially the highest parts of the old temples, representing the future movements of the heavens, were now the present, and so could be incorporated into the new temple, so that it would always be an accurate representation of the heavens. Even the old materials were used as the foundation out of which the new picture of the heavens could grow.

If such is ever shown to be the case it will mean at least that true astronomical secrets were still known to the Egyptian priesthood of the time of Rameses, and of course it will dispose of the modern theory that the older temples were despoiled to glorify the new temples and their creators.

For the present state of the controversy, and bibliography, see A. Rousseaux, "La Querelle des égyptologues," *Mercure de France*, July, 1951, pp. 418–439.

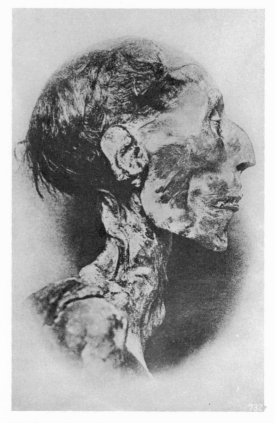

*Head of Pharaoh Rameses II from his extant mummy. Rameses died at an advanced age after more than sixty years on the throne.*

their onslaughts into Asia Minor and Syria. Rameses III of the Twentieth Dynasty won the last great victory of Egypt in Palestine.

## FOREIGN CONQUEST BY ETHIOPIANS, ASSYRIANS, PERSIANS

Thereafter the Pharaohs were content to retire within their own boundaries. There are indications of temporary interruptions in the kingship, and even usurpations by foreign officials. Later there was widespread anarchy, followed by invasions from the south by Ethiopians who took over the monarchy and called themselves Pharaohs and divine. It was only a question of time before the still rich but slowly disintegrating Egypt would fall prey to the rising empire of the invincible Assyrians. Esarhaddon of Assyria conquered Egypt in 670 B.C., but a few years later, with the aid of Greek mercenaries, she recovered her independence. There was a brief renewal of life for a century, and she feebly tried to intrigue in Palestine, incidentally serving, by her alliance with the kingdom of Judah, to bring down the armies of Babylon upon Jerusalem. With the conquest by the Persian Cambyses in 525 B.C. her independence was over for almost twenty-five hundred years until our own twentieth century A.D. As Ezekiel had prophesied, "there shall be no more a prince of the land of Egypt.[24]

GRADUAL SENESCENCE OF EGYPTIAN
CIVILIZATION—ANTIQUARIANISM

It was inevitable that the decline of national spirit should be reflected in all aspects of Egyptian life. Even up to the time of Rameses II, though there had been more fear and less emphasis on the joyous nature of the hereafter during the empire than in earlier days, there had been at least some emphasis on the continuance of the excellent life known on earth. But with the Twentieth Dynasty a great change is visible. Death suddenly became a welcome release. Autobiographies of the owners of the tombs, characteristic of earlier times, disappeared almost entirely. Their place is taken by hymns, rituals, and ever longer magical and religious texts used for protection against the dangers and terrors of the afterlife. There is an emphasis on humility and piety, and there are even confessions of inadequacy, closely resembling our Judaeo-Christian conception of sin, and mercy is sought from the gods: "Come to me, thou who protectest millions, and rescuest hundreds of thousands, the protector of the one who cries out to him."

There is an extraordinary return to the old documents of their ancestors as if these had known a truth hidden from themselves. Many of the important documents of the Old Kingdom are known to us only from copies made in the last centuries of Egyptian independence. There is apparent a gradual fossilization into the set forms described by Herodotus, including even the mummifica-

[24] Ezekiel 30:13.

tion of animals, which had never in earlier times been actually worshiped.[25] The *power* in animals, their changeless part in the cosmic scheme was no doubt what made the Egyptians revere them and use the animals as symbols of some power associated with them. But in these last days the form was retained without the living substance of their religion. As Herodotus succinctly puts it, "They keep the ordinances of their fathers and add none others to them."

[25] Herodotus, Plutarch, and other Greeks were misled by Egyptian animal worship into believing that the Egyptians thought that human souls passed after death into animals. This idea, however, is certainly incorrect.

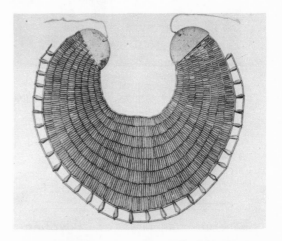

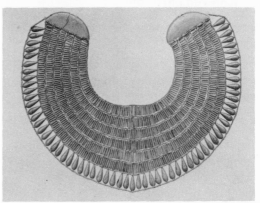

*Two collars of beads. The one at the top dates from the XIth Dynasty, the one at the bottom from the XVIIIth. More than seven hundred years separate these two collars, yet the design is the same, suggesting something of Egyptian conservatism.* (COURTESY THE METROPOLITAN MUSEUM OF ART)

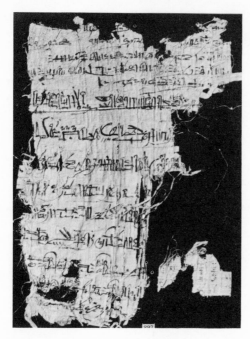

*At the left is a fragment of an Egyptian legal document written in hieratic, the common official script. At the right is a fragment of an Egyptian papyrus of the Roman period written in demotic, the common Egyptian writing for everyday use. Contrast these two writings with the hieroglyphic used for sacred texts, as shown on the obelisk of Thutmose III, which appears earlier in this chapter.* (COURTESY THE METROPOLITAN MUSEUM OF ART)

## ▶ General summary of Egyptian achievements

WRITING, MATHEMATICS, MEDICINE,
ARCHITECTURE

The form of exposition adopted in this chapter has emphasized throughout the intimate connection between the social and religious history of Egypt and the political. In the course of recounting this history we necessarily have taken account of the changes in religion, in art, in science and technology in response to the social and political experience of the people. We believe that our procedure was necessitated by the fact that in ancient Egypt religion, art, and science were inseparable as they have not been in later civilizations. In Greece, science becomes emancipated from art, though art remains tied to religion. In the later Western civilization all three have become separate and can

be treated separately. Art for art's sake in either Egypt or Greece was unthinkable. It only remains therefore here to summarize in a more convenient form the major discoveries and contributions to the history of civilization made by the Egyptians.

The Egyptians did not invent writing; so far as we know, this honor rests with the Sumerians. But very early the Egyptians developed a distinctive form known as hieroglyphic (sacred carving), with simplified forms known as hieratic and demotic. It is possible that at one time they used plain pictographs, each representing the object in question, and that these later became conventionalized and stylized, as in Mesopotamia. But, curiously enough, even the earliest Egyptian writing known to us had already adopted a syllabic system based on sounds. This so-called rebus principle (the classic English example is *be-lief,* the picture of a bee combined with the picture of a leaf) was already in use in Mesopotamia before the earliest examples in Egypt. Though the Egyptians used Egyptian rather than Mesopotamian pictures, the borrowing would seem probable. It is still uncertain whether there was ever a true consonantal alphabet of twenty-four letters in Egypt, for although the determinative (the initial consonant) in a word was sometimes used for a particular sound, the Egyptians themselves did not develop this principle further and make an alphabet. For some reason they seem to have known the alphabetical principle without using it. Perhaps the best explanation for this failure is that the alphabet was used only for the spoken words when vowels could be inserted by the speaker, and that the absence of vowels was an insuperable obstacle to the use of the alphabet. It is not obvious that a vowel is also a *letter*. If the alphabetical phonetic system was in use in the spoken language, it is hardly surprising that one of the subject peoples of the Egyptians should have developed it into a written alphabet, using the Egyptian signs but their own Semitic names—*alif*, the ox, and *bet*, the house, becoming later the alpha and beta of the Greek system. It is not yet known for certain which people was the first to do this, though the Phoenicians usually receive the credit for it. The Egyptians also invented writing materials far superior in everything except permanence to the clay tablets of the Mesopotamian peoples; they used papyrus, from a reed found near the Nile, ink from various gums, and pens of pointed reed.

The Egyptian system of arithmetic seems clumsy to us, but it was used with modifications in certain parts of Eastern Europe and Asia until comparatively recently. Being unable to multiply or divide by more than two, they combined these two procedures in an ingenious manner in such a way that they were able to do a complicated multiplication slowly but quite accurately. The two numbers to be multiplied are written in separate columns; then one column is multiplied by 2 and the other divided by 2. Disregard all even numbers on the side divided, and add only those in the other column opposite the odd numbers. The answer will be the required number.

*Example:* To multiply 44 by 28.

| 44 | 28 |
|----|----|
| 22 | 56 |
| 11 | 112 |
| 5 | 224 |
| 2 | 448 |
| 1 | 896 |
| | 1,232. |

The Egyptians could not use complex fractions, and, like all peoples before the last few centuries of Western civilization, were hampered by an inadequate system of notation. For fractions they reduced all the numerators to one, and then added.

This, of course, does not exhaust the mathematical, as distinct from the arithmetical, ability of the Egyptians, since, as we know, they were remarkably efficient at surveying, and could build such precisely calculated figures as pyramids. It has been pointed out by a mathematician that, to build the Great Pyramid, they must have known the G ratio, the formula for which was a nineteenth-century discovery, i.e., the ratio between the sides of a regular decagon and the radius of its circumscribed circle, and also the Golden Section, i.e., dividing a line segment into two unequal parts in such a manner that the smaller part has to the larger part the same ratio as the larger part to the total. The Great Pyramid has the G ratio between its triangles and the base.

As far as our present knowledge goes, the Egyptians had no theoretical knowledge of mathematics at all in the modern sense. Their notebooks are filled with practical examples, but the universality of a mathematical principle was unknown to them. They did not invent a single geometrical proposition, e.g., *all* triangles have such or such a property, whereas the first Greek mathematicians were able to *abstract* the universal principles from the particular examples, and thus could formulate valid theorems or propositions.

In medicine the Edwin Smith Surgical

Papyrus has already been mentioned as an example of the best Egyptian medical knowledge of the Old Kingdom. And we know from the developed Egyptian mortuary practices how skillful they were in preserving the human body after death. The Ebers Medical Papyrus, probably dating from the Middle Kingdom, possesses much herbal lore, too many magic formulas and strange magical medicines; but it also has a fairly accurate account of the workings of the human heart.

In architecture the Egyptians were the first people to make a really successful use of mass when dealing with stone. Their structures, it has been pointed out, imitate the solid mass of the desert cliffs and mountains, and they planned that their buildings, like these cliffs, would last for eternity. There can be little doubt that classical Greek architecture borrowed the idea of floral capitals from Egypt, but it is not as clear why the Egyptians themselves used them, as they are singularly inappropriate functionally. Why should a powerful stone column sprout flowers and buds? It has been suggested that they are a survival from the days when bundles of reeds with flowers or tufted heads would appear at the top of the pillar, being used as supports instead of timber which was lacking. The explanation, however, seems hardly convincing. The obelisk as well as the pyramid is a distinctive Egyptian form, copied self-consciously by other peoples for purposes of self-glorification. But they always seem native to, and at home only in, Egypt.

NATURE OF EGYPTIAN LITERATURE—ABSENCE OF MUCH NARRATIVE IN A CHANGELESS WORLD

Egyptian thought and literature have been sufficiently dealt with in the main body of this chapter not to require much further mention here. It may only be pointed out that the Egyptian, at least in the written literature that survives, was only very slightly interested in narrative. In such a tale as The Eloquent Peasant, the bulk of the story is taken up with what we consider tedious and repetitive teachings and platitudes. Yet these were what gained it its popularity; not the brief story of the loss of the peasant's goods and their eventual restitution, which is what we should relish. Modern digests of this tale too often give the wrong impression by omitting all but the few lines of "story." It would seem probable that this lack of interest in mere events is connected with the Egyptian sense of time and eternity. The "platitudes" were timeless truths, while the events were ripples in the ocean of eternity. For the same reason, the Egyptian lacked a sense of history and too often did not bother to record it, or record it accurately. As we know, the same deeds are repeated of different monarchs, and interest is directed away from these mere details to the—to us—monotonous record of victories which were only to be expected of a divine monarch and recurred whenever he took the field. There is nothing that can possibly be called an epic in the whole of Egyptian literature.

*Composite capital from an Egyptian temple of Amon. Capital represents papyrus plant.* (COURTESY THE METROPOLITAN MUSEUM OF ART)

THE VALUES OF EGYPT—HER LEGACY TO LATER
CIVILIZATIONS

The Greeks considered Egypt the repository of all ancient wisdom, and they accorded to her a respect which was perhaps undeserved. While we may now admire the civilization of the Egyptians, it sometimes makes us impatient that they made so little progress, that the great achievements of the Old Kingdom were not treated as the beginning of an ascending path, a fine start to be built upon rather than a Golden Age of glory to be looked back upon and forever imitated.

What we have tried to present in this chapter is a picture of a civilization that looked backward and decayed, as distinct from the picture familiar to us of a Western civilization that looks forward and strives forward, but is chaotic and unstable, and is even now able to destroy itself and all its works by the destructive use of a science which was brought to its present perfection through that very desire to progress which is the essential feature of this civilization. If we assume that it is an inborn characteristic of man to wish to advance, it is perhaps as well to realize that it was not a characteristic of the ancient Egyptians. Toynbee, in studying Egyptian civilization, was hard put to it to discover his challenges and responses and succeeded in devising a pattern satisfactory to him only by doing grave violence to the facts of Egyptian history, as has already been pointed out by many historians. The Marxian interpretation of history finds little confirmation in Egypt, as was pointed out in the early pages of this chapter. We are thus left with a phenomenon which seems ultimately to be explained only in terms of itself—that the Egyptians, unlike ourselves, neither wished to advance nor succeeded in doing so after a brilliant start. Yet their civilization did not die until twenty-five centuries had elapsed.

We wish to point no moral and to draw no conclusions. We have merely presented the phenomenon. To study it should be an exercise in that historical imagination spoken of in the introductory chapter, without which there is neither understanding nor appreciation of history; and it may serve to help us view our own civilization in perspective. We, like the Greeks, must respect the Egyptians for what they accomplished in the light of their own ideals and their own aims, with so little, and so early in the world's history. And even though we may not share their ideals nor respect their aims, we can hardly deny that it was one of the few great civilizations of the world.

▶  Suggestions for further reading

There are no first-rate, up-to-date histories of ancient Egypt in English. In spite of certain deficiencies, the best are still J. H. Breasted, *A History of Egypt* (2nd ed.; New York: Charles Scribner's Sons, 1909), and A. Baikie, *A History of Egypt from the Earliest Times to the End of the XVIIIth Dynasty* (New York: The Macmillan Company, 1929). The first-named of these works was an outstanding pioneer effort in its day, but it has never been revised in the light of modern discoveries, although the older edition is still kept in print. Baikie's book was a painstaking work and made use of the best sources, but it was written by one who was not himself an expert in the field. A notable attempt to bring Breasted up to date for the period of the Egyptian Empire was Georg Steindorff and K. C. Steele, *When Egypt Ruled the East* (Chicago: The University of Chicago Press, 1942). This work is especially valuable for its first-rate illustrations, which really do illustrate the text and are not mere decorative appendages.

As indicated in the chapter above, various efforts have been made to interpret Egyptian civilization as a whole, especially by the scholars attached to the Oriental Institute in Chicago. Since this chapter has made extensive use of these researches and interpretations, the student is advised to consult the original works published by The University of Chicago Press. The most complete is by the former director of the Institute, J. A. Wilson, *The Burden of Egypt* (Chicago: The University of Chicago Press, 1951). Egyptian kingship is studied in the first half of Henri Frankfort, *Kingship and the Gods* (Chicago: The University of Chicago Press, 1948). Egyptian religion is studied by the same author in a little book which offers many stimulating insights, Henri Frankfort, *Ancient Egyptian Religion* (New York: Columbia University Press, 1948). Various scholars of the Oriental Institute collaborated in a pioneer work, Henri Frankfort *et al., The Intellectual Adventure of Ancient Man* (Chicago: The University of Chicago Press, 1946), but the chapter on Egypt, written by J. A. Wilson, is greatly inferior to this author's later complete book, *The Burden of Egypt.* However, the 1946 symposium is reprinted in convenient form in a Pelican book, Henri Frankfort *et al., Before Philosophy* (Harmondsworth, Middlesex: Penguin Books, 1951), and it should certainly be read if *The Burden of Egypt* is not available.

The pyramids are carefully considered in another Pelican book, I. E. S. Edwards, *The Pyramids of Egypt* (Harmondsworth, Middlesex: Penguin Books, 1947). Here the author gives most of the known facts about the pyramids, explaining how they must have been built, while indicating the numerous problems still to be solved. The Pyramid Texts are translated in a recently published work, S. A. B. Mercer, *The Pyramid Texts in Translation and Commentary* (New York: Longmans, Green & Co., Inc., 1952), Vol. 1, but on the whole these difficult texts are not recommended for beginning students. A useful account of Egyptian life is to be found in A. Moret, *The Nile and Egyptian Civilization* (New York: Alfred A. Knopf, Inc., 1927).

By far the best collection of easily available source material in translation is J. B. Pritchard, ed., *Ancient Near Eastern Texts Relating to the Old Testament* (Princeton, N.J.: Princeton University Press, 1950). Though the size of the collection is limited by the requirements of the subject matter, the editor has interpreted his mandate generously, and most of the best-known and interesting Egyptian documents are included, in spite of a rather remote connection with the Old Testament.

# 4

# Mesopotamia

*General characteristics of Mesopotamian civilization • The Sumerians • Semitic conquests of Mesopotamia • Mesopotamia under Hammurabi • The Empire of the Assyrians • The Chaldeans and New Babylonia • The Persian Empire • Conclusion: the influence of Mesopotamia*

---

## ► General characteristics of Mesopotamian civilization

Throughout the country today known as Iraq two great rivers, the Tigris and the Euphrates, flow southeastward to the Persian Gulf. To the north and east of these rivers are mountains, to the south is the great Arabian desert. The fertile valleys of the Tigris and the Euphrates form the eastern arc of what is usually called the Fertile Crescent, the western arc of that crescent stretching down through Syria and Palestine to the borders of Egypt. In both these areas of fertility civilizations sprang up in ancient times, but the Tigris-Euphrates valleys hold priority. For here, in all probability, is the real cradle of western civilization.

Though there are still some scholars who argue for Egypt, the weight of the evidence seems almost conclusive that any early borrowing of cultural elements was by Egypt and not vice versa.

There is no one name which can be applied to the whole area drained by the Tigris and the Euphrates rivers. The word "Mesopotamia" really refers to the northern area only, while "Babylonia" refers to the southern part. But neither of these is an exact term, though during the long period of Babylonian supremacy the whole southern part of these valleys was under the control of Babylon. The ancient land of Sumer and Sumerian civilization, which was the parent of all other civilizations in this area, were absorbed, and even the Sumerian language died out. Our only justification, then, for using the word "Mesopotamia" to cover all the area in question is that its use has become conventional. The word itself means "the land between the rivers" and this is the general meaning we wish to convey.

The area, unlike Egypt, does not form a natural entity, and the boundaries are not clearly defined. No warrior could ever say he had conquered Mesopotamia; he would never be able to boast that he had reached its natural frontiers and was prepared to defend them, as an Egyptian could say of his country. Yet the continuity of culture in this area is remarkable. All the conquerors and successors of the Sumerians adopted the main features of the original Sumerian culture, their gods, their festivals, their writing, their art and architecture. The late Assyrian was in all respects far closer to his Sumerian forebears than to his Egyptian contemporaries.

This total civilization, in fact, stands out in marked contrast to that of the Egyptians. The Egyptian civilization was grand and magnificent; but, as was shown in the last chapter, it was isolated, and it was totally alien to us. It was therefore studied as a whole for itself, rather than for its "contributions" to world civilization. Mesopotamian civilization, on the contrary, seems far closer to ours. The line of descent from ancient Sumer to ourselves is clear. Though the Children of Israel were in bondage in Egypt, their Egyptian heritage was small. And though they were not taken into captivity in Babylon until their civilization had flourished for hundreds of years and had taken on its most characteristic forms, there can be little doubt that it was influenced by Mesopotamian ideas and institutions. Even Hebrew religion itself is concerned with questions raised by the Mesopotamian peoples, and in its own special way gives answers to them. The Egyptian idea of a static universe found no adherents in Mesopotamia, nor was its supreme self-confidence or its king-god found acceptable.

In this chapter, therefore, it will be possible to adopt a more conventional treatment of the material than was suitable for Egypt. The rise and fall of Mesopotamian culture does not present a similar object lesson to us, for it merged insensibly into the whole cultural stream of mankind, and never collapsed with its foundations undermined, as happened in Egypt. For in Mesopotamia there never were any fixed foundations, there never was any psychological security to be destroyed. The Mesopotamians had no great expectations of good to be obtained in life; they expected change on earth and were prepared to endure it. They had no expectation of a blessed hereafter. The Mesopotamian view of life was more in keeping with our own view of life than with the Egyptian view. Their relatively pessimistic attitude toward life was certainly more ap-

propriate for them than the naïve optimism of the Egyptians. At all events, their view of life as a vale of tears has almost always prevailed since their time.

It has already been pointed out that the kind of river rather than the mere fact of a river should be considered when attempting to trace the effect of a river valley upon its civilization. Both the Tigris and the Euphrates rise in flood each year in the spring, but the floods are unpredictable and vary greatly from year to year. Sometimes they are very severe and break the dikes, wreaking havoc upon the lands and submerging the crops and villages. At other times they are insufficient to ward off drought. Famines due both to flood and to drought are therefore not uncommon. There are scorching winds and smothering dust storms which wrack the throat and may even suffocate. There are occasional torrential rains which turn the ground into mud, making travel impossible. The sun in summer has no appearance of being a beneficent force giving life to the crops. It is savage, fierce, and blistering, and the land often lies parched under it, or blows away in dust. The sublime, life-giving sun of cloudless Egypt could never have become the all-pervasive god of Mesopotamia, however strongly the people might be impressed with its power and force. In addition to these doubtfully benevolent forces of nature, the land was militarily indefensible as an entity, and time and again was conquered, either by outside invaders or by one or another of the Mesopotamian peoples. At any time a city might be destroyed in war if it did not take care of its defenses; or if, as the Mesopotamians themselves put it, the gods were for any reason angry with them and wished to destroy it. This complex of forces, as we shall see, tended to breed in these peoples a deep sense of insecurity and inadequacy, which found expression in a pessimistic view of life utterly at variance with the Egyptian optimism, and in a religion which stressed man's helplessness against the arbitrariness and unpredictable wrath of the gods. But it did not prevent them from creating an earthly civili-

# ▶ chronological chart

| | |
|---|---|
| Neolithic Age | *ca.* 6000–4500 |
| Early Copper Age | *ca.* 4500–3000 |
| Invention of writing | *ca.* 3500 |
| Primitive Democracy | ? |
| Early Sumerian cities (Bronze Age) | 3000–2400 |
| Temple communities | |
| Semitic conquests of Mesopotamia | |
| Akkadians (Sargon) | 2400–2200 |
| Guti | 2200–2000 |
| Independence of Sumerian Cities | 2300 |
| Gudea of Lagash | 2300 |
| Dungi of Ur | 2275 |
| Amorites | 2000–1750 |
| Hammurabi Code | 1800 |
| Kassites | 1750–910 |
| Assyrian Empire | |
| Conquest of Babylon | 910 |
| Conquest of Samaria and deportation of Ten Tribes | 721 |
| Conquest of Egypt by Esar-Haddon | 670 |
| Library of Assurbanipal | 660 |
| Fall of Nineveh to Medes, Chaldeans, and Scythians | 612 |
| Battle of Carchemish—End of Assyrian Empire and annihilation of Assyrians | 606 |
| Chaldeans and New Babylonians | |
| Conquest of Jerusalem by Nebuchadnezzar | 586 |
| Reign of Nabonidus | 555–538 |
| Fall of Babylon to Persians | 538 |
| Persian Empire | |
| Zoroaster the Prophet | *ca.* 600 |
| Cyrus of Persia accepted as king by Medes | 549 |
| Conquest of Lydia by Cyrus | 547 |
| Conquest of Babylon | 538 |
| Conquest of Egypt (Cambyses) | 525 |
| Reorganization of Persia by Darius i | 522–486 |
| First Persian expedition to Greece (Darius) | 490 |
| Second Persian expedition to Greece (Xerxes) | 480–479 |
| Persian influence in Greece | 410–338 |
| Conquest of Persia by Alexander the Great | 330 |

Dates are before Christ. Earlier dates are disputed; others may be a year out.

Chief authority used: G. E. Wright and F. V. Filson, eds., *Westminster Historical Atlas to the Bible* (Philadelphia: Westminster Press, 1945).

zation which, from our point of view, compares in many respects favorably with that of the Egyptians.

## ▶ The Sumerians

EARLIEST GOVERNMENT—PRIMITIVE DEMOCRACY

Mesopotamia, as has been said, was indefensible against invaders. In discussing the Mesopotamian civilization we shall therefore be dealing with several distinct peoples who ruled the territory, though without necessarily displacing those who had settled there before. The first of these are the Sumerians, followed in succession by Akkadians, Guti, Amorites, Kassites, Assyrians, Chaldeans, Medes, and Persians. For details of the chronology of these periods the chart on page 77 should be consulted.

There is still difference of opinion as to the origin of the Sumerians. It is now generally believed that they were not the original inhabitants of the land, but migrated into

the area of Mesopotamia nearest the Persian Gulf from Central Asia. Many elements in their culture are similar to those of the Indus civilization to the southeast, though the borrowing appears to have been done by the Indians and not by the Sumerians. In the fourth millennium B.C. the Persian Gulf came much further inland than it does today, for the rivers carry deposits of silt to the sea every year, thus increasing the area of land. The seaports of the Sumerians are now as much as 150 miles inland. It is certain, however, that their language was not Semitic, so we can state safely that they were not Semites (we have already said that the term "Semitic" is primarily a language differentiation). The unknown earlier inhabitants of the area are supposed to have been Semites.

From the beginning of the present century there have been many archaeological investigations in Sumer, and we now have a considerable amount of information about the great Sumerian "city-states" of Ur, Lagash, Uruk, and others, though the evaluation of this information is still very far from complete. Few of the theories of the original investigator, Sir Leonard Woolley, are now accepted, and it is possible that much of what is said here will still require reconsideration in the future in the light of new finds.

As in the case of Egypt, we lack information on the transitional stage from primitive village life to the civilized life of the larger villages and cities, and to the organized government that knew how to direct the large-scale irrigation. For in these early days in the first cities of Ur there already were irrigation and canals, together with fine art work and craftsmanship, facts which presuppose a previous period of technical development of which we know little. But it is now believed by many that the earliest government in the independent "city-states" characteristic of the Sumerians was a kind of democracy. Kings and central governments came later only when imperative need arose for them. These democracies do not seem to have evolved from the family or clan, for

Nineveh

Assur

AKKAD

*Euphrates R.*

*Tigris R.*

Babylon

E  L  A  M

S  U  M  E  R
⊙ Nippur
Lagash ⊙
Uruk ⊙   Eridu ⊙
Ur ⊙

Present
Coastline

*Persian*

*Gulf*

### SUMERIAN
### CITY
### STATES

⊙ City States

50    0         100
Miles

the democratic institutions were based on locality rather than on family. The heads of families, however, were of importance in the assemblies and councils, and were always called the "fathers," as in the later Roman Senate. It is possible that the Sumerians brought these institutions with them from their original homes; at all events it is certain that they were of considerable antiquity and had considerable prestige. The councils of the Sumerian gods functioned in this democratic manner long after there were kings in the cities of men.

In this Primitive Democracy there were a general assembly of all adult men and a council of elders. In time of danger a king was chosen by the assembly who was to rule for only a limited time. When the danger passed he became a private citizen again, much like the election of a dictator under the early Roman Republic. All decisions were reached after discussion, "asking one another," as it was called, and decisions had to be reached unanimously before action could be taken. Hence the need for an overriding authority when immediate action was needed. Majority rule and voting were unknown at this early stage of society. It is not known at what time Primitive Democracy in its pure form was in existence, since in historic times there were already leaders

of a more or less permanent nature. If we are to judge from the councils of the gods as they appear in Sumerian mythology, the prestige of certain elders was the deciding factor in reaching decisions, for the seven great gods who "determine destinies" were the ultimate arbiters in heavenly affairs. This very early stage of government developed into the temple community discussed in a later section.*

LANGUAGE AND WRITING

In these early days so-called cuneiform writing had already been invented; at the same time were developed the characteristic Mesopotamian art and architectural forms which persisted throughout the whole civilization. The evolution of writing from the original pictures can easily be traced in Mesopotamia, these pictures becoming more and more conventionalized and stylized as time progressed. So it is impossible to determine from the later writing the earlier forms, as in the case of our own writing, without first examining the intermediate between the picture and the conventional sign. Thus, although we are ignorant of the exact period and the details of this epoch-making invention, it can in all probability be assigned to the Sumerians as perhaps the greatest of their many achievements.

| Sumerian | Babylonian | Assyrian |

The cuneiform symbol for a bird, showing its evolution from the picture of a bird. The original bird symbol, however, is not actually known, but the later forms as shown above allow us to presuppose that in very early times a definite picture of a bird, similar to this, was used.

* The details given in the last two paragraphs have not been accepted by all scholars, and it must be admitted that the evidence is not of a kind that commends itself to all types of historians. The evidence is summarized in Thorkild Jacobsen's chapters in Henri Frankfort, et al., *The Intellectual Adventure of Ancient Man* (Chicago: The University of Chicago Press, 1948).

*Cuneiform tablet recording expenditure and distribution of grain and animals.* (COURTESY THE METROPOLITAN MUSEUM OF ART)

The writing was not done by scratching some form of pen over a paperlike material, as in Egypt, but was made by impressing soft clay with a square-tipped reed, and then baking the clay into a kind of brick. This made a permanent record of considerable bulk. This method of writing determined the form, as it was impossible to use much artistry with such tools. The writing is called cuneiform ("wedge-shaped"), from the form of the finished characters. Enormous quantities of these tablets have been found in the ruins of Mesopotamian cities, not all of which have even now been read. The language was phonetic, each of the 350 or so signs representing either a syllable or an entire word. The rebus principle described in the chapter on Egypt was first developed by the Sumerians. There was, however, never at any time a cuneiform alphabet, as far as we know.

The language was not deciphered until the middle of the nineteenth century. A huge rock inscription at Behistun in western Iran, written in three cuneiform scripts—Old Persian, Elamite, and Assyrian—had long been known; but the ascent to this rock was difficult, and would have been useless until some progress had been made at the ground level in the knowledge of what to look for in the inscription. When Sir Henry Rawlinson, an Englishman, had discovered three names of kings in the simplest of these writings, the Old Persian script, and thus identified fourteen Persian characters, he climbed the Behistun rock and made copies of the inscription. On his descent to the ground he was able to complete his Persian investigations and turn to the more complex Mesopotamian writings. With the aid of other investigators who were able to note the similarity to the later Hebrew and Arabic languages, he was at last able to complete the knowledge of Assyrian. With this tool it was possible to read the records of the Sumerian civilization when these records were unearthed at the end of the century.[1]

ART AND ARCHITECTURE

The characteristic form of monumental architecture in Mesopotamia is the ziggurat, built of brick, unlike the Egyptian temples. All architecture, domestic and monumental, was limited in this region by the nature of the only available building material, mud and clay, baked into bricks. Since this material is not permanent and is easily damaged and made shapeless by the elements, nothing has survived to our time in its original form; in fact, in ancient times there was constant replacement of buildings. Cities are found superimposed upon one another, and Mesopotamian cities have to be carefully excavated to see the traces of each successive city. Before excavation a buried city is nothing but a sand-covered mound in the desert.

A ziggurat was usually built on an artificial mountain of sun-dried bricks rising out of the plain. Upon this base was erected the temple itself, a kind of tower with several stories, or terraces, each stepped back and smaller than the one on which it rested.

[1] The Assyrian language is an offshoot of the Akkadian which itself is the direct successor of the Sumerian.

A great stairway led to the summit. On the shrine itself all the resources of the country could be used. As early as the First Dynasty of Ur[2]—a city now far inland, but then close to the Persian Gulf—there were fine friezes in relief and inlay work of the highest craftsmanship. The brick columns were overlaid with copper and mother of pearl. The archi-

[2] 3500 B.C., or earlier.

tects used their ingenuity not only in solving the technical problems of building in sundried brick, but in suggesting the central nature of the temple by making all the lines lead up to the shrine at the top. It was not possible to use the post and lintel, as in Egypt, with this material; when trying to span large openings with small pieces of material they developed the arch with its

*These two pictures show the mound of Tepe Gawra in Assyria at different stages of excavation. Tepe Gawra, in the words of Dr. Speiser, the director of the excavation project, "furnishes the longest continuous record of superimposed occupations known to science." The latest of the settlements was abandoned at least 3,500 years ago, and the great majority of the settlements date from the third and fourth milleniums B.C.; over half are demonstrably prehistoric.* (COURTESY OF E. A. SPEISER)

Model of the City of Ur about 2000 B.C.; constructed by the American Museum of Natural History. (COURTESY AMERICAN MUSEUM OF NATURAL HISTORY)

Ruins of the Ziggurat of Assur from the south.

*Jewelry from the graves of two ladies-in-waiting of the Queen of Ur, 3500–2500 B.C. Made of gold, carnelian, and lapis lazuli, this jewelry is the oldest known in the world up to the present time, but the skill shown presupposes long development in craftsmanship from prehistoric times.* (COURTESY THE METROPOLITAN MUSEUM OF ART)

*Steatite (soapstone) vase carved in relief. Sumerian, about 3000 B.C.* (COURTESY THE METROPOLITAN MUSEUM OF ART)

*White gypsum figure from a Sumerian temple, about 3000 B.C.* (COURTESY THE METROPOLITAN MUSEUM OF ART)

blocks of different shapes to take the stress. The vault and dome were also used by the Sumerians, but in their private architecture rather than in the conventional ziggurats.

The craftsmen of ancient Sumer must have been by far the most skilled in the world of their day. They carved gems, and understood a great deal more about alloys and the casting of metals than did any of their contemporaries. The graves at Ur, excavated by Woolley, are full of finely sculptured ornaments, usually in precious metals, and stone. These are imaginative and varied, excelling especially in the representation of human and animal life.

PRACTICAL INVENTIONS AND THE
ECONOMY—MATHEMATICS

The Sumerians seem to have been an eminently practical people, and they developed many useful devices for use in their economy and daily life. Their calendar suffered from the disadvantage of all lunar calendars in that it needed to be adjusted to the solar year at irregular intervals by intercalating an extra month when necessary. In this practice, too, they influenced later peoples. The Hebrews and the Muslims later adopted a lunar calendar rather than the more effective Egyptian one. At an early date the Sumerians had already achieved skill in practical mathematics, adopting a positional notation for the use of large numbers which influenced indirectly even our own system. They used 60 as their basic number, instead of 10 (the decimal system). Since 60 has more factors than 10, especially 3, which presents so much difficulty in our decimal system, this had some practical advantages. To use this system one must remember that each position counts for 60 and not for 10. Thus 123 in our system $= 1 \times 10^2$ plus $2 \times 10^1$ plus 3. A similar notation in Mesopotamia ′ ″ ‴ would give $60^2$ plus $2 \times 60^1$ plus $3 = 3,723$, while 123 would be written in two positions as ′ ′ ‴ or $2 \times 60^1$ plus 3. For numbers under 60, however, the notation is clumsy, as a

dividing line had to be used for the tens and integers:

$$\prime\prime < \prime\prime\prime = 26.$$

Fractions, however, could be handled by the use of another sign, it being understood that the denominator in each case would be 60:

$$\prime \lessgtr \prime\prime \ \prime = 1 \text{ plus } \frac{2}{60} \text{ plus } \frac{1}{60^2}.$$

Later Mesopotamian civilizations, using the same method, divided the circle into $6 \times 60$ degrees, which has remained the standard to this day. The unit of weight was the mina (or pound) which was divided into 60 shekels.

A flourishing trade exchanging the surplus agricultural and industrial produce of this usually fertile area especially for metals not found in Mesopotamia was the basis of the prosperity of the Sumerian cities. Almost all the simple methods of transacting business known today were already in use—bills, receipts, notes, and letters of credit. Such large quantities of this commercial material have been preserved that much of it has never been read. The investigator can at once see that a tablet concerns a business transaction of a familiar kind, and he needs to go no further. For a comparatively small sum the private collector can buy such a tablet, thousands of years old, knowing that, even if he could read it, it would change nothing of our knowledge of this ancient civilization.

Extensive regulations for international and domestic trade were early developed, and there is no doubt that the famous Hammurabi Code, to be discussed later, had its basis in Sumerian law, and was issued as a new code by Hammurabi only because his dynasty had conquered Babylon and Sumer, and he wished to establish a common law for all his dominions. This fact, of course, accounts for the extraordinary unevenness of the code; as will be seen, its ancient customs and, in some instances, its more enlightened provisions are all inextricably woven together.

SOCIAL AND POLITICAL SYSTEM AND RELIGION

## Relation between Sumerian religion and the social order

As noted earlier, the first form of government known to us in Mesopotamia is a Primitive Democracy, details for which are largely lacking, but whose existence is inferred from later material, especially from extant accounts of the behavior of the gods in council. The first historical records tell of simple temple communities, ruled by a *sangu*, or steward of the gods. Larger communities, with several temples, are ruled by an *ensi*, who is also a steward of the gods, but he is responsible to the god of the whole community, whereas the earlier *sangu* was responsible only to the god of his particular temple. The last form of this development is the emergence of a king or *lugal*, who was usually the ruler of many cities, or at least of a considerable number of temple communities. The *lugal* ruled a fairly advanced type of community which may, not improperly, be called a town or a city. It is no longer merely an agricultural community; and though the temple may be the principal building, the whole life of the community no longer centers around it, as in the more primitive society. But the *lugal*, like the earlier rulers, remains only the chief representative on earth of the gods, who are the theoretical owners of all the land. There is therefore no such thing as a secular state, nor does a truly secular state at any time develop in any Mesopotamian country. So it becomes necessary, if Mesopotamian government is to be understood, to study the religion of the Mesopotamian peoples in some detail in order to see how the rulers came to occupy such an unusual position.

It has already been suggested that the Mesopotamian peoples feared their gods, while they worshiped them as beings commanding respect and submission. They did not love them, as the Hebrews in later times were taught to love their God, and they did not regard them as just and powerful protectors, looking after their land and seeing that it was prosperous, as did the Egyptians. The reason for this Mesopotamian view has already been hinted at. The gods of the Mesopotamians in fact did not protect their land, nor could the people think their gods behaved justly to them. Instead, these deities made demands upon them, while giving them little in return, and this little was given quite arbitrarily. The bounty of the gods depended upon the sacrifices given to them by the people and the duties performed in their behalf. Yet the gods did not tell man unequivocally just what they wanted of him; man had to find out for himself and he might be wrong. Herein lies the profound difference between the Sumerian and the Hebrew conceptions of the divinity. Both required man to perform certain duties; but the Hebrew God told his people in no uncertain manner what these duties were. He gave them the Law, and thus provided the Hebrews with a sense of security always lacking in Mesopotamia.

Moreover, the Mesopotamian gods not only omitted to tell their people what was required of them but punished them for their ignorance. This was the arbitrary act of an unpredictable and unjust master—in short, the behavior of a human master to his slave. This master-slave relationship was the central feature of the theology in Mesopotamia, and was adopted first by the Sumerians, and then by all the peoples who followed them in the Land of the Two Rivers. Man was born to be the slave of the gods. This conception permeates not only the religion and myths of these peoples, but their whole social order.

The Mesopotamian peoples, unlike the Egyptians, did not have many different stories of creation, all giving a different point of view. Creation was not to them the one supremely important fact, the only thing in history which could properly be called an *event*, as it was in Egypt with its static conception of time. It was certainly not a theme for religious meditation. There is, in fact, nothing really religious in the Mesopotamian story of creation;[3] it did not inspire awe or reverence, but was merely true, something to be accepted and taken into consideration by man in all his earthly actions. Like all Mesopotamian religious stories, it represented conditions in heaven as being the exact counterpart of what occurred on earth, a conception which, as we shall see, permeated Mesopotamian thinking and ultimately gave birth to the great Chaldean science of astrology.

We have a fairly complete account of creation dating from the period of Babylonian supremacy, and we have others from Assyrian records. The Babylonian god Marduk is the hero in the Babylonian story and Assur in the Assyrian. But both these gods perform the same function in the myth that the young god Enlil, god of wind and storm, the executive of the heavenly powers, performs in Sumerian mythology. We should therefore be justified in assuming that the myth existed also in Sumerian times even if we did not possess fragments dating from that period. And these Assyrian and Babylonian hero-gods also possess the natural powers always ascribed to Enlil by the Sumerians.

This story, known as the *Enuma Elish* (When Above), tells how Marduk, or Assur, supplanted the older gods by conquering Tiamat, the goddess of primeval chaos. The earthly position corresponding to this is clear. As soon as a conqueror took over a new city, his conquest was in a very real sense the victory of his god as well as of himself. When Babylon extended its rule over the Sumerian cities, this was the supplanting of the older gods of Sumer by Marduk of Babylon. As we shall see, the city-god was entirely responsible for the welfare of his city, and his power rose and fell with the success or failure of his city.

In the beginning there is primeval chaos, Tiamat, says the story; with her is Apsu her consort (the sweet waters) and

attendant hosts. They beget the earliest gods, and in two generations the sky, Anu, comes into being, the supreme lord of the world above. And Anu engenders En-ki, or Ea, the earth, the most cunning and skilled of the gods. But the gods have to work with pick and shovel on this small piece of earth because as yet there is no man, and no place for man to live. The movement of the gods, however, upon the belly of Tiamat disturbs her and Apsu, so that she proposes to destroy them "that peace may reign and we may sleep."

It is clear that the begetting of these gods is also a nature myth explaining how land is indeed created in Mesopotamia "upon the bosom of the deep" by the meeting of the sweet waters (Apsu) and the salt water (Tiamat) and the formation of silt. But this aspect need not be treated in detail here.

So Tiamat prepares for war, and the gods, disturbed, send En-ki down to forestall trouble. He is successful in killing Apsu by a word of command (the sweet waters now held immobile forever afterward). Tiamat is furious, but temporarily quiescent until her attendants rouse her again to action. Meanwhile she marries a new consort, Kingu. The gods again send En-ki down to deal with Tiamat, but this time he is impotent. Even the great Anu finds he can do nothing against her. The gods are now in despair until En-ki proposes that his son Marduk (in the Babylonian version) be authorized to do battle with her. The gods are at first doubtful but, having tested Marduk's power, are willing to concede him authority on his own terms, namely, that thereafter he shall be the executive power of the gods.

Marduk, thus fortified, then marches against Tiamat, and envelops her and her hosts in a net. When Tiamat, pictured as a great sea monster, opens her mouth to swallow him, he sends in the force of the winds, preventing her from closing her mouth while he shoots an arrow which pierces her heart and kills her. Her followers are held in the net and taken captive. Marduk returns to the upper world and claims his position, which is conceded. Then he takes the body

---

[3] There are variations known of the creation myth given here, but basically they are the same, though the particular gods responsible for the creation vary according to the place and period.

of the dead Tiamat, cuts it in two, and lifts half of it up to form the sky, making sure that the waters above the earth are guarded by locks to prevent its escape.[4] The lower part of her body exactly corresponds to the upper, and on it Marduk makes his own dwelling. He sets stars in the sky to determine the days and months of the year and special openings for the daily entrance and departure of the sun, moon, and planets.

Finally comes his last task, how to relieve the gods of their toil "that they may freely breathe," and he says: "Arteries will I knot, and bring bones into being. I will make a savage, 'Man' be his name. I will form a savage—man. Let him be burdened with the toil of the gods." So Kingu, the defeated consort of the dead Tiamat, is executed, and "they condemned him, severed his arteries, and from his blood they formed mankind."[5] And Marduk divides the gods, assigning some to heaven under the direction of Anu and assigning others to earth. The gods take pick and shovel in hand for the last time to build Marduk a city; then they confirm his titles and status, and the poem ends by a recounting of his many names.

So mankind was created out of the blood of the defeated consort of the forces of chaos, than which there was nothing lower in the universe; and he was created as a slave to perform the menial tasks of the gods, relieving them of their work. This conception of the place of man in the universe permeates Mesopotamian thought. The king is the chief human representative of the gods upon earth, but even he is a slave of the gods. He may be all-powerful in earthly things, but he is not himself a god, and his titles in early days mean steward or governor. He is a viceroy rather than a true king. He is the head of an underprivileged group in the cosmic state, rather than the giver of rights to the people.

## The temple-community

In theory, then, it is clear that the gods were the owners of all the land, with the king or *ensi* their steward or bailiff. In practice we find that the temple had the first call upon the services of all the people, but those services were strictly defined by law and custom. And the temple had a large portion of the land under its direct control. Nevertheless the king was not subordinate to the priestly power as he was in later Egypt, except in matters considered purely religious; and these matters were carefully defined according to a prescribed set of rules. The kings appointed the high priests and not vice versa, though in some Sumerian cities the high priest is, in the absence of an *ensi* or steward of the gods, himself the chief secular authority also. From Assyrian documents to be discussed later it is clear that the religious knowledge of the priesthood could have lent itself to considerable abuse. But there was always the safeguard that the king also knew the rules to be observed in determining the will of the gods, and the priests had to point to specific omens which required a certain line of conduct from the king before he would agree to abide by their decisions. This was one of the great advantages of a written law in curbing the power even of those who administered and executed it.

The temple estates in the Sumerian cities were really conceived of as the estates of the gods who owned them, who themselves had subordinate gods under them, even to the divine bailiffs in charge of operations, divine inspectors of fisheries, and divine gamekeepers. Only the menial labor was done by human beings, organized under the chief human overseer, the *ensi*. His position was that of a steward in relation to the god. He was supposed, like an earthly steward, to consult the god on all important and

---

[4] There might seem to be a contradiction between the presence of Anu, the sky, and the new creation of heavens and earth by Marduk. This is usually explained by the suggestion that Anu is no longer only the sky, but the power and authority symbolized by the sky. This theory is supported by his function in this myth, not as sky-god but as king of the older gods.

[5] These quotations are from J. B. Pritchard, ed., *Ancient Near Eastern Texts Relating to the Old Testament*, tr. E. A. Speiser; Princeton, N. J.: Princeton University Press, 1950, p. 68.

even unimportant occasions, and to administer the law for him, according to contracts entered into with the god. He had to negotiate with the *ensi* of other city-gods, since each city had its own particular city-god. These city-gods, as a rule, were comparatively minor deities. The great gods had more to do than bother with one city-state, but their power extended through all of the communities according to their particular functions in the universe. The wife of the *ensi* had similar duties to perform for the wife of the god.

At once this question arises: How did each god communicate with his *ensi?* Was it left entirely up to the priesthood to decide what the gods wanted?

The chief method was through the interpretation of omens. However, these were not interpreted according to the judgment of individual priests, but from long catalogues in which all possible omens and their meanings were listed. In other cases, when a particular question had to be answered, the liver of some sacrificial animal would be inspected. The liver of a sheep, for example, has certain markings on it, which, like the lines of the human hand, differ widely from each other. Most personal of all methods of communication with the god was the dream. The king would go to the temple, sacrifice and pray, then lie down to sleep, and the god would appear to him and give him his orders. From these methods it can be seen that the priesthood, though it acted as interpreter, remained the servant of the god and the king, and could not abuse its power readily. And the duty of obedience to the gods' wishes seems to have been so deeply impressed upon all Mesopotamian peoples that a manipulation of these wishes for political purposes was probably at most periods unthinkable. If even the Assyrian kings with their militarist peoples behind them could not act against the will of the gods, much less would the priests have had the audacity to do so.

The whole conception of the close relationship between the processes of nature (as represented by the gods) and the activities of man seems to have been the ruling thought of Mesopotamian culture at all times. What happened in heaven was the counterpart of what happened on earth. The heavens and natural events could be consulted to see what must happen on earth, and, if possible, human beings might try to avert dangers and disasters foretold there. Nothing in nature happened casually. Any movement of birds or animals, any eclipse or conjunction between one star and another —these did not happen by chance, but by design of the gods, as the earth itself was created as the direct counterpart of the heavens. When astrology largely took the place of divination by omens, the conception was in no way changed. Chaldean astronomy and astrology belonged to the same view of the world, and were just as natural. It is clear that astronomy was an incidental by-product of astrology and must have been so, for astrology itself was only a more scientific method of discovering the will of the gods and coming events on earth than the earlier techniques. The dream was the least effective of these methods because it could not be compelled, and there could be no interpretation until there was a dream to interpret. But when every natural event could be read as an omen, and every movement of the heavens portended some event on earth, it is clear there was no lack of information on the will of the gods for their earthly slaves to carry out.

The chief figure, then, in the Sumerian city was the god, and his chief human attendant was the *ensi.* In human terms title to the greater part of the land would be vested in the temple of the city-god. If the city were a large one there might be several estates belonging to different local gods and their families, together with the larger estate of the chief city-god, which would exercise some jurisdiction over the estates of minor gods. In the case of administrative units of two or three towns and villages, the chief god of the chief city, and his *ensi,* would be the paramount authority of the unit. Each temple had its own serfs and tenants working on a sharecropping basis, with the lion's share of the produce going to the temple-landowner. The temple also had its own servants, the priests and their assistants, who were devoted to the strict service of the god. The work of a temple community might be directed either by the *ensi* if there was one, or by the high priest of the particular god in person as the chief local temple authority. In practical terms this seems to have meant that the land was owned by the community and that everyone within the city-god's estate had a definite position with definite duties to perform for the community. The serfs had no rights except that they were protected by their master, in this case the temple, and the tenants had a certain amount of land whose produce they could keep for themselves. The rest they cultivated on behalf of the temple-community. Other land seems to have been rented out by the temple-community for money. Everyone, whatever his status, was liable for certain community services, e.g., for building temples, public works, roads, and irrigation projects.

In larger communities, in addition to the *ensi* there was a real king, a *lugal*. As servant of the god of the city or groups of cities, he had an overriding authority over both minor *ensis* and the high priests. But his position, in theory and apparently, at least in the early days, in practice, was only temporary. If the gods gave a sign that he should be replaced or that kingship should cease in the area, then it was his duty to retire or submit to being deposed; or as a last resort, in the Sumerian phrase, he could be "smitten by weapons." No doubt this deposition would be carried out if the king had lost the support of the community; or, if the religion had sufficient hold on the minds of the people, this loss of support by the community would result from his having been abandoned by the gods.

### Attitude of the people to the gods

These gods of the Sumerians were so closely identified with the civil administration that they must have commanded little worship from their adherents beyond formal obedience and submission. They could not be approached by individuals for help. So the individuals also had personal gods, usually some minor deities who were believed to have shown personal interest in the worshiper by some special mark of distinction. Believing as deeply in his own powerlessness to change events as the Sumerian did, he could only hope that his personal god would be influential enough to achieve something in his behalf in his own field of activity. There are many examples of letters written to these personal gods by their adherents, asking for their assistance in ordinary worldly affairs. And these gods are even threatened with desertion by their worshipers if they do not lend their aid. Naturally the great gods would be chosen as helpers if they were available. But the Sumerian was only too well aware of the remoteness of such deities. So it was safer to choose some minor god and try to persuade him to use his influence with those higher up. Unhappily, in spite of law codes and the paraphernalia of justice, it seems probable that this practice also reflects contemporary experience. For it is often only elementary justice that the worshiper petitions from his god; and if he needed a god to influence other gods to obtain it, and this god could be bribed, threatened, or cajoled into exercising it, the inference is clear!

Once the basic premise has been grasped, it is not too difficult to understand this world of the Sumerians. If we abandon the belief that heavenly affairs are the counterpart of earthly—a belief abandoned by the Hebrews with their conception of a righteous and transcendent god—we shall readily find the substrata of our Judaeo-Christian heritage, especially the powerlessness of man in the face of God. The Mesopotamian religion certainly offered few grounds for optimism. If the gods are arbitrary and man is created only to do their will, everything in life is made to hinge upon the knowledge of what the gods want from man; they do not instruct man in this, so that at any time he is liable to make a mistake. Disagreements in heaven are decided solely on the basis of rank; and man has to pay the price for it. When the city of Ur was destroyed by foreign invaders, it was because the gods in council had so decreed it; and the protective goddess of Ur had herself been forced to acquiesce in the decision. In the description of the destruction of Ur the goddess mourned, but was unable to save it; and the decree is carried out by Enlil, the executive of the heavenly state. Nowhere is the crime imputed to the actual invading armies, who were only the earthly tools of the gods. Had the gods not decreed it, these tools would have been powerless. The Hebrews also looked upon their enemies in this manner. The Babylonians could not have destroyed Jerusalem if God had not so decreed it. But the Hebrews had a consolation denied to the Sumerians. They knew that the reason for the destruction was that they had committed sins, and were being punished for them. The Sumerian had no such faith. The best he could hope to do was to discover in advance that the gods were contemplating destruction; and then try his utmost to appease them, and so prevent it. But there was never any certainty that he had correctly diagnosed the situation or understood what the gods required of him to avert it.

### The position of the Mesopotamian kings as representatives of gods

This uncertainty affected the position of the king in a remarkable manner at all stages of Mesopotamian history. We have evidence on this point from the middle of the third millennium B.C. right down to the age of the Assyrian conquerors. Being the chief representative of the gods on earth, he had also the chief responsibility. When Lagash was defeated, the responsibility was at once placed on the personal god of the king who had proved too weak to protect it. It was the king's duty above all to discover what the gods wanted and then do it, at whatever personal cost and inconvenience to himself. No one but the king could stay the anger of the gods, though there is evidence that his mantle, and even a substitute king, could function for him on occasions. King Gudea of Lagash, when the gods had indicated that

*Head of Gudea, ensi of Lagash.* (COURTESY THE METROPOLITAN MUSEUM OF ART)

a new temple should be built, had to look in all directions for a sign as to where it should be built and the exact moment for it. An extant cylinder seal records the extraordinary precautions taken by the king before he could be certain that he had correctly understood the message. Then at last he had to purify himself thoroughly and then mold the first brick with infinite care. Correspondence exists from the Assyrian kings to their priests, in which a powerful king complains that the gods' demands seem unreasonable, and requests them to examine the omens again. He is made to undergo ritual shaving, a considerable ordeal for men who had beards such as are shown in the Assyrian reliefs and paintings. On another occasion he was made to live in a reed hut in the desert for several days in order to avert a threatened disaster to his people. When an eclipse took place he prayed: "In the evil eclipse of the moon which took place in the month of Kislimu, on the tenth day; in the evil of the powers, of the signs, evil and not good, which are in my palace and my country, I fear, I tremble, and I am cast down in fear! . . . At thy exalted command let me live, let me be perfect, and let me behold thy divinity. Whenever I plan, let me succeed! Cause truth to dwell in my mouth."[6] When the Assyrian King Sennacherib impiously destroyed rebellious Babylon, he forgot that he was destroying a city of his empire, for which he was responsible to the gods. His successor, realizing the fact, humbly rebuilt the city and built new shrines for the god of the city, hoping to appease him. In all the great festivals of the year the king had to be present, performing his ritual part, especially in the great spring festival of the New Year, which begins with the special Day of Atonement for the king, and is followed by his ritual humiliation. It was clearly no light burden to be a king in Mesopotamia.

GENERAL PESSIMISM OF SUMERIAN AND MESOPOTAMIAN PEOPLES—EPIC OF GILGAMESH

We have no evidence that the Sumerians were disturbed by the arbitrary nature of their gods to the extent of repudiating them or criticizing them. But their later successors within Mesopotamia have left several documents in which the gods are shown as unjust, oppressing man on earth, demanding service, and giving nothing in return. And when man dies there is no hereafter to compensate. All go alike to Aralu, the abode of shades. Why must this be? Although the two best examples of this thought are not Sumerian, they are of interest as revealing the insoluble nature of the problem within the framework of Mesopotamian religion, and so will be discussed here. But it should not be thought that such ethical emphasis as appears in these texts is as early as the Sumerian civilization.

In one dialogue, which may have been the prototype for the later Hebrew Book of Job, a sufferer is afflicted by the gods, but can see no reason for it. He has sacrificed, prayed, and worshiped; he has performed his duties for the king, and looked after the prescribed ritual. Yet he is suffering from a loathsome disease, he has been whipped with

[6] Quoted by H. Frankfort, *Kingship and the Gods* (Chicago: The University of Chicago Press, 1948), p. 248.

a lash, and his enemies rejoice over him. There should be a reason, he feels, but in typical Mesopotamian fashion he is simply bewildered, until, without any explanation, Marduk heals him and all is well again. So he praises the Lord of Wisdom, but has gained no understanding of why it happened in the first place. However, it is clear that this thinker believed that there should have been some clear connection between his suffering and his life on earth, during which he had always correctly performed his duties to the gods.

The Epic of Gilgamesh undoubtedly dates back in some form to the Sumerian times, though our copies are of a later date; the ethical form in which this version is cast is probably a product of later thinking. This famous epic is the first known to deal with the adventures and trials of a great hero, though it has had many successors, from the *Odyssey* to *Parzival*. The quest of Gilgamesh in this version is for the plant of immortality, which he seeks because his friend has died without apparent reason and the hero refuses to be comforted. The problem, thus insistently posed, is why man does not have immortality.

Gilgamesh hears of an ancestor of his who did indeed have eternal life, one Utnapishtim, who now lives beyond the waters of death. So he sets out on his quest, wanders through the mountains, goes where the sun travels at night. But everyone tells him of the uselessness of his journey. He will never find Utnapishtim, for he lives beyond the waters of death; he might as well abandon the quest. But at last Gilgamesh gains passage over these waters and finds his ancestor. But Utnapishtim has no hope for him. The only reason he himself lives on is because he had saved himself, his wife, and pairs of all living things when Enlil decided to destroy the earth by flood. Then Enlil had repented of his act and, though angry with Utnapishtim at first, granted him immortality for his deed. After the conversation Gilgamesh falls into a magic sleep, which would have turned into death had not Utnapishtim's wife awakened him just in time. She then persuades her husband to give him a parting gift. This gift turns out to be information about a plant which grows on the bottom of the sea, and would bring renewed youth to anyone who should eat it. With the aid of Utnapishtim's boatman Gilgamesh discovers the whereabouts of the plant, dives down beneath the sea, and brings it up. Without eating it himself he makes haste back to the city of Uruk. But, as he nears it, he sees a pool, and, being tired, he goes for a swim, leaving the plant on the bank. There a snake smells it, and snatches it away, thus winning the power of everlasting renewal by shedding his old body and growing a new one. There is, however, no happy ending for Gilgamesh. He bewails his loss and all the trials he has undertaken. He has found no answer; and man cannot gain immortality.

Fundamentally this is the mood of Mesopotamian civilization. There *is* no answer. Man is the plaything of the gods; there is no reason in anything. Man's duty is only obedience and submission in this life, and there is nothing beyond the grave.

▶ **Semitic conquests of Mesopotamia**

Some time in the third millennium B.C. the independent city-states of Sumer fell victims to the first conqueror from the north, Sargon of Agade. This is usually described as a Semitic conquest, and there is no doubt that the conquest meant the gradual absorption of the non-Semitic Sumerian language by the Semitic Akkadian. But it is strange that there is as yet no evidence that the Sumerians realized they were being conquered by an alien people. To the Sumerians it was a conquest like all others. The Akkadians absorbed the culture and religion of the Sumerians, giving them only a more effective administration than the separate regimes of the city-states had ever afforded. Sargon then proceeded to conquer the Elamites and northern Syria, thus establishing the first great empire of historic times. However, after his death the Sumerian cities

revolted, and within a few generations the empire passed under the domination of a northern barbarian tribe, the Guti, with local administration resting in the hands of the Sumerians, until about 2300 B.C., when the city of Ur was able to throw off their yoke altogether. Ur then became the chief city of Sumer and kept the other states under its control. The greatest of the rulers of Ur was Dungi, who issued a law code which was the precursor of, and the foundation for, the more famous Code of Hammurabi, though later discoveries have unearthed even earlier codes than that of Dungi. About 2000 B.C. the whole country was conquered and pacified by the rulers of a desert tribe, the Amorites (Amurru), who captured the village of Babylon and made it into a great city. Then they extended its rule over the whole of Sumer, and elevated the Babylonian city-god Marduk into the ruler and supplanter of the old gods as already described. Hammurabi was the sixth king of the Amorites to rule in Babylon, and it was he who finally consolidated the whole country.

From this time the independence of the Sumerian city-states was permanently lost, and henceforward "Semitic" Babylon was the center of Mesopotamia civilization. The original Sumerian language died out altogether, to be replaced by the Akkadian of Babylon.

Shortly after the death of Hammurabi, about 1750 B.C., Babylon came under the control of the barbarian Kassites, who ruled it and the greater part of Babylonia, with occasional lapses from power, for over eight hundred years, but made few further advances in civilization beyond the introduction of the horse. During this time the Hittites, to be dealt with in the next chapter, were the predominant power in Asia Minor, though they do not seem to have tried to extend their power as far east as Babylonia, contenting themselves with sporadic raids. Not until the rise of Assyria to the domination of the entire Near East were the Kassites finally overthrown, and Babylon captured in 910 B.C.

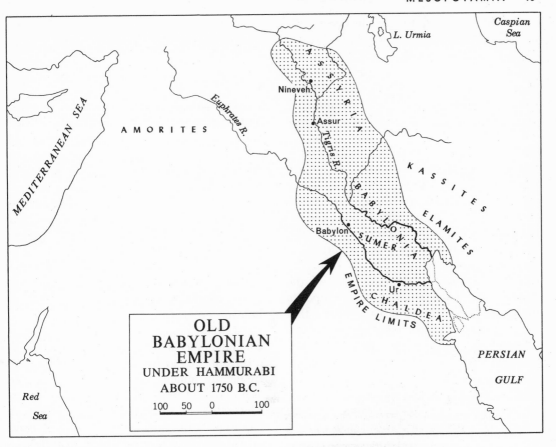

OLD
BABYLONIAN
EMPIRE
UNDER HAMMURABI
ABOUT 1750 B.C.

100  50  0  100

### ▶ Mesopotamia under Hammurabi—The Hammurabi Code

The rule of Hammurabi in Babylonia and the elevation of Marduk, the god of Babylon, to the chief position in the celestial universe were marked by no great cultural advances. But we are well informed about the life of the times, and the political and economic administration of the period, through our possession of the great Hammurabi Code and some of the official correspondence of the great king.

The code was given to him by Shamash, the god of the sun and of justice. It was therefore this god who inspired him; but Shamash is not given credit for the authority to execute the laws, which is specifically ascribed to the old Sumerian gods Anu and Enlil, and to Marduk, who has just replaced the latter. "When lofty Anu . . . and Enlil . . .

determined for Marduk, the first born of En-ki, the Enlil functions over all mankind . . . called Babylon by its exalted name, made it supreme in the world . . . at that time Anu and Enlil named me to promote the welfare of the people, me, Hammurabi, the god-fearing prince, to cause justice to prevail in the land, to destroy the wicked and the evil, that the strong might not oppress the weak . . . ."[7]

If we translate these theological terms into earthly conceptions, we shall find that this is a very accurate description of the nature of the code, which is a mixture of old barbarous custom and more modern attempts at administering an evenhanded justice. The old arbitrary gods were still accepted, but Marduk and Hammurabi were anxious to establish themselves as supreme overlords

[7] Pritchard, *Ancient Near Eastern Texts,* tr. T. J. Meek, p. 164.

of the country, and to give justice to the people, as far as was compatible with sanctified custom. No doubt the new ruler recognized the value for his dynasty of having justice enforced by the state rather than by private vengeance; but it was not possible to abolish this latter at one blow in the face of the conservative customs of the people. It is also noteworthy that Hammurabi at least acknowledged that the laws ought to be just, in response to the wishes of the gods. He was still the representative of the gods on earth.

Any selection from this famous code is likely to give a false impression. Only by judicious but unfair selection would it be possible to produce any general theory of the nature of law in the early part of the second millennium B.C. But the composite nature of the code does at least suggest that a serious attempt was being made to improve it. And a knowledge of how the law was administered is lacking. We do not know

A stela showing Hammurabi receiving his code of laws from the sun god Shamash, who was also the god of justice. The code itself is inscribed on the stela. (COURTESY THE LOUVRE)

if the older and more barbarous parts were ever put into effect. These, however, would appear in any codification carried out without respect to usage. It must always be remembered that the Hammurabi Code is a codification and not a new series of laws, and suffers from all the defects of codifications.

One barbarous survival is the so-called lex talionis, applied in a manner which hardly seems to accord with any abstract conception of justice. If a man kill another man's son, his son shall be put to death. If this provision is not merely repeated because it was in the old law, then it would show an extreme sense of property in a family, the children belonging like chattels to the father. But this is at variance with other more humane provisions of the same code.

Capital punishment in the code is very common, especially for offenses against property. But we do not know whether it was frequently inflicted or was intended to act as a deterrent to theft and misappropriation. The code of the Twelve Tables with its barbarous penalties remained the basic law code of the Romans. But we know that Roman citizens for hundreds of years were always permitted to choose exile instead of death, and that when Julius Caesar as high priest tried to revive some of the old laws and their strange penalties, it outraged the feelings of even the most conservative senators. In the early nineteenth century in England, capital punishment could be inflicted for the theft of property worth more than a shilling. But we also know that juries refused to convict when the law made such a penalty mandatory.

But certain features of Babylonian society do emerge clearly from the code. Justice was unequal. The population was divided into three classes, nobles, free commoners, and serfs and slaves. Crimes against nobles were dealt with more severely than those against the lower classes; but nobles themselves were also in many cases dealt with more severely if it was they who committed the crime. Property seems to have been rated above human life—crimes against property being usually treated more severely. Even accidental homicide was regarded as a crime against the victim's family and compensated accordingly. Murder was not a crime against the state but against the person. Aliens were treated liberally, women held a relatively high position, and there were extensive regulations for industry and trade, as might be expected in a commercial civilization. Noteworthy is the fact that private tenure of land seems to have been the rule, unlike the system described for the Sumerian city-states. Peasants were sharecroppers or serfs as before; but, in addition to the priests, the government and nobles now owned the land. This probably reflects the changed conditions under a conquering house of invaders who would not necessarily respect the arrangements made by deities for their sustenance, even while they accepted the general divine order decreed by them. The sharecroppers were protected by law against eviction before the end of the contract year—as before under the regime of the gods—and against obligation to pay full rent if the crop failed.

There are many provisions governing marriage in the code. Evidently it was a legal contract in Babylonia. Though the wife was the legal property of her husband and brought a marriage gift to him, she had some rights, being permitted to return to her father if ill treated by her husband. Although marriage was ordinarily for life, divorce was permissible; the bridal gift would be returned with her, and she would keep the custody of the children. Women were allowed to engage in business, and had as many business rights as the men. However, if the husband fell into debt the wife could be sold as payment for it. There are severe penalties for adultery and other sexual offenses.

If we knew more about the earlier law codes and, as said earlier, if we knew how it was administered, we could comment with more confidence upon the significance of this code and how far it represented an advance upon earlier thinking. But the correspondence

of Hammurabi shows at least that he took his duties very seriously. Quite trivial disputes he investigated himself, and there are several instances of his sending back cases for retrial, as well as handing down decisions himself. There can be little doubt that the parts of the code which stem from Hammurabi and Babylon represent a codification of existing practices in the commercial civilization of Babylonia. It cannot, however, be described truly as the first secular legislation. It is significant that it was represented as having divine sanction and as being unalterable, and that it was enforced by the authority both of the ruler and the gods. Legislation that was truly secular, and subject to change by duly authorized legislators, did not arise until the time of the Romans. Even the Greeks entrusted their basic legislation to individuals, and those who proposed to modify these laws ran the risk of severe penalties if the proposals were turned down.

It is certain that both the Hammurabi Code and the whole Mesopotamian legal tradition had a marked influence upon the Hebrew law of a far later epoch, especially upon those parts of the Hebrew codes which seem to be the most ancient. Here no fewer than thirty-five provisions out of fifty are similar. Even the language in both has marked resemblances. The probable explanation is the influence the legal tradition had upon Canaanites and other peoples of Palestine rather than any direct borrowing by the Hebrews. The Hebrews would naturally adopt some of the customs of the Canaanites; and if, as seems probable, there were already Israelites in Palestine before the exodus of the captives from Egypt, during the reunion of the two branches of the people after the exodus each would absorb customs and laws from the other.

▶ **The Empire of the Assyrians**

THE RISE OF THE ASSYRIANS TO POWER IN THE NEAR EAST AND IN EGYPT

When Babylon fell about 910 B.C. to the Assyrians, the conquerors were not a newly established people, but had been settled in northern Mesopotamia as early as 3000 B.C. During the period of Sumerian and Babylonian ascendancy they had been a pastoral, and then a trading, people, but had always been in danger from their neighbors. We know of wars they fought against Babylonians, Hittites, and Mitanni, as well as against mountaineers and Aramaeans who overran their defenseless frontiers.

The whole history of Assyria is relatively well documented from the records of the great library of Assurbanipal at Nineveh, and inscriptions which have been excavated since the middle of the nineteenth century in other Assyrian cities. From these records we can see the gradual turning of a peaceful people into a nation of warriors, sudden periods of domination over their neighbors followed by periods of quiescence when their enemies were too strong for them. Then, at last, the building of the greatest empire the world had yet seen by the use of methods that have made the Assyrians the byword in later times for ruthless and unprogressive militarism and imperialism. In the Assyrian records there is no attempt to hide the ruthlessness of the conquerors. On the contrary, they boast of it, evidently considering it to be the most effective imperial policy.

We also have the records of the Hebrew prophets and chroniclers, who seem to have looked upon Assyria as the necessary scourge of God, and with a kind of horrible fascination at their wickedness. The delirious delight of Nahum at the destruction of Nineveh, unmatched anywhere else in the Bible, gives some measure of the hatred it had inspired: "Woe to the city, bloody throughout, full of lies and booty. I will strip off your skirts to your face. . . . I will throw vile things at you. And treat you with contempt and make you a horror; so that everyone that sees you will flee from you."[8]

[8] Nahum 3:1, 5–7. This and other Biblical translations in this text are taken from J. M. P. Smith, E. J. Goodspeed, and others, tr., *The Complete Bible, an American Translation* (Chicago: The University of Chicago Press, 1939).

Once the Assyrians had embarked on their aggressive policy they went into it thoroughly. By devoting all their capacities to military invention they far surpassed the technical abilities of their opponents. Few as they were in numbers, they were never defeated in battle until the very end, when their resources were too thin to permit defense on all fronts. Conquered countries were made to pay tribute; if the tribute was not forthcoming at the proper time a lightning expedition would be made against the defaulters, who would pay dearly, as an example to other would-be offenders. All rebellions were crushed ruthlessly, Sennacherib razing the great city of Babylon to the ground and turning the waters of the Euphrates over the site. In the Assyrian records there is mention of wholesale massacres, terrible tortures, public exhibition of the bloody heads of corpses on the battlements of conquered cities, even by those kings, like Assurbanipal, who devoted themselves also to peaceful pursuits. They used iron on an extensive scale for weapons, the first nation to do so; they made use of a mounted cavalry, they invented the battering ram and special siege machinery capable of overcoming the brick cities of Mesopotamia and Palestine without too much difficulty. They conquered the whole of Mesopotamia and most of Palestine, deporting the inhabitants of Samaria and sending in immigrants from elsewhere so that there would be no further disturbance—a policy used by them frequently elsewhere. They did not conquer Judah, however, the deliverance being ascribed to the angel of the Lord who destroyed the Assyrian army of Sennacherib. Judah did, nevertheless, become tributary to Assyria, as the records show. Esarhaddon also conquered Egypt, as already related, but the Assyrians could not rule such a vast land with so few men, and they had to abandon it soon afterward.

ORGANIZATION OF THE EMPIRE

The rule of the Assyrians was not, however, entirely without its compensations for the conquered peoples so long as they submitted and continued to pay tribute.[9] Local wars between their subjects came to an end, an efficient provincial administration was developed to keep a close watch on governors and subject kings, who had to keep in continuous correspondence with the capital. Roads were built, and a regular royal postal service was inaugurated. A considerable amount of self-government was permitted to the subject cities, and, in particular, trade, in which the native Assyrian of imperial times took little interest, flourished, mainly in the

[9] Their work has also been valuable for *us,* in that they carefully collected the records of earlier civilizations of Mesopotamia, preserving them in their libraries. Once destroyed, Nineveh, their capital, unlike Babylon, was never again refounded, as the very site was cursed; and their records remained there intact until they were uncovered by archaeologists more than two thousand years later.

hands of the Aramaeans, a people who will be briefly discussed in the next chapter.

### CULTURAL ACHIEVEMENTS

The Assyrian kings were great builders, living in fine palaces with pleasure gardens, and constantly building and rebuilding temples. There was little original in their work, and they did not make much use of stone although it was abundant in their empire. Their whole culture and religion was, as already mentioned, Babylonian, and, through Babylon, Sumerian in its basis. In fact, toward the end of the Assyrian imperial age Marduk seems to have been almost as important as their native god Assur. They made use of Babylonian science and patronized it, altering the cuneiform script by the addition of more symbols. Their many reliefs

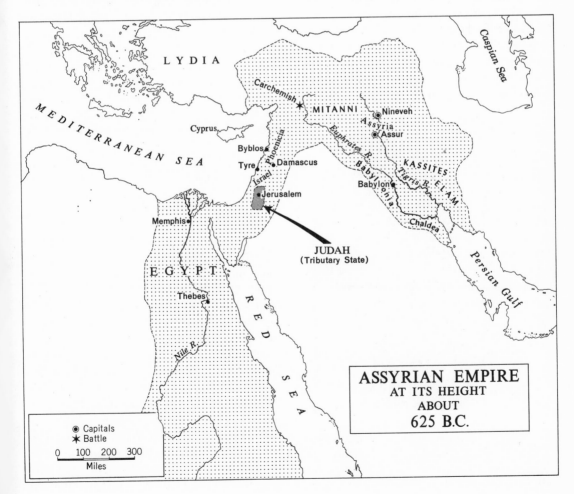

ASSYRIAN EMPIRE
AT ITS HEIGHT
ABOUT
625 B.C.

⊙ Capitals
★ Battle
0   100   200   300
Miles

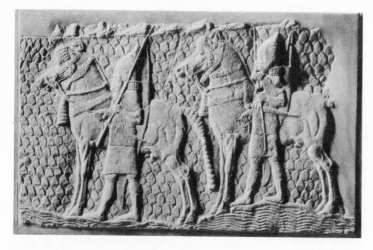

*Wall slab (alabaster) from the palace of Sennacherib at Nineveh, showing the king's cavalry in the mountains.* (COURTESY THE METROPOLITAN MUSEUM OF ART)

in their monumental architecture were well executed but Sumerian in inspiration.

It would seem that the Assyrian rulers were more conscious of the past of the Mesopotamian peoples than were the Babylonians whom they supplanted. It has already been mentioned how many of the old stories are known to us only through Assyrian versions, and how frequently the Assyrians copied them. The Babylonian kings of the

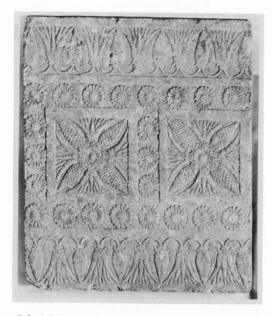

*Slab (alabaster) from a pavement in the palace of Sennacherib at Nineveh. The design shows lotus blossoms, palm cones, and rosettes.* (COURTESY THE METROPOLITAN MUSEUM OF ART)

Hammurabi Age were far less attached to the idea of the king as the representative of the gods on earth and responsible to them than were these even more powerful monarchs. Never were the temples in Mesopotamia so prosperous as under the Assyrian despots. Perhaps the more civilized of their kings may have felt the hatred of the conquered peoples and realized the weak foundations of their empire, and desperately tried to ward off the evil day. Military conquerors in all ages, not excluding the twentieth century A.D. have been superstitious, playing their luck and looking to omens and astrologers for reassurance.

### FALL OF THE ASSYRIAN EMPIRE

However this may be, the final destruction of the Assyrians was sudden and merciless. It was believed impossible to defeat them in battle if the numbers were at all equal. An exiled prince from Babylonia tried to raise a coalition against them but failed repeatedly. Nevertheless the peoples to the east of Mesopotamia were able to advance slowly and relentlessly, Medes and Chaldeans, and Scythians from the north—all sure of the support of the conquered peoples if the Assyrian hold should weaken. The Assyrians fought back, still winning every local engagement, until suddenly the coalition took Nineveh and razed it to the ground, thus destroying the basis of the state. Still the Assyrian remnants fought on from the old capital of Assur until Nebuchadnezzar, son of the new Chaldean king of Babylon, defeated them and their Egyptian allies decisively in 606 B.C. at the battle of Carchemish. The Assyrians received no mercy as they had shown none. The very people disappeared from history, killed or absorbed into the population of their conquerors.

Subsequent peoples from that day to this have pointed to the fate of the Assyrians as an object lesson for imperialists, and as a people they have had few admirers. Nevertheless they did prepare the way for a great flowering of civilization in Mesopotamia, first under the Chaldeans, then the Medes, and finally the Persians. The East had moved into an era of great empires, and the civilization thus built up was absorbed into the heritage of the West when Alexander the Macedonian three hundred years later conquered the last feeble Persians and founded the Greco-Oriental civilization which exercised such a profound influence on the Romans, and through them and through Christianity upon ourselves. By uniting the Mesopotamian people after a long period of disunity the Assyrians blazed the way for their more constructive successors.

▶ **The Chaldeans and New Babylonia**

PIETY, ANTIQUARIANISM—ASTROLOGY

The new empire of the Chaldeans at Babylon quickly showed signs of wishing to inherit the mantle of Assyria. Nebuchadnezzar tried to take Tyre and failed, but he succeeded in defeating Egypt severely in several battles, though he did not conquer it. He was at first content with installing a tributary king in Jerusalem; but after repeated rebellions he took the leading Jews captive to Babylon, and Judah was incorporated into his empire. Thus he became overlord of almost all Palestine, and for the rest of his reign retired to his capital of Babylon, which was then enjoying a cultural renascence, in many respects the most brilliant of all.

The people who controlled Babylonia at that time were called Chaldeans, both by

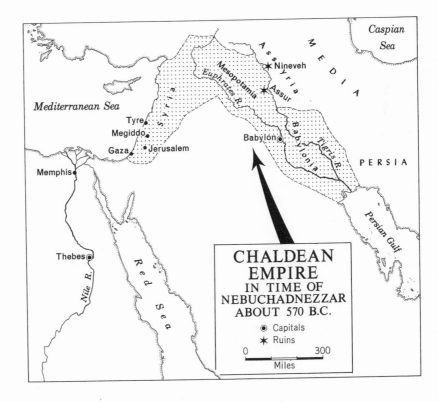

CHALDEAN EMPIRE IN TIME OF NEBUCHADNEZZAR ABOUT 570 B.C.

◉ Capitals
★ Ruins

0    300
Miles

the Hebrews and by the Greek historian Herodotus. In Mesopotamian records the name appears only toward the end of the Assyrian Empire. As far as can be judged they do not seem to have been a people different from the Semitic Babylonians of earlier times, though it is possible that exiles from the Assyrian domination now returned to Babylonia from regions to the East, bearing with them astronomical knowledge which gave a new impetus to the study of the stars, which increased greatly in this period of Chaldean rule. The Chaldean kings made every effort to restore the ancient Mesopotamian heritage, and there was a pronounced trend toward antiquarianism. The Chaldean attitude toward religion bears a strong resemblance to the piety of the later Egyptians. It was as if all life had left it, and the only thing that remained was to try to blow upon the old fires and hope to revive them. The result, as in Egypt, was formalism—the revival of the form without the living substance.

Submission to the gods had always been a characteristic of Mesopotamian religion. But now it became a simple matter of resignation and humility before the unalterable decrees of fate. It was still not an ethical religion such as the one the Hebrews developed; sin, as before, was the failure to behave in the manner prescribed by the gods, and had no relation to moral behavior on the earth. As explained earlier, the study of astrology would fit in naturally with the Mesopotamian world-conception; but it was even further removed from the reach of the people, since no one could understand the star lore without instruction. In earlier days they could at least recognize omens. But with the enthronement of astrology as the supreme science the ordinary people were too far removed from the gods to do more than offer humble submission to their decrees. So arose the conception of fate and destiny which was to play such a large part in Oriental thought thereafter.

Chaldean interest in astrology, however, did give rise to the science of astronomy, which reached heights far beyond anything previously achieved by the Mesopotamian peoples. They charted the entire heavens, they worked out a system for the recording of time which was the best so far achieved, and they calculated the length of the year with an error of only twenty-six minutes. All celestial occurrences were recorded with meticulous care. The planets were equated with the old Babylonian gods, and given their names. All this work was continued under the Persians, Greeks, and Romans; from the ancient Chaldean astrologers has come not only all subsequent astrology, especially as developed by the Muslims; but also our own astronomy.

## THE CITY OF NEW BABYLON

The absence of a living religion did not prevent the building of great temples in the new Babylon of Nebuchadnezzar. The great temple of Marduk excited the enthusiasm of Herodotus, the Greek tourist and historian, and his description of the ziggurat in the temple and the whole city corresponds very exactly to the results of modern archaeological investigation. It was probably the largest ziggurat ever built. Nebuchadnezzar's palace, with its Hanging Gardens, was for the Greek one of the seven wonders of the world. The famous gardens were a terraced roof garden high above the ground with tropical plants growing in it in great profusion. The city of this king, devoted to peaceful arts and a thriving trade, was one of the greatest, perhaps the greatest city in the world of the day, larger by far than any previous Mesopotamian city. This was the city where the final ethical religion of the Jews was developed, the city whose luxuries tempted them so sorely, the city whose inhabitants to the more puritan among them seemed to symbolize everything they must avoid, the very essence of wickedness and worldly vice. "Daughter of Babylon who art to be destroyed, happy shall he be that rewardeth thee as thou hast served us. Happy shall he be that taketh and dasheth thy little ones against the stones."[10]

[10] Psalms 137:8.

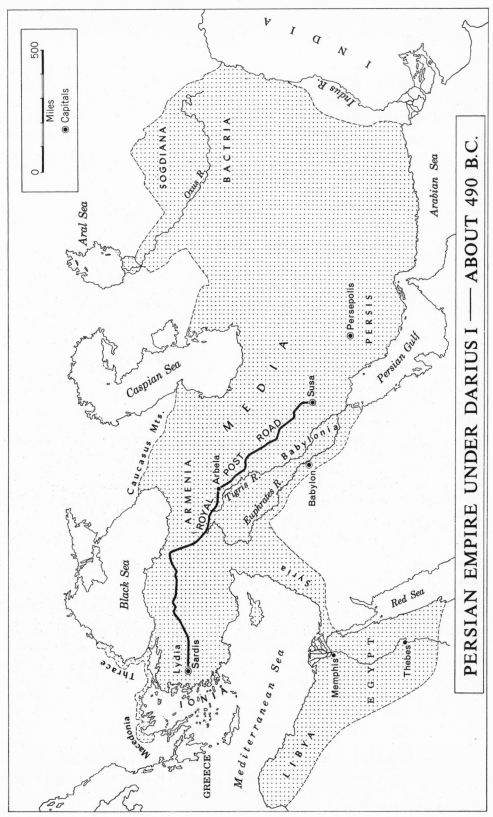

PERSIAN EMPIRE UNDER DARIUS I — ABOUT 490 B.C.

▶ **The great Persian Empire**

CONQUEST OF BABYLONIA

To the northeast of the new Babylonia a warlike power was gathering strength. The Medes, a people of an Indo-European and not Semitic language, had already joined forces with the Chaldeans in the destruction of Assyria. But thereafter friendly relations had not been maintained, and the Medes extended their empire further east, bringing another Indo-European people, the Persians, under their rule. The Persians, however, under a young and adventurous prince who went down in history as Cyrus the Great, revolted from the Medes in 549 B.C., and the Medes, apparently without serious opposition, accepted him as king. Thus was formed a strong imperial power, a potential threat to the rapidly weakening Chaldean regime. The story of the "conquest" of Babylon by Cyrus is told in the Book of Daniel—how Belshazzar the king was feasting when he saw the writing on the wall which told him that his kingdom was to be divided and given to the Medes and Persians; and "the same night" Cyrus entered the city and fulfilled the prophecy. However this may be, Cyrus in his own records declared that he took Babylon "without a battle and without fighting" and there can be no doubt that he experienced little opposition from the Chaldeans. The incorporation of Babylonia into his empire made it the greatest that the world had yet seen, stretching as far east as the borders of Turkestan and India, and west to the Aegean Sea. For before proceeding against Babylon Cyrus had conquered Lydia, the chief power in Asia Minor, and expanded his power equally in Central Asia.

In Babylon Cyrus was hailed as a deliverer by the influential classes as well as by the Jews, who were permitted to return to Jerusalem and build their temple. Although his religion was quite different from the one he encountered in Babylon, he had the political good sense to proclaim himself the servant of Marduk and accepted the throne as a gift from Marduk and his priests.

The city became henceforth one of the capitals of the Persian Empire. It had to pay taxes to the Great King (as the Persian emperor was always called) like all the conquered lands; but in return the whole of Mesopotamia for the first time enjoyed the benefits of a comparatively enlightened administration and an internal peace which endured until the conquests of Alexander the Great. These benefits, however, were not, for the most part, the work of the great conqueror Cyrus, who was killed in battle while still a fairly young man, nor of his successor Cambyses, who conquered Egypt, but of Darius the Great who usurped the throne when Cambyses died on the way home from Egypt.

GOVERNMENT AND PROVINCIAL ADMINISTRATION

The problem of organizing this vast empire presented many great difficulties. Sardis, the capital of Lydia, an outpost of the empire, was fifteen hundred miles from Susa, the chief imperial capital—a tremendous distance when the difficulty of communication is considered. And though the Persians did not attempt to interfere with local customs, they were still a conquering people and regarded as such. A show of force was necessary to ensure obedience and payment of the taxes required from their subjects. Persians, moreover, had special privileges in the matter of taxation and officeholding in the imperial administration. Nevertheless, the organization set up by Darius did endure for two hundred years in spite of local rebellions by dissatisfied subjects and disobedient governors.

For administrative purposes the country was divided into provinces, each under an official called a satrap. He was head of the civil administration and led the king's armies in the province in the event of war. But the military establishment in other respects remained under the direct authority of the king. The satraps also had to submit to inspection by other officials who were appointed by, and were directly responsible to, the king and who were supposed to keep him informed on the efficiency and loyalty of the satrap. The satrap was responsible for collecting the taxes of the province, which were realistically set at a figure which enabled the satrap to remit to the monarch less than he collected. The system, therefore, was a mixture of local and centralized government like the republican provincial administration of Rome. The chief difference, however—and it is perhaps in favor of the Persian system—was that the satrap could remain in office only as long as he performed his duties capably, and he was always liable to dismissal by the king; whereas the Roman official was restrained only by the threat of legal proceedings by the provincials *after* he had laid down his office, when he had the proceeds of his tenure at his disposal to bribe the juries.

THE ARMY

The army commanded by the Persian king was formidable in size, but motley in its composition, and of doubtful loyalty outside the famous band of Immortals—a picked body of Persian nobles—and the standing army of native Persians who formed the personal bodyguard of the Great King. The difficulty experienced by the Persians in their wars with Greece, especially when attacked by Alexander the Great, was that the levies liable for service belonged to all the subject peoples of the empire, with different military customs and different traditions. Moreover, they could not be assembled at a moment's notice, but required time both for assembly and for training together. It was possible for Xerxes to recruit a mighty army when he was the aggressor and could choose the moment for his expedition; but even so the army was seldom a match for the smaller numbers of well-trained, disciplined, and patriotic Greeks. But it was not possible for the later Darius who had to face Alexander to assemble his army all together at one time when he was on the defensive against the vastly smaller Macedonian forces. So Alexander was able to defeat him piecemeal. One thing, however, the Persians always possessed —money; and with this they could afford to hire Greek and other foreign mercenaries,

and could intrigue, as the later Persian kings did, to prevent the union of Greek city-states in a possible offensive alliance against themselves. They were also able to mobilize a large fleet, manned for the most part by Greeks and Phoenicians, some of whom were in the empire and some of whom were hired as mercenaries. With this fleet the Persians explored the southern Asiatic coast to the borders of India, and restored the canal, newly built by one of the last Egyptian Pharaohs, between the Nile and the Red Sea.

Darius also restored and greatly improved the postal system of the Assyrians. He built new roads to connect with the imperial capital, and along these he stationed relays of fast horsemen to carry messages. By this means the time for news to travel from Sardis to Susa was cut from three months to less than two weeks. The new roads were also a great assistance to trade and general intercourse within the empire. In spite, therefore, of the local variations within this empire the culture became authentically Persian over the centuries, though the dominant language in its western half was Aramaean, with its alphabet from which a new Persian alphabet of thirty-nine letters was formed. The cuneiform languages gradually died out under this competition.

RELIGION

### Zoroaster and the traditions of the Avesta

While for the most part the Persians adopted and developed the culture of their predecessors, as was to be expected of a people only recently emerged from barbarism, and while in Mesopotamia and Palestine they did not interfere with local religions, adapting their religious policies as required, they brought with them an entirely new religion of their own, many features of which were in the course of time to supplant the older ones, and to exercise a profound influence upon all later religions, including Christianity and Islam.

The origins of what is called Zoroastrianism lie far back in the remote past, and it is impossible to determine how much of the

*One of the rich finds of the University of Chicago expedition, near Persepolis, was this sculptured relief on a stairway. Persepolis, the Versailles of ancient Persia, was burned by Alexander the Great during a drunken debauch.* (WIDE WORLD PHOTO)

Persian religion was of recent origin, how much was due to the influence of the prophet Zoroaster or Zarathustra, who lived perhaps as late as the sixth or seventh century B.C., and how much came from remote antiquity. The prophet himself was always a mysterious figure, and the teachings of his religion, as propounded by himself and enlarged by the Magian priests of the Persian religion, were not collected in one book, the *Zend-Avesta,* until the early Christian Era. As with the religion of India, there was a considerable religious tradition handed down by word of mouth for centuries before it was found necessary to record it in writing. Even in the *Zend-Avesta* itself there is so much that is mysterious and difficult to comprehend that it cannot be used directly as a book of religious teachings without a key which is missing and will probably never be known. The very century of the prophet's birth—whether in fact he ever lived at all—is not known for certain, in spite of many studies by Westerners. And the apparent teaching that Zarathustra was to return again in nine thousand years to bring about a new age in the

history of mankind, and that his appearance was to be a constantly recurring phenomenon, has led some students to believe that the "historical" Zarathustra assumed the name only because of some earlier Zarathustra who lived thousands of years earlier and was the traditional founder of Persian civilization. Persian tradition claims that a prophet Zarathustra initiated the Neolithic Revolution, and the many references to agriculture and its importance in the *Zend-Avesta* are adduced as support for the tradition.

However all this may be, and however little we may be able to use the cryptic writings of the *Zend-Avesta* as historical source material, it is clear that Zoroastrianism in the form in which we find it during the Persian Empire and in its many important successors, was a religion which was well suited to supplant the older Mesopotamian religions which, as has been seen, were already in their death throes. For this reason alone, if for no other, the existence of a comparatively late prophet, who at the very least refounded and reinterpreted the traditional religion, would seem probable. For

Zoroastrianism was clearly an ethical religion, one that appealed to the developing spiritual capacities of mankind, and fitted to command the faith and allegiance of individuals rather than the devotion of the state, and the people as members of the state. It was deeply concerned, as the older religions were not, with the problem of good and evil, ethical good and evil, and not merely with the failure to observe prescribed ritual practices or to understand what the gods required of man and his integration within the order of the universe.

### Dualism—The spirit of light and the spirit of darkness

The world had been created by Ahura-Mazda, the god of light. But though he would ultimately triumph, he was not omnipotent, and was engaged in a constant struggle with the god of darkness, Aingra-Manu, or Ahriman, who was the embodiment of all wickedness, treachery, and deceit and possessed of almost equal powers. Each of these gods had his attendant host of spirits ceaselessly working for him. It was man's duty—within limits he had free choice—to aid the god of light in his struggle with the god of darkness and help to overcome him. The Persian kings all claimed their position by the grace of Ahura-Mazda and conceived it as their duty to support the rule of light upon earth, administer justice, and rule according to righteousness. Darius expressed this ideal in the Behistun inscription referred to earlier. The priests of Zarathustra, usually called the Magi, kept alive the sacred fire, the symbol of Ahura-Mazda in their temples.

### Ethical system and the belief in immortality

Zoroastrianism contained a definite and clear belief in a future life. In the process of time the good powers would overcome the evil, and then a messiah would be born to prepare the end of the world. The last great day would then come when Ahriman would be finally vanquished, and the souls of the dead would be judged according to their deeds, the justified would at once enter Paradise, while the wicked would be cast into Hell with their master Ahriman. There they would serve him until they too would be redeemed in a far distant future. There can be little doubt that the Christian story of the Wise Men of the East who visited the infant Jesus in Bethlehem to worship him was intended to show that the priests of Zarathustra had recognized in him the Messiah whom they awaited.

The sins which lead to damnation are catalogued—pride, gluttony, sloth, and other of the Christians' "deadly sins,"—as are also the virtues—keeping contracts, obeying rulers, tilling the soil, showing mercy, giving alms, and not doing to others what one did not wish done to one's self. Early Zoroastrianism, unlike the later religions which developed from it and stressed the evil nature of the material world, did not approve of asceticism, self-inflicted suffering, and excessive fasting or grief.

### Successors of Zoroastrianism—Mithraism, Manichaeism, medieval heresies

The elements of this new revealed religion which affected later Judaism and Christianity are obvious; and it may be said that many of its best features found their fruition elsewhere than in those religions which developed directly from it. In Mithraism, which in the Roman Empire presented such competition to Christianity during the first centuries of the Christian Era, there is far more stress laid on Mithras the Redeemer, as also upon the evil nature of the world, than in Zoroastrianism, with the resultant emphasis on the corrupt nature of mankind and the means of overcoming it in self-mortification. By the time of the rise of Manichaeism in the third century A.D. the world has been altogether corrupted by the god of darkness, with all its terrible consequences; and matter itself is conceived of as evil. From this teaching came the beliefs of the Cathari and Albigensians in medieval Europe. But these religions and their influence upon Christianity will be kept for a brief discussion in a later chapter.

► **Conclusion—The influence of Mesopotamia**

We have now traced the history of Mesopotamia until the coming of the Greeks. The greatest direct contribution of these peoples to Western civilization was probably their science, which became mingled with Greek science and so was passed on to the West after the conquests of Alexander. The art of writing was discovered by them, they did important work in mathematics, and they laid the foundations of astronomy. Indirectly their work was of the greatest importance for the Hebrews, since they gave them their basic law, and from them sprang the whole tradition of submission and obedience to the gods who ruled the universe. The Persians added an ethical emphasis which affected both later Hebrew thought and Christianity, with their conception of the Last Judgment and rewards and punishments in the next world, and new thoughts on the nature of good and evil. The Assyrians provided a great object lesson on the dangers of undiluted imperialism which was appreciated and profited from by the Persians and Greeks who followed them.

In bulk the contribution of Mesopotamia does not begin to compare with the legacy to the West of the Greeks and Romans, though it probably surpasses the legacy of Egypt; but in the depth of its influence it is surpassed by few civilizations. Without the pioneer work of the Mesopotamian peoples in science and religion the lives of all later peoples would have been substantially different. And Mesopotamia itself did not cease to be a center of civilization, but again rose to power and influence under the Parthians, the Sassanid Persians, and the Muslim Abbasids. But by this time the independent civilizations of the West were growing up and the civilizations of the Near East had only a minor influence upon them. When Harun-al-Rashid of Bagdad and Charlemagne of Aachen exchanged courtesies in the eighth century A.D., each knew almost nothing of the other. The East and West had embarked on their independent journeys.

► **Suggestions for further reading**

For the interpretation of Mesopotamian life used in this chapter the author is again indebted to the work of the Oriental Institute in Chicago. The Mesopotamian chapters written by Thorkild Jacobsen in Henri Frankfort *et al., The Intellectual Adventure of Ancient Man* (Chicago: The University of Chicago Press, 1946), present the evidence for the general pessimistic outlook of the various Mesopotamian peoples, while the position of the Mesopotamian kings is studied in greater detail in Henri Frankfort, *Kingship and the Gods* (Chicago: The University of Chicago Press, 1948). The first-mentioned of these two books is reprinted, as far as the material on Mesopotamia is concerned, in Henri Frankfort *et al., Before Philosophy* (Harmondsworth, Middlesex: Penguin Books, 1951). Many of the original documents showing the relationship between the Assyrian kings and their priests are printed in R. H. Pfeiffer, *State Letters of Assyria* (New Haven, Conn.: American Oriental Society, 1935). An up-to-date account of the daily life in Mesopotamia, excellently illustrated, based on the latest archaeological investigations, is contained in G. Contenau, *Everyday Life in Babylon and Assyria* (tr. K. R. and A. R. Maxwell-Hyslop; New York: St. Martin's Press, 1954).

There are, however, no really satisfactory histories of Mesopotamia in ancient times. Perhaps the best for a beginning student, and sufficient to give him a general orientation in the subject, is G. S. Goodspeed, *A History of the Babylonians and Assyrians* (New York: Charles Scribner's Sons, 1921). Better histories of Assyria and Persia are, however, available. The standard work on Assyrian history is A. T. Olmstead, *History of Assyria* (New York: Charles Scribner's Sons, 1923), which may appear to some to be too favorable to imperialism, though the author defends his thesis by claiming that other empires have been just as bloody if more hypocritical. The book is very well written, and the author's enthusiasm for his subject is visible on every page. A suitable antidote may be found for his point of view in the brilliant attack of Arnold J. Toynbee on Assyrian imperialism in *A Study of History* (London: Oxford University Press, 1935), IV, 468–488. Here Toynbee offers the thesis that Assyrian specialization in militarism brought about the utter destruction of the state, and cites its downfall as a horrible example of suicidal warfare unredeemed by any success in the creative arts of civilization. Albert Olmstead's posthumously published *History of the Persian Empire* (Chicago: The University of Chicago Press, 1948) takes into account modern archaeological investigations, and is as brilliantly written as his *History of Assyria.* But it has several important defects, which would probably have been remedied if he had lived to revise it himself. Especially is he not sufficiently critical of his sources in dealing with Zoroastrianism. Curiously enough, a high priest of modern Parseeism has written a much more convincing and critical account of Zoroastrianism, which is probably the best work on the subject up to the present time, M. N. Dhalla, *History of Zoroastrianism* (New York: Oxford University Press, 1938). The most readable and analytical account of the organization of the Persian Empire is Clément Huart, *Ancient Persian and Iranian Civilization* (New York: Alfred A. Knopf, Inc., 1927), though modern archaeological investigation will probably need to add important details to this work, and change it in some particulars.

On the early civilization in Mesopotamia a useful short work is Henri Frankfort, *The Birth of Civilization in the Near East* (Bloomington, Ind.: Indiana University Press, 1951), while a standard pioneer work, many times reprinted, is Charles Leonard Woolley, *The Sumerians* (Oxford: The Clarendon Press, 1929), though it is to some degree marred by certain overhasty conclusions. The Hammurabi Code, together with much other important material, is printed in J. B. Pritchard, ed., *Ancient Near Eastern Texts Relating to the Old Testament,* with numerous valuable footnotes giving the comparable passages in the Old Testament lawbooks. The best commentary on the Code is S. R. Driver, *The Babylonian Laws* (New York: Oxford University Press, 1952), Vol. I, but much of this book will be found too difficult by the beginning student.

Books on the various special achievements of the Mesopotamian peoples which may prove useful are I. J. Gelb, *A Study of Writing* (Chicago: The University of Chicago Press, 1952); Howard Eves, *An Introduction to the History of Mathematics* (New York: Rinehart & Co., Inc., 1953); and Otto Neugebauer, *The Exact Sciences in Antiquity* (Princeton, N.J.: Princeton University Press, 1952). The last-named book contains an entire re-evaluation of the contribution of the Babylonians to science, which is difficult and technical, but very well worth while for any student interested in the origins of science who has the required technical ability to understand it.

# 5

# Maritime and Other Civilizations
# of the Ancient World

*General characteristics of the minor civilizations of the Near East • The civiliza-*
*tion of Asia Minor • The trading civilizations of the Near East • The peoples*
*of Palestine • The Hebrew contribution to civilization • Aegean civilization*

---

► ### General characteristics of the minor civilizations of the Near East

It has already been pointed out in an earlier chapter that the conventional classification of early civilizations into river-valley and maritime is not altogether an accurate one. Nevertheless, the civilizations to be discussed in this chapter all made a large part of their means of subsistence through foreign trade and industry, though the basis of the economy in most cases remained agricultural. The people known as the Aramaeans were independent only for a short time, with a state based on Damascus; thereafter they continued to be an important people acting as land traders under various masters, spreading their language until it became the predominant spoken tongue far beyond the original borders of their country and influencing every country in the Near East. The Phoenicians also knew only short periods of independence and power, but remained active as sea traders under their masters, performing a similar service for the greater empires that the Aramaeans performed on land. The Hittites and the Lydians, on the other hand, were strong states in Asia Minor and owned considerable territory; but both lost their in-

dependence, and to a large degree their national identity, after their empires fell.

The Hebrews, after building with great difficulty a strong state covering a fairly extensive territory, split into two parts, one of which lost its national identity after conquest by the Assyrians. The other, a tiny upland state with a hinterland of sparsely inhabited desert and based on the city of Jerusalem, but situated in a strategic position on an important trade route, maintained a precarious independence for a century and a half longer before being itself overthrown. The national identity of the Hebrews was preserved only because of the strong religious cohesion. Without this it could hardly have survived the destruction of the state, since the people as a whole had not developed a distinctive activity sufficient to keep that identity through so many misfortunes.

Finally, the Aegean civilization, unlike any of the others in this chapter, not only built up a powerful and distinctive culture, based securely on the island of Crete, but maintained independence for nearly two thousand years, thanks to the mixed economy of a balanced agriculture and industry combined with command of trade routes through a powerful navy. When it finally fell it had extended its influence through the mainland of Greece and the coast towns of Asia Minor, and its heritage was absorbed by the younger barbaric people who conquered it. This is the only civilization to be discussed in this chapter which can be considered great in its own right, though individual contributions of the other peoples have been of importance in the history of civilization, and the religious heritage of the Hebrews exercised an incalculable influence on all religious thought thereafter.

## ▶ The civilizations of Asia Minor

### THE HITTITES

It has just been said that the Hittites built a strong state in Asia Minor and held much territory under their control. Yet little was known about them until the twentieth century; and a hundred years ago no one considered them to be of any account. They were mentioned occasionally in the Old Testament, but always as if they were a minor people. The reason for this is that their great empire had already fallen into decay before any of the Hebrew records were committed to writing.

The first indication of their importance came from a few chance finds in Syria in an

*Hittite hieroglyphs, recently deciphered.* (COURTESY THE METROPOLITAN MUSEUM OF ART)

unknown language, in 1870, which excited the interest of archaeologists and stimulated the search for more. By 1907, when a great Hittite city was discovered near Boghaz-Keui in Anatolia, there was enough information available to show something of the scope of this Hittite Empire; and with the excavation of the city and the finding of extensive documents in the ruins the stage was set for an archaeological development as promising as that of Crete, which was in the same years being unearthed for the first time.

The great obstacle in both cases was the decipherment of the writing, which in the case of the Hittites was both cuneiform and hieroglyphic. The cuneiform was successfully deciphered in the second decade of this century but the hieroglyphic still remains unread.[1] It is now virtually established that the Hittite language is Indo-European in origin, though superimposed upon an earlier Semitic language.

On the whole, the Hittite discoveries were disappointing, except insofar as they served to fill in the serious gaps in our knowledge of the period. The people seem to have entered Asia Minor from northern highlands late in the third millennium B.C. By 1900 B.C. they had built an empire extending east from Asia Minor into the upper reaches of the Euphrates. At one time they were one of the conquerors of the early Assyrians, and they joined the Kassites in the conquest of Babylon, though it was the Kassites who inherited the kingdom of Babylonia. The Hittite Empire seems to have contracted for two centuries or so, then expanded again southward into Syria, competing with Egypt for the control of all Palestine until definite spheres of influence were arranged by the treaty of Kadesh in 1297 B.C. Perhaps its long wars with Egypt had exhausted the country, for about 1200 B.C. the Hittite Empire was suddenly overwhelmed by hordes of northern barbarians. The remnant of the Hittites retired to Carchemish on the Euphrates, where it maintained a commercial rather than an imperial independence until it was finally

[1] A recently discovered bilingual inscription may provide the long-awaited key.

## ▶ chronological chart

| Hittite Empire | | Aramaeans | | Phoenicians | |
|---|---|---|---|---|---|
| Migration into Asia Minor | *ca.* 2200 B.C. | | | In Palestine before 2000 B.C. | |
| Largest extent of Empire | 1900 | | | | |
| | | In Palestine | 1500 B.C. | | |
| | | | | Conquest by Egypt (Thutmose III) | 1447 |
| Battle of Kadesh and treaty with Rameses II of Egypt | 1297 | | | | |
| Fall of Hittite Empire (remnants around Carchemish) | 1200 | | | Independent Phoenician cities | 1200–1000 |
| | | | | Leadership of Tyre —maritime supremacy of Phoenicians | *ca.* 1000–774 |
| | | Kingdom of Damascus | *ca.* 1000–732 | | |
| | | Fall of Damascus to Assyrians (Tiglath– Pileser III) | 732 | Phoenicians tributary to Assyria | 774–625 |
| **Lydian Empire** | *ca.* 950–547 B.C | | | Phoenicians tributary to Persia | 538–332 |
| Fall of Sardis to Cyrus the Persian | 547 | | | Conquest of Phoenician cities by Alexander the Great | 332 |

*Sources:* G. E. Wright and F. V. Filson, eds., *Westminster Historical Atlas to the Bible* (Philadelphia: Westminster Press, 1945), and W. L. Langer, ed., *Encyclopaedia of World History* (rev. 3d ed.; Boston: Houghton Mifflin Company, 1952).

## Hebrews

| | |
|---|---|
| Wanderings of Hebrew patriarchs (?) | 2000–1700 B.C. |
| Family of Jacob migrates to Egypt (?) | 1700 |
| Exodus of Hebrews from Egypt (?) | 1260 |
| Period of Judges in Israel | 1225–1020 |
| Saul, king of Israel | 1020–1004 |
| David | 1004–965 |
| Solomon | 965–926 |
| Division of kingdom of Israel | 926 |
| Fall of Samaria to Assyrians | 721 |
| Fall of Jerusalem; Exile in Babylon | 586 |
| Return of Jews to Jerusalem | 538 |
| Building of the new temple | 520–516 |
| Conquest of Palestine by Alexander the Great (part of Ptolemy I's domain) | 332 |
| Palestine conquered by Antiochus III of Syria | 198 |
| Revolt of Maccabees against Antiochus IV | 167 |
| Conquest by Romans under Pompey, ruled by family of Herods, clients of Romans | 63 |
| Direct rule by Romans   A.D. | 6–41 |
| Jewish revolt against Romans | 66–70 |
| Destruction of Jerusalem by Titus | 70 |
| Jerusalem rebuilt under name of Aelian Capitolina; Jews not permitted to live in it; Judaea remains Roman province | 135 |

## Aegean Civilization

| | |
|---|---|
| Early Bronze Age in Crete  before | 3000 B.C. |
| Minoan civilizations in Crete | 3000–1400 |
| Mycenaean civilization on mainland | before 1600 |
| Conquest of Crete by Achaeans (?) | ca. 1400 |
| Conquest of Crete by Dorians | ca. 1200 |
| Fall of Troy to Achaeans and others | ca. 1184 |
| Dark Age in Crete and on mainland | 1100–800 |

absorbed by the Assyrians and neighboring peoples.

There is still not enough evidence from the excavations, and from such of the Hittite writings as have been deciphered, to make any just estimate of the Hittite civilization.[2] The Hittites are usually credited with the development of iron, which they obtained from Armenia or, in the opinion of some authorities, from Europe, where deposits are much richer than in Asia. At all events, they were the first Oriental people to make extensive use of it; and the superiority of that metal for warlike purposes may go far to explain their successes. They maintained a jealous monopoly of iron as long as they could, and there are records of presents of iron made to foreign potentates which were apparently much prized. They themselves also mined silver, copper, and lead, and carried on an extensive trade in metals. That they were not exclusively a warlike people but relied upon trade at least as much as on war for their penetration into foreign countries is suggested by the many Hittite products discovered far beyond their own borders. Moreover, the great bulk of the documents and clay tablets so far examined are legal and commercial, with some religious legends and stories, derived largely from Mesopotamian sources.

Their government was strongly centralized, with the king or the local governments owning all land and demanding services in return for its use, with wages and prices fixed for most commodities, and all services compensated at rates regulated by the state. An extensive Hittite law code has been translated, which is in many respects superior to the Babylonian, though apparently reflecting its influence.

Their architecture has few original features, though the palaces, with porch supported by two columns, with square towers guarded by great stone lions, have become familiar to Westerners through many pic-

[2] It may be mentioned that Hittite exploration at the present time is very active, supported wholeheartedly by the Turkish authorities, so that much of the information given here will probably soon need, if not revision, much supplementation.

tures. Their art was comparatively crude, consisting mostly of sculptural reliefs showing scenes of war and mythology. The latter was very inclusive, and we find a great number of stories familiar throughout the Near East adopted by the Hittites without important changes or originality. The great importance of the Hittites in history, apart from their introduction of iron, and probably the horse and chariot, was their function as intermediaries between Mesopotamia and Western Asia. The Hyksos were probably indebted to them, and it is possible that Troy in Asia Minor came under their influence. The Lydians, who inherited the Hittite power in Asia Minor and themselves influenced the Greeks in a later age, almost certainly learned from the Hittites the business methods which they used so effectively themselves.

### THE LYDIANS

The Lydians grew to power in Western Asia Minor at a time when the great ancient empires were in decline and the newer and more efficient empires had not yet arisen. They may have migrated from Europe and intermingled with the existing peoples, probably after the fall of the Hittites. They became prosperous by the exploitation of the natural mineral wealth of the country, including gold and electrum, a mixture of gold and silver found in river sands. The electrum gave them the opportunity to make their greatest contribution to civilization for which they are chiefly remembered—the coining of money. Prior to this time precious metals were usually weighed and the currency unit corresponded to a given weight. Now the Lydians began to stamp the electrum with its value and used it as money in

*The earliest coined money in the world. Invention attributed to the Lydians, three of whose coins are shown here.* (COURTESY THE METROPOLITAN MUSEUM OF ART)

our modern sense. The practice was quickly adopted by other countries which used gold and silver, thus considerably helping international trade. The Lydians established a strong and wealthy state based on Sardis, their capital, and extended their empire into the Greek (Ionian) coastal cities, but apparently without disturbing too much local self-government, as long as the subject cities paid their taxes regularly. The great age of Ionian science began during the Lydian rule. The last great king of Lydia was the famous and fabulously wealthy Croesus, about whom the Greeks wove many legends; and the sudden loss of his empire to Cyrus the Persian was the theme of many moral stories. Sardis, the Lydian capital, fell in 547 B.C. and the Lydian Empire was absorbed into Persia.

## ▶ The trading civilizations of the Near East

### THE ARAMAEANS

The Aramaeans, a Semitic people, were probably originally descended from nomad desert tribes who infiltrated into Syria during the decline of the Hittite Empire, and who, after its disappearance, established a number of small but prosperous kingdoms, the most important of which was Damascus. Biblical records tell us much of the relationship of the Hebrews with the kings of Damascus; on one occasion the prophet Elisha was even sent by God to instigate the murder of one king and anoint his murderer as king to the vacant throne. At all events, the kingdom of Damascus was very useful to the Hebrews, acting as a buffer state to absorb the shocks from Assyria and the north. It was not until Damascus had been taken that the full fury of the Assyrian onslaught was felt in Israel.

After the fall of Damascus the Aramaeans engaged in extensive trade, acting as factors for the uncommercial Assyrians, and surviving them. It was from the Aramaeans' alphabet that the new Babylonian state which rose on the Assyrian ruins had its first experience of an alphabet; and it was their language, spoken and written, that finally became the common language of the Near East. Jesus Christ spoke Aramaic, and some of the latest books of the Old Testament were written in this language, which displaced Hebrew even in Palestine itself. The Aramaeans are an interesting example of a people which made all its conquests by peaceful means after it had lost its national independence, thus providing a precedent for the later history of the Jews.

### THE PHOENICIANS

The Phoenicians were settled in northwest Palestine at a very early date in history. They are mentioned in Old Kingdom Egyptian records as shipbuilders and traders, and Sargon of Agade, the first conqueror of the Sumerians, claimed to have conquered them. They were frequently under foreign domination at all periods in their history, and no doubt this fact to some degree affected their prosperity; but all their conquerors found them too useful to allow their talents ever to be completely suppressed. They seem, however, to have suffered also from competition in the carrying trade from Minoan Crete and the maritime cities of Greece. For it was when these cities declined and when Hittite power which had controlled Phoenicia disappeared that they rose to their greatest heights of power and prosperity. At this time the chief Phoenician cities, Tyre, Sidon, Byblos, and Beirut, which had previously been separate and all relatively small, joined together for a period under the monarchy of Tyre, and all became prosperous and wealthy together. It was during this period that Hiram, king of Tyre, helped Solomon to build his temple. The Phoenicians did not, however, move far inland, where the Aramaeans were established in force, but preferred to make their living from industry and the sea.

They are usually credited with having sailed as far as Britain in search of tin for bronze, and it is certain that they traded with Spain. By tradition they were hired by one of the last Egyptian Pharaohs to circumnavigate the African continent, and they are said to have accomplished the mission successfully. They founded colonies through-

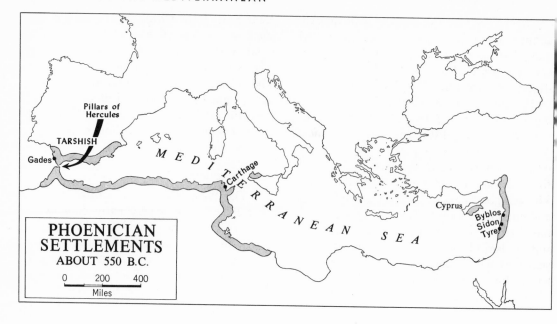

PHOENICIAN
SETTLEMENTS
ABOUT 550 B.C.

0     200     400

Miles

out the Mediterranean, the most important of which, Carthage, survived the fall of its founder and dominated the western Mediterranean until destroyed by Rome. They were evidently still the chief sea power in the Aegean and Mediterranean area in the Homeric epoch, and their wealth and skill in manufacture were proverbial.

In spite of a desperate resistance against the Assyrians, the union of Phoenician cities was unable to maintain its independence, and passed under the Assyrian yoke. They were also conquered by the Chaldeans of New Babylon, and by the Persians. Alexander captured Tyre after a long siege, then after the Phoenicians made another effort at independence one of his successors recaptured the city. The Phoenicians always retained their maritime skills, and their sailors and ships were always put to use by their conquerors. But they never again recovered the trade they had possessed before the Assyrian conquest. The Greeks who had remained free, and the Greek cities in Asia Minor in the Lydian and Persian empires, captured the bulk of Phoenician trade and never again lost it.

In addition to their seafaring and their

function as distributors of goods, especially the luxury products of Egypt, they had a thriving industry of their own, for the most part learned from Egypt. They were especially noted for their dye, the Tyrian purple, which was exclusive to them, being made from a Mediterranean shellfish. But they also excelled in glassware, textiles, and metalwork, with designs mostly borrowed from Egypt.

The Phoenicians have also usually been credited with the invention of the Semitic alphabet, from which the Greek and Roman alphabets were derived. The earliest known Phoenician alphabetic inscription is dated about 1300 B.C., and was found at Byblos; but much older alphabetic inscriptions are now known, so that it is no longer clear whether it was the Phoenicians themselves who developed the alphabet from Egyptian hieroglyphic signs, or whether they merely adopted it and transmitted it to Greece and elsewhere in the course of trade. At present most scholars seem to think that it was a Canaanitish people in Palestine that saw the value of alphabetic signs and made the alphabet. Its usefulness in Phoenician and Aramaean hands assured its adoption elsewhere. The Greeks in adopting it—probably, as they said, from the Phoenicians—found that there were more letters than they needed for the Greek language. So they used the surplus Phoenician consonants as vowels, which were not used by the Phoenicians at all.

▶ The peoples of Palestine

THE EARLY INHABITANTS

South of the Aramaean state, extending to the desert of Sinai, stretched the land of Canaan, fought over for centuries, its early inhabitants Semitic but mingling with its various conquerors, so that the resulting amalgam was as polyglot as any in the ancient world. This was the land "promised" to the Hebrews by their God, but not "given" to them until they had for centuries fought for it. Egyptians conquered it in the time of Thutmose III (1470 B.C.); Hittites penetrated into it in the later days of the Egyptian Empire (thirteenth century B.C.); from the twelfth century B.C. Philistines from over the sea settled in the southern coastal plain. Before the desert Hebrews conquered it, the people whom we call the Canaanites built up a considerable civilization in the land, founding several important cities, including Jebus, the later Jerusalem. The Canaanites were strongly influenced by Mesopotamian culture, with a law not dissimilar to that of the Babylon of Hammurabi, while they used the Hittite horse and chariot and iron weapons.

Though to the invading Hebrews from the desert the land of Canaan seemed a "land flowing with milk and honey," it is in truth a hard and rocky land, especially in the south, and the rainfall is scanty. Only the coastal plain is adequately supplied with water, and only in comparison with the deserts of Sinai and Arabia can it be considered a fertile and fruitful land. But for its unequaled importance in the religious history of the world it has become the "Holy Land," and since World War II it has become once more a haven of refuge for Jews under its ancient name, held in antiquity for but a few centuries and now revived—Israel.

THE HEBREWS

The persisting significance of Hebrew history

There is little doubt that the Hebrews would have occupied but a small place in history books if the impression they made upon the external world in their own time were the sole criterion for their importance. Yet this history is familiar to us in the Western world probably beyond that of any ancient people. The names of outstanding Hebrew individuals are familiar to us as household words, and a modern encyclopaedia boasts that it contains every Biblical character with an appropriate Biblical reference. Medieval scholars with their love of allegory tried to extract a secondary religious meaning from every event recorded in the historical writings of the Hebrews.

This astonishing success of Hebrew historians arises not only from the fact that they were the great pioneers in the historical art, and may rightfully be considered as the founders of systematic historical study. It is above all the result of their way of regarding history as *meaningful*. To a Hebrew historian there was no such thing as a chance event. If a pestilence decimated the people this was an act of God, arranged by God either to teach them a lesson, or to punish them for some sin against him. God was ceaselessly watchful, tirelessly guiding his chosen people on their path. The peoples of Mesopotamia, as we have seen, attributed their disasters to divine powers who had been insufficiently courted and appeased; but the Hebrews tried to make sense of every event, even of some that might seem to us trivial or resulting from quite adequate natural causes, and always as revealing some new facet of the relationship between man and God. And because man likes to think that his sojourn on earth has significance, the Hebrews' belief in divine Providence has permeated the writings of numberless historians since their day, and even those in our time who merely search for laws of history are in their debt for having been the first to deny that it is "told by an idiot, signifying nothing."

It will, of course, at once be realized that a history designed with the purpose of setting forth the relationship between man and God, intended to instruct the people in their duties toward God, and in what happens when man disobeys the divine injunctions, must be treated with some caution, since both events and their interpretation are inextricably interwoven, and events selected for recording will be those that lend themselves best to this particular interpretation. Nevertheless such events as archaeologists and scholars have been able to check have tended with remarkable consistency to confirm the Biblical record. And if we must regret the shortage of information on the lives of kings, such as Omri of Israel, who played an important part in the external affairs of their time but were unimportant in religious history, this is a small price to pay for the incomparable color and life imparted to their historical writings by the fervor and conviction of these ancient Hebrew writers.

It has not been possible to check most of the early history of the Hebrews against either the contemporary writings of other peoples or archaeological records. In this book, therefore, the story will be told as the Hebrews themselves told it, a procedure we shall also adopt with the early Christian stories recorded in the Gospels and the Acts of the Apostles, adding only a few explanations not considered necessary by the Hebrews themselves. We are the more justified in refraining from criticizing the probabilities in the case of both the Hebrews and Christians because the belief of these peoples that their own history was true served itself to mold their later history. The teachings and actions of Christ and of medieval Christians would surely have been different had they not believed, for instance, in the sojourn of the Hebrews in Egypt and their miraculous escape through divine interven-

tion, just as Christian history would unquestionably have been different had there been any doubt in Christian minds of the absolute truth of the Gospel story.

### External history of the Hebrew people

The scriptural tradition of the Hebrew people, or, as they called themselves, the Children of Israel, begins with the patriarch Abraham to whom God promised that his seed would endure for ever. Abraham came from "Ur of the Chaldees," but migrated into Palestine with his flocks, setting up altars to his God, Yahweh, and digging wells. It is very likely that this tradition is true, and that Abraham did indeed found the worship of Yahweh in Palestine. His son Isaac and his grandson Jacob, also called Israel, continued his work, digging the wells again and finding "living water," growing prosperous and powerful in the land through alliances with the local Canaanites. Joseph, one of the sons of Jacob, was "sold into Egypt," where he became later the vizier of the Pharaoh, from which office he was able to befriend his brothers and father when they emigrated there to escape a famine in Canaan. The descendants of Jacob in Egypt were all enslaved by a subsequent Pharaoh "who knew not Joseph," and made to work on his extensive building program. From this servitude they were rescued by Moses, who led them back into Canaan after they had spent forty years in the wilderness of Sinai. Moses taught them to worship Yahweh and welded them into a powerful and united fighting force capable of conquering the country. Moses himself did not live to lead them personally into the promised land, this task falling to his successor Joshua.

There is nothing inherently improbable in this tradition in spite of the fact that only minor corroboration of parts of it can be obtained from Egyptian records. It seems clear, however, that a people named Habiru (from which comes our word "Hebrew") continued to inhabit Palestine during the period of the sojourn in Egypt, and that they were one of the Canaanite peoples, or, if originally distinct from them, that they had intermingled with the Canaanites. During the period of Egyptian imperialism numbers of these Habiru had been taken captive and made to work for the Pharaoh, and Egyptian records show that they were still present in Egypt sixty years after the first and only Egyptian mention of the Israelites as a Palestinian people. The probability would therefore seem to be that a party of Habiru either voluntarily emigrated to Egypt or were taken there as prisoners, and perhaps already were united through their worship of Yahweh. Later they were enslaved, a condition from which they were rescued by Moses, who reminded them of their worship of Yahweh and unified them during the desert wanderings. But some of the kinsmen of the Habiru remained in Palestine, while yet others did not take part in the Exodus but remained in Egypt. It is possible that the invaders, now called the "Children of Israel" after their ancestor Jacob, or Israel, were able to unite in Palestine with the remnants of the Habiru whom they found there, and who were willing to accept Yahweh as their God since he had so miraculously delivered their kinsmen out of the land of Egypt.

But the promised land was, as has been said, by no means uninhabited. It required several centuries of fighting before the Israelites were able to conquer it, subduing first the peoples of Moab and Ammon across the Jordan, then the various Canaanite peoples who resisted them, and ultimately the Philistines. The Israelites themselves were rarely united, preferring to fight by tribes in a loose alliance. The Song of Deborah, perhaps the earliest document in the Old Testament, celebrates the victory of one such alliance, and treats with contempt those Children of Israel who had been too timorous to join it.

The early Israelites were ruled by judges, who were religious leaders with only a local authority. In the course of the wars with the Philistines, who for many years kept most of the Hebrews in subjection, it was realized that a king would best serve as a rallying point for the whole people. The prophet and judge Samuel therefore chose a certain Saul, of the tribe of Benjamin, as king, and anointed him as the chosen of Yahweh, thus conferring upon him both a secular and a religious responsibility. Throughout Hebrew history the king had a special task in that he had to set an example in worshiping Yahweh as well as leading the people in their secular affairs.

According to the Biblical narrative Saul failed in his religious duties, and was abandoned by Samuel in favor of a young man named David of the tribe of Judah, who was anointed king even before he had reached manhood. Thereafter David went to the court of Saul, and acted for a time as Saul's armor-bearer and married Saul's daughter. But Saul became jealous of the military prowess that David showed and forced him to go into exile, where he engaged in guerrilla warfare against the common enemy the Philistines. When Saul was killed in battle against the Philistines, David was proclaimed king. In this new capacity he broke the Philistine yoke for good, captured Jebus, which he made into his new capital, and founded a strong unified kingdom stretching as far as the Aramaean and Phoenician cities in the north and in the south to the borders of the Arabian desert. The Canaanite peoples of Moab and Ammon and Edom in southern Palestine were kept under control, though retaining their nominal independence. This Israelite kingdom lasted through the reigns of David and his son Solomon.

But the price was heavy. Solomon tried with his limited resources to live like an Oriental despot, and at the same time to engage in an extensive building program, including the famous temple of Yahweh in Jerusalem. His resources were not sufficient, and he was compelled to enter into an agreement with the Phoenician king of Tyre to send Israelites to work in the forests there in exchange for materials and assistance in the building program at Jerusalem. The result was a rebellion of the northern tribes of Israel on the accession of Solomon's son.

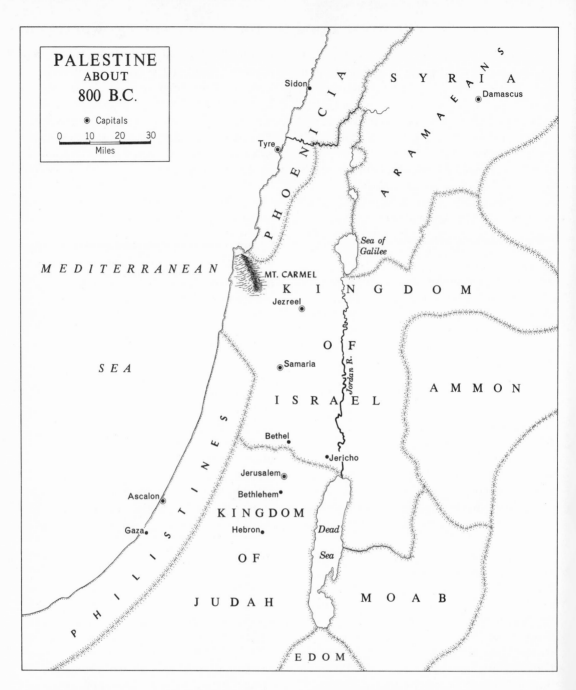

PALESTINE
ABOUT
800 B.C.

◉ Capitals

0   10   20   30
Miles

MEDITERRANEAN

SEA

PHOENICIA

SYRIA

Sidon

Damascus

Tyre

ARAMAEANS

Sea of
Galilee

MT. CARMEL

K   I   N   G   D   O   M

Jezreel

O   F

Samaria

Jordan R.

AMMON

I   S   R   A   E   L

Bethel

Jericho

Jerusalem

Bethlehem

Ascalon

KINGDOM

Gaza

Hebron

Dead

PHILISTINES

O   F

Sea

JUDAH

M   O   A   B

P

EDOM

Thereafter there were two kingdoms, the north, which took the name of Ephraim or Israel, and the south, which was composed of only two tribes, Judah and Benjamin, and which centered around what had been the national capital of the united kingdom. The northern kingdom was the more prosperous and sophisticated, but at the same time more subject to foreign influence and penetration. It enjoyed several periods of prosperity, even though the priestly chronicler does not admit that one single king "did what was right in the sight of the Lord." Everyone walked in the ways of the first king of the north, Jeroboam the son of Nebat "who made Israel to sin." In other words, he adopted most of the customs of the local religion and deserted Yahweh. But it was the northern kingdom that fell first (in 721 B.C.) to the conquering

Assyrians, while the southern, which was more defensible and not so close to the great conquering powers of the age, maintained a precarious and usually only nominal independence. It, too, fell, to the Chaldeans, in 586, after its rulers had vainly allied themselves with the decadent and powerless last Pharaohs of Egypt. From the southern kingdom a number of Jews, as they were called by this time (from Judah), were taken as prisoners to Babylon, where under the inspiration of at least one great prophet they kept alive the worship of Yahweh and probably intrigued against their captors. When the Persian Cyrus took Babylon, they received their reward, and were allowed to return to Jerusalem, where, after encountering much opposition but supported by their Persian overlords, they were able to rebuild the temple as a center for their religion.

Palestine remained in Persian hands until the conquests of Alexander, after whose death it fell to Seleucus, one of his generals. When Antiochus Epiphanes, a descendant of Seleucus, tried to enforce the Hellenization of the country, he encountered stiff opposition from the more orthodox Jews who, under the leadership of the family of the Maccabees, asserted their independence until the whole country fell to the Romans. Thereafter the land was ruled by client kings of the Romans until it was converted into an imperial province A.D. 6. When it rebelled against the Roman rule, Jerusalem was captured by Titus A.D. 70 and the inhabitants dispersed. There was no Jewish nation again until the middle of the twentieth century.

► **The Hebrew contribution to civilization**

THE EVOLUTION OF HEBREW THOUGHT

This account of the external history of the Jews, bald though it is, does serve to bring out one remarkable, almost unique phenomenon—the extraordinary persistence of the national and religious tradition, and the tenacious refusal of the Hebrews to be absorbed permanently into any other culture. Though thousands of them—no doubt an enormous majority of those born into it through the centuries—abandoned their heritage, nevertheless a nucleus always remained who "remembered the god of their fathers." So when Jesus of Nazareth was born a few years before Judaea became a Roman province, he was able to sum up the whole Hebrew and Jewish heritage in such a way that it could be passed on by his followers as the foundation for the great militant religion of the West. Even if the Jewish religion itself had not survived, this transmission to Christianity alone would justify the tremendous efforts and concentrated thought devoted by generations of Hebrew prophets and priests to the great problems of life, destiny, and the duty of man toward God.

We have purposely refrained from treating the evolution of the Hebrew religion in terms of the changing social experience of the Hebrew people partly because there is still so much controversy about it, especially concerning the dates of the various documents which comprise the Old Testament, and partly because this religion has never died, and is still regarded by millions of Christians and Jews as permanently true: there *is* one God, not many; he *is* just and righteous and omnipotent; he *did* create the world; and he does rule it through his Providence. In such circumstances it is needlessly offensive to suggest that the Bible was arrived at by addition and subtraction, a kind of Darwinian process of the survival of the fittest—this idea having been pilfered from Babylon, this from Egypt, and this from Persia—or that the Hebrews, having suffered so much, wanted so urgently that a god should punish their enemies that they came to believe in a God of the whole earth, using even the terrible Assyrians as his tools. Yet it is clear that there are such differing concepts of Yahweh in the Old Testament that it is impossible to believe that the concept in the Book of Isaiah, for instance, was held at the same time as the concept in the Book of

Exodus or the Book of Numbers. So it would seem best to attempt to trace Hebrew thought in regard to the same great problems with which their contemporaries also contended, and to see what solutions were worked out by different Hebrew writers at different times, without relation to the events that may be supposed to have suggested these solutions. In this way we shall treat the thought as a whole, dating the writings from the standpoint of maturity and richness of conception, instead of trying to relate this thought to particular social experiences. The student will have enough material at his disposal to enable him to judge this relevance for himself.

THE NATURE AND UNITY OF GOD

### Monotheism versus polytheism

The Hebrews are, of course, credited above all with the formulation of monotheism, the worship of one God; and this monotheism has been transmitted both to Christianity and to Islam, so that it is the fundamental religious belief of the West. But it is not always recognized that they are also responsible for the precise definition of the nature of sin; and their thought upon the question of sin and punishment has permeated Western thought as deeply as has the concept of monotheism itself. The evolution of Hebrew thought on these two subjects will therefore be treated in some detail in this chapter.

The Hebrews did not come all at once to their idea of a transcendent God ruling the universe. In the period of the desert wanderings we find them given the commandment that they are to have no other gods beside Yahweh, but there is as yet no suggestion that other gods do not exist. He is their special God, their protector and rock of defense, who will keep his promises to his chosen people; but as yet nothing more. It is only in relatively late times that the great prophets picture him as the God of the universe, with all peoples alike subjected to him, and the gods of other peoples as nothing but idols of wood and stone.

They were perhaps driven to this conclusion through their belief that God used foreigners to punish his own people, and thus must control these foreigners also.

In early times also it is clear that the Hebrews believed in a rather primitive anthropomorphism, that Yahweh could walk the earth and talk to men, and that he needed an earthly habitation. By the time of the end of the kingdom of Judah the priests were emphasizing that God could neither be seen nor heard by human beings, but that He was a spirit, infinitely remote from man, though caring for him like a father, dwelling in heaven and not on earth. Ultimately both these concepts—the unity and the spiritual nature of God—were fully accepted by the Jews, and it was in this form that the Hebrew ideas about God were transmitted to posterity.

It should be pointed out, however, that there is no reason to assume that this evolution from polytheism to monotheism is a necessary progress in religious thought, as has already been suggested in connection with the Egyptians. The best Hindu religious thought is far from primitive; yet it is polytheistic, and it shows no signs of developing into monotheism. To a Hindu all gods are an aspect of the great whole which is Brahma; but this does not mean that the others do not have a separate existence. The process of subtracting from the powers of lesser gods and adding them to Brahma is not considered necessary to the Hindus, as it was by the Hebrews—and it is perhaps not surprising that ancient legend should have attributed the invention of mathematics to Abraham. For Hebrew thought on God was eminently logical, and, in a sense, mathematical; whereas the Hindu approach to religion, as was the case also with the ancient Egyptians, is emotional, enriching their feeling for the Divine by indefinitely multiplying their gods, in accordance with their reverence for all the works of God. Monotheism conceives of God as a person, on the analogy of an omnipotent and omniscient ruler, whereas the Hindu thinks of Brahma as present in all the works of his creation, a divine element in all phenomena, rather than separate from them and responsible for their existence.

### Importance of monotheism for morality— Contrast with Mesopotamian polytheism

The supreme consequence of the Hebrew concept is in the field of human morality. Because God is a person, he can take part in human affairs, guiding them, rewarding and punishing his children, thus upholding the moral order.[3] This monotheism is clearly an advance on Mesopotamian thought, since the many gods of the Babylonians were conceived of as so many arbitrary but powerful beings competing for man's worship. Each man had a personal god who was expected to use his influence with the higher gods on behalf of his protégé, as human beings use political influence to ensure personal favors. And among the higher gods it was impossible for a man to choose which to petition. He could not tell which one he had offended, nor did he know what was demanded of him.

Polytheism cannot escape the dilemma that the different gods may issue contradictory demands; unless these gods may be said to have agreed among themselves on what to demand from man, their different commands will necessarily at some time conflict with each other. The separate gods can only reward and punish in accordance with their limited power, and thus cannot command obedience from man and insist upon it on pain of punishment. Shamash, the Babylonian god of the sun and of justice, might give Hammurabi a code of laws, but it was only by virtue of his function as lawgiver among the numerous Babylonian gods. The Babylonian did not regard him as the enforcer of the laws, nor did he pray to

Shamash to mitigate his severity. This was the task of the personal god of the Babylonian, who used his influence among his superiors in the pantheon.

But the Hebrew God, being one, not a force of nature but a transcendent being, separate from the world, could act as ruler and governor, first of his chosen people and then of the whole world. He could issue a law which instructed the people as to exactly what he expected of them, could define disobedience to the law as sin, and could take steps to see that he was obeyed. The law thus removed any doubt in the sinner's mind as to what he was expected to do, and what was forbidden him, and held out the hope that if he fulfilled these duties toward God he would be prosperous and happy. We shall see in the next section how the Hebrews were forced to modify this simple conception in the light of their actual experience, but the following quotations from Babylonian and Hebrew documents will serve to point the contrast between the two attitudes, and reveal at the same time how greatly the Hebrew felt he had been privileged when God gave him his Law.

The Babylonian: "What is good in one's sight is evil for a god, what is bad in one's own mind is good for his god. Who can understand the counsel of the gods in the midst of heaven? Where has befuddled mankind ever learned what a god's conduct is?"[4] Again: "Man is dumb; he knows nothing. Mankind, everyone that exists—what does he know? Whether he is committing sin or doing good he does not even know."[5]

The Hebrew: "I have stored thy message in my heart that I may not sin against thee . . . . With my lips I recount all the ordinances of thy mouth. In the way of thy decrees I delight, as much as in all wealth. I meditate upon thy precepts, and I observe thy paths. I find joy in thy statutes, I will not forget thy word . . . . At midnight I rise up to give thee thanks because of thy righteous

[3] The Hindu Brahma does none of these things. The moral order is conceived of as a part of the whole universe. The consequences of a man's deeds affect his life in the spiritual worlds after death, and determine the character of subsequent lives on earth (reincarnation). No transcendent God is needed to guide this process; the deeds themselves are the cause, and the character of subsequent lives is the effect.

[4] Pritchard, *Ancient Near Eastern Texts*, p. 435. Translated by R. H. Pfeiffer.

[5] *Ibid.*, p. 392. Translated by F. J. Stephens.

ordinances . . . the law of thy mouth is worth more to me than thousands in gold and silver."[6]

Hebrew monotheism, then, with its consequent belief that God rewarded and punished men in accordance with their deeds, has been of incalculable importance in the religious and psychological history of mankind. Nevertheless, the conception of morality, enforced by God in his capacity as judge, even tempered by mercy shown by him as a loving father who "rebukes and chastens" his children, is ultimately a sterile one, negative because it does not (indeed, cannot) prescribe goodness, and because it does not touch the more difficult matter of human ethics, or the art of right action.

This aspect too did not escape the best Hebrew thinkers. Some of the prophets saw that the commands of the Law limited morality within a too rigid framework. When Micah spoke of the task of man as to "do justice, love mercy, and walk humbly with God," he extended the boundaries of those actions favored by God to cover less circumscribed activities. And Jeremiah had an inkling of the need for escape from the bondage of the Law when he made this promise in the name of the Lord: "Behold I will make a new covenant with the house of Israel . . . . I will put my law in their inward parts and in their hearts will I write it . . . . And they shall teach no more every man his neighbor and his brothers, saying, 'Know the Lord'; for they shall all know me from the least to the greatest of them."[7] Paul, converted from Judaism to Christianity, but thoroughly conversant with the Law, explained that the Law was given to the people because of offenses, that they might know what was sin, and could strive to avoid it. The Law, he said, was a schoolmaster, to prepare the people for Christ: "A man is not made upright by doing what the Law commands, but by faith . . . the Law has nothing to do with faith; . . . We, by the Spirit, through faith wait for the uprightness we hope for . . . . What the

Spirit produces is love, joy, peace, patience, kindness, goodness, faithfulness, gentleness, self-control."[8] When we were children, he says, we needed such a schoolmaster, but when we became men we put away childish things.

This conception of the schoolmaster seems to suggest the true place of the Law in the history of human morality. It was an advance on the arbitrariness of the Babylonian gods who kept mankind in ignorance. When man did not yet know from within what he must do, then his behavior must be prescribed from without. When the Law was written within the heart, or was replaced by faith, then there was no longer need of the schoolmaster. Here, as we shall see, Greek and Hebrew thought meet, in Socrates' experience of the "little god" within, and in the search for the positive good carried out so unwearyingly by himself and his pupil Plato.

### The idea of a Universal God

The third great development in Hebrew thought concerns the total activity of God in the world. In early times the whole conception of God expressed in Hebrew writings was as protector of the Children of Israel, his chosen and peculiar people. But if he was all-powerful, then he did not have to fight with other nations; he would deliver them into the hands of Israel. What, then, did this deduction mean, from the point of view of other nations? Was he not their god also? Once this problem was posed, and it did not arise so long as Yahweh was only one god among many, the answer must follow. But it did arise when the logical consequences of his supreme power were considered. If his power were not supreme, then he had to fight on behalf of Israel against the gods of their enemies. If he was supreme, then he was their *enemies'* protector too; or else they were unfortunately left without a true God at all, which would be unjust. There was no way out of the dilemma; the other nations must somehow fit into the world order. It was all very well

---

[6] Psalms 119:11–16, 62, 72.
[7] Jeremiah 31:31–34.

[8] Galatians 2:15, 3:12, 5:5, 22–23.

to denounce Assyria and Egypt, call their gods false gods, and prophesy destruction for them. But could any prophet with a sense of justice allow such a one-sided arrangement and say it was the work of a just God?

The answer might be, and was, given in terms of Israel's mission. God was using the foreign nations for purposes of his own, for the disciplining of Israel. He could have prevented the Assyrians from oppressing Israel, as he prevented them from taking Jerusalem in the time of Hezekiah; or he could use them to punish Israel's sin, as when the northern kingdom was deported. But to the more thoughtful among the prophets even this seemed rather a cavalier treatment of foreign nations. Were they not judged and punished for their sins; or did only Israel's sins count?

The question was no sooner posed in this manner than it must be answered in the only way possible. If Yahweh were indeed the God of the whole earth, then all the peoples were responsible to him equally, even if Israel had special tasks and special responsibilities as the only people of the earth to whom he had revealed himself and his Law. But the Assyrians were responsible when they broke the ordinary unrevealed natural law, and could be punished for it.

And so we have the Book of Jonah, which tells how the prophet was sent to Nineveh to urge the Assyrians to repent. It is nothing short of astounding how daring this thought was that a prophet from the despised nation of Israel should go up to the capital of the mightiest world empire at the height of its power and prophesy its destruction (if it did not repent). And the writer shows that Jonah was well aware of his temerity. For at first he did not dare to go, but took a ship going in the opposite direction. Then the Lord sent a storm upon the ship and did not calm it until the sailors had cast Jonah into the sea. Here he was swallowed by a whale, and not released from the belly of the whale until he had repented and promised to fulfill his mission. So at last he went up to Nineveh and

*A medieval impression of Jonah praying to God for deliverance from the belly of the whale. Evidently the illustrator's knowledge of zoology left something to be desired! From a manuscript, Pseudo-Rudolf von Ems, Weltchronik, ca. 1400.* (COURTESY THE PIERPONT MORGAN LIBRARY. Ms. 769, folio 223)

preached. And, lo and behold, the Assyrians did repent, and the Lord spared them.

But the story does not end here. Jonah is angry because God has forgiven the Assyrians, thus making him a false prophet. So he sulks in the sun by the gate of the city. A gourd grows to protect him from the sun, and then, at God's command, the gourd withers, showing him by this sign that God has everything in his power, and that Jonah himself would not survive against God's will. And the book ends with the stern rebuke, "Should I not have compassion on Nineveh, that great city, in which are more than a hundred and twenty thousand people who know not their right hands from the left, and also many cattle?" Their ignorance saved them, for they had not been chosen and so had not known of God; when at last they were warned and heard, then God turned from his original purpose.

It should not be thought from this emphasis on the logical thought of the Hebrews that there was anything cold or abstract about their religion or their God. On the contrary, their whole thinking represented God as a person impossibly high above man, but recognizably akin to him, and with the feelings of man. It was thus possible not only to worship God but to love him, and God loved man in return. Man was in a real sense to the Hebrews the son of God, who must occasionally be corrected, but always with a fatherly hand. "Those I love I rebuke and chasten," says the writer of the Proverbs. But the emphasis was not always in the chastening. "I taught Ephraim to walk, I took him in my arms . . . with human bonds I drew him, with cords of love. How shall I give you up, Ephraim, how shall I let you go, Israel? My heart turns within me, all my tenderness is kindled. I will not perform my fierce anger. I will not turn about to destroy Ephraim. For I am God and not man."[9]

SIN AND PUNISHMENT

It has already been suggested that later Hebrew thought was disturbed by the discrepancy between the promises made by God to his people seen by the Hebrews as a special Covenant between God and his chosen people—and the experience of life on earth as they knew it. If they obeyed the Law they should have been rewarded, and if they ceased to obey it, then they should have been punished. But only rarely did this happen; and it was the apparent happiness of the ungodly, and the undoubted occasional suffering of the manifestly righteous that probably persuaded the later Hebrews to adopt the idea of a future life where justice would be vindicated.

It does not seem that the Covenant itself was ever seriously questioned. But later thinkers realized that it could not comprise the whole duty of man, nor could the simple theory of rewards and punishments on earth for keeping or breaking it suffice for them. More thought was needed on this central problem of the relationship between God and man, and much of the profoundest thought of mankind went into the effort to understand it—which thought, embodied in the Old Testament, became part of the imperishable heritage of Western man.

God had created man, not as a slave

[9] Hosea 11:3–8.

of God, but in the image of God. He had made man only a little lower than the Elohim (one of the Hebrew words for God, but sometimes translated by the timorous who do not appreciate the grandeur of the Hebrew aspiration, as "angels"); he was God's special favorite among all living creatures, a child of God. And God was for man a Rock of Defense. If this were so, and God was all-just, all-righteous, and all-powerful, demanding equal righteousness from man, how could he sometimes seem not to care, and deliver man over to destructive forces of nature or to his earthly enemies? Was this the protection to which he was entitled by the Covenant?

The answer varied in different stages of Hebrew civilization, and according to whether the fate of the Hebrew people or the individual man was being considered. But both problems were thoroughly explored.

The most prevalent early view, the one expounded by the priestly writers when they considered the history of the people of Israel, was that in fact the people had not obeyed the Law and were rightly punished for disobedience. The individual kings were also punished for leading Israel into sin. But this theory was far from accounting for all the facts. Jeroboam II of Israel and Manasseh of Judah, both wicked kings according to the priests, had long and apparently prosperous reigns. Josiah of Judah, in spite of his reform of the religion in accordance with priestly desires, met an untimely death in battle. These matters are not satisfactorily explained by the writers. But much is made of the miraculous prolongation of the life of King Hezekiah of Judah and his deliverance from the Assyrians because "his heart was right with the Lord." It can be seen, therefore, how great a temptation it was for these priestly writers to slur quickly over those reigns which pointed no moral lesson, thus in some degree distorting their history.

According to the priestly tradition, then, the sins of the people of Israel and Judah were responsible for the destruction of these independent kingdoms; but Judah, because it was the home of David, to whom God had made special promises, would not be destroyed forever, because of God's mercy and because of his oath to David. God therefore was able to act unilaterally on behalf of his people out of his mercy, though the people had not in fact deserved it. The people sinned and deserved punishment; God sometimes spared and sometimes condemned them. Yet this was still not arbitrariness on the part of God, as he was bound by his oath to spare the house of Judah. This tradition is naturally characterized by concentration upon the deeds of the kings because it was primarily they who led the people astray and "made them to sin." Though there were individual righteous men in Israel and Judah, and schools of prophets continuing to keep the First Commandment, they were far outnumbered by those who followed the king in his aberrations.

The great prophets, deeper thinkers than the priests, and gradually moving away from the strict tradition of the Law as comprising the sum total of human duties, would not accept the traditional answer; and some of them came to the thought that the sufferings of the people were not the result of sin, but a preparation, a testing, for an even higher destiny. At the time of the fall of Jerusalem to Babylon, and during the exile, this thought alone seemed to fit the circumstances. It was not only because of God's mercy that the remnant was saved; it was because God had need of them. Not all of them, but those who had continued to worship him in spite of all their disasters. From the idea of suffering as the due recompense for sin, it became instead a discipline, a purification in the fire, so that those who survived were fitted for this great destiny. And so ultimately, fully in accord with this thought, followed the idea of a Messiah who should redeem the world, sometimes conceived of as an earthly king who would inaugurate the rule of righteousness on earth, and sometimes as a suffering servant, "the man of sorrows and acquainted with grief," who would take upon himself the sorrows of the world. In both cases the mission of the whole Hebrew people had been

to prepare themselves to be ready to receive the Messiah, forming an elect body of righteous men to leaven the great masses of wicked humanity in the new age.

Once again it will be seen that these prophets returned the only answer that was logically possible unless the whole Hebrew tradition were to be abandoned as false. The suffering of a people, if it is to have a meaning—and the Hebrews could not deny meaning to it without abandoning their faith in the justice and righteousness of God —must be either punishment for the past or discipline for the future. There is no other alternative.

It did not, however, need a prophet to give the answer to the other parallel problem, the sufferings of the individual. To the logical mind, if the man who keeps the Law suffers, there must be some reason. Conversely, if the man who fails to keep the Law is not punished, why not? Here there are more possibilities, and the Hebrews explored all but one—the possibility of a future life of rewards and punishments— very thoroughly. And this last possibility as soon as it was suggested was abandoned by all the thinkers included in the canonical books of the Old Testament. Moreover, even when it was accepted by some Jews, it did not attain the dignity of a revelation, and was still not accepted by the priestly party at the time of Christ.

We see a suggestion of the problem very early; and already in the Law there is a typically primitive answer. The sins of the fathers are visited upon the children, an answer scornfully rejected by the prophets Ezekiel and Jeremiah: "The fathers have eaten sour grapes, and the children's teeth are set on edge." It is posed frequently in the Psalms: "Why do the ungodly flourish like a green bay-tree?" Look to the end of their life, suggests one answer. Their good fortune will change. But manifestly this is not always the case. They will suffer inwardly from the knowledge of their crimes; but no, there are instances where this does not happen. The problem treated from this point of view is insoluble. And the righteous man? The Psalmist stoutly affirms that he has never seen him in poverty and his seed begging their bread. But he must be honest with himself; he *has* seen them. And in case the conception of sin contained in the Law is too narrow, the Psalmist makes it clear that he is considering just dealing in its broadest sense, and not only as obedience to the Law. After wrestling with the problem without receiving an answer he goes into the sanctuary of the Lord, and there it appears he receives the only possible answer—he must just continue to believe and throw himself on the mercy and trust to the wisdom of God. And as for the ungodly man, he must believe that God will punish him "in the latter end."[10]

Substantially this is the same answer given in the Book of Job, an old Babylonian legend in a new guise, with all the depth of Hebrew thought built into it. Here the problem is presented in dramatic form. The book opens with the Devil boasting in Heaven of his accomplishments. There is, thanks to him, no righteous man upon earth. God asks him to consider "my servant Job," a man "after my own heart." The Devil complains that Job has never been properly tempted, and receives permission first to take away his wealth; then, when this has failed, to afflict him with "boils." Job's wife advises him to "curse God and die," but he refuses to accept such a counsel of despair. God remains just, and there is some reason for his action, but Job cannot find it. Three "friends" visit him, and with varying arguments they try to convince Job that he must have sinned, and must repent before God will forgive him. Job replies stubbornly that he is not conscious of any sin, either of breaking the Law or of sinning in any other way. He considers all the possible alternatives, including the possibility of an afterlife but rejects them all, finally being almost driven to the conclusion that God is ruled by caprice, that he is arbitrary and unjust, afflicting man without cause. And so at last he appeals to God himself to answer him. God answers out of the whirlwind with

the unanswerable argument. Job, he asks, can you make a crocodile—or a horse—or even a hippopotamus? And these chapters give the Hebrew poet a wonderful opportunity to describe these animals, the marvelous works of God. But Job can only answer no. "Can you make any of my works?" The answer is still no. So Job is at last convinced that man can find no answer, and God is so tremendously far above him that he cannot attempt to find understanding. And he "repents in dust and ashes" for ever having dared to question. At which God shows mercy to him, heals him, and gives him twice as much as he had before. So this magnificent book ends on a note of the deepest pessimism as far as man is concerned. There is an answer, but it is not to be understood by man's weak faculties. God remains just, but "his ways are past finding out."

### THE CANONIZATION OF THE LAW

It should be emphasized that the bulk of Hebrew thought on the relationship between man and God was achieved by prophets and independent thinkers rather than by the priests. But in the last days of the kingdom of Judah a book of the Law was "found" in the temple and became the basis of a thoroughgoing religious reform carried out by King Josiah and the priests. This book is almost certainly the one called Deuteronomy, and from it we can see that as yet there has been no great change in the conception of sin and punishment held in earlier times, no emphasis on righteousness beyond the dictates of the Law. God will prosper the people if they keep his Law. "If you will but heed the commands that I am giving you today, to love the Lord your God, and serve him with all your mind and heart, he will give you rain for your land in due season . . . and he will produce grass in your fields for your cattle, and you will eat your fill."[11] This is the tone of the whole book, as was indeed to be expected in a religious reform carried out by the aid of the priesthood. The emphasis was on the

---

[10] See especially Psalm 73.

[11] Deuteronomy 11:13–15.

tribulations that had come upon the people because they had not kept the Law, and the material rewards that would be their lot if they returned to it.

A short time afterward the kingdom was conquered by the Chaldeans, and some of the leading Jews were taken captive and brought to Babylon. There, in spite of great prophets to lead them who laid little emphasis on the Law, they were held together as a people by the Law, and on their return to Palestine under Persian auspices, it was the priests who supervised the return and rebuilt the temple. As can be clearly seen especially from the book called *Ecclesiasticus,* or the *Wisdom of Sirach,* the Law had become the cement binding together both the Hebrew religion and the Jewish nation. The Law in its now conclusive form was sufficient for all human purposes. The Torah or Pentateuch (the first five books of the Old Testament) was canonized as the revealed word of God. It was not earthly but divine; and it was unchangeable. It remained for Jesus Christ and his followers to return the emphasis to the *spirit* of the Law as suggested by Jeremiah, and allow scope for human ethics beyond it.

## THE INFLUENCE AND IMPORTANCE OF THE HEBREW RELIGION

The importance of the whole Hebrew religion to the world is incalculable. Once the problems of man's relationship with God and the resultant ethics had been wrestled with and certain conclusions reached, the world would never be the same again. One may deny the original premises[12] and ask for the evidence for the existence of any God at all; one may say that the Hebrews projected their own highest aspirations into their imagination of a supreme ruler of the universe. But one cannot deny the aspirations nor that the conclusions, as far as they go, follow from the premises. Not only did Christianity, the predominant religion in the West, base itself upon Hebrew thinking, but Islam also adopted the idea of the single

transcendent God and much of Hebrew social thought. The teachings of the Old Testament became the standard of conduct and even provided some of the law for the Protestant reformers in the sixteenth century, especially for those who followed the teachings of Calvin. And the Jews themselves have preserved their heritage and their belief in the promised land even thirty centuries after the death of Moses, and over nineteen hundred years after they ceased to exist as a separate nation. But more important than all this may have been their belief that man is answerable to God for his deeds on earth, that there is a divine sanction over man's activity. Whether we forget this, or believe with Aristotle /that man cannot be happy unless he is good and that no divine sanction is necessary, since man must seek for happiness, we cannot deny that the concept has profoundly influenced all subsequent civilization, and that few men in the West have not at some time in their lives been forced to consider the possibility of its truth.

## THE HEBREWS AS LITERARY ARTISTS

After this extended study of Hebrew religion it is hardly necessary to dwell further upon Hebrew literature. The Hebrew religious documents, with very rare exceptions, are couched in language of considerable beauty and are rich with concrete images; many of them, such as the Psalms, are the purest poetry. The ancient Hebrew clearly had a discerning eye, and took a delight in this world. The famous description of the horse in the Book of Job; the Psalmist's panegyric on the way God provides for the animals; Isaiah's prophecy of the heavenly world of peace among men and beasts; and even the Deuteronomic priest's lyric description of the land of Canaan—all spring to mind. The so-called Song of Songs is one of the most beautiful love lyrics in any language. "The time of the singing of birds is come and the voice of the turtle dove is heard in our land."[13] But

[12] The author of *Ecclesiastes,* a canonical book, even puts this point of view forward himself!

[13] *Not* "turtle," as in the King James version. *Song of Songs* 2:12.

even this is included in the Old Testament. There is no secular literature known to us until a very late date, simply because only literature that concerned man and God was worth preserving in a canon of Scriptures, and to the Hebrew almost any poetry concerned some aspect of this relationship.

The Hebrews contributed little to political theory or practice outside what is implied in their religon. Kings, of course, could never be, or be made into, gods because there was only one God, and only one God was conceivable. The kings of Israel were chosen because they were needed for government and warfare; but they as well as, or more than, their people must obey the Law. They were not above the Law, and they could be and were frequently recalled to their duty by outspoken prophets, who were protected from kingly anger either by divine protection (as with Elijah) or by the prestige of their calling (Micaiah before Ahab). The priest Jehoiada kept a king of Judah from "sinning" as long as he was his guardian.

In all the other arts and in science the Hebrews were singularly lacking in accomplishment. The famous temple of Solomon was Phoenician in design and execution. It was a great wonder to the Hebrew chronicler, but it would hardly have ranked as a second-class building in Egypt. Sculpture was abhorred and forbidden by the law; no scientific invention is to be ascribed to the Hebrews. There can be no doubt that the whole of their creative genius was concentrated on their religion and thought and, incidentally, their literature. More could hardly be expected of one small people.

▶ **Aegean civilization**

MINOAN CRETE—A TRIUMPH OF ARCHAEOLOGY

The discovery and excavation of the Aegean civilization is one of the great romances of archaeology. It began when Heinrich Schliemann, a retired businessman, organized an expedition to Asia Minor to search for the site of Troy. In spite of discouragement from scholars, he firmly believed that the Troy of the Iliad was not an invention of Homer and Greek bards, but a real city which had had a real war with the Achaean Greeks,[14] even if the war had not concerned the theft of Helen from her husband's palace in Sparta. He succeeded in finding nine cities superimposed upon one another, the last dating from Roman times; and though he was too anxious to identify the Troy of Homeric fame, and chose the second instead of the seventh city, his work excited the imagination of the whole scholarly world. Homer was now taken much more seriously as historian as well as poet, and Schliemann himself turned his attention to the Greek mainland and to Mycenae, the supposed home of Agamemnon. New discoveries of tombs were made here containing great treasures belonging to a civilization then still unknown, which were later identified as offshoots from a great Bronze Age Cretan Empire. Soon after 1900 the headquarters of this civilization was uncovered on the island of Crete by Sir Arthur Evans, and an international group of archaeologists set to work on one of the richest remains from the ancient world ever found, uncovering gradually the history of a whole civilization whose existence had hardly been suspected a brief fifty years before.

It is extremely unfortunate that the Cretan language has not yet been deciphered,[15] and the whole history has to be inferred from the material remains, supplemented by Egyptian records and the stories of Homer and later writers. And in making use of the latter it must be constantly remembered that these writers were interested in telling a tale rather than in recounting sober fact, and in any case they lived hundreds of years after the great period of Cretan civilization. If the language is ever deciphered it is more than possible that our whole present tentative historical reconstruction will have to be drastically revised. All that can be determined with

[14] See pages 130, 180–187.
[15] On the subject of the possible decipherment of the language, however, see further remarks later in this chapter.

*A reproduction of the Phaestus disk, with Cretan writing from the period of Mycenaean domination. With the recent success in deciphering the Mycenaean script, it is hoped that this disk will soon yield to translation.* (COURTESY THE METROPOLITAN MUSEUM OF ART)

some accuracy at present are the various phases of culture—and even on these scholarly opinion is far from unanimous. These are based primarily upon the types of pottery, which are found also in Egypt where it can be dated more accurately. Knowledge of Egypt is thus applied to the Cretan remains. As indicated in earlier chapters, it would be most unsafe to date the remains on the basis of aesthetic considerations alone, for we have seen that much of the early work in these ancient civilizations is greatly superior to the later work, for reasons that have been discussed. And there are many periods of flowering and decline in all civilizations.

A word should be said on the names used for these cultural phases, and for the Aegean civilization in general. While the archaeological record is still far from complete and excavation is still continuing, more evidence is continually being found of the extensive area influenced by this culture. But the earliest phases, as far as we know, are certainly Cretan, and there is no doubt that this is the parent civilization. However, the conventional term used to describe it is not Cretan, but Minoan, after the mythical

King Minos, famed in Greek legend (though probably he was also a historic king.) The phases of the culture are called Early, Middle, and Late Minoan, and they are each given three subdivisions. The mainland Greek civilization which sprang from the Cretan center is usually called Mycenaean. As a rule when the Mycenaean civilization is referred to the reference is to the period after the island civilization had fallen and only this offshoot survived. The whole complex of this civilization, covering primarily the lands surrounding the Aegean Sea, is called Aegean, and this will be the name used for the civilization in this book.

RISE AND FALL OF CRETE

The Minoan civilization is of great antiquity, hardly, if at all, subsequent to the unification of Upper and Lower Egypt; and there are extensive Neolithic remains prior to 3000 B.C. It is also one of the most long-lived civilizations known to us, as Crete apparently never lost her independence between 3000 and 1400 B.C. After 1200 B.C. she was unable to recover any of her former greatness and she declined into the comparatively unimportant Greek island that she has been ever since. It was for this reason that her ancient civilization remained unknown for so long. No one suspected her past glories from her drab present.

Yet Crete in ancient days had all the elements necessary for the flowering of a great civilization, as long as the human inhabitants made the necessary "response." It had fertile land as well as marginal uplands, enough to support a prosperous agriculture; it had several fine harbors if the people wished to take to the sea. The Cretans were close enough to the willfully isolated Egyptians for a profitable commerce to be maintained which the Egyptians did not care to undertake themselves; moreover, Crete had resources of gold, silver, copper and lead, and fine building material. Tin could be imported for bronze from Spain, Britain, and possibly Asia Minor. About 2400 B.C. the Cretans began to use bronze extensively, and thereafter they were probably the greatest producers of bronze implements in the world. They maintained this supremacy for a thousand years, and it is possible that their ultimate decline was due to the supersession of bronze by iron. At all events their final conquerors from Greece were warlike peoples who used iron, and the day of the more expensive bronze was over.

It is in its middle period that Minoan civilization rose to its greatest heights of power and commercial influence. It was during this period that the great cities of Cnossus and Phaestus were built on a grand scale, and when even private houses surpassed anything similar elsewhere, including those of contemporary Egypt. Though an earthquake, probably followed by revolution, destroyed the great palace of Cnossus about 1700 B.C., this was only a temporary setback; new and finer palaces were built, and trade and colonization spread to Mycenae and Troy. Mycenae, inhabited now by the warlike Achaeans, learned quickly. Their civilization never equaled that of their teachers; also, they were not as peaceful. Their cities were fortified strongly, and probably they chafed against Cretan restrictions and tribute. The Cretans had a strong navy, but from the evidence it would appear that they never had any land force of importance. It is thus usually assumed that when Cnossus and its palace and the other cities of the island were suddenly and ruthlessly destroyed by invaders, it was by the Myceanaean Achaeans, who were trained to war and over the centuries had built up a navy capable of defeating the Cretan masters—as even landlocked Sparta under Lysander was able, with the aid of Persian gold, to defeat the maritime Athenians in 404 B.C.

Thereafter the ancient position was reversed, and the Cretans were subservient to the Mycenaeans. They rebuilt their cities, but on a smaller scale, and the palaces now became fortresses. Achaean figures appear in Cretan art, and Achaean place names replace the Cretan; and throughout the whole Aegean area Achaean influence is predominant. It was during this time no doubt that the famous expedition of Agamemnon to the Asiatic stronghold of Troy took place, and we know from Egyptian records that Achaeans were repulsed in the Egyptian Delta by the Pharaoh Rameses III.

But the Achaean domination did not endure beyond 1200 B.C. The semibarbaric Dorians were already penetrating into western and central Greece, probably from Illyria and further north. The Dorians had iron weapons, and were not interested in Cretan or Achaean culture. They completed a thorough job of destroying both the Mycenaean civilization and what remained of the Cretan. Thereafter the Aegean area went into a decline from which it did not recover until the beginning of the classical age of Greece. By that time the Dorian, Ionian, and other invaders had altogether eclipsed the Achaeans, but not without absorbing some of their culture, and making some of the elements of their history into the background of their own tradition.

MINOAN GOVERNMENT, RELIGION, AND SOCIETY

The Cretan people were evidently closely related to the Egyptians in physical type as well as in culture. They cannot be classed as Greeks, of whom the Achaeans were the earliest known. Nevertheless, their art, while perhaps mainly Egyptian in inspiration, resembles in many respects that of the later Greeks, as will be shown. The Minoan civilization therefore was an important link between ancient Egypt and classical Greece. Even Minoan government seems to have been much more similar to later Greek institutions than to Egyptian, though it is difficult to speak with much conviction in the absence of written records. Their writing, unfortunately, was original, though the earlier script was pictographic in the Egyptian style. Knowledge of Greek or Egyptian has not as yet been of any help in deciphering it.

The kings of Crete seem to have held a position unparalleled elsewhere in early times. Attached to their palaces were great factories, which turned out pottery, textiles, and metal goods, suggesting that they were

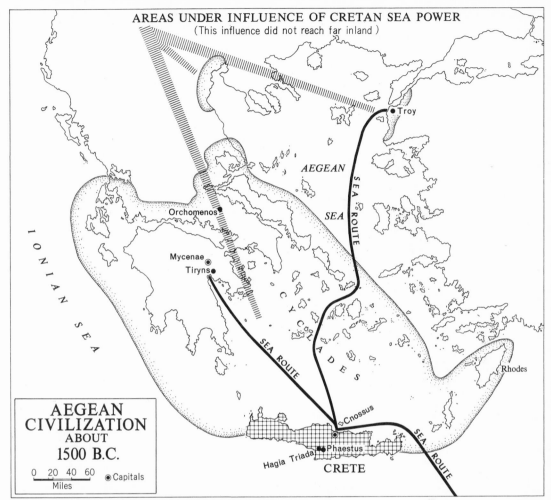

AREAS UNDER INFLUENCE OF CRETAN SEA POWER
(This influence did not reach far inland)

AEGEAN
CIVILIZATION
ABOUT
1500 B.C.

0  20  40  60
Miles

● Capitals

merchants as well as kings; and that perhaps their power was based on their commercial position at least as much as on any reverence paid to the throne as such. But even in the capital cities there were apparently private enterprises, as there were certainly in other cities of the island. Until Late Minoan times there was little centralized government, each city being at least partly self-governing. In the later ages of commercial penetration and colonization the government was centralized and the kings ruled the whole island from Cnossus. It is during this period that Minos himself is believed to have ruled, entering into Greek legend as a tyrant who required the sacrifices of Greek maidens to his bull, shut up in his famous labyrinth. Greek legend also placed him as judge in the underworld. The question of Minos,

however, has never been settled, and other scholars think that Minos was only a title comparable to that of the Pharaoh in Egypt.[16] In Minoan art the later kings are shown with symbols indicating that the king was military and naval commander, legislator, judge, priest. Like Hammurabi he is shown receiving the code of law from the gods.

The chief deity of Crete was not a god but a goddess, represented in art as the symbol of fertility, sometimes carrying a child in her arms, and accompanied by a serpent and a dove. She brought storm and destruction as well as fertility, and was apparently the source of evil as well as good. The dead were buried with all the articles they had

[16] See also the note on "Menes" of Egypt, page 36.

*Ivory statuette of Cretan snake goddess, with a golden snake in each hand and hair entwined with snakes. The unusual facial features of the goddess have given rise to suggestions that the piece is a modern forgery, but opinion still seems to incline toward its acceptance as genuine.* (COURTESY BOSTON MUSEUM OF FINE ARTS)

used in life, the hunter with his spear and the sailor with a miniature boat. A prominent feature of the religion was the sacrifice of large numbers of animals, together with fruit and grain offered up to the gods. There is, however, no sign of human sacrifice, as suggested in the Greek legend; but the Minotaur, half bull and half man, is prominent, as are the bull and the stag, and sacred trees and symbolic objects. All information about the religion itself, however, and any meaning it may have had, has to be inferred from the painting and reliefs. But there are, most surprisingly, no temples at all nor buildings devoted exclusively to religious purposes. The Cretans used high places

open to the sky, or sacred caves, and there were altars, and chapels in the palaces. Each house had its own corner devoted to worship, and miniature statues were kept in them.

The Cretans seem to have been precursors of the Greeks in their love of athletics and all forms of games. The national game was bull-leaping. The bull, however, was not killed; the toreadors, men and women, would catch a horn of the animal, spring to his head and turn a somersault, trying to land on their feet to the rear of the bull. A comrade stood ready to catch the athlete in case of mishap. They engaged in boxing contests, running matches, and dancing, and they built fine stone theatres for their games, processions, and music. In all these things they were far closer to the Greeks than to the Egyptians.

There seems to have been substantial social equality, and little if any slavery. Women were evidently in a social position superior to that held by them in classical Greece. The kings possessed no harems, and women took a prominent part in religious festivals as priestesses. In addition to engaging in the athletic contests—including prize-fighting!—we see them working side by side with men in the factories, and even hunting with them. But they remained feminine, as evidenced by the remarkable changes in fashion, puffed short sleeves and bare forearms, tiered skirts, even bustles, their many hats, and their attention to the art of hairdressing. Though an Egyptian might not feel too strange in Crete, any stray visitor from Palestine or Mesopotamia would find himself sadly out of place in this atmosphere; and even a classical Greek straying back into the past would find much to wonder at, and perhaps to condemn.

The foregoing information is based solely upon the archaeological record. But hopes have recently been raised that before very long we shall be able to read the Cretan writings, which are numerous, being found extensively even in the houses of the poorer classes. Toward the end of 1953 an English amateur succeeded in deciphering one of

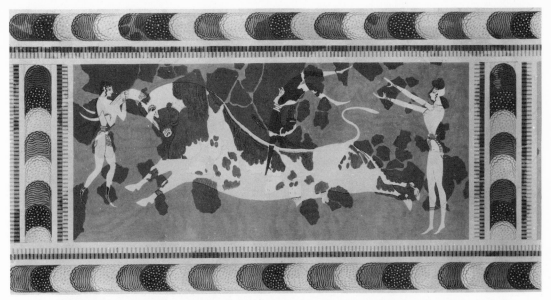

*Reproduction of a Cretan fresco from the palace at Cnossus, showing the sport of bull leaping. Evidently the man uses the bull's horns as an aid in leaping over the bull, to be caught by his female partner on the other side.* (COURTESY THE METROPOLITAN MUSEUM OF ART)

*Reproduction of a fresco from Cnossus, "Men and women in garden."* (COURTESY THE METROPOLITAN MUSEUM OF ART)

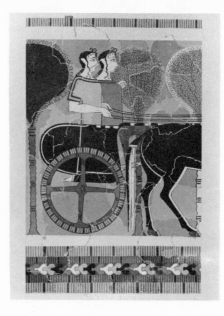

*Reproduction of a fragment of a Cretan fresco, showing the head of a young girl. Note the elaborate hair styling, with a modern-looking "spit curl."* (COURTESY THE METROPOLITAN MUSEUM OF ART)

*Reproduction of a fresco from the mainland of Greece (Tiryns); two women watching a boar hunt. Note the mainland use of Cretan technique.* (COURTESY THE METROPOLITAN MUSEUM OF ART)

the two scripts in use during the Aegean civilization. The script deciphered is the later of the two known to us and was in use on the mainland of Greece during the Mycenaean Age, and on the island of Crete during the period of Achaean domination. The language is now known to be definitely Greek, and can thus be understood by classical scholars. However, as yet no connection has been established between this Achaean script and the earlier purely Cretan script, an example of which is the Phaestus disc, illustrated in the text. But scholars believe that this connection will be able to be made with further work, and then perhaps at last we shall be in a position to know how far the picture of Cretan civilization available to us from the archaeological record corresponds with what the Cretan people tell us about themselves.[17]

[17] A useful and informative account of the deciphering of the script is easily available in a popular magazine. J. Johnson, "The Language of Homer's Heroes," *Scientific American*, May, 1954, pp. 70–75.

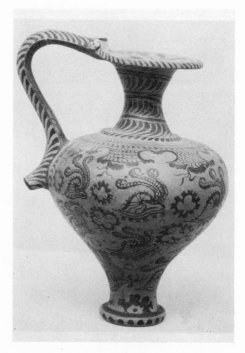

*Reproduction of a Cretan jug exported to Egypt.* (COURTESY THE METROPOLITAN MUSEUM OF ART)

*Reproduction of a fragment of a wall fresco from Hagia Triada in Crete. This famous fresco, showing a cat hunting a pheasant, is the earliest of the frescoes shown in this chapter.* (COURTESY THE METROPOLITAN MUSEUM OF ART)

## MINOAN ART

But the greatest glory of Minoan Crete was its art, one of the few really great arts of the world. It was delicate, and at the same time spontaneous and natural, and continuously creative; beautiful objects, as in the Greek world, were to be found everywhere and not only in the houses and palaces of the great. As with the Greeks, art seems to have been a necessity of their lives. Though the Cretans learned much from the Egyptians, in certain respects they far surpassed their masters. While their architecture was not especially distinguished, even the great palaces being designed at least partly for comfort and utility, the interiors

*This picture of an ordinary Cretan household drinking cup shows how ancient is the design of cup and handle that we use today.* (COURTESY THE METROPOLITAN MUSEUM OF ART)

of their buildings were beautifully decorated, especially with paintings. Painting was the supreme art of the Minoans, although sculpture and pottery were not far behind. It is typical of this culture that it developed sanitation more thoroughly than any Oriental people. Flush toilets were already known, and there was a sewage system, with main and subsidiary drains, for the streets as well as for the palaces. No ancient people surpassed the Minoans in such refinements until the Romans.

Minoan painting, mostly in the form of mural frescoes, shows a strong instinct for the dramatic, and for the naturalistic portrayal of plants, and of animals in action. Their wonderful pictures of the frightened deer and the stalking cat have become famous in reproductions in the Western world. Human figures appear only in late times, and they are largely stereotypes, and conventional. The sculptor did not make gigantic statues but concentrated upon miniature objects of exquisite workmanship in clay, ivory, and metal, which were used in individual homes. Only in very late Minoan times did the quality of these fall off, possibly with mass production, to fulfill the huge demand for domestic and foreign consumption. In ceramics there was constant development and improvement in technique as well as creative inspiration, and new

forms were continually produced until the late period, when the same decline is seen as in sculpture. The old forms were used again and again; and at last after the fall of Cnossus the workshops were reduced to the production in quantity of common ware. The art of the goldsmith and jeweler was as highly developed as sculpture and ceramics. Exquisite jewelry of all kinds has been found, and finely decorated swords and daggers; and gaming boards are known with inlays of gold, silver, and crystal.

It is difficult to appreciate the impression made by the remains of this ancient civilization, and the extraordinary enthusiasm kindled by it unless one examines a large number of its art objects. It was a civilization that remains all light and color and beauty, in the absence of written records which might contradict that impression. It is hard indeed to forgive the ruthlessness of those peoples who learned so much from it, if it was indeed they who destroyed it.

For the art of the Mycenaeans is derivative and inferior by comparison, in spite of its own great superiority to what followed before the classical age of Greece. And their civilization, with its concentration on war and defense, bears no comparison at all. Marvelous gold weapons, crowns and swords belonging to the treasure of their kings, were found in the six shaft graves of Mycenae,

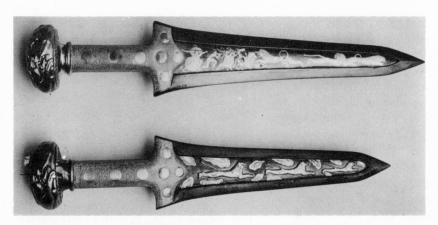

*Reproductions of two inlaid daggers from Mycenae. This mainland center was especially noted for the fine bronze weapons it produced.* (COURTESY THE METROPOLITAN MUSEUM OF ART)

as well as bracelets, cups, necklaces, and alabaster vases. But the art of making these was learned from Crete, and many of the best specimens were imported from there. Literacy seems to have been uncommon among the Achaeans, and it was the kings and princes for whose benefit the weapons and ornaments were made. It is therefore not necessary to go into the achievements of the Achaeans and Mycenae and Orchomenus and the mainland cities separately.

INFLUENCE OF AEGEAN CIVILIZATION

It is not possible to assess accurately the influence of Aegean civilization in general upon the world. The Achaeans remained in Greece and were absorbed or worked as serfs for their conquerors, especially in Laconia, the main center of Doric penetration, though some cities remained independent for a long time. The memory of Minoan and Mycenaean civilization was retained by the Greeks and found its echoes in Homeric poetry, and some Greek gods were known by Cretan names. Probably the festivals of Greece and certainly their devotion to athletics were derived from this earlier pre-Hellenic age. In spite of the dark age that followed the Dorian invasion, much of the past was retained without a distinct break, and this especially in the cities of Asia, peopled by Ionians and living for centuries under the mild rule of Lydians and Persians. Philistines who settled in Palestine introduced a few elements of Aegean culture into Palestine. As traders the Aegean peoples spread Egyptian culture as well as their own, and they formed a kind of cultural bridge between Egypt and Europe.

But, as far as our present information goes, the Aegean peoples were not thinkers, and their influence on Western civilization has been incomparably less than that of the Hebrews or the Mesopotamians—a fact which provides an interesting reflection on the requirements for cultural immortality. But it is good to think, until written evidence can serve to suggest the contrary, that at least one people *enjoyed themselves* in antiquity.

## ▶ Suggestions for further reading

The most up-to-date book on the Hittites for general use is the recently issued Pelican, O. R. Gurney, *The Hittites* (Harmondsworth, Middlesex: Penguin Books, 1952), which, unlike some of the Pelican series, has also some useful and informative illustrations. Gurney is both a Hittite linguist and archaeologist, and his book is a reliable survey of what is presently known about the Hittites. The Phoenicians are studied in R. Weill, *Phoenicia and Western Asia to the Macedonian Conquest* (tr. E. F. Row; London: G. Harrap & Co., 1940). This book collects within a manageable compass much information difficult to find together elsewhere and is especially interesting for its study of Carthage as a Phoenician outpost rather than as one of the enemies of Rome. The book, however, illustrates at the same time the difficulty of dealing adequately with a people whose written records are meager, and much of the work is taken up with a study of the other peoples of the Mediterranean world, including some pertinent information about the Israelites and Canaanites which takes into account the most modern researches.

On the Hebrews there is an enormous amount of material available, and the main difficulty is to select what is most valuable for the beginning student. The Pelican book by W. F. Albright, *The Archaeology of Palestine* (Harmondsworth, Middlesex: Penguin Books, 1949), is an excellent survey of the various peoples who inhabited Palestine from the earliest times, written entirely from the point of view of an archaeologist, leaving the reader, for the most part, to reconcile this material with the Old Testament records. The best general history of the Hebrews, a carefully planned, judicious, readable study, which takes full account of the history of the other peoples with whom the Hebrews were in contact, and uses all the material available at the time of writing, is T. H. Robinson and W. O. E. Oesterly, *A History of Israel* (2 vols.; Oxford: The Clarendon Press, 1932). Two well-organized books by Adolphe Lods give a very thoughtful, interesting account of the religious, intellectual, and social history of the Hebrews, using primarily, but not exclusively, the Old Testament records: *Israel from Its Beginnings to the Middle of the Eighth Century* (tr. S. H. H. Hooke; New York: Alfred A. Knopf, Inc., 1932) and *The Prophets and the Rise of Judaism* (tr. S. H. H. Hooke; New York: E. P. Dutton & Co.,

1937). A brief (117 pages) but stimulating interpretation of the work of the Hebrew prophets from a social point of view is W. C. Graham, *The Prophets and Israel's Culture* (Chicago: The University of Chicago Press, 1934).

The pioneer work on the Old Testament documents which was constantly reprinted until most of it had been generally incorporated into other men's work, but still worth reading, is S. R. Driver, *Introduction to the Literature of the Old Testament* (9th ed., rev.; New York: Charles Scribner's Sons, 1914). The author of the present text has made much use of W. A. Irwin's essay on the Hebrews in the University of Chicago symposium already referred to, H. Frankfort *et al.*, *The Intellectual Adventure of Ancient Man* (Chicago: The University of Chicago Press, 1946), which essay, however, was not reprinted in the Pelican *Before Philosophy*. This is a very provocative piece of work, in which the writer looks again with fresh eyes upon the real contribution of the Hebrews to human thought. From another point of view, the English historian Butterfield examines the Hebrew attitude toward history and traces the influence of Hebrew ideas on the meaning of history in several superb chapters: H. Butterfield, *Christianity and History* (New York: Charles Scribner's Sons, 1950). A good survey of the influence of Hebrew thought is to be found in W. G. De Burgh, *The Legacy of the Ancient World* (Harmondsworth, Middlesex: Penguin Books, 1953), I, 50–95.

Finally, of course, as much of the Old Testament should be read as possible, including the Apocrypha, but preferably in some modern translation such as J. M. P. Smith and E. J. Goodspeed, eds., *The Complete Bible: An American Translation* (Chicago: The University of Chicago Press, 1939). In the author's view, it is a great mistake for the student anxious to ascertain and understand the meaning of the Bible, to read it in the early seventeenth-century translation known as the King James version, in spite of the extreme beauty of the archaic diction. The familiar words, no longer in current usage, serve to obscure the true meaning, and prevent too often the serious attempt to understand the subject matter. Moreover, in most editions of the King James version the insistence on the use of verses printed separately in a quite arbitrary manner, rather than paragraphs designed according to the required sense, is an additional hindrance.

On the Aegean civilization undoubtedly the most comprehensive work is still G. Glotz, *The Aegean Civilization* (New York: Alfred A. Knopf, Inc., 1925), although in detail some of Glotz's views are no longer acceptable. A. R. Burn, *Minoans, Philistines, and Greeks* (New York: Alfred A. Knopf, Inc., 1930), is an interesting attempt to write a chronological history of the Aegean world from records available in 1930, and is certainly a fair summary of the work done by archaeologists up to that time. The book, however, is also an illustration of the difficulties inherent in the writing of any history without access to contemporary written records. Sometimes Burn blandly assumes the truth of highly disputed hypotheses and states them as facts without mentioning that they are hypotheses. The coming decipherment of Cretan records, now confidently hoped for, may make all these earlier books obsolete. But meanwhile Burn is still worth reading, if only for the attempted synthesis of legendary, semimythical, and archaeological material.

The best account of Minoan art is probably J. D. S. Pendlebury, *The Archaeology of Crete* (London: Methuen & Co., Ltd., 1939), which is well illustrated, though somewhat technical for the general reader.

# 6

# Far Eastern Contrasts with the Western World

*Reasons for inclusion of the Far East • India: the land and its history • China: the land and its history • Similarities between China and India • Contrast of both with the West*

---

▶ ## Reasons for inclusion of the Far East

In a book intended to deal with the heritage of the West, there would at first thought seem no reason to discuss China and India, whose influence on Western civilization has been relatively slight, certainly not important enough to justify an extended treatment. These countries, however, are now influencing and being influenced by the West, with tremendous and far-reaching consequences for each. So it has seemed worth while to offer a brief study here, not of these civilizations as a whole, but primarily of the great differences between East and West which prevented any extensive diffusion of culture in either direction until the nineteenth century of our era. There was always some trade between East and West, sometimes on quite an extended scale as in the period of the Roman Empire. But such trade was almost entirely in scarce luxury goods, and the traders had only minor contacts with the peoples with whom they traded.

The Indian and Chinese civilizations, indeed, have been astonishingly self sufficient, even to this day. It is barely a hundred years since the Chinese emperor learned to

his cost that Queen Victoria of England was not a tributary princess owing him allegiance; and though the Indian rulers bowed to the superior might of the British a century earlier, few Indians thought they had anything much to learn from their masters in any of the major arts of civilization. Although China in earlier times occupied much less territory than now, it usually formed one political unit; the civilized part of China has always been one cultural unit, in spite of invasions, and even of rule by foreign conquerors. These conquerors, with few and short-lived exceptions, adopted the customs and language of the people they ruled, and quite consciously built their regimes upon the cultural foundations of the native Chinese they displaced. India has only rarely been a political unit, in part because of the presence of natural boundaries within the territory; but again the conquerors of India have usually been unwilling and always unable to impress their alien religions and customs upon the native inhabitants. Either the conquerors conformed to the practices of the natives, or they maintained themselves as a foreign island in the sea of Hinduism. In our own day, when India was partitioned between Muslims and Hindus into India and Pakistan, a considerable number of believers in the religions which were held by the minority in each segment chose to leave the land of their ancestors and make a home anew in those parts of India given to their co-religionists. In the process more than a million people died. The Muslims, descendants of the conquering bands that set up the Mogul Empire, like the British who supplanted them, kept to their own religion and customs. And though over a period of centuries there were some converts to Islam[1] who carried over some of their customs into their new religion, on the whole their numbers remained small. Neither people effected any profound change in the nature of Hinduism, nor did they in any way break down the general self-sufficiency of Hinduism.

In this chapter, therefore, the history of the Indian and Chinese peoples will be kept to a minimum, only enough to give some indication of the greatness of these civilizations in the past, which is so often ignored by Westerners who know only of the drab present of the East at a time when it suffers from poverty, overpopulation, and exploitation. What will mainly be stressed are the social and cultural differences between the East and the West. This procedure, it is hoped, will bring out the self-sufficiency of the Eastern cultures and the limited nature and extent of their contribution to the heritage of the West.

## ▶ India—The land and its history

### THE LAND

India is usually called a subcontinent, a fair description when it is recalled that her population is only a little less than 400 million, and her territory is as large as all Europe without Russia. The high mountains to the northeast, shutting India off from Tibet and western China, have served to keep contacts with China to a minimum, although the way into southeastern China is not so strongly protected by natural bar-

riers. But the mountains to the northeast are not altogether impassable, and the northwest frontier, which was always guarded carefully by the British, has been the historic route for land invasions of India. The British, however, with their command of the sea, conquered India from over the sea, a feat that could hardly have been accomplished if India had been united against them, or if they had been compelled to bring land armies over the Khyber Pass from Afghanistan.

The land of India falls naturally into four well-defined sections—the northern hill country stretching up to the Himalayas; the north central plain, partly desert but mostly well watered by India's great rivers; the south central plain known as the Deccan, south of the hills called the Vindhyas which formerly were covered with thick jungle; and the southern maritime plains known as Tamil Land. The two northern regions have usually provided India with its conquerors. In ancient times the small Vindhya Hills were sufficient to protect the Deccan from any but the best equipped and most militant of empire builders, and the Deccan was the first to be lost when the emperors of the north fell on evil times. The narrow southern plains have usually been ruled independently. At certain times in Indian history one language could be understood from coast to coast, and from northern mountains to the southern tip. But in modern times countless dialects are spoken throughout India, though scholars everywhere may be able to read Sanskrit, the language of Hindu learning and the Hindu scriptures. The great religions of India have their believers in the whole territory, and help to give the people an awareness of their cultural unity.

The land is a violent one, and there are everywhere violent contrasts. Many parts of the country are extremely fertile and have a very high rainfall; others are chronically short of rain, dependent upon a specially favorable monsoon, and much of the northern territory is semidesert. Except for the highlands, the climate is torrid and enervating, and there is always danger in India

[1] The religion of Islam and the earlier history of the Muslims are dealt with in Chapter 16.

from animals and reptiles as well as from hunger and starvation. Nevertheless, before the last centuries of gross overpopulation, India was a relatively prosperous land. China and India were both envied by Westerners as lands of riches and luxury for most of the centuries of their history.

HARAPPA OR INDUS VALLEY CIVILIZATION
(*ca.* 3000–1500 B.C.[2])

Not so many years ago there was no suspicion in the minds of historians that there had been a flourishing civilization in the Indus Valley before the invasions of the people usually called the Aryans in the second millennium B.C., and little was known of the pre-Aryan inhabitants. But in recent years two important sites have been exca-

---

[2] These dates differ considerably from earlier estimates and are based primarily upon the recent work of S. Piggott and the latest archaeological investigations. See especially his "A Forgotten Empire of Antiquity," *Scientific American,* November, 1953, pp. 43–48, and *Prehistoric India* (Harmondsworth, Middlesex: Penguin Books, 1950).

vated and thoroughly explored by archaeologists, and many others are known. These two sites are at Mohenjo-Daro and Harappa in the northwest of India, and the civilization is now usually called the Harappa after the name of the modern village over one of the ancient sites. It appears to have been a civilization at least as far advanced as those of its slightly older contemporaries in Egypt and Mesopotamia, with a bronze and copper technology, buildings made of a fired brick superior to that used in Sumer, and a pictographic script. The latter, however, has not yet been deciphered, though it is not now believed there was any extensive literature. All the records so far discovered are short, and probably concern details of personal property. There are far fewer recognizably different characters than in Sumer or Egypt, although the script is nonalphabetic. This fact has suggested to scholars either that the script represents an advanced stage of writing, or, alternatively, that there was little use for many signs because few

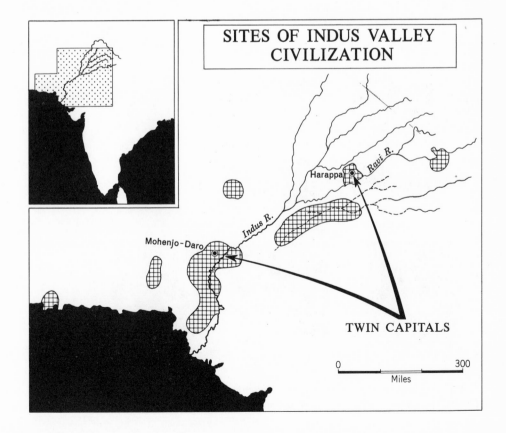

SITES OF INDUS VALLEY CIVILIZATION

Harappa

Ravi R.

Indus R.

Mohenjo-Daro

TWIN CAPITALS

0                               300
Miles

*This picture of the site of the prehistoric Indian city of Mohenjo-Daro gives some idea of the size of this ancient center of the Indus Valley civilization.* (COURTESY GOVERNMENT OF INDIA INFORMATION SERVICES)

*A group of representative seals from Mohenjo-Daro with pictographic script.* (COURTESY GOVERNMENT OF INDIA INFORMATION SERVICES)

things needed to be expressed in writing. Archaeologists now believe that this civilization developed almost entirely independently of its Western contemporaries, and there are no certain evidences of diffusion in either direction.

But it is not the details of this early civilization that concern us here. What is most suggestive is the discovery of the archaeologists that so many of the features of later Hindu society were found at these ancient sites and apparently survived the Aryan invasions. The area of the Harappa civilization was considerable, more than seven times the extent of Sumer. More than seventy towns and villages have been discovered in addition to the two main sites, which themselves were four hundred odd miles apart. It is clear that it was not a confederation of cities but an organized kingdom with a central government. Both cities were in all essentials similar, planned urban units, well built, rectilinear, and without any of the crooked narrow streets and slums characteristic of later Oriental (and Occidental) towns. What is of great interest is the quite extraordinary conservatism of these ancient Indians. Several times Mohenjo-Daro was actually destroyed by the flooding of the river Indus; but on each occasion it was rebuilt exactly as before, with no apparent changes, even the houses rising again on exactly the same spot as before. In the citadel at Mohenjo-Daro there was an open bath surrounded by verandahs, complete with disrobing rooms. The bath was apparently the central feature of the building, just as in later sacred sites of India—suggesting the importance even to the ancient Indian of a ritual bath, which may indeed, as now, have been prescribed by his religion. The art and architecture of the Harappa civilization are quite distinctly Indian. There are several statuettes of gods and goddesses which resemble their later counterparts, especially one of a god which could easily be taken for the later Siva.

In the whole civilization there is no sign that there was ever any warfare. There are no war implements, no strong points for defense. The leading cities never went to war with each other. It seems to have been a truly peaceful civilization, and it was perhaps this very feature that made these early Indians incapable of defending themselves when at last they were attacked and defeated by invading Aryans. All this suggests that the authority wielded by the central government was moral and religious, not military, and that already there were priest-kings who ruled by virtue of their sanctity and their connection with the gods. Such rulers, the basis of whose power was their moral ascendancy over their people, are less rare in Indian history than in any other known civilization, and the example of Gandhi in modern times shows that the tradition is not yet dead. However, such suggestions cannot yet be confirmed and must await further excavation and possibly a deciphering of the script.

THE ARYAN INVASIONS—THE VEDIC AGE

Invaders from the northwest began infiltrating into India early in the second millennium B.C. They probably destroyed the Harappa civilization about 1500, moving on gradually into the south, driving many of the earlier so-called Dravidian peoples into the south of the peninsula. These invaders, who are called the Aryans, established effective dominion only in the northern part of the country. They produced a remarkable heroic literature, especially two long epic poems known as the *Mahabharata* and the *Ramayana,* which are comparable in many respects to the poetry of the Heroic Age in Greece to be described in the next chapter. This early poetry, which included also many hymns, was incorporated in the Vedas probably many hundred years later. These Vedas have given their name to the whole age, which is usually called the Vedic age.[3]

[3] It is difficult to tell in exactly what order these epics were composed since for a long time the Vedas were considered too sacred to write down, and in any case the great epics, the *Mahabharata* and the *Ramayana,* contain material evidently from different periods. The most sacred book of the Hindus, the *Bhagavad Gita,* is incorporated, for instance, into the *Mahabharata.* The poems and the hymns together give a fairly complete picture of early Aryan society.

In due course the marauders settled down to a life of agriculture. They began to live in villages, as their descendants have lived until today. The larger Aryan towns were usually fortified, and wars were constant. To these invaders is ascribed the caste system, perhaps originally devised for the purpose of maintaining their separateness from the earlier inhabitants, though in early times the castes were not so highly stratified as they became later. It is not known whether the Aryans found a caste system already in existence among the people they conquered or whether they developed it themselves. At all events by the end of the Vedic age it had already crystallized into a closed system without freedom of movement between the castes. The system will be fully dealt with in a later section of this chapter.

PERSIAN AND GREEK INVASIONS—THE MAURYA DYNASTY (322–185 B.C.)

Under the Persian ruler Darius I, an expedition succeeded in entering India from the northwest, and a Persian satrapy was set up which did not survive for very long. The Persian admiral sailed down the Indus to the ocean, a feat duplicated by the next invader, Alexander the Great of Macedon in 327–326 B.C. Alexander defeated the local Indian chieftain at the battle of the Hydaspes, mentioned in a later chapter, but was forced to turn back when his troops refused to follow him further into the unknown. The expedition had no lasting effects on the Indian government or social structure, though some of Alexander's successors again penetrated into the Punjab and for brief periods set up independent kingdoms in that area. Greek influence, however, can be discerned in Indian art, and Alexander himself became a heroic figure of Indian legend under the name of Iscander.

The year after Alexander's death an Indian ruler named Chandragupta Maurya (322–298 B.C.), who is believed to have met Alexander and even fought against him, began to unify northern India, and ultimately was able to establish a firm rule over all India north of the Vindhyas. The dynasty that he founded was sometimes disturbed by Greek inroads from the Bactrian kingdom to the east of the Persian Empire, but those Greeks who penetrated to the court of Chandragupta were welcomed there. The new kingdom was peaceful and well organized, and extremely rich by comparison with any of the other kingdoms of that day. The Brahmin priests were influential and the Hindu religion, enriched some while earlier by the profound speculation of the Upanishads, was the official religion of the realm.

Chandragupta's grandson Asoka (273–232 B.C.), however, was converted to Buddhism, with its more ethical teachings and its charitable emphasis. This monarch deserves more than a passing attention.

After adding the Deccan in southern India to the lands that he had inherited, Asoka underwent a conversion to Buddhism, as a result of which he realized that he had caused unnecessary suffering to millions of people. Thereafter he eschewed war and became a model ruler, tolerant in matters of religion in spite of his conversion, helpful and compassionate, determined to convert others to Buddhism by example rather than by coercion. Asoka, in this respect, is unique

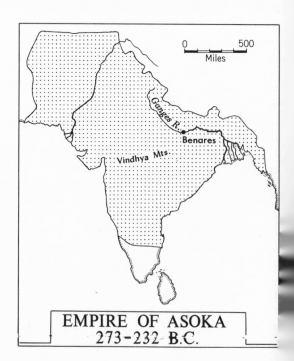

EMPIRE OF ASOKA
273–232 B.C.

# ► chronological chart

| India | | China | |
|---|---|---|---|
| Harappa civilization | *ca.* 3000–1500 B.C. | | |
| Aryan invasions | *ca.* 1500 | | |
| | | Shang dynasty | 1450–1050 B.C. |
| | | Chou dynasty | 1050–256 |
| Death of Mahavira | *ca.* 528 | | |
| Life of Gautama Buddha | *ca.* 563–483 | Life of Confucius | 551–478 |
| Expedition to India of Scylax the Persian | *ca.* 518–517 | Era of the "Contending States" | 481–256 |
| Alexander's invasion of India | 327–326 | | |
| Maurya dynasty | 322–185 | | |
| Chandragupta Maurya | 322–298 | | |
| | | Ch'in dynasty | 256–207 |
| | | Reign of Shih Huang Ti | 221–207 |
| Kushan monarchs | *ca.* 40–A.D. 220 | Han dynasty | 206 B.C.–A.D. 220 |
| | | Reign of Wang Mang | 9–A.D. 23 |
| Gupta Empire | 320–647 | | |
| Reign of Chandragupta II | 380–415 | | |
| Reign of Harsha of Kanauj | 606–647 | T'ang dynasty | 618–906 |
| Era of Rajput princes | 700–*ca.* 1100 | | |
| | | Sung dynasty | 960–1279 |
| Muslim invasions | 1175 on | | |
| | | Mongol conquest of northern China | 1234 |
| | | Mongol conquest of China completed under Kublai Khan | 1279 |
| | | Mongols driven from China | 1368 |
| | | Ming dynasty | 1368–1644 |
| Sack of Delhi by Tamerlane | 1398 | | |
| Conquest of India by Babur | 1526 | | |
| The Great Mogul Empire | 1526–1857 | | |
| Reign of Akbar the Great | 1556–1605 | | |
| | | Manchu dynasty | 1644–1911 |

in history. India has had many rulers of high character, the mainspring in whose lives was the desire to put into practice the ethics of Indian religion, which insist upon nonviolence, peacefulness, and government in the interests of all, and who have believed that the king himself must set an example of humility and responsibility. But none appears to have equaled Asoka, and his attitude is an ideal which has been alien to the West, especially in his humility and tolerance. The best Western monarchs have had a deep sense of responsibility. But the dynamism and activism which are characteristic of the West have usually led to intolerance of opposition and to the attempt to gain adherents by force, rather than by love and compassion, so greatly emphasized by Asoka. It is difficult to imagine any Western ruler insisting that the poor serfs should be won over by kindness, as Asoka attempted to win over the jungle folk, comparing himself to a nurse. "The skilled nurse," he said, "is eager to care for the happiness of her child. Even so have my governors been created for the welfare and happiness of my country, and their task is to be pursued with patience and perseverance."

Asoka sent Buddhist missionaries into countries to the west, as well as throughout India itself. These missionaries converted Ceylon, which became and has remained to this day primarily a Buddhist country. Tibetans, Burmese, and Siamese similarly received his message and kept it. Difficult also is it to imagine a Western ruler, even a pope, insisting that "although a man injures him, the Emperor believes that as far as possible it must patiently be endured," although this has been the teaching of the Founder of Christianity. Asoka proclaimed the *Dharma*, or Law of Piety of Buddha, as the ideal to be followed, with its virtues of compassion, liberality, truth, purity, gentleness, and saintliness of life, and he endeavored himself to live up to it. Wars of religion were to be stopped, all religions were to receive toleration and even royal support, no more animals were to be slaughtered, and animal sacrifices were to be abandoned. The emperor abolished the royal hunt as an example.

Fundamentally the Buddhist ideal, preached and demonstrated by the emperor, rested upon the belief that all men equally were subject to the law of *karma*, or repeated earth lives. Life was suffering, as the Buddha had proclaimed. No man could escape from this suffering, which was the lot of men upon earth, but each man had the task on earth of helping others, alleviating and not adding to this suffering, knowing that he was in his present position on earth as the result of his former lives, and each equally was worthy of pity and compassion, as on the same path as one's self. Parenthetically, it may be added that, according to Western ideals, Asoka should have made an attack upon the caste system. But it is symptomatic that we should know

nothing of any such attempt. We know of his tolerance of the Brahmins, although they were not of his religion, and we know of his efforts to mitigate the hard lot of the lowest members of society. But the caste system, as we shall see, was not looked upon as discrimination, but rather as the conferring of a definite status and definite responsibilities upon all members of society; and the system was deeply rooted in all Indian religion of the time, whether Hindu or Buddhist. A man was in his particular caste in this incarnation because of his deeds in a previous life, and he encountered the opportunities and suffered the restrictions imposed upon him by it. In an individualist society which believes in "getting on in the world" this notion would be intolerable; but India of this age was not individualist. Indian philosophers and holy men did not even believe the world itself to be real, but an illusion, a *maya* which had to be endured and ultimately understood for the illusion that it was. The bond with earth had to be severed by the achievement of a state of being without desire for it; the thirst for existence had to be overcome.[4]

It can therefore be seen why even the most enlightened of reformers would not wish to interfere with a system believed to be part of the whole universal order. A man's place in life was not only divinely ordained, but was for the ultimate benefit of the individual man himself. For only by being tested and by suffering in the position he had merited by his deeds, and needed for his development, could he hope to rise into the state called Nirvana by the Buddhists, which would make unnecessary any further incarnation upon earth. This question has been entered into briefly by anticipation here because it invariably arises in a discussion of Asoka. Hinduism and Buddhism will be dealt with in more detail later in this chapter.

[4] This system was only fully developed in the Sankara school of philosophy about A.D. 800, but it is implicit in many of the Upanishads which had already been composed well before the time of Asoka.

LATER INDIAN HISTORY TO THE ONSET OF ISLAM

The Maurya dynasty did not long survive the death of Asoka. The next period is poorly documented—the Indians themselves were not interested in writing history until a much later period—but it is certain that the control of the monarchy declined. The Deccan became independent for several centuries under one dynasty (Andra), and was never fully conquered again, in spite of sporadic campaigns from the north, until the coming of the Muslims. Invaders again poured into the north, including Greeks from Bactria who became Indianized, and in many cases accepted Hindu religion. A dynasty of nomads, called the Kushans (*ca.* A.D. 40–220) controlled much of the north fairly effectively for two centuries or so. As close neighbors of the Roman Empire to the west, the Kushans imitated Roman coins and engaged in trade with them. Many of the Kushan rulers became Buddhist, but under their rule Buddhism became a theist religion, in the form of Mahayana Buddhism, to be discussed briefly later. Buddha himself became a god, and was represented as such in Indian sculpture.

Following the breakup of the Kushan Empire there was a further dark age which ended in the establishment of the so-called Gupta Empire (320–647) which under Chandragupta II (380–415) again became a benevolent despotism, with the country well ordered, peaceful, and prosperous. Though apparently an orthodox Hindu himself, he and his family always granted full and complete tolerance to the Buddhists. It was this circumstance that gives us our knowledge of his reign, since he was visited by a Chinese Buddhist pilgrim, one of many devoted and learned Chinese who made the difficult pilgrimage from China to visit the shrines and holy places and monasteries of their religion. Another glimpse of a great ruler of this time is given by a seventh-century Chinese pilprim, who was also much impressed by the Emperor Harsha (606–647). He especially noted the excellence of the administration and the high standard of living enjoyed by all classes. Both Brahmins and Buddhists he found to be living up to the best precepts of their religions. During the Gupta Empire there was considerable trade with the West over the caravan routes, but much more with China. Occasional Indian merchants voyaged to the West by way of the Red Sea. But it seems that the voyages were mostly in the easterly direction, while the Indians themselves went east and planted colonies in Burma, Java, Sumatra, and Indo-China, taking both Hinduism and Buddhism with them.

During all this time southern India and Ceylon were entirely free from domination by the northern region, and they themselves did not expand, but seem to have been content with their own very fertile territory. The government usually seems to have been decentralized. Most of the people made their living by agriculture. But the tropical products which grew there in such profusion were much in demand in the West, and a very extensive trade was carried on with the Roman Empire. The Romans and Greeks, however, had little to offer to this prosperous people. The West, therefore, had an extremely unfavorable balance of trade with southern India, which had to be made up by the export of currency, of which there was a great shortage in the later days of the empire. About A.D. 900 southern India fell under the rule of an efficient but warlike series of monarchs who unified the whole of the southern region and maintained the unity for several centuries. They were great builders. Hinduism and Buddhism flourished together for a long time in the southern area, but in later times several rulers instituted persecutions of Buddhists and Jainists. The result was the eventual triumph of Hinduism except in Ceylon, which was ruled by native Singhalese monarchs until the fourteenth century. Tamil invaders from southern India then entered Ceylon: they tried to extirpate Buddhism but only succeeded in driving it from the coastal areas into the highlands, where it persisted until the present time.

THE MUSLIM INVASIONS AND THE
ESTABLISHMENT OF THE MOGUL EMPIRE

After the fall of the Gupta Empire in the north the country fell into the hands of small princes until the Muslims began to make serious invasions in the twelfth century. Orthodox Islam detested the polytheism of the Hindus. By this time Hinduism had largely superseded Buddhism in India.

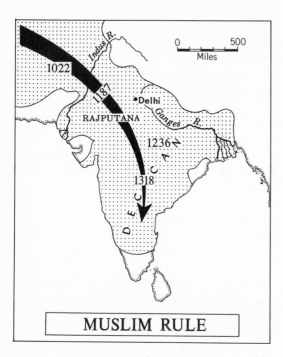

The old Hinayana Buddhism of Asoka had, as has been seen, been replaced by Mahayana Buddhism with its personal gods, among whom was the Buddha himself. Perhaps this latter form of Buddhism seemed to be too little distinguished from orthodox Hinduism to be worthy of a separate existence in the country of its birth. The Buddhist monasteries, with their praying monks, may well have been a social evil, in addition to presenting a serious competition to the Brahmins who were dominant in Hinduism. At all events, it seems that the new Rajput princes who followed the Gupta emperors allied themselves with the Brahmins and together they vanquished Buddhism, so that

today it is almost extinct in the territory of India. Hinduism was made more formal and ritualistic than ever and the caste system was defined and enforced. So the Muslims were faced with a polytheistic religion which was by this time marked by a number of rather horrible rites, which, incidentally, did not conduce to effective defense against a courageous and fiercely aggressive enemy. In particular the *jauhar*, a mass suicide of the vanquished, or those who believed themselves to be vanquished, became not uncommon. The Hindus, rather than allow themselves to be captured or defiled by ritually unclean peoples, cremated themselves on a gigantic funeral pyre. Suttee, or the suicide of a widow on her husband's funeral pyre, had always been expected of a Hindu woman who wished to stay with her husband in the afterlife. But during the ascendancy of the Rajputs and during the Muslim invasions it became ever more prevalent and was even enforced instead of being left to the choice of the widow. The Hindus invariably outnumbered their adversaries, but their military tactics were outmoded. The elephants, on which Hindu military rulers had always relied, were defeated time and again by mobile horsemen, and were made to turn back upon their own army, as had already been done centuries before by Alexander at the battle of the Hydaspes. But the Indians did not change their tactics, and the numerous Hindu kingdoms refused to unite against the common enemy. The only breathing space they had against the Muslims was when the latter withdrew of their own accord, or there were internecine rivalries between Muslim rulers. Almost never did the Hindus win a battle, until at last the Muslims came to stay, and organized the enduring empire of the Moguls.

Although this period lies outside the scope of this book, a few words should be devoted to Akbar the Great (1556–1605). This extraordinary man, though an alien conqueror, ruled in the tradition of Asoka. If he was not quite as saintly in his private life, and if he sometimes lost his temper and

*Portrait of Mogul Emperor Shah Jehan.* (COURTESY THE METROPOLITAN MUSEUM OF ART)

meted out severe punishment to his enemies, he nevertheless stands out as a ruler with few equals in the history of the world. Like Asoka he realized that it was his duty as monarch to care for the interests of his subjects, Hindu and Muslim alike. Completely tolerant in matters of religion, and himself a striver after religious truth, he tried to devise an administrative system for his subjects that would be based upon the principles of order and justice. During his reign there can be no doubt that the Mogul Empire was the best-governed territory in the world, there was the least corruption, the greatest equity in matters of taxation, and equality for all under the law. The administrative system that he devised lived for centuries after him. And it is said of him, too, that he loved children; and he is remembered for the saying "Children are the young saplings in the garden of life; to love them is to turn our minds to the Bountiful Creator."

For more than a century not all the vices and bigotry of his successors could destroy the structure that he had built. The dynasty itself did not officially end until after the so-called Indian mutiny in 1857, though the British had been virtual masters in India for a century before.

## ▶ China—The land and its history

### THE LAND

China is a land of great contrasts. Larger than India, it stretches in the north into temperate and even cold climatic zones, while in the south it is subtropical. Thus the crops are varied, depending not only upon the differences in temperature, but upon the rainfall. Many parts of the north and northwest are arid, and the land needs more water than it obtains by nature. Though irrigation is practiced, China nevertheless suffers from famine because of insufficient rainfall and damage due to floods—sometimes both in the same year. Parts of the land, especially in the south, are rich, but on the whole it is not a rich country, and the soil is always in danger of severe erosion. But very careful

attention to the land, the building of terraces, and controlled irrigation have always made possible a high yield per acre of cultivable land, whether of northern wheat or of southern rice. But it has also necessitated the hard and constant labor of many people, and at all times the very large majority of Chinese have been tied to the land. Until a few centuries ago China was underpopulated in relation to its resources, and the comparatively few inhabitants probably enjoyed as good a standard of living as anywhere else in the world. Only in these last few centuries has the population begun to mount, enforcing a grinding poverty only equaled by the similarly overpopulated India and parts of the Near East.

The two greatest rivers in China have not been an unmixed blessing. The Hwang Ho, or Yellow River, in the north has had to be heavily diked to spare the surrounding countryside the floods which would otherwise have overwhelmed it and it is as a rule not navigable owing to the swiftness of its current; yet, when kept under control, it brings down with it enormous quantities of life-giving and soil-building mud. The Yangtze River is the main artery and waterway and means of communication in China, and upon it have grown up the great commercial cities which have always served as industrial centers and entrepôts of trade. Southern China has also its great river, the Si, on which is situated the great commercial city of Canton. The Chinese are not a homogeneous people. Most of them belong to the race classified as Mongolian; but there are large Turkish elements, Tibetans, and others which have been kept united by the all-pervading and absorbent Chinese culture, which, by any known criterion, must surely be considered to have been the greatest in the world for almost two thousand years of the world's history. At most periods in this history a considerable percentage of the area now called China has been ruled by a single "Son of Heaven," in this differing in a marked manner from India, which until modern times was never ruled entirely by any single government.

## PREHISTORY

For various reasons which will be discussed later, the Chinese have always been very conscious of their history, and the historical records of China are more complete and continuous than those of any other nation. Yet the bulk of the earlier records are so seriously refuted by the evidences of archaeology that many scholars are inclined to abandon them as utterly worthless. There are legends of celestial emperors reigning for impossibly long periods of time, ruling over highly civilized peoples during ages when the archaeological records show little beyond small primitive Neolithic settlements. The earliest really historical records confirmed by archaeology only begin in the middle of the second millennium B.C., at a time when Egyptian civilization was already growing old and entering on its long period of decline, when Hammurabi had long been gathered to his fathers and the Sumerian language had already become extinct. Yet China had its prehistoric "Peking Man,"

*Sinanthropus Pekinensis,* already referred to in Chapter 2, and archaeologists have found in this ancient type of man certain physical traits similar to those of the later Mongol peoples. But the long interval between this ancient Chinese and the Neolithic Chinese of 4000 B.C. is not as yet filled save by a few stray remains, the age and significance of which are still greatly in dispute.

The Chinese histories are extremely detailed on these prehistoric epochs. They name the kings and give anecdotes from their lives, even to the words they are supposed to have spoken. If these are only the results of the working of fertile human imaginations of later times, they still remain interesting; but their significance has yet to be established.

## THE SHANG AND CHOU DYNASTIES
(*ca.* 1450–256 B.C.)

History proper, then, begins with the Shang dynasty, and with the first known use of writing. Yet this is already a highly developed civilization, with excellent glazed

*Two bronze vessels from the first historical dynasty of China, the Shang. The vessel below is called a kuang, that at the right a ku.* (COURTESY THE METROPOLITAN MUSEUM OF ART)

pottery which is very close to the later porcelain, an advanced bronze technology, and the use of that characteristic Chinese material, silk, which was woven into garments and material for decoration. All these things must have been developed in the earlier prehistoric times, and indeed there are traces of their use in excavated villages and towns belonging to an earlier epoch. There were already hundreds of gods, local deities attached to particular places, and gods of every element of nature from rivers to thunder and lightning. There was divination, especially by means of "oracle bones," that is, bones which were burned on one side in order to make cracks on the other which were believed to have significance. There were human sacrifices, apparently, for the most part, of captured prisoners of war. The ruler of the Shang state was already an emperor, who was chosen to rule by the "mandate of Heaven." All the names of the Shang rulers can be found on contemporary records as well as in history books, and the historians of later ages have their names correctly. This suggests the careful work of the scholar, thus making the mystery of the earlier rulers whose existence has not been confirmed even more baffling. The Shang dynasty, however, did not rule over the whole of China, but primarily in the province of Shensi in the northwest, though their dominion was later extended farther toward the south. Rebellion brought the dynasty to an end about the year 1050 B.C., and the Shang dynasty was replaced by the Chou, which held the mandate of Heaven for over eight hundred years.

As has happened so often in China, the new ruling house does not seem to have been Chinese in origin, but rather nomad Turkish. However, the rulers soon identified themselves with their subjects. For the long centuries of their rule the Chou monarchs were rarely effectively in control of their lands. As a comparatively small group of interlopers, they were forced to share their rule with powerful lords, and sometimes the reigning monarchs were puppets of these lords, kept with an honorary title but without effective power. It was during the period of their weakness in the fifth century B.C. that Confucius taught his political and social ethics, elaborated on especially by his follower Mencius, and left substantially unchanged by generations of political theorists, though some schools of thought did develop that disagreed with a few of the basic tenets of Confucius. Confucius and his followers elaborated precepts of behavior for rulers and subjects that were based on conditions of the Chou period when there was no effective centralized state. Yet the rules for the moral behavior of emperors in name were not found to be too much different even when the rulers were effective absolute monarchs. All rulers, in Confucius' view, being dependent upon heaven for their thrones, should act with responsibility towards their subjects. Thus Confucian ideas, derived from the social experience of an earlier epoch, could be used in later centuries as a real limitation on the arbitrariness of absolute monarchs.

THE CENTRALIZED MONARCHY OF THE CH'IN (256–207 B.C.)

The last years of the Chou are known as the period of the "Contending States." In this period whatever authority the Chou had exercised collapsed, and more than a thousand petty Chinese states engaged in almost unending warfare. None of these states proved able to dominate the whole. Alliances were made and remade, war lords aligned themselves first on one side and then on the other; but gradually in the stress of military competition many war lords found they could no longer survive in independence. They offered their swords and services to others more powerful than themselves. By the middle of the third century B.C. there were only fourteen states left that could lay claim to and enforce any effective degree of independence. At the same time peaceful and military penetration into southern China increased, the natives of these regions putting up little resistance, either to the merchants in search of new food supplies and ready to provide their industrial wares in exchange or to the military adventurers in search of new land. The result was that the stage was set for the unification of all China under the short-lived military dictatorship of the Ch'in (256–207 B.C.).

The state of Ch'in in the northwest of China had been one of the "Contending States," but differed from most of the others in that a large proportion of the people of Ch'in were not Chinese, but had a considerable admixture of Turks and Tibetans. The other states regarded the Ch'in as barbarians. Nevertheless before the final downfall of the Chou dynasty the Ch'in had put their house in order, and the state was ruled by real leaders who had effectively subordinated the feudal lords in their territory. For about thirty-five years the Ch'in waged an organized warfare against the feudal lords of the rest of China, until at last the emperor Shih Huang Ti became Emperor of all China (221–207 B.C.), ably assisted by an extraordinary minister, Li Ssu.

These able and energetic men, who had a few key ideas as to how the empire was to be administered, were backed by an efficient army and supported by a school of realistic political philosophers (the Legalists). They succeeded in the short period of less than twenty years in remaking China in such a way that the work was never undone in spite of the fall of the Ch'in themselves. The key policy was one of unlimited centralization in every field, and the destruction, as complete as possible, of the decentralized feudal system. The entire administration of the country was to be carried out by officials in a graded hierarchy, the higher members appointed by the emperor himself, and the lower responsible directly to imperial appointees. Weights and measures were to be standardized throughout the country, and a uniform tax system instituted.

These plans were duly put into effect with considerable energy and brutality. Feudal lords were forcibly transferred from their previous domains when necessary. The greatest difficulty experienced was in finding enough competent officials, but the Ch'in did at least firmly lay the foundation for the bureaucratic rule which has been so characteristic of China ever since. In the effort to obliterate all memory of the destroyed feudal states and the philosophy that had underpinned earlier Chinese society, the Ch'in decreed a gigantic holocaust of books throughout the country, especially books of history and of Confucian philosophy, which latter had stressed the responsibility and virtue of rulers rather than the power politics of the Legalist School, which was now in the saddle. This literature had to be laboriously pieced together again by later rulers who returned to Confucian principles in their government; and there can be little doubt that this great burning has been in large part responsible for the unreliable nature of earlier Chinese history.

Finally the Ch'in built the so-called Great Wall, which already existed in part, a remarkable effort to keep out the constantly invading nomads from the north, as well, perhaps, as to seal in Chinese civilization against disruptive forces from without. The huge rampart, made partly of brick and partly of stone, now stretched from the personal kingdom of the Ch'in in the northwest, right to the sea. According to Chinese tradition, the loss of life in the building was enormous, but the Ch'in cared nothing for this and pursued the work with the utmost thoroughness and determination. The wall was completed before the dynasty fell.[5]

## THE HAN DYNASTY—RULE BY THE BUREAUCRACY AND GENTRY (206 B.C.–A.D. 220)

The Emperor Shih Huang Ti was no sooner in his grave than the reaction came. But it was found impossible to reverse the centralizing process. The revolution, once made, could not be undone, and the new imperial system was so tempting for other autocrats that it is not surprising that the first ruler of the Han dynasty who came to the

[5] It has, of course, often been remarked how similar the whole process was to recent twentieth-century revolutions, and efforts have been made to predict the future accordingly. There is no doubt that the Russians, certainly unconsciously, have used many of the techniques of the Ch'in, and the present Chinese revolutionaries are returning to the same tradition.

*A part of the Great Wall of China.*

throne in 206 B.C. built his empire upon the foundations laid by the Ch'in and changed nothing of importance. It is true that the Han proceeded to give out new feudal estates to their friends and relatives. But the new independent landowners, who possessed both wealth from their land and valuable official positions in the state, were able to prevent the recrudescence of the old-style feudal system based solely upon landownership and the military power that went with it. The old system was completely dead within a hun-

dred years of the accession of the Han. The new, independently wealthy landowners united with the emperors to form the real governing class of China from the time of the Han until the Chinese Revolution of the twentieth century. They became the scholars and officials of the empire, and their numbers were constantly augmented from others of the same class. These officials are usually called in Western literature the "gentry class," although some Chinese historians have objected to the term as misleading. They

PREHISTORIC
CHINA

0    1000    2000
Miles

Neolithic Remains    Peking Man

Gobi Desert

Yellow R.

Yangtze R.

CHOU
DYNASTY
1122-249 B.C.

CH'IN
DYNASTY
221-207 B.C.

HAN DYNASTY
206 B.C.-220 A.D.
Lo-yang

TIBET

T'ANG DYNASTY
618-906

Canton

THE
SUNGS
960-1279
(Striped area controlled
by the Chins,
1127-1279)

REGIME OF
KUBLAI KHAN
1259-1294

Karakorum
Great Wall
Peking
Grand
Canal

MING
CHINA
1368-1644
------- Grand Canal

THE GROWTH OF THE KINGDOM OF CHINA

have pointed out that these men were closely tied to the interests of their own local communities, and did not in any way identify themselves with lords and officials in similar positions in other communities. They never took action as a class either for or against the emperors. However this may be—and some attention will be given to the matter later in the chapter—the scholar-bureaucrats did in effect become the mainstay of the Chinese throne for the remainder of Chinese history.

LATER CHINESE DYNASTIES TO THE COMING OF THE MONGOLS (220–1279)

In a chapter primarily devoted to contrasts between East and West it is unnecessary to go into the details of the successive dynasties of China after the Han. The Han dynasty was broken by a brief interlude under a usurper, Wang Mang (A.D. 9–23), who was backed by a powerful clique of gentry. But in spite of extreme measures to perpetuate his power (often termed "socialist," but erroneously, since the sole object was to strengthen the power of the monarchy), he failed after a few years of power, and was replaced by more rulers of the Han dynasty.

Following the final fall of the Han in A.D. 220, the kingdom was divided into three independent domains, and considerable territory to the south was added. Larger areas were penetrated by Chinese language and culture. From Han times onward there were continuous wars in the north, especially with the Hsiung Nu or Huns, a nomad people, about half of whom finally settled in China and became Chinese, while the remainder turned west and formed the nucleus of the Hun hordes that poured into Europe in the fifth century (see Chapter 14).

At last China achieved stability again under the T'ang dynasty (618–906), whose founder instituted a series of far-reaching administrative reforms which tied the gentry-bureaucrats more closely to his person and greatly improved the collection of taxes. In the T'ang period the famous Chinese civil service examination, already instituted by the Han, became the invariable method of recruiting new members of the bureaucracy.

Theoretically all the people of China were entitled to sit for this examination, which was given in literary and philosophical subjects, the so-called Classics. But the examination was extremely difficult, and was divided into three parts, all of which had to be passed successfully. Then the candidate was eligible for an imperial appointment, which was usually forthcoming, especially to those whose grades were highest. As few could afford the considerable time needed for the study and memorization required of the candidates, the highest positions in the state were virtually barred to the peasant class. But at least the system prevented purely hereditary appointments and thus kept the power of the bureaucracy from falling into the hands of the hereditary nobility. It may be added that even the passing of the first part of the examination conferred local prestige on the candidate, who had been forced at least to become literate in order to sit for the examination at all.

After a century and a half of power, during which the boundaries of the empire had been considerably extended, the T'ang dynasty had to cope with a number of serious revolts by their Turkish subjects as well as with invasions by foreigners. For a time these outsiders controlled the throne. Then, soon after the restoration of the T'ang, the dynasty was again threatened by a peasant revolt, the first in Chinese history, brought on by famine and military exactions. The revolt became a full-fledged civil war, with the government depending upon the alien Turks for support. Finally a Chinese leader emerged who successfully deposed the last T'ang, and proclaimed himself Emperor Chu Chuan-Chung (A.D. 906). Again China became divided, with the south enjoying under a series of military rulers a greater prosperity than the north. This period was followed by the rise of the great Sung dynasty, which was able in the process of time to defeat the northerners who had set up a separate state under Mongol leadership. The Sung, however, never established any lasting and effective rule over north China. Their power was really consolidated only in the south, though they are officially credited with being the rulers of China from 960 to 1279.

## MONGOL RULE (1259–1368)

The Chinese now had to face the onslaught of the Mongols, Jenghiz Khan and his successors. This nomadic horde, which is dealt with briefly in Chapter 15, was able with the aid of its central Asiatic resources, its tremendous army, and for the day, its advanced military technique, to conquer and subdue the whole of China for the first time. Kublai Khan (1259–1294), the final conqueror of China, who also attempted even to conquer Japan, was an efficient organizer and administrator as well as soldier. But his power could not rest upon anything but the sword in view of the racial policy he adopted. There were hundreds of thousands of Mongols and their allies to be supported, ultimately by the Chinese peasantry; and every Mongol employed in a supervisory capacity meant a Chinese bureaucrat disgruntled and out of work, a further burden to be supported by the same overburdened peasantry. However, as long as the Mongols had control of other areas in Central Asia and could be sure of military reinforcements and supplies, they were able to hold China in subjection.

Legislation favoring Mongols, and adopting a generally racialist policy, was enforced. The capital was moved for the first time to Peking, which was laid out by the Mongols without regard for expense, and with the aid of a forced *corvée* of the Chinese peasantry. It remains the most brilliantly planned capital of the world, not excelled by any European capital city, since it could be built without regard for any existing rights of the former inhabitants. Tremendous palaces and temples were erected, far larger than anything China had boasted previously. The life of the court of the Mongols, described by Marco Polo, was of a style and grandeur never before seen.

Yet Peking was not really the center of the country. It was in the wheat belt, whereas most of the Chinese were now subsisting on rice, and the land around Peking was not especially fertile. So again huge quantities of food for the capital had to be imported at great cost, and transportation had to be improved. Hence the Grand Canal, a tremendous engineering project of the sixth century A.D. which links the Yellow River with the Yangtze, had to be made fit for the heavy traffic of this age. All this was necessarily at the expense of the peasants; the bulk of the

*The summer palace at Peking built by the Yuan (Mongol) dynasty.* (COURTESY THE METROPOLITAN MUSEUM OF ART)

gentry accepted the inevitable and joined the Mongols. They were allowed to keep their estates but were deprived of their privileged political position, which was naturally reserved for the Mongols.

It was therefore not surprising that with the first signs of weakness in the Mongol rule the peasants again revolted against the oppressions of the tax collectors and the ever-increasing *corvée*. Whenever the Mongols tried to collect *corvées*, even when in the interests of the people as, for instance, when the dikes of the Yellow River burst, they were met by armed resistance. A peasant leader who in his youth had been a Buddhist monk finally organized these scattered revolts into a really national resistance movement. Such of the Chinese gentry as had not been murdered by the peasants again switched sides and joined the adventurer, and the Mongols at last retired from China to their northern domains without attempting any serious resistance. The peasant leader Chu became the founder of the great Ming dynasty (1368–1644).

The last years of Mongol rule were embittered for the Chinese by stringent racial laws put into effect against them, with the consequence that what had started as simple resistance to Mongol exactions became in effect a war of national liberation. From this time onward the Chinese have had a certain sense of Chinese nationality, missing in earlier times, combined with a detestation of foreigners. The Mongol period of rule has always been distorted by Chinese historians, although in fact it left for the Ming rulers the heritage of a united China which the Chinese themselves had never been able to organize.

MINGS AND MANCHUS

After a brief brilliant period of rule, the Ming emperors became puppets of the court cliques, while the more virile Mongols and Manchurian tribes (Manchus) from the north began to penetrate China again. By the early part of the seventeenth century they were entering northern China almost with impunity, and in due course numbers of im-

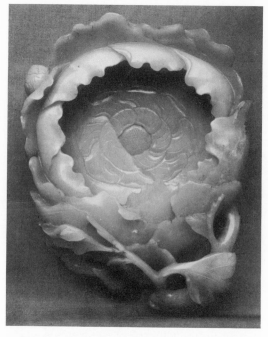

*Jade dish, Ming dynasty.* (COURTESY THE METROPOLITAN MUSEUM OF ART)

portant Chinese war lords and gentry deserted to them. Invited to take part in the siege of Peking against a usurper who had forced the last Ming emperor to commit suicide, the Manchus stayed. Though few might have expected their rule to survive the century, especially as they revived the racial laws against the Chinese and forced them to wear the pigtail as a badge of servitude, the Manchus did manage to survive by skillful diplomacy and effective military measures until they, too, lost the "mandate of Heaven" in the late nineteenth century, assisted in their defeat by the "barbarians" from the West.

▶ **Similarities between China and India—Contrast of both with the West**

GENERAL SIMILARITIES

The two great countries of the East, with a population between them of over 800 million, not much less than half of the entire human race, are in many respects extremely similar. They have never fought with each other as nations, the only clashes between them occurring in districts in Southeastern Asia in which both peoples competed for spheres of influence. Each has at many periods of history admired and imitated the other. Numerous Chinese, in particular, visited India in ancient times, often for the purpose of worshiping at Buddhist shrines and holy places in the land of the founder of their religion. It is to Chinese pilgrims that we owe much of our knowledge of such paternal Indian monarchs as Asoka, Chandragupta II, and Harsha, all of whom these pilgrims greatly admired, and whose rule appeared to them to be in accordance with the moral principles they themselves accepted. Both countries are now heavily overpopulated. This overpopulation, however, seems to be a phenomenon only of the last few centuries, a fact which accounts for the relative prosperity of these countries in earlier ages.

The religions and patterns of social behavior of each country are based upon a different conception of time from those of the West, on an understanding of the continuity of human existence rather than of the importance of the self-realization of particular individuals in one incarnation upon earth. In all history they have lacked the dynamism and drive of the West, and their influence upon the West, if not quite negligible, is nevertheless very small indeed. Until recent times the influence of the West upon the East was likewise small. The Macedonian-Greek Alexander the Great was able to win victories in India,[6] but left little there beyond a legend; the Muslims, with their dynamic monotheistic religion which they wished to force upon the world, conquered India, but did not convert very many—and the bulk of these were only casteless persons who were not accepted as equals in India itself. Thus the Muslims always remained a separate community, and under the present partition still inhabit a territory carved out of India, instead of allowing themselves to become assimilated with the Indians. The British were never more than a small com-

[6] See Chapter 9.

pany of administrators and soldiers who introduced India to the West but remained incurably alien. The Mongol conquerors of China lost their nomad dynamism under the Manchu regime and became as Chinese as their subjects, the same people having failed to hold the throne in an earlier century because they insisted on remaining alien and practicing racial discrimination. It is only now that both China and India—and of course Japan—are being forced by the manifest superiority of Western techniques and armaments, and the shrinking of the world under modern methods of transportation and communication, to realize that they cannot remain isolated and insulated from the impact of the West.

Japan imitated the West with a forced march into the twentieth century. China is engaged in the same process, first under the influence of the Western democratic powers and presently under the influence of Russian communism. India, after a long period of tutelage and preparation under the British, in her new independence is now trying to increase the tempo of change gradually, and hopes to accomplish the necessary revolution in cooperation with the West rather than being forced violently into a mold imposed upon her either by the West or by Russia. Each country has reacted in its own way, and all deserve the utmost sympathy and understanding that the West can give them. But the basic problem is the same for all—how to modify their ancient cultures without succumbing to the dynamic expansionism of the West.

THE SOCIAL STRUCTURE IN THE ORIENT

### The village as center of the community

The basic social unit in China and India is the family, and the basic political unit is the village. This has been the case from the most ancient times, and is still true at the present time. The village is made up of a number of families, almost all of whose members are engaged in agriculture. The villages are largely self-sufficient. As in medieval Europe, but unlike modern Western countries, the farmers do not live in isolated farms in the middle of their land; on the contrary, the village is the center of the cultivated land. Each family owns or leases some part of the land and keeps it in cultivation, but the family actually lives in the village. Thus what affects one person in the village affects everyone else, though the family, or the several closely related families under one roof, has its own private life. And, especially in China, the houses, when possible, are built in such a way as to insulate this small community within its walls; the windows in many cases face inward onto a court and not outward to the street. But in almost all the affairs of life, community cooperation is a necessity, and both Indian and Chinese societies are fundamentally uncompetitive. The individual person obtains his entire psychological security from his position in his own family and community rather than from the possession of wealth or a thriving business; and any prestige he may gain in the course of his life is worthless to him unless it is recognized by his family and community.

The possession of enough land for the family is, of course, required. Loss of land entails the breakup of the family. But a business—unless, as is so often the case in these countries, it is a family business based on the ownership of property—does not serve to keep the family together, and its loss is only a loss of money, not of security. A bankrupt merchant always has his family to fall back upon. The persistent conservatism of these peoples, which is the despair of the West, is primarily due to the lack of incentive provided by the society; whereas in the West, where prestige is bound up with success, and especially financial success, there is always a pressing incentive to "get on," which increases as small successes are won, and is, in the nature of things, ultimately insatiable. When a member of the Chinese family leaves the shelter of his home community to make his way in the world, any success is nothing to him unless he can return to the community, use his wealth to help his family, and can be pointed out in his town or village as a great man. It is no use merely being a great man

at Peking or Nanking or Shanghai, for he can enjoy that success with no one whose good opinion he really desires.

### The caste system in India

In these respects China and India are similar, in contrast with the West. In their methods of achieving this social control their methods are different, though the results are not too unlike. The caste system in India has been briefly referred to above, but will now be dealt with in more detail. As has already been said, the early Aryans do not seem to have had a fully developed caste system, though in the later Vedic age the lines of differentiation had already been established. At about the beginning of the Christian Era the system was formulated clearly and written down in the so-called Laws of Manu, named after a mythical lawgiver of the ancient past. These laws, which prescribe the duties of each caste, making clear in particular the central position of the Brahmin, have been accepted since that time as authoritative until the present century, when the Indian government, under the inspiration of Gandhi, outlawed untouchability in its constitution.

The highest caste is the Brahmin, whose members perform all the priestly and religious duties of the society; the second is the Kshatriya or warrior caste; the Vaisya caste, the third, is made up of herdsmen, farmers, and tradesmen. The lowest caste is the Sudra, whose duty it is to perform the menial work for the others. But not all Indians belong to these four castes. There are others, in some cases composed of foreign slaves and their descendants, and the offspring of mixed marriages; and in other cases perhaps of people who had disobeyed the laws of their castes and have been expelled from their former castes. These—in recent times as many as one sixth of the whole population—were the outcastes, pariahs or untouchables, the very contact with whom by men of superior castes meant defilement. They carry on occupations which themselves are considered defiling and, unlike orthodox Hindus, can eat meat, and by this very act become defiled. The caste system has tended to divide and subdivide into rigid occupational groups, all distinguished from each other by the nature of their work, which it is impossible, or at least very difficult, for any members of the family to leave in order to better themselves.

It should be emphasized that the members of each caste have their duties and responsibilities as well as their privileges. The Brahmin performs all religious rituals for which he may receive payment as well as prestige from the rest of the community; but at the same time he must rigorously observe the regulations of his caste, and these are not simple or easy. He may not eat meat, he must constantly purify and repurify himself, especially from the slightest contact with untouchables, or even the shadow of an untouchable. He must bathe several times a day in running water; his clothes must always be scrupulously clean. There are thousands of things he is forbidden to do. He is not necessarily a professional priest, and there are holy men in India from every caste. But if he is not a priest, and is only called upon occasionally to perform priestly functions which he is entitled to perform by reason of his birth, he must still at all times act in such a way as not to defile himself or in any way disqualify himself from those duties for which he was born. It is doubtless in many ways more difficult for the Brahmin to live up to his high responsibilities than for members of the lower castes to live up to their lesser ones.

The religious system of Hinduism as developed by Hindu philosophers makes clear the basis of the caste system. Every human being holds his caste in this earthly life as a result of his acts in a previous life. It is not simply an arbitrary decision on the part of the gods. Over the course of many incarnations he has worked himself up to the position where it is possible for him to be born, for instance, as a Brahmin. And it is equally possible to degrade one's self by one's acts so that one may be born another time as a member of the lower castes or even as an untouchable. In honoring a Brahmin,

therefore, a lower-caste Hindu is not honoring primarily the Brahmin himself, nor even paying tribute to his present holiness. He is honoring the whole process of development of the individual soul in previous incarnations which have led the Brahmin to his present position of social superiority.

The social consequences of the caste system have been immense. In such a system there was, of course, no equality of opportunity. Birth determined the nature of the career, and, whether in a village or in a great city, there was an upper limit beyond which one could not progress. As marriage between castes was forbidden, there was no free choice of marriage partners. This did not trouble the member of a higher caste, but it might be serious for a Vaisya or a Sudra (though there was at least one family of Sudras which occupied the throne). If there had been no subdivision of castes then there would have been plenty of opportunity, even within the caste. But with the proliferation of the castes in later centuries opportunity for promotion and social mobility became scarcer. Discrimination between castes worked enough hardship upon the lower castes, but it was serious indeed for the untouchables, who were kept in their lowly position by the united pressure of all the persons of caste. They could not enter a temple, they could not take part in festivals, they could not receive an education. It was these manifest disabilities and the visible evidence everywhere of their enforced degradation that made Gandhi undertake so many fasts on their behalf in the effort to force his fellow religionists to relax their laws. His triumph came when the Indian Constitution at last outlawed untouchability, though common practice has not as yet caught up with the provisions of the law.

Yet the caste system did have one redeeming feature besides its stress on responsibilities and duties. It gave each man and woman of caste a secure position in society, and it strengthened the bonds of community between persons of the same caste or subcaste. When the bonds of family and village were broken, the city dweller could find fellow caste members who accepted him as one of themselves, and to some extent overcame the psychological disease of loneliness which may afflict a Western man in similar circumstances. The ordinary Indian, unprepared by the nature of his closely knit family life and the lack of stress upon individuality in his upbringing and education for living by himself in the alien world of the big city, nevertheless found a natural milieu in which he would be socially accepted.

### The family in the Orient

The caste system, important though it is in India, is not as important as the family considered as a social and economic unit, both in India and in China. The caste system could probably be entirely abolished without disrupting the general social basis of Indian life. Not so with the family structure. Within the village the families, as has been said, tended to congregate under one roof or in several houses built close to each other. In both countries the chief element that served to keep the family together was the observance of ritual presided over by the male head of the family. The family property was held in common, that is, none of the land could be alienated or in any way disposed of without common agreement between the males. When the father died, if there was enough, the land would be divided, thus starting another family group, though the eldest son remained the head of the family. But under the Laws of Manu they had no right even to this division while the father still lived. Likewise all the earnings of individual members were considered to belong to the family as a whole. It was therefore of the utmost importance for every man to have sons to carry on his line, and especially to take care of his funeral rites. This applied in both countries in spite of the difference of actual religious beliefs. If there was only one house for the family, it was presided over by the head of the family; if the family was large enough to possess more than one house, then all members of the family would gather for common worship, as far as feasible, at the house of the head of the family. Women who married into the family were regarded as part of it, and therefore had to be chosen with the greatest care and found acceptable to the head of the family and its other more prominent members. Unmarried daughters remained in the parental home until they were married.

Modern conditions have wrought various changes in this stable social structure in both China and India, especially with the growth of industrialism, and the new opportunities offered for both men and women in factories and other establishments far from the control of parents. The Chinese Communists are trying by military and political means to force its destruction from above. But a structure that has endured for centuries can clearly be neither destroyed nor even radically changed in a few short years, much less in a moment.

For such a social order is very stable, and it presents certain advantages not always apparent to Westerners. And even though under the impact of the West it is bound to change, it is not yet certain that the whole structure will go. The child from his earliest years is under the influence of his elders of both sexes, by whom he is automatically accepted and from whom he learns. He does not look especially to one parent for protection; still less does he expect them to compete for his favor. He is just one of the family, a junior because he is its youngest. He is not encouraged to be an individual and to express himself, and no psychological problems arise from excessive competitiveness, as in the West. He is expected to show respect to his elders, and he sees others in his family doing the same. In China this even extends beyond the surviving parents to the ancestors who are now no longer on the earthly plane, but are believed to retain an interest in the affairs of their earthly family, and who are informed of these at regular intervals by the survivors. These members have only changed their form but continue close to their household as protecting spirits. When the child grows up he knows that his first duty is still to his elders, and above all to his father, who has no worries about being neglected in his old age, having to survive alone and unloved and uncared for. The old men and women have no need to seek for old-age pensions and retirement pay; they have the first call upon their children's earnings as these latter will be able to look to their children when they in turn come to their own old age. The Western isolation of the individual has no place in Oriental society. Unemployment and old age may be hardships, but old age holds the compensation of greater respect and attention, while unemployment is at least shared by the whole family, and in many cases by the whole community. It thus becomes more bearable, and any member who is able to find work will become the mainstay of the rest of the family. For this he will be repaid in prestige and gratitude—which for an Oriental may be better reward than "enjoying himself" with the fruits of his labor.

There is no outsider in an Oriental family. If there is only one house and fifteen persons to live in it, they at least know that there are always a few square feet available for them. If they have but one bushel of wheat, no stronger member will steal from the others and leave the weakest to starve. Clearly it is a system which gives little incentive to an individual to outshine the others, and this may be in part a reason for the grinding poverty of their lands. But it is also a system in which poverty can be more easily borne than in a society where it is regarded as a measure of ill success and of failure to make the grade in a competitive world, and is despised accordingly.

THE ROLE OF THE RULER IN THE ORIENT

It is no accident that both Oriental peoples should have produced thinkers who stressed virtue, above all, in their rulers. Perhaps the bulk of the rulers of these lands were in practice no more virtuous than rulers in the West. But it is significant that the ideal ruler in the theory of both peoples should have been pictured as a wise and benevolent father, and performing the functions of a father. It is hard to match the deeds of Asoka, Harsha, or Akbar anywhere in the West at any time. Asoka, as we have seen, after a

destructive conquest of the people of the south, was horrified at what he had done and became a convert to Buddhism. Then he proceeded not only to preach the enlightened doctrines of Buddhism but to practice them. He actually did renounce war, he did execute justice as far as he could possibly conceive it, he did enforce upon his subordinates the same canons of morality as he obeyed himself. In the whole record of his reign after his conversion it is impossible for the most carping critic to find one act in which he was untrue to his ideals of justice, mercy, and humility, and even nonviolence to animals, the hunting of which had been the traditional royal pastime until his day. Harsha of Kanauj followed in his footsteps, granting tolerance to all, discharged all his duties with never-failing care and courtesy, tried to mitigate the rigors of the caste system, and gave away the surplus of the imperial treasury to the poor as an act of charity. When there was nothing to distribute it was said of him that he wore a secondhand garment until there was again a surplus. Akbar stated publicly that his gratitude to his God could only be shown by preserving a just government with due recognition of merit. Though an alien conqueror, he refused to treat his Hindu subjects as unequals, severely punished any attempt to humiliate them, and gave them complete equality of treatment in his appointments. He abolished the tax on pilgrims to the sacred shrines of India though he was not a Buddhist, and he not only devised an administrative system that was one of the most equitable ever yet put into practice, but he saw to it that each position, as far as was humanly possible, should be filled on the sole basis of merit.

The Chinese rulers, according to Confucian theory, held the "mandate of Heaven" only as long as they ruled well. It was always understood that revolution was justified if the ruler failed to maintain his own virtue. It was the theory of Confucius and his follower Mencius that virtue was handed down from the ruler to the people. He must rule by the force of his moral example, not by the use of crude force. "An intelligent ruler," says

Mencius, "will regulate the livelihood of the people, so that they shall have enough to serve their parents, wives, and children." Then he "may urge them, and they will proceed to what is good, for in this case the people will follow this good example." Confucius says that the rulers, "when they wished to order well their own states, first regulated their families." In order to do this they must first "rectify their hearts, and be sincere in their thoughts."

We do not know of any Chinese rulers who were, in practice, the equal of the greatest Indian rulers. But constantly their scholars urged the path of virtue upon them; no Chinese ruler, under pressure from his society which believed that the gods would overthrow him if he ceased to follow it, could afford to be completely arbitrary if he hoped to maintain his position. Moreover, it was expected of the emperor that he would take the blame for any natural disasters that overtook the empire, and attribute them to his own lack of worth. Cases are known of emperors obeying this prescription. Alien conquerors such as the Manchus were early taught by their scholars and bureaucracy what was expected of them when they took over the "mandate of Heaven." Many of them did their best to live up to it. There is no instance in Chinese history of the restoration of any emperor who had ruled badly and thus lost that mandate. Once they had shown themselves to be lacking not only in power but in "virtue" they were never able to obtain the necessary support for their restoration. Apparent disloyalty to a particular ruler and wholesale switching of sides in China is not to be judged, therefore, altogether by the standards of the West. Recent history has tended to show that this ancient Confucian principle has not been forgotten even by men who have ceased to read the works of the sage himself.

While benevolence has sometimes been the Western kingly ideal, as in eighteenth-century monarchy,[7] on the whole, Western doctrine has taught rather the responsibility of the ruler to God, with an emphasis on the

right to rule ("divine right of kings") rather than on the responsibilities entailed by the position. Moreover, the power to win the throne and the prestige attached to a particular family have generally been regarded as sufficient justification for the tenure of Western rulers. The Hebrews are a possible exception. But for Hebrew historians and religious theorists, the kings' responsibilities were primarily in the matter of religion. Hebrew history shows little evidence that the rulers themselves regarded the matter in the same light. The priests put pressure on them to observe the Law, and when the kings were unsuccessful they blamed it on royal disregard for the Law. But there is no sign that any priest threatened the king with divine displeasure or interpreted his failure as evidence of the lack of that "virtue" extolled by Confucius.

It should be added that one important school of Chinese political philosophers, the Legalists, rejected the theory of the virtue required of rulers. They insisted instead on the proto-Machiavellian theory that the king rules by rewards and punishments (one reward against nine punishments!) and impresses his will on the people by keeping them weak and the army strong and obedient. It is perhaps instructive to note that the only dynasty that ever officially adopted this philosophy was the Ch'in, which came to an untimely end, the shortest rule of any of the recognized Chinese dynasties.

ORIENTAL CONCEPTION OF TIME AND HUMAN LIFE—REINCARNATION

### Chinese religion and philosophy

There are many important differences between Chinese and Indian religion and art, but both are based upon the conception of time and continuity held in the East. Each people expresses its time sense in different ways. Chinese art is impressionistic, suggest-

[7] In extolling the excellence of benevolent despotism, Voltaire used, in fact, the extensive Chinese literature on the subject, which was just being translated in his time, assuming for the purposes of his argument that the Chinese rulers had always lived up to the ideal.

*Painting attributed to Ma Yuan (Sung dynasty). As often portrayed in Chinese paintings, the sage is shown in contemplation. Note the contrast between the suggestions of landscape in this picture and the care for detail shown in the flower painting (below) of the same period. Evidently the purpose of the second painting is to induce a mood, and the painting might therefore be termed "impressionistic."* (COURTESY THE METROPOLITAN MUSEUM OF ART)

*Flower painting of Sung dynasty, showing the Chinese exquisite care for detail.* (COURTESY THE METROPOLITAN MUSEUM OF ART)

ing tranquillity; even silk, the material used for the painting, enhances the effect. The painter or sage often paints himself in the picture as part of the landscape—not differentiated, however, as an individual, as in such Western masterpieces as the Rembrandt and Van Gogh self-portraits, but rather to suggest that the human being, too, is a part of the natural scene, any human being, not especially the painter. Chinese poetry has a similar tendency. Much of it is nature poetry, usually short and descriptive, not full of dramatic action, but pictorial, the images having no inner symbolism, making no connection with other allied thoughts in the reader's mind.

It is no accident that the Chinese symbol for time is a pool. A stone thrown into a pool spreads ripples ever wider and wider, and then the water is as it was before. To an Oriental, time is not something to be hoarded or spent, time is not money, and it is not something which is fast running out and must be enjoyed because it is going by so quickly. A life on earth is a short space in years, but it is a part of eternity, without beginning and without end except in some unimagined, far-distant future. It is not exactly true, as is so often said, that the Chinese worship their ancestors. Their ancestors are only an earlier phase of their continuing family, as the "celestial" emperors who gave China her first rulers are likewise a part of the continuity of China herself. The heavens are peopled by millions of gods under the Supreme Lord Shang Ti, who corresponds to the emperor on earth. The worshiper, as in ancient Babylonia, does not expect to interest the supreme god in his very minor affairs on earth. Rather he deals with minor functionaries who are chosen as his special protectors, who may be bribed and cajoled like men on earth. In China also it has always been important to find what these gods wanted and appease or placate them; hence the need for the ubiquitous soothsayers and diviners still to be found plying their trade in every Chinese village. The excellence or failure of harvests is due to interventions by the gods, who may

be persuaded not to attack a particular community if their intentions are known in advance.

After death there are numerous rewards and punishments, but this life after death is not of unlimited duration, as in Western thought. Soon there will be a return to life on earth in a position commensurate with one's behavior in the previous life. Life is an endless cycle; to be born in a fortunate position is due either to one's own merits in a previous life or to the merits of one's parents who had deserved to have such a dutiful son. The ancestors then are only temporarily sojourning in the spirit worlds during the period between death and rebirth. Soon their imperishable spirit will return to inhabit a new body. But meanwhile they need sustenance during their period of death, and this must be provided for them by the living. If there are no living to provide for them, then death for them is a sorry affair. Hence the importance of having a dutiful family. These ancestors can reciprocate by helping the living.

There is thus no clear distinction between the living and the dead, as there also may not have been in ancient Egypt. But the Chinese are not depressed by this belief, nor by their ignorance of what the gods desire of them. For these spirits are not altogether arbitrary. The members of one's own well-loved family live as spirits in the spirit land, and it is possible to receive aid from them and to give them aid in return. This attitude seems to have taken away from the Chinese all horror of the hereafter and allowed them to concentrate their attention on earthly affairs. The orientation of the Chinese toward the earth, their philosophy of this world, and their religion are rooted in the belief that nothing changes fundamentally after death. Even a natural disaster such as an earthquake could affect the dead ancestors equally, and the living were expected to give them special aid and relief as if they were alive. At death only one change occurred: the body was dropped and the spirit pursued its path without it, needing sustenance as before but satisfied with food and paper models of furniture and other requirements of earthly life.

This folk religion is of immemorial antiquity and is almost universal in China except among the minority for whom one of the more highly developed religions such as Buddhism, Islam, or Christianity has been found acceptable. But, as we shall see, Buddhism in the form in which it was accepted in China (Mahayana Buddhism) was in no way contradictory to basic prevailing beliefs. For most Chinese, Buddha became merely one of the gods, as Christ and Mahomet were also accepted into the pantheon without grave difficulty. Every town, and nearly every village, has more than one temple, and the worshiper may use any or all of them as he wishes, in the hope of finding the solace and protection he needs from one, if not from another. Some temples will house Confucius, Buddha, and Lao-tzu as gods. This fact has one important consequence, religious toleration. The Westerner may wish to oust all the other gods in favor of his single all-powerful one; but the Chinese is quite willing to be hospitable to the gods of other peoples. In his system there can never be too many gods. Any or all of them may work evil upon him at any given time and for any given offense; but they are not intrinsically evil except those demons whose business it is to cause natural catastrophes. Yet these, too, can be kept in order by their superiors.

It is never therefore as an enemy of any particular religion that the Chinese in history have sometimes shown signs of intolerance. Organized religions may lead to social abuses as did the increase of Buddhist monasticism in the ninth century A.D., with its attendant evils of idleness and celibacy. For the practices of Buddhist monks could only be considered by most Chinese as damaging to the whole of their society, not least because when the monks died their spirits wandered aimlessly with no descendants to take care of them, causing some disruption in the social order in the spirit worlds and consequent harmful effects on the living. Similar social and political disturbances followed the introduction of Christianity; but any persecution visited upon missionaries was the result of their Westernism, not of their religion. As emissaries, and sometimes the vanguard, of the hated Western powers in the nineteenth century they received the

*A Chinese Buddhist temple.*

same treatment as their conationals, and thus they are treated today by the Chinese Communists.

Chinese religion, as this account has made clear, has been conspicuous for its dearth of any systematic theology or religious speculation. It is for this reason that it has been dealt with first in this book before coming to the profound and extensive Indian thought on the subject, which was adopted, often *in toto*, by Chinese religious thinkers. There has, however, been at least one important Chinese religious philosophy, although its appeal was limited. This is the philosophy of Lao-tzu, usually called Taoism. Systematic Confucianism was a political and social teaching. When, many centuries after the death of Confucius, it became a religion, it was absorbed into the popular cult and Confucius was accepted merely as one of the many gods. Lao-tzu was likewise received into their company, as was even Buddha himself, except among the sophisticated monks and philosophers, some of whom made the pilgrimage to India already mentioned.

The Taoist writers stressed the unity and transitoriness of all worldly phenomena. All things change their form but return in the process of time to their starting points to take up the ceaseless round. This is the "Tao," or the Way of the universe. Man who pursues the Way must give up striving and realize the relativity of all things in the universe, including action, and he must not strive to interfere with their harmonious workings. He must contemplate and become one with the world by direct experience, not trying to force change upon it by his puny efforts. The Taoists, therefore, wished to retire from active interference with nature, take no part in government, and, if possible, even avoid the ordinary social duties of private life. It is not surprising that in later centuries the Taoists became interested in the transmutation of elements, the science of alchemy. It became the chief concern of many of the followers of the cult to find the philosophers' stone or the elixir of life; for this stone had the power of hastening the

ceaseless process of the Tao. All things were slowly changing in their endless cycle. Base metals would certainly one day become gold. Why should a good Taoist not cooperate to his own profit?

This philosophy bears very remarkable resemblances to the Hinduism of the Upanishads and later Hindu philosophy, though apparently of independent origin. But both, as will be seen, derive from the same view of life and the same understanding that man's life on earth is but a small part of his sojourn in eternal duration.

### Indian religion and philosophy

*The wheel of rebirth*—The Hindu thinkers from very early times gave serious attention to the fundamental problems of religion. Even in the Vedic hymns there is speculation on the nature and existence of the gods. In the popular religion of India

*The Indian goddess Durga, with ten arms each holding a weapon, accompanied by lions, overcoming a demon.* (COURTESY THE METROPOLITAN MUSEUM OF ART)

traordinarily alien to our own, and, indeed, appear to be so contradictory to the realities of life that only mystics in the West have ever interpreted our earthly experience in similar terms.[8]

[8] It should, perhaps, be noted that while the discussion in the text describes the general cast of Hindu thought, Hindu philosophy is so rich that it would be possible to cite other thinkers who have followed paths of thought less alien to ours, and more similar to certain schools of thought in the West. Nevertheless, these have not been the really influential schools of thought in India, perhaps in part, at least, because of the fact that the "illusionist" philosophies have been more in accord with traditional Hindu religion and the way of life based upon it.

Indian god Vishnu, the preserver. (COURTESY THE METROPOLITAN MUSEUM OF ART)

there have always been many gods representing various powers of nature. Today, while there are still many gods, there are three who are almost universally worshiped: Brahma the all-embracing Lord of the Universe, Vishnu the Preserver, and Siva the Destroyer. But this did not prevent Hindu thinkers from striving to penetrate behind even these gods and speculate upon the nature of Brahma and in what way he was present in all created things, even in the other gods, and upon the universe of Brahma. The teachings of these thinkers are to be found especially in the Upanishads (written down from about the sixth century B.C.) and their numerous commentaries in later centuries. Their assumptions, which seem to have been shared by all the Indian peoples, even those far removed from philosophical and religious speculation, are ex-

Seated statue of the great god Brahma, represented in later Indian sculpture with three heads. Actually, in Indian philosophy Brahma is purely spiritual and impersonal, and thus could not have been represented in sculptured form. (COURTESY THE METROPOLITAN MUSEUM OF ART)

For to many Hindu thinkers, and not only to the thinkers but to some of the ordinary believers, the world itself is an illusion, a *maya*. Man is not an earthly being who may hope to win immortality in a different kind of existence after death, but a spiritual being who incarnates from time to time on earth, in exile from his natural heavenly abode. The eternal being of man is indestructible; it does not have to win immortality, for it is already immortal; it is the deeds of this being in earthly life which chain him to that life and make his reincarnation on earth necessary. At different times in Indian thought it has been held that this eternal being can also incarnate in the lower kingdoms of nature; probably at all times some people have believed this, though it has not been held by the greater teachers, who have always insisted that reincarnation must be into another human being, not into an animal or plant. The soul or spirit of man indeed creates for itself a new body when required and chooses those parents who can best help him to achieve his destiny.

If, then, the world itself is an illusion, the task of the man who would become wise is to try to understand the nature of the illusion, and at the same time free himself from dependence upon it. Man has become dependent upon the earth for his sustenance by being born on earth for the first time. This has certain inevitable consequences. He begins to desire earthly things for their own sake, and while on earth he performs certain deeds which bind him to other people and to the whole destiny of the earth. These deeds can never be undone, and they constitute man's *karma*. After his death when he is freed from his body these deeds are relived and spiritually understood; but they still must be compensated on earth, which is the only testing ground provided for man. So his *karma* attracts him back to earth to a milieu suitable for the task which he has to perform, which may be a particular family in a particular caste; or, indeed, he may be born as an untouchable if the task which he has to perform is one that demands persecution or enforced humility. He may

also be required to compensate personally for evil deeds he has performed toward a certain person, in which case he will be born close to a person with whom he has lived on earth before. Thus a Hindu can never be sure that he is meeting another person for the first time in this incarnation; on the contrary, he may have a special task to perform for any person he meets, a task which must be performed if he is to redeem himself from some important part of his *karma,* and thus continue on the path of spiritual progress. There is thus, according to Hindu thought, a long procession of births and rebirths, usually pictured as a kind of wheel. But in all these incarnations the eternal spirit of the particular man, which, incidentally, is not itself truly real but appears to be subjectively real for the duration of the incarnations, should continue to strive upward to reach *moksha* or enlightenment, by freeing itself as far as possible from the desire for earthly things.

It is at once clear how exactly the caste system fits into this scheme. The Brahmin and the untouchable equally hold their status by virtue of their previous lives on earth, and the task which has been laid upon them by their *karma* to perform in this particular life. Interference with the caste system, even the improvement of the lot of an untouchable, is, in this scheme, an interference with the destiny that the man has chosen on earth for himself, and which he really needs for his spiritual development. It is a scheme perfectly fitted for a static social order where man's task lies not in trying to improve his position on earth but in accepting this lot as unchangeable. Instead he must try to help others whom he may have wronged in a previous life, while in patience and resignation he now strives to build up less *karma* for himself to be redeemed in a later incarnation.

Though most Hindus are unaware of all these subtleties in their religion, nevertheless some elements of it are almost always understood in all classes of Indian society. This accounts for an atmosphere in India which is quite different from any known in the West, a kind of widespread gentleness and tendency toward resignation and non-violence, a respect for holiness and moral purity, and a willingness to follow the example and advice of a holy man who really lives out his principles in daily life. The "go-getter" of the West rarely commands such admiration as is accorded to an apparently lazy holy man. And though Gandhi may have been a shrewd politician as well as a holy man, it was his holiness and not his shrewdness that gave him his unique hold upon Indian minds and hearts and made his spectacular fasts so effective. Few were prepared to take responsibility for his death if they had refused to do what he wanted, even though it meant adopting a policy of which, as political men, they disapproved. The extreme nationalists who at length murdered him had to replace in their own minds the old religion of India with their nationalism, a modern variety of religion which they themselves held fanatically before they could have dared to lay a hand upon him.

A further aspect of nonviolence should be noted which is equally bound up with Indian religion. All created things, as has been said, were considered an aspect of Brahma and thus sacred. Especially sacred are certain animals, above all the cow, which provides the perfect food for man in the form of milk. The cow, therefore, must not be killed. The strict Hindu must eat no food that comes from a dead animal, and the Hindu religion does not permit animals to be killed for food at all. The doctrine of nonviolence (*ahimsa*), though imperfectly observed at all times in Indian history, is the necessary consequence of the understanding of all nature as being one. "Thou art That," says the Hindu sage.

*Escape from the wheel of rebirth—Yoga, Jainism, Buddhism*—In their desire to dispense with the almost endless round of rebirths which put such a premium on resignation, many schools of thought in India have wished to speed up the process of acquiring enlightenment. One, very well known to the West because of its often spectacular manifestations, is the practice of Yoga, which has developed certain ancient Hindu practices to an extreme, though its detailed regulations are of comparatively recent date.

The theory of Yoga is that a man must endeavor by special exercises to make himself as little dependent upon earthly things as possible. He must cultivate his latent spiritual powers, especially by intense concentration and exclusion of worldly thoughts. In this way the yogi achieves enlightenment by learning to understand the illusionary nature of the world; moreover, by developing his spiritual powers, he becomes less dependent upon his physical environment. He lives as simply as possible and fasts often; he may become a hermit, able to bear solitude and physical discomfort, or he may return to the world, be in it but not of it, giving advice and aid to others. There are different practices in Yoga according to the task which the yogi conceives to be his. Some practices are intended to fit him for prolonged work in the world, administering loving care to others, while different practices may fit him rather for a life of solitude. In all cases the yogi is expected to acquire control of his physical organism and dominate it through his developed spiritual powers. Since self-control, with its accompanying enlightenment, is admired by all those in India who have refrained from attempting it, the yogi is widely regarded as a holy man and honored accordingly. Not all holy men who are thus honored, however, have actually attained any degree of self-control or enlightenment, and there are many who prey upon the superstitions and beliefs of the people, and are sometimes willing to admit that fact to strangers. Many are simply charlatans, professional beggars who make their living performing feats of "magic," but the prestige accorded to them undoubtedly rests upon the general belief that the yogi has genuinely renounced the world for the purpose of attaining that freedom from earthly ties and the lessening of *karma*, which is the main task of all men upon earth.

But long before Yoga had been systematized there appeared about the same time (sixth century B.C.) the two chief "heretical" religions of India, Buddhism and Jainism. Both built upon the earlier Hindu foundations and were based upon Indian life experience. Perhaps they are best thought of as reform movements in Hinduism which later became distinct religions. They arose at a time when Hinduism itself had not yet become as systematized and carefully formulated as it was later in the different Hindu schools of religious philosophy, though it was already filled with carefully prescribed ritual.

Jainism was founded by Mahavira, probably an older contemporary of Gautama Buddha, who after years of meditation emerged from his seclusion to become a prophet and teacher. While accepting the general religious ideas of Hinduism, including, of course, the doctrine of *karma*, he lowered the number of incarnations to be endured by human beings to nine provided that they were lived in strict asceticism, that certain vows were taken and kept, such as sexual abstinence and the renunciation of worldly goods, and that continuous attention was paid to the achievement of enlightenment. After nine such incarnations the soul could attain a state of desirelessness and freedom from earthly entanglements which was called *Nirvana*. But according to Jainist teaching not all souls who had attained the right to Nirvana did in fact accept it. They could, if they so wished, return to the earth and help others toward the same salvation. Before long Jainism divided into two sects, the stricter one composed of ascetics who practiced nudism as part of the effort to separate themselves from earthly things and contact with matter (the "air-clothed"), the members of the other sect distinguished by white clothes, symbols of the purity they sought. The Jainists, as ascetics, were often persecuted in later times, and several rulers tried to extirpate the sect. Nevertheless, it still exists in India, with an estimated million and a half believers.

Buddhism, on the other hand, is almost extinct on the mainland of India, though, as has been seen, it is still strong elsewhere, if in a form that its founder would scarcely have recognized. Thousands of legends have sprung up about Gautama Buddha, which it is impossible at this late date to disentangle from the truth. But the main lines of his life are fairly well established.

He was the son of a ruler variously described as a king or a chieftain. Brought up in his father's palace, he was kept shielded from the realities of life until he was an adult. Then suddenly he was exposed to the sight of death and poverty, which made such a profound impression upon him that he spent the next years of his life wandering through India ministering to the poor and sharing their suffering. At last in his twenty-ninth year he fell into a deep meditation as he sat under a bo tree, from which he emerged as an "enlightened one," a Buddha. Soon afterward he went to Benares, where he delivered a famous sermon which laid down the teachings which became the core of what was later called Hinayana Buddhism (the "Lesser Vehicle"). It was this form of Buddhism that was acepted by the Emperor Asoka and spread by his missionaries. Thereafter Gautama Buddha spent the rest of his life as a wandering preacher and teacher, gathering around himself a devoted band of disciples who were the first Buddhist missionaries.

The fundamental teaching of Buddha was that all life is suffering, and that man's task on earth is to overcome it by following the Eightfold Path. The choice of these particular eight means of overcoming suffering shows how deeply indebted Buddha was to his Indian predecessors, and to the Indian view of the nature of the world. For one must not simply alleviate suffering, although this is a part of the task; one must perceive the illusion that it is. The Four Noble Truths of Buddha describe the nature of suffering: that all existence is suffering, that the origin of suffering is desire, that suffering ceases when there is no longer any desire, and that the way to overcome suffering is to follow the Eightfold Path. This path consists, in this order, of Right Belief, Right Resolve (to renounce all that leads to increased desire and to cultivate nonviolence), Right Speech,

Right Conduct, Right Way of Living, Right Effort, Right Contemplation, Right Meditation (or Ecstasy). The path thus leads from faith to action, and ultimately to Contemplation and Meditation, ever further away from the world into a mystic unity with the Divine. Thus each individual could progress in accordance with his own spiritual potentialities, first believing, then doing, ever moving upward to the highest form of earthly existence, to contemplation and meditation at which point he would be coming close to that desirelessness which was sought as an end. The end itself was Nirvana, the same state of being (or, more truly, nonbeing) which was pursued by the Jainists, when it would no longer be necessary to incarnate on earth, and all *karma* had been redeemed.

But Buddhism, by stressing the gentleness, compassion, and nonviolence which characterized the lower rungs of the ladder to Nirvana, put the emphasis more strongly upon ethical behavior than was customary in other Indian religions. Moreover, by emphasizing the fact that all human beings are equally born to suffering, the Buddhist paid less attention to the caste system, which may lead to pride in one's own status and in one's own spiritual achievements which have led to the present privileged position. For Buddha the lowest casteless man is as much a human being as the highest Brahmin; all alike are doomed to suffering and can only reach Nirvana in the same way as other men. Moreover, ritual held no importance in his teachings, nor was worship of the gods enjoined upon Buddhists. The only god in Buddhism was that divine essence (called Brahma in the Upanishads) which embraces every earthly phenomenon, living or dead, as the ocean embraces the waves.

It is one of the extraordinary ironies of religious history that this earlier Hinayana Buddhism should, in its later form of Mahayana Buddhism (the "Greater Vehicle"), have become theistic, that Buddha himself should have been metamorphosed into a god, and that statues of him should have been made in vast profusion in all the lands into which Buddhism penetrated. Though

Buddha had not advocated asceticism, or separation from the world, Buddhist monasteries living under rules formulated by ascetics, grew up in India, and especially in Tibet, where they flourish till this day, even though the religion, as has been seen, was driven out of India. Mahayana Buddhism was far more active, seeking for converts in a dynamic manner not characteristic of its early adherents. There is no doubt that many of Buddha's teachings lent themselves to this treatment when in other hands than his. If one stresses the last steps on the Eightfold Path, then for meditation and contemplation it is clearly best to retire from the world; if the overcoming of all desire is the primary end to be pursued, then asceticism, the denial of all ordinary human desires, may seem to be the best way of achieving it: and if the Divine is present in everything, then it is not out of place to glorify the particular aspects of the Divine as manifested in Buddha himself and in such other great men as Confucius and Lao-tzu, especially when it is seen how human beings crave for something less abstract than Brahma for the exercise of the human feelings of reverence and desire to worship. Finally, when the Buddhists had realized that their own leader had progressed to the status of a Buddha by his life on earth, prepared for him in previous incarnations, the possibility that other men might do the same led the Mahayana Buddhists to look for new appearances of other men (called bodhisattvas, a lower grade of adept than a Buddha) who would become Buddhas in their turn. Thus they introduced the idea of a Maitreya Buddha, as a messiah who would appear at the appointed time.

### Influence of Indian religions

*On Indian life*—There is no doubt that these religions of India are, as they have been called, "life-denying." They are all based on the assumption that the world is an illusion, a place for the testing of human souls, but not a field for human enterprise nor a territory to be mastered to yield a life that is to be enjoyed for its own sake—

certainly not a place which is so beloved that the greatest wish of men is for heaven to be its replica, as in Old Kingdom Egypt. For the Indian, death is a welcome escape and release, a period between two lives when the soul can be truly itself.[9] When such beliefs are widely held, as they are in India, it is evident that there will be little incentive to earthly progress, little emphasis on personal success, and little earthly ambition. And yet India has many virtues which may be thought to compensate. Gentleness, compassion for men and animals, nonviolence to others and realization of the sacredness of all living things, gratitude to divine powers and recognition of their gifts to man, and above all the strongest of all incentives toward well-doing in the doctrine of reincarnation and *karma,* the impossibility of escaping judgment for one's evildoing in the next life on earth—these are not virtues to be entirely disregarded in these days of the ascendancy of the Western way of life with its self-assertiveness and aggression. But one has to look no further than these teachings of resignation, humility, and renunciation to see why the West has been able to exploit and dominate the East from first contact until the revolutions of the twentieth century.

*Influence on Western thought*—It has

[9] It is instructive to contrast the *Odyssey,* the great epic of the West, with the Indian *Ramayana.* The entire mood of the Indian epic is almost the polar opposite of the Greek. At the close of the *Ramayana* the heroine, Queen Sita, has been justified and it has been proved that she had, in spite of appearances, been faithful to her husband. But just at the moment of what for a Westerner would be triumph, Sita calls upon her Mother, the Earth, to take her back to herself, since she cannot bear the shame of having ever been doubted.

If unstained in thought and action I have lived
   from day of birth
Spare a daughter's shame and anguish, and
   receive her, Mother Earth!
If in duty and devotion I have labored undefiled,
Mother Earth who bore this woman, once again
   receive thy child.
If in truth unto my husband I have proved
   a faithful wife,
Mother Earth! relieve thy Sita from the
   burden of this life!"
   —Translation by Romesh Dutt (*ca.* 1880)

always been a fascinating question as to how far, if at all, the West has been influenced by these Oriental teachings. No direct influence has ever been proved in any of the major Western philosophers. Yet Plato's teaching, and even more the philosophy of his later follower Plotinus, who certainly had access to Oriental philosophies, insisted upon the inferior if not illusionary nature of the physical body and the physical earth. Plato, indeed, called the body the prison house of the soul, and the world as an inferior copy of the heavenly reality. The myth of the cave in the seventh book of his *Republic* comes very close to the Hindu teachings on the nature of reality, though Plato draws different, and Greek, conclusions from his story. The thought of Plato and Plotinus deeply influenced Christian philosophers, especially Paul and Augustine. Stoicism, the late Hellenistic Greek philosophy, also stressed resignation and the equality of all men through suffering, as had Buddhism; and the Stoic teachers could certainly have been in direct contact with Buddhist missionaries or with Buddhism itself in India. Moreover, the Stoic god of Divine Reason bears a recognizable resemblance to the Brahma of the Indians. Probably there is some influence on these key philosophies of the West which has penetrated into much of Christian thought. We know also that Indian mathematics, with its numerals miscalled Arabic and its zero (often suggested as a typical Hindu conception, a consequence of Hindu desire to recognize and attain nonbeing), influenced the West through the Muslims, as we shall see in a later chapter.

But whatever the underlying influences on Western thought that have been accepted from the Oriental world, one can hardly deny that the Western attitude toward life on earth as a field for human activity is profoundly antithetic to the attitude developed in the East, and that the importance of individuality is emphasized in the West in a manner that is still unaccepted by the East. This chapter, in striving to bring out these contrasts, may therefore be found to

*Ornate interior of Indian temple in Baroda during the Mogul Empire.* (COURTESY THE METROPOLITAN MUSEUM OF ART)

have been justified in a book devoted to Western civilization, for we often see ourselves most clearly in contrasts.[10]

[10] This account has purposely omitted more recent influences, which are numerous in the last two centuries even if they have not been very profound. New commodities, such as silk, muslins, brocade, and porcelain, and new foods such as tea, have been found desirable by Western countries. In a footnote to page 164 there is a mention of

Voltaire's interest in the supposedly benevolent character of Oriental rule; other eighteenth-century thinkers, such as Rousseau and Montesquieu, were greatly interested in, and to some degree were affected by, Chinese thought, and they studied Chinese institutions. Western art has frequently admired and imitated some features of Chinese art. Finally, the importance of the wealth of India should not be underestimated, especially its effect on the rise of the British Empire. But these instances do not belong in a book which closes in the year 1500.

▶ **Suggestions for further reading**

Undoubtedly the best one-volume presentation of the Chinese people, their history and present-day problems, is J. K. Fairbank, *The United States and China* (Cambridge, Mass.: Harvard University Press, 1948). In this book China of the present time is admirably explained in relation to her history, even though this necessarily entails severe compression in the chapters on the ancient Chinese. Another book in the same vein, also recommended, is L. C. Goodrich, *A Short History of the Chinese People* (rev. ed.; New York: Harper & Brothers, 1951). A useful short history, somewhat opinionated and laying heavy stress on an economic interpretation, is W. Eberhard, *A History of China* (tr. E. W. Dickes; Berkeley: University of California Press, 1950). The standard longer work is K. S. Latourette, *The Chinese; Their History and Culture* (3rd ed., rev.; New York: The Macmillan Company, 1946).

A very effective presentation of the outstanding differences between Chinese and Americans is given by a Chinese anthropologist long resident in America, F. L. K. Hsu, *Americans and Chinese: Two Ways of Life* (New York: Henry Schuman, 1953). C. P. Fitzgerald, *China, a Short Cultural History*, attempts with considerable success to explain the relationship between Chinese history and culture.

Many histories of India exist, but none is wholly satisfactory. W. H. Moreland and A. C. Chatterjee, *A Short History of India* (2nd ed.; London: Longmans, Green & Co., 1944), is moderately successful in achieving its aim of presenting Indian culture within its historical framework, based on modern researches. But many chapters are so short that they raise more questions than they answer. Though much longer, R. C. Majumdar, N. C. Raychaudhuri, and K. Datta, *An Advanced History of India* (London: Macmillan & Co., 1950), may therefore perhaps be recommended more highly, even for beginning students, who can of course select the parts they wish to read, in the certainty that the authors have made a serious attempt to handle their subject adequately, in spite of the limitations of space. A book which is primarily devoted to modern India has some excellent early chapters on the country, peoples, and religions of India, and attempts, like the text, to draw contrasts and make comparisons with the West; this is P. Spear, *India, Pakistan and the West* (Home University Library; London: Oxford University Press, 1952). Stimulating and provocative are the chapters devoted to India in H. J. Muller, *The Uses of the Past* (New York: Oxford University Press, 1952), and those on China and India in F. S. C. Northrop, *The Meeting of East and West* (New York: The Macmillan Company, 1946). Though Northrop's case is undoubtedly overstated, the book has special value for those who are trying to determine what East and West can contribute to each other in the twentieth century. Finally, a popular book written by a thoughtful American who was in the O.S.S. in India during World War II, E. Taylor, *Richer by Asia* (Boston: Houghton, Mifflin Co., 1947) gives a very sympathetic account of present-day India and suggests many ways in which we could still learn from this "backward" culture.

On special subjects handled in this chapter S. Piggott, *Prehistoric India* (Harmondsworth, Middlesex: Penguin Books, 1951), gives a clear account of the excavations at Mohenjo-Daro and Haruppa, while H. G. Rawlinson, in *India: A Short Cultural History* (4th imp. rev.; London: Cresset Press, 1952), presents an admirable survey of Indian culture, showing its relationship to Indian history. Hinduism and Buddhism are not easily understood in the West. There is a Pelican book on Buddhism, C. Humphreys, *Buddhism* (Harmondsworth, Middlesex: Penguin Books, 1951), but it concentrates rather excessively on explaining the difference between the various Buddhist sects, so that it may be better, even for the beginning student, to try the clear but detailed account in such a book as C. Eliot, *Hinduism and Buddhism* (3 vols.; London: E. Arnold & Co., 1921). Finally, there is a recent book written about Hinduism by a number of representative Indian scholars, much of which may be found helpful, K. W. Morgan, ed., *The Religion of the Hindus* (New York: The Ronald Press, 1953).

# III Classical Civilization in the West

*This photograph of the Parthenon as it appears today suggests the commanding position of this unique temple on the Acropolis at Athens.* (COURTESY ROYAL GREEK EMBASSY)

# 7

# Greek Civilization

*Physiography • The peoples of Greece • The Homeric Age • General characteristics of the Greek peoples • Political evolution • Intercity relations • The economic basis of Athenian imperialism • Athenian society*

---

## ▶ Physiography

### CLIMATE AND TERRITORY

The mainland of Greece is a land of many contrasts, now, as in antiquity. There is wild mountain country, there are fertile river valleys and plains, and there are bustling seaports. Communication between the different areas has always been difficult, making for regional self-sufficiency and independence; political unity, though perhaps always desirable, was never essential for the maintenance of an orderly life, as it was in Egypt. Every city in classical times was at least partly dependent upon its local fertile area, while there were certain mountain districts where primitive conditions persisted throughout the whole period of Greek greatness. The fertile area of the country, however, amounts to hardly more than one fifth of the total acreage of the country, making poverty the general rule in the absence of nonagricultural methods of subsistence.

The pressure of poverty and population in Greece has always stimulated emigration; in classical times it also stimulated enterprise. In general, the valleys run in a southeasterly direction and the harbors face southeast. Hence there was no great open expanse of sea to be crossed before contact could be made with foreigners. There are chains of islands, welcome havens for the sailors of antiquity, each with its own harbor, inviting trade and transshipment. Before the Greeks became seafarers the Minoans and the Phoenicians came sailing into the Greek ports; when the Phoenicians declined in power it was natural for the Greeks to take their place.

The climate of Greece is equable; there are land and sea breezes to temper the heat of summer, and winter, except in the mountains, is not cold and remains sunny, as in all Mediterranean lands. As early as February the Athenians held an outdoor festival. There is little or no rain in summer, but in most areas there is sufficient rain in spring and fall. Severe storms, however, are known (the thunderbolt of Zeus was not only a poetic imagination); but they are local in incidence and never damage all the country's crops equally.

### POVERTY OF THE NATURAL RESOURCES

The fertile areas themselves present contrasts. There is the lush plain of Boeotia, suitable for grain and cattle, and there is the stony soil of Attica, suitable for vines and olives but, as Solon insisted, not suitable for grain. The greater part of Greek soil was heavily eroded even in the time of Solon, perhaps because of excessive cutting of timber. There is a striking contrast between the comparative wealth of the life described by Homer and the life of an Athenian of the fifth century, still more with that of the Spartan. There were no oxen roasted whole in Athens; in fact, there was little meat at all, and even fish, despised in Homeric times, was a luxury. Timber was in short supply, metals were rare, and there was no iron. Gold, silver, copper and lead, though present, were not abundant; but there were many varieties of excellent building stone, and a good quality of clay for pottery.

In short, the most outstanding physical fact of Greece was and is the shortage of means of subsistence. Yet the Greek of antiquity was able to make such good use of what he had that extreme poverty was very rare, and he was able to build up a civilization on a fairly secure economic base. The process was a simple one, and has much to recommend it—learn to do without. If the Greeks had needed three meals a day with meat as a regular diet, they could not have had them; alternatively a favored few could have satisfied their own demands, but would have been forced to build a political organization that ensured their special position. In an equalitarian and democratic society all equally had to do without. Breakfast was unknown; two meals, both of them simple, sufficed. And the remarkable number of long-lived men in Greece suggests that the regimen did them no harm. Bernard Shaw outlived Sophocles, but only by three years; John Dewey outlived Plato by only seven; and the examples cited are exceptions in our society. Winston Churchill has to survive two more decades if he is to reach the age of Isocrates. If the Greeks had needed luxurious houses, central heating, and spring beds they could not have had them. Fortunately their climate made the first two unnecessary, and their lack of taste for our kind of luxury spared them the other.

The grain that the Athenians had to import at the time when they were specializing in the culture of the vine and olive was paid for not only by these products but also by their craftsmanship. Clay was cheap and plentiful, but vases required skill and artistry. Taken into the right market by enterprising traders, they were worth much grain. But, even so, the only time Athens became really rich was when she was able to draw upon the surplus of her island confederacy. Then again, she provided skill in seamanship, and some political organization, as her invisible export to keep her economy balanced.

The Greek civilization then was far different from the material civilization of the Minoans, or of the modern Americans. But fourth- and fifth-century Athens nevertheless presents a roster of great names in every field of activity that would be hard to match in any civilization at any time in history, and we have continued to try to imitate her art with imperfect success to this day.

▶ **The peoples of Greece**

The Greeks called themselves Hellenes, and their land Hellas.[1] In historic times they regarded themselves as a peculiar people, different from the rest of the world, which indeed, as we shall see, they were. Others were "barbarians," a descriptive term originally used for those who spoke foreign languages, but certainly intended as a term of reproach. The Greeks were in no sense ethnically a pure "race," nor ever pretended to be. It was their customs that set them apart.

There is no consensus as to who the Greeks were, nor where even they came from. They are presumed to have come from Central Europe, penetrating slowly over the course of centuries toward the south. It is also unknown who the original inhabitants of Greece were before the waves of immigrants arrived, nor what proportion

[1] The word "Greek" is first used by the Romans in referring to the civilization of southern Italy.

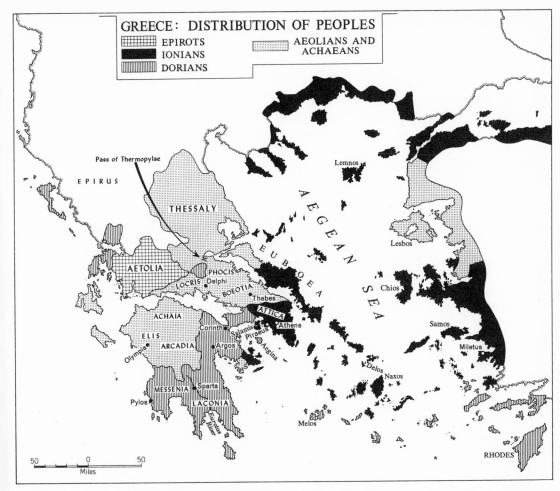

GREECE: DISTRIBUTION OF PEOPLES

EPIROTS
IONIANS
DORIANS
AEOLIANS AND ACHAEANS

of the original stock survived. There is little doubt that the least civilized of the conquering groups, the Dorians, arrived last in Greece, as already described. Ionians, as well as Achaeans preceded them, together with smaller groups such as the Aeolians. The Dorians themselves were followed by the always imperfectly civilized Epirotes, who did not penetrate into southern Greece at all. It seems probable that the Ionians were contemporary with, or even earlier than, the Achaeans, but that the latter were more warlike and came to grips therefore with the Minoans in the parts of the country to which they penetrated. The Ionians settled in Attica and southern Euboea. Then, either of their own accord at an early date, or later when driven to it by the Dorians, they populated the majority of the Aegean Islands and pushed across to Asia Minor, where they

settled near the coast and maintained some contact with their Greek motherland at the same time as they absorbed some of the higher culture of the Orient.

The Athenians were proud of their Ionian heritage, and had many legends which boasted of its antiquity; in later days they regarded themselves as superior to the rude Dorians, whose virtues were certainly dissimilar to theirs. But both had great virtues, and these two were the leading peoples in Greece throughout the classical era.

## ▶ Homeric Age

### INFORMATION FROM ARCHAEOLOGY

We have already spoken of a Dark Age that fell upon Greece with the fading of the Mycenaean civilization and the invasions of the Dorians. It was not altogether dark, as the age that followed the fall of Rome was also not altogether dark. There are, indeed, resemblances between these two periods. In each case barbarians had taken over a civilization that was alien to them, and which they could neither understand nor appreciate. They could not at once take it over and put their own energy to work on it. There was, so to speak, a long period of incubation, during which all political organization was primitive and intellectual activity feeble. Then suddenly, in each case, intellectual activity was reborn, different in direction from what went before; and the characteristic genius of the new people sprang to life. It was not altogether new in either case—indeed after the fall of Rome the chief surviving institution, the Church, was careful to preserve the ancient tradition as far as possible—but such of the old heritage as survived was used in a new way. This historical phenomenon is like a kind of dissolution into chaos, all the elements being mingled together and then finally coming forth in a new shape.

The only archaeological information we have for the four hundred years of incubation merely shows some development in the working of iron, and a decay in the other arts. This information, however, is not all that we possess. For a literary phenomenon of the first magnitude must also have been composed in these years—Homer's immortal epics, the *Iliad* and the *Odyssey*.

The two poems are so familiar to most students in the Western world that little need be said of them here. The *Iliad* tells of the war between the Achaeans and the Trojans, fought because Helen, wife of King Menelaus of Sparta, was abducted by Paris, one of the sons of the king of Troy. The poem details at great length the deeds of the heroes on both sides, culminating in the death of the Trojan prince, Hector, and the ransoming of his body by his father Priam. The *Odyssey* tells of the wanderings of the Achaean hero Odysseus after the fall of Troy, his belated return to his home at Ithaca, and his revenge upon the unwelcome suitors of his wife, Penelope, who had tried to force her to acknowledge her husband's death and choose one of them as his successor.

If, as the Greek historian Herodotus insists, Homer lived not more than four hundred years before his own time, and as scholarly consensus on a much disputed question would seem to agree, Homer must himself have lived during the Dark Age just described. Unquestionably he wrote about a period much earlier than his own, so that we cannot use his poems as direct evidence for his own times. What scholarly ingenuity therefore has concentrated upon in the study of Homer for historical purposes has been to see what he writes between the lines, what he unconsciously gives away. This process has been made possible by our knowledge of Mycenaean civilization through archaeology. We assume that where Homer did not know of the details of this earlier period he has filled in with material from his own. Nevertheless, the whole that we can learn does not amount to a very impressive body of knowledge.

We discover, for instance, such things as that the dead were now cremated as well as being buried, that iron had now to some extent taken the position of bronze, that

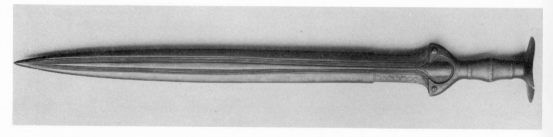

*This bronze sword of the Homeric age in Greece might have been used in the Trojan War.* (COURTESY THE METROPOLITAN MUSEUM OF ART)

# ► chronological chart

Period of invasions
| | | |
|---|---|---|
| Conquest of Crete by Achaeans (?) | B.C. | 1400 |
| Early period, Achaeans, Ionians, Aeolians, etc. | | 1300–1100 |
| Conquest of Crete by Dorians | *ca.* | 1200 |
| Fall of Troy to Achaeans and others | *ca.* | 1184 |
| Dorian invasions | | 1200–1000 |
| Settlements in Asia Minor (Aeolians, Ionians, Dorians) | | 1000–900 |

Homeric Age in Greece
| | | |
|---|---|---|
| Homeric poems | *ca.* | 850 |
| Hesiod | *ca.* | 700 |

Expansion of Greece
| | |
|---|---|
| Colonization of Sicily and southern Italy | 760–700 |
| Black Sea (Euxine) settlements | 756–747 |
| Byzantium colonized by Megara | 660 |
| Great age of Miletus | 750–550 |

Here the "Expansion of Greece" heading has 800–600.

Sparta
| | |
|---|---|
| First Messenian War (first enslavement of Messenians) | 736–716 |
| Second Messenian War | 650–630 |
| "Lycurgan" reforms | 610? |
| Peloponnesian League | 560 |

Athens
| | | |
|---|---|---|
| Rule of Areopagus and archons (abolition of kingship) | *ca.* | 683 |
| Draconian Code | | 621 |
| Solonian reforms | | 594 |
| Regime of Pisistratus | | 561–527 |
| Constitution of Cleisthenes | | 508 |
| Ascendancy of Pericles | | 457–429 |

Intercity relations
| | |
|---|---|
| First Persian invasion—Battle of Marathon | 490 |
| Second Persian invasion—Salamis and Plataea | 480–479 |
| Organization of Confederation of Delos | 477 |
| Persians defeated at Eurymedon | 467 |
| Treasury of the Confederation removed to Athens | 454 |
| Peloponnesian War | 431–404 |
| *Knights* of Aristophanes—Ascendancy of Cleon | 425 |
| Athenian expedition to Syracuse | 415–413 |
| Battle of Aegospotami—Defeat of Athenians | 404 |
| Regime of Thirty and Ten "tyrants" | 404–403 |
| Restoration of the democracy | 403 |
| Trial and execution of Socrates | 399 |
| Spartan hegemony of Greece | 404–371 |
| Battle of Leuctra—Defeat of Spartans by Thebans | 371 |
| Freedom of Spartan helots and organization of Arcadian League | 370 |
| Hegemony of Thebes | 371–362 |
| Plato at the court of Dion in Sicily | 366 |
| Philip II becomes king of Macedon | 359 |

agriculture and sheepherding were the chief means of making a living, that the common method of distribution and exchange of goods was by barter, aided by war and plunder, that the Greeks were not as skilled as the Phoenicians at making industrial products, that slavery, except for domestic purposes, was relatively uncommon. And we can gather that family ties were strong, that respect for parents and age was the general rule, and that strangers were expected to be treated hospitably.

### INFERENCES FROM THE HOMERIC POEMS

We are on less certain ground when we insist on the aristocratic nature of Homeric society. It is true that in the *Iliad* the common man is hardly mentioned, though he may be presumed to have done most of the real fighting against the Trojans, and even Thersites, who used to be cited as the one example of the common man, was not really one, but the son of a barbarian king. Eumaeus, the noble swineherd of the *Odyssey,* was also the son of a king, who had in his youth been enslaved by Phoenicians. But the purpose of Homer has to be considered before we can make inferences on the nature of the society of his day. He was not writing history, nor even a systematic story of the Trojan War. He does not begin at the beginning nor end with the fall of Troy. He is primarily interested in telling, as he himself informs us, of the wrath of Achilles and his quarrel with Agamemnon, and the evils to which they led. It was a moral poem, and was always recognized as such; and it is difficult to see where the common man could have been brought into it. Similarly in the *Odyssey* the story is of the cunning and craft of Odysseus, and the wickedness of the suitors who cared nothing for the gods nor for the traditional ideals of good faith and hospitality and common humanity, and so met with punishment from the returning master. Finally we must always remember that Homer's audience was probably largely aristocratic, interested in listening to the deeds of heroes and not of common men.

There are, nevertheless, some inferences that may safely be made. There is a complete absence in the Homeric poems of anything resembling the divine kings of the Orient, or even of absolute rule by a monarch. Agamemnon, "the king of men," is the leader of the expedition to Troy, and no one ever thinks of deposing him, in spite of the disasters brought upon the Achaean host by his willfulness. Achilles is able to retire and refuse to go into battle, though he cannot keep his prize, the maiden Briseis, once Agamemnon has decided to take her to compensate for the loss of his own prize. Achilles does not defend her by the might of his own sword because the goddess Athena counsels him against doing so, and he obeys rather than incur divine wrath. Put into secular terms, this sounds as if Agamemnon had a certain prescriptive right to rule which had nothing to do with his personal valor; and that he had a kind of overriding authority over the whole expedition which he was not expected to exercise in matters not affecting the expedition. He could, however, do so, even in the face of public opinion, which was all on the side of Achilles; no one except the aggrieved party could stop him, though all might counsel against a misuse of kingly power. On the other hand, there are many divine sanctions preventing Agamemnon's use of arbitrary power; the gods could punish his host, and prevent the success of the expedition. Indeed, he had been forced to give up his own prize because she was the daughter of a priest of Apollo, and Apollo knew how to protect his own.

In both the *Iliad* and the *Odyssey* we have examples of councils and assemblies called by the rulers. Here there is considerable freedom of speech, even against these rulers. Anyone is permitted to speak, but he must convince the whole assembly and the ruler if he is to have his policy adopted. Telemachus, son of Odysseus, has apparently the right to call a council in the absence of his father. The suitors may meet among themselves, but in the absence of the actual ruler they cannot call a council of all the people. These customs do not look unlike those of the Primitive Democracy discussed under Mesopotamia where the elders and heads of families were listened to with respect. But in Homeric times the chief elder has become a king, as we saw he did in Mesopotamia in historical times. But the king in Greece never developed into the absolute monarch of the Orient; on the contrary, he lost his power to the nobles and ultimately, as we shall see, to the people.

THE HOMERIC EPICS

### The authorship of the poems

But the Homeric poems are far more important for what they are in themselves and for what they became in Greek culture than as source books for the history of the Dark Age in Greece.

There is no unanimity of opinion on who Homer was, when he lived, whether he wrote both the *Iliad* and the *Odyssey*, whether they were written in one piece or assembled at a later date—or even whether there was ever a Homer at all. The question will certainly never be settled to the satisfaction of everyone, and, on the whole, it does not seem necessary that it should. In spite of passages which seem to have been added to each poem, both have an impressive unity of idea; and this unity could best be attained by the activity of a great poet working over a considerable mass of earlier material. There is nothing immature about either poem; both are finished works of art, the despair of all later imitators. "Homer" would seem to come at the end of a long line of poets and minstrels rather than to have created both his epics out of nothing. But it was he who gave form to the material. Whether the *Iliad* and the *Odyssey* were written by the same poet is an even more thorny question. Longinus, the best critic of antiquity, did not doubt the authorship. His famous remark, "Homer in the *Odyssey* is like the setting sun; the grandeur remains but not the intensity; it is as though the Ocean had shrunk into its lair and lay becalmed within its own confines," has found many adherents among modern critics, while

others are equally certain that the same poet could never have written both, so marked are the differences. The arguments put forward by Samuel Butler trying to prove that the author of the *Odyssey* was a woman make an impressive total; and even these cannot be refuted on the basis of our information.

### Homer as "the Bible of the Greeks"

But whatever the answer to this "Homeric Question" there can be no doubt of the enormous influence of the poems on all later Greek thought, and the remark that Homer was the Bible of the Greeks is apt. Above all he was their common heritage; in spite of the differences between the individual city-states, Homer served, like the great Greek festivals, to remind them that they were one people. Painters, poets, men of action, and philosophers alike turned to him for inspiration. Every schoolboy could recite long passages by heart, and any allusion to Homer would at once be understood, as any allusion to the King James Bible was understood by every educated Englishman and most Americans before the twentieth century.[2]

### The *Iliad*—The first tragedy of destiny

Why did Homer become such a bible? The evidence shows it was not his language, magnificent though it is, but primarily his thought. Not that the later Greeks believed in the gods of Olympus in any literal sense —and there is no reason to believe that even Homer did. This was his conventional framework. He describes the activities of the gods, but he is really speaking about the human beings. When Achilles refrains from attacking Agamemnon and swallows the insult offered him, the good advice he receives is credited to Athena. But Achilles is not a puppet in the hands of Athena; it is he who receives

[2] Toynbee in our day represents the tradition. There are few pages in his six volumes which do not have at least one Biblical allusion, which—alas, mistakenly—he seems to think will be appreciated at once by his readers, though he is careful to give the necessary chapter and verse, even for the most familiar passages.

the inspiration and acts upon it, and this is the impression gained by the reader. Achilles is the greater man for his self-control, and this impression is undoubtedly intended by the poet. When Diomede is filled with super-human vigor in the fifth book of the *Iliad* and attacks and puts the goddess Aphrodite to flight, and even takes on the great god Apollo himself, the god first defends him-self. When Diomede continues to try to dis-patch Aineias the Trojan against the god's will, Apollo finally forces him to desist with the words "Be not so fain to match thyself with God. The immortal kind ranks not with mankind." This is the message to the reader. Man is not a god. Elsewhere we are shown Apollo pleading for the life of Hector against Athena, who claims it for Achilles. Zeus, though sorry for Hector as a human being, cannot override the Fates who have decreed his death. So even Zeus is not all-powerful. He, too, must bend to the unalterable law of fate.

What, then, Homer taught the Greeks was above all that man is not a god, that pride, especially pride that would make man equal with the gods, will lead to destruction; and that the laws of the universe are not of man's making but must be obeyed. Homer has an unsurpassed feeling for the tragedy of man's life, the *lacrimae rerum* never far from the Greek consciousness. Hector is portrayed with the utmost sensitivity, and his scenes with his wife Andromache are unsurpassed in all literature for their human tenderness. Homer understands what it will mean for her when Hector is killed and Troy captured. Yet Hector must die; we know, and the poet knows, that this is a de-cree of destiny and it is no fault of his. It is no sin of Hector's that is to bring him to destruction, and there is no moral to be taught. And Hector knows his fate, too, but he cannot avoid it. Because he, as a hero, must be true to himself. He cannot avoid the battle and play the coward, even at the entreaty of his beloved wife.

So in the *Iliad* we have the heart of Greek thinking already presented to us in a magnificently dramatic and human form.

Man is living in a framework of necessity which he cannot change. It is his delusion that he should exult in his own strength, and believe it is his, when in reality it is given him by higher powers. He can always abuse it by making himself the equal of the gods, and this is the deadly error which will lead to his destruction. But within the given framework he has a duty also to be himself, to seek for the only immortality that he will ever know, a glory among men that will live after him. Then he will have played his part on earth with nobility. All classical Greek thought is included in this ideal. The gods disappear as persons, but the ideal re-mains. Socrates, refusing to go into exile rather than stand trial because his daemon has not counseled it, and drinking the hem-lock because he is not above the law, is in the same tradition. Man's morality is not required of him by the gods. The gods make no demands upon him, and so have been thought immoral in Homer. But neither do they make demands in any Greek thought. The laws of the universe are there from the beginning, and the gods adminster them. But it is man himself who creates his own ideal of what is befitting him as man, and his reward is on earth in the approval of himself and his fellow men. Even in Plato and Aristotle this humanism is present. The gods of Olympus have disappeared, but the search for the good remains human good. The duty toward one's self missing in He-brew thought is balanced by the Greek ideal of humanism; and because it was pres-ent in Homer, he was never outmoded, even while the gods of Olympus disappeared into higher regions.

### The Odyssey—The Greek mind in action

In the *Odyssey* we see revealed the second great gift of the Greeks to humanity, the means by which the ideal is attained —the Greek mind. Odysseus, above every-thing else, is a man of "many wiles." There is no future for Achilles, who belonged only to the old world of warriors, relying on his strength and fleetness of foot, remain-ing true to himself—for he had chosen a short life of glory in preference to a long life of ease—but a man of swift anger and without compassion, almost a force of nature, living by instinct rather than in full self-consciousness. It is Odysseus who *thinks out* how to take Troy, with the wooden horse. And it is noticeable that the inspirations of Odysseus are not provided him by the gods; they are his own. It is he who thinks out how to outwit Polyphemus, not Athena, though Athena does guide him on other occasions. We must, however, remember also that Athena is the goddess of wisdom, and sprang, fully armed, from the *head* of Zeus. Odysseus boasts of *his own* cleverness, and in so doing draws upon himself the vengeance of the god Poseidon, who leads him into so many unnecessary dangers and hardships. But he is also a mighty man of valor and strength. It is only he who can string his bow; all the suitors have tried and failed. So in Odysseus we have the combination of mind and body which became the ideal of the classical Greeks.

The *Odyssey* has been described as a novel, and many recent translators have had this in mind as they worked. But it is far more than this, or it could never have commanded a position in Greek thought equivalent to that of the *Iliad*. It is the story of a wandering hero who passes through trials of fortitude to reach his home and execute judgment upon those who had been eating up his substance and breaking the sacred customs of the land. The suitors are godless men who think they can treat his wife and son with contempt, and they are punished with death, even those who had shown some signs of common humanity. Those survived who remained faithful to the wanderer and would not believe him dead. And Odysseus himself is clearly chastened by his wanderings and his bitter experiences during his long time in disguise in his homeland, living as a beggar and submitting to humiliation at the hands of the suitors. He knows he will destroy them when the time comes, but he has to wait for the right moment. The plan is carefully laid and carried out; the goddess Athena plays her part in this finale, guiding him at every turn. It does not seem that all this framework is present just for the purpose of making a good tale, though it is certainly that too.

What we have here is a story of the Homeric hero as a grown-up man, no longer ruled by elemental passions needing a god to control them; but ruled now by his own mind. And Homer shows how this cleverness and lack of moderation and wanton boasting destroyed his innocent companions, and led Odysseus himself to his trials and his humiliation. Only when this had been fully experienced could he take up his bow and with the help of Athena kill the suitors and recover his position as king. The divine framework is still there; man is still to beware of his pride which will bring destruction. He must still be true to himself and seek his ideal—which is not here conjugal bliss with Penelope but recovery of his rights as king, filched from him by the suitors and their families. Odysseus has all the qualities admired by the Greeks: valor, decision, presence of mind, and intelligence. Achilles lacked the last; he didn't need it in the world of the *Iliad*. But in the new world of the *Odyssey*, when the hero is cast alone on the deep, when at the last he is thrown up naked and without one companion on the shores of Phaeacia, then a man must rely upon his own inner strength, his mind, and not only his martial prowess. Though few would claim that the *Odyssey* is superior to the *Iliad* in passion, sublimity, or humanity, it is a worthy companion and complement; and it is a fitting prologue to the drama of Greek history, which is in essence the coming to maturity of the human mind.

## ▶ General characteristics of the Greek peoples

GREEK HISTORY AS UNIVERSAL HISTORY ON A MINIATURE SCALE—THE STUDY OF EXTREMES

The mature ideal of the Greeks was *sophrosyne,* or moderation, a quality for which they strove, but which was comparatively lacking in their original make-up. We study the history of Athens and Sparta, the two most renowned of Greek city-states, because they were extremes. If we want to examine the nearest approach to a full democracy, completely logical, permeated through and through by the mind, we study Athens. If we want to study the opposite, the most completely logical example of a closed state, unwilling to accept a new idea, a civilization fossilized and arrested by intelligent design, we study Sparta. When Aristotle wanted to find a golden mean, a moderate state, neither too progressive nor too conservative, he looked for the halfway point between Athens and Sparta.

The Greeks impressed their minds on everything they undertook. Their political history is worth studying in some detail because it was an experiment in miniature with human nature. How much democracy and freedom can human nature stand? Or, on the other hand, how much self-sacrifice can it stand for an accepted ideal enforced on all members of the society? Though the conditions for each experiment were peculiar to the time and place and can never be exactly repeated again, we can learn something of the limitations of human nature from the efforts of these peoples. We can almost see the exact moment when the pressure of outside events proved too much for it—especially when we have with us as a guide a man who lived through the crucial times and recorded them with a self-consciousness and depth of understanding rarely, if ever, equaled in a historian.

The problems the Greeks had to deal with are universal problems, transcending the limitations of time and place. When we read in Thucydides' histories of the debate in the Athenian Assembly between Cleon and Diodotus on the efficacy of capital punishment as a deterrent to treason, we cannot say that times have changed or that human nature has changed essentially from the fifth century B.C. When we read Demosthenes' speeches in the same Assembly excoriating Philip of Macedon—warning against the dangers of self-delusion in the face of a determined enemy—we are transported forward to the 1930's. When we read

of the deterioration of Athenian character under the influence of fear and desire for party gains, we are unhappily again in our own world of the 1950's. The only great difference is that today we are no longer living in a small *polis,* or city-state. The laboratory experiment has been transferred to the great world of superstates. So, necessarily, our particular problems are different, and the particular Greek solutions are not relevant as solutions to the problems of our world. But we can still return to the Greeks for an understanding of the dignity and the limitations of man; and the unanswered questions raised in the city-states of ancient Greece are with us still in our superstates. The refinements of a technical civilization, of which they never dreamed and which it is doubtful they would have appreciated, do not change the nature of the fundamental human problems with which man is confronted, today and twenty-five hundred years ago.

THE SEARCHING MIND OF THE GREEK

All knowledge, said the Greeks, begins in wonder, wonder about the world, and wonder about man. The Hebrews asked only one question about man, his relation to his God. The Greeks asked not only this question, but all other questions. They were the greatest people for questioning that the world has yet seen, or at all events until our own time. When Aristotle came to write his *Politics* he felt obliged to ask a great many fundamental questions before he dared to generalize. He had amassed material on 158 constitutions, constitutions evolved by generations of men struggling with the problem of how men could best be governed. None of the constitutions was perfect; all had failed in some respects. But the people themselves had discovered the defects, and by asking why and considering the alternatives they had tried to remedy them. So Aristotle conceived it to be his task to classify these constitutions, to see if he could evolve a system that would have the most merits and the fewest weaknesses even if it would not be ideal. Plato, on the other hand, was looking in his *Republic* for an ideal state. So it was necessary for him to inquire first on what principles an ideal state could be built, and then try to find institutions through which it could be expressed. This took him a long way. For, having discovered that it must be based on justice, he then had to find out what justice was. Neither Plato nor Aristotle ever thought for a moment that it was not the duty of man to improve his institutions, as the ancient Egyptians had thought. And it is this willingness to seek new knowledge and to stake their lives upon the result of ever-continuous experiment based on the best thinking of which they were capable that distinguishes the Greeks from their predecessors.

The Greeks wondered about the physical world. What was the underlying stable substratum in a world where everything appeared to be in flux—was it water, air, fire, or atoms? Clearly everything changed in appearance; but they did not doubt that this change was only an apparent change. Underneath was a unity. When Thales saw the Egyptian notebooks which told of the measurements of the angles and sides of a triangle, his mind leaped ahead to the universal idea underlying all these particulars. And he is credited with the famous pons asinorum theorem—in *all* triangles, the angles subtending equal sides are equal to one another.

They wondered about man—his nature, the seen body and the unseen soul that gave life to it. They assumed the existence of the soul, but they tried to find the relationship between soul and body. How does man acquire knowledge? What is the nature of the mind that knows it? What are the laws of thinking? How does one idea connect with another? What is an idea? What are the activities proper to man? What is morality?

In all these questions except the last, the Greeks were pioneers in human thinking; and even in the last they were different from the Hebrews in that at least the later Greeks accepted nothing, even the gods, as final arbiters. While they might admit that the fear of the Lord was the beginning of wisdom, this to them would only be one more reminder that they were men and not gods. The last thing a classical Greek would do would be to enter the sanctuary and there receive a comfort which would save him the necessity of questioning further.

### THE REVERENCE FOR MAN AND ALL HIS WORKS

But the Greeks were not a people of philosophers and questioners alone. Their interest in man excited not only their inquiry but also their reverence. The sudden panegyric of man voiced by the chorus in Sophocles's tragic drama *Antigone* seems ready to burst out of the Greek at any moment. What a wonderful thing is man, of all things most wonderful. He can navigate the seas, he can curb the horse, he can tame the wild beast; with his thinking mind he is the lord of creation. And so with loving hands they modeled man in stone and clay, the discus thrower and the athlete and the runner, sculptured him in movement, breathing the living activity into him as no people has ever done since; and they put crystals in his sockets for eyes, put color on his face and sheen on his limbs. And the victor in the games was crowned with a laurel wreath, and poets extolled him for his achievements and gave him immortal fame.

Believing in the dignity of man, the classical Greeks were singularly uncorrupt in everything they did; and though they were later corrupted by exposure to the hard facts of life and found it beyond their powers to retain the purity of their ideal, as artists it was impossible for them to be insincere and shoddy. Though they all worked equally for a wage of one drachma a day, the nameless artists of the Parthenon and the Erechtheum did work that has been the despair and admiration of later ages. High above the ground and only dimly illuminated by such light as filtered through the translucent marble roof, the Parthenon friezes were a worthy offering to Athena, while the foundations beneath the unique building are as honestly laid as anything in the temple that was visible. The artistry of the workmen, as well as the apparent ability of all the people to appreciate and understand the tragic drama, encourages us to believe that this was not a society where only the noble or the rich could play an active part in the culture of their city. It is therefore necessary to try to understand the nature of those institutions which provided them with something hitherto unique in world experience.

## ▶ Political evolution

### THE ORIGIN AND NATURE OF THE POLIS

"The man who can live without the polis is a beast or a god." This dogmatic statement of Aristotle, an alien resident in Athens, sums up admirably the attitude of a Greek toward his characteristic institution —the polis, or city-state. It is an enlargement of Aristotle's other famous dictum about man in society: "Man is an animal whose characteristic it is to live in a polis."[3] Any other kind of state was unthinkable for Greeks, or indeed for complete men. The main distinction in Greek minds between barbarians and Greeks was that the barbarians lived under a monarchy, not in a polis. When Alexander, after his conquests, invited Greek immigrants into his Empire, they at once founded a polis. But it was an alien institution in Asia; the environment necessary for its proper functioning was absent. And it is sad to read of the immigrants with the forms of the polis around them but unable to breathe life into these forms. The polis existed for only a short time in history, and it was never possible anywhere else or at any other time to duplicate those conditions in which it flourished. Yet even such a thinker as Aristotle regarded it as the only possible form of social and political organization in which freedom and democracy could exist.

The word "polis" refers both to a city and to the people living in it; it refers also

[3] Frequently less accurately translated as "Man is a political [or social] animal."

to the countryside around the city which supports it. The polis should be self-supporting as an entity. Though it could be very small it could not be so small that it ceased to be able to support itself, nor so large that the citizens would not know each other by sight and could not take part effectively in public business. It would have its own city-god, a kind of patron saint, who would receive special honor in it. The polis, of course, was self-governing, and it provided everything necessary for the good life through the joint communal activity of all the members. Every freeborn Greek was born as a member of a polis; his whole life centered around it. If he lived elsewhere he would be excluded from the polis, but he would have certain legal rights such as the right of trade, but probably not the right to intermarry or own property—and certainly without the right to take part in the Assembly. It was the all-embracing nature of the polis that made exile such a terrible punishment for the ancient Greek. He ceased to "belong," he ceased to be acceptable in his community, and save in rare circumstances he could not be taken into another.

The polis therefore is a combination of a political and a social unit. In a barbarian empire, said the Greeks, a monarchy is no doubt suitable; but it bears no comparison with a polis. How could you express yourself? How could you be free in an empire? And what would all the paper rights in the world be worth if you don't govern yourself, if you are told by others what to do? What above all the Greek loved in his small polis was the sense of participation in everything that was going on, and the sense of responsibility that went with it. Every man was as good as another. If a man grew rich he would have more responsibilities and duties to the polis. He would have to provide a warship or some part of a warship out of his own means—man it, even command it if he wanted. Expensive, no doubt, but he would have the honor among his fellow citizens as some compensation. On the other hand, a poor man would not feel himself excluded by his poverty from the community life. Socrates was neither rich nor wellborn; nor did he build himself a career. But no one despised him. He took his turn in the Council with other citizens, and was president of it for one day like everyone else. He fought as a hoplite, or heavy-armed foot soldier, in the army. He voted in the Assembly and could speak when he wanted. He sat on the popular juries; he could be present at all the festivals. He lived the rich full life of the community. Though the theater was not free of charge, the polis provided a fund to pay for seats for those who could not find the small price of admission; and in later days a fee was paid to jurors and citizens attending the Assembly so that no one should be barred by poverty from his civic duties and privileges.

So when we compare our own representative government with that of the Greeks we have no real basis of comparison. We say that the Greeks did not invent representative government—implying that such clever people ought to have thought up such a progressive innovation—and certainly they did not. But why should they? They wanted to participate themselves. They were not interested in efficiency, and doing things in the most economical manner. Of course, Greek government was wasteful and expensive. There was gross overgovernment, and doubtless a streamlined administrative system could have saved them much wasted energy. But the Greek loved to talk and listen. Parrhesia—freedom of speech—was a necessity of his life. These prerogatives would not be possible in an empire of the Persian type, however smoothly it worked.

But it was also important for the Greek that his polis should be effective in action. It was useless for the Roman consul Flamininus in later days to proclaim the freedom of all Greeks. The Greek did not want just to talk; but effective action was no more possible under the Roman eagles than it had been in the empire of Alexander and his successors. Only for one brief period when no empire threatened could such a

tiny unit as the polis survive. But this proved to be the time of the flowering of the Greek genius. If Aristotle could not imagine any community other than this for the best realization of human capacities, perhaps he was right.

But it is clear also that the polis is a very delicate organism, capable of disintegrating from within as well as breaking down under external pressure. All Greek poleis (plural of polis), with their highly local patriotism, and each sovereign in its own domain, would be the natural competitor of every other. As long as this competition was confined to peaceful pursuits, it could do nothing but good; but trade rivalry could lead to attempts to damage the trade of another polis, and in a passionate people quarrels of honor could lead to test by battle. In the absence of any overriding authority, any dispute could lead to war, and any war between the larger and more powerful poleis would drag in those who were bound by common interest or treaties. On the other hand, within the polis itself the common interest must always take precedence of party advantage, which is a lot to ask of human nature. And when the individual puts *his* interest first, and feels that *his* wealth, happiness, or prestige is more important than that of the polis, then the polis becomes only an aggregation of individuals, and ceases to be a true community. In fifth-century Athens, when Pericles was leader of the democracy, we have the polis at its best; in the sordid Athens of Demosthenes (385?–322 B.C.) we have it at its worst, disintegrating before our eyes, with the orator himself at times able to bring the city back to its better self by his eloquence, while the intriguers with Philip by their self-seeking politics undermine his work.

The polis appears to be a unique transitional stage between the old tribal and clan society, and the modern administrative state made up of individuals who more or less accept the form of government they have but cannot all participate directly in it, and who have legal rights assured to them by the state, which in turn enforces various duties upon them. The loss of the feeling of integration within the small society and the development of individual, as distinct from community, interests necessitated a different form of government, even in Greece itself, and nowhere else has it been found possible to revive the Greek ideal, save in certain local communities, as during the settlement of America.

The origin of the Greek polis is still a matter of opinion, since there are no written records. But it is assumed that during the invasions the clan, or group of families with a common ancestor, tended to settle in the same place; that clans united into brotherhoods, and brotherhoods into tribes; and that the union of tribes formed a nation—and we have Greek words for all these subdivisions. It is unfortunate for the theory that we have evidence of quite close kinsmen settling in different areas, but the rule may still have been as described. Coming into a certain area the tribes, or union of tribes, settled in scattered agricultural villages, and joined together around some fortified strong point, the *acropolis.* Here the leader of the clans, chosen, or holding his position by prescriptive right as the closest in kin to the common ancestor, would be the king. But other clan leaders would be as important as he, and these would form the class of nobles. The villages, needing a means for common defense, would need the fortress, and with the gradual division of labor would come to require a common market. This market—the agora of all Greek cities—would soon grow beneath the acropolis and the fortified place would also be the natural center for assembly.

This general theory fits the circumstances well enough. We know of the hero or divine ancestor of the cities, we know of the division into clans and tribes which persisted even after the full organization of the polis. We know of the tradition of kings whose power was usurped by the nobles, and we know of the occasional assemblies for the consultation of all the people. What is not known is why the development, not a unique one, nevertheless stopped short at the polis. The physical barriers of Greece might favor the polis as the ultimate unit of government, but certainly did not determine it, because even when the barriers did not exist the polis persisted. On the whole it can only be stated that the Greeks found it favorable to their own particular genius, and liked the small unit; and there was no external power at this time capable of forcing a larger unit upon them. Not all poleis, however, moved on to democracy—by progressively limiting the power of the king and the nobles and giving it to the people. Some were ruled by individuals who evidently satisfied their subjects, others were ruled by oligarchies (rule by the few) or aristocracies (rule by the best), or by the old nobles, more or less controlled or accepted by the people. Some had oligarchies, tyrannies, and democracies at different times. And all had parties favoring one or the other form of rule, the foundation for internal rivalries within the states themselves that almost ruined them.

So far we have been speaking only of freeborn citizens. In addition to these there were resident aliens (called at Athens *metics*) without full rights, and there were slaves. All the cities were too poor in resources to support a wealthy leisure class. Not even by extensive slave labor could enough surplus be produced to give this leisure to any substantial number. So it is entirely inaccurate to imagine any Greek city-state as composed of a small leisure class creating the high culture while slaves toiled to provide the means for it. Almost every Greek, slave or free, had to work for his living, with the possible exception of the inhabitants of Sparta, where the free citizens, or Spartiates, were heavily outnumbered by their slaves, and were required to do a large amount of unproductive supervisory work. There was almost no agricultural slavery outside Sparta. It was difficult enough on most Greek land for anybody to make much of a living, and the slave had to be fed. For the most part slaves worked in industry or in domestic employment. The well-to-do Athenian liked to have one or two

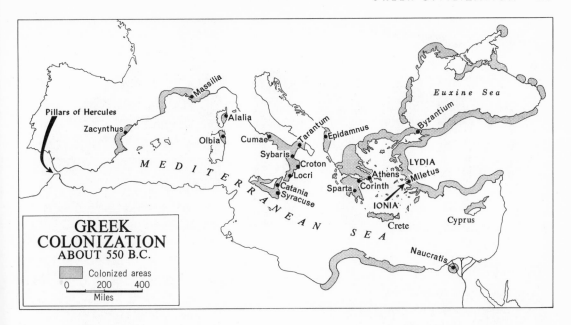

**GREEK COLONIZATION ABOUT 550 B.C.**

Colonized areas

0     200     400
Miles

Pillars of Hercules
Zacynthus
Massilia
Alalia
Olbia
Cumae
Sybaris
Croton
Locri
Catania
Syracuse
Tarantum
Epidamnus
Sparta
Corinth
Athens
IONIA
Crete
Byzantium
LYDIA
Miletus
Cyprus
Naucratis
Euxine Sea
MEDITERRANEAN SEA

domestic slaves, who could be more accurately described as his unfree servants. The Old Oligarch, a disgruntled aristocrat who did not like the Athenian democracy, complains in his work on the Athenian constitution that in Athens it was difficult to distinguish a slave from a freeman, so it may be assumed that slaves were not badly treated. Nearly all industry in Athens, as we shall see, was small, as was to be expected of a people all of whom liked to be in business for themselves. But factory owners employed slaves, a few each as workers. The slaves also were paid, and beating them was not permitted—another complaint of the Old Oligarch. So, on the whole, it is more accurate to regard the slave as a worker with no political rights, and under a permanent contract with his employer—which contract could be sold to another employer without consulting the worker.[4] While the slavery certainly detracted from the purity of the democracy, it was more of an economic evil, tending to keep the freeman's wage down to the level of that of the slave, than the social evil it has been elsewhere.

[4] The only great exception to this rule was the worker in the mines, where conditions were terrible and few freemen could be found to do the work.

## EXPANSION OF GREECE—EARLY COLONIZATION

Before proceeding to the internal development of the individual Greek poleis, mention should be made of the great movement to colonize other lands in which all the peoples of Greece took part. This colonization antedated the political and social reforms in the cities which gave the latter their characteristic shape. Although we know little about the reasons for the colonization movement we do know that at least the early colonies were not trade settlements like those of the Phoenicians, but were the result of land hunger. This suggests the pressure of an expanding population which could find little outlet in Greece itself. With the nobles in possession of the land, and enslavement for debt the common result of failure to make a living, the younger sons of small farmers would be anxious to leave and try somewhere else. Moreover the polis was not yet the ideal place to live in, and for the poor there was as yet no participation in the community life. If they started again somewhere else, there was always more hope.

Along the shores of the Mediterranean and Black Seas, along the whole west coast of Italy, colonies were planted, each of them

*The temple of Poseidon at Paestum, one of the Greek colonies in Italy. In spite of being located in Italy, this temple is older than the Parthenon, and is the best-preserved Greek temple in the world. These Greek colonies were conquered by the Romans and absorbed into the Confederation of Italy at the close of the wars with Pyrrhus.* (PHOTO BY MRS. JOSEPH E. WISAN)

a little Greece beyond the sea. At first the ventures were rather haphazard, and organized by private enterprise. Then the mother cities themselves organized the emigrating parties, often inviting the participation of other cities in the venture. Before a colony was decided upon the participants usually took the precaution of consulting the Delphic Oracle, which acquired much knowledge and experience in colonization and so was able to give useful advice. A colony, however, did not remain subject to the mother city, though it had provided the colony with a human founder and its own gods. One or two cities, such as Miletus and Corinth, tried to keep some control of their foundations, but were never permanently successful. The ties between the colony and its mother city were religious and sentimental; and though these ties counted for much with the Greeks, they were never decisive, and colonies not infrequently in later years joined in wars against their founding

cities. This action was never regarded as rebellion, even though Greek public opinion was against it as unnatural strife. At the beginning the colony always had every reason to maintain good relations with its sponsor, especially when it had been formed for trade purposes, since in its early years it had little energy to spare in seeking out new markets for its product.

Many of the colonies became greater and more prosperous than the motherland. The small rocky polis of Megara founded Byzantium on the Bosporus, and Chalcedon on the Asiatic shore opposite; Miletus made the Black Sea area almost a Milesian lake, with ninety colonies in the area according to tradition. She even established a colony at Naucratis in the Egyptian Delta. Corinth founded Corcyra and Syracuse, the latter destined far to surpass her in prosperity. Even Sparta founded the chief city in southern Italy, Tarentum, though there were special reasons for this venture. Athens, however, developed later and took no part in the early colonization movement. She was more engaged in affairs at home. Having the territory of Attica, larger than that possessed by most cities, to settle, her energies were occupied with this during the formative period.

The results of the colonization movement, though not visible at once, were momentous for the future of Greece. Though the colonies were founded from land hunger, the immigrant Greeks, with their always keen business sense, soon entered into trade relations with their neighbors, who in most cases were inferior in culture to themselves, but had foreign products to sell. Thus a new trade sprang up, bringing prosperity to the motherland as well as to themselves, and providing more employment and stimulating movement to the cities from the overpopulated countryside. Some of the most lasting work of Solon in Athens was his stimulation of the Athenians to look overseas, produce goods suitable for export, and so relieve the pressure on the land. Being eminently fitted for this task, Athens was soon able to compensate for her late start.

SPARTA

### The type of the closed society

It has been already remarked that the Greeks, in spite of their ideal of *sophrosyne* or moderation, tended to go to extremes, and that Athens and Sparta represent the extreme cases of their particular forms of government. The contrast between Athens and Sparta makes an eternally fascinating study. Sparta has been called a classical example of a fossilized static state, a militarist state, a communist state, a fascist state, even an imperialist state, and none of the terms is altogether inaccurate. Yet, on the other hand, such essentially humane non-Spartans as Plato, Aristotle, Xenophon, Plutarch, and Polybius all in some degree approved of her constitution on theoretical and even practical grounds. Did these men, then, approve of fascism, militarism, and the rest?

Toynbee in one of his finest studies presents the history of Sparta as a classical instance of an arrested civilization; and there is no doubt that it fits perfectly into this classification. Sparta was proud of the fact that she had not changed for centuries; she revered as a god her mythical lawgiver Lycurgus. She was ultimately forced by circumstances to emerge from her isolation, and she had to change her way of life when at last her state slaves, known as *helots,* revolted successively. But the changes were grudgingly made; and in spite of increasingly difficult conditions the constitution was continuously restored, with only minor changes down to the time of Cleomenes III in the third century B.C. By this time the conditions that gave rise to it had completely disappeared.

For, as will be seen, it is clear for what purpose the supposed lawgiver "Lycurgus" issued his famous laws.[5] What is not quite so clear is on what earlier foundations he was building that the laws should take such a tenacious hold on the people. The Spartans were the most nearly pure Dorian stock in Greece. The Dorians penetrated to the southeastern portion of the Peloponnesus, where they had to contend with the old Myceneaean stronghold of Argos. The process of conquest seems to have been slow and arduous, but it was at last successful, and the Dorians finally subdued the whole of Laconia, a fertile plain bounded by mountains. They enslaved the native population, making them, however, not into domestic or industrial private slaves but into state slaves, working on the land and contributing half their produce to the citizens who had charge of them. The Dorians themselves lived in Sparta, and a ring of villages around Sparta was peopled by free inhabitants not belonging to the dominant group and of mixed ancestry. These were called perioeci (neighbors). They were not permitted to intermarry with the true Spartans, called Spartiates, and they had no political rights.

[5] It has never been established by historians whether any man Lycurgus ever existed, even though Plutarch wrote his biography, which is mainly an account of the Spartan Constitution.

*Two views of a Spartan kylix (terracotta). The painted interior depicts the apotheosis of Heracles. This piece shows that by 580 B.C., the date of the kylix, the Spartans were still able to produce works of craftsmanship comparable to that of the other Greeks.* (COURTESY THE METROPOLITAN MUSEUM OF ART)

It will therefore be seen that long before the constitution of Lycurgus, Laconian society was increasingly stratified. It could, however, have developed more on the lines of other Greek cities had not events of supreme importance occurred—the Messenian Wars. At the time of these wars Sparta was well abreast of the other Greeks in artistic production. The Dorian style was more simple and severe than contemporary Ionian, but it was creative and beautiful. Poets and artists still lived in Sparta. There were music and luxury in the city, and the Dorian choral lyric was developed there. Foreigners were welcomed who could entertain and enliven the lives of the highborn Spartiates.

### The conquest of the Messenians— Establishment of a rigid militarism

But land hunger attacked the noble lords of Sparta, as it attacked others in Greece, and they were not content with Laconia alone. Colonization was not her answer—the only important colony she sent out, to Tarentum in Italy, was peopled by the offspring of Spartan women and perioeci, an illegitimate union in Spartan eyes—for she had a military tradition, and unlike other Greek cities, a standing army. So she invaded Messenia to the west, a country more fertile and more thickly populated than herself, and conquered it. Many Messenians fled and founded colonies elsewhere; and

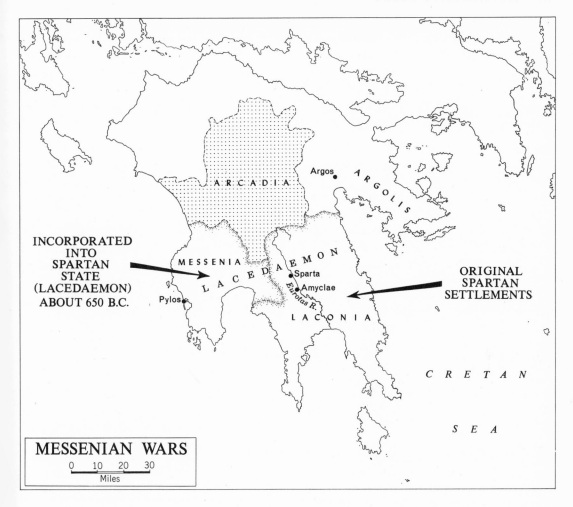

INCORPORATED
INTO
SPARTAN
STATE
(LACEDAEMON)
ABOUT 650 B.C.

ARCADIA

Argos

ARGOLIS

MESSENIA

LACEDAEMON

Sparta

Amyclae

Eurotas R.

Pylos

LACONIA

ORIGINAL
SPARTAN
SETTLEMENTS

CRETAN

SEA

MESSENIAN WARS

0    10    20    30

Miles

Sparta was faced with the problem of what to do with this new territory. She decided to annex it, and made the whole population into helots working for Spartiate masters. We have little knowledge of how this system worked; but we do know that toward the end of the eighth century B.C. the Messenians, allied with Argos and other Peloponnesian cities, revolted, and a desperate and bloody war ensued. Victory at first went to the allies, who pressed on into Laconia. Then, with the death of the Argive leader, the tide of battle turned, and the Spartans, spurred on by Tyrtaeus, their last poet, won the final victory. It had taken twenty years of warfare. It seems almost certain that the laws of Lycurgus date from this time, and

were directed to the problem of what to do about Messenia.

The Spartiates were now outnumbered by their subjects by about twenty to one. These subjects would be a constant menace to their masters unless held under tight control—or allowed self-government. In the latter case they would soon have slipped from Spartan jurisdiction altogether. The answer was, to our view, inhuman, but it was strictly logical. The Spartiates, according to the laws of Lycurgus, were to be supported as a professional military class by the helots and perioeci. The perioeci could live in Laconia as before and handle all the economic affairs of Sparta. They were not to become professional soldiers, nor intermarry with Spartans, nor have any political rights. They could make an adequate living, but not participate in any Spartan activity, except that in case of war they served with the Spartan heavy infantry. The remainder, the vast bulk of the population, was to be held down by the Spartiates by military force and secret police. Each Spartiate would be allotted a certain number of helots to work for him, and from their produce he and his family would live. The professional military class would devote itself to nothing but war and preparations for war. This class would be rigidly selected. Children who were weak and puny would simply be exposed at birth. Education for boys was to consist of all forms of athletics, military instruction, and physical exercise. Boys were made to go barefoot and ill-clad in winter, to sleep without coverings, and to prepare all their own meals. Girls being fitted to be mothers of Spartans had to undergo a similar regime of athletics and games, and were taught courage, endurance, and patriotism. Boys lived at home with their mothers till they were seven years old. Then they went into military training in groups under the charge of older boys, and lived in barracks. At the age of twenty marriage was compulsory, but the husband continued to live in barracks, and could visit his wife only on rare occasions. According to Plutarch, it was hoped that this continence would serve to procreate more healthy children, and in any case protected the Spartiate from a possible weakening caused by contact with home comforts. From the labor of his helots each adult had to supply his share of the food eaten at the public mess. If a Spartiate for any reason could not supply his share, he lost status, and became an inferior citizen, with reduced political and social rights. To prevent contamination with foreign ideas and people, aliens were rarely admitted to the city; and those who received permits were periodically expelled. To prevent the accumulation of wealth the Spartans maintained a heavy iron currency which was not exchangeable anywhere else.

The helots were not personal but state slaves, as mentioned above. They were therefore possessed of certain elementary rights. They could not be put to death except by the state; though it was customary to allow the Spartiate youths approaching manhood to complete their education by spying on the helots. If the youths found any sign of conspiracy, they were armed with the authority of the state and could put the alleged conspirators summarily to death. A helot, provided he farmed well and furnished his particular master with the necessary supplies, could keep the remainder of his produce for himself. He was personally free, and could raise a family in the normal manner. Though in some respects his life appears less dismal to us than that of his masters, we do know that the helots were constantly seething with revolt. For they were true Greeks, with a Greek detestation of any limitation on their freedom; and it must have been galling indeed to know that all other Greeks were living the full life of the polis, while they were kept under by a military state. Helots were naturally not permitted in the Spartan army except on rare occasions of danger, until the Spartiate population had dropped below the point where it could keep its position in Greek affairs without the aid of the helots. But by this time the helots were on the verge of freedom. It says much for the persistence of their independent spirit that when they were ultimately freed by the Thebans in the fourth century, they were able to set up a Messenian state independent of Sparta, and maintain it until all Greece was subdued by Macedonia.

This logical "Lycurgan" system fulfilled its purpose. The helots were kept under control for more than two hundred years, and Sparta possessed an army which was able to play a noble part in defeating the Persians. Its heavy infantry was unbeaten by any Greek city in battle until the rise of Thebes in the fourth century, and was the most highly disciplined and efficient body of troops in Greece. However, it should be understood that the main purpose of this army was for internal control, and not for foreign imperialist adventures. The Spartans were always hesitant to go to war abroad for the obvious reason that this would lessen their control over the helots. Besides, Sparta could not afford to lose many of her citizens, for they were irreplaceable. If any sizable body of Spartiate prisoners were taken, as at Pylos in the Peloponnesian War, she would at once sue for peace, and pay almost any price to gain it. Moreover, the leaders of the army, once outside the borders of Sparta, were in full control, away from the social sanctions of the city. Several Spartan generals showed initiative in their campaigns and came at once under suspicion. The Spartans preferred not to take the risk of military adventures away from the Peloponnese and not until after they had emerged as victors in the Peloponnesian War did they adopt any truly imperialistic policy. And then this policy led rapidly to the freeing of the helots and the breakdown of the Spartan state. The only consideration that could lead the early Spartans to make war was fear of encirclement, or aggression by others. Athenian democracy and the Athenian empire presented a grave threat, not only by reason of their dangerous ideas, but because of the possibility that Athens was aiming at the unification of all Greece. Oligarchies were much safer as neighbors than democracies. The Corinthian envoys who finally persuaded Sparta to make preventive war on Athens played shrewdly upon these Spartan fears; but that Corinth should have been compelled to produce such arguments is conclusive proof of Sparta's lack of interest in further expansion.

### Institutions of Spartan state—Kings, ephors, Senate, Assembly

None of the Greek philosophers knew quite what to make of the Spartan constitution, as distinct from her social system. There were two kings from different families, relics of earlier times, who had little power at home but had the hereditary right to lead the army in the field. When with the army, the king had absolute power, unless the two kings were with the same army, in which case one had a veto on the other. In general each king served to limit the power of the other, but at home neither had very much authority, their function being primarily religious. So Sparta, though it had kings, was not a monarchy. The most important ruling body in the state were the five *ephors*, who were chosen annually by the Assembly. They had supreme power over the helots, handled foreign affairs, interviewed ambassadors, acted as censors of public and private morals, and could call anyone in Sparta to account for his actions, including the kings. The Council or Senate (*Gerousia*) was composed of twenty-eight members of old and noble families. The Senate acted as the supreme criminal court, and it prepared legislation for the Assembly. With the ephors, it also composed the executive of the state. The Assembly of all Spartiates (*Apella*) was the legislature; it also elected the ephors. It could not, however, debate, and it did not vote in the usual manner. Elections and legislation were carried by the loudest shout, as in modern radio programs. Aristotle gave up trying to classify this remarkable mixture of new and old constitutional elements, and called it a "mixed constitution." Broadly speaking, it had many of the characteristics of an oligarchy. But the Spartan constitutional forms are of minor importance in comparison with the social system—the laws, as the philosophers called them—which was the really effective control in Sparta.

### Social pressures molding Spartan character—Approval of the philosophers

Why, then, did the philosophers approve of this system, and why did so many contemporary Greeks turn to it with a kind of envy, and at most with only a half-hearted disapproval? Probably few of the contemporaries knew of the historical reason for the system, and all believed in the laws of "Lycurgus." There is no reason to suppose that the enslavement of the helots was regarded as a particularly heinous offense. What they did see was the Spartan prowess in war, which, as warlike people themselves, they admired; at the all-Greek festivals, they saw the Spartans carrying off many of the honors; and they saw the Spartan girls and women, who were famous in Greece for their modesty, physique, and beauty. And they did not hear Spartan grumbling, if there was any. The Greeks of the other cities did not have as high an appreciation of their own art as we do, and the Spartan lack of artistic achievement probably was not considered specially blameworthy. Spartan heroism, however, was proverbial, and undoubtedly real. The social sanctions ensured it, for no Spartan dared go home in disgrace; he dared not even leave the battlefield to take news home. The Spartan anecdotes and sayings recorded by Plutarch illustrate the kind of reception his fellow citizens, and especially the women of Sparta, would give him.

The other Greeks, with their high ideal of civic virtue and duty, recognized that on this score the Spartans were their superiors. Civic duty, though in Sparta it was of a military nature, was nevertheless imposed by the polis and accepted by the citizens. This condition, to them, was not slavery, because obedience to laws was the whole ideal framework of the polis, as obedience to divine laws was a similar duty for the individual. The other Greeks did not think the Spartans lived under a tyranny, but under a regime chosen for them by Lycurgus, and accepted by them. The Athenian would not have accepted such laws for a moment, nor would he have put up with the Spartan food and frugality, which were the object of frequent jests among citizens of other states, frugal as they were themselves by our standards.

It was the privilege of the Spartans to choose their laws and to obey them; and to all appearances they did obey them. We do not hear of Spartans leaving their city to enjoy the delights of Athens or Corinth until after the Spartan victory in the Peloponnesian War (404 B.C.). It was perhaps the heroic nature of their extreme and narrow ideal and the heroic way in which they lived up to it that excited the admiration of their neighbors; while the philosophers admired the way they used their laws to form character

and the logical nature of the laws themselves. The vulgarity, boasting, and propaganda of modern fascist states distinguish them effectively from Sparta. It was the Spartan's pride that he was a man of few words; and the word "laconic" has passed into our language. And a "Spartan" regime means, not an imperialist, fascist, communist, or oligarchic state, but a regime of simplicity and abstinence.

### The Peloponnesian League

Sparta with her new professional army became the leading power in Greece after Argos had been defeated in the Second Messenian War. Her power in the Peloponnesus was beyond question. Her late enemies either joined voluntarily, or were forced into an alliance with her. The independent cities of northern Peloponnesus, including the trading center of Corinth, applied to her for protection, which she was willing to grant. Thus came into existence the first and the most long-lived of all Greek leagues, containing all the Peloponnesian poleis except the mountain areas, most of Achaea, and the city of Argos.

Within this league Sparta was the acknowledged leader; but when the members met for discussion, the Spartan vote counted for no more than any of the others. No member was allowed to secede, and there was a binding offensive and defensive alliance between all the states. There was no interference with local government, though most of the states were oligarchic. There was no common treasury and no funds, though all agreed to contribute in the event of war. It was in no sense a Spartan empire, and the variety of separate and largely complementary interests, plus the dominance of Sparta in prestige and military power, prevented most of the internal jealousies which broke up other Greek political organizations. Nevertheless there were weak links in it among the trading cities in the north. The secession of Megara, which put in a democratic government in the early days of the Periclean empire, and the defeat of Aegina in open warfare by Pericles, who forced her into the

*This model of the Agora shows Athens in the second century A.D. rather than in the period covered by the text. Many changes were made during the period of domination by the wealthy Hellenistic monarchs; however, the model will serve to give some idea of the layout of the Agora. Although the buildings of the fifth century B.C. were less sumptuous and costly and the arrangement was less orderly, the style of architecture was not greatly different.* (COURTESY AMERICAN SCHOOL OF CLASSICAL STUDIES AT ATHENS)

Athenian Confederation, gave the Spartans their first serious suspicions of Athenian imperialism, and were an important contributory cause of the Peloponnesian War, even though the seceding states returned to Sparta repentant before the actual outbreak.

### THE ATHENIAN DEMOCRACY

#### The early beginnings—Rule by aristocracy

The difference between Athenian political development and that of all other Greek states, as far as we know, was the willingness of the Athenians to go forward to a complete democracy. If the landowners and nobles had insisted on being stubborn and recalcitrant, they might well have prevented this development; then there would have been no Athenian democracy, and probably no Athenian creative achievement. But time and again the aristocrats in Athens gave way, talked things over in a reasonable manner, abstained from violence to gain their own

ends—and throughout the great period of Athens it was they who were the accepted, democratically appointed, political leaders. In all Athenian history there is but one real oligarchic revolution, and it lasted for barely a year. It came into existence only on Spartan insistence, when Athens had been disastrously defeated in war.

We do not know even in what century the small villages and poleis of Attica united into the one polis of Athens, nor do we know the name of the statesman responsible for this first constructive political act of the Athenians—though Athenian legend attributed it to Theseus. The union was celebrated by a festival in later times (*Synoikia*); though not remembered as vividly in Athens as the similar act of "Menes" in Egypt, it was no less important. For it was the real foundation of Athenian greatness.

The date at which kingship disappeared from Attica is likewise unknown, but there was probably a gradual process under which the king became a civilian magistrate. We

find a record of a king with a ten-year term
of office; following this period there were
chief officers of state called *archons,* one of
whom was called a "king-archon," which
title remained to the days of the democracy.
Another was the *polemarch,* leader in war.
The legislative and judicial body of the state
became the Areopagus,[6] and though in these
early times an assembly had a shadowy kind
of existence it does not seem to have had
much power. Only the nobles, heads of the
traditional clans, were eligible to election
for office. The next stage was the taking into
political partnership of the more wealthy
landowners, and a property qualification was
substituted for the sole qualification of birth.
The law was administered arbitrarily, the
large landowners were squeezing out the
small farmers, and economic depression was
rife. In the absence of colonies the small
farmers unable to make their living on the
poor soil of Attica were becoming tenants
and sharecroppers. They fell heavily into
debt; unable to pay the debts, they sold
themselves into slavery. Then, as slaves, these
former freemen and citizens were kept on
the same land which had once been theirs,
or were even sold abroad.

### The reforms of Solon

About 621 B.C. one of the causes of discontent was attacked when the nobles gave
authority to a certain Draco to codify the
law. The law he published was extremely
severe (Draconian), but at least it was some
check on the old blood-feud method of settling murder cases, and was the foundation
of Athenian law. Distinction was made between voluntary and involuntary homicides.
But none of the other important grievances
was settled.

It was at this point that most Greek states,

unable to work their way out of their
troubles, allowed the situation to degenerate
into bloody revolution. But in Athens the
aristocrats and wealthier merchants who
formed the powerful class in the state realized that something constructive must be
done. So they called upon Solon, a merchant
and much-traveled man, a poet who had
written fiery attacks on greed and injustice
and who was noted as a wise man. They
elected him as archon in 594 B.C. with full
powers to reorganize the state in any way
he saw fit.

Solon was a remarkable statesman. He
saw the close connection between the economic and social discontent, and set Athens
on the path to curing both. Hitherto the
Athenians had tried to make a living growing grain in the unsuitable soil of Attica;
they had even exported grain for cash, though
the price they obtained could hardly cover
the cost of producing it. This was the basic
reason why so many of the peasants had
fallen into debt, why the large landlords had
swallowed up the small ones. Unable to
make a living on the land, they had been
forced to borrow first on the security of their
farms and then of their persons. Solon now
realized that it was not only "greed and injustice." He at once prohibited enslavement
for debt, but accompanied this with a prohibition of the export of grain. He brought
back those who had been sold as slaves
abroad and annulled all debts for which the
security was either the land itself or the
person of the borrower. He did not redis-
tribute the land as the more radical reformers were demanding. While he dissuaded
farmers from growing grain as unsuitable for
Attic soil, his experience told him that the
olive and vine could be cultivated successfully and required less space; and that the
products themselves were more profitable.
On the other hand, the specialized agriculture would release more men from the land,
who would then, in company with the newly
freed slaves and the farmers who could not
make a living, need an alternative occupation. The production of wine and oil required containers, giving work to the potters,

---

[6] The Areopagus, a body made up of aristocrats
and the wealthy, was all-powerful, and from its ranks
all the magistrates of the state were chosen; the poor
farmer was unrepresented and at the mercy of his
superiors and creditors, who had the monopoly of
the police power of the state. And there must have
seemed no chance of improvement, for the land
could not be made to produce enough for himself
and his insatiable oppressors.

but not enough. There must be a large-scale expansion of industry, and foreign markets must be secured. So Solon promised Athenian citizenship to skilled foreign craftsmen if they would settle in Athens, and he decreed that every father must teach his son a trade. Finally he adopted or stimulated the use of the best coinage available in Greece at that time.

The economic reform of Solon therefore was designed to solve the agricultural problem and build up the city at the same time. Dispossessed farmers, or farmers who could no longer make a living because fewer men were needed for the new crops, could go to the city to learn a trade, and craftsmen were to be found who could teach them. Slaves freed by their masters need not return to the country, but could become craftsmen in the city. And the traders would have

more goods to sell and more incentive to seek foreign markets. Only the landed aristocracy might suffer, deprived of the easy sale of wheat, wrested from a starving peasantry; and even these might sometime hope to make profits from wine and olives. If they cared to, they, too, could become merchants and traders. That many of them did not become reconciled to Solon's "New Deal" is shown by the forcible ejection of large numbers of them from their land in the time of Pisistratus, as we shall see.

Though such reforms could not bear fruit at once, and few were immediately satisfied, they laid the basis for all later Athenian prosperity.

Having dealt with the economic problem Solon turned to the political. The new industrial and commercial class required political rights; and all the citizens needed a

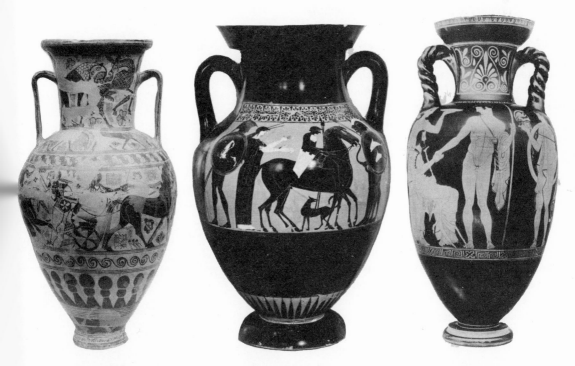

*Each of these three amphorae is from a different century. The one on the left is from the seventh century B.C. and is a product of inferior technique; also, note that the decoration still shows some Oriental influence. The center amphora is from the great age of Pisistratus when Athens was striving hard against severe competition in the export market. The amphora on the right is from the age of Pericles when Athens was secure and prosperous and these amphorae were often used for the home market; note the ornateness of this amphora.* (COURTESY THE METROPOLITAN MUSEUM OF ART)

new status, and some sense of participation in the life of the community. The old Assembly was therefore put on a new basis, and apparently became a full legislature. Every male citizen, of whatever class in society, was entitled to sit in this Assembly. The archons, on the other hand, the executive of the state, retained their high property qualifications. But they were now to be elected indirectly by all the people. Each of the four traditional tribes elected ten eligible citizens, and out of these forty, nine were elected by lot as archons. The old Areopagus, which was recruited from former archons, was kept intact, but some of its legislative powers were taken away from it by the formation of a new Council, the *Boule* of four hundred chosen by lot from an eligible list elected also by the tribes. The poorest classes of the city were not as yet, however, eligible for the Boule. The chief business of the Boule was to prepare legislation for the Assembly.

Finally Solon introduced the popular law court, the *Heliaea*, which was a large body elected by the whole people to act as a court of appeal from the decisions of the magistrates. It could also try former magistrates for their activities while in office. Since this typical Athenian institution was naturally not used during the regime of the tyrants who followed Solon, it will be discussed more fully in its later form as revived by Cleisthenes.

### The age of Tyrants—Pisistratus—Economic advance

Having produced this constitution, Solon then went into voluntary exile from Athens to see how the state would function without him. It soon became evident that this moderately democratic constitution had one serious defect, apart from the time required to put it in full operation with any chance of success. The tribal system of election was a relic of old clan days, and the tribal leaders were sure of election. Moreover, they were situated in definite geographical areas. Thus party politics based on economic interests were possible and to be expected. Two old clan leaders, both nobles, organized groups

known as the Shore and the Plain, presumably the traders and the landowners. They then proceeded to engage in a political and family struggle, making government in Athens for a time impossible. A third noble, Pisistratus, then organized a new party of his own from the rural groups, which he called the Mountain; and with this he bid for the support of the Shore. By a number of ingenious devices he succeeded after several abortive attempts at making his political machine supreme and establishing himself in supreme power in Athens with the solid support of the Mountain and the Shore.

His first task was to silence opposition from the Plain. He did not try to liquidate his opponents, but he took hostages, and imprisoned and exiled others. Then he settled down to constructive work. His rule raised Athens to prosperity and laid the eco-

*Terra-cotta oil flask, recently discovered in Athens, in the shape of an athlete with much of the original paint preserved. The flask gives a good impression of how the Greeks looked in the age of Pisistratus.* (COURTESY AMERICAN SCHOOL OF CLASSICAL STUDIES AT ATHENS)

nomic basis for the later political freedom; moreover he was careful also to behave in a scrupulously correct manner toward his fellow citizens, observe the laws, and keep to such forms of the constitution as could be permitted; and he died in his bed. The Greek word "tyrant" merely means one-man illegitimate rule, as distinct from a hereditary monarchy. It was the misrule of Pisistratus' son, not his own, that gave the word its later meaning which we have inherited.

Having disposed of the largest landowners, Pisistratus divided their lands among the landless and the small holders, stocking them with vines and olives with the aid of funds obtained from new mines which he worked, and from a small income tax on the rich. By these means he satisfied most of his friends of the Mountain. The remainder he set to work on the first great beautification of Athens, with a huge temple of Olympian Zeus which was not finished until the time of the Roman Emperor Hadrian. Among other public works, he gave Athens a new water supply by building a new aqueduct. He patronized the drama, and supported its development into a popular spectacle with annual contests in tragedy.

For his friends of the Shore Pisistratus built a strong navy, entered into foreign commercial alliances, and sent out a few colonies to important strategic points. He maintained a policy of peace and alliance with the Peloponnesian League. Athens prospered under his rule, and fully recovered from her hesitant start. By the time of his death Athens was the recognized leader of the Ionian peoples, and one of the greatest— if not the greatest—polis in Greece.

## The Constitution of Cleisthenes— Establishment of political democracy

Pisistratus was succeeded by his two sons, who for a time continued his policies. But when one was murdered in a private quarrel, the other, Hippias, hired mercenary troops, paid for them by levying high taxes, and became a tyrant in the modern sense. It was not long before a group of exiled nobles was able to enlist enough out-side support, including Sparta, to overthrow him. But when these nobles attempted with Spartan help to establish an oligarchy and regain their old aristocratic privileges they were met with determined resistance from the Athenians. One of the noble leaders, Cleisthenes, turned against his fellow nobles and supported the people. The Spartan soldiers were expelled, and after some delay decided not to contest the issue further. So Cleisthenes was left supreme, supported by virtually the whole Athenian people. It was a magnificent opportunity for constructive statesmanship, and he grasped it to the full. The constitution of Cleisthenes remained the fundamental constitution of the Athenians; and though it was modified in a few relatively unimportant points later, it survived all stresses for the rest of the period of Athenian independence.

What was primarily needed now was political reform, for the economic base had been securely laid by Pisistratus. The tribal jealousies and the possibility of political manipulation had to be overcome. Though the reform of Cleisthenes looks too ingenious to work, it was made to work by the public spirit of the Athenians and their desire to make it work. The finished system could be abused, and was greatly abused later. But in theory and practice it was probably the most democratic constitution ever devised and put into effect (if one disregards those who, like the women, the noncitizens, and the slaves, were always disfranchised). Its abuse is a commentary upon human nature in the difficult circumstances of later years rather than upon the constitution itself.

The four tribes were replaced by ten new ones, each with a mythical ancestor as patron. But not all the tribes were geographically next to each other any more. Each was made up of about ten *demes* (townships or parishes), a third of these coming from the Mountain, a third from the Plain, and a third from the Shore. The deme was the real local unit. Each would-be citizen and boy growing up to manhood would have his credentials examined by the demesmen, and they would probably know enough about the candidate to handle his application. But it was the tribe, that apparently theoretical organization with a fictitious ancestor and no fixed abode, that voted in the Assembly. The members of the tribe, which was composed of its widely scattered demes, would have to sit together in the Assembly.

The purpose of this reform was probably almost as much social as political. Citizens from different areas would learn to know each other, and they were united by their common aims and common citizenship in the Athenian polis. Moreover, the Athenians also now fought by tribes, and dramatic and other contests went by tribes. In spite of their artificiality, rivalry sprang up between them. Indeed the comparison with army regiments is a very accurate one. Regiments in modern wars contain members from every part of the country. Yet rivalry springs up between them and, with rivalry, loyalty.

The next step for Cleisthenes was to restore to full power the Assembly, the Council, and the law courts of Solon, and reform them to meet the new conditions.

The Boule was to be chosen by lot, fifty members of each tribe. It is not agreed whether this meant complete reliance upon the chance of the lot, as there is some evidence to suggest that the demes provided an eligible list to the tribes. But probably this only means that the eligible list contained the names of all who could be elected. Though we know of exceptions, ordinarily citizens did not sit in the Boule more than once in their lives, so that many each year would be ineligible. In practice, in any case, the result was that a considerable majority of all the citizens actually sat in the Boule during their lifetime. The Boule of five hundred was considered to be too large to transact business efficiently. So a committee, composed of all the fifty members of one tribal delegation (a *prytany*) did the work for one tenth of the year each. Every day a new chairman of the prytany was chosen by lot to be president of the Assembly and titular head of the state for that day. This means that thirty-six out of every fifty tribal delegates would be president of the polis for one day apiece in their lifetimes.

The Boule took care of all administrative matters, looking after shipping, foreign affairs, finance, and public works, and prepared legislation for the Assembly. Individual members would be chosen by lot from the Boule to occupy all the public positions in the state, with a few exceptions. These officers of the state, however, could be excluded from their position before entering on it by action taken against them in the law courts; they had to submit to examination in the law courts after leaving it; and all their accounts had to be audited before they could leave Athens or sell property.

The Assembly (*Ecclesia*) was the sovereign legislature. It could initiate legislation, but it did not often do so. It met at least once every prytany (later four times), and could be called specially by the Boule in matters of urgency. Though the chairman of the Boule for the day presided, anyone could speak, anyone could make a proposal, and the measure was decided upon by majority vote. The citizens, however, had to be present in person to vote.

The only control over the people was exercised by the *Heliaea,* or law court. Six thousand members were chosen by the demes each year, and of these the number required for the juries was chosen by lot as occasion demanded. The juries were very large, sometimes as many as 1001, and apparently never less than 101. In these courts the acts of magistrates and their characters were reviewed, private and public cases of all kinds were tried, and in later times even a law could be tried, and sustained or quashed, in spite of the fact that the Assembly had voted for it. There was no public prosecutor, and of course there could be no higher appeal than that to the sovereign people. Anyone was permitted to bring a case against anyone else, whether he was the aggrieved party or not; but he risked both losing his case and then being punished himself by the vote of the jury. There were no lawyers, and the parties to the case had to plead personally; though professional speech

*Klepsydra, or water clock, recently discovered in Athens. The jar was full of water when a speaker either in the Boule or Heliaea started to talk. When the water was gone the speaker's time was up (about six minutes for this clock). "Antiochidos" was the name of one of the Athenian tribes, which held the prytany for one tenth of the year. This jar was evidently used during the prytany of that particular tribe.* (COURTESY AMERICAN SCHOOL OF CLASSICAL STUDIES AT ATHENS)

writers were available, the pleader had to learn his speech by heart and speak it himself. Since his case was decided by majority vote, and the jury decided both on the guilt of the accused and on the penalty to be imposed, much depended on the ability of the speaker to convince by his oratory. But is was certainly the logical development of the theory that the whole polis had the right to rule, and had the last word on everything in the state.

Two further innovations were introduced by Cleisthenes or a few years later. A board of *strategi*, or generals, came into existence; they were the official chief magistrates of the state, but their primary purpose was to take command of the army and navy.

Since these offices required special competence, appointment for them was not decided by lot but by election. The office, furthermore, though annual, could be held by the outgoing general. And indeed it became customary for the generals to be re-elected. No general, however, had the right to command the army or navy in any particular campaign. The Assembly made the decision on the military leader when the time came, but as a rule the command fell to the leading general. Pericles held the position of general for over thirty years, and during this time he was able by his personal control of the Assembly and this position to rule the Athenians almost as he liked. But at any time in the annual elections he could have been ousted, as indeed he was for a brief period at the beginning of the Peloponnesian War.

The other innovation was ostracism, a clumsy device to prevent any man from becoming too powerful and possibly becoming tyrant. Once a year the Assembly might hold a referendum to see whether any citizen should be sent into an honorable exile for ten years. No specific name was mentioned; and any citizen's name could be written on a potsherd, or *ostrakon*, by the voters. If any person or persons received more than six thousand such votes he had to go into exile, with no further penalty attached. The last ostracism occurred during the Peloponnesian War, when it was in fact used as a piece of political maneuvering. It was evidently clear to the Athenian people by this time that it was an ineffective weapon for the purpose for which it was intended, and it fell into disuse. Moreover, the people were so thoroughly accustomed to the rule of law by then that a tyrant could hardly be expected to be able to get into power by political manipulation. Far more effective weapons were now available to serve the same ends.

### Characteristics of Periclean democracy

When Cleisthenes had finished his work, the democracy was still not quite complete.

*Ostraka, or ballots, used for ostracism in Athens in the fifth century B.C. Note the names of prominent Athenian statesmen written on them: Kimon, Themistokles, (A)risteid(es), Perikles, Miltiades.* (COURTESY AMERICAN SCHOOL OF CLASSICAL STUDIES AT ATHENS)

The Areopagus retained some power, and the archons who entered the Areopagus after their year of office were still elected with minor property qualifications. They had some important duties to perform, especially the supervision of the law courts and the festivals. But it was in the hands of the Assembly to deprive them of these duties at its pleasure. In the years after the Persian Wars when the democracy was riding the crest of its success, the Areopagus was stripped of all powers except the right to try homicide cases, which were essentially religious offenses to the Greeks; the archonship, moreover, was opened to all but the poorest class in the state and election was by lot. Jurymen were now for the first time paid for their services, so that all citizens were equally able to serve on the juries if elected by their demesmen. Payment for attendance

at the Assembly, however, was not instituted until some years after the death of Pericles. Everyone was, of course, eligible to attend and was expected to do so. But when the number of meetings was increased to between 30 and 40 a year, not including special sessions, attendance required a considerable expenditure of time. It seemed only fair to later Athenians to compensate the citizen for attendance.

Unfortunately for the democracy this well-intended reform meant that those to whom the small pay was attractive attended regularly, while busier persons with greater means often stayed away. The regulars included not only retired farmers and others unable to work, but also the city proletariat who knocked off work for the day when the Assembly was sitting. This group of unemployed and low-paid workers in time came to dominate the Assembly, especially during and after the Peloponnesian War, ensuring some class legislation and exploitation of the propertied classes. Moreover, all the evidence would seem to show that the Assembly took an excessive interest in policies which could be made the basis of emotional appeals, such as imperialistic adventures. The philosophers and conservatives alike regarded the Assembly's susceptibility to emotional appeals as a radical defect in democracy itself. However, during the regime of Pericles, the masses were willing to follow him—but then, as well as being an enlightened statesman, he was also an imperialist; and his empire paid handsomely.

The last feature worthy of mention in this account of the Athenian constitution was the writ of illegality (*graphe paranomon*), an effective device that was destined to take the place of ostracism. As suggested earlier, the Athenian did not regard his fundamental laws as alterable for any temporary reasons of expediency. His respect for law was too great, for the laws of a polis were the expression of its ideals. Anyone who proposed a law could be attacked in the courts for proposing an unconstitutional law. If he were acquitted, the law was passed; if not, the proposer was fined or otherwise punished according to the will of the jury. This procedure not only effectively discouraged rash innovators but gave the people a chance to think again, since the law could not be put into execution until the case had been decided. It should be understood that there was no definite criterion as to whether the law was really unconstitutional or not, though the proposer would also try to produce evidence that it was not contrary to previous laws and customs. Such evidence would be weighed by the jury together with all other considerations and the verdict rendered accordingly; the device therefore amounted substantially to a judicial review and a trial of the law itself.

The details of the constitution of the Athenians have been gone into at such length because this was the system under which Athens in the great "Classical Age" of Pericles

lived, and the system survived for several hundred years. Even under the Macedonians the Athenians still kept substantial self-government though the franchise was restricted. During the Classical Age all the great Athenian masterpieces of art and literature were produced. Such a constitution would be unthinkable in the modern world; indeed, except in the special circumstances of the polis it could not succeed at any time. In spite of its defects even in Athens—and there were many, especially during the Peloponnesian War and in the fourth century B.C.—its many virtues probably outweighed them.

The constitution was predicated upon the belief that every citizen both wished to take, and was capable of taking, an active part in political life, that the judgment of one citizen was as likely to be right as that of another, that nearly all offices of state could be administered as easily by one citizen as another. It gave no consideration to the specialist—and indeed the Athenian ideal was of the gifted and versatile amateur rather than the specialist, as being nearer to the whole man. At least a majority of the citizens under this system held administrative office in the Boule at some time in their lives. It has been estimated that at any given time at least one sixth of the citizen body was engaged in public activity of some kind, either in the Boule, in the juries, or in one of the numerous minor administrative positions in the state—apart from the Assemblies, where all citizens were expected to be present. This political activity was the real breath of life to the Athenian citizen; it was something that suited his temperament, with his love of talk and social intercourse. And this explains his extreme attachment to the form of the polis, and why no other kind of state was thinkable for a freeman, as Aristotle understood. It also explains why the polis could not absorb other poleis, and why no representative system could be developed, as this would rob the citizen of what he valued most.

It made for strength under adversity, as a general rule. Though the Assembly might be subject to occasional emotional sprees, every man in it knew that his decisions in the Assembly would affect him personally. There was no idea of "they" and "we" about his attitude toward the government. Time after time in the hard years of war we see Athens recovering from a defeat, even after the disastrous Syracusan expedition—though on this occasion there was a brief period of fear and a brief suspension of full democracy. Almost miraculously she then produced a fleet and citizen sailors to man it, aristocrats and slaves rowing together. Even in the decadent fourth century B.C., when Athenian fighting was mostly done through mercenaries, the eloquence of Demosthenes, his strong sense of patriotism, and the democratic tradition of responsibility were able to recall the Assembly to its duty, and create a citizen army. Though the errors of judgment of the period were enormous, and Athenian power had dwindled, the soul of the city remained. It took defeats by Philip, Alexander, and Antigonus Doson to quell the democratic spirit; and even then it died slowly, and never altogether until the coming of the Romans.

The usual criticism of the Athenian democracy—that it rested on foundations of slavery—is based upon a misunderstanding, as is also the second line of attack—that women were disfranchised. The theory of the Greek polis was that it was an enlarged family, an association of kinsmen. A Greek slave could therefore ultimately hope to be freed and become a citizen, while a barbarian slave—in the Greek view—could never understand the working of a polis. If the latter were freed, he must remain an alien. The slave could not exercise the functions of a citizen until he had been freed and educated. If slavery had been abolished, in spite of the economic conditions that bred it, then political rights for the Greek freedmen would have followed as a matter of course. Slavery cannot therefore be regarded as a blot on Greek democracy as a political ideal, whatever we may think of slavery as an economic and social evil. *Metics*, or resi-

dent aliens, could win full citizenship on occasion, but to do so was difficult. As foreigners they were not expected to understand the concept of the polis as an enlarged family until they had been resident in it for a considerable time. They had rights, but they could not perform the duties of a citizen without understanding very fully the relationship of these duties to the whole ideal of the polis. The enfranchisement of women was, of course, unknown in the Greek world, though we can infer from the fact that Aristophanes devoted a whole play to a lampoon on women in government (*Ecclesiazusae*) that it was an issue of some interest to the citizens. The position of women in Athens will be discussed later. Here it need only be said that the duties of men and women were rigorously circumscribed. If the status of women had been different, the logic of the situation would have demanded that they be given a vote; but it was their social status that determined their political position. It would have been quite alien to Greek political conceptions that the vote should be, or could be, used to improve social status, as in our own age.

It is fortunate that the entire ideal of the Athenian polis and political life can be inferred from the institutional evidence without touching what is perhaps the most eloquent expression of a political ideal ever made—the Funeral Speech put into the mouth of Pericles by Thucydides. In this speech in honor of the citizen soldiers who have been killed in the first year of the Peloponnesian War, Pericles, instead of praising the dead as was the custom, praises the ideal for which they have died. So his speech becomes a panegyric of the Athenian polis. An Athenian citizen, he says, "does not neglect the state because he takes care of his own household; and even those of us who are engaged in business have a very fair idea of politics. We alone regard a man who takes no interest in public affairs, not as a harmless, but as a useless character; and if few of us are originators, we are all sound judges of policy. . . . When a citizen is in any way distinguished, he is preferred to the public service, not as a matter of privilege, but as the reward of merit. Neither is poverty a bar, but a man may benefit his country whatever be the obscurity of his condition."[7]

It is impossible to deny that these virtues are to be found in the developed Athenian constitution. Within all Greek states there were oligarchic and democratic factions, even in Athens; though in the days of her greatness the aristocrats, on the whole, supported the democracy, and one of its most outstanding members led it. During the Peloponnesian War the oligarchs twice came to power briefly, as we shall see; but only because the democracy had discredited itself through failure in the war. There was always a natural antagonism between the cities with democracies and those with oligarchies, the latter tending to concentrate in the Peloponnesus. The other cities and colonies usually had their parties fairly equally balanced. The result was frequent revolutions, with the oligarchies appealing to Sparta and the democracies to Athens, for help, which was usually given. This situation accounts partly for the divisions and antagonisms between the cities. Trade and other rivalries also caused local wars. Spartan fears of encirclement and Athenian imperialist policies in the fifth century also made for dissension, and local, followed by general, war. There is hardly any period when the Greek cities, each claiming and maintaining full freedom of action on foreign policy, were not engaged in some hostilities against other cities. These intercity rivalries and quarrels are a sad commentary on the Greek political systems which gave rise to them, but they do not compel us to say that the form of government was a failure when it obviously had so many merits in the eyes of its own citizens and was able to manage its internal affairs with such marked success. The national state also has not so far succeeded in abolishing wars.

[7] Thucydides, II, 39 ff.

## ▶ Intercity relations

UNIFYING FORCES IN GREEK LIFE—THE
RELIGIOUS LEAGUES AND FESTIVALS

But there were also unifying forces in Greek life. All Greeks looked with contempt upon barbarian kingdoms as unfit for free men, and, as we shall soon see, some unity of purpose was achieved against the attacks of Persian "barbarians." There were several all-Greek festivals, the best known of which were the Olympic games. Here Greeks forgot they were citizens of different poleis, and sat together in amity. Though each city had its patron god or goddess, the great gods were gods of all the Greeks equally, as were the Orphic and other mysteries. The great oracle of Apollo at Delphi in Phocis was a neutral, giving advice impartially to all comers, protected by its sacred position, with even its treasure safe until the late fourth century B.C. Though the Delphic Oracle was in Phocian territory, a league called the Delphic Amphictyony made up of the different states and tribes of Greece was responsible for its protection, and a kind of international law prevailed, neutralizing the sanctuary in the event of war. Even this Amphictyonic League, however, was later manipulated for political purposes, especially by the non-Greek Philip of Macedon. Another league of Ionians protected the sanctuary of Apollo at Delos. On the whole, the political leagues accentuated the division between the states rather than helped to unite them. The great political failure of the Greeks was unquestionably in interstate relations, and it was not until more than a century after the conquests of Macedonia that there appeared any serious likelihood of unification brought about by the free efforts of Greeks themselves.

THE PERSIAN WARS

### Unity in face of external danger

The only occasion in classical times that a majority of Greeks made an important united effort was in the early fifth century against the Persians.

### The campaign of Marathon

The struggle began with the revolt of the Ionian cities of Asia Minor against Persian expansion under Darius the Great. Darius and his Persians had already expanded into Europe and conquered Thrace, and suppressed some of the liberties of the Ionian cities conquered from Lydia by Cyrus.[8] The moment for the revolt was badly timed. Though the war lasted a long time, Darius at last was able to bring his superior forces to bear, especially the Phoenician navy, and defeat the cities. He destroyed the ringleader Miletus; but the remainder he treated leniently, even allowing them to have democratic governments if they desired them. But he did not forget that the Athenians and Euboeans had sent a small expedition to help their Ionian kinsmen. The expedition had returned home after aiding in the destruction of the local Persian capital, Sardis; but, according to Herodotus, the historian of the Persian Wars, Darius cherished thoughts of revenge. Urged on by Hippias, the exiled tyrant of Athens who was at his court, Darius prepared an expedition against Athens and Euboea, and sent heralds to other Greek cities demanding submission. Several, including Thebes, sent the token earth and water to the Persian king.

In 490 B.C. the expedition set sail for Athens across the Aegean Sea, under the command of the generals Datis and Artaphernes. After chastising the Euboeans the Persians anchored in the Bay of Marathon, only a few miles to the northeast of Athens, intending to land troops and march directly to the city. Few preparations had been made to meet the Persians, though the young Athenian democracy had a well-trained citizen infantry under the polemarch Callimachus, with an experienced general, Miltiades, a hater of Persia, as strategic adviser. When they heard of the landing at Marathon, and apparently not before, the

[8] See above, Chapter 4.

Athenians sent a runner to Sparta requesting aid, which was duly promised. Unfortunately, however, the omens in Sparta were not favorable and the army was not sent immediately. The result was that Athens had to face the Persian host with the aid only of fewer than a thousand men from the neighboring city of Plataea. The total army facing the Persians was at the most ten thousand; and the Athenians might not have even engaged in battle if they had not thought that Spartan help would soon arrive.

However, the Persians were so sure of victory that they did not trouble to throw in their whole force. It has also been suggested that the account given by Herodotus can be explained only on the assumption that the Persians were awaiting a signal from traitors in Athens sympathetic to the exiled Hippias. However this may be, it seems that the Persian fleet with a large part of the army watched the battle without taking part in it, prepared at the first sign of victory to make for Athens by sea. Nevertheless, the Athenians, assisted by superior knowledge of the terrain, and superior tactics, inflicted an overwhelming defeat on the Persians; then, immediately the battle was over, without waiting to bury the dead, they returned to Athens and marched straight through to Piraeus, the port of the city, a few miles to the southwest. They arrived just as the Persian fleet made its appearance, and the latter, not anxious to engage the victors of Marathon in battle so soon after their own defeat, returned to Persia. Darius died soon afterward, and the Greeks had a breathing space of ten years before Xerxes, his son, could prepare a really formidable expedition, this time not only to punish Athens but to conquer the whole of Greece.

The interval was marked in Athens by the rise to power of Themistocles, who realized the extent of the danger and the only way to combat it. He persuaded the Assembly to use the profits of a new silver mine for the expansion of the navy. Thus, when the Persians struck, Athens had an efficient, well-trained navy, which was to prove one of the decisive factors in the war.

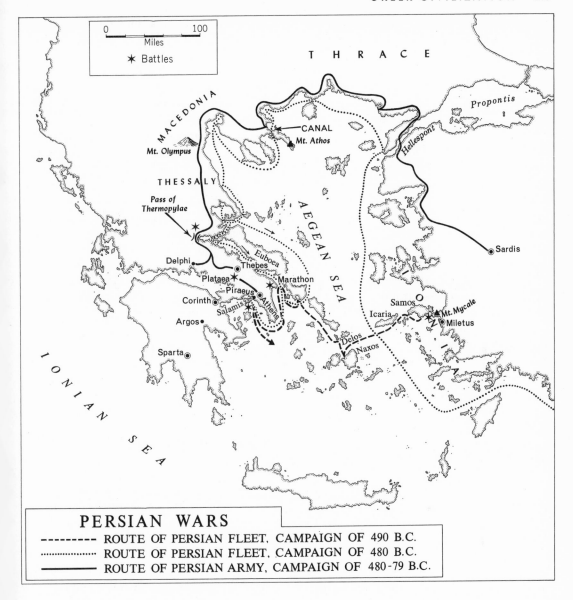

PERSIAN WARS

- - - - - - - - - ROUTE OF PERSIAN FLEET, CAMPAIGN OF 490 B.C.
················· ROUTE OF PERSIAN FLEET, CAMPAIGN OF 480 B.C.
————————— ROUTE OF PERSIAN ARMY, CAMPAIGN OF 480-79 B.C.

## The full-scale invasion of Xerxes

In 480 B.C., Xerxes, at the head of a huge, motley army, and accompanied by a navy, partly Phoenician in origin, which hugged the coast ready to lend support, marched through Thrace to the borders of Greece. Sparta, for once taking the initiative, called a congress to consider a joint defense. Thebes followed her previous policy of immediate submission to the Persians (called "Medizing" by the Greeks), other cities wavered, and ultimately submitted

when the Persians approached. Nevertheless this congress at Sparta was attended by delegates from almost all the major cities of Greece, an impressive demonstration of unity never again duplicated. The results, however, were not equally impressive. In view of her naval commitments, Athens found it impossible to spare men to help defend the passes into Greece. Ultimately only three hundred Spartiates with some auxiliary helots, and several more or less unwilling allies, marched to Thermopylae under the leadership of Leonidas, king of Sparta. This army nevertheless withstood the Persians for several days until a traitor revealed a side path which was inadequately guarded. Sending most of the allies home, the Spartiates fought to the last man[9] in one of the most famous and heroic defenses of history. The army of Xerxes poured through the pass, the Spartans and the Peloponnesian League proceeded to build a wall across the Isthmus of Corinth, and Themistocles and the Athenians prepared to evacuate Athens and Attica and take to the ships. The army of Xerxes entered Athens, sacked and looted it, and burned the temples.

The navy, meanwhile, under the command of Athens but not manned entirely by Athenians, was having trouble in arriving at a decision. The allies wanted to retire to the Peloponnesus, as did the Spartans. But Themistocles threatened to take the Athenian part of the fleet and sail to the west and found a new colony. This sobered the Spartans and the allies, and Themistocles was reluctantly given permission to engage in naval battle with the Persians at once. Baiting a trap with a supposed traitor who succeeded in deceiving Xerxes, he lured the Persians into the narrows of Salamis, where the Greek fleet won a resounding victory. Xerxes rèturned home, leaving Mardonius with his brother-in-law to carry on the campaign. He retired north for the winter, but again advanced on Attica in the spring. Athens appealed frantically for help to the Spartans, who were now safely holed up in the Peloponnesus; and after much delay the Greeks decided to take the offensive north of the Peloponnesus. At last a really representative allied army brought the army of Mardonius to battle on fairly equal terms. The discipline and valor of the Spartan hoplites won the battle of Plataea (479 B.C.) and Mardonius and almost the whole of his army were killed. This was the decisive battle. The allied fleet won, traditionally on the same day, the final victory of the war at Mycale,

off the coast of Ionia, and the Ionian cities were freed.

The Persian Wars revealed, as usual, the prevalence of local jealousies and the extreme difficulty of obtaining any kind of unity, even in the face of the overwhelming threat of submersion within a barbarian empire and the loss of all Greek liberties; nevertheless, by the end of 479 B.C. there had been an impressive cooperation and a unified command. Although more than half of it was Athenian, the allied navy had submitted to the control of a Spartan admiral, and won the final victory under his leadership. But no one in Greece after Mycale would have dared to prophesy a permanent unification of all the city-states for any purpose; and indeed, as far as we know, not one man ever thought of such a thing. The nature of the polis, as we have seen, precluded any more effective arrangement than glorified leagues; the kingdom or empire was universally regarded as a barbarian form of government. The Spartans were only anxious to go home; they had done their duty and had won their glory, but more pressing needs were now paramount.

### THE CONFEDERATION OF DELOS—ATHENIAN IMPERIALISM

In general all the other mainland city-states except Athens were of the same opinion; but the Ionian cities of Asia Minor, just freed from Persian rule, and the islands of the Aegean did not feel themselves so secure. All Greeks knew that an expedition of the type manned by Xerxes was impossible for years to come, and in any case could probably be beaten off by improvisation as before. But it was not too difficult for Persia, with its immense financial resources and the seamen of Phoenicia at its disposal, to put together a fleet which could do severe damage in the Aegean. So when the Athenians proposed to keep the maritime part of the recent league in being, the islands were willing. The guiding spirit behind the naval policy was undoubtedly Themistocles, the hero of Salamis. He alone among the statesmen of Greece had a clear vision of the future

---

[9] According to Herodotus, one man alone escaped, who was held by the Spartans in such infamy that he sacrificed his life in ostentatious deeds of valor later at Plataea.

*An inscription, found on the Acropolis, dealing with the assessment of tribute from one of the Athenian allies in the Confederation of Delos (425 B.C.).* (COURTESY THE METROPOLITAN MUSEUM OF ART)

and prepared for it, converting the Athenian democracy in the years after the wars to the understanding that its future lay on the sea. But the league itself was organized by Aristides the Just, a more trustworthy person, with a reputation for incorruptibility which was accepted by the cities of the new league.

So came into being the Confederation of Delos under the leadership of Athens. The purpose and constitution of this league were admirable in theory; but one clause was capable of abuse, and led the way to Athenian domination and empire. In any case Athens was always the dominant power, and could have made the league an empire, with or without the legal rights on her side. But the league itself would probably never have come into being in this dangerous form had the allies not trusted Aristides, who made the naval and financial assessments for each member. The Confederation was more than the offensive and defensive alliance of the Peloponnesian League; it was a full collective security program backed by a joint navy, and under the protection and sanction of the god Apollo. Those members

who were wealthy enough to provide ships could do so; the remainder could contribute money proportionate to their means. The money was to be deposited in Delos, a small island sacred to Apollo, and at Delos was to be held every year a congress, in which each state would be equal, each having one vote. Athens guaranteed the independence of each member, including its foreign policy, and freedom to rule itself under whatever form of government it wished. But, no state could withdraw without the consent of all.[10]

The form of this constitution is, of course, democratic enough. But in substance the Athenian veto on withdrawal and the right of the Athenians to make the assessments, combined with her command of the allied navy, gave her a power too great to be opposed by anything except the alliance of all the members together; and this was impossible. In any case most of the members profited by the alliance, and their trade and wealth increased; and they could hope, each individually, that they would not incur the displeasure of Athens nor have their taxes increased. As time went on, almost all the members found it more convenient to pay money instead of providing ships; and this, too, played into the hands of Athens, since the ships bought with the money were built by the Athenians and commanded and manned by them.

In 467 B.C. the Persian navy ventured into Aegean waters and was soundly defeated by the confederation at the battle of the Eurymedon. Thereafter the Aegean became a Greek lake. And though the fleet was used in other imperialist ventures by Pericles later, the real danger was over. It was therefore not unnatural that some of the members should seek to withdraw. The Athenian democracy under all its leaders set itself against this trend with stubbornness and determination, and never in any circumstances gave its consent. When a member seceded, the joint navy, partly paid for by

[10] An instructive modern parallel is the 1834 *Zollverein* of German states under the leadership of Prussia, which emerged as the German Empire.

*Bust of Pericles, the Athenian statesman.* (COUR-TESY BRITISH MUSEUM)

### THE PELOPONNESIAN WAR

Though Pericles was a high-minded statesman, and a true democrat as far as his own polis was concerned, his foreign policy was that of a confirmed imperialist. Moreover, his consistent anti-Spartan policy was bound to bring him into conflict with the greatest Greek land power and with the maritime cities in the northern Peloponnesus which found their trade slipping from them. When he tried to interfere in the Peloponnesian League itself, and force and cajole members away from that alliance, it was clear that he was aiming at a complete domination of Greece and that Sparta was indeed in danger. There were several clashes on land before the Spartans could be finally convinced by her allies that war was inevitable, and that she must really enter into it as wholeheartedly as the Corinthians and others who were directly threatened by Athenian aggression. But on the outbreak of full-scale war she sent her incomparable army directly against Attica.

The Athenians knew that it would be impossible to defeat the Spartans in open battle. But the city and harbor were now encircled by the Long Walls, built by Themistocles; and as long as Athens maintained command of the sea she could not be starved out and no Greek army could breach the Long Walls until the fleet was conquered. But the policy of keeping all citizens within the Long Walls meant the loss of Attica, and it could not be expected that such a policy would prove popular. In the crowded conditions of the city plague broke out, and Pericles and his policy were briefly repudiated by the people. He failed to be re-elected as general, and peace was considered. However, the tide soon turned, since the people found they could not do without him, and he was given supreme powers to carry on the war as he saw fit. But he died a year later, and soon afterward the Assembly fell into the hands of Cleon, the villain of Thucydides' history, advocate of a strong policy toward the doubtful allies and the counteroffensive against Sparta on land.

the seceding member, was used against it; and the state itself was regarded as rebellious. When the revolt was quelled it was made into a subject state and its taxes were increased. Finding that the revolts were usually the work of oligarchs, the Athenians then insisted upon having democratic governments throughout the Confederation, contrary to their original undertakings when this league was founded. This insistence, however, did not always have the intended results. The members began to realize that Athens was not the lover of liberty in others that she pretended to be; and gradually it came to be said that she was "the enslaver of Greek liberties." However, revolts were few and sporadic until the Peloponnesian War, and on the whole the cities were probably content. Even when the treasure of the Confederation was removed from Delos to Athens in 454 B.C. by Pericles, a specious excuse was made, and it was not Athens herself who proposed it. But the Confederation had clearly become an empire; and Pericles and the Athenians were thoroughly aware of the fact, and prepared to exploit it to the full.

431 B.C.
GREECE AT THE
BEGINNING OF THE
PELOPONNESIAN WAR

ATHENS AND ALLIES
SPARTA AND ALLIES
NEUTRAL

The details of this long war are no longer of importance to us, though the incomparable history of Thucydides has made it of perennial interest both to military historians and to all those fascinated by the behavior of human beings under the stress of war. The Athenians built up their army and were able to defeat the allied Peloponnesian forces, even if not the Spartan army itself; though on one occasion the feebleness of Spartan strategy and tactics allowed a fairly large force to be surrounded and captured. Thereupon the Spartans made overtures for peace on the basis of the *status quo* of the beginning of the war, which terms were rejected by Cleon and the Athenian Assembly. The cities in the empire, as a whole, remained loyal, though evidently with increasing reluctance. The war was none of their making, and did not concern their vital interests. The Athenians at the height of their power sent an expedition to Syracuse, the powerful Corinthian colony in Sicily, and might well have captured it had it not been for the incompetence of the commanding general. A Spartan adviser was instrumental in helping the Syracusans to the decisive victory; and the Persian king saw his chance to break up the hated Athenian empire as well as recover the Ionian cities. Thereafter he supported Sparta with the money she had been lacking, and Sparta found in Lysander an able admiral. The Persian navy, with Phoenician and Peloponnesian sailors, proved too strong for the Athenians and their now largely disloyal empire. In 404 B.C. Athens was decisively defeated by sea at the battle of Aegospotami, and her resistance was over.

The Spartan army prepared to enter the defenseless city, and the Spartan fleet entered Piraeus Harbor. Terms were dictated to the Athenians. The Spartan allies, Thebes and Corinth, wanted to raze the city to the ground, but the Spartans refused. Athenian services to all Hellas during the Persian Wars, they said, had been such that they could never be forgotten (a nasty and typically Spartan reminder to the Thebans of their disgrace in having "Medized"). The terms, however, were severe enough. The Long Walls were to be pulled down, Athens was to lose all her foreign possessions and to keep only twelve ships, and she was to submit to Sparta as a subject ally. Moreover, the democracy was to be replaced by an oligarchy, which afterward became known in Athenian history as the rule of the Thirty, and, in its last stages, the Ten, Tyrants.

These oligarchs, long unused to power, created a reign of terror, and maintained themselves only by the aid of Lysander and the Spartan army. A group of Athenian refugees won some local victories, and other small towns expelled their Spartan garrisons. Sparta, whose losses in the war were serious, realized that it would be either perpetual war or the restoration of the democracy. She chose to permit the latter, and Athens was free again. But she had yielded supremacy in Greece to Sparta, and, though she was able in due course to rebuild her navy, she never again became the leading power in Greece.

CORRUPTION AND DECLINE IN FOURTH-CENTURY GREECE—HEGEMONY OF SPARTA AND THEBES

Fourth-century Greek history is a sordid tale of intrigues, first by Persia and then by Macedon, that effectively prevented Greek unity, which in any case few in Greece were looking for. Spartan supremacy was marked by the excesses to be expected of a people only just released from isolation, and whose leaders could not be controlled by the ephors and their social system when beyond Spartan borders. As the price for Persian support Sparta allowed the Great King to take back the Ionian cities in Asia Minor, which remained subject to him till the expedition of Alexander; and he dictated a peace to Greece. His money, however, was spent in intrigues of all kinds. For a time he transferred it to Thebes, and Thebes became the leader in Greece, thanks also to the ability of two of the greatest generals in Greek history, who defeated Sparta decisively in the open field and freed the helots. But Thebes, too, lost Persian support, her generals were killed in battle, and leadership in Greece fell into the hands of the semibarbarian Macedonians. But the fall of all Greece to Philip of Macedon, and the expansion into Asia under Alexander will be left to a later chapter.

▶ **The economic basis of Athenian imperialism**

AGRICULTURE—COLONIZATION, CLERUCHIES

In the course of the preceding survey mention has been made where necessary of the economic foundations of Athenian society. Though the empire was not of as much benefit to the farmer as to the merchant and manufacturer, and though he was the first to be hit by the war, he must in general have supported the imperial policy of Pericles, or have been unable to vote against it through the requirement of Athenian democracy that he vote in person. Agriculture remained the foundation of Athenian life. There were probably as many small farmers in Attica as there were permanent inhabitants of the city.

The poverty of the soil and the small

size of the farms always made living on the land difficult. Large farms were very rare; a farm of sixty-five acres in the fourth century was considered enormous. After the reforms of Solon little wheat was grown in Attica. More than two thirds of the whole grain supply had to be imported, mostly from the Black Sea area; and 90 per cent of the grain grown in Attica was barley. Vines and olives remained the principal crop. Slavery on the farms was almost negligible. Few farmers could afford the price; and a slave had to eat and could not produce much more than his keep in return for his labor. But though life on the farms was hard, it at least assured economic independence and prevented the working for wages, which was disliked by all Greeks except in the service of the state.

During the imperial period a new policy, already found for the first time at the beginning of the fifth century, was encouraged, which took some notice of the permanent land hunger of the farmer. It has been seen that Athens was backward in overseas colonization because of her late development. But it became the custom in imperial times to establish small colonies called *cleruchies,* in the conquered lands, which played a similar part to the Roman republican colonies to be discussed later. These cleruchies were outposts of the Athenian empire, and their inhabitants retained their Athenian citizenship and, of course, were always ready to support Athenian policy. Pericles sent over six thousand colonists or cleruchs to members of the Delian Confederation which had seceded and required to be disciplined. While some of these cleruchs were traders and merchants, the cleruchies were definite allotments of land, and they were sufficient for the small Athenian farms. As well as helping to solve unemployment in Athens and Attica, they provided a means of military control. The cleruchs were usually well able to take care of themselves and at a pinch could always call on the Athenians for support. All through the Peloponnesian War the policy was continued, and was revived occasionally afterward. It was one of the few uses to which the otherwise usually barren military victories were put.

The agriculture of Attica was, however, not necessarily primitive. Though we do not possess much information on agriculture in classical times, the high production of wine and olives, especially the latter, could not have been obtained without very considerable knowledge and intelligent management of the soil. We know that when the Greeks went into Egypt after the conquests of Alexander they were able to introduce there far more scientific soil management than had been known before. As early as the time of Homer we know that vine management was understood, as a famous descriptive passage in the Odyssey makes clear. It was the grain farming that was inefficient and unprofitable rather than the specialized crops. But on the small farms which were expected to provide a living the cultivation had to be highly intensive, or even this meager living would not have been possible.

COMMERCE AND TRADE

There is no doubt that the Athenian empire was highly profitable to the individual Athenians, and to the state. Empire was not indulged in for the sake of prestige. In spite of their enjoyment of glory, it is improbable that any Greek cities would have thought it worth while to quarrel over which should first set up its flag on a stretch of barren desert or a swamp, or to prove to themselves or their enemies that they were better men than their opponents; least of all would they have indulged in imperialism because they thought that barbarians were entitled to the privilege of being made Greeks, even against their will, or should be made to worship Greek gods. We must remember that the Greeks, though passionate, were rationalists, and modern excuses for imperialism would not have moved them. Greek imperialism was as rational as other Greek activities. They were willing to fight to preserve their independence—meaning, ultimately, for their self-government and social order; and they also fought for material gains without bothering to apologize.

*This gold bow case was found in Scythia (South Russia). It was evidently an Athenian export item of special interest to the barbarian princes in this area on whom the Athenians were dependent for imports of grain.* (COURTESY THE METROPOLITAN MUSEUM OF ART)

All the Greek maritime cities needed their trade. The country as a whole was not self-supporting in foods; and Athens, after the reforms of Solon, had deliberately chosen not to be, as England chose after the repeal of the Corn Laws in 1846. Grain was mostly imported from the Black Sea area, where Persia could always be a danger. In addition Athens was dependent on outside sources for hides, for most metals, for timber for ships, and for hemp for ropes. With a constantly increasing population to be fed, grain imports had to be rigorously controlled, and both its price and its sale were regulated. Protective tariffs were unknown. There was only a regular 2 per cent customs and excise duty for revenue purposes. But to encourage the export of grain to Athens, regular quantity shippers of grain were not required to pay import duty on all their other exports to Athens. Cleruchs and metics were not permitted to ship grain anywhere except to Athens. Very heavy penalties fell upon all

who speculated in grain, and the officials who regulated imports were made to report ten times a year to the Assembly. These measures show something of the importance of the grain trade for Athens; they show also that the problem was simply to ensure the physical supply of grain rather than to make the trade profitable for the grain merchants. It is true that most of the evidence dates from the fourth century after Athens had lost her empire. But it suggests at least one of the chief reasons for the existence of the Athenian imperial navy and the empire itself.

In order to pay for grain and a large variety of minor imports Athens in the Periclean age had little enough to export. The physical import trade was far larger than the export, and the problem of return cargoes for the grain ships must have been important. Hence the need for some kind of coercion. During imperial days Athens kept a consular officer on the shores of the Hellespont to see that grain ships were headed in the right direction. While she was mistress of the seas, no doubt grain went safely to Athens, and was paid for not only by exports but from the imperial treasury of the Delos Confederation. There was no possibility of substantially increasing the exports, which consisted of olive oil and various olive products, pottery, marble, weapons and armor, artistic metalwork, and similar luxury products, in addition to some wine, though probably at this time more wine was imported than exported. The only other valuable visible export was silver from the Laurian mines. It is clear, therefore, that with such an enormous trade deficit Athens either had to compensate with an equally large invisible export or had to increase her production of industrial products and sell them. In the age of Pericles she did indeed possess this invisible export—her shipping services, and the protection she extended to the Aegean islands for which she was handsomely compensated by the expropriation of the treasury of the Confederation.

INDUSTRY

As far as we know, if Athens had decided to increase her industrial production by importing raw materials and manufacturing them, as England did in the second half of the nineteenth century, she might well have been able to find a market. But, as in so many other phases of Athenian life that we might wish to criticize, there was a very good social reason why she did not. Every man wanted to control his own business. Not only was it regarded as derogatory to the dignity of a citizen to accept private employment, but if he worked for someone else he was being cheated out of something that gave him great pleasure, namely, running his own business. For a people with such a passion for any form of creative activity to work for another was to work at a disadvantage. Even the building of a great temple, as we know, was carried out by thousands of small contractors, not by one large contractor working efficiently with a gang of workmen, nor by the direct activity of the state. If an Athenian had decided to enlarge his business to make it more efficient and to take better advantage of the division of labor he would have been forced to employ large numbers of slaves, which might have been possible; but he would also need citizen overseers, all of whom would have preferred to be in business for themselves. The largest industrial concern known to us from Greek sources is a shield factory owned by a metic, with 120 slaves; and the largest for the fourth century that we know of employed only 60. One considerable area of Athens was devoted to the manufacture of pottery, but again in small separate concerns. The marble quarries and the silver mines belonged to the state but were rented out in small concessions. In the fourth century the evidence shows a greater division of labor, a fact mentioned with approval by the great philosophers of the time; but the number of slaves in fourth-century Athens also increased, and examination of the records shows that in the factories both foremen and workers were usually slaves. Probably this fourth-century development was forced on the people by the loss of their empire; but there can seldom have been a city of comparable size which had so many citizens working for themselves. This is just one more aspect of the way in which the Greek polis was able to satisfy, by its peculiar social and economic system, the needs and desires of its citizens. But the result unquestionably was that the total product was remarkably small for such a large population; and in Periclean times there was even less than usual to export because the artisans worked for the city, and almost their whole industrial production was consumed at home. For even the most ardent individualist who would refuse to work for a fellow Greek employer was happy to work for the state. In the next chapter we shall see something of what these men accomplished.

BUSINESS ORGANIZATION AND PUBLIC FINANCE

Most of the improvement in business methods dates from the fourth century, when the need for better methods was greater. There was a considerable development in banking. Not only were more mines being exploited but the subsidies of the Persian kings kept a constant flow of money into the Greek world. In earlier times there were always money-changers who used to sit at a table near the harbor of Piraeus, changing the coins of different states. The value of these coins was largely determined by the intrinsic worth of the coin itself. The Athenian "owls," however, were acceptable almost anywhere in both the fifth and fourth centuries at their face value, for the Athenians were very careful never to debase their currency. It was boasted that foreign merchants were always content to take payment in cash at Athens, knowing they could use it elsewhere. Bankers replaced the money-changers to a large extent, especially during the fourth century, accumulating supplies of money and lending it out, usually at 12 per cent per annum paid by the month. Loans on voyages in which the ship had to face many dangers were at much higher rates. But this was also a kind of insurance, since the money did not have to be repaid if the ship were lost. Bankers also furnished letters of credit, and sometimes financed large transactions and contracts with ready money.

There was no regular tax system in most of the Greek cities. Taxation was on a hand-to-mouth basis. Temple treasures were frequently borrowed, but usually they were carefully repaid. Special assessments were made in times of emergencies, and the rich were expected to make "voluntary" contributions, which in time became compulsory. Athens in imperial days had many extra expenses for public works, but the wage paid by the state was very low, and was the same in nearly all cases for all kinds of work. In later times after the empire, when civic spirit was declining, a new expense had to be met, the pay for the mercenary soldiers who largely replaced the citizen armies. Direct doles to the poor and the unemployed also increased. Moreover, the old system whereby ships were voluntarily contributed by the wealthy was rapidly

disappearing, so that recourse to higher taxes was necessary. Sales taxes and a heavy income tax seldom filled the fourth-century Athenian treasury, and the state was constantly in arrears with tax collection, and not infrequently on the verge of bankruptcy. Nevertheless, as soon as efficient and honest administrators were appointed, the city quickly became solvent again, suggesting that some of the tax money went into private pockets.

## ▶ Athenian society

### DAILY LIFE IN ATHENS

The whole social life of Athens, and indeed that of all other Greek cities, reflects, above all, the extraordinary poverty of material resources, which was not only accepted philosophically by the Greeks but regarded as the natural, and even desirable, order of things. The ordinary man remained a frugal liver, both in imperial times and in the fourth century. Even what he considered luxuries would be to the imperial Roman very little indeed. Everything must be judged by Greek standards. When Pericles boasts that luxuries from the whole world stream into Athens we must set this against the background of the known national income, and the known social life as shown by the inscriptions, by the artistic remains as well as by the literature. All Greeks wore clothes of the utmost simplicity at all times, an undergarment fastened with a safety pin, and an outer garment draped about their person. The same garment served as a blanket. Beds were usually planks, without springs. The average house, unlike the temples, was made of sun-dried brick, and houses were built closely together. The walls were not decorated, the furniture was crude and utilitarian. When Pericles insisted that Athenian homes were beautiful and elegant, he may have been speaking the truth, because the artistic decorations that the Greek knew so well how to make may have been in use. If so, we know nothing of such decorations; but a list of the furniture in the house of the most fashionable young man of Athens in his day which we do possess is singularly unimpressive. The houses themselves were adequate for living in, but bear no comparison at all with those of pre-Greek Minoan Crete.

The reason for this utter lack of luxury in the private homes of the Athenians is simple enough. The Greek lived primarily in the open air. More hours of the day were spent in the gymnasium, the agora, or the streets than in his house. When it was dark he went to bed, and at dawn he usually rose and went into the street, without breakfast. We hear nothing from any source of any great mansions of the Roman type in classical times, nor of palatial private gardens and pleasure grounds. Rich men contributed their wealth to the polis, and did not use it so much for their own pleasure; but even their riches were small enough by Roman or Minoan standards. There were no gargantuan feasts; food was scarce and lacked variety. Meat was rarely eaten.

The truth seems to be, hard as it may be for us to believe, that the Greek really did not care for luxury, or not enough to give up his leisure to gain it; and it was frowned upon by public opinion. A contrast sometimes made between Athenian luxury and Spartan simplicity is extremely relative. Both lived simply; but the Spartan cultivated simplicity, wearing only one garment in winter and going barefoot, while the Athenian had sandals. The Athenian was able to decorate his city superbly because he cared for it rather than for his home; and to the service of his gods and his city he devoted all his unparalleled artistic talents. No doubt it was a temptation to distribute, as a dividend to all citizens, the hundred talents unexpectedly gained from a city-owned silver mine; but he was also willing to spend it, as he did on the advice of Themistocles, on a navy instead.

The kind of freedom that resulted from this doing without is one that is unique in history, and can never be repeated. But if one delights in free talk, assemblies, festivals, plays, the development of the mind and the body, self-government, and civic glory, the logical thing to do is to avoid cluttering one's self up with possessions useless to this kind of life. But the loss of the city life—not necessarily even the city itself, for this could be rebuilt—would be irreparable. The life of the expatriated Greek in Alexander's empire was such that he could gain luxury without difficulty; but from the evidence it appears that he was lonely, rootless, bored, inclined to suicide, to the worship of Tyche, goddess of chance, and to mystery religions, even though he tried his best to re-create the forms of the polis around him.

## CLASSES IN ATHENIAN SOCIETY

The classes in Athenian society were definitely marked out on the basis of property, not birth. The three main subdivisions, of course, were the citizens, the metics, and the slaves. From the time of Pericles, citizenship was limited to those Athenians both of whose parents were also citizens. This restriction was later to some extent relaxed, though the officials of the demes who examined credentials were naturally jealous of the privilege of citizenship, which meant much to the citizens and was a considerable expense to the state, for citizens, as a rule, were more lightly taxed than metics. The Assembly, as sovereign body of the state, could, of course, grant citizenship in certain cases, sometimes en masse, as to the inhabitants of Samos who remained faithful to the Athenian alliance under adversity.

About 6 per cent of the citizens were enrolled in the two highest classes of the state, the nobles and the knights. The majority of the population were small farmers (*zeugitae*), a solid middle class which served to balance the radical democrats of the *thetes,* or lowest class, who possessed little or no property, and were mostly artisans and other city dwellers. Some state offices, such as the archonship, always had a property qualification, and the thetes were excluded from them.

Ordinary temporary residents of the city had no rights in it and no privileges. After a certain period of residence an alien could be given the official status of metic, which entitled him to pay taxes, serve in the army, and perform the other duties of citizens. He was not permitted to own land, nor plead in the courts except through citizens. But metics were on a level of social equality with the Athenians, could take part in the festivals, and in certain circumstances could hope to obtain citizenship. Aristotle was never an Athenian citizen, but was able to study and teach there as long as he wished. His ultimate exile as a friend of the hated Alexander could have been imposed with no more difficulty on a citizen.

The position of women in Athenian society has given rise to some controversy among scholars. The literary and legal evidence is clear enough. They could not attend the Assembly or hold office; they could not hold property; they could not plead in the courts. In all public affairs a man—her husband or her nearest male relative—had to act on behalf of a woman. If she were an only child and her father died intestate, her nearest male relative could claim her in marriage, even being permitted to divorce his own wife for the purpose, or he became her guardian. The Athenian houses were divided into men's and women's quarters, marriages were arranged between parents without consulting the girl, women were not formally educated; and, finally, Aristotle claims that "by nature" men are superior and women inferior, and Pericles, in a famous passage, advised the women in his audience that their "best reputation is not to be spoken of for good or evil."

But much of the literary evidence can be construed differently. Pericles's advice may mean no more than that women should not provide food for gossip, an unexceptionable and common sentiment in all societies. When Xenophon shows us a middle-aged man giving advice to a young girl while she makes approving and respectful noises in return this may be only a piece of wish-fulfillment on the part of the middle-aged writer. The whole evidence taken literally seems to conflict with the happy pictures of family life shown in the tomb reliefs and on decorated vases; and other indications

*Early fourth-century marble relief, a gravestone in the form of a lekythos. Note the intimate but solemn family relationship, which suggests that the position of women in Athens was not exactly what it has been depicted by Greek writers.* (COURTESY THE METROPOLITAN MUSEUM OF ART)

from the literary sources suggest different conclusions. There are noble heroines in Euripides, and Sophocles' Antigone is one

*Farewell scene from another gravestone, with a significance similar to that of the scene on the lekythos shown previously.* (COURTESY THE METROPOLITAN MUSEUM OF ART)

of the great feminine characters of all literature, an ideal of a loving and tender-hearted girl who by her courage and integrity puts all the other characters in the play to shame. There is no suggestion of inferiority here. If women did not vote in the Assembly it was because their menfolk had to make important decisions on public policy which they themselves, and not the women, would have to carry out. Even so, Aristophanes in a famous comedy (*Lysistrata*) suggests that women would be less likely to push the state into unnecessary wars than stupid men.

Probably the explanation of the conflicting evidence is that the spheres of men and women were clearly demarcated in Athens. The woman took care of the home and family, while the man engaged in other work. But the women were not in any way secluded, and there is no reason to believe

that family life was not as normal as elsewhere. There is, however, certain evidence that romantic love was not a Greek ideal, at least as between man and woman. Passionate love between men and women is treated by the serious writers as if it were a dread disease, as in the *Hippolytus* and *Medea* of Euripides. On the other hand, there is much evidence that love between members of the same sex was treated as an ordinary and natural thing, and no Greek writer condemns it as likely to lead to the same tragic disturbances as passionate love between man and woman.

EDUCATION

The standard education of the Athenian boy consisted in reading, writing, and practical numbers. This included the learning of much of the best Greek poetry by heart. Musical training was given, especially in the lyre, to those who could afford it. This was accompanied by games, contests, and physical exercises, directed, not as in Sparta, to military ends, but toward the development of a healthy body and physical beauty. Up to the age of fourteen the boy was under the direction of a *paidagogos*, a private tutor, usually a slave, who also tried to instill moral principles into his charges. From fourteen to eighteen the boy's education was primarily physical and conducted in the public gymnasia where athletes were also trained for the games. Here he had his first real opportunity for contact with older men; in the gymnasia he engaged in the public discussions so dear to the Athenians.[11] At eighteen the youth became a citizen by taking an oath to obey the laws and the constitution and not "to disgrace my sacred weapons." From ages eighteen to twenty the first three classes of citizens engaged in compulsory military training from which, as in early Rome, the poorest class was exempt.

[11] In the time of Pericles the Sophists also taught for money, much to the disgust of the more conservative Athenians. The subjects they taught were more "practical." But, of course, the Sophists were not sponsored by the polis. Socrates, incidentally, though accused of being a Sophist, was not a professional, and always refused to take pay.

This kind of education, it may be noted, was not suitable for women, who received such education as they had privately. Since they were permitted to go to the theaters and take part in festivals, and as the theater, at least, required a considerable understanding, it may be supposed that feminine accomplishment was, in such matters as reading and writing, not far behind that of their sons and husbands. In the matter of education, as in everything else, the polis was realistic. It sponsored what it deemed to be useful, and, for the rest, it left the citizen entirely free. It provided athletic instructors and gymnasia, but private persons contributed the paidagogoi. But the men who talked and discussed in the gymnasia did so from the love of it, and the youths took part if they wished. It was probably entirely possible—but very boring—to be as badly educated in Athens as it is now. What on earth would one do when all that one could see at the theater was a performance of the *Frogs?*

▶ ## Suggestions for further reading

There is no substitute for the reading of as many Greek works as possible in translation, and secondary sources should always take second place to the Greek writers themselves. Some useful works of interpretation will be suggested in this and the following chapters, but attention will also be drawn to those translations which seem best fitted for the student. In reading Homer, one should remember that the *Iliad* and the *Odyssey* are magnificent heroic poems; and the present writer is unsympathetic to the modern tendency, to be observed, for instance, in the Penguin and Mentor editions destined for a large public, to treat them as if they were merely tales, almost the equivalent of modern novels. On the other hand, self-consciously archaic language goes to the other extreme and is often irritating to the modern student. In the author's view the most satisfactory translation of the *Iliad* is R. Lattimore, *The Iliad* (Chicago: The University of Chicago Press, 1951). For the *Odyssey* the student may select any that suits his fancy. The present writer will make no recommendation.

In general, the translations published in the Loeb Classical Library (Cambridge, Mass.: Harvard University Press) are the most accurate and reliable, though they are sometimes pedestrian. All the Greek works mentioned in the text are available in this series, though of course other editions exist. New translations of Herodotus and Thucydides have recently appeared in the Penguin Classics series which are both modern in diction and, as far as I have checked, accurate. These are almost certain to supersede the older nineteenth-century translations, which were difficult to read: Herodotus, *The Persian Wars*, tr. Aubrey de Selincourt, and Thucydides, *The Peloponnesian War*, tr. Rex Warner (Harmondsworth, Middlesex: Penguin Books, 1954). These works, being written in prose, do not suffer so much as the *Iliad* and *Odyssey* from colloquialism, which is in any case not so marked. For this chapter the treatise of the aristocrat known as the Old Oligarch should be read. It is to be found in G. W. Botsford and E. G. Sihler, *Hellenic Civilization* (New York: Columbia University Press, 1915), pp. 222–239, although the nineteenth-century translation, even when revised by Sihler, leaves a good deal to be desired in certain places and is distinguished by excessive and unnecessary circumlocution. Some of the biographies of Plutarch should also be read, especially those of Themistocles, Pericles, Cimon, Alcibiades, Aristides, and Nicias. Aristotle, *Constitution of Athens* (tr. K. von Fritz and E. Kapp; New York: Hafner Publishing Co., 1950), is a succinct account by the great philosopher of the political history of Athens, and should not be missed.

Two classics among the secondary sources are G. L. Dickinson, *The Greek View of Life* (22nd ed.; London: Methuen & Co., Ltd., 1949), and A. Zimmern, *The Greek Commonwealth* (5th ed., rev.; Oxford: The Clarendon Press, 1931), though both are perhaps excessively favorable to the Athenians. Zimmern contains a great deal of important economic and financial material not easily found elsewhere, though a more strictly economic work of considerable merit is J. Toutain, *The Economic Life of the Ancient World* (New York: Alfred A. Knopf, Inc., 1930). A very good short survey of Greek life, which includes a specially interesting section on women in Athens, is H. D. F. Kitto, *The Greeks* (Harmondsworth, Middlesex: Penguin Books, 1951). A suitable antidote for the general praise of the Athenians prevalent in most books may be gained by examining the section on freedom and tyranny in the ancient world, written by the present author in K. Setton and H. Winkler, eds., *Great Problems in European Civilization* (New York: Prentice-Hall, Inc., 1954), Chapter 1, in which differing opinions of both ancient and modern authors are placed side by side. The chapter on the Athenians in F. D. Marsh, *Modern Problems in the Ancient World* (Austin, Texas: The University of Texas Press, 1943), may also be profitably examined, as also the classic study of Greek imperialism, W. S. Ferguson, *Greek Imperialism* (Boston: Houghton Mifflin Co., 1913). Comprehensive studies of the Greek city are G. Glotz's two works, *The Greek City* (New York: Alfred A. Knopf, Inc., 1930) and *Ancient Greece at Work* (New York: Alfred A. Knopf, Inc., 1936). A brilliant study of Sparta as the classic case of an arrested civilization is to be found in A. Toynbee, *A Study of History* (London: Oxford University Press, 1935), III, 50–79. The primary sources upon which all studies of Sparta are based are Xenophon, *Constitution of the Lacedaemonians,* and Plutarch, *Lycurgus,* which may be read in any edition available.

# 8

# Hellenic Culture

*The originality of Greek thought • Wonder about the world • From religion to philosophy • Religion: early forms, maturity • Philosophy; the advance of rationalism; philosophy becomes science • Hellenic art of the Classical Age • Literature*

---

## ► The originality of Greek thought

CONTRAST WITH ORIENTAL THOUGHT

Many efforts have been made to trace Greek thought back to its origins and relate it to its Oriental forebears. The Greeks themselves had a great respect for Egyptian thought and science; certain elements in Greek mystery religion obviously derive from Oriental conceptions. Early Greek art shows traces of Egyptian, and certainly Minoan and Mycenaean, influence; gods and goddesses, myths and legends, are also often of foreign, especially Minoan, origin. But when all is said and done there is something definitely and clearly new in Greek thought, something which is not present even in the profound and important Hindu philosophy (most of which does not in any case certainly antedate Greek thought). The new element is wonder and curiosity about this world and everything in it, particularly man.

The Hebrews, the Hindus, and the Chinese were all interested in discovering what man's position was in this world, and his proper behavior toward the gods. The Hindus saw clearly man's possibility of self-development; but they lacked admiration for man. They examined his psychology, but their emphasis of his immortal part above his mortal led mature Hindu thought to conceive of earthly existence as *maya,* and the body as a prison house. Self-development therefore to the Hindu was a process of freeing one's self from earthly desires, and becoming as far as possible a spiritual being while still on earth (the *Atman*). The Greeks, on the other hand, respectfully and admiringly inquired into the nature of man on earth, admiring both his body and his mind. The union of body and mind (or soul) was perfection. Hence a culture of *this* world was created, and the next world was pictured as a shadowy existence, hardly imaginable, without solidity, and no substitute at all for the joys and sufferings and growth of this.

THE ATTEMPT TO FIND ORDER AND PATTERN IN EARTHLY PHENOMENA

Since man was anchored securely in this world, everything about this world was of interest and importance to him. The great questions *why* and *what* were always on his lips. No one thing should be examined alone, for this was specialization and meant neglect of all the other good things to which his attention might turn. "We have a happy versatility," said Pericles. All the great Greek philosophers were men of action, or willing to be; all took the whole realm of knowledge for their field of inquiry, or tried to find huge universal explanations which covered all phenomena, and explained the whole, not only the small visible parts. They were fortunate in that a great deal of empirical material existed as the heritage of previous civilizations, and into this they attempted to put order. Later philosophers such as Aristotle tried to put order also into the speculations of their earlier Greek predecessors. But the great characteristic of all Greek thinkers is an attempt, consistently pursued, to find order and pattern, to discover the real harmony in things by the use of their minds, to replace the recalcitrant phenomena of sense perception by the precise and orderly mental conceptions which form their counterpart. In this Plato and Aristotle are at one with the Ionian cosmologists, as well as with Aeschylus and Sophocles, who strove to fit the deeds of men into the framework of human destiny.

### THE GREEK LANGUAGE—ITS UNIQUENESS

The Greek genius is reflected in its remarkable language, which is in many ways unique among the languages of mankind, as an instrument for expressing all the different possible shades of meaning. It is the most fully inflected of languages, the inflections being used where we employ the less effective and less precise auxiliaries "to have" and "to be," accompanied by participles. In the Greek language, unlike the Latin, there are no missing forms—there are, for instance, present participles in the passive, and active participles in the past. There are three voices, the active, the passive, and the middle, the last reflecting the shade of meaning required when something is done on behalf of the subject, not unlike the French reflexive verb. There are three numbers, the singular, the plural, and the dual, for every

verb and for every noun, reflecting the shade of meaning which distinguishes acts done in company with many from those performed with only one companion. There are a host of particles used to create an internal balance within a sentence, and to point to the logical connection between one sentence and the one which follows it. Perhaps the most useful feature of the language for all later peoples who have borrowed words from it is the multitude of prepositions, which can be used also as prefixes for verbs and nouns, to reflect slight changes in meaning, as, for instance, between psychology (*psyche*—soul, and *logos*—discussion, both Greek words) and parapsychology (by the side of psychology), a word needed in the English language when the suggestion had to be voiced that certain new theories in psychology did not strictly belong to the original science. The vast bulk of our scientific terminology is Greek in origin, and daily we add new compounds, usually formed from the Greek.

### ▶ Wonder about the world

PRE-SOCRATIC COSMOLOGISTS—SEARCH FOR THE UNDERLYING SUBSTANCE—MONISM

It was in the Asiatic Greek cities that speculation about the natural world first arose. Though there were certainly thinkers before Thales of Miletus, he is the first of whom we have knowledge. He has therefore been called the father of philosophy, although, in view of the object of his speculations, we should prefer to call him the father of natural science. He is said to have traveled in Asia and Egypt; he was a practical man and a statesman.

Thales (born about 620 B.C.) is credited with several theorems, including the proof of the proposition that the angles at the base of an isosceles triangle are equal to one another, and that a circle is cut into two equal parts by its diameter. The particular theorems, however, are of secondary importance. But it is of the utmost significance that at last, and apparently for the first time, a universal mathematical proposition was formulated and proved. No longer would it be necessary to draw triangles and measure them, as the Egyptians appear to have done until the close of their civilization. The truths of geometry hold good for all triangles, whether drawn or merely existing in the human mind. It is impossible to believe that any triangle could ever be drawn that would prove an exception to the general rule. It was the Greeks who first perceived this fact, and geometry is undoubtedly the greatest scientific achievement of the Greek genius.

But Thales is of great importance also in the history of science for his speculations on the subject of change, speculations in which he was followed by a whole series of thinkers who came up with different answers to the question he posed. It was, of course, obvious to Thales that there was a great diversity in all perceivable phenomena. But, he asked, is there some fundamental substance which merely changes its form in the different phenomena but remains in essence the same? Thales assumed that there must be one such substance, and he suggested it was water, or moisture, perhaps on the basis of a correct observation that water does appear on earth in solid, liquid, and gaseous form. In postulating one substance, Thales, like the other Ionian thinkers, was a "monist" (Greek—*monos*, one).

It may be added that the kind of speculation initiated by the Ionian Greeks was totally different from any thought on the physical world that preceded them. All these Greek thinkers, though not necessarily rejecting the idea of God, rejected the gods as an explanation for earthly phenomena. Hesiod and earlier poets had explained the world solely in terms of the activities of gods, and in his account of the creation of the world there is no natural causation. But the "water" of Thales changes its form by evaporation or solidification, and the explanation is self-subsistent without need for the agency of gods.

Anaximander (born about 630 B.C.), also of Miletus, was not satisfied with the fundamental substance proposed by Thales, though he agreed that there must be such a substance. He suggested that it must be indeterminate, and not any recognizable earthly "stuff." This he called the "boundless thing," an indeterminate substance, "ungendered and imperishable." All phenomena periodically returned to the condition of indeterminacy, and then evolved into new forms. Anaximander, in pursuance of this thought of evolution, produced an imaginative picture of how one animal evolved from another which has remarkable similarities with the modern Darwinian theory, although of course the Milesian had little evidence on which to base his theory.

Anaximenes (born about 590 B.C.), the last of the three great early Ionian thinkers, was dissatisfied with the "boundless thing" of Anaximander, since to him it was a mere verbal explanation without real meaning. He preferred to return to a more real substance which, as he could see, did change on earth. He chose air for this substance, which at its rarest became fire, and at its densest became earth. A stone was the most condensed form of air, and even the stars are "pushed by condensed resisting air."

Rather later than these early pioneers came Heraclitus of Ephesus (born about 530 B.C.), many of whose dark and cryptic sayings have survived and have exercised the ingenuity of numerous interpreters since his day. It is difficult indeed to reconcile all his statements into a coherent and consistent whole. In his search for a fundamental substance underlying all changing appearances he hit upon "ever-living fire, which is kindled, dies and then is kindled again." But, though he stated this unequivocally, he concentrated more than his predecessors on the changes in form rather than on the attempt to find the substance which changes, drawing attention to the fact that "everything is flowing," and that "you cannot step twice in the same river." This led him to the understanding that beneath all change and disorder is the great underlying order of the Divine Intelligence or Logos, which he also did not hesitate to call God, seeming to see it as the power which harmonizes all opposites in the universe. There is a hidden harmony between opposites: "From what draws apart results the most beautiful harmony."

From such fragments as we possess it would seem that Heraclitus was filled with admiration for the world as an orderly process, with opposites being harmonized, the unlike acting as the complement of the like, not dissimilar to the thesis, antithesis, and synthesis of Hegel, who was certainly influenced by him. But it was not yet possible to express such an idea in an abstract manner, so that he was forced to fall back upon fire as an inadequate but suggestive image for what he was trying to convey.

Though he is sometimes called a dualist because he spoke of the principles of the world as being the unit and the infinite, another virtual monist was Pythagoras (born about 590 B.C.), of whom we know very little, though we know more of the work done by his school in Italy. To these thinkers number was the essence of all things, and they thought and experimented with numbers to the exclusion of ordinary physical inquiry. They discovered the mathematical laws of musical harmony, the relationship between the length of the string of a lyre and the sound produced by it, that a string of half the length will produce the same note an octave higher. Certain combinations and numbers were harmonious, they found, while others were not. Harmony itself was therefore mathematical. There is no reason to suppose that they arrived at the practical conclusion that everything in the world was capable of being numbered; it seems rather that they devoted their attention exclusively to discovering the mathematical relations between the phenomena of the world (a similar approach to that of the seventeenth-century astronomer and mathematician Kepler) and regarded the ordering activity of God as expressing itself in the numerical harmony of all things created. Pythagoras, of course, is also universally credited with the famous theorem that bears his name.

The last of the early monists was Parmenides of Elea in southern Italy (born about 515 B.C.), who did not attempt to define any fundamental substance but contented himself with calling it "the One." The basis of Parmenides' thought was that it is manifestly inconceivable that there should be such a thing as nothing. There can be no coming into existence or passing away, since the one must have arisen in nothing, and the other must end in nothing. Matter is uniform and indestructible, or it would have to be mixed with nothing. Change does not really exist and must be an illusion —for since there is no creation and there will be no end, everything is as it has always been, whatever the appearances may suggest. This theory had important consequences. Sense perception, which gives untrue information, must be untrustworthy, and only thought, which can perceive the truth, is real. Hence reason is superior to sense perception as a means of knowing, and what is known in the mind can alone be considered true, a fundamental assumption in Greek mathematics, and the basis of Euclidean geometry. When Plato considered the archetypal heavenly ideas, to be perceived by the human *Nous* or Mind, as the source of all earthly knowledge, the inferior copy of which can alone be perceived by the senses on earth, he was showing himself a disciple of Parmenides.

Moreover, the logical criticism of Parmenides put an end to the attempt to discover a single underlying material substance which changed its form. Since Parmenides' argument that there was no such thing as nothing was accepted, everything must then be made up of combinations of already existing things, which neither came from nothing nor dissolved into nothing, but merely changed their forms by making different combinations. Now, therefore, we have the pluralists, believers in many substances, of whom the earliest was Empedocles (born about 510 B.C.)

PLURALISM—THE SEARCH FOR MANY
SUBSTANCES IN CHANGING COMBINATIONS

Empedocles posited the existence of four basic elements, earth, air, fire, and water, and two types of motion, Love and Strife. Love unites these elements together into compounds, while Strife forces them apart. Empedocles' pluralism was criticized by the Ionian Anaxagoras (born about 500 B.C.), on the grounds that he had not properly explained how any objects of sense could come into being from these elements, nor how they combined. "How can hair come from what is not hair, and flesh from what is not flesh?" Anaxagoras accepted the suggestion that there was such a process of combination, but it was of an enormous number of separate seeds, each homogeneous, flesh being made up predominantly of flesh "seeds," in combination with other invisible seeds of different substances. These seeds were combined by the activity of Mind, which was responsible for all motion.

This speculation left the way open for the atomists. Leucippus, a contemporary of Anaxagoras, may have been the first to suggest the theory; but as we possess no certainly authentic fragment of his, the theory is usually credited to Democritus (born about 460 B.C.), a considerable number of fragments of his work being extant. Democritus, still trying to solve the problem of how there was so much diversity in the world of phenomena, while reason seemed to suggest that there could be no real change, no coming into being and passing away, came to the conclusion that there was nothing in the world except atoms and the void (filled space and empty space). The atoms differed not in quality but in shape and size and they combined into different observable phenomena on a simple quantitative basis. They could move, because there was space to move in, and they could be separated from each other by space, thus altering their visible appearance in combination. Democritus did not apparently try to account for motion, but his imagination suggested many different kinds of combinations of atoms and space to account for the various qualities of all phenomena. The theories of Democritus were elaborated by Epicurus (born about 342 B.C.), who used them as a basis for a moral philosophy, and by the Roman Lucretius, whose ideas will be dealt with in a later chapter. The atomic view of nature was not accepted, however, by Plato or Aristotle, and, as a materialistic philosophy especially as developed by Epicurus and Lucretius, was hardly likely to be acceptable in its own or later ages for a long time to come. As a physical theory, however, even though it was only a guess and could not be supported by experimental inquiry as in our own times when atomism has been revived, it was a respectable answer to the questions raised by Thales, and no better one was provided by any of the Greeks. Interest in the problem itself became dormant as philosophers and thinkers turned to other problems.

## ▶ From religion to philosophy

RELIGION—EARLY FORMS

### Pervasiveness of religion in all Greek life

In studying Egypt we found it impossible to separate religion from government; and there was almost nothing that could be studied in Egypt without an understanding of the religious framework. The Greeks are usually thought of as a secular people—indeed as the founders of secularism because of their exclusive interest in this life, and their special interest in man. If this interest be conceded, we still should not confuse Greek secularism in this limited sense with modern secularism. All religion is not concerned with the next world, and all religion does not require a canonical book, churches, and priests. The sole necessity for religion is the belief in gods or divine powers which are concerned with man and the universe. And this religion was not only present among the Greeks but suffused all their activities until late in Hellenic times.

Disregard for, and disbelief in, the gods was uncommon before the fourth century B.C. even among intellectuals; and a truly secular attitude to life can be detected only from the middle of the fifth century B.C. at the earliest, concurrent with the rise of individualism and the decline of the polis. At this time art became to some degree emancipated from religion, and the tragic drama, not only religious in origin but providing the deepest of religious experiences for all those privileged to be present, came to an abrupt end. The Sophists questioned the very basis of all received beliefs, and Socrates and his followers Plato and Aristotle tried to build a new ethic upon the ruins. The communal life of the polis, based upon beliefs and rituals held and performed in common, slowly gave place to self-seeking and the pursuit of personal wealth and happiness.

The decay of religion should not be thought of as the *reason* for the decay of civic life and other manifestations of the secularist revolution, but as its necessary accompaniment. It will be misleading, however, to study the religion in total isolation, as if it were kept for Sunday and were not a central element in Hellenic culture. We shall therefore in this chapter study first the early and fifth-century Greek religion, paying special attention to its most mature expression in the tragic drama, and then deal with the Sophists and thinkers of the later period under the general title of philosophy. Then we shall return to Greek art and such of Greek literature as has not hitherto been considered, and when necessary relate these also to the dominant religious conceptions. It is hoped that this unorthodox procedure will be justified by a greater understanding of the total Greek spirit than is provided by a study of each realm of achievement in isolation.

Our understanding of Greek religion and appreciation for it has been seriously dulled by the way in which most people have learned of it; and this applies to the Romans as well as to ourselves. When the Greek religion ceased to be a living force, the scholars and storytellers began to find it naïve and amusing, and to tell not very edifying stories of the Greek gods on Olympus. Though there was still a substratum of the original myth left, the story was heightened by the art of the teller. We heard of the amours of Ares and Aphrodite, and of the many wives, children, and grandchildren of Zeus, the rape of Persephone, and the story of the pomegranate seeds—there are thousands of them, and most of them appear in the *Metamorphoses* of the Roman poet Ovid. But those stories that become "cute" in Ovid are not cute in Homer or even in Euripides. We have tended to present the story of Greek religion according to the tales of Ovid or the scholarly investigations of the Alexandrians, but not often enough as the Greeks themselves looked upon their gods. It is certain that they never snickered at them. We have said that the common people needed a popular religion, and no doubt they and not the intellectuals believed in the gods of Olympus; but it is too often forgotten that the same common people were able to appreciate the tremendous tragic drama of Aeschylus and Sophocles, and awarded a first prize to that comedy of Aristophanes (*The Frogs*), the heart of which was a technical discussion of the poetry, meter, and thought of Aeschylus and Euripides. Aristophanes continued to win prizes to the end of his days. Can it be imagined that the little people who built the Parthenon and carved the friezes snickered at the stories of the gods and heroes, the subjects of their work?

### The nature of Greek polytheism— The gods as powers of nature

As with other polytheistic peoples, the gods were powers. Some of the older myths about the ancient gods and Titans were concerned with the creation of order out of chaos, and the supersession of this order by another, which was more moral than the first. Of such a kind is the story of the ancient sky-god Ouranos, who was defeated by his son Chronos, when Time first came into existence, and then his later defeat by his son Zeus. The vast bulk of the Greek gods were associated with special places; and with the conquests of one people by another it is possible that the old god and the new united, and a myth told of the fusion of peoples as of their gods. Few gods were ousted altogether, for Greek religion was very hospitable to gods; but at all times they were kept in order by Zeus, and belonged to his family—tribal gods, river and place gods, and even abstractions like Themis (Justice), and Dike (Law). All gods were regarded as more powerful than men, like them insofar as they had mortal passions, and unlike them insofar as they were immortal.

We can only write vaguely about the *beliefs* of the Greeks in their gods because such beliefs, as is evident from the dialogues of Plato, vary markedly from man to man. But their ritual and manner of worship did not vary to the same degree, and from them we can realize the general respect in which the gods were held, whatever the individual belief. The god is both a power who can bestow help and a being worthy of man's worship. The Greeks do not seem to have propitiated their gods or even asked favors of them; on the contrary, they honored them, and waited for the blessing of the gods in return, without presuming to make suggestions to them. Temples were built not for worship but as homes for the gods. At a festival the citizens made a solemn procession to the temple, and expressed gratitude for all the god had done for them. They did not kneel, but stood upright, with hands outstretched. The Greeks never abased themselves, before either god or man.

### The belief in destiny (*Moira*)

To thinking peoples, however, the gods, even in the time of Homer, were never all-powerful. There is a greater power behind the world, the force of Destiny (*Moira*). To this even the gods are subject. Human life follows an inevitable destiny; man cannot understand it, and neither the gods nor man can change it. This is the true order in the universe. It is not arbitrary, as with the Mesopotamians; it is merely incomprehensible by man. Oedipus had no say in his fatal destiny. It was decreed before he was born; it was foretold, and those who knew of it tried to avoid it—but the destiny was fulfilled. Yet to mature Greek thought Oedipus was in no sense the plaything of the gods. He had to live as a man within the framework of this destiny, and his nobility lay in the human qualities he showed in facing it. In time Moira became incorporated among the powers of Zeus who "orders fate," but this did not alter the conception of fate itself.

### Apollo and Dionysus—Mind and emotion

Beneath Zeus were the great powers of Apollo and Dionysus. Apollo was the serene god of light, supreme patron of the arts, of beauty, and of music; his ideal was moderation, self-control through the mind, *sophrosyne*, everything the Greek wished to be. Upon the shrine of Apollo at Delphi were inscribed the words "Nothing too much." Through his knowledge of destiny and of the hearts of men Apollo knew what was to come. At Delphi he could be consulted through a priestess whom he inspired. Any devotee could inquire the future from him and ask his advice. But he could not be petitioned or asked to change the future.

There was an old legend that for three months in the year Dionysus should rule at Delphi, and not Apollo. This was a profound psychological perception of the Greeks, for they knew as well as anyone else that man is not always ruled by reason and moderation, but often by passion. And Dionysus was the god of passion and inspiration. The worship of Dionysus is closely connected with the Orphic mysteries, a form of religion which does not seem, to the traditional way of thinking, characteristically Greek, and was certainly known under various guises in the Orient. Throughout Greece and the Near East were mystery centers where individual human beings were initiated through ceremonies, rituals, and trials, into the knowledge of death, resurrection, and immortality which was otherwise unknown to them. Unfortunately our own information on these mysteries must be inferred from the representations in Greek art, and the type-myths which were enacted during the celebration of the mysteries. Plutarch spoke of the initiation of his own day, centuries later, as an unforgettable experience, after which no initiate could ever be the same again. Innocent happiness dwelt in the darkness, we are told, and no one should receive knowledge which he is not strong enough to bear; hence the preparations and trials before initiation, and the well-kept secrets of the knowledge imparted there.

Dionysus, we know, had a miraculous rebirth after being torn to pieces (reminding us of the Egyptian Osiris myth); Demeter (celebrated at Eleusis) mourns the loss of her daughter Persephone to Hades, king of the underworld; Orpheus goes to the underworld to rescue Eurydice who had died on her wedding night, and by his sweet song so charms the lords of the underworld that he is permitted to rescue her on condition he does not look back. He fails to fulfill the condition, Eurydice returns, and Orpheus is torn in pieces by the Bacchantes. All these myths suggest the trials of initiation and the knowledge of immortality. Pindar, the Theban poet, was deeply influenced by these mysteries, as was Plato, and, traditionally, Aeschylus the tragic poet, who was accused of betraying them in his plays and was forced to take sanctuary and clear himself before the Areopagus by swearing he had never been initiated. We cannot at this date reconstruct the mysteries. From its representation in Athenian art we know of the procession of the initiates along the sacred way to Eleusis, and we know from Pindar of the certainty of immortality given there. It was the only really personal religion of ancient Greece, and to those who could take part it must have offered something that even the most beautiful of civic festivals could not match. But it was at the great annual festival in honor of the god Dionysus that the last great religious creation of the Greeks came to full expression, in which all the people participated to gain that catharsis of the emotions through pity and fear of which Aristotle spoke—the tragic drama of Aeschylus and Sophocles.

GREEK RELIGION AT ITS MATURITY— THE TRAGIC DRAMA

### The beginnings of drama—Relationship of man to the gods—Aeschylus

There is an extraordinary certainty about the drama of Aeschylus and Sophocles that reveals a profound faith in the divine moral order of the universe, and the framework within which man must live, that suggests an accepted and unquestioned faith among the Athenians of their day; though there is nothing of the idea of immortality associated with the mysteries, as found in the poetry of Pindar. Aeschylus is concerned only with the great problem of man on earth and his relationship with the gods; not with man's ultimate fate. The Greek tragic drama had only recently emerged from its beginnings in the dithyramb or sacred hymn to Dionysus, and the sacred dance. But with Aeschylus it has now become a true drama, with few characters and long, beautiful choric odes. For sheer magnificence it has not been surpassed by any later drama. The human beings are drawn on a heroic scale, never individuals such as one would meet on the streets, but types of all humanity. And in what is perhaps his profoundest play, the *Prometheus Bound,* there is no human being at all. A Titan, or demigod, is the hero.

The play, the only one we possess of the original trilogy, is simple; it is only in its religious implications that it can be comprehended at all. Prometheus has stolen fire from heaven and given it to man; he glories in his deed, refusing to submit, even though Zeus threatens him with endless tortures. He has a secret which Zeus would know. But he refuses to divulge it, though Hermes comes from Zeus with threats, though Oceanos bids him submit for his own good because it is useless to fight with Zeus, and though Io, driven endlessly over the earth from jealousy of the gods, visits him on her journey. The play ends with the descent of Prometheus to the underworld, still defiant, and still glorying in his deed.

At one level of thought Prometheus is

the type of rebellious, proud, and independent *man,* who cannot be coerced by threats, though the gods threaten to destroy him. The will of man, sovereign on earth, cannot even be compelled to submission to the gods when they are unjust. But at another level of thought it is also clear that we have not yet exhausted the meaning of Aeschylus, and that the secret that Prometheus knows and Zeus does not is the heart of it. It is impossible to interpret this play in strictly rational terms. It is a long meditation on the theme of the creation of man and his purpose in the world; it has its Hebrew analogy in the story of the Tower of Babel which tells how man tried to ascend to Heaven, and God was jealous and destroyed the tower and confounded the tongues. The thought of Aeschylus seems to be that man, by the use of his freedom, is potentially equal to the gods and can even destroy them; and for this reason they withheld that gift which ensured freedom to man—they withheld fire. So Prometheus stole the fire and gave it to man. The gods cannot take away the gift from man, once he has received it; but they can still punish him for his presumptuousness, and man will remain in the power of the gods—Prometheus will not be freed— until one of the immortals sacrifices himself, giving up his immortality to free him. Though we do not possess the *Prometheus Unbound,* the myth is known, and the play must have contained something of it. Surely these teachings about immortality and the relationship between the gods and man are close to what must have been imparted in the mysteries; and if tradition is correct this was probably the play which brought the dramatist to trial before the Areopagus.

In the trilogy of the *Oresteia,* the theme is not so much the presumption of man which leads him to madness and destruction, though this is also implied when Agamemnon treads on the purple carpet, forgetting that his deeds of valor are granted him by the gods and are not his own. Returning from Troy, Agamemnon is murdered by his wife, Clytemnestra, her excuse being an earlier crime of Agamemnon in sacrificing their daughter

Iphigenia to ensure the success of the expedition to Troy. Orestes, their son, is instructed by Apollo to avenge his father by murdering Clytemnestra and her paramour. He obeys, but is pursued by the Furies, beings whose task it is to pursue those guilty of matricide. Orestes flees over the earth before the Furies, at last appealing to Apollo to save him. But Apollo is powerless. Orestes was indeed right to murder his mother; it was an ancient duty to avenge his father. But by the laws of the universe he incurred the penalty of pursuit by the Furies. The case, however, is tried before the Athenian Areopagus, the votes are equal, and Athena, the judge, gives the casting vote to Orestes. The Furies refuse to accept the verdict until they are pacified by the gift of a new home at Athens, and they are now to become the kindly ones (the Eumenides), and henceforth act as guardian deities of Athens.

Clearly Aeschylus tells here of the passing of an old order. The crime of Orestes has been forgiven, and the sequence of murders is at an end. But it is significant that the avenging deities have now become the guardians of law and order in the city of Athens. The sanctions on a man's actions are still divine; but they are no longer arbitrary. Punishment does not follow automatically; it is no longer a law of the universe, crime breeding punishment and the punishment itself entailing another crime. Order has been made out of chaos, and the gods withdraw a step, leaving punishment to the laws of the city, sanctified by Athena and the old gods.

But presumption against the gods still earns its punishment as a law of the universe. Man is not a god, and he must not think that he is. In the *Persians,* the history of the Persian War is made into a drama of man's presumption against the gods. Xerxes has been too fortunate, he is king of the world. He experiences *koros* or satiety, and he presumes upon it by attempting to conquer Greece without divine sanction. This is *hybris.* He is led into folly (*ate*) and the result is *nemesis,* or destruction. This theme of the sequence of *koros, hybris, ate, neme-*

*sis,* which runs through the bulk of Greek tragedy (it is even implicit in the *Prometheus*), through the poetry of Solon, and through the histories of Herodotus and Thucydides, is essentially the Greek conception of sin. In Herodotus the Persians commit *hybris,* while in Thucydides it is the Athenians. The good fortune of Athens leads her to the sin of *hybris* in barbarously destroying the neutral and unoffending Melians, thus denying the power of the gods to punish, and the common laws of humanity. This leads to the expedition against Syracuse with its grand folly of deposing the general who urged the expedition and appointing as general its chief opponent, and the inexcusable delays out of sheer superstition—this was *ate; nemesis* followed when the entire expedition was destroyed. The dramatic juxtaposition of these events in Thucydides shows the way his mind was working.

### Sophocles—The human drama—Search for the meaning of life and purpose of suffering

With Sophocles we are at the height of the human drama. The gods are always present, but no longer on the stage, while man moves within the framework of his destiny. In the *Ajax,* the hero is presumptuous, he thinks he has the better right to the arms of Achilles, which are awarded to his rival Odysseus; he plans to murder his enemies and rivals, but a god sends madness upon him, and he only butchers the animals belonging to the Achaean army. When Ajax recovers he is so ashamed that he dies by his own hand. He had not the right to boast of his own prowess, and *claim* the arms, and it was this presumption that led to his madness and destruction.

In the *Oedipus* trilogy Sophocles moves on to an even more profound problem, the problem of human suffering, and its relation to human destiny. And to this problem he was unable to give any solution until in his old age he completed the trilogy with the *Oedipus at Colonus.* In the *Antigone,* the first of the plays to be written—though the last in the sequence of events—Antigone re-

fuses to accept the right of the tyrant Creon to make a law which infringes "the immutable, unwritten laws of heaven." For this she has to die, and she meets her death nobly. Yet her death is not meaningless, for she has vindicated the sacred rights of humanity and earned a glorious name; while, on the other hand, Creon, in trying to change the divine law, has committed *hybris.* In folly he condemns Antigone and spurns the pleas of his son, and destruction comes upon him with the suicide of his wife and son and the abandonment of his throne.

In the *Oedipus Rex* the hero has been destined to murder his father and marry his mother; but he commits these crimes in ignorance, and in any case he could not have avoided them since they were decreed by his destiny. Nevertheless, after he discovers what he has done he blinds himself, and wanders through the land, led by his daughters. What, asks Sophocles, is the purpose of such a destiny? He gives us the answer in the *Oedipus at Colonus.* Oedipus has now grown old, and is ready to die, and an oracle has foretold that the land in which his bones rest will be blessed. He chooses to die near Athens, whose king, Theseus, gives him his own tomb. Theseus accompanies him into the tomb and leaves him. And suddenly Oedipus is no longer there, and a great wonder falls upon the messenger who relates that fact. The sufferings are no longer meaningless. The king has been purified by them, and his bones will bring good fortune upon Athens.

These plays have not been described for their dramatic quality, nor has any mention been made of the wealth of imagery in the poetry, nor of the extraordinary dramatic irony, especially in Sophocles, nor of the spectacular effects and the tragic atmosphere created in these masterpieces; rather has Greek tragedy been described here to bring out the religious nature of the whole. The audience knew all the stories, there were no surprises for them; plot was of little importance. The purpose of this drama was, as Aristotle stated it, to win a catharsis through pity and fear; to arouse appreciation of the moral grandeur of the universe, ruled by the unalterable moral laws of the gods. The audience was made up of the ordinary men and women of Athens, but they were present at a festival, the festival of Dionysus, god of inspiration. Time and again they awarded the prize to Sophocles; he gave them the kind of experience they expected of a drama. When Euripides began to exhibit his plays, the Athenians consistently refused to award him the crown. They did not want plays about ordinary people, however pathetic; they did not want to question the gods, doubt the myths, and be generally left with a feeling of mental discomfort. They wanted to appreciate the nobility of man in the face of his destiny. Tragedy is only possible when a good man meets misfortune undeservedly, or beyond his deserts. If a villain receives his just deserts or a good man finds happiness, what of it? And the contrary would be morally repellent, as Aristotle points out. But if a good man suffers, the gods are at work; the laws of the universe are being manifested, and there is a mystery. In short, man can rise above his suffering, and in so doing he shows himself worthy of his position as the crown of creation—a true man.

### Transition from religion to philosophy— Euripides, the questioner—Are the gods unjust?

Into this world enters Euripides and he has lost his faith. The gods do play their part in earthly affairs, they do punish man; but without reason. The gods have authority and power but, according to human standards, no justice—and yet this fact appears to be a law of the universe. Heroes do not really suffer nobly. They are human, like you and me, and they rage against the tyranny of the gods. They have to make the best of things, but do not call that justice. There is no such thing, says Euripides, as absolute justice, or god-directed justice. Man is the measure of all things.

But Euripides is a man of deep feeling. He realizes the pathos of a human being who is afflicted by destiny and arbitrary misfortune. He shows how some characters bear misfortune nobly, like Polyxena, Iphigenia, and Hippolytus, while others rage against it like Hecuba, queen of Troy, and Medea.[1] He is acquainted with all the human passions, and does not hesitate to show them on the stage. His plays are problem plays, appealing to the mind, not to religious feeling. Not a single play is really a tragedy in the sense that it purges the emotions, leaving the audience in a religious awe at the nobility of man in the face of his destiny. There may be awe at the gods, as in the *Bacchae;* but the question at the end is always, What kind of gods are these?

The real tragedy is that Euripides himself did not know. His is a work of the critical, rational mind, a destructive work which was necessary in the process of human evolution, and ushered in the age of individualism and reliance on the mind alone, without benefit of gods. His drama concerns the behavior of men in an unknown world, a world without morality, in which men are not rewarded for their good deeds nor necessarily punished for their evil ones. Heracles in the *Madness of Heracles* is a much-tried man who has been obeying the orders of the gods, but through no fault of his own has incurred the anger of Hera, who sends madness upon him so that he murders his own wife and children. Even Madness herself complains of her task but is forced to perform it. Similarly, Hippolytus is a virtuous young man who wants to devote himself to Artemis, but in so doing incurs the jealousy of Aphrodite; the Trojan women, in the play of the same name, are victims of a war which was none of their making and in which they had no say; Pentheus, in the *Bacchae*, does his duty as king and warns the women of his country not to indulge in the orgies of Dionysus, and after the god has induced a frenzy in him he is torn in pieces by the women; Medea is a violent murderess but escapes through her magic powers. So the list could go on.

[1] Polyxena and Hecuba appear in the play called the *Hecuba;* Iphigenia behaves nobly in the play called *Iphigenia in Aulis;* Medea and Hippolytus are in the plays named after them.

Euripides has a vast pity for man in these circumstances, but only very rarely does this become respect. Man, according to his experience, is not dignified by his sufferings; on the contrary, he usually becomes querulous, though sometimes he may have twinges of conscience for evil deeds he may have committed. Indeed, the first use of any Greek word for conscience is found in Euripides—interestingly enough, in a play where we can make a direct comparison with Aeschylus. In Euripides' *Orestes*, after the hero has murdered his mother, he wanders over the earth; but there are no Furies following him. He is just ill at ease. Menelaus asks him why he is troubled, and he replies: "It is my *synesis* [the Latin word *con-scientia* is an exact translation of this word], because I realize I have done terrible things." No longer are there Beings sent by the gods of the universe to pursue him; on the contrary he is inwardly troubled.

The tragedy of Euripides is that he is not an atheist, he cannot deny the gods; he has lost the old faith and has acquired no new one. Though a destructive critic, he cannot be a complete rationalist. He is still searching for a solution. And to crown the tragedy there seems to be only one immortality that he can recognize—the immortality of the individual man through his children. But children in the plays of Euripides are shown as defenseless, and time and again they are murdered uselessly. There is a vacuum in the thought of Euripides that cannot be filled. It was left for Socrates to fill it, to show that conscience could take the place of external sanctions, that if all the baggage of the old gods were discarded and man searched himself he could find the good and the just; that the intellect was the crown of man's faculties, and man could live and die by his own inner light.

So religion became philosophy.[2]

---

[2] For this interpretation of Euripides, which, incidentally, necessitated a rereading of all his plays, I am greatly indebted to the masterly monograph by A. Rivier, *Essai sur le tragique d'Euripide* (Lausanne: 1944), which seems to be far too little known.

## THE ADVANCE OF RATIONALISM

### The Sophists—"Man is the measure of all things"

About the middle of the fifth century B.C. wandering teachers called Sophists, began to visit Athens, already the center of Greek culture, and at the height of her prosperity. They were given a mixed welcome, for they struck at the roots of traditional thought; moreover, contrary to the accepted Athenian notion that talk was free and that the best education for the young was listening to the wisdom of their elders in the gymnasia, these newcomers taught for pay. They were, in short, professionals in an amateur world. It was often suggested that they should be expelled from the city. All manner of offenses were charged against them. They taught how to make the worse case appear the better, without any regard for what was just; indeed, they questioned the very idea of any justice. They were said to ridicule the gods, and to give purely physical explanations of the world. Anaxagoras had publicly stated that the Sun was not the god Helios but an ignited stone, the moon had hills and valleys, and all the planets were of the same substance as the earth. They were quick witted and could catch the unwary in verbal contradictions, and make fools of them in public. The old wise talk of the gymnasia, when boys sat listening to their elders, was being replaced by clever brilliant talk without substance. But the young intellectuals flocked to the Sophists to learn and gladly paid the fees; these young men were able to acquire the tricks which were of great use to them in the law courts, and they learned professional rhetoric—how to make convincing speeches in the Assembly and elsewhere. But in addition to this they also learned something of inestimable value—criticism; above all, criticism of the validity of all received knowledge and tradition, even when this went so far as the statement ascribed to Alcidamas: "The gods made all men free, nature has made no man a slave," and that there was no "natural" difference between a Greek and a barbarian.

We have most of our knowledge of the Sophists from their enemies, though Plato recognizes the value of their work, and distinguishes between the great teachers like Protagoras, and the fakes and show-offs. Aristophanes, the conservative writer of comedies, lampoons them mercilessly and with quite conscious unfairness—not only to gain a laugh, but because he cared for the old Athens and recognized the destructiveness of most of the Sophists' work. From extant fragments we can also judge the trend of other arguments. Antiphon wrote a pamphlet *On Truth,* in which he stated that all law is conventional; that it is wise to show respect for it before witnesses, but otherwise one should follow one's own advantage. Plato attributes to Thrasymachus the doctrine that justice is only the interest of the stronger, and to Callicles the idea that a man who is sufficiently powerful can break the law with impunity, and that laws are only made to protect the weakling. It was Protagoras who stated the principle of the new criticism in the most succinct manner; though, in antiquity and since, his famous sentence has usually been abbreviated to make it look more radical than it is. What he said was: "Man is the measuring rod for all things, of things which are, that they are, of things which are not, in what manner they are not."[3] This is not quite the same as simply, "Man is the measure of all things."

The contemporaries and successors of Protagoras, however, drew the full consequences from this teaching. Man cannot tell whether what he sees in the world is, in fact, there or not, or whether it really has the form it appears to have. The senses may deceive. Thus there is no absolute, but only relative, knowledge. We cannot, said Protagoras himself, know whether there are even any gods, as absolute truth is unattainable to man. Truth is what man thinks it is. We should

therefore follow what seems to be best for man. Socrates and Plato, in denying that knowledge is merely the possibly inaccurate data of sense perception, and trying to find an absolute and heavenly knowledge attainable by the human mind, as distinct from his senses, are thus engaged in an all-out struggle with the relativism of Protagoras and the Sophists.

There can be no doubt that the influence of the Sophists was primarily destructive. That it was not wholly so is at least partly due to the presence of Socrates; we have seen what influence Sophistic teachings had on a man like Euripides of great human feeling, but with no similar power of constructive thought. The Sophists were a typical product of their time. The imperial splendor of Athens had created a confidence in Athenian superiority that was rudely shattered in the Peloponnesian War. Imperialism itself obviously created ethical problems; an aggressive policy, though unquestionably *hybris,* according to the old manner of thinking, nevertheless did seem for a time to pay off. It is one of the purposes of Thucydides, himself a rationalist, and understanding very well the arguments of ethical relativism, to show that the gods do not forget, and laws cannot be flouted with impunity.[4]

At this time there was in Athens a growing tendency to seek for individual wealth. There was a loss of faith in the old communal ideals of the polis. There was a growing disrespect for age. Theories of communist utopias were rife. All these signs of the moral disintegration of the old polis were pilloried in the comedies of Aristophanes, upholder of the old order, who hated to see it passing and blamed the Sophists in large part for its deterioration. In his play the *Knights,* Cleon is the villain, a typical representative of the new style of Athenian politician, trained in demagogic rhetoric and without moral principle. In the *Clouds* Socrates and the Sophists come under direct

---

[3] There is doubt as to whether Protagoras himself used the Greek word meaning "that they are," or "in what manner they are," for different writers quote him differently.

[4] See especially the dialogue between the Melians and the Athenian envoys, Thucydides, v, 85 ff.

attack for undermining public morality and teaching sons how to get the better of their fathers. Yet it is hardly fair to blame the Sophists for all the ills of their time. Representative of the new order they may have been; but the soldiers of fortune, the mercenary armies, and the corrupt politicians of the fourth century can hardly be considered the offspring of the Sophists so much as of the loss of social control within the polis first observable in the stress of the Peloponnesian War.

### Socrates—Search for a new ethic through self-examination

The insight of the oracle of Apollo at Delphi into the intellectual current of the age can never be sufficiently admired. For it declared publicly that Socrates was the wisest man in Greece, and second to him was Euripides. That Socrates, the son of a midwife and a stonemason, who never wrote a line, who spent all his life talking in the streets of Athens to anyone who would listen, only leaving it twice to perform his military duty, should have been thus singled out is nothing short of a miracle of clairvoyance. Plato tells the story that, because of this encouragement from the oracle, Socrates started out on his quest for a man wiser than himself, a quest which led him to the conclusion that he alone was wise because he alone knew that he knew nothing. This profound paradox is the heart of Socratean thought. It is, of course, already implied in the dictum of Protagoras; and insofar as Socrates stresses the ignorance of those who profess to know, and the unproved nature of all traditional thinking, he is one with the Sophists. But he goes further than they; and this marks his constructiveness as a thinker. We must not indeed take received opinion on trust; but man *can* know through self-examination.

In order to discover this truth, which every man knows inwardly, it is necessary to bring knowledge to birth. For this purpose Socrates developed a method of question and answer, ever since associated with his name, by which it is gradually discovered first what is *not* true; and thereafter the truth is built up stage by stage, allowing no definition to stand until it has been examined, and no questionable statement to pass without criticism. When the process has finished, the questioner will then find that he really knows something, however little, that he was not aware of knowing before. Socrates thus calls himself the "midwife" of knowledge in that he has brought knowledge to birth through the labor of the dialectic (the technical term given to the Socratic method).

Clearly this method is above all applicable to the realm of ethics; and the greater part of the Platonic dialogues where Socrates seems to be himself and not the mere mouthpiece of his pupil is devoted to inquiry into the nature of the good, and how it can be pursued by man. Furthermore, can virtue (*arete*) or moral excellence be taught? If the code of right behavior is not to be dictated by tradition, received opinion, and the supposed will of the gods, then it must emanate from man. An individual ethic based on man's own best knowledge must replace the traditional one. It is Socrates' belief that if we rid ourselves of all prejudice and previous thinking on the subject, then by constant criticism followed by constructive thought we can obtain an idea of the good which will be the same for all; because the human being is so constituted that he *can* know the good. And, knowing it, he can follow it; for no one who truly knows the good would deliberately choose to follow the evil. This is a typically Greek notion, and is attractive to all rationalists. The greatest medieval rationalist, Thomas Aquinas, goes with Socrates as far as *knowledge* of the good is concerned; but, being a Christian, he also stresses the infirmity of the human *will*, which, being evil as the result of original sin, cannot carry out without divine grace what the intellect indicates as the good. And most medieval Christians would not even allow a true knowledge of the good without grace. It follows, therefore, that virtue is knowledge and ignorance is the root of moral evil; from which conclusion Socrates and his pupil Plato drew out the full consequences.

*Socrates. This statue suggests the reason why Alcibiades, in Plato's* Symposium, *compares Socrates with Marsyas the satyr, the Greek model of ugliness. Yet the artist has also contrived to show the deep seriousness of the master engaged in a problem which requires concentration of thought.* (COURTESY BRITISH MUSEUM)

In dealing with the Sophists, Socrates deliberately points out the inadequacy of their aim of teaching "useful knowledge." He asks pertinently, "Useful for what?" and has no difficulty in showing that the only truly human aim is the pursuit of the good, to which all else is subordinate. He denies their premise that knowledge is relative; but he admits that it must be tentative. No one knows, or can know, the final truth about anything (Plato excepts mathematics); and the frequency with which Plato shows him as dissatisfied with his preliminary destructive criticism, and the tentative conclusions that fill the vacuum he has created by it, suggest the real humility before knowledge which entitled him to the accolade of Apollo of Delphi, god of wisdom.

In spite of his apparently individualistic ethics, Socrates was a profoundly social being, and lover of his polis. He had a high opinion of the truth that lay behind the religious traditions of Greece, though he always interpreted them in his own way, as spiritual rather than physical truths. It was not his task to destroy the law and government of his polis, even though they were based on tradition; he fully accepted the right of the democracy to put him to death under its laws. These laws provided the whole framework for his social life; they were not unchangeable and their ethical content might no doubt be improved. But if it happened that he was the victim of the laws in their present state, then it still behooved him as a citizen to abide by them.

Within himself he only answered to the call of his own inner knowledge. He understood very fully that others might be moved by tradition and prejudice; but this was no excuse for him to follow their example. Very gravely and accurately he describes the activity of the human conscience which never tells him what to do but only what not to do. And he calls this his "daimonion," his little god—as indeed for him it was, since it took the place of the sanctions of the gods and the traditional piety associated with them.

His teachings may have been too heady for many who were not of the highest moral fiber. Alcibiades, traitor and loose liver, was one of his pupils; so was Critias, oligarchic leader of the Thirty Tyrants who instituted and carried out a bloody proscription of the democratic leaders—though it is not altogether reasonable to blame the master for the human frailties of his pupils. We can see in the Platonic dialogues how easily Socrates' method lends itself to misconstruction, and how quickly an enemy could take his gently objective criticism as personal disbelief. In the *Meno,* for instance, Socrates has been showing that no virtuous man has been able to teach virtue to his son. Anytus, one of his accusers at his trial, at once jumps to the conclusion that Socrates is maligning these men instead of using them to prove his philosophical point. In the political conditions of the restoration of the democracy after the oligarchic revolution, it was difficult to believe that any man could be searching for philosophical truth. Yet Socrates continued in the only activity that for him made life worth living.

In 399 B.C. his enemies brought him to trial before the people's jury on a charge of atheism and corrupting the youth. It was a clever charge, for it was, in appearance, true. Socrates took part in all the festivals and performed all his religious observances, but he did speak of his daimonion, a strange god, and he did teach—indeed the whole of his teaching led inevitably to the conclusion —that a new dispensation had come when man was to be free, to rule himself, not be ruled by the gods. And insofar as this was his instruction to his pupils, then he "corrupted the youth."

The account of his trial in Plato's *Apology* shows his moral courage and his confidence that his own path was right. He defends himself against the charges only by affirming them. Convicted by a small majority and asked for a suggestion as to what punishment he deserves, with the same serene confidence he tells them that he ought to have a pension and be supported at the city's expense for the rest of his life. This irony is too much for human endurance, and by a larger vote the jury condemns him to death. Instead of going into exile as his friends urge, an exile which would undoubtedly have been winked at, he accepts his sentence, not in stoical resignation but with dignity, tenderness for his friends, and good humor. While he awaits the fatal hemlock he discourses on immortality, still with the same calm reason that he had shown during his life. There is, he believes, an inner self in man, his divine part; this, being of the same nature as the divine, cannot die, and will dwell forever with the gods. But he will soon know. He shows no fear and no regrets. And so he drinks the hemlock; and by the manner of his dying he truly ensured his immortality on earth. For it was a turning point in the life of his pupil Plato, then a young man of about twenty-eight years of age.

### Plato—The "idea" and its application in life

Plato, unlike Socrates, was an aristocrat by birth, and had lived through the later years of the Peloponnesian War and the oligarchic revolution. He tells us himself that he had lost all personal political ambitions by the time of the death of Socrates. Disgusted equally with democracy and oligarchy, he went abroad to Egypt and Italy before returning about 387 B.C. to Athens and founding the famous Academy, in which he taught with occasional breaks for over forty years. All his known works have survived, and there is no other Greek mind which we have been permitted to explore so thoroughly. While his thought has evidently been influenced by Oriental and Orphic mysticism more than that of any surviving writer of the classical period, and for this reason there are some things in his works which seem to us un-Greek (for instance his condemnation of poetry and music and especially his contrast between soul and body), nevertheless the main line of his thought, with its emphasis on the supremacy of the mind, is characteristically Greek, and he follows the lines of investigation traced out by Socrates.[5]

Plato presents his thought in the form of dialogues, often very dramatic, with Socrates as protagonist discovering knowledge by means of question and answer. In other dialogues, however, the device only thinly conceals Plato's own thoughts; and one or another of the characters will then lecture on the subject, with the interposition only of a few expressions of assent or enjoyment. This art of the dialogue has been imitated frequently in the years since, but it is a very difficult one to master; at its best, as in the *Republic,* it is incomparably more effective and alive than straight exposition. But it is clear that we can never be quite certain what is Plato's own thought. Did Plato himself, for instance, really believe all that he puts into the mouth of Timaeus in the dialogue of that name? Since we shall never know, we must in our ignorance call the whole "the philosophy of Plato," though it is never classified or organized into a comprehensive system.

The heart of Plato's teaching stems from the original conception of Socrates that the human being can know the good; and that, knowing it, he can do it. What Plato seeks to discover is *how* he can know it, and *what* it is exactly that he knows. And by using the dialogue form he shows us the whole process by which he arrived at his conclusions; hence the endless stimulation that Plato has afforded to all subsequent mankind. All that we must do is hitch up to his thought at one place, and either follow him to the same conclusions, or, by casting aside some of his thoughts as based on assumptions which we

will not accept, proceed to arrive at different conclusions.

Assuming, then, that man can know the good, with what faculty does he know it, and what is the object of this faculty? To this Plato answers that man is possessed of the power of thinking (*Nous*), and that this spiritual element in man can recognize the spiritual element akin to it—the Idea. And this Idea is not in the physical world, but in the spiritual world, forever hidden from every faculty in man save the Nous. Following this thought further, he concludes that everything we see in front of us is a *particular,* a single example of something, the Idea or archetype of which is really spiritual, and not to be found on earth. We see, for instance, a single plant; but the Idea of the plant is in the spiritual worlds. From this it is but a short step to the value judgment that the earthly example is necessarily an inferior copy of the ideal plant. That the spiritual reality is more beautiful, more worthy of contemplation than anything on earth.

The next step is to consider how we can recognize this earthly copy as indeed a copy of an Idea. And to this Plato's answer is that the soul, with its active faculty, the Nous, existed before incarnation on earth in a human body. Before it descended to earth it glimpsed these Ideas, which were implanted forever in the soul. Thus knowledge of the universal behind the particular appearance on earth is simply *recognition.* This, it will be seen, completely accounts for man's possession of innate knowledge, which Socrates had shown man did possess.

Here then, in a different, more spiritualized form, and serving different ends, we find the Oriental (Mesopotamian) thought that the earth is a copy of the heavens; and therefore it is no surprise to find also in the cosmogony and physiology of the *Timaeus* the thought that man is a microcosm, an earthly human counterpart of the heavenly macrocosm. The crucial—and typically Greek —difference was that for Plato the heavens themselves were endowed with a body, a soul, and Reason.

[5] It has been argued, and will no doubt be argued as long as Plato is read, that there is very little of Socrates in Plato, and, conversely, that everything worth while in Plato stems from Socrates. We can never know the truth, for Socrates did not write himself; and our two main authorities, Plato and Xenophon, supplemented by a few remarks in Aristotle, are both highly selective, putting into the mouth of Socrates whatever arguments they please. It has always been necessary, therefore, for later readers to separate in their own minds what was genuine Socrates and what belonged to the writers themselves. Aristotle credits Socrates with the inductive method and with universal definition.

It is clear that this "idealist" philosophy gives an enormous scope to the philosopher. He is not compelled to examine the phenomena in front of him but may reason a priori; indeed, since it is only human thinking that can perceive the Ideas, there is no other method of reasoning than a priori. Thus by reasoning, the moral and political philosopher must try to discover for himself the ideal good, and not the practicable good. It is for this reason that Plato placed on the door of his Academy "Let no one without geometry enter here," for this is precisely the method of geometry. The mind at once perceives the universal Idea, which is true (the axiom), from which the consequences are deduced by the reason. And it is the same thought when Plato says: "God geometrizes without end."

The *Republic* is the Platonic masterpiece of this kind of reasoning. But by this it should not be thought that Plato had no practical ends in view. He tells us specifically that he has. No political state of which he has knowledge has been *thought* out; all are defective. But in his view these defects need not be inevitable. For if men know the good they will not deliberately prefer the evil unless they have been warped beyond cure. Since "virtue" may be taught, men can be educated to admire the best, and not choose a second-best polity to live in.

His method, then, is to discover what is the bond which holds society together (justice), and then try to arrive at a definition of justice. He comes to the conclusion that justice in the citizen and in the state is identical, and that if each man is given a position in the social order which enables him to do that for which he is best fitted, and he performs this task properly, then the ends of both the citizen and the state will be fully served, and the society will be a just one. Plato then proceeds to inquire into how human potentialities can best be realized in a social framework, and what will be the nature of the social institutions required.

Given his premises, the whole work, built up on these lines, is logically impeccable. Its value in all ages has been its suggestiveness, and the joy of following the thought of a truly creative mind, willing to pursue the argument wherever it will lead, without deference to conventional Greek notions, as, for instance, on the inequality of women. It is not native conservatism or a preference for oligarchy—though these may have been present, they are irrelevant—that forces him to the conclusion that the enlightened despotism of a board of professional guardians (philosopher kings and queens) is the only possible "best" government. These alone have been able to discover the good, and they must be dedicated utterly to its pursuit, without the warping of judgment which would arise from the possession of either material goods or family. With such a body of truly scientific professionals there would be no need for laws or for the exercise of power; for at all grades in the society each man would have received the education, and hold the position, for which he was best fitted.

It has often been pointed out, justly, that Plato makes a number of assumptions which are extremely questionable—for instance, that public and private virtue are identical, and that a state made up of good individuals will be able to function harmoniously as a state. But it will usually be found that these assumptions are the result of his fundamental belief that no one, knowing the good, would deliberately choose to do evil. If the state is a just one, its duties will be just and good; the individual, if he is good, will desire to do this duty. Duty and inclination must coincide. If they do not, then either the state needs to be corrected or the individual needs to be improved— by development and adjustment, not by repression and force.

Plato may also be accused of neglecting the psychology of man, as it *must* have been known to him from experience. What was the use of theorizing about an ideal state when he knew of its impossibility in real life? Again the answer must be that by showing men the ideal good which was, for him, having regard to his assumptions, not impossible of realization but only extremely difficult, he was pointing out a direction for the aspirations and endeavors of man. And that it was not his last thought on the subject is shown by his later works, the *Statesman* and *Laws,* in which he outlines the "second-best state," the state ruled by laws, laws which are directed to the ethical improvement of man, but cannot be as scientifically impeccable as the personal guidance of the philosopher kings. And elsewhere he shows that he is not unaware of human psychology. He recognizes the irrational part of man, but does not consider it incurable. The desires are controlled by reason, which, in the light of its knowledge of the good, will give man the power of evaluating his desires at their true worth.

As with the state, so with man. The harmonious functioning of all the parts that go to make up the full man, this is self-realization under the guiding power of the Nous. It is a psychology the truth of which would be vehemently denied by both Christians and Freudians, who both deny the power of the mind to control the will unaided. Perhaps to these the psychology of Plato would seem naïve; but it was the fullest and most complete expression of the Greek ideal of harmony and *sophrosyne,* and of the Greek belief in the efficacy of human thinking. If it is a glorification of the one specifically human power, this to the Greeks would have been a recommendation. Oedipus to the Greeks was not a complex but a human being, proud and erring but undefeated; and they were glad to be considered of his company.

PHILOSOPHY BECOMES SCIENCE—ARISTOTLE

### The universality of his genius

Aristotle was the son of a Chalcidian physician in the service of Philip of Macedon. He studied at the Academy of Plato and was unquestionably his most brilliant pupil. He was tutor of Alexander, son of Philip, for several years, returning to Athens and opening a school himself (the Lyceum), where he taught for twelve years. Forced into exile on the death of Alexander, he died a year later in 322 B.C. at the age of sixty-two.

Thus Aristotle stands at the end of the Classical Age of Greece before the great emigration to Asia that followed the conquests of Alexander; and in a very real sense he completed it. While he left one or two things undone which were repaired by Theophrastus his pupil and successor (for instance, a work on plants and another on human character) and he contributed nothing to Greek mathematics, which followed an independent course, in other respects he took all the varied speculations of his Greek predecessors, brilliant and disorganized as they were, and by the giant force of his capacity for system, order, and classification, discharged them from his hands as sciences, a body of work that could be communicated to others in comprehensible form. Once he had laid down the principles of scientific inquiry, the work would not have to be done again. He was the first true scientist in the history of mankind; and few who have really studied his work would dispute his title to be the greatest the world has yet known. And now that we have passed beyond recovery into a world of specialists, there never will be anyone again who will be able to lay claim to the universality of his learning. Any one of half a dozen of his mental achievements would have entitled him to an undying fame. The sum total is almost beyond belief.

### The laws of thinking—Logic

If this seem excessive praise, let us consider for a moment a few of Aristotle's achievements. Basing his observations upon Plato's theory of ideas, he formulated the laws of thinking, the relation between the universal and the particular, the formal procedure required for arriving at conclusions and correct reasoning, giving in passing a different solution to the problem of the origin of the universal; disturbed by the way in which objects are described without including all their features, he formulated a method for describing them inclusively (the "categories of being"); stimulated perhaps by Socrates' remark that he himself knew that his will prevented him from going into exile and not "his bones and sinews," as Anaxagoras would have claimed, he formulated a system for dealing accurately with causation and had to invent a new vocabulary for the purpose; faced with a mass of biological data, he evolved a system of classification into genus and species which has been followed with modifications ever since.

## The foundation for classification of phenomena—Genus and species

Aristotle is usually praised in these days rather patronizingly for his excellent and careful observation and description of the animal world, and his early recognition of facts which modern science with its greater knowledge and improved instruments has shown to be true—as if anyone with the time and the patience could not observe correctly! And he has been criticized for premature guesses on the basis of insufficient information, for his doctrines of purpose, for his denial of the atomic theory, and in general for having held back medieval scientists from more correct theories while they elaborated on his incorrect ones instead. But insufficient attention has been paid to the gigantic mental effort required to create order out of chaos, and to make the world *intelligible,* which was his primary purpose. No one before his time had seen the need for a method of inquiry, or classification of knowledge. Philosophers had speculated, and looked for universal principles, every now and then carrying out a few desultory experiments; but always jumping to theoretical conclusions of little value beyond their aesthetic appeal. But to watch Aristotle at work trying to determine how to deal with zoology with no previous guide, as in the first book of his *Parts of Animals,* is to see the enormous difficulties that faced him in the struggle to order the material; and to read any part of the *Metaphysics* is to realize his extraordinary ability to handle the most difficult abstractions of thought with the utmost delicacy and sureness—in which again

he had no predecessor. Plato charms us because of his artistry and imagination, and because there is no word that we cannot understand, no thought that we cannot follow. He flatters our ignorance, making us believe we are not as ignorant as we are; in reading Plato we all imagine ourselves philosophers. But Aristotle is hard work, and he makes no concessions to us; even when we think we have grasped one of his thoughts it quickly eludes us again. Then suddenly it becomes clear and fruitful and applicable in a hundred other ways, and we possess a tool for understanding the world.

In following the Aristotelian method as we have all followed it since his time without acknowledgments, our work has been made easy. But it was not easy for him. He had first to invent the tools of analysis, and then with these to set to work on all the phenomena of knowledge available to the Greek world. Both parts of his work he largely accomplished. His nephew went with Alexander on his expedition, and Alexander himself sent back data that he thought would be of interest to his old tutor. His students collected material for him, and he analyzed and classified it, no doubt with their assistance. For his *Politics* he analyzed and digested the constitutions of 158 different states, this analysis enabling him to classify the different kinds of states on the basis of evidence. He viewed the plays of his own age and the tragic drama of the great era, and in his *Poetics* classified the results, together with his findings in general terms of the requirements of tragedy. He did the same thing for the animal world in his three great works in zoology, the *History of Animals, Parts of Animals,* and *Generation of Animals;* and so on. Certainly in some cases he generalized and theorized too soon; but only very rarely did he fail to offer good reasons for the theories, and for his acute criticisms of his predecessors. And never did his analysis fail. His successors could have built always upon his foundations, and revised his theories when necessary.

It was a tragedy that Aristotle of all men should have been regarded as an authority and the last word on any subject, he who was the most ready of all the ancient investigators to base his theories on the observed facts. And it is now the prevalent opinion that when at last the late medieval scholars did begin to work on his findings at the University of Padua without accepting him as infallible, then they only had to revise his groundwork, and criticize some of his conclusions on the basis of their improved knowledge of the facts, and it was possible for Galileo, who studied at Padua, to lay the basis for modern science. Aristotle was not abandoned, save by the ignorant; but adapted, improved upon, and commented upon until at last he emerged as the great pioneer he was, but no longer "the master of those who know," which he was not.

If we examine the conclusions reached by Aristotle in all the numerous fields of inquiry to which he gave his attention, we shall find that they were almost always inspired by common sense, which has not been regarded as a useful tool in modern exact science with its powerful mathematics and instruments of research. Almost none of the findings of modern science, from the electron to the Copernican theory, from the physics of Einstein to the corpuscular-wave theory of light is validated by common sense or direct sense observation. For this reason Aristotle's conclusions in the physical sciences have to be interpreted very spaciously and charitably if they are to be in any way acceptable, while his conclusions in the social sciences may be as valid as in the days they were written.

### The physics of Aristotle—Excessive reliance on common sense

From the observed motion in the world Aristotle concluded that all motion was communicated from the moving agent to the thing moved. The movement of the sun and planets around the earth was accounted for by motion communicated from the "sphere" of one planet to the next. This had the important logical consequence that there must be an ultimate mover, the origin of all motion, itself unmoved.[6] This he was willing to call God. This God, however, was not personal; and medieval philosophers, followers of Aristotle, were not content with his treatment of creation. It appeared that the world had always existed, though not always in the same form.

### The metaphysics of Aristotle— The final cause

Having taken back all motion to its origin, Aristotle then had to account for motion within the world, or change. For this he used a human analogy—purpose. He reasoned that if man takes an action, the beginning of the action is the purpose or intention of the person. This he called the Final Cause, that "for the sake of which" a thing is done. Logically prior, then, to all change is the thing *into* which it changes, not the thing *from* which it changes. The new form was always present, but previously it was potential. Change, therefore, is the actualizing of a potential; and the cause of the change was the necessity for the new form to come into being. The reason, for instance, that an object falls to the ground is that this is its natural place; acceleration is due to the increasing operation of the final cause, i.e., its natural place (perhaps by analogy of the horse when it gallops the last mile to the stable).

Throughout the world of living things, purpose, the Final Cause, is operative. The egg, the whole, is logically prior to its parts, the protoplasm, and so on. The form of the complete egg governs the organization of the constituents; they were, in other words, organized in this way in order that they might become an egg. The egg was of such a nature in order that it might become a chicken by actualizing its potentialities, the chicken that it might become a hen, the hen that it might take its necessary place in the world scheme—feeding of other animals, and so on. Thus the organization of all things in the world, living or dead, was

[6] The theory was not original with Aristotle, but was taken from the Greek mathematician Eudoxus. The logical conclusions, of course, are his own.

orderly, each fitting into its natural surroundings. It can be seen how well this scheme would fit into the Christian teaching of Divine Providence, and how it gave a natural and metaphysical explanation for Plato's mystical teachings concerning divine creation. "Nature does nothing in vain," was Aristotle's aphorism, setting his followers to the task of discovering reasons for the existence of natural phenomena which conform to human conceptions of purpose, rather than seeking with the moderns the efficient causes, i.e., the immediate *how* or sequence of events by which the egg becomes what it is, and the material causes, i.e., the constituents from which it is made up; while the moderns deny the ability of the human reason to determine "that for the sake of which" the phenomena are as they are. But it will be admitted that Aristotle's procedure, invalid as it may be, does create an orderliness in the phenomena which they seem to the common sense in fact to possess.

### Political observations of Aristotle— Practicality and empiricism

Where purpose really rules, and common sense is of more value than theories and conclusions, in the realm of the social sciences, Aristotle is at his unequaled best. In his *Politics,* under the influence of Plato, he first tackled the question of an ideal state, and at once discovered the formidable practical difficulties. While admitting that the purpose of the laws and the state is to train citizens, it is also to ensure good government. Which brings him to the question, Good government for whom? And from this point on[7] he examines carefully all forms of government known to him, classifying them here and seeing similarities there, taking into account the advantages and disadvantages of each and how each works, the relative importance of property and human rights, and so on, until order begins to emerge. The constitution of an ideal

[7] The *Politics,* like all Aristotle's works, was never organized for the public, and the present arrangement is neither logical nor chronological and is probably due to technical considerations on the part of the ancient compiler.

state is then abandoned, and he gives his rules for the best kind of state practicable, bringing in here his favorite biological analogy of the plant which needs the right soil and the right cultivation if it is to realize its potentialities. Even here, however, his conclusions are tentative, for he recognizes that circumstances always alter cases. While his study is confined to the polis, as the only kind of state adapted to develop the potentialities of men, he also informs the tyrant how to rule and keep his power. No later student of political science has ever attempted such a comprehensive work, backed up by such a multitude of examples; and Aristotle's method of first studying the constitutional history and from this formulating conclusions on the structure and functioning of states in the light of this history and his contemporary observation has been the model followed by most competent political scientists since his time.

### Ethical observations of Aristotle— The supremacy of reason

His (*Nicomachean*) *Ethics* was a work of similar nature; though his primary data were the observations he had made of human beings in society, he had also to consider the nature of the human being, his possession of soul and body, and his highest faculty, the Nous, which alone distinguished him from the animals. His principal conclusion is that man must seek for happiness, which consists in the fullest development of the Nous, and is the Final Cause which draws out all the potentialities of man. The Nous, to Aristotle, is not only intellectual but moral. All ethical values are determined by reason; good acts therefore depend upon their motivation. Since all parts of the human being need to be developed and used for the highest happiness, they must be developed harmoniously. The mean between two extremes is the best kind of harmony; one should be neither timid nor irascible, but good-tempered. The ability to love or feel friendship toward another depends upon the development of the self. Excessive altruism is as bad as excessive egoism; the mean between the two is necessary for a communal good in which we all share.

### Aristotle—The culmination of Greek desire to know and understand

These descriptions of various parts of Aristotle's work are intended only to suggest the universality of his genius, and something of the scope of his mind. Both Plato and Aristotle had an advantage over later thinkers in that the known world was small, and the whole range of knowledge was not very great. So it was still possible for one man to try to encompass it. Frequently throughout the work of Aristotle we find him making the statement that any science or art ought to cover the whole of a subject; and it is true that he makes the attempt. But not only this; he tries also to cover the whole of *all* subjects, using his key of logical analysis and systematic organization. This no successor has ever been able to do, and few have tried—though, as we shall see, it was the aim of Roger Bacon in medieval times. But even he did not find it necessary to go over a subject again once Aristotle had "completed" it; though toward the end of Bacon's life he suggested that a corps of specialists should be organized for the purpose of producing the necessary compendium. It is certain that no single person will ever try again.

This work of Aristotle was therefore unique, a last and most complete expression of the Greek desire for an orderly and harmonious whole, one of the greatest intellectual monuments in the history of mankind. If the highest praise is to be given, let us say that his work is worthy of the Greek genius.

### SCIENCE—HIPPOCRATES AND THE BEGINNING OF SCIENTIFIC MEDICINE

The age that followed Aristotle was an age of science rather than philosophy. Even the chief philosophical schools were primarily interested in ethics and consolation, and speculation itself became less disinterested. This notable flowering of science will be discussed in the next chapter, and reasons for it will be suggested. With the exception of mathematics, which will be dealt with as a whole under Hellenistic science, only the practical art of medicine can really be said to have flourished in the Classical Age.

It is here called an art (or craft) intentionally since this was what the Greeks themselves insisted it was. They objected very strongly to premature attempts to establish it as a systematic science until enough material was available for proper theorizing. In this they were very much in accord with modern medicine, as were the methods employed. Until very recently medicine always seems to have stood somewhat apart from the other sciences, and owed little to them. This also seems to have been the case in Greece of the time of Hippocrates, although Empedocles the Sicilian, with his four elements derived from his philosophical speculations, provided medicine with a theory of four humors which persisted in various forms even into modern times, and was accepted by the school of Hippocrates.

Early Greek medicine began in the temples, as probably also in Egypt, and much of it returned there in the Hellenistic and Roman ages. Here the patient, under the direction of the priest, lay down to sleep; and while he was asleep the god Aesculapius approached him and healed him. Charms, spells, incantations, and other forms of magic were also practiced by the priests.

Hippocrates of Cos founded in the fifth century an outstanding school of medicine, breaking away from the priestly traditions in which he himself had been reared. His chief principle was that "every disease has a natural cause, and without natural causes nothing ever happens." He and his students and followers made it their rule to study the progress of every disease very carefully, note the symptoms, and use previous experience in diagnosis and therapy. Most of the therapy of this school seems to have consisted of proper care and improved diet; for, as Hippocrates insisted, "nature is the best healer." Nevertheless, most of the herbal healing drugs were known, and presumably used when necessary. A large body of so-called Hippocratic writings have survived, some of which are probably by the great doctor himself; though others are polemical tracts which read more like the work of professional orators with an interest in medicine (evidently this species was a pest then as now). The famous Hippocratic oath, a masterly formulation of the ethics of doctors, is still taken by medical students on their graduation as doctors.

## ▶ Hellenic art of the Classical Age

### FULFILLMENT OF IDEAL OF MODERATION AND HARMONY

The Greek ideal of balance, of *sophrosyne*, and harmony found a perfect expression in art—perhaps its most perfect expression. For in art alone the human being has not to contend with the difficulties in the everyday world of a too complete idealism. In art man is a creator, not a discoverer. His materials are at hand; they are the given world, but as yet without necessary form. It is he that gives it its form; as the soul, in Greek thought, is the form of the body, so the Greek conceived that he must give soul to the as yet inanimate material. To do this was to repeat, as far as it was possible for man, the act of the Creator.

The Greek of the Classical Age did not dream of art as useful; and he was content to live in houses that were singularly uncomfortable by the standards of any of his successors. This was not because he was poor, though he was; under a democracy the fruits of empire could have been distributed to the citizens, and the same artists could have designed a graceful home as well as a temple. Rather was it because artistic creation was a sacred act, reserved for the service of the gods.

This is not to deny the artistic creations of the Greek world in the production of humbler objects than temples or statues. But even these are as perfect as they are because of the dedication of the artist to his task. The Greek did not self-consciously set out to create something "artistic." Though the Greeks are supposed to have a word for

everything, they do not have a word for our conception of the "artistic" as something somewhat higher than, and to be distinguished from, the "useful." The Greek word for art is *Techne*, which is nearer to our conception of craft. It was the product of craftsmen, ordinary hand workers. But even in painting a vase for export to a Persian barbarian king the Greek always knew he was creating, giving form to material according to the nature of the material and the purpose for which it was used.[8]

We know that the Greek artisans all received the same low wage when they were at work for the city, just enough to maintain their wives and families for one day. And we also know that it was the highest honor to work for her; and those who scorned private employment as unworthy of free men welcomed the opportunity. And—a very strange thing indeed—the masterpiece among all Ionic temples, the Erechtheum at Athens, dedicated to Athena, protectress of Athens, and to Erechtheus, her first ancestral king, was built in the last days of the Peloponnesian War, when the expedition to Syracuse had been defeated, and there were no longer any spoils of empire and victory available. The love of the Greeks for their polis and their reverence for their gods combined to make the building of a temple the very highest expression of all that was in them as men.

### CLASSICAL ARCHITECTURE—THE TEMPLE AS HOME FOR THE GODS

At first the Greeks worked within the framework of tradition and inheritance from other cultures. We can see this process with the early Greeks, the Doric temples built like the Mycenaean palaces, the stiff sculptures in the Egyptian style with square shoulders and one foot slightly advanced, and the crude anatomy. Then, suddenly, as early as the tyranny of Pisistratus, the Greek spirit breaks through, and first the detailed representation of hair and drapery and then the human form become true to life. And away

[8] Vases and a bow-case destined for export are illustrated in Chapter 7.

in Ionia the Ionic temple takes shape, and the sculptured figures become mobile and graceful. Then come the Persian Wars, and Athens is sacked and destroyed, leaving to a new generation a new city to be built.

The city was the work of Pericles and his democracy, the full flowering of the Greek genius in works of harmony and beauty that have been the despair of later ages, imitated but never equaled. For, whether we like it or not, it is impossible for machines, however skillfully directed, to do the creative work of man; and never again shall we have the compelling religious desire to create beauty, nor the skill of hand and integrity of purpose of those unnamed craftsmen at a drachma a day. The economic resources came from the new commercial prosperity of Athens and her empire, and from the surplus treasure of the Delian Confederacy; the human resources, the architects and the sculptors, were free men of Athens who had experimented and worked on lesser masterpieces until the city could recognize them as the supreme exponents of their art.

The style of the Greek temple was one of the simplest structural forms known to man. Essentially it was composed of the *cella,* a rectangular chamber, the dwelling place of the statue of the god; the columns surrounding the cella and forming a porch; the lintel which rested on the columns and supported the roof; the gabled roof itself; and the pediment, the triangular section under the roof. The difference in the style of temple is determined by the column, of which three were in use—though the third was not known in Periclean Athens. The Doric column is a strong, heavy, sharply fluted column, crowned with a plain capital. The Ionic is more slender and graceful, with flat flutings,

*Athenian head of Heracles (conventional archaic style, sixth century B.C.).* (COURTESY AMERICAN SCHOOL OF CLASSICAL STUDIES AT ATHENS)

*Early Athenian statue, showing marked Egyptian influence (seventh century B.C.).* (COURTESY THE METROPOLITAN MUSEUM OF ART)

*Model of the Parthenon, now a semi-ruin, constructed by The Metropolitan Museum of Art. Note the Doric columns.* (COURTESY THE METROPOLITAN MUSEUM OF ART)

*Church of La Madeleine (Paris), constructed in the reign of Napoleon I, showing the persistent copying of Greek design. Clearly this church is modeled after the Parthenon, though Corinthian—more ornate—columns were preferred.*

*Part of the temple of Hephaistos at Athens, formerly called the Theseum. This is the best-preserved temple on the Greek mainland. Note the Doric columns. (Built 449–444 B.C.)* (COURTESY AMERICAN SCHOOL OF CLASSICAL STUDIES AT ATHENS)

*Doric triglyphs and sculptured metopes on the Temple of Hephaistos. The frieze is Ionic.* (COURTESY AMERICAN SCHOOL OF CLASSICAL STUDIES AT ATHENS)

and a scroll or volute capital; while the Corinthian has similar flutings and a very ornate capital. The Corinthian order appealed to the Hellenistic Age and to the Romans.

The temple, then, is the house of the god. Unlike the medieval cathedrals, it is not intended for worshipers, and the god or goddess is not lighted except by such sunlight as penetrates through the transparent marble of the roof. The frieze and the pediments of the temples are decorated with scenes from mythology or history, and it was in these reliefs that the sculptor joined hands with the architect to build a fitting home for the god.

Though his work was not confined to the Acropolis of Athens, the hill which stood in the center of the city, it was the restoration of the temples that was the crowning work of Pericles—above all the Parthenon, the temple of Athena, the protecting goddess of Athens. This unique building is constructed entirely of marble, with eight Doric columns at the ends and seventeen along each side. There are also six internal columns at each end. But the Doric columns are more graceful and slender than usual in this order. One of the wonders of the Parthenon, noble still in its ruins, is that it is made to *live* by the slight curves given to every part of the building, from the columns which lean slightly inward and taper toward the top, to the steps leading to the temple. The temple itself was the work of Callicrates and his younger contemporary Ictinus, the bulk of the work being ascribed to the latter. The sculpture was directed by Phidias; and the marvel of his work lies not only in the general design, which is a long continuous theme in glorification of Athens and her goddess, but in the way in which each part fits so perfectly into the whole. There is no dullness or monotony in it, with the horses prancing, and their young riders in perfect control, or Athena springing in full panoply from the head of Zeus while the other gods are calm and commanding, having not yet heard the momentous news. Some of these reliefs many feet above the ground were not meant to

*Volute of Ionic column, showing detail.* (COURTESY THE METROPOLITAN MUSEUM OF ART)

be seen by any mortal, but they are all executed with the utmost honesty.

### SCULPTURE—HARMONY OF BODY AND SOUL

The human body for the first time was appreciated, indeed loved, by those sculptors, great and small, of the Hellenic Age. Every muscle is perfectly rendered, whether in tension or repose. There was no striving after effect, as indeed there was no realism in the sense of contortion and strain as we find it in real life. There were ideal figures, harmonious and perfectly proportioned, the Greek ideal of man as a harmony of body and soul. Everyone who examines any of the smaller sculptures—the large sculptures for this age are all lost—is at once struck by the way the artist has been able to suggest life, and somehow conjure it out of his marble or ivory. In their original forms all the sculpture and the buildings themselves were painted, and it is difficult to imagine the effect the whole must have created, especially when we always view what remains to us in the cold white of the original marble.

Phidias is generally considered the greatest sculptor that Greece produced. In addition to his statue of Athena for the Parthenon,

he is known for his forty-foot figure of a seated Zeus at Olympia in Elis in the Peloponnese, which is described in detail by Pausanias, a Greek traveler of the Christian Era. No work known to be by him survives, though the Parthenon friezes give some indication of his style of work, and some of them may be by the hand of the master. The only sculpture by one of the really great Greek sculptors which is certainly identified is the Hermes of Praxiteles, an Athenian of the fourth century B.C., when art had been modified from the complete idealism of the Age of Pericles. This is a real youth, alive, though in repose. Though he is called a god, no one could mistake him for one. Many of the great sculptors, however, are known through Roman and later Greek copies. This at least serves to suggest the kind of sculpture and the methods and character of the sculpture of a particular artist. From this we know how great a loss we have sustained in having none of the genuine work of Lysippus, whose

*Marble relief of a Maenad. Classical period, fifth century B.C.* (COURTESY THE METROPOLITAN MUSEUM OF ART)

*Two slabs from the Parthenon frieze known as the Elgin marbles after the English lord who carried them off to England. Note the mastery of the riders in the Panathenaic procession, and the absence of any sense of the strain which is noticeable in some of the realistic sculpture of the Hellenistic Age shown in the next chapter. The riders are caught in a moment of eternity rather than individualized as riders taking part in one particular procession at one particular moment. The frieze was designed by Phidias and carried out at his direction though by different craftsmen.* (COURTESY BRITISH MUSEUM)

which are of great value for the information they give of life in the Greek cities, as well as for incidents of mythology and religion. It was a kind of specialized miniature painting, and often done with great skill. But this art was already decaying before the fourth century, and the later pottery was more strictly utilitarian; but, as always in Greek art, a special effort was made to draw each figure with full regard for the group in which it appeared, and for the shape of the vase itself. The vases are painted in red and black, and are made of clay turned on the potter's wheel.

*Head of a young athlete (fourth century B.C.). This is a fragment of a statue contemporary with the Hermes of Praxiteles, and shows the trend toward increasing realism.* (COURTESY THE METROPOLITAN MUSEUM OF ART)

portrait of Alexander the Great, known in a copy, has fixed his features and demeanor indelibly upon later generations.

### PAINTING

Of painting, as such, unfortunately we know only what Roman and Greek tourists have told us. We know of the great Polygnotus of Thasos, who was invited to Athens before the time of Pericles to do frescoes, and who depicted scenes from the Trojan War with Athenian notables in the likeness of their Achaean forebears; and we know that in the individualist fourth century was the beginning of portrait painting, with stress on fidelity to nature. Zeuxis and Apelles were the great masters in this genre.

But though all the great painting is lost we possess thousands of examples of vase painting from the earliest times, examples

*The famous Hermes of Praxiteles, the only almost complete statue extant from the fourth century B.C. Note how the god is given truly human features, which should be contrasted with the less differentiated features of the participants in the Panathenaic procession shown in the Parthenon frieze (Elgin marbles).*

## Literature

LYRIC POETRY—THE CHORAL LYRIC

In the classical Greek period there was, as far as we know, no literature produced for the sole purpose of entertainment, and none that was not intimately connected with the social and political life of the polis. There were no self-conscious "men of letters" until the breakdown of this social life after the conquest of Asia. Several of the more important writers have therefore already been dealt with in the course of these chapters, leaving only formal classification and a few supplementary remarks for this section.

Epic poetry inevitably suffered a decline after Homer. The heroic deeds which it celebrated were now far in the past, and new forms of poetry were better fitted to express the great deeds of the present. There was no attempt to recover it until the Hellenistic Age, when some scholars made the effort to tell the legends of the past again in a manner fitted for contemporary consumption. But Hesiod, a Boeotian farmer of the seventh century B.C., is known to us from two long poems, *Works and Days* and the *Theogony*. The latter is our chief source for the Greek myths and legends about the gods, and was, with Homer, often learned by heart by later Greeks and taught to every schoolboy. The former is a conservative peasant's glorification of his own way of life, and a sustained and bitter attack upon the new power and importance of commerce and trade, and the exploitation of the farmer that results from it. The poems are marked by few graces of style or poetic feeling. They are more important to us, and evidently also to the later Greeks, for the subjects treated; as yet there was no Greek prose writing, and Hesiod therefore naturally wrote in verse.

Greek lyric poetry, as such, belongs pre-eminently to the age before the Greek genius had reached full maturity. The great choral lyrics of tragedy and comedy thereafter took its place. Very little of these earlier lyrics survive; but enough to tell us of the incalculable loss sustained. Most of them are known to us only through quotations by later scholars and critics which have been assembled by modern Western scholars into a collection substantial enough to give us some idea of the richness and variety of this almost lost treasure.

This poetry can best be classified into the elegy and the personal lyric. The elegy was not pre-eminently musical, though many varieties of meter were used, and was closely connected with the social life of the time. Calls to action were sounded in elegy, and social criticism by Solon and Theognis. This later developed into the epigram, which was used extensively for epitaphs and dedicatory offerings in the temples. These are short, and often packed with thought and feeling, especially when composed to honor the glorious dead.

THE PERSONAL LYRIC—PINDAR AND THE
EXALTATION OF THE GREEK GAMES

The personal and choral Greek lyrics were sung to the music of the lyre or cithara. Many of them, such as the passionate poems of Sappho, sing of love; others, of the beauties of nature. The greatest work makes a marvelous use of the musical Greek language, which was perfectly fitted for song. These poems have given inspiration to thousands of poets in other tongues who have copied their meters, their themes, and their images without ever being able to approach the originals. Nevertheless, those odes of the Roman Horace which were inspired by the Greeks are among his best work in spite of the different virtues of the Latin tongue. The personal lyric developed into the great odes celebrating the winners in the games, which reached their climax in the Theban poet Pindar, who was able with a wealth of images and often profound thought to elevate the whole theme of glory and victory into a paean of praise of man and the gods, and the life of man upon earth among the beauties of the natural world. The Greeks acclaimed Pindar as their greatest poet after Homer, and Alexander, when he razed Thebes as a terrible example of the fruits of rebellion, spared Pindar's house in deference

*A lady playing a cithara, popular Greek musical instrument. This fresco is from Bosco-reale, a southern Italian city destroyed in the same earthquake that destroyed Pompeii and Herculaneum.* (COURTESY THE METROPOLITAN MUSEUM OF ART)

to this esteem. For us, our ignorance of the music that accompanied the odes is a loss that cannot be fully overcome; but if we imagine the atmosphere of the games, and can enter a little into the Greek spirit that animated them, it becomes possible to understand the honor in which the poet was held, why he was the most honored poet in Greece during his lifetime, and why he became a classic at once when he died.

The choral lyric found its early home in Sparta, and was designed to express the spirit of a civic festival. Usually it glorified the mythical or historical past of the city, its ancestral hero, and its god; and for this reason was specially suited for martial Sparta, though it was equally at home at Athens in the days of her glory. It found a natural continuation in the tragic drama and the Old Comedy; both Aristophanes and the great tragic dramatists were all wonderful exponents of the choral lyric, the singing and the dancing enhancing the atmosphere of the festival, and the lyrics themselves giving the poets opportunity to point to the universality of the solemn themes which were the heart of their plays.

### THE OLD COMEDY—ARISTOPHANES

Of Greek drama, which has already been dealt with extensively, it only remains to treat more fully Aristophanes, the master of the Old Comedy. Fragments exist from other writers of comedy, although insufficient to enable us to form a judgment on his competitors; but Aristophanes failed to win the first prize at the annual festivals often enough for us to surmise that the works of other dramatists were of the same high standard as the extant works of the master himself. To appreciate Aristophanes today it is absolutely necessary to re-create in the imagination the circumstances of the time. Notes on the meanings of the great number of allusions to current events can hardly take the place of this knowledge. He was an extremely acute social critic, with a love of Athens which shines through all his work. He has been called an arch-conservative, incapable of understanding the changing times; but this is a one-sided judgment. He understood the changing times only too well, and he did not like the change. Spending his youth in the bright days of the Periclean empire, and living through the Peloponnesian War and the oligarchic revolution, he was in a position to estimate the magnitude of what was being lost; and his comedies should be read in conjunction with the history of his contemporary Thucydides, as a parallel picture of the disintegration of the democracy under the scourge of war—and Thucydides is not usually accused, after his famous Periclean Funeral Speech, of being a hater of democracy.

Aristophanes saw Euripides destroying the tragic drama (the *Frogs*); he saw Cleon and the demagogues destroying the balance and order of the Periclean democracy (again the *Frogs,* but especially the *Knights*); he saw the dignity of the law courts being destroyed by corruption and blackmail (the *Wasps*); he saw faith in the old gods and the old unquestioned basis of society being destroyed by the Sophists (the *Clouds*); and he saw from the beginning that imperialism was not worth the price and would lead to what in fact followed (the *Acharnians*). With an unsurpassed gift for caricature and comic invention and a rich sense of verbal repartee, he brings forth his satires, one after another, criticizing his polis and its leaders unsparingly—and yet the Athenian comedy was produced out of public funds. The plays make use of dozens of different meters chosen with such obviously meticulous care for the effect they create that we could recognize a master poet in spite of his medium, even if we could not see this from the exquisite choral lyrics.[9] They were rich entertainment for a politically alert citizenry; but once the social and political conditions of the old polis had changed, this kind of comedy had outlived its purpose and there was never any serious attempt to revive it. In the so-called Middle Comedy of the fourth century B.C., the old uproarious satire takes on gentler tones, and the ordinary foibles of private life come increasingly to the fore, to emerge in the comedies of manners and character which reach full fruition in Menander and the New Comedy of the Hellenistic Age, which will be dealt with in the next chapter.

### PROSE

### The historians—Herodotus and Thucydides

Prose writing finds its beginning in the two great histories of the Classical Age. Enough references have already been made to Herodotus, the "father of history," for the reader to be already familiar with his work and methods. Ostensibly his book (the *Persian Wars*) deals with the Persian Wars; but he was also so much interested in the peoples who took part in them, even remotely, and he traveled so extensively and made so many inquiries, that his work is almost a universal history. The customs and history of Persia

[9] The English-speaking reader in need of a translation should always use those of B. B. Rogers, who catches beautifully the spirit of Aristophanes, as well as rendering the lyrics into the same meter as the original.

and Egypt, as far as he was able to ascertain them, fill a large portion of his work, which is a mine of interesting stories as well as material for social and cultural anthropology. For the age in which he wrote, before the advent of rationalism and the critical spirit of the Sophists and their followers, he was not especially credulous, as has sometimes been stated. The trouble was that he had as yet no proper tools for criticism. When a story was told him, he either accepted or rejected it on the grounds of its own inherent credibility or lack of it. He could not check it by comparing and evaluating sources, but only by making more inquiries from more people, so that the problem of credibility remained unsolved. The story of the Persian Wars itself is told in a masterly narrative form, and primarily as an example of the destruction that awaits the presumptuous. From this point of view the Persian Wars were indeed a tragic drama, and Aeschylus, as we have seen, used it as a theme for one of his own. Written in the days when faith was still unshaken in the justice of the universal order and with an incomparable theme to celebrate, the later part of his book has unity and solidity; and with its charming style and the fund of delightful as well as heroic stories, it is a work of perennial interest, and has never failed to find appreciative readers in all the ages since.

But with Thucydides, son of Olorus, we are in the presence of one of the great minds of the world, one of the greatest that has ever turned to the writing of history. The defects, from a modern point of view, are easily stated, and detract little from its value. His book (*History of the Peloponnesian War*) is too little concerned with economic and social life, and too much occupied with politics and political psychology; and it says nothing of the great Greek art and the flowering of Athenian culture. And occasionally the style is artificial and crabbed (a characteristic also of his great English pupil Gibbon). But it was not the purpose of his work to deal with Athenian culture. He was not even writing a formal history of Athens during the Peloponnesian War; but

of the Peloponnesian War itself, the interstate rivalry and imperialism that caused it, and the defects and virtues of Athenian democracy that caused it to take the course it did. If we grant this framework as the legitimate field for a historian, and further take into account that he was writing the most difficult form of history, the study of the contemporary scene, the magnitude of his achievement remains without parallel in the whole field of history.

Thucydides himself was at one time an Athenian general, but because of ill success in a campaign and suspicions arising from it he was exiled, and while still in exile he wrote his *History*. He made it his business to gather together all the information he could, and he is severely critical in his use of sources. But most of the facts he recounts were quite familiar to him, and only needed his interpretation. As a true Greek he always tries to see the universal in the particular, and on almost every page we find magnificent generalizations which have remained permanently true, and make his history a mine of wisdom for the politician and the soldier and the citizen. He is so impartial and objective in his descriptions and criticisms that he sometimes seems like the voice of the Greek gods themselves commenting on the presumptuousness of man, the overconfidence born of success, and the madness and destruction that follow. Intensely dramatic in the structure and emphasis of his writing, Thucydides, as no historian has ever done since, laid bare the psychology of a whole people perfectly—the Athenian ideal as proclaimed by Pericles, the cold realities of the rule by the people, the oratory that moved them and the considerations of power that shaped their imperial policy, the party strife between oligarchs and democrats that destroyed the polis from within and was finally responsible for the follies of the war.

The drama is revealed especially in the speeches, not heard by Thucydides himself; but the emotions felt and the arguments used are those of the occasion, re-created by the imaginative understanding of the historian, heightening the drama and relieving the somber realism of the narrative. The Peloponnesian War may have been a small one between small states of little political importance in the history of the world, and (unfortunately) later wars greater in magnitude have sometimes suggested that this was a lot of fuss about little; but it was, like other Greek experiences, an archetype, the history in miniature of all other wars. And because it found its historian of genius it has remained till our own times, with its warning and its lesson, as vivid as in the day it was written.

### The orators—Demosthenes, Isocrates, Aeschines

Another form of prose writing sprang up in the fourth century, the written and published speeches of professional orators. The Sophists, as has been seen, first showed the value of careful professional training in speaking, which already with them in practice meant the careful planning of the effects of the speech, the use of a carefully calculated diction, the building up of dramatic effects as well as the employment of doubtful arguments of the kind satirized by Plato and Aristophanes. The effect of this self-conscious examination of what had always no doubt been applied half-consciously in practice is to be seen in Thucydides; but the full impact of this new education was not felt until the fourth-century schools of oratory attained their maturity and their resounding success. No longer could a pleader hope to win his case in the law court or a speaker command the attention of the Assembly without the assistance of planned artifice; and by the second half of the fourth century almost every politician of note had been trained by the orators. But in addition to public speaking the demand also arose for publicists, men who could make their appeal to an informed public by the written word.

All fourth-century prose writing was dominated by the art and craft of the orator. It was apparently impossible to find an audience for anything except fine writing, artificial, perhaps, but carefully balanced and elaborated, thoroughly orderly in the Greek manner, and thought out, rather than merely poured out, in words. Even the appeal to the emotions was planned, though with such an orator as Demosthenes the fire of his patriotism and the real emotion behind his words removed any hint of the artificial. Because he himself and his art were so intermingled that the masterly technique is concealed, he has been regarded as the greatest exponent of political oratory in history; and his speeches remained the model for Romans and Western Europeans until very recent times.

Isocrates is the great example of the scholarly orator, who wrote his speeches and rarely delivered them because, as he explains, his voice was too weak to be effective in public. His was for the greater part of the century the most influential school of oratory, and the most promising students of the Greek world came to study with him. While not aloof from politics he strove to look at them with a detached eye, and he alone of Greek publicists recognized that the future of the world did not lie with the individual polis, and that the necessary unity of Greece could best be attained by a joint expedition under Greek leadership against the barbarian world of Persia. From early in his long life till almost the end he urged this policy and his *Letter to Philip,* in which he exhorted the Macedonian king to undertake the leadership of the Greeks against the Persians was an act of political courage in the days of the ascendancy of the superpatriot Demosthenes. Isocrates always seems to have had a circle of friends around him who held similar views, though they were men of little political influence. But their very existence and the way in which the independent politicians were able to find thoroughly respectable arguments to justify the appeasement of Philip are a commentary on the detached and excessively rational attitude of the Athenian democracy in its declining days.

A considerable number of orations, private and public, are known for this period, but most of them are hardly to be classed as literature, valuable though they are for the insight they give us into the social conditions of the time. Aeschines was a brilliant writer and a brilliant speaker, though lacking sincerity and without profound political insight. If he had not been a contemporary of Demosthenes he, instead of his implacable enemy, might well have become the model for later times. When we read his speech against the man who had proposed a crown for Demosthenes, we marvel how he could have failed to win his case. Then when we read Demosthenes afterward we see why there could have been no other verdict. Demosthenes had every art of the orator at his finger tips in addition to a burning sincerity. On whether his policy was a wise one in the circumstances there can be difference of opinion; but on whether he was a worthy exponent of it, and of his passionate love of and belief in the idea of the polis and of Athens there can be none at all. But of this the reader will better be able to judge when the struggle between Demosthenes and Macedonian imperialism has been considered in the next chapter.

▶ ## Suggestions for further reading

Again, the same observations should be stressed as in the suggestions for the preceding chapter: there is no substitute for reading as widely as possible in the primary sources. Many translations are available of the works of all the writers mentioned in this chapter; if no specific translations are recommended, the reliable Loeb Classical Library translations are always available. As mentioned in the text, translations of the plays of Aristophanes by B. B. Rogers are reprinted in the Loeb series, and should certainly be used for this writer. There are several good collections also available containing the works of several writers. Strongly recommended are T. F. Higham and C. M. Bowra, eds., *The Oxford Book of Greek Verse in Translation* (Oxford: The Clarendon Press, 1938), and W. J. Oates and Eugene O'Neill, Jr., eds., *The Complete Greek Drama* (2 vols.; New York: Random House, 1938). The introduction to the latter volume by O'Neill is especially valuable. F. R. B. Godolphin, ed., *The Greek Historians* (2 vols.; New York: Random House, 1942), is a comprehensive work, but the Penguin translations of Herodotus and Thucydides referred to at the

end of Chapter 7 may be preferred. M. C. Nahm, ed., *Selections from Early Greek Philosophy* (3rd ed.; New York: Appleton-Century-Crofts, Inc., 1947), with a useful introduction by the editor, collects in one volume a substantial number of the fragments of the writings of the pre-Socratic philosophers which are difficult to find together elsewhere in English. Until very recently the most easily available complete translation of the works of Plato, that of Benjamin Jowett, led many students astray in their attempts to understand exactly what Plato had said. In spite of the real excellence of Jowett's work as a whole, much fault could be found in detail. Now, however, a new edition of Jowett's work has just been issued, substantially revised where necessary by a number of distinguished scholars. This new edition, B. Jowett, *The Dialogues of Plato*, revised by D. J. Allan and H. E. Dale (4 vols.; Oxford: The Clarendon Press, 1953), should certainly be used when available. The standard edition of the works of Aristotle, on which most other editions have been based, is that of W. D. Ross, who also edited an abridged version for students, *The Student's Oxford Aristotle* (6 vols.; London: Oxford University Press, 1942). There are many convenient anthologies containing some of the more important works of Aristotle. Among the most useful is R. McKeon, ed., *Introduction to Aristotle* (New York: The Modern Library, 1947).

It would be a hopeless task to attempt to make a list of even all the first-rate works on different aspects of Hellenic culture. All that will be given here is a list of a few books that the author thinks are specially relevant to the exposition he has offered in this chapter. On Greek tragedy, contrary to much modern opinion, he is inclined toward the view of Nietzsche, which emphasizes the relation of tragedy to Greek religion, and regards it as having been destroyed by the rationalism of the Sophists. This view has been eloquently expounded in Nietzsche's *The Birth of Tragedy*, which is excellently translated by Clifton Fadiman, in C. Fadiman, ed., *The Philosophy of Nietzsche* (New York: The Modern Library, 1927). For a careful analysis of the extant plays, with a standpoint differing substantially from that of the author, the reader is referred to H. D. F. Kitto, *Greek Tragedy* (Garden City, N.Y.: Doubleday & Co., Inc., 1954), an Anchor book. A well-organized history of philosophy which gives, on the whole, a very fair summary of all Greek thought is W. T. Jones, *A History of Western Philosophy* (New

York: Harcourt, Brace & Co., 1952), Vol. 1. A summary of Greek thought, paying special attention to the problems with which Greek thinkers were wrestling, which has always seemed to the writer to be one of the very best books of its kind, is J. M. Warbeke, *The Searching Mind of Greece* (New York: Appleton-Century-Crofts, Inc., 1930). A fine, though highly controversial, criticism of Thucydides as a prose tragedian is the old classic, F. M. Cornford, *Thucydides Mythistoricus* (London: Edward Arnold & Co., 1907). A vivid and easily available picture of Hellenic culture is provided in Edith Hamilton, *The Greek Way to Western Civilization* (New York: The New American Library of World Literature, Inc., 1948). On political theory a very convenient and thoughtful summary is given in the first six chapters of G. H. Sabine, *A History of Political Theory* (New York: Henry Holt & Co., 1937). Another good summary of the special nature of the Greek contribution to the history of thought, emphasizing its relation to the Hebrew thinkers and Roman and Christian thinkers, including also a few pages on the Hellenistic contribution, is to be found in the Pelican book already recommended at the end of Chapter 5, W. G. De Burgh, *The Legacy of the Ancient World* (Harmondsworth, Middlesex: Penguin Books, 1953), I, 96–224.

# 9

# The Hellenistic Age

*The end of the independent polis in Greece • The career of Alexander the Great • Results of the conquests • The Hellenistic Age in Greece • The Hellenistic Age in Egypt • The Hellenistic Age in Asia: Pergamum and the Seleucid Empire • Hellenistic culture • Transition to the Roman world: Hellenistic "conquest" of Rome*

## ► The end of the independent polis in Greece

DIVISIVE CITY-STATE POLITICS VERSUS THE UNIFIED IMPERIAL STATE

The struggle between the polis and Macedonian imperialism deserves more space than is usually given it in a textbook. Looking back from this distance of time it is clear that all the advantages were on the side of Philip, and that Demosthenes and his party were always fighting a losing battle. The polis as a unit of government had outlived its usefulness, and as a social unit it had outlived its creativeness. The weakness of the barbarian empires, possessed of a potential power that the Greek poleis could not command, had allowed the latter to make their outstanding contributions to civilization. Now again it was the turn of the great empires, and the future lay with them, until once again the civilization of Europe was destroyed by primitive barbarians unfitted to manage their inheritance of empire.

All this may be so, but it did not seem so to Demosthenes; nor even, so far as we can tell, to Aristotle, who, as tutor of the young Alexander, ought to have known better. The social organization of the polis was dear to its inhabitants; the collaborators with Philip were probably not pining for a great strong master and an enlightened or powerful despotism. They were merely shortsighted self-seekers who failed to see the danger. And in fact the polis in Greece did survive for a couple of centuries more, even though it had lost its full political autonomy. It is thus as a case history of unpreparedness, political ineptitude, and the willingness of a democracy to be hoaxed that this period has a melancholy interest, rather than merely as a struggle for an inevitably lost cause.

The Greek political genius had not been fully spent, even if the leadership of Greece had passed from Athens. There are sporadic attempts at federations and leagues of cities, each maintaining its social autonomy and yielding some of its political autonomy. The problem was again not dissimilar to our own in the twentieth century, with the political unit in ancient times being the polis, and in modern the national state. The heart of the matter in ancient times was that the cities wanted to eat their cake and have it; they wanted to remain the arbiters of their own destiny and at the same time to have the advantage of "collective security"; they did not want a different social organization from that of the polis, nor to give up the patriotism associated with it. As it turned out, events were too strong for them, and the more hopeful leagues had only brief moments of growth and prosperity before being destroyed from within by traitors or unredeemed polis patriots, or from without by armed force.

### THE RISE OF MACEDONIA—PHILIP II AND THE PIECEMEAL CONQUEST OF GREECE

One of the most interesting of these attempts at intercity organization led directly to the rise of Macedon, and so is worth a brief mention here. About 387 B.C. the democracy of the city of Olynthus in the Chalcidian peninsula at the borders of Macedonia suggested to the local smaller cities that they hold certain well-defined rights in common,

in particular those of property and intermarriage. There should also be a league citizenship in addition to the citizenship of the individual polis. All citizens would therefore hold a dual citizenship, one of their own polis and one of the league. The league and its new idea quickly spread outside the original peninsula and began to incorporate other local cities against the will of their governments. It also began to make military advances with a joint army, capturing the Macedonian capital of Pella. Macedonia at that time was only a semibarbarian kingdom with a weak army and constantly beset by dynastic feuds. The two Greek cities with oligarchic governments within the sphere of influence of Olynthus naturally appealed to the chief upholder of oligarchies and the leading power in Greece at that time—Sparta.

The Spartan government decided to take action, backed as usual in the early fourth century B.C., by Persian gold, proceeded to besiege Olynthus, and after four years forced her capitulation. The league was nominally dissolved. Shortly afterward, however, Sparta

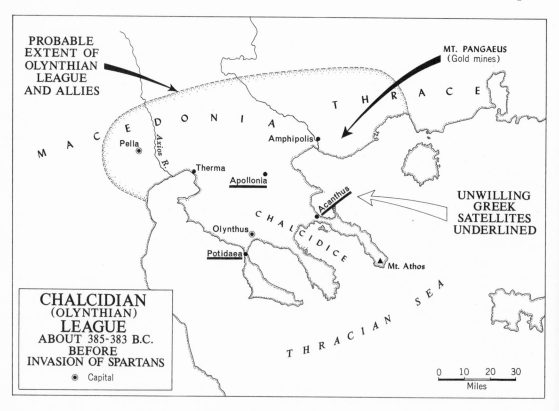

PROBABLE EXTENT OF OLYNTHIAN LEAGUE AND ALLIES

MT. PANGAEUS (Gold mines)

T H R A C E

M A C E D O N I A

Pella

Axios R.

Amphipolis

Therma

Apollonia

Acanthus

C H A L C I D I C E

Olynthus

Potidaea

Mt. Athos

UNWILLING GREEK SATELLITES UNDERLINED

T H R A C I A N   S E A

CHALCIDIAN (OLYNTHIAN) LEAGUE
ABOUT 385-383 B.C.
BEFORE INVASION OF SPARTANS
⊙ Capital

0    10    20    30
Miles

herself was defeated by Thebes, and the league came to life again. But the Macedonian king, Amyntas, a minor victim of the Olynthian expansion, had learned his lesson and proceeded to re-establish his kingdom, build up an army, and try to ensure that he would be able at least to defend his kingdom against a few aggressive cities of Greece. At his death the kingdom was rent for another ten years by internal struggles until his third son, Philip, came to the throne in 359 B.C.

In his youth Philip had been taken to Thebes as a hostage and there he had taken careful account of the Theban improvements in military organization, and had gained a firsthand knowledge of the internal weakness of the Greek city-states. This knowledge he was to put to good use in his drive for supreme power in Greece. This remarkable man, who has never received from history a fame commensurate with his achievements, succeeded, in the comparatively short reign of twenty-three years, in converting Macedonia from a weak, disunited, and unimportant kingdom which had remained on the fringe of Greek civilization and taken no part in its affairs, into the dominating power in the Greek world, with every state save Sparta submissive to him, and with a strong, well-trained body of troops which under the leadership of Alexander was to conquer Asia. All his life Philip seems to have been a genuine admirer of Hellenic culture, though he had nothing but contempt for its outmoded government. Time after time his knowledge of Greek political weaknesses enabled him to divide and rule; but even when he had won his final victory he imposed easy terms on Athens, and did not even demand the banishment of his unyielding opponent Demosthenes. He seems genuinely to have desired the cooperation of the Greek states in his Asiatic venture, and probably hoped for it till the end. Even though he knew the lukewarm nature of Greek support he took the trouble to organize a league for the conquest of Persia and had himself elected its leader.

In his dealings with the Greek city-states he showed himself master of the art of power politics.[1] He was completely faithless, he regarded a treaty as a move in the game, to be abandoned whenever it seemed advisable; he knew equally the value of a well-placed bribe and soft and soothing words. He knew exactly what his ultimate aim was, and, being one of the most brilliant opportunists in history, he could always take advantage of a momentary weakness or division among his opponents. To assist him he had a personally trained professional army, by far the finest in the Western world of his day but small in size; he could use it exactly when and where it was needed, confident of its loyalty. He was altogether too formidable an opponent for the Greek cities, even though the material means were usually in their favor, and at any time in his career until the last, a united front must have overwhelmed him. Even after the Athenian defeat by land at Chaeronea in 338 B.C., the Athenian navy could and did defeat singlehanded any navy he was able to put together.

Philip's first need was money to pay his army. He looked covetously at some gold mines which belonged to Amphipolis, a city which did not exploit them properly. Some shrewd diplomacy to hold off interference from Athens, a lightning blow of his army, and the gold mines were his. With these funds he organized the famous Macedonian phalanx, a new and effective formation which remained the master military unit of the Western world until the Roman legion defeated it. The Chalcidian cities and Olynthus barred his way to the sea, and with the considerable resources of the revived league, they presented probably the most formidable single opposition in Greece, far too strong for a direct attack at this point. Thebes was still a strong land power, with the best army. Athens had the best navy. But Athens in the fourth century had grown accustomed to using mercenary soldiers under generals of fortune, and her reputation for regular payment was not of the best.

The Athenian, in fact, at this time had

[1] It will be realized by the student that the detailed account of the strategy of Philip given here is intended to draw attention to an instructive modern parallel.

a good reputation for nothing. When the Assembly, under the influence of some war-minded demagogue, decided to engage in a military expedition, the usual procedure was to appoint a general and tell him to go out and raise some troops on credit. This he might do if he were otherwise disengaged; then someone else would offer a higher rate or more swift payment, and Athens would suddenly find herself at war but without an army. And as the war was usually to be fought with some ally, the ally would then be left in the lurch. Even the navy was semi-professional and dependent upon spasmodic outbursts of generosity by the citizens or upon a good orator to urge its support. The ready cash accumulated in the city treasury from the good years, which were rare enough, was put into a so-called festival fund which was sacrosanct, not to be touched; for out of it the poorer citizens were given money to attend the festivals, and the poorer citizens were in full control of the Assembly by the late fourth century B.C.

The incessant struggles between the city-states brought Philip actively into Greece for the first time. Thebes accused Phocis, the custodian of the Delphic Oracle and its treasures, of some sacrilege, and proceeded to invade the small state. The Phocians, who no doubt thought they might as well be hanged for the sheep as the dog, then became really sacrilegious, and stole the god's treasure, with which they purchased the bulk of the unemployed mercenaries in the country. They started to expand northward; and Thebes, frightened at the hornet's nest she had stirred up, appealed to Philip for assistance. Delighted to oblige, he descended with an army and inflicted a decisive defeat on the Phocians. At this point he was almost in the center of Greece; and the Athenians, suddenly scared, sent an army to Thermopylae. Philip, not having secured his rear and not yet ready to take on a major foe, retired gracefully. His services to the god Apollo were rewarded by an invitation to take the place of the sacrilegious Phocians on the Amphictyonic Council,[2] which meant

[2] See page 211, above.

that Philip was now a Greek by adoption—and, more important, if another "sacred" war could be incited, he was the proper agent to defend the god and his property.

At this juncture Athens found herself a leader—Demosthenes, who had realized before his countrymen what a danger the Macedonian king represented to all Greece and her cherished liberties. He proposed in his first *Philippic* (his speeches against Philip have received this name from posterity) the creation of a national army, citizens as well as mercenaries, and a policy of uncompromising hostility to Philip, and he gave exact indications as to the number of men required and how they should be financed. But the Athenians thought he was taking the situation too seriously. No one questioned his figures, but they said that Philip was just a kind, cultured gentleman; in any case he was "far away"—and, besides, he might die.

Back in Macedonia, enriched by a little privateering against Athenian vessels, Philip suddenly struck at his real enemy, Olynthus and the Chalcidian League, in the meantime fomenting a small rebellion in another Athenian dependency nearer home. Demosthenes in his *Olynthiac* orations now urged the use of the festival fund for troops; the opposition, some of its members now probably in the pay of Philip, countered with the usual arguments. Philip made short work of the confederate cities and laid siege to Olynthus. At this point Demosthenes had his way, and some two thousand troops went north. But they were too late. Philip had some well-placed traitors in the city, and it fell without too long a resistance. It had been too dangerous to Philip, with its constructive ideas of federation, it had shown too marked an ability to recover. There must be no mistake this time. It was razed and its inhabitants were sold as slaves, shocking all Greece into the realization of Philip's power and ruthlessness. This was not the kind of thing that happened in the enlightened fourth century.

But Philip had calculated correctly. The shock was not enough to awaken the Athenians to activity, but it was just enough to scare them into good behavior. When he

# ► chronological chart

The end of the independent polis
| | |
|---|---|
| Expansion of Olynthus in Chalcidice | 400–379 |
| First conquest of Olynthus by Spartans and Macedonians | 379 |
| Philip II becomes king of Macedon (Macedonia) | 359 |
| *Olynthiacs* of Demosthenes | 351 |
| Destruction of Olynthus by Philip | 348 |
| Sacred (Phocian) War | 355–346 |
| Philip conquers Phocians | 346 |
| Philip invited to take part in further Sacred War | 339 |
| Demosthenes, *Third Philippic* | 339 |
| Battle of Chaeronea | 338 |
| Congress of Corinth and foundation of Hellenic League | 338–337 |
| Murder of Philip | 336 |

The career of Alexander the Great
| | |
|---|---|
| Alexander crushes revolts in Greece | 335 |
| Alexander invades Asia—Battle of Granicus | 334 |
| Battle of Issus | 333 |
| Expedition to Egypt and submission of Egyptians | 332–331 |
| Battle of Gaugamela (Arbela) | 331 |
| Murder of Darius—Alexander becomes Great King | 330 |
| Indian campaign of Alexander | 327–324 |
| Death of Alexander | 323 |
| Deaths of Demosthenes and Aristotle | 322 |

Results of the conquests
| | |
|---|---|
| Ptolemy I Soter seizes Egypt | 321 |
| Civil War between the generals | 322–301 |
| Battle of Ipsus—Final division of Alexander's kingdom | 301 |

Hellenistic Age in Greece
| | |
|---|---|
| Formation of the Aetolian League | 290 |
| Formation of Achaean League | 280 |
| Revolution and reforms in Sparta | 245–235 |
| Philip V of Macedon engages in first hostilities with Rome | 215 |

Hellenistic Age in Egypt
| | |
|---|---|
| Foundation of Museum of Alexandria | 286 |
| Romans intervene to save Alexandria from Syrians | 168 |
| Cleopatra (VII) on Egyptian throne | 51 |

Hellenistic Age in Asia
| | |
|---|---|
| Seleucus I founder of Seleucid dynasty | 305–280 |
| Eumenes I founds independent kingdom of Pergamum | 263 |
| Antiochus III defeated by Romans at Magnesia | 190 |
| Revolt in Palestine against Antiochus IV (Judas Maccabaeus) | 168 |
| Attalus III of Pergamum bequeaths kingdom to Rome | 133 |
| Syria made a Roman province by Pompey | 64 |

Dates are before Christ.

invited them to discuss a peace treaty, he played the charming host at his Macedonian capital, and convinced them that he was a good, cultured Greek after all; and they signed the peace. But Demosthenes had now made his influence felt in the Assembly. *He* had not been charmed by Philip, and he was backed by a strong party who had realized the danger presented by Philip and that only force would defeat Philip. Backed by the Assembly Demosthenes proceeded to organize a pan-Hellenic league against Philip. But most of the cities were powerless and were hardly capable of making any appreciable contribution to a joint army. Only Thebes had such an army, and Thebes was still in uneasy alliance with Philip. At this point an opposition leader in the Assembly committed either an inexcusable blunder or deliberate treachery.

Philip, it will be remembered, was now in the Amphictyonic League of all Greeks. It was thus very probable that there would somehow be another extremely profitable "sacred" war. No one ever could prove that the fine hand of Philip was behind the "Second Sacred War," and perhaps he was just in luck.

At all events, Athens gratuitously and publicly insulted Thebes on the old matter of Theban collaboration with the Persians a century and a half before, and was herself accused in the Amphictyonic Council of sacrilege by Amphissa, a small city friendly to Thebes. Athens replied by the counter-charge that Amphissa had been committing a much worse sacrilege by cultivating the lands of Apollo (she had been doing so with impunity for at least a hundred years). The Athenian orator Aeschines was so effective in the ensuing debate that the Council declared war against Amphissa. Philip was invited to undertake the job, which he accepted with alacrity.

With an unnecessarily powerful army he moved into central Greece past the gates of Thermopylae, was welcomed as the defender of the god of Delphi, and took up a position commanding the road to Thebes. The Athenian Assembly, apparently not having ex-

pected this, now turned once more to Demosthenes. He personally went to Thebes, armed with full authority and funds from Athens, and succeeded in persuading the Thebans at last that they must either fight together or be picked off separately. By his eloquence he persuaded the Thebans to throw off their long-standing alliance with Philip, and just at the moment when they were in the greatest danger. Philip, now safely in central Greece, was in no hurry. He took a trip to Amphissa and settled the affairs of the god in a swift and relentless campaign; then suddenly turned on the army of the alliance and routed it at Chaeronea in 338 B.C. The Theban Sacred Band, the crack troops of the city, fell to the last man, and the harshest terms were imposed upon her—a Macedonian garrison in the citadel, and slavery or death for her leaders. Athens was spared, either for the sake of her glorious past and her culture or because she still had a navy.

### PHILIP AS THE GREEK LEADER AGAINST PERSIA— HIS MURDER

Philip then proceeded to call a congress of all Greek states to which only Sparta, now almost impotent, who had not fought in the recent war, refused to go. He dictated his terms. No state should be allowed to go to war on its own, and each must contribute troops and arms for his projected war against the barbarian Persians. In return Philip offered them his protection. No one was interested in his campaign, and, as the sequel showed, the hope was general that he would overreach himself, and perhaps be put out of the way by some barbarian.

As it happened, within a year he was murdered, probably in a family quarrel; and his son Alexander succeeded him. Demosthenes sprang to the attack again and persuaded the Athenians to send envoys even to Persia for support. Thebes expelled the Macedonian garrison. But Alexander in a lightning march took Thebes by assault, razed it, and enslaved the inhabitants. The Athenians, faced with a similar fate and not knowing what to expect of this terrible young man, passed a motion of congratulation on

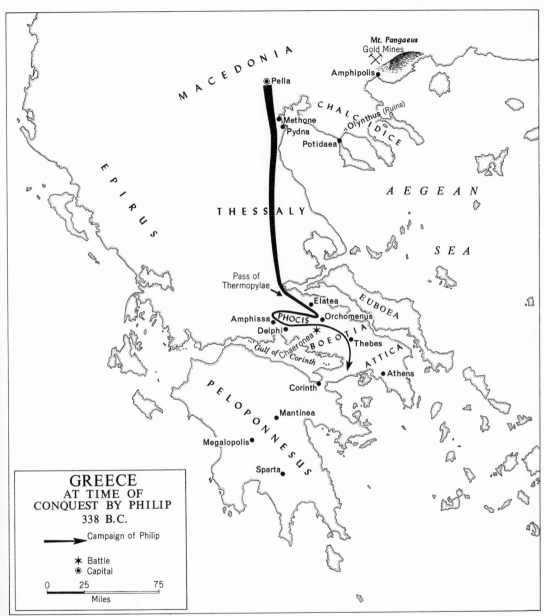

GREECE
AT TIME OF
CONQUEST BY PHILIP
338 B.C.

Campaign of Philip

✳ Battle
◉ Capital

0    25    75
Miles

his punishment of Thebes! Alexander was reinstated as leader of the Greeks, and prepared for his expedition to Persia.

### ▶ The career of Alexander the Great

THE INFLUENCE OF ARISTOTLE

Alexander the Great was one of the most remarkable conquerors in history. Yet he was much more than a conqueror. A man of wide learning and genuine enthusiasm for all that was Greek, something of a poet and a very considerable idealist, he seems to have been imbued with a sense of mission, and an exact knowledge of what he was going to do and how he was going to do it, even before he started on his expedition. It is tempting to ascribe at least some of this to his association with Aristotle, who had tutored him privately for at least three years—and Aristotle, as we have seen, was both the most learned man in the world of his day and the best exponent of all things Greek that could have been found. The evidence shows that Alexander and Aristotle were in close contact with each other all through the campaigns, and that the association was not broken even when Alexander found it necessary to execute his tutor's nephew. But, at the same time, Aristotle in his *Politics* is critical of monarchies, and regards the polis as the only fit form of government for human beings. How can these apparent contradictions be reconciled?

Alexander's regard for reason and balance, his belief in the control of the body by the mind, his disinterested love of knowledge, and his spirit of inquiry could have been instilled into him by his tutor. Alexander's first thought in entering a foreign country was to visit the shrines and initiation centers, and to inquire into the customs and beliefs of the people. But he persistently refused to regard the conquered as barbarians and in any way different from Greeks, much to the annoyance indeed of his own soldiers. In this he might appear to be ahead of Aristotle. The truth seems to have been that as a practical man he needed a policy, and that he used what he could of his teachings from his master, put them into effect wherever possible, and improvised the rest of his policy on the basis of his growing understanding of the problem of an empire builder in a territory in which the Greeks would necessarily be outnumbered by foreigners.

Though, as we shall see, he consolidated the empire under a central administration, this governmental technique he took over intact from the Persians; but in addition he founded new poleis wherever he went. To these he gave the institutions exactly as they were found in Greece itself. And though in many respects these cities could not function effectively as political entities, as social entities they were far nearer the Greek ideal than anything formerly to be found in Persia. A king over barbarians, Aristotle had said, must at least pretend to an interest in public welfare, avoid the exhibition of a tyrant's vices, and rule as little like a tyrant as possible. As far as his imperfect control over his own temper permitted him—for unhappily, like too many Greeks, he lacked moderation (*sophrosyne*)—this is what Alexander

seems to have attempted. He did not accept Aristotle's more cynical suggestions as to how the tyrant could rule without the consent of his people and still maintain himself in power. For the rest he did his duty by his old tutor by taking along with him a corps of specialists, collecting specimens of strange plants and animals and sending them back to him. No military campaign in history has been so much like a scientific expedition. But the question remains: Did Aristotle know of the expedition in advance, and did he approve of it? If so, why did he not give his pupil special instructions on how to carry it out, and why did he not give more attention to the special needs of the situation, giving more detailed instructions, for instance, on monarchy?

While there is always the possibility that Aristotle's works on this subject are lost— tradition says that he was asked for books on colonization and monarchy—even if we assume these books were not written, it can hardly be doubted that Aristotle knew of the planned expedition. Everyone in Greece knew of it for a considerable time before, and it was certainly known at the Macedonian court. Probably the best conclusion is that the expedition itself was the plan of Philip, inherited by his son Alexander. Isocrates, the Athenian orator and political philosopher, had urged it upon Philip. When the latter chose Aristotle as tutor for his son, he may have only wanted him to have the best education that money could buy. But Aristotle succeeded in giving his pupil an enthusiasm for Greek culture that was later to bear much fruit, though details of his personal advice on how to conquer and rule a barbarian people are missing and probably were never committed to writing.[3] For Aristotle was hoping to return to Athens, and public support of the policy of the Macedonian king was hardly likely to endear him to Athenians.

Aristotle was a student of politics, and particularly of the Greek polis as a form of

[3] Plutarch, writing four centuries later, declared that Aristotle did give Alexander such private personal advice. But we do not know whether Plutarch had any definite information on the subject.

government and as a medium for social life; he probably hoped that something of the values of the polis, as he saw them, could be transferred to an alien territory. And Alexander, as we have seen, tried his best to transfer the polis to Asia, and it was no personal fault of his if it failed to take root within a monarchical system, and in a foreign land permeated by Oriental culture. What Alexander seems to have appreciated, and Aristotle did not, were the values of Oriental culture in themselves. This was the result of the conqueror's own experience, which, of course, Aristotle lacked.

### FLEXIBLE POLICY TOWARD THE CONQUERED PEOPLES

Alexander was a consummate master not only of military strategy and tactics but of publicity. This was of vital importance, especially in the initial stages of his campaign. For though Philip had made nearly all the preliminary preparations for the campaign, he had not yet taken care of financing it. The Persian treasury was a more formidable enemy than the Persian native manpower, for it meant that he would be opposed by Greek mercenaries who were as tough fighters as his own Macedonians, and originally more numerous. There seem to have been, in fact, more Greeks fighting against Alexander at the beginning than were fighting for him. However, they were scattered throughout Persia, and not all of them could be brought to bear upon him at the same moment. Alexander's policy, as it revealed itself, was therefore to pose as a champion of Hellas, and to try to arouse Hellenic patriotism. Moreover, if he could demonstrate to the world that he was an invincible conqueror the mercenaries might be persuaded to desert. And above all if he could acquire the treasury of Darius, the Macedonian himself could hire troops and put them in the field against the Persian king. Alexander's policy, with a force vastly inferior in numbers, though of excellent quality, varied in each country he entered. He had to pose as the champion of liberty

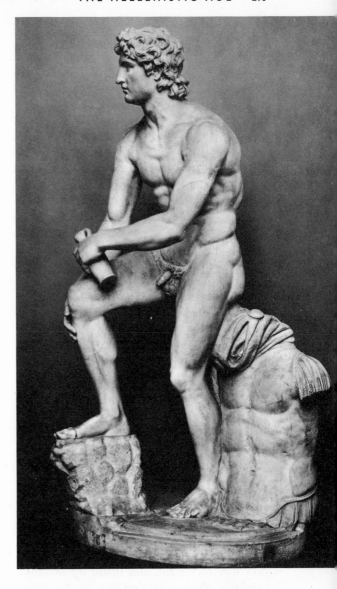

*Statue of Alexander the Great, artist unknown.*

in a country such as Asia Minor which appreciated that pose; he had to pose as a god-king appearing in majesty in Egypt where god-kings were acceptable, and for this purpose he had to win over the priesthood; and in Persia proper he had to be an invincible conqueror and appreciative of Persian valor and traditions. His brilliant propaganda seems to have been an important element in his success. His policy and campaigns have always been of great interest to students of the Greek mind and civilization because not only did he have the physical appearance of an ideal Greek, but in every act that he performed, except when he could not control his passions, we see the evidence of a trained and logical Greek mind, master of itself and its environment.

### THE CONQUESTS

He started on his conquest of Asia with only thirty days' provisions for his army and with only seventy talents in his treasury; and he was already heavily in debt. He dared not leave Greece without an effective garrison, so that he had to leave nearly half his army behind in Macedonia to keep order and prevent revolt in the Greek cities. As it happened, the garrison was very necessary since Sparta suddenly revived, and for a while tried to unite the cities against him. The revolt caused considerable trouble to the regent, but was ultimately suppressed. The Greek "volunteers" in Alexander's army amounted to fewer than eight thousand men, and he only had enough cash and credit to hire a further five thousand. The "Hellenic League," so carefully provided by Philip, was of little use to him until it could be seen that he would be successful. The Macedonian nucleus is estimated at about eighteen thousand infantry and three thousand cavalry, with a valuable unit of Thessalian cavalry which had really volunteered and was of inestimable value to him. His fleet was very small and made up of undependable allies. The Persians, on the other hand, possessed almost unlimited gold and silver, which was, however, virtually useless to Darius once his original mercenaries were expended, since he could not hire any more foreign manpower after Alexander had secured the coasts. Darius also had the services of a large Phoenician navy. Potentially he had a very large Persian army made up of feudal levies, but these were not, for the most part, well trained, as he had relied in recent years too heavily on Greek mercenaries, and could not organize an effective army from his polyglot empire in the short time available to him.[4]

The first battle in Asia Minor was a resounding victory for Alexander (Granicus, 334 B.C.). The propaganda was working well enough for most Greek mercenaries to be doubtful, and so take little active part in the battle. Those who did take part and were captured were sent as slaves to Macedonia, causing some consternation among the remainder. They finally chose their sides; but the remnant that opted for the Persian king and his treasure was too small to be effective, and was wiped out by Alexander's victorious troops in a local engagement. The Persians retired from Asia Minor, and most of the non-Persian inhabitants offered their submission, the Ionians naturally hailing Alexander as liberator. The remainder were quietly mopped up, and suitable forms of government granted to them.

Darius by this time had assembled what he could of the Persian armies, including Greek mercenaries from his Persian provinces, and advanced to meet Alexander in Syria; and though Alexander's army had also increased in size it was no match in numbers for the Persian. This time everything seemed to be in Darius's favor. His Greek mercenaries, knowing that Alexander would show them no mercy, fought loyally and stubbornly. But Alexander's cavalry won the day and Darius himself fled into the interior (battle of Issus, 333 B.C.). Alexander captured his camp and enough spoil to be able to pay his troops, hire more, and still have something in hand. In no hurry about pursuing Darius, he proceeded to capture the Phoenician coast and secure the sea; then he went on what was largely a triumphal tour into Egypt, sacrificed to the Egyptian gods, rebuilt a number of temples, and founded the city of Alexandria, destined to become the greatest city of the world. Greek architects, artists, craftsmen, and plain immigrants flocked to it. At last Alexander had the support of some of the Greeks. His tolerant and Hellenizing policy was beginning to pay off. He made a state visit to the Greco-Egyptian oracle of Zeus-Amon

[4] See also Chapter 4 for the organization of the Persian Empire.

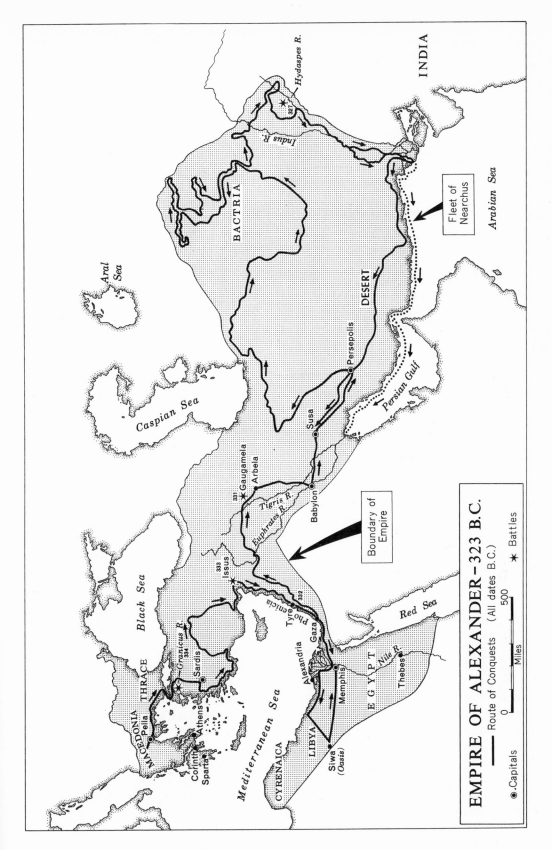

# EMPIRE OF ALEXANDER – 323 B.C.

—— Route of Conquests   (All dates B.C.)

⊙ Capitals    ★ Battles

Scale:
0 ........ 500
Miles

INDIA

Hydaspes R.

327

Indus R.

BACTRIA

Aral Sea

Caspian Sea

DESERT

Persepolis

Susa

Gaugamela
Arbela
331

Tigris R.

Euphrates R.

Babylon

Arabian Sea

Fleet of Nearchus

Persian Gulf

Boundary of Empire

Black Sea

Issus
333

Granicus R.
334

Sardis

Phoenicia

Tyre
332

Gaza

MACEDONIA
Pella

THRACE

Corinth
Sparta

Athens

Mediterranean Sea

Alexandria

Memphis

EGYPT

Nile R.

Thebes

Red Sea

CYRENAICA

LIBYA

Siwa
(Oasis)

away off in the desert, and left everyone to this day speculating what the god told him that was so "agreeable to his desire."

Having settled Egypt to his satisfaction without opposition, he took up again the pursuit of Darius, who had now gathered together his motley troops into another powerful army, which still greatly outnumbered anything Alexander could muster. But again by superior tactics and discipline he was successful on a battlefield chosen by his opponents, a wide plain near Nineveh, former capital of the Assyrian Empire (battle of Arbela, 331 B.C.). Alexander now adopted the Persian title of the "Great King," successor to the "abdicated" Darius, who had again fled into the interior, and took possession of the remaining three capitals of Persia, together with their enormous hoards of treasure. The avenging of the ancient expedition of the Persian Xerxes, the official reason for the war, was now complete, and Alexander dismissed all his allied Greek forces with thanks and handsome rewards. He then took steps to capture his predecessor, who was still at large; instead he found Darius's corpse, slain by the latter's own satraps. Furious that these men could have committed such· sacrilege upon his own predecessor Alexander proclaimed a man hunt for the murderers. After burying Darius with all the honors befitting a Great King, he adopted Persian court ceremonial, and began to treat Persians as his subjects rather than as his enemies, much to the annoyance of the Macedonians. They also disapproved of his man hunt for the murderers, since this meant a further campaign into far-distant lands. Before he was able to catch up with them he had to cross the mountains of the Hindu Kush and conquer Bactria, developing new tactics as he went along to cope with a kind of warfare he had never known. He was, however, uniformly successful. He assumed Oriental manners more than ever before, demanded the Persian custom of prostration before him even from his Macedonians, and married Roxane, a native princess. Callisthenes, nephew of

Aristotle, refused to prostrate himself and was later put to death for plotting against the king.

Pushing south, Alexander made his way next into India, and again won a desperate battle with a formidable force, including elephants, by developing other new tactics, and the Punjab was his (battle of the Hydaspes, 327 B.C.). But at this point his exhausted army refused to go any further, and at last Alexander decided to return to Susa and Babylon. The homeward journey was made very difficult by Alexander's insistence on returning by way of the deserts of Baluchistan, apparently for scientific and exploratory reasons only. At last, however, he reached Susa, where he held a five-day marriage festival with ninety of his leading Macedonians marrying Persians, and he himself taking as an extra wife the daughter of Darius. All previous Greco-Persian marriages, amounting to about ten thousand were registered, and the bridegrooms rewarded with royal presents. Alexander also distributed some thirty thousand noble Persians throughout the Macedonian army, causing a revolt which was settled after an eloquent speech by the commander. After a few months he went to Babylon, where he contracted swamp fever and died at the age of thirty-three (323 B.C.). He had changed the face of the ancient world and never lost a battle.

Since he had left no provisions for a successor, and he had as yet no children—though Roxane later gave birth to a son—the inheritance was disputed among several of his more capable generals. There were a few attempts to hold the empire together; but no one general was strong enough to take over the whole, and the efforts ultimately collapsed. Egypt fell to Ptolemy Soter, the greater part of the Asiatic provinces to Seleucus, and Macedonia, after a long struggle between several contending generals, was consolidated under Antigonus Gonatas. Each of these men founded dynasties, and such of their history as is necessary will be recounted elsewhere in this chapter.

## ► Results of the conquests

THE FUSION OF GREEK AND ORIENTAL CULTURE

The effects of the conquests of Alexander were momentous in world history, not so much politically as culturally. The empire did not last as a single unified governmental unit, but the rule of Macedonians and Greeks over Oriental peoples was secured. Extensive immigration from Greece made the conquest more real than if an alien power had established political control only, as has happened in other periods of history. The barriers between Greek and barbarian had been broken down forever, and the resulting interpenetration of cultures determined the future pattern of all later civilization in the West. It is impossible to estimate whether Greek or Oriental culture predominated in the resulting complex. Both Oriental and Greek civilizations were already developed, and neither could be said to have absorbed the other; on the contrary, both contributed to a new, distinct amalgam. And it was left to the Romans, who entered this world in the guise of semibarbarians with a gift only for law, government, and military science, to spread this amalgam into a Western Europe which had been largely untouched by the Greeks and the Orientals themselves.

The period following the death of Alexander (usually called Hellenistic, as distinct from the earlier Hellenic) is therefore one of the great formative periods in the history of mankind, and should require extensive study. But since we have studied separately the elements that went to make it up, it is only necessary here to discuss the fusion, and the new trends in human civilization that resulted from it. Thereafter we shall move to the beginnings of the Roman state which inherited it, though it would have been quite possible, and perhaps even preferable, to have discussed Rome as a late comer in the Hellenistic civilization to which it contributed a few distinctive features.

The outstanding element making for unity in the whole Hellenistic world was the penetration of the Greek language as the common language of all educated men and of all those engaged in any form of commercial or trading activity. The old cuneiform and hieroglyphic writing quickly disappeared. The Greek language lost its ancient purity and became hospitable to any useful Oriental expressions that were needed. The language in which the New Testament, for instance, is written is the *Koine*, the "common language," which could be understood from Central Asia west to Italy and beyond. Other languages and dialects were, of course, spoken, especially Aramaic in the Near East, as has already been described; but the possession of a second language made it possible for the Italian and the Bactrian to carry on commercial and literary activities together. We find Armenian and Parthian kings as connoisseurs of Euripides and even writing plays in Greek, and we find a king of far-off Ethiopia having at least a nodding acquaintance with the language centuries after the conquests of Alexander. This powerful instrument of cultural fusion was perhaps the greatest single Greek contribution to the Hellenistic world civilization.

COMMERCIAL AND INDUSTRIAL CIVILIZATION OF THE HELLENISTIC WORLD

The Greeks had always been good traders, though the peoples of the Near East had been no novices. But the Greeks had developed more useful devices for the furthering of trade, and these now appeared in the Hellenistic world and were developed on a far larger scale than had been required before. Greek traders made themselves at home in the new world-cities founded by Alexander and his successors and were often granted special privileges. The greatest stimulus to trade was the release of the enormous hoards of gold and silver accumulated by the Persian kings, but never allowed to enter circulation. The chronic shortage of precious metals was therefore relieved, with a remarkably fructifying influence upon all trade and industry. For the first time throughout a large area taxes were paid in coin, and the states paid out their own wages in coin, especially to the armies. Banks sprang up everywhere, credit expanded far beyond anything previously known, and the check became a usual method of payment, though Egypt was ahead of the Asiatic empire in this. The new, largely money, economy, however, had a serious effect upon the poorer classes, as will be seen.

Insofar as the economic situation can be generalized, it may be said that the numerous new cities and the greatly expanded old cities were characterized by a commercial and industrial civilization more like our own than in any period prior to the sixteenth century. However, as was to be expected in an economy where slaves were present in large numbers, there was a very distinct cleavage between rich and poor. Profits were very high, while wages remained extremely low. The upper classes had access to all the luxuries of the ancient world and took full advantage of it. The poor, with the price of their labor determined by supply and demand, and the latter determined by the available slave labor, found themselves at the mercy of economic forces over which they had no control. Slaves actually declined in number, but this was no advantage to the poor freeman; slavery declined only because slave labor was more expensive than free labor. Slaves had to be fed and housed and treated as a valuable property, while the free laborer could be exploited without limit and it was of no interest to the employer whether he lived or died. The upper classes in the early period were predominantly Greek and Macedonian, but increasingly local nobles and traders were admitted into their company. Intermarriage continued in Persia, though in Egypt it was not so common and was hedged by restrictions. The distinction between rich and poor was far more important than that between Greek and barbarian. The peasant continued to work as from time immemorial, he gave crops and services to the state under the Seleucids and the Ptolemies as he had given them to Persian kings or Egyptian Pharaohs. The money economy of the cities hardly affected him; nor did the cultural radiation from the Greek cities, with their imported political institutions and their literature, philosophy, and science. The improved agricultural practices of the Greeks were passed on to him and when he was compelled to do so, as in Egypt, the peasant adopted them.

But there were several important differences, both political and economic, between the different parts of the Hellenistic world, and these require some separate mention.

## ▶ The Hellenistic Age in Greece

CONTINUED POLITICAL EXPERIMENTATION—
THE NEW LEAGUES

The cities of Greece were usually politically subject to Macedonia, but Macedonia did not interfere with their economic activities. Indeed, the Macedonians performed a notable service to them by protecting them from barbarian invasions from the north, and by insisting that they keep the peace. Corinth, however, now far surpassed Athens in trade, being a more important industrial and manufacturing city, while the Aegean islands and ports on the Hellespont and in Asia Minor knew their greatest period of prosperity during the Hellenistic Age. But there was a constant drain of the population of the mainland into Asia and Egypt, and the prosperity was on a small scale, enjoyed mostly by the upper classes. On the land, owing to the depopulation, the estates became much larger than in classical times, with severe consequences to the small farmer, who could not compete with them and was often evicted for debt and lost his land permanently. There was a great increase in agricultural unemployment, and many parts of the country became desolate. Free distributions of grain became the rule in those cities which could collect enough in taxes to afford them.

Two promising political organizations were developed during the centuries after Alex-

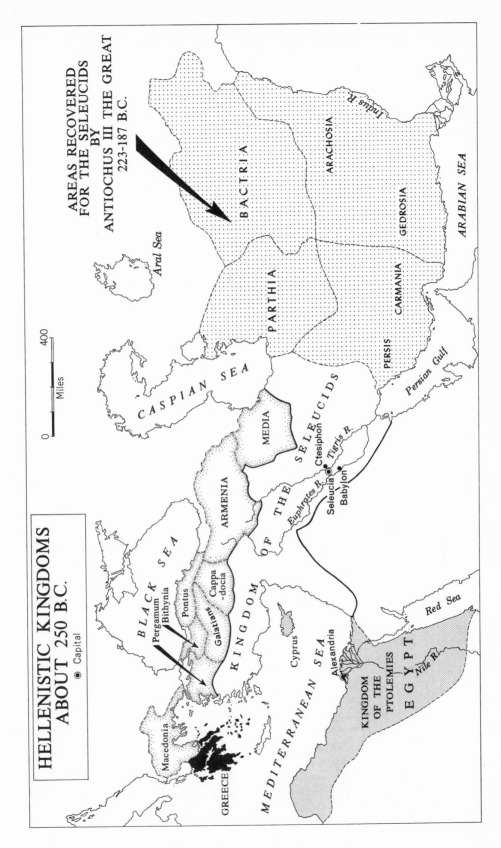

HELLENISTIC KINGDOMS
ABOUT 250 B.C.

● Capital

AREAS RECOVERED
FOR THE SELEUCIDS
BY
ANTIOCHUS III THE GREAT
223–187 B.C.

Aral Sea

0    400
Miles

CASPIAN SEA

BACTRIA

ARACHOSIA

Indus R.

ARABIAN SEA

PARTHIA

GEDROSIA

CARMANIA

PERSIS

Persian Gulf

MEDIA

ARMENIA

KINGDOM   OF   THE   SELEUCIDS

Ctesiphon

Tigris R.

Seleucia

Babylon

Euphrates R.

BLACK   SEA

Pergamum
Bithynia

Pontus

Cappa
-docia

Galatians

Cyprus

MEDITERRANEAN SEA

Red Sea

Alexandria

KINGDOM OF THE
PTOLEMIES

EGYPT

Nile R.

Macedonia

GREECE

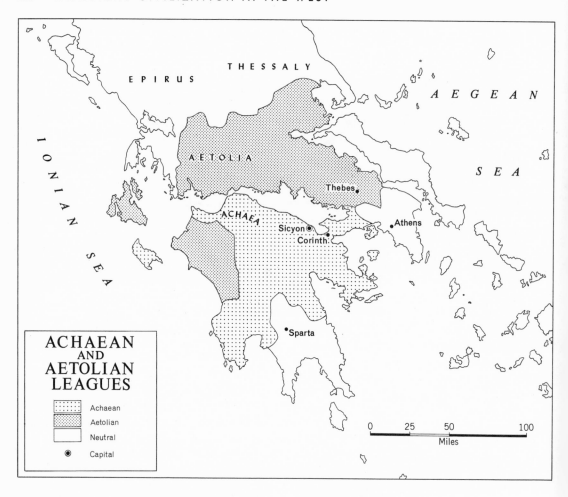

ander, but unfortunately they were usually antagonistic to each other. Moreover, the superior power of Macedonia in the north was a disturbing factor, since it tempted the leagues to apply for help to Macedonia when they quarreled with each other. But these leagues had genuine federal, or confederate, constitutions, and were the nearest approach the Greeks ever made to any organization larger than the polis. Their special contribution to federal unity was the abolition of the leadership of the most powerful city, leadership which had been the downfall, for instance, of the otherwise promising Chalcidian League of Olynthus. The capital cities of both the Achaean and the Aetolian leagues were small and unimportant. The constitutions of the two leagues were substantially similar. In their most advanced forms they had a federal

council on which each constituent city was represented on a proportional basis and to which had been delegated the power to take joint action without referring back to the cities. There was also an Assembly of all the citizens of all the cities, who voted by city, each of which had only one vote. The vote cast by the city was determined by a majority of all the citizens attending the Assembly who belonged to it. This Assembly elected officials and had to decide on peace and war and a number of other important questions concerning its own league. A general of the whole league was elected, but he could not succeed himself in office, though he could be elected in alternate years. The Achaean League at its height was made up of more than half of the cities in the Peloponnesus; the Aetolian League was made up of the cities of central Greece with the exception of Athens and some cities of Thessaly.

The only other power of importance in Greece was Sparta, where the old spirit reasserted itself and found expression in the division of the land, cancellation of debts, reform of the army, and re-establishment of discipline. The distinction between rich and poor that had grown up during the period of Spartan imperialism was abolished, together with the ephorate and council. But when the kings, under whose leadership these reforms were instituted, tried to expand their power in the Peloponnesus they came into contact with the Achaean League, which appealed to Macedonia rather than to the Aetolian League, which thereupon joined Sparta. The superior alliance squeezed out Sparta for the time, the revived Spartan kingdom was abolished, and the old constitution was restored. The Aetolians, left to the mercies of Macedonia, appealed to Rome, which ultimately conquered both Greece and Macedonia. As always, the internal strife in Greece prevented any chance of an all-Greek government, until, with the conquest by Rome, their liberties were lost for good.

## ▶  The Hellenistic Age in Egypt

MACEDONIAN EFFICIENCY IN AGRICULTURE

Egypt under the Ptolemies was for several centuries probably the most prosperous area in the world, at least as far as the upper classes were concerned. We are exceptionally well informed on the period because of the continuous discovery in recent years of Greek papyri preserved by the dry climate of the country. With the exception of Alexandria, which became a metropolis of more than half a million people and lived a full and relatively independent life of its own, the whole land of Egypt was the personal estate of the new Pharaoh, who made it a definite policy not to found any new Greek cities, preferring to exploit the political and economic heritage of ancient Egypt, which, as will be remembered, was accustomed to a god-king. First, however, it was necessary to restore the agricultural system to prosperity.

An extensive program for the improvement of irrigation and cultivation was put in hand for the benefit of both ruler and sub-

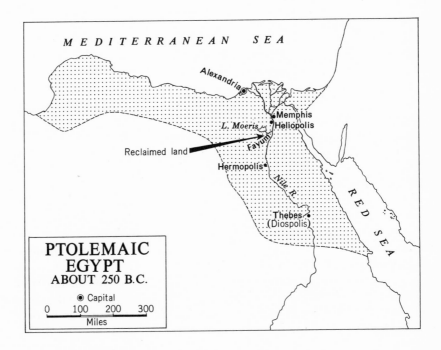

MEDITERRANEAN    SEA

Alexandria

Memphis
L. Moeris    Heliopolis
Reclaimed land    Fayum

Hermopolis

Nile R.

RED SEA

Thebes
(Diospolis)

**PTOLEMAIC
EGYPT**
ABOUT 250 B.C.

⊙ Capital

0    100    200    300

Miles

jects. Most of the best soil in the country was farmed as the Pharaoh's personal estate through royal appointees or by tenants of the crown, who were not permitted to leave their land and had to supply services and produce in exchange for the right to farm and for seed. In the reigns of the earlier Ptolemies this did not bear too hard on the tenants, but later the taxes and exactions were raised so high that it was almost impossible to make a living. Moreover, each village was collectively responsible for the taxes and had to make up any deficit on the part of individual tenants. Though we hear of several strikes and attempts to leave the land, the police and the military system were in every case strong enough to suppress them and enforce obedience. The lands let out by the Pharaoh, including temple lands, were farmed in the same way. Loyal soldiers, generals, nobles, and other favorites were sometimes freed of all taxes and allowed to exploit their tenants so long as they kept the land in good condition in case the king-god should have need of it himself. This was one of the methods used for pensioning soldiers and ensuring a new supply when required.

The Ptolemies also maintained a tight monopoly of all industry. Either directly or indirectly through concessionaires, usually Greeks, and carefully supervised by the state, all important businesses were under royal control, with gangs of inspectors checking to see that the established price was maintained. Even retailing was controlled, with the individual retailer buying the right to sell at a fixed rate of profit. The crown also subsidized voyages and exploration, and transportation was a royal monopoly. Directly or indirectly the Pharaoh had his hand in everything; his subjects were allowed to make a living, but only by his permission and under his control. Though there were organizations of workers, these were mostly for social and religious purposes, and not for the purpose of coercing their rulers. The theory of ancient Egypt was now put into thorough practical operation as it probably had never been, even in ancient times, under the efficient management and with all the necessary police control

of a dynasty descended from a Macedonian general who had once more appeared as a god on earth.

## ► The Hellenistic Age in Asia—Pergamum and the Seleucid Empire

On the conditions in Asia we have less information. One important part of Asia, northwest Asia Minor, was separated from the Seleucid Empire very early and became an important and very prosperous small kingdom, the kingdom of Pergamum, more urban than the other Hellenistic kingdoms, and better situated for maritime trade, with royal monopolies in the key industries and private enterprise in the others. This was almost a model small kingdom under the Attalids, who were great builders and patrons of art. Many of the finest specimens of Hellenistic art and architecture come from Pergamum. The whole kingdom was bequeathed to Rome by the last of the Attalids, as we shall see.

Central control in the Seleucid Empire was far less effective than in Egypt, for the rulers had continuously to fight with pretenders to their throne, with military adventurers, and, by the second century B.C., with the Romans. Their kingdom increased and decreased in size according to the fortunes of war. The old kingdom of Persia was largely worked by royal serfs, and temple lands were added to the royal property. The kings also made it a policy to dispossess nobles when possible. The Seleucid monarchs established royal monopolies in several industries, but private enterprise in industry was far more widespread than in Egypt, owing to the difficulty of central control in such a vast country. The royal post roads and the postal system of the Persians were expanded and improved, and for the first time many of the Asiatic rivers were made navigable; fleets of ships under royal protection and supervision carried the products of industry over long distances in shorter time than before.

Most of this system in the western part of Asia was taken over intact by the Romans. Internally, as in the Persian days, the area was usually at peace; the warring armies of

*Ruins of the temple of Zeus at Pergamum as they appear at the present time. The size of the ruins will give some indication of the scale of the work of the Hellenistic monarchs of this commercial state.* (COURTESY TURKISH INFORMATION OFFICE)

the monarchs did not affect the ordinary life of peasant and trader. Ships regularly plied the seas and rivers all the way from Persia to Italy, some armed with catapults against enemies and pirates. There was already substantial peace in this part of the world before Rome, with fanfare of trumpets, established a Pax Romana.

▶ **Hellenistic culture**

GENERAL CHARACTERISTICS—COSMOPOLITANISM AND INDIVIDUALISM

The cosmopolitanism of the Hellenistic world is the dominant characteristic of all Greek thought and society during this period. We have seen the rise of individualism in the fourth century, B.C., and how this tended to break down the old, close-knit social organization of the polis. Although the polis was now transferred to new surroundings and many formal elements of self-government were retained, the self-determination of the state was irretrievably lost, and with it community duties and responsibilities. In fifth-century Athens a citizen was content to live in a humble house on a tiny income because he valued participation in the social life of the community more than individual wealth and "self-expression"; his religion was part of the life of the community rather than a means of individual comfort, much less salvation. His art and his architecture were expressions of his love for his city and were the result of great communal efforts. When the polis life disintegrated, everything the earlier Greek had valued disappeared with it. The transition was, as we have seen, gradual through the fourth century. The conquests of Alexander only put the seal on the already accomplished fact.

It is useless to try to discover whether

individualism was the cause or the effect of the social breakdown. Both were always present at the same time. And, since there no longer was a community, it became necessary for each man to take care of himself, whether he liked it or not. A great temple of Zeus built by a monarch was not his, and he felt no civic pride in it. But he could still feel pride in a piece of fine craftsmanship of his own making. He could hope to get rich by struggling, necessarily to some degree at the expense of his neighbor and fellow citizen. If he were wealthy, he could take advantage of the good things, the luxuries offered by this cosmopolitan civilization. He could be entertained in the theater by amusing slices of life, seeing other people fighting to reach the top like himself; he could read books of an entertaining nature, not the kind to make him think, but worth reading to keep himself from contemplating the fact that something was missing in life that his ancestors had known, some secret of happiness withheld from him. Or, if he were a scholar, he could try to discover what it had been that these ancestors had had, he could diligently peruse their works, editing them with fine fidelity, taking care to catch the exact wording of the original, and write ponderous histories about them. If he were practical he could try to increase the sum of useful knowledge instead of speculating about things that could never be known. Or, finally, he could decide that life was not worth living anyway, with this vacuum at the heart of things, and so he could turn to the Persian religions or the religions of the mysteries, or he could become a Stoic philosopher.

All these different manifestations of individualism we find in the Hellenistic world; it only seems to have needed the Industrial Revolution, which was already well on the way with the latest technical developments of the Greek scientists, to transform it into our own society. But the creativity of the early Hellenistic civilization gradually spent itself for reasons which still elude the investigator. There was too much revolt perhaps against the relatively new individualism, too little real interest in the workings of the material world, too much respect for nature to wish to interfere with it for the satisfaction of the material needs of human beings. Too recently had these peoples emerged from the belief that they were powerless against the gods for them to be able to take the whole step of usurping the position of the gods without drawing upon themselves *ate* and *nemesis*. They had to go through a long apprenticeship before they could come to believe that man was the lord of creation, and that only the individual human being and his welfare on earth counted in all creation, and explain satisfactorily to themselves that this indeed was the intention of the gods. In the Hellenistic Age they lacked the compelling assurance of the value of this life for the individual man that proved to be the great strength of Western civilization in its struggle to understand and control nature; and so when the new religions promised salvation in the next world after a period of trial and testing in this, their teachings fell on willing ears. When Bishop Theophilus in A.D. 390 destroyed the bulk of the library of Alexandria, the greatest collection of Greek books ever assembled, he was only symbolizing a choice that had been made centuries earlier in the Hellenistic Age.

PHILOSOPHIES OF DOUBT AND PESSIMISM

### The Cynics

The thought of the Hellenistic Age is in strong contrast with that of earlier days. The Academy of Plato and the Lyceum of Aristotle continued their work, the latter patiently assembling more facts and writing histories of special fields, the former moving at first into some of the more mystical aspects of Platonism and then into Skepticism. But the original philosophies of this age were more directly influenced by the new social experience of individualism and cosmopolitanism.

The earliest of these was Cynicism, founded by Antisthenes; its most notorious early member was the famous Diogenes, who lived in a tub and cultivated rudeness and self-sufficiency. Though it arose out of the discontents of the fourth century before the conquests of Alexander, the germ of developed Stoicism is already to be found in this philosophy. Everything in society, said the Cynics, is foolishness; nothing in life is worth having. What men pursue is not worth the trouble; whether you are rich or poor, Greek or barbarian, is of no importance to the wise man. Only the wise man can appreciate the uselessness of possessions. He alone can be self-sufficing, and his own thought and character are all that count. He can think and he can be moral only if he is completely indifferent to possessions. The wise men in the world form a world community, a city of the world, as Diogenes called it, based on contempt for everyone and everything.

The Cynics did not form an organized school of philosophy but became wandering beggars and preachers, often cultivating uncouthness and rudeness in order to show their superiority to all conventions. The only positive action that the wise man would take would be what his personal sense of duty dictated, for he was bound by no social convention nor by any other of man's inventions for leading people away from the philosophic life. The equality in Cynicism, the world-city of wise men, and the cultivated indifference to worldly things were all to be found later transformed in Stoicism; therein lies its only permanent importance, for the philosophy was obviously not designed to attract a numerous following.

## Epicurism

The philosophy of Epicurism was founded by Epicurus, who began to teach in Athens about 306 B.C. Though Epicurus took over the atomistic science of Democritus, the core of his teaching was his insistence on indifference (*ataraxia*—literally the condition of not being shaken). "Be happy with little, for being interested in, and needing, much, brings unhappiness." The goal of men is the attainment of happiness. But for Epicurus and his disciples happiness consisted primarily in freedom from physical pain, worldly cares, and fears. Since congenial friendship was one of those pleasures

which can be obtained with the least difficulty, the early Epicureans especially cultivated it, living a simple life and discoursing on philosophy in the famous "Garden of Epicurus."

In Epicurean thought everything was subservient to the pursuit of happiness. It was better to cultivate the virtues than the vices because the latter usually involved pain—which should be avoided. But there was no need to cultivate virtue too assiduously, since this would lead to self-denial—which was unnecessary and prevented enjoyment. In general the philosophy in its original form was more negative than positive—a tired man's travesty of Aristotle's Golden Mean—and a mild asceticism was the usual practice of the personal followers of Epicurus.

In order to justify such a worldly philosophy the gods were relegated to a far-off sphere, primarily to provide man with an example of how to live perfectly. They paid no attention whatever to man, and all religion was simply superstition. Astrology, divination, and other outgrowths of religion were the result of man's ignorance. The truth was, according to Epicurus, that we live in a purely material world of atoms in constant motion, and the whole world has come into existence by chance and not by divine decree. It is not known whether Epicurus himself, or his Roman disciple Lucretius, introduced the famous "swerve" of the atoms so that they would move from their regular perpendicular downward path and strike each other; at all events this swerve was also fortuitous in the atoms, though its occurrence made free will possible in human beings.

The philosophy of happiness, although with Epicurus it led to a gentle asceticism, in later times, especially in Rome, became a simple philosophy of hedonism, or the pursuit of pleasure, even of the grosser varieties —likely to lead to pain. The same lack of interest in social responsibilities was maintained, and the same indifference to worldly success; but happiness was considered to be attained best by enjoyment of all that the

The Stoic philosophers were so called because they congregated in the great stoas of Athens to discuss philosophy. One of these stoas is at present being restored by the American School of Classical Studies in cooperation with the Greek government. This picture shows a corner of the restored stoa, originally built by King Attalus II of Pergamum about 150 B.C., and gives an impression of these long porches frequented not only by the Stoics but by earlier philosophers such as Socrates. The size of such a stoa can be gauged from the reconstruction of the whole Agora shown in Chapter 7. (COURTESY AMERICAN SCHOOL OF CLASSICAL STUDIES AT ATHENS)

world offered, even to excess, rather than by the moderate enjoyment of Epicurus, and the consequent lack of the penalties of excess.

### Stoicism

Stoicism was unquestionably the greatest philosophy of this age, and in its many aspects went far toward answering the difficult problems arising out of the new social experience. It was a philosophy that continually grew in scope as the centuries passed; much of it was woven into the fabric of Christian philosophy and ethics, and much also into Roman law. As a philosophy it was still vital in the last centuries of the Roman Empire, and at times it provided the only moral anchor for those who could not accept the salvationist religions, and yet would not lapse into the negative or hedonistic indifference of Epicurism, or complete Skepticism. Its founder, Zeno of Citium, supposedly a "Phoenician," founded a school at Athens about 300 B.C., but Stoicism was never centered on a single school, and never held deep roots in old Greece. It was from the beginning Hellenistic rather than Hellenic. Zeno, like the Cynics, his forebears, taught that there is only one world-state, with all men equal in it, united by no race or class but only by virtue—as with the Cynics, a world of wise men united by their wisdom. We know very little about Zeno himself beyond his teaching on the ideal state, for his writings have not survived. Indeed, most of our knowledge of the Stoics comes from Roman sources.

Chrysippus, a Cilician who taught at Athens some seventy years after Zeno, is regarded as the second founder of Stoicism. He it was who gave it its systematic theology and its ethics. The purpose of Stoicism, as with Epicurism, is to give man individual well-being and self-sufficiency. It is therefore primarily a philosophy of *this* life. Throughout the history of Stoicism there are many who interpret the ideal of self-sufficiency as justification for the withdrawal from life, including even suicide in certain circumstances. But Chrysippus taught resolution, fortitude, and devotion to duty, combined with indifference to all temptations of ordinary earthly pleasure and enjoyment. Every man on earth has his part to play, assigned by Divine Providence, and this he must seek to play with dignity, answering only to his own conscience for his lapses from rectitude. The world order is created by God and it is working for good; the wise man should understand the goodness and seek to work in accordance with the divine plan. Not only man, but the animal kingdom, is part of this great world order, and animals also have their part to play. But man is different because he has reason; and reason is an attribute of God. Hence the world order is reasonable, and it is man's duty to discover this Divine Reason as far as he can, and try to make his human laws approximate to it. Therefore above the laws of any earthly state are the divine laws, or what is henceforward to be called Natural Law. Every man possessed of reason is equal to every other man; there are no natural inequalities. A slave is a "laborer hired for life," and should be treated accordingly, not as a subhuman implement.

This dogmatic teaching, so much at variance with earlier Greek rationalism, laid itself open to practical criticism, which it received primarily from Carneades, the Skeptic who devoted the greater part of his life to attacks on Chrysippus. The chief ground for criticism was that the wise man indifferent to things of the world, inhuman in his attempts to get rid of all natural feeling, could be found nowhere in nature. And Carneades complained that there was no evidence for divine justice whatever, and there could be no agreement even between reasonable human beings on what justice is. On the contrary, Carneades insisted that on the evidence man is governed by self-interest only; and it is nothing but fear of the consequences that prevents him from pursuing his own interests altogether without regard for others. He disagreed that this could be called justice. This and other criticisms led Panaetius of Rhodes to modify the early Stoicism into the philosophy of the so-called Middle Stoa, restating it in a form palatable to the Romans, among whom Stoicism was now finding most of its adherents. The Romans were imperialists; and the Stoic idea of a world-state, the old Stoic virtues of devotion to duty and public spirit, and the idea of natural law were able to appeal to them, once Panaetius had brought the philosophy down to earth by eliminating the superhuman wise man, and replacing the asceticism by public service and humanity. But this aspect of Stoicism in the Roman world will be briefly discussed in a later chapter.

In the East, Stoicism became more religious in tone, with Divine Reason being exalted almost to the status of a God. Cleanthes in his famous *Hymn* petitions this one universal God not for anything worldly but for a virtuous mind. The traditional gods were also absorbed into the Stoic system as attendants upon the Divine Reason, even astrology and magic finding their home in it. But in whatever form it appeared, and whatever religion it influenced, always the central ethic remained—be indifferent to worldly success and strive to cultivate the moral life, for man's first duty is to fulfill the demands of his moral nature. Externals can never be worth anything in comparison with the self-sufficiency of the consciously upright man. This was clearly a thought to which all religions that stress morality could be hospitable.

### The Skeptics

The Skeptical school was founded by Pyrrho as early as the end of the fourth century B.C. We know little of the founder beyond the fact that he seems to have been the first to make criticism of other theories the goal of his philosophy, denying that knowledge was possible. All sense perceptions are illusions, and against every statement that can be made an opposite is equally probable. The wise man therefore will make the best of the world of illusion, and by suspending all judgment not strive after the impossible, but take the world as he finds it. Later Skeptics continued to emphasize criticism, which in a world of superstition and dogmatism was necessary enough; and their work was on the whole salutary, as we have seen from its effect on Stoicism. But Skepticism as a philosophy made little impression on the less rational philosophies and religions. It was too austere to command much general success, though for a while its spirit dominated, of all places, the Platonic Academy at Athens. A philosophy without positive content can be a valuable tool for the reform of others, but in a religious age even the indifference which Skepticism preached found more arguments in its support within other philosophies than Skepticism alone could offer.

THE RELIGIOUS VACUUM—MYSTERY RELIGIONS

In philosophy Greek thought still predominated, but Greek religion of the Classical Age was so closely associated with the polis that it could not be expected to survive in the Hellenistic world. The religious vacuum was filled by the mystical Oriental religions; and the mystery religions of old Greece, which themselves had developed out of an earlier Oriental tradition, received a new lease on life. The more intellectual upper-class Greek probably despised the new "barbarian" religions, and many of them took refuge in atheism and skepticism, or in the Greek philosophies. The goddess Tyche or

chance, which indeed seemed to rule Hellenistic life, was widely worshiped, and astrology from the Chaldeans was both believed in as a science and used as the basis for a kind of star worship. On the whole, even when the Greeks accepted the Oriental religions they were inclined to make the gods abstract, representing universal principles rather than the *persons* they were to their Oriental adherents. The Stoic god, for instance, was never a person, which has led students to characterize the philosophy as pantheism. For the Greeks there were divine persons, but they did not fulfill the functions of Oriental gods. The Greeks had no objection to deifying kings, especially after they were dead. It was even explained in the Hellenistic Age that this was what had happened to the Olympian gods: they were ancient kings who died and had been deified (Euhemerism).

A more extended discussion of the Hellenistic mystery religions of this time will be deferred to Chapter 12, when they will be considered as part of the background for Christianity.

SCIENCE

### Growth of exact science and scholarship —The Museum of Alexandria

The classical polis had never been an especially good soil for the development of exact science. There had been much speculation, as we have seen, and there had been a significant development of mathematics, largely as a by-product of philosophy. But the practical sciences did not come into their own until the Hellenistic Age, when the professional scholar who devoted all his time to his study first became socially respectable. The earlier Greeks had abhorred professionalism of all kinds as likely to detract from social usefulness and ability to participate in political life. In the fourth century there had been an increase in professionalism especially in the army and in public life; but in the Hellenistic kingdoms the pure scholar was for the first time fully appreciated. The patronage of the wealthy monarchs often enabled scholars to spend their lives in one activity without the distraction of political life. Alexandria with its famous Museum was the chief center of study, and all the Ptolemies gave their support to this great headquarters of research. Its four departments of literature, mathematics, astronomy, and medicine were both research centers and schools, with a library of four hundred thousand books to support them which later increased to an estimated seven hundred thousand.

In the Hellenistic world facts could now for the first time be systematically collected, and the bases thus laid firmly for correct deductions and even experimentation. Archimedes of Syracuse in the third century B.C. even made use of the scientific method, the combination of induction and deduction which has been found acceptable in modern times, though it was neglected for nearly two thousand years after him. The scientists, however, being Greek, were more interested in theory than in practice, and several inventions that might have been greatly developed in other hands were regarded as ingenious toys and of far less importance than the theory which led to their construction. But the addition to knowledge in these years was nevertheless considerable.

### Astronomy—Influence of Babylonia— Heracleides, Aristarchus, Hipparchus

The most notable advances were made in astronomy.[5] Here the Greeks had the enormous stimulus of contact with the Chaldean astronomy and astrology which had hitherto been almost unknown to them. The observations of Chaldean and Babylonian astronomers had been carefully recorded for hundreds of years, and formed a basis for theoretical work by the Greeks, just as Tycho Brahe's observations in the sixteenth century laid the basis for Kepler's theories. The significant advances in geography due to the voyages financed by the Hellenistic rulers also led to new conceptions of the move-

ment of the earth and the planets. Only a brief note on the many achievements of the Hellenistic scientists can be attempted here.

About 350 B.C. Heracleides of Pontus propounded the theory that while the sun and outer planets move round the earth, Venus and Mercury move round the sun. Aristarchus of Samos about a hundred years later, on the basis of his observation of eclipses of the moon, came to the conclusion with the aid of geometry, that the sun is much larger than the earth. Although we do not know on what arguments he based his theory, Aristarchus also concluded that "the earth moves round the sun on the circumference of a circle, the sun lying at the center of the orbit."

To make this point of view, so obviously contrary to common sense, possible, Aristarchus was forced to assume that the fixed stars were enormous distances from the earth. The theory, according to Plutarch, was found acceptable only by Seleucus of Babylon a century later, who tried to prove it and failed. Other astronomers preferred the view of common sense and appearances, in spite of its obvious difficulties of which they were not unaware. By Aristarchus' scheme it was impossible to predict any celestial events, and there was as yet no telescope to show similar movements of the satellites of Jupiter which were later to convince Galileo of the truth of the theory of Copernicus. If Aristarchus had been willing to abandon circular movement he might have convinced his fellow astronomers. These Greeks were not wedded to the geocentric theory from religious, but for scientific reasons.

Hipparchus of Nicaea, who worked in Alexandria most of his life, finally cleared up the difficulties of the geocentric theory insofar as they presented themselves at the time. He propounded a theory of epicycles, minor orbits of the heavenly bodies which combined with the major orbit or cycle around the earth. This accounted satisfactorily for all the phenomena, and he was able to establish tables which predicted fairly accurately future eclipses of the sun and moon. Hipparchus also invented several

---

[5] Not all the work described below was done at Alexandria; but it seems more convenient to classify by subject than by the place of the research.

astronomical instruments, used the Mesopotamian division of the circle into 360 degrees, and discovered (or possibly restated the Chaldean discovery of) the precession of the equinoxes, though his estimate was slightly at fault. He made a very nearly accurate estimate of the size of the moon and its distance from the earth. Since he also invented both sphere and plane trigonometry he can be regarded as the greatest astronomer and one of the greatest mathematicians of antiquity. His work was summed up by Claudius Ptolemy and improved in some respects in the Christian Era. Ptolemy wrote several important works of synthesis which provided the Muslims and medieval Christians with the bulk of their knowledge of Alexandrian science.

### Mathematics—Euclid, Archimedes

In geometry, of course, the great name is Euclid, who collected all the work of his predecessors in this predominantly Greek science, and added many propositions of his own. His work has never needed revision insofar as it defines the qualities of a certain kind of space (three-dimensional), though later mathematicians have found that other kinds of space are also possible, in which case Euclid's geometry does not apply.

Archimedes of Syracuse was not only a creative geometer, but made extensive use of geometrical principles and the deductive method in his other work. The idea of specific gravity he discovered while in his bath, when he noticed that he displaced water equal in volume to his body; he then proceeded to deduce it mathematically. He also considered the lever, which in practice had been used for millennia before him, and deduced mathematically from self-evident axioms why it must behave as it does. This, however, was not a new discovery, but was due to the straightforward use of the syllogism, or the combining of two different pieces of known or evident information to demonstrate a new conclusion. In the field of pure geometry Archimedes discovered the ratio of the volume of the cylinder to that of the sphere inscribed in it, and this he

characteristically regarded as his chief claim to fame, and had it recorded on his tombstone. He was, however, also responsible for many ingenious inventions: pulleys, hydraulic screws, and various engines of warfare, which he did not regard as important, though his science was able to keep the Romans from capturing Syracuse for three years.

Apollonius of Perga, by geometrical means, put the study of cones on a sound basis, giving the well-known Greek names to the various sections—hyperbola, parabola and ellipse.

### Geography—Eratosthenes

Allied to geometry and astronomy was geography which, as has been said, supplied information to the theoretical sciences. The most famous of the geographers, Eratosthenes, was librarian of the Alexandrian museum for many years. He calculated the diameter of the earth, which he regarded as a sphere, with a comparatively small error, and he estimated the distance to the sun with an error of only 1 per cent. He also produced an improved map with lines of latitude and longitude. He made it clear that the known world of three continents was a great island, and suggested that India could be reached by sailing west. His latitudes and longitudes were corrected by Hipparchus.

### Medicine—Herophilus, Erasistratus

In the field of medicine at Alexandria Herophilus was the first to undertake human dissection for the purpose of discovering the facts of anatomy, making several important discoveries, as might be expected. He corrected the erroneous conception, among others, that the arteries were filled with air. For the most part his work was simply descriptive. His pupil Erasistratus continued his work, and is regarded as the founder of physiology; his many suggestions on the functions of the various organs and the damage done to them by certain diseases entitle him to this honor. On the basis of his findings he deplored excessive bleeding and preferred diet and regimen as suggested by the earlier school of Hippocrates. Later

Greek medicine, however, did not follow these promising lines, but turned more to therapy on the basis of the usual trial and error, though a number of new drugs were added to the pharmacopoeia.

ART

### Architecture—The beginning of the cult of magnificence

In accordance with the tendencies observed elsewhere in the Hellenistic Age the architecture of this period turned from temples to palaces, theaters, libraries, and private homes, which were now far more elaborate than had been considered suitable in the classical period. Temples were still

*The temple of Zeus at Içel in Asia Minor. Note the ornate Corinthian columns of this temple of the Hellenistic period.* (COURTESY TURKISH INFORMATION OFFICE)

*When the ruins of Pergamum were excavated, the altar of Zeus from the temple was carried away by the Germans, who restored it. This picture shows the restoration, which is located in Berlin.*

built, some of very great size. Probably, like the great altar of Zeus at Pergamum, a commemoration of Pergamene victories over the barbarian Gauls, they were regarded less as an honor to the gods than a symbol of the power and success of their builders. Certainly they were not built by voluntary co-operation. The result was that for beauty and harmony there was nothing in the Hellenistic Age in any way comparable to the Parthenon, though technical skill and design were not lacking. The architecture of the Hellenistic Age is a herald of the Roman taste for magnificence rather than a continuation of the classical, though Greek artistry, especially in Pergamum, still succeeded in producing far more balance and harmony than Rome ever attained. The most notable structure in the Hellenistic world, characteristically, was the famous Pharos or lighthouse of Alexandria, a storied building rising to four hundred feet, with eight columns supporting the light at the summit. The Corinthian column, as already remarked, came into vogue at this time, though it was not yet as popular as it became in Rome. Many buildings have combinations of the three orders, though Ionic was still probably the most prevalent, with some Hellenistic modification.

### Sculpture—Realism, contrast with classical sculpture

By far the greatest number of Greek sculptures known to us belong to the Hellenistic rather than to the earlier period. It is possible to prefer these to the classical, if one prefers realism to idealism. The character of the person sculptured now comes to the fore, the muscles are less smooth and rhythmic, and closer to our own experience of human bodies. There is much experimentation visible, and much striving after effect; often there are thoroughly dramatic pieces which the classical artist would have scorned. We have a dying Gaul with blood flowing, and we have a fallen giant from a frieze in Pergamum who expresses a pathos that the sculptor has truly imagined.

What is missing in Hellenistic sculpture

is a sense of the intimate relationship between soul and body; and there is a lack of balance and harmony which is compensated by individual disharmonies realistically portrayed. Both, in a sense, are true art. The aims and perceptions of the two ages are different, and we can condemn the one as decadent and praise the other as "perfect" only by making a subjective judgment on these aims and perceptions. There was certainly no loss of technical ability in the later age; on the contrary, it is very doubtful if so perfectly executed a statue as the Nike of Samothrace, with its "Winged Victory" alighting on the prow of a ship could have been produced by any sculptor of the time

*Hellenistic realism. This statue of an old market woman, discovered at Rome, dates from the second century B.C. and was perhaps looted from Greece by the Romans.* (COURTESY THE METROPOLITAN MUSEUM OF ART)

*Opinion has varied remarkably at different times on the merits of the Laocoön, a late Hellenistic group showing the priest Laocoön and his two sons grappling with snakes. The impression of strain and power has appealed to many as one of the finest expressions of Hellenistic realism, while others have found the whole composition theatrical and forced and, from the Greek point of view, "bad art."*

of Phidias. But again the observation is meaningless, for the earlier sculptor would not have thought of it and could not have experienced it. The suggestion of motion, so wonderfully portrayed in the Nike, would no more have appealed to Phidias as an effect worth realizing in sculpture than it would to an Egyptian of any age.

There was a great growth of portrait sculpture for private purposes in the Hellenistic Age, and evidently a great commercial demand for it. The realistic sculpture of the

*Bronze figure of Eros (god of love) sleeping; third to second century B.C.* (COURTESY THE METROPOLITAN MUSEUM OF ART)

*Goddess Aphrodite of Hellenistic period discovered at Smyrna. The statue was broken when found, but most of the parts were retrieved and assembled as shown here.* (COURTESY TURKISH INFORMATION OFFICE)

*The Nike (Victory) of Samothrace, a statue (now in the Louvre) in the form of the prow of a ship. Note how the Nike suggests speed and movement, unlike the static figures of the Parthenon.* (COURTESY THE LOUVRE)

The Aphrodite of Melos (so called because the statue was discovered on the island of Melos) is widely regarded as the finest statue of a woman ever made. The artist is unknown, but the figure probably dates from the second century B.C. No photograph can do justice to this masterpiece. Located in the Louvre, it is displayed to perfection—especially at night, when it is most effectively lighted. (COURTESY THE LOUVRE)

*Portrait head of a man, late Hellenistic period (second to first century B.C.).* (COURTESY THE METROPOLITAN MUSEUM OF ART)

an earthquake in the first century A.D., was largely a Greek city, we cannot safely infer from its remains much about the earlier Hellenistic painting. Only the cameos, a new art developed in Alexandria, are known to us, and mosaics for walls and floors, most of which, however, were made out of naturally colored stones. We probably know enough about the painting to say that it was more distinctly Greco-Oriental than the predominantly Greek sculpture and architecture of the time. Mosaics in particular were usually made in Egypt and Syria by native workmen.

## LITERATURE

### Growth of literary scholarship

The entire later world is very greatly in debt to the learned Alexandrians who were the chief instrument in the preservation of the classical heritage. The important scholarly science of philology had its beginnings here. In classical Greece, books were something of a rarity. But an enormous demand grew up in Alexandria and elsewhere for books of all kinds and on all sorts of subjects —mostly entertainment, but also serious and learned literature. The scholarly Alexandrians, without accurate knowledge even of the dates when their masters had lived, invented a system for dating them which to us seems fantastic. They assumed that a writer's greatest period of production was around the age of forty; on this basis they assigned the birth and death dates which passed into later tradition and are still in use. They were meticulously careful in the copying and editing of manuscripts; and much of their work in this field was invaluable to us, though we have now no means of checking their accuracy. These men were subsidized by the Hellenistic rulers, who were proud of "their" ancestral heritage, and we owe them also a debt, especially for the library of the Museum of Alexandria, which was a hive of industry for many centuries.

day was of course alone suitable for this— no one wanted an ideal figure in the home. Sculptured portraits could be turned out in the later years of the period according to a more or less simple pattern, and the technique of making them became fixed. The result, especially with the Romans as patrons, who in their expansive days could hardly tell good sculpture from bad, was the degeneration of sculpture into a pure business activity. And though fine pieces, showing technical mastery if not inspiration, were still turned out, they seem to have declined in number, probably owing to the parallel decline of taste. Roman art had many virtues, but few would care to suggest that the requirements of the Roman bourgeois or noble patron of art would be likely to promote a renaissance.

### Painting—The cameo, mosaics

Almost no Hellenistic painting has survived; and though Pompeii, destroyed by

### Popular literature

In the Hellenistic Age the upper classes

really had time to read, including upper-class women who knew far more freedom and education than women had enjoyed in earlier days. Apparently the upper classes also had the desire to write. No fewer than eleven thousand names of writers are known to us, and there must have been thousands more. While in classical days reading was subordinate to the perhaps more liberal education through educated talk and discussion and the development of mind and body, now that this earlier ideal associated with the polis was no longer relevant, the hours were whiled away with books, produced by slaves and low-paid freemen who copied manuscripts for the market. Biography was popular, romantic and realistic, with a tincture of polite moralizing; legends of gods and heroes were turned out by the hundreds, frequently emphasizing the misfortunes of human women mated to gods. There was a great vogue for sentimental and pastoral stories and poems about shepherdesses and the like, and, as more solid fare, a new crop of utopias suitable for such improbable creatures to dwell in. Some of this great bulk of material was both imaginative and attractive, though, as far as we can tell, a considerable majority was not intended to do more than help the reader pass the idle hour with some enjoyment.

There is no great literature, or at all events no literature that we consider great. The supreme works of the earlier Classical Age have appealed to all ages since and many are by common consent looked upon as unequaled of their kind. Nothing of this stature appears in the Hellenistic Age, perhaps because it was the political and cultural conditions of the polis that could alone, for the Greek, call forth the deep and passionate involvement that is the hallmark of the greatest literature. It is certain that such a writer as Thucydides would not have flourished in Alexandria, nor could the tragedy or the Old Comedy of Athens have grown out of such soil. Euripides was still appreciated and admired in Athens, but probably for the reason that he put ordinary people on the stage; as Nietzsche pointed out, it

would not have required much change to make Euripides into a writer of comedy. Had he chosen different characters and less pathetic plots, he would have written those amusing and realistic slices of life that the Athenians regarded as comedy.

### New Comedy of Athens

Athenian New Comedy, as represented primarily by Menander, is concerned directly with the life lived in the Athens of his day. It was never transplanted to Alexandria or elsewhere in the Hellenistic world. Naturally Menander does not use the gods as Euripides uses them; he is not interested in the Euripidean quest for a lost certainty. But he gives us the lineal descendant of the *deus ex machina* who comes in at the end of a Euripidean tragedy to straighten out a situation that has got beyond control—Menander gives us the happy ending, usually a happy marriage. His themes are the sorrows and joys of romantic love, intrigues, recognitions, and other devices from the old drama, but all now on the everyday level. He created human types which became stock figures of all later comedy, the old seducer, the clever slave, the boastful soldier, and so on. Menander himself was far greater, however, than any of his Roman and later imitators, as far as we can judge from the many fragments that remain. And, of course, his comedy is valuable for the insight it affords into one section of Athenian society, as again most good comedy has continued to do since his day.

### Pastoral poetry and the literature of escape

Most of the Hellenistic poetry comes from Alexandria, where learned scholars studied meters and forms of earlier poetry, and then tried to do their best with their limited poetical equipment. The result is often interesting as storytelling, though feeble enough as poetry. And it is difficult to be enthusiastic about the passions of these erudite lovers if one is unkind enough to look back for one moment to any of the extant lyrics of, say, Sappho or Alcaeus. But fortunately these scholars were also interested in the great lyricists of the past, if only enough to try to imitate them; and it is often from their quotations alone that, ironically, we know their elders and betters. Apollonius of Rhodes revived the long epic, and in his *Argonautica* he has given us in detail, ample detail, the story of the Golden Fleece. There are some romantic passages, especially the story of Jason and Medea (the original models for Vergil's Dido and Aeneas), which approach poetry, and have been considered superior to the Vergilian counterpart.

The pastorals of Theocritus, not an Alexandrian but a Sicilian, belong to a form of poetry which excites the most varied reactions among readers and critics. One either likes it or dislikes it, usually beyond reason. There can be no doubt at all that Theocritus, the inventor of this form of poetry, is far better than any of his imitators; and it is hard to see how these exquisite idylls could be improved or surpassed. They are not pedantic, but quite natural. But their progeny in later ages has killed the appreciation for them in many people. One thinks of the fashionable eighteenth-century French gentleman grinding out between breakfast and lunch a piece about shepherdesses and their loves and the pipes of Pan, then adjusting his periwig and going out to recite it at Madame's salon. But such a picture is not at all fair to Theocritus and in particular to his really perceptive impressions of natural beauty, while the French gentleman would not even have a nodding acquaintance with a cow. Theocritus also wrote short epics, some of which show again a genuine natural feeling; and he wrote more realistic mimes, designed to be read at the *soirées* of the time. These, in the hands of Theocritus, present a section of life unfamiliar to the scholars of Alexandria, and are sketched with great perceptiveness. Incidentally, Theocritus was the only poet after Homer who had any real success with the Greek hexameter.

There was little serious prosewriting, as far as we know, in the Hellenistic world except in scholarly or semischolarly fields; and almost nothing of it has survived. But there was one great Greek historian, Polybius, probably the greatest after Thucydides —though his style is rather dull and not to be compared with that of his great master, who, though involved and difficult in places and occasionally striving too deliberately for effect, often rose to heights of unmatched eloquence. But Polybius wrote almost exclusively of Rome, and during his stay as a hostage in Rome. A brief mention of his work appears in Chapter 12.

▶ **Transition to the Roman world— Hellenistic "conquest" of Rome**

There is, as has already been suggested, no definite break between the civilization of the Hellenistic world and the Roman civilization that followed it. The Romans, while developing their characteristic institutions of law and government in Italy and the West, were from the first dependent upon the Greeks for almost every other branch of culture. It was contact with the Greek cities of southern Italy that inspired their first poetry and their first art; and the Greeks gave them their first taste of philosophy and literature—even though it was long before they could comprehend it. In a very real sense Rome was simply a cultural colonization by the Greeks, the last important western center to be added to their cultural empire. So when the Romans conquered the Hellenistic civilization by force they were only inheriting the task that Macedonia had undertaken earlier. Nevertheless, they did have a distinctive Latin language which differs in many important respects from the Greek language, and this they did impose upon the Greeks as a necessity in the sphere of law and government.

But the Greek language and Hellenistic civilization were deep rooted and so far ahead of anything the Romans had to offer that the Hellenistic world remained predominantly Greek. In dealing, therefore, with Rome we shall stress primarily its original contributions in law and government, and the political history and social experience that gave rise to these contributions. And when we come to Roman culture, the reader should always remember the civilization which molded it, and examine the new fusion in the same sense in which we have in this chapter studied the Greco-Oriental fusion which composed the Hellenistic world.

## ▶ Suggestions for further reading

The speeches of Demosthenes, especially the *Philippics,* the *Olynthiacs,* and the speech *On the Crown,* should certainly be read, if only to make the inevitable comparisons with the speeches of Winston Churchill during the 1930's. Some of the speeches of Aeschines, especially the *Against Ctesiphon,* and Isocrates' *Letter to Philip* should also be read. They may be found most conveniently in the Loeb Series. Still perhaps the best secondary account of the last years of Greek independence is A. W. Pickard-Cambridge, *Demosthenes and the Last Days of Greek Freedom* (New York: G. P. Putnam's Sons, 1914).

On the conquests of Alexander, Plutarch's Life of Alexander is worth reading, in spite of the invariable moralist's bias in this author's work. But the best primary source is Arrian, whose work is to be found in F. R. B. Godolphin, ed., *The Greek Historians* (New York: Random House, 1942). Biographies of Alexander are numerous. Most of them, if not all, are to a greater or lesser degree marred by the particular prejudices of their authors. This is natural in the case of such a romantic figure about whose inner thought we really know almost nothing. C. A. Robinson, Jr., *Alexander the Great* (New York: E. P. Dutton & Co., Inc., 1947), is certainly not free from visible defects, and some of the author's assumptions are not really to be sustained by the evidence; but on the whole it is a simply written, well-balanced work by a fine classical scholar, and is to be recommended. A thoughtful study of Macedonian imperialism is to be found in P. Jouguet, *Macedonian Imperialism and the Hellenization of the East* (New York: Alfred A. Knopf, Inc., 1928).

There are two really outstanding studies of the Hellenistic world which should be attempted by any students interested in this crucial period of history. These are M. I. Rostovstzeff, *Social and Economic History of the Hellenistic World,* a long but well-written study which is not as formidable as it looks (Oxford: The Clarendon Press, 1941), Vols. 1 and 2, and W. W. Tarn, *Hellenistic Civilization* (3rd ed.; London: Edward Arnold & Co., 1952). At the other extreme from these two detailed studies is the masterly brief exposition of the nature of Hellenistic civilization by W. L. Westermann in *Encyclopaedia of the Social Sciences* (New York: The Macmillan Company, 1930), I, 31–41.

The extant writings of Stoic and Epicurean philosophers may be read in W. J. Oates, ed., *The Stoic and Epicurean Philosophers* (New York: Random House, 1940). The political thought of the Stoics is dealt with in a thoughtful and convincing manner in G. H. Sabine, *A History of Political Theory* (New York: Henry Holt & Co., 1937), pp. 123–158.

For many years B. Farrington's work on Greek (especially Hellenistic) science, *Greek Science: Its Meaning for Us* (Harmondsworth, Middlesex: Penguin Books, 1944), was the only nontechnical work on Greek science available easily. It was therefore widely read, in spite of the author's explanations, which seemed to many to be highly oversimplified. Now, however, there has recently appeared a very full, careful, and scholarly work, the product of many years' research, which should supersede Farrington, even for the general reader who will no doubt skip some of the more technical parts of this new book: G. Sarton, *A History of Science* (Cambridge, Mass.: Harvard University Press, 1952), Vol. 1. O. Neugebauer's book, recommended also at the end of Chapter 4—*The Exact Sciences in Antiquity* (Princeton, N.J.: Princeton University Press, 1952), is also excellent, especially in the sections on Hellenistic science and the contributions made to it by the earlier Babylonian science.

Finally, a special study of Egypt in the Hellenistic Age and the influence of Hellenism on native Egyptian culture is well worth study as a pioneer work in a very interesting field, H. I. Bell, *Egypt from Alexander the Great to the Arab Conquest* (Oxford: The Clarendon Press, 1948).

# 10

# The Roman Republic

*Divisions of Roman history: republic and empire • Roman history as the classical case of a democracy destroyed by its own imperialism • Early Italy • Early political evolution • The ruling oligarchy of the mature republic • External history • The collapse of the republic*

---

▶ ## Divisions of Roman history—Republic and empire

Roman history proper can be said to begin only with the expulsion of the kings, about 509 B.C. Previous to this date it can only be reconstructed with difficulty from archaeological remains and such facts as can be tentatively inferred from later Roman legend. Imperial Rome fell to a barbarian ruler in A.D. 476; and thereafter a Roman emperor ceased to rule in the West.

A natural dividing line during the period 509 B.C. to A.D. 476 occurs in 31 B.C. with the battle of Actium. Previous to 31 B.C. the form of government was *republican;*[1] after 31 B.C. it may be called *monarchical* (Greek *monos*—one, *arche*—rule = rule by one man). Traditionally we speak of the earlier period as the period of the *Roman Republic,* and of the later as the period of the *Roman Empire.*

It should be clearly understood that this division into republic and empire refers to the *form* of government. Confusion is often

[1] The Latin word *respublica* means only the "state." It is we who have given our word "republic" its modern meaning of a state without a monarch.

caused by the fact that it was the Roman Republic that conquered most of the lands beyond Italy which were later administered by Roman emperors; and this rule of foreign peoples is in modern times called an empire. But, to avoid confusion in this text, the word "empire" will not be used in this modern sense, and will only refer to the *period* and *form* of government after 31 B.C. The word "expansion" or other words suitable to the context will be used to refer to the conquests of the Romans which took place primarily under the republic.

▶ ## Roman history as the classical case of a democracy destroyed by its own imperialism

THE INVOLUNTARY NATURE OF THE MARCH TO EMPIRE—CONTRAST WITH GREEK POLITICAL FORESIGHT

During the whole of the period from 509 B.C. to A.D. 476 the Romans were never subjected to domination by others. On the contrary, it was the rulers in Rome, whether the people, the senatorial oligarchy, or the emperor, who made their will felt and respected by others. In studying Roman history we are frequently struck by the fact that there seems to have been something inevitable about the march of the Romans to domination of the Mediterranean world, and that the individual men responsible for Roman policies never seem to have planned anything the way it turned out. The Senate did not want to expand beyond Italy, but the relentless pressure of events forced that expansion; the citizens of the Roman republic did not want to destroy their republic, any more than did the soldiers of fortune who made its fall inevitable. We who live so many centuries later can see the majestic sequence of cause and effect, how each change in the form of government, each province added, was dictated by necessity, so that these self-governing, responsible, dominating Romans appear almost as puppets, doing what had to be done and nothing else. The Christian Fathers regarded the Roman Empire as a necessary preparation for their establishment of the Catholic Church; and we can see how they were able, even with far less evidence available to them than we have and working with a preconceived notion of Divine Providence, to reach such a conclusion and defend it. The Athenians *thought out* a constitution, logical and appropriate to themselves, which they proceeded to make work; Alexander *thought out* the policy appropriate to his empire, which had been quite self-consciously planned by his father and himself. The Greeks imposed mind upon matter, in their political life, in their art, and in their philosophy; the Romans *felt* their way along, modifying, adapting, improvising. Conservative to the core, they tried to retain every old form they had ever known far beyond its limit of usefulness, responding to each challenge as it presented itself to them. Thus the Romans remained empirical, practical, illogical, but uniquely effective, without producing a truly creative mind throughout the whole of their history comparable to any one of a dozen Greeks. It was no wonder that the Roman augurs consulted the gods every day, for no great people ever owed less to their own minds and more to their

gods than they. That they should have conquered the Greeks was the triumph of character over intellect, and it is salutary for us to remember that fact. That it should have been Plato and Aristotle who took over the theology of the Roman church, and the Greeks and the Syrians who developed the Roman law in the final form in which it could be transmitted to posterity, is an ironic commentary upon the ability of even character, important though it is, to substitute for mind in the long sweep of history.

The history of the Roman Republic is the classical case of a potential democracy destroyed by its own imperialism. The Roman Republic was never a true democracy as Athens was, for the people never used the power that formally belonged to them, although it had taken centuries of struggle to acquire it. They were not really interested in participation in the government so much as they were anxious to secure equality of rights due to citizens, an equality which was taken for granted in Athens and never became a problem. The Roman oligarchy, the ruling class (a conception foreign to the Athenian polis altogether), was interested in government and extremely competent in it, and did not want to give the less competent masses any opportunity of acquiring it. Instead, the oligarchy made way for competent and distinguished *individuals* to enter its ranks. But the expansion beyond Italy which necessarily followed the expansion within Italy had such momentous results for the now enfranchised people and for the oligarchy that the former were compelled to use their voting power against the oligarchy to ensure their rights; while the oligarchy in defending itself won the day, but lost its morale and the respect of the people. Thereafter, as the problems of the expansion remained unsolved, both yielded power to the military, and the republic itself yielded to the one-man rule of the emperor.

In studying Roman history, therefore, the foregoing is the sequence of events to be observed. At no time in the history of the republic does it seem possible to say that if A had been wiser or B more conciliatory or C had had a bright idea, the republic would have survived. The very form of the republic carried within itself the seeds of its downfall. The Roman Republic, with its oligarchy and its magistrates and its solid farmer-soldiers, proved itself incompetent to rule beyond Italy; competent though it was in conquering, it could not manage its conquests. If we are to discover the reason for this fact, we must examine the nature of Roman institutions and how they functioned, and watch the influence that the Roman possessions beyond the seas had on the home government.

THE REPUBLIC AND ITS SUCCESSES AND FAILURES AS THE NECESSARY PRELUDE TO WORLD RULE

And yet without the republic there would have been no effective empire. An Oriental empire which had never known free institutions might have conquered, but it could not have consolidated its possessions into a form of government as stable as that of the Romans. The heart of the empire was its self-governing cities; the means of government was the professional army and its officers, and the administrators with their long tradition of public service. These carried over from the great republic, the builder of character and the developer of institutions. Without the republic the empire would have been just another despotism, not a world organization that called forth such an unexampled loyalty from its citizens. When that organization fell, it seemed even to Christians who hated its gods and deplored its morality that the world itself had lost its foundations.

► **Early Italy**

PHYSIOGRAPHY

The land of Italy is a peninsula extending southeast into the Mediterranean, divided by the Apennine chain of mountains, high in the north and dwindling away into foothills only in the extreme south. The largest fertile area in the country suitable for grain growing is the Po Valley in the northeast; but as this is separated by the mountains from the coastal plains of the west, communications have never been easy between the two areas, and in republican days the region of the Po was not regarded as a part of Italy at all but as the separate province of Hither Gaul. The second largest expanse of fertile land in ancient times was in Latium and Campania, though the surface soil was early exhausted, and the land became more suitable for vineyards and orchards than for grain. The greater part of Italy was best suited for pasture, either of sheep or cattle; but the basic agricultural unit, except when political and social conditions prevented it, has always been the small mixed farm.

There are many variations in climate, from the Po Valley, which has cold winters and warm summers, to the semitropical climate of the southwest. The east coast in ancient times was almost barren of seaports; Italy is not too well blessed with them, even now, in spite of her long coast line. The best harbors in the country were in the south and southwest. Ostia, the harbor of Rome, was never a good one, and needed constant dredging to keep it usable. The Tiber, which leads from Rome to Ostia, is a swift-flowing river, and suitable only for small boats and lighters. Rome, disadvantageously situated for water traffic, never became a great commercial or industrial city.

Italy on the whole was far richer in agricultural resources than Greece, and Greek travelers to Italy in early imperial times always emphasize the abundance of produce, the fine timber, especially the hardwoods, and the animals pasturing on the rich lands. But she was and is short of metals, with iron in significant quantities only to be found on the island of Elba, and small deposits of other metals scattered throughout the country; and even in arable and pasture land she is greatly inferior to France, and was inferior to almost any land in her empire in ancient days.

Rome itself was situated on the left bank of the Tiber, about fifteen miles from the sea, with the fertile hinterland of Latium to the south, and the more broken but still fertile land of Etruria to the north. Her famous Seven Hills are really three separate hills with four adjacent spurs. Rome at its most extensive filled the whole space between the hills and had a settlement on the right bank of the river. The only real advantage of the situation of Rome was that it was in central Italy and could usually prevent the northern and southern areas from uniting against her. The immediate neighborhood of Rome was unhealthful, and even the land covered by the city had to be artificially drained before it was habitable. It was primarily her man-made system of roads, all leading out of Rome, that enabled her to keep military control of Italy. It was, then, the work of her people that made her mistress of Italy rather than any special advantages of geography. In the Middle Ages, and in modern times, Milan, with a far better natural situation, has always tended to grow naturally and surpass Rome; it has always required special man-directed efforts, almost contrary to nature, to build Rome up to equal or surpass her upstart daughter in the north.

### PREHISTORIC SETTLEMENTS IN ITALY

Several prehistoric cultures are known in Italy. Skulls of Neanderthal man have been found not far from Rome, and Neolithic settlements of a people who domesticated animals but did not yet know agriculture have been excavated. An extensive Bronze Age culture of people who lived in pile dwellings similar to those found in Switzerland (the so-called Terramare culture) was followed by the "Villanovan" people who used iron. These last two groups are generally supposed to have been migrants from the north who mingled with the neolithic inhabitants to form the Italic people of the peninsula in historic times. But there is as yet no final certainty on the matter, and excavations may still turn up enough evidence to establish the original homes of these settlers and to determine whether the Terramare and Villanovan cultures are distinct, or the latter developed from the former. It seems quite possible that some tribes of

Indo-European people went into Greece, where they found the advanced Mycenaean civilization already existent, and so were able to progress more quickly themselves till they ultimately became the Hellenic peoples of history. At the same time another offshoot went into Italy, but were slower in developing a characteristic culture of their own, having less to build upon. At all events by 1000 B.C. the Italic peoples were already speaking the language that ultimately became Latin, though they could not yet write it. About 1000 B.C. also the first settlement on the Palatine Hill of Rome was founded.

### THE INVADERS OF ITALY—CELTS AND ETRUSCANS —INFLUENCES ON ROMANS

Into the Italic peninsula during the next three hundred years came three groups of invaders: Celts, who formed a permanent settlement in the valley of the Po and were called Gauls by the Romans; Greeks, who came from the mainland from the eighth century onward, as we have seen, whose settlements were for the most part in southern Italy close to the sea; and a group of people called the Etruscans, "people of the sea," probably coming from Asia Minor after the destruction of the Mycenaean civilization by the invading Dorians. These Etruscans were considerably more advanced culturally and militarily than their Italic neighbors, and they maintained contact by sea not only with the Greek cities in southern Italy but with Carthage. They gradually expanded northward in Italy to control the Po Valley, as far as the Alps, and through Latium to Capua, ruling Rome itself intermittently. Though their language is almost unknown to us, archaeologists have made very extensive finds, so that we are familiar with the material elements in their civilization. We know that they had developed urban life to the extent that their nobles had fine houses and enjoyed athletic contests, feasts, and dancing, that the women had elaborate dresses with considerable ornamentation, and used cosmetics and make-up. In material comfort and luxury the civilization was far ahead of anything the Romans or Italians achieved for

An Etruscan biga, a kind of chariot, dating from the sixth century B.C., the period of the Etruscan domination of Rome. (COURTESY THE METROPOLITAN MUSEUM OF ART)

many centuries afterward. There was, however, no single centralized Etruscan state, but many self-governing cities which frequently engaged in intercity warfare. We cannot, therefore, speak of an Etruscan Empire so much as of the expansion of the Etruscans, though there is evidence that the Etruscan cities sometimes united into leagues. From the Etruscans the Romans learned the use of hewn stone for their public buildings, temples, and walls, and probably gladiatorial games. One feature in Roman religion, divination from the entrails of animals and augury from the flight of birds, was taken from the Etruscans, but the principles were apparently never fully understood by the Romans, for even in Cicero's time (the first century B.C.) Etruscan diviners were employed by the priests and augurs of Rome. Some Roman gods take their names from their Etruscan counterparts.

Etruscan influence on Roman political development was crucial, but not long lasting. Rome was conquered by the Etruscans and dominated by them for a period of uncertain duration. During this time the small villages which occupied the area of the Seven Hills were consolidated into one city. Naturally the Romans never gave credit to their conquerors for this creative act; the city in Roman tradition had been founded in 753 B.C. by Romulus, who had come from Alba Longa in Latium. The founder of that city had himself come from Troy as a child with his father, Aeneas, one of the Trojan heroes mentioned in the *Iliad*. Romulus, according to this tradition, was the first king of Rome. But, as we have seen, there was already a settlement at Rome by 1000 B.C., and though there is some evidence that emigrants from Alba did found it, the famous date of 753 does not seem to represent any event of significance. The tradition, in fact, is not older than the fourth century B.C. The last king, and possibly the last three kings, of Rome were Etruscans; they did not endear themselves to the Romans, who hated the name of king forever afterward.

## ▶ Early political evolution

### EXPULSION OF THE KINGS

About 509 B.C., according to tradition,[2] the kings were driven out of Rome. Again, it is not certain that the Romans themselves drove them out. Some scholars are of the opinion that it was the neighboring Latin cities who were ruled from Rome by the Etruscan monarchy who united to defeat the Romans and the Etruscans together. It is also probable that Rome was retaken by the Etruscans for a time after the fall of the monarchy. However this may be, the Romans did soon succeed in gaining their independence, but found themselves at war with the Latin League, a league of cities of Latium. Presumably Rome was trying to assert her rule over these cities on her own account, as during Etruscan days. This war was brought to an end by a Roman victory at Lake Regillus in 486 B.C., and a treaty was signed under which Rome and the Latin cities entered into a virtual partnership which lasted for nearly 150 years, and which enabled Rome to become the recognized leader of all central Italy.

### THE ASCENDANCY OF THE NOBILITY

In addition to making the villages of Rome into a city from which it dominated Latium, the Etruscan monarchy had been able to keep order between the classes in Rome. Almost every Roman was a farmer, for though the Etruscan kings tried to support industry, there was very little, and most manufacture, for instance of weapons and pottery, was done in the home. Three kinds of land were available to the farmer, his own plot belonging personally to him, public land which he might rent, and common

[2] Roman tradition is represented to us above all by the first historian of the Roman Empire, Livy, who makes no secret of his purpose to show how the gods guided the destiny of Rome from the beginning, and to remind his generation of Romans of their glorious past. In line with this purpose he quite consciously exalts the heroic virtues of the Romans to more than life size. The tradition, of course, is older than Livy, but does not go back to within even two centuries of the Etruscan kings.

land where he could pasture his flocks and herds. But certain customary rights were held by the old noble families; and when they had the power they constantly encroached on the rights of the smaller farmers, who had no means of defending themselves. The noble families, or patricians, jealously guarded their rights, and were divided from the plebeians, the remainder of the population, by a rigid class distinction. While the kings ruled in Rome the nobles were kept in check. But when the kings were expelled from Rome and the nobles ruled the state in their place, the latter held arbitrary power over the plebeians which they abused to the utmost. Public land was sold to the highest bidder as long as he was a patrician, or let out at a nominal rent; or it was pre-empted for the sole use of the patricians. Thus the poorer farmer fell into debt or was driven from his land. Moreover, with the wars that followed the breakdown of the monarchy and with the ill success that often attended Roman arms at the beginning, especially when the Etruscans tried to retake the city, the farmers would go on the annual campaigns and return to find their land ravaged and their property ruined by the war.

### THE STRUGGLE OF THE ORDERS—FIRST STAGE

Revolt against the patrician power seems to have been ill organized at the beginning, and took the form of occasional acts of violence, which were avenged speedily by the more powerful patricians, armed with all the authority of the state. The magistrates were able to inflict any legal penalty at will, and creditors were entitled to sell the debt-ridden farmers across the Tiber; if there were several creditors, under primitive custom they could divide the debtor's body in pieces.

There was only one recourse for the more numerous plebeians. In one thing their numbers counted, even though the machinery of the state was controlled by their enemies. They were needed as soldiers— the patricians could not fight the Etruscans or the Latin League all by themselves. So about 494 B.C., according to the story in Livy, the plebeian troops, called out for a campaign, marched to the Sacred Hill where they presented demands, in particular for some security against arbitrary acts of magistrates. They were granted the right to have their own assembly of plebeians which would elect two tribunes (later increased to four, then to ten), whose persons were to be sacrosanct, i.e., anyone offering violence against them could be put to death without trial. The tribunes could forbid any act of the magistrates by pronouncing the word "veto" (I forbid).

### THE GOVERNMENT OF EARLY ROME—PRIMITIVE DEMOCRACY—MAGISTRATES, SENATE, AND ASSEMBLIES

In order to understand how the nobles had acquired such power after the expulsion of the kings it is necessary to examine the institutions of the Roman state during and after the kingly regime, and then to see how they were modified by further acts of the plebeians through their assembly and officers, and through further use of their potent weapon, the military strike.

The early government of Rome was probably a Primitive Democracy of the kind previously described in the chapter on Mesopotamia. But, as in the case of the Greeks, the king ceased to hold his position instead of developing into an absolute monarch, as in the East. The Council in Rome was known as the *Senate,* and was composed originally of the heads of clans (*gentes*), and the Primitive Assembly was the *Comitia curiata.* In this Assembly each man had a vote; but the whole Assembly was divided into thirty *curiae,* and it was the majority of the curiae rather than the majority of the total vote that counted. In the time of the kings, the Senate was an advisory body only, and in the event of the death of the king administered the state until the new one was chosen. The Assembly chose the king and conferred his authority (*imperium*) upon him, and would occasionally be consulted, if called by the king, on important matters of legislation. The

king was the sole executive, leader in war, chief priest, and judge.

These bodies and their functions, then, were substantially similar to those discussed in earlier chapters. In Rome all the later governmental organizations retained their basic character, and in fact, long after it had been superseded by other assemblies which had real powers and could use them, even the old Comitia curiata continued to exist, with no powers beyond solemnly meeting to confer the imperium upon magistrates. The Senate always remained in theory an advisory body, could be called only by the magistrates, and had no power of legislation. Although it encroached upon the powers of the other governing bodies of the state so that it became for a long time the actual ruling body, these powers never belonged to it in theory, and could be taken away from it by determined action by the Assembly and magistrates as soon as the Senate lost its indirect control over them.

The first great change in this system was, of course, the expulsion of the kings. Their place was taken by two magistrates, first called *praetors,* then *consuls.* The important feature of the supreme magistracy in the state was that, as the name suggests, they consulted together; to prevent arbitrary and absolute power from going to either, each had a veto on the acts of the other. These consuls were primarily leaders in war, and they alternated authority in the field; in practice this did not make for too much difficulty as there were usually two armies in the field at once. The consuls were elected annually by the Assembly, and they appointed the members of the Senate from among those who were eligible. In important matters it was customary for them to consult the Senate; but it was with them and not with the Senate that responsibility rested. Consuls at this time were always chosen from the number of existing senators, and they returned to the Senate after their year of office; this fact no doubt was of considerable influence on their behavior while in office, as they would not wish to antagonize unduly their future colleagues. The consuls could also call the Assembly when necessary, and neither Senate nor Assembly could be called by anyone else except in the case of a dictatorship. The only appeal against the decision of a consul was in a case involving capital punishment of a citizen; then by custom an appeal to the Assembly was permitted.

In times of grave danger to the state a *dictator* could be appointed for six months, with a *master of the horse* as his second in command. For this period the dictator had supreme power, and his appointment was therefore the equivalent of six months under martial law, unless the crisis was over before this time, in which case the dictator automatically retired.

It will be seen at once how this election of consuls instead of the king would work to the detriment of the plebeians. The consuls always came from the noble class, and were to some degree responsible to their class owing to their annual term of office; whereas the king held his office for life and was above the nobles, and thus need not be in any way subservient to their interests.

The priestly power of the king was not transferred to the consuls, but to a college of priests and augurs, also patricians, who were headed by a chief priest (*Pontifex Maximus*) who was elected by the Assembly. The priestly function was of considerable importance since most public acts were preceded by religious ritual. Knowledge of this ritual was necessary, and ignorance of it kept plebeians from transacting public business on their own account.

Almost at the same time as the election of consuls—the exact date is uncertain—the need for a new kind of Assembly became apparent. The old Comitia curiata was not, however, reformed or abolished. Instead, an altogether new Assembly was formed to which the powers of the old were assigned, together with some new ones. This was the Assembly by centuries (a military formation), the *Comitia centuriata*. The whole population of the state was divided into various classes, according to the military equipment each could provide. Thus the first class,

which could provide horses, weapons, and armor, was superior to the second class, which could not provide horses; and so on. The largest number of centuries was allotted to the first class; the propertyless citizens of the lowest class, who were excused from fighting except in cases of extreme danger to the state, were all put into one century. The centuries of the first class, who provided most military equipment and paid the highest property tax, amounted in number to 98 out of a total of 193 centuries. Since voting went by centuries and not by numbers of individual soldiers, the wealthy classes were able to dominate the Assembly if they voted together (see the chart on opposite page).

To this Assembly were transferred the right to make war and peace, the right to elect magistrates, the right to hear appeals of citizens against the death sentence, and the right to accept or reject proposals for legislation offered by the magistrates. It could not, however, discuss or amend such proposals; no Roman Assembly ever had this right. The vote was always taken in Roman Assemblies by the presiding magistrate's calling for the vote of each century (or, in the Tribal Assembly, to be discussed later, of each tribe) one by one. When a majority was obtained, the bill was declared passed, and the opinion of the remaining centuries was not taken. So the poorer classes were virtually disfranchised, their opinion not being heard and their vote not counted. The only way open to them to make their voice heard was to acquire enough wealth to enable them to be enrolled in a superior century. This Assembly, though it lost much of its power later to the Tribal Assembly, remained throughout the Roman Republic a factor making for conservatism; even when it was re-formed about 240 B.C. and its composition changed, it was still largely a vehicle for the men of property.

THE STRUGGLE OF THE ORDERS—SECOND STAGE

### Tribal Assembly

We have seen how the plebeians first seceded about 494 B.C. and demanded some check upon the arbitrary power of the magistrates. The result of their action was the right to appoint tribunes. The tribune was a new civilian official who held no military powers and only the limited civil authority (*potestas*) already described. These tribunes were to be elected by the plebs alone, in an assembly of their own (*Concilium plebis*). This Assembly was also allowed to legislate in matters that concerned the plebs alone (*plebiscita*). Very soon afterward—though the details of the operation are not clear— the composition of this new Plebeian Assembly was regularized by its conversion into an Assembly of the People by Tribes (*Comitia tributa*), of which three tribes were urban and seventeen were rural, later rising over the course of the next 250 years to four urban and thirty-one rural. The new Assembly could be called into session either by the tribunes or by the consuls. Later, when the title of praetor was revived and praetors were elected to undertake some of the duties of the consul, these magistrates could also summon the Assembly of the Tribes.

The result of these changes was that the Romans now had three Assemblies; obviously there was no real need for all three. The Comitia curiata of the kings fell into disuse, retaining no powers but a few minor duties, mostly of a religious nature. The Comitia centuriata controlled by the wealthy classes gave place to the Comitia tributa, theoretically controlled by the majority of citizens. This change was accomplished by the Valerio-Horatian laws of about 448 B.C., under which all legislation passed by the Comitia tributa became binding on the people if ratified by the Senate. Thus the Comitia centuriata lost its powers of legislation but retained its other powers, especially the election of magistrates and the declaration of war. It remained the last court of appeal in death sentences.

### The first codification of the law— The Twelve Tables

The appointment of the tribunes and the enlargement of their numbers were a help to the plebeians but not enough. Presumably the arbitrary acts continued and the magistrates interpreted the customary law as they wanted. Moreover, the wealthier plebeians felt themselves discriminated against in the matter of magistracies, which were still confined to the patrician class. And they were not allowed to intermarry with patricians. Around the middle of the fifth century several advances were made under severe pressure from the plebeians. First came the appointment of a body of decemvirs (ten men) to codify the hitherto unwritten law. Since they did not produce a law code within their first year of office, the plebeians agitated very violently, and perhaps staged a second full-dress secession. The result was the issue of the Twelve Tables, which was followed by the Valerio-Horatian laws just described, giving the power of legislation to the Comitia tributa. By then or even earlier this Comitia also enrolled the Roman patricians in its ranks, though of course they were numerically inferior to the plebeians in this Assembly. Agitation for the consulship was settled by a compromise under which a new office, military tribunes, was substituted for the consulship, and to this office plebeians could theoretically be elected. When the number of military tribunes reached six, and the Romans were engaged in a deadly conflict with the Etruscans at the end of the fifth century, a few plebeians were at last elected by the patrician-controlled Comitia centuriata. But the agitation still continued for the return of the honored consulate, and for the election of plebeians to it.

### Piecemeal concession of rights and offices to plebeians

Meanwhile a gain had been registered by the plebeians in the first important breach of the social stratification of the classes. Permission to intermarry with patricians was granted a few years after the codification of the law. At the same time the patricians created a new office for themselves, that of *quaestor,* an assistant to the consuls, whose duties were mostly financial, including the administration of the treasury and the division of war booty. The office, however did not remain for very long exclusively in patrician hands, no doubt because the booty was being unfairly divided. The plebeians obtained the right to be elected to the quaestorship about twenty-five years after it had first become an elective office.

By the end of the fifth century, then, the plebeians had obtained some important concessions. They could be elected military tribunes, though they were not often in fact elected; they could be elected quaestor. They had an Assembly which could legislate, though the Senate had a veto; they had succeeded in obtaining a written law code; and they were allowed to intermarry with the patricians. But they were still far from

---

► **chronological chart**

### THE ETRUSCAN MONARCHY

| Internal history | | External history | |
|---|---|---|---|
| Terramare culture | *ca.* 2000 | | |
| Villanovan culture | *ca.* 1000 | | |
| First settlements in Rome | *ca.* 1000 | | |
| Etruscans appear in Italy | *ca.* 900 | | |
| Traditional date of founding of Rome | 753 | Greek colonization in southern Italy | 760 |
| Traditional first four kings of Rome | 753–616 | | |
| Tarquinius Priscus (Etruscan king) | 616–578 | | |
| Servius Tullius | 578–534 | | |
| Tarquinius Superbus (Etruscan king) | 534–510 | | |
| End of Etruscan domination | 509 | | |

# THE ROMAN REPUBLIC

## Internal history

| | |
|---|---|
| First secession of plebs—Election of tribunes and establishment of Concilium plebis (plebiscites binding on plebs) | 494 |
| Establishment of Comitia tributa (Assembly of Tribes) | *ca.* 460 |
| Twelve Tables | 450–449 |
| Valerio-Horatian Laws (legislation by plebs binding on state if accepted by Senate) | 448 |
| Intermarriage permitted between plebeians and patricians | 445 |
| Suspension of consulship, substituted by military tribunes, open to plebeians | 444–367 |
| Licinian-Sextian Laws—Consulship opened to plebeians | 367 |
| First plebeian dictator | 356 |
| One of consuls *must* be plebeian | 340 |
| Censors to give preference to ex-magistrates in drawing up list of senators | 310 |
| Loss of senatorial veto on all legislation | 287 |
| Reorganization of Comitia centuriata (electoral assembly) | *ca* 242 |
| Tiberius Gracchus elected tribune | 133 |
| Murder of Tiberius Gracchus | 132 |
| Re-election of tribune made legal | 125 |
| Tribunate of Gaius Gracchus | 123–122 |
| Death of Gaius Gracchus | 121 |
| Marius elected consul | 107 |
| Reorganization of army on volunteer basis by Marius | 106 |
| Sixth consulship of Marius | 100 |
| Return of Sulla to Italy—Proscriptions | 83 |
| Sullan Constitution | 83–80 |
| Pompey given extended command against pirates | 67 |
| Pompey given extended command against Mithridates | 66 |
| Consulate of Cicero and conspiracy of Catiline | 63 |
| Return of Pompey to Rome | 62 |
| First Triumvirate | 60 |
| Caesar appointed to command in Gaul | 58 |
| Return of Caesar to Italy | 49 |
| Caesar as dictator | 46–44 |
| Murder of Caesar | 44 |

## External history

| | |
|---|---|
| Battle of Lake Regillus—Roman victory over Latin League | 496 |
| Treaty with Latin League—Promulgation of Latin rights | 493 |
| Rome leader of Latin League—Gradual expansion | 490–430 |
| Conquest of Veii (southern Etruria) | 396 |
| Invasion of Italy by Gauls—Sack of Rome | 387–386 |
| Wars with various Latin and other local cities | 362–345 |
| War with Latin League | 340–338 |
| Defeat of Latin League—Roman Confederation | 338 |
| Samnite Wars | 327–290 |
| War with Pyrrhus and Magna Graecia | 281–272 |
| First Punic War | 264–241 |
| Sicily becomes first Roman province | 227 |
| Sardinia and Corsica become second Roman province | 227 |
| Second Punic War | 218–201 |
| Spain divided into two provinces | 197 |
| Defeat of Antiochus III (king of Syria) at Magnesia | 190 |
| Wars with Macedonia | 200–197; 171–168 |
| Third Punic War | 149–146 |
| Destruction of Carthage and sack of Corinth | 146 |
| Macedonia becomes Roman province | 146 |
| Jugurthine War | 112–106 |
| Marius defeats Cimbri and Teutones | 102–101 |
| Social War in Italy | 90–88 |
| Murder of all Romans and Italians in Asia by Mithridates VI | 89 |
| Sulla undertakes war with Mithridates | 87 |
| Wars with Mithridates (Lucullus) | 75–66 |
| Slave War in Italy | 74–71 |
| Conquest and reorganization of Asia by Pompey | 66–62 |
| Caesar conquers Gaul | 58–51 |
| Crassus defeated and killed in Parthia | 53 |

Dates are before Christ.

being first-class citizens. And, as we shall see, whenever the patricians made a concession, they tried to recover their lost power by other means. The background of the struggle remained primarily economic. The successful fifth-century campaigns of the Romans added a great deal of public land to the state, which was divided unfairly by the patricians as long as they had a monopoly of government. And, since the possession of land also determined the position of the owner in the Comitia centuriata, which elected magistrats, the plebeians still had no legal redress. To reduce their agitation for reform there were occasional land divisions which helped them, and in conquered territory colonies were planted in which the poorer citizens could take part.

But after the sacking of Rome by the Gauls in the early fourth century B.C. and the extensive wars in Italy that followed, it became clear that the patricians could no longer maintain their complete monopoly of government. So in 367 B.C. the Licinian-Sextian laws were passed admitting plebeians to the consulship, which was now restored, and limiting the amount of public land that could be held by any citizen. The land law, however, seems to have remained a dead letter, as we find land tenure still a problem for the next two centuries. Following these laws there was intensive agitation for a scaling down of debt, and by the end of the century, after a few minor reforms, slavery for debt was abolished.

The patricians, as usual, had another card up their sleeves. Two new magistracies were instituted after 367 B.C., the *praetorship* and the *curule aedileship,* the latter occupied primarily with the administration of the city of Rome, the former undertaking some of the civil, and if necessary, military powers of the consul. The praetor became the chief judge in Rome, but he could also command armies in the absence of the consul and could summon the Senate and the Assemblies. Needless to say, these offices were reserved for patricians, as some compensation for the loss of their exclusive right to the consulate.

The plebeians realized that it was useless to have the right to be elected consul if the Centuriate Assembly never elected them, though in practice a few wealthy plebeians were elected who were acceptable to the patricians and who usually had intermarried with them. So in 340 B.C., since the election machinery could not be tampered with, a law was passed that one of the consuls *must* be a plebeian; two years later the praetorship was opened to the plebeians, and at the same time a law was passed that the highest dignity in the state, the *censorship,* must be shared between plebeians and patricians.

A word is now necessary on the censorship, which had been established soon after the Twelve Tables. Every five years two ex-consuls must be elected by the Military Assembly to take a census of the citizens, and decide on the property classification for this Assembly. This work usually occupied about eighteen months, after which the censor (or census taker) laid down his office. During the expansion of Rome the censors came to exercise many important financial functions, including the auctioning of tax contracts and the letting out of contracts for public works. In the early days senators had been appointed by the consuls, but this duty soon devolved upon the censors, who had, in any case, all been consuls. It was, of course, impossible for plebeians to be censors until they had obtained entry into the consulate; but when one consul had to be a plebeian, one of the censors could be a plebeian ex-consul. In 310 B.C. the censors were instructed by the Ovinian Law to give preference to ex-magistrates in drawing up the list of senators, so that it became the custom for all magistrates to enter the Senate automatically. The censors, however, assumed as part of their function the right to purge the Senate for breaches of public decorum and for other offenses (hence our word *censorious*).

In 300 B.C. the last patrician stronghold fell with the admission of plebeians into the college of pontiffs and augurs, thus giving them access to the secrets of religious ritual necessary for the management of the state.

## Abolition of senatorial veto on legislation

Only one victory now remained to be gained—the abolition of the senatorial veto on legislation. Again it was the question of public land and the pressure of debt during the Samnite War that fanned the agitation that was to lead to the concession. Under the leadership of the plebeian Hortensius, a third secession of the plebs was staged in 287 B.C. Hortensius was made dictator, and the final authority in legislation was handed over to the Tribal Assembly. All laws passed by this Assembly became law with or without the consent of the Senate.

It might appear that the constitution was now well balanced, as the Greek historian Polybius thought it, with a fairly even division of powers between the patricians and plebeians. Yet in fact for the next 150 years the balance was only on paper; in practice rule was by a senatorial oligarchy in spite of the fact that the Senate remained in theory what it always had been—an advisory body.

## ▶ The ruling oligarchy of the mature republic

INDIRECT SENATORIAL CONTROL OF THE ASSEMBLIES

The two potentially democratic elements in the constitution, the tribunate and the Tribal Assembly, were both indirectly controlled by the patricians; and such strife as we hear of during the next centuries, not even excluding altogether the revolt of the Gracchi, was more an interfamily struggle for power among the patrician families and their respective plebeian connections than a true struggle between patricians and plebeians. It was, on the whole, only the richer plebeians who were interested in obtaining office; and these were frequently allowed to marry into the patrician families, not only because of their wealth but because they could, as plebeians, be elected tribune. As tribunes they were extremely useful to the ruling classes because they were able to veto legislation introduced into the Tribal Assembly. There were now ten tribunes, and the veto of any one of them was sufficient to hold up legislation for a year. The tribunes, moreover, now sat in the Senate and had gained the privilege of calling it. So the practice grew up of calling the Senate first and consulting it before taking any measure to the Tribal Assembly. Unless it were called by a magistrate, the Assembly could take no action, and it could neither debate nor amend. So through the control of one or more tribunes the Senate was able to gain an indirect power at least the equal of what it had lost in 287 B.C.

But the patricians had a further indirect control of the Assembly. In the Tribal Assembly the votes were distributed inequitably. It has already been mentioned that there were originally twenty tribes. Over the years the number had been increased to thirty-five, only four of which were urban, while the remainder were rural. Moreover, all new citizens were enrolled in the urban tribes, where their votes counted for little or nothing. It might be thought that in a system where votes could only be cast in person the urban vote would swamp the rural, since genuine farmers could not afford the time to come to the city to vote except on rare occasions. This, however, was not the case; for anyone who had been born in the country retained his vote in a rural tribe even after he had come to live in Rome and the tribal vote could be cast by the few members of the tribe who were able to be present. The votes for the rural tribes were therefore cast by rich landowners whose interests lay with the senatorial oligarchy, and by the clients of these landowners who were evidently organized into an effective political machine, no doubt being paid their expenses for living at Rome in exchange for their vote. Only when the small farmers themselves were dispossessed or had such an important grievance that they thought it worth while to make their journey to Rome to vote could this machine be broken, as it was in the time of the Gracchi.

## DIRECT POWERS OF THE SENATE

In addition to these indirect powers which enabled the senatorial oligarchy to control legislation, the Senate also had important powers of its own. Being the only deliberative body in the state, and made up of all those who had held office and high command in the army, it discussed foreign affairs, appointed and received ambassadors, appointed commissions to discuss treaties and ratified them, allotted military commands to the consuls and praetors, and later prolonged the commands of consuls (with the title of proconsuls) and praetors (propraetors). It had to approve the public contracts let out by the censors, and it had almost complete charge of finance. Later it claimed to be able to decree martial law when the state was in extreme danger, and to call upon the consuls to enforce it. Though the Senate did not formally have the right to declare war, its policy could make war inevitable, aside from its general control of the Assembly.[3] Finally, the Senate could always refuse to finance any legislation, so that such legislation would remain a dead letter. Thus the Senate had still another means of preventing the execution of the popular will.

## SENATORIAL CONTROL OF THE REPUBLIC
## DURING THE PERIOD OF EXPANSION

The whole result, therefore, of the plebeian agitation for reform was that certain plebeians were now admitted to office and its rewards, while the people were in the same position as before, though they now had the formal power to break the oligarchy if they could gain sufficient cohesion within their class and find the necessary leaders. But, although a few such leaders did arise, they were rare, for they had to resist all the blandishments that were available to the oligarchy for their seduction. A tribune who wanted to fight on behalf of the people would need to organize the farmers' vote to

---

[3] There are, however, at least two important cases where the Senate did not wish for war, but the consuls were willing to defy it and cajoled a declaration out of the Assembly.

break the political machine, he would have to ensure that all his colleagues were of the same mind and could not be corrupted or persuaded to veto his measures, and he would have himself to possess a private income, which in the early days meant the possession of land—for officers of state were not paid. Finally, he would probably be called upon to resist temptation in the form of a marriage into one of the best families, who were quite willing to use their daughters as pawns in the political game, marrying and divorcing them with alarming suddenness to cement a political alliance. It is not, therefore, surprising that most of the tribunes who did in fact espouse the cause of the people were themselves aristocrats or allied with the aristocracy already, even though they might still be classified as "plebeians."

From this account it should not be concluded that the Senate was unworthy of its responsibilities and position of power. For several centuries it was really the only possible government of Rome, containing, as it did, all the men with experience in public office, military command, wealth, and education. It retained its position primarily because of its enormous prestige, its long series of victorious wars, its successful diplomacy, and its real sense of responsibility and tradition of public service. Not only was the Senate unpaid; it was not even allowed to engage in commerce or industry or to contract for provincial taxes. It was only when it failed in war and later when it lost its prestige through corruption and mismanagement in the conquered provinces, and when a new class arose which was wealthier than the landholding Senate and willing to use its wealth to promote its material interests, that the Senate began to lose its grip and become a jealous and embittered oligarchy fighting every inch of the way against all reform.

But for nearly 150 years of expansion the Senate's power was unchallenged by any other class in the state, and during this time Carthage was defeated and destroyed and the bulk of the Mediterranean world was added to the possessions of Rome. Some of the material proceeds of this expansion filtered down to the people who fought the wars, and for a long time no Roman citizen had to pay any tax, since the whole state was financed by its booty from wars and its taxes from the unfree provinces.

## ▶ External history*

THE UNIFICATION OF ITALY

### General Italian policy—Roman, Latin, and allied rights

The constitutional development has taken us forward by several centuries in time, and we must now return to the external history of Rome, which had so much influence upon this development. Here again Rome showed the ability to compromise and improvise which made her capable of ruling so many foreign peoples with efficiency and considerable success, at least until she went beyond the borders of Italy.

After the treaty with the Latin League following the battle of Lake Regillus she was quickly able, with the assistance of the Latin cities, to subdue the local hostile tribes until at the beginning of the fourth century B.C. she had extended her dominion over southern Etruria. Toward the peoples she conquered she adopted a military and civil policy which became the model for all her conquests in Italy. She never made permanent peace with an enemy before she had put herself into a position to dictate terms. The terms were always of the same type. A colony of Roman citizens with a garrison was to be established on land ceded to Rome, and a treaty was signed regulating the status of the conquered. Some cities near to Rome were granted full citizenship, including the right of trade and marriage, and the right to vote. This status, however, was rare. The so-called Latin rights were the usual concession, which left the city in full possession of its self-government (*municipia*), with the exception of its foreign policy, of which Rome thereafter took full charge. The city provided Rome with specified numbers of troops under

their own commanders to fight in the Roman wars, and a comparatively low tax. Trade and intermarriage with the Romans were permitted, but not the right to vote. This last lack was not felt to be of importance in early days, though later full Roman citizenship meant the first share in the spoils of victory, while the Latin allies only received what was left. Even then it was not the right to vote, as such, that was appreciated so much as the other privileges that belonged to the full Roman citizen. The allied Latins were allowed to send out special Latin colonies within Italy after Roman victories, and these colonies, as well as the cities themselves, were always protected by Rome.

On the whole the arrangement was a distinct gain for these Latin allies. No longer were they in danger of defeat and destruction at the hands of local enemies; and the cost of protection was far less than the maintenance of a separate army capable of self-defense. And for a long time they retained all the important elements of self-government. The cities were united with Rome by the famous network of Roman roads. Each city was bound to Rome by a separate treaty, but the cities themselves did not have treaties with each other; frequently the rights of one Latin city were not enjoyed by all other Latin cities. The purpose of this direct connection with Rome was, of course, to prevent alliances from springing up against her; already the principle of "divide and rule" had been adopted with success.

The third type of treaty was the treaty for federate allies, substantially a defensive alliance. Again the cities were in direct relationship only with Rome; they also kept their self-government but lost the right to make war on their own. They furnished troops to the Roman army under local officers. The Romans paid for their subsistence when on campaign, and they had a share of the booty; they were not otherwise taxed.

If we consider this general policy more carefully we shall see that in the wars for the control of Italy Rome was in an exceptionally favorable position. For Rome had a policy, while the Italian cities were fighting only for complete independence without any

* The chronological chart (page 311) for this chapter is of special importance for the understanding of Roman expansion and its effects on the internal organization of the republic.

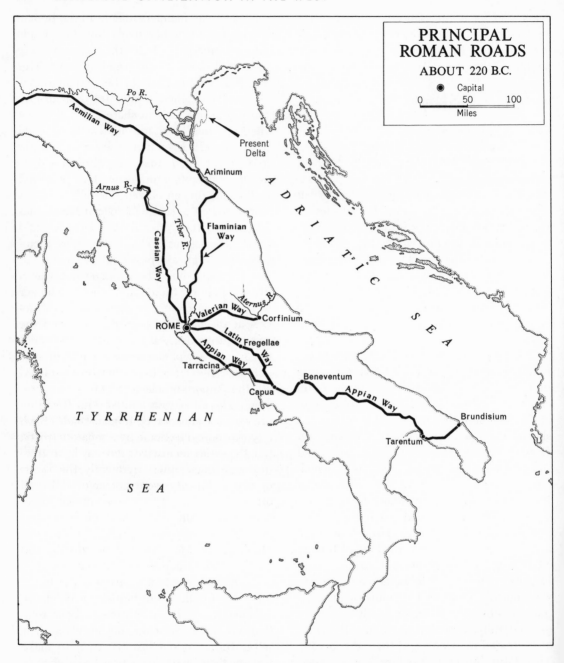

dictation from Rome—a rather intangible good, when it is remembered that this in substance only meant the right to make war and run their own foreign relations. And it was soon learned that when Rome fought, she would never give up, short of outright victory. Her enemies knew that they had only to submit and they would receive her usual terms. So Rome was never without allies; there were always cities that were content with their position and did not want to make foreign wars at the high cost of having to fight Rome for the privilege. Moreover, her enemies had no comparable policy; if they defeated Rome, even captured her, what could they do that would be of permanent value? It is significant that the Samnites, the most persistent of Rome's enemies in

Italy, had to form another confederation of their own to oppose her, with a similar constitution and with similar rights. So it became merely a question of confederation under the Samnites or confederation under Rome. In either case complete independence was over for the cities in Italy.

### Wars with Gauls, Etruscans, and Samnites—The Latin League

In 387–386 B.C. the terrifying Gauls descended upon Rome from Gaul and the Po Valley on a plundering raid. The Roman armies panicked at the battle of Allia, and the city was captured except for the fortified Capitol. The Romans were forced to ransom their city, and the Gauls retired, having no further use for the territory. But it was a considerable blow to Roman prestige and leadership; the Etruscans revolted, as did some of the Latin cities. But more important than these was the competition for leadership in Italy offered by the Samnites, a fierce and determined group of fighters from southeastern Italy, more numerous than the Latins. When the Samnites threatened Campania and its capital Capua, the Campanians appealed to Rome and the Latin League for help. This was given, and in the first round the Romans and Latins were successful. But the Romans annexed the territory themselves and did not share it with the Latins; whereupon the latter revolted, demanding full Roman citizenship and their share in the spoils that went with it. Rome refused concessions and was able, with the aid of some

*The Appian Way, the most famous road in Italy, built by the censor Appius Claudius during the fourth century B.C.* (COURTESY ITALIAN STATE TOURIST OFFICE)

UNIFICATION
OF ITALY

DATES (B.C.) INDICATE
FINAL CONQUEST
BY ROMANS

◉ Capital       ★ Battle

0          50          100
Miles

loyal allies, to defeat the Latin League before the Samnites were ready for the next round. By not reducing the Latin rights and making a few minor concessions, Rome pacified her ancient allies and was able to use their help when the Samnites attacked again in full

force. At times the Etruscans and at times the distant Gauls helped the Samnites in the long wars that followed, which became almost the final struggle for Italian independence. Often the Romans lost battles, but their persistence finally wore the Samnites and their allies down, and at last, by 290 B.C., the war was over—the Romans victorious.

## The conquest of Magna Graecia— The confederation of Italy

Too late the cities of Magna Graecia in southern Italy, which had been giving desultory aid to the Samnites, realized their danger. These ancient Greek colonies had enjoyed independence and prosperity for centuries, but they were never united and, as usual with Greek cities, they frequently indulged in petty wars with each other. During the course of one of these, some cities had appealed to Rome, and one city, Thurii, had been taken into the Roman Federation. The very year after the final defeat of the Samnites, in 289 B.C., Thurii was attacked by its neighbors who were allied with the chief city of Magna Graecia, the old Spartan colony of Tarentum. Having no force of her own, Thurii appealed to Rome, but the Senate, weary of the Samnite Wars, refused help. The consuls, however, refused to accept this senatorial decision as final and called the Assembly, which then authorized the war.

The operations of the Romans soon brought them into conflict with the Tarentines, who invited Pyrrhus, the Greek king of Epirus, a military adventurer, to help them. Pyrrhus agreed, and with a formidable army including elephants, crossed to Italy and defeated the Romans in two battles but lost so many men that he became discouraged (whence our term "Pyrrhic victories"). Unable to get much assistance from the unwarlike Italian Greeks, Pyrrhus left Italy for Sicily, whose cities were appealing for his aid against Carthage. This brought Carthage, a maritime Phoenician city of North Africa, and the greatest power in the western Mediterranean, by chance onto the same side as the Romans, and a treaty was signed which called for Carthaginian financial and naval aid to the Romans. Pyrrhus was now in difficulties. He was at first very successful in Sicily, but the Romans began to capture the Greek cities in Italy one by one. So he decided to return to Italy, and on the way

the Carthaginians sank half his ships. Rome meanwhile improved her army, adopted new tactics to withstand the elephants, and was able to defeat Pyrrhus comfortably at the battle of Maleventum ("ill chance"), thereafter called Beneventum ("good chance"). In 275 B.C. Pyrrhus went home to Epirus, intending to return some day, but he was killed by a skillfully (or luckily) aimed tile from a woman's hand while he was besieging a small town in Greece a few years later. Tarentum gave up the struggle in 272, entering the Italian Federation with an obligation to provide ships to Rome when required, and Carthage quietly gobbled up most of Sicily again without too much difficulty.

## Consequences of Italian conquests— Infiltration of Greeks—Beginnings of money economy

Rome was now mistress of the whole of Italy, with a confederation of free cities, especially among the last series of acquisitions, which enjoyed wide contacts with the Mediterranean and Oriental world. From this time on, the influence of Greek culture on the Romans was gradual but persistent. The nation of farmers now had contact with all the riches of Hellenic and Hellenistic culture. Greeks began arriving in Rome, and Roman literature appeared for the first time, a poor imitation of Greek, but at least in the Latin language. Roman primitive religion was gradually transformed, the Greek gods receiving Roman names, and some of the Greek ritual even penetrated into the Roman festivals. But these developments will be discussed in a later chapter.

Economically Rome began for the first time to live in a money economy. This was a considerable hardship to the poorer farmers, who had already suffered enough from the encroachments of the nobles, and had already ceased to grow much grain. Land was no longer the only form of property. Various plebeians who preferred wealth to office began to enter into trade relations with southern Italy. But this was a cumulative process, and became more marked with

*Ruins of the temple of Mars in the Roman Forum.* (COURTESY ITALIAN STATE TOURIST OFFICE)

the organization of the first Roman province of Sicily after the First Punic War.

### THE CONQUEST OF THE MEDITERRANEAN LANDS

#### Reasons for expansion beyond Italy

A few words are necessary on the reasons for the expansion of Rome beyond Italy which was to have such momentous effects for Rome and the whole world. Rome was now one of the two great powers in the western Mediterranean, and she was bound by certain treaty obligations to her allies by reason of the fact that she had prevented them from defending themselves and their interests. One of the unpalatable facts that all powerful states, however isolationist in

sentiment they may be, have to learn is that it is impossible not to use their power. The southern Italian cities which had trading interests with the rest of the world could not be simply left to their fate and not permitted to defend themselves though they had a defensive alliance with Rome. Moreover, the very existence of Rome as a great power meant that she would be constantly appealed to for protection and arbitration between smaller warring cities. In the next centuries Rome was often anxious to spread no further; she tried to grant self-government to conquered peoples and to the leagues of Greece. But when the leagues quarreled with each other, one of them would always appeal to Rome or to one of the other great powers in the East for assistance. Rome had either to refuse or to allow the other great power to come too close to her borders for comfort.

Carthage in the third century B.C. was the second great power in the western Mediterranean. A Phoenician colony, she had obtained her independence when Phoenicia fell, first to Assyria and then to Persia. Expanding into the hinterland of North Africa, commanding the North African coast, part of Spain and Sicily, and controlling Corsica and Sardinia, she had a formidable naval and military as well as financial and commercial strength. However, she remained primarily a sea power. Her trade policy was mercantile, that is, she maintained a monopoly on all overseas trade, and taxed even her own colonies and dependencies mercilessly. With the resulting financial resources she could afford to hire huge armies of mercenaries, whom she paid fairly well but whom she allowed to supplement their wages with booty. The Greek cities which also lived by trade objected very strongly to Carthaginian policy, especially in Sicily, which had usually been ruled by Greek tyrants with a more lenient trade and tax policy. It is probable, therefore, that sooner or later these cities would have tried to enlist Rome in an effort to weaken the Carthaginian hold on their natural markets.

### The First Punic War

It is unlikely that the Roman Senate fully understood all the implications of Rome's defensive alliances with the southern Italian cities, since we find it refusing to entertain a request for help from some Italian mercenaries besieged by the Carthaginians in Sicily in 265 B.C. It is true that this incident in itself was an insufficient cause for outright war with Carthage, but Rome could not look with equanimity on the presence of Carthaginian troops in Messina, which commanded the strait leading to Italy. The consuls, in any case, went to the Assembly and secured a declaration of war in which the Senate acquiesced. So began the First Punic War, which lasted for more than twenty years and started Rome on the path to world empire.

Carthage proved at first too strong for the Romans, who had no navy of importance and who did not altogether trust the Greek cities they had so recently conquered. So the Romans built a special kind of navy with ships which could grapple with those of the enemy at close quarters, turning what should have been a sea battle into a hand-to-hand fight on the decks of the ships. By these tactics they so disconcerted the Carthaginians that they defeated them in every battle but one that was fought at sea during this war. On the other hand, the Romans had very little idea of navigation and apparently did not take full advantage of the skill and experience of their allies in the confederation. They lost more than a hundred thousand men in storms, a far greater number than they lost in battle, and were forced to modify their system of annual commands to some degree when they found that admirals did not all come from the best families, and in any case could not be trained in a year. Though Rome's allies were extremely restive at the losses, they remained loyal until the Carthaginian mercenaries, depressed at the lack of booty provided by the Roman farmer-soldier-sailors, and not receiving their pay from Carthage regularly, began to fight with diminishing enthusiasm as the war progressed. When the Romans finally defeated these soldiers of fortune and Carthage made peace, ceding Sicily to the Romans, the mercenaries decided to take matters into their own hands by sacking Carthage, where there was certainly enough booty; and the Carthaginians were hard put to it to defend themselves.

### The first provinces—Organization and tax system

Rome now was faced with the problem of what to do with Sicily, whether to incorporate it into the confederation, annex it, or make some other arrangements. She finally decided on a combination of all three plans. Some cities were given to a loyal king of Syracuse, a few were incorporated into the confederation, and the remainder were organized as the first Roman *province*. Since the provincial system was used for the bulk of her later conquests, it needs a brief description here.

The most important person in the province was the Roman governor, at first holding the rank of praetor; then, when it became the custom to send out magistrates after their year of office at Rome, he was called a propraetor. Other provinces were governed by ex-consuls, called proconsuls. The governor was head of the state and chief judge; he was commander in chief of the Roman army which was permanently stationed there. He held office for only one year unless he had to undertake a prolonged military campaign. In this case his command could also be prolonged. As always with Roman magistrates, he was unpaid. The individual cities in the province were allowed municipal self-government under Roman protection, but they had to pay taxes to Rome. The governor, however, had no staff capable of assessing the taxes and making the collections. This task was therefore handed over to private enterprise in the persons of *publicani,* tax contractors who bid for the provincial tax contracts in Rome from the censors, who made the assessment for each whole province. Sometimes the provincial city itself bid for its own tax contract, and this was the usual custom in Sicily. If the contract fell to the publicani, they were supposed to make only a profit of 10 per cent on the contract price. The publicani had the support of the governor and his army in case of necessity. If the provincials thought the governor had been extortionate, they could prosecute him in the Roman senatorial courts.

Now this system made considerable demands on the character of the governor and the courts to which he was responsible; and it is a tribute to the still honest senatorial class that complaints in early years were so few. It need only be pointed out here that there was a natural community of interests between the publicani and the governor, which might be made to pay off at the expense of the provincial. And since the courts were composed of men of the same class as the governor, who hoped to govern a province themselves later, it might be difficult to secure a conviction. And even if a conviction were made for the sake of public appearances, the ex-governor was always permitted to live in some other part of the world, comforting his declining years with his ill-gotten gains. Moreover, when it is considered that for only two years in his life, the year following praetorship and the year following the consulate, could he hope for a province to govern, there was an undoubted temptation to make the most of those years. We shall see how this system did indeed tend to ruin the morale of the senatorial class after we have briefly followed the progress of the imperial expansion.

### The Second Punic War

Carthage, having with difficulty beaten off her rebellious mercenaries, soon returned to the war again, this time with a new and brilliant leader. Hannibal, one of the great generals of history, came through Spain over the Alps into Italy, defeating every Roman army that was sent against him. But he did not take Rome, even though after the battle of Cannae he came almost up to her gates. He took Capua and ravaged Campania, remaining in Italy for over fifteen years. But he could not gain many allies in Italy, and he was insufficiently supported by reinforcements from Carthage. Ultimately the Second Punic War was decided by a brilliant young Roman general, Scipio Africanus, who with a prolonged command conquered first Spain, and then landed in Africa with a new army. He first defeated the local Carthaginian army, and then defeated the returning Hannibal decisively at the batta of Zama (202 B.C.). Carthage received severe terms, losing all territory except the capital and surrounding areas. Rome became the protector of the North African coast, and Spain was made into a province.

### Interference in Greece—Conquest of Macedonia

The war with Hannibal involved Rome in another war with Macedonia and interference in Greece. Even before the Second Punic War the Romans had been forced to intervene on behalf of the traders of Italy to put a stop to piracy on the Adriatic Sea. When the pirates were cleaned up, the Romans naturally had to prevent their reappearance by occupying the coastal area of western Greece (Epirus and Illyria). This annoyed the Macedonian king, who regarded this as his sphere of influence. So when Hannibal appealed to him for help he joined the alliance against Rome. The Romans, however, in spite of their preoccupation with Carthage, were still able to spare enough troops to force Philip v of Macedon to make peace.

Meanwhile the Hellenistic kingdom of Seleucia had been extending its boundaries in Asia under Antiochus III (the Great) and was beginning to look westward. Antiochus entered into a private agreement with Philip of Macedon to partition Asia Minor (the

kingdom of Pergamum), the Ionian cities, and possibly Egypt. The important commercial city of Rhodes and the king of Pergamum at once sent envoys to the only power capable of preventing the partition. They arrived at Rome with a request for help in the last year of the Second Punic War; and this time it was the Senate who wanted to go to war with Philip v and Antiochus, while the people hesitated. The Senate quite correctly pointed out that the Romans might be able to defeat Philip before he could get help from his ally, and thus stop the whole scheme before it had started. The people allowed themselves to be persuaded, and Rome, with the assistance, for once, of both the leagues of Greece,[4] defeated Philip decisively. The Roman consul Flamininus, amid scenes of great enthusiasm, solemnly proclaimed freedom for all the Greeks for the first time since the conquests of Alexander.

[4] See above, page 280.

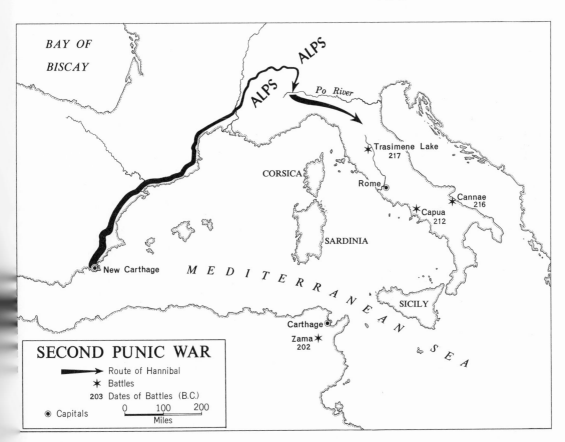

SECOND PUNIC WAR

→ Route of Hannibal
✳ Battles
**203** Dates of Battles (B.C.)
◉ Capitals

0     100     200
Miles

The gesture, unfortunately, was useless, for the leagues began quarreling again soon afterward, and the Aetolian League invited Antiochus into Greece. The Romans, now freed from the war with Carthage, defeated him, chased him back into Asia, took Asia Minor from him, and added the bulk of the northern part of the old kingdom of Seleucia to the territories of their allies, Pergamum and Rhodes. The Aetolian League surrendered, and Greece was now in Roman hands. But again Rome did not annex, preferring to keep all the existent governments too weak to present a threat to herself, but unfortunately, also too weak to maintain order. Macedonia, which had remained neutral during the war with Antiochus, soon began to intrigue against Rome until she was defeated decisively at the battle of Pydna in 168 B.C. Still she was not annexed, being divided into four "autonomous" republics, with newly devised constitutions.

It is not likely that this Roman policy of making no annexations was dictated by any special concern for Greek liberties; it seems to have been simply a refusal to take the responsibility of maintaining order in these countries as she kept order in Italy. The problem was not so simple for the Roman ruling class as it might seem to us. It was already clear that the Roman armies were not as well disciplined and efficient as they had been in the past. The Romans now fought with considerable superiority in troops and resources at their disposal, but the campaigns were no longer sharp and decisive. What had happened was that both the soldiers and their generals now realized the great profits to be won from the conquests, and too frequently they went as plunderers rather than as disciplined soldiers. The booty gained from the battle of Pydna was enormous, but it had taken several years to defeat the greatly inferior Macedonian army, and even the disunited Greeks could not be overcome in one short campaign. And at the other end of the Roman territory, Spain, inherited from Carthage, was very far from subdued, even though its armies were composed of poorly armed barbarians. If Rome then annexed these territories outright, they would have to be governed; and experience elsewhere showed how difficult it was to keep the governors under proper control by the Senate.

### Hardening of Roman imperial policy—Destruction of Corinth and Carthage

After Pydna there is noticeable a definite hardening of the senatorial policy under the influence of men like Cato the Elder, who hated foreigners, and especially Greeks, and no doubt also of the capitalists who had so much to gain from the conquests. The lack of a clear policy combined with exploitation soon drove the Greeks to rebellion again, and at last they were defeated for good in 146 B.C. The chief commercial city of Greece, Corinth, was ruthlessly sacked and Macedonia was annexed and made into a Roman province. In the same year Carthage was razed and the site cursed, even though she had scrupulously respected her treaty obligations, and even aided the Romans with troops and ships. There was no question of trade competition, for Rome was still not interested in commerce; this destruction has always been difficult to account for rationally, though we know that it was the ultrapatriotic party of Cato that urged it tirelessly until it was accepted as a policy. Greece was made into a protectorate under the governor of the new province of Macedonia. At last Rome had accepted responsibility for Greece's defense; but it was a looted and declining country that remained. Spain also was finally pacified a few years later, after barbarous cruelties, and in callous disregard of treaties.

By 133 B.C., therefore, when the Roman Republic entered on the last century of its existence, the whole state was already far on the road to complete demoralization. It is time now to deal more systematically with the effects of the expansion upon the Roman people and their constitution.

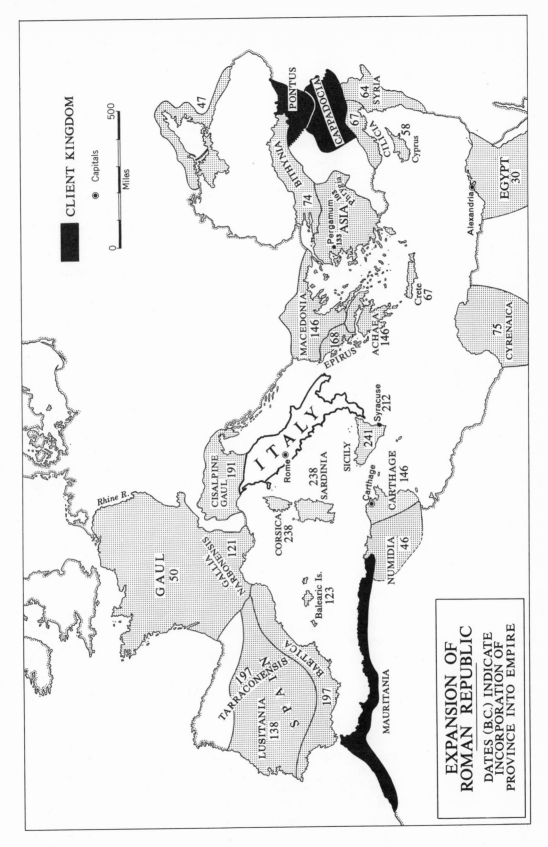

EXPANSION OF
ROMAN REPUBLIC

DATES (B.C.) INDICATE
INCORPORATION OF
PROVINCE INTO EMPIRE

CLIENT KINGDOM

● Capitals

Miles

0          500

GAUL
50

NARBONENSIS
121

CISALPINE
GAUL 191

Rhine R.

SPAIN

TARRACONENSIS
197

LUSITANIA
138

BAETICA
197

Balearic Is.
123

CORSICA
238

SARDINIA
238

ITALY

Rome ●

SICILY

Syracuse
212

241

Carthage ●

CARTHAGE
146

NUMIDIA
46

MAURITANIA

ITALY

MACEDONIA
146

EPIRUS
168

ACHAEA
146

Crete
67

BITHYNIA
74

PONTUS

CAPPADOCIA
67

ASIA
133

Pergamum
133

Phrygia
105

CILICIA
64

SYRIA
64

Cyprus
58

Alexandria ●

EGYPT
30

CYRENAICA
75

41

325

### The profits of empire

Rome still remained a city without much industry beyond the supply of goods necessary for the maintenance of the armies and ordinary daily needs of the citizens, and she suffered from an extremely unfavorable visible balance of trade. The exports consisted of some wool, wine, olive oil, and iron implements, and very little more. The Romans were not in the least interested in the carrying trade, never inserted any commercial clauses in their treaties, and allowed other seafaring peoples to attend to all the details of shipping the necessary grain and other imports to Rome. But the profits of empire were so enormous in the form of booty and regular tribute that the city and its more prosperous inhabitants had a handsome surplus, some of which went into new buildings and private estates. By 133 B.C. Rome was beginning to look somewhat like a Greek city; for the contact, first with southern Italy, and then with the Hellenistic world, brought thousands of Greeks, both free and slave, into Rome, where they made themselves useful to their masters in organizing more businesses, especially the retail trade, and introducing Hellenistic financial improvements. At the same time the stolid Roman began to be influenced by Hellenistic culture, which took on a new lease of life in Rome. Greek and Oriental luxuries began to flow into Roman hands, causing old puritans like Cato to bemoan the decadence of the old Roman character and the loss of old Roman manners. Some of the Roman families became educated in the Greek style, and even studied Greek philosophy, especially the circle around the Scipios, who were strong patrons of all forms of Greek culture. More and more interesting things could now be bought for money than in the hard old days. Cato was certainly far from wrong when he viewed this taste for luxuries with alarm; for it did indeed play an important part in the ultimate downfall of his republic.

### The rise of the equestrian order

The class that profited most from the expansion was the group of wealthy plebeians, never very many in number, who did not seek office but preferred wealth and the indirect influence that went with it. These men, who belonged to the first class in the Centuriate Assembly and therefore could have been enrolled in the cavalry, were called *equites,* or knights. These were the men who bid for contracts for public works on which they made profits, but their main source of income was from handling the provincial tax contracts. Most governors could be bribed, for reasons to be discussed shortly, with the result that taxes were stepped up far beyond the permissible rate. When the provincials were unable to pay and faced eviction or worse at the hands of the governor, other capitalists, called *negotiatores,* offered to lend them the money at high rates of interest, thus ensuring double profits for the equites of Rome. These capitalists soon began to exercise a sinister influence on Roman imperial policy, partly through suborning the senators, and partly through political influence over magistrates and the Assemblies by means of well-placed bribes.

### Dispossession of the peasant proprietors —Latifundia

Meanwhile the senators themselves, forbidden by law to handle tax contracts or, indeed, to engage in any other business, could increase their wealth only by capitalizing in some way upon their monopoly of office. They had three methods open to them: winning booty in military campaigns, exploiting the provinces in cooperation with the equites during their terms as governors, and by increasing their landholdings, mostly in Italy. The Punic Wars, while ruinous to the small farmers, had helped the large landholders. Much land had been devastated, especially in southern Italy, and only wealthy men could bring it back into cultivation and make it pay. They were able to buy this land at very low prices, or rent it at a nominal figure, and thereafter work it profitably with slaves on a plantation basis. The resulting large estates, called *latifundia*, were mostly given up to sheep, which required the least labor, though olive orchards and vineyards also lent themselves to large-scale cultivation.

### The growth of the city proletariat

The social results of the growth of these large estates were catastrophic. The poor farmers who found themselves ousted could only go to Rome, where there was very little employment for them. The Latins and Italians, who were the chief victims, were not permitted, as noncitizens, to bid for the public land even if they had had the money to do so. These allies had won no rights for centuries even though they had loyally supported Rome in all her wars. They began to agitate for Roman citizenship, and the poorer among them went to Rome, where they had an even more precarious existence than the impoverished Roman citizens.

In Rome there was little to do. For those who were skilled there were new public and private buildings to work on, others might be able to pay court to the rich, citizens could sell their votes when the oligarchy needed them. With the influx of slaves, often better educated and more capable than the Roman farmer in the city, wages fell till it was barely possible to live on them. The total result was the creation of a vast proletariat, most of whom had the vote and full rights but felt no responsibility for the state. They were, however, potentially very dangerous to the oligarchy; for many of them came from the rural tribes, and could at any moment break the senatorial political machine in the Tribal Assembly if they were not fed and amused and otherwise bribed.[5] The office seekers began to provide them with great public games and spectacles, and the state began to supply them with grain at very low prices. But all these distractions did not prevent the ex-farmers from agitating

[5] The Roman citizen retained his vote in the tribe into which he had been born, even when he took up residence permanently in the capital.

for the breaking up of the large estates and for the founding of colonies where they could start life again. For the majority of them there was nothing else; the army still required some property qualification, so that even this last resort was closed to many.

### ▶ The Gracchan revolution

THE LAND LAW OF TIBERIUS GRACCHUS— THE CONSTITUTIONAL ISSUE

This was the background of the Gracchan "revolution." There had been several attempts in the years before 133 B.C. to have the land redistributed, often sponsored by members of the Claudian family, which had always cultivated the proletariat for political purposes; but Tiberius Gracchus, the elder of the two reforming brothers, though connected with this family, was undoubtedly sincere himself. In 133 B.C. he was elected tribune, after a campaign in which he promised the redistribution of the land.

When he brought forward a comparatively mild law in the Tribal Assembly, the senatorial party, now generally called the Optimates, played its usual card: a tribune, one of the colleagues of Tiberius, vetoed the bill. Legally Tiberius had no recourse. He could only wait for the next year and hope to have a full board of tribunes elected to support his program. But he himself could not be elected tribune two years in succession. Rather than abandon his program he chose to appeal to the people to depose the recalcitrant tribune. The people backed him, but the deposition was undoubtedly illegal. The law was then declared duly passed.

In ordinary circumstances the Senate could have resisted further by refusing to provide funds to put the law into operation. But, as it happened, it was just at this moment that the last king of Pergamum, in Asia Minor, left his entire kingdom to Rome in his will. Tiberius summoned the Assembly and instructed it to accept the gift on behalf of the people of Rome. This act was not illegal, but for centuries this had been regarded as the task of the Senate and not of the people, and thus was deeply offensive to that august body, which saw a future in which a determined tribune with the aid of the proletariat could wrest from it all its long-cherished privileges. Only one safeguard remained—the tribune could not be re-elected. But Tiberius did not have time in his year of office to put his law into execution, and he chose to stand again for office the second year. On the election day the Pontifex Maximus, a Scipio and an opponent of the Claudian faction, led an armed band of senators and their clients against Tiberius and succeeded in murdering him and three hundred of his followers. Some reaction against this violence followed, and the law of Tiberius was put into effect, showing perhaps that the opposition was rather against rule by the proletariat than against the law itself. And a law seems to have been passed during the next ten years that a tribune could succeed himself in office.

### THE TRIBUNATE OF GAIUS GRACCHUS— SENATORIAL RESORT TO DEMAGOGUERY AND VIOLENCE

In 123 B.C. the younger brother of Tiberius, Gaius Gracchus, was elected tribune with a much more comprehensive program than his brother had sponsored. But it was not uniformly popular with the people, thus giving the Optimates a chance to defeat him by strictly legal means. The first item on Gaius's program was to provide grain for the people below cost price. This was probably not new, and was of no special importance, except that Gaius also made careful administrative arrangements for the import and distribution of this grain. All later tribunes who tried to persuade the people to pass laws included such bills in their program. Gaius also proposed an extensive colonization scheme in the conquered lands, including one on the "cursed" but incomparable site of Carthage. The colonists, however, had to possess some means, as the sites were often, like Carthage, capable of commercial as well as agricultural development. This was therefore not very interesting to the quite penniless proletariat. He proposed a program of public works, especially roads; and he also

re-enacted his brother's land law, although there was by then not much land available for distribution. To gain the support of the equites he made special arrangements for a graduated tax system in the provinces, and he handed over the new rich province of Asia to them alone as taxgatherers; although this system was already substantially in effect elsewhere, the new law gave it official sanction. The whole provincial tax was now let as a unit at Rome, and not to separate groups as had been the earlier custom in Sicily, thus necessitating the formation of large and profitable corporations in Rome. Gaius also substituted equestrian juries for senatorial juries to try cases of corruption in the provinces, a move which involved the recognition of the equites for the first time as a separate order in the state. The new juries were certainly no improvement on the senatorial juries, since both classes were equally engaged in the fleecing of the provincials.

Gaius now stood for re-election and was successful, though far from the top of the poll. As one of his colleagues he had an Optimate sympathizer, one Livius Drusus, who had discovered a new and effective weapon against Gaius. For Gaius wanted to introduce, and may have already introduced in his first term, a bill which he was certain would not be popular—the full enfranchisement of the Italians. This could never please the Roman proletariat, which saw various treasured privileges shared with "foreigners," especially such minor but personally important matters as good seats at the games and festivals. Drusus proceeded to veto this bill, even though it probably had little chance of passing, and proposed instead a bill which might have passed and would have removed one important grievance of the Italians, namely, discrimination between Italians and citizens when on military service in the matter of discipline. But Drusus went on to show his real intentions by playing upon mass superstition, warning the people of the terrible results that would come from settling a cursed site; and he proposed also that the new colonies should be opened equally to propertyless citizens. There was doubtless no intention whatever of putting such a proposal into effect, but he was successful in defeating Gaius, who was not elected for the third year.

As his term neared its end the Optimates made obvious preparations to deal with Gaius personally as soon as he had ceased to be sacrosanct. Incidents were numerous, and Gaius surrounded himself with a bodyguard drawn from his own political party, the Populares, as they were called. When one of his followers was tricked into murdering an opponent at the end of the year, the Senate declared martial law and called upon the consul, a ruffian elected for the special purpose, to take steps to defend the state. The consul did so by killing a large number of Populares, and Gracchus himself was either killed or committed suicide. Three thousand more were condemned to death by a senatorial judicial commission without allowing the traditional appeal to the people and without even a trial. The Senate had declared publicly its moral bankruptcy; and though it did not take further steps against such of the Gracchan laws as had passed, it had set the example of violence which was to be followed by senators, demagogues, and generals alike until the republic itself collapsed.

▶ **The collapse of the republic** [6]

THE ENROLLMENT OF A VOLUNTEER
PROFESSIONAL ARMY—MARIUS

The instrument which was to destroy the republic was forged by a general who certainly had no idea of the ultimate future consequences of his handiwork, and was directly due to the corruption and rapacity of knights and senators. A young African prince named Jugurtha, who was well acquainted with Rome, decided to use the venality of the governing classes in Rome to carve himself out a large independent kingdom in Africa. Since this meant the deposition of

[6] This section is given in considerable detail for its value as a case study of the dangers to free institutions of refusal by an entrenched oligarchy to grant timely reforms which could perhaps have preserved them.

an ally of Rome, he evidently hoped that the judicious placing of bribes would persuade the Senate to wink at his activities. Unfortunately for him, an eloquent tribune succeeded in keeping the issue before the people, or Jugurtha might well have been successful. Several armies were sent against him, but all met with unexplained difficulties, and Jugurtha openly proclaimed that everything in Rome was for sale. Though our only account of the war is from a source unsympathetic to the Senate, there can be little doubt that the earlier generals were bribed; at last Metellus, a member of the ruling clique, himself went out and made some progress in the war. But even he was unable to finish it, thus giving the opportunity to one of his subordinates, C. Marius, to suggest that his superior, too, was lagging for private reasons, and to insist that he himself should be given the command as consul.

Marius was a man of the people, a rugged soldier, no doubt; and with the ability to win popular support in Rome, where his friends prepared the ground for his consulship. When all was ready he demanded a leave from his superior officer to go to Rome and stand for the consulship. This ultimately had to be granted, and Marius was duly elected. But the Senate, which, by custom, distributed the commands, refused to appoint him to Africa. The Assembly, working smoothly under his supporters, passed a special law giving it to him, and the Senate had to acquiesce. It was now that Marius adopted the military policy that led to the downfall of the Republic. He abolished the property qualifications for military service altogether, and proceeded to recruit his army from the proletariat. This army was now made up of volunteers, men who looked to their general for payment of their wages, as well as for booty, and for pensions when they had completed their service.

It is hard to overestimate the importance of this innovation. Property qualifications had been consistently lowered for centuries, and this was only the final logical step; but the soldier-citizens now recruited were those for whom the Roman Republic meant nothing but a hostile oligarchy and "bread and circuses" on occasion. They had no loyalty to it, and only contempt and dislike for the ruling oligarchy which made such a good thing out of it. Now they could recover their self-respect in the army; it was not, however, the army of the Roman Republic but the army of the general. One thing only was necessary as qualification for this general. He must be successful, capable of delivering pay, booty, and pensions—or the equivalent of pensions, land. This last could only be secured at the expense of the republic, by political activity.

It was easy for a general with an army at his back to cow the Senate and the people once he was in command; but he had first to be appointed to this command. And he had to be sure that there was no rival general of equal power with him. So it became necessary for the prospective general to maintain a political machine which would ensure him his first and subsequent commands, and would see to it that his rivals did not surpass him. And in order that there might be suitable commands available, the conquests must be expanded, with or without causes of war.

It was clear that the Assembly was now a more suitable instrument than the Senate for this purpose. If the Senate was favorable, well and good; but if not, the Gracchi had shown where the real power in the state lay. And the army belonged to the proletarian class. The power of the Senate rested on the acquiescence of the people and its willingness to abide by the constitution; the new army, being an extraconstitutional power, was hampered by no constitutional inhibitions, and needed to have no compunction about intimidating a few hundred senators and their clients. From this time onward the government of Rome was to be in the hands of the tribunes and the Assembly, aided by such funds as were necessary for bribery, and by the threat of the return of the army commander to enforce his will on any opponents of his regime. While the commander was away the Senate was still able to function, and even assert itself on occasion.

But the oligarchy knew well enough that the power in the state had gone elsewhere; its only hope was to be able to persuade a successful general to lend his support to it, rather than to the people. But the Senate was never able again to function as an independent, responsible body, without the support of some general; it could be a nuisance to the general who wanted to act constitutionally, but it could no longer overrule him if he decided to act in opposition to it.

Doubtless none of these consequences were foreseen at the time that the army was organized on a volunteer basis, but they followed inevitably. The republic was doomed.

Marius himself with his new army made considerable headway in his campaigns against Jugurtha. But the latter had gained an important ally in his father-in-law, another African ruler, and it was not until one of Marius's own officers, Sulla, persuaded the father-in-law to betray Jugurtha that the war could be finished. Marius flew into a jealous rage against Sulla; but since the people gave Marius credit for the victory and since he, not Sulla, celebrated the triumph over Jugurtha, the consul remained the most popular man in Rome. At this moment Rome was suddenly threatened by an invasion of German barbarians from the north. Marius stood illegally for re-election as consul, and was successful, receiving the supreme command against the Germans. It took him several years to recruit and reorganize a larger and more effective army, and finally defeat the enemy, and during this time his supporters in the Assembly continued to elect him every year as consul. But when the war was over, he needed lands for his veterans and he wanted to be elected consul for the sixth time. He had to obtain some political support, for he was no longer an indispensable man; the Senate was anxious to put an end to his illegal consulships, and the proletariat was not interested in his program of lands for veterans.

The only party possible for him was the Populares, led at this time by a pair of unscrupulous demagogues whose price was high. By grain doles and wholesale bribery he was duly elected consul for the sixth time, but his supporters proceeded to rule Rome by violence and open murder. When the Senate called upon him to suppress them and declared martial law, he decided to disown the demagogues, who were themselves murdered by supporters of the oligarchy. Marius, his usefulness to the Senate over, and naturally deserted by the populace, retired to exile in Africa, where he plotted how to obtain revenge as well as how to achieve the seventh consulship promised him by a soothsayer.

DISCONTENT OF THE ITALIANS—THE SOCIAL WAR

Meanwhile the Italians, who had fought loyally against the Germanic invaders, were subjected to new indignities and discriminations. Italian soldiers in the armies of Marius had not been permitted to take part in the colonization schemes put through for them by the Assembly; and civilian Italians found that some of the colonization, as usual, was at their expense. For years they had been trying to overcome this discrimination by the use of the vote, since they were allowed to vote if they came to Rome to live. But the Senate and people were united in their desire to prevent this, and in 95 B.C. a drastic law was passed expelling all Italian noncitizens from Rome. From this moment the Italians began to plot a rebellion, actual secession from Rome, and the setting up of a new confederacy independent of Rome.

In 92 B.C. new evidence of the debasement of justice, one of the few remaining reasons for Roman pride and Italian loyalty, gave further ammunition to those agitators who claimed that Rome had outlived its usefulness. A certain Rutilius, who had refused to allow the equites to exploit his province of Asia, was himself accused of extortion and bribery and convicted by the equestrian jury as an example to governors to keep their hands off the capitalists. On conviction he went into exile in the province that he was supposed to have exploited, which supported him in comfort for the rest of his days.

In 91 B.C. the last effort was made to satisfy the Italians by a tribune named Drusus the Younger, who brought in a bill for their enfranchisement. Knowing that it had no chance of passing by itself, he included it in an omnibus bill which also contained provisions for cheap grain and new colonies for the proletariat. The Senate claimed that he had ignored the auspices, that earthquakes and other portents showed divine displeasure, and declared the legislation invalid. The people refused to re-elect him, and the next tribune proposed to prosecute him and all his friends. Drusus was murdered, and the Italians, their last hope of succeeding by peaceful means gone, rose in revolt.

With armies the equal of any the Romans could command in Italy, they won several victories, and set up a new state called Italia. But the Romans were no longer exclusively dependent upon the Italians. They recalled Marius and sent for veterans from the provinces who knew nothing of the grievances of the Italians. With these, and under the generalship of Marius and Sulla, his rival and lieutenant from African days, they began to make headway. But progress was slow, and the Romans at last decided to take some action on the grievances in the hope of dividing the Italian ranks. They passed a law giving citizenship to all Italians who had not revolted, and followed it up by another law offering citizenship to anyone whose home was in Italy and who would lay down his arms within a stipulated period. This move was successful, for the Italians had never been fully united in their desire to leave Rome altogether. Indeed, the upper class among the Italians had sometimes profited from Roman rule, and had from the beginning opposed Italia. The Roman armies were now able to make much better progress and at last, with the death of the Italian leader, the revolt was suppressed. But, as usual, the oligarchy had a card up its sleeve. The new citizens were all enrolled in eight tribes out of the thirty-five, and, though they gained some privileges, they were unable to make their influence felt in the Assembly.

### THE RIVALRY BETWEEN MARIUS AND SULLA— THE TRIUMPH OF SULLA

Meanwhile the opportunity for a most important command in the East had arisen. While the Romans were busy elsewhere, Mithridates VI, king of Pontus in Asia Minor, had just massacred all Italians in Asia within his dominions, and he had enlarged his kingdom to the point where it was dangerous to Rome. Both Marius, although he was sixty-seven years old, and Sulla wanted the command. But Sulla, the more successful general in the Italian war, had been elected consul and appointed by the Senate to the command before Marius was able to summon enough political strength to dispute it.

At this point a tribune Sulpicius, evidently a real statesman but condemned by the violence of his times to stoop to violent and demagogic methods, wanted to give the full franchise to the Italians, and enroll them in all the tribes. But the only political support he could gain was from Marius and the worst group of the Populares, including slaves, whom the old man was willing to recruit for his army. When the bill was brought forward in the Assembly, there was a riot, and Sulla was caught in Rome, many miles away from his army, the veterans of the recent Italian war. Sulla was forced to hide, of all places in the house of Marius, until he could escape to join his troops. The bill for the full enfranchisement of the Italians passed, under the threat of the soldiers of Marius, and the latter was then given the command against Mithridates by the Assembly. Sulla, however, escaped to his army.

It was at this point that the domination of the generals became evident to all. Sulla had been appointed to the command by the Senate, Marius by the Assembly. Each had an army in Italy, but Sulla's army was greatly superior to the rabble of Marius—if he could hold its loyalty to himself. The Assembly requested Sulla to turn over his legions to Marius, but they decided to stick to their general, and he marched on Rome. Marius fled, Sulpicius was murdered, and Sulla hastily passed a number of laws taking power away from the Tribal Assembly and giving it to the older Comitia centuriata, which was still, at least to some extent, in the hands of the propertied classes. But he could not stay long in Rome, since he was anxious to go on to his command; he contented himself, therefore, with extracting from the new consul an oath to keep the laws he had just forced through, and departed for Asia.

Needless to say, as soon as he had left, his laws were rescinded; and some courageous or troublemaking tribune again brought forward a law for the full enfranchisement of the Italians. The result was another riot, and once more Marius was recalled. With a band of hastily recruited slaves he entered Rome and started a bloody massacre of senatorial supporters. He was at last elected for his seventh consulship, but died after one month in office. The Assembly formally deposed Sulla from his command, and an army was recruited to take it over from him. This army, however, after meeting Sulla in Greece, decided that he was more likely to provide it with booty, and most of its members deserted to him.

As the menace of Sulla's return grew nearer after a series of successful campaigns against Mithridates, the Populares, knowing what awaited them, tried to raise revolt elsewhere than in Italy. Supporters in Spain, Sicily, and Africa, together with still unreconciled groups in southern Italy, took up arms and prepared to resist him. But Sulla made a solemn declaration that he would support full and equal citizenship for all Italians, thus splitting the opposition in Italy; and with some severe fighting he was able to subdue the other revolts, though Spain continued for a long time to resist successfully under the moderate Marian, Sertorius. After a brief but bloody battle Sulla captured Rome, and instituted another set of proscriptions against the popular leaders. Then he made a determined effort to revise the constitution, and save, if possible, the republic.

### THE LAST EFFORT AT REFORM—THE CONSTITUTION OF SULLA

Sulla was an accomplished general, and one with a remarkable faculty for keeping the loyalty of his troops. He belonged to the senatorial class, though he did not owe his position to his family connections; he had had to make his own way to the top by hard work and undoubted military talent. He was now to make the last attempt to restore the republic to a workable condition, and he showed a considerable insight into the problems that had to be solved if it was to survive. He could unquestionably have made himself sole ruler and founded the empire then and there; but he was now fairly well advanced in years, and, even if he had so desired, he could not himself have undertaken the enormous work which later Augustus performed in a long reign of forty-five years. It may be added also that the republic had not as yet fully demonstrated its incapacity, and public opinion had not yet been prepared in a people as conservative as the Roman for any form of government other than that under which they had grown to greatness and power. Having then decided on reform rather than abolition, Sulla put a very capable mind to work on the real problems. The military had been overriding the civilian elements in the government, and the rule by the Roman proletariat, with power but without responsibility, had been shown to be both incompetent and corrupt. Yet the Senate, the only alternative body, had degenerated into a narrow, self-seeking oligarchy, and needed a thorough overhauling if it were to be a fit alternative to rule by the proletariat.

In order to reform the constitution Sulla first had himself appointed dictator for an unlimited period; since both consuls were dead and the appointment was carried out with due formality, there was nothing unconstitutional about it beyond the unlimited period of office. Then he had a series of laws passed (the Cornelian Laws) which were directed to the main problems. He had decided that the most hopeful approach was the reform of the Senate and the partial abolition of the powers of the incompetent and unrepresentative assemblies. He would also restrict prolonged army commands and strictly enforce the laws.

He increased the membership of the Senate to six hundred, and prevented it from being a self-perpetuating body by taking away from the censors all power of choosing its members. The new senators chosen by Sulla were mostly from the equites and upper-class men who had held no previous office. Instead of being replenished at the discretion of the censors, the Senate was now brought up to its full establishment by the addition of quaestors—the lowest rank in the *cursus honorum*. Since quaestors were elected, the Senate thus became virtually an elected body. Twenty were elected each year, none below the age of thirty. Minimum age limits were also set for the praetorship and consulship (thirty-nine and forty-two, respectively), thus ensuring that praetors and consuls had several years' service in the Senate before being elected to their offices. The number of praetors was increased to eight. Each praetor and each consul, after his year of office, proceeded at once to take command of one of the ten provinces. No consul could be elected a second time to his office without an interval of ten years, thus spacing his provincial commands in such a way that he could not gain much personal loyalty from his troops. The Senate through these reforms became more nearly a parliament than anything the Romans had previously known.

In order to give civil powers back to those magistrates who had been losing ground to the tribunes in the last centuries, Sulla disqualified tribunes from holding any other office afterward, thus ensuring that men of ambition would not stand for the tribunate. He probably also took away from the tribunes any power of introducing legislation to the Assembly, and it is fairly certain that the Senate had to agree to the legislation before it was presented. Finally he forbade re-election to the tribunate except after an interval of ten years.

In order to handle military adventurers, he relied upon a redefinition of the law of treason. Under this, no governor of a province was permitted to leave it or march beyond its borders with an army; he might not start a war on his own initiative; and he could not invade the territory of a client king without permission from Rome. No governor could stay in his province more than thirty days after the arrival of his successor. To enforce this redefinition he reformed the law courts —a permanent reform—abolishing appeal to the people, and putting them entirely in the hands of senatorial members under the presidency of a praetor.

It was obviously a well-thought-out reform, provided that the Romans had continued to be a law-abiding people, provided that anyone had seriously intended to keep to the new rules, and provided that no enemy of Rome appeared who could not be handled by annual generals of the old type—necessarily without much military experience but capable of commanding the loyalty of professional troops with guaranteed pensions. What was needed was the conception of a *state,* and state responsibility for pensions and pay. Then the army could have provided an honorable career properly rewarded by the state, with all booty appropriated by the state and not by the generals. The reform of the Senate was on the right lines, and its method of recruitment endured even under the empire. There was no further trouble from consuls and praetors except twice when they also had armies in Italy; and there was no trouble from ordinary provincial governors, but only from special prolonged commands given in defiance of the constitution by the Senate or the people. In short, the military dangers necessitated prolonged commands, and prolonged commands, in the absence of loyalty to the state, continued to mean political power for the commanders. The new Senate, even though it may have been a better body, less restricted and less narrowly oligarchical than before, did not command respect from the soldiers; its authority as a *parliament,* in view of its history and the circumstances of the time, was accepted by no one.

Sulla, having put this new constitution on its feet, then tried to settle his veterans on the land, mostly in Italy, at the expense of rebellious Italians, and founded at least fourteen new colonies. But most of the soldiers recruited after the Marian military reform were no longer even farmers; many of them drifted back to Rome, selling their new

land to the eager land speculators in Rome, while others, faced with armed resistance from the recently dispossessed, gave up the attempt to take over their allotments and drifted back too. Sulla, however, did not live to see what happened to his reforms. He gave up his dictatorship, retired to the country, and died soon afterward.

## THE BREAKDOWN OF THE SULLAN CONSTITUTION—THE FIRST TRIUMVIRATE

The sequel to the establishment of the Sullan Constitution showed that no important body in Rome really wished to give it a fair trial, and the problems connected with the taking over and managing of foreign lands required professional military commanders to deal with them. Sulla had not been long in his grave when it seemed necessary to the Senate to appoint one of his generals, a popular young soldier named Pompey, to a long-term command to subdue some persistent rebels in Spain; and while he was away a slave revolt broke out in Italy which again needed attention from a tried general. This was Crassus, a capable soldier who had become rich through buying up property confiscated from Sulla's victims, and who was to become better known later as a capitalist and banker than as a general. Neither Pompey nor Crassus had gone through the usual offices of state before receiving their special commands, thus infringing already the Sullan Constitution. When the slave war in Italy was at an end, these two men, though jealous of each other, combined to force the Senate, which had, as noted, now become a virtual legislature, to pass bills to legalize their joint election as consuls. As part of the program on which they ran for election they promised to restore power to the tribunes and to give the full legislative power back to the Assembly. This promise they fulfilled, the Senate in 70 B.C. ceasing to be a legislature after a bare ten years in this capacity.

Having restored power to the tribunes and the people, Pompey proceeded to take steps to control them by political manipulation. For many years afterward he always had sufficient friends among them to ensure the passing of legislation favorable to himself. The opportunity soon arose for another command. The pirates in the Mediterranean had long been a serious menace to the Roman grain supply, and ordinary commands by proconsuls seemed to be ineffective. Pompey's friends therefore introduced legislation in the Assembly proposing that he should be given a three-year command of a very special nature, requiring governors in the provinces to assist him, and giving him an official staff of fifteen men of praetorian rank. The Senate objected strongly, but was now powerless to prevent him from receiving the command, and he was duly appointed.

He completed the work with his usual prompt efficiency, and within three months he was ready for another command. The obliging and grateful populace, now assured of its grain supply, voted him a proconsular command in the East, superseding the senatorial general Lucullus, who, after several successful campaigns, had bogged down because of a mutiny by his troops, who found him too niggardly with the distribution of his booty. Pompey soon remedied this situation, and proceeded to reorganize the East, a task his predecessor had already substantially done. There could now be no doubt in anyone's mind that Pompey was the supreme arbiter of the Roman world. His troops were secured to him by his open-handedness; and when at last he returned to Rome, there would be no one to contest his supremacy.

At Rome his rivals did their best to undermine him, and at times his agents found themselves hard put to it to defend his interests against the wholesale bribery of Crassus, who was trying desperately to find some alternative candidate for power. The notorious Catiline, known to generations of Latin students for the speeches made against him by Cicero, was one of Crassus' protégés who overreached himself and was deserted by his backer. Julius Caesar, a popular demagogue, seemed a more hopeful candidate, for he was obviously a man of considerable talents and resolution, and his poverty gave Crassus a chance to put him

in his debt by lending him the money for sumptuous games, which, of course, endeared him to the voters. Crassus' support of Caesar later paid off handsomely, as we shall see. But meanwhile, as long as Pompey was successful in the East and his political agents looked after his interests adequately, everyone in Rome had to bear in mind his eventual return and take it into account in their political calculations. During these years Cicero, a parvenu lawyer, was able to have himself elected consul as a compromise choice, and chance gave him the opportunity to "save the state" by suppressing the ill-planned conspiracy of Catiline. Cicero's piece of self-assertion seems to have annoyed the supporters of Pompey, who would have preferred that their hero had been recalled to restore order in Rome. As it was, when Pompey finally did return there was no crisis in Rome. Everything was quiet and peaceful, and there was no legitimate excuse available for illegally bringing his army to Rome.

But Pompey, if he chose not to force his way into power by the use of his loyal troops, was in need of some political support. The leader of the Senate was a die-hard republican named Cato (called the Younger to distinguish him from a similarly die-hard ancestor, pages 324–326), and he was supported by the disgruntled general Lucullus, who had been superseded in his Eastern command by Pompey. When Pompey, therefore, disbanded his army at the coast and proceeded peaceably to Rome, these senators thought they would teach him a lesson, and refuse to grant pensions to his veterans, while at the same time they would also refuse to give legal sanction to his administrative settlements in the East—this in spite of the fact that Pompey had sent an enormous quantity of booty to the Senate for the use of the treasury.

This incredible piece of stupidity and shortsightedness on the part of the senators was the death warrant for the republic. Pompey, a man of great administrative and military capacity but apparently not politically ambitious, could at this moment have been won over to the senatorial party, and

Crassus and Caesar would have been impotent. As it was, Pompey was forced to look to these two for political support, and he had much to offer in exchange for it. His land-hungry veterans would naturally follow him in any venture which he demanded from them, in spite of the fact that they had been formally disbanded.

Nevertheless the price of Caesar and Crassus was high, though Pompey seems not to have realized at the time what would be the personal cost to himself. The money of Crassus had partially undermined Pompey's previously unchallenged popularity with the voters, and the banker's support was pledged to his protégé Julius Caesar, whose year it would ordinarily be for the consulship. But there was a legal obstacle to Caesar's election. He had just returned from his first command of importance in Spain, and he desired a triumph for his work there. But, if he were to have his triumph, then legally he could not enter Rome and stand for the consulship. Reasonably enough, he asked the Senate for permission to stand for the consulship by proxy. Cato filibustered the proposal out, and permission was refused. Caesar abandoned his triumph, which had social rather than political value, and was duly elected consul with the support of Crassus. The Senate, still rushing on blindly to its destruction after the manner of a Greek tragedy but well aware of Caesar's military ambitions and believing that it still wielded the powers of ancient days, gratuitously insulted him by allotting him as his proconsular command, to which he was entitled after his year as consul, the sinecure of control of the lands and forests of Italy. This drove Caesar into the arms of the only man who could get him what he wanted.

Pompey needed ratification of his acts in the East and he needed lands for his veterans, Caesar needed a command to satisfy his newly discovered military genius, Crassus needed a pay-off from Caesar whom he had financed so faithfully while waiting for this moment. All these needs were taken care of by an unofficial and extralegal agreement known as the First Triumvirate (60 B.C.). When Caesar proposed that the Senate should satisfy Pompey's demands and it refused, Pompey offered the consul the use of a few of his veterans. The Senate house was surrounded and of course the Senate had to give way. When Caesar asked for a five-year proconsular command in Gaul, Pompey, not fearing any danger from such a recent and militarily unknown rival, supported him. Crassus was entirely happy at the distribution of land to Pompey's veterans, as he had been quietly buying up all the good land in Italy which he could now sell to the state at substantial profit to himself; while for good measure a tribune was permitted to propose that there should be a one-third reduction in the price of all tax contracts for the year (the tribune was paid off in shares of Crassus' corporation). Finally, Caesar and Pompey accepted a gift of six thousand talents from King Ptolemy of Egypt in return for a senatorial resolution that he should be allowed to keep his throne! But Caesar also had what he wanted most, a five-year command in Cisalpine Gaul where there were a few local disturbances. Later Transalpine Gaul was added to his command when a more real danger appeared from invading northern tribes. The year ended, and Caesar went on his epoch-making command, while Pompey and Crassus stayed in Italy.

### CIVIL WAR—THE DICTATORSHIP OF CAESAR

The story of the next ten years is the story of the gradual supplanting of Pompey by Caesar. In the early years of the triumvirate Pompey was still supreme, but his veterans were aging, while Caesar was building up a strong army of disciplined legionaries loyal to himself. Crassus was eliminated from the triumvirate when he insisted on being appointed to a military command against the Parthians in the East and was killed in a disastrous defeat at Carrhae (53 B.C.). For most of the time Pompey held no official position, though his services were occasionally called upon to suppress riots in Rome and to organize the grain supply. He was in command of troops in Spain and elsewhere, and the navy was under his control, but he did not rule these forces personally, preferring to stay in the vicinity of Rome. When reports of Caesar's successes reached Rome, for a long time he took no action to sustain his earlier supremacy over all rivals. And the Senate, realizing that it was now in greater danger from Caesar than from Pompey, proceeded to woo the older man away from his partner. In 51 B.C. it tried for the last time to make use of constitutional republican safeguards against an aspiring general, and this ill-timed maneuver precipitated the civil war which destroyed its independence forever.

Caesar spent nearly ten years campaigning in Gaul. The Gauls or Celts were by no means a barbarian people, but had developed a distinctive civilization of their own, though they retained their primitive tribal governments. They were, however, seriously disunited, and it had been Caesar's task to take advantage of this disunity to offset his comparatively small army. He never had to fight with many Gauls at the same time; and though, even so, he was usually outnumbered, he always emerged successful in the end. There was very little excuse for the whole campaign, since the Gauls were not troubling the Romans; but once Caesar had intervened, the disunity of the various groups made possible the exercise of the customary Roman imperial policy of divide and rule. By slow degrees Caesar was thus able to conquer the whole country. In the process he built up a very strong body of legionaries, personally devoted to himself, though several of his senior officers later deserted him as soon as they had the opportunity, and a number of them joined in his murder. His administration of the province and his military acumen were clearly of a very high order, although our only account was written by himself.

At this crisis of the Roman Republic in 50–49 B.C., one thing stands out clearly. Caesar, in addition to being a slightly younger man than his rival Pompey, had obviously a greater resolution; he had tasted supreme military power for ten years and was at the height of his glory and self-confidence. He had no intention of allowing himself to be dictated to by the constitution,

by his rival, or by the Senate, though he would probably have preferred to avoid civil war, especially when he had little strength beside his own legions in Gaul. He was not sure how strong Pompey and the Senate would actually prove; for on paper Pompey had the Spanish and African legions, a legendary reputation in the East which could be converted into troops, and undisputed command of the seas. Clearly it was better to behave legally if possible.

But the Senate seemed determined to drive Caesar to illegal action, evidently with the intention of summoning Pompey to take drastic legal steps against him. Pompey, who could have taken supreme power for himself earlier, had refrained from doing so. He might therefore as a last resort be relied upon to defend the republic against Caesar, who might well be intending to destroy it. There were many charges that could be made against Caesar. There were undoubted illegalities in the conduct of the war in Gaul. He had extended his authority without permission, he had massacred prisoners contrary to accepted rules of war, and if these real crimes were not enough, many others could be manufactured, quite sufficient to ensure his exile and punishment should he ever permit himself to be tried by Roman courts. Caesar, of course, was well aware of what was planned against him; hence his insistence that he must continue to keep his command or another one which would carry with it immunity from prosecution. But the Senate had no intention of permitting him such immunity; on the contrary, before he even returned to Italy, it declared martial law and called upon Pompey to defend the republic, thus forcing Caesar's hand. Caesar, hearing the news, is said to have cried, "Alea jacta est!" ("The die is cast!") and crossed the river Rubicon, the boundary of Italy, with his army, thus putting himself at once legally in the wrong, as no general was permitted to enter Italy with an army.

Pompey did his best. But when he summoned troops to his standard, too few responded. His active legions were far away, and his reputation was no longer what it had been. The bulk of the senators and the aristocrats in general were with him; but in the campaign that followed they were a hindrance rather than a help, forcing him into battle before he was ready. With a properly planned campaign he should have won, but he was never allowed to plan his strategy; the navy, which was entirely on his side, was used to poor advantage. Leaving Italy for Greece, he tempted the impetuous Caesar to follow him, but then allowed the rebel to escape from the consequences of his rashness. In the end Pompey was defeated at the battle of Pharsalia (48 B.C.) and escaped to Egypt, where he was murdered. Caesar followed him there and was nearly brought to an untimely end by a sudden uprising of the Egyptians under the last of the Ptolemies. Surviving this misadventure by the fortunate arrival of reinforcements, he defeated and killed Ptolemy and spent the winter with his widow, a young beauty named Cleopatra. The following year he set out again in pursuit of the last supporters of Pompey. Though some of the campaigns were strenuous and hard fought, Caesar was uniformly successful, and was able to return to Rome at the end of the year 46 B.C. and turn his attention to affairs of state.

ESTIMATE OF THE WORK OF JULIUS CAESAR— ADMINISTRATIVE REFORMS AND POLITICAL INEPTITUDE

Caesar spent the last two years of his life in trying to create order in the empire of which he was now undisputed ruler. Unquestionably he had a very considerable grasp of the administrative problems involved in this task, and his administration, as far as it went, was enlightened. He extended Roman citizenship to many provincials and he stopped the tax-farming system, making the governors responsible only to himself. He put the municipalities of Italy on a uniform basis. He planned and put into execution an extensive program of public works, draining of marshes, and building of roads; and he planned an immense program of colonization in the provinces. He reformed the calendar, putting into use the Egyptian solar calendar of 365¼ days. He

took measures to diminish the population of Rome, and he instituted a public works program for the remainder, which was greatly superior to the privately sponsored building programs of his predecessors in that it was better planned and less haphazard. He undertook an important reform in the free municipalities of the empire in the hope of ensuring a regular supply of officials to undertake public duties, he substituted a graduated land tax in some of the provinces instead of the much-abused irregular collections. He was able to carry out these reforms because, for the first time, there was a real public authority in Rome in the person of himself. Rome was, in his day, on the verge of becoming, for the first time, a true state.

It was a good beginning, and a very considerable body of achievement for the short time that he held absolute power. There is no doubt that Caesar was a military man of immense energy and outstanding attainments, and as an administrator he was equal to any in Roman history, though perhaps not surpassing his great-nephew and successor. He was, of course, also one of the best military writers of all times, and a master of the Latin tongue. It is, however, doubtful if he deserves the enormous reputation that he has acquired in the centuries since his time, as a kind of universal genius. If he had survived longer than two years after his final return to Rome, we would be better able to come to an informed judgment. It was to the interest of Augustus, his great-nephew and adopted son, to exalt the reputation of his "martyred" predecessor, as we shall see; and it may well be that this propaganda and the use of the name Caesar by all the imperial rulers of Rome have tended to obscure the real defects in the vision as well as in the character of the great dictator.

For Caesar, above all, lacked political insight. The visible and tangible problems of Rome and the empire were clear to him but not the more subtle political realities of which the founder of a stable regime must take account. What was so vitally important in his time was the regularization of his own position, and about this he seems to have had no ideas whatever. He had himself elected dictator for life, but, unlike Sulla, he made no attempt to reform the constitution, and then abdicate his emergency power. He accepted every honorific title offered him by a cowed and obsequious Senate, and even suggested more. He did not know whether to make himself king—a few trial balloons were sent up on this notion—or stay in his present position. He allowed no one to approach him in power, and was content to hand over administrative tasks to his military subordinates. It would seem that the only thought he had on the matter of his position was that he should become something like a Hellenistic king, with divine attributes, ruling by divine right.

This, in a city which had known self-government for nearly five centuries and had risen to be mistress of the world by her own efforts, and especially by the activities of her noble families, a city, moreover, as conservative and enamored of tradition as Rome, was certain to arouse all classes against him. The Senate was "reformed" by the introduction of recently enfranchised provincials and by some of his own veteran soldiers, down to the rank of centurion. This "reformation" may have improved the quality of the Senate, but it is far more likely that Caesar instituted it in order to satisfy his own sardonic sense of humor, since he pointedly gave the Senate nothing to do. But why waste such an institution? Though it had fallen on evil days it still counted for something, and a statesman, like Caesar's successor, Augustus, was able to put it to work. The result of Caesar's tactlessness, which could easily have been foreseen, was that the senators were furious, even though they had to conceal their feelings, and the Senate became the focal point for the conspiracy which cost Caesar his life. Sulla had been much more careful. Though he knew as well as anyone else how feeble the Senate had become, he tried to make use of it, striving to improve its quality by increasing the number of officeholders and making entry into the Senate mandatory for officeholders. Caesar, of course, realized that the time had come for one-man rule, and that a reform of the Sullan variety was no longer feasible. But a dictatorship, based on military power alone, could never have been permanent. And it was the height of folly to plan a new campaign in Parthia, on which he was to take his intended heir, leaving a city full of enemies behind him. As it happened, the conspirators against his life seized the opportunity to murder him before he left.

Caesar always prided himself on his "clemency," and it is true that he did not proscribe his enemies as did Sulla and Caesar's own successors. He could be ruthless on occasion, while at other times even his enemies admitted his personal charm. There can, however, be little doubt that Caesar did regard himself as in some degree superhuman, not subject to human failings, and altogether removed from the ordinary run of men. He trusted his destiny, and in all his career never bothered to take elementary precautions. Probably it was for this reason that he did not care to trouble himself with the subtle arts of the statesman. His treatment of his enemies must have wounded them in their dignity; there are different ways of forgiving one's enemies, and even Caesar's most determined apologists have never credited him with tact. When he returned from his victories over Roman citizens in Spain he celebrated a triumph, and forced the Senate to vote him a thanksgiving. Several of his most trusted officers deserted him, even when he was victorious, and the conspiracy against his life included such soldiers as Decimus Brutus and Cassius, who had served through long campaigns with him. It would seem, then, that in the end it was his inhuman or superhuman arrogance that was responsible for his death, and prevented him from being the founder of the empire.

On the Ides of March in 44 B.C. Caesar was murdered in the Senate house as he sat listening to petitions. Marcus Brutus, his longtime friend, and reputed illegitimate son, led the conspiracy, and, according to Suetonius, Caesar gave up the struggle with the famous words, "Et tu Brute!" when he saw Brutus among his enemies. The conspirators had no program, and it was an act of folly to murder the man who had become the state without any idea of what was to replace him; but on personal grounds the act was entirely understandable. It can hardly be denied that Caesar in a sense invited his own murder. If, like Augustus, he had taken the Senate into partnership, or even spared its dignity by pretending to do so, he would probably never have been murdered. Something new had to be thought out, some way of ensuring continuity between the dying past and the future not yet born. In this Caesar failed, and it was left to the political genius and the unsurpassed tact of Augustus to achieve this result in the forty-five years of absolute power that he enjoyed. Certainly Augustus profited by Caesar's mistakes and untimely end. But nothing in Julius Caesar's career or in the ideas that he revealed during his few years of supreme power suggests that he could have founded an empire that would last for five hundred years, even if he had had twenty more years to live and had returned victorious from Parthia with the eagles lost by Crassus at Carrhae.

▶ **Suggestions for further reading**

There is one excellent modern source book which gives many pertinent extracts from the primary sources, including inscriptions. This is N. Lewis and M. Reinhold, *Roman Civilization* (New York: Columbia University Press, 1951). Aside from these readings, the Loeb Classical Library translations may be used, and the student is urged to try at least some of the letters and speeches of Cicero, and the political work of Polybius. Though Livy as a historian has to be treated with caution, the student should read at least a few of the earlier books of this writer. If he does so, it might be interesting to examine the way in which a renaissance Italian historian and statesman interpreted Livy, by looking into Niccolo Machiavelli's comments on Livy, recently published in a cheap edition: N. Machiavelli, *The Prince and the Discourses* (New York: Carlton House, n.d.). Plutarch's biographies of such Romans as Marcus Cato, Cato the

Younger, Crassus, Marius, Sulla, Cicero, Caesar, Pompey, and Marcus Brutus may also be consulted.

In Roman constitutional history there is one outstanding summary which is a masterpiece of compression and clarity. It is, however, difficult to obtain except in good libraries, since it was published in South Africa. This is J. K. Wylie, *Roman Constitutional History from the Earliest Times to the Death of Justinian* (Cape Town, South Africa: African Bookman, 1948). If this is not available, perhaps the best book is F. F. Abbott, *History and Description of Roman Political Institutions* (Boston: E. Ginn & Co., 1911). Very clear, but sometimes suppressing some of the difficulties, is L. Homo, *Roman Political Institutions* (New York: Alfred A. Knopf, Inc., 1929).

This reading list does not, as a rule, recommend text books for further study. But an exception should be made for a really outstanding piece of clear exposition which will serve admirably to fill out some of the gaps in the text. This is R. Geer, *Classical Civilization* (2nd ed.; New York: Prentice-Hall, Inc., 1950), Vol. 2, *Rome*.

For the last century of the Roman Republic there is available an excellent study which deals with all the factors that entered into the decline and final fall of the Republic—F. R. Cowell, *Cicero and the Roman Republic* (New York: Chanticleer Press, 1948). This book is graced also with a number of colored charts which well repay study, once the technique has been mastered. A clear and interesting essay on the fall of the Republic is also to be found in F. D. Marsh, *Modern Problems in the Ancient World* (Austin: University of Texas Press, 1943). A pioneer study, sometimes truculent and ill-tempered, highly destructive of earlier romantic traditions about the great men of the last age of the Republic and the early Empire, but solidly based in the most recent scholarship, is R. Syme, *The Roman Revolution* (Oxford: The Clarendon Press, 1939). No serious student of the Roman Republic, however, can afford to neglect this work, even though he is cautioned to treat it with some reserve. A well-balanced and judicious account which may serve to complete the study of this period is F. D. Marsh, *The Foundation of the Roman Empire* (2nd ed.; London: Oxford University Press, 1927).

# 11

## The Foundation of the Roman Empire

*The Civil War and the establishment of one-man rule • The problems facing Augustus and his solutions • The successors of Augustus: Tiberius and the decline of the Senate; Julians, Flavians, and "Good Emperors" • The provinces in the first two centuries • Influence of the Roman imperial idea*

---

### ▶ The Civil War and the establishment of one-man rule

Caesar had been successfully murdered, but the murderers had no idea how they were to replace him. There is no evidence that any of them had grasped the magnitude of the difficulties with which the republic had to contend if it was to survive. Only Cicero, a lifelong supporter of constitutional government, showed any real signs of leadership in the crisis. But even Cicero, who was not himself one of the actual conspirators against Caesar, had no positive policy for dealing with it. He seems to have hoped vaguely for an end to the military dictators and a restoration of the republic through a new concord between the warring classes. Though he gave leadership to the senators, his practical policy was one of opportunism, trying to play one leader against the other. He failed to appreciate the real abilities of Caesar's adopted heir, and this underestimation cost him any chance he might have had of success, and ultimately his life.

The murder of Julius Caesar was not greeted with any enthusiasm by the proletariat, who had always regarded Caesar as their champion, and who naturally appreciated his openhandedness. But their sullenness presented no immediate danger to the conspirators. The danger was from the Caesarian armies led by Mark Antony the consul, and by Lepidus who held the title of master of the horse, second in command to Caesar as dictator. Another important army in northern Italy was commanded by Decimus Brutus, one of the conspirators. If these commanders could hold the loyalty of their troops, a new civil war was inevitable. Lepidus succeeded in escaping from Rome and joining his army, but Antony was trapped at the time of the murder, being forced to barricade himself in his own house. In spite of the realization by some of the conspirators that Antony ought to have been murdered with Caesar, they failed to secure him. Instead, they negotiated with him, and he at once came to terms, hoping for time to come to his aid. But no sooner had an agreement been patched up when an opportunity presented itself to Antony for getting rid of them. On the occasion of Caesar's funeral he made an impassioned speech which was followed by a riot, and the conspirators suddenly found Rome too hot to hold them. They fled across the Adriatic, and began to recruit armies in Greece and the Near East among those who had been supporters of Pompey and were willing enough to put an end to the Caesarian rule. Pompey's son Sextus, who was in Spain, also proceeded to raise an army and a formidable fleet. But Antony was left with the priceless advantage of possession of the capital and control of the machinery of government. Lepidus went off to Spain on a lucrative command.

Cicero and the Senate were for the moment helpless. It was not therefore surprising that they gave a warm welcome to a new candidate for power who showed promise of becoming the only possible champion against Antony. Gaius Octavianus, Caesar's great-nephew, had been adopted as the dictator's personal heir by the terms of his will, and the will had been proclaimed and accepted by Senate and people alike. Antony had disregarded many of its terms, and embezzled for his own use part of the money. He had also hesitated to fulfill the bequests of lands to Caesar's veterans until the situation was easier. It was natural that Antony had paid little attention to his chief's adoption of a young and unknown man of eighteen, although the consul had hoped to be made Caesar's heir himself. But Octavian was no ordinary young man. Caesar had paid sporadic attention to him and provided for his education. But he too could have had little idea of his qualities, having had little opportunity for personal contact with him. Octavian was known to be sickly and he had had little military experience. His father's family was an obscure one, and if he had not been adopted by Caesar, he would have been regarded as an Italian rather than a true Roman. At the time of Caesar's death he had been undergoing training in preparation for accompanying the dictator on his Parthian campaign.

But Octavian in fact possessed certain personal assets of his own which were in most respects wholly contrary to those of Caesar, and would probably have failed to rouse the latter's admiration if he had known of them. Octavian had political gifts of the first order, a natural tact and understanding of people, an appreciation of their strengths and weaknesses, including his own, and he seems to have been entirely free from the arrogance that was the undoing of his great-uncle. At the same time he had great personal courage, and at this period in his career he could be as ruthless as any of his opponents, with a farsightedness and flexibility in action denied to them.

With an astonishing resolution and grasp of the realities of the situation and of the possible sources for his own power Octavian proceeded to capitalize on his only real asset, the act of adoption in Caesar's will which enabled him to add the names of Caesar to his own. Realizing that Antony had lost the loyalty of some of Caesar's troops by not carrying out his bequests, Octavian proclaimed that he personally would honor them, and indeed he paid some of them out of his own pocket in the name of Caesar. The gamble succeeded. On his arrival in Italy from Greece, where he had been in training, several legions joined him. In due course others deserted to him, even from Antony. Cicero offered him the support of the Senate. Antony, occupied with preparations for the campaign in northern Italy against Decimus Brutus, treated him with disdain, but did not take effective measures against him, and ultimately left for the north. This was Octavian's chance. Cicero delivered a series of orations against Antony (the *Philippics*, so called from their resemblance to the famous speeches delivered by Demosthenes against Philip of Macedon). Antony was declared a public enemy, and the consuls of the year, with the aid of Octavian and his legions, took the field against him. The consuls were killed in the fighting, but Octavian was left in possession of the field. Antony escaped across the Alps, where he defeated Decimus Brutus and recuperated from his losses.

The Senate under Cicero's leadership then repeated the mistake it had made on Pompey's return from the East. Octavian was slighted and refused the consulship on

## ► chronological chart

The Civil War and establishment of one-man rule
Second Triumvirate—Proscriptions and death of Cicero  B.C.  43
Battle of Philippi—Death of Brutus and Cassius  42
Antony goes to the East  42
Defeat and death of Sextus Pompeius  37
Renewal of triumvirate for five years  37
Battle of Actium  31
Death of Antony and Cleopatra  30

The work of Augustus
Augustus given *proconsulare imperium* and *tribunicia*
  *potestas* for life  23
Augustus becomes Pontifex Maximus on death of Lepidus  12
Danube frontier established for empire  15
Rhine frontier accepted after defeat of Varus  A.D.  9
Death of Augustus  14

The successors of Augustus
Reign of Tiberius  14–37
Reign of Caligula (Gaius)  37–41
Reign of Claudius  41–54
Reign of Nero  54–68
Year of the Four Emperors  69
Vespasian and the Flavian dynasty  69–96
Nerva chosen emperor by Senate  96
The "Good Emperors"—Nerva, Trajan, Hadrian, Antoninus
  Pius, Marcus Aurelius  96–180

technical grounds, while the conspirators, who had now prepared a formidable force in the East, were honored with official commands. But these forces were not in Italy, where Octavian still had his loyal and victorious legions, which he did not hesitate to use against the Senate. Rebuffed by the Senate, Octavian decided to make advances to Antony and to Lepidus, who still had troops under his command which could not be ignored. The three met in northern Italy, and on the first day of the year 42 B.C. began a triumvirate which, unlike the first private agreement of 60 B.C., was proclaimed the official government of Rome.

The first act of the Triumvirate was the proscription of three hundred senators and two thousand knights. While the private vengeance of the triumvirs was sated against the murderers of Caesar and their own political enemies, the chief purpose of the proscriptions seems to have been to secure money for the necessary campaign against Marcus Brutus and Cassius. Estates of the proscribed were confiscated and the proceeds used to recruit an army. Even this was insufficient, and the triumvirs resorted to arbitrary requisitions and forced loans. But at last the army was ready, and in the brief campaign of Philippi, Brutus and Cassius were defeated and committed suicide. The credit lay mostly with Antony, for Octavian showed poor generalship and was intermittently confined to his bed by sickness.

There was now only one formidable enemy left, Sextus Pompeius, who had a fleet of ships active in the Mediterranean with which he was able to threaten and at times cut off the grain supply of Rome. Antony had allied himself with him before the Triumvirate, and afterward tried to use him against Octavian; and even Octavian several times was forced into an agreement with him. It was not until 37 B.C. that Octavian, by then in sole command in Italy, was able to dispose of this naval menace and restore Italy to normal life.

After Philippi (42 B.C.), Antony, still the leading partner in the Triumvirate, was given the chief command in the East to undertake the Parthian campaign projected by Caesar, while Octavian had to be content with Spain, and Lepidus with Africa. Control in Italy was divided between Antony and Octavian. But Octavian did not find it necessary to go personally to Spain and was actually present for several years in Italy, while Antony left for the East. His absence from Rome proved to be the older man's undoing.

It will never be known whether it was the infatuation of Antony for Cleopatra, queen of Egypt, that destroyed them both, or whether Antony had a coherent and potentially successful plan for an Eastern Roman Empire with its capital at Alexandria, in the most prosperous area of the empire. But it is certain that his absence from Italy during the crucial period of his rivalry with Octavian presented the latter with an opportunity for the display of his unique political gifts, which at this moment in history were more necessary than any possible military talents. Octavian had at least one first-rate general in Agrippa, but it was not Agrippa's talents that won Caesar's nephew the empire. His gradual ascendancy over his rival was due to his building of an effective political party loyal to himself, and to an unexampled use of propaganda to which Antony had laid himself open by his own policy.

Cleopatra had become queen of Egypt in her own right when her brother (and husband) Ptolemy had been killed in the time of Julius Caesar.[1] But her country's independence was only nominal while the Romans ruled the Hellenistic world. She was a woman of great ability as well as beauty, she was thoroughly conversant with Roman politics, and she had unbounded ambition. A useful asset was a son Caesarion, who was presumed to be the son also of Julius Caesar, and therefore a real rival for Octavian, who was only the adopted son of the dictator. She was not, however, of Egyptian ancestry, being descended on both sides from Ptolemy Soter, the general of Alexander who had taken Egypt after the untimely death of his master. She was therefore a Macedonian princess who happened to be queen of Egypt. But the Roman people looked upon her as an Oriental, an Egyptian, and there is no doubt that the vast majority of the Roman people were made to believe by Octavian that she was a foreigner who had captivated Antony and charmed him out of his senses.

Antony met her first at Tarsus when he set out on his Parthian campaign. He followed her to Alexandria, and thereafter with brief intervals of military activity which was far from successful, and occasional visits to Italy to renew his alliance with Octavian, he remained in Egypt, formally marrying Cleopatra and divorcing Octavia, the sister of Octavian, whom he had married in 40 B.C. He proclaimed Caesarion as "King of Kings," joint ruler of the East with Cleopatra, while kingdoms were also given to her two children by Antony. This procedure was not in itself unprecedented. Many Roman territories for years to come were ruled by "client kings," nominally independent, with many real duties to perform but under the overlordship of Rome. Herod the Great held such a position in Judaea at the time of the birth of Jesus. But it was easy for Octavian to represent these administrative arrangements as gifts of Antony to his lover and to frighten the Romans with stories that An-

---

[1] Soon after the death of this brother, she had married another younger brother, but after a short time had him murdered.

tony intended one day to conquer Rome itself with the aid of Egyptian resources, and to make Cleopatra queen of the Roman Empire with himself as king. Italy would be dethroned from her proud position as the seat of empire.

It should be remembered that Egypt possessed vast resources, but its troops were now Roman. Antony could not rely upon foreign or Oriental troops alone in any trial of strength with Octavian. It was essential to him to keep both officers and men loyal to himself, or they would desert to the enemy; and not all his superior generalship could help him against Octavian if he had no troops to support it.

Evidently Octavian saw that this was his supreme chance. He did not dare to challenge Antony for many years, during which he was patiently building up his own strength in Italy. Though Antony was suspicious, he also could no longer afford to quarrel with his rival, and the Triumvirate was always formally renewed until the end of 33 B.C.

Antony then made his bid for power in Rome, but now it was too late. Octavian had the support of the people, inflamed against Antony by the publication of his acts in the East, colored by the young triumvir's own interpretation of them. And though perhaps even a majority of the Senate still supported Antony, they soon began to desert to what was clearly to be the winning side. The conclusion was by this time inevitable. Cleopatra dared not let Antony venture too far from Egypt lest he make terms with Octavian which would be insupportable for her. On the other hand, if she accompanied Antony in a military attack on Octavian, then the Roman troops would believe the propaganda of Octavian that Antony had fallen victim to the wiles of an Oriental princess. The naval battle of Actium, therefore, in 31 B.C., such as it was, was a foregone conclusion. The bulk of Antony's forces deserted him, and shortly afterward both he and Cleopatra committed suicide.

Octavian was now in all but name the supreme ruler of the Roman world. That he had matured greatly and that his early ruthlessness had been softened can already be seen by his immediate acts. There were no more proscriptions. Where the triumvirs had mercilessly expropriated land in Italy for Caesar's veterans, Octavian now gave his veterans land outside Italy. The administrative arrangements of Antony in the East he disturbed as little as possible, though Egypt was annexed as his personal property. A subservient but perhaps also grateful Senate, purged of some of its less reliable members, a few years later voted Octavian the title of Augustus, by which he will henceforth be known in this book. One-man rule had begun, and the new ruler was faced with the enormous task of making it permanent, in spite of the five-hundred-year tradition which had been too strong for all previous aspirants.

## ► The problems facing Augustus and his solutions

### THE SCOPE OF THE PROBLEMS

The magnitude and scope of the problems facing the young ruler (he had been born in 63 B.C. and was thus thirty-two at the time of the battle of Actium) can hardly be overestimated. The old Roman Republic had clearly failed to live up to the responsibilities of empire, and had collapsed from its own weaknesses. Yet some form of government must replace it which was capable of enduring. And this government, whatever it might be, must also be able to keep under control the vast territories which had fallen to Roman arms during the previous three centuries. Rome had a responsibility to them also. It was impossible simply to decree their freedom and independence, even if the idea had ever occurred to Augustus. Their earlier forms of government had been destroyed beyond recall and could not be restored by a mere imperial fiat. In the last century of the republic the governors of the provinces had been political appointees of the Senate, anxious only to make their fortunes and return to Rome. By corruption and extortion they had advanced themselves; moreover, they were in league with the equestrian class of Rome which had milked the provinces for the sake of its own financial interests. The provinces had suffered abominably from this regular regime, and in many cases had been driven into bankruptcy by the more recent civil wars and irregular extortions by would-be rulers of Rome. There was little encouragement to honesty or efficiency, qualities rarely found in the governors. Was it possible for Augustus to reward these qualities and so improve the provincial system that they would become the rule rather than the exception?

We have seen that the enrollment of volunteer armies by Marius had led directly to the fall of the republic, since the troops relied upon their generals for pay and pensions, and their loyalty was given to these generals rather than to Rome. Moreover the various armies had swollen to such an extent in the civil wars that there were probably at least half a million men under arms at the time of the battle of Actium. Augustus had to consider what was the real purpose of an army in the Roman Empire, where the various legions should be stationed, how they were to occupy themselves during peacetime, how they could be persuaded to be loyal to Rome rather than to generals; and yet at the same time the armies must continue to have those professional military virtues, the absence of which in the earlier armies had compelled Marius to introduce long-term volunteer service.

Behind the great political and administrative problems was the ever-present social and economic background. Rome was not a great manufacturing city, not even a trading center of importance comparable to its size and population. There were far too many people in Rome unable to make a living and requiring public support. Yet these men were citizens and possessed the right to vote. The votes of this urban proletariat had always been for sale to the highest bidder in the last century of the republic. Could they be made into a self-respecting citizenry by any means available to a capable administrator? How could the numerous slaves live side by side

with a free citizenry without depressing wages? In spite of the fertility of much of the soil, Italy had never really recovered from the depredations of Hannibal nearly two centuries earlier. The small estates had been swallowed by senators and capitalists and made into large specialized agricultural units worked usually by slaves under overseers. Moreover, the small landholders who survived suffered from chronic insecurity of tenure, their properties often being sequestrated for the benefit of veterans. And throughout the length and breadth of Italy, especially near Rome, rich men built their villas, too often neglecting the land itself and its cultivation.

The cleavage between rich and poor had undermined the old Roman traditional virtues, and the search for ever-increasing luxury among the upper classes had replaced the stern frugality of the earlier republic. Family life in the upper classes had almost disappeared, with divorce to be had for the asking and marriage used for political and financial advancement. The birth rate among the free Romans had naturally been declining. Was it possible to arrest this process, at least the decay of public morality, even if the ancient virtues had disappeared forever?

These were a few of the problems with which Augustus had to contend. If he did not solve them all, at least he perceived their existence, and made an attempt to solve them. And the organization of an empire which endured for many centuries, the most enduring indeed that the Western world has yet seen, is almost entirely his work. The essential administrative structure was built by him, though the conquests themselves were bequeathed to him by the Roman conquerors of the republic.

THE WORK OF AUGUSTUS

### The establishment of a legitimate government

The most difficult problem of all was undoubtedly the reorganization of the government: and it was the most fundamental. Julius Caesar's inability to make any constructive contribution to this problem marks his inferiority to his successor as a statesman. Not even a provincial reorganization, the establishment of an equitable system of taxation, nor the enlargement of the conception of Roman citizenship, all of which were in the mind of Julius and well within his capacity, would have been of any permanent value without a governmental system which was capable of controlling the empire and which was at the same time acceptable to the people. Any dictatorship or arbitrary military rule can be cut short by assassination, as Caesar's own career had shown. It was a measure of the genius of Augustus that he made his government both acceptable and legitimate. Though he did not solve permanently the method of succession, this may only be because, as will be discussed later, the problem may well be insoluble within the framework of absolute monarchy.

According to the tradition believed by the Romans, Rome had existed as a city for more than seven hundred years. For almost five hundred it had been free and self-governing. Though occasionally defeated in individual battles, it had never lost a war and had never been compelled to sign a peace with an undefeated enemy. For five hundred years magistrates had been elected and the noblest of the citizens had sat in the Senate and given their advice to the magistrates. It was a body of incomparable prestige, even though in the last century, often through its own incompetence, it had been forced to bow to arbitrary military men with armies at their backs. And the people of Rome had accepted its supremacy and shared in the glories won by their arms under its leadership. Though Rome was not a state, the Romans were truly a people, and Roman citizenship was prized by everyone who possessed it; and those who did not possess it valued it and sought to win it for themselves. During all these years the name of *rex* or king had been detested. The Romans no less than the Greeks regarded it as an office fit only for barbarians.

Yet Augustus realized that he must be king in fact, even though he did not hold

*Bust of Augustus at the prime of his manhood.* (COURTESY BRITISH MUSEUM)

the title. It would never have occurred to him —nor indeed would it have been possible— to have ruled the empire with its many different peoples of varying degrees of culture, through any kind of representative government. The empire was too vast and heterogeneous for any such experiment. But if the government had been returned to Senate and people as under the republic, the same weaknesses would have led to the same breakdown of government. Only a monarch could hope to hold it together.

Augustus solved his dilemma by one of the great creative compromises of history, a species of legal fiction which bridged the gulf between the fallen republic and the monarchy which had to come. In time the republic was forgotten, the monarchy supplanted it, and the necessity for the fiction disappeared. But in the competent hands of Augustus, who understood it, the reasons for it, and the behavior required of him to maintain it, the fiction worked. Though thinking Romans of course knew that he was the sole ruler and that his power was ultimately based on the army and the treasury, nevertheless to the mass of the people the republic still survived. They felt at home in the new Roman state. The magistrates were still elected by the same procedure as before, though no candidate would even have run for office without the approval of Augustus; the Senate and the Assemblies still met for debate and legislation; and though there was now a Princeps, or first citizen, a title and office unknown to the republic, he was not obtrusive, he scrupulously respected all the old republican forms, and his public and private life were beyond reproach in the best tradition of the early days of the Roman Republic.

Augustus confined the offices held by himself personally to the minimum required for his possession of the reality of power. He had a permanent proconsular military power (*proconsulare imperium*) conferred upon him, giving him supreme command of the army; he was granted a permanent civil power as previously exercised by the tribunes (*tribunicia potestas*), which gave him the power to introduce legislation and veto it. He became chief priest (*Pontifex Maximus*), giving him authority in religious matters; but, characteristically, he did not assume this office until the death of Lepidus, who had been ousted from his position as triumvir in 36 B.C. and consoled for his loss of power by appointment to this honored position. Occasionally Augustus allowed himself to be elected consul in the early years of his rule, feeling that he needed the civil as well as the military power inherent in this office. But consuls, praetors, aediles, and even tribunes were elected as before to perform the specific duties of these offices under the guidance of the Princeps.

Augustus tried his best to maintain the dignity of the Senate. He encouraged it to give him advice, and he presided over it personally as *Princeps Senatus*. The judicial functions of the Senate were maintained and even increased under his rule. By setting aside certain provinces to be ruled by ex-

magistrates under the direct control of the Senate and not of himself, he made it worth while moving through the full sequence of offices (*cursus honorum*) to the exalted position of consul. The Senate also had its own treasury. As under the Constitution of Sulla, the quaestors on being elected automatically became senators, though under Augustus their duties lay primarily in the provinces. From the equestrian order he recruited a body of public officials, paid out of the imperial treasury (*fiscus*) but with the same duties as taxgatherers and tax assessors that they had performed in their own interests under the republic. Under later emperors these men became part of the imperial civil service.

When it was proposed that he should be worshiped as a god (his adoptive father had already been deified), he refused the honor, but permitted his Genius to be worshiped instead. According to old Roman belief every man had a guiding Genius, and the Genius of the head of a family guided the fortunes of that family. In allowing a cult to be set up to his Genius, Augustus was therefore directing Roman worship toward the state of which he was now the controlling Genius. Later this indeed became the worship of the living emperor as god, a state cult to which all had to subscribe on pain of treason. But Augustus in his lifetime never claimed to be a god except in the Hellenistic world, which had for centuries been accustomed to a divine monarchy.

The greatest difficulty inherent in his position as sole ruler, the difficulty of the succession, Augustus never solved. There were only a few possibilities open to him. Since the Roman ruler had to be a supremely capable man, the vagaries of heredity made this natural and traditional method of succession dangerous for the welfare of the state. Augustus himself had no sons, and his one daughter Julia was the scandal of Rome, from which Augustus was ultimately forced to banish her. He had grandsons and several relatives by marriage, but all died before him. He also had two stepsons, both extremely competent men, the younger of

*Mausoleum dedicated to Gaius and Julius Caesar, grandsons of Augustus who died before him, to the great grief of the ruler, who had hoped that his position would be inherited by members of his family (St. Rémy, France).*

the right was an empty one, never independently exercised during the empire except when the Senate was called upon for an election by its military masters. So for the first two dynasties the succession was hereditary within the Julian and Flavian families. The so-called "Good Emperors," Nerva, Trajan, Hadrian, Antoninus Pius, and Marcus Aurelius (A.D. 96–180), were all childless except the last-named, and adopted the best men they could find in the empire as their successors. Marcus, however, chose his son, who happened to be incompetent and a wastrel, and under him the empire declined precipitately. It always remained true that the ultimate power to choose an emperor rested with the army. But there was not only one army. The legions stationed in different provinces favored their own particular leaders, and as early as the death of Nero in A.D. 68 these legions joined battle with each other on behalf of their respective choices.

If, therefore, an emperor chose his successor and granted him military power while he was still alive, then this successor would probably accede to the throne without difficulty as long as he had taken the precaution to promise suitable bonuses to the army. When, however, an emperor died before nominating his successor and without having transferred to anyone a part of his power, a free-for-all usually resulted, and the most powerful army leader won the throne. If the hereditary principle had been strictly observed, as in modern monarchies, there would have been no doubt in anyone's mind as to who was the rightful successor. But in that case the risk of having an incompetent ruler, and the chance of the death of an emperor without sons, would have to be run. Even under a strict hereditary monarchy, the possibility of a civil war over the succession is not avoided altogether, but it is greatly minimized. On the whole, therefore, it would seem that the hesitancy of Augustus to face the problem of succession was inevitable in the circumstances of his time, and the combination of adoption and heredity was as good a choice as any available to him.

whom was accidentally killed while on campaign in Germany. The surviving stepson, Tiberius, did indeed succeed him, but not by virtue of his own relationship to the Princeps. Tiberius was forced first to divorce his wife and marry the profligate Julia. Later Augustus adopted him as his son, and conferred on him the two great powers held by himself as Princeps. So on his death there was no doubt as to who had been designated as his successor; and Tiberius, already possessing proconsular and tribunician power, could have mastered any possible rival with ease.

But the principle of adoption or heredity was not yet established. Theoretically the Senate was entitled to elect the ruler; but

## The reorganization of the provinces

The reorganization of the provinces was a further example of Augustus' efficient use of such opportunities as existed. He saw at once that it was not necessary to keep armies in every province, as had been the custom in the later years of the republic. Those that had long been pacified and had no frontiers to be defended against barbarians needed no more than enough troops to ensure local discipline. These provinces (see the map for details) he entrusted to the Senate, which was given the power of appointing governors and administering the tax monies. These provinces, as under the republic, were reserved for ex-magistrates, and constituted a reward for those who had progressed through the cursus honorum. In addition the arrangement gave the Senate some real work to do and served to maintain its prestige as a body. And though Augustus exercised a final supervisory jurisdiction over these provinces, he left them largely to themselves. Those provinces, however, which needed legions of trained troops, and whose frontiers had continually to be defended against enemies, were under his direct control, which he ex- ercised though the appointment of salaried legates, personally responsible to him, who could hold their positions as long as they proved efficient. This arrangement gave them the opportunity to gain a real knowledge of their provinces and to win the loyalty of their troops, but in later times it proved a serious danger to the state in the event of a disputed succession to the throne. Egypt, as the richest province, the primary source of the grain supply for Rome and Italy, was given a special status in keeping with its history as well as its present importance. As in the past, the ruler was divine and the owner of all the land. Augustus, therefore, was a Pharaoh in Egypt, with all the privileges of this office, although he did not perform his duties as king-god there himself, but entrusted them to a prefect of equestrian rank, responsible to himself. The country, however, was farmed as an imperial estate rather than as a province with a certain degree of self-government, and its revenues accrued directly to the ruler. No one of senatorial rank was permitted within the territory without the permission of the Princeps. Finally, a number of kingdoms on the outskirts of the empire were permitted self-government

*Triumphal arch of Augustus, set up near the present St. Rémy de Provence, in southern France.*

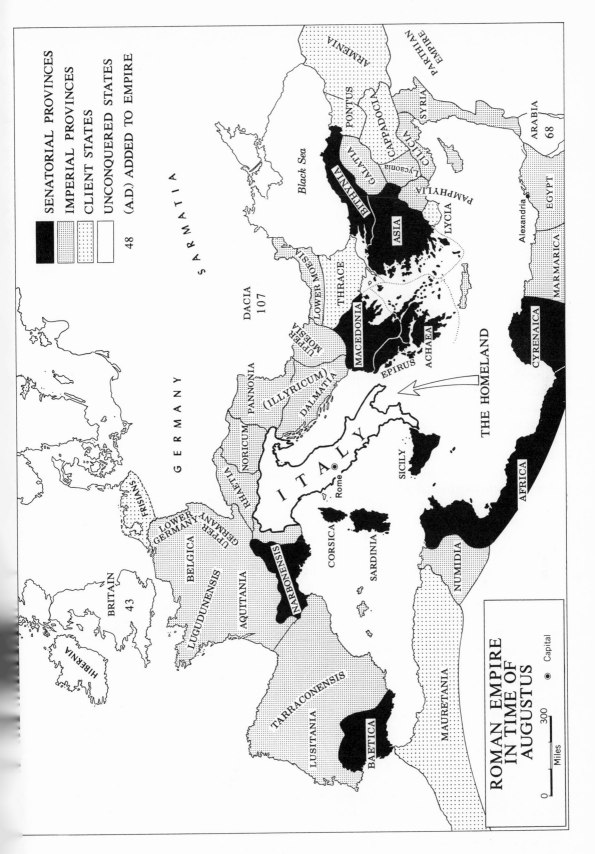

ROMAN EMPIRE
IN TIME OF
AUGUSTUS

SENATORIAL PROVINCES
IMPERIAL PROVINCES
CLIENT STATES
UNCONQUERED STATES
(A.D.) ADDED TO EMPIRE

⊙ Capital

0    300
Miles

351

under their kings, who became clients or vassals of Rome.

The provinces of the Roman Empire had always been made up of more or less self-governing municipalities, city-states on the Greek model, together with a number of other communities whose position had been defined by treaty, usually without full self-government. Augustus encouraged as much local administration as was compatible with the imperial relationship, thus saving the burden of direct administration. The corrupt tax system of the republican period was not abolished by Augustus, probably for lack of any alternative method of collection. His successors, especially Claudius and Hadrian, developed a regular civil service which gradually supplanted the tax companies. Meanwhile the abuses of the system were checked through more efficient supervision by the Princeps, even in the senatorial provinces. Penalties for extortion were severe, and even senatorial governors were far too much under control to be able to lend the efficient aid to the tax farmers that had been the custom under the republic in its last years. And the nucleus of the later civil service was formed with the inclusion of treasury officials in the staff of the governors.

The entire system of provinces was reorganized thoroughly by Augustus, with new boundaries, chosen for the sake of efficient administration and defense (see map). In the process a number of minor conquests had to be undertaken to round out many territories which had been acquired haphazardly by the republic according to the needs of the moment. Augustus always hoped to make the northern boundary the Elbe rather than the Rhine, as shorter and more easily defensible. Such a boundary, however, would have necessitated the conquest of a large part of Germany. Though progress with this conquest was made in the earlier years of his reign, his armies suffered a severe defeat toward the end of his life, and the conquest was abandoned. The Rhine became the northwestern frontier, while Augustus maintained the Danube in the East, refusing to move into Dacia to the north of the Danube

(the modern Rumania) on the grounds that it was indefensible. This policy was maintained until Trajan A.D. 98–117, who not only took Dacia but engaged in extensive wars in the East, the spoils of which had to be abandoned by his successors, as Augustus had predicted. The empire was held together by the great Roman roads, which were constantly extended throughout the imperial period and over which the imperial post traveled, bringing news to the emperor and his instructions in return.

The provincial system proved to be the most enduring of the reforms of Augustus. Whatever happened at Rome, the life of the provinces went on much as usual, under good rulers and bad alike. Only when the burden of taxation was heavily increased and prosperity declined in the third century A.D. with the continuous civil and foreign wars was the strength of the provinces slowly sapped. But while the Roman peace (*Pax Romana*) gave them a respite from war they had never previously enjoyed, their prosperity increased and with it the ability to pay the taxes which ensured the continuance of that rule.

*Two bronze plates of a military diploma granting citizenship to honorably discharged soldiers and their wives.* (COURTESY THE METROPOLITAN MUSEUM OF ART)

Augustus himself, as has been said, was an Italian rather than a Roman, and always regarded Italy as the center of his dominions, the homeland with special privileges, with Rome as first the capital of Italy and then of the empire. The inhabitants of Rome, however, were no longer exempt from all taxation as had been the case under the republic for all Roman citizens. But their taxes always remained lighter than those of the provinces. Every native freeborn Italian was a Roman citizen with all the privileges attached to the position. The provincials could achieve Roman citizenship, but Augustus regarded it as a privilege to be earned and not a right to which they were entitled by birth. This policy was gradually abandoned by his successors until in A.D. 212 citizenship was granted to every free inhabitant of the empire.

### The reform of the army

By virtue of his proconsular power the Princeps was naturally commander in chief of the army. Augustus, drawing upon the experience of his predecessors and especially of his adoptive father, laid down a permanent basis for recruitment and for the composition of the army, which survived in its essentials throughout the whole empire. The regular troops or legionaries were drawn from Italians and the most Romanized provincials, who received citizenship on enlistment if they did not already possess it. They served for twenty years, receiving a regular salary and a pension on retirement. In addition to these were auxiliary troops who received citizenship only on retirement. These were also salaried men, but drawn from the less Romanized provinces, and serving primarily within these provinces. Their officers also were originally drawn from the same territory, but later, after it had been shown that these troops were capable of rebellion in the interests of their own provinces, Italian officers were substituted. The armies were by no means always engaged in active warfare, although the legions might at any time be transferred to a danger spot on a distant frontier. During the first two centuries, however, the general practice was for the legionaries to live in camps behind permanent fortifications which were built by themselves. There were strategic roads to be built, ditches and moats to be dug, walls to be erected, and many of the troops necessarily became skilled artisans as well as soldiers, not unlike the modern corps of Army Engineers. These men, holding Roman citizenship, speaking Latin, imbued with Roman tradition, enjoying even on the frontiers the comforts of Roman civilization, such as warm baths, naturally mingled with the peoples among whom they were stationed, and served therefore as an important instrument for the Romanization of the empire. The army, however, in its own estimation, was rarely well enough paid in proportion to its value to the state. Its chronic dissatisfaction and its sporadic insistence on bonuses gave ambitious generals the opportunity to make lavish promises in exchange for support of their candidacies to the throne.

In Italy itself no regular troops were stationed except the Praetorian Guard, which in the early centuries was drawn from Italians alone. This was a body of about nine thousand men under its own prefect and living in special barracks just outside the city of Rome. Being the only body of troops with easy access to the capital, it was often instrumental in the elevation of an emperor, and its prefect at all times wielded an authority far greater than could be justified by his actual position. As early as the reign of Tiberius the praetorian prefect, in the absence of the Princeps himself on the island of Capri, was the virtual ruler of Rome, with actual power quite sufficient to dominate the Senate. Nevertheless at this time the power of the Princeps was hardly to be challenged if he cared to exercise it, and a letter of Tiberius to the Senate with a concealed threat was enough to ensure the fall of the ambitious prefect.

### Social and economic policy

Rome had never been an important industrial center, and even as a commercial

*Reconstruction, by the Metropolitan Museum of Art, of a bedroom from the southern Italian city of Boscoreale, which was buried by the famous eruption of Vesuvius in A.D. 79. Note the frescoes on the three walls. The room is furnished with authentic pieces from the same city dating from the period of the eruption.* (COURTESY THE METROPOLITAN MUSEUM OF ART)

city its usefulness was impaired by its lack of a good harbor. The muddy Tiber had constantly to be dredged to keep the harbor of Ostia at its mouth open for commerce at all. Puteoli, where Paul landed on his journey to Rome, became the regular seaport for Roman trade, and developed into a great city, largely peopled by Greeks and other foreigners, who remained the leaders in maritime commerce as under the republic. But in spite of the absence of large-scale industry, there were innumerable small manufacturing shops in Rome and throughout Italy. For centuries Italy was the chief manufacturer for the Western world, though its

products were far surpassed in quality by those of Alexandria and the East. Nevertheless, the Italian balance of trade was always unfavorable, if Rome is included with Italy, since Rome remained a parasite on the economy.

Augustus did not take any active interest in the economy as such. Except for Egypt, industry in the Roman Empire was overwhelmingly in private hands. There was no state industry, nor monopolies of the kind that later developed in the Eastern Roman Empire of Constantinople. But indirectly the establishment of the Pax Romana, with its network of roads and safe transportation, increased prosperity for all classes throughout the empire. And Augustus used the tax money that came from the provinces to pay for an enormous program of public works, chiefly temples and other public buildings, gardens, and baths; and in this the majority of those emperors who had the money available and were not too heavily engaged in unproductive warfare followed his example. These public works provided a market for numerous products made by small industry throughout the empire, and direct work for the large army of unemployed in Rome itself. The provincial municipalities also engaged in similar programs on their account, and it became a matter of civic pride for wealthy citizens to improve their cities with gifts of parks, gardens, temples, and other public buildings.

But social and political conditions throughout the empire and especially in Rome itself militated against any real and lasting prosperity for all. In a world without machines, hand labor must be efficient indeed to produce any surplus for luxuries over and above the ordinary daily needs. Agriculture, the backbone of the imperial economy, improved in efficiency, it is true, with the introduction of rotation of crops and the use of leguminous plants. But it was severely hampered by many disabilities, especially absentee ownership; and it had to feed an enormous urban population. The real life of the Roman Empire, as life had been in the Hellenistic world, was concentrated in the cities, and every encouragement was given by the authorities to create ever more and more municipalities. The inhab-

*A house at Pompeii as it appears today, partly restored. This house belonged to the Vetii family.* (COURTESY ITALIAN STATE TOURIST OFFICE)

itants of the cities never produced by their inefficient industrial techniques goods proportionate to the large number of people engaged in their production, and these goods in any case were luxuries rather than essentials. Moreover, there were large numbers of people who did no productive work at all, but lived on the proceeds of farms and small industrial establishments owned but not worked by them. In addition there was a growing army of public servants engaged in important work but not contributing directly to production. The reason why it was possible for so many men and women to be idle from the point of view of production was that there was also a large army of slaves, manumitted slaves, and freemen, all of whom consumed far less than they produced. Most slaves in the imperial period could look forward to being manumitted (freed) by their masters as a reward for good service, and in many cases they could earn enough to buy their own freedom. On ordinary farms the slave was also to some degree protected as a valuable property and at least fed enough to live on. But slaves engaged in mining and contract labor were in a different category. They cost less to buy than domestic and agricultural slaves, whose skills were appreciated. The work of these men and women was·supervised by overseers who drove them mercilessly to obtain the maximum work from them. In the last days of the republic enormous numbers of slaves were captured and sold (Caesar sold 53,000 as the result of one campaign alone, the proceeds from slave sales forming an important item in his estate), but with the decline of foreign wars this source gradually became less productive. More slaves at most periods of the empire were probably obtained by natural increase (the child of slave parents being a slave himself) than by capture.

Nevertheless, in the time of Augustus a large part of the population of Rome and indeed of the whole empire was made up of slaves who, as always, served to depress the wages of free labor, which had to compete with them. But at the same time the low

wage rate for free workers also served to promote the manumission of slaves, since a slaveowner not only had to buy and support his slave throughout his lifetime, but also by custom had to allow him to keep some of his earnings for himself. On the other hand, a free laborer could be laid off work in slack times and left to fend for himself, and his employer had to make no initial investment in him. Economic causes therefore worked in the direction of free labor rather than slave, and slaves became fewer. Furthermore, with the decline of prosperity in the upper slaveholding classes, fewer men could keep the armies of domestic slaves retained for prestige purposes in the early days of the empire. But, however socially desirable the freeing of slaves may seem to us, it should be emphasized that it was only because free labor was so cheap that slavery declined, and that emancipation did not result in any economic improvement in the lot of the ex-slave or of the laborer in general.

For social and political reasons Augustus attempted to place some restrictions on the manumission of slaves, as part of his general effort to make Roman citizenship a privilege and prevent the Orientalizing of the Roman populace. But it seems to have been impossible to halt the natural process by imperial decree.

For the poor of the city of Rome, who were grossly underemployed, he found no remedy beyond his public works programs and a continuance of the republican practice of providing them with cheap or free food. In addition he, and more particularly the later emperors, provided lavish public spectacles to keep them amused. This program was called by the later satirist Juvenal "bread and circuses." Since the elections were arranged and laws were now really made indirectly by the Princeps, the Roman people, so powerful in the last century of the republic when their votes were necessary for the election of magistrates and army officers, lost their power. Riots could be dangerous on occasion, but they could now be easily suppressed. On the other hand, all the rulers were anxious to keep the people as contented as possible, and tried to provide for their needs. Augustus, recognizing the irresponsibility that went with their unemployment and dependence on imperial handouts, tried to give them some status in the community and in their own eyes by incorporating them formally into an order, the plebeian as distinct from the equestrian and senatorial orders. But since they had no real duties in addition to their privileges, it is probable that the gesture remained an empty formality. We are not told what the plebeians themselves thought about it.

The city in the time of Augustus was efficiently policed, and a fire brigade was established, first under elected officials and then under appointees of the Princeps.

In agriculture Augustus strove to increase the number of small farmers. He gave security of tenure to those who had farms already, and he made an effort to instill a real love of the Italian countryside into the free peasantry. In this effort he was ably assisted by the poet-farmer Vergil, whose *Georgics* are a long paean of praise of the rural life. But the tendencies of the time were against Augustus. It was difficult to arrest the growth of large farms and estates which could be more economically worked than the small unit. The exodus of farmers to the cities which had been such an important feature of the last years of the republic continued. Not all the praise of the rural life could prevail against the hard necessities of making a living. Though there was, as has been seen, chronic underemployment in Rome, at least the citizen could scrape a living somehow, and free bread and circuses were available, as nowhere else. Not until the Industrial Revolution in modern times did it become possible to work farms efficiently with a small labor force, and at the same time keep millions employed in the large cities through the production of machine-made goods and the provision of multifarious services. The problem of Rome itself was almost certainly insoluble by Augustus, however great his power and intelligence.

## Cultural and religious policy

There is no doubt that Augustus thoroughly understood the Roman ideal and the Roman tradition. Though in his earlier days he was no model of virtue, in his principate he strove by example and legislation to revive the old Roman virtues which had made her great. Seriousness, hard work, frugality, piety, family solidarity, public spirit—these were the traditional virtues, and Augustus did not believe they had disappeared forever. The desire for luxury and ostentation, overeating and overdrinking, skepticism, public and private immorality had been no part of the earlier Roman tradition. But it was quite another matter to try to put the clock back and revive the old virtues against all the cultural pressures of the age. Still less was it possible to do this by legislation, although Augustus has had some distinguished successors in the attempt in many times and places. His cultural and religious policy, therefore, though partially successful in some directions, must on the whole be accounted a failure. Trying to restore the sanctity of private life, he decreed compulsory marriage at a certain age, and for all citizens. Later, when he was forced to modify this decree he laid special disabilities on the unmarried and he offered preference to certain state offices to fathers with three children. He legislated on the size of houses, and the quantity of food and drink to be consumed at banquets. He even encouraged informers against those who offended against his laws. Naturally these laws were extremely unpopular, especially among the upper and middle classes who could afford luxuries, and they were completely ineffective against the other social evils at which they were directed. And, as far as we know, bachelors remained as numerous as ever, and the birth rate was not increased.

The more positive aspects of his policy, however, seem to have had some effect. He tried to revive some of the old Italian rural religious festivals, and regenerate the old primitive religion of the countryside, which had never altogether died out. And he undoubtedly succeeded in reviving patriotism and a reverence for the Roman heritage, as evidenced by the success of his great patriotic poets, especially Vergil and Horace, and even of the old republican historian Livy, whose history exalts the Roman virtues at the expense, it is feared, of historical accuracy. The court poets and writers, dealt with in the next chapter, for the first time found a patron in Maecenas, who subsidized and encouraged them with the full backing of the Princeps. But, above all, the imperial cult really did take hold of the people and persisted for several centuries in the form of emperor or state worship. It does not seem to have been the empty formality that we, with our higher religions concerned with the relationship between man and God, might have expected. It was building on traditional foundations, both the reverence paid to the gods of the household and family, and to the Genius of the father of the family. What Augustus did was enlarge the conception to include the whole Roman family and state, and institute rituals designed to capture this reverence for the protective deities of the state and the ruler himself. In addition he exalted the older gods Apollo, Mars, and, above all, Jupiter, building great temples for them in their capacity of protectors of the state. The new era of peace was his greatest helper in the program; for it did seem to all at this time that the gods had indeed had the protection of Rome within their care, and brought her through a long age of civil war and anarchy to a secure haven. And though Livy's history was designed to show that the gods had always protected those Romans who had kept their virtue, every reader could see for himself that it was for this purpose, for the purpose of bringing into being the Roman Empire, that the Romans had been tried and purified—that it was their *destiny* to rule, as Vergil had stated more explicitly in his *Aeneid*, and had always been since the day when Aeneas completed his long journey to Italy and his descendant Romulus laid the foundations of Rome.

## Estimate of the achievement of Augustus

It is difficult to find in the records of all history a greater political and administrative genius than the first Princeps of Rome, the "architect of Empire," Augustus Caesar, and there are few who have approached him. He has suffered in comparison with his great-uncle, who was undoubtedly a more impressive personality with more spectacular and captivating qualities. He has also suffered from his biographers in ancient times, who could not appreciate at their true worth his farsightedness and understanding of the real problems involved in the transition from republic to monarchy, and who paid too much attention to minor failures, such as his sumptuary legislation.

He was conservative, cherishing the old virtues and the old institutions, and appreciating their value; and he devised means to continue what seemed good in them. He did not try to set back the clock in his governmental reforms, nor yet leap forward rashly into impossible experiments forbidden by the nature of the times. The most difficult and rare art of the statesman is to see the limits of the possible and pursue only the possible. And his monument was the Roman peace and the Roman Empire, which endured for hundreds of years in the framework which he had invented. The empire did not collapse after his death as did Charlemagne's, nor fall to pieces by military overextension as did Napoleon's.

Augustus had a tremendous job to accomplish in which all his predecessors had failed; and yet once he had achieved supreme power he substituted, almost without friction, a legitimate and acceptable civil government for civil warfare and domestic anarchy. There is a tale that a man was brought before him who had attempted a conspiracy against him. Augustus reasoned with the man, asking him how he proposed to replace him, and succeeded in convincing him of the impossibility of any alternative. Thereupon he forgave the would-be murderer and even promoted him in the public service. Perhaps Augustus was fortunate in that he was still a young man and had many years of life in front of him to make full use of the opportunity with which he had been presented. But he was never a healthy man, and it is one of his titles to greatness that he was able to overcome the handicap. He lived without ostentation, and never let anyone believe that he had any other ambition than to be first citizen in a restored and transformed republic. He is the most eminent disproof in history of the famous dictum of Lord Acton that "all power corrupts, and absolute power corrupts absolutely."

## ▶ The successors of Augustus

TIBERIUS AND THE DECLINE OF THE SENATE

It is not necessary in a book of this compass to go into detail on the achievements of the successors of Augustus. The reign of Tiberius (A.D. 14–37) was marked by excellent provincial administration but a growing disharmony between the Princeps and the Senate. Our chief authority for this period is the great Roman historian Tacitus, a man of senatorial rank who lived almost a century later, who, in the opinion of many scholars, described the conditions of his own time but placed them earlier in the age of Tiberius, as this was less dangerous to himself. But Tiberius most certainly lacked his step-father's tact, and he was already a morose and disillusioned elderly man when he became Princeps. It was not surprising that the senators for the first time now realized the potentialities for an *imperial* tyranny that had been masked under the principate of Augustus. And many of them began to look back nostalgically to the lost republic, viewing it through rose-colored glasses since few of them had actually experienced it. Brutus and Cassius, the tyrannicides, became their heroes, for they had defended with their lives the dignity of senators. Throughout the reign of Tiberius there were constant intrigues over

the succession, even while his son, later poisoned by the orders of his favorite, the praetorian prefect Sejanus, was still alive. Betrayed by the one man he had trusted, Tiberius countered the opposition to him with new laws against treason, and new rewards for informers, setting a precedent followed by too many of his successors. There were many real conspiracies against him, but, more than anyone else Sejanus, master of Rome when Tiberius retired to Capri for a little peace in his old age, betrayed him; and though Tiberius was strong enough to crush this conspiracy, the aftermath of treason trials and executions was always remembered against him by later historians and posterity.

The position of the Senate was indeed unenviable. It had had a long tradition of power under the republic, and its position even at its worst was always one of dignity. Augustus had given the senators work to do, but there was no doubt that all real power had been taken from them, and they were deeply offended. Tiberius would preside over the Senate; and though even the anti-imperial historian Tacitus admits that, at least in the early part of his reign, he encouraged the senators to speak freely, most of them were careful to catch every sign of approval or disapproval, so that they would not be found on the wrong side, in opposition to the Princeps, with all the danger that this entailed. This subservience wounded them in their dignity. They were forced out of fear to agree, and their true opinions were not valued. As long as any republican tradition remained, as it did at least until the death of Nero, A.D. 68, they were bound to regret their lost freedom, human dignity, and respect. Not all the outward dignity of a special toga could compensate them. Only the Stoics in the reigns to come provided any real resistance to the rulers, since they had a philosophy to sustain them, and at the last a sword to fall upon; and it was no accident that the tyrannous emperors especially singled out the Stoics as their enemies and treated them accordingly.

At last Tiberius died, and was succeeded by Caligula (A.D. 37–41), a young man of no ability and no experience who soon became insane, his insanity revealing itself in an undisguised tyranny and sadistic cruelty. When he was murdered in a praetorian conspiracy he was succeeded by Claudius (A.D. 41–54), an able administrator and student of history who effected many valuable reforms in the provincial administration but was unable to keep order in his own house, being ruled by his successive wives. He was murdered by his last wife, who thus succeeded in securing the succession for her son Nero (A.D. 54–68), who was only the stepson of Claudius. Nero lost no time in getting rid of his stepbrother, who was a real son of Claudius, but for five years he allowed his praetorian prefect Burrus and his tutor Seneca to exercise the actual rule of the empire. Thus the first five years of Nero's administration became proverbial for excellent administration at home and abroad. Then Nero began to show himself as the misfit he was on the throne, a second-rate artist, anxious only for the plaudits of the crowds for his theatrical performances and careless of his administration. The people loved him for his spectacular games and gladiatorial shows, but he degraded the imperial dignity, emptied the treasury, and won only contempt and enmity from the upper classes, contempt which culminated in conspiracies against his life. Thereafter no one in Rome was safe from his vengeance, and especially not his former friends. His tyranny in his last years equaled that of the madman Caligula. When he was overthrown by an open revolt and perished at the hands of a freedman when he lacked courage to take his own life, no provision had been made for the succession and no direct heir remained of the Julian house (called Julian after Julius Caesar). First the commander of the Spanish legions took the throne, then the praetorian prefect, then the commander of the German legions, none surviving the year (A.D. 69). Finally the commander of the Eastern legions, a plebeian general of rural ancestry, gained the throne and restored order.

Vespasian (69–79) ruled sensibly and restored some of its earlier dignity to the principate. He was succeeded by his two sons (the Flavian dynasty), one of whom died after two years, while Domitian, the second son (81–96), a suspicious tyrant but a good administrator, fell to a conspiracy. This was the end of the hereditary principle for nearly a century. For the first time no obvious candidate was available for the throne, and the choice fell into the hands of the Senate, which selected Nerva (96–98), a mild, elderly man whose most important act was the adoption of the best general in the empire as his son. Thus the adoptive principle superseded the hereditary, and the result was the period known as the era of the "Good Emperors." Each of the four emperors who reigned between 98 and 180 was a good administrator, and Trajan (98–117) was a great general, though it is not certain that his policy of enlarging the empire was altogether a wise one. The province of Dacia, north of the Danube, acquired by him, in addition to territories in Asia had to be abandoned before most of the rest of the empire, but not before it had been civilized by the Romans. The old Roman province of Dacia, the present-day Rumania, still has a language based upon Latin. Hadrian (117–138) was one of the ablest of the Roman emperors as an administrator. He it was who systematized the civil service, the most competent body of bureaucrats outside China in the ancient world, recruiting its members almost exclusively from the equestrian order, which was now entirely dependent upon himself. Hadrian also gave impetus to the study and codification of the Roman Law by abolishing the edicts of the annually elected praetors (see the next chapter). By Hadrian's time it was recognized that the word of the emperor was the true source of law for the empire, and it may be said that with Hadrian disappeared the

*Bust of the Emperor Antoninus Pius. Note the Greek influence and the careful attention to detail characteristic of this period, as shown in the treatment of hair and beard.* (COURTESY THE METROPOLITAN MUSEUM OF ART)

remnants of the old republican tradition. Antoninus Pius (138–161) further improved the law and provided a long reign of almost unbroken peace. Marcus Aurelius (161–180), the Stoic writer of the *Meditations*, was compelled to spend most of his reign defending the empire against barbarian tribes who were threatening the frontiers, but maintained the record of his predecessors in the administration of the empire.

All these emperors were chosen by their predecessors and adopted as their sons. The Augustan title of Princeps, though still formally used, no longer seems appropriate for these absolute rulers. Unfortunately, as has already been mentioned, Marcus Aurelius was not, like the others, childless, and chose as his successor his worthless son Commodus (180–193), whose reign marked the beginning of the serious decline of the empire, as will be narrated in a later chapter. But, whatever the principle of succession used, there was no thought now of restoring the antique republic. The monarchy as an institution had proved itself; the republic was a fit subject only for historical study.

## THE PROVINCES IN THE FIRST TWO CENTURIES

Life in the provinces was rarely affected by the disturbances in the capital. The chief annoyance undoubtedly was the arbitrary increases in taxation necessitated by the spendthrift habits of some of the early emperors, especially Caligula and Nero. Imperial governors usually remained over from one regime to another, and senatorial governors continued to be appointed as before unless the emperor was especially interested in the appointment. The Roman peace was maintained in almost the whole empire without a break. The only power in the first two centuries that presented any danger was the Parthian Empire in the Near East. But it was already on the decline in the second century, and Trajan inflicted several severe defeats upon it, altering the Augustan settlement in this region by annexing several new provinces. But his successor recognized the great difficulty of holding them, and the fact that the expense involved could ill be afforded. For this reason he returned some of the new provinces to client kings. Not until the reign of Marcus Aurelius was the Roman peace seriously threatened by the first movements of barbarians against the frontiers; and even this was of no moment to the interior provinces, save for increases in taxation to pay for the wars.

The first two centuries of the empire were characterized by an increasing centralization of the government, above all through the growth of the bureaucracy or imperial civil service. Hadrian brought every official under direct imperial control, including those in Italy, even in some cases nominating the governors of senatorial provinces, who were in any case by now the prisoners of the bureaucracy provided for them by the emperor. The municipalities also lost some of their responsibilities. Though the "Good Emperors," including Hadrian, were not personally tyrants, and indeed kept on very good terms with the Senate, being themselves drawn from the senatorial class, their policies tended toward an increasing absolutism which was ultimately recognized by the formal changes in the nature of the monarchy brought about by Diocletian at the end of the third century A.D. It should be added, however, that the Senate no longer provided any opposition to the absolutist tendency, for it had been itself enrolled by previous emperors, and the old qualification of nobility of birth alone had long ago disappeared. The tyrants Caligula, Nero, and Domitian had paid careful attention to see that it should.

The Romanized provinces by the end of the second century had become the real heart of the empire, though Rome, of course, remained the capital. The rank and file of the legions was made up exclusively of provincials, and the officers now came as much from the Romanized provinces as from Italy. One of the reasons why Trajan's wars in the East were ultimately so dangerous to Rome was that the most thoroughly Romanized provinces, Gaul and the two Spanish provinces, provided so many of his troops, who too often did not return to their homelands; if they were not killed in the East they were likely to settle there. All the emperors after Nero had had long experience in the provinces and recognized their importance; Trajan and Hadrian were both Spaniards. The Italian patriotism of Augustus was therefore slowly replaced by the wider patriotism of the citizen of the Roman Empire itself. This reality was ultimately recognized in the famous edict of the Emperor Caracalla in 212, which granted Roman citizenship to every freeman of the empire.

INFLUENCE OF THE ROMAN IMPERIAL IDEA

The Roman Empire, then, by the end of the second century had become fully established and accepted as the natural order of things. Internal opposition had disappeared, and the idea of the Roman Empire now had such a hold on the hearts and heads of men as no empire in the past had ever achieved, with the possible exception of the Chinese Empire under the Hans. There was some excuse for the belief that it was eternal, that it had even been willed by the gods. It was in this atmosphere of eternity and impregnability that the foundations of the

Christian Church were laid, and this Church, the spiritual successor of the Roman Empire, was deeply influenced by it.

The achievements of the empire had already been enormous. It had always given tolerable and often excellent administration and an equitable law to a vast area, and it had given this area a peace it neither knew before nor has known since. If liberty was missing, this was a lack not felt by the people of the time. No one alive had known it from experience. It survived, at most, as a philosophical ideal. In the next chapter we shall see the other contributions to the cultural heritage of the world made by this hard-headed, efficient, practical, but hardly inspired people who first unified and ruled the Western world.

▶  Suggestions for further reading

Every student should make the effort to read at least some part of the great history of Tacitus, which is conveniently printed in the Modern Library series in the standard translation, M. Hadas, ed., *The Complete Works of Tacitus* (tr. A. J. Church and W. J. Brodribb; New York: The Modern Library, 1942). The *Annals* covers the Julian Age; and the *Histories* covers especially the period of anarchy following the death of Nero and the re-establishment of the principate under Vespasian. Other worthwhile authors are Juvenal, some parts of Seneca, Lucan, and, with caution, Suetonius. These may be read in the Loeb Classical series.

For the differing views on Augustus and Tiberius, the present author's chapter on "Freedom and Tyranny in the Ancient World," in K. Setton and H. Winkler, eds., *Great Problems in European History* (New York: Prentice-Hall, Inc., 1954), will serve to introduce the problem and give some idea of the varying views of contemporaries and posterity. The last half of R Syme, *The Roman Revolution* (Oxford: The Clarendon Press, 1939), already referred to at the end of the previous chapter, and J. Buchan, *Augustus* (Boston: Houghton, Mifflin & Co., 1937), should be read, preferably in conjuction, since they represent opposite points of view. F. D. Marsh, *The Reign of Tiberius* (London: Oxford University Press, 1931), is a masterly attempt to rehabilitate the second princeps, whom the author feels to have been much maligned by Tacitus.

Almost all the information the beginning student will wish to know on the actual workings of the early Empire are to be found in the pages of M. I. Rostovtzeff, *The Social and Economic History of the Roman Empire* (New York: Oxford University Press, 1926), though the reader should be warned that not all scholars agree with his conclusions. The book is also excellently illustrated. For the more conservative opinion, the old classic, T. Mommsen, *The Provinces of the Roman Empire* (2nd ed.; New York: Charles Scribner's Sons, 1909), is still worth consulting. For a briefer picture of the Roman Empire, in-cluding its cultural achievements, a valuable work is M. P. Charlesworth, *The Roman Empire* (Home University Library; London: Oxford University Press, 1951).

The standard book on Roman society of the early imperial period is S. Dill, *Roman Society from Nero to Marcus Aurelius* (London: Macmillan & Co., Ltd., 1904), which may be supplemented by a more lively account by J. Carcopino, *Daily Life in Ancient Rome* (tr. E. O. Lorimer; New Haven, Conn.: Yale University Press, 1940). A useful survey, which contains also much cultural material, is F. G. Moore, *The Roman's World* (New York: Columbia University Press, 1936).

# 12

# Roman Culture

*General characteristics of Roman culture • Religion • Philosophy: transformation of Greek thought by the Roman spirit • Science • Architecture and sculpture • Rhetoric • History • Law • Literature*

▶ **General characteristics of Roman culture**

CONTRAST WITH CREATIVENESS OF THE GREEKS

It is one of the ironies of history that, in spite of our admiration for the Greeks, Western civilization has always been nourished far more by Roman ideas and institutions than by Greek. With the recovery of Greek literature in recent centuries and the opportunity to study some of the masterpieces of Greek art in the original we have been able to make a comparative estimate of Greek and Roman contributions; and few would today claim the Romans to have been qualitatively superior in any single field of cultural endeavor to which the Greeks turned their attention. Roman architecture made use of far more forms than the Greeks had found necessary for their simpler needs, Roman engineering solved practical problems that were outside Greek experience. But though we are impressed by the grandeur of the Pantheon in Rome and admire the excellence of Roman roads, bridges, and aqueducts, it is to the Athenian Parthenon that we go for an ideal of architectural beauty. Yet our own public buildings are copied from the Romans, we are inclined to use the Corinthian rather

than Doric or Ionic capitals, and our columns, like Roman columns, too often support nothing and are merely superfluous decorations. But remove a Greek column and the building will collapse. To us the Greek world is remote, to be admired but not imitated, whereas the Romans are close to us. We feel we understand them. They are people like ourselves. To enter the Greek world requires an effort of the imagination; but the Romans, nearly as far away from us in time, can be understood, it seems, without any such rare and difficult mental activity.

It would appear that even to the Romans themselves the Greeks were a people apart. They admitted that in every branch of cultural activity the Greeks were their teachers and masters, and they did their best to imitate them. But they never seriously tried to think in the way the Greeks had thought. It is impossible to conceive of any Roman with whom we are acquainted taking time out to consider the fundamental problem of the early cosmologists, what it is that is stable in a world of changing appearances. No Roman could speculate like Plato or reason like Aristotle. The more simple ideas of these masters they could understand, at least in part. But whenever they tried to explain

*The Pantheon at Rome, a much-imitated building, where the deified emperors were buried. Note the combination of dome and Corinthian columns.* (COURTESY ITALIAN STATE TOURIST OFFICE)

*One such imitation—the Low Library at Columbia University, New York.* (COURTESY COLUMBIA UNIVERSITY)

what they had read—and many Romans, notably Cicero and Seneca, made a real effort to cope with the problems of philosophy— the result always appears as oversimplification, not touching the root of the matter, in some way debased. The truth seems to be, however it may be explained, that the Roman mind simply *could* not think in the Greek manner. Not that such thinking died out in the Roman period. The Greeks, Claudius Ptolemy the astronomer and Galen the physician are recognizably Greek in their thinking, though they lived in the second century of the Roman Empire.

### PRACTICAL NATURE OF THE ROMAN GENIUS

The great Roman contribution to world culture therefore lies not in the field of thought, but in the application of thought in the ordinary world of men. In this way they served as a complement to the Greeks. They reaped the harvest of whatever had been thought before them, putting it to practical use. Where the Greeks had been concerned with ethical speculations, the Romans translated these into practical everyday morality; where Democritus had speculated on the constitution of matter, and Epicurus had drawn the conclusion that in such a cosmology there was no need for gods, the Roman Lucretius makes a passionate attack on religion and superstition as the prime causes of human suffering; where human morality is conspicuously missing in the adventures of Odysseus as told by Homer, the Roman Vergil in his *Aeneid* emphasizes the filial devotion of his hero, and the glorification of Rome and its destiny—the purpose of the voyage of Aeneas—breathes in every line of the poem.

### ASSIMILATION AND TRANSMISSION OF GREEK CULTURE

The Romans, then, were the greatest transmitters of culture the world has yet seen, though to a lesser degree the Arabs later performed the same function. But the Roman spirit is nevertheless imprinted on every line the Romans wrote, every idea they took up and put to use. They should not be regarded as mere copiers. Moreover, when the Greeks left no model, the Romans showed themselves quite capable of developing new forms of their own, as in satire, epigram, letter writing, and perhaps even fiction. If anyone had ever had the temerity to translate a Roman work into Greek, it would at once have been recognized as Roman handiwork.

What is especially worth studying, therefore, in a survey of civilization is the process of cultural assimilation from the Greeks, the working of the Roman genius upon the material, and then the advances, if any, made by the Romans themselves in the same field. This chapter, then, will take the various fields of cultural activity one by one, and try to show this process at work rather than attempt a strictly chronological account of republican, Augustan, and Silver Age (the second century A.D.) achievements; external circumstances surrounding particular works will be mentioned only when they have a special relevance. In this way it is hoped that the student will perceive something of the nature of cultural assimilation in general, since every culture, now and in the future, will necessarily build upon the achievements of its predecessors, adding, like the Romans, the impress of its own distinctive genius, and thus carrying it forward into the future.

### THE LATIN LANGUAGE

A word, however, is first necessary on the language of Roman literature. The Latin language is a native product of Italy. Though it has many virtues, it cannot compare with the Greek for flexibility, variety, and subtlety. It has comparatively few tenses, it lacks the middle voice, the dual number, and above all it lacks the Greek particles and prefixes which make Greek a language capable of expressing so many different shades of meaning. In this it shows itself as a suitable vehicle for Roman expression. The Romans did not make fine distinctions, they were not subtle; they, like their language, said what they meant, clearly and distinctly, with no nonsense about it. Moreover, the Latin language also lacks the invaluable auxiliary verbs, "to have" and "to be," which are so useful in the modern languages. It is defective in many parts, lacking, for instance, the present participle passive and past participle active in transitive verbs. Classical Latin makes use of what seem to us awkward circumlocutions when dealing with reported speech and past events (this defect was remedied in medieval Latin). And while it has one useful case, the ablative, unknown to the Greeks, this hardly compensates for what is missing. However, it has a wonderful terseness and brevity which make for precision and clarity, and in the course of time it developed a wealth of abstract nouns, which made it in medieval times an admirable vehicle for the formal logical philosophy of the scholastics. It also has the qualities of dignity and stateliness which made it especially suitable as the language of church and government. Medieval Latin, though derided by the humanists of the Renaissance, had gone far toward remedying the language's earlier defects, and out of medieval Latin developed not only all the Romance languages of the West, but much of the English language in its present form. For more than a thousand years it was the universal language of educated men, and until the present century was probably read by more people in Western Europe than any other. It is still the official language of the Roman Catholic Church.

## ▶ Religion

### NATIVE AND ETRUSCAN

Native Roman and Italian religion reflects the social structure of the primitive Romans, but it is difficult to look upon it as in any sense a religion in our sense of the word. If the Romans had not become in later times a great people, few students of religion would probably have troubled to examine their religion. It conforms very closely in its primitive beliefs and rituals to those discovered by modern anthropologists working with uncivilized tribes. It explains, however, much in the early Roman character, and makes it easy to understand why the Romans were always so hospitable to im-

*A lar, one of the household gods of the Romans.* (COURTESY THE METROPOLITAN MUSEUM OF ART)

ported religions which made a greater appeal to religious feeling.

The early Romans evidently regarded all nature as animate, and gave names to the spirits, of particular areas and of natural phenomena such as rivers, as also to various agricultural functions such as plowing and sowing. These natural forces were called *numina*, or spiritual powers, and the farmer had to propitiate these powers by sacrifice. In addition there were certain protective deities, especially the *lares*, protectors of the home, the *penates*, protectors of the household stores, and the *genius*, protector of the family itself who worked through the head of the family. There was no kind of morality or ethics in this religion, as the spirits merely required specified attentions from members of the family. If these duties were fulfilled then the spirits were bound by a kind of bargain to support the family. Ironically enough, this binding contract is the original meaning of the word "religio," from which comes our word "religion." After death the spirits of human beings survived, but apparently without any individuality, and wandered in a featureless underworld, similar to the Babylonian Aralu. In addition to these nature spirits, Jupiter, god of the sky, and Mars, god of war, were worshiped from an early time and seem to have been native Italian deities. They possessed greater power than the lesser spirits, but the latter were closer to the individual man, like the personal gods of the primitive Sumerians and Babylonians. The household gods, especially the *lares* and *penates*, served to keep the Roman family together, and were very close to all its members, while the greater gods only came into prominence when the Romans became a real people, and families acquired a wide loyalty to Rome itself.

The Etruscans influenced the early religion in several important ways. The father of the family was originally the only priest required for household worship. But as the state grew in importance, especially under the Etruscan monarchy, it became necessary to know more about the will of the gods of the state so that they might be propitiated in times of danger. Hence developed, as in Babylonia, the art of reading the future through the inspection of the livers of animals, and later the interpretation of various omens such as lightning and the flight of birds. For these specialized functions colleges of priests came into existence, whose duty was to keep officials advised of the will of the gods. This gave the college of pontiffs and augurs a considerable political power in later days, for the Romans were legally unable to transact any business on unlucky days. Bibulus, the colleague of Julius Caesar in his first consulship, refused to take any part in the triumvir's transactions, and laid the legal basis for nullification of his laws by retiring to his house to watch the omens every day the Senate sat. Since these omens were all declared by the stubborn consul to be unlucky, the laws were officially null and void. When Caesar decided to cross the Rubicon rather than face as a private person charges of illegal acts committed during his consulship, no doubt he remembered the process by which they had been made illegal. Under Etruscan influence the gods of the state were first furnished with temples, and

these gods gradually became established in public esteem, with the addition of Juno, as a wife for Jupiter, Minerva, goddess of the artisans, and others. Temple building, however, was slow to take hold in Rome, and several gods were worshiped only in the open air until a late date in Roman history. The state religion was looked after by a college of pontiffs, under the chief direction of the Pontifex Maximus, an official elected for life, and exact rules were drawn up for public ceremonial and worship.

GREEK INFLUENCE

With the conquest of the Greek cities in Italy a great change came over this primitive religion. Perhaps the first effect was the acceptance of one of the Greek oracles, the Sibyl of Cumae, as inspired. Her prophecies were contained in the sacred Sibylline Books, which were consulted by the pontiffs in times of crisis. The Greek gods were early grafted onto their Roman counterparts, and the Romans took over intact the very considerable Greek mythology and applied it to their own gods. By the end of the third century B.C. the new Hellenistic religions were already flourishing in the Near East, the worship of Cybele, the great Earth Mother, and various mystery religions. It was not long before these penetrated into Italy, and the greater requirements of the new gods seemed to meet a need on the part of many Romans. The Sibylline Books aided in this process, for when they were consulted the advice usually was to introduce a new cult from the Near East. Since consultation coincided with an actual crisis in Roman affairs, the entry of these new gods was greeted with emotional fervor and elaborate festivals were held. The older and more conservative Romans looked upon these innovations with disgust, and Cato the Elder (234–149 B.C.) led a special campaign to drive all Greeks from the city. But he was behind the times and never met more than a temporary success. On the whole the Romans remained tolerant of all religions unless they presented, like later Christianity, a danger to the state or offended Roman conceptions of morality.

## ORIENTAL INFLUENCE

As we have seen already, when Augustus became princeps he tried vainly to revive the old agricultural religion. But he was only successful in the countryside, which had never fully abandoned its old primitivism. Bringing rural deities to the city was hardly sufficient to satisfy the now apparent emotional needs of many Romans. Only emperor-worship among Roman cults took any real hold of the people, and even this was supplemented by other more emotional religions which offered more to the individual worshipers. All the religions imported during the empire taught individual immortality and purification of the soul in this life in preparation for the next. It is therefore clear enough that many Roman men and women by the time of the principate were thoroughly dissatisfied with the old traditional ceremonies and the cold formality of the state religion. The worshipers themselves did not take part in these ceremonies but only watched them, whereas in the new Oriental religions the worshipers themselves were initiated with mystic rites and ceremonies. Moreover, with the assumption by the emperor of so many of the duties of private citizens in earlier times, local patriotism began to die out, together with the religion that had sustained it. For some few the semi-religious philosophy of Stoicism with its high ethical content (dealt with in the next section) was sufficient, but the new Oriental religions claimed far more adherents.

The two earliest and most important of these were the revived religion of the Egyptian Isis and the Persian Mithraism. The Egyptian religion now included more definite teachings on immortality, initiation ceremonies, and festivals of mourning for the dead Osiris. It was also highly organized into a cult of priests and worshipers, providing a sense of community missing in both Stoicism and the state cult. Mithraism had developed out of Zoroastrianism, and retained its central belief in the two great

spirits, Light and Darkness. But now it was made clear that the worshiper must struggle against the Spirit of Darkness. In the struggle he is aided by the god Mithra, who is nearer to man than the original Sun-god, Ahura-Mazda, with whom indeed Mithra intercedes for the human soul. This religion, which has so many striking elements in common with Christianity, made tremendous advances within the empire in the early centuries, especially through dissemination by the Roman legions. But it suffered from one handicap that was insuperable. Unlike the religion of Isis and of Christianity, it did not admit women, whose influence in early Christianity was so strong. Very similar to Mithraism was the worship of the Unconquered Sun, of which very little is known, in spite of the fact that one emperor (Elagabalus, 218–222) was a priest of the cult, and another (Aurelian, 270–275) established it as the official religion of Rome. The rival of Constantine for the throne, A.D. 312, fought under the banner of the Unconquered Sun (*Sol Invictus*) but lost to Constantine, who had chosen before the decisive battle to fight under the sign of the cross of Christianity. Thereafter Christianity, discussed more fully in the next chapter, became the official religion of the emperors, and before the end of the fourth century the only permitted religion in the empire. The competitive religions gradually died out, though elements of Mithraism survived in Manichaeism, which influenced many important Christian thinkers, especially St. Augustine, and Manichaeism itself survived in various heretical groups in Bulgaria and later in southern France, where we shall meet it again among the Cathari or Albigensians, suppressed by Pope Innocent III in the thirteenth century. The essential element in these religions of Persian origin was always dualism, or the almost equal power of good and evil, and human life as the scene of the struggle between these powers. Christianity, while admitting Satan into its religion, nevertheless always stressed his complete inferiority to God, and denied him any part in creation.

▶ **Philosophy—Transformation of Greek thought by the Roman spirit**

STOICISM

Until the introduction of Greek thought into Rome there was no philosophy among the Romans, and they found no need for it. As an active and practical people they were inclined to despise all forms of speculation. However, in the first flush of enthusiasm for all things Greek in the second century B.C. a number of Greeks were invited to Rome by a distinguished Roman gentleman of the highest rank, Scipio Aemilianus, around whom formed a circle of young Romans interested in Greek culture. Among those who came to Rome was a Stoic philosopher Panaetius, who had already done much original thinking on the traditional Stoic material of which mention was made in Chapter 9. Stoicism, it will be remembered, postulated a Divine Reason which pervaded all nature and was indeed identical with it. All human laws are attempts to legislate in accordance with the Divine Reason, which must be discovered by men. Thus arose the persistent belief in the existence of a natural law in accordance with which positive law on earth must be made. No law is really just unless it conforms with this natural law. All men are equal and brothers, said the Stoics, and this fact necessitated full equality before the law, a lasting principle of Roman jurisprudence. These ideas exercised an enormous influence upon Roman jurists, the greatest of whom were thoroughly at home with Stoic philosophy, which thus found practical application in Rome rather than in its own Hellenistic world.

It will be remembered also that Stoicism taught that the task of man was to achieve indifference to worldly success, and emphasized the dignity and worth of the individual human being, standing alone and without support from the gods, but secure because his wants were few and he could willingly relinquish all earthly desires. Though such a thought was no doubt too demanding for most Romans, and indeed for most human beings of any national origin, it nevertheless did appeal to something deep-seated in the Roman character, his willingness to undertake unpaid public service as a duty laid upon him simply by virtue of the fact that he was a Roman. Throughout Roman history we find many such self-reliant men, devoted to the service of their family and of the state, willing to expend themselves in it without hope of material reward. Such men found their philosophical justification in Stoicism. It was a philosophy only suited to the strong, for it offered no hope of reward in this world or the next. It is no accident that the greatest opponents of the absolute power of the emperors were the Stoics, whose regard for human dignity made them also willing to commit suicide rather than submit to indignity and loss of freedom.

We possess the writings of several Roman Stoics, but none is of first-rate quality. Too often lacking the capacity for sustained original thought, they are inclined to fall into platitudes, and little moral sermons. Cicero interprets Greek Stoicism fairly effectively, but makes no claims to originality. Seneca in the early empire sometimes utters ethical teachings worthily and has a few moving passages much appreciated by the early Christians, who believed him to have corresponded directly with Paul. But too often he lapses into commonplaces; and when we remember his own personal fortune acquired in public office, his sincerity is too often open to doubt, spoiling the effect of some of his preachments. On the other hand, the lame freedman, Epictetus, born Greek but thoroughly Romanized, neglects philosophical speculation altogether and concentrates his attention on how to lead a good life on earth in accordance with Stoic principles. All through his work the sincere moralist is evident. In the *Meditations* of Marcus Aurelius we see the effect of Stoicism upon a man who happened to be an emperor but would have preferred to be an ordinary humble human being. Possessed of a true humanitarian spirit, and really imbued with the theoretical Stoic love for all mankind, there is no doubt that he felt the burden of empire a heavy one. But Stoicism helped him fulfill his imperial duties, and the *Meditations,* written (in Greek) for the most part when he was on campaign and under the most difficult circumstances, shows both the man and the philosophy at their best.

## EPICURISM

In the hands of the republican poet Lucretius, Epicurism appears as one of the great scientific philosophies of history. Lucretius, however, had a practical aim, to save human beings from their unreasonable fear of death, and free them from the bonds of superstition and religion, which he regards as synonymous and tending to destroy what little happiness is possible in life. Basing his science upon the teachings of Democritus and Epicurus—that the world is made up of atoms which come together by a chance swerve—Lucretius concludes with his masters that gods are unnecessary. Even if they do exist, they live apart at ease, and take no account of human affairs. It is therefore irrational to fear them, or to worship them. Death is not an evil, but a rest from earthly suffering. It is man's task to live without fear, and without any particular hope for happiness.

The beautiful poem *De rerum natura* is unique in all literature in that the greater part is true poetry, with many imaginative passages of great power, especially in the account of the creation of the world and all living creatures; yet it remains thoroughly scientific according to the best scientific principles of the time. It achieved wide popularity again in the European Enlightenment before its science was fully outmoded. Even Lucretius' science was taken seriously for a time, especially by Gassendi in the seventeenth century.

The form of Epicurism as found in Lucretius was not the form in which it was accepted by most Romans. Always implicit in the teaching, "Be happy with little, for desire is likely to bring unhappiness, and we shall all soon be dead"—the teaching of Epicurus himself—is the further thought that we ought to be happy now while we can, and

not trouble about tomorrow. And it was in this form that the Romans accepted it as a philosophy of eating, drinking, and being merry. Horace, the Augustan poet laureate, is a gentle Epicurean, content with his loaf of bread and his bottle of Falernian wine on a Sabine farm, and many are the praises he sings of the harmless life of simple pleasures. Others were not so restrained, and ultimately it became the fate of Epicurus to act as the philosophical sponsor for Roman hedonism, the cult of excessive eating and drinking for which Rome is too often remembered.

## ECLECTICISM

It was the custom for many centuries for upper-class Romans to go to Greece for the completion of their education. Here they came in contact with many schools of philosophy, and, as in modern universities, they had the opportunity to develop their own philosophy after listening to the best that was offered by their predecessors. The best example of this eclecticism, or choosing parts from various philosophies as one's own personal philosophy, is to be found in the great lawyer Cicero, who was a thoroughly educated man, but not himself a thinker of the first order. He did not even claim to be, preferring to consider himself as an interpreter of the Greek schools, putting their ideas into attractive Latin dress. It is characteristic of Cicero, as of Romans in general, that Plato and Aristotle are, on the whole, beyond his comprehension, though he admired them greatly. He prefers the later Hellenistic thinkers and philosophies, and again he is more interested in the practical side of their work. He discusses virtue at great length, but the more profound thoughts of Plato and Aristotle on the subject of the Good he lays aside in favor of discussions on how to live a happy life. On the whole, Stoicism seems to be interpreted with the greatest sympathy, and Cicero is one of our best sources for the Stoic teachings current in his day. He pays special attention to the Stoic idea of divine providence, thus endearing himself in a later day to the Christian Fathers. But he always remained to some degree skeptical, and he appreciated Greek Skepticism, but in a busy life it was natural that that philosophy never engaged his full attention.

Cicero's philosophical writings have had a career far beyond their intrinsic merit, for they were well known throughout the medieval period, and were still appreciated in the Italian Renaissance. Their simplification of the more profound problems of human life has always appealed to those who do not wish to struggle with the metaphysical issues involved, and his practical advice can be appreciated without excessive mental strain. The clarity of his language, even in his philosophical writings, is always a delight; indeed, he was responsible for the development of a philosophical Latin language capable of conveying Greek thought to posterity.

### ▶ Science

In pure science the Romans contributed not a single figure of any importance. In mathematics they were encumbered with numerals which present insuperable difficulties to any advanced calculations. Although they understood techniques based on mathematics and were extremely competent engineers and surveyors, they had no interest whatever in the fundamental Greek science of geometry, the theoretical basis of these techniques. Indeed, science actually degenerated in Roman hands and the few works written by them were far inferior to work already done before their time.

The elder Pliny was a man of considerable scientific curiosity but no talent. And even though he is said to have lost his life in an attempt to investigate at firsthand the eruption of Vesuvius which destroyed Pompeii, his enormous encyclopedia of *Natural History* betrays no critical sense. It is nothing but a repository of all the information available to an inquiring Roman in his day, without much serious attempt to discover whether it is true or not. Yet this work remains extremely valuable to us, as it is the primary source for Roman scientific knowledge in all the many fields it covers. The book was also greatly valued in the Middle Ages, since, with the Bible, it provided most of the information available to that period before the more advanced Muslim science and the works of Aristotle became accessible in Latin translations.

The Romans were diligent astrologers but had little interest in astronomy. The Greek Ptolemy in the second century A.D. wrote a highly competent synthesis of the work of previous astronomers, but no Roman name is known in the history of astronomy. When Caesar needed a competent astronomer for the revision of the Roman calendar, a Greek had to be hired for the purpose.

The history of medicine among the Romans is typical of their attitude. Theory was almost entirely neglected, though Galen, a Greek contemporary of Ptolemy, summed up earlier Greek theory and added much of his own. But the Romans were greatly interested in public health and sanitation. The emperors also established a hospital service for soldiers and officials in the provinces. If, however, the remedies used in these hospitals were those described by Pliny, it would seem probable that the doctors who served in them played but a small part in the eventual recovery of the wounded.

In technology the Romans made progress beyond their masters. Even in early republican days they developed a new technique for making roads, the best ones paved with stone, while secondary roads were surfaced with gravel. They built their roads up carefully from a depth of several feet below the surface of the surrounding country, using small stones and even concrete. It seems to have been by accident rather than through any scientific knowledge that the Romans discovered how to make a real concrete composed of lime and a volcanic ash which happens to contain the necessary ingredients. This discovery enabled the Romans to construct their public buildings out of a readily available material instead of using only the always expensive marble, which was then freed for use as a veneer.

The Romans knew how to construct strong bridges through the extensive use of the arch; they made tunnels through difficult

*This famous Roman aqueduct, the Pont du Gard in France, gives some idea of Roman engineering skill and the gigantic size of Roman public works of the imperial period. Such construction is even more impressive when one realizes it was carried on with only the most primitive machinery.*

mountain terrain; and they understood, but rarely used, the principle of the siphon for their baths and aqueducts. The many Roman remains, not only in Italy but throughout Europe, are an ample testimony to the strength of the materials used and the effectiveness of the Romans as engineers.

▶ **Art**

ARCHITECTURE—CULT OF HUGE AND
GRANDIOSE, CONTRAST WITH GREEK HARMONY

Oswald Spengler, when he put forward his theory of the rise and fall of cultures and their different stages of development from "spring" to "winter," suggested that the winter stage was characterized always by the cult of the gigantic, the mania for huge buildings and engineering projects rather than the more delicate, beautiful, and truly artistic works of the earlier stages. Since he regarded the Roman civilization as the "win-

ter" phase of Greco-Roman culture, one of his most important pieces of evidence was Roman architecture (the colossal buildings of Rameses in Egypt and American skyscrapers were others). Whether this preference for the huge may be better explained by other theories or not, it is certainly true that the Romans had a taste for the large and ornate rather than for the simple and unpretentious. Whereas the Greeks excelled especially in temples and other religious buildings which were intended only to house the god, much of the best Roman architecture has more practical uses. The greatest successes of the Romans are to be found in their public buildings, baths, theaters, and amphitheaters, and in their monumental imperial architecture.

It was the Etruscans who first taught architecture to the Romans, and Etruscan influence always persisted. It was they who instructed the Romans in the use of stone and brick, and they who gave them the arch. But the Etruscans had themselves been influenced by the Greeks, and they used Greek columns in their public buildings and had houses of Greek design. After the Punic Wars, Greek influence became predominant in Rome, and during this period Roman buildings, public and private, were usually copies of those in Hellenistic cities. But even in this copying the Romans knew what they liked, which was invariably the ornate and the grandiose. The Corinthian column was preferred to the more severe Ionic and Doric, and the post and lintel construction was abandoned as unsuitable for large buildings constructed for practical needs, for which the dome, vault, and arch were more suitable. Gradually the Greek forms which the Romans, like ourselves, felt to be "artistic," became merely decorative on Roman buildings. They solemnly inserted useless columns, supporting nothing, they carefully fluted their columns although the fluting served now no practical purpose. The volutes at the top of the columns became more and more luxuriant and decorative, the Corinthian and Ionic capitals now being welded into a new composite. Not until twentieth-century architecture was the Roman practice looked upon with disfavor, and even now it is far from ousted, as a glance around any of our large cities will confirm.[1] But it is now believed by architectural theorists that the function should dictate the form and not the reverse. This principle, of course, had been fully understood by the Greeks.

When the spoils of war began to flow into Rome during the last century of the republic, private houses, often built by successful bankers and generals, became larger and more ostentatious, and still for the most part constructed by Greek architects, and often furnished with Greek works of art looted during the successful campaigns. Pompey built the first permanent Roman theater out of his spoils, Julius Caesar from his Gallic booty built a new Forum and repaved the old. Roman taste at this time, as usual with the new rich, ran to the extravagant and splendid, with elaborate ornamentation and

statuary (copied from the Greek, of course) in wild profusion.

With the advent of Augustus, Roman architecture came into its own, and we begin to hear of Roman architects and engineers, even though Greek influence was still strong and perhaps predominant. The rebuilding of Rome by Augustus, and the construction of vast new temples in accordance with his religious policy, influenced provincial cities also to take advantage of the new prosperity and rebuild their cities. In the imperial period every city of any importance had its baths, and even the smaller cities were able to build theaters, amphitheaters, and basilicas which were used for public business and to house the law courts. The best known of the Roman amphitheaters is the Colosseum, constructed by the first two Flavian emperors, much of which is still standing today, a huge round structure with a great arena for the spectacle. Underneath the arena is a network of passages, enabling performers—beasts and men—to reach any part of the arena as required. The basilica is a typical Roman structure, the plan of which, with nave, aisles, and clerestory windows, was adapted by the Christians for their early churches.[2] The cross-vaulting of the Romanesque cathedrals seems to have been a Roman invention, and allowed far greater size to the buildings.

Roman architecture reached its zenith in the time of Hadrian in the second century A.D. Thereafter there are still many huge and impressive buildings, especially the Baths of Caracalla, the Basilica of Constantine, and the palace of Diocletian at Split on the Adriatic Coast. But these only showed that the Romans had not forgotten how to construct. The materials, as was natural at a time when prosperity was declining, were now inferior, and there is no significant architectural innovation. Diocletian's palace was more of a fortress than a royal residence of the earlier ages, and indeed many of the villas and palaces of this declining period paid more attention to strength than to style.[2] It is true that in the Constantinople of Justinian there

[1] For example, New York General Post Office.

[2] A Christian church in the style of a Roman basilica is illustrated in Chapter 20 (Cathedral of Pisa), while the palace of Diocletian at Split is shown in Chapter 14.

*A Roman theater at Arles, in southern France, as it appears today.*

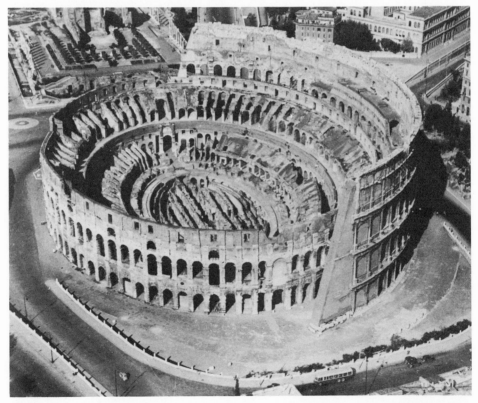

*Aerial view of the Colosseum at Rome, built by the Flavian emperors for the display of such public entertainment as gladiatorial fights.* (COURTESY ITALIAN STATE TOURIST OFFICE)

*Left, a Roman of the third century B.C. (portrait bust in bronze). Right, a Roman of the first century B.C. Note how the Roman sculptors strove to express character in their subjects' faces. It would appear from their literature that the Romans indeed believed character showed in a man's face. This may perhaps account in part for the relative frequency of the bust over the full-size statue. (*COURTESY THE METROPOLITAN MUSEUM OF ART*)*

*The Colosseum seen through the Arch of Titus, a triumphal arch built by the conqueror of Palestine. (*COURTESY ITALIAN STATE TOURIST OFFICE*)*

*The Arch of Constantine in Rome, a triumphal arch for which he is said to have pillaged materials from other such monuments. The workmanship is greatly inferior to that of earlier works of the same kind, though its size remains impressive.* (COURTESY ITALIAN STATE TOURIST OFFICE)

was a real rebirth of architecture, but this can no longer be called Roman, and will be considered in its place under Byzantine art.

### SCULPTURE—REALISM

Like architecture, Roman sculpture was first influenced by the Etruscans and then by the Greeks. Indeed, the Romans had such a high opinion of Greek (almost exclusively Hellenistic) sculpture that to the end of the empire many sculptors were employed simply at making copies of Greek statuary for the Roman market. But aside from these copies there is a pronounced difference between Roman and even Hellenistic sculpture, which is in full keeping with the Roman character

as we know it. The Romans liked their sculpture to be realistic, thus completing what was only a tendency in the Hellenistic world. In this preference they followed the Etruscan tradition also. The Romans therefore developed the art of realistic portraiture far more than the Greeks. When the Greeks, even Hellenistic Greeks, carved a portrait they were always conscious of the harmony between body and mind or soul, between life itself and the material it informed. So the Greeks preferred to carve the whole body, of which the head and face were only a part. When, at the request of the Romans, who usually desired merely a portrait bust, Greek artists took to portrait sculpture, they remained aware of the mind which lay behind the mere features, and thus strove to reveal character through the features and the harmony of the whole composition. The details thus fitted into place as part of the whole, but were not insisted upon, and perhaps the Greek sculptor did not care too much whether he caught the actual features to be observed on the model. This tendency is what is usually meant when we speak of the idealism of Greek sculpture.

The Romans, on the other hand, as always, were preoccupied by the outer appearance, which they carved exactly as they saw it, including lines of anxiety and unruly hair, which in most cases had no relation at all to what the Greek was trying to portray. For a period in the early empire the two tendencies fully harmonized, the realistic detail being combined with the psychological penetration of the Greek. Then the tendency again disappeared, and this time it was the Greek spirit alone which triumphed, late imperial and other portraits often being only suggestive of the subject rather than realistic likenesses. In noting the insistence of the Romans on this detail in the portrait busts, one is reminded of the way in which Tacitus describes the senators watching the emperor Tiberius for any change of facial expression, trying to discover what he was thinking from the outward appearance. It is clear that the Romans believed that the outward face was the true expression of a man's individuality, lines of anxiety and the set of the eyes included, and they probably did not wish any detail to escape them, however apparently unimportant. Hence this emphasis on what we call realism.

The same tendency is carried over into Roman sculpture en masse, the enormous reliefs of the imperial triumphal monuments. One has only to look at the Elgin marbles and then at, say, Trajan's column or the arch of Titus, to perceive at once the difference, though again the tendency toward realism was already visible to some degree in the Hellenistic world. The horses and riders in the Elgin marbles are magnificent, but they are not individualized. Though a mythical story is told, it is done in a series of scenes of a certain static beauty. But Trajan's column tells a true story, with real men fighting and dying. One can follow the Dacian campaign from beginning to end—and indeed the column has been used to supplement the historical accounts. The Romans tried also to add a third dimension to their relief sculpture by carving in depth, unlike the Greek reliefs where the background is flat and the figures are merely carved on it, all parallel to each other. The Roman technique in reliefs is sometimes very effective. No one would imagine an actual procession in motion from the Greek reliefs, while the best Roman work succeeds in creating this illusion.

Sculptural skill seems to have been lost by the Romans in the troubled third century A.D. Constantine, when building his famous Arch of Triumph, was forced to steal panels from the work of his predecessors Trajan and Marcus Aurelius, and these present a marked contrast to the figures made by his own workmen on the same arch. All illusion of movement has gone from them, and they are stiff, badly executed and designed figures of no artistic merit whatever. Constantine fared no better when he sought for a sculptor to make a statue of himself. The statue is huge but we do not know what the first Christian emperor looked like nor even whether the sculptor was attempting to make an ideal image. An ideal image may have been in his mind, but, though he was presumably the best sculptor in the empire, he lacked the skill to execute it.

## ▶ Rhetoric

### INFLUENCE OF RHETORIC ON ROMAN LIFE AND CULTURE

Roman rhetoric deserves a section to itself as the art which the Romans most diligently cultivated, and a full study of its rise, influence, and decline would be a comment on the whole history of Rome. In the world of the republic words were powerful. A man could sway the Assembly, the Senate, or the law courts by his oratory, which could mean both a lucrative private profession or election to a magistracy, with a possible

ommand of an army and a fortune awaiting
im at the end. It could even mean the
ontrol of the republic itself. The Greeks,
oo, had been noted orators, and toward the
nd of the period of Athenian independence
ll the orators had studied carefully how to
ompose their speeches. But whenever a
peech is carefully composed, it may tend to
veremphasize its calculated psychological
ffect on an audience, while true sincerity
nay be lacking. The Sophists had been the
irst teachers of rhetoric in Athens, and the
radition they began was carried to perfec-
ion in the fourth century B.C.

When, therefore, the Romans began to
e self-conscious about their speeches and
eased to speak directly out of their mo-
nentary inspiration, they naturally turned
o the Greeks, whose schools were already
stablished. Even the conservative Cato the
Elder studied the speeches of Demos-
henes for self-improvement. The Greeks
oon began to teach rhetoric for the new
narket, and the Romans were apt pupils.
Unfortunately there are many dangers in
he art, dangers of which too few Romans
vere aware. Demosthenes had possessed
uch a burning sincerity that his speeches
vere relatively free from ornate and studied
laborations. Isocrates, on the other hand,
ad never delivered his speeches, and flow-
ry phrases and circumlocutions abound in
hem. Too many of these airs and graces
lipped into Roman rhetoric, especially when
he speeches were intended for publication
ind not for delivery. In the empire, when the
nost effective of spoken speeches could have
ıad no practical effect, since the real deci-
ions were always made by the emperor,
hetoric became ever more polished and arti-
icial and entirely concealed any possible
incerity of the speaker.

Indeed, rhetoric, the principal subject
n Roman education under the empire, found
ts way into all Roman writing of this period.
Lucan wrote an epic, with Pompey as its
iero, in which a theme that could have been
iobly presented was utterly spoiled by the
triving after effect. A few passages are still
ioteworthy, even many, for Lucan had the

makings of a first-rate poet, but the whole
is now almost unreadable. A further danger
exists in the too thorough study of rhetoric.
The student goes back to the great speeches
of the past and examines carefully the form,
the pregnant pauses, the rhetorical questions, the moments of drama. And, since it
is impossible really to reimagine the circumstances of the original speech, he painstak-
ingly analyzes the form and then tries to use
the same form in his own compositions and
prepared orations. He is thus working at
secondhand, and all sincerity and directness
of his own are lost, and his speech becomes
merely a lifeless artifice, convincing to no
one, but polished and worked over to the
last comma. The too exclusive study of
rhetoric in the schools of imperial Rome
has often been given as one of the most
potent reasons for the general decline of
Roman culture. And though the study of
rhetoric may have been primarily a symptom
rather than a cause, it certainly reacted upon
the writers, and helped prevent the emergence of a new style suited to the times
and more expressive of the spirit of that age.

### CICERO, THE MODEL ORATOR

Cicero, of course, was the model for all
later would-be orators. He himself had studied in Greece and claimed that his speaking
style was based on both Demosthenes and
Isocrates. But however powerful these formative influences may have been, he used a
different language and his speeches were
dictated by the needs of his own day, so
that his work was truly original. Fifty-seven
full orations and many fragments have come
down to us, a greater bulk of work than from
any other orator, Latin or Greek. Until very
recently these were the possession of every
educated man in the Western world, especially the well-known ones, such as those on
Catiline. Cicero was not at his best in legal
argument, and in this many great lawyers
have surpassed him. But few in any language
have equaled his capacity for irony and invective, carefully controlled rhythm, and the
use of the telling word. He was the complete master of the Latin tongue, and it is

not to be wondered at that his works became classics in the empire and again in the Italian Renaissance, which looked back to him as the master who should be imitated, while despising the medieval Latin which was still in daily use.

### RHETORIC UNDER THE EMPIRE—SENECA— QUINTILIAN

Perhaps the best example of false rhetoric is Seneca, whose writings are consistently bombastic and always striving for effect, especially by the use of antithesis. Against the tendency of Seneca, the greatest teacher of rhetoric, his fellow Spaniard Quintilian, set himself. Quintilian looked to Cicero as his model, and regarded rhetoric from an ideal standpoint as part of a whole liberal education. To him rhetoric was rather eloquence, which is something not to be produced solely by technical training but by study of the humanities. His work on oratory therefore is a treatise more on education than on oratory, and is the only first-rate Roman contribution to this subject.

Orators in the next century turned more and more to artificial diction, archaisms, and stilted mannerisms, and reacted against Cicero, returning to even earlier writers for inspiration. Their work, however, need not detain us here.

## ▶ History

### UNDER THE REPUBLIC—SALLUST AND CAESAR

History was one of the earliest forms of writing to be attempted in the Roman Republic, but mostly in the form of annals, factual accounts of events written for information. The earliest histories known to us were written in Greek, though evidently for Roman consumption. But in the middle of the second century B.C. Polybius, a Greek hostage in Rome, wrote one of the great histories of the ancient world, analytical, thorough, containing above all a really admirable analysis of the Roman republican constitution, which he greatly admired.

The first strictly Roman historian of the first importance was Sallust, whose history was clearly modeled on that of Thucydides, showing the same interest in human and social psychology, and using fairly effectively Thucydides' device of introducing speeches verbatim, even when he had not heard them. We possess only two monographs of Sallust, enough to show the quality of his work, but the *History* on which his Roman reputation was based is lost.

Contemporary with Sallust was Julius Caesar himself, whose two monographs on the Gallic and Civil Wars are masterpieces of their kind. Caesar writes about his own exploits in a clear, lucid, military style, speaking always of himself in the third person in an effort to appear impartial. No more effective propaganda device could have been invented; for his reputation, at least as a soldier, has been secured primarily on the evidence of these works. Although few would deny the military prowess of the great dictator and the thought and care that he put into his campaigns, it is possible to remain unconvinced that he was always as justified and unerringly right as he claims—possible, but difficult.

### THE AUGUSTAN AGE—HISTORY WITH A PURPOSE—LIVY

Mention has already been made of Livy, the prorepublican historian of the Augustan age. Not all his *History of Rome* survives, but enough for us to realize how valuable the work would have been if complete. It was the first systematic attempt at covering all republican history; and evidently Livy had a real enthusiasm for his subject. Unfortunately no one in his day knew any certain facts about the kingdom and early republic, nor had any histories been written within centuries of this early age. What Livy gives us, then, is the tradition as it was known in the Augustan period, and this tradition centered round certain great heroes, whose lives had conformed, or were made to conform, to the best republican ideals of seriousness, courage, fortitude, and selfless service to Rome. The work thus served as a kind of supplement to the *Aeneid* of Vergil, which showed how the gods had, from the end of the Trojan War, always planned for the greatness of Rome and her imperial destiny. Livy shows how the virtues of the Romans had made them worthy of this high destiny. Its republican bias was therefore all to the good in a work of this kind. Livy was in no sense a scientific historian like Polybius or Thucydides, and was barely indebted to them at all, and he had done no research beyond studying the works of his predecessors. But it is his picture of republican Rome that captured the minds and hearts of posterity rather than the more difficult and thoughtful Tacitus, who was not known in the Middle Ages, and has never attained a tithe of Livy's popularity in the centuries since.

### TACITUS—THE PSYCHOLOGIST AS HISTORIAN

Tacitus was a republican at heart, but born out of his time into the age of the Flavians and early Antonines, and his experience as a senator in this difficult period for men of his class undoubtedly embittered him. He made no real attempt at objectivity (though he did not realize his bias himself), but his work is nevertheless one of the world's historical and literary masterpieces. Tacitus had evidently been trained in rhetoric and he wrote in a terse epigrammatic style which is extremely effective in Latin, though it would be entirely unsuited to Greek. Time and again his thumbnail personality sketches hit the mark, summing up an emperor or an official with deadly accuracy.[3] For Tacitus is primarily a psychologist writing history. His *Annals,* as far as we have them, cover the reigns of Tiberius, Claudius, and Nero, while the *Histories,* of which we have only the first part, cover the Year of the Four Emperors. In addition there is a famous and often-quoted monograph on the primitive Germans, whom it was his intention to contrast with the effete Romans of his day. There is also a biography of his father-in-

[3] Well known is his characterization of Galba, for a few months emperor in A.D. 69: "Omnium consensu capax imperii nisi imperasset." ("By universal consent he was fit to rule only had he never ruled.")

law, a Roman official whom he greatly admired, and who served in Britain.

Tacitus' thesis throughout his work is that the decay of public and private morality in his age was due to the absolutism of the emperors and to the suppression of human freedom. As far back as Tiberius this tendency was visible, and it is inherent in the very nature of absolutism. Tacitus movingly describes the way in which the moral fiber of the senators must have been undermined by their subserviency, and describes how as members of the highest law court in the land they were forced to agree to the condemnation of entirely innocent men by Domitian, on pain of having to suffer the same fate. Nowhere do we get such an impression of what it was really like to be a noble in the days of the tyrannous emperors. Yet it is only fair to point out that this was not the whole story of the empire, and that Tacitus quite intentionally blinded himself to any merits the system might have had in other respects. But for a modern reader these passages nevertheless remain the vital parts of his work, and Tacitus can be read with profit in our own age, even by those who have no other interest in Roman history.

### THE LATE EMPIRE

Suetonius, who lived in the reign of Hadrian, may be classed as a historian only by courtesy. His gossipy biographies of twelve emperors have been very influential in forming later opinion of these men and usually stress the facts about them that are of the least historical importance. The information may be reliable as far as it goes, since for a time he had access to the imperial archives. But his selection of what was important leaves almost everything to be desired, and there can be little doubt that the scandalous anecdotes which fill his work are precisely those that would *not* have appeared in the imperial archives, and were probably selected from Roman gossip, in many cases more than a hundred years after the events described. The reliability of this part of the work may therefore be seriously questioned.

Ammianus Marcellinus, the last Latin historian of importance (there were other minor historians who wrote in Greek) lived in the fourth century A.D. His history starts where Tacitus left off, but we possess only that part which covers the second half of the fourth century. Accurate and painstaking, there are several vivid passages describing the corruption of the period, though he did not seem to appreciate sufficiently the fact that the empire was doomed, and so sometimes conveys an air of unreality to the modern reader.

Epitomes of history were also written in considerable number, and are sometimes of considerable value, since they digest passages of historians now lost. One of the best of these is Florus's *Epitome of Livy*.

▶ **Law**

CONTRASTS WITH EARLIER SYSTEMS OF LAW

The greatest of Roman glories, and Rome's supreme legacy to mankind, is the Roman law, the development of which we are fortunately able to trace almost from the earliest times, owing to the extant writings of so many great jurists, and to the firsthand description of the working of republican courts derived from such men as the practicing lawyer Cicero.

As was seen in an earlier chapter, the first codified law of Rome was the Twelve Tables, drawn up by a committee of ten in 449 B.C. under the stimulus of the second secession of the plebs. This committee is said to have visited Greece to study existing systems of law and especially the constitution of Solon. But if the visit was ever made (it is recorded by Livy many centuries later), it was singularly unfruitful, for the Twelve Tables bear no evidence of Greek influence, being an extremely primitive document as far as we are able to judge from what has survived. They remained the basic statute law of the Romans. In addition, statute law was made from time to time by the Assembly. These laws, however, covered primarily constitutional and criminal law, which have only limited importance. They were applicable only to Rome herself and her citizens. Since no principles were involved they were incapable of wider application.

To understand the epoch-making character of the Roman contribution to the science of law, it should first be contrasted with what went before it. Until late times the Egyptian law was the word of the Pharaoh as revealed to him by the gods (*Ma'at*). In other words, each case was decided by a person, whether the Pharaoh or a judge appointed by him, not necessarily in accordance with any law or legal principles. Personal justice of this kind is common throughout the East, even to the present time. It has nothing to do with law in the Roman sense.

The Hammurabi Code of Babylonia is a series of statute laws, some criminal and some social and commercial, which name definite penalties for their contravention. Individual judges could no doubt decide whether to enforce the full penalty, but since the penalties were clearly stated, the minimum room was left for the exercise of their personal discretion. The code, in fact, was clearly designed for the purpose of preventing judges from making arbitrary decisions. The Hebrew codes were of the same nature, with the addition of certain prescribed religious practices.

The Greek city-states, in addition to possessing basic constitutional laws, had a number of statute laws of the same kind as those mentioned above. But in ordinary private litigation each particular case was decided on its merits by appeal to a jury. The jury did not have to take into account decisions made by earlier juries in similar cases. There was as yet nowhere any science of jurisprudence or principles of law which could be applied to each case as it arose, regulating the decisions of the judges. Nor did the Romans have it at the time of the Twelve Tables, which was a primitive code of the type of the Code of Hammurabi, though much simpler, as befitted a primitive society.

## THE RIGHTS OF THE ROMAN CITIZEN— JUS CIVILE

But the Romans did have a new and quite original conception of citizenship, which covered certain well-defined rights, already discussed in Chapter 10. The rights belonged to the man who was a citizen, they were inherent in his person, wherever he might happen to be. This is the first time these particular rights, which in earlier times accrued to a man only by birth, were believed to be vested in a *person*. In Athens the city gave certain privileges to its citizens, but there was no kind of contract between them and the city, and naturally they possessed no privileges unless they were living in the particular city which gave them. But the Romans guaranteed certain definite rights to their citizens, and these they retained even when abroad. These rights collectively were known as *jus,* and a Roman citizen was entitled to have any case tried under the *jus civile,* or civil law.

Now this law was rarely affected by statutes (*leges*) passed by the Assembly. It was built up ordinarily in early times by the priests, who stated on authority what the law was. This task then passed to a special official called the *praetor urbanus* (city praetor). The praetor, however, was an elected official, probably a would-be general rather than a jurist. It was hardly possible for him to state what the law was, or to decide all cases personally, and it was not his duty to do so. He had as assistants judges who came from noble families, and who were in charge of the actual trial. But even these judges were not as a rule trained lawyers, though they had more experience than the annually elected praetor.

When, therefore, a civil case was brought to trial, it was necessary for the parties to the case to have some knowledge of what the law was likely to be in their case. So it gradually came about that the praetor every year on assuming office made a public statement of the law that he would use while in office. This was called the *edictum,* and it was made up largely of the instructions that he proposed to give to the judges. These instructions were called *formulae.* And the edict was made up, for the most part, of decisions that had been made by his predecessors in office.

It will be seen, then, that in this way a collection of decisions would be built up which would really have the force of law, even though no statutes had been made on the subject. Statute law would, of course, be taken into consideration by the praetor, but even this he could interpret, as our judges and higher courts interpret law today. And this interpretation would probably be incorporated in the edict of the next praetor and so be binding for the future, unless a praetor for good reasons decided to depart from it —as our judges may also on occasion depart from interpretations of their predecessors.

## THE RIGHTS OF FOREIGNERS—JUS GENTIUM

This, then, was the system for public and private law for Roman citizens, and it lasted for a considerable length of time. But cases also arose where one party to a lawsuit was a Roman citizen and one was not, and where two resident noncitizens might engage in litigation with each other in the Roman courts. If the case concerned a foreigner's personal status, it would clearly be impossible to settle it through the *jus civile,* applicable only to citizens. So in 242 B.C. a *praetor peregrinus* or foreign praetor, whose task was to look after such cases, was elected for the first time. Thus the idea arose that foreigners also had rights, and the new law under which they were judged was called the *jus gentium,* or law of peoples. Both praetors now issued annual edicts covering the cases for which they were responsible.

## INTERPRETATION OF THE LAW—BEGINNINGS OF JURISPRUDENCE

As the Roman state grew in importance and undertook more and more responsibilities, and legal decisions of wide significance had to be made by unqualified persons, an innovation was made which proved to be the real foundation of Roman jurisprudence. It became the custom for certain skilled lawyers, who had also held high office in the state, to assist the praetors in drawing up their edicts and in answering questions put by judges. They could also give advice to litigants. These men were not paid, nor did they hold any official position, but undertook the work from a sense of duty and for the prestige involved. Since these *juris prudentes* (men skilled in the law, hence our word "jurisprudence") were appealed to for advice, especially in cases where the law was doubtful, they became specialists in interpretation, and theirs was now the chief responsibility in the building up of new law for the future. It was among these men that the conception of equity (*aequitas*) grew up as a principle which could override a strict interpretation of the law. In time, especially under the empire, certain individuals among them became known for the excellence of their opinions, as certain Supreme Court Justices of the past may still be quoted and accepted in the United States even though they have been long dead.

### INFLUENCE OF PHILOSOPHY—JUS NATURALE

Many of these *juris prudentes* were strongly influenced by Stoicism, with its conception of the natural law of divine reason (*jus naturale*), which became a commonly accepted ideal, a kind of ideal law in accordance with which all statute law should be made and all legal decisions should be rendered. The strongly humanitarian viewpoint of the Stoics thus became incorporated into Roman law.

Under the early principate the same system was maintained. But naturally the edict of the praetor and the opinions of the *juris prudentes* had to take account of the new influence of the princeps; and with the increasing absolutism of the emperors the decisions in public law tended to reflect the increasing importance of the state. There was also far more statute law in the empire than under the republic. The Assembly declined as a lawmaking body after Augustus,

but the Senate now became for the first time since 448 B.C. a real legislative body, though its laws were naturally in accordance with the emperor's wishes. The emperors after Augustus also issued decrees which had all the force of law. Under Hadrian the praetors' edicts were codified into a perpetual edict, leaving the *juris prudentes* and their interpretations of still greater importance than before. After Hadrian many of them began to hold official positions in the imperial service, often serving as advisers to the emperor, who now felt in need of skilled legal assistance. The law continued to develop, often in accordance with newer Greek and Oriental philosophical ideas.

By this time there was virtually no distinction between the *jus civile* and the *jus gentium,* since the vast majority of the inhabitants of the empire by the time of Hadrian, and all by A.D. 212, were Roman citizens. It was the principles of the *jus gentium,* which had always been more universal and thus more in accordance with philosophical principles, as well as more in accordance with contemporary requirements in law, which prevailed. In the last stage of the empire, the great codification of the law began. Creativeness declined under the absolutist emperors, and the opinions of the great *juris prudentes* of the past were taken as actual law, and a number of dead jurists were named whose opinions must prevail. In the event of a tie, the opinion of the supposed greatest, Papinian, was to be decisive.

### THE GREAT CODIFICATION OF THE LAW AND ITS INFLUENCE

The Theodosian Code of A.D. 438 was a collection of imperial edicts binding in the Eastern and Western Empires. This was followed in the sixth century by the great definitive code of Justinian, drawn up by Trebonian and a group of distinguished jurists in Constantinople. This code, known as the *Corpus Juris Civilis,* had four parts: the Code, which consisted of the imperial edicts of all the emperors *(constitutiones);*

the Digest, which contained the decisions of the great *juris prudentes;* the Institutes, primarily a manual on legal principles for use in schools; and the Novels, a series of new laws which Justinian found necessary to complete the whole structure. Naturally the Digest was the most important part of the code for posterity, since these opinions, based on the best thought of the greatest jurists in accordance with their conceptions of the natural law, were to a large extent free from limitations of time and place. This law code, however, differed from earlier ones in that Christian influence had now been admitted to it. Religious crimes, such as heresy, were included, but on the whole the Christian influence was a gain, especially the legislation on slavery.

The influence of Roman law is almost incalculable. It is not so much that codes of law in many modern countries are still largely Roman, nor that the canon law of the Church is almost exclusively Roman; but that this civilizing work was done by the Romans once and for all, and there was no need ever to do it again. The primitive laws of the barbarian invaders of the empire were so far behind Roman law in principles and sheer intellectual grasp of the problems involved in any law code that all took freely from the Romans, and no code in the Western world has not been influenced by it. It was used as a political tool to help the development of the national state by medieval monarchs. It was so patently superior to feudal law that when the king's justice was modified Roman, and the local law was feudal, every litigant, if he had the choice, would prefer the king's justice. When Napoleon needed a new law code for France in the early nineteenth century, it was to Roman law that he went for a model.

And, as we shall see in a later chapter, the great tradition of the *juris prudentes* was carried on by the jurists of the University of Bologna from the eleventh century onward. Indeed, the university itself only came into existence as a law school with the rediscovery of the *Corpus juris civilis* of

Justinian, which had been lost in the ages of barbarian domination of Europe.

## ▶ Literature

### POETRY

In the field of literature as such the influence of the Greeks was for a long time paramount. But three new fields were exploited by the Romans—satire, the satirical epigram,[4] and letter writing. They may also have invented the novel, of which the earliest example known to us is the *Satyricon* of Petronius, though among the vast lost literature of Alexandria, much of it written for pure entertainment, there may have been precursors.

### THE EPIC

Much has already been said of the great epic of Vergil, the *Aeneid.* The story is concerned with the voyage of Aeneas to Rome after the fall of Troy, but the real purpose is to extol the glory of Rome, founded by a descendant of Aeneas. It thus becomes a patriotic poem, the first in history, and perhaps still the greatest. Since Aeneas is also a wanderer, and several of the scenes in the poem are direct imitations of Homer, the whole poem is bound to invite comparison with the *Odyssey.* This, in view of his purpose, is unfair to Vergil, for his work is on the whole original, with most of its best episodes not even paralleled in the *Odyssey.* The work is very uneven—Vergil himself intended to polish it if he had lived—and the hero is by all standards a failure, never holding either our interest or our sympathy. But the incidental scenes, and especially those in which the hero is forced to wrong innocent people in the pursuit of his mission, are moving. And there is a great grandeur in the poem, especially in the account of the fall of Troy. Vergil was a great literary artist, certainly a master of the Latin lan-

---

[4] The Greeks had also composed epigrams, but these were, as a rule, short panegyrics of famous people and events, rather than the pointed, usually witty and often biting thumbnail sketches of Martial.

guage. But the *Aeneid* is not an easy poem to appreciate in any language but the original, and without some understanding of and sympathy for his purpose. The medievals, with their special feeling for Rome, regarded Vergil as not only the greatest of the pagans, but as almost superhuman, a prophet as well as poet, and in Rome itself he was a classic as soon as he was dead, to be studied by every Roman schoolboy. His influence until the present century was probably greater than that of any writer of the ancient world.

## LYRIC POETRY

The Greeks had been such masters of lyric poetry that the Romans never escaped fully from their influence, and many excellent Latin lyrics are little but paraphrases of Greek originals. Yet the subjects chosen are frequently Roman, and it was early found that the Latin language could be effectively used for lyric and that the principal Greek meters could be turned easily into Latin. Catullus is the greatest early master of the Latin lyric. Much of his work is on conventional Greek subjects, but his odes to Lesbia, a noble Roman lady who was probably also the most profligate and notorious of her generation, are deeply felt. Horace, a poet of the age of Augustus, composed his odes very carefully, and they are not always entirely successful as poetry. But most of his odes, composed both in light and serious vein, are highly polished and apparently sincerely felt. Horace's remarkable felicity of phrase has made him perhaps the most translated of ancient poets, and his poems render well into any language. The Greek influence is mostly to be found in his choice of meters, which are nearly always of Greek origin.

## PASTORAL POETRY

Theocritus, the Hellenistic Greek, was the model for all pastoral poetry, and, in the opinion of many critics, he has never been surpassed. But Vergil composed a number of poems in this style, which are collectively called the *Eclogues*, though they are not all concerned with shepherds and shepherdesses and the usual material of the pastoral. Several of them are charming, though recognizably imitations. But the fourth eclogue is of a different kind, containing a prophecy of the birth of a child who was to usher in the Golden Age. Christians, of course, took this to be a prophecy of the birth of Jesus, and this was probably the chief reason they looked upon Vergil as inspired. The details of the prophecy as they appear in the eclogue do not apply very closely to any child known to us, but it expresses clearly Vergil's semi-mystical temperament, and the hopes that had been aroused in him by the era of peace inaugurated by Augustus, his patron.

## DIDACTIC POETRY

The most original didactic poem in the Latin language is certainly the *Georgics* of Vergil, a long, sustained hymn of praise of the rural life, which really succeeds in recapturing the atmosphere of the Italian countryside in which the poet was reared. The occupations of the farmer are accurately detailed, but always with the halo of romance upon them. The poem is more finished than the *Aeneid,* and within its chosen compass in many ways more effective, and much of the poet's best work is in it.

Ovid, after Vergil the most popular of Latin poets in the Middle Ages, was the most versatile and facile of all poets in his versification. In view of the variety of his subjects, he cannot be easily classified. Amongst his didactic poems are the *Fasti,* in which he takes up the various feast days of the Roman year and tells of the rites celebrated and their origin. His most famous, or notorious, work also falls into this classification, the *Ars amatoria,* or the art of loving, in which he explains the art of seduction, with many witty and intentionally sententious digressions. His *Metamorphoses,* one of our chief sources of information on the subject—and sometimes our only source—is a handbook of Greek mythology. These Greek stories he tells very entertainingly. His *Amores* are love poems addressed to passing loves, written as ever, without any real feeling, but with great facility. Ovid was finally banished from Rome by Augustus, perhaps for his *Ars amatoria,* which was hardly in keeping with the Princeps's policy for restoring the sanctity of family life, but possibly for a more than usually outrageous exploit with Julia, the daughter of the Princeps, who was banished about the same time.

## DRAMA

The Romans had no sense of tragedy in their make-up, and it is not surprising that there are no first-rate writers of tragedy in Latin. The tragic dramas of Euripides, however, as the reader will realize after recalling the discussion of this writer in an earlier chapter, lent themselves to imitation fairly well. Early in the republic various writers tried to adapt Euripides to the Latin stage, and the first important Roman poet, only fragments of whose work remain, wrote a few plays based on Roman history. The only poet whose tragedies are extant, Seneca, was not eminently fitted for his task as a tragedian, as he was unable to rid himself of his sententiousness and his addiction to false rhetoric. Occasionally a speech rings true, and there is some verbally dexterous dialogue, but very little that can be called truly tragic. And it was almost ludicrous to attempt, as he did, to imitate the Greek paraphernalia of gods when in his day no one had any belief in them. Unfortunately his influence was strong in European tragedy before Shakespeare, and the medievals, knowing nothing better, admired him. He is seldom admired now that we have the Greek tragedians in the original, and never performed.

## COMEDY

The Romans do not seem as a people to have been gifted with a natural facility for laughter. There was always some cruelty in their wit, and they did not possess the urbanity required for comedies of manners. Doubtless a people who could be entertained by gladiatorial shows would not take so easily to the more polite entertainment of true comedy. The only comedies extant were written in the first days of Greek influence under the republic, and both the playwrights, Plautus and Terence, are heavily indebted to the New Comedy of Athens. The scenes and characters of Plautus are invariably Greek, but to make a greater appeal to his Roman audience he combined elements from the Roman society of his day. They were written solely for entertainment, and in this they are on the whole successful, and revivals and adaptations of Plautus have even been successful in modern times. Shakespeare and Molière were indebted to him for some of their plots, though these, of course, also came from the New Comedy of Athens. Since we possess only fragments of the New Comedy, the plays of Plautus have a certain additional value for us. The other writer of comedies, Terence, who belonged to the circle of Scipio Aemilianus at Rome, was not interested in adding Roman characteristics to his plays, since his audience was made up of pronounced Grecophiles. They are therefore simply adaptations of the New Comedy in Latin. His style was more polished than that of Plautus, and he is more quotable. And he is believed to have added a new feature to the drama, the use of plot to sustain interest. Though this device may have already been used in some plays of the New Comedy of which we know nothing all the plays prior to Terence of which we have knowledge, tragedy and comedy alike, used only plots and situations to which the audience possessed the key. The audience knew, and the characters did not, what was going to happen, so that the entertainment consisted in watching the characters make errors which full knowledge would have avoided. The use of a plot which was unknown to the audience provided it with a new interest to hold its attention to the end of the play.

## CHARACTERISTIC ROMAN FORMS

### Satire

The same qualities which made the Romans unsuccessful at comedy, their seriousness, their interest in moral questions, and their caustic wit, led them to develop a new form of literature unknown to the

Greeks. A man like Aristophanes could criticize his society bitterly enough, but beneath it all there was a real love of Athens, in addition to a wild and irreverent inventiveness and boisterousness altogether alien to Roman character. When the Romans wished to criticize their society they did it as moralists and realists, and with full seriousness, and they were really indignant at what they criticized, however they might sweeten the pill with wit and even humor. The form most suitable for this is satire, which was developed for the first time by the Romans. An early satirist of whose work we possess only fragments is Lucilius, who presented scenes from the life of his time in verse, usually criticizing its vices, though some of his satires are merely descriptive of contemporary life. This simple descriptiveness disappears in the more developed form of the satire as it appears later. Horace, who acknowledges himself as the follower of Lucilius, is still genial and without personal bitterness. But most of his satires are concerned with the follies and absurdities of mankind, though some are also devoted to incidents in his earlier life. Vivid and often extremely funny, they lend themselves well to translation. Perhaps the best known is the satire about the bore who tried to coerce the poet into introducing him to his patron Maecenas, and Horace's attempts to get rid of him.

The satirists of the Silver Age of the early second century A.D. had far more, it would appear, to criticize in their society than had Horace. Persius seems too often to be insincere and his themes are stock ones. But Juvenal, unquestionably the greatest of Roman satirists, whipped himself into a continual fury at what he saw around him, and he did not hesitate to put it on paper. No doubt his portrait of Roman society, with its clients, its legacy hunters, its gluttons, and its crooked contractors, is overdrawn, and Juvenal was a bitterly disillusioned man who took little joy from his life. But the portrait is vivid and convincing as far as it goes. It is from Juvenal that we get the famous expression "bread and circuses" for

the life of the proletariat, and from Juvenal that the stereotype of the decadent society of the imperial capital has been taken by subsequent writers. He has been the model for satirists ever since.

## Epigram

The Latin language was eminently suitable for epigram, and in Martial, an earlier contemporary of Juvenal, it found its master. Most of his epigrams are extremely witty and pointed, and defy translation with the same condensation in any other language. Martial was quite objective about his own work. Most of the epigrams were composed to order for anyone who would pay him, or hold out the hope of paying him. His picture of the decadent society of Rome coincides in all essentials with that of Juvenal, and all classes of Roman society came within range of his biting wit. Like Juvenal, he succeeded in making himself the model for later generations in his particular field.

## Letter writing

The Greeks, for want of a postal system, did not take naturally to letter writing, although some letters attributed to Plato are extant. So this art can be credited to the Romans, and above all to Cicero, whose voluminous correspondence, which also includes some of the replies he received, presents an extremely valuable picture of the Rome of his day and of Roman politics of the late years of the republic. More than this, it presents a picture of Cicero himself which is unequaled by that of any other man in all Roman history. For Cicero did not intend the letters to be published, and he made no effort to edit them. So they reveal him with all his faults, which are apparent on the surface, while the virtues are more concealed, but still visible to the discerning reader.

In contrast, Pliny the Younger's letters seem a little precious, having been carefully edited by the writer to show off his virtues, and more polished than is usual with people who write letters in the ordinary course of the day's activity. But they, too, give us a valuable picture of the life of the early second century A.D. in Rome and the provinces and are especially important in that this is the same period covered by the satirist Juvenal. Curiously enough, none of the vices castigated by the satirist are so much as mentioned by Pliny. His letters to the Emperor Trajan show him as an honest official, who in accordance with the conditions of his appointment as a "trouble shooter," consults his master on every point and elicits replies that are a model of imperial patience. Among these is the famous letter from Trajan telling him not to seek out the Christians and punish them although the laws against them are still in effect, but rather to leave them alone until they are accused and then only to take appropriate action in punishing them.

### Fiction

Though the *Metamorphoses* of Ovid, already dealt with, might be classed at least as storytelling, the only real novel we possess is by a writer named Petronius, who is thought by most critics to be a friend of the emperor Nero mentioned by Tacitus as sharer of Nero's pleasures. This man was ultimately made to commit suicide by his master, and sent him a detailed list of his imperial crimes in revenge. The incident provided the inspiration for the famous novel *Quo Vadis* by Sienkiewicz, twice used as the basis for spectacular motion pictures. However, there are dissenting opinions as to the authorship of the *Satyricon,* and the novel could also describe the society of a much later age than Nero's. The novel relates the experiences of a trio of adventurers wandering around southern Italy. The largest part of the *Satyricon* that has survived is concerned with a gargantuan feast given by Trimalchio, a new-rich freedman. Petronius tells his story in an urbane, detached manner, quite unlike the fury with which Juvenal describes a not dissimilar scene, and the book is also notable for its effective use of conversation, giving us our only real knowledge of how Latin was spoken among the people of Rome and Italy in the early empire.

This brief account of Latin literature, which is far from inclusive, may fittingly end with a mention of the *Metamorphoses* of Apuleius, a prose writer of the second century A.D. The writer was a professional orator who turned his hand to the composition of tales based on subjects taken from the Greeks. The famous *Golden Ass* and *Cupid and Psyche* are still known and still retranslated today, and have never lost their popularity. But the Latin scholar is amazed at the work of Apuleius, wondering how it could be possible as early as that day for such antiquarian zeal to be employed in the writing of anything designed to be read by contemporaries. It is full of strange words, still stranger turns of phrase, and other exhibitions of what seems to be simple verbal fantasy. He coined words and phrases which we find in no other writing of his time, and no other extant writer has imitated him.

It would look as if the virtuosity of Apuleius was carefully calculated to attract the interest of the bored Roman of his day (like some *avant-garde* writers in the 1920's), which would not have been excited by an ordinary composition in a tongue familiar to readers. Most of the verbal ingenuity is lost in translation into any tongue, though many translators have made the attempt, in part, perhaps, accounting for his continued popularity with them, for they were thus enabled to play amusing tricks with their own languages also. The highly sophisticated and calculated artificiality of the tales of Apuleius renders them sometimes most charming in translation, but is certainly a sign that the creative period of Roman writing was over. Latin literature did not recover its vitality until the descendants of the invading barbarians took up the use of a greatly modified Latin once more in the early Middle Ages.

### ▶  Suggestions for further reading

The most noble poem in the Latin language, the *Aeneid* of Vergil, is available in many translations. A new translation in an inexpensive edition, which steers a safe path between modern and archaic language and is highly recommended, is K. Guinagh, *The Aeneid of Vergil* (New York: Rinehart & Co., Inc., 1953). Other Latin authors who should be read are Lucretius, Horace, and Ovid, in addition to those mentioned at the end of the two previous chapters. There are many good translations available, especially two Classics Club editions of the two first-named poets.

On Latin literature there are two outstanding works by J. W. Duff, one of them recently reprinted. There is no other history of Latin literature which will begin to compare with these masterpieces: J. W. Duff, *A Literary History of Rome to the Close of the Golden Age* (ed. A. M. Duff; New York: Barnes and Noble, Inc., 1953), and J. W. Duff, *A Literary History of Rome in the Silver Age from Tiberius to Hadrian* (New York: Charles Scribner's Sons, 1927).

An interesting effort to isolate the "Roman Spirit" and distinguish it from the "Greek Spirit" and Greek influence is provided in C. Grénier, *The Roman Spirit in Religion, Thought, and Art* (tr. M. R. Dobie; New York: Alfred A. Knopf, Inc., 1926), but, in general, books on Roman culture have, perhaps naturally, tended to fall far below the level attained by books on the achievements of the Greeks. R. Geer, as he did with the political life of the Romans, has done an excellent job in presenting Roman achievements in a brief compass, with first-rate illustrations, in his text book, *Classical Civilization* (2nd ed.; New York: Prentice-Hall, Inc., 1950), Vol. 2, *Rome.*

On Roman law, J. Declareuil, *Rome the Law-Giver* (tr. E. A. Parker; New York: Alfred A. Knopf, Inc., 1927), is a masterly presentation of Roman law which stresses and explains its uniqueness and importance, but the book is not easily obtainable. Otherwise the books on Roman law are too technical for the general student. A brief survey is given in R. H. Barrow, *The Romans* (Harmondsworth, Middlesex: Penguin Books, 1949), pp. 209–217, and in Geer's book, just mentioned, pp. 347–357. Barrow's book is otherwise recommended for its excellent first chapter on ancient Roman religion and traditions, but elsewhere it is too thin to be even adequate as a survey.

On the city of Rome itself mention should be made of the well-written and well-illustrated G. Showerman, *Eternal Rome* (New Haven, Conn.: Yale University Press, 1924), Vol. 1, which tells much of the history of Rome from the point of view of the city of Rome, an original idea well sustained and carried out.

Since, above all, Rome was famed for its buildings and engineering feats, many of which still survive today, the interested student should consult W. J. Anderson and R. P. Spiers, *The Architecture of Greece and Rome* (New York: Charles Scribner's Sons, 1927), Vol. 2, *Rome,* which should be available in all good libraries.

Finally, mention should be made of the *Meditations* of Marcus Aurelius, available in many editions and translations. This little book, though written in Greek and therefore not forming part of Latin literature, was written by a Roman emperor, and tells much not only of the emperor himself but of Stoic philosophy as it was understood in the Silver Age.

# 13

## The Rise of Christianity

*Religious conditions in the Roman Empire at the beginning of the Christian Era • The life and death of Jesus Christ • The early Christian Church • The organization of the Church • The establishment of Christian doctrine • The persistent ideal of poverty and holiness: monasticism*

---

► **Religious conditions in the Roman Empire at the beginning of the Christian Era**

Mention has already been made in the last chapter of the new religions that arose in the Orient and penetrated into the Roman Empire. This chapter will be concerned with the religion that was the last to arise but was destined to supersede all the others and finally, as an organized religion, to become the successor to the Roman Empire itself.

THE GREEK BACKGROUND

In order to understand the setting for the new faith it is first necessary to review briefly the religious conditions in the Roman Empire, and especially in the Hellenistic world. With the loss of independence suffered by the Greek city-states, the old civic pride, and with it civic religion, had declined; but the Greeks had not lost their vitality and creativeness, nor their intellectual curiosity. The whole Hellenistic world had become the field for their activities, and under their stimulus a momentous change had come over the native Oriental peoples. No people in the whole Near East had remained untouched by the Greek spirit, and Greek restlessness had communicated itself to the others.

But the whole vast field of political activity which had taken so much of the energy of the Hellenes in the days of independence was now closed to them. The Hellenistic monarchical system had altogether replaced democracy, and when these monarchies themselves succumbed in turn to the Roman expansion, there was still no outlet for political aspirations save for individuals in Roman service. Roman influence in the Hellenistic world, however, was primarily in government and military affairs. The Romans usually protected and ruled this world efficiently enough, but the cultural influence was all in the other direction. The Greeks absorbed the Romans into their culture, which continued to expand ever further westward as the Romans provided the means.

Deprived of what had been the joy of his life in earlier times, the restless Greek engaged in commercial activity, transforming the economy of the Near East; he introduced his language, his art, his literature, his philosophy, his sports, and his whole way of life wherever he went. But still he was

391

not satisfied. Something essential had gone from his life, and for all the great show of activity too often he felt his existence was empty. The gods were pleasant myths to be explained away and Chance ruled now; but though she could be wooed, she could hardly be loved or worshiped. Nor could philosophies hold the allegiance of the Greeks. The Skeptics were busy showing that all philosophies were based on untenable assumptions and that the truth could not be known. The vacuum could only be filled by a religion which appealed to the heart, giving a meaning to the aimless life of the now cosmopolitan and rootless Greeks.

First came a revival of the native Greek mysteries of Eleusis and Samothrace, which, as Plutarch tells us, left the initiate feeling as if he had indeed had an experience of divinity. These mysteries had always demanded much of their devotees, but in return had assured them of immortality, through the undergoing of certain trials which purified the soul. And throughout the Hellenistic world the Oriental religions all experienced a revival, the cults of Cybele and Isis and of Mithra offering impressive ceremonial, festivals, ritual, and initiation, as well as purification and redemption of the soul with the aid of a mediator who sacrificed himself for the salvation of men. At last the Orient ceased to accept from the Greeks without giving in return. Now the culture became truly Greco-Oriental, with the Romans as outside conquerors, resisting or succumbing to the allurements of this culture, but always alien in the Hellenistic world.

THE JEWISH BACKGROUND

But there was one Oriental people which held itself aloof, for the Jews had already received their separate promises. The Jewish religion had absorbed elements from the other Oriental teachings, and the more orthodox Jews now believed in the future life, and they believed in the Satan and demons of Persian Zoroastrianism and Mithraism; but they also held fast to their more ancient law and ritual which, with the ascendancy of their priesthood, had become

ever more strict and rigid. They remained monotheists, believing that all other gods than Yahweh were either demons, idols, or nonexistent. And above all they were looking for a Messiah who would come to redeem the faithful people of Israel; for him they must remain apart, a chosen people, the only righteous ones on earth, the only ones ready to greet him when he came. The center of the Jewish religion was the holy city of Jerusalem, which had retained a precarious independence under the Maccabees, only to fall to the arms of Pompey, and thereafter submit, first to a client king, Herod of Idumaea, and then to the direct government of Rome under an equestrian procurator. The Romans had never been able to understand the Jews. From sad experience they knew that they could not drive them into making any compromises with polytheism, not even the formal acknowledgment of the divinity of the emperor. So at last they accepted the fact and let them alone, giving them religious privileges withheld from any other subjects of Rome, for the Romans felt that the Jewish faith did not constitute any real danger. It seemed impossible that such a small and exclusive sect could expand so far that it could undermine the loyalty of the vast population of the empire.

But the Jews in Jerusalem were by no means the only Jews in the Hellenistic world. Elsewhere, in every city of importance, there was a Jewish colony which sent representatives to the great festivals at Jerusalem, willingly acknowledged the temple there as the headquarters of their religion, and from their greater wealth often sent donations for the poorer Jews of the religious capital. The widely scattered Jews of the Diaspora (Dispersion) lived in Greek cities, and were subject to the all pervading influence of Greek culture. They could not all be so strict in their religious observances as their brethren of Jerusalem. Though they studied and loved the Hebrew Law, they also studied Greek philosophy at Greek schools; they were familiar with all the intellectual currents of the Greek world. Such a one was Saul of Tarsus, who was to became the first great Christian missionary.

Even in Jerusalem itself not all the Jews had kept themselves free from Greek influence. In the days of Antiochus Epiphanes, there were Jewish collaborators, and though these had lost power in the time of the Maccabees, others were still ready to collaborate with the Greeks and Romans when the Jews lost their independence. It was necessary for these men to play a very careful game with the Romans, for the ultimate benefit, as they no doubt felt, of the whole Jewish people. These men provided the high priest at the time of the Crucifixion, and probably a majority of the Jewish Council (Sanhedrin or Synedrion), which was entrusted by the Romans with local government, subject only to the general supervision of the Roman procurator.

But these Hellenized Jews (Sadducees) who accepted realistically the Roman rule differed in one important respect from their fellow Jews the Pharisees. They did not believe in the resurrection of the body and in immortality.

With many fervent men and women looking for a Messiah, and with no certainty of when he would come, nor how he would reveal himself, it was natural that there were many who claimed to be the Messiah. These men gathered around themselves fanatical bands of disciples, who were too often determined that their Messiah should prevail, if necessary by force. But all failed, and by the time of the birth of Jesus there was none who had been able to command the faith and allegiance of all the Jews. The Sadducees had found it necessary to suppress these would-be Messiahs, for they were held responsible by their masters for all riots. Other Jews, like the Essenes, had gone into the desert, purifying themselves by ascetic practices, but they too were waiting for the Messiah to reveal himself. And again others, like the Pharisee Hillel, had begun to teach the people that the true religion was a religion of the heart, one that emphasized love for one's neighbor, rather than only an affair of religious observances and ritual.

Such, then, was the atmosphere in Judaea and Palestine when Jesus was born.

## ▶ The life and death of Jesus Christ

THE NATURE OF THE SOURCES

We do not know as much as we should like about the early history of Christianity, and the actual life and work of its founder, for reasons not unlike those already discussed in connection with the Hebrews. And though the traditions about Jesus Christ grew up far closer in time to his actual life than the traditions about Moses, and indeed some of the writers may have known him on earth and participated in his work, the chief difficulty remains that these men were not concerned with writing a history so much as with presenting a picture which would captivate the minds and hearts of their readers. The four Gospels (the Greek word is "evangelion," meaning "good news," hence the writers were called Evangelists), which tell of the life of Jesus all present this unique personality in terms sufficiently alike for us to recognize the authenticity of the general portrait. But each Evangelist selects from Jesus' life and teachings those elements which the writer personally has felt to be essential. The portrait is thus colored by the understanding and purpose of the Evangelist himself. Matthew and Luke record the birth, and, very briefly, the childhood of Jesus, while Mark is apparently only interested in the mission of Christ. Mark therefore begins his Gospel with the baptism in the river Jordan, where this mission received its public divine approval—one of the few incidents described by all four Evangelists. John also writes only of the mission of Christ, but every word in his Gospel is deeply concerned with the divinity of Christ and the inner meaning of the impulse of love that he came on earth to proclaim.

None of the Evangelists shows any signs of having done any historical research, nor would it seem to have occurred to any of them to do so. While Matthew and Luke make brief mention of an important event in the life of Jesus at the age of twelve, both are silent on the years between this event and the baptism at the age of thirty; and this period can only be filled, if at all, by the use of much later legends, which may have some basis of truth behind them.

Apparent contradictions in the accounts have always been difficult for commentators to explain, as, for instance, the different genealogies of Jesus which appear in Matthew and Luke, and the voyage to Egypt described by Matthew, which seems inconsistent with the Luke narrative. Yet these Gospels are all that we possess in the way of external record, and from them must be constructed such consecutive history as we can. The personality of Jesus Christ shines out so clearly from all four narratives that there has never been any real question as to their general truth and authenticity.

After the death of Christ the records become more plentiful. For the years immediately after his death the book of the Acts of the Apostles, probably also written by Luke, comes much closer to being a historical narrative than do the Gospels. Contemporary with this book are the letters of the apostle Paul to the churches which he founded. Most of these are certainly authentic. In the early second century we have the first mention of Christians from Roman sources, and from the middle of the second century there are enough Christian records for a consecutive account to be framed with some accuracy. But most of first-century Christianity and even the question whether St. Peter was the first bishop of Rome and was martyred there are not yet entirely historically established.

*The Evangelist St. John writing his gospel. The eagle, always associated with St. John, symbolized, according to the inscription, the evangelist's yearning toward the heights. From a book of gospels (Anglo-Frankish), ca. 850.* (COURTESY THE PIERPONT MORGAN LIBRARY, Ms. 862, folio 144)

# ► chronological chart

The life and death of Jesus Christ
    Birth of Jesus         (probably) B.C. 4
    Mission of Jesus Christ     (probably) A.D. 26–30
    Crucifixion of Jesus Christ     (probably)    30

The early Christian Church
    Missionary journeys of Paul         ca. 34–60
    Paul appeals to Roman emperor     60
    Fire of Rome—Massacre of Christians     64
    Pliny's correspondence with Trajan about Christians     111–112
    Rescript by Marcus Aurelius against Christians     169
    General persecution of Christians by Emperor Decius     249–51
    "Diocletian" persecution     303–13
    Constantine succeeds to throne     312
    "Edict of Milan"     313
    Council of Nicaea     325
    Conversion and death of Constantine     337
    Conversion of Goths to Arianism (Bishop Ulfilas)     340–348
    Julian the Apostate     361–363
    Theodosius I forced to do penance for massacre at Thessalonica     390
    Proscription of pagan religions by Theodosius     392
    Death of Augustine (*City of God, ca. 425–430*)     430
    Invasion of Italy by Attila the Hun     452
    Western bishops subjected to Pope Leo I by Emperor Valentinian III     455

Monasticism
    Rule of St. Basil         ca. 360
    St. Patrick's mission to Ireland     432
    Rule of St. Benedict     529
    Irish monasticism of St. Columba     533–597
    Columba founds monastery of Iona and Scottish Church     563
    Missionary work of St. Columban in Europe     590–615
    Pope Gregory I the Great     590–604
    Conversion of England to Catholic Christianity     597
    Synod of Whitby—Submission of Irish Church     664

The story, therefore, that follows will necessarily be drawn from the Gospels and the other books of the New Testament, with the reminder that it may not be fully accurate, and it cannot be independently verified by any means now available to us.

### THE GOSPEL ACCOUNT

Jesus was born in Bethlehem of Judaea, as prophesied by the Hebrew prophet Micah. He was born through the influence of the Holy Spirit to Mary, whose husband was Joseph of the lineage of King David. Mary had been informed by an angel that the child was to be born, and was to be a "son of the Most High." Thus far the story parallels that of Mithra, who was born by a similar divine dispensation.

While only a few days old Jesus was visited by representatives of the Oriental religions in the form of three wise men or kings, who followed a star to the cattle barn where he was lying (Matthew), and by humble shepherds to whom the birth had been revealed by a choir of angels (Luke). After a journey to Egypt to escape from persecution by King Herod, who had heard of the visit by the wise men (Matthew), Jesus returned to Nazareth, where he was brought up in the Jewish faith. At the age of twelve he was taken to Jerusalem by his parents, who found him after some days in the temple disputing with the Jewish rabbis. The Evangelist records that his parents were astonished at his learning, thus making it clear his knowledge of the Jewish Law had been acquired by divine dispensation, and not through their instruction. When they found him he returned with them to Nazareth, where in due course he took up his father's trade of carpentry.

Thereafter there is a break in the narrative until all four Evangelists record a visit to an Essene prophet, John the Baptist, who has been preaching the imminent coming of the Messiah, and urging the people to change their way of thinking in preparation for this event.[1] John has already declared that he himself is not the Messiah. When he sees Jesus coming he immediately recognizes him as the one who should come, "the latchet of whose shoes I am unworthy to unloose," and baptizes him in the river. A voice is heard from heaven saying, "This is my beloved son in whom I am well pleased," and the Holy Spirit is seen descending from heaven in the form of a dove.

This is the beginning of the Messianic mission of Christ (the word "Christus" means the "anointed one"). For the next three years he preaches to the people and heals the sick, giving many signs of his Messiahship.[2] Sometimes he teaches straightforwardly, attacking above all the strict Pharisees, whose religion is mere outward show. At other times he hides his true message within parables, sometimes adding, even as he gives one interpretation, the words, "Let him hear who has ears to hear." He chooses twelve men to be his special aides, and these are called apostles; around him gather many more who come to listen to him. Those who decided to follow him are called disciples.

Throughout Christ's teaching there is always the emphasis that true religion comes from the heart, and that "the Law and the prophets" are comprised in two commandments, the love of God and the love of one's neighbor. Though these teachings, with their evident wealth of hidden meanings, have inspired Christians ever since, nevertheless it is not the teachings of Christ so much as his life and death and whole personality as revealed by the Gospels that have been taken by the Christian Church and Christian believers as the truest evidence for the divine origin of his mission and for the divinity of his person. The Gospels thus gave Christianity some of its human appeal over such competing religions as Mithraism and the Egyptian mystery religions in that the central figure of Christianity was a man who had actually lived on earth, and had been seen and could be remembered by his followers. The teachings have been expressed by others almost equally well, and there is nothing profoundly new in their ethics. But the inspiration of the death and resurrection has been constantly renewed in countless Christian hearts in all the centuries since.

The Gospel accounts are in substantial agreement with each other on the death and resurrection of Jesus Christ. After three years of preaching and healing he had aroused the resentment of many Jews who had not been convinced by his signs or his teachings. But it was one of Christ's own apostles, Judas Iscariot, who betrayed him to the leading Jews, who thereupon sent a guard to take him prisoner. Christ made no attempt to defend himself, and indeed forbade his disciples to use any violence against the guard. He had already warned them that he would be put to death and raised from

---

[1] The Greek word "metanoeite" used means literally "change your outlook" or "change your way of thinking." This conveys a different sense from the word "repent," by which it is usually translated.

[2] The Greek word used for what have since been called miracles is "semaion," which means a sign. The Greek therefore stresses the symbolic nature of the acts rather than their "wonderful" or "miraculous" nature.

*The crucifixion of Jesus Christ painted by the Dominican Friar, Fra Angelico (fourteenth century).* (COURTESY THE METROPOLITAN MUSEUM OF ART)

the dead after three days, but they had not understood him. When therefore they saw that he was captured and would not defend himself, they deserted him. The leading apostle, Peter, even went so far as to deny publicly that he had ever known Christ, thus again fulfilling a prophesy of his master.

Christ was then examined by the High Priest, and admitted that he was the Son of God. The High Priest and Council, declaring that this admission was a blasphemy, wished to put him to death in accordance with Jewish law, but to do so they needed confirmation of the sentence from the Roman procurator, Pontius Pilate. Pilate then questioned him, but finding that his offense seemed to be only a religious one, was anxious to release him. However, when the Jews insisted that Christ wished to make himself "King of the Jews," Pilate became afraid, no doubt remembering that Tiberius was on the throne, and had recently passed severe laws against treason. He therefore confirmed the sentence and Christ was crucified. A rich follower claimed the body, and buried it in the tomb prepared for himself.

At this point it must have seemed to anyone alive at the time that Christ's mission had failed. The new Messiah had been put to death, and his followers, mostly men and women of the lower classes and of no influence, had deserted him. Like other Jewish Messiahs, of whom there had been many, he would be forgotten.

## ▶ The early Christian Church

THE CONVERSION OF ST. PAUL AND THE NEW
MISSIONARY IMPULSE

This time, however, there was a strikingly different outcome. On the third day after his death Peter, John, and a woman follower of Jesus named Mary Magdalene went to the tomb and found it empty. Then they saw their master once more alive in the body, and he showed himself to his disciples several times. This experience gave them new hope and energy, and after they had seen the resurrected Christ received into heaven, they all awaited the last fulfillment of his promise—the coming of the Helper or Holy Spirit who, according to the promise, could only come to them after Christ had died and had been resurrected. One day, when the apostles had gathered together in an upper room and after they had chosen by lot a twelfth apostle to replace Judas Iscariot, who had, in remorse, hanged himself, there was suddenly "the sound of a rushing mighty wind," and they were all filled with the Holy Spirit, and began to prophesy, and speak each in the tongue of the land of his origin. The onlookers thought them drunk, but with new inspiration they began to preach the resurrection of Christ and to make converts. One of the disciples, Stephen, addressed an assembly of Jews, accusing them of always having maltreated, rejected, and put to death their prophets. The Jews, goaded beyond their endurance, stoned him to death, making him the first Christian martyr (Greek for "witness"). Apparently the Roman officials looked the other way and did not interfere

Present at the stoning was Saul of Tarsus, a Roman citizen, an orthodox Hellenized Jew of the sect of the Pharisees, who at once saw the danger from these new fanatical believers in a Messiah who had failed and died without fulfilling the mission expected of him. Saul therefore, with a band of determined helpers, proceeded to lead an expedition of extermination against the Christians, presumably with the aid, or at least the connivance, of the authorities. Having done his best in Jerusalem, he set out on a journey to Damascus in Syria to continue the persecution of converts in the north. On the road to Damascus he had an experience in which the crucified Christ appeared to him in a vision. This experience gave him an absolute conviction from which he never afterward wavered, leading him to regard and speak of himself as an apostle called out of due time. At first, however, he was paralyzed and struck blind; his servants brought him to Damascus, where his faculties were restored by a Christian. From this moment Saul, whom the records thereafter call Paul, was as strongly for the Christians as he had previously been against them. After a period of retirement during which he was apparently coming to an understanding of his experience on the road to Damascus, and the realization of his mission he went to Jerusalem, where he was naturally received with some distrust by his late enemies. But, even without any real authorization from the body of Jewish Christians who had now formed a church in Jerusalem as headquarters of the new religion, he set out on a missionary journey, during the course of which he took the epoch-making decision to baptize Greeks and other non-Jews as Christians without making them become Jews first, sparing them the Jewish rites and ritual which Peter had been insisting on in Palestine.

Returning to Jerusalem, Paul reached a compromise with Peter that Gentiles outside Palestine need not become Jews, while the church in Jerusalem would continue with the requirement. Then Paul set out again, making converts everywhere, especially among the Greeks to whom he, with his Greek education, was able to speak in their own language and in their own terms. At Athens itself, finding an altar dedicated "To the unknown God," he showed the Athenians who this God was, and why he hitherto had been unknown to them. With rare organizing ability and drive, he founded churches in all the places he visited, and kept in touch with them afterward by correspondence. His letters, the earliest authentic Christian documents, expounded the new Christian theology, which seems to have been almost entirely his own work, and answered the numerous questions put to him. In all the cities Paul visited in Asia Minor and Greece, his most determined opponents were always the Jews.

#### OPPOSITION OF THE JEWS TO CHRISTIANITY

It cannot be stated categorically why the Jews were so determinedly hostile as a body to the Christians, although individual Jews were of course converted, especially in the Hellenistic cities. The Jewish leaders, Pharisees and Sadducees alike, had instigated the proceedings which led to the Crucifixion, but only a few took an active part in this event. The usual explanation is that the Jews were looking for a Messiah of an entirely different kind from Jesus Christ, one who would give them temporal power and not merely redeem them through suffering. Their prophet Isaiah had devoted his matchless eloquence to a description of a "suffering servant," a "man of sorrows and acquainted with grief,"—but it was not certain that this prophecy referred to an actual man, a Messiah. It might only refer to the people of Israel as a whole. Moreover, by no means all Jews had yet accepted the idea of a future life. If there was no such future life and no heavenly kingdom, then clearly such a Messiah as Christ was worse than useless, since his religion tended to create a schism within Jewry which could not be tolerated. All through Hebrew history there had been such schisms, and in Jewish belief these had been punished by Yahweh. They had, indeed, been responsible in part for Yahweh's continual postponement of the fulfillment of his promises. The temptation offered by Christianity, therefore, was just one more test of their faith. And even those Jews who took account of political rather than religious realities could see that Christianity represented a grave danger to the privileged status of their religion in the Roman Empire. They realized that the Romans would look upon Christianity as a Jewish sect—but potentially dangerous not only because of its exclusive monotheism but because of its zeal for conversion from which the Jews themselves had usually been free.

Christ had been a Jew, thoroughly grounded in the Law and the prophets. But he had claimed that the Law itself had to be newly interpreted, not in the manner of the rabbis, but through breathing a new spirit into it. Many were impressed by the authority with which he spoke, even daring to criticize Moses—"Moses said to you, but *I* say." Now St. Paul, claiming a similar authority as an apostle, was even more explicit. The Law, he wrote in a letter, is a schoolmaster to bring us to Christ. The Law had been given to the Hebrews because at that time they did not know right from wrong, nor did they know how God was to be worshiped and what he required of them. Now, however, under the new dispensation of Jesus Christ, they were no longer children, needing to be kept under discipline, but "sons," with their knowledge of right and wrong coming from within, through faith and love. Therefore, although Hebrew thought, formerly an exclusive possession of the Jews, was spread throughout the whole Western world by Christianity, the orthodox Jews took no pride in this dissemination of their heritage, for if this heritage was to be a possession of the world, then their mission as a chosen people was over.

#### ST. PAUL AS THE FOUNDER OF CHRISTIAN THEOLOGY

On the whole Paul met with little opposition from Greeks and Romans unless, as at Ephesus, he offended the priesthood of a powerful Greco-Oriental mystery cult. But regularly the local Jewish community tried to prevent him from preaching. Several times he was thrown into prisons by the Roman authorities for causing riots, but in general it was the Romans who protected him. When at last he returned to Jerusalem, opposition to him was so strong that he was first taken into protective custody by the Romans.

Then, when he was about to be punished for his part in the riots, he used his right as a Roman citizen and appealed to Caesar (Nero). The local governor was thus forced to send him to Rome, where he was allowed a limited freedom even before his trial came up. We know nothing further of his life for certain, but tradition has it that he was beheaded during the first organized persecution of Christians in Rome about A.D. 65.

St. Paul was the real founder of Christianity as a universal religion. If the other apostles, who wished to confine Christianity to the Jews, had been successful it hardly seems possible that it could have survived. Paul also deserves to be considered as one of the most influential thinkers of history. It was no mean feat to transform what was, after all, to external eyes nothing beyond the life and death of a great prophet, into a system of theology, logical, clear, and compelling, which has stood the test of time, and is still the fundamental theological doctrine of all Christian churches, Catholic and Protestant alike.

Christ, according to Paul, had been the Son of God—a God-man—though he was also fully a man by virtue of his incarnation into a human body. Every man born into the world suffers from the sin of Adam. ("As in Adam all die, so in Christ shall all be made alive.") Man would have been doomed only to hell if it had not been for the voluntary sacrifice of Christ upon the cross, which redeemed mankind through his blood, and made possible man's salvation and reception into a blessed immortality in heaven. For Paul the necessity for man was to believe in Christ, which faith effected an inner transformation of his whole being, freeing him from the bonds of original sin, and enabling him to be good also on earth. Thus man was not saved through good works, but the good works were the fruit of his faith. The symbol of the washing away of the original sin of Adam was baptism, by which a man of his own free will declared his faith in Christ, and was received into the Church.

It should be added that, although Paul founded churches as communities of Christians who had all accepted Christ and been baptized, it was not the reception into the Church which was decisive for salvation, but the inner act of "putting on the whole armor of Christ," allowing Christ to live within the inner self—the symbol for which was the baptism in water, which symbolically washed away the sins of the convert. Only in later days with the growth of the Church did the belief come to be accepted that the Eucharist and the other sacraments were necessary to salvation, and that the transubstantiation, the miracle of the turning of the bread and wine into the body and blood of Christ, was the supreme need of all human beings. The baptism then became a rite to be performed in infancy, and not an affirmation of faith by a believer; from childhood, then, a Christian was cleansed from original sin and was thus eligible for Heaven even though he never lived to participate in the other sacraments.[3]

## THE APPEAL OF CHRISTIANITY IN THE ROMAN WORLD

Christianity, as it emerged from the mind and heart of St. Paul, was eminently fitted to make the deepest appeal to religious men and women throughout the world. It promised salvation in the hereafter to all who would accept Christ, and this acceptance was simply an act of faith. Thus, in spite of its complex theology, perhaps never understood by more than a small minority of its adherents, it was basically simple. It was no respecter of persons. The meanest slave was eligible for salvation, and to him it also offered the fullest compensation for his hard life on earth—which was merely a testing ground for the hereafter. No distinction was made between men and women, and there were no difficult trials and initiation ceremonies to be undergone by the convert. And in early days there was a belief in the imminent second coming of Christ to judge the world, so that the faithful Christians might not even see death. No religion

[3] It should be pointed out that there are other varying interpretations of the teachings of St. Paul, and that what has been said here is still in dispute among theologians.

in the world of the time, not even the mystery religions, could offer as much to its converts—community fellowship, a sense of mission and urgency, a promise of a blessed immortality, and a systematic theology and philosophy which could satisfy even the Greek mind when later it set to work on it. And if at first Christianity lacked gorgeous ceremonial, this was later added in full measure by the Church. And in the recorded sayings of Christ it had a fund of ethical and moral teachings which could satisfy even the Roman feeling for active morality.

Yet it did not appeal in early times to the upper classes among either the Romans or the Greeks; indeed, for centuries it was primarily a religion of Greeks and Orientals, with comparatively few Roman converts, no Roman pope for two centuries, and hardly a single Roman martyr. The Romans, even when they were correctly informed about it, regarded it as a religion for slaves and foreigners, and it was difficult for them to accept as a redeemer a man who had belonged to a despised people and had suffered a slave's death in a remote part of the empire. His origin and manner of dying offended their class consciousness and pride of race, while the Greek intellectuals considered his teachings at first as philosophically negligible. In time, however, as the Greeks learned more about the religion, many of them began to take an active role in the formulation of Christian theology, and, especially in the early days of the Byzantine Empire, they entered passionately into theological controversy.

Physical conditions in the Roman Empire, however, were ideally suited for the spread of Christianity. The establishment of the Pax Romana made it possible for missionaries to travel in perfect safety from one end of the empire to the other, and the strategic Roman roads provided an ideal means of communication. The common languages of Greek and Latin could be understood everywhere. And Roman protection was extended to all without discrimination, at least until the new religion was proscribed as a subversive organization. And, as we have seen, any missionary like Paul who happened to be also a Roman citizen had special privileges in addition to the general protection extended by the Roman Empire to all its subjects.

### ROMAN MEASURES AGAINST CHRISTIANITY TO THE CONVERSION OF CONSTANTINE

In general, as we have seen, the Romans were tolerant of all religions, and gave hospitality in their shrines to the gods of all their subject peoples. They would have been entirely willing to include Christ among these divinities. But the Christians refused to acknowledge the existence of the other gods, or else categorically condemned them as demons. And this intolerance made the Christians refuse even to pay formal obeisance to the dead emperors as gods. This refusal was, to the Romans, not a religious but a political offense, and when it became dangerous it had to be severely punished. The Jews had long been known to possess similar subversive views, but since they made no attempt to convert, and did not make themselves conspicuous, they were generally tolerated except by such a mentally unbalanced emperor as Caligula. But the Christians kept themselves apart in small communities, with simple ceremonies such as common meals during which they celebrated the last supper of Christ and his disciples. Few Romans could believe that Christian practices were really as simple and harmless as they appeared, and it was easy for their enemies to say that they performed hideous rites in secret. Even the eating of bread and the drinking of wine, which in the early days of the religion they seem to have regarded simply as symbolic of the body and blood of Christ, brought accusations of cannibalism upon them. And since many of their early communities held all goods in common, they were accused of undermining society.

So when Nero, after a serious fire had broken out in Rome (A.D. 64), was himself accused of setting it, it was not too difficult for him to turn the accusation against the Christians, inspiring the first important persecution. Tacitus, who recorded the fact of the accusation, did not think the Christians set the fire, but he did regard them as "haters of the human race," and for this reason worthy of punishment. The Roman citizens among those condemned, traditionally including Paul, were beheaded, while of the remainder most were killed by wild beasts in the arena, the Roman method of execution which economically served for entertainment as well as satisfying the needs of justice. St. Peter also probably perished in Rome at this time, but, according to tradition, by being crucified upside down. Yet even in this persecution, as at all times in Roman history, anyone who recanted, and was willing to prove he was no Christian by formally acknowledging the divinity of the emperors, was spared.

The laws against Christians remained on the statute books, but were only sporadically enforced. Pliny, governor of Bithynia in the early second century, asked his master Trajan if he should enforce them, and was told that he was not to seek Christians out, but that he must punish them if they were brought before him for trial and either confessed or refused to recant. In the reign of Marcus Aurelius (A.D. 177) forty-eight Christians were executed in Lyons, but this seems to have been done by the Roman authorities at the demand of a mob, presumably drawn from adherents of competing religions. This massacre was followed by a decree against all subversive religions which were likely to lead to riots. In the middle of the third century the emperors Decius and Valerius, in an attempt to halt the anarchy of the time and revive loyalty to the throne, issued a number of decrees ordering the Christians to take part in the official state worship. But though there were some martyrdoms and recantations, the laws were soon abandoned with the deaths of their authors, and the decrees were even officially rescinded by their successors.

In the early fourth century, just before the acceptance of Christianity by Constantine, a new series of decrees were issued by Diocletian and Galerius, which were this time put energetically into effect. Diocletian's new oriental absolutism (to be described in the next chapter), with the monarch a god on earth, obviously could not tolerate the state within a state that the Christian sect had now become. But though many Christians fell away from the Church at this time, the faithful remained steadfast, and it was soon seen that the religion was too powerful to be exterminated merely by force. In 311 Galerius issued an Edict of Toleration, and the following year Constantine won his battle of the Milvia Bridge under the sign of the cross. In 313 he and the Eastern Emperor Licinius jointly prepared the so-called Edict of Milan,[4] granting equal toleration to all religions in the empire.

Constantine, though not baptized a Christian until he was on his deathbed, took an active interest in the religion, presiding over the important Council of Nicaea, which defined the doctrine of the Trinity. During the fourth century, under imperial protection, except for two years under Julian the Apostate, the Christian religion in spite of considerable opposition to it throughout the empire, made rapid progress, even in rural areas where the old gods had never altogether lost their appeal. When at the end of the century (A.D. 392) Theodosius I decreed that henceforth Christianity was to be the only religion in the empire, the countryside perforce had to submit and adopt at least the forms of Christianity. But it would probably have been difficult for any observer to detect much difference. Instead of pagan deities, Christ was enthroned; instead of the pagan shrine, a church was erected. But it is clear that these folk knew little enough of the teachings or theology of Christianity, and the festivals and ceremonies of paganism for the most part were incorporated directly into the new official religion.

[4] Most modern opinion holds that there was no actual Edict of Milan. The matter was discussed by the two emperors, and Licinius later issued an imperial rescript on the subject from his headquarters in the East. Constantine had already made clear his own position.

# ▶ The organization of the Church

IN THE PROVINCES

As the Church grew, so naturally did the complexity of its organization. St. Paul himself, as we have seen, kept in touch with all the congregations he had founded, giving them advice and visiting them when he could. As yet there were no priests or Church officials of any kind, and the simple ceremonies and meetings did not require the services of men set aside for purely religious duties. The affairs of the churches were managed by elders, active men in the congregation who took the initiative in matters of religion. But as ever more congregations were organized and it was realized that they might drift apart both in doctrine and in practices if left to themselves, it became clear to the leaders that some kind of more elaborate organization was necessary to keep them united. Living, as they did, within the Roman Empire, there was obviously one particular pattern of organization that could best be imitated, the organization of the empire itself. Within the congregations three hierarchies differentiated themselves in the process of time: deacons, whose task was to give help to Christians in their ordinary daily affairs and especially to take care of the administration of charity; presbyters, who looked after religious affairs of the church; and then an individual leader, called an overseer or episcopus, from which comes our word "bishop."

In early times neither presbyters nor bishops were in any way superior to the ordinary layman, nor did they go through any special ceremony when they were elected to their position. But by the end of the second century, with the elaboration of the ceremonial of the Church, and the growth of the belief that its services were needed for salvation, these clergy became set apart as a class of real priests who were *ordained* by the bishops. And this ordination, like baptism and the Eucharist, had now become a *sacrament*, while the ceremony of ordination had now become a ritual conferring special sanctity upon the holder. For several centuries more it was the congregations who chose their bishops; but once chosen, these men had full monarchical power within their churches. As time went on, it became necessary to have archbishops whose seats were usually in the Roman capitals, or chief cities, of the provinces and who were in charge of all the churches in their respective provinces. These men were called *metropolitans*. The bishops in the whole empire met from time to time in ecumenical (universal) councils, presided over by the metropolitans or by the Bishop of Rome (later called *Pope*[5]), to consider doctrinal problems and to discuss matters which concerned the Church as a whole.

IN ROME—THE BISHOP OF ROME—
PETRINE SUPREMACY

The bishop of Rome had a peculiar position as the head of the Church in the capital city of the empire. Probably as early as the second century A.D. the Roman congregation was the largest in the empire. The Church in Rome, according to tradition, had been founded by the apostle Peter, who had been martyred and buried there. He thus became the first bishop of Rome. Though there is as yet no certain documentary evidence of this fact, there is no reason why it should not be true; at all events, it was generally believed by the middle of the second century A.D., since lists of the bishops of Rome were compiled about this time, and the first name on the list was always that of Peter. The tradition was also confirmed by a passage in the Gospel of St. Matthew, in the course of which Christ himself had said to Peter: "Thou art Peter (Greek for *rock*), and upon this rock I shall found my Church." Then he had given to Peter "the keys of heaven" and told him, "Whatever you bind on earth shall be bound in the

[5] The Latin word *papa* merely means "father," a title given by courtesy to other priests than the pope. It is not known for certain when the word "pope" was first applied exclusively to the bishop of Rome.

heavens, and whatever you loose on earth shall be loosed in the heavens."[6]

But it was a long time before St. Peter's position was supposed to confer any supreme authority upon his successors. Other bishops claimed to be the equal of the bishops of Rome, and it was usually the reputation and personality of individual bishops which gave them whatever authority they might possess in spiritual matters. Ambrose, bishop of Milan in the fourth century, was clearly the most influential bishop of his day, and was able to force the emperor himself to do penance for a massacre he had committed. Augustine, the great bishop of Hippo, tells us in his *Confessions* that he himself would never have accepted the authority of the Church if it had not been that he discovered from this passage in Matthew that the Church had been founded by Christ, who had delegated authority to Peter. Peter then had delegated this authority to his successor, and so on down to Augustine's own time. This gradually became the accepted doctrine of the Church. The Catholic Church today still derives its authority from the fact that the popes are traced back in a direct line to St. Peter (Petrine succession).

As long as an emperor ruled in Rome, the bishop's authority was naturally limited to his spiritual domain. But when Honorius, Emperor of the West, removed his court to Ravenna at the end of the fourth century, the bishop was left as the chief dignitary in Rome, and at times he performed the functions of a Roman ruler in the city. One great pope, Leo I, negotiated with Attila the Hun, and succeeded in diverting him from the city, and the same pope negotiated for the safety of its inhabitants during the sack of Rome by the Vandals. As the Roman provincial administration gradually collapsed in the fifth century, under the impact of the barbarian invaders, the bishops in many of the

provinces took over from the helpless Roman governors, and tried to protect the interests of the people as best they could. They looked increasingly to the pope (as we may now call the Bishop of Rome) as their chief guide in political policy as well as for spiritual leadership. Pope Leo I was given official recognition by Emperor Valentinian III of Ravenna, who conferred upon him full authority over all the bishops in the empire, an authority which he did not hesitate to use, demanding implicit obedience from them and pronouncing final decisions in matters of doctrine.

## ▶ The establishment of Christian doctrine

### THE QUESTIONS NOT ANSWERED BY ST. PAUL

St. Paul, as already mentioned, was the founder of Christian theology; but his teachings, usually given in response to definite questions put to him by his churches, were very far from satisfying the inquiring minds, especially of his Greek audience. Early in the history of the Christian Church his authority was accepted as that of an apostle chosen by the resurrected Christ to explain the nature of his relationship to God the Father and other mysteries of the religion; and by A.D. 170 his letters, together with letters of the other apostles, the four Gospels, the Acts of the Apostles, and most of the present books of the New Testament were accepted as canonical or inspired books. These are the basic books of Christianity, and nothing else written by any later Christians has quite the same authority. Other men might add to this theology, but these men were not apostles;[7] they had never known Christ personally on earth, and there was no inherent reason why one man's ideas on the subject should be better than any other man's. Yet clearly all the questions that could be asked had not been answered by Christ, Paul, or the other apostles. And it was equally

[6] This is the literal translation of the Greek (Matthew 16:19). It should be added that some scholars have rejected the whole passage as spurious, while Protestant theologians deny the interpretation placed upon it by the Roman Catholic Church, since there is no reference to the word "sin" always associated with it in Catholic doctrine. The Greek merely says *"whatever* you bind, . . ."* (ὅ ἐὰν δήσῃς).

[7] Neither, of course, was Paul one of the original apostles. But he claimed to have been personally chosen as an apostle by the resurrected Christ, and his authority was accepted by the second century A.D. by all Christians.

clear that some questions really did need answering. Moreover, many men came into Christianity after earlier experience in the mystery religions, and they were not all ready to abandon what they had been taught before conversion.

While most Romans, as was to be expected from such an unphilosophical people, were more interested in the organization of the Church and its day-to-day activities, the Greeks and Orientals were by no means content simply to believe. They wanted to *understand*. At the heart of Christian theology, however, there is a mystery. The religion was monotheistic, like its predecessor Judaism. But yet at the same time there is a Trinity of Father, Son, and Holy Spirit—a belief which later led the Muslims to attack the Christians as tritheists (having three Gods). This central Christian mystery was, of course, accepted by most Christians as a mystery not to be resolved by reason, and some of the early Christian teachers instructed their congregations not to think about the matter at all. Tertullian, for instance, an African bishop, stated openly that the more absurd an idea appeared to be to the unaided human reason, so much the more meritorious it was in the eyes of God to believe it, since such faith involved a purposeful humbling of the rational faculty, and humility had been enjoined upon his followers by Christ himself. But questionings would not be stilled, especially among Greek converts to Christianity. What was the true relationship between the Father and the other persons of the Trinity? How did the Father-God beget a Son? Where was the Son of God before he became a man? If he was really a God, then did he suffer when he was crucified?

In the first four Christian centuries there was endless division between different Christian thinkers on these problems. At the one extreme were the Gnostics, who insisted that Christ was a spiritual being whose physical body was only a phantom, while at the other extreme were the Arians (followers of Arius of Alexandria), who claimed that Christ was only sent from God, possessed divine sub-stance, but was in no sense coequal with God. In the middle was Athanasius, whose opinion was finally accepted as orthodox (literally—correct opinion), and who stated substantially the present doctrine of the Catholic Church on the nature of the Trinity.

But questions concerning doctrine were by no means the only ones to be considered in the first few centuries of the Christian Era. When it became a settled belief that the sacraments of the Church (to be more fully explained in a later chapter) were necessary for salvation, the question naturally arose as to whether the faithful partaking of the sacraments was alone necessary for salvation. If a man sinned and yet partook of the sacraments, would he be saved? Paul had already been forced to deal with the question of whether faith alone without good works was sufficient for salvation. An affirmative answer might be taken as permission to sin, as Paul's opponents insisted. If God knew in advance who was to be saved, and God by definition must be all-knowing, then how could man be said to have free will? If everything had been predetermined, then man was not a free being at all, but only a kind of puppet in the hands of God. Would it not be better, argued Pelagius, to say that man must work his way into heaven by his deeds? Then, Augustine retorted to Pelagius, what became of God's saving grace? How could man force God to save him if God were omnipotent? If God's son had sacrificed himself for the sins of the world—and this was the central teaching of Paul's theology—then salvation must be a gift of God. What was man's own share in his own salvation?

DOCTRINAL HERESIES

By the time of the conversion of Constantine many of these differing opinions had already been stated publicly by their proponents, but there was no evident way of establishing the truth. Constantine himself, however, anxious to put an end to the strife, called a council at Nicaea (A.D. 325), over which he presided. Here the bishops of the empire assembled and a statement of beliefs, or a creed, was agreed upon. Majority opinion was against Arius, whose teachings had been making considerable headway in recent times. The result was that Arius himself was banished and Christians were forbidden to preach his doctrines on the nature of the Trinity.

However, this proscription of Arianism was not final. During the same fourth century some of the emperors of Constantinople preferred the simpler teaching of Arius and had Arianism proclaimed as the true doctrine. This temporary ascendancy of Arianism had momentous consequences, for it was during this period that many of the barbarian peoples were converted to Christianity, and it was the Arian *heresy* (from the Greek word for choice) that was accepted by them in preference to the teaching which Athanasius had proclaimed and ultimately became orthodox. The popes in Rome had never accepted Arianism at all—a fact which probably contributed to the later acceptance of the pope as final arbiter in matters of faith and doctrine.

The heresies, however, were far from suppressed, and struggles over doctrine constantly broke out during the next centuries, especially in Constantinople. The chief Church official in Constantinople, the patriarch, who was appointed by the emperor, frequently differed from the pope in Rome. Backed by all the prestige of the empire, the patriarch and his master frequently adopted theological positions at variance with those of the pope, while the latter considered himself, and was considered generally in the West, as having a spiritual authority far above that of the servant of an emperor who might be only a successful warrior of no learning whatever. In the eleventh century there was a final split between the Eastern and Western Churches, ostensibly over a theological question, but complicated by a real question of jurisdiction between the Churches of the East and West which will be discussed more fully in Chapter 15. The split between the Churches persists up to the present time, though for a period in the thirteenth century they were briefly united by force when Constantinople was captured by a party of crusaders from the West. The Coptic Church of Abyssinia parted company with both the Eastern and Western Churches on a theological question as early as the fifth century A.D. and is still independent.

## NEW AUTHORITATIVE DOCTRINE—THE CHURCH FATHERS

Gradually the doctrine of the Petrine supremacy became accepted in the West, and by the end of the fifth century few would have questioned the right of the pope to declare the true doctrines of the Church by virtue of his authority as the successor of Peter. By virtue of this authority he could state which of the early Christian writings had to be accepted as containing correct teachings, which among them were in the direct tradition of the apostles themselves and thus had access to directly inspired information, if not themselves inspired. Thus grew up the authority of the so-called "Apostolic Fathers" of the Church, both Greek and Latin, whose teachings were to be regarded as orthodox. Certain creeds were adopted as correct formulations of Christian faith; the Latin Vulgate version of the Bible, translated by St. Jerome, became the authoritative Latin text; and in later times such doctrines as Purgatory and the immaculate conception of Mary the mother of Jesus became accepted as part of Church doctrine, though not appearing in the Bible itself.

The earliest of the Latin Fathers of the Church was Ambrose (339?–397) Bishop of Milan, a powerful churchman who was especially important because of his insistence on the right of the clergy to discipline offenders, a right of cardinal importance in the attempt of the Church to maintain the unity of Christendom. He was also a preacher of great persuasiveness who was instrumental in converting many leading pagans, and bringing them into active work in the Church. One of his converts was Augustine. In his sermons St. Ambrose, like Pope Gregory the Great in a later century, gave a great deal of practical advice which was accepted as authoritative in the life of the early Church. St. Jerome (*ca.* 340–420), another Latin Father, translated the authoritative version of the Bible, and wrote many tracts on theology. He was a supporter of the orthodox position on the Trinity, and attacked and refuted heresy.

But by far the most influential of these Latin Church Fathers was St. Augustine (354–430), who was made bishop of Hippo in North Africa by his congregation, and then devoted his life not only to the duties of his bishopric but to evolving a theology which became in its essentials the accepted doctrine of the Church, even though some of his most extreme views were not stressed owing to their momentous consequences for human free will. Augustine has left us in his *Confessions* a complete account of his intellectual and spiritual struggles before his conversion, which are of the greatest importance for our understanding of the conflicting intellectual currents of the time. Always conscious of his own guilt and sinfulness, like Martin Luther, who resembled him in so many respects, he could only believe in a real conversion of the heart. But for a long time he could not bring himself to accept Christianity, which he was inclined to despise because it left too many questions unanswered. Tempted by the dualistic doctrine of Manichaeism, he never really freed himself from it, believing most fervently in the power of evil, which he had experienced within himself. Then he immersed himself in the last great pagan philosophy of Neoplatonism,[8] which also taught the evilness of matter, and

[8] This philosophy, whose founder was an Egyptian named Plotinus, was derived from Plato, but it is a far more systematic idealism than that of the Greek. Fundamentally it is an attempt to bring mysticism within the scope of philosophy, and is both a philosophical explanation of the experience of the human soul when it finds union with God (called by Plotinus the One), and an "otherworldly" ethic which emphasizes the desirability of this union. It is impossible in a brief space to do any justice to the philosophy, which had an immense influence on both Christian and Muslim thought, though a few further remarks will be devoted to it in later chapters, especially in connection with the philosopher John Scotus Erigena in Chapter 20.

the necessity of overcoming all material desires for the purpose of attaining a mystical union with God. This also finds its place in Augustine's theology; and there is an extraordinarily moving passage in the *Confessions* where he describes such an experience, which came to him as the result of his conversion.

The real question, therefore, for Augustine, it will be seen, was what need there was for a Church as mediator between man and God, and why there should be a Church at all. Indeed, Martin Luther, a deep student of Augustine, did break away from the Catholic Church, while not deviating from St. Augustine save in this one matter. The human will, said Augustine, following St. Paul, is not free, and the human being is bound by original sin. He cannot even acquire any true knowledge merely out of himself. But Christ's sacrifice had redeemed mankind, and thereafter it had become possible for man to receive grace, as a heavenly gift. Grace alone can enable man to know the truth, and to do good. And he accepts the Church teaching that grace can be obtained only if a man truly believes and receives the sacraments. The Catholic Church alone can administer these sacraments. Where did the Catholic Church receive this power? Directly from Christ to St. Peter, as we have seen, and so through the succession of popes.

This, however, does not mean that man is necessarily saved by faith or by receiving the sacraments, for God has infinite foreknowledge and infinite power. Augustine therefore comes to the conclusion that God has predestined some men for salvation and some to damnation. Man can never know for certain whether he is saved, since this is entirely in God's hands, and within his knowledge alone. In logic this position is irrefutable, and Thomas Aquinas and the medieval scholastics were forced to wrestle with the problem again. But predestination was never stressed in the Catholic Church, and not until John Calvin in the sixteenth century was it stated in this extreme form again. The remainder of the doctrine—the powerlessness of human thinking and willing, and the necessity for grace—became part of orthodox Christian thought.

Augustine was also a pioneer in another field of thought at least as influential as his theology. An earlier Christian Father, Eusebius, had written an *Ecclesiastical History* which interpreted all the events of his own and earlier times in the light of the Old Testament, and especially of Hebrew prophecy. But Augustine went much further, and in his *City of God* wrote a history designed to show that with the coming of Christ an entirely new phase had opened. Attacking the pagans who claimed that the sack of Rome by Alaric was due to the desertion of the old gods by their worshipers, Augustine declared that this was part of God's scheme. Rome belonged to the "City of Man," which was only temporary and must pass away, to give place to the "City of God" on earth, which will endure forever, the beginnings of which had already been made under the Hebrew theocracy, and now from the coming of Christ must be continued by the Christian Church. And Augustine with great passion and power describes God's whole plan for the world, the creation and fall of man and the old dispensation, followed by man's redemption in the new age and the building of the City of God. It need hardly be pointed out how much this conception owes to the Hebrew interpretation of history, already discussed in an earlier chapter.

In Augustine's own thought it is clear that the perfect City of God can never exist on earth; but it is the ideal to which all Christians should aspire, and the beginnings of the building can be made in the here and now. Christians in subsequent ages, however, took it to be the ideal of Chistendom, a working plan for all Christians to follow, justifying the extirpation of heresy as treason to the City of God, and later justifying also the extermination of infidels as a fulfillment of God's plan for the unity of all men on earth in the Christian religion. The *City of God* was perhaps, after the Bible, the most influential book in the medieval world.

## ▶  The persistent ideal of poverty and holiness—Monasticism

From very early times there was opposition to the Church as an organized institution, and especially in the East, where Roman organization had not been so greatly admired as by its inheritors in the West. These dissenters could point to the teachings of Christ himself on poverty and its spiritual value, and to his advice to the young man who asked him what was necessary to salvation. Christ had replied that he should sell all his goods and follow him, "but the young man went away sorrowful because he had great possessions." These men were deeply influenced by Oriental thought, and indeed by the mystery religions, which taught that the true path of salvation was by purification on earth and an inward acceptance of the Divine. They did not believe in the machinery of salvation, as propounded by the Church, regarding it as too complex and too legal, too much in the nature of a Roman contract to be the real path to salvation. Yet at the same time they fervently believed in Christ and the central truths of the Christian religion as taught by Christ himself. Determined on self-purification, some went alone into the desert, fasted and prayed and inflicted tortures upon themselves, trying to mortify their evil nature. Others lived in small communities, holding their possessions in common, and aiding each other in their self-mortifying practices. These ascetics were regarded by all the people as holy men, so that it was difficult for the official Church to say that they were heretics.

But they did present a real problem for a Church which had chosen a different path, one that entailed organization, material resources, and political power. Their lives were a standing reproach to such a Church gradually becoming immersed in worldliness. Both in the East and in the West, however, the Church proved flexible enough to accept popular opinion of these hermits and anchorites, sometimes canonizing them as saints, even the famous St. Simeon Stylites, who lived on a pillar for more than thirty years without even space to lie down. But it did attempt also to organize them. By the end of the fourth century the moderate Rule of St. Basil was adopted, which prescribed an orderly, regular life for these monks, as they were called. They no longer lived in the open air or in the desert or in caves, but in a communal dwelling house or monastery, in which each did a share of the work required for their subsistence. Most monks of the Eastern Church still live under the fourth-century Rule of St. Basil.

In the West asceticism of the kind possible in Egypt and the East was more difficult, as the climate in most parts is not conducive to a solitary outdoor life throughout the year. But the ascetic practices found favor with those who wished to devote their whole lives to prayer and worship, and we know of many solitary hermits and hermits already living in communities in the time of St. Jerome, who spent much of his eloquence in defending the practice. It met severe opposition from those who objected to the monks on the ground that they were too often merely escaping their social responsibilities; and when women also began to organize themselves into monasteries or nunneries

Jerome had to take up the cudgels on their behalf also. St. Martin of Tours (316–397), who spent most of his life destroying the last remnants of paganism in France after the decree of Theodosius forbidding the practice of any religion but Christianity, was criticized sharply by his superiors for his own personally ascetic regimen, although he never was a monk. But in time the monasteries became institutionalized, both for men and for women; and it became a recognized sign of holiness that a man or woman should submit to mortification of the flesh while on earth, even if such people did not live according to a recognized Rule. If they lived by a Rule they were called "regular" clergy, or sometimes just "religious," since they devoted their whole lives to religion. They were distinguished from the "secular" clergy, whose duties lay in the outer world.

At the beginning of the sixth century an acceptable Rule which was applicable to all Western monasteries was drawn up by St. Benedict, who had begun his religious career as a hermit. When, however, his fame as a holy man began to attract many followers, he changed his manner of living and founded the monastery of Monte Cassino, instituting an orderly regimen which was blessed by

*The monastery of Monte Cassino, in southern Italy, as it was before it was destroyed during World War II. It is now being rebuilt.*

Pope Gregory the Great. The monks at Monte Cassino and all those who lived by the Benedictine Rule had to take vows of poverty and obedience to the abbot, the head of the community. They had to cut off all ties with their families and their previous lives before entering the monastery. Periods were set aside each day for prayer and worship; the rest of the day was to be spent in manual labor, either in the fields, which were cultivated with great care and made to yield all the food required by the community, or in the monastery itself. No monk was permitted to own anything at all; everything was to be handled by the abbot, whose word was law within the monastery. Monks slept in a common dormitory and ate in a common dining room.

By the eighth century the Benedictine Rule was adopted by the vast majority of monasteries in the West except the Irish, and for centuries it was the model life for the religious, and faithfully observed by those who had chosen it. Even when abuses began to creep in, all those who undertook reforms returned to the Benedictine Rule or some modification of it, as the ideal Rule for a religious community. There was no doubt that in spite of its initial reservations the Church was wise to permit and ultimately take the lead in organizing these communities of monks. For if it was necessary to institutionalize the Church, and the papacy had no doubts on this necessity, then it was also necessary to take care of those deeply earnest men and women who wished to devote all their lives to their religion, and to live a communal life of poverty that seemed to them more in accordance with the teachings of Christ. As long as the monks continued to live holy lives they were a standing example of the virtues of Christianity; they troubled no one, and at the same time they absorbed into their communities all those who might have attacked the Church for its institutionalism and worldliness. It is surely no accident that those later medieval heresies which stressed poverty and asceticism as the true Christian ideal never arose while the monasteries were still truly religious communities

and practiced poverty and abstinence; but that when they no longer fulfilled this function and the monks became notorious for laxity in morals, idleness, and luxurious habits, such a heresy as that of the Poor Men of Lyons obtained numerous adherents and for a long time constituted a real threat to the Church, calling forth a St. Francis and a St. Dominic to set the example once more of saintly lives spent in the earliest tradition of Christianity.

The Irish monasteries alone did not conform to the Benedictine Rule and some monasteries founded by Irish missionaries persisted for a long time on the Continent. The reason for this situation is to be found in the manner in which the Irish had been converted to Christianity. Ireland had been a land of clans, with a very primitive system of government; it had never been conquered by the Romans. St. Patrick, who had been attracted by Oriental monasticism before going to Ireland, succeeded in converting many of the savage chieftains and with them their clansmen. Instead of setting up a church on the Roman model, he allowed the clan to become the congregation. There were no priests except monks, and these did not live in the same isolation from their fellow men as in Western Europe, since they had also to perform the same functions as the secular clergy. They undertook the task of converting the other clansmen who had remained heathen while at the same time they lived in monasteries, practicing austerities, and gaining a great reputation for both piety and learning. Remaining for centuries unconnected with the Church in Rome, they were unaware even of many of the newer teachings of the Church. The result was that they developed a Christianity that was never institutionalized in the Roman manner, and they retained a fervor, especially in missionary activity, that had begun to disappear from Europe. St. Columba converted some Celtic tribes in Britain before they had yet been visited by official emissaries of the Church, St. Columban penetrated into Gaul and made converts in places where Christianity had as yet no foothold and founded monasteries there; another Irishman founded the great monastery of St. Gall in what is now Switzerland. Moreover, once the first monks had gained a knowledge of Greek, it continued to be taught in the monasteries, and was never allowed to die out in Ireland. The only great philosopher of the Dark Ages in Europe, John Scotus Erigena, was an Irishman.

But this progress was rudely checked in Britain. Pope Gregory I (the fourth and last of the officially recognized Latin Fathers of the Church), of whom more in the next chapter, at the end of the sixth century sent a missionary to Britain named Augustine, who succeeded in converting the South. As this Catholic Christianity progressed northward it came into contact with the communities converted from Ireland, which had quite unknowingly adopted a different form of ecclesiastical usage. Both sides agreed to accept the decision of a synod at Whitby (664), presided over by the king of Northumbria. The question hinged upon the Petrine supremacy. The Irish could point to no such authority as that of the pope, descended from St. Peter. Their failure was decisive. The Roman Church received the award, the new English Church was organized after the Roman manner and the monasteries accepted the Benedictine Rule; in time even the Irish themselves accepted the inevitable, and adopted the discipline and organization of the central Church in Rome.

## ► Suggestions for further reading

Every student should of course read as much of the New Testament as possible—the Gospels for the story of the life and death of Jesus Christ, the Acts of the Apostles for the only near-contemporary account of the foundation of the Christian religion and the missionary journeys of St. Paul, and the epistles of various apostles for the first efforts to build a Christian theology and to deal with the practical problems that came up in the first century A.D. in the light of Christian ethical teachings. For translations to be used, see Chapter 5, where the Old Testament translations are considered.

Study of the development of early Christian doctrine is made difficult by the personal beliefs of the authors of books on the subject. Naturally, Catholics and Protestants interpret both history and doctrine from divergent points of view. There is probably no work available which would satisfy all parties. Moreover, Christian doctrine was never simple, and any books that attempt to make it simple are likely to be misleading. One of the best is certainly G. P. Fisher, *The History of Christian Doctrine* (New York: Charles Scribner's Sons, 1923), but the student should have a real interest in the subject if he is to read the book fruitfully. It cannot be skimmed through. A very simple account, entirely accurate but limited in scope, of the rise of Christianity, with no visible bias, is E. R. Goodenough, *The Church in the Roman Empire* (Berkshire Studies in European History; New York: Henry Holt & Co., Inc., 1931). This book, which barely attempts, however, to define or deal with Christian doctrine, achieves what it sets out to do, that is, to give a clear and simple account of the facts, about as well as it can be done.

There are many books which give the primary sources for early Christian history. One such book, easily available, is H. S. Bettinson, ed., *Documents of the Christian Church* (New York: Oxford University Press, 1947). Very valuable for its collection of primary documents on the growth of the papacy and the gradual acceptance of the bishop of Rome as the head of the Church is J. T. Shotwell and L. R. Loomis, eds., *The See of Peter* (New York: Columbia University Press, 1927).

Many students will no doubt have obtained a great deal of their information about early Christianity from novels, or from movies made from these novels. Most works of this sort are neither historically accurate, in so far as we possess the facts, nor anything but misleading. In general, they are sentimental rubbish. An exception might be made, however, for the sympathetic, non-Christian works of Shalom Asch. In particular, *The Apostle* (tr. M. Samuel; New York: G. P. Putnam's Sons, 1943), which tells, although necessarily with fictional embellishments, of the life and work of Paul, is a real aid to the effort to re-imagine the atmosphere of the first Christian century. Asch sticks closely to the known facts, and his additions and interpretation are believable.

The epoch-making and influential work of Augustine should certainly be studied, especially the *Confessions* (which throw a revealing light on the great bishop himself and on the struggles an intellectual pagan had to make before he could bring himself to accept Christianity, a religion which was, as yet, rather anti-intellectual) and the *City of God*. Far the best available translation of the former is *Confessions of St. Augustine* (tr. F. J. Sheed; New York: Sheed & Ward, 1943). Several translations of the *City of God* are available, but none is entirely satisfactory. Much of the book is repetitious, but since it remains probably the most influential work in the field of political thought, it should be attempted. Easily available is the *City of God* (tr. and ed. M. Dods, 2 vols.; New York: Hafner Pub. Co., Inc., 1948). For a good though brief commentary on the political thought of Augustine, the student is referred to Chapter 10 of G. H. Sabine, *A History of Political Theory* (New York: Henry Holt & Co., Inc., 1937).

Finally, attention should be drawn to a masterly study of the problems involved in the conversion of Constantine to Christianity, and of the political and religious issues of the time, in Setton's chapter, "The Triumph of Christianity," in K. Setton and H. Winkler, eds., *Great Problems in European Civilization* (New York: Prentice-Hall, Inc., 1954); here a judicious selection from primary and secondary sources is made which permits the reader to make up his own mind on the matter.

(See also under Duckett in the Readings for Chapter 14.)

# IV The Centuries of Transition

*Church of the Holy Wisdom (Hagia Sophia, Sancta Sophia) at Constantinople, built by the Emperor Justinian. This building embodied altogether new principles of architecture. Especially difficult was the erection of the huge dome. The angle of this photograph sets off the commanding position of the church, which is often obscured from other directions by the modern Turkish buildings. The minarets close to the church are later additions dating from the period when the church was used by the Muslim Turks as a mosque. In the foreground is the Mosque of Sultan Ahmed, one of the minarets of which appears just in front of the camera.*
(COURTESY TURKISH INFORMATION OFFICE)

# 14

## The End of the Roman Empire, and the Establishment of Successor States

*The beginning of the end • Re-establishment of discipline: totalitarianism • External dangers to the empire • Barbarian conquest of Italy • Barbarian kingdoms of the West • The end of an era*

---

### ▶ The beginning of the end

THE MILITARY AUTOCRACY OF SEPTIMIUS
SEVERUS (193–211)

The murder of Commodus in 192 was the signal for the opening of a period of outright domination of the Roman emperor by the army, which was to last till the fall of the empire. The first half of this period, up to the accession of Diocletian, was characterized by the increasing disintegration of the civil government under a series of military usurpers whose chief, and sometimes only, ability lay in the military sphere. The empire itself was, on the whole, successfully defended against external pressure on the boundaries, but at tremendous cost to its internal stability. The second half was characterized by the development of a totalitarian state under a civil administration backed by a usually obedient professional mercenary army, directed by an absolute emperor. Without going into the question at this stage of whether wiser policies on the part of the emperors could have prevented this sequence, which culminated in the fall of the empire and the survival of a truncated East-

ern Empire under absolutist government, it is clear that it was the policies of the early third-century emperor, Septimius Severus, that set the process in motion.

He himself owed his position to his military ability alone, which was sufficient to enable him to defeat several other contenders. African by birth but Roman in education, and with a Syrian wife, he had no personal or sentimental attachment to Rome and her institutions. He frankly despised the Senate, and showed no understanding of the political and economic basis of the empire. Certainly the pretense that the government was a principate with himself as first citizen, that it was a partnership between ruler and people, had long been outmoded. And it was demonstrably true that the ruler was made and unmade by the various armies of the state. But the armies still had to be fed, paid, and clothed; and if their requirements were not to be always forcibly taken directly from the people that provided them, then some basis of consent must be retained. Moreover, since the empire's prosperity, such as it was, was based to such a large extent upon the production of the cities, and it was the cities which provided the bulk of the tax money for the troops, it was not wise to destroy the urban middle classes for the sake of the army, the peasants, and the urban proletariat. Whether the policies of Severus had any such intention or not, their result was to set in motion the process which led inexorably to the impoverishment and ultimate destruction of the middle classes and the independent municipalities which had provided the solid substructure of the older empire.

To pay for his increased army it was necessary both to increase taxes and to take more active steps to see that they were paid. Severus therefore kept a very strict watch upon all provincial governors, brought many provincials into the imperial service, and in this respect his administration was superior to those of his immediate predecessors. His object, however, was not in any way to lighten the burdens of the provinces and municipalities, but to see that his treasury was full. For this purpose he initiated the policy of making municipal magistrates personally responsible for the collection of the taxes. If they were not paid in full, the magistrates themselves had to make up the difference. To see that all sources of income were tapped and that all officials were kept to their duty, he inaugurated a secret police to report directly to himself on any failure to fulfill obligations and to warn him of any tendencies toward treason. On the other hand, he won the approval of the proletariat by increasing its dole from the state, and passed other special legislation which protected its interests.

THE ASCENDANCY OF THE PEASANT ARMY

But the real danger of the policy of Severus was in the favoritism he showed to his legions. Their pay was considerably raised, and many concessions were made to them which had the effect of impairing their usefulness to the state, while incidentally lowering their efficiency. Married soldiers were allowed to live with their wives in towns behind the lines, auxiliary divisions were given permanent lands, and social clubs

in the army were encouraged. This policy made the troops relatively immobile and unfit for service on an endangered frontier. It also made them less willing to fight and less amenable to discipline. Time after time in the third century we hear of mutinies and of the assassination of military leaders when they called upon the troops to fight in defense of the frontiers or tried to instill some discipline into them. Moreover, Severus now made it possible for all provincial soldiers to rise to the position of centurion, which carried with it equestrian rank. Since this was the class favored both by Severus and by his successors for all posts in the imperial bureaucracy, the result was that a military career became the best means of entry to the highest positions in the state, and civilian rule was gradually replaced by military. The very highest offices in the imperial service brought their holders within the senatorial aristocracy, which carried special privileges. Thus the senatorial order became increasingly filled with successful soldiers who acquired large tracts of land and settled down, unencumbered by taxation, having in their progress from the ranks avoided any payment of taxes whatever, and having acquired a vast contempt for those more productive members of society upon whom fell the whole burden of their upkeep. Thus the army became a privileged career, and the military caste, pampered and favored by Severus and all the third-century emperors, became a state within the state, entirely irresponsible, and giving its support only to those rulers who perpetuated its position and catered to its demands.

By opening to soldiers from the ranks the way even to the crown itself, the emperors might have attracted into the army men from the upper and middle classes. But, though Italians and provincials of equestrian rank did continue to provide some of the officers, the bulk of the army was recruited, by design, from the peasantry. It has even been suggested that this was a deliberate policy to increase the class struggle between the peasantry and the urban middle classes. It would seem more probable, however, that the conscript army could only find recruits in sufficient number from the peasantry, and that the concessions made to them were of the kind more likely to appeal to a largely illiterate and semicivilized peasantry which had always found it difficult to make a living from the land. The result of the whole policy, as doubtless intended, was to undermine the position of the upper classes and infiltrate them with uncouth but able soldiers; but it was probably not foreseen that the army itself would become progressively barbarized, nor that it would prefer its privileged life behind the lines to defending the state. The soldiers preferred to follow only those leaders who promised them the most at the least cost to themselves in military activity. So many emperors were assassinated by rebellious troops during fifty years of the third century that only one of eighteen such "emperors" died peacefully in his bed.

FIFTY YEARS OF ANARCHY—THE "BARRACK EMPERORS" (235–284)

There is no need to dwell on the lives, activities, and sudden deaths of these "barrack" emperors. No real rule of succession was observed, though on a few occasions fathers were in fact succeeded by sons who had made appropriate donatives to the legions; frequently there were several competing emperors supported by their own troops but not accepted by any others. On several occasions the Germans penetrated into Gaul, once even passing the Alps and only meeting ultimate defeat in northern Italy. For ten years there was a separate kingdom of Gaul with complete independence. Without effective central administration, tax collecting was by the rough-and-ready method of requisition of supplies and forced levies of money. Almost the whole of Roman Asia acquired a virtual independence for a time (267–273) under the leadership of a desert city named Palmyra, and its queen, Zenobia. The middle classes and active peasants were progressively impoverished; it hardly seemed worth while to plant crops or to engage in any commercial activity when so little could be kept from the insatiable maw of the army.

Near the frontiers the Germanic barbarians at times were able to enter the empire and plunder at will.

But at last a succession of emperors from Illyria was able to re-establish discipline in the armies. And though the greatest of these, Aurelian, was himself murdered (275) after enjoying only five years of supreme power, it was not before he had restored Asia to the empire, defeated the Parthians, brought Gaul back to her allegiance and unified the old Roman Empire almost within her ancient boundaries, though the province of Dacia added by Trajan had been lost forever.

▶ Re-establishment of discipline— Totalitarianism

THE ESTABLISHMENT OF ABSOLUTE GOVERNMENT—DIOCLETIAN AND HIS ASSOCIATES

When Diocletian (285–305) became sole ruler of the empire in 285, having vanquished his only serious rival, he was faced with problems beyond the capacity of any ruler to solve. The years of anarchy had impoverished the middle classes to such an extent that desperate measures to ensure their continued service to the state and payment of taxes had already been put into effect; the industrial and agricultural workers were already being regimented in a similar manner. Trade had been meeting increasing difficulties, not only because of the insecurity of transport but because of constant depreciations of the currency. The Illyrian emperors had been driven to the expedient of inviting warlike barbarians to serve in the imperial armies for pay, and even in the ranks of the officers barbarians were rapidly becoming as frequent as Roman citizens. But at least these barbarians were usually willing to serve; and, being professional soldiers, they fought better than the peasantry of the earlier part of the century and were better disciplined, not having yet grown to look upon the army as a privileged existence, entitling them to live indefinitely off the civilian economy without giving services in return. On the other hand, they owed no

# ► chronological chart

## Roman Empire

| | |
|---|---|
| Murder of Roman Emperor Commodus | 192 |
| Reign of Septimius Severus | 193–211 |
| Edict of Caracalla—Extension of Roman citizenship to virtually all free inhabitants of the empire | 212 |
| Murder of Emperor Alexander Severus | 235 |
| "Barrack Emperors" | 235–284 |
| Palmyra declares independence under Queen Zenobia | 267 |
| Capture of Zenobia and sack of Palmyra by Aurelian | 273 |
| Murder of Aurelian | 275 |
| Accession of Diocletian | 284 |
| Diocletian chooses Maximian as colleague (Augustus) | 285 |
| Appointment of two "Caesars" | 293 |
| Edict limiting prices of goods and labor | 301 |
| Persecution of Christians | 303–311 |
| Abdication of Diocletian and Maximian | 305 |
| Galerius emperor of the East, Constantius of West | 305 |
| Death of Constantius in Britain, Constantine saluted as emperor | 306 |
| Death of Galerius | 311 |
| Battle of Milvian Bridge, death of Maxentius | 312 |
| Constantine emperor of West, Licinius of East | 312 |
| "Edict of Milan" | 313 |
| Execution of Licinius | 324 |
| Constantine sole emperor | 324–337 |
| Council of Nicaea | 325 |
| Foundation of Constantinople | 330 |
| Conversion and death of Constantine | 337 |
| Advance of Huns into empire, defeating Goths | 372 |
| Goths permitted across Danube by Emperor Valens | 376 |
| Battle of Adrianople—Death of Valens | 378 |
| Stilicho the Vandal becomes imperial master of troops | 400 |
| Honorius moves Roman capital to Ravenna | ca. 400 |
| Sack of Rome by Alaric and Visigoths | 410 |

## Roman Empire (cont'd)

| | |
|---|---|
| Aetius becomes master of the troops under Valentinian III | 430 |
| Aetius defeats Visigoths in Gaul | 436 |
| Rise of Attila to power among Huns, moves west | 445 |
| Battle of Chalons—Partial victory of Aetius over Attila | 451 |
| Aetius defeats some Franks, remainder permitted into Gaul | 451 |
| Attila invades Italy | 452 |
| Death of Attila | 453 |
| Murder of Aetius by Valentinian III | 454 |
| Sack of Rome by Vandals under Gaeseric | 455 |
| Puppet rulers in Rome | 455–476 |
| Odoacer deposes last emperor ("Fall of Rome") | 476 |

## England and France

| | |
|---|---|
| Roman legions leave England | 407–442 |
| Franks penetrate into Gaul | 431 onward |
| Aetius defeats some Franks, remainder permitted into Gaul | 451 |
| Clovis consolidates Franks into kingdom | 481–511 |
| Merovingian kingdom | 481–754 |
| Conversion of Clovis and Franks to Roman Catholicism | 486 |
| Invasions of England by Angles, Saxons, and Jutes | 5th and 6th centuries |
| Mission of St. Augustine of Canterbury to England | 596–597 |
| Conquests of Angles, Saxons, and Jutes completed by | 615 |
| Influx of Celtic Christianity into England from Iona | 633 onward |
| Synod of Whitby—Triumph of Roman Catholicism over Celtic Christianity | 664 |
| Charles Martel "mayor of the palace" in France | 714–741 |
| Pepin crowned king of the Franks (Pepin the Short) | 754 |

loyalty whatever to the empire. Serving for experience and pay alone, they were loyal to their paymaster the emperor, but to no one else.

Finally, there was no acceptable method of succession to the throne, and no apparent way of preventing usurpation by the strongest commander.

Diocletian was in no sense an innovator. But he was a disinterested ruler, with no personal ambitions—he abdicated later in accordance with a plan he devised for a succession without bloodshed—and he had many years of life in front of him in which to accomplish his reforms. His general plan was to accept conditions as they were and to create formal institutions in keeping with them, and, by instituting a strong government, try to preserve the empire at least from the anarchy of the previous fifty years. In this he was, on the whole, successful, in spite of the failure of his new principle of succession. The empire did survive in form for nearly another two hundred years, and a substantial part of it, the later Byzantine Empire, ultimately gained a new lease of life and survived for a further thousand years.

In a word, his plan was to make of the whole empire one centrally administered state of the kind now called totalitarian.[1] This necessitated the final abolition of the principate in theory as well as in fact. But Diocletian also realized that the administration of the empire and the defense of its boundaries against the increasingly dangerous barbarians were far too much for one man. He therefore invited Maximian, another Illyrian general, to act as his colleague in the empire, sharing the title of Augustus. Maximian and he then chose two seconds-in-command, with the title of Caesar. The two Augusti were to retire after twenty years in office, to be succeeded by the two Caesars, each then naming a pair of Caesars who would in turn succeed them. Unfortunately

---

[1] The system has often been called "oriental absolutism," but the latter is a very vague term, since the Orient has known many different degrees of absolutism, while the analogy with modern totalitarian states, with their emphasis on guns instead of butter, is clear.

not all these potentates were as disinterested as himself, nor were the sons of the Augusti willing to be discarded in favor of generals of greater experience, even under parental pressure. The scheme actually never worked at all except when Diocletian was able to compel the Augusti to keep to their agreement, and civil wars continued until Constantine (312–337) established for good the hereditary principle, in spite of the danger that the empire might fall into childish or incompetent hands.

The division of the empire into two parts, however, survived the abdication and death of Diocletian, though without the refinement of the two added Caesars. And the scheme of the two Augusti and the two Caesars proved effective enough in his own lifetime to enable him to put into effect the necessary administrative reforms that made the empire into a totalitarian state. The frontiers were guarded, a number of minor revolts were quelled, and the expanding Persian Empire was held in check.

REORGANIZATION OF ARMY AND PROVINCES
UNDER IMPERIAL CONTROL

The army was considerably enlarged, friendly barbarians were allowed to settle in frontier districts with an obligation to military service, companies of barbarians, sometimes even under their own chiefs, were welcomed, while the more warlike sections of the empire provided further conscripted recruits; if not of high quality their discipline and training were better than they had been for years. Diocletian also organized a force of picked men who could be moved from one part of the empire to another as danger threatened, helping to stiffen the resistance of the resident legions. The army was under the direct command of the emperor and his associates, who were all experienced generals, so that there was less opportunity for local armies to revolt and try to set up a new emperor.

The number of the provinces was increased by subdivision to 101, with every governor an appointee of one of the emperors, and subject to control by vicars who

had about seven provinces each (dioceses), who in their turn were responsible to four prefects, personal representatives of the four rulers. The vicars, however, had the right of direct appeal to Diocletian, as senior emperor, against decisions of the prefects. Thus was established a graded hierarchy responsible to the emperor and his associates alone.

Diocletian and Maximian as Augusti now took divine titles although they did not call themselves actual gods. They withdrew as much as possible from direct participation in public life, instituting an elaborate court ceremonial of an Oriental kind, including prostration and kissing the hem of the emperor's robe when the privilege of an audience was granted. The persecution of Christians which accompanied the elevation of the monarchy has been discussed in the last chapter. Many new temples were built to the old gods, while there was an insistence on greater observance of the imperial cult.

REGIMENTATION OF PUBLIC AND PRIVATE LIFE

### The imperial bureaucracy and its task

It was clear at once that the expenses of the new administration could not be less than the old. The increased burden of the army and the building program could be met only by increased and more efficiently collected taxes. And this collection must also entail an increase in the unproductive army of imperial bureaucrats whose task it was to see that the taxes were paid. Diocletian's solution was simply to use his army and his bureaucrats, including secret police and paid informers, to ensure the collection, and hope to keep up the necessary agricultural and industrial production by all the legal weapons available to him, enforced by his officials and his army.

### Compulsory agriculture—The *coloni*

The armies during the period of anarchy had been accustomed to requisition supplies. Diocletian now took away the arbitrary and casual requisitioning and made it regular and legal. Having little idea of the productive value of the various lands in his empire, he assessed them in accordance with

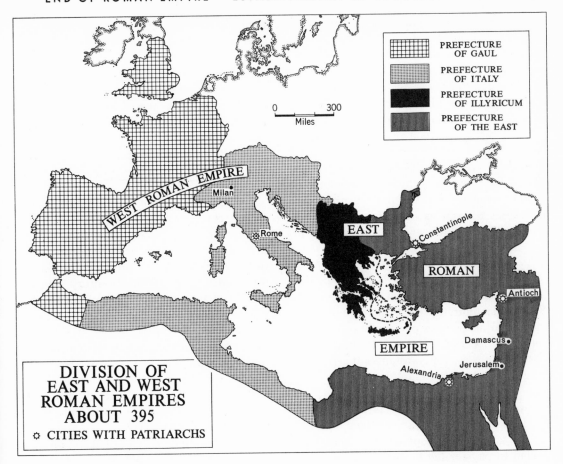

**PREFECTURE OF GAUL**

**PREFECTURE OF ITALY**

**PREFECTURE OF ILLYRICUM**

**PREFECTURE OF THE EAST**

WEST ROMAN EMPIRE

Milan

Rome

EAST

Constantinople

ROMAN

Antioch

Damascus

EMPIRE

Jerusalem

Alexandria

DIVISION OF
EAST AND WEST
ROMAN EMPIRES
ABOUT 395
☼ CITIES WITH PATRIARCHS

the numbers of cultivators employed and the land under cultivation, irrespective of the fertility of the soil and the probable yields, which were more difficult to measure. This tax was then collected by his officials, regardless of the actual ability to pay or the hardship payment entailed upon individual farmers. Since many farmers tried to escape their obligations and left the land, by the time of Constantine they were forced to remain on it, whether they were owners, tenants, or sharecroppers. If they left they were still liable for the tax on the land they had left, and if found they were returned to it. Though still theoretically freemen, they were practically serfs. These farmers were called *coloni*. Manumitted slaves were now free only in name also. They remained tied to their masters and bound to work for them. If they did not pay their masters due "reverence," a phrase which could be made to cover

any refusal to obey instructions, they could be returned to their status of slaves.

### The privileged landowners

On the other hand, the large landowners who still employed some slaves, and had always a number of *coloni* on their lands, were often able to avoid taxation altogether, as they were in many cases too powerful for the imperial officials to dare to antagonize them. During the period of anarchy these landholders had often been able to increase their estates when the small farmers had fallen irretrievably into debt or had had their livestock driven off by the rapacious armies. From this time onward the large landowners were the only people to profit by the imperial policy, and many of them, who had been soldiers or imperial officials themselves, had obtained legal immunity from taxation. Assisted by slaves and *coloni* who were completely dependent upon them, they were rarely forced by even the strongest emperors to pay taxes commensurate with their income, for a squadron of troops would have been needed to enforce the collection. Many of the luxurious villas of these privileged aristocrats still survive, especially in France, some of them with their own manufacturing establishments which produced a variety of goods, even luxuries, with large storehouses for provisions, the whole fortified as if for security against possible imperial emissaries as well as against invading barbarians. These villas are the forerunners of the medieval manors.

### Compulsory state service—The *curiales*

We have already seen that Septimius Severus inaugurated the system of making municipal magistrates personally responsible for the collection of taxes. Naturally few wished in these circumstances to become magistrates, however much prestige the position might bring them. Diocletian made it compulsory for men of a certain property qualification to hold these positions. In addition to taxes to the emperor, they were compelled to pay for local games, public buildings, and their repairs, and were personally responsible for seeing that all such work was carried out satisfactorily. Constantine laid the burden of this taxation upon the whole body of people eligible for these offices, who were called *curiales*, once a title of honor but now a badge of municipal serfdom.

The only way for the *curiales* to escape their onerous position would have been to rise to the senatorial class and receive tax immunity. But this also was made impossible by decree in the century after Diocletian. If they left their class, then their children would have to undertake the curial obligation instead. If they tried to escape by joining the army, they were summarily returned to their previous duties. And, forced to find means to pay the taxes and other obligations, they naturally tried to obtain as much as they could from their own tenant cultivators or *coloni;* thus the class struggle was intensified more than ever. With no chance of escaping

their involuntary servitude, faced on the one side by the imperial officers and on the other by a bitterly hostile peasantry, and with a complete lack of incentive, this middle class, which had previously been the backbone of the empire, was mercilessly crushed. Its gradual disappearance was one of the chief causes for the economic decline and ultimately the fall of the empire.

### Compulsory industry—The *collegia*

The regimentation in industry was equally severe. As early as the second century urban workers had been encouraged to form themselves into guilds or *collegia*, according to the particular goods produced or services rendered. An early third-century emperor organized into monopolies under state control all collegia suplying goods to the capital. The same control was exercised over merchants and manufacturers engaged in purveying supplies to the army. Under the Illyrian emperors and Constantine, all city workers were finally organized into castes under strict state control, with each worker bound to follow the trade of his father. We know of hereditary castes of bakers, shippers, millers, and others, but it is not known whether all industry was thus regimented or if any escaped. None, however, escaped the ubiquitous tax collectors.

Thus with *coloni, curiales,* and artisans all forbidden to change their occupations and unable to improve their status, the entire class structure of the state was stratified, and the totalitarian empire firmly established. The only way of avoiding one's obligations was to bribe the tax collectors; and we hear of numerous cases of such corruption in the following two centuries. But even bribery amounted to nothing more than an irregular alternative to taxes, and could only modify the impositions for a brief period.

### CONSTANTINE AND THE PERFECTING OF TOTALITARIANISM

### Economic and military policy

After his prescribed twenty years of rule Diocletian celebrated a jubilee in 305, and

*A reconstruction of the huge palace which the Emperor Diocletian built for his retirement after he abdicated. The palace is at Split, Yugoslavia.* (COURTESY YUGOSLAV STATE TOURIST OFFICE)

then retired, dying much later in 313. His colleague Maximian, however, was not yet tired of power. Diocletian at last persuaded him to relinquish it, but Maximian preferred to hand it over to his sons rather than to the properly appointed Caesars. An intermittent civil war then broke out which was concluded by a great victory in 312 won by Constantine, son of a man who had been Caesar while Diocletian was still on the throne. Diocletian, who survived these brief wars, contented himself with exhortations issued from his huge fortress-palace at Salona (now Split, in Dalmatia). For a further twelve years after Constantine's succession to the empire in the West the new emperor tolerated an Eastern colleague, Licinius, in charge of the empire in the East. Then they came to blows, in part because of the latter's studied policy of persecuting Christians and trying to restore the old religion. Constantine prevailed and in 324 became sole emperor.

The policies of Constantine were in full accord with those of Diocletian, but after over thirty years of experience it was now possible to see in what respects they had failed. Constantine concluded only that they had not yet been carried far enough. He increased the imperial bureaucracy still further and clamped the machinery of repression still tighter. By the end of his reign the totalitarian state was complete, and the hereditary caste system no longer had any loopholes in it. Each man was securely fixed in the position in which he had been born; and his obligation to fulfill his quota of work and provide a surplus for the ever more insatiable needs of the army was absolute. The police and the bureaucracy were ubiquitous in ferreting out any source of income, returning escapees to their duty, and requisitioning food and supplies when money was unavailable.

Though Constantine reformed the coinage it is clear that there was not enough precious metal available even to keep the wheels of trade and industry revolving, much less to provide the agricultural workers with hard cash. As we now know, some of it had left the empire altogether for distant places such as India, which had always had a favorable trade balance with the empire. Increasingly taxes were paid in kind, and there was a gradual return to a barter economy and self-sufficiency on the large estates. The surplus of raw materials thus collected by the emperors presented a further problem, which was solved in the classic totalitarian manner. The emperors set up industrial establishments of their own with conscripted hereditary workers manufacturing for the needs of the emperor and the army. These factories were under the control of imperial bureaucrats, and formed the pattern for the great imperial monopolies of the later Byzantine Empire.

Constantine completed the barbarization of the army by carrying Diocletian's policies to their logical conclusion. The old frontier legions which had been at least recruited from Roman citizens, even though they had been little enough influenced by Roman civilization, were now degraded to a local militia, and troops still drawn from the citizen body were made inferior in status to the German mercenaries. The real army was a mobile field army, recruited from the neighboring barbarians, chiefly the Germanic tribes in the West, and the Sarmatians on the Danube. The elite corps of cavalry, the crack troops of the empire, were entirely composed of German mercenaries. It was possible for the foreign mercenaries to reach the highest position in the army and become *magistri militum,* or masters of the troops. From the time of Constantine onward, and especially in the fifth century, we find German masters of the troops far more powerful than their puppets who wore the purple and were still called emperors. As a rule the barbarian leaders did not aspire to the throne themselves—a possible reason for the choice of barbarians for the supreme military position. But this army, at least in the hands of Constantine, was the most efficient instru-

ment the Romans had possessed in centuries for its two primary purposes—the defense against unauthorized barbarian immigration and armed attacks into the empire, and the enforcement of discipline upon the civilians who paid for its upkeep. Always increasing as defense needs grew more imperious, it devoured the substance of the civil population, laying its heavy, unproductive hand upon all enterprise until the Roman empire collapsed from within under the impact of foreign peoples with a population almost certainly far short of theirs. But the army at least served to introduce many of the most able barbarians to the civilization of the empire, which trained them and gave them military experience—which many of them used in later years against the empire itself.

### New Rome on the Bosporus

The most significant act of the reign of Constantine, however, was the founding of a new capital near the incomparable site of ancient Byzantium on the Bosporus at the entrance to the Black Sea. This city, called Constantinople, quickly grew to surpass Rome. The eastern provinces of the empire, though equally ground down by taxation, never sank to the level of the more agricultural West. Some cities continued to thrive and trade continued, if less luxuriantly than in the past. It was certainly for this reason that Constantine founded his new capital in the midst of this area. The western provinces hardly served to support themselves and their defense, while the defense needs in the East were not so vast. Moreover, the provinces themselves provided some surplus for luxuries appreciated by the now entirely Orientalized court of the first Christian monarch.

Constantinople was also a port, which Rome had never been; it could be made impregnable by sea and strongly fortified by land. Not very far from the capital was the river Danube, more easily defended than the distant Rhine. Time and again the barbarians threatened the Danube, and on some occasions they crossed it and reached almost to

Constantinople. But faced with the formidable bastion of the city itself, they realized they could hardly conquer it with their crude weapons. When, therefore, the emperors suggested to them that the West was an easier target, Alaric, Theodoric, and other barbarian leaders took the hint, and Constantinople was left in peace. Not until the barbarian "crusaders" from the West took it in 1204 against what was little more than a token defense did it ever succumb to an external invader.

For the adornment of his new capital Constantine sent for the best artists and craftsmen of the empire. But their talent proved to be far from adequate to the opportunity. Constantine then proceeded systematically to pillage Greece. The ancient Greek shrines were made to yield up their sculpture of the glorious age of Hellenic art. Trophies of the battle of Salamis, marble columns from temples to the Greek gods, possibly even the Olympian Zeus of Phidias, by all accounts the noblest sculpture the world has yet seen, priceless manuscripts from Alexandria and other Hellenistic cities were brought into Constantinople, where they survived for many more centuries, cheek by jowl with the inferior, badly built, and artistically tasteless artifacts of the age of Constantine. The bulk of these works was destroyed in the early thirteenth century by Latin "crusaders" ignorant of art and interested primarily in the precious metals of which so many of these works of art were made. What was not stolen at this time was largely destroyed by fires set by both the "crusaders" and their victims.

Constantine himself ruled over the united empire, and he ensured the succession of his sons to the throne. But he realized it was too vast for efficient rule by one man; and, having two sons, he divided it. Thereafter, though in theory they were each co-emperors of the whole, the empire was in fact divided between two emperors, one resident in Constantinople, the other with an official residence in Rome, but more often living in Milan, Trier, or Ravenna, an impregnable city in the marshes of north-eastern Italy where, amid the invasions of the Goths, the emperor felt safe enough to neglect the interests of the empire with impunity.

## ▶ External dangers to the empire

BARBARIAN INFILTRATION

### The Germanic tribes, general characteristics

We have already had occasion to refer to the infiltration of barbarians into the Roman Empire. Naturally this description of the invaders is not the preferred term in Germany and Northern Europe where the whole process, which occupied several centuries, is known as the *Völkerwanderung*, or the migration of peoples. Without attempting to pronounce on the native excellences of these peoples, it is clear that they were imperfectly versed at this time in the practices of civilization which had grown up in cities, of which these peoples had none.

Julius Caesar and Tacitus among the Roman historians had described the manners and customs of the German peoples in their day—Caesar briefly from the point of view of an alien conqueror; Tacitus actuated, in part at least, by a desire to contrast the noble savage with the effete and decadent Romans of the capital at the beginning of the second century. These accounts, valuable as they are, need to be treated with some caution. Tacitus himself had probably never been in Germany, and his picture, convincing though his incomparable style makes it, is only based on information received from others. Nevertheless the facts of his *Germania* coincide in essentials with later records based on the firsthand observations of later times.

In physical characteristics the Germans were, as a group, taller than the Roman peoples from the Mediterranean area; many of them had reddish or blond hair which they wore long. The country which they inhabited was infertile, swampy, and heavily forested; to the Germans, therefore, life was a constant struggle for survival. Their chief joy in life appears to have been fighting, and many of them knew no other occupation. Though by the fourth century they had moved from "savagery" to "barbarism," and cultivated some crops, their chief occupation remained hunting and food gathering. They possessed large numbers of domestic animals, especially pigs and cattle with which they supplemented their food supply. Their agricultural practices were wasteful. When one piece of land was exhausted they moved on to another. However, like the Dorian peoples who invaded and conquered Greece, they had the use of iron, and the weapons of at least the leading warriors were made of that metal. Both in their manner of living and in many features of their political and social organization they strongly resembled the North American Indian as he was known to the Americans of the colonial era.

As in all primitive societies, their basic unit was the family, and a number of families composed a clan or tribe. The clan had a hereditary chieftain who was the leader in war and peace. There was also a tribal assembly of all free men who met in council to decide policies suggested by the chief. If they agreed they showed their assent by clashing their shields. In later times many tribes would unite under a king; as a rule when the Romans came in contact with them it was with the king they had to negotiate, and the kings and the tribes consolidated under them with whom they had to fight. The only distinctive organization not to be found in the other primitive peoples studied in earlier chapters was the *comitatus*, or league of companions. In a fighting people it was to be expected that powerful warriors would sometimes arise who held no hereditary position. These men would attract around themselves others who looked to them for leadership. Such organizations were encouraged by the Germans. They fought together, and if necessary died together. The leader looked first to the needs of his men, and they in turn were bound to him by the strongest ties of loyalty. In this institution we evi-

dently have the germ of the later feudal relationship between lords and the vassals who were tied to them by an oath of fealty, and owed military service to them.

Such law as these peoples possessed was based upon the tribal relationships. It was the duty of a family or tribe to avenge the death of its members or exact monetary compensation for it. The tribal council might act as arbiter but without considering so much factual evidence as the number and quality of the oaths taken by supporters of both sides. In cases of doubt, single combat might be prescribed, the loser thus being proved guilty; or, in the case of men of inferior status and women, an ordeal would be called for, from which if the victim emerged without serious damage he could safely be presumed to be innocent.[2]

The men of the German tribes spent most of their lives in fighting or looking after the animals, the women stayed home and looked after the household, while the slaves, who had some personal freedom though tied to the land, looked after such crops as the tribes possessed. Not being closely attached to any piece of land, it was not difficult for whole tribes or nations to migrate, either in search of better pastures or crop land or from simple restlessness. None of the Germanic peoples had moved very far from the nomadic life; while other barbarian peoples who now began to endanger the empire were still truly nomads, who pushed the more settled peoples before them, and, as a result, set an even larger migration in motion.

These migrations of people are as old as history. We have already noticed the Achaean, Ionian, and Dorian invasions of Greece. In the fourth century B.C. the Celts migrated all over Europe and into Asia, and

---

[2] It has been thought by some that the institution of compurgation (joint swearing) by "oath-helpers," mentioned here, was the origin of the modern jury, especially since twelve was the number of oath-helpers most commonly used. However, it is now generally believed that the jury system in England originated in the medieval French practice of sending out officials to inquire into various matters of interest to the kings, about which evidence was taken on oath.

were defeated by the Romans only with great difficulty, not before Rome itself had been thoroughly sacked. At the turn of the first century B.C. the Germanic Cimbri and Teutones had penetrated far into Italy, and could not be defeated until the Romans had reorganized their army. The rulers of the early Roman Empire after a few abortive efforts, decided that it was impossible to civilize and conquer the barbarians beyond the borders of the empire, and contented themselves with building fortifications to defend its boundaries. For several centuries this defense was successful.

When at last new groups of barbarians began to threaten again, the danger came from Eastern Europe rather than from the land known to the Romans as Germany. But the threatening peoples were still Germanic in origin. By this time they were a far more formidable enemy than the earlier primitive Germanic tribes, having learned new methods of warfare from contact with less primitive peoples. Many of them now fought on horseback and used the lance and improved armor. These were the Goths, Vandals, Burgundians, and Alemanni. They in turn were followed by native Germanic groups who had never migrated to Eastern Europe, and were armed with pikes and battle-axes, with wooden shields carried on their left arms, fighting on foot and lacking mobility, but powerful in defense, and terrifying when they appeared in large numbers. These peoples were the Franks, and the Angles and Saxons who conquered Britain. Among them only the leaders rode on horseback; and they lacked the ability to produce the superior military equipment used by their less primitive predecessors.

Behind the Germanic groups were the Sarmatians, a warlike people who gave much trouble to the Byzantine Empire with their raids into the Balkans, but who for the most part remained in southern Russia; and the Slavs, who at this time lived in a more primitive manner than any of the other groups, but whose capacity for resisting and absorbing conquerors enabled them to survive when most of the more warlike groups had disappeared. These Slavs moved into eastern Germany and Central Europe in the wake of the migrating Germanic peoples, and stayed there, many of them to this day, as well as infiltrating into the Balkans. Behind all these peoples, again, were the Asiatic Huns who relentlessly moved westward, pushing the other peoples in front of them.

### The Goths

*Relations with the empire*—A great island of civilization into which they were not permitted to penetrate naturally exercised a powerful fascination on those barbarian peoples who were closest to the Roman frontiers. Within the empire were settled towns, law and order, luxuries, and a way of living entirely alien to them but nonetheless attractive for that. The disciplined legionaries of Rome were always more than a match for them save in exceptional circumstances, and they hesitated to try conclusions with them unless pressure from the rear forced them to violate the Roman boundaries in spite of themselves. On the other hand, they fiercely defended themselves against attacks from the Roman side. While they may have at all times expressed contempt for the civilized Romans on the other side of the barrier, great numbers of them seem to have hungered for a different kind of life, and not only for the plunder of a successful raid. When the Roman emperors found that they could no longer rely upon the empire and the citizen body to defend their boundaries, and especially during the half century of anarchy when individual Roman generals seeking the supreme power would take troops wherever they could find them, then it was natural to turn to these barbarians whose trade it was to fight, who were strong and warlike, though lacking the training which would enable them to defeat the Roman legionaries.

So from the third century we find individual barbarians and whole tribes being enrolled into the army, receiving training, and acquiring some knowledge and understanding of Roman civilization. They were not, of course, at first loyal to Rome or to the empire, impersonal entities quite alien to their experience, which was always of men rather than institutions. Few indeed can ever have grasped the idea of the Roman Empire. But they did take to disciplined military life, and did not lose their warrior spirit; and they were far more loyal to their new leaders than most of the Roman peasants who had been conscripted into the army, were scarcely more literate than the barbarians, lacked warlike spirit, and yet looked upon themselves as a privileged caste.

It was, therefore, natural for the Roman soldier-emperors to look more and more to the barbarians, especially to the Goths, and, in the East, to the Sarmatians, for the real core of their armies. As long as they needed troops there were unlimited numbers of barbarians available to them, who served for pay, who obeyed orders, who did not want to set themselves up as emperors, and who in their simplicity would put up with more hardships than would the citizen conscripts. Thus arose the military policy of the late emperors, especially Constantine. They were managers of a totalitarian state which had to be kept down by an iron rule, and whose citizens had to be forced to work and to pay taxes. Many of these emperors no doubt believed in the Roman Empire, believed that no price was too high to pay for its formal preservation. And few indeed probably realized what the result would be: that instead of the Romans civilizing the barbarians and making them into good civilized servants of the empire, it was the empire that would be barbarized by the Goths and their successors, and that the whole superstructure of an imperial universal state would collapse from within, when the real cement that held it together, the free municipalities and the economy and culture based on them, finally crashed and gave way. The Romans, as has been said, were not an imaginative people, and few were their thinkers who perceived the inevitable end even when it was almost upon them.

The policies adopted by the emperors were dictated by the immediate circum-

stances of each case. There never was a settled, agreed policy for keeping the barbarians in check. The earliest Goths were recruited for the army as individual soldiers, perhaps a comitatus, or even a tribe. When in later times large bodies of barbarians clamored for entry into the empire, with their wives and children, they were allowed to come in as *coloni,* were given land to cultivate which they were not permitted to leave, and agreed to give military service for the privilege. When in the late fourth and fifth centuries the boundaries became increasingly difficult to defend, whole tribes and even nations with their kings violated the frontier openly and settled down in land that had been Roman territory. When the emperors got around to it they legalized the position by giving these peoples the status of allies, *foederati,* bound by treaty to Rome and expected to defend their newly acquired lands against the next comers. This they often did, the Goths having little friendship for the Franks, and even the West Goths (Visigoths) little enough for the East Goths (Ostrogoths), and vice versa. And all united, as we shall see, against the Huns. Other groups applied for permission to come in as allies in advance, and were allowed in, upon the signing of a treaty; but these in many cases found the Roman officials unbearably patronizing and predatory, reluctant to carry out the terms to which their masters had agreed.

*Gradual barbarization of the Romans*— It was to be expected that once the boundaries were defended by barbarians, some at least of their kinsmen would be admitted without formalities, and that gradually the frontier provinces would become predominantly barbarian. As a privileged caste also the soldiers would have little respect for the Roman citizens who were living in virtual slavery under constant threat from themselves, the emperors, and the imperial bureaucracy. If they were not paid promptly they could always loot a few cities, for which they had little respect but much envy. The Romans, whose cities had been destroyed by the Goths, could not hope to recover in the circumstances of the fifth century. Thus, gradually, and especially after the invasion of the Huns which forced ever more peoples over the imperial boundaries, the peoples of the empire became themselves barbarized, sometimes joining the hordes and plundering their neighbors, protected only by some of the assimilated barbarians who now regarded themselves as Romans and by those few landholders who could still maintain their independence in spite of barbarian infiltration.

*Conversion of the barbarians to Christianity*—One softening influence, however, should be noticed. For much of the fourth century Bishop Ulfilas (*ca.* 311–383), of partly Gothic ancestry himself, but educated in Constantinople, had been working in the Gothic vineyard. He gave the Goths their first writing, including a Gothic Bible, and converted great numbers of the West Goths, who passed the new religion on to many of the East Goths and Vandals who were in close contact with them. The type of Christianity, however, to which he converted them was Arianism, which had been the accepted doctrine in Constantinople during the good bishop's period of study, and which in any case was far more likely to be acceptable to the simple barbarians than the more mysterious teachings of orthodox Christianity. Thus all the earlier barbarian peoples who invaded the Roman Empire were converted to Arian Christianity, ultimately bringing upon themselves difficulties when an orthodox pope and an orthodox emperor used their heresy as an excuse for the invasion of Italy and the destruction of the East Gothic kingdom. The organization of the Arian Church in the areas inhabited by these peoples was also of material help during the most severe period of the barbarian invasions when the imperial government broke down. In Gaul, later Frankland, however, most of the bishops remained orthodox, giving great help to the orthodox Frankish King Clovis at the end of the fifth century in the establishment of his authority over most of the territory which had been Gaul.

## THE BARBARIAN INVASIONS

### The advance of the Huns (372–451)

While the first stage of the entry of the barbarians into the West is marked by slow infiltration, with the agreement, if not always active support of the emperors, the second stage consists of true invasions, not intentional on the part of the invaders, but forced by the westward advance of a central Asiatic people, the Huns. These people, according to the records of their enemies, were a group of short, squat, strong warriors who came riding into Europe on horses, which they seldom left, being believed by the Goths even to sleep on them. Their numbers do not seem to have been overwhelming; but they could move very rapidly, giving the appearance of great numbers. They were yellow-skinned, beardless, and to the Westerners incredibly ugly, and terrifying. They showed no mercy.

### Involuntary advance of the barbarians into the empire

The Goths and other Germanic peoples were unable to hold their own against the assaults of the Huns. Most of the Ostrogoths were penned in near the Black Sea, while others escaped to the Carpathian mountains. Large numbers of the Visigoths, pushed by the Huns, congregated on the Danube, the boundary of the empire, and petitioned the Eastern emperor to allow them to cross into safety. The emperor, Valens, faced with such massive immigration, was uncertain what policy to adopt. At last he made up his mind to accept them as *foederati;* but as soon as the Goths were in Roman territory the imperial officials proceeded to plunder them, carrying off some of their people as slaves, and refusing to supply the remainder even with food. The fiercely independent and numerically superior Goths finally took matters into their own hands and made their way towards Constantinople, plundering and ravaging as they went. The emperor called to the West for aid. But his young nephew Gratian, who had succeeded to the throne in 375, was fully occupied with a campaign against the Alemanni. After a few successes won by his generals, Valens became more confident and rejected the advice of his nephew, who urged him to wait for the arrival of his own force. Taking the field himself, Valens was disastrously defeated in the battle of Adrianople, and was killed shortly afterwards while trying to make his escape (378). His successor promptly made terms and tried to carry out the original treaty. But the Goths were now firmly ensconced in the empire, with their own kings and leaders, a constant menace to the emperors, sometimes paid salaries and serving in the imperial armies, sometimes taking the law into their own hands, wandering up and down Europe.

But the Eastern emperor held two trump cards denied to the emperor in the West. The heart of his territory was defensible. His important towns were strongly fortified, and Constantinople itself was impregnable to barbarian arms. And the emperor, commanding the resources of the only remaining prosperous area in the empire, had access to ready money. The combination of these two was sufficient to enable the Eastern Empire to survive the worst that the barbarians could do. The emperor was willing to take them into the army and pay them well; and they could not, on the other hand, hope to conquer him unless he should be as foolhardy as Valens. There can be no doubt also that the Oriental splendor of the imperial court made a deep impression on the barbarians and convinced them that the emperor possessed power greater than he actually had at his disposal. At all events, it was possible for him to convince the ambitious barbarians that pickings were easier elsewhere.

*The barbarian invasions in the West— Visigoths, Vandals, Franks, Burgundians, Bretons*—So it was upon the now greatly enfeebled empire in the West that the Goths concentrated their attacks, opposed for a few years by a Vandal general in the service of Rome, then on his death marching into Italy and sacking Rome, as will be described in more detail in the next section devoted to the fortunes of Italy. From Italy they moved into Gaul and thence into Spain,

where in 419 they were allowed to form their own kingdom as allies of the empire. They were later driven from Gaul by the Franks.

At the beginning of the fifth century the Vandals, themselves driven relentlessly by constant pressure from the westward advance of the Huns, moved into Gaul without meeting much opposition, plundering and burning as they went. From the fact that the Roman prefect a few years earlier had been transferred to southeastern Gaul it seems clear that the empire had given up hope of defending the Rhine and the North. It took three years (406–409) for the Vandals to eat up the resources of Gaul ("the whole of Gaul burnt like a torch," as a contemporary poet described it) and cross over into Spain. After a few years in Spain, they were driven by the Roman armies and their Gothic allies into the extreme south. Here they found in Gaiseric a great leader who, through the treachery of the Roman governor in Africa, was allowed to cross the strait of Gibraltar into Africa, where he founded a kingdom (429). This kingdom was later recognized by the Roman emperor as another ally. But by this time the emperor exercised hardly even a nominal sway over his numerous barbarian allies.

Behind the Vandals came the Franks and the Burgundians. The last great Roman general, Aetius (magister militum, 430–454), permitted the Franks to stay in northern Gaul, again as allies; while the Burgundians moved, also with his assent, into southern Gaul along the valley of the Rhone, and into the area now known as Savoy. Taking advantage of the general movement, a group of Celts, severely harassed by the activities of another Germanic group, the Saxons, who had sent expeditions to Britain from about 440, passed over from their home in Britain into northwest Gaul, the land now called Brittany.

## The lifting of the Hun menace

In the early fifth century the Huns, who had been largely responsible for the barbarian movement in the first place, united under the leadership of a chieftain named

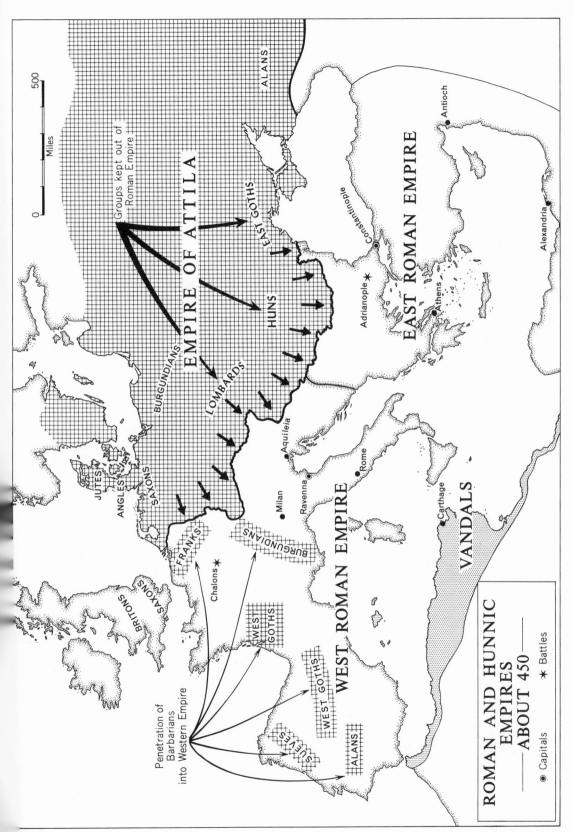

# ROMAN AND HUNNIC EMPIRES — ABOUT 450 —

◉ Capitals   ★ Battles

**WEST ROMAN EMPIRE**

**EAST ROMAN EMPIRE**

**EMPIRE OF ATTILA**

**VANDALS**

Penetration of Barbarians into Western Empire

Groups kept out of Roman Empire

ALANS

EAST GOTHS

HUNS

LOMBARDS

BURGUNDIANS

JUTES

ANGLES

SAXONS

SAXONS

BRITONS

FRANKS

BURGUNDIANS

WEST GOTHS

WEST GOTHS

SUEVES

ALANS

Chalons ★

Adrianople ★

Constantinople ◉

Athens

Antioch

Alexandria

Aquileia

Milan

Ravenna ◉

Rome

Carthage

500

0

Miles

Attila, and resumed their westward drive (445). For some time they had hovered near the frontiers of the Eastern Empire, forcing the emperors to pay them an annual tribute. But when at last one of them refused, Attila, possibly realizing he could not hope to do more than carry out sporadic raids for plunder, or perhaps acting on a suggestion from some Eastern traitor, decided, like the Goths before him, that the West offered more scope for his enterprise, and he invaded Gaul. In the crisis all the barbarian tribes remembered their duty to Rome, and, spurred by terror of the Hun, they stood and fought under the Roman imperial general Aetius. This was the battle usually called Chalons (451). It was not a clear-cut victory for either side; but Attila deemed it prudent to retreat to a prepared position, from which he began to threaten Italy. But he died the following year, and the Hunnish confederation dissolved, remnants settling down in Europe but others returning to Asia, where later they became part of the Avar horde. Their only permanent settlement in Europe was in Hungary, later to be settled by another group of barbarians, the Magyars.

Thus was the Hun menace lifted, leaving those barbarians who for nearly a century had been forced by the relentless pressure of the Huns to defend themselves at the expense of the Roman Empire, now able for the first time to take charge of their own destinies.

## ▶ Barbarian conquest of Italy

NOMINAL IMPERIAL RULE FROM RAVENNA

After the death of Constantine, as we have seen, the Western half of the empire had its own co-emperor, but, without access to the more prosperous part of the Roman dominions, it fell into a swift decline. For brief periods during the century the East and West were again united, and the façade of empire was successfully maintained for most of the fourth century until the pressure of the Huns started the barbarian movements again. When the dangers became acute at the end of the century, Honorius, the west-

ern emperor, moved his capital to Ravenna (ca. 400), leaving the pope as the real ruler of Rome. Thereafter most of the emperors were either children, feeble-minded, or both. They lived in a hothouse atmosphere of intrigue, surrounded by eunuchs, courtiers, clergy, and women. But they were still officially rulers of the empire, and it was with them that the barbarians negotiated. Secure in their stronghold of Ravenna, which, fully fortified and surrounded by marshes, could not be conquered with the resources available to the barbarians, many of these emperors behaved with an astounding lack of foresight and sense of responsibility. Beset by fears of treachery and even ignorant of what was going on in their territories, they still imagined themselves the potentates that earlier emperors had actually been. They treated the barbarians, including their own generals, too often with a lordly disdain. The result was that the generals were forced to take matters into their own hands, and do the best they could to preserve the empire. And yet the emperors, on at least two occasions, rewarded them, in the one case with execution, and in the other with assassination. By the end of the fifth century the last of these successors of Constantine was deposed by the barbarian general of the day, who merely assumed the kingship without opposition. This was the so-called fall of Rome in 476.

ROME UNDER PAPAL RULE

### The position of the pope

In Rome itself the pope was the real, but not the nominal, ruler of the city. Only his influence was able to temper the ferocity of the barbarians who invaded Italy three times during the century, twice sacking Rome. The imperial generals were away from Italy, defending the northern provinces. On each occasion it was the failure of these generals that allowed the barbarians to enter the defenseless peninsula. The popes organized such defense as there was, negotiated with the enemy, and superintended the reconstruction. The old Senate, now only a municipal council of Rome, gave occasional aid; even consuls continued to be elected, but they were not allowed to exercise any real power. The only well-organized and effective body in Rome was the clergy, under the authority of the pope.

### Sack of Rome by Alaric (410)

The first attack came from Alaric the Visigoth, who had marched over from the Danubian provinces. The barbarian imperial general Stilicho twice defeated him; but the emperor Honorius suspected his general's loyalty, and had him executed. The Goth was thus given a free passage into Italy. No army was there to meet him, the emperor remaining safely defiant in Ravenna when Alaric asked him for land in Italy for the settlement of his people. The Roman citizens offered Alaric a ransom for their city, but he wanted land, not cash. Exasperated with the stubbornness of Honorius, Alaric then appointed an emperor of his own, a Roman noble. But when this gentleman also was either unwilling or unable to grant his demands, Alaric and his troops lost patience and sacked Rome for three days. But the Gothic king died within a year, and the emperor patched up a treaty with his successors. The Visigoths moved off to greener pastures.

### The invasion of Attila (452)

For forty years Rome survived, and was partly reconstructed under papal direction. It was now little more than a defenseless provincial city, no longer the seat of empire, and grievously depopulated; but it still housed the spiritual head of Christendom.

After his check at Chalons Attila looked around for an area for his next year's campaigns, and Italy looked like an easy conquest. It is said that he hoped for a marriage into the imperial family, a suit not altogether discouraged by the lady herself, who was tired of her nunnery and wrote him letters whose content can only be guessed. But Attila could gain no satisfaction from her brother, the emperor at Ravenna. He therefore took matters into his own hands, invaded Italy, and approached the gates of Rome. Here the pious legends say that he was checked by Pope Leo I, who appeared with all the regalia of his office, and a procession of acolytes bearing candles. The barbarian was dismayed—or perhaps bought off with the remains of the treasures of the Church. At all events he retired to winter quarters in the north of Italy, gave up hopes of a bride from the imperial family, and satisfied himself with a beautiful barbarian princess. He died shortly afterward and his empire vanished with him.

### Sack of Rome by Vandals (455)

But the barbarians were not yet through with Rome. Only three years later, at a moment when Aetius, the Roman victor of Chalons, had just been assassinated by the emperor Valentinian III (a murder quickly avenged by friends of the general), Gaiseric, the terrible king of the Vandals, sailed from Carthage with a fleet of barbarians bent on plunder. Sailing unmolested up the Tiber in their shallow-bottomed boats, the Vandals entered Rome. Again Pope Leo interceded, but was able to win nothing but the lives of the citizens. The Vandals then sacked the defenseless city for two weeks. When their ships left, laden with booty, Rome was little but a desolate ruin, her temples pillaged, her palaces sacked and burned, and everything of any value that had not been hidden from the barbarians was on the way to Africa.

THE BARBARIANS IN ITALY—THE END OF IMPERIAL RULE ("FALL OF ROME," 476)

For another twenty years the imperial rulers in Ravenna exercised a nominal sway over Italy. But the real rulers were the barbarian chieftains who bore Roman titles and commanded the army, which was still Roman in name. Emperors were made and unmade at will until one of the generals, Odoacer by name, finally decided to put an end to the solemn farce. The last emperor, a child rejoicing in the name of Romulus, the little Augustus (Augustulus), was formally deposed, his imperial insignia confiscated and sent to Zeno, the crafty emperor of the East, as a token that there was no further emperor in the West. Though he proclaimed himself king of Italy, Odoacer thus showed himself willing to acknowledge the overlordship of the Eastern emperor, who was theoretically still lord of the whole united empire. Doubtless Odoacer thought him sufficiently far away and sufficiently occupied to be of no danger to his Italian sovereignty. Thus was the fall of Rome, which had stood for almost a thousand years in proud independence, consummated by the simple act of a barbarian general, without fighting, and with little noticeable change even in the form of the government. For a long time the imperial officials had been powerless, with the clergy alone keeping their Roman-inspired organization intact. Even under Odoacer, the Senate still sat as the municipal council of Rome, a position of honor but no authority; and even consuls continued to be solemnly elected. But all real power was now in the hands of the army and its generals. The army itself was made up of various Germanic tribesmen under the leadership of Odoacer himself, whose origin is unknown. He has been thought by some scholars even to have been a Hun, though he was originally called Herulian. High positions in the state were reserved for the barbarian rulers. Relations with the papacy were correct but not cordial, for these barbarian peoples were all heretical Arians and thus unacceptable to orthodox Christians. Not until Justinian's reconquest of Italy, to be described later, was the papacy to be freed from its difficult position as an island of orthodoxy within a sea of heresy.

OSTROGOTHIC KINGDOM OF ITALY—
THEODORIC (493–526)

But Odoacer was not to enjoy his new crown in peace. His army, though loyal to him, had no united body of tribesmen behind it. It was a formidable enough body of military men, but not strong enough to defend itself against a powerful united people. And such a people under Theodoric, prob-

ably the greatest of all barbarian generals and administrators, this army was now to be called upon to meet.

We have seen that the Ostrogoths (East Goths) had early submitted to Attila, and had been penned into a territory near the Black Sea. When this menace was lifted the Ostrogoths began to stir again and look for land for settlement. They made a treaty with Constantinople under which they became allies of the empire, and a young prince named Theodoric was sent to the capital as hostage. Thus he was educated in Constantinople, learned to understand and respect Roman institutions and even Roman law, and gained military experience. When his father died and he became king of a section of the Ostrogothic people he continued friendly relations with Zeno, emperor at Constantinople, was made a Roman citizen, and a master of the Byzantine troops. But later, when Theodoric consolidated all the Ostrogoths under his rulership, the emperor began to worry, and thought it would be safer to divert Theodoric and his people to the West, where he had no objection to the expulsion of Odoacer. Theodoric, taking the hint, led his people over into Italy and drove his opponent into Ravenna, from which, however, he found it impossible to dislodge him. Resorting to treachery under cover of peace negotiations, Theodoric was able to murder his rival, and became sole ruler of Italy, with a united Ostrogothic people behind him (493).

His reign of thirty-seven years was a remarkable example of the importance of good government to the prosperity of a country, even one as ill-used as Italy had been in the last centuries. Unencumbered by an imperial heritage, facing no enemies who could not be easily handled, keeping Constantinople at a safe distance and without cause for complaint against him since he scrupulously acknowledged the overlordship of the emperor, Theodoric gave a government to the Italians such as they had not known for centuries. The Goths were assigned land in Italy, apparently by the simple expedient of dispossessing a few large pro-

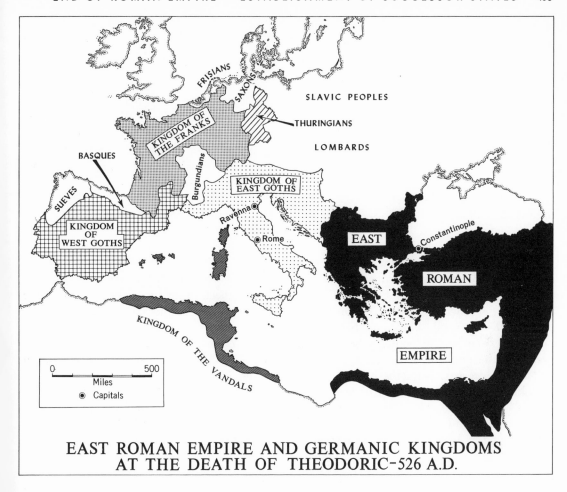

## EAST ROMAN EMPIRE AND GERMANIC KINGDOMS
## AT THE DEATH OF THEODORIC-526 A.D.

prietors and repopulating land that was not being worked for lack of cultivators, while those who were not in the army settled down as farmers. The Roman administration of government and justice was maintained, the Senate remained, on the whole, loyal to the king, and taxes were drastically reduced, as there was no longer such need for them. Agriculture and commerce revived; even private enterprise began to appear. Theodoric dredged the harbors, rebuilt aqueducts, and restored the cities as far as he could with his limited means. No longer having a vast empire to maintain, and with a greatly reduced population to support, Italy became the self-supporting territory that she has always had it in her power to be. The pope continued to maintain correct relations with the king though he was an Arian; and Theodoric in

return made no attempt to convert his orthodox Roman subjects to Arianism.

There was even a brief revival of culture, with the two great scholars Boethius and Cassiodorus the chief ornaments. Boethius, foreseeing correctly the certain loss of all Greek culture in the West under the barbarian monarchy, spent much of his life translating the logical works of Aristotle into Latin, and writing textbooks based on the dying Greek knowledge, but suitable for the barbarians and barbarized Romans who alone would remain to study them. Unfortunately he became suspected of treasonable designs against the throne, and was cast into prison. Here he wrote the *Consolations of Philosophy*, which has been read ever since, and was especially popular in the Middle Ages. Ultimately he was executed by order of Theodoric. His shade, however, may have been compensated by the knowledge that his textbooks and translations did indeed survive to become the chief intellectual diet of generations of medieval students. Cassiodorus, however, long outlived the Gothic king, supervising the translating and copying of manuscripts in a monastery which he founded on his own estate. He also wrote a *History of the Goths.*

### RECONQUEST OF ITALY BY THE BYZANTINE EMPIRE

#### Italian policy of Justinian

Theodoric's kingdom, however, did not survive his death. It was evidently only his personality that held it together. Civil war disrupted the kingdom, the succession, as so often in the Germanic kingdoms, being disputed between several contestants; in 535, Justinian, the emperor of the East, decided that the time was ripe for the restoration of the old Roman Empire, as it had been and always ought to be. The emperor Justinian was also a strong zealot for the orthodox faith as long as he was allowed to interpret it himself. In the laudable aim of extinguishing Arianism, he had the moral support of the papacy in Rome, and whatever more tangible support it could give him—at least until the popes recognized that Justinian's authoritarianism extended to the field of religion also.

#### Destruction of Ostrogothic kingdom— Economic and strategic consequences

In a long-drawn-out and ruinously expensive war, Justinian's generals, Belisarius and Narses, reconquered Italy piecemeal. Behind them came the imperial bureaucracy and the tax collectors from whom the fortunate Italians had been free for a generation. The Ostrogothic nation resisted to the last, and was virtually destroyed, Italy was devastated; twenty years of warfare in which neither side showed any mercy was the final crippling blow to a country which had been able to recover from so many in the past. From this she never recovered for centuries.

Justinian, leaving an *exarch,* an imperial official, to rule Italy from Ravenna on his behalf, and a pope grateful for his orthodoxy but disliking intensely his autocratic manner of dealing with spiritual matters which he had acquired in his own capital, turned his attention to other affairs. He died soon afterward, having saddled his empire with a territory almost useless for exploitation, and incapable of self-defense against any barbarian horde that wished to enter.

### INVASION OF ITALY BY LOMBARDS (568) —PARTITION OF ITALY

#### The Lombard conquests (568–605)

This was not long in coming. Justinian had not been in his grave three years before the Lombards, another Germanic people, but by far the least civilized of any that had hitherto penetrated into Southern Europe, nominally Arians also, but in fact nearer to heathenism, swept into northern Italy, where there was no one left to oppose them. This time they made no compromises with the emperor, nor were they interested in Roman civilization. The Italians lost their estates, which were simply sequestrated by the Lombards. Northern Italy was consolidated under their rule in seven years, and they began to push southward. The exarch of Ravenna maintained his stronghold, still theoretically the ruler of Italy under the emperor; but neither he nor the rest of Italy could obtain any support from the various emperors of Constantinople, who were fully engaged elsewhere. Nor did the emperors give any aid to the other isolated areas in Italy under their nominal rule. And there was no such partly civilized king as Theodoric over the Lombards. They were united only for conquest and plunder. Thereafter their separate leaders (dukes) took what they could, and maintained it as their own private possession. By 605 all Italy except Ravenna, Naples, Rome, and parts of the extreme south were in the hands of the barbarians.

#### Remnants of Byzantine rule

What remained to the empire from the

warfare of Justinian was the isolated and useless Ravenna, and the south. Rome acknowledged the overlordship of Constantinople on the principle that a distant overlord is better than a local one, especially if he is powerless to intervene. Since such acknowledgment carried with it no obligation to obedience, the popes were content to make it for centuries to come. And the pope of Rome was now at last in fact its temporal lord also. He was the spiritual lord of all Christendom, the owner of many scattered estates in Italy which had been given to the Church in the troubled times, and the defender of Rome against the barbarian Lombards from whom he had managed to keep his city intact.

### Position of the papacy—Gregory I (590–604)

This was the work of one man, one of the greatest of the popes, a Roman by descent, a saint, and a gifted administrator and diplomatist, Gregory i, the Great.

It is possible that the Lombards, vastly superior in numbers as they were, could have taken Rome by force if they had united against it. But they seem to have respected the person of the pope, and perhaps the sanctity of the city, in spite of the fact that they were only nominal Christians, and a heretical sect at that. At all events, they never made any serious effort to do so, perhaps in part because of their internal disunity. Thus for centuries the popes were able to exist, often isolated and always precariously, until they were rescued in the eighth century by the orthodox Frankish kings. Gregory, who had at an earlier stage in his life been an official agent of the papacy in Constantinople, knew how useless it was to look for help from this quarter. He therefore accepted the position, and negotiated directly with the Lombards, while the emperor continued to bid him resist, and for many years refused to accept his arrangements. Ultimately the empire recognized the conquests; and Gregory through the negotiations was allowed to keep his city and the territory around it.

Such a position, in spite of its precariousness, had certain manifest advantages. As a temporal ruler the pope continued to owe a nominal allegiance to Constantinople, an allegiance which could not be enforced, but still gave him legal title to his position, and perhaps served to keep the Lombards away from his city. As a spiritual and temporal leader he had just shown himself as a true shepherd of his people, thereby greatly enhancing his prestige. He began to improve his position still further by directing missionary enterprises, especially the successful mission of St. Augustine to England (596), and a further mission to Spain, where the Visigothic king was at last converted from his Arianism to orthodox Catholicism. Gregory took careful thought for the position of the clergy in Christendom, and wrote several works giving them guidance and practical advice on the care of souls. His instructions to bishops remain the fundamental work on the subject, explaining in a simple manner the different kinds of cases with which they would be called upon to deal, and how the instruction varied in each case. As explained already, he also fully supported the work of St. Benedict in his reform of the monasteries.

Perhaps the most important of Gregory's work was his insistence that all the clergy of Europe should obey the papacy and receive instructions from it. He was not too successful in France, where the appointment of the clergy was largely in the hands of the Merovingian kings, but the bishops nevertheless listened to him with respect, and later popes could quote Gregory as authority for their own claims. Newly converted Spain and England accepted the overlordship of the papacy from the first. And wherever there were orthodox clergy in Italy, they too accepted his supremacy. Though Gregory could not actually alter the domination of the Church by the state in Constantinople, he constantly repeated his claim that all the Eastern bishops and the Patriarch of Constantinople were subordinate to the Holy See by virtue of the Petrine supremacy. In all these things he gave a lead to the popes

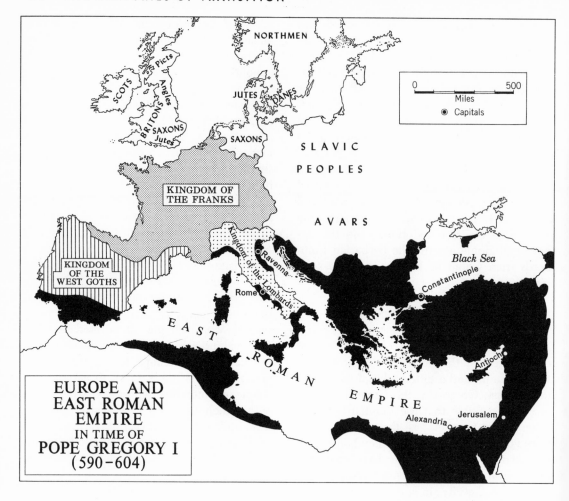

NORTHMEN

SCOTS

Picts

Angles

JUTES  DANES

BRITONS

SAXONS

Jutes

SAXONS

SLAVIC

PEOPLES

KINGDOM OF
THE FRANKS

AVARS

0                500

Miles

⊙ Capitals

KINGDOM
OF THE
WEST GOTHS

Kingdom of the Lombards

Ravenna

Rome

Black Sea

Constantinople

E A S T

R O M A N

E M P I R E

Antioch

EUROPE AND
EAST ROMAN
EMPIRE
IN TIME OF
POPE GREGORY I
(590–604)

Alexandria

Jerusalem

who followed him. For, though the practice of appointing bishops by lay rulers was never abandoned in France and Germany, and discipline could hardly be enforced, the clergy nevertheless did look to the papacy for guidance in spiritual affairs when they felt the need for it; and this dependence largely remained even when the papacy fell into weak hands, and when Constantinople and the Eastern Empire drifted entirely away from papal rule.

## ▶ Barbarian kingdoms in the West

### THE ASCENDANCY OF THE FRANKS

#### Conquest of Gaul by Clovis (481–511)

When we last mentioned the Franks, they were following the Vandals into the land that was then called Gaul but thereafter was to be known as Frankland or France. Meeting little opposition from the few remaining Romans, the Franks first set up several kingdoms in the north under separate kings. But in 482 a young prince named Clovis became the ruler of one small kingdom clustered around the modern Tournai. Able and ambitious, he began to expand his kingdom to the south by judicious murders, treachery, and open warfare. France at the time was peopled by Visigoths, Burgundians, Alemanni, as well as the old Gallo-Romans, including a Gallic noble who called himself king of Rome. Defeating this pretender first, Clovis then drove the Alemanni back across the Rhine into Germany (to which they gave their name, Allemagne in the French language) and incorporated their kingdom into his; then he turned south and drove the Visigothic remnants into Spain to join their fellow tribesmen; and at last, having disposed also of his fellow Frankish kings, he consolidated a kingdom not much smaller than the present-day France (481–511).

### Conversion of Clovis to orthodox Catholicism

Clovis, as it happened, had a Christian wife, Clotilda, who was orthodox and not Arian; after his victories he allowed himself to be converted by her clerical adviser and with him his Franks, thus being the first barbarian group to deviate from the otherwise universal Arianism. Publicly baptised at Rheims by a Catholic bishop, by this act he gained the support of the entire clergy of France, who now rallied to his aid. This was no mean help, since they controlled what was left of the old Gallo-Roman administration, while the remainder of the old Gallo-Roman population, also orthodox Christians, offered Clovis at least their moral support. From this time onward the Frankish monarchy remained the papal favorite among secular powers, and it was to the Franks that the papacy looked for help and military aid when it became involved with the Lombard kings, in preference to the official overlord of Italy away in Constantinople who was too prone to lapse into heresy and was inclined to treat papal claims to supremacy with disrespect.

### The Merovingian kingdom

After the death of Clovis, his kingdom, according to Germanic custom, was divided between his four sons, who spent most of their lives fighting against each other, though they united against all non-Frankish outsiders, consolidating their total dominions by the addition of almost all the remainder of modern France. The Merovingian kingdom (418–754, so called after Meroveus, grandfather of Clovis) was sometimes under the rule of one member of the family and sometimes subdivided. But until the eighth century at least one of his descendants occu-

pied the throne, though in later years the authority of the kings was only nominal and the real power was in the hands of hereditary officials, chief stewards, who are usually, and incorrectly, called mayors of the palace (*major domus*). Ultimately, as we shall see, one of these officials deposed his titular master with papal approval and became king of the Franks himself.

It is difficult to generalize about the state of the country in Merovingian times. Some of Gaul had been thoroughly Romanized, and remained so, even under alien monarchs. On the whole, it can be said that the Latin element tended to prevail. The French language has barely four hundred words of Germanic origin, all the remainder being of Latin origin. Much of Roman law and even Roman governmental system remained, especially in the center and the south, while in the north German customs prevailed. On the other hand, the barbaric habits of the kings; their addiction to murder, wholesale and retail; their lack of care for commerce and trade so long as they were able to have the Oriental luxuries, especially of dress and ornament, in which they delighted; their general propensity to treat their territories as if they were private estates to be exploited for their own gain; and their failure to control the rapacity of local, semi-independent chiefs called counts—all these tended to push the unhappy country further into barbarism, which historians have politely called a fusion between German and Gallo-Roman culture. This fusion undoubtedly existed, and the result, after many centuries, was the modern kingdom of France, but far more Latin than Germanic—in this showing once again how the superior culture tends to absorb the lesser, if the lesser, like the Frankish culture of this period, has less to offer. The best that can be said for the Merovingian monarchy is that, by providing government of a sort and by not interfering too drastically with institutions they were incapable of understanding and with a culture that meant nothing to them, they preserved France for a brighter future when the Dark Ages which had fallen

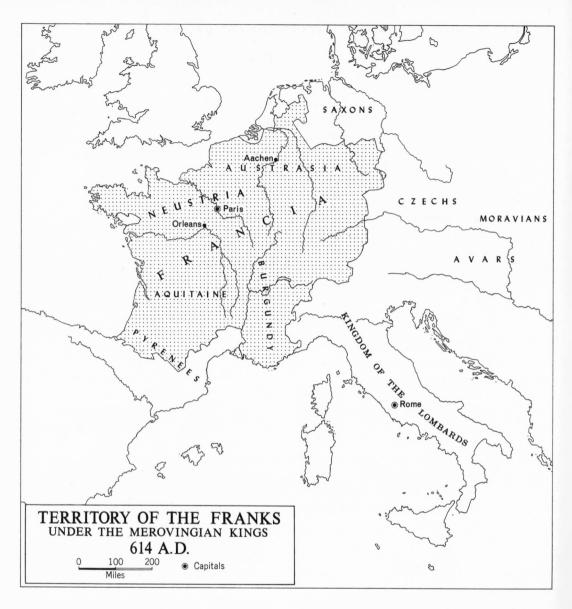

**TERRITORY OF THE FRANKS**
UNDER THE MEROVINGIAN KINGS
**614 A.D.**

0   100   200   ◉ Capitals
Miles

on all Europe at last should come to an end.

As in all other matters the Merovingian kings were dictatorial and arbitrary in their policy toward the Church. They insisted on making all higher appointments themselves, or at least in supervising them. The result was that the choice was not always suitable, and morality does not seem to have been one of the more important qualifications for office. However, there were many good choices among the bad, and there can be little doubt that, on the whole, the bishops were several degrees better than the counts, with whom they shared the authority within

the territories under their control. While we hear of bishops who publicly boasted of their adulteries, who adopted the trade of highwaymen in addition to their spiritual duties, who daily used to drink themselves into a stupor and celebrate Mass without taking the trouble to recover their sobriety, of bishops who went to war in full armor and of at least one who admitted to regicide, the record would be incomplete without mention also of many who spent their lives looking after the poor and humble and defending them against the secular power, many who administered justice faithfully, and many who were true shepherds of their

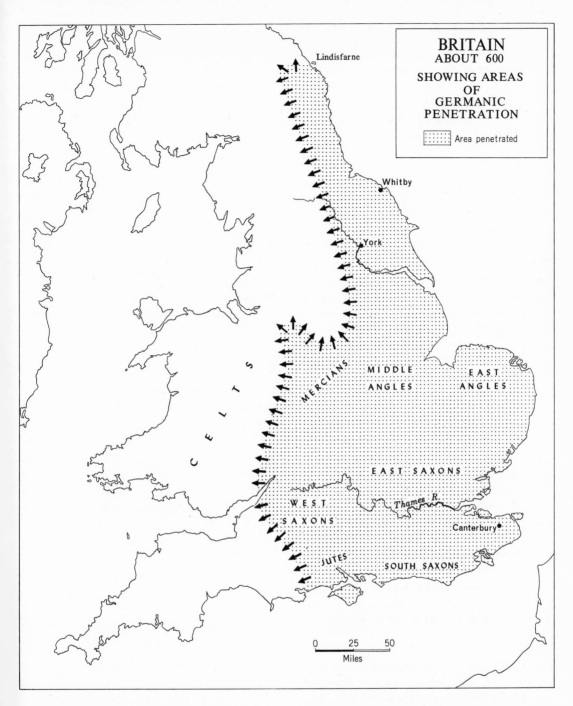

BRITAIN
ABOUT 600

SHOWING AREAS
OF
GERMANIC
PENETRATION

:::::: Area penetrated

Lindisfarne

Whitby

York

MERCIANS

MIDDLE
ANGLES

EAST
ANGLES

C E L T S

EAST SAXONS

WEST
SAXONS

Thames R.

Canterbury

JUTES

SOUTH SAXONS

0      25      50
Miles

flocks. The bishops and clergy were a reflection of the times in which they lived and of the monarchs who appointed them.

### THE ANGLO-SAXON KINGDOM OF ENGLAND—INVASION (440–615)

In the early fifth century the Roman legions in Britain revolted, and finally left the country to its fate (442). The northern walls which had protected the country from the Celtic Picts were promptly overrun by these invaders, while other Celts from Ireland, called the Scots, came over by sea. Saxons from Germany, and later a people called Angles, usually collectively known as Anglo-Saxons, together with some Jutes from Denmark, invaded Britain from the east, driving the Celtic population, including the recent arrivals from Ireland and Scotland, into the west of the country, and setting up kingdoms of their own, the Angles and Jutes in the north and east, and the Saxons in the South. These conquests were completed by 615. The original Celts, who had never fully accepted Roman culture, though they had been, for the most part, converted to Christianity, fled into the extreme west of the country, and relapsed into barbarism, retaining their Celtic language to this day (Welsh); they were not reclaimed into England until the fourteenth century. The Celts (Britons) who remained in England were thoroughly Germanized by the invaders, and the country became in all essentials a Germanic one. This Anglo-Saxon realm was even able to survive the fierce raids of the Northmen, who invaded repeatedly from the late eighth to the eleventh century, and at one time gave England, as the country came to be called, one of the greatest of its kings (Cnut). The Irish and Roman Churches soon competed for converts among the English, as described in the last chapter, the Roman Church finally obtaining one of its most constantly faithful clergy and people, subject to discipline from the papacy. The English kings made no attempt to defy the Church or interfere with clerical appointments until after the Norman Conquest in the eleventh century. This was the most successful and permanent of the Germanic kingdoms, of all that the barbarians invaded during these migrations the only country which survived as a truly Germanic entity.

### THE VISIGOTHIC KINGDOM OF SPAIN (507–711)

The Visigothic kingdom of Spain, conquered after many efforts in other directions by the Visigothic people, remained under Gothic control until the beginning of the eighth century, with the exception of a small area in the south which was conquered by Justinian in 554 and held by the Byzantines for a few years. Being the most civilized of the German barbarians, they fused more easily with the Romanized Spaniards than did the Franks with the Gallo-Roman peoples of France. This was especially true after the

conversion of the Visigoths to Catholic Christianity in the late sixth century. Roman law was maintained as well as elements of the Roman government, with the Goths providing the ruler, though they remained a small minority in the country. The Spanish language has very few words of Germanic origin, remaining almost as close to Latin as is Italian.

But the Goths declined in military ardor during their two centuries of rule, and were no match for the invading Muslims under Tarik (711), even though the latter were only one comparatively small unit among the numerous Muslim armies. As soon as the Muslims brought over their first reinforcements the kingdom succumbed without serious resistance. The consolidation of this kingdom by the Muslims will be described in Chapter 16.

### THE VANDAL KINGDOM IN AFRICA—ITS EXTINCTION BY JUSTINIAN

The Vandal kingdom in Africa, founded by Gaiseric, survived only until the early sixth century. After the death of the great leader the government disintegrated, with civil war and disputed successions among the chiefs. One such dispute gave Justinian, the Emperor of Constantinople, the opportunity to interfere and add this Arian kingdom to orthodox Christendom. This was accomplished in one expedition under the brilliant Byzantine general Belisarius (533).

## ▶ The end of an era

With the fall of the Roman Empire we reach the end of an era. Though the successor-state in the East, known as the Byzantine Empire, survived for almost a thousand years longer, this civilization was so different from the old Roman Empire that it will be discussed separately in the next chapter, together with its own offshoots.

The achievements of Greco-Roman civilization were far from lost, even in the West; but the destruction of its political system and the decline of its culture as a iving creative force threw Europe into a condition of political, social, and cultural degradation which used to be called the "Dark Ages." If these centuries are not believed by modern scholars to be as dark as earlier historians thought them, the term remains not altogether inappropriate. It was a period of fermentation which ultimately proved to have in it the potentiality for new life and creativity; but while the fermentation was in process life was dark indeed, and no one could have foretold what would arise from it. Other countries which have had great cultures in the past have never emerged from their stagnation, and it was possible that Europe might have followed their example.

The conditions which made possible the Greek and Roman achievements had disappeared, as it proved, forever. The Roman Empire had survived as long as it had because it was able to make use of the old city-state culture which was the distinctive achievement of the Greeks. The empire had succeeded in the one field in which the Greeks had failed; it had provided a political framework under which the ruinous intercity warfare was no longer possible. But the later empire had destroyed the basis for its own government when, by relentless pressure, it undermined the ability of the cities to survive as independent entities. It was not possible to force them to produce in the same way as they had produced under their own impetus; and though the peasant has always been ready to work his land under the most tyrannous oppression, either by landlords or by monarchs, Europe was too vast to treat as if it were an Egypt, and no emperor could be strong enough to keep every landlord in Europe directly subject to him and obedient to his orders. So no basis remained for absolute government; the army could not be maintained with the cities refusing to work, and with the peasants out of the control of the absolute monarchs. The army was merely an instrument for compulsion, and it could not itself produce.

With the destruction of the cities, land alone remained; and for the next few centuries the rule of Europe was in the hands of landlords, sometimes nominally subject to monarchs, but actually exercising almost independent control of comparatively small areas which were not beyond their capacity to rule. With the subsequent rise of cities it again became possible for monarchs to unite with them and subject the landlords to control; but it has never been possible up to this time to exercise this dominion in areas as large and with as wide and varied a culture as the territory ruled by the Roman Empire.

This is not to say that this fact was ever understood by contemporaries. To the people who could remember, or whose institutions had been formed by the Roman Empire, it seemed that the natural form of government was a huge universal state ruled by an emperor who, at least according to Christian thought, was responsible to God, or perhaps to God's spiritual representative on earth, the pope. If this no longer suited the new condition of Europe, then it must be imposed by force. Charlemagne, as we shall see, succeeded by the force of his personal genius in subjecting most of the landlords to discipline in his day and compelling them to acknowledge his authority. But all they had to do was to sit out his lifetime and throw off his out-of-date despotism as soon as he was dead. In this they were backed by all the effective force of the times.

The papacy, seeking a similar restoration of the empire in a different form, would probably have liked an emperor, obedient to itself in spiritual matters but exercising supreme authority in the secular sphere. This arrangement would have been more convenient, but the basis for such an authority was nowhere to be found. The emperor of Constantinople before the division of the Eastern and Western Churches refused to accept the overlordship of the papacy, even in spiritual matters. And the Holy Roman Empire was usually only a shadow empire, unable to maintain undisputed authority even within Germany, and could not even aspire, after Charlemagne, to the rulership of Europe.

So the papacy had to fall back upon the dream of a spiritual dominion, its ruler trying to dictate to the separate governments of Europe in spiritual matters, the only universal authority in a Europe split into many separate and warring states. But in the Middle Ages, when the Church fulfilled so many functions now considered the prerogative of secular governments, it was impossible to draw a dividing line between the realms of each. The secular governments, trying to establish their own power within their states, could not tolerate what came to seem foreign intervention in domestic matters, and conflict ensued between them and the spiritual authority exercised from Rome. And the latter, in an age of declining faith and increasing interest in worldly matters, was, at the last, unable to substantiate its claims.

So there was no restoration of the Roman Empire, either by secular or religious powers. It had served its purpose in history. Its achievements had been many; it had given to the Western world its first long experience of peace, it had spread Greek culture, with its ability to deal with abstract thought, its thirst for experimentation and explanation, and its tendency to think of life in terms of this world; and it had itself introduced mankind to the idea that each human being has rights which should be embodied in a law which ought to be just, clear, and not arbitrary, and as far as possible in accordance with what man could discover about the Divine Reason. It had given hospitality to an Oriental religion which gave man hope of a blessed hereafter, and explained this life as a proving ground for a world to come; and it has been contended that it also laid the impress of its own thought on the ancient Hebrew idea of man's atonement for sin by making it into a contract between man and God with salvation as the reward; and it certainly gave the organization of this Church as a gift to the religion. And it provided a language for this Church which could be understood throughout Europe, and has remained its chosen language to this day.

If little that was authentically Roman survived outside the Church in the Dark Ages Roman and Greek rationalism was not lost forever. When the human mind awakened again—when, with Anselm, it was first found necessary to *prove* the existence of God—the process was set in motion that led to modern Western civilization. And the work of the Greeks and Romans, gradually recovered and assimilated, had no mean share in it.

## ▶ Suggestions for further reading

There have been so many studies on the fall of the Roman Empire that it is impossible to make a really satisfactory choice. Each book is inclined to stress some factors to the exclusion or minimization of others, as, indeed, this text itself has been forced to do. In the author's opinion the most adequate account within a reasonable space is F. Lot, *The End of the Ancient World and the Beginnings of the Middle Ages* (tr. P. and M. Leon; New York: Alfred A. Knopf, Inc., 1931). This book offers a useful synthesis of causes for the decline and fall, with a very thoughtful evaluation, and the whole is presented with an admirable clarity. H. St. L. B. Moss, *The Birth of the Middle Ages, 395–814* (Oxford: The Clarendon Press, 1935), offers a good brief general picture of Roman civilization in the last centuries of the Roman Empire, and gives much essential information on the barbarian invasions and the establishment of the barbarian kingdoms, with a clarity not usually found in books about this confusing period. From the point of view of a classical scholar primarily interested in the culture of this period, Miss E. S. Duckett gives an admirable survey, country by country, of the new barbarian kingdoms and the interaction of the Romans and barbarians, its effects upon the old Roman culture. There is a particularly sympathetic account of Boethius, and a picture of the world of Pope Gregory i which should be read in connection with the material at the close of Chapter 13. This book is E. S. Duckett, *The Gateway to the Middle Ages* (New York: The Macmillan Company, 1938). Utilizing in particular the Latin writings of this period, Miss Duckett succeeds in giving a very fresh and interesting account, with many quotations not easily found elsewhere. Dill's masterpiece, long a classic in this field, should also not be missed, especially the long quotations from the writers of the fifth century which show so clearly the decadence of the time and the surprising ignorance of the Romans that their Empire was on the verge of collapse: S. Dill, *Roman Society in the Last Century of the Western Empire* (2nd ed., rev.; London: Macmillan & Co., Ltd., 1921). Finally, the heritage of Rome and what it meant to the world are well handled in C. Dawson, *The Making of Europe* (New York: The Macmillan Company, 1932), which is described more fully under Chapters 15 and 17.

All students should read *Germania*, the fundamental study of the German barbarians by the Roman historian Tacitus, available in many different editions. One easily available edition is M. Hadas, ed., *The Complete Works of Tacitus* (tr. A. J. Church and W. J. Brodribb; New York: Modern Library, Inc., 1942).

For students interested in the Merovingian kingdom of Gaul there is a very complete study by Dill also in this field, *Roman Society in Gaul in the Merovingian Age* (New York: The Macmillan Company, 1926). This book appears to be slightly misnamed, since it does not exclusively deal with, nor even especially emphasize, the remnants of Roman culture in Gaul, as might be expected. It is, nevertheless, an exhaustive study of Merovingian society, as far as it can be described from the numerous literary sources extant, and there is as yet nothing in English which will supersede it, though in France there has been much study in recent times of the extant nonliterary sources which will in time round out the picture more fully. A competent survey of Anglo-Saxon England, adequate for the general student, will be found in the Pelican book, D. Whitelock, *The Beginnings of English Society* (Harmondsworth, Middlesex: Penguin Books, 1952).

# 15

## The Byzantine and Slavic Worlds

*The Byzantine Empire • Byzantine relations with Eastern Europe: Bulgar and Slav invasions; the Russians • The disputed territories of Eastern Europe: Hungary, Bohemia, and Moravia; Prussia, Poland, and Lithuania*

---

### ► Introductory

The last great successor-state of the Roman Empire, the empire we call Byzantine after the ancient name of its capital Byzantium, survived, as we have seen, the fall of the empire in the West, and for many centuries was the only civilized power in all Europe. The cultural radiation from this center spread not only over the lands in the eastern Mediterranean that had formed part of the old Roman Empire, but also over lands inhabited previously only by barbarians, altogether untouched by any civilizing influences from Rome.

It is still of great importance to us today that the eastern Slavs were converted to Christianity by missionaries from Constantinople, and that they knew their first taste of luxury at the Byzantine court. These peoples were unmoved by papal decrees from Rome, and they lived far beyond the bounds of the Holy Roman Empire. Some Slavs moved west, were absorbed by Western Christianity, and came within the orbit of the emperors of the West; but the vast majority either raided into Southeastern Europe, ultimately settling in the Balkan peninsula within the orbit of Constantinople,

or remained in their own vast steppes in Eastern Europe, defending themselves against Christian knights from the West or Mongol and other invaders from the East. No attempt will be made in this chapter to recount the full history of either the Byzantine Empire or of the numerous Slavic peoples introduced to civilization by it. Only as much will be given as is necessary to provide the essential medieval background for the study of the Slavic peoples in the period after 1500.

### ► The Byzantine Empire

THE SOURCES OF BYZANTINE STRENGTH

#### Economic basis

As we have seen in the previous chapter, the Eastern Roman, or Byzantine Empire survived the fall of the West not so much through the excellence of its rulers as through the fact that it had been able to take control of the most prosperous part of the empire. The fall of the West, which had been deprived of its main economic resources, can almost be considered as a necessary consequence of the recovery of the East.

The totalitarian heritage of the later

empire, the severe taxation, the huge imperial bureaucracy, and the mercenary army were retained in the Eastern Empire. But there were significant differences. Far less money was needed for the defense of its much shorter boundaries, the capital of the empire was also its greatest industrial city and port, and there was a constant flow of trade between this capital and many other large cities in the empire. Most of the best agricultural land of the old empire was in the new, including the granary of Egypt. The East, moreover, was not burdened with the huge estates, virtually exempt from taxation, which had been such a source of weakness in the old empire. The people were highly civilized, with a far smaller admixture of unassimilable barbarians; they were, on the whole, far more enterprising, especially in commerce, than the Romans; and there was no such serious proletarian problem as in the previous capital, since there was far more profitable work to be done. In a word, the new imperial unit was more manageable than the old, and, high though the taxation was, except in periods of external danger it fell upon an economy that could bear it.

It was primarily the strength of its economy that enabled the Eastern Empire to survive—with a brief interlude of Latin occupation—for almost a thousand years; for the inefficiency and extravagance of so many of its rulers and the corruption of its bureaucracy would have ruined a less resilient economy many times over. Yet in spite of intrigues over the succession, numerous foreign wars, rule by dissolute women and incompetent and irresponsible men, the state never went bankrupt in all its history; and several times it was able to produce an effective ruler from most unpromising sources, just when to an outsider it would have seemed that all was lost.

### Administrative system

The Byzantines called themselves Romans (though they wrote the word in the Greek language), but the language and culture were overwhelmingly Greek, with strong Oriental influence. Looked at from a Greek point of view, the Eastern Empire was the restoration of a united Hellenistic monarchy after a three-hundred-year interlude of barbaric Roman occupation. But the Roman rule had also left its influence in the one field in which the Romans had been creative—in law and government. The Byzantine administrative system had been directly inherited from the later post-Diocletian empire, and it did not change its nature. The people of the empire were all equally the subjects of the monarch; they had no rights against him except the protection afforded by the law. He could raise and lower the taxes, his word had the force of law, and he could enforce obedience through his bureaucracy and his army. The cities had only such self-government as the emperor wished to allow them. The backbone of the state was no longer the free municipalities. City magistrates were imperial officials, who collected taxes on the basis of imperial needs. So there was nothing of the Roman Republic or the Augustan principate in the new empire; the system of Diocletian and Constantine prevailed.

The Roman law, with its Stoic admixture and its concept of natural law and equity, remained the law of the Byzantines, as has already been explained. But already, long before the fall of the West, Greek and Oriental thought had been incorporated in it. Under Theodosius, Justinian, Leo III, and the other legal reformers and codifiers, it now became more Christianized, but it was still recognizably Roman law.

In spite of the authoritarianism of the administration, it cannot be said that the peoples of the empire felt themselves to be slaves. The government was neither liked nor disliked. It was a fact to be accepted, and made the best of. Political factions came into existence, satisfying the Greek love of politics. But they were not divided on matters of principle. All accepted the inevitability of the absolutist regime; there were no attempts at revolution, or the restoration of any kind of republic or free institutions. The factions supported rival contenders for the throne, but not the overthrow of the monarchy itself.

For the rest, the Byzantine world, like the Hellenistic world, offered many incentives to enterprise and hard work, either in the imperial service or in commerce and industry. Many fields of activity were left open to the private citizen in this empire so honeycombed with prosperous cities. If one became rich, one paid heavy taxes; but at least, with the surplus, life could be made more pleasant. There were luxuries to be bought, there were innumerable forms of entertainment, new and old, especially horse and chariot racing in the Hippodrome at Constantinople. And, for the pious and those who felt the emptiness of a pleasure-seeking life, there was now the Christian religion, as there had not been in the Hellenistic world.

RELATIONS BETWEEN CHURCH AND STATE

### The position of the patriarch

The chief official in the Church of Constantinople was called the patriarch. He was an imperial nominee, subject to dismissal by the emperor at any time. This fact, however, does not mean that he was totally subservient to the emperor during his term of office.

It would take us too far afield in this survey to go at length into this important question of how it happened that an imperial nominee, the patriarch of Constantinople (later called the Ecumenical, or universal, Patriarch) could obtain such power as he undoubtedly possessed after his appointment. But a few indications must be given, since they are essential for the understanding of the relationship between the Byzantine Empire and the Slavs, who were rarely within the political boundaries of the empire, but came within its cultural and religious sphere of influence—an influence which has had momentous consequences even to the present time.

The emperor, as has been said, could replace a stubborn patriarch with a more pliable official. But if a patriarch thus ousted could keep the support of his clergy and monks, even the most powerful emperor would soon find himself in trouble, for he could not dispense with the services of the clergy for very long. On several occasions in Byzantine history a patriarch who stood up to the emperor commanded greater support, even in the imperial household, than the emperor himself. Such was the case at all stages in Byzantine history. Furthermore, in later centuries the patriarch often was actually in a far stronger position than the emperor, because the patriarch commanded the allegiance of believers outside the empire, whereas the emperor was often hard put to it to maintain his political authority within the boundaries of his supposed empire. He had to fight Turks and other barbarians as well as occasional Westerners, while the spiritual domain of the Ecumenical Patriarch might stretch on the one side far into Russia and on the other beyond the Danube into Central Europe.

The fact that the patriarch, with such a vast territory subject to his spiritual rule, was nevertheless appointed by and subject to dismissal by the emperor entailed some remarkable consequences, especially in the borderlands between the spheres of influence of the Western Church and the Eastern. A monarch who was politically independent of Constantinople would think twice before accepting the Eastern rite, when acceptance must mean that the emperor in Constantinople, who was often his political enemy, could exercise some control upon him through the patriarch. There was always the thought that membership in the Eastern Orthodox Church entailed some degree of political subservience to the emperor.

Yet, on the other hand, if these distant peoples chose to submit in religious matters to Rome instead of to Constantinople, there were other disadvantages of a different kind, not political but religious. The Roman Church insisted on the use of Latin, a language incomprehensible to most of the Slavs, whereas the Orthodox Church not only permitted but encouraged the use of a liturgy in the Slavonic vernaculars. Moreover, by the ninth century, the Orthodox Church differed in a very important dogma (on the "proces-

# ► chronological chart

## The Byzantine Empire

| | | | |
|---|---|---|---|
| Foundation of Constantinople | 330 | Byzantine emperor killed in battle by Bulgarian khan, Krum | 811 |
| Theodosius the Great last emperor of East and West | 379–395 | Krum at the gates of Constantinople | 813 |
| Reign of Justinian | 527–565 | Thirty years' peace with Bulgars signed | 817 |
| *Corpus juris civilis* of Justinian | 533 | End of iconoclastic controversy; image worship restored | 843 |
| Conquest of North Africa | 533–543 | First appearance of Varangians at Constantinople | 860 |
| Conquest of Italy | 535–554 | Mission of Sts. Cyril and Methodius to Slavs | 863–885 |
| Great Persian War | 540–562 | Renewal of wars with Bulgarians | 889 |
| Fifty years' peace with Persia— Justinian to pay tribute | 562 | Reign of Basil II the Bulgar-Killer | 976–1025 |
| Loss of Italian possessions to Lombards (except Rome, Ravenna, and Naples) | 568–571 | Bulgaria incorporated into Byzantine Empire | 1018 |
| Reign of Heraclius | 610–641 | Final schism between Rome and Constantinople | 1054 |
| "Flight" of Mahomet from Mecca to Medina | 622 | Reign of Alexius Comnenus | 1081–1118 |
| Persian Wars of Heraclius | 622–630 | The First Crusade | 1096–1097 |
| Conquest of Syria by Muslims under Khalid | 635–641 | Latin Conquest of Constantinople (Fourth Crusade) | 1204 |
| Conquest of Egypt by Muslims | 639–655 | Latin Kingdom of Constantinople | 1204–1261 |
| Blockade of Constantinople by Muslims | 673–678 | Reconquest of Constantinople by Michael VIII | 1261 |
| Thirty years' peace concluded between Byzantines and Muslims | 678 | Rise of the Ottoman Turks in Asia Minor | 1326 |
| Conquest of Carthage by Muslims | 698 | Serbs under Stephen Dushan at the gates of Constantinople | 1355 |
| Second siege of Constantinople by Muslims | 717–718 | Siege of Constantinople by Turks under Bayazid I | 1391–1397 |
| Reign of Leo III (the Isaurian) | 717–740 | Defeat of Turks by Tamerlane at battle of Angora | 1402 |
| Beginning of the iconoclastic controversy | 726 | Council of Florence—Agreement by Byzantine emperor to religious union with Rome | 1439 |
| Promulgation of *Ecloga* by Leo III | 739 | Siege and Capture of Constantinople by Ottoman Turks | 1453 |
| Conquest of exarchate of Ravenna by Lombards | 751 | Marriage of Ivan III, Grand Duke of Moscow, to Zoë, niece of last emperor of Constantinople—Ivan takes title of Tsar, and adopts Byzantine court ceremonial | 1472 |
| Defeat of Lombards by Pepin the Short, king of the Franks | 754–756 | | |
| Donation of Pepin of Lombard (Byzantine) lands to pope | 756 | | |
| Reign of Charlemagne in the West | 768–814 | | |
| Peace between Byzantines and Charlemagne (Byzantines retaining southern Italy, Venice, and Dalmatia) | 803 | | |

## Bulgaria

| | |
|---|---|
| Movements of Bulgars to the south of the Danube | 650 onward |
| Tervel, Bulgarian khan, advances to gates of Constantinople—Byzantine emperor agrees to pay tribute | 712 |
| Bulgarians subjugated by Byzantines | ca. 775 |
| Battle of Marcellae, defeat of Byzantines by Bulgars, refoundation of Bulgarian state under Kardam | 792 |
| Krum, Bulgar khan, at gates of Constantinople | 813 |
| Foundation of Preslav, Bulgarian capital | 821 |
| Reign of Boris I | 852–888 |
| Conversion of Bulgars to Christianity | 865 |
| Reign of Tsar Symeon—Constant wars with Byzantines | 893–927 |
| Reign of Tsar Peter | 927–969 |
| Raids on Bulgaria by Magyars and Patzinaks | 934–962 |
| Invasion of Bulgaria by Sviatoslav and Russians | 967 |
| Defeat of Russians and Bulgarians by Byzantines—End of Bulgarian Empire | 969–972 |
| Reign of Tsar Samuel | 976–1014 |
| Re-establishment of Bulgarian kingdom | 976–989 |
| Reign of Byzantine emperor Basil II (the Bulgar-Killer) | 976–1025 |
| Battle of Balathista—Defeat and death of Tsar Samuel | 1014 |
| Bulgaria incorporated into Byzantine Empire | 1018 |
| Bulgaria in Byzantine Empire | 1018–1185 |
| Refoundation of Bulgarian kingdom by John and Peter Asen | 1185 |
| Defeat of crusaders (Fourth Crusade) by King Kaloyan, and capture of Latin emperor, Baldwin I | 1205 |
| Peace with Latin kingdom of Constantinople | 1213 |
| Reign of John Asen II | 1218–1241 |
| John proclaims independence of Bulgarian Church | 1232 |
| Ottoman Turks cross into Europe | 1345 |
| Shishman, Bulgarian king, becomes vassal of Turks | 1372 |
| Battle of Kossovo—Bulgarians, with allies, totally defeated by Turks | 1389 |
| Incorporation of Bulgaria into Turkish Empire | 1393 |

## Serbia

| | |
|---|---|
| Conversion of Serbs to Eastern Christianity | end of 10th century |
| Expansion of Serbs at expense of Byzantines | 1280 onward |
| Reign of Stephen Dushan | 1331–1355 |
| Subjection of almost whole Balkan peninsula by Stephen | 1331–1344 |
| Stephen proclaims himself Emperor of Serbs, Greeks, Bulgars, and Albanians | 1346 |
| Death of Stephen en route to Constantinople | 1355 |
| Battle of Kossovo—Defeat of Serbs and allies by Turks—Serbia vassal of Turks | 1389 |
| George Brankevitch, despot of Serbia, escapes vassalage of Turks | 1436–1444 |
| George recognized by Turks as independent | 1444 |
| Turks conquer and incorporate Serbia in empire | 1459 |

## Poland and Lithuania

| | |
|---|---|
| Conversion of Mieszko I of Poland to Christianity | 966 |
| Boleslav I organizes a Polish state | 992–1025 |
| Boleslav becomes king of Poland | 1025 |
| Heathen reaction in Poland and persecution of Christians | 1034–1040 |
| Casimir I restores Christianity | 1054 |
| Teutonic Knights' efforts to convert Lithuanians | 1230 onward |
| Teutonic Knights raid into Poland | 1326–1333 |
| Olgerd, Duke of Lithuania, defeated by Teutonic Knights | 1360 |
| Jadwiga elected queen of Poland | 1384 |
| Marriage of Jadwiga to Jagiello, Duke of Lithuania | 1386 |
| Lithuania converted to Christianity by Jagiello | 1387 onward |
| Lithuania separated from Poland under Grand Duke Witold | 1398 |
| Battle of Tannenberg—Defeat of Teutonic Knights by Jagiello | 1410 |
| Poland and Lithuania again united by Casimir IV of Poland | 1447 |
| Wars against Teutonic Order | 1454–1466 |
| Second Peace of Thorn—Teutonic Order vassal of Polish crown | 1466 |
| Constitution of Radom—National Diet becomes supreme legislature of Poland | 1505 |
| Diet passes laws establishing serfdom in Poland | 1511 |

## Russia

| | |
|---|---|
| Traditional date of rule in Novgorod of Rurik | 860 |
| First recorded appearance of Varangians in Constantinople | 860 |
| Novgorod and Kiev under rule of Prince Oleg | 880–912 |
| Russians (Varangians) extract trade concessions from Constantinople | 911 |
| Conversion of Grand Duchess Olga of Kiev to Christianity | 957 |
| Rule of Sviatoslav as Grand Duke of Kiev | 964–972 |
| Expeditions of Sviatoslav into Byzantine Empire and against Byzantines | 965–971 |
| Reign of Vladimir I as Grand Duke of Kiev | 978–1015 |
| Conversion of Russians to Christianity | 990 |
| Disintegration of Duchy of Kiev, forming especially the territory of Novgorod in north and Grand Duchy of Moscow | 1054 onward |
| Conquest of Kiev by Andrei Boguliubski, prince of central Russia | 1169 |
| Foundation of Livonian Knights | 1202 |
| Teutonic Knights commissioned to conquer Prussia | 1226 |
| Union of Livonian and Teutonic Knights | 1237 |
| Mongol conquest of most of Russia | 1237–1240 |
| Mongol conquest of Kiev | 1240 |
| Defeat of Swedes and others by Alexander Nevski of Novgorod at battle of the Neva | 1240 |
| Defeat of Teutonic Knights at battle of Lake Peipus by Alexander Nevski | 1242 |
| Ivan I Grand Duke of Moscow (vassal of Mongols) | 1325–1341 |
| Battle of Kulikovo—Defeat of Mongols by Russians | 1380 |
| Ivan III, the Great, Grand Duke of Moscow | 1462–1505 |
| Conquest of Novgorod by Ivan III | 1470 |
| Marriage of Ivan to Zoë, niece of last emperor of Constantinople | 1472 |
| Incorporation of territory of Novgorod and dissolution of the Hansa in Novgorod | 1494 |
| Expansion of Russians into Lithuania and incorporation of some Lithuanian territories | 1503 |
| Ivan IV, the Terrible, becomes Tsar of Russia | 1547 |

## Croatia

| | |
|---|---|
| Croats under Frankish domination from | 9th century |
| Tomislav becomes king of Croatia, accepting crown from pope | 924 |
| King Peter defeated by Ladislas I of Hungary | 1091 |
| Croatia and Hungary in dynastic union | 1102 |

## Hungary, Bohemia, and Moravia

| | |
|---|---|
| Hungarians raid into Europe | end of 9th century |
| Gradual conversion of Hungarians to Eastern and Western Christianity | 972–997 |
| St. Stephen I crowned king of Hungary with crown sent by pope —Forcible conversion to Roman Catholicism | 1001 |
| Conquest of Croatia and Bosnia by St. Ladislas I | 1091 |
| Invasion of Hungary by Mongols | 1241 |
| End of native (Arpad) Hungarian dynasty (thereafter kings were mostly foreign potentates) | 1301–1308 |
| Sigismund king of Hungary (Luxembourg House) | 1387–1437 |
| John Hunyadi (frontier lord in Hungary) defeats Turks | 1437 |
| Hunyadi leads crusade against Turks | 1456 |
| Reign of Mathias Corvinus, son of Hunyadi | 1458–1490 |
| Mathias king of Bohemia as well as Hungary | 1470 |
| Turks advance into Hungary | 1521 |
| Battle of Mohacs—Defeat of Hungarians and allies by Turks | 1526 |
| Most of Hungary vassal state of Turks | 1540 onward |

## Mongols

| | |
|---|---|
| Reign of Jenghiz Khan | 1206–1227 |
| Reign of Ogodai Khan | 1229–1241 |
| Reign of Batu Khan | 1242–1255 |
| Reign of Kublai Khan | 1260–1294 |

sion of the Holy Spirit") from the Western Church, and the clergy from the West were very stubborn in their insistence upon the correctness of the Western interpretation—sanctified, of course, by the authority of the incumbent of the Chair of Peter.[1]

Furthermore, the Patriarch of Constantinople, whatever his pretensions to the designation Ecumenical, was always theoretically subject to the spiritual leadership of the successor of Peter, the pope in Rome. But at the same time these very popes acknowledged the theoretical overlordship of the emperor as the true heir of Constantine, in matters not concerned with religion, even though the emperor seldom had much effective power in Italy, and never in Rome itself. This relationship was more convenient for the pope than for the emperor since the latter, after the time of Justinian (sixth century), was not interested in exercising any rights over the pope, while the pope frequently called upon the emperor for military assistance against his enemies the Lombards (and was, as frequently, refused). But when, in the ninth century, a western European outpost of Slavs petitioned the emperor to send missionaries to convert them to Chris-

tianity, and the emperor duly obliged by sending them St. Cyril and St. Methodius, the pope (Nicholas I) decided that the new Moravian converts should belong to the Western Church, though he allowed them, at first, to use a Slavonic liturgy. The emperor gracefully accepted the decision, but his clergy were not so happy about it, since the territory was lost from their jurisdiction, while the emperor had never hoped to add such a distant land as Moravia to his empire. On the other hand, when, for political and economic reasons, as well as religious, an earlier emperor, Leo III (717–740), and his successors forbade the use of images in churches (the iconoclastic controversy, dealt with in more detail below, page 459) and a series of popes defied them, the emperors refused to accept papal dictation, and the patriarchs were forced to obey their immediate masters in Constantinople rather than their spiritual superiors in Rome.

In the last centuries of the Byzantine Empire the Orthodox Church was often more powerful than the emperors. The Church continually interfered with the imperial policy of maintaining correct relations, as far as possible, with the papacy. The final split in 1054 between the Orthodox Church and the papacy, ostensibly over the theological question of the procession of the Holy Spirit (whether the Holy Spirit descended from the Father or from the Father and the Son), was deliberately provoked by the Patriarch Michael, in spite of the fact that the emperor had a political alliance with the papacy at the time which he was anxious to preserve. The emperor found himself unable to discipline his recalcitrant official, who was supported by the clergy and people, who were fanatically anti-Western and anti-papal.

A patriarch excommunicated an emperor in 1262 for blinding a defeated enemy. The emperor deposed him, but the patriarch, who was living safely in a fortified monastery some distance from the capital, refused to consider himself deposed, even though the emperor appointed a successor to him in Constantinople. Even in the last century of the empire, when it was in mortal danger

---

[1] Illustrative of the difficulties involved in conversion is the case of the Bulgarian khan, Boris I (853–888), who was too close to Constantinople for comfort, and would have preferred, on political grounds, to accept the overlordship of the distant pope, which carried with it no stigma of political servitude, and would have permitted him to carry out inroads on the Byzantine Empire without fear of spiritual reprisals. But, on religious grounds, both he and his people preferred the Eastern rite and the Eastern dogma. He switched allegiance several times, and was given the free right to choose by the Byzantine emperor, Basil I, who was evidently fairly sure of the khan's final choice, and confident that the Western clergy would overreach themselves. As the emperor had foreseen, the Western clergy made a sufficient nuisance of themselves by insisting on the Latin Liturgy and on their own version of the procession of the Holy Spirit, so that the Bulgarian khan at last threw in his lot with the emperor and patriarch even though he was aware that this gave the emperor the opportunity to intervene in Bulgarian affairs. The position became so intolerable to the Bulgarians that the younger son of Boris, Symeon, who had originally been a monk in Constantinople, made a serious effort to obtain the imperial crown for himself, at least, in part, for the satisfaction of appointing his own patriarch.

*The monastery of Mt. Athos occupies a commanding site. From close up it is very similar to the monastery of Monte Cassino shown in Chapter 13.* (COURTESY ROYAL GREEK EMBASSY)

from the Ottoman Turks, the Orthodox clergy refused to recognize the union with the papacy which had been contrived by the diplomacy of the emperor in the hopes of obtaining aid from the West.

When at last Constantinople fell to the Turks in 1453 the Orthodox Church and its clergy survived. The Turks adopted a tolerant policy toward the Christians, and believed they could make use of the clerical hierarchy. They made the Christian patriarch the official leader of all Christians in the Turkish dominions, with all minor patriarchs in the East subordinate to him. He had at last become an "Ecumenical" Patriarch, and the patriarchate had survived the empire itself.

### The nature of the Byzantine religion

The strength of the Byzantine religion, however, did not depend on the nature of Church government in the empire, as is seen by the continued creativity of Byzantine religious art, and even to some degree in the endless theological controversies in which the Greeks took a passionate interest. Byzantine religion was always more mystical, less formal and rational, than in the West, and thus less dependent upon the quality of its priesthood. The gorgeous ceremonies and rituals performed in the Byzantine churches, with their magnificent interiors, ablaze with light and rich with incense, were the heart of the Byzantine religion, as was the extreme veneration of holy pictures, and icons, which had tempted the iconoclastic emperors to suppress their use for a time (see page 459). Finally, those who wished for a deeper religious life and revolted against the materialism and pleasure seeking of the Byzantine world could always go into the monasteries, especially the great religious center of Mt. Athos, which were less orderly and more ascetic than those of the West, with less emphasis on community living, but at least as much devoted in their prime to earnest pursuit of the spiritual life.

## THE REIGN OF JUSTINIAN (527–565)

### Conquests—Africa, Spain, Italy

Until the sixth century the Roman influence was strong and the Latin language was still known. But after the long reign of Justinian, with the loss of contact with Italy and strained relations with the papacy, this influence quickly disappeared; soon even the law code of Justinian had to be translated into Greek. The reign of Justinian is notable for the last effort, by a Roman of Illyrian descent, to re-establish the old Roman Empire as a totality. He came to the throne in 527, after having already been the power behind his uncle's throne for some years previously, and reigned till 565. Justinian was a man of great energy combined with an interest in giving close attention to detail, thoroughly imbued with the imperial spirit of the later Roman Empire, but with no real grasp of the problems of his time. He was immensely successful in his own lifetime but he left a heritage to his successors which was disastrous for his empire and might well have wrecked it altogether.

His conquest of North Africa, Italy, and part of Spain has already been noticed. The Spanish province was quickly retaken even by the enfeebled Visigoths; most of Italy, weakened by the destruction of the Ostrogoths and impossible for the successors of Justinian to defend, fell a prey to the Lombards; and though Africa survived for a while, it collapsed at the Muslim assault in the next century almost without a struggle.

### Persian and Balkan policy

But the cost to the Eastern Empire of these expeditions can hardly be calculated. Not only were the taxes increased in the worst later Roman manner, to the point where distress became widespread, in spite of commercial and industrial prosperity, but Justinian was forced to weaken the defense of his eastern frontiers and even give large donations to the newly vitalized Persian Empire to stave off invasion. Moreover, remnants from the Hunnish invasions and numerous Slav peoples, who had hitherto been held back by more warlike groups of barbarians, began to approach and threaten his northern boundaries.

Justinian, indeed, perceived this danger. He built a considerable number of forts to defend the Balkans, but these ultimately proved useless when inadequately defended by troops. He invited barbarian chiefs to his Oriental court at Constantinople, impressing them with his splendor and giving them sumptuous gifts. He tried all the arts of diplomacy—and in Greek hands these were not inconsiderable—to foster dissension among the various tribes. But it is questionable whether these were as effective as an army, and there is no doubt that the barbarians, while accepting his hospitality, were hardly too simple to perceive that these riches could also be enjoyed through conquest. If Justinian had not been so obsessed with his Roman dream he would have seen that his eastern hinterland and the Danube frontier were far more vital to his empire than anything the West could offer. Indeed, if there had been any attempt by his successors to defend his conquests, nothing could have saved even Constantinople itself in the seventh century.

### Administrative and legal reforms, economic policy

However questionable Justinian's military policy may have been, his administrative capacity is undoubted. We have already mentioned in Chapter 12 ("General Charac-

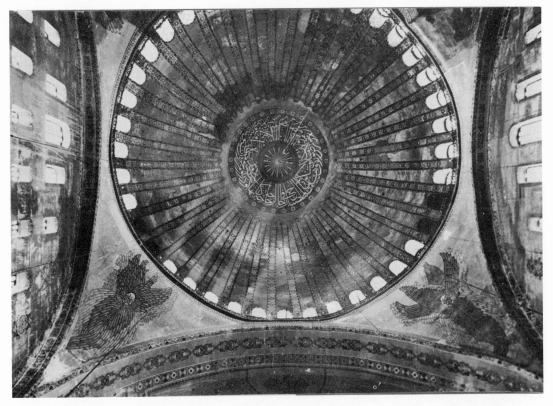

*Summit of the dome of the Church of the Holy Wisdom in Constantinople (See also picture of the Church facing page 412).* (COURTESY TURKISH INFORMATION OFFICE)

teristics of Roman Culture") his great codification of the Roman law, always associated with his name. He also pruned the imperial bureaucracy for greater efficiency in tax collecting at less expense, he fixed regular salaries for all his officials, and inaugurated a more regular method of recruiting them. He established state industrial monopolies in various luxury goods, including silk, the secret of which was stolen from the Chinese during his reign. The mulberry trees necessary for the cultivation of silkworms were planted on an imperial estate. Justinian also issued new and effective regulations for traders in the great cities of his empire. All these measures contributed to the absolute power of the emperor, and all survived his reign, forming the basis of the Byzantine administrative system which survived so many dangers in the following centuries substantially unimpaired.

## Religious and cultural policy—Consequences

In his dealings with the Church, Justinian was equally autocratic. He refused to accept the claims of the pope to spiritual supremacy, and he insisted on dictating Church policies, and even giving decisions on theological questions wherever his power extended. His concern for the right opinions of his subjects was reinforced by a measure that none of his predecessors had considered necessary. He closed the last pagan center of learning, the School of Athens, which had been continuously in existence since the time of Plato and Aristotle, where the classical philosophies were still taught and where commentaries on Aristotle, which later medieval Christian scholars found of the utmost value, were still being written. Simplicius, one of the best of the Aristotelian

*Main façade of the Byzantine Church of St. Marks in Venice.* (COURTESY ITALIAN STATE TOURIST OFFICE)

commentators, and his companions were warmly welcomed, however, by the king of Persia, who gave them a home, as his predecessors had given a home to philosophical heretics driven out in earlier years. But philosophy apparently was a hothouse growth in Persia, and the exiles were not happy, preferring even silence in their own land. Yet the Persian efforts nevertheless bore a surprising fruit in later years; for the Muslims, coming upon the Persian academy of Gondisapur, founded by the distinguished Persian emperor Sapur I, were fired by enthusiasm for the Greek philosophy and science, especially medicine, taught there. So by devious routes, through Avicenna and Averroës and numerous other scholars, the

works of Aristotle came to the West through Syriac, Arabic, and sometimes Hebrew versions until they became absorbed in medieval scholasticism.

Justinian also spent enormous fortunes on his capital of Constantinople, building the great church of the Holy Wisdom (Hagia Sophia) in a new style of architecture, owing much to Roman experience but incorporating new designs perfected by two architects of genius who discovered how to rest a round dome gracefully on a square opening. This great church, the largest in Christendom, became the model for what is known as the Byzantine style in architecture, examples of which are to be found throughout Eastern Europe from Venice to Moscow.

## THE DISASTROUS LEGACY OF JUSTINIAN

### Loss of western provinces

By permitting his finance minister to use every unscrupulous device he could discover for gaining new sources of income, as well as by really improving the system of tax collection, Justinian managed to survive these unprecedented expenses without bankruptcy; and though at his death its treasury was empty, the Eastern Empire had enough resilience to make a partial recovery which carried it through the next forty years. Yet the country was too poor and too greatly weakened in the face of new threats to be able to make any effort to defend the western provinces so recently won at such cost. The decision not to accede to the desperate requests of Gregory the Great and other Italian emissaries was undoubtedly a wise one, even though, as we have seen, it forced Gregory to make his own terms with the invading Lombards, and made the papacy from this time on virtually independent of its imperial overlord in Constantinople.

### Wars with Persia and the Avars— Heraclius (610–641)

Justinian had kept the Persians quiet by his gifts, but these were discontinued by his successors. The Persians, taking advantage of the murder of an emperor and a disputed succession, invaded the richest territories of the empire, and within a few years the Avars swept over the Danube, Illyria, and the Balkans. The Persians made light of such imperial armies as attempted to defend the eastern provinces, conquered Syria, invaded Egypt, and marched almost to the gates of Constantinople, shearing from the empire almost the whole of its Asiatic hinterland on which it was dependent. To make matters almost hopeless for Constantinople, the Persian emperor Chosroes made a treaty with the Avars which would enable him to put Constantinople under fire from two sides. The Byzantine emperor Heraclius (610–641), who had previously been governor of Africa and who had seized the throne of Constantinople from another usurper, tried vainly to stem the double attacks, while he feverishly attempted from what remained to him to build up new resources for the defense. At last, when the Avars were almost at the gates of Constantinople, and the Persians were across the Bosporus at Chalcedon, Heraclius gave up hope, and determined to return to the safer refuge of Africa.

At this juncture, the patriarch, a militant priest named Sergius, undertook to breathe new life into his master. With a combination of threats and pious exhortations he shamed Heraclius into remaining, and together they prepared to put Constantinople into a condition to withstand the inevitable siege. When the city was strong enough, Heraclius himself left by sea to take the Persians in the rear, while Sergius superintended the defense of the city against the Avars. The maneuver was successful. The Persian emperor had to turn back to face his unexpected assailant, and Heraclius, after inflicting several defeats upon him, marched into the interior of Persia and succeeded in capturing the capital, Ctesiphon. The war between the two fairly evenly matched adversaries went on for years, exhausting both parties equally. The new empire of Chosroes was ruined, at enormous cost not only to himself but to the Byzantines. The story is told that Chosroes, encamped by the banks of a river, received a letter from an unknown Arab named Mahomet, commanding him to acknowledge that there was only one God, whose name was Allah and whose prophet was Mahomet himself. The emperor is said to have torn up the letter and thrown it into the river. When Mahomet heard of it, he prophesied that "thus God would tear the kingdom and reject the prayers of Chosroes." At all events, this incident (ca. 628) was shortly to be followed by an invasion of Persia by the followers of Mahomet, though Chosroes himself was not alive to endure it. His name is held in abhorrence by all pious Muslims for his blasphemous act in rejecting the appeal from the Prophet.

At last Heraclius defeated the Persians

*Most Byzantine icons were destroyed during the iconoclastic controversy by order of the emperors. This picture shows a fifteenth-century Russian icon, with Christ enthroned. Painted in oil on wood, these pictures received a reverence from pious worshipers that the Byzantine emperors claimed was close to idolatry.* (COURTESY THE METROPOLITAN MUSEUM OF ART)

and made a treaty which restored all the imperial territories so recently wrested from the empire. Returning to Constantinople he found that the Avars likewise had been driven back by the efforts of Patriarch Sergius. The Byzantine Empire had been given a new lease of life, but at appalling cost. The Avars, an Asiatic people akin to the Turks, and the Slavs who had followed in their wake, had occupied the Balkans and had overrun Illyria, the home of so many great Roman and Byzantine emperors, from which they would never again be dislodged. In the southeast, Mahomet and his successors were gathering their strength for a new assault on the empire. All that remained to Heraclius were the seacoasts of Greece, Macedonia, and the Adriatic, together with the few remaining territories reconquered less than a century before by Justinian. The Danube frontier was lost; and though the land around Constantinople and the heartland of the empire in Asia Minor (Anatolia) remained,

they did not have time to recover from the ravages of the wars before the Muslims fell upon them.

The first attacks by the Muslims were carried out by sea, after Syria and Palestine, together with important islands in the Mediterranean and the Aegean, had fallen to them. Year after year the Muslims returned to the attack, but Constantinople proved impregnable. The Byzantines used "Greek fire," some unknown explosive compound, with devastating effect. In 677, the Muslims gave up the attempt until after they had conquered Asia Minor. In 717, when this conquest had been completed, they attacked Constantinople by land on the European side, and by sea. But again they were unsuccessful, the defense being carried out by one of the greatest of the Byzantine emperors, Leo III, the Isaurian, who at last drove the Muslims back to the line of the Taurus Mountains in southeast Asia Minor. It was the last great effort of the Muslims until the inroads of the Turks in the eleventh century, and by that time the West was able to lend aid to save the empire (the First Crusade).

## THE REIGN OF LEO III (717–740)

### The restoration of the empire

The work of Leo III has sometimes been regarded as a second foundation of the empire. The policy of Justinian had been abandoned, once and for all. There would be no further expansion into the West, and much of what had formerly belonged to the Byzantine Empire was lost to the Muslims forever. Most of the Christians in this part of the world had embraced Islam, and the minor patriarchs in the Muslim Empire only continued to exist by the permission of the rulers of Islam. But the lands now controlled by Leo the Isaurian were compact and manageable, and an economic base for an empire, even if the empire was perforce much smaller than before, still existed. Constantinople recovered her prosperity under the reigns of Leo and his son, who between them ruled over fifty years, the tax system was reformed from top to bottom, and the army was put on a new basis stressing military efficiency and permanent professional service. A new revised law code (the *Ecloga*) was promulgated, a more humane and Christian code than that of Justinian, which remained the dominant law code in the empire, with minor revisions, until its final destruction.

### The iconoclastic controversy

Brief reference has already been made to an action of fundamental importance in the relations between the Eastern and Western Churches, the condemnation of images by the Byzantine emperors, an action known as iconoclasm. The first prohibition of images was made by the emperor Leo III in 725. Until this time images and icons, as well as naturalistic representations of Christ, had been very popular in Constantinople, and numerous monks had made their living by manufacturing them. Leo claimed that this practice was gross superstition, a survival of ancient pagan practices, and equivalent to idol worship. In this stand he was probably supported by most Greek theologians, who objected to any representation of the divine in human form, and it is probable that the Muslims and Jews, who both forbade the use of "graven images," had influenced the emperor against icons. (Leo was not himself a Greek, but a Syrian.) Nevertheless there was naturally a great outcry from the monks who made their living out of the images, and the people who used them no doubt gave little support to the emperor's policy. Leo retorted that the monks were idle and should be busy cultivating the land, and he did not mind at all if the monasteries were closed and their inhabitants turned to more useful occupation. His soldiers were then instructed to break all the images they could find.

The pope, who was the theoretical leader of the whole Christian Church, defended the use of images, claiming that they were aids to true devotion, but was unable to deflect the emperor from his policy, a fact which deeply embittered relations between Rome and Constantinople. Leo's successors for more than a century, with one exception, the empress Irene, continued the edicts against the images (the Iconoclastic Emperors), and councils were called in Constantinople to support the edicts. Several of the emperors, realizing that the chief opposition centered in the monasteries, persecuted the monks and closed the monasteries. During this period the popes had as few dealings as they could with Constantinople, calling in the Franks, as we shall see, to protect them against the reviving Lombards in the middle of the eighth century.[2] The struggle was brought to an end at last in 843, when the regent Theodora of Constantinople called another council which restored the use of images. Iconoclasm was dead, and the monks had triumphed. But even so there were no more sculptured icons in the Byzantine Em-

[2] It is curious, however, to note that the idea of imperial overlordship over the West was still so strong, even during the Iconoclastic Controversy, that Pope Stephen II did first appeal to Constantinople, and its "super-iconoclast" Constantine V, for help against the Lombards, though he must have been relieved at the failure of his efforts.

pire; flat images took their place. By this time Charlemagne had been crowned emperor in the West (800); there has always been doubt if the pope would have dared to defy Constantinople by crowning an emperor in the West if there had not been a long heritage of strife between popes and eastern emperors during the Iconoclastic Controversy.

## ▶ Byzantine relations with Eastern Europe

### BULGAR AND SLAV INVASIONS

The last chapter described at some length the invasions of the barbarians who delivered the *coup de grâce* to the old Roman Empire; the later invasions of Northmen and Magyars will be dealt with in Chapter 17. Mention now needs to be made of another great people who followed behind these warlike spearheads, and who inherited many of the lands vacated by those who finally settled in the empire. The origin of the Slavs is still not known, nor is it known for certain when they settled in Europe east of the Elbe. By the sixth century A.D. the most westerly groups of Slavs were already in that part of eastern Germany later known as Bohemia and Moravia. They had not yet been converted to Christianity. Unlike the bulk of their contemporaries, they seem to have been a peaceful people who possessed no political unity and were content to work for whatever masters dominated the lands they inhabited. Forced by pressure of Asiatic nomads, Slavs were also infiltrating into the Balkan peninsula, again settling there peacefully until the nomad warriors caught up with them and on some occasions forced them into open hostilities with the Byzantine Empire. Nevertheless, it was the Slavic culture and language that survived, an impressive demonstration of the formidable superiority of endurance over mere militancy. The Avars swept into the Balkans and were absorbed, while those offshoots from the Avars who remained north of the Balkans were defeated by Charlemagne (see Chapter 17) and disappeared from history. The

Bulgars from Western Asia, originally a people akin to the Turks and with a Turki language, made fierce inroads into the Balkans also, and became serious competitors of Constantinople itself, which they almost captured on several occasions; but though they gave their name to a country which still exists today, their culture and language became entirely Slavic, and today, despite their origin, the Bulgars are a Slavic people. And though Rurik, a Viking Swede, founded the state of Russia in the ninth century, the sea of Slavs again absorbed the handful of Swedes, and Russians today also are Slavs.

The Byzantine Empire was in no position before the end of the tenth century to resist this penetration into the Balkans had it wished to do so. The European hinterland of the empire became Slavic to the Adriatic Sea. The Slavs learned from Constantinople the arts of civilization, and the powerful radiation from Constantinople so attracted them that almost all the eastern Slavs joined the Byzantines and their patriarch in the escape from papal discipline in the eleventh century. And, in the end, with their Byzantine teachers, the eastern Slavs fell to the Ottoman Turks, from whose domination they escaped only in the nineteenth and twentieth centuries. A brief summary of the medieval history of these Slavic peoples will serve to remind the student that Serbs and Bulgars as well as Greeks have roots as nations in the distant past, and that they did not spring full-grown from the decaying body of the Ottoman Empire in the nineteenth century.

### THE CONVERSION OF THE SLAVS TO CHRISTIANITY

A brief mention should be made at this point about the conversion of the western Slavs to Christianity. About 862 Rostislav, Prince of Moravia, asked that missionaries be sent to his country to instruct his people in Christianity. It may be supposed that the decision was not taken suddenly. The Slavs in Central Europe had been in contact with Christianity on their western boundaries for a considerable time, and the German clergy

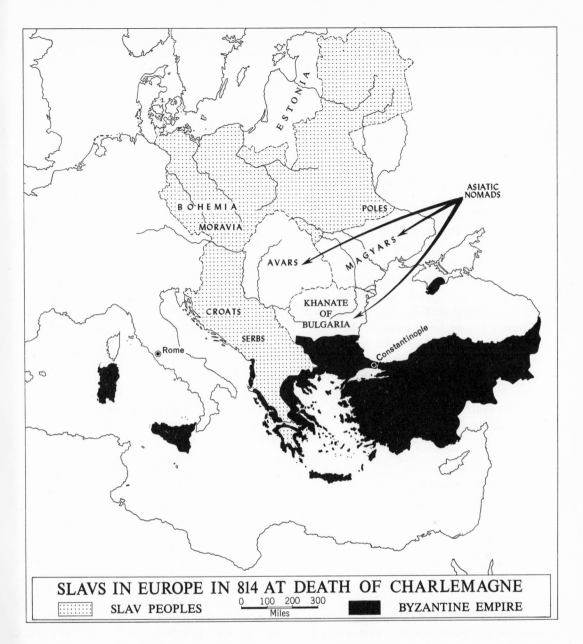

# SLAVS IN EUROPE IN 814 AT DEATH OF CHARLEMAGNE

| :::::: | SLAV PEOPLES | 0 100 200 300 Miles | ■ | BYZANTINE EMPIRE |

had been making efforts to convert them, at least since the reign of Charlemagne (768–814). But the Moravians could not resist all blandishments from the Christians indefinitely, and it must have seemed safer to Rostislav to receive instruction from distant Constantinople rather than from the comparatively local German clergy. The Byzantines took the request seriously, and two missionaries, St. Cyril and St. Methodius, set out, bearing with them a new Slavonic alphabet (called Cyrillic after St. Cyril, though probably it was not his own inven-

tion) based on the Greek letters, into which the Bible and the Byzantine Liturgy could be translated for the use of the Slavs, who had not yet a written language. The mission was successful, but it naturally aroused the opposition of the German clergy, who complained to Rome. The two saints were summoned to Rome by the reigning pope, Nicholas I, who had already successfully asserted his authority over Constantinople.

They were received graciously by the pontiff, but both Nicholas and his successors insisted that the new Christian principalities

461

(the Moravian, Bohemian, and Slovak tribes of the Slavs) must be subject to the German clergy and, of course, to the papacy; but the converts were permitted the use of the Slavonic Liturgy, which was provided in the following years by Methodius. This privilege, however, was withdrawn in 885 at the insistence of the German clergy, and the Slavs thereafter were forced to use the Latin tongue for their services. The Slavonic clergy, who had been ministering to the needs of the converts for more than twenty years, were allowed to go to Bulgaria by courtesy of the Byzantine emperor, and the Slavonic Liturgy, devised for the use of the western Slavs, was introduced to the eastern Slavs, who were not yet converted to Christianity, and was no doubt a potent instrument in their conversion. The western Slavic Churches, thus rudely thrust into the bosom of the West, remained under papal rule in later centuries and to this day, even after the division of the Eastern and Western Churches in the eleventh century.

RISE OF BULGARIA

### Conversion of Bulgars

Meanwhile the Bulgar khan, Boris I (853–888), also desired that his people be converted to Christianity, but he, for reasons already suggested (see note 1 on page 452 above), preferred to take his instructions from distant Rome. But the pressure of geography was too great for him, and his people ultimately became subject in religious matters to the patriarch at Constantinople, though at times the Bulgarian Church was virtually independent. At first the Bulgars had to use the Greek Liturgy of Constantinople, though, as has been seen, after 885 they were permitted to use the Slavonic tongue, which by this time had become the vernacular of the whole Bulgarian people, including the non-Slavic ruling class.

### First wars with Constantinople

When Boris abdicated and went into a monastery (888), to be succeeded by his two sons in turn, the Bulgars reversed his policy of peace with the Byzantine Empire, and made a serious effort to conquer the whole of the empire in Europe, including Constantinople. Symeon, the younger son of Boris (893–927), who in the last years of his reign proclaimed himself to be Tsar (Slavonic form of "Caesar") and not a mere khan, ravaged the peninsula with a formidable army right up to the gates of the great city; and toward the end of his reign he attempted to secure the succession of the empire for himself by marrying his daughter to the reigning emperor. But in the end his policies collapsed, he lost to barbarian nomads lands held across the Danube (part of modern Rumania), while the Serbs, another Slavic people to the west, and the Croats, yet another Slavic people to the northwest, resisted continuously, backed by Constantinople. Symeon's empire collapsed before it had been properly consolidated into a unity, though his reign marked the golden age of old Slavonic literature, and the Tsar encouraged the translation of many Greek works into Slavonic. After his death Bulgaria remained politically independent, but the immediate dream of being the successor in Europe of Constantinople was over.

### Incorporation of Bulgaria into Byzantine Empire—Basil the Bulgar–Killer (Basil II, 976–1025)

The war was resumed before the death of Symeon's son Peter (927–969). On this occasion the Byzantine emperor invited the pagan Russians under Sviatoslav to discipline the Bulgars, but Sviatoslav proved unmanageable. He destroyed the Bulgarian Empire altogether, but then turned on Constantinople. The Byzantine emperor John I at last defeated him in 972 and assumed the Bulgarian throne. But soon afterward the Bulgar remnants in western Bulgaria discovered a leader (Tsar Samuel, 976–1014) and returned to the attack. The result was a devastating war which lasted for forty-three years, during which countless atrocities were committed, and a large part of the population of both empires, including the best troops of the Byzantines recruited in Anatolia, were killed.

The Byzantine emperor who conducted this war to the death gained the honorific title of Basil the Bulgar-Killer from his successes, and after the war was over he gave a mild peace to the survivors. For a time the Byzantines ruled triumphantly from the Euphrates to the Adriatic, and included parts of Italy under their sway. But within fifty years the Seljuk Turks began moving into Anatolia, disastrously defeating a motley imperial army at Manzikert (1071), and the oppressed subjects of Constantinople began to convert en masse to Islam and to the less oppressive Turks.

### Restoration of the Bulgarian kingdom

In 1186 the Bulgars rose again under a new dynasty, and the Byzantines, fully oc-cupied elsewhere, were unable to prevent the restoration of the kingdom. When the Latin crusaders took Constantinople in 1204 (see Chapter 18), the Bulgars at once conquered almost the whole Balkan peninsula except Greece from the crusaders. But again the Bulgars were unable to hold their possessions for long. In the early fourteenth century they were subdued, first by their fellow Slavs, the Serbs, to the west, and then by the Ottoman Turks at the decisive battle of Kossovo in 1389, which extinguished the independence of all the Slavs in the peninsula until the nineteenth century.

### SERBIA AND CROATIA

Brief mention has already been made of Serbia. This Slavic country in the north-

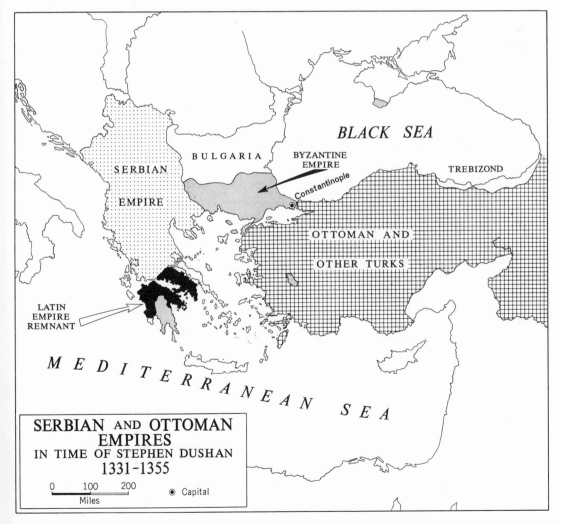

BLACK SEA

BULGARIA

SERBIAN

EMPIRE

BYZANTINE
EMPIRE

TREBIZOND

Constantinople

OTTOMAN AND

OTHER TURKS

LATIN
EMPIRE
REMNANT

MEDITERRANEAN SEA

SERBIAN AND OTTOMAN
EMPIRES
IN TIME OF STEPHEN DUSHAN
1331-1355

0    100    200
⎯⎯⎯⎯⎯⎯
Miles

◉ Capital

western part of the Balkan peninsula was converted, like Bulgaria, to Orthodox Christianity in the ninth century. In the twelfth and early thirteenth centuries the various Serbian princes united under a monarch, and the kingdom, free of foreign control, was ruled by the descendants of Stephen Nemanja for two centuries. In the fourteenth century, when the Greek empire of Constantinople had been restored (see Chapter 18) after the Latin interlude, the Serbian king, Stephen Dushan (1331–1355), made a bid for the control of the whole Balkan peninsula once more. But he, like so many of his predecessors, was unable to capture Constantinople, and shortly after his death his great kingdom, which extended from the Danube to the Gulf of Corinth, began to fall apart. The Serbians joined in the battle of Kossovo in 1389 against the Ottoman Turks, and their king, Stephen Lazar, whose defeat and death are celebrated in so many Serbian poems, was killed. Nominal independence was permitted to the Serbian kings for another seventy years until the country was finally incorporated into the Turkish dominions in 1459. The patriotic Serbs today, a militant people still, the majority group in Yugoslavia, have not ceased to remember their few days of glory under the heroic Stephen Dushan.

The Croatian Slavs to the north of Serbia were converted to Christianity in the ninth century, but, unlike the Serbs, from the beginning they accepted the leadership and authority of the Roman Church. After a short period of independence Croatia was conquered by the Magyars from Hungary (1091), though permitted to retain some measure of local autonomy under the Hungarian crown. The Ottoman Turks absorbed Croatia, as well as most of Hungary, in 1526, but never fully subdued it. When Hungary escaped the Turkish yoke, Croatia escaped too. Thereafter the fortunes of this Slavic people were bound up with those of Hungary until Croatia became part of the new south Slavic kingdom (Yugo-Slavia) in 1918. The Croatians, owing to their allegiance to the Roman Church and their long-standing con-

nection with the West through rule by Hungary (later Austria-Hungary) have always considered themselves superior to the Serbs and other south Slavs, and the feeling is reciprocated by the latter. The medieval schism between these Slavic peoples has still not been healed today in spite of the existence of the state of Yugoslavia.[3]

### THE RUSSIANS

#### Conversion to Christianity

The vast bulk of the Slavic peoples are Russians. As has already been noted, the Russians obtained their name from the Swedish Vikings,[4] those Varangians (dealt with also briefly in Chapter 21) who settled in western Russia, first at Novgorod, and then at Kiev. The descendants of Rurik, the Viking captor of the old Slavic port of Novgorod, became grand dukes of Kiev, extending their power eastward over most of the Russian plain. By the early tenth century these Russians, who were by this time completely a Slavic people, had not yet been converted to Christianity. However, the Grand Duchess Olga of Kiev, mother of the formidable Sviatoslav, for whom she was regent for many years, was formally converted in a great ceremony at Constantinople about 957.[5] On her return to Kiev she seems to have tried to convert her people (for which act she was later honored with canonization as a saint), but was unsuccessful, perhaps because of the necessary political as well as religious connection with Constantinople that would have followed. Sviatoslav thus made his fierce inroads into the Balkans as a pagan, and even Olga's grandson Vladimir I (St. Vladimir) spent his early years as duke fervently trying to restore fully the old pagan religion with its blood sacrifices.

---

[3] Present-day Yugoslavia of course includes also the Roman Catholic Slovenes, but as Slovenia was never an independent state, its history has not been included in this chapter.

[4] The name "Russian" is believed to come from "Ruotsi," the Finnish word for Swedes.

[5] Constantinople conferred upon the duchess the title of "archon-ess," thus, as Gibbon puts it, "Whimsically borrowing the title of an Athenian magistrate with a female termination, which would have astonished the ear of Demosthenes."

RUSSIA BEFORE
MONGOL INVASIONS
ABOUT 1200

But either because of the efforts of the Greek missionaries in Russia, or because he wished to marry a Greek princess for the prestige the alliance would give him and for the sake of improved trade relations with Constantinople, Vladimir allowed himself at last to be converted, and, with as much fervor as he had hitherto supported them, proceeded to make a public destruction of the images of the old gods. The Russians were obdurate and it was a long time before all Vladimir's subjects were duly baptized; but from their conversion onward they were the most faithful and orthodox of Christians. Kiev and Novgorod became cities of churches, especially Kiev, which for a time became second only to Constantinople as a great and prosperous city in the whole of Europe. Furs, honey, hides, wax, and slaves were the principal articles exported. But from its commanding position on the Dnieper, Kiev was also a port of transit and transshipment for goods destined from Scandinavia to Constantinople, thus altogether by-passing feudal Europe. In the middle of the twelfth century the rule of the grand duchy of Kiev was at its height. Then, in the early thirteenth century it was all destroyed, and Kiev was a

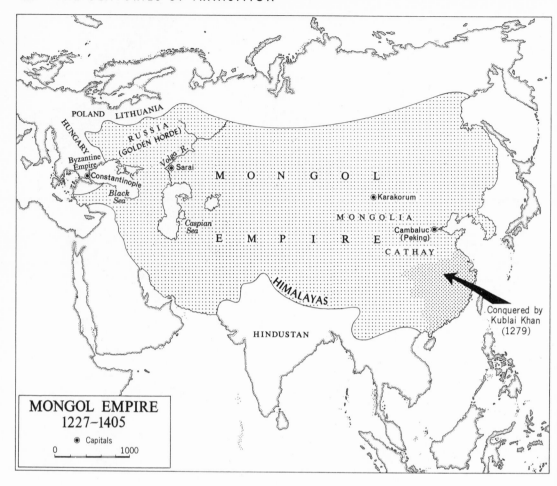

MONGOL EMPIRE
1227–1405

◉ Capitals

0 _____ 1000

blazing ruin; and the whole of Russia was cast back into a barbarism which prevented the country, for all its large and diligent population, from taking its place until recent times with the nations of Europe.

### The Mongol invasions

The fall of Kiev was the result of the invasion of the Mongols (or Tatars). Sporadic invasions of nomadic Mongols from Central Asia had occurred in the twelfth century. Then in 1206 a great Mongol ruler arose, Jenghiz Khan, who united the scattered Mongol tribes into what was perhaps the most formidable band of warriors the world had yet seen. This Mongol khan was the first such leader since Attila the Hun. Jenghiz Khan and his successors carved out for themselves the largest empire in territorial extent so far seen in the world's history. By the time of the death of Jenghiz in 1227 northern China had been taken, together with almost the whole of Central Asia; even Russia had been briefly raided. The death of Jenghiz, however, meant a short respite for Europe since all the sons of the khan had to return to Asia for the election of his successor.

The successors of the great Jenghiz, however, were hardly less formidable than he. During the reign of Ogodai Khan and later during that of his cousin Batu, Europe was invaded in force—Poland, Silesia, and Hungary being overrun; and in each case Europe, which was unable to provide an army capable of resisting the Mongols, was saved only by the death of the khan. After the death of Ogodai, the Mongols returned,

*When the great Khans died, their sons had to return to the capital of Karakorum to receive their inheritance. This picture is taken from a manuscript illustration in a sixteenth-century book, and shows Jenghiz Khan dividing his kingdom, prior to his death, between his sons.* (COURTESY THE METROPOLITAN MUSEUM OF ART)

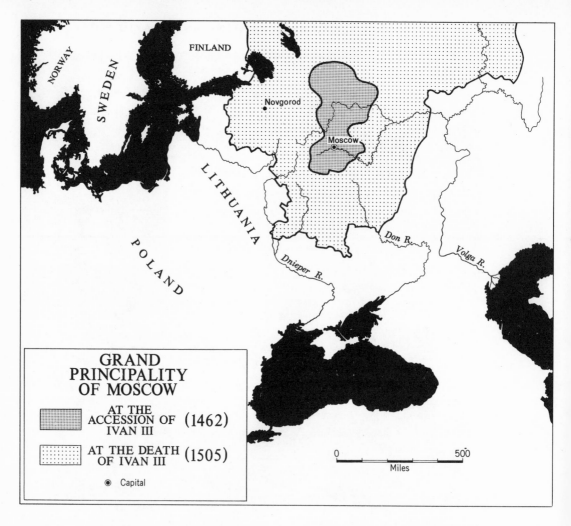

GRAND
PRINCIPALITY
OF MOSCOW

AT THE
ACCESSION OF (1462)
IVAN III

AT THE DEATH (1505)
OF IVAN III

◉ Capital

and the Golden Horde of Batu Khan encamped on the banks of the Volga in southern Russia, having captured and ruthlessly
sacked every important city in Russia save
Novgorod, which at this time escaped into
the Western orbit, becoming later an independent Hanseatic trading city, while the
rest of Russia groaned under the Mongol
yoke. The Golden Horde remained as an
Asiatic occupying army for two centuries,
demanding and receiving tribute from the
Russian princelings. The Mongols, after some
hesitation, were converted to Islam, but, in
accordance with traditional Muslim religious
policy, permitted the Orthodox clergy in
Russia to remain independent. The clergy,
unlike the secular lords, were not made to
pay tribute, and they thus were enabled to
reach a unique position of power and influence under the Mongol occupation.

The western provinces of Russia, as we
shall see in the next section, gradually freed
themselves from the Mongols, and the earlier
great cities in what is now the Ukraine,
which never recovered from the pillage and
ruin inflicted on them by their conquerors,
ceased to be a part of Russia. It therefore
fell to one of the minor principalities,
Moscow, to become the leader in the new
state. In due course its ruler, Grand Duke
Ivan I (1325–1341) became the chief collector of taxes for the Mongols, with the duty
of forcing the other principalities to pay
them. This position made the grand dukes
virtually puppet rulers under the Mongols;
but when the power of the latter at last
declined it was they who were in the best
position to assert leadership. With the whole-
hearted assistance of the clergy, who constantly preached liberation from the Golden

Horde, the grand duke won an ephemeral victory in 1380, but slavery was reimposed in two years. At the beginning of the fifteenth century, Tamerlane, another Mongol ruler bent on world conquest, severely defeated the Golden Horde, weakening its power so that it could no longer control its Russian vassals. Ivan III, the Great (1462–1505), Grand Duke of Moscow, united the greater part of modern European Russia under his absolute autocratic sway, incidentally reabsorbing the independent city of Novgorod. Then he took other important cities in the west from the kingdom of Poland-Lithuania to be described in the next section.

### "Holy Russia"

In 1472 Ivan married the niece of the last emperor of Constantinople, a symbolic act of which he proceeded to take full advantage. Moscow under Ivan and his successors proclaimed itself the true successor of Constantinople, the "third Rome," with a Church that had remained consistently "Orthodox," a powerful and efficient clergy, under ducal control, with a "metropolitan" who was the protector of all Orthodox Christians everywhere and the natural successor of the Patriarch of Constantinople, now the puppet of the Turks. The Muscovite court was Byzantine, the architecture of the great Russian cities was Byzantine, and the religion was Byzantine. As far as was possible in such a vast domain, the government and administration were Byzantine. When Ivan the Great proclaimed himself sovereign of all Russia, he ruled the only territory in Eastern Europe comparable with that of the Turks. If the Ottoman Turks had inherited the body of Constantinople, Ivan the Great had surely inherited the soul. And if today the Russians still do not possess the body, it has not been for want of trying.

### ▶ The disputed territories of Eastern Europe

#### HUNGARY, BOHEMIA, AND MORAVIA

As we shall see in Chapter 17, Hungary, in South Central Europe, was settled by the conquering Magyars in the period after the death of Charlemagne.[6] For a long time they remained pagan, but were converted to the Roman Church at the beginning of the eleventh century by St. Stephen I (1001–1038). Stephen was granted the title of "apostolic king," by Pope Sylvester II (Gerbert), who sent him a crown, preserved as a sacred symbol of Hungarian independence until 1945, even during the time Hungary was in subjection to foreign powers. For centuries the Hungarian kings had difficulty in maintaining a position much superior to that of the great nobles, who preferred a feudal state; and many of the kings had to submit to feudal domination. Hungary was continually drawn into the politics of Central Europe, and its throne was frequently occupied by kings who also possessed foreign thrones, and were often enough not Hungarian at all. Living in the eastern borderlands of Europe, the Hungarians frequently also had to bear the brunt of invasions from the East. The Mongols occupied the whole country for a year (1241) until the usual retirement on the death of the khan, and the Hungarians had to defend Europe also against the onset of the Ottoman Turks. Together with the Serbs and other Slavs, the Hungarians were defeated by the Turks at the battle of Kossovo in 1389. In spite of several victories in the fifteenth century which postponed the evil day, at last they were defeated by the Turks at the battle of Mohacs in 1526, and were condemned to partition between the Austrians and the Turks, since the country was not strong enough to survive as an independent nation. Though the Turkish part was recovered at the end of the seventeenth century it was only to fall to the Hapsburgs of Austria, who remained the rulers of Hungary until 1918.

Farthest to the west of all the Slavic peoples were those of Bohemia and Moravia.

[6] Hungary, of course, is not a Slavic country, but it has always possessed a large Slavic minority, especially in Slovakia, which was a part of Hungary from the tenth to the twentieth centuries, was incorporated into Czechoslovakia in 1919, and was nominally independent for a short time under the regime of Hitler.

These territories were already settled by Slavs in the sixth century, who were called Czechs and spoke the Slavonic dialect of Czech. At the time of the mission of St. Cyril and St. Methodius, already described, the two countries were united under Moravian rule, and both were converted to Christianity. After a brief period of struggle they accepted the ecclesiastical rule of Rome. Thereafter their history lay with the West. In the tenth century Bohemia became dominant over Moravia under St. Wenceslas I (died 935), king of Bohemia, and Bohemia itself became the vassal of the Holy Roman Empire, after Otto I had repelled from Moravia the invasions of the Magyars (Chapter 17). German influence grew constantly in the country, the towns prospered, and the country became Westernized and altogether out of touch with the eastern Slavs, similar to them in language, but not in culture.[7] At times Bohemia was the largest of all the territories of the Empire, though its king remained the vassal of the emperor. On several occasions the king of Bohemia was also emperor, and with the Golden Bull (1356) the king of Bohemia was formally recognized as an elector of the Empire. The country remained predominantly Catholic, although, as described in Chapter 19, the earliest movements which led to Protestantism occurred in Bohemia (the Hussite Wars), and there is a substantial Protestant minority to this day.

PRUSSIA, POLAND, AND LITHUANIA

In East Central Europe, east of the boundaries of the Holy Roman Empire, and extending far up the Baltic Sea, were the Baltic peoples of Prussia and Lithuania, the Slavs of Poland, and the Finnish people of Livonia. The Poles had become Christians in the tenth century under their Duke Mieszko I (962–992) of the Piast family, which reigned, later as kings, in Poland until 1370. But the Prussians and Lithuanians

[7] The (Sudeten) Germans whom Hitler discovered to be oppressed by the Czech majority in 1938 had lived in Bohemia peacefully side by side with the Slavic Czechs since medieval times.

remained obstinately pagan until the Teutonic Knights were invited by a Polish prince to help him with a campaign against the Prussians. The Teutonic Knights were a crusading order of militant "monks" dedicated, like the other orders to be mentioned in Chapter 18, to a life of fighting. After the failure of the Third Crusade they returned to Europe, settling in Hungary until they were called upon for action against the Prussians. A group of these Knights joined another missionary order (Livonian Brothers of the Sword) and proceeded to conquer and convert Livonia (present-day Esthonia and most of Latvia). Cities were founded in the newly converted land which became flourishing members of the Hanseatic League; but by far the greater part of the territory was given to German nobles, who thus extended the feudal system into these Baltic borderlands, creating a permanent German aristocracy which has only been expelled by the Russians since World War II. The Livonian Knights, unable to move further east after a defeat at the Neva by the Russians under Alexander Nevski (1242), amalgamated with the Teutonic Knights and together the two orders proceeded systematically to subdue and convert the Prussians. Under their Grand Master Hermann of Salza, the Knights made considerable conquests, settling, however, as feudal lords in the new territories, and owing only nominal allegiance to the popes, to the discomfiture of the Poles who claimed the territories. Prussia was thoroughly Germanized, and the earlier Slavic population almost exterminated.

When the Knights pressed on into Pomerelia, to the northwest of the kingdom of Poland, the Poles tried to organize resistance, but did not have any great success until the Teutonic Order fell into decay, in part owing to excessive material prosperity. Then in 1386 the heiress to the Polish crown, Princess Jadwiga, married Jagiello, Grand Duke of Lithuania, who thereupon became King Ladislaus II of Poland, and a huge if short-lived kingdom was thus created which stretched from the Baltic to the Black Sea.

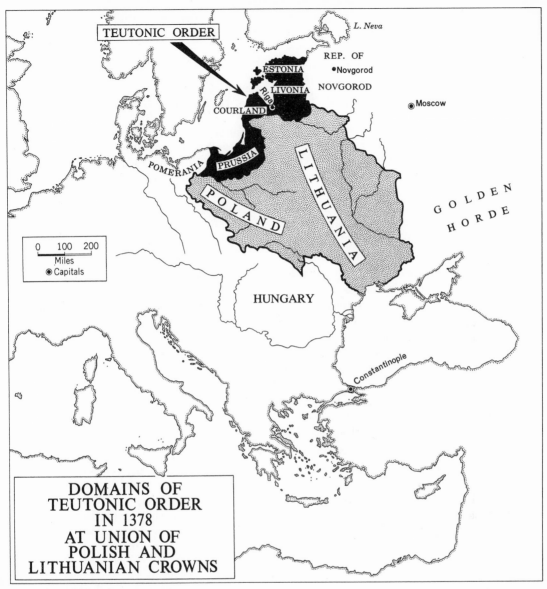

TEUTONIC ORDER

L. Neva

REP. OF
●Novgorod
NOVGOROD

ESTONIA
LIVONIA

⊚Moscow

Riga

COURLAND

LITHUANIA

POMERANIA

PRUSSIA

GOLDEN

POLAND

HORDE

0    100    200
Miles
⊚ Capitals

HUNGARY

Constantinople

DOMAINS OF
TEUTONIC ORDER
IN 1378
AT UNION OF
POLISH AND
LITHUANIAN CROWNS

Up to this time Lithuania had remained stubbornly impervious to the best efforts of Christian missionaries. Her dukes had created a huge, ramshackle state, much of it carved out of western Russia, which the dominant Mongols were unable to defend. After the union with the Polish crown the new king at last accepted Roman Christianity for himself and his people, with the exception of the Russian and Ukrainian people in his state, who were already Christians but of the Orthodox faith. This new state had resources formidable even for the militant Teu-

tonic Knights, upon whom it inflicted an overwhelming defeat at the battle of Tannenberg (1410). Thereafter, however, with the freeing of the Russians and the ascendancy of the duchy of Moscow, the eastern provinces of Poland-Lithuania fell away, following their coreligionists into obedience to the metropolitan of Moscow. In 1569 the Lithuanians merged with Poland in the Union of Lublin to protect themselves from the inroads of Ivan IV, the Terrible, the Tsar of Russia.

During the Jagiello dynasty (1386–

1572) the Poles experienced the greatest age in their history, the arts and sciences flourished, and the University of Cracow (founded 1364), where Nicolas Copernicus studied, was one of the leading centers of learning in Europe. Toward the end of the dynasty, however, the nobles began to gain much power over the kings, forcing Alexander I in 1505 to reorganize the Diet of nobles and gentry as a legislature. Lacking the protection of the king, the peasants were reduced to serfdom by the nobles. The later kings were elected by the Diet, but had little power, especially since the jealousy of the Polish nobles frequently resulted in the bestowal of the throne on foreigners with their own separate dynastic interests to pursue. The greater part of that section of the country which had formed the old state of Lithuania was lost to Russia, while Poland itself was cynically partitioned in the eighteenth century among the European powers, only emerging again into independence in the twentieth century.

This chapter has taken us a long way ahead in time. But since the remainder of this volume is concerned with development in the West, it was thought more convenient to sketch, once and for all, the history of eastern Europe until the period when it again became important in modern times. The accompanying maps, and the chronological charts (pages 449–451), if carefully studied, should provide the student with as much as he needs to know of this too often neglected medieval history of important modern states. It is truly impossible to understand the nationalities problem in modern Europe, the compelling urge for "self-determination," and the strivings of minorities, unless ancient glories as well as recent dominations are appreciated at their full value.

▶ **Suggestions for further reading**

There are several good surveys of Byzantine civilization as a whole. Excellent is N. H. Baynes, *The Byzantine Empire* (Home University Library; London: Oxford University Press, 1925), many times reprinted, which covers the various fields of Byzantine activity topically and has a large bibliography. Rather fuller, but still eminently readable, is S. Runciman, *Byzantine Civilization* (London: Edward Arnold & Co., 1933). Covering a more restricted field is a survey of early Byzantine civilization, in P. N. Ure, *Justinian and His Age* (Harmondsworth, Middlesex: Penguin Books, 1951). An extremely interesting work, not all of which has yet been translated into English, is C. Diehl, *Byzantine Portraits* (New York: Alfred A. Knopf, Inc., 1927), in which the author, a noted Byzantine specialist, selects a number of representative Byzantine men and women of different classes and presents a rather impressionistic character and life study of each. The whole serves to give an admirable impression of Byzantine society at different periods of time. A thoughtful summary of Byzantine accomplishments, which is especially intended to show the civilization centered round Constantinople as a separate civilization in its own right, and neither a continuation of the Roman Empire in a different setting nor even a specially Greek empire in spite of its language, is to be found in a few chapters of C. Dawson, *The Making of Europe* (New York: The Macmillan Company, 1932), which are well worth reading.

On the other countries dealt with in this chapter there are two very good special histories: S. Runciman, *A History of the First Bulgarian Empire* (London: G. Bell & Sons, Ltd., 1930), by a leading scholar in this difficult and almost unknown field, a lively and well-written piece of work which concludes with the death of Tsar Samuel and the final victory of Basil the Bulgar-Killer; and H. W. V. Temperley, *A History of Serbia* (London: G. Bell & Sons, Ltd., 1917), the first 106 pages of which are devoted to the history of Serbia as far as the Turkish conquest. This latter book is free from the excessive nationalist bias which has marred other more recent books on modern Yugo-Slavia, though the book is, rather naturally, keenly sympathetic to Serbia's struggle against the central European powers, which was at its height in 1917. Within its limits the book is as accurate as could be expected at that time. For the Turks an old work, E. S. Creasy, *History of the Ottoman Turks* (2nd ed.; London: Richard Bentley and Son, 1878), has never been superseded, while there is a valuable modern study of the whole Balkan Peninsula in F. Schevill, *The History of the Balkan Peninsula* (rev. ed.; New York: Harcourt Brace & Co., Inc., 1933).

With the growing interest in Eastern Europe which has resulted from World War II, a number of books have appeared in recent times which have dealt with the early history of these peoples in a way comprehensible to the West. J. Roucek, ed., *Central-Eastern Europe, Crucible of World Wars* (New York: Prentice-Hall, Inc., 1946), attempts to do on a larger scale what Chapter 15 of this text has attempted, that is, to give a severely compressed historical background which may serve as a necessary minimum of knowledge for the general student, and thus to provide an introduction to be filled in by fuller study. Such a fuller study is given in a really outstanding account of this difficult and little-known history, in O. Halecki, *Border Lands of Western Civilization* (New York: The Ronald Press Company, 1952). This book will give the student a fine introduction to the history of Poland and Lithuania and other border countries, including the expansion of Russia at the end of the medieval period. The information contained in this book is to be found only with the greatest difficulty elsewhere, and, as far as the author knows, Halecki's book is the one thorough work in English on the subject.

For the early history of Russia the standard book is G. Vernadsky, *A History of Russia* (4th ed., completely rev.; New Haven, Conn.: Yale University Press, 1954).

# 16

# The Muslim Empire

*Arabia before Mahomet • Mahomet and Islam • Progress of Islam in the time of Mahomet • Expansion of Islam • The nature of Muslim culture • Decay of Muslim civilization: the Turks*

---

▶ ## Arabia before Mahomet

THE ARAB PEOPLE

It was noticed briefly in the last chapter that the Persian Emperor Chosroes, while engaged in war with the Byzantines, received a letter from an unknown Arab informing him of the existence of a new prophet, whose message, accepted by millions to whom Christianity made no appeal, was to change the world hardly less profoundly than Christianity's own founder. And even before Heraclius was dead he already knew that his long and exhausting war with Persia had been fruitless; for the prophet of Mecca and his followers were surely to enter into his heritage.

The peninsula of Arabia had hitherto played little part in history. A small area in the north had been a Roman province; but the great desert lands of the south had supported only Bedouin, nomad tribesmen who wandered from oasis to oasis with their flocks, warlike, hospitable, illiterate but with a remarkable natural shrewdness and understanding, fiercely loyal to their tribes, families, and chiefs (sheiks), but quick to take offense and as quick to avenge a slight as an injury. The sheiks were independent chief-

tains, owing homage to no man, and their country was without political organization of any kind; the few families who made up a tribe were part of no larger unit.

Along the coasts of Arabia, however, the land was more fertile, and a few cities had grown up. Jidda was the seaport, Mecca and Yathrib were trading cities, with their bazaars selling the products of the country—meat, dates, nuts, palm oil, and other foodstuffs, luxuries imported by sea and caravan as well as made by local industry. And from these cities set out camel caravans to the north, south, and through the desert to the east, manned by shrewd Arab traders and Jewish merchants. The cities, like the Bedouin tribesmen, were dominated by local families. One of the greatest of these was the Kuraish, which dominated Mecca, the chief commercial and religious center of the country. Though often warring among themselves, the Kuraish, with their many collateral branches, could be relied upon to unite when family interests were threatened.

Probably such a people as this would never have been united by political means; no king had yet arisen among them as in the other states with a similar early society that we have studied. Loyalty from such a people

474

could not be commanded or enforced. But what could and did unite them and make of them one of the greatest fighting forces the world has yet seen was a new and dynamic religion whose early successes, often against overwhelming odds, must have seemed to doubters proof indeed of its divine origin.

RELIGION BEFORE ISLAM

Before the days of Mahomet, Mecca was already a religious center. A stone, believed to have fallen from heaven (a meteorite?) around which a temple, the Kaaba, had been built, was the chief object of veneration. Arabs from distant lands came to pay homage at it, to the financial advantage of the trading community. Idols and other sacred objects were worshiped. Both in the holy city of Mecca and elsewhere there seem to have been many varieties of sacrifice offered both to deities and to deified forces of nature. But, as far as we can tell, no synthesis of beliefs or religious practices existed which would justify our calling it in any way a religion. And this was surprising since Judaism and even Christianity were known to the Arabs from traders and wandering missionaries, who must have been astonished at their lack of interest when they had so little positive religion of their own. And yet, as we shall see, the religious spirit was there, quiescent, waiting for the words of inspiration that would kindle it. This task was the lifework of Mahomet.

▶  Mahomet and Islam

RELIGIOUS EXPERIENCE OF MAHOMET

Mahomet (the name is spelled in even more different ways than Shakespeare's) was born in Mecca in 570 of one of the poorer and less influential branches of the leading Kuraish family. His childhood was spent in the shadow of poverty, it would appear. But when he was twenty-five he began to work for a widow Khadija, older than he, a business woman of ability and in comfortable circumstances, whom he later married. By her he had his only child, Fatima. From this time on Mahomet prospered as a trader, leading his wife's caravans, once as far as Syria, and until the age of forty gave no indication that he would

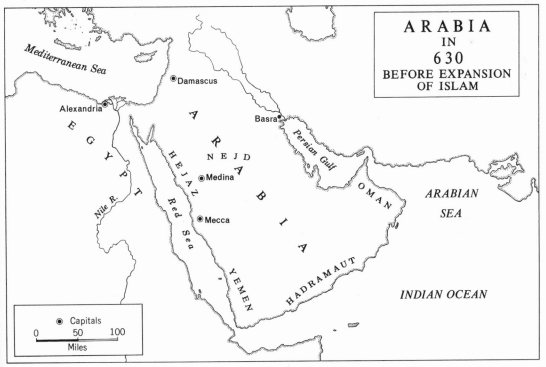

ARABIA
IN
630
BEFORE EXPANSION
OF ISLAM

Mediterranean Sea

Damascus

Alexandria

EGYPT

Nile R.

Red Sea

HEJAZ

Medina

Mecca

YEMEN

NEJD

ARABIA

HADRAMAUT

Basra

Persian Gulf

OMAN

ARABIAN
SEA

INDIAN OCEAN

⊙ Capitals
0    50    100
Miles

later preach a new religion. But it seems clear that he must have pondered long on what he knew of the other religions of the Near East and often have thought of the religious backwardness of his native land. And it is said that for a month each year he went into the desert, and there his thoughts became clearer, and he prepared himself so that at last, when the revelation came to him, he was ready. The revelation was that there was only one God, Allah, and that he, Mahomet, had been chosen to be God's prophet. Islam therefore stands firmly on the revelations to Mahomet, as Judaism stands upon the revelations to Moses. It is consequently a religion that calls for faith, with all the dynamism that such a religion entails. And although Islam contains much from the older religions, commingled with observations growing out of the customs of the desert tribes, it should not be regarded as a religion that was simply tailored by the keen intellect of Mahomet to fit the circumstances of his country. Students of history should avoid such an easy assumption, which is sometimes made when we speak of *syncretistic* religions, or those which draw their chief elements from several others of the day.

### RELATION TO OTHER RELIGIONS

The fundamental belief, therefore, in Islam (Arabic for "submission") is monotheism of the strict Judaic kind. For the Muslim,[1] there is no Trinity of Persons in God. Mahomet did not claim to be a god, but a prophet of God. There had been, in his belief, other prophets before him, among whom he numbered Moses and Jesus Christ; but he himself was to be the last, revealing the whole truth as it had been partially revealed to his predecessors. There was thus no reason for despising these earlier religions, or for denying their teachings; but they were not complete, and not fully understood. Islam therefore does not wish to exterminate the other religions; those who

[1] The word "Muslim," also Anglicized as "Moslem" or "Mussulman," means one who "surrenders himself to God."

converted to Islam showed that they were a chosen people insofar as they had been able to accept the higher revelation, and for this reason in a Muslim country would be entitled to special privileges. Those who preferred to keep their second-class religions could do so, but they must then expect to be treated as second-class citizens in a religious state. As "people of the Book," believers in other religions were permitted to keep their Books. Only those who had no Book and no religion were to be converted by force. This attitude always remained the religious policy of Islam, which was reflected in its political policies. A holy war (*jehad*) could only be proclaimed against heathen, or when Islam was forced to defend itself against other religions which attacked it. A holy war, enjoined upon the faithful only in certain well-defined circumstances, could never be arbitrary, or for the sake of simple conquest; the true religion must be endangered first by the enemy.

### THE KORAN—HADITH, ULEMA

Mahomet from the time he began his mission received many revelations from, as he proclaimed, the angel Gabriel. These were given to the people orally, but collected after his death in the sacred book of Islam—the Koran. Each revelation (or sura) is separate, and the compilers assembled them only in the order of length. There is thus no logical, chronological, or other order in the Koran, and if read consecutively by an unsympathetic critic, it appears to be a medley of unrelated teachings, most of them concerned with everyday life and behavior. This appearance of confusion is the natural result of the fact that Mahomet did not trust to his own judgment to answer the innumerable questions put to him in his earlier years. When asked for an authoritative answer, he meditated in the desert until the answer came. This was then a new revelation later to be incorporated in the Koran. It may be added that throughout the book the language is beautiful, the words are chosen with masterly care, and the whole betrays a poetic imagination which makes

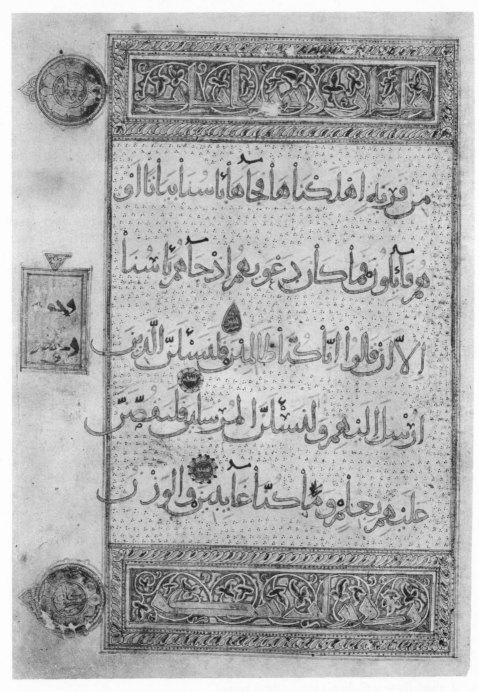

*Leaf from a thirteenth-century Koran.* (COURTESY THE METROPOLITAN MUSEUM OF ART)

it not unworthy to stand beside the Hebrew Scriptures. And it has never been difficult for any believing Muslim to accept it as inspired, in spite of occasional contradictions between various instructions to the faithful, which are explained as a progressive understanding of his mission by the Prophet, who, after all, was not divine but partook of some of the frailties of mortals.

The Koran contained all the positive teaching given by Mahomet in his lifetime; but, as with Christianity, not all points of Islamic theology had been cleared up by the Prophet himself. And since the Koran was also a guide to ethics and ordinary worldly activity, it early became necessary to have authoritative rulings on knotty points of doctrine. Moreover, Mahomet had also given oral instructions to his disciples which were not direct revelations like the suras in the Koran but were almost equally authoritative. Thus were added to the teachings of the holy book itself the *Hadith,* or traditions, which derived directly from the Prophet; and a number of learned men, the *ulema,* became recognized as the interpreters of the sacred text and the Hadith. These ulema still exist today with the same tasks in orthodox Muslim communities, even though there is no priesthood.

ORGANIZATION AND DOCTRINES OF ISLAM—
SIMPLICITY, APPEAL TO JEWS

In Islam there has never been any recognized priesthood. Each community may have an *imam,* who leads the prayers while there is also a *muezzin* who summons the faithful at sundown to turn toward Mecca and pray. The prayers are regularly prescribed, as are also fast days; and a whole month, Ramadan, is set aside during which no Muslim may break his fast between sunrise and sundown. In addition, there are moral duties to be performed, such as giving alms to the poor, showing hospitality to strangers; and there are injunctions against pride and worldliness and taking advantage of the difficult position of one's neighbor. There are laws of ritual cleanliness to be observed, following the general pattern of the Jewish codes: the pig is unclean, and there are ritual washings to be performed. No wine or strong drink must be taken, and there must be no images or idols of any kind, since these will divert the faithful from the strictest monotheism, persuading them to believe that other beings beside Allah have godlike attributes. The articles of belief are few and equally simple. There is a resurrection of the body and Paradise for the righteous, and an unending suffering in Gehenna for the wicked; both places are eloquently described in the Koran. There are also angels of God and evil beings, emissaries of the Devil.

Thus the religion is essentially simple. It does away with the complexity of Christianity, with its Trinity and doctrine of the Redemption, and concentrates on the few essentials which proved acceptable to the simple people to whom these were preached. The simple elements of Jewish ritual were alone retained, while the whole of Jewish legalism was abandoned. And the ancient desert morality at its best—such virtues as simplicity, straightforwardness, hospitality to friends and even enemies—was enshrined now as moral law, binding on the faithful, so that little change was needed from what was already practiced. The religion, there can be little doubt, was intended to appeal to Jews as well as to the heathen, and much of early Hebrew legend is incorporated in the Koran as fact. Although in the process of time many Jews within this culture were indeed converted, on the whole Islam did not succeed in weaning them from their Law. In early times there were many wars against Jewish communities, but the communities were not destroyed; and within a Muslim state Judaism was tolerated in the same way as Christianity. And Mahomet, who always regarded Jerusalem as a holy city, and indeed chose it himself as the place from which he ascended to Heaven, ultimately did not adopt it as the chief, but only the second, holy city in Islam, the place of supreme honor being reserved to his birthplace Mecca.

▶   **Progress of the religion in the time of Mahomet**

OPPOSITION IN MECCA

Mahomet's first convert appears to have been his wife. But progress was very slow in the early years of his mission when its appeal was exclusively religious. He was unable to obtain the support of his own Kuraish family, who were apparently afraid for the future of the lucrative tourist trade

# ► chronological chart

Islam in the time of Mahomet
  Birth of Mahomet                                                                  570
  "Flight" of Mahomet to Medina from Mecca                                          622
  Organization of the commonwealth of Islam in Medina                               622–630
  Return to Mecca of Mahomet                                                        630
  Death of Mahomet                                                                  632

Expansion of Islam
  Caliphate of Abu Bekr                                                             632–634
  Caliphate of Omar                                                                 634–644
  Conquest of Syria                                                                 634–641
  Conquest of Persia                                                                635–641
  Conquest of Egypt                                                                 639–644
  Conquest and slow subjugation of North Africa                                     643–711
  Ommeyad caliphate founded by Moawiya                                              661
  Blockade of Constantinople                                                        673–678
  Peace with Constantinople                                                         678
  Civil wars between rival sects and dynasties                                      680–699
  Conquest of Transoxania and part of Turkestan                                     705–712
  Conquest of Punjab                                                                708–715
  Conquest of Spain                                                                 711–715
  Invasions of southern France                                                      715–732
  Battle of "Tours"                                                                 732
  Conquest of Georgia                                                               727–733
  End of the Ommeyad caliphate                                                      750
  Abbasid caliphate                                                                 750–1258
  Independent Ommeyad dynasty under Abdu-r-Rahman in Spain                           755
  Caliphate of Harun-al-Rashid                                                      785–809
  Ommeyad caliphate in Spain (Cordova)                                              756–1031
  Fatimid dynasty of Egypt                                                          968–1171
  Capture of Bagdad by Seljuk Turks                                                 1055
  Capture and sack of Bagdad by Mongols,
    execution of last Abbasid caliph                                       1258

to Mecca, since there was as yet no suggestion that Mecca would continue to be a holy city. Naturally Mahomet's uncompromising monotheism offended all those who had a vested interest in the old religion; and there are always difficulties in the way of accepting as a prophet a man one has known all one's life. It was not surprising, then, that most of the earliest converts were gained in a city other than his birthplace, the city of Yathrib. Mahomet then made up his mind to leave his birthplace for Yathrib, and his followers began by political intrigue to prepare for him there a position of honor. When all was ready, he left Mecca, having been preceded by all his Meccan converts, and was given command of the whole city, the name of which was shortly afterward changed to Medina, the "City of the Prophet." This migration was the famous Hegira, of 622, from which year the Muslim Era is counted.

## PROGRESS IN MEDINA

The date is truly an epochal one, since from this time Islam began to forge ahead as a religious and political movement. The support of the Bedouins of the desert was enlisted, while the Jews in Medina whom Mahomet had been hoping to gain as converts finally refused to join him and were rewarded with confiscation of their property for the benefit of the faithful. In addition, Mecca was now an idolatrous enemy, a fit target for a holy war, in which the Bedouins engaged with enthusiasm, since one of their most pleasurable and profitable occupations was the raiding of caravans. The Meccans tried to defend themselves, but were beaten on several occasions by the growing army of Muslims. Finally Mahomet judged the time ripe for the forcible conversion of the people of his birthplace. He gathered an army of about ten thousand men and marched on the city.

## VICTORIOUS RETURN TO MECCA—CONVERSION OF ARABIA

The Kuraish looked at this vast army, far larger than anything they could hope to muster, and decided that it was better to make terms and follow the Prophet to victory rather than resist him. Mahomet entered Mecca in triumph, destroyed the idols and all remnants of the old religion, but maintained the sacred Kaaba and the stone from heaven, which remained for Islam the most holy place of pilgrimage. Thus the commercial interests of the Meccans and the religious imperatives of Islam were both respected.

Meanwhile, the religion had also been spreading. The Bedouins accepted it without murmur, and the people of Mecca and Medina and the other Arabian cities at least outwardly conformed. It now became allied with Arab expansionism, and its future was assured by its early successes. Mahomet himself died two years later (in 632), when Arabia itself was only half converted, and without making clear provisions for a successor. There was no central government for Arabia; and at this point few could have predicted the astonishing career that awaited the new religion under the leadership of the successors of the Prophet. In fact, there never was a stable central government for Arabia, as the Bedouins cherished their independence too closely. But after a series of minor wars a loose overlordship of Medina was accepted, and the Bedouins were perfectly willing to follow the military leadership of the faithful in their attacks upon foreign countries.

▶ **Expansion of Islam**

## THE SUCCESSION TO THE PROPHET—ALI, MOAWIYA, OMMEYADS, ABBASIDS

At the time of Mahomet's death in 632 little thought seems to have been given as to how Islam was to be propagated and by whom. Mahomet himself had always acted as the absolute and infallible leader, and his followers had been able to rely upon his revelations. Now there were to be no more revelations, and it was not yet known whether his spiritual mantle would fall upon his family or upon his disciples. And to this day there is still a major schism in Islam on this very point. Mahomet's daughter Fatima had married his own cousin. Clearly this man was the nearest male heir in the immediate family. But Ali, the cousin, was overshadowed as a warrior by many of the other followers, and it did not seem probable that he could give the leadership required. So the followers passed him over and chose the elderly father-in-law of the Prophet, Abu Bekr, who survived only two years (632–634). The second leader (called caliph, a religious and political title) was the great warrior Omar, who ruled for ten years and added Syria and Persia to the growing empire. The next to be chosen belonged to the Ommeyad family, one of the most important of the Meccan families, whose leaders had been faithful to Mahomet from the first. But while all these caliphs reigned, opposition had been gathering around the person of Ali, the son-in-law and cousin of Mahomet, who wished to keep the caliphate in the family of the founder and keep intact the Koran as the only inspired book, without the Hadith or traditions.

On the murder of the Ommeyad caliph by supporters of Ali, war broke out between the latter and the Ommeyad family, with its new head, Moawiya; and though Ali was proclaimed caliph, he was murdered not long afterward. Moawiya then became caliph (661). The followers of Ali became a dissident sect within Islam, the Shiites, which remained the leading group in Persia and later in Egypt. Other descendants of Ali and Mahomet from time to time set themselves up as independent caliphs, and the next great dynasty of the Abbasids was predominantly Shiite in contrast to the orthodox Muslims called Sunni. The Shiites still persist today, especially in Persia and Afghanistan.

The dynasty of the Ommeyads (661–750) removed the capital of the religion and empire to Damascus in Syria, and it was during their caliphates that Islam expanded farthest. In 750 the descendants of Abbas, a cousin of Mahomet, overthrew the Syrian Ommeyads and established the Abbasid dynasty, with the new capital at Bagdad in Mesopotamia. This dynasty, which officially ruled till 1258, saw the Oriental courts of such potentates as Harun-al-Rashid and Al-Mamun, which fell heir to the ancient traditions of Persia, and Persian influence was predominantly throughout. For the last few centuries of the Abbasid rule in Bagdad the caliph was the prisoner of his Turkish mercenaries, who overran his territories and ruled in his name. These were the Seljuk Turks, whose conquest of Jerusalem led to the Crusades.

### THE FORCES BEHIND EXPANSION— OVERPOPULATION, RELIGION, INSPIRED LEADERSHIP, TOLERATION

The successful expansion of Islam should not be credited altogether to the nature of the religion, which, as we have seen, was far from fanatical in its beginnings, and never was inherently expansionist. This was not the first time in history that the Semites of the desert penetrated into the richer lands of the north. The usual explanation for this new drive is given as the increasing desiccation of the desert and the drying up of oases on which the Bedouins had been dependent. There is, however, no evidence for this, though of course it is possible. There can be no doubt that the Bedouins had always been condemned to a low standard of living in view of the meager resources of their country. And being trained in the hard school of the desert and naturally warlike, with nothing to lose, they would follow any successful and inspired leadership. If the unifying and dynamic force of Islam had not been provided just at that time there is no reason to suppose that they would have erupted out of the desert to conquer a world empire at that particular moment. But the spark was provided by Mahomet and his religion; and the brilliant success of the initial enterprises against weak and divided opposition brought ever-increasing numbers of converts to swell the expanding armies. The Arabs from the desert alone could never have conquered such an empire, but they did provide the effective leadership for all the heterogeneous forces that joined them and embraced their religion.

It is quite untrue to picture these invading Muslims as a fanatical horde bent on attaining Paradise at the cost of their lives and ready to die in battle for this immediate reward. The Koran did indeed promise such a reward, but it is not to be supposed that this was the passage in the sacred text that claimed their exclusive attention. The Koran had also told them what policy to adopt toward the unbelievers; and this policy was worth far more to the faithful than any fanatical self-sacrifice. Briefly, as noted before, the unbelievers could keep their religion, could even keep their churches and their synagogues and their priesthood; but they had to pay dearly for the privilege. Anyone who converted to Islam was freed of all taxes, though, of course, he accepted voluntarily the obligation to give alms to the poor as prescribed by the Koran. The taxes were borne by the unbelievers, and until the era of conquest was over no faithful Muslim had to pay any. Moreover, the Muslims were not at all interested in destroying the civilization of the peoples they conquered. On the contrary, they had the most endearing trait of being extremely interested in the native cultures and wishing only to learn from them and contribute to them what they could—in this respect putting to shame many of the conquerors of history and imitating only the greatest, Alexander the Great. It was this quality of cultural tolerance which made the Muslims and the civilization they created the most influential transmitters of culture that the world has yet seen, superior to the Romans in that these new imperialists took also from the best that India and the Far East could give. Only when the barbarous Turks entered into the Muslim heritage, after it had been in decay for centuries, did Islam become fanatical and destroy more than it created and preserved.

The governments of Syria and Bagdad were Oriental despotisms of a familiar kind, owing much to the example of Constantinople. Their courts were centers of luxury and culture; but both were, on the whole, more creative than Constantinople, with its ancient Greek heritage on which it too exclusively relied. The subjects of the caliphates of Syria and Bagdad were kept under central control as far as it was possible for the monarchs to establish such control. But the Bedouin tribes of Arabia, whose dynamism had been responsible for the upsurge of Islam in the first place, were unwilling to submit to any kind of central rule. Nor were the warlike tribes in Africa. So the despots made only sporadic efforts to enforce their authority over these tribes, which, for the most part, remained independent under local leadership, retaining to this day the religion of Islam, but never more than nominal subjects of the Muslim political empires. Islam as a religion was congenial to them and did not interfere with their way of life; but the political system of the Muslim Empire interfered with their traditional independence, and it is not surprising that they rejected it.

## WEAKNESS OF OPPOSITION TO MUSLIM EXPANSION—THE BYZANTINE AND PERSIAN EMPIRES

At the outset of their career the Muslims found an inspired general, Khalid, the "sword of Allah." Though his armies were small in comparison with those of his enemies, they were determined; and Syria was oppressed by Byzantine taxes, having been only recently recovered by the Byzantine from the Persians. The Syrian armies hardly put up more than token resistance, and the population, itself Semitic like the Arabs, positively welcomed the relief from Byzantine tyranny and was, for the most part, entirely willing to submit to the formality of conversion with its privileged status. Another army marched on Persia, where it met the same situation. Persia, too, had been exhausted by the recent wars, the Persian religion had long ago fallen into decay, and the king had for a long time been unable to make his authority felt against his nobles. It took only three battles to conquer the Persians and thereafter many of the Persians joined the army of conquest. The victorious Muslims spread out to the East, carrying their religion with them. They usually had to fight against the great cities, but opposition was not prolonged, and at last they reached the limits of the ancient Persian Empire and the confines of China and India. Here they halted, and their expansion took a different form.

Aided by the Persian converts, they built fleets and sailed the Persian Gulf down into the Indian Ocean, trading and engaging in missionary activity for Islam wherever they went. Part of India was converted, and almost the whole of what is today called Indonesia, and the Malay Peninsula. They established colonies even in the chief cities of China itself. These areas were never part of the political empire of the Muslims, though as Muslims the inhabitants looked to the caliph as their religious leader. The vast majority of these converts made in the Far East have remained Muslims to this day.

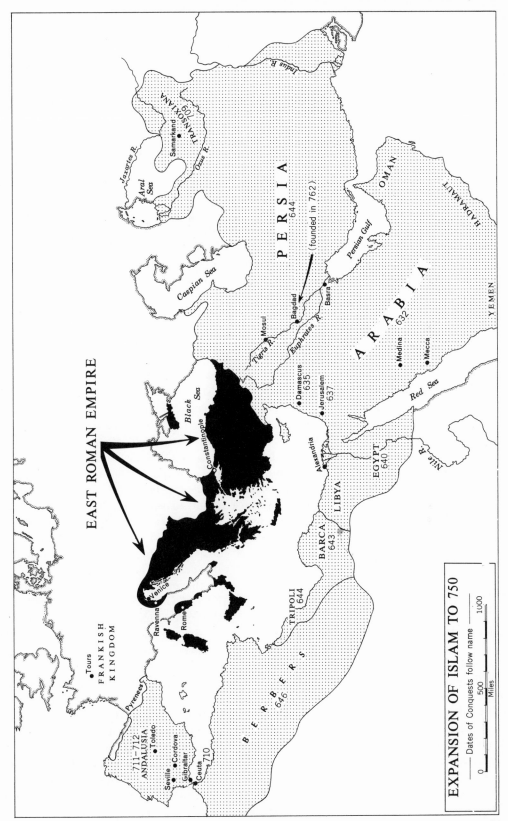

EXPANSION OF ISLAM TO 750

Dates of Conquests follow name

0     500     1000
Miles

EAST ROMAN EMPIRE

PERSIA
644

(founded in 762)

TRANSOXIANA
709

Jaxartes R.

Aral Sea

Samarkand

Oxus R.

Indus R.

Caspian Sea

Bagdad

Basra

Persian Gulf

OMAN

HADRAMAUT

ARABIA

YEMEN

Tigris R.
Mosul

Euphrates R.

Medina
632

Mecca

Damascus
635

Jerusalem
637

Red Sea

Black Sea

Constantinople

Alexandria

EGYPT
640

Nile R.

LIBYA

BARCA
643

Venice

Ravenna

Rome

TRIPOLI
644

BERBERS
646

Tours

FRANKISH
KINGDOM

Pyrenees

711–712
ANDALUSIA

Toledo

Cordova

Seville

Gibraltar

Ceuta
710

THE CONQUEST OF NORTH AFRICA (639–711)

Egypt and North Africa still belonged in name to the Byzantine Empire when the Arabs began their career of conquests. But the Byzantines, with their limited resources, were unable to hold them against this new menace. Egypt succumbed quickly, leaving its rich lands in the possession of the Muslims and cut off forever from Constantinople, which never recovered fully from the loss. Carthage, the old capital of the Vandal kingdom, in the hands of the Byzantines since Justinian, resisted the outlying bands of Arabs which attacked it for a few years until the Arabs could bring up sufficient reinforcements. Then it, too, was lost to Constantinople, while the Arabs pressed on to the West.

Here, however, they met solid resistance from the Berbers, desert people like themselves, just as fiercely independent, and with a tradition as warlike as that of the Bedouins. But at last the Berbers were defeated, accepting Islam at first reluctantly, and then with a fanaticism that outmatched that of their conquerors. Perhaps, too, they were not uninfluenced in their decision to embrace Islam by the prospects it held out for further plunder. At all events, it was the Berbers who formed the bulk of the expeditions into Spain, which succeeded in adding that country also to the dominions of the Ommeyads.

THE CONQUEST OF SPAIN AND THE EXPEDITIONS INTO FRANCE

In 711 the Berbers, led by a general named Tarik and a small number of seasoned Arabs, moved across the Pillars of Hercules and captured the Rock of Gibraltar, which received its new name from the Arab leader (Jebel Tarik). Conditions in Spain since the Visigothic conversion to Orthodox Christianity had deteriorated until the Church had become the chief power in the realm, far more important than the Visigothic kings, who had lost most of their authority and could not at this late stage regain it in time to muster an effective defending army. Moreover, the heretical Christians and Jews, persecuted by the Orthodox Christian Church, positively welcomed the Muslims, who were, of course, willing to tolerate them; and it is said that much of Tarik's army was composed of refugees from ecclesiastical persecution. The Muslims, therefore, met with little more than token resistance except from the Basques in the north, who indeed fought them with such stubbornness that during their whole rule in Spain the Muslims never troubled to conquer their small strips of Basque land.

Having disposed of Spain, the victorious Muslims moved on into France. But here progress ceased to be so easy. The Arabs were a long way from home, and had to rely on the Berbers for reinforcements; the latter seem to have been content with Spain, and were also engaged in revolting against the Arab rulers in Africa, whose authority they resented. So the Arab army in France was not strong enough to conquer the country against the much more determined resistance of the Franks under the Merovingian "mayor of the palace," Charles Martel. Defeated at the so-called battle of Tours in 732 ("so-called" because it seems to have been fought near Poitiers, many miles away), the Muslim armies moved to southwestern France, where they remained until finally being driven from the country in 759. Not many years afterward Charlemagne, by then king of the Franks, launched a counteroffensive and established the Spanish March, a frontier state in Northern Spain which served as the outpost for the reconquest of Spain by the Christians in a later century. Since the expedition to France could hardly have conquered the country against Frankish resistance even under a lesser captain than Charles Martel, the battle of Tours is perhaps not so epoch-making as it has sometimes been described. Its significance rather lies in what it meant in the way of prestige for the family of Charles Martel and the leadership in Europe that it gave to the Franks. However, the Muslims had at last been checked and the limits for their expansion determined. In Spain the usual tolerance was shown to the Christians, but in a Muslim

KINGDOM

OF

L E O N

Kingdom

of

Castile

Kingdom
of Navarre

P Y R E N E E S

Ribagorza

County of Barcelona

Barcelona

Douro R.

Ebro R.

Tagus R.    Toledo

C A L I P H A T E

Valencia

Guadiana R.

Lisbon

O F    C O R D O V A

Cordova

Guadalquivir R.

Cartagena

Seville

Str. of    Gibraltar

### CALIPHATE
OF
### CORDOVA
IN
10th CENTURY

⊙  Capitals

0      50      100

Miles

country they were cut off from contact with the papacy. They developed a form of worship quite distinct from papal Catholicism, with their own separate Liturgy, called the Mozarabic Liturgy. The spirit of this Christianity was curiously Muslim in its attitude toward heresy and its taste for secular literature; and it did not take altogether kindly to the Christian crusaders, emissaries of the papacy, who returned in a later century to enforce orthodox Catholicism upon them again. But after the conquest of Toledo by the Christians in the eleventh century the Arabized Spanish Christians entered with enthusiasm into the work of translating Aristotle and the Arabic commentators into Latin for the benefit of their new masters.

### THE MUSLIM FAILURE AGAINST
### CONSTANTINOPLE

The greatest prize in the civilized world was, of course, Constantinople; but the Muslims of this age never succeeded in conquering it. This was reserved for their Turkish successors as late as 1453. With the aid of a fleet built in Egypt and using the old Byzantine naval base of Alexandria, the Muslims took the Byzantine bases of Cyprus and Rhodes in the Eastern Mediterranean, and they were able with their fleet to pass the

Hellespont and besiege Constantinople by sea. They also overran Asia Minor in the early eighth century. But they could not take the impregnable city at any of their many attempts, being unable, as we have seen, to overcome the Byzantine secret weapon, Greek fire, which seems to have been a kind of primitive flame thrower with an explosive compound which set fire to the enemy's ships and, according to the descriptions, would even burn on the water. Soon afterward the Muslims withdrew from Asia Minor also, and Eastern Europe was saved. Two centuries later the Byzantines recovered much of what had been lost, including the command of the Eastern Mediterranean, but for a period the whole sea was a Muslim lake.

CONQUEST OF THE MEDITERRANEAN—
CONSEQUENCES

The eastern Mediterranean was conquered early, as has been seen, in accordance with the Muslim plan for conquering Constantinople and maintaining safely the possession of Syria. Crete was the next to fall. But it was another century before the Muslims of a new strong state in modern Algeria and Tunis began to move across the Mediterranean, taking Malta and Sicily. They advanced into southern Italy, capturing from the Byzantine Empire the last of the conquests of Justinian. And though this was again restored to the Macedonian dynasty of Constantinople (ninth and tenth centuries), Sicily remained a Muslim land until its conquest by the Normans in the late eleventh century.

This conquest of the Mediterranean cut off all sea trade between Constantinople and the kingdom of the Franks. For a long time before the actual conquests Muslim pirates had made trade difficult, working out of the North African ports. Some important ports had retained sea trade with the East long after the fall of the Roman Empire, trade which, in turn, had kept up some prosperity in the cities of France and in neighboring lands. With the important sea-borne luxury trade cut off by the Muslims, who did not view the Christian lands in Europe with any favor, and were in any case fond of piracy, European towns were hard hit, although some trade in later centuries was carried on with the Muslims themselves, especially from the Italian port of Amalfi. Not until the Byzantines reconquered the eastern Mediterranean and Venice began to trade with them was the West again able to enjoy in quantity the superior goods of the East. Sicily remained an outpost of Muslim culture and was able to exercise a considerable cultural influence upon the Normans who conquered it. It was from Sicily and Spain that, from the eleventh century onward, the European Christians gained their first real knowledge of Muslim culture, which became so influential in the next centuries. In the East during the Crusades these Christians were in contact only with the Seljuk Turks, far behind both Spain and Sicily in the arts of civilization.

THE SPECIFICALLY ARAB CONTRIBUTION TO THE
EXPANSION OF ISLAM

In general it may be said that the higher civilizations conquered by the Arabs absorbed their masters, thus following the rule that we have observed already. And indeed the Arabs made no effort to impose such culture as they had upon their new subjects. The Persian and Byzantine systems of government, with their bureaucracies and their absolutism, were taken over intact by the Arabs. A similar system with modifications, under a dynasty of Ommeyad caliphs, independent of the Abbasid caliphs of Bagdad, prevailed in Spain. Elsewhere the Arabs were rarely complete masters in their own realm and made use of what was at hand, not developing any new bureaucracy where none existed already. But the Arabic religion was accepted everywhere, if in a heretical form in some parts of the empire, and Islam spread in the Far East without benefit of conquest. The religion of Islam was a truly native product, with its desert origin plainly marked upon it. But the subtle minds of the Persian theologians transformed even this religion, developing a true theology out of it, while continuing to maintain the integrity of the Koran and its divine inspiration. The other great contribution, in addition to the dynamism and leadership provided, was the incomparable Arabic language. The Koran may not be translated into any other language, according to the law of Islam. And the Koran must be read by all the faithful. Therefore it was necessary to learn Arabic, which became, as Greek had once been, the common language of the whole empire and of the whole area converted to the religion of Islam. It is true that the original language was greatly altered in its transmission through these lands. But it proved capable of meeting the demands made upon it. Words when necessary were imported from Greek, and words were invented to express the conceptions never needed in the lands of the desert. Arabic, with its delicate signs used so beautifully in decorative work designed in Muslim lands, has remained one of the great languages of the world, strengthened and enlarged through the centuries, but retaining still the marks of its Arab origin.

▶ **The nature of Muslim culture**

ATTITUDE OF THE MUSLIMS TOWARD LEARNING

As has already been said, the Arabs, unlike the Romans, were genuinely interested in learning. As a practical people, the Arabs were chiefly interested in science. But there were also many learned philosophers in the new Muslim Empire, though their influence was probably not as great as the quality of their work would have justified. Philosophy never seems to have become a regular subject of instruction in their universities, perhaps because of the difficulties that have always arisen when philosophy and revealed religion must be reconciled. The Muslims took from the people in their empire what interested them, and neglected the remainder. They did not, for instance, show any interest in Greek literature and poetry, probably because there was already a long Arab tradition in these fields and the work in the ancient Hellenic tradition did not lend itself to translation in the Arabic. Moreover, Greek

religion, which suffused Greek literature, would not be acceptable to confirmed believers in the Koran. No Roman work except the law seems to have come into their hands at all, showing that, with the exception of Spain, Latin knowledge had died out in the territories which they controlled.

In every field that they touched the Muslims added something of their own. Though they regarded Aristotle as the real master of philosophy, calling him simply "The Philosopher," they nevertheless tried to understand him, and the great Muslim philosophers took his work as the starting point and added commentaries, trying to explain and enlarge his often brief and cryptic remarks. They took the great synthesis of Greek scientific knowledge written by Claudius Ptolemy in the second century A.D. as the point of departure for their own science, and then added numerous observations to it, especially in the fields of optics and astronomy. And, being in contact with Hindu thought also, they added the mathematical knowledge of the Hindus to the work of Euclid and the great Greek geometricians, and they advanced trigonometry beyond the point that Ptolemy had reached in his fundamental work. These instances are only given here to suggest the kind of work that the Muslims performed; a later section will give more detail on their specific contributions. The Muslims were the heirs of all the ages up to their own time; and though little that is really new can be credited to them, they preserved the Greek and Persian heritages, added something of Hindu achievements, and even took a fundamental invention from China, paper. And this they handed on to the Western civilization intact and improved. And though much in Western civilization owed little to the Muslims, and their influence should not be exaggerated, nevertheless in theoretical and applied science their influence was crucial, as the large number of scientific words incorporated into Western languages sufficiently demonstrates, most of them words in daily use such as "algebra," "alcohol," "zenith," and "zero"; while Muslim commercial invention and innovations made possible the voyages of discovery, the exploitation of which led directly to the modern world.

### Philosophy

If one reads through the work of a medieval thinker, such as Roger Bacon, who was interested in Muslim thought, one is at once struck by the very considerable number of Muslim philosophers whom he quotes as authority. But the two philosophers whose names appear most frequently are Avicenna and Averroës, as the Latins called them. Both men wrote extensive commentaries on Aristotle, but also did much serious thinking of their own.

Avicenna was a Persian who lived in the early eleventh century, and is known chiefly for his great *Canon* of medical knowledge. As a philosopher he was very popular with medieval scholars, since his ideas, which were almost as much Platonic as Aristotelian, were more easy to reconcile with religious teachings than were those of Aristotle. Plato's theories on the creation of the world, as given, for instance, in his dialogue the *Timaeus,* are not too far from those of medieval Christians, whereas Aristotle does not seem to have believed in a creation of the world by God at all. Astrology, a subject of absorbing interest to many medieval scholars, is also more easily fitted into a Platonic framework. Avicenna, when apparently commenting on Aristotle, introduces a considerable number of the ideas of Plato and the Neoplatonists, and his work did not arouse as much opposition in Christendom as that of Averroës, who was a more strict Aristotelian. Perhaps the most interesting original work of Avicenna concerns the nature of the human soul, where he uses his considerable knowledge of human physiology to supplement his philosophical considerations on the nature of the soul and its relation to the body.

Averroës was a Spanish Muslim who lived in the twelfth century, at a time when Spain was in the process of being conquered by the Christians, and the last defense was being put up by semicivilized Muslim immigrants from Africa. These fanatical Muslims disapproved of the work of Averroës, and it is said that they drove him from his native city of Cordova; they cared neither for his Aristotelian philosophy nor for its implications for Islam. So it happened that Averroës was never as highly regarded in the Muslim world as in the Christian, where his works were translated and appeared in Paris some forty years after his death. Averroës wrote what many consider even today as the best of all commentaries on Aristotle, and his reputation was such that medieval scholars called him simply "The Commentator." Very faithful to the original spirit, his writings are extremely objective and openminded, following the Master according to no preconceived ideas as to how he should be interpreted, in this differing from the medievals, who wished to reconcile him with Christian thought. Averroës came to some conclusions rather startling to medieval Christians, for instance, that Aristotle did not believe in the creation of the world. This would not have been so serious—and indeed Thomas Aquinas agreed that this was the correct interpretation of Aristotle—but Averroës also seemed to deny individual immortality. For him there was one great world soul into which all individual souls merged after death, thus admitting collective but not individual immortality. Whether this could be deduced from Aristotle is questionable; but at all events it was a theory which naturally offended both Christians and Muslims. Averroës, in defending his theory, was forced to the conclusion that there were different degrees of truth, the truth of religion to be accepted on faith, and the truth of philosophy which could be ascertained by the natural reason of man, and these sometimes appeared to be contradictory. This point of view was later in the medieval world known as Averroism, after the great Muslim philosopher. His theories caused considerable trouble at the University of Paris in the second half of the thirteenth century, and were later the basis for much original speculation in many fields at the University of Padua, which bore fruitful results in the scientific renaissance in Italy of the fifteenth and sixteenth centuries.

## Science

*Theoretical—Mathematics, physics, astronomy—*The Muslims, curiously enough, are remembered in the field of mathematics chiefly for the "Arabic" numerals. These numerals, however, were not invented by the Arabs, nor, in fact, are the actual signs used of such supreme importance. Any signs whose meaning would be universally accepted would suffice, but, of course, preferably not letters, which were used as numbers by both Greeks and Romans. The signs themselves are modified from the Hindu. The importance of the numerals, however, lies in their combination with the zero, which may or may not also be Hindu. Spengler has argued interestingly that the Greeks, with their conception of geometry as the chief mathematical science and their tendency to regard all geometrical figures as actual substantial segments, bounded by lines, could never come to a conception of anything that was not, in some sense, a body; whereas the Hindus with their urge toward self-obliteration in nothingness, and their conception of the world as really nothing, an illusion, would naturally arrive at the idea of zero. So he insists that the Greeks could subdivide 1 an infinite number of times but never could conceive of zero being ever reached. However this may be, it is not as yet possible from records to determine whether the Hindus or the Muslims had priority in the invention of the zero. But at all events the epoch-making work in which the nine numerals and the zero are used, with the decimal positional system that had been known in a different form to both Babylonians and Egyptians, was written by one Al-Khwarizmi (flourished 810, from whose name comes our word "algorism"), and were later introduced to the Western world by Leonardo of Pisa at the beginning of the thirteenth century. The same Muslim mathematician wrote a basic textbook in algebra, which seems to have been largely a Muslim invention (the word "algebra" is also Arabic), combining work done by the later Greek mathematicians and Hindus. The symbols used in algebra in the Western world were the work of a sixteenth-century Italian, Vieta. The elements of musical notation and the measurement of time values in music are also to be credited to Muslims, especially Al-Farabi (died 950). In the field of trigonometry, impressive work was also done by many Muslims using the basis laid by Ptolemy in his fundamental work on the subject.

In the field of physics the single great philosopher of the Arabic people, Al-Kindi (ninth century), wrote over two hundred works, especially in meteorology and optics. But he also worked out a complex theory concerning lines of force, or what the medievals called the "multiplication of species," based primarily upon optical observations. The physicist Al-Hazen (Al-Haitham, *ca.* 965–1039), wrote extensively on optics, including the reflection and refraction of rays, and put forward a theory of the manner in which the human eye is able to perceive objects which has many merits; it was accepted by most medievals who gave their attention to the subject, and perhaps is not altogether disproved today, though it is not presently in fashion. The great medieval bishop Robert Grosseteste was deeply indebted to Al-Hazen as was Roger Bacon.

The Muslims were greatly interested in astronomy, and many of their scientists wrote on the subject. But though they made many observations, they did not add much to the theoretical side of this science, since Ptolemy was regarded still as the great authority. Ptolemy's work was early translated under the title of the *Almagest* (Al-Majisti), by which it was known to the medievals when it was translated at the beginning of the thirteenth century. More Muslims were probably interested in the less scientific aspect of astronomy, preferring to draw astrological horoscopes for which, it would appear, there was a considerable demand in the Muslim world. Their astrology was also the basis for the medieval work in this field, which oc-

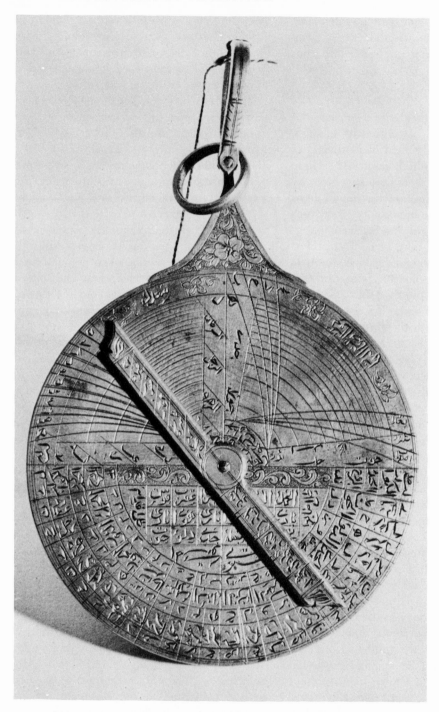

*An Arabic astrolabe. This instrument, which was suspended by the ring at its top, was used to take bearings by the stars. The crosspiece, called the alidade, was directed toward a particular star, and the navigator or astronomer took his bearing by sighting along it. By the fourteenth century it was customary to use two alidades and thus take a double bearing and calculate exactly the position of the ship.* (COURTESY THE OWNER, MR. BARNEY OF NEW YORK. PHOTO BY MORTON A. BERGER)

cupied the minds of enormous numbers of people till at least the late sixteenth century, though it was never approved of by the Church. The Muslims also perfected an astronomical instrument of great value, the astrolabe, with which to observe the movements of heavenly bodies.

*Practical science—Medicine, chemistry, agriculture, geography—*It has already been mentioned that heretic Christians, driven from Constantinople, founded an academy of medicine under Persian auspices before the Muslim invasions. These Hellenized Christians were soon persuaded to turn their accumulated learning into the Arabic language, and by the early ninth century the Muslims had at their disposal the whole body of Greek medical writings, including all the work of the school of Hippocrates and Galen. The Persians of Bagdad were the best physicians, and studied especially the diseases of the eye, which were so common in the Near East. But they were very careful observers of all diseases, and the greatest of their practicing physicians, Rhazes (Al-Razi), wrote more than a hundred separate medical works including a twenty-volume compendium of all the medical knowledge of the time. These books were in use in the Muslim world until as late as the nineteenth century. The most comprehensive of all the Muslim medical books was the *Canon* of Avicenna, who has already been referred to as a philosopher. In this work, in addition to careful descriptions, there is much very intelligent theory, having regard to the material at his disposal. It is not surprising that Jews and Muslims were greatly sought after in the Western world, whose own medicine even by late medieval times was a terrifying compound of superstition and quackery.

Muslim chemistry is not always judged fairly, owing to the prevalent belief in the transmutation of elements, the search for a universal catalyst (the philosopher's stone), and the diversion of intellectual and practical effort to these unprofitable pursuits. And in the practice of this science of alchemy there was much that we should call excessively mystical, even in the hands of the Muslims. But if we have lost our wonder at the marvelous transformations possible in the world of chemistry, this is not because there is nothing wonderful in it but because we have been so accustomed to think of all scientific wonders as commonplace. The fact remains that in their experimentations the Muslims discovered how to isolate many important chemicals, including sal ammoniac, saltpeter, and a number of oxides, and learned how to prepare sulfuric and nitric acids. There can be no doubt at all that Muslim alchemy laid the basis for modern chemistry by performing this pioneer work, whatever the objectives of their experimentation.

The Muslims made considerable progress in agriculture, especially in the science of irrigation. They improved the irrigation system in Egypt by carrying the Nile water further from the river and up slopes to higher ground; in Spain they brought water from the higher regions down to the plains which had always been arid. It is possible that Spain was never so well cultivated at any time in her history as under the Ommeyads. Vineyards were planted, and scientific methods of terracing were used, perhaps learned from the Far East. Cordova was noted for beautiful landscape gardening made possible by irrigation.

Muslim voyages into areas previously unknown to the West and the Near East made possible a great increase in geographical knowledge, and an improvement in map making. The best-known geographer, Al-Idrisi (1099–1154), was employed by the Normans in Sicily in the twelfth century, thus introducing the best geographical knowledge of the day into the West. The Muslims also introduced, if they did not invent, the crucial mariner's compass. The actual inventor is unknown.

## Art

*Architecture—*The most characteristic Muslim structure is the mosque, which differs essentially from the Christian church or the Greek temple in that no provision had to be made for the celebration of the

*Interior of Sultan Ahmed Mosque in Constantinople.* (COURTESY TURKISH INFORMATION OFFICE)

*Exterior of Mosque of Selim at Edirne (Adrianople). Note certain elements of similarity between this typical mosque and the Church of Hagia Sophia, which influenced so much of Muslim architecture. From the minarets the muezzin called to prayer.* (COURTESY TURKISH INFORMATION OFFICE)

sacraments, nor was there, of course, any god to be housed in it. The Muslims, keeping strictly to the law against "graven images," allowed no representation in their mosques of either human beings or animals, thus limiting sculpture to flowers and leaves, but above all to geometrical patterns which reached a high degree of intricacy and beauty of design (arabesques). On the other hand, since the Koran must be read publicly, a pulpit was necessary; a place must be provided for the ritual washing; and from the mosque the muezzin called to prayer. For the last-named function the Muslims added to their mosques the graceful minaret, so characteristic a feature of all Muslim ecclesiastical architecture— which was, as usual, copied by other peoples who did not use it for any such purpose.

In other hands the minaret, when used, became mere decoration, like the Roman and Renaissance columns which supported nothing. The campanile, or bell tower, of Christian churches, however, was often imitated from the design of the Muslim minaret. The Muslims used many different forms of the arch, especially developing the horseshoe arch, almost a signature of Muslim architecture. For decoration the Muslims, like the Byzantines, excelled in mosaic, the use of colored glass, stone, and other materials fitted into a decorative design. This seems to have been a Persian invention taken over by both Byzantines and the later Muslims. The dome, brought to perfection by the architects of Justinian, was almost universal in Muslim architecture.

*Applied arts*—Muslim craftsmen were

*Decorated introductory page of a sixteenth-century Persian book. The geometrical patterns are called arabesques; they were much used by the Muslims, who were forbidden by their religion to use so many forms approved of in other religions.* (COURTESY THE METROPOLITAN MUSEUM OF ART)

A Moorish temple in Tetuán, Spanish Morocco, features a horse-shoe arch typical of Moorish architecture. (COURTESY THE SPANISH STATE TOURIST DEPARTMENT)

Arabesque decorations on a fourteenth-century Persian tombstone. Note the similarity between these decorations and those on the book shown previously. (COURTESY THE METROPOLITAN MUSEUM OF ART)

*The Persians have always been noted for the exquisite design of their rugs. Here is a sixteenth-century example.* (COURTESY THE METROPOLITAN MUSEUM OF ART)

noted throughout the world for the excellence of their handwork, their only competitor being the Byzantine Empire. The process known as damascening, the inlaying of gold and silver on cheaper metals, was called after the city of Damascus and was a Muslim invention. Persian carpets are still famous today. The tooling of leather was a specialty (morocco, cordova), and swords and rapiers of Toledo steel were valued by Christian knights as the finest weapons in the medieval world. The designing of silks, brocades, muslins, and other materials was brought to high perfection and many of the materials used still keep their Arabic names (damask, muslin).

### Literature

When we think of Arabic literature we think almost automatically of the *Rubáiyát* of Omar Khayyam and the *Arabian Nights*. The former, written by a Persian mathematician, gives expression to the refined hedonism and polite fatalism of late Muslim Persia, and is, of course, known to the West through its very free translation by Edward Fitzgerald, so that the poem is better known perhaps in English-speaking countries than in its native Persia, where Omar was only one of many great poets. The *Thousand and One Nights* reflects the society of Bagdad in the time of Harun-al-Rashid, who appears in many of the tales in person. Arabs had always been fond of storytelling, even in the days before Mahomet, and this is one of many collections which was to exercise a considerable influence upon medieval and even modern storytellers. Boccaccio especially was influenced by the mode; though as a rule he wrote on contemporary themes, nevertheless many of his stories made use of those of his Arabic predecessors. The minstrels of Spain had a decisive influence on Provençal medieval poetry associated with the troubadours, and for a long time the whole civilization of Provence, so ruthlessly destroyed in the Albigensian Crusade, was indebted to the Muslim culture of Spain.

Throughout Muslim civilization there were always historians of talent, culminating, long after the civilization was in full decay, in the first great secular philosophy of history written by Ibn Khaldun (1332–1406), the great merits of which are only in very recent times beginning to be discovered, having been reintroduced to the Western world in part by the efforts of Toynbee, whose work lies in a similar field. Ibn Khaldun wrote a penetrating study of the causes for the success of the original Arab invasions, which is as full of remarkable generalizations as the works of Thucydides, though, for the most part, it is concerned with the nature of nomad peoples and their peculiar ethos, and why they were able to conquer the sedentary peoples with so much ease. He came to the conclusion that it was impossible for such conquests to survive unless the conquerors were held together by a religion, in spite of the fact that the nomads possessed an *esprit de corps* (*'asabiyah*) and unity of purpose denied to the sedentary peoples. The study of the growth and decay of the Muslim Empire leads him to make further generalizations about the rise and fall of all empires in terms of the degree of *'asabiyah* of the people and the corruption of the bourgeoisie by luxury and lack of opportunity for dangerous living. Ibn Khaldun's experience and knowledge of history were limited in scope, and it would be impossible for us to sustain his generalizations on the basis of our fuller knowledge. But Thucydides also had an equally limited experience and knowledge, and it is with the great Greek historian that Ibn Khaldun may not unfairly be compared. It is enough to say that it is by no means certain that, having regard to the material available to each, the Muslim historian would come off second best.

▶ **Decay of Muslim civilization**

Muslim civilization was unable to recover from the political disasters that overtook it from the eleventh century onward. The Seljuk Turks from Central Asia took over the Abbasid Empire of Bagdad, as we have seen (1055–1258). These Turks remained imperfectly civilized, although there was still enough cultural resilience in Islam for Islamic civilization to hold its own for some centuries. Then an even more barbarous group, the Ottoman Turks, took over from their Seljuk brethren. They consolidated much of eastern Europe and the Near East into a new political unit known as the Ottoman Empire, already briefly discussed in the previous chapter. Though in some respects the Turks took over the worst features of the Byzantine Empire, with corrupt and despotic provincial governors and oppressive taxation, in other respects the government was distinctively oriental. The sultan was an absolute ruler and his officials and soldiers were his slaves. An important contingent in his army was the corps of Janissaries, Christians who had been forced into his service when children, and later converted to Islam and trained as warriors. Soon after the subjugation of the Byzantine Empire the Turkish sultan became the caliph, called the "Commander of the Faithful."

But they laid a dead hand upon Islam. They themselves were strict Muslims, and under their rule the fatalism that was always implicit in Islam became increasingly the dominant attitude among Muslims. Some of the great cities survived, but grievously depopulated, while the implacable hostility of the Christians, whose civilization was growing as Muslim civilization declined, also served to prevent the cultural interpenetration that might have infused new life into the ancient Muslim civilization. Only in the present century have there appeared signs of a cultural renascence in Islam, though now under the spur of nationalism.

► Summary and conclusion

The achievements of Muslim civilization have sometimes been minimized and sometimes exaggerated, especially by scholars who have enjoyed contrasting medieval European backwardness, lack of science, and superstition with Muslim enlightenment. The Muslims were not on the whole great creators and innovators, but they were incomparable imitators and assimilators. For many centuries they acted as the sole bridge between East and West. They studied Greek science, neglected and almost unknown in the West of the day, and they studied and translated Greek philosophy. They did not add much to Plato and Aristotle beyond commentaries, but they added a great deal to Hellenistic science from their own thinking and observations. And they were able to make use of Hindu speculation and discoveries hitherto unknown in Europe. Their medicine, both theory and practice, was renowned in Europe, and the first European medical school at Salerno was originally staffed by Muslims.

They were an extremely mobile people, and their traveling merchants carried more than news and gossip and geographical information over the thousands of miles of their trade routes. They carried Persian techniques and manufacturing processes into Spain and Sicily and so ultimately into Christian Europe. They navigated the seas and brought the perfected astrolabe, quadrant, and mariner's compass to the West. Their storytellers provided the basis for much of medieval European literature. If the West had had to discover for itself all that the Muslims taught it, Western civilization might have been delayed for centuries.

But it is hardly fair to judge the Muslims by what they gave to the West, great though our debt is to them. Anyone who visits southern Spain today and sees the ruins of the great works of the Muslims, who looks at the arid lands which were made to blossom by Muslim genius and are now desolate, does not need to be reminded that this was a great civilization in its own right, and that the peoples who worshiped the one God Allah, whose prophet was Mahomet, do not need to fear comparison with the greatest there have been—even though their genius has been overshadowed in recent centuries by the expansionism and 'asabiyah of the Christians, and of the Western civilization which has flourished as it has, at least in part by virtue of its own heritage from the Muslims.

► Suggestions for further reading

It is very difficult to find western studies of Islam which are free from the besetting sin of the West, that is, underestimating or even despising Islam as an inferior and derivative religion, in spite of the undoubted fact of its survival as a living force after so many centuries. Likewise, accounts written by believing Muslims are inclined to take the western attitude into consideration and to assume the form of apologetics if addressed to the western world. Perhaps the most successful attempt at objectivity is the admirable short survey in the Home University Library, by H. A. R. Gibb, *Mohammedanism, a Historical Survey* (London: Oxford University Press, 1949). Another recent survey by a noted Arabist is A. Guillaume, *Islam* (Harmondsworth, Middlesex: Penguin Books, 1954). A series of lectures by a well-known oriental scholar, T. W. Arnold, *The Caliphate* (Oxford: The Clarendon Press, 1924), gives a succinct account of the relation between Muslim political life and Muslim religion. It is difficult to extract this information from the fuller books available on the subject, in spite of its great importance. Another series of lectures, by a well-known legal writer, D. S. Margoliouth, *The Early Development of Mohammedanism* (London: Constable & Co., Ltd., 1926), explains in a clear and concise manner the relationship between Islamic law and the teachings of the Koran. It goes without saying that some parts of the Koran itself should be read, though none of the translations known to the author is really adequate, and it is perhaps truly untranslatable into any western tongue.

In general, the series of books with such titles as the *Legacy of Greece* and the *Legacy of Rome* are not recommended for the beginning student, as they are either too full of unknown names, too technical in content, or too compressed to be really useful. An exception must be made, however, for T. W. Arnold and A. Guillaume, eds., *The Legacy of Islam* (Oxford: The Clarendon Press, 1931), in which many sections are admirably done; the material is difficult, if not impossible, to find elsewhere in English except in highly specialized works. The chapters on geography and commerce, and especially those on the minor arts in which the Muslims excelled, are highly recommended. Those on law and literature are also first-rate and do not suffer from excessive profusion of names, in spite of being reasonably comprehensive. It is still difficult to find in English any accounts of Mus-

lim science that are at all adequate. An old nineteenth-century work which was extremely influential in drawing attention in the West to our astonishing neglect of this subject is still worth looking into, although it is extremely pugnacious and although the author was deliberately overstating his case, especially against the medieval thinkers who had, in his now outmoded view, neglected and even persecuted science. This is J. W. Draper, *History of the Intellectual Development of Europe* (2 vols., rev. ed.; New York: Harper & Brothers, 1899), especially Vol. I, Chap. 13, and Vol. II, Chap. 2. On the whole, in spite of certain inadequacies, the two books by DeLacy O'Leary, *Arabic Thought and Its Place in History* (rev. ed.; New York: E. P. Dutton & Co., Inc., 1939), and *How Greek Science Passed to the Arabs* (London: Routledge & Kegan Paul, Ltd., 1949), are probably the best introduction for the English-speaking student. The thumbnail sketches of the great Muslim scientists given in G. Sarton, *Introduction to the History of Science* (Baltimore: The Williams and Wilkins Company, 1931), Vols. I and II, are always well considered, and if further study is desired, this great historian of science refers to as many works as were available in 1931. Lynn Thorndike, *A History of Magic and Experimental Science* (New York: The Macmillan Company, 1923), Vols. I and II, offers a fuller account of a number of outstanding Muslim scientists.

# V Civilization of the Middle Ages in Europe

*Manorial tenant touching his cap to his lord.*
*From a* Book of Hours *(Flemish),* ca. *1515.*
(COURTESY THE PIERPONT MORGAN LIBRARY. Ms.
399, folio 4)

# 17

## Political and Social Structure
## of the Early Middle Ages

*The Frankish kingdom in the eighth century • The Papacy in the eighth century • The Carolingian Empire • The successors of Charlemagne • Renewed invasion by barbarians in the ninth century • The feudal system • The manorial system: economic basis of feudalism*

---

### ▶ The Frankish kingdom in the eighth century

In Chapter 14 we saw that the Merovingian kingdom of the Franks had fallen under the control of stewards of the king's household (mayors of the palace), a position which had become hereditary. Charles Martel, one of these mayors, had succeeded in uniting the Franks under his command against the Muslims, defeating them, with the aid of the Lombards from northern Italy, in 732 at the battle of "Tours." The prestige gained by this victory enabled Charles to maintain his ascendancy over both the feeble kings and the warring lords of his realm. He also added to his kingdom by further victories against various Germanic peoples which had hitherto never been brought under Frankish control and were still pagan. He worked closely with the great English missionary and church organizer St. Boniface, who himself admitted that his work of conversion could hardly have proceeded without the aid of the sword of Charles.

When Charles died, leaving his position and lands to his two sons in accordance with Frankish custom, his work might have come to a sudden end. Fortunately one of these sons abdicated his position and went into a monastery, leaving the kingdom, of which Charles had been king in everything but name, to Pepin the Short (Pepin III) (752–768).

It should be recognized that it was a work of the utmost difficulty to keep together the Frankish kingdom, which, in the centuries since Clovis, had sometimes been split into as many as three separate kingdoms, each under a Merovingian king and his mayor. Furthermore there were many powerful nobles scattered throughout the country whose allegiance to the crown was, as a rule, only nominal, and who exercised almost complete control within their dominions. All through the Merovingian age there had been a gradual growth of feudalism, a decentralized form of social and political organization under which military protection was provided locally by landowners. The rise of feudalism, in other words, was a process of decentralization, in the course of which real power slipped into the hands of noble landowners, who alone were in a position to provide protection. Such protection, of course, was the theoretical pre-rogative of the king, but too often he was not in a position to assert it. Since, however, the process of feudalization was held up to some degree under the effective rule of the Carolingian family (so called from Char-lemagne, or Carolus Magnus, its greatest representative), it can be better discussed after the collapse of the Carolingian Empire.

Charles Martel had been content with the real power in France, and had not troubled himself about the title of king. One of his ancestors had tried prematurely to dispose of the reigning Merovingian monarch and had been killed by the outraged nobles, who evidently preferred a puppet to a real monarch; so Charles may have thought it wiser not to stir up gratuitous trouble for himself. But Pepin, his son, wanted to reg-ularize his position. The Merovingian mon-archs had held their office by descent from Clovis, who had been supported by the papacy after his conversion to Christianity, and had been crowned king by an arch-bishop. It occurred, therefore, to Pepin that the act which he proposed of setting aside this legitimate king could best be sanctioned by the pope as head of Christendom; and Pepin was prepared to pay a high price for this sanction. Hence he did not at once pro-claim himself king, preferring to send the

pope a message gently inquiring whether it was fitter for the one who held the power to be king, or the one who held the title but no power. This message, ostensibly a re-quest for a ruling from the head of Christen-dom on a question of abstract justice, had evidently been carefully prepared by Pepin and his advisers, probably including St. Boniface; in a masterful manner it gave the pope time to think over all the implications, while at the same time it did not require him to interfere in a political matter out-side his competence, thereby perhaps set-ting an unwelcome precedent.

▶ **The Papacy in the eighth century**

RELATIONS WITH CONSTANTINOPLE

**The iconoclastic controversy**

It is necessary here to consider the posi-tion of the papacy at this time in some detail, since from this request of Pepin on-ward the pope was deep in European poli-tics. The favorable answer he gave to Pepin had momentous results for the Church, set-ting in motion the train of events which ultimately precipitated the contest between the Church and the State for the successor-ship of the Roman Empire.

As explained in Chapter 14, Pope

▶ **chronological chart**

| Frankish kingdom and Carolingian Empire | | Papacy | |
|---|---|---|---|
| Merovingian kingdom | 486–751 | Lombard conquest of Italy | 568 |
| Charles Martel becomes Mayor of Palace | 714 | Leo III of Constantinople forbids use of images | 726 |
| Battle of "Tours"—Victory of Charles over Muslims | 732 | Iconoclastic controversy | 726–843 |
| Pepin the Short elected king by Frankish nobles | 752 | Aistulf becomes king of Lombards | 749 |
| Donation of Pepin to papacy | 756 | Pope Stephen II crowns Pepin king of Franks | 754 |
| Muslims retreat over Pyrenees | 759 | Charlemagne crowned emperor by Pope Leo III | 800 |
| Accession of Charlemagne | 768 | Otto the Great crowned emperor by pope | 962 |

## Carolingian Empire

| | |
|---|---|
| Charlemagne defeats Lombards and assumes title of king | 773–774 |
| Battle of Roncesvalles—Defeat of Charlemagne's army under Roland in Spain | 778 |
| Charlemagne completes conquest of Saxons | 785 |
| Charlemagne conquers Bavarians | 787–788 |
| Charlemagne conquers Avars | 795–796 |
| Charlemagne crowned emperor by Pope Leo III | 800 |
| Establishment of the Spanish March | 801 |
| Introduction of system of *missi dominici* | 802 |
| Treaty with Constantinople—Recognition of Charlemagne by Nicephorus, Byzantine emperor | 803 |
| Death of Charlemagne | 814 |

## The successors of Charlemagne

| | |
|---|---|
| Louis the Debonair (814–840) agrees to the division of his kingdom among his three sons | 817 |
| Louis makes second division of kingdom to include youngest son, Charles the Bald | 838 |
| Death of Louis—Succession of Lothair as emperor | 840 |
| Oaths of Strasbourg | 842 |
| Treaty of Verdun | 843 |
| Division of Empire at death of Lothair | 855 |
| Charles the Fat, emperor and king of East and West Franks (West Franks 884–887) | 881–887 |
| Paris defended by Odo against Northmen | 886 |
| Deposition of Charles the Fat | 887 |
| Robert, Count of Paris and brother of Odo, elected king of France | 922 |
| Death of Robert | 923 |
| Hugh Capet king of France | 987 |
| Henry the Fowler king of Germany | 919–936 |
| Accession of Otto the Great | 936 |
| First expedition of Otto to Italy | 951–952 |
| Second expedition of Otto to Italy | 961–964 |
| Otto the Great crowned emperor by pope | 962 |

## Invasions of Magyars

| | |
|---|---|
| Magyars cross Carpathians into Central Europe | ca. 895 |
| Magyars defeated by Henry the Fowler | 933 |
| Battle of Augsburg—Magyars defeated by Otto I | 955 |
| Magyars accept Christianity (missionaries from East and West) | 974 onward |
| St. Stephen I king of Magyars (Hungary)—Completion of conversion of Hungarians to Roman Catholic Christianity | 997–1038 |

## Invasions of Northmen

| | |
|---|---|
| First invasions of England by Northmen (Danes) | 787 |
| Continuous invasions of England | 856–875 |
| Foundation of Novgorod by Swedes | 862 |
| Alfred the Great, king of England—Danes checked | 871–900 |
| Colonization of Iceland by Northmen | 874 |
| Siege of Paris by Northmen | 886 |
| Foundation of Kiev by Swedes about | 900 |
| Rollo becomes Duke of Normandy | 911 |
| Colonization of Greenland by Northmen | 981 |
| Sweyn (Sven) Danish king of England | 1013–1014 |
| Canute (Cnut) king of England | 1017–1035 |
| Normans conquer southern Italy from Byzantines | 1042–1068 |
| Invasion of England by Harold Hardrada of Norway | 1066 |
| Defeat and death of Harold Hardrada at Stamford Bridge       (September) | 1066 |
| Invasion of England by Duke William of Normandy—Battle of Hastings       (October) | 1066 |
| Normans conquer Sicily from Muslims | 1072–1091 |
| Norman sack of Rome (Robert Guiscard) | 1084 |
| Norman kingdom of Sicily | 1091–1266 |

Gregory I and his successors acknowledged the temporal overlordship of the Byzantine Empire, while refusing to admit that the emperor had any right to interfere in spiritual matters. Nevertheless, as we have seen in Chapter 15, the emperors continued to appoint their own patriarchs in Constantinople, and regarded themselves as head of both church and state in their own realms, which included the extreme southern part of Italy, where they usually exercised effective jurisdiction. Relations between pope and emperor were rarely cordial, especially when the emperors set themselves up as theologians; but there were few open quarrels until the emperor Leo III took a step of such importance in a field clearly outside his competence as a mere temporal ruler that the Pope felt himself obliged to make vehement protest, and mobilized all his forces to resist. This, of course, was the iconoclastic controversy, already described, set in motion by the decrees of Leo in 725.

The papacy, which never had any sympathy with the iconoclastic movement, did everything in its power to stop it, ultimately even excommunicating all iconoclasts. But the emperors, with the exception of two women who held the throne, were for a century iconoclasts, and the whole movement deeply embittered the papacy against the Byzantine Empire.

Thus it happened that in 751 when, as has been noted, Pope Zacharias was in difficulties with the Lombards, and his request for aid went unheeded by the emperor Constantine V, one of the strictest of the iconoclasts, the pontiff was certainly relieved to find an alternative and more acceptable champion in Frankland.

### THE DANGER FROM THE LOMBARDS

For thirty years the papacy had been in danger from a revived Lombard kingdom in northern and central Italy. The Lombards since their conversion to Catholic Christianity were no longer so barbarous as at the time of their invasion of Italy in the years following 568. Indeed, they had been largely assimilated with the Italians and were already adopting the modified Latin which ultimately became the Italian language. They presented, however, a serious danger to the temporal power of the papacy, which had been reasonably undisturbed during the period of Byzantine overlordship. Yet, as we have seen, the papacy could hardly expect much help from Constantinople when the throne was occupied by an iconoclast, even though the request was formally made, on this as on several other occasions. There was only one direction to turn—and the pope had already turned there soon after the battle of "Tours." But Charles Martel had refused, not wishing to fight the Lombard king who had done yeoman service on his behalf at that battle.

With the accession of a new Lombard king, Aistulf, who conquered Ravenna, the last foothold of the Byzantine Empire in northern Italy, and was evidently preparing a march on Rome itself to round out a complete conquest of northern and central Italy, the papal position was serious indeed. It was at this opportune moment that Zacharias received Pepin's request for a ruling on the Merovingian kingdom. This request must have seemed like an answer to prayer.

### PAPAL ACCEPTANCE OF FRANKISH HELP

Of course the papacy could have become, as it finally did in 1870, a purely spiritual power, with no claim to earthly rulership over any territories whatever. But, as earlier chapters have shown, for centuries it had actually ruled over Rome and the area around Rome, as well as over various scattered lands in Italy. These secured to it an income which, if not sufficient for its needs, was at least safe, and could be collected without difficulty. In that age when communications were always threatened, when obedience to the papacy was by no means universal, when local prelates could hold up donations to the papacy made by the faithful, it would have seemed madness to rely upon anything except the effective possession of land for the expenses of the Holy See. To have allowed Rome to be captured by the Lombards, however faithful to the Church they might be, would have been to put the papacy in perpetual danger from a secular power, and would have made even spiritual independence impossible. Lombards could have forced whatever appointments from the papacy they wished. If the popes must be dependent upon any secular power, then it would surely be better to have that power a distant one, allowing at least intervals of independence when direct force was unavailable.

Zacharias must have known at once that it would be possible to persuade Pepin now to undertake the task refused by his father. He therefore sent back the message that he who held the power should also have the title. Pepin took the hint, was formally elected king by his nobles, sending the young incumbent to a monastery. Then, a few weeks later, the new king was crowned, probably by St. Boniface himself (752). The throne was in the eyes of all a gift from the Church; in return the throne was expected to constitute itself protector of the Church. The Frankish kingdom had always been a useful support for the papacy since the days of Clovis; now, in the hour of danger, it was to take its full position of leadership.

It was two years before the Lombards made any dangerous move. Then, when they suddenly became threatening, Pope Stephen II himself voyaged over the Alps and anointed Pepin with the sacred oil, a supreme gesture, for Pepin was the first king ever to be anointed by a pope. Pepin cooperated with an assault on the Lombards which was completely successful. After his victory he presented the pope with symbolic keys, and gave him the overlordship not only of papal lands taken by the Lombards, but of the exarchate of Ravenna taken by the Lombards from the Byzantine Empire. Pepin himself took the title of *patricius* of Rome, a late imperial title given to successful generals. This made him the official protector of the Papal States.

## DONATION OF PEPIN—PSEUDO DONATION OF CONSTANTINE

The pope, by this donation of Pepin, was now the temporal monarch of a compact kingdom in central Italy which cut a swath across the Lombard possessions and for centuries made the unification of Italy impossible under any secular ruler. The popes held onto this kingdom, with brief intervals when some of it was temporarily conquered, for over eleven hundred years.

The pope may have had some misgivings about the cavalier manner in which the Byzantines had been robbed of their territory. It seems probable, therefore, that it was about this time that the famous forged document known as the Donation of Constantine was made known. This curious document purported to have been written by the great emperor Constantine I, the founder of Constantinople. The emperor, so the document stated, having been healed of leprosy by the pope, embraced Christianity and decided to leave Rome forever, giving it, together with all his western dominions, to the pope and his successors. While the forgers were about it, they took the opportunity to emphasize that, in Constantine's view, the pope was to be "highest and chief of all priests in the whole world," superior to the throne of the emperor, and with rule over all the other sees in Christendom. "The sacred see of Peter shall be gloriously exalted above our empire and earthly throne." Anything less likely to have come from Constantine the Great, the father of all Caesaropapists, and perhaps the most authoritarian of all Roman emperors, can hardly be imagined; but this pious forgery was believed by the faithful to be genuine until Lorenzo Valla, a fifteenth-century humanist, showed conclusively that its Latin was not the Latin of the Age of Constantine. But for many centuries to come numerous popes were to quote it as authority for their claims.

Pepin was succeeded in 768 by his two sons. But one died early, leaving Charles, known as Charles the Great or Charlemagne (or, in Latin, Carolus Magnus), as sole ruler (768–814). When the Lombards attacked the papal possessions again, the new pope again called to the king of the Franks for aid. Charles descended swiftly on Italy, deposed the king of the Lombards, took all the remaining Lombard possessions, and became king of the Lombards himself. He confirmed the Donation of Pepin, but also made it clear that his new Italian possessions belonged to the Frankish Empire, with the pope holding the Papal States under his authority. Of the relationship between the pope and the secular ruler as Charlemagne conceived it, we shall have occasion to speak in a later section.

▶ **The Carolingian Empire**

THE IMPERIAL DREAM

### The feudal reality

By all odds, Charlemagne, son of Pepin, is the most considerable figure of the Dark Ages, whose name became legendary within a few years of his death. As a conqueror and administrator he was the equal of all but the very greatest in history. And yet the bulk of his work died with him. He set back the growing tide of feudalism for a few generations, he forced the heathen Saxons into the fold of Christianity, and by his imperial patronage of education he helped to reawaken the desire for learning which had for centuries been slowly dying on the continent of Europe. These achievements, great as they may appear in relation to those of others in the Dark Ages,[1] are small in comparison with his fame. For it was not given to any in his own day to realize the general futility of his policy; and only with the hindsight of the historian can the inevitable failure of his out-of-date Roman imperial dream be judged.

[1] The term "Dark Ages" is by no means acceptable to all scholars, but for various reasons it seems to the present writer to be justifiable. It is used in this book to designate the period of time between the fall of the Roman Empire and the eleventh century.

It is sometimes said that the destruction of his work was simply a consequence of the fact that the Germanic practice of dividing an inheritance among all the sons was not abandoned in favor of handing it intact to the eldest (primogeniture). But, even if this reform had been possible, a question begged by holders of that view, the causes of Charlemagne's ultimate failure lie deeper. It was not possible to impose an imperial system upon a decentralized agricultural society, as has already been pointed out in the chapter on the fall of Rome. The strong hand and watchful eye of Charlemagne, combined with his imperial prestige, might compel the landowners into obedience for a time; but the real power was theirs, not his. They possessed the means for enforcing law in their realms; all the wearer of the crown could do was try to make them enforce it on his behalf and in accordance with his wishes, something they would only do as long as it suited them. Charlemagne's army was drawn from his own lands, the lands over which he was the effective chief. Outside these he was dependent upon what the landowners were willing to provide him. He could hold their loyalty while he was alive; in some cases it had been he who first gave them their land out of his conquests and endowed them with the rank necessary to make their rule legitimate. They would be grateful to him, loyal to him while he lived, but their separate interests were diametrically opposed to those of any monarchy, and their gratitude could not be expected to extend to his successors.

So monarchy or empire could not be a solution to the political ills of the time; it could not be superimposed upon a feudal structure and survive. In the later years of the Merovingian kingdom civil wars were incessant—and not simply due to the quarrels between rival kings. Rival lords quarreled too, joining one king or another according to their separate interests, but involved in the quarrel only because of local gains they hoped to make. After the death of Charlemagne the civil wars returned, more virulent and destructive than ever. The new national states had to be born before these civil wars could be quelled by superior power imposed by monarchs.

### Caesaropapism—Supremacy of secular over spiritual power

But Charlemagne was a Christian as well as a secular ruler. And his biographer tells us that one of his favorite books was Augustine's *City of God.* There can be no doubt that he was greatly impressed by it, and what he gained from it is clearly to be seen in his policy. He conceived of a great Christian Empire, including, if possible, Constantinople, whose empress Irene he desired to marry. At all events the empire was to comprise the whole of his lands in the West, with himself exercising the temporal power; while the pope, approved of by him if not

his own nominee, would exercise the spiritual power, and the emperor would see that the pope's commands were enforced.

Unfortunately the popes had a different version of the same dream. Their theory was exactly the opposite to that of Charlemagne. The pope, wielding the spiritual power, was naturally above the temporal, as the soul is superior to the body, and eternal life is superior to the temporal life on earth. As we shall see, this assertion of papal superiority ultimately brought the papacy into an irreconcilable conflict with the Empire, which forced it to use temporal as well as spiritual weapons. With these it was able to ruin the Empire, but in doing so it destroyed its own basis for even the universal spiritual dominion it had been offered by Charlemagne. Charlemagne was

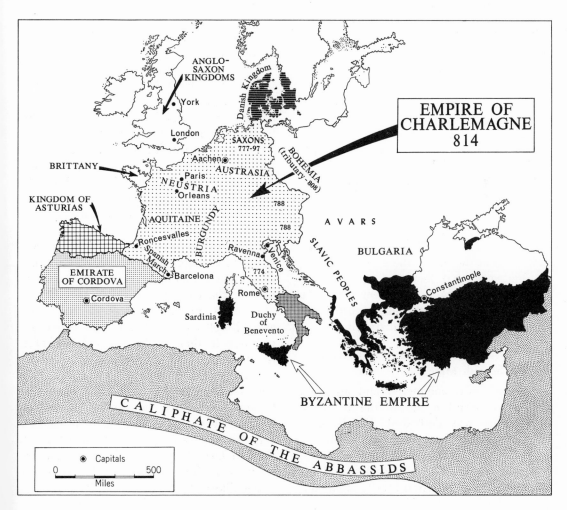

the only really effective Caesaropapist in the West, as his Empire was the nearest approach to a restored Roman Empire. But the dream died hard, and many war-filled centuries were to pass before it was abandoned.

## THE CONQUESTS OF CHARLEMAGNE

### The Saxons

Although Charlemagne was engaged in almost continuous war throughout his reign, his main efforts were devoted to the conquest of the heathen Saxons. This Germanic people seems to have remained faithful to the ancient pagan gods, worshiping them to the accompaniment of many rites repulsive to the Christians. They resisted Charlemagne with cunning as well as force, frequently agreeing to a peace and submitting to conversion, and then breaking it as soon as his back was turned. It took thirty-two years of hard campaigning, fearful proscriptions of the Saxon leaders, massacres, and wholesale transfer of the population, before they were finally subdued and allowed the Christian churches to be organized in Saxony. If any Saxon refused to be baptized, or even broke some of the Christian customs such as fasting in Lent, he was to be put to death, according to the regulations of Charlemagne. Unfortunately for his successors, the campaigns were so exhausting to the Franks and so deeply embittered the Saxons that when new waves of barbarians broke upon the Empire from the north, these new enemies, the Vikings, found their task much easier than it would probably have been if the two peoples had not wasted their resources and man power in their fratricidal strife.

### Other conquests—Bavaria, the Avars, the Spanish March

Bavaria was conquered and absorbed into the Frankish Empire, and the Avar state in Hungary was destroyed. Charlemagne also attempted the conquest of Muslim Spain, but was unable to make much headway, his rear guard being attacked and cut to pieces on one occasion by the independ-ent Christian Basques at Roncesvalles. The death of the Frankish commander Roland was immortalized in the earliest French epic, the *Chanson de Roland.* However, Charles was able to take some territory on the other side of the Pyrenees, which he organized into the Spanish March, later to be a bridge-head for the conquest of Spain.

To defend his new empire Charles made all his frontier territories into Marches, the defense of which he assigned to newly created Counts of the March (margraves, marquises), who became entirely independent in their new homes under his successors, though most of them were effective enough in their primary task of defending the empire against external enemies. He also founded monasteries in the newly conquered territories to assist in their conversion and purification.

## THE ORGANIZATION OF THE CAROLINGIAN EMPIRE

### Personal versus institutional government

Charles gave much thought to the internal organization of his vast empire; but, as has been indicated, it could not endure without his personality to guide it. Unlike the Romans, the Germanic peoples had no experience of, and no natural inclination for, rule by impersonal institutions based on an impersonal law. In an impersonal system, when an official dies there is another to take his place at once, and the institution continues to function. All our institutions today are of this character. When even the President of the United States dies, his office is at once assumed by his successor, and taxes are still collected, rents are paid, diplomats continue in their posts; essentially nothing is changed. This impersonality was the strength of the Roman system, and, as we have seen, the provincial administration continued even under the worst of emperors and during years of civil war. The Church was the only system of the Roman type in the Frankish Empire, and it could and did continue to function without great change under different rulers.

But the Germanic system was personal, and it was many centuries before institutions took over from persons. Government was based on a personal relationship between the governor and the governed. Loyalty was a personal thing, symbolized by oaths of allegiance and fealty. There might be a loyalty to a family, set apart as especially sacred, such as the families of chiefs and kings, but the relationship was still personal. The knight or noble held his sword at the disposal of the king, but not of the institution of kingship. Hence the extreme importance of having a king from a particular line; when the line failed, the necessary loyalty of the subject too often failed with it.

Another interesting contrast between the Frankish and Roman conceptions is the importance given in Frankish life to the officers of the household who performed personal and direct services for the monarch, and were thus in close daily association with him. As we have seen, Charlemagne's own family rose to power through holding the office of chief steward of the Merovingian king. The emperor's own chief official was the chamberlain or governor of the palace; next in line came the seneschal, who managed his goods and estates; the marshal, who was in charge of his stable and came to have command of the army; and the butler, who had charge of his wine cellar and vineyards. These tasks were considered by the Germanic peoples as the greatest honor the king could bestow, and the positions were of the highest importance and prestige. At Rome such tasks would have been considered beneath the dignity of nobles and reserved for freedmen and slaves. The German tradition, however, was maintained in Europe, and to this day such positions as the king's chamberlain and the queen's ladies in waiting in England are reserved for the highest nobility.

### Administrative regulations of Charlemagne—Capitularies

Charlemagne was a very energetic man, and we are fortunate to possess his instructions ( *capitularies* ) to his officials, by which he tried to govern his vast realm. But few

hold more than a passing interest, since no one considered himself bound by them once Charles was no longer there to enforce them. Many of them are concerned with the management of the emperor's many estates, and go into the greatest detail in such matters as the furnishings for the rooms in his manor houses and palaces, methods of keeping accounts and taking inventory, useful no doubt as showing the best custom of the time and probably followed by many managers of large estates. He issued regulations for the conduct of courts, and stated who should attend them. He divided his empire into counties, marking the boundaries of the jurisdiction of each court. He codified the laws for the different peoples of the empire who had as yet no written codes, though the Germanic basis was, of course, retained.

### The *missi dominici*

To see whether his interests were being properly looked after, Charles sent out two officials whose task it was to inquire whether justice was being properly done and to listen to complaints. These men, called *missi dominici,* or royal messengers, were armed with his own personal authority. One was always a cleric, usually a bishop, while the other was a layman. It is possible that in this system, though it died out with Charles, lay the germ of the idea of itinerant justices, first sent out in England by the Norman King Henry I, probably following Norman custom of the day. Out of these circuit judges developed the English system of regular assizes, the basis for the administration of criminal law in England to this day.

CROWNING OF CHARLEMAGNE AS ROMAN
EMPEROR—SIGNIFICANCE

Toward the end of his reign Charles reached the height of his prestige on being crowned Charles Augustus, Emperor of the Romans, by the pope. Einhard, his biographer, says that he was so averse to receiving the title at the hands of the pope that he would not have gone to the church that day if he had known what to expect, although it was the day of a great festival.

*A medieval illustrator's idea of the coronation of Charlemagne. From* Christ-Herre Chronik, *ca. 1400.* (COURTESY THE PIERPONT MORGAN LIBRARY. Ms. 769, folio 340)

This remark has given much trouble to scholars, many of whom have found themselves unable to believe that Charles knew nothing about the event until it happened, and have doubted whether the reluctance was anything more than a piece of assumed modesty. To understand his position it is necessary to consider in some detail the circumstances of the crowning.

Pope Leo III had been subjected to many indignities at the hands of his council and local nobles. They justified themselves by accusing him of perjury and adultery. Finally escaping from them, Leo made his way over the Alps to Germany and threw himself upon the mercy of Charles himself, pleading for protection. His accusers followed him there to repeat the charges in front of the king. Charles, as we have seen, regarded himself as protector of the whole Church; with his ideas on the proper function of the papacy as the regulator of the spiritual life of Christendom, he thought it of the utmost importance that the pope's authority should not be questioned except by the protector. So he placed the suppliant under his protection and sent him to Rome to await his arrival, when he would hear the case in front of a council. On reaching Rome at the end of the year 800, Charlemagne had evidently decided that

it would be a dangerous precedent if a pope were to be condemned by any council. He therefore allowed Leo to declare his innocence under oath, according to German law; then, regarding him as acquitted, he reinstated him as pope. Two days later, on Christmas Day 800, Leo anointed Charles Emperor of the Romans, at a time when Charles was unable to escape, during the Christmas service in the cathedral.

Now it seems at first sight inconceivable to us that Leo would not have consulted Charles in advance, when he was so obviously in the king's power. But at the Christmas festival Charles was in no position to refuse the pope's honor, because for once it was the pope's day; he was in charge of the service and not the king. It is possible that Charles would some time have proclaimed himself emperor, and would have called upon the pope to crown him, thus avoiding any appearance of granting the pope the right to make emperors, with the corresponding right of refusing to make them. But Charles would hardly have chosen that particular moment, when it looked to the whole congregation that the pope was conferring a dignity upon the emperor of his own free will. From Leo's point of view, it would seem that he could strengthen his own position by anointing the emperor without permission, for Charles could not repudiate him without repudiating the crown at the same time. And since he wanted the crown, that alternative was closed. Henceforth the emperor must support the pope against the latter's personal enemies, or admit that he had been crowned by unworthy hands.

The coronation had the effect that Leo had probably foreseen. Once the precedent had been established, it was accepted throughout Christendom that the pope had the right to crown the emperor; and many popes used this power as a lever to extract concessions from imperial candidates before agreeing to perform the ceremony. In a later time the papacy used the precedent to prove that the Church alone possessed from God the power to crown emperors and kings, and

*The coronation chair of Charlemagne at Aachen.* (COURTESY GERMAN TOURIST INFORMATION OFFICE)

was thus superior to them, even claiming that Leo had, by virtue of his spiritual authority, transferred the crown from the unworthy head of the notoriously dissolute Empress Irene of Constantinople to the loyal son of the Church who ruled the Western world from Aachen. That Charles had understood the implications of his coronation is confirmed by the action that he took the year before his death in having his own son crown himself emperor rather than accept the crown at the hands of a pope.

Having accepted his title, Charles now realized it would have to be made legitimate, for, after all, there was another theoretical emperor of the Romans at Constantinople. And as Irene was deposed in 802 he could no longer hope to unite the empires by marriage. Charles hastened to make a treaty with her successor. In exchange for some of his eastern territories his title was recognized, and the Roman Empire was duly established as it had been after Constantine, an emperor in the East and one in the West dividing the actual rule, while the empire itself was, as always, theoretically one and indivisible.

This monumental piece of archaism, this desire to return to a past which could never be restored, is a tribute to the hold that the old Roman Empire still had on the minds of men, and speaks volumes for the political conservatism of both the clerical and lay leaders of the time. It also demonstrates the power of an idea to create and mold institutions; but its sequel also demonstrates in an unexceptionable manner a further truth which has not lost its validity—that an idea cannot prevail unless it is in accordance with the political, social, and economic realities of the time. For Charles's empire almost immediately disintegrated after his death, and not all the efforts of his successors could put it together again.

"THE CAROLINGIAN RENAISSANCE"

The educational work of Charlemagne will be left to a later chapter. All that is necessary to say here is that, in conformity with his policy of using clerics in his govern-

ment, these must at least be able, unlike the emperor himself, to read and write. The monasteries under the Benedictine Rule did not emphasize learning, though the monks received the rudiments of education, and many spent their spare time copying manuscripts. It was possible for students to go to a monastery to study, but it was inconvenient. Though the monasteries were usually far from the important centers, for the next few centuries they continued to hold their own until they were to a large degree replaced by the cathedral schools, which will be dealt with in Chapter 20. Charles encouraged the monasteries to devote more time to teaching and study, but he also founded an important school of his own which was attached to his palace at Aachen (Aix-la-Chapelle). Since at that time he was the only patron of learning on a large scale, this school served to attract scholars from all over the empire and from outside it. In particular he skimmed the scholarly cream from England, the country which was at the time most advanced in scholarship. This movement is sometimes grandiloquently called the "Carolingian Renaissance." It was certainly a step in the right direction, though on a very small scale, and entirely dependent upon the patronage of the monarch. The real medieval renaissance had to wait for a few more centuries, as we shall see. But such as it was, the Carolingian Renaissance will be discussed in the chapter on medieval culture.

## ▶ The successors of Charlemagne

THE DIVISION OF THE EMPIRE

Charles had not been long in his grave before the Empire began to break up into semi-independent segments, as was to be expected. Since he had only one surviving son, the Empire passed intact to him, with the title of Emperor, which as has been seen, he had Louis assume without benefit of the papacy. Louis, however, called the Debonair, later allowed himself to be recrowned by the pope, and immediately afterward took steps to regulate the succession. He was no longer a young man, and he had three grown-up sons, Lothair, Pepin, and Louis. In a solemn assembly in 817, attended by churchmen and the nobility, he declared that the Empire was to go to the eldest, Lothair, while the two younger sons were to have two territories of their own, one in the east containing Bavaria and the Eastern March, and one in the west, Aquitaine and the Spanish March, with the title of king which they could pass on to their successors. Both, however, were to be subordinate to Lothair, were forbidden to carry out an independent policy, and were to contribute to his expenses from their own revenues. This scheme, evidently an attempt under clerical influence to mitigate the Germanic system of dividing an inheritance into equal parts, was approved by all present at the assembly who swore to uphold it. Then Louis proceeded to spoil it all by marrying for the second time. The new empress, a self-willed young Bavarian girl, apparently chosen by the emperor in the ninth-century equivalent of the modern beauty contest, provided him with another heir, who was later to be known as Charles the Bald. The young empress then insisted on a kingdom for her son, too, a request which her fond husband found it impossible to refuse. But the bishops insisted that he keep to his arrangements, the elder sons also had something to say on the matter, and the nobles began, rather naturally, to fish in the troubled waters. But Louis and his empress were adamant.

In the course of a confused twenty years Louis was deposed, publicly confessed his sins and was restored; intermittent civil war broke out in different parts of the realm; and Charles the Bald grew up to manhood, presumably losing his hair in the process. Meanwhile one of the emperor's sons, Pepin, had died; but the arrangement of 817 had long ago been abandoned. Louis himself died in 840. The Empire was divided between his surviving sons; but, though Lothair still retained the title of Emperor, he no longer had the supreme position guaranteed to him twenty-three years before.

Discontented with the division, the two younger brothers made an alliance against him, making an oath to be faithful to each other, each swearing in the vernacular language of the other. These Strasbourg Oaths (842) are of fundamental importance for the study of the evolving language of the period, since Charles swore in German and Louis in Gallicized Latin. The purpose of taking the oath in different languages seems to have been to enable the soldiers on each side to understand the nature of the alliance, for the two brothers themselves must have spoken a tongue they both could understand.

Louis and Charles succeeded in inflicting such a defeat on Lothair that he quickly came to terms, embodied in the Treaty of Verdun in 843. Under this arrangement Lothair kept his title of Emperor, but the territory of Charlemagne was divided into three parts, more or less equal in area, but with no regard to the defensibility or compactness of the segments. The emperor took both capitals, Rome and Aachen, and his territory was a comparatively narrow strip stretching all the way from the modern Netherlands almost to Naples in Italy (see map). The kingdom of Charles the Bald included everything to the west of Lothair's land, and the kingdom of Louis everything to the east. It has been suggested that the areas were chosen in this way in order to include the greatest possible variety of agricultural resources, since all the European varieties of climate are represented in each segment; it has also been suggested that it was divided according to the number of estates directly controlled in each by the Carolingian family. Possibly it was a combination of both these considerations. Nevertheless, it was a disastrous settlement on account of the lack of natural and defensible boundaries, and because it paid no attention to growing national differences. Ancient Gaul had to yield up part of its territories to Lothair, and it lost its Rhine boundary. The monstrous territory of Lothair, its northern part later to be called Lotharingia and still retaining the name of Lothringen (French, Lorraine), was to be disputed between

DIVISION OF
CHARLEMAGNE'S KINGDOM
AT TREATY OF VERDUN–843

0      100     200
⊙ Capitals
Miles

France and Germany even into the present century. The Italian part, separated from the German by the Alps, had to be reconquered by many generations of Germans under their emperors; for the tenacious efforts of the emperors and the popes to hold on to their territories in Italy was to prevent the formation of any national state of Italy until the nineteenth century. A case can be made out for this settlement as the most important treaty in the whole history of Europe, since it was signed at a period when the national state was not yet born, but the gestation process was already far advanced. This arbitrary division of the Treaty of Verdun forced the nations into a mold not designed by nature, and which the ensuing wars were never able to change once and for all. The monarchs did not take the results of such subsequent wars as final, citing the ancient treaty as their authority for renewed efforts to change them. It is perhaps not altogether fruitless to speculate how different the future of Europe might have been if Louis the

Debonair had not been so debonair and had eschewed beauty contests, and if he had thus been survived by two sons instead of by three.

Lothair was able to hold his kingdom together till his death in 855, dividing it again in his will—the eldest son Louis taking Italy and the title of Emperor, while the others took the northern and southern halves of the remainder. Upon the premature death of Lothair ii, king of Lotharingia, his uncles Charles the Bald (France) and Louis, perhaps better called by the German equivalent Ludwig, since he was the ruler of Germany, fought for the territory of Lotharingia. First one gained it, and then the other, thus setting an example for later kings who disputed the possession of the fair lands of Lorraine. Sundry premature deaths succeeded in uniting the whole territory for a brief period under Charles the Fat of Germany, but his cowardice in the face of the Viking invasions persuaded the nobles to depose him, bringing the Empire in the west to an inglorious end in 888. Thereupon the western kingdom was given to Odo, the defender of Paris, while the Germans gave their half to a more valiant nephew of Charles. The imperial title, such as it was, was frequently disputed by several claimants, none of whom was accepted by the others. By the early tenth century it had ceased to be of any importance, no ruler of any distinction even bothering to claim it.

## THE EMERGENCE OF THE FRENCH MONARCHY

But out of this anarchy emerged Odo as king of the Franks; and though the Church and Frankish nobles returned after his death to another Carolingian, the family of Odo was strong enough to reinstate his brother by 922. His grandson was the first of the continuous line of French kings, Hugh Capet (987–996), who was thus no descendant of Charlemagne, laid no claim to any imperial title, and possessed little but his own county of Paris. His claim to the throne rested on the valor of his great-uncle Odo, and the choice of his grandfather as king was the work of the nobles of France who elected him. This was the Capetian dynasty that was to unite

France and provide, with the aid of the collateral branches of Valois and Bourbon, monarchs of legitimate descent until the French Revolution, and still provides a pretender to the French throne whose title, like that of Hugh Capet, is still the Count of Paris.

## RESTORATION OF THE EMPIRE AS A GERMAN PRESERVE

The title of Emperor was extinguished when the last of the descendants of Charlemagne, Ludwig the Child, died in 911. The German nobles would hardly have looked to the last Carolingian now on the French throne (Charles the Simple) to set up as an emperor over them. They were by now entirely independent, and intended to remain so. But habit was strong and they returned to their ancient practice of electing a king as a kind of leader of the independent tribal duchies. After the death of the first of these they turned to the most powerful lord, Duke Henry (Henry the Fowler) of Saxony (919–936). He justified the choice by leading the Germans against the invading Magyars and thoroughly defeating them. He was also successful in incorporating the whole of Lorraine within his territory. When he died he left the throne to Otto i, who was formally elected without opposition.

But without any dangerous enemies abroad, Otto's lords became rebellious, and, while still quite young, Otto had to decide how he was to make himself an effective king and not be a king in name only, a king to be overthrown by rebellion as soon as his lords combined against him. He was by far the strongest lord in Germany, as far as his lands were concerned, and his feudal army was perhaps the equal of any two that could be brought against him. But he could not fight them all alone if they united against him. He needed powerful allies, and there was just one place open to him. This was the Church.

The Church had certain manifest advantages as an ally. It possessed the best administrators in the realm, it had an efficient working organization, and it was controlled by the higher clergy under the nominal, but not in this age effective, control of the papacy. What was necessary if the Church organization were to be used for the benefit of the kingdom of Germany was that Otto as king should make all the appointments, without the approval of the papacy. The obvious way to accomplish this was to constitute himself, like Charlemagne, the protector of the papacy, and control the appointment even of the popes themselves. The higher clergy in Germany were drawn from the feudal families, but their position could not be inherited, in part owing to the canon law against the marriage of the clergy, which was not too strictly observed, and because in any case all appointments lapsed at the death of the incumbent. Otto here was in a strong position. He had the right to appoint all the higher clergy in his realm, and they needed the land which he alone could give them, since they had no other regular source of income.

Thus was inaugurated the policy of what was later called lay investiture, which, though it was not new with Otto, was carefully systematized by him. The bishops were tied to him by feudal tenure, required to provide both military and financial aid from their territories. Certainly the Ottonian bishops were not noted for their piety, but he was careful to appoint competent and loyal administrators, his first appointments, indeed, being made from his own very competent family. Many of these clerics actually went to war themselves on his behalf, some of them becoming noted warriors, no doubt the envy of Otto's brother rulers in Europe. In short, the German Church, though partially independent, like other feudal magnates, usually lent its aid to the monarch, helping him to keep the lay feudal nobles in their place.

In 951 the first opportunity occurred to interfere in Italy. The Lombards had revived their kingship, but it was ineffectual, and the greater part of Italy had become the prey of rival lords. Taking advantage of a dispute over the Lombard crown, Otto made short work of the pretender, married the widow of the previous king, and became king of the Lombards himself, a title, it will be remembered, once held by Charlemagne. Recalled to Germany by renewed pressure from the Magyars, he was summoned for aid by a pope (John XII) in 961 against, as usual, the Lombards. This time after his customary victory over the Lombard nobles he forced the pope to crown him emperor, later to be called the Holy Roman Emperor. At the same time he extracted a formal promise, from a council called for the purpose, that his confirmation was to be required for all elections to the papacy.

The Roman nobles who for many years had been accustomed to this privilege, usually electing one of the feeblest of their own number, objected; and as soon as Otto had left they proceeded to elect a pope of their own. Otto returned, ousted the Roman choice and put in his own nominee. When this one, too, was driven out the new emperor lost his patience, returned with yet another army, and inflicted a sanguinary punishment on the rebels. Thereafter Rome was quiet. The emperor had established the right to approve of the election of popes, he was likely to be untroubled by papal interference with his choice of the German clergy, and he was now the accepted overlord of Germany and Italy. And the Roman dream of Charlemagne had once more been revived, to the irreparable damage, as we shall see, of both countries.

The papacy still possessed its estates in Italy, now under the overlordship of the German emperor, but it had lost what authority it had over the German clergy, being no longer able to choose the appointees or invest them. A pope could not even hold his own office without imperial approval. He was as much a servant of the secular power as were ever the popes under Charlemagne. Yet, from the papal point of view, there was one advantage, slight as it was, that Otto had over Charlemagne. He was no theologian, and his appointees were not chosen for their piety. The Empire was thus vulnerable on religious grounds; a movement for the reform of the clergy would have the support of true Christians throughout Germany and the Christian world, and might even be fortunate enough to find some day a successor of Otto the Great who was himself a Christian before he was an emperor. And already, even in the darkest hour of the papacy, when the Holy See itself was a plaything of the Roman nobles, the reform movement had been set in motion which was ultimately to lead to the re-establishment of the authority of Church and papacy, and to the destruction of the Empire itself. This movement and its consequences will be described in the next chapter.

▶ ### Renewed invasions by barbarians in the ninth century

MUSLIM PIRACY AND MAGYAR RAIDS

We have been discussing the political changes in Europe, but the other causes and results of the long anarchy have yet to be considered.

Soon after the death of Charlemagne, Europe was again threatened by barbarian invaders; and this time there was no effective centralized monarchy to hold them

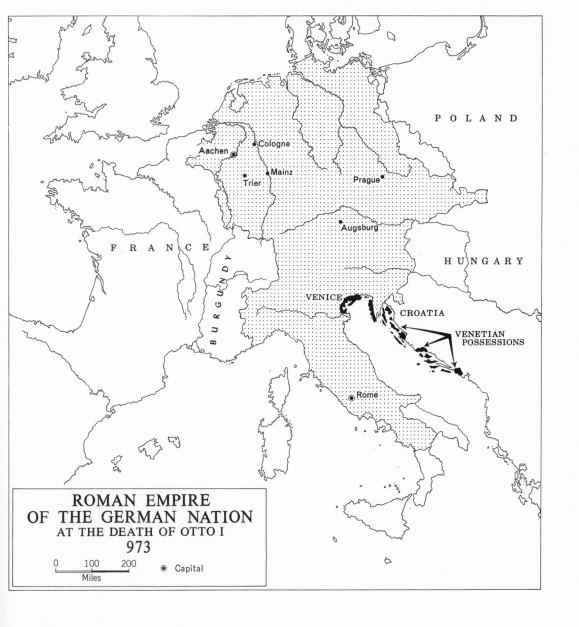

ROMAN EMPIRE
OF THE GERMAN NATION
AT THE DEATH OF OTTO I
973

0    100    200
Miles

◉ Capital

back. The Germanic peoples had become sufficiently civilized for them to be able ultimately to absorb the invaders; but their defense against them was scattered, and for more than a century at least the Northmen could move into most parts of Europe without meeting serious resistance. The Muslims, working out of Tunis, terrorized the Mediterranean, occupied much of southern Italy until driven out by the "Macedonian" dynasty of Constantinople, which in the tenth century suddenly sprang into renewed activity; and for extended periods the Muslims also occupied parts of southern France, establishing centers from which they could prey upon unguarded cities and caravans, paying particular attention to parties of Christian pilgrims. Though they succeeded, as has been seen, in finally cutting off all Mediterranean trade from Constantinople, they were the least dangerous of the new invaders within Europe itself.

Magyars (dealt with in more detail in Chapter 15 above), another Asiatic people akin to the Huns, made repeated inroads into Europe, finally settling down, after they had on occasions penetrated even as far as the left bank of the Rhine, as a ruling class of warriors in Hungary, and accepting Christianity and the authority of the Roman Church.

## THE NORTHMEN

### The period of looting and destruction

By far the most dangerous and destructive of the invasions were made by the Northmen, a seafaring people from Scandinavia and of Germanic origin. These invasions were not migrations of peoples, at least not in the beginning. Rather were they well-planned forays of freebooters led by individual chiefs, sometimes called sea kings. The Scandinavian countries can only with difficulty support an extensive agriculture, and it was natural that their inhabitants should take to the sea for a living, and there is evidence that in early times they confined themselves to their role as traders. But from the ninth century, no doubt having seen the defenselessness of Europe, and driven by population pressure

on their limited resources, they expanded all over Northern Europe, including parts of Russia, where a Swedish inland state was set up which lasted for centuries; while in the West they settled the Faroes, Iceland, and southern Greenland; discovered America; and occupied parts of western Scotland and the Isle of Man.

In boats which would hold sixty warriors and using both sail and oars, these bands of still heathen Northmen, clad in chain mail and using the sword and the battle-ax, crossed to England, where for centuries they terrorized the population, at one time occupying and ruling most of the country; then they advanced to the mainland of Europe, where they ascended the rivers in their boats, pillaging and sacking without discrimination. When the season was over they would return to their own countries, leaving desolation behind them. They early learned that the Christian monasteries possessed the largest quantities of movable wealth, so these bore the brunt of their attacks. Almost every city in Western Europe was sacked at one time or another; it was useless for farmers to raise crops for they knew that soon the Northmen would fall upon them and rob them. Agriculture was neglected save in the large defended feudal estates; the only remedy seemed to be prayer, which was for a long time ineffective, though repeated daily in the Litany. The nobles were unable to unite against the common enemy, occupied as they were with trying to defend their own estates against each other, and in any case finding it exceedingly difficult to defeat such a mobile enemy with their earth-bound methods. The Vikings did not bother to wait to fight; if any army approached, it was easy to go off by water at a pace that could not be matched in the difficult roadless terrain. The policy favored by the nobles was simply to buy the Vikings off, sending them, if possible, in another direction.

### The period of settlement

*Normandy*—But at last, not through great victories by Christian arms, but

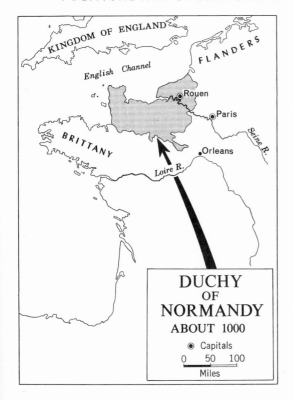

KINGDOM OF ENGLAND

FLANDERS

English Channel

Rouen

Paris

BRITTANY

Seine R.

Orleans

Loire R.

DUCHY
OF
NORMANDY
ABOUT 1000

⊚ Capitals

0    50    100

Miles

exchange for permission to live peaceably on his territory. As no one but these Northmen now owned it, Charles was glad to oblige. And though the actual homage ceremony was turned into a farce by the proud Northmen, Rollo did become the vassal of the French king, he and his descendants accepted Christianity, and a new state within the Frankish kingdom was formed.

*England under the Northmen (Danes)*— From the early ninth century the Northmen, called Danes by the English, began to send expeditions to England in force, sacking the principal towns throughout the south and east of England, including London. They defeated one king of the divided country after another until Alfred (871–900) king of Wessex (southwest England, West Saxons) began to build up an army of resistance, and ultimately to advance into the territory to the east, which had been altogether subdued by the invaders. At last he was able to sign a peace with them, under which he granted them the eastern lands of England which they had already acquired, on condition that they recognized him as king of all England, agreed to be his vassals (a similar arrangement to that made between Rollo and Charles the Simple), and formally accepted Christianity. The land was to be known henceforth as the Danelaw.

Neither party, however, was prepared to accept the division as permanent. The Danes encouraged continuous migration from their homeland, while the successors of Alfred, fired by his resistance, prepared to reconquer it. That work was completed in the first half of the tenth century, only to be endangered again when Ethelred (the Unready) became king of England while a new Danish pagan monarch made preparations for conquering not only the Danelaw but all England. Once again Ethelred started paying Danegeld (Winston Churchill in recent years used the same term to describe the appeasement of Hitler); whenever he ceased paying it the Danish king Sweyn (Sven), who had by now added the resources of Norway to his realm, descended upon England in force. At last he conquered the whole, and his son Canute

through the lack of further resources to plunder, the Northmen began to settle down, to bring their families with them, and to carve out territories where they would live permanently. They still sent out forays from their new homes into surrounding lands, but less regularly. And the Christians had begun to learn how to deal with them. The defenses of the riverside cities were strengthened, defensive castles were built by the nobles, and on a few occasions some great warrior would inflict a local defeat upon them. We have seen how Paris was defended by its count Odo; and though the emperor Charles the Fat raised the siege by paying unnecessary ransom (Danegeld) as usual, and directing the Vikings toward Burgundy, his cowardice cost him his throne, this very fact showing that the Franks now felt themselves strong enough to handle the invaders.

In 911 Rollo (Hrolf), who had taken possession of a part of northern France, later called Normandy, offered his allegiance to Charles the Simple, king of the Franks, in

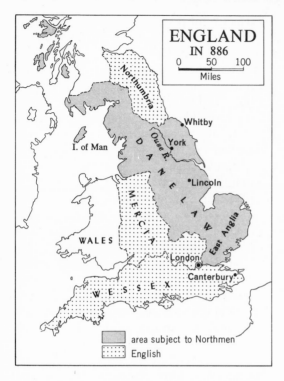

**ENGLAND IN 886**

0    50    100
Miles

▓▓ area subject to Northmen
∷∷ English

*The kingdom of Sicily and southern Italy* —Late in the eleventh century a further venturesome band of Normans, tired of peaceful life in Normandy, went in search of new land and adventures in Italy, under the leadership of Robert Guiscard (the Sly). The Byzantine Empire, which at that time ruled southern Italy, was having trouble at home with Turks and other peoples from the steppes of Asia. Robert had little difficulty in carving himself the duchies of Apulia and Calabria from Byzantine domains. The papacy, looking for allies against the German emperor, recognized the conquest, and Robert was willing to do homage to the pope in return for recognition. Thereafter the Normans, reinforced from home, began to expand into Sicily, winning the island from the Muslims by 1091. The nephew of Robert Guiscard was crowned in the ancient Muslim capital of Palermo on Christmas Day 1130 as King of Sicily, Apulia, and Calabria. Thus was founded the great Norman kingdom of "Sicily" of which we shall have occasion to speak later.

### The Northmen—An estimate

The Northmen, Vikings, or Normans, were an extraordinary people. They came into a semicivilized world as wild heathen barbarians, the terror of all. Yet once they decided to accept the religion and civilization of the kingdoms they had so recently plundered, they showed a genius for government and administration hardly equaled by any other people in history. For centuries the kingdom of *Sicily* was the most tolerant, enlightened, cultured, and far the best governed state in Europe, though based on a decaying Muslim civilization. The Normans breathed new life into this Muslim culture, not destroying but assimilating it. With their ancient talent for seafaring and trade, they made full use of the commanding strategic position of Sicily in the Mediterranean Sea and developed the Sicilian capital of Palermo into the greatest and richest city in Europe outside Constantinople.

*Normandy,* the first territory granted to this gifted people, became quickly one of

(Cnut), now a Christian, ruled over an England that was part of a large Scandinavian Empire (1017–1035).

After the death of King Canute's sons, who also sat briefly on the English throne, the Scandinavians allowed the succession to pass to an Englishman, a descendant of King Alfred the Great (Edward the Confessor, 1042–1066). When Edward died, however, leaving no direct heirs, the Norwegian king of the day, Harold Hardrada, decided that he would like to be king of England as well as of Norway, and launched an expedition against the nominee of the English lords, Harold the Saxon, son of Godwin. At the same time Duke William of Normandy, himself also a descendant of the Vikings, but lord of a far more civilized realm than the Norway of that era, claimed the English throne. The issue was decided by battle. Harold the Saxon defeated and killed Harold Hardrada, king of Norway, at Stamford Bridge, but succumbed in turn to the Norman knights under Duke William at the battle of Hastings (1066). Thus was founded the Norman monarchy of England, to be discussed at greater length in the last chapter of this volume.

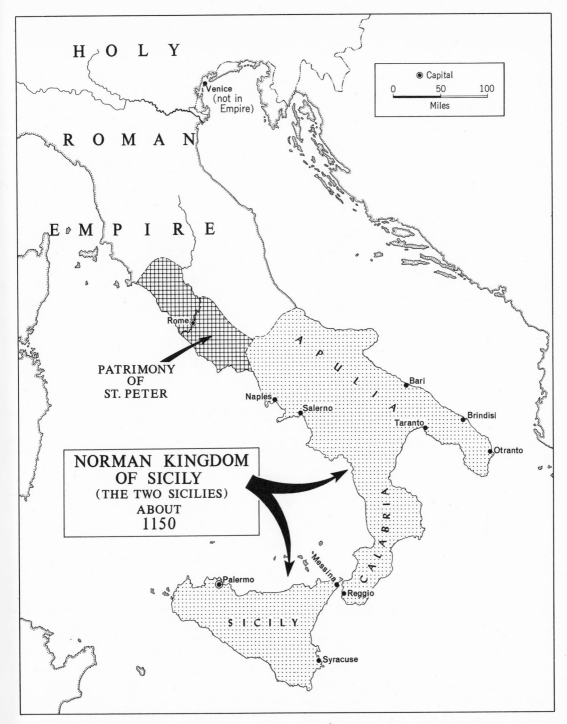

HOLY

ROMAN

EMPIRE

Venice
(not in
Empire)

⦿ Capital

0    50    100
Miles

PATRIMONY
OF
ST. PETER

Rome

NORMAN KINGDOM
OF SICILY
(THE TWO SICILIES)
ABOUT
1150

A P U L I A

Naples

Salerno

Bari

Taranto

Brindisi

Otranto

C A L A B R I A

Messina

Palermo

Reggio

S I C I L Y

Syracuse

the best organized parts of France, the Norman rulers adapting to their use many of the ancient institutions of France which had not been effectively used since the eighth and ninth centuries, when France had been a part of Charlemagne's empire. *England* became a great nation primarily because Duke William of Normandy and his successors on the English throne were able to give it a strong feudal government, much stronger than that of their Anglo-Saxon predecessors, while at the same time they put to use what was best in the Anglo-Saxon heritage.

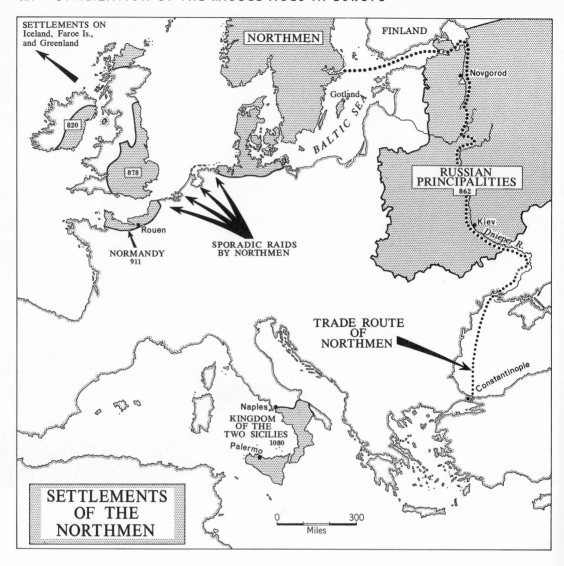

SETTLEMENTS ON Iceland, Faroe Is., and Greenland

NORTHMEN

FINLAND

Novgorod

Gotland

BALTIC SEA

820

878

RUSSIAN PRINCIPALITIES
862

Rouen

SPORADIC RAIDS BY NORTHMEN

Kiev

Dnieper R.

NORMANDY
911

TRADE ROUTE OF NORTHMEN

Constantinople

Naples
KINGDOM OF THE TWO SICILIES
1080
Palermo

SETTLEMENTS OF THE NORTHMEN

0          300
Miles

Northmen in *Iceland,* far away in the north Atlantic, produced the earliest great European literature, the Eddas. Northmen, meanwhile, led by Rurik and his successors, founded a trading state in *Russia* which ultimately became a Slavic empire; Northmen in Constantinople were recognized as the finest warriors and were recruited to form the emperor's bodyguard. Normans distinguished themselves in the Crusades, and were usually the acknowledged leaders; they were responsible for the Norman style of architecture (a modified form of Romanesque), and their monuments are still to be seen today dotted through the English and northern French countryside. It is difficult to find a people among all the invaders of Europe who were evidently so naturally gifted or so versatile, or who have left their characteristic mark in such an unmistakable way upon European institutions as these ex-Vikings from Scandinavia.

▶ **The feudal system**

THE NATURE OF FEUDAL AUTHORITY—
ARBITRARY LOCAL POWER MODIFIED BY CUSTOM
AND MORAL SANCTIONS

Having seen the anarchy of the period after the death of Charlemagne and the breakup of his Empire, we now need to examine in more detail what it was that filled this political vacuum. Power, as always, continued to exist; but it was now widely diffused, and no longer exercised by a responsible government. Put briefly, the power relapsed into the hands of landowners who each possessed a private army supported from his own resources. But the power was not exercised in a completely arbitrary manner; there was a network of customary and legal sanctions upon its exercise which, though perhaps not as strong as sanctions exercised by monarchs who had armies and bureaucracies at their disposal to enforce their will, were nonetheless adequate to keep powerful landowners from doing everything that their fancy dictated.

We have already seen that in Egypt what has been loosely called a Feudal Age replaced the Divine Monarchy of the Old Kingdom. We know too little about this remote period to be able to state what sanctions there were upon the arbitrary power of Egyptian landowners. All we know is that the landowners appear to have assumed power after the breakdown of the monarchy. In the absence of such essential information we cannot call the age truly "feudal" in the way that the early Middle Ages were feudal. If we wish to be accurate, we must say that the only truly feudal age known to us is this medieval period, characterized by the holding of *feuda,* or fiefs.

The relationship between lord (suzerain)[2] and vassal, between the bestower and receiver of the fief, is the heart of the medieval feudal system; and the duties imposed on each party to the transaction by feudal law and custom are the chief sanctions on the arbitrary use of their power by either. A vassal had the power to go to war against his suzerain, and, indeed, only too frequently he did so; but, if he did, unless the suzerain had failed to perform his own duties, the vassal not only broke the feudal law and could be called to account for it in the feudal court of his lord, but also broke an oath of fealty which he had taken. And this itself,

[2] The word "suzerain" is used in this chapter to denote the superior lord in a lord-vassal relationship, although the word has in certain countries a definite technical meaning not applicable to all such overlords.

in an age when an oath was taken upon the Cross or upon holy relics, and was considered sacred, was enough to brand him as a false knight and hold him up to infamy.

So the sanctions in the feudal system were both material and moral, as under any effective law. The difficulty was that too often the law could not be enforced, and it never could be enforced without war; hence a man might brave the moral sanctions if his material interests were involved and he thought he had a chance in the ensuing war. It was thus an ineffectual system rather than an arbitrary or immoral one; and since it was also an unequal one in that the peasants and lower classes had few rights, and those unenforceable without military power to back them, it was not one that would obtain the assent of more than a small minority. It was only likely to endure as long as the effective power could be kept within the small class of nobles. Later medieval and modern history can be viewed largely as the attempt to destroy the privileges of the upper class and replace them with a more equitable system giving more rights to ever-increasing numbers of people. The national state, under a monarch backed by a middle class which hardly existed in earlier medieval times, provided such a system, however imperfectly; and the establishment of national states in several European countries, coincident with the destruction of the greater part of the feudal system, will form a fitting climax to this account of the Western heritage from ancient times. With the establishment of national states modern political history really begins.

THE ORIGIN OF FEUDALISM

## The Roman heritage

To trace back into the past the origins of such a mass of irrational customs and laws as the feudal system is not a very profitable task, though many scholars have devoted their lives to it without coming to any agreed conclusions. It would seem tolerably certain that feudalism derives from both Roman and Germanic sources. We have already seen that in late Roman society, when the barbarians were invading and the ordinary small landholders found difficulty in surviving without military protection, these latter would ask the nobility to protect them in exchange for what services they could give. This practice was called *patrocinium*, or patronage. As a rule military services were not required so much as cultivation of land, whether such land was given to the farmer by the lord or already belonged to him. This relationship between patron and client is entirely a late Roman feature, and has little to do with the patron-client relationship in earlier days, when the client was usually of the same social class but inferior in worldly goods.

During the period of the Merovingian kings there was as much danger to a small independent man as in the late Roman Empire. So we find in the early Middle Ages an established practice of *commendation* by a poor and landless man, who asked for protection from a noble in a better situation. The more powerful nobles could gather large bands of followers in this way; the greater they were, the more men would commend themselves to them, for the safer would be the protection. Some of these were lesser nobles themselves and not farmers, but for some reason they had lost their land. In these cases the patron after commendation would take them into his service as military followers.

Another heritage from Roman times was similar. A free farmer who suffered from insecurity or had fallen into debt could yield up his land either to his creditor or to some noble, and ask for it back again as a tenant. This was called *precarium*, or requesting. Another form of precarium was simply the prayer by a landless farmer for some land to cultivate in exchange for goods and services. Since the noble had far too much land to cultivate himself, it was to his advantage to give it out to a good tenant. So the precarium helped him to take care of his needs, and was mutually advantageous. The Church, in particular, found the system valuable. It was forbidden to alienate Church lands altogether, but a precarious tenancy permitted it to have its lands cultivated without losing them; and in feudal times it had enough sanctions of its own peculiar kind at its disposal for it to be as well able as the secular lord to protect its tenants.

The precarium by the eighth century had largely been replaced by the *beneficium*, or benefice, which was practically the same thing under a different name. Both were tantamount to leases of land for a limited period; but the later benefices rarely took land from freeholders and gave them back, for there was little such land available by this time. Benefices were given frequently by the great nobles to their officials and assistants in lieu of a money income. They were also given to lesser nobles who could provide great nobles with troops paid for out of the proceeds of the benefice. The Carolingian kings gave out such benefices freely, in many cases including an *immunity* from taxation and the performance of feudal services; then the land was held as a virtual freehold.

### The Germanic heritage

The development from Roman times seems to be fairly clear. But in the system described above there seems to be an obvious parallel with the German custom of *comitatus* already noticed. Here, it will be remembered, the old warrior bands of Germans used to join the troop of an independent chieftain to whom they were bound by ties of honor and fealty and for whom they were ready to fight and die. It would seem that in the early feudal period before Charlemagne, Roman custom was predominant, and that the precarious system noted above arose in response to the definite needs of the time. But the necessity, under Germanic influence, became converted into a virtue; and all the ancient sanctions of the comitatus were gradually invoked to tie the lesser landholder and benefice holder to his lord. The moral sanctions now became established instead of sanctions that were only legal and instead of the ordinary ties of self-interest as between landlord and tenant. The vassal, as he shortly came to be called, owed loyalty and allegiance to his lord, a virtue conspicuously missing in late Roman and Merovingian times. This development corresponded with the increasing militarization of the whole society and with the rise of a class of nobles whose interest ceased to be in land. Though of course he had to own land, the noble gave out most of it again to vassals in exchange primarily, not for goods and ordinary menial and farming services, but for military service under his command.

It is now in this post-Carolingian period that feudalism based on the possession of fiefs comes to the fore. A fief was really only a hereditary benefice;[3] but almost invariably the obligation upon the vassal or fief holder was to supply warriors. Knights who could ride on horseback and provide their own equipment were the most valued. Anyone who could not do this was unlikely to be given a fief. Hence fief holders finally became warriors belonging to the class of the nobility, or churchmen with such warriors under them, who could perform the same service.

RELATIONSHIP BETWEEN LORD AND VASSAL

### The theoretical relationship—Practical complications—Subinfeudation

The developed feudal system thus contained the lord or suzerain who held his land, originally or theoretically, by gift from the king, who was in theory the owner of all the land. This suzerain let out most of his land to vassals in exchange for military and certain other stipulated services to be described later; but he retained some land as a demesne from which he obtained the subsistence required for himself, his family, his personal landless military retainers, and his servants. The land received as fiefs by his vassals could also be subdivided, and let out again as fiefs to yet other vassals who would perform for them the same services as they themselves performed for their suzerains. This was a method of passing

[3] A fief was not necessarily even land. Some honor or right could be held as a fief, entailing the usual obligations of a vassal.

on some of the military obligations to others, and was called *subinfeudation*. At times the greater lords tried to check excessive subinfeudation, since by it they tended to lose control of their subtenants, who owed them no direct allegiance, and could be reached only through their own personal vassals.

At this stage the process is not too complicated. Diagrammatically it would look like this:

King
↑
Suzerain 1
↑
Vassal 1 (himself a suzerain in relation to Vassal 2)
↑
Vassal 2
. . . . .

But unfortunately it was not in practice so simple. Any vassal could hold any number of fiefs from different suzerains; and sooner or later it would happen that, say, Vassal 2 in the above diagram would have let out part of his land as a fief to Suzerain 1, and would thus be in the relationship of a vassal to the vassal of this suzerain (Vassal 1), and yet be a suzerain in relation to the suzerain of his own suzerain! If this appears complicated, it is only a reflection of the actual state of feudal society, and may be illustrated in a more complex diagram (arrows indicate the direction of the services rendered).

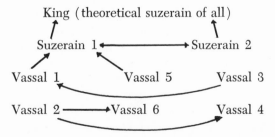

(part of Suzerain 2's land is held as a fief from Suzerain 1, and another part in a different locality he has let out to the same suzerain)

Puzzle: What happens when Suzerain 2 decides he will cease performing feudal services for Suzerain 1, and what will Vassal 3 do when called out by his respective suzerains?

The answer to the puzzle is that, if a vassal was anxious to do the right thing, he would give his own personal service to one lord while allowing his own vassals to perform the remainder of his service. But clearly this would not hold good if he were called out by two lords at the same time who happened to be at war with one another.

It can be easily seen from these diagrams and examples that there was endless occasion for feudal wars. These could hardly have been avoided even if the feudal aristocracy had not in any case regarded war as a positive pleasure, their one great vocation in life, while they were content to hand over the management of their estates, from which they obtained their subsistence, to baseborn hirelings.

### The legal structure—The feudal court

In order to enforce these rights the lord would periodically hold a court to which he summoned all his vassals. If any vassal did not appear without sufficient excuse, or if his equals in the court condemned him for failure to perform his proper feudal services, his fief could be forfeited. If he was accused by another vassal in his lord's court, he could claim the right to single combat with his accuser. If he lost, he was presumed to be guilty.

The enforcement of the decree, however, was another matter. There was no means for driving him from a fief which he held in actual possession save by war. It was thus of importance that all the vassals should sit on the court, since it was they also who would have to enforce the decree. If the guilty vassal had no greater lord to protect him, it was probable that the other vassals, fighting in unison under their suzerain, would succeed in compelling him to yield up the fief. It need hardly be emphasized how rough and ready such justice was; nor need it surprise us that many of the lesser

nobility in later centuries supported the efforts of the kings to establish a king's justice, containing elements of Roman law, in preference to the feudal variety.

### The duties of the lord toward his vassal

The lord, of course, provided the vassal with his land in the first place. But it was also his duty to protect this land and the vassal from other lords or invaders. In this he was, in theory, only protecting his own land. It was also his duty to protect the vassal in other ways. If, for instance, a vassal were summoned to the king's court for an offense, as became possible when the kings began to hold courts for the administration of justice, it was the lord's duty to defend him. In theory, if the lord did not fulfill his obligation to protect the vassal, the contract was terminated, and the vassal no longer owed him allegiance. We find Pope Gregory VII later using this as an excuse for his deposition of the German Emperor, and it is the basis for the much later idea of the supposed Social Contract, under which, as expounded by the English theorist John Locke, the people were released from their allegiance to the king if he did not maintain their "natural rights."

### The duties of the vassal toward his lord

The first duty of the vassal to his lord was allegiance, symbolized in the (Frankish) ceremony of homage. On being given or on inheriting a fief the vassal would kneel, place his two hands within those of his lord and declare himself his man. If the lord accepted the homage he kissed him as a sign of recognition of his vassalage. Since in theory a fief was not hereditary, an heir on coming into his father's estate had to do homage for his fief, which could, in theory also, be refused. In practice, the eldest son of a vassal inherited the fief of his father, and merely had to do homage for it, perform certain special services, and pay special dues, the equivalent of an inheritance tax. If a vassal died without male heirs, then the fief theoretically escheated to the suzerain, even if there was a surviving daughter.

But in practice this daughter inherited it, though the suzerain took her under his protection and saw that she was provided with a suitable husband, who then undertook the duties of the vassal. If there were no heirs, male or female, then the land did escheat, that is, it returned to the suzerain. The fief was not subdivided between many sons, but passed down intact to the eldest (primogeniture), who could, of course, let it out by subinfeudation if he desired.

The chief duty for most fief holders was to provide a stipulated number of knights, mounted warriors, calculated in accordance with the size of the fief. The custom, however, varied in different parts as indeed, did all the feudal arrangements. These warriors were bound to serve only for a definite, quite limited period, a fact which made long campaigns difficult. The period, as a rule, was forty days in each year. However, the lord could promise booty or other rewards and then have his vassals follow him voluntarily, as, for instance when William the Conqueror invaded England on the understanding that there would be new fiefs for all. In later medieval periods the military service could be commuted for a sum of money called *scutage*. This arrangement was more convenient for towns, in particular, if they happened to form part of a fief; and the money was often more appreciated by the lord than military service, since it enabled him to hire mercenaries who could serve for a longer period of time. The Church also on occasion paid scutage instead of military service, since it had more easy access to money than to warriors. Nevertheless, most ecclesiastical fiefs had some military service to perform, which was usually done by subinfeudation to lords who were willing to undertake the service.

The vassal had the duty of providing hospitality to his lord when he visited him. As this visit might be very expensive if the lord arrived with a large retinue, it was limited by custom and sometimes was commuted for a regular sum of money. The vassal also, as we have seen, had to attend the lord's court when requested.

When the lord was in financial difficulties, as for instance if he were trying to raise money to go on a crusade, the vassal could be called upon for a gift, known as an *aid*. At other times the aids were given for the ransoming of the lord, for the knighting of his eldest son, and for the marriage of his eldest daughter. These again were limited by custom according to the size and value of the fief.

A further sum of money was provided by the vassal on certain specified occasions, which was known as a *relief*. When an heir inherited his fief, it was customary to pay a relief, which might amount to as much as a whole year's revenue. When the lord himself died and was succeeded by his heir a relief was also paid. Finally when a vassal wished to transfer his fief to someone else, the equivalent of a sale, then he had to give a relief to the lord in exchange for his permission to the transfer. All these reliefs were fixed by custom, and when the money economy began to take the place of the earlier commodity economy the reliefs usually took the form of money payments. An heiress who wished to marry without the consent of the suzerain might persuade him to give it by offering him a sum of money. One of the best, if most irregular, sources of income for a lord was from the fief of a minor, or of an unmarried girl, whom he looked after till he or she came of age. The child for the time gave up what would have been his rights had he been of age to become a vassal, and the lord took the income from his estate. The lord did not have to reimburse the child for any losses that were sustained by such a child during his infancy.

It should be emphasized that the lord did not live off the income provided him by his vassals, which was quite limited and only given at irregular intervals. He lived off the income from his demesne, which contained his personal manors run by his servants. These will be dealt with in a later section. Every vassal belonged to the feudal nobility himself, and he always possessed a demesne of his own unless he were a personal retainer living with his lord, a situation which became rare in the later feudal age. The primary purpose of the feudal system was to provide warriors for protection and prestige. It was the manorial system, the private demesnes of these feudal lords, which provided the economic base for the feudal system. The feudal nobility therefore was a military aristocracy which incidentally owned land, rather than a landed aristocracy, which occasionally had to defend its property by military means, but at other times lived quietly, attending to its rural concerns. With the exception of the lord himself, the managers of the estates were of a different class from the nobility, were hired by them, and were treated as social inferiors. Most of the lords felt themselves too superior, and were too busy with their military affairs, to pay much attention to their estates. If this had not been so, they would not have given out so much of their land in financially unrewarding fiefs; they would, like the later Roman nobles, have lived in the lap of luxury from the intelligent exploitation of huge estates worked by laborers who could not rebel and could not leave the land.

### The special position of the feudal king

In view of the later importance of kings a few words are necessary here on the anomalous position they occupied during the feudal age. Theoretically, as we have seen, the kings owned all the land, and every noble in a given country owed allegiance to his king. But, as a matter of historical fact, the greater nobles, perhaps the majority of them, had never even received their land from a king in the first place, but had taken it for themselves during the period of disintegration following the breakup of the Carolingian Empire. And the king exercised very little power over them. The king's effective power was only what he derived from his own feudal estates, which were often, as in the case of France, by design of the nobles smaller in extent than those of many of the lords who owed nominal allegiance to him. The French lords, in choosing their king

from the Capetian family, had probably agreed on the choice for the simple reason that he was less powerful than they, and thus likely to present little threat to their power.

The king's position was naturally different in each country, according to the local conditions found there. The German king, who was usually also at the same time the Holy Roman Emperor, was elected from among the German nobles; and, though there was a tendency to keep the office within certain families for long periods at a time, it never did become formally a hereditary position, and his power, as elsewhere, was derived from the estates of his house. After he had been elected king by the chief nobles, and later by certain of the higher clergy of his realm, he had only prestige in addition to what he had before, with two important exceptions. He had in his hands the appointment of the bulk of the higher clergy, a patronage that an astute monarch could manipulate to great advantage, and land left without heirs altogether would escheat to him and not to any other noble. His prestige and title gave him the first refusal of the command in any all-German or all-European war, such as the Crusades. When the emperors tried to make good their claim to Italy, and sent a regular "Roman expedition" of German warriors over the Alps, their leadership was not challenged. For the rest, the only real feudal tie between the nobles and their elected monarch was the oath of allegiance which they took to him after election; and, as we shall see, the right claimed by the papacy to absolve from oaths by virtue of its spiritual power was also used as a political instrument for the deposition of an emperor. When Gregory VII wished to depose Henry IV of Germany, a prerogative naturally contested bitterly by this emperor, he solemnly absolved all the German nobles from their oaths of allegiance so that they could elect another emperor.

In England after the conquest by Duke William of Normandy, the kings of his line actually did own all the land, since it had been acquired by conquest. They gave it out as fiefs, with certain restrictions on the raising of private armies which will be discussed in a later chapter on the rise of the English national state. It is only important here to notice that in England the theory corresponded to the actual facts, with incalculable advantages for the monarchy.

The position of the French king, however, is of the most interest, since the Capetian kings used their theoretical powers and their prestige to such good effect that they were ultimately able to unify France under their rule. Hugh Capet and his successors actually owned only a small compact area around Paris. They owned this as counts, and their armies were only such as could be drawn from this comparatively small territory. Yet, as kings, they were socially of a higher rank than any of the more powerful lords in their realm. They were solemnly anointed as kings by the archbishop of Rheims, and made to swear a coronation oath under which they promised to defend the humble, help the oppressed, preserve peace, maintain justice, and perform a number of other functions which were fantastically outside the scope of their real powers. But in theory they were expected to do this, and in their efforts they could usually count on the full support of the Church and the ecclesiastical officials, who had nothing, as a rule, to gain from the lawlessness created by the independent nobles. In addition the king held in his hands much of the best patronage of the Church, especially in northern France.

The king as theoretical owner of all the land in the territory vaguely called France was owed allegiance by all the lords in his realm. His prestige was such that most nobles, at all events those of French origin, usually did perform the act of homage once in their lives; it cost them nothing, since the king was not in a position to take away their fiefs, and they did not have to give him anything substantial unless he was in a position to compel them. He was theoretically entitled to the usual military service from them, and could summon them to his court for the administration of justice. None of

these rights was worth much as long as the kings were unable to enforce them. But in a society which laid so much store by custom and loyalty they were not negligible. And the king had one immense advantage which was ultimately to prove crucial; if any lord did not obey the summons issued by him, then the lord was in the wrong. The king had the feudal law on his side if he went to war with the rebellious noble, and he had the right to call upon all the other lords in the kingdom to aid in punishing the rebel. Naturally the other nobles would consult their own interests in deciding whether or not they would obey the king; but it happened frequently enough that these interests would best be served by joining him and dispossessing the rebellious vassal. Philip Augustus used this power with extreme skill and effectiveness against his English vassal, John, king of England, who considered it beneath his dignity to attend the court of a man he considered his inferior and who owned far less land even in France than John himself. When John refused to obey his summons Philip called upon the other French nobles to dispossess him; and since John was regarded as an interloper in France and commanded few French sympathies, Philip was able to take away the bulk of his lands and bestow them on his own followers as fiefs; but with the great difference that Philip was now their real overlord and not merely a theoretical one.

Finally the king had all the social prestige belonging to his title. His wife would be queen, unlike the wife of any other noble, a position naturally sought after by heiresses; and their lands would serve to extend the feudal estates of the monarch while land without heirs would escheat to him. The king was often chosen as the most fitting protector of minors and of young women who had not yet found a suitable husband. And, like the German emperor, the French king[4] was the natural leader for a crusade or other foreign war if he wished to go. It

---

[4] The last chapter in this volume will deal briefly with other states than Germany and France, as well as go into more detail on the French monarchy.

can be seen, therefore, that in shrewd and able hands the position of king, in spite of his relative poverty, had certain manifest advantages over the rest of the feudal nobility; and perhaps it will no longer seem so strange that from these small beginnings the French monarchy was ultimately able to unify France and effectively control that feudal nobility which had elected him in the first place with far different expectations.

### The feudal castle—Structure and purpose

The primary task of the feudal noble, as we have seen, was the provision of protection for his dependents. If he failed in this duty not only would he lose his retainers but he would also lose his very land to more warlike enemies. Especially during the invasions of the Northmen this duty was far from easy to fulfill. With only a small band of retainers he could not hope to meet an army in open combat, and there might be occasions when he could look for no help from either his lord or his fellow vassals. His only recourse, then, was to wall himself in, and keep the invading warriors out. Thus his home had to be fortified as strongly as his resources would permit.

The early castle was primitive enough. As a rule there had to be a moat or fosse, as an outer protection against invaders. Over the moat there had to be a bridge which could be raised and lowered at will. Invaders who tried to cross were at a disadvantage, for the defenders were able to discharge their weapons at them while keeping as far as possible out of sight themselves. Any house that could satisfy these conditions could be called a castle, although the earliest examples were only wooden affairs, not very large, with dark rooms and with slits for windows. Gradually, with the improvement of technique, the castles began to be

*An impressive feudal castle in southern France (Les Baux en Provence) now in ruins. The castle commanded an extensive valley and was considered impregnable until it was captured in the time of Cardinal Richelieu. The village around it, which used to house some five thousand people, is now populated by a bare fifty.*

*This castle at Óbidos (Portugal), only slightly restored, is now a government hotel. A picture of the town of Óbidos, which still has its medieval walls intact, appears in Chapter 21.*

built of stone and to be larger and larger. A castle that was meant to withstand a siege had to contain within its walls storehouses for food, sufficient weapons and missiles and the means for making them, and shelter for all the defenders and their horses. While this was the minimum needed for purposes of defense, the castle was also the home of the lord and his family, and therefore needed some amenities. Later castles, therefore, were quite elaborate structures, serving for defense but also for display. Every castle maintained its inner portion in addition to the donjon or keep, a wooden or stone tower protected by its own portcullis (a grating made of strong bars of wood or iron, sharp pointed, which could be dropped suddenly in case of an attack) a drawbridge, and a moat. Here the last stand would be made in case of assault. The outer battlements were protected from attackers by walls which had smaller towers on them at intervals from which the defenders could discharge their missiles, and pour down boiling oil and other dangerous substances as well as rocks upon the besiegers, who were at a distinct disadvantage down below. Before the days of gunpowder and the cannon ball it was very difficult to storm a castle. Scaling ladders had to be used to reach the battlements, and

all the time that the besiegers were trying to place them in position and climb them the defenders were more or less immune from attack, and could use all the resources at their disposal to destroy the battering rams, the siege machines, and the other paraphernalia used against them. The usual way to take a castle in earlier days was to sit down in front of it and starve the defenders into submission. Hence the importance of making the castle as nearly self-sufficient as possible and thus continually increasing its size. There might be enough room even for the peasants of the noble to escape to the castle in the event of an attack.

In the later Middle Ages, when feudal warfare had been brought under some control, the castle became more of a home, the central point for the administration of the fief. Here the lord usually lived, surrounded by his officials and administrators, who stayed there permanently; but the lord himself, if he owned many estates, could live in one of his lesser manor houses if he preferred it. He had access to whatever luxuries were available, a diet largely of meat, cooked on open fires of charcoal or roasted on a spit above the fire, washed down by plenty of wine. Furnishings in the castle were primitive until trade with the East was opened

*A medieval deer hunt. From* Book of the King Modus *(French), ca. 1460.* (COURTESY
THE PIERPONT MORGAN LIBRARY. Ms. 820, folio 12)

up after the Muslims had been driven from
the Mediterranean; especially after the Crusades, rugs and tapestries became more frequent, and in the later Middle Ages fine
tapestries were also manufactured in the
West. But the castle rooms always remained
rather dark and cheerless, though the great
hall had dignity and spaciousness which in
some degree compensated; and on the occasion of a feast, with minstrels and musicians
and storytellers plying their arts, a feudal
noble could feel that he had at hand everything that truly made life worth living.

### Amusements of the feudal nobility

The chief amusement of a noble was
warfare, in which he took a delight that was
never altogether assuaged. If he could not
indulge in this, then, in later ages, he made
mock fights, called jousts or tournaments. In

these elaborate imitations of the real thing
all danger was not removed. Neither single
combat between horsemen armed with the
lance, nor mock battles between groups of
knights on horseback lacked danger for the
participants. In early times the armor consisted only of a shirt of mail reaching to the
hips, and a helmet. But in later ages, when
in fact the armored horseman was becoming an anachronism, vanquished by the crossbow, the longbow, and finally gunpowder,
the armor became more elaborate and well
made than ever, with the horse and its rider
protected in every possible place. The result,
of course, was that an unfortunate horseman
became also immobile, and a fall from his
horse might even have dangerous consequences. But it was when the feudal tradition
was dying, and there was less serious warfare, that the tournaments reached their

*Falconers show off their birds to a queen. From* Book of the King Modus *(French), ca. 1460.* (COURTESY THE PIERPONT MORGAN LIBRARY. Ms. 820, folio 55)

*Game of backgammon—not too dissimilar to our own game. From a miniature, Hugo von Trimberg,* Der Renner, *fifteenth century.* (COURTESY THE PIERPONT MORGAN LIBRARY. Ms. 763, folio 134)

*Woodcut from a Caxton printed book, showing a game of chess. From Jacobus de Cessolis,* The Game and Play of Chess, *ca. 1482.* (COURTESY THE PIERPONT MORGAN LIBRARY)

*This medieval miniature shows the Israelite general Joab entertaining Abner, whom he is planning to murder. As in all these miniatures, the picture faithfully represents the illustrator's contemporary experience, and the feasting scene depicted here is no doubt authentically medieval. From a* Picture Bible *(French), ca. 1250.* (COURTESY THE PIERPONT MORGAN LIBRARY. Ms. 638, folio 37)

height. And if the dates of the armorial collections in our museums are ever examined, it will be noticed how many of the most decorative are fourteenth- and fifteenth- and even sixteenth-century manufactures, while the battle of Crécy in 1346 had already shown that the feudal chivalry of France was no match for the yeomanry of England armed with the longbow.

If they could not fight men, the nobles hunted animals. Every noble learned to hunt, not for food—though this was important too—but for pleasure and for the chance to exercise his skill in what became, and has remained, a ritual and a cult, reserved only for the feudal nobility. Above all in the later Middle Ages hunting with the falcon became the highest of skills; Emperor Frederic II

devoted a remarkable and scientific book to the *Art of Hunting with Birds,* in which he explains the ritual of hunting and goes into considerable detail on the different kinds of falcon and how they should be bred. Few activities of the noble were more damaging to his peasants, since all game was protected and there were very stringent and strictly enforced laws on the preservation of forests and woodlands. Moreover, the peasant was not allowed to touch even a rabbit himself, while the hunt was likely to destroy his standing crops if it passed through them. The practice of hunting has persisted in Europe long after other feudal vestiges have disappeared, and it has always remained the hallmark of a class. One does not need to be reminded of the late Marshal Goering's visits to Poland or the passion of the Archduke Francis Ferdinand for the chase (the prince who was murdered at Sarajevo), or the importance of August 12 in England and Scotland before the world wars (the opening of the grouse season) to realize how persistent this feudal prerogative has been.

Among less sanguinary sports could be mentioned games of dice, such as backgammon, and the mock battle of chess, introduced into the West at the end of eleventh century. An amusement seldom found among the feudal nobility, however, was reading. As a class nobles were not noted for their literacy, though there were some famous exceptions, notably Emperor Frederic himself.

### The noble lady

The wife of the feudal lord, even though she had probably been married for her family connections and possible estates, nevertheless had a most important and no doubt insufficiently appreciated part to play in feudal society. The entire household arrangements of the castle fell within her province. And this, in an economy that tried to be self-sufficient, was no small task. She had to supervise the making of clothing and furnishings, she had to apportion tasks among the women of her entourage, and not infrequently she had to undertake the administrative duties of her husband as well. If he went on a crusade she had to manage the fief; if he were killed on campaign she had to undertake all his duties until she found herself a new husband or one was found for her by a relative or her husband's suzerain; or she would have to negotiate with her lord so that he gave her permission to remain a widow. She had to visit the peasants and tenantry on the estate, acting as Lady Bountiful, occasionally nursing the sick herself, or at least making arrangements for nursing care. In her spare time she plied her needle in embroidery and decorative work. Finally, at a pinch, she must be prepared to defend the castle in the absence of suitable males and to direct the lesser-born warriors on the battlements.

If a noble lady did not find a husband she could go to a convent; if she did not bear a child to her lord, preferably a male, then there was usually not too much difficulty in finding some cleric who would declare that the marriage was within the prohibited degrees and thus null and void from the beginning. This annulment was not hard to reconcile with a clerical conscience, since so many members of the privileged nobility were indeed closely related to each other. Marriage to a first cousin was considered too close, and it was likewise forbidden to marry various relatives who were related only by marriage.

In the later Middle Ages a movement sprang up, under the inspiration of some of the greatest of these ladies, especially Eleanor of Aquitaine, which made use of more romantic conceptions of womanhood than were current in real life. These tended to raise the ideal of womanhood, if not the status of women. This new ideal, called *chivalry*, will be discussed, however, in a later section of this chapter.

THE POSITION OF THE CHURCH IN THE FEUDAL SYSTEM

### The Church as captive of the system

In the discussion of the relationship between the German emperor Otto I and his clergy, reference has already been made to the way in which the appointment of the higher clergy fell into the hands of the secular powers. In general, throughout Europe in the early Middle Ages the king and the nobility were the patrons of the Church and made all appointments, right down to the parish priests, who had the actual task of ministering to the spiritual needs of the people. The local higher clergy might have some say in the appointments, but since they too were drawn from the noble class this choice would probably not have been much improvement over the appointments made by the noble lords themselves. The quality of the clergy under these conditions was not likely to be high. Most appointments were made to relatives, to friends, or to those who could afford to buy them. The reason for this system of patronage was simply that the clergy, like everyone else, had to live. And they could live only if they were assured of a continuing income. This they could only gain from the possession of land; and the possession of land meant that they had to fulfill the feudal obligations that went with it. Otto I may have intentionally tried to recruit potential warriors into the Church hierarchy, but other rulers and nobles certainly chose their appointees from those who were noted for competence rather than for piety.

So the Church itself became part of the feudal system, with the higher clergy drawn from the feudal class and performing feudal duties in addition to their tasks as clerics. On the other hand, the Church did have one manifest advantage in a rude age; it had at its disposal all the powers of compulsion wielded by the nobility. The clergy could discipline their flocks, even if they had to bow to their own feudal overlords; and they had their own courts in which to try offenders against ecclesiastical law and regulations. They could enforce their decisions either by exacting spiritual punishments (penances) or by handing over offenders to the secular authorities. And on the whole, with certain notorious exceptions, it would seem that their influence was exercised in a more humane manner than the nobles used theirs; moreover, their influence on the nobility was not negligible, and probably greater than it would have been had they belonged to a different and more despised class.

### Attitude of Church toward feudal system

For the papacy, as we shall see, feudalism was an enemy, to be controlled and if possible destroyed; but this point need not be labored further here. The papacy was naturally opposed to any decentralized system into which its own monarchical framework could not fit. Above all the clergy disapproved of the unlimited warfare of the feudal classes and tried their best to restrain it. They had no power to compel obedience; all they could use was moral suasion and the fact that the lords themselves were professing Christians. The first effective effort in this direction was the proclamation by councils throughout Europe of several "Peaces of God" which tried to protect certain classes of the people from the rapacity of the nobles. Merchants were to be protected, and, above all, the churches, the monasteries, and their inhabitants. Curses were also called down upon those who robbed the poor. These Peaces, proclaimed in 989 and on several occasions thereafter, had some effect, since certain Christian nobles took oaths not to do any of the forbidden things, at least for part of the year.

A further effort was made in the early eleventh century with the "Truce of God." Under threat of excommunication[5] private warfare was forbidden from sundown on Wednesday to sunrise on Monday, and for certain specified periods of the year. The hope was that the peasants would at least be able to undertake their planting and harvesting work without molestation. Again the edict was not everywhere, or perhaps even in most places, observed; but it had some effect, since at this time the kings were gaining more power and prestige, and it was to their advantage also to curb feudal warfare, except in their own interests. These efforts, at all events, showed that the Church was alive to some of the tasks required of it as a spiritual institution. The Church also made serious efforts as far as it could to mitigate the evils of the warfare when it could not stop them, and many cases are known of charitable efforts to help and protect the poor, orphans, and other unprotected members of feudal society. The warfare, however, was satisfactorily curbed only when the papacy was able to direct the more warlike spirits against the Muslims in Spain and Palestine; such warfare against infidels could be approved of wholeheartedly for the sake of its good cause.

It has already been noted how the French clergy gave continuous support to the king in his efforts to deal with his nobles.

[5] This and other Church penalties will be explained in the next chapter.

*A jongleur and a medieval lady.* Chansonnier Provençal *(Paduan), thirteenth century.* (COURTESY THE PIERPONT MORGAN LIBRARY. Ms. 819, folio 57)

This support was given even by some of the clergy who were appointed by other lords than the king. When there was a chance to support the king they did, but it was too difficult to quarrel with one's overlord for such clergy to be ready to take the risks involved in following a feeble king. When, however, the French kings began to increase in power, they had no more faithful supporters than the higher clergy.

## Chivalry

As the Middle Ages approached their height a curious movement arose, partly literary in origin, which began to glorify the feudal ideals and separate them from the practices of the day, which were far from "noble" in our sense of the word. And this movement in turn had its effect upon the feudal practices, softening them and making them in fact more "noble," in this sense, than they had been. This movement was the cult of chivalry.

We have seen that in the ancient Germanic comitatus, loyalty was the highest virtue, and the personal relationship between the vassal and his lord was always sustained by the pledge of allegiance and

*Two knights do battle for a demoiselle, who is seen watching the combat. From a miniature, Tristan, ca. 1450.* (COURTESY THE PIERPONT MORGAN LIBRARY. Ms. 41, folio 49)

loyalty. This element naturally appealed to the minstrels and poets, even while too many actual feudal nobles by no means observed the pledge. The troubadours of southern France, the minnesingers in Germany, and the trouvères of northern France all combined to sing the praises of this virtue, but at the same time they also began to raise the ideal itself. Gradually a whole code of honor was evolved for the noble, and thus the ideal of knighthood was born.

There had always been much ceremony attached to becoming a knight when the age of twenty-one was reached. But in earlier times the ceremony had been performed by any noble, and though it was a formal act, there were no special preparations for it and no code of honor to be sworn to and solemnly observed beyond those involved in the ordinary duty of vassal to lord. But in later times it was only the king or great nobles who could perform the ceremony, and the youth had to undergo severe trials, purifications, and rituals, and then had to swear an oath of fealty upon the Gospels or upon holy relics. His training had to start at the age of seven, when he went as page to the court of a noble, usually the suzerain of his father, where he learned to serve and took training in the manners of his class. At fourteen he began to be trained in military duties, sports, and hunting, and perhaps in some of the social graces. From a youth he was among women as well as men, especially during the period from seven to fourteen; and it gradually came to be accepted that he should form a romantic attachment to the lady of the court, or one of her attendants, who was to be his ideal and for whom he was to perform deeds of gallantry. He was always to observe perfect courtesy toward her, including the courtesy of loving and cherishing her above all women. When he went out into the world it was the custom for the knight to defend her honor, and challenge any word spoken against her. He also had to keep faith, speak the truth at all times, protect the weak, and practice numerous other virtues.

It is clear that the Church had a hand in this, although the hand was concealed. It is a feudal and class ideal, but it is not exclusively this. The Church had gradually allowed into its worship a special reverence for Mary, the mother of Jesus, which had never been present in earlier Christianity. But she became the great religious ideal of the Middle Ages, an ideal of the heavenly feminine, called Our Lady, and a mediator between the sinner and Christ with whom she intercedes on his behalf. It seems clear that the connection between the new ideal of chivalry and courtesy toward womanhood and this new element in Christianity is close. And it is also clear that it must have raised the status of women in this particular society, even though the Christians elsewhere showed no more regard for women than before. It was not surprising that Eleanor of Aquitaine, Marie de France, and their twelfth- and thirteenth-century followers among the women writers and poets took up the cause with enthusiasm. And the whole romantic ideal of Western civilization, which does not yet seem to have spent its force, is its heritage.

▶ **The manorial system—Economic basis of feudalism**

THE MANOR AS AN ECONOMIC UNIT

### Origin of manor

In the feudal system ultimately the entire noble class was supported by the labor of the peasantry, the sole producers in feudal society outside the few towns. In this section the organization of the peasantry for production will be discussed, and how it was possible for a small class of hereditary nobles to compel the enormous majority of human beings in the society to produce a surplus large enough for them to live as economic parasites, whatever valuable political and cultural services they may have performed.

Since the agricultural unit was the manor, the system is usually called the manorial system. As usual in medieval institutions, both Roman and Germanic origins can

*Farm animals. From a miniature,* Petrus Crescentius, ca. *1460.* (COURTESY THE PIER-
PONT MORGAN LIBRARY. Ms. 232, folio 212)

*Sowing and reaping on a medieval manor. From a* Book of Hours *(Flemish), ca. 1515.*
(COURTESY THE PIERPONT MORGAN LIBRARY. Ms. 399, folios 9 and 10)

be traced. The large agricultural estate of the Roman Empire was called a villa. Attached to the villa were slaves and *coloni*, both working the land, the *coloni* in theory freemen, but in later Roman times forbidden by law to leave the land. The medieval manor had rarely any actual slaves, but the serfs were unable to leave the land, and were thus the equivalent of the *coloni*. There were also freemen on the manors who found it, as a rule, impossible to leave the land for lack, in early times, of anywhere else to go, and who were tied by debt and other obligations to the lord of the manor. These freemen were called in most places *villeins*, from the Latin *villa*. Medieval estates were sometimes the very same that had been villas in Roman times. Probably more estates, however, had originally been villages worked by communities of freemen who had been forced by the need for protection to seek it from some feudal lord, who had thereupon reduced the status of the freemen to virtual or actual serfdom.

542

### Relation of feudal to manorial system

As we have seen, most feudal lords gave away the greater part of their land to vassals in exchange for military service. But all lords, whether owning large or small estates, were compelled to keep some land which was cultivated for their own use. From this land they obtained the bulk of their income, since the feudal incidents and reliefs were comparatively small in total and only reached them at irregular intervals. The income from their own estates or manors was, on the contrary, entirely regular, and under their own control, either directly or through officials appointed by and responsible to themselves. And only from the proceeds of their manors could they pay for the soldiers they were forced to furnish for their lords, together with the various feudal payments described above. It was therefore necessary for every lord to keep in his hands as many manors as was necessary for the purpose. A wealthy lord, with large obligations, might have a

considerable number of manors, quite beyond his ability to supervise personally even
if he had the competence. These manors
would be supervised by bailiffs and stewards, who in every respect drew their authority from him, and carried out his orders
as his representative.

### Manorial self-sufficiency

*The lord's demesne*—Every manorial
estate had on it a manor house inhabited
by the lord or his officials, a certain amount
of arable and pasture land, and probably
some forest land. There was probably also
a parish church, whose priest lived in his
own house, and was appointed to his position by the lord. There was a village where
the peasants lived, and other workers required by the estate but who did not work
on the land. Such men would be blacksmiths, wheelwrights, shoemakers, and other
specialized workers.

A portion of the land, fixed by custom,
like everything else on a manor, was set
aside as the lord's personal demesne. It was
seldom more than a third of the whole property and might be as little as a sixth. This
land was worked for him by the peasants
under the direct supervision, as a rule, of
one of their number chosen by the other
peasants, and according to the instructions
of the lord or steward. When they were
working on the lord's land the supervisor had
authority to beat the peasants if they did
not work hard enough. All the produce from
the lord's demesne belonged to the lord and
constituted the major source of his income.

*The land of the peasants*—The remainder of the manorial land was worked by
the peasants for their own account, whether
they were freemen or serfs, and was subject to taxation, which will be discussed
in detail in a later section. Each peasant
had a certain acreage allotted to him varying from a half dozen to about thirty acres
each. But the acres were not all together,
making up a self-contained farm. They
were in strips, each strip containing about
an acre, and each of the length that a
team of oxen could plow before it needed

to take a rest (from which comes the measure "furlong"—furrow long). A peasant's
strips were separated from each other, sometimes by quite a considerable distance, perhaps in order to give each peasant his fair
share of the best and the worst land. Among
these strips were also the strips belonging
to the lord which had to be cultivated by the
peasants without profit.

The strip system, however, was not so
uneconomical in medieval as it would be
in modern times, for the cultivation was done
on a cooperative basis. No peasant was
likely to own enough oxen to pull through
soil that was at all stubborn the very primitive plow that was in use. Usually a team
of eight of these scrawny, ill-fed animals
was necessary to pull it. Thus the strips
would all be cultivated together, though the
produce of each strip went to the individual
owner. The meadow and pasture land was
kept for hay, necessary to keep the animals
fed over the winter; when the hay crop had
been taken off, the land then became common property, and all the peasants might
pasture their animals on it. Likewise, when
the crops had been harvested from the arable
land the stubble could be used as rough
pasture for the beasts. Pigs were allowed
to gather what nourishment they could from
the forest land, which remained in the hands
of the peasantry after the lord had set aside
what he needed for his own use. Since
the strips were divided from each other only
by a rough path or perhaps a double furrow, this system is known as the open-field
system.

A scientific rotation of crops, though
known to the ancient Greeks and Romans,
was unknown to the medieval peasant. But
it was recognized that the fertility of the
soil needed to be renewed, and that the
manure from the few domestic animals was
insufficient for the purpose. The only method
known to the peasants was the practice of letting the land lie fallow. In some parts of the
country a full half of the arable land was
allowed to lie fallow every year, being
plowed twice in the month of June, the only
use for the land for that year being for

rough pasture in the fall. Elsewhere it was found that only a third of the land need lie fallow and that two crops could be safely taken off in succession before the fallow. Naturally the frequency of fallow depended upon the fertility of the soil, but in most areas of Europe if in one year a spring crop was planted and in the next year a fall crop, sufficient fertility was maintained. These systems are known as the two-field and three-field systems, and they remained the common practice until the agricultural discoveries of the seventeenth century which led to the agricultural revolution of the eighteenth and nineteenth.

The peasant lived in the village in a small thatched hut which had a small plot of land attached to it which he could use as he wished. In this he grew vegetables, and kept a few chickens or geese which could pick up enough feed to sustain life and yield a few eggs a year. He lived on black bread, fresh vegetables if he was thrifty enough to grow them, porridge,

*This medieval illustration of the building of a biblical city again reflects authentic medieval practice. From a* Picture Bible *(French), ca. 1250.* (COURTESY THE PIERPONT MORGAN LIBRARY. Ms. 638, folio 3)

cheese, and very occasionally meat or fish, and wine. The staple field crops to which he had access were rye and wheat, planted in the fall, and barley, oats, beans, peas, and sometimes spring rye, planted in the spring and harvested in the fall of the same year. Rye was the cereal used most for the peasant's bread, wheat for his lord's.

*Subsidiary workers on the manor*—Many of the menial tasks were done for the lord by free peasants and serfs. In the lord's mill millers were needed, and bakers for the lord's household. These men might receive full-time employment from the lord, or they might also have a few strips to cultivate. The blacksmith, carpenter, mason, and the rest had their houses in the village and might combine their other specialized work with agricultural labor. The aim of the lord was naturally to be as self-sufficient on his manor as possible, for money was scarce and there were some items which must be imported, such as salt, spices, and all the luxuries for which he could pay. Moreover, it was only the surplus of the manor that provided him with such money as he had, and therefore it was not to his interest to keep more peasants working on the land than could be profitably employed. It was better to use any surplus labor on the manufacture of goods that could be exported and bring him some cash income. Indeed, one of the reasons for the later improvement of the status of the peasantry was the taste for luxury acquired by the lord, which forced him to improve his system of production; this often meant hiring free laborers, organizing them more efficiently, and allowing the manufacturing part of the village to become specialized into a town.

*Status of the peasant*—In practice, the peasant was not altogether without rights though in theory his lord could do almost anything he wished with him. The lord could if necessary enforce his own rights in the manorial court, presided over by himself or his steward. Here also could serfs obtain justice against other serfs, and villeins

*This medieval blacksmith is no ordinary smith, but St. Eloy, patron of all blacksmiths. When the Devil tormented him, he tweaked the Devil's nose. When the horse would not stand still to be shod, the saint cut off his hoof, shod it, and put it back. From Bonifacius Calabrensis, Of the Care of Horses (Italy), ca. 1400.* (COURTESY THE PIERPONT MORGAN LIBRARY. Ms. 735, folio 3)

against villeins.[6] But no class had any rights against a higher class.

The sons and daughters of a serf remained serfs. In a "mixed marriage" between a serf and a freeman, the new status was determined by the custom of the manor, subject to the decision of the lord in the particular case. As a rule it was the freeman who reverted to the status of the serf rather than the other way round. On the other hand, a serf was protected against eviction by the very fact that he was the property of his lord. Individually he could not be sold if he

were a cultivator of the land, though there are instances of the sales of sons of serfs, and occasionally of serf cultivators who had probably in some way offended their lord and were punished in this way, contrary to the usual custom. The serf was not allowed to marry except with the permission of the lord, for which permission he paid a small fee; if he wanted to marry outside the manor he might be refused permission. If it were granted the fee would be larger, and probably the woman would also have to pay a fee to her lord for the privilege.

The same regulations applied to the children of the serf. Though we know of cases where peasants' sons attained to high rank in the Church, perhaps including the great

---

[6] A villein by derivation means simply a villager. Customarily it is used to designate a peasant who was theoretically not a serf, but was at the same time not wholly free, owing to his lord special manorial services not owed by the real freeman.

Pope Gregory VII, permission had first to be obtained from the lord and a fee paid. If the serf left the land without permission he could be brought back by force if the lord could catch him, which was not always easy. And if he were able to stay away for a year and a day without recapture the lord's right lapsed, and the serf became free. Hence arose the saying that "town air makes free," for many a serf escaped from his bondage to the towns and was never recaptured.

*The parish priest on the manor*—As a rule the Church division of a parish (a term still used in many countries) corresponded exactly to the area covered by a manor. There was thus one priest required for each manor, whose duty it was to provide for the spiritual needs of the peasantry and the lord. Appointed by the lord, he was as much his servant as any of his officials; and he had some of the rights of the lord within his parish. He had a separate house and small plot of ground of his own; he was also provided with a certain number of the strips which had to be cultivated by the peasants in the same way as the lord's. His income was provided by a tax of one tenth (tithe) of the income of every peasant in the parish. However, the better priests, often themselves drawn from the ranks of the peasants, lived very close to the people; and the priest's services at every important crisis in the peasants' lives to administer the sacraments, as well as his regular visits and giving of

*Dances in the street. From a* Book of Hours *(French),* ca. *1474.* (COURTESY THE PIERPONT MORGAN LIBRARY. Ms. 677, folio 137)

spiritual comfort, were appreciated. Sometimes, but not always, he had had at least the rudiments of education and could impart these to the younger peasants, thus preparing them for a wider life either in the Church or in the towns. His church was provided for him by the lord, with the aid, of course, of the labor of the peasants.

*Amusements of the peasantry*—The peasant's life was hard, and, as we shall see, a very large percentage of the fruits of his labor was yielded up to the lord. But there were certain compensations of a simple kind. He did not have to work, and was indeed forbidden to work on Sundays, and on the festivals of a considerable number of saints. On these festival days there was always dancing in the village—in the parish hall if there was one, if not, in the streets or even in the church itself. Two or three times a year most lords entertained their peasantry, especially at harvest time or after bringing the hay in, after sowing and at the great festivals, especially Christmas, when the peasants decorated the manor house and were allowed to enjoy themselves in it afterward. In wine country there was always a vintage festival. Sometimes jugglers and acrobats came through the village and performed for the villagers either in the manor house or in the parish hall. In the later Middle Ages fairs became common to which the peasants could take their produce and enjoy themselves in the towns for the day.

Though these occasional joys did not compensate for the hardness of the peasants' work and the scantiness of their reward, they did mitigate their lot. We should remember also the fact that every peasant had a secure place, however humble, in his society, that he belonged to the same religion as his neighbors and had to cooperate with them every minute of his life. He was dependent upon them as they upon him. When one considers all that this means for psychological security, it can be more easily understood why, even in our own century, those who were compelled by circumstances to come to America have not always made their peace with it until the second generation.

## THE INCOME OF THE LORD OF THE MANOR

### From his demesne land

The lord's land was cultivated by his peasants, and he took the produce from it. Though the lord in theory could make unlimited demands upon the labor of his peasants, custom usually regulated the limit placed on it in fact. The regular work was called *week work,* and limited as a rule to not more than three days a week. The time depended naturally upon the size of the lord's land and the number of peasants available. At certain times the peasant could be called upon for additional work, as at harvest time. This was called *boon work,* and included such extra duties as bringing in firewood and hay for the lord. Finally, the peasant was made to do forced labor on the estate such as digging ditches and making roads, while his wife and children might be called upon for housework in the manor. This labor was called *corvée.* The amount of *corvée* required was again regulated by custom as well as by the need of the lord, and depended upon the status of the peasant, whether he was a serf or technically a freeman. The building and repairing of a castle were a very heavy burden on the peasant, but they were done by *corvée.*

### From the peasants' land— Different forms of taxation

The lord was not content with having his peasants work his own land for his benefit. In numerous ways he levied toll upon what the peasant produced from his own land. The levies were not arbitrary, but fixed by custom; this, however, did not prevent them from being very heavy, and there was nothing except the probable resistance of the peasants, perhaps by armed revolt, to prevent the lord from increasing them.

There was usually a head tax paid annually by all serfs, and there was a direct tax upon the property of every peasant, known as tallage (French *taille*). There were many "gifts" to be made at specified seasons of the year, and there was a special tax to be paid when a serf inherited his land. The last two were similar to feudal aids. These taxes were seldom excessive, and could be regarded as the equivalent of rent, while the tilling of the lord's land could be regarded as a form of sharecropping—though a modern sharecropper does not have to pay rent too!

But far more annoying and probably more costly in actual cash or produce paid out were the payments that had to be made for the use of various facilities provided by the lord, whether the peasants wished to use them or not. The lord, for instance, provided a bake oven, and the peasant was not permitted to make one for himself. He had to use the lord's bake oven and pay a fee for the privilege. He was not permitted to grind his own wheat, but had to use the lord's mill and the services of his millers, who usually cheated him. He was made to buy wine whether he wanted it or not, use the lord's winepress, and use the lord's bull for breeding; moreover, the lord erected toll houses on his roads and bridges which everyone had to use. These nuisance taxes were called *banalités* and were extremely difficult to get rid of. The French nobles never gave them up till the French Revolution, and they were largely responsible for the fact that the conservative peasants helped to foment it. And always the lord could enforce the payment of fines for breaking his regulations, and impose fines for any other breach of the peace or misdemeanor brought to him for trial.

It is impossible to say what percentage of the actual produce of his manor went into the lord's pocket by one device or another, but it was certainly a large one, and kept the peasants from accumulating much that they could call their own. And it sufficiently accounts for the ability of the feudal nobility to engage in their pleasant pursuits in spite of the low-producing nature of the manorial economy.

### THE PEASANT'S INCOME

What he had left over after paying all taxes and fines belonged to the peasant.

Though it was not much, there would be something if the land were fertile and he and his wife were good managers. He could convert his produce into cash at the fairs, and we do know that enough agricultural produce found its way into the towns to feed the townsmen, though some of it also came from the lord's demesne and what he had collected in kind from the peasantry. There might be enough in the peasant's sock or mattress to pay a small amount to the priest to educate his son or to pay the apprentice's fee for his son to learn a trade in a town. But seldom do we hear of any luxury in the peasant's home. It would, in any case, have only invited unpleasant attention from his lord.

### THE ATTITUDE OF THE CHURCH TOWARD THE PEASANT

The theory of the Church was no different from the theory of the lord as far as the serf was concerned. He was a piece of property. Yet he was also a human soul, and as likely to go to heaven as his lord. The Church believed that the needs of the peasant's soul could be taken care of by the priest with his sacraments, but that Divine Providence had arranged that each man should be born into a certain position in life in which he should remain. Life was not supposed to be a bed of roses, but a hard testing ground in preparation for the world to come. There were three estates in the world, two privileged and the third unprivileged whose duty it was to work for the two privileged classes. The two upper classes or estates were the clergy and the nobility. The townsman or bourgeois belonged to the third estate, along with the peasant. No distinction was made between the bourgeois and the peasants in medieval theory; it was the bourgeois themselves who assumed the title of the third estate as referring only to themselves in later years, when these estates became the first French approach to a Parliament.

Yet there were individual churchmen who recognized the parasitic position of the nobility, and some preached thundering sermons against their exploitation of the peasantry. Jacques de Vitry, a thirteenth-century clergyman, famous for his sermons, once caustically pointed out that "what the peasant takes a year of hard labor to produce the noble consumes in an hour." But in general the clergy recognized that everything that could be said of the nobles could equally be said of themselves, and that it was as well not to disturb the established order. Monasteries and higher clergy were also lords of the manor, and exploited peasants themselves, often more severely than the worst of lords because they were more efficient. It was only reformers and parish priests who seriously tried to improve the lot of the manorial peasants, and their efforts in an entrenched system had little effect. The Church was hardly at all responsible for the ultimate improvement of the peasant's lot through emancipation.

EMANCIPATION OF THE PEASANT

It has already been explained that if a serf stayed away from his manor for a year and a day he had earned his freedom. This was perhaps the principal loophole through which he finally escaped his servitude. With the growth of towns there was some other place for him to go. When Crusades were called the lords were under great pressure from the Church and public opinion to allow them to leave. Few returned alive from the Crusades, especially the First Crusade, when large numbers of peasants were massacred in trying to make their way overland to Palestine. Those who did survive naturally did not return to the manors.

The lord's desire for luxuries beyond what an ordinary manor could provide under its generally inefficient management was also an aid to the peasants. More efficient management meant fewer serfs and large numbers were freed, especially from the thirteenth century onward. In later times it was found that sheep farming earned larger dividends. This gave rise to the enclosure movement which turned many former manors into estates run by few laborers, though at the cost of great hardship to peasants who found themselves deprived by legal means of their strips. When the kings began to establish their authority over the feudal nobility they found themselves in constant need of mercenary soldiers. These again came from the ranks of the peasantry, and no lord could pursue and bring back a peasant who had joined the king's army.

The manorial system itself survived for many centuries, but greatly transformed. The servile status and the legal power of the lords over their peasants disappeared first, and in most Western countries did not survive the thirteenth century. Tenant farmers and small proprietors took the place of serfs, the former still bound by the ancient customs and the ancient taxes, and still forced on occasions to do *corvée* and to pay the *banalités*. But when the taxes were raised the peasants soon learned that they had the power to revolt. And though the revolts were usually mercilessly suppressed, reforms did come in time, for the lords as well as the peasants were the losers by them.

More than anything else it was probably the inefficiency of the early manorial system that condemned it; with the growth of towns and the commercial revolution a more efficient use had to be made of the land, and this could be provided neither by the warrior class of feudal nobility nor by the manorial system which nourished it.

▶  Suggestions for further reading

Books on the political and social structure of the early Middle Ages are numerous. There are several good chapters on the early centuries in Dawson's book, already referred to, *The Making of Europe* (New York: The Macmillan Company, 1932). There is a fine survey in short compass in a book in the Home University Library series, which, though written in 1911, was considered worthy of a reprint in 1948: H. W. C. Davis, *Medieval Europe* (London: Oxford University Press, 1948). This little book studies especially those medieval topics likely to be of most interest to the beginning student, though everything in it has clearly behind it the lifetime learning of a great scholar on the medieval period. Another short popular survey by a noted scholar is S. Painter, *Medieval Society* (Ithaca: Cornell University Press, 1951). A more extensive survey, not entirely up to date but very thoughtful and well organized under topics of interest to the student, is G. B. Adams, *Civilization during the Middle Ages* (New York: Charles Scribner's Sons, 1914). A much fuller book, no doubt used as a text but readable in itself, fully up to date, and with proper attention paid to Byzantine history and to the relations of Constantinople with the West, is J. L. La Monte, *The World of the Middle Ages* (New York: Appleton-Century-Crofts, Inc., 1949).

On medieval society of this period there is a very interesting recent book based on the actual observations of Alexander Neckam, a medieval traveler and indefatigable student; H. T. Holmes, *Daily Living in the Twelfth Century* (Madison: University of Wisconsin Press, 1952). Numerous books by G. G. Coulton, all based on original research which will bring the student close to the actual writings of the period, are available. Probably the best to use is *Medieval Panorama* (New York: The Macmillan Company, 1943), which should, however, be judiciously skipped. The student will easily discover for himself the parts which are really familiar to the author, and worth reading, and he can neglect chapters which are thin and derivative. Coulton, in spite of a lifetime's research, was not able to keep up with all the work done by other medieval scholars. He is always at his best in

social history. The same author's *The Medieval Village* (Cambridge, England: Cambridge University Press, 1926) is a full study of certain aspects of village life, particularly in England, based on original records and literature; it shows clearly the relationship between the various classes in rural society. While Eileen Power's classic *Medieval People* (9th ed.; London: Methuen & Co., Ltd., 1950) contains some elements that are undoubtedly fictional, it is based on solid research and brings vividly to the imagination various medieval individuals and the milieu in which they lived.

Although this particular book, J. B. Ross and M. M. McLaughlin, *The Portable Medieval Reader* (New York: The Viking Press, Inc., 1949), is not perhaps quite up to the standard of some of the others in its admirable series, and although some of the selections are of minimal interest, there are enough good selections to make it well worth reading, with some skipping. An imaginative picture of a French seigneury is given in W. S. Davis, *Life in a Medieval Barony* (New York: Harper & Brothers, 1923), which, in spite of its derivation from different sources, all, of course, authentically feudal, will give the student a good impression of the actual nature of feudalism in the Middle Ages. A special study of chivalry is to be found in S. Painter, *French Chivalry, Chivalric Ideas and Practices in Medieval France* (Baltimore: Johns Hopkins University Press, 1940).

# 18

# The Growth of the Papacy
# to Innocent III

*The church in the tenth century • The Cluniac reform • Conflict between the papacy and secular powers • Unification of Christendom against the Muslims • The Crusades • Reaction to the worldliness of the Church • Reaction of the Church to the rise of heresy • The issue of apostolic poverty*

---

## ▶ The Church in the tenth century

ECCLESIASTICAL ORGANIZATION IN EUROPE—
LAY INVESTITURE

It will have been realized from the last chapter how completely the Church had become integrated into the feudal system. Throughout Europe the emperor, kings, and chief nobles appointed the bishops and the archbishops; the clerical assistants in the episcopal sees (cathedral chapters), who were responsible for the administration of the diocese, were appointed by the bishops, while the parish priests, chosen by local lords, usually from their own free peasantry, were ordained priests by the bishops whenever the latter found time for it, without too closely inquiring into the qualifications of the priests. There was no way in which the papacy could interfere in the process, though in theory all the high clergy were at least subject to confirmation from the Holy See. If the rulers desired to sell the offices of the Church or give them to their friends and relatives, no papal wrath could stop them; if the bishops accepted fees illegally for the performance of their ordinary duties, if they

inflicted fines as penance and put the proceeds into their own pockets, perhaps to pay the sum exacted from them by the kings in exchange for their appointment, no one could insist on their obedience to the laws of the Church which forbade such practices. If the parish priest had no qualifications for his office, knew no Latin, permitted gaming and dicing in his church, was unable to celebrate the Mass with due order and dignity, and betrayed the secrets of the confessional for private gain—if his manorial lord did not discipline him, no one else would. All these practices were common, and there was not much that anyone in high authority in the Church could do about it.

THE PAPACY IN THE FEUDAL SYSTEM

The papacy itself was in no position to institute reforms. When the pope was not chosen by the local Italian nobles and people, he was chosen by the emperor. If he offended the emperor, he could be deposed; if he offended the local nobles, they also could depose him by force unless the emperor objected. The revenues of the Papal States in Italy were collected through the papal

## ► chronological chart

### The Cluniac reform and its consequences

| | |
|---|---|
| Foundation of monastery of Cluny | 910 |
| Growth of Cluniac influence | 910–1050 |
| Otto the Great crowned emperor | 962 |
| Henry III emperor | 1039–1056 |
| Henry III appoints four successive reform popes | 1046–1054 |
| Schism between Eastern and Western Churches | 1054 |
| Domination of papacy by Hildebrand (later Gregory VII) | 1054–1085 |
| Death of Henry III, accession of boy Henry IV | 1056 |
| Synod of the Lateran—Popes to be elected by College of Cardinals | 1059 |
| Synod of Melfi—Condemnation of clerical marriage | 1059 |
| Treaty of Melfi—Robert Guiscard invested with southern Italy by pope Nicholas II | 1059 |
| Saxon rebellion against Henry IV | 1073–1075 |
| Gregory VII becomes pope | 1073 |
| Synod of Rome—Decrees against simony, clerical marriage, and lay investiture | 1075 |
| Henry IV quells rebellion of Saxon nobles | 1075 |
| *Dictatus papae* by Gregory VII | 1076 |
| Synod of Worms, called by Henry IV, deposes Gregory | 1076 |
| Penance of Henry IV at Canossa | 1077 |
| Renewed Saxon wars in Germany | 1077–1080 |
| Defeat and death of Rudolph of Swabia | 1080 |
| Second deposition of Henry IV by Gregory VII | 1080 |
| Henry invades Italy | 1081 |
| Sack of Rome by Normans | 1084 |
| Death of Gregory VII | 1085 |
| Proclamation of First Crusade by Urban II | 1095 |
| Compromises over lay investiture in England and France | 1107 |
| Concordat of Worms | 1122 |

### Rise of Hohenstaufen family

| | |
|---|---|
| Conrad III first Hohenstaufen emperor | 1138–1152 |
| Frederic I (Barbarossa) emperor | 1152–1190 |

### Rise of Hohenstaufen family (cont'd)

| | |
|---|---|
| Frederic states claims on Italian cities at Diet of Roncaglia | 1158 |
| Formation of Lombard League | 1159 |
| Destruction of Milan by Frederic | 1162 |
| Battle of Legnano—Defeat of Frederic by Lombard League | 1176 |
| Peace of Constance | 1183 |
| Marriage of Henry (son of Frederic) to Constance of Sicily | 1186 |
| Death of Frederic Barbarossa on Third Crusade | 1190 |
| Henry VI emperor | 1190–1197 |
| Capture of Richard I of England by Henry and payment of heavy ransom | 1192–1194 |
| Birth of Frederic Hohenstaufen (Frederic II) | 1194 |
| Death of Henry VI | 1197 |
| Civil War in Germany | 1197–1212 |
| Pontificate of Innocent III | 1198–1216 |
| Frederic Hohenstaufen becomes king of the Romans | 1212 |
| Frederic crowned emperor | 1220 |

### The Papacy and England

| | |
|---|---|
| Conquest of England by Normans with papal approval | 1066 |
| Compromise over lay investiture | 1107 |
| St. Thomas Becket becomes Archbishop of Canterbury | 1162 |
| Constitutions of Clarendon | 1164 |
| Murder of St. Thomas Becket | 1170 |
| John King of England | 1199–1216 |
| Innocent III appoints Stephen Langton Archbishop of Canterbury | 1207 |
| Innocent lays interdict on England | 1208 |
| Innocent excommunicates John | 1209 |
| Innocent deposes John and invites Philip Augustus to execute the sentence | 1213 |
| John submits, doing homage to Innocent for throne | 1213 |
| Battle of Bouvines—Victory of Philip over allies of John | 1214 |
| Magna Carta | 1215 |
| Deaths of John and Innocent | 1216 |
| Louis, son of Philip Augustus, abandons efforts to gain English crown | 1217 |

bureaucracy; but this also was composed of local nobles who could direct them into more suitable pockets than the pope's.

In such circumstances few would have ventured to predict that in little more than a century a pope would have brought an emperor to beg his forgiveness in the snow, still less that in two and a half centuries Pope Innocent III would be successfully disciplining every monarch in Europe. Such an achievement therefore deserves a careful analysis in itself as a political event of the first magnitude. Moreover, the swift collapse of papal power that followed Innocent's triumphs may also reveal the necessary limitations on the exercise of political authority by a power whose claims were spiritual, and whose sanctions depended on moral rather than on military and political force.

## THE THEORY OF SALVATION

### The means of salvation

In our modern age, when Christianity has been split into numerous sects, when a large number of people are religious skeptics, and when power rests firmly in the hands of secular authorities, it is clear that the moral reform of the individual can only be enforced, if at all, by secular authority through legislation. A Church can only hope to induce moral reform by persuasion and by the threat of cutting off such ecclesiastical comforts as it can supply. In the Middle Ages, however, Catholic Christianity was a religious monopoly, and there is no evidence that anyone in the whole of Christendom in the tenth century doubted its main teachings, so far as they were understood. The central teaching understood by all was that there was a God in Heaven, a Devil in Hell, and that after death human beings went to either Heaven or Hell according to a verdict given by God in his capacity as judge. The supreme aim of man's life on earth was to win a favorable decision at this last judgment. And it was universally believed that the purpose of the Church was to help man win the decision and thus attain Heaven.

Largely on the authority of Pope Gregory I a further important doctrine had been propounded for the belief of the faithful, though it was not widely understood: the doctrine that there was an intermediate place between the earth and Heaven through which those who were destined for Heaven would pass. This was called Purgatory, the place where sins were purged through punishment, leaving a purified soul to pass on to Heaven. It was only a temporary abode, but the period passed in it varied according to the sins committed on earth. The Church could also help mitigate the punishment in purgatory.

### The role of the Church in the attainment of salvation

*The sacraments*—According to the theory of salvation put forward by Augustine in the fifth century, modified by Gregory I, and generally accepted as the true teaching of the Church, man was saved only through grace, bestowed as a heavenly gift by God, a gift made possible only by the sacrifice of Christ. Grace, however, was given to man only through the medium of the sacraments of the Church, which had been founded by Christ for this purpose.

There were seven sacraments: baptism, by which the newborn child was redeemed from original sin, with godparents accepting Christianity on his behalf; confirmation, when a child of about twelve accepted Christianity for himself; the Eucharist, the most sacred and important of the sacraments, offered daily, in which through the miracle of transubstantiation bread and wine were made into the body and blood of Christ; matrimony; penance; and extreme unction, which prepares the Christian for death and wipes away what is left of his sins. The seventh sacrament (holy orders) was the ceremony by which a layman was made into a priest, setting him apart from ordinary men, and enabling him to celebrate the Eucharist and grant absolution from sin.

*Penance—Indulgences*—The sacrament of penance needs a few words of explanation because of its role in the disciplining of the Christian by the Church, and the consequent power conferred by it on the clergy. In theory the Church could not guarantee salvation; all that was sure was that salvation could not be won without the aid of the Church—a distinction not always clear to the unschooled Christian. But the Church could save the Christian sinner from having to suffer the consequences of his sin in Purgatory—provided always that God had chosen to grant him salvation and an entry into Heaven. Christ and his saints, according to Church doctrine, had made full satisfaction to God for the sins of every man on earth, and thus a treasury of merits had been accumulated which was at the disposal of the Church for helping repentant sinners through Purgatory.

If a sinner repented truly and confessed his sins to a priest, then it was the duty of the priest to absolve him. This was the sacrament of penance. But the consequences of the sin still remained, and in the absence of any intervention by the Church, full punishment for it would be exacted in Purgatory. But the Church could remit the punishment by assigning some temporal punishment on earth, in the form of the repetition of a certain number of prayers, the undertaking of special fasts, the performance of a useful social work such as building a bridge, or even a pilgrimage to some sacred place such as Rome or Jerusalem. Such an act would relieve the sinner of some period of punishment in Purgatory. The statement of this remission of punishment was called an *indulgence*. A plenary indulgence, which was the chief inducement offered to crusaders, remitted the whole time of punishment in Purgatory. If, therefore, God had chosen to save a sinner who had been given a plenary indulgence, then he would enter Heaven at once without having to spend any time in Purgatory.

It is clear that this complex theory would not be understood by the ordinary ignorant layman. It is not, therefore, to be wondered at that only too often the sinner who possessed an indulgence regarded it as a safe passport to Heaven; and it is also not too surprising that the temptation to abuse the sacrament of penance and sell the indulgences for money was sometimes too much for a Church that had many uses for money. It was the flagrant abuse of the indulgence in the sixteenth century that was the principal factor in the rebellion of Martin Luther against the Church which began the Protestant Reformation.

*The withholding of the sacraments—The disciplinary powers of the Church—*Since the receiving of the sacraments was necessary for salvation, the most severe penalty that could be meted out to a Christian was to withhold them, a penalty known as excommunication. Complete excommunication, which could be pronounced by the higher clergy or by the pope, meant that the offender was severed from all services performed by the Church. No Christian might have any dealings with him on pain of excommunication himself, he could not attend services of the Church or receive any sacraments, and he could not be buried in holy ground. If the state accepted the excommunication it would sometimes withdraw the benefits of secular law from him also, making him an outlaw. He then could be killed with impunity, and by the Church action he was necessarily condemned to Hell. If excommunication was to be lifted by the Church the offender would be expected to make a complete submission, and undergo severe penance.

As a supplement to excommunication when directed at a monarch or an independent feudal lord, the Church could also declare an interdict upon his whole territory. This was a kind of excommunication en masse of a whole population, and its purpose was to bring the pressure of public opinion to bear on the offending ruler. In a land laid under an interdict the Church performed none of its duties at all—though exception might be made by special dispensation for some of the essential sacraments such as baptism and extreme unction. When it is remembered how many duties the Church performed in the Middle Ages that we now regard as functions of the state, it can readily be seen how effective this weapon might be in the hands of a Church obedient to its leaders.

Clearly neither of these disciplinary powers, however, would have any effect at all if the local clergy did not cooperate. When, as in the tenth century, the clergy were nominated by local lords, they could not be used; and probably no cleric could even be found who would read a bull of excommunication of a high noble or a monarch.

In addition to these weapons, the pope, who alone could pronounce an interdict, claimed the right to depose a king, who, theoretically, could not hold office from the moment of his excommunication; and the oath of allegiance made to him by his subjects became automatically void. Naturally this right was never admitted by the rulers, who themselves claimed to hold their power from God and not from the Church. The pope's ability to make his decree effective depended entirely upon the conditions in the country concerned—as, for instance, whether there was any rival for the throne, or whether any foreign king could be induced with papal support to overthrow the offending and deposed monarch.

### THE CHURCH AS REGULATOR OF CHRISTIAN MORALITY—CANON LAW

The Church had always claimed jurisdiction throughout Christendom in all matters which concerned faith and morals. In the early centuries of Christianity authoritative creeds—statements of what Christians must believe—had been drawn up by councils. But gradually it was recognized that a single authority must be accepted in such matters, and this, after many centuries of doubt as to where the authority lay, was granted by consent in the Western world to the pope. From time to time popes also promulgated new dogmas which must be believed by the faithful. Those who refused to subscribe to these beliefs could be charged with heresy, and handed over to the state for punishment. If they did not recant they could be put to death by burning (without the shedding of blood, forbidden to churchmen). Before the establishment of the Inquisition in the thirteenth century heresy trials were in the hands of the bishops. By such means the Church attempted to guard the purity of the faith.

In the realm of morals, which covered a very wide field and which the Church in the days of its power sought to make ever wider, the authority was the canon law, the rules laid down by the early councils, combined with decrees made by various popes. These were codified by Gratian in the twelfth century.

Canon law stated that all clerics, both regular and secular, and even those in minor orders—assistants of the higher clergy, even, later, students at universities—were subject only to the jurisdiction of the Church and were not to be tried for any offense whatever by the temporal powers. It claimed that all crimes against religion, whoever committed them, were to be tried by the Church. This included not only heresy, simony, and blasphemy, but sorcery, adultery, and sexual crimes, usury, and even the illegal fighting of duels. If these were not punished by the state of its own accord—and in the early Middle Ages many of the chief offenders were rulers and nobles in high position who did not even recognize these acts as crimes—then the Church claimed the right to try the offenders instead.

Finally, canon law regulated all civil cases connected in any way with one of the sacraments, as, for instance, marriage settlements and divorces, wills, and civil contracts which concerned inheritance. The canon law, observing Roman principles and taking into account such things as motives, not recognized as important under feudal law, did serve to mitigate some of the evils of feudal law, as well as adding to the power of the Church.

Again, however, it must be emphasized that the Church was able to regulate such matters only if the State permitted it to do so. In general, the Church was allowed to have its way in matters that were not of too great moment to the rulers, and the higher courts were always crowded with legal business at a time when feudal law was only rudimentary, and incompetent to deal with much that occupied the Church. The Church, however, was rarely allowed much say in the matter of feudal inheritance; but when a quarrel was precipitated with Henry II, a strong king of England, over his efforts to establish a uniform law for clerics and laymen alike, it was the Church, not the king, who won the victory.

## THE REQUIREMENTS FOR THE ESTABLISHMENT OF PAPAL AUTHORITY IN EUROPE

From the above it can be seen what relation the claims of the Church had to the reality of its power in the tenth century. It remains to be considered what were the essential changes that must be made if the pretended power were to become real. First, and underlying all the remainder, it must re-establish its moral supremacy in Europe, so that Christians throughout the whole area could see that the Church was not just an oppressive secular institution demanding tithes and feudal dues and contributions, but a body with a true spiritual mission and able to help in the saving of souls. It must renew the faith of the people both in Christianity itself and in the mission of the Church.

Second, and as a consequence of this, it must attract to itself as a body sufficient voluntary financial support to enable it to carry out its duties and maintain some independence from the feudal lords. Voluntary support would only be forthcoming if the people believed in its efficacy for salvation. And the Papal States, the best immediate source of income, must be thoroughly subjected to the pope and firmly administered.

Third, the papacy must free itself from the domination of the German emperor and the Roman nobles and people, thus enabling it to carry out a consistent policy, dependent not on imperial or local desires, but upon what it considered best for the Church. The most obvious way was for a pope to name, or have a large share in naming, his successor.

Fourth, the control of appointments to the higher clergy must be taken out of the hands of the feudal lords and kings and put under the control of the papacy. If the higher clergy were papal appointees, then the lower clergy would likewise become responsive to papal policy through these nominees. This meant, of course, the suppression of such practices as the sale of Church offices (simony), the bestowal of them on relatives (nepotism), and incelibacy, since a church office might become hereditary if a clergyman had sons to succeed him.

This tremendous program was substantially carried out in the next few centuries. Its instrument, as so often in the reforms of the Church in the Middle Ages, was found in the monastic system, which had for a long time ceased to play any important part in the public life of the Christian world, but was now to show itself capable of a self-renewal that was as unexpected to the papacy as it was welcome. And in the end, as it happened, it was the monastic reform that took over the papacy instead of the papacy's taking over and exploiting the reform.

## ▶ The Cluniac reform

### THE CLUNIAC SYSTEM

In 910, a Duke William of Aquitaine, desiring to have Masses said for his soul, and dissatisfied with the existing monasteries, although they had for a long time been striving to reform themselves, left land for a new monastery or abbey to be established at Cluny in eastern France (Burgundy). This abbey, under a distinguished churchman, was to be entirely free from either royal or feudal jurisdiction and subject only to the papacy. It was to be a reformed monastery, returning to the strict Benedictine Rule.

Under its first abbot, Odo, and a subsequent series of remarkable abbots, it did indeed return to the Benedictine Rule, but with certain innovations. There was not so much stress on manual labor or even on scholarly pursuits—though many of the abbots and monks were in fact as learned as any in

Christendom—as there was stress on a strict return to canon law in such matters as chastity and celibacy and the proper election to Church offices. It is clear that such a program was intended from the beginning to be influential in the reform of the whole Church, and from the beginning it attracted all those serious Christians in Europe who hoped for and wanted to work for Church reform.

Soon the mother abbey began to expand and found daughter-houses and the bequests of land began to come in; for it need hardly be stressed that if a noble was thinking of giving an estate to the Church for the benefit of his soul the most likely place to find clergy competent for the purpose would be at Cluny, where the monks were chaste, where they spent many hours of the day interceding for the souls of the living and the departed; he would not be likely to bequeath it to his brother whose appointment to the office of bishop he had influenced, or to a monastery noted only for the excellence of its food and liquor. The same principle as in the foundation of Cluny itself was observed in the foundation of the daughter abbeys called *priories;* the land must be unencumbered by feudal privileges, and each priory must be obedient to the abbey at Cluny. This obedience was enforced through the priors of each of these houses, who were appointed by the abbot of Cluny and regularly visited by him.

### CONSEQUENCES OF CLUNY REFORM

#### Growth of elite and educated clergy

The first important consequence of the reform was that at last a monastery attracted not only monks who wished to escape the world but ambitious and sincere clergymen who wished to reform it. They knew that at Cluny they would receive training for the job that was to be done—above all ecclesiastical reform. It was much easier to obtain appointment from a king or a lord and enjoy personally the fruits of office; but it was the dedicated men who went to Cluny. Under the supervision of the abbot who had uncontrolled authority—for real control by the tenth-century papacy was unthinkable—ability would have a better chance of being recognized than anywhere else. Once monks were trained, they could preach safely without being made to submit to feudal dictation; even though they ran the risk of being manhandled by the lords and their henchmen, public opinion would be on their side. Above all, there was a practical and realizable goal to be striven for, and if the movement grew, the results of their work would be visible to all.

For all these reasons there can be no question that the Cluny monasteries for nearly two centuries, until excessive worldly success undermined their original high purpose, received the pick of the crop of those who sincerely wished for the reform of Christianity and the elevation of the Church to a position of honor and independence. And, as we know from the influence of the low-born Hildebrand, Cluny was able to call upon all ranks of society for its members and not only upon the feudal nobility, as in the higher positions within the secular clergy.

### Independence from lay control

The secret of the success of the reform movement lay in its independence from lay control. Set down as an independent body in the heart of the feudal system, it was in the highest degree revolutionary, threatening to overthrow the entire established order without fear of reprisals, except crude and violent ones which could only hurt individuals but not the system. The king could not dismiss them; he could not take away their land and revenue for it was not his; even the imperial control of the papacy did not help, for the abbot of Cluny could no more be made to obey a pope than a feudal bishop or archbishop. So a corps of elite clergy was gradually recruited, of great potential danger to the secular clergy and to the prized patronage of the monarch—and they could do nothing about it.

### Growth of Christian spirit among the laity

Even more dangerous to the nobility and to the monarchs, had they been able to real-ize it, was the fact that for the first time in centuries there was a genuine spiritual revival that affected all classes of society. Here were some clergymen who were personally moral and chaste, who preached with fervor and conviction, and who said just what most people had been thinking about the Church for a long time—that it was unspiritual, interested only in its own comfort, careless of the spiritual needs of the people, unchaste, simoniac, and not fit to be considered the Church of God. Though the opinion of the serfs on the manor might not be important, and unless they were close to a Cluny priory they would know nothing of the reform, other men of importance, even among the feudal nobility, did not approve of the practices of the secular clergy. Such men were often in a position to influence the appointment of bishops. Reformers at all times in history have been able to make a genuine appeal to disinterested persons; and no Christian could afford to stand against reform if he really believed in Christianity and the importance of the Church—unless his personal interests in this world were too deeply involved to pay an equal attention to the next.

So it began to happen that some noblemen who had the gift of bishoprics chose to appoint reformers from Cluny to these offices. The first foothold in the secular world had been won. It remained for the reformers to develop a complete program for the Church and to use their influence to put it into effect.

### CLUNY AND THE ESTABLISHMENT OF PAPAL AUTHORITY

#### Release of the clergy from secular control—Reform of abuses in appointment, simony, nepotism, incelibacy

The second stage of the Cluniac reform involves the reform of the papacy itself. Since this is associated with the name of Pope Gregory VII (1073–1085), it is sometimes called the Gregorian Reform, though it was a natural consequence of the Cluniac reform and involved no change in policy.

As mentioned earlier, the main line of the attack on secular control of the clergy was

*The monastery of Montmajour (twelfth century), in southern France.*

directed verbally against the abuses in appointment, against simony, nepotism, and incelibacy. This had for a long time little effect. The secular clergy had been accustomed to living openly with their wives or concubines, and considered the monkish demand for celibacy inhuman. Most rulers also were not willing to give up their patronage so easily, though there were some notable exceptions who greatly advanced the cause of the reform.

But slowly and carefully the ground was prepared and at last it was possible for the popes, several of them from Cluny, to decree that only the pope was entitled to appoint the higher clergy. There must be no more appointments to church positions by the laity. Thus was precipitated the quarrel between rulers and the papacy over lay investiture.

It was a demand for more than the popes could hope to gain. The clergy required an income, and income could at this time only be obtained from land. The Church had no land to give to its clergy. Hence the feudal lord must give the land, and the Church was willing to allow him to invest with the symbols of sovereignty, which right it could hardly take away. But the reformers nevertheless went boldly ahead and demanded the abolition of lay investiture altogether.

### Release of papacy from secular control —Election by cardinals

It was not possible for the papacy itself to be independent until it could free itself from control by the emperor. The reformers therefore waited patiently for a suitable opportunity to throw off the shackles. This presented itself when a child (Henry IV) was elected emperor. The papacy then announced (1059) that the pope henceforth would be elected by the College of Cardinals. The cardinals were originally assistants in the papal court of Rome and the heads of certain Italian churches. In time they came to be chosen from all the clergy of Christendom, and the title became an honorary one, carrying great prestige and power because of the cardinal's role in the election of a pope, but held in conjunction with any other office in the Church he might possess. The importance of the announcement at this time was that cardinals could be appointed only by the pope, and they held office for life. Thus continuity of policy could be maintained. The papal appointees of the previous few reigns chose the next incumbent; and the emperor had nothing to do with it.

### Role of the papal legates—By-passing of the secular clergy

A third feature of importance and fundamental to the program was the growth of a new position in the Church, the papal legate. The legate was a personal representative of the pope and had precedence over any clergyman in the country to which he was sent. The local clergy and nobles might not like these ambassadors, but they could neglect them only if they also intended to defy the pope. And legates could proclaim the announcements of the pope in the churches of their diocese, they could read the bulls which the local clergy might have wished to suppress, and they could excommunicate or lay an interdict upon the country by the direct authority of the pope himself; by means of the legates the pope could make a direct appeal to public opinion over the heads of the clergy.

The reform movement could not now fail for want of publicity given to the decrees of the pope in the countries for which they were intended.

THE EMERGENCE OF A STRONG PAPACY UNDER CLUNIAC INSPIRATION—HILDEBRAND (GREGORY VII)

From the middle of the eleventh century all the popes were serious reformers, the first being chosen, against his feudal interests, by the German emperor, Henry III, who approved of the reform for religious reasons. The power behind the papal throne from 1054 onward was a monk named Hildebrand, who did not himself take the chair as

Gregory VII till 1073. But as assistant to one pope after another he was largely responsible for policy. When Henry III died, his son was only a child, and during the regency of the child's mother the popes were able to prevent the Germans from playing any active part in papal affairs. This, then, was the opportune moment for proclaiming the new procedure for election. Some German bishops protested, but the dowager empress did not make an issue of it.

Since the first and most long-drawn-out struggle with the secular authorities by the papacy was with the German emperors, a full section will be devoted to this conflict, which will reveal the nature and efficacy of the weapons at the disposal of both sides and will show clearly how and in what circumstances the pope was able to make his authority effective. Subsequent sections will treat more briefly the effectiveness of these same weapons against the other secular powers until the age of Pope Innocent III.

## ▶ Conflict between the papacy and secular powers

THE STRUGGLE WITH THE EMPIRE

### Ecclesiastical policy of the successors of Otto I

*Realization of need for papal reform*— Otto the Great, who, as we have seen, became emperor some fifty years after the foundation of Cluny (962), was anxious to be another Charlemagne, keeping effective control of the papacy and permitting no pope to reign who did not support his policy. But his grandson Otto III (983–1002), who came to the throne at a very tender age, was sincerely in favor of ecclesiastical reform, even at the cost of his imperial interests. And by this time Cluny had become a power to be reckoned with in Europe. Otto appointed two popes who, though not themselves educated at Cluny, were strong believers in reform, the second being the finest scholar in Christendom, Gerbert of Aurillac (Pope Sylvester II), whom we shall have occasion to meet in a later chapter. After Otto III's pre-

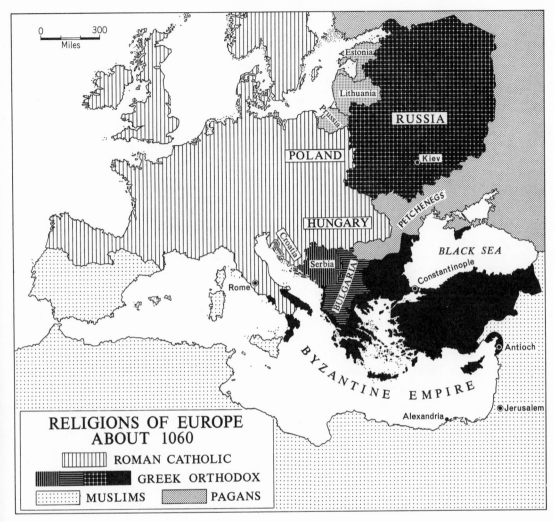

RELIGIONS OF EUROPE
ABOUT 1060

▓▓▓ ROMAN CATHOLIC

███ GREEK ORTHODOX

░░░ MUSLIMS     ▒▒▒ PAGANS

mature death the emperors returned to the policy of Otto I, permitting only subservient popes.

This continued until a new dynasty took possession of the imperial throne (the Salian or Franconian). The second of these rulers, Henry III (1039–1056), became seriously interested in the Cluniac reform. Not realizing how dangerous the reform was to his royal interests in Germany, he supported several reforming popes; moreover, he tried to prevent simony in his own dominions and refused to practice it himself. As a result, by the time of his death in 1056 the papacy was greatly strengthened, to such an extent that it was now prepared to go ahead with its program on its own, even if to do so meant coming into conflict with the empire. But the

new emperor, Henry IV, was only six years old, and the regency was in the hands of a French noblewoman, his mother, who was herself in favor of the reform. Nevertheless, perhaps in preparation for the inevitable struggle, the papacy during this period took the opportunity to provide itself with some reliable lay support by recognizing the Norman conquests in southern Italy (see Chapter 17 above), making the Normans theoretically vassals of the papacy. This in itself was a challenge to the empire, which still maintained a claim to the whole of Italy; but Henry IV was too young to know anything about it, and his mother did not care.

*Reaction under Henry IV—Restoration of abuses in ecclesiastic appointment—*As soon as he grew up Henry IV saw the dangers involved in the reform policies of his father and mother and tried to reverse them. But throughout his reign he was always in trouble with the German nobles, who constantly rebelled against him. He wished for a united Germany under his leadership, and full control of his own clergy and the nobility. He saw at once that he needed his clergy to help control the nobles in the manner of Otto the Great; and he also needed money, most easily obtained by simony, for the purpose of keeping always at hand a body of faithful servants who would help him when necessary to crush the feudal nobility, especially the Saxon lords, who resented the fact that they no longer provided the emperors.

It was thus very difficult to retain control of Italy as well, nor could Henry usually find the time to curb the reformers. Indeed, it was necessary for him even to recognize the reforming popes, in spite of the fact that, in his view, they had been illegally elected since 1059, when election was handed over to the College of Cardinals without his permission. But in Germany he continued to ignore the fulminations of the reformers. He did nothing about clerical marriage, he continued to sell church offices for money for his campaigns; and of course he made all clerical appointments without reference to the popes. He thought he could afford to wait to deal with the papacy; when it suited him he could always repudiate his recognition of the popes since 1059, and claim they had all been illegally elected, including any pope who tried to discipline him.

### Weakness of feudal empire in relation to absolute papacy

To understand the sequel, it is necessary to consider briefly the weaknesses of the empire in all its dealings with the papacy. Though since Otto I the crown had always descended from father to son, when the Saxon line of Otto had died out the nobles had chosen Henry IV's grandfather after the old Germanic custom; the hereditary principle had been by no means established. When the crown passed to the Salian line the Saxons in particular felt slighted; and there were always disgruntled nobles who felt that it should have passed to their own families. The only tie between the emperor and these nobles was the oath of allegiance they made to him when he was elected. Although he was theoretically ruler of the whole Empire, his real power was based only on his feudal possessions, whose lords owed him direct allegiance as vassals, and on his control of such bureaucracy as there was, at this time only his own servants and the higher clergy and their staff. He could not therefore voluntarily relinquish his hold on the clergy, as this would mean losing a large part of his effective power.

An elected monarchy meant always the presence of a large number of possible alternatives to a ruler, unlike the situation in a national state where the hereditary monarchy has been fully accepted. And the oaths by which the nobles were bound to the emperor could be dissolved by the Church for good reason, thus safeguarding such conscience as the dissident nobles might possess.

### The pontificate of Gregory VII

*Views on papal supremacy*—The disadvantages of the imperial position had never been lost on the monk Hildebrand who, after probably refusing the position at least once, at last ascended the papal throne in 1073, with the title of Gregory VII, just at a moment when Henry had become involved in a serious Saxon rebellion. Henry could therefore neither give effective support to his German clergy nor devote any energy to dealing with the pope far away in Italy. It was the moment for decisive action by the papacy, and the new pope was certainly the man for the job.

Gregory, as we shall hereafter call him, left behind him many writings from which it is possible to determine with certainty his views on the relative positions of Church and State. Two famous forgeries supplied him with theoretical support, though there is no reason to believe that Gregory doubted their authenticity himself. These were the Donation of Constantine, already referred to, under which the first Christian emperor had given to the papacy overlordship over the whole Western world and full authority over its clergy, and the so-called Isidorian Decretals (False Decretals), a document first published in the ninth century. This went into details of the papal control of the clergy, and made the explicit declaration that the Church was superior to the State, as a more holy institution than the evil and unholy secular authority.

This was precisely the position taken by Gregory. He regarded himself as the spokesman for God on earth, beyond the judgment of anyone on earth, responsible to God for the good behavior of his clergy, and entitled to demand obedience from any secular power in the world. At the beginning of his reign he expressed these principles in a document known as the *Dictatus papae*, and proceeded to use to the full every instrument of power that had been built up by himself and his predecessors. He wrote letters to kings all over Christendom informing them of the authority of his office, and commanding them to acknowledge it, and even pay him tribute. His legates went forth with instructions to kings and nobles, proclaiming them regardless of any objections from the local clergy. But his real task, as he knew, was to establish his authority over the highest power in Christendom, the emperor. If this could be done, then lesser men would fall into line.

*Prohibition of lay investiture*—He began by excommunicating and deposing from office certain of the German higher clergy who had refused to obey his decrees against simony, nepotism, and unchastity. He followed this up in 1075 with a decree prohibiting lay investiture altogether, thus, of course, making simony forever impossible unless the pope himself sold the offices (not an unheard of thing in later centuries). Unfortunately 1075 was just the year that Henry IV finally succeeded in putting down his Saxon rebellion, leaving him at last free to deal with the papacy. He retained the excommunicated German clergy in office, continued to invest new German bishops, and finally named an archbishop and several bishops in Italy itself.

*Excommunication and deposition of Henry IV*—Gregory reacted confidently. His legates were instructed to threaten Henry with excommunication if he persisted in lay investiture. Henry then summoned the German clergy, who owed their appointments to him and who in any case resented the highhanded actions of the pope. Under the direction of the emperor they wrote an offensive letter to Gregory, addressing him as Brother Hildebrand and informing him that they had never considered him as pope and owed no obedience to him. Henry added a still more offensive note of his own, calling him "no Pope, but false monk," and calling upon him to descend from his throne "and be damned to eternity."

These amenities over, Gregory, who was entirely confident of success, explained the position to his own overlord, St. Peter, telling him that for rebellion against his Church he was depriving Henry of his kingdom, releasing all Christians from their allegiance to him, and excommunicating him (1076). He also excommunicated the chief prelate in Germany and his schismatic bishops.

*Rebellion in Germany—The dilemma of Gregory at Canossa*—Gregory's confidence was based on his understanding of the political situation in Germany. The majority of the German clergy, he felt sure, would return to him if he succeeded in defeating their protector. He knew of Henry's unpopularity with his feudal lords, the result of his determined effort to make Germany into a real monarchy; and he must have guessed that a German noble named Rudolph of Swabia would be elected in Henry's place by the lords, although he afterwards claimed that Rudolph's election was made without his knowledge or approval. As Rudolph later gave Gregory very explicit guarantees not to engage in many of Henry's reprehensible practices, and as he would undoubtedly owe his crown to papal support, Gregory certainly must have thought that his intervention in Germany would lead to satisfactory political results.

Gregory was also sure that the solemn excommunication, the first to be used against such an exalted personage, was bound to create a profound sensation, quite sufficient to turn both nobles and people against their ruler; and that the people, forbidden to have any dealings with an excommunicated person, would probably obey, since it endangered their salvation too. Against all this what had Henry to rely on? A wavering clergy, and his own personal vassals, but little else.

Yet Gregory in his calculations forgot one thing, which was to be his undoing. He forgot that he was also a priest, and that his authority was not the equivalent of secular authority. He could not afford to be branded in the eyes of Christendom as a priest who forgot his religious duties in pursuit of political ends.

The effect of the excommunication was all that he had hoped and foreseen. The German clergy, thoroughly frightened, put up no defense of their monarch, while the German nobles took him into custody, saying that if he did not make his peace with Gregory within a certain time, they would no longer recognize him as king. When he refused to make his peace, the nobles invited Gregory to come to Germany in person to preside over the new election. Henry had only one chance; and it seems that he had recognized the Achilles' heel of the pope as Gregory himself had not. He escaped from custody, crossed the Alps in dead of winter, and made his way to the castle at Canossa where Gregory was staying with Countess Matilda, a faithful supporter, on his way to Germany to preside over the election. Clad only in a coarse woolen garment and barefooted, he stood outside the castle in the snow, begging forgiveness. And this was the one thing that Gregory as a priest could not refuse.

It was one of the cruelest dilemmas in history. If he forgave Henry, all his work went for nothing. The clergy and most of the nobles would return to Henry, the rebellious nobles would certainly be victimized, and a civil war would be inevitable. Gregory could not extract any promise from him that he could not break as soon as he regained his power; and he could never excommunicate or discipline him again with a similar

effect. Only a first excommunication could hope to draw the attention of all Europe, and gain the publicity which would make it effective.

Yet he could not refuse. The sight of the highest ruler in Christendom begging for forgiveness in the snow had already shocked all Europe who knew of it, and especially the Countess Matilda and her entourage who witnessed it. Even if he did not fulfill his Christian duty of forgiving an apparently repentant sinner, he must lose the moral support of Christendom and thus endanger the whole reform and undermine its theoretical foundations. So, in the final analysis, he had no choice.

But it seems from his correspondence that the cruelty of the dilemma and his difficult decision unnerved him, and robbed him of the decisiveness he had shown throughout his life. It would seem possible for Gregory to have given Henry some drastic penance, as, for instance, sending him on a pilgrimage to Jerusalem, which would have removed him from Germany. This idea does not seem to have occurred to Gregory. And while relieving Henry of the ban of excommunication Gregory did not say whether he was to be restored to his throne or not, thus leaving Rudolph and the nobles in an impossible position. All he did was extract an oath from Henry that he would not hinder Gregory's own journey to Germany, and would "give satisfaction in the matter of the German clergy." Rudolph wrote an agonized letter to Gregory asking for instructions, but did not receive a straightforward answer. Gregory merely said that he had not restored Henry to the throne, but he did not say that he was still deposed and that the nobles should bestow the crown elsewhere.

*Recovery of Henry IV—Flight of Gregory* —Henry returned to a divided Germany. Legates were busy trying to repair the situation, and preparing for the election of a new king. But Henry immediately assumed his old authority, and nobles and clergy began to return to him. By 1080 Gregory had made up his mind, but by this time the position had deteriorated beyond retrieving.

He excommunicated and deposed Henry again. Rudolph and the rebellious nobles took up the challenge, but they were too few and they had lost their moment. Before the end of the year Henry had crushed them and killed Rudolph. He was now ready to deal with Gregory. At a council of German clergy called by Henry, Gregory was formally deposed, and an antipope was proclaimed in his place.

Gregory now only had one resort while Henry was collecting an army to invade Italy and make his deposition effective. He called upon his Norman vassals to protect Rome. They could not answer at once, however, and Henry arrived first, in 1084. He had himself crowned by his antipope, while Gregory fled.

*Sack of Rome by Normans—Death of Gregory VII*—No sooner had Henry left for Germany than the Normans appeared, furious with the Roman nobles and people for having yielded Rome to the Germans without a fight. Using this as an excuse, they thoroughly sacked Rome, and took Gregory back with them to Monte Cassino. He died shortly afterward at Salerno, his whole policy apparently a failure; he was detested by the Germans for his interference in imperial affairs, and by the Romans for having invited the barbarous Normans into the city to sack it. And there was an antipope still officially on the papal throne.

*Consequence of this attempt at control of secular power by the papacy*—This important episode in the rise of the papacy to power has been dealt with in such detail because it reveals so clearly both the strength and the weakness of the papal claim to temporal authority. At a crucial moment the pope could not disregard the fact that he was head of Christendom and not a secular ruler. And his position as arbiter in the affairs of Europe depended on his ability to make use of German disunity. When he was no longer able to make use of it, he had to depend on an army which consulted only its own interests. Pope Innocent III, who in a later century brought papal power to its height, was likewise dependent on a similar German disunity for the free hand he was allowed in his reign, as we shall see; and his ability to discipline English and French rulers was dependent upon the fact that they were at war with each other. The successors of Innocent could no longer hope to divide and rule at all. The papal support was not worth enough troops unless the contending forces were fairly equal. These successors had to enlist the support of towns and independent feudal lords with armies; but in so doing they lost their moral authority, and were treated as the secular lords whose weapons they were using.

This, stripped of theories and pretensions, is the inner story of the rise and fall of the papacy as a universal state within the territory of Europe; and it could already have been predicted in the time of Gregory VII from a close observation of the significant details of his victory and defeat.

### Diversion of interest to Crusades under papal leadership

Though Gregory himself was defeated and died in exile, his work did not die with him. Henry in Germany was still excommunicated and, in the eyes of the papacy, still dethroned; and rebellions continued against him for the rest of his life. Finally his son was elected king by the nobles with papal support, and Henry died a year later, really without a throne. The new king once interfered in Italy to ensure his imperial coronation, but the College of Cardinals continued to elect the popes without hindrance, establishing enough precedent for the practice to make it impossible for an emperor later to question its legality. But meanwhile papal interest had shifted to the Crusades, which increased their authority in a different way, as related in a subsequent section.

### Concordat of Worms—Compromise on lay investiture

The popes and the new emperor, Henry V, continued to negotiate on the matter of lay investiture, usually in a more cooperative manner. One pope, Paschal II, even admitted the logic of the situation—that if the popes wished to control the clergy they should not rely upon lands bestowed by the emperor but should make other arrangements to support them. This admission naturally raised an outcry from the clergy, who had no desire to lose their fiefs and become dependent on charity. At last a compromise was arranged, embodied in the Concordat of Worms of 1122. Under this settlement the emperor invested the clergy with land and secular authority, symbolized by the scepter; while the pope invested them with spiritual authority, symbolized by ring and staff. Thus each had a veto on the other's appointments, a clear gain for the papacy, for it now gained something it had never previously held, while the emperor lost his right to make nominations without reference to the papacy. As long as the popes remained reformers, simony and incelibacy could be held in check, since they could always refuse to invest any priest who did not fulfill their moral and religious requirements.

### The rise of the Hohenstaufen family to the imperial throne—Renewal of conflict

*Basis for increased power of the Empire* —In the later twelfth century the struggle between Empire and papacy changed its character. A new family, the Hohenstaufens, took over the German kingship; and by a shrewd policy of divide and rule within Germany its leading representative was able to gain the support of enough great feudal lords to keep his power intact through his lifetime and hand it over, fortified by the great prestige of his name and successes, to his son. The second great family in Germany, the Welfs of Saxony, at first conciliated and then ruthlessly suppressed by Frederic Barbarossa of the Hohenstaufens, remained an outstanding competitor for a century. The names of these two families became so well known in Europe that, even in Italy, the Welfs were always regarded as anti-imperial, and the name "Guelph" (corruption of Welf) was used for all anti-imperialists in Italy; while the imperialist supporters were called Ghibellines from the corrupted name of the

imperial estates of the Hohenstaufen family (Waiblingen).

The first Hohenstaufens were supporters of the papacy and the cause of religious reform. But perhaps the greatest king of the line, Frederic I Barbarossa (1152–1190) was interested in the papacy and reform only when they collided with his ambitions. His main task in life was the establishment of a real Holy Roman Empire (the title seems to be his), with full control not only of Germany but of Italy. For most of his life he was able to keep the support of his German clergy and make use of their services for his imperial aims. But the basis of his power was feudal and military. He and his son and grandson were able to bring the Holy Roman Empire to the height of its medieval strength.

*Italian policy of Frederic Barbarossa—* It was certain that these ambitions would come in conflict with the papal secular interests in Italy, especially since Frederic coveted Rome itself. And the whole reign of Frederic Barbarossa was occupied in a skillful rear-guard action by the papacy, now with one ally and now with another against what seemed until the end to be overwhelming military power.

Northern Italy in the last hundred years had become dotted with prosperous towns, in part as a result of the Crusades. These towns had originally been feudal possessions under the nominal overlordship of the emperor, and ruled directly either by his nobles or by higher clergy who were often hardly distinguishable from the nobility. While the nobility in these towns felt their interests to be bound up with the feudal system and the emperor (Ghibelline party), the bourgeois and the lower classes deeply resented any feudal interference whatever (Guelphs). And when Frederic began to insist that feudal dues be paid to him, an extra burden which had been laxly enforced, if at all, in earlier days, some of the towns overthrew their local feudal overlords altogether, bringing imperial wrath and armies down on their heads. The papacy at first sided with the nobles, especially when bishops and archbishops were attacked; then, quickly realizing where its own interests lay, preferred to support the towns against the emperor.

Frederic precipitated the conflict by stating imperial claims in an extreme form at the Diet of Roncaglia in 1158, including the collection of dues and direct administration of the towns through imperial nominees. Many of the Italian towns, including Milan, made armed resistance to the decrees with papal support. Frederic razed Milan, marched on Rome, denied recognition to Pope Alexan-

der III, and installed an antipope. But Alexander himself escaped, and with support from Venice, the Normans, and, of course, the Italian towns, re-entered Rome as soon as Frederic was gone. He then helped organize the Lombard League of Italian towns, including a new Milan, rebuilt by the efforts of the league.

When Frederic in 1176 was able to give full attention to Italian affairs again, he was met by the united resistance of the league, and his German army was heavily defeated

HOLY ROMAN EMPIRE
AT DEATH OF
FREDERIC BARBAROSSA
1190
★ LOMBARD LEAGUE TOWNS

ADDED TO EMPIRE
UNDER HENRY VI
1190-97

at Legnano, the first major defeat of feudal cavalry by infantry. Frederic at once came to terms with Alexander, recognizing him as the lawful pope, and a few years later signed the Peace of Constance with the towns (1183). By this treaty he retained his less important rights, carrying prestige but little power, while virtual sovereignty was granted to the towns (as described in more detail in a later chapter). But, perhaps of more importance for the future, Frederic also made peace with the Norman kingdom of Sicily and southern Italy, and married his son to Constance, the niece and heiress of the reigning king.

*Menace of Henry* vi *to papal interests in Italy*—When Frederic Barbarossa suddenly died in 1190 while leading the Third Crusade,[1] his son Henry was elected without opposition to the imperial throne. But he was also the king of Sicily through his wife Constance, who had just inherited the Sicilian throne. Sicily under the Norman kings had been made into a powerful compact kingdom, with revenues carefully organized, and supplying everything that the German Empire lacked.

Henry, however, was not to be allowed to resume his Sicilian kingdom peacefully, for a pretender was on the throne, supported by the Welfs and the local Sicilian nobility. He marched into Italy, meeting little resistance, had himself crowned emperor by the pope, and received the fortunate news that the king of England, Richard i, had been captured by one of his vassals on the way back from the Third Crusade. Using this valuable hostage as an argument in his negotiations, he forced the Welfs, who were allied to the English royal house, to give way. And just at that moment the pretender in Sicily providentially died, so that Henry's campaign into Sicily became a triumphant procession.

[1] In later centuries Frederic became a heroic legendary figure who was not dead, but lay in an enchanted sleep in the German mountains awaiting the day when Germany again needed him. Nineteenth-century German nationalists revived the legend and it played no small part in the rise of modern German nationalism.

At this point Henry, in control of a temporarily submissive Germany and a united kingdom of Sicily, thus held the Italian peninsula in a pincer grip. There was nowhere for the pope to turn to for allies except the towns, which were now engaged in bickering among themselves, with Guelphs and Ghibellines struggling for control of the individual cities and attacking each other according to whichever party gained control. While Henry vi had apparently no immediate plans in Italy and no quarrel in progress with the papacy since he had been recently crowned, there is little doubt that the papacy could have become his prisoner if he had wished to make the effort.

*Premature death of Henry* vi—*Internal conflict in Empire promoted by papacy*— Then, in a moment, the whole situation changed. Henry died at the early age of thirty-two, leaving a son of three in Sicily, and no one of his family strong enough to hold the Empire together. And one year later, in 1198, Innocent iii ascended the papal throne.

Innocent's policy was thus all prepared for him. His task was clearly to prevent Sicily and the Empire from ever falling into the same hands again, and to keep the two chief German families at each other's throats. He accomplished the second not very difficult task by throwing his support first to one family and then to the other, while Germany fell into the throes of a civil war. He kindly took the infant Frederic Hohenstaufen of Sicily, son of Henry vi, under his personal patronage, made him his ward, and promised to keep the kingdom of Sicily for him until he was grown up—with the determination that at all costs he must be kept from the Empire.

In the century since Gregory, the papacy had gained no new weapon; it could exercise its influence to disrupt, and hope to make incidental gains from the discord. Nevertheless, the breathing space after the extreme danger of the reign of Henry vi was enough for Innocent to display the papacy at the height of its temporal power; even though to hindsight its foundations were no stronger than the temporary division among the natural opponents of papal prerogatives in the secular realm.

## PAPAL POLICY IN FRANCE—RELATIONS WITH CAPETIAN KINGS

### Lay investiture

Papal prohibition of lay investiture was not confined to Germany, but was directed against all monarchs equally. Philip I, the French king in Gregory VII's time (1060–1108), like all the poverty-stricken kings of his line, regarded simony as one of his necessary sources of income. He had to be excommunicated three times before he finally submitted; his own feeble position as one of the less powerful of French feudal lords made him vulnerable to papal attack. The question was not of sufficient importance to him to make him wish to endanger the careful work his family was engaged in—trying to expand its feudal domain into a real kingdom. A compromise was agreed to under which the investiture by ring and staff was dropped by the king; but he was permitted to postpone appointments until a suitable candidate was found whom he was ready to confirm, and his right to confirm such candidates was guaranteed by the papacy. This was substantially what was agreed to for Germany at the Concordat of Worms in 1122 as already described.

### Philip Augustus and Innocent III

The later Capetian kings chose their clergy wisely and with a regard for their ability rather than for their birth, including the indefatigable Abbot Suger, who was the virtual ruler of the kingdom while his master was on a crusade. Such men, owing their positions altogether to the monarchs, served them far more faithfully than the nobles who were always seeking the advancement of their families and the expansion of their lands.

Philip Augustus (1180–1223), the real unifier of France, a master of political strategy, understood very clearly the strengths and weaknesses of his position. In his dealings with the papacy he showed also that he knew the limitations of its power, and how far he could safely go with Innocent III. In 1193 he repudiated his wife, Ingeborg of Denmark, without papal permission, later marrying another wife. Innocent commanded him to take back Ingeborg and give up his second wife; when Philip refused he laid an interdict upon the country. Thereupon Philip submitted; he was heavily engaged in taking the English king John's possessions in France and could not afford to have the pope and the English king in alliance against him. Innocent continued to object to Philip's conquests of John's territories, but Philip paid no further attention to him, and in due course the pope himself became embroiled with John over the appointment of the Archbishop of Canterbury.

Now Philip's submission paid off. The pope began to support him; and when at last he deposed John, Philip was his chosen successor for the throne of England. Nothing more was said about Philip's conquests in France. If John had not submitted to the pope Philip might well have gained his throne—or at least have been able to bargain with him for all his French possessions in exchange for it. Philip also refused to take part in the Albigensian Crusade proclaimed by the pope against heretics in southern France, although the territory was not yet part of his domains, and denied that the pope had any right to call the crusade at all. In short, outside the minor matter of the divorce, which did not concern his kingdom, Philip pleased himself in France, without caring what Innocent desired, but he was not above making use of Innocent when it seemed profitable to do so. The kingdom thus unified by Philip was to prove itself invulnerable to serious attacks by the papacy at the end of the thirteenth century, the first of the national states to win a complete and enduring victory, as will be seen in the next chapter.

### Struggle with the Norman kings over lay investiture

When Duke William of Normandy wished to conquer England at the height of the reform movement, he took the precaution of sounding out the papacy first. He was rewarded with a banner and confirmation of his claim to the throne. The pope was able to justify this action since Harold, the Saxon nominee to the English crown, had sworn an oath that he would not claim it, and so could be regarded as perjured.

But when William had conquered England, he was determined to make his rule absolute, with no interference from any outsiders, however exalted. Papal bulls could not be published in England, the pope himself would not be recognized without the king's consent. William chose and invested with both temporal and spiritual power all the higher clergy, and paid no attention whatever to decrees which forbade such a practice. At the same time he appointed Lanfranc, one of the greatest churchmen of the day, as Archbishop of Canterbury. Lanfranc, who had been an abbot under William in Normandy, was in full sympathy with the greater part of the reform. Not needing the cash, William did not engage in simony, and clerical celibacy was enforced. Though Gregory VII admonished him on lay investiture, the main purpose of the reform was in any case accomplished; papal control of the clergy was not so necessary if the king would truly control them himself. In any case, Gregory's hands were full with Germany, and he had absolutely no power over William in his compact country entirely subordinated to himself—and Gregory knew it.

William Rufus, however, son of the Conqueror, had no Lanfranc at hand, was not interested in the welfare of the Church, and was unable to control his nobles as effectively as his father had. Declaring he would be head of the Church himself, he refused to appoint any successor to Lanfranc. Since this was the period of difficulty after the death of Gregory VII, no action could be taken, until William, of his own accord, stricken by an illness, gave the position to another abbot from Normandy, St. Anselm. But on the recovery of the king, Anselm found his position impossible and left the country, while William continued his lay investiture to which Anselm had objected. Even under William's successor, Henry I, Anselm continued to object, and refused to accept the king's appointees. After Anselm was absent from England several times to plead the case at Rome and gain papal support, his position was vindicated in part. The pope negotiated an agreement with Henry in 1107 under which the king gave up the right to invest with ring and staff, but could receive homage from his appointees on granting them their land.

### Henry II and St. Thomas Becket—Royal jurisdiction over the clergy

This question of lay investiture in England having been settled by the usual compromise, during the period of anarchy that followed the death of Henry I the Church became as independent of the king as the feudal nobility; and Henry II felt impelled to reduce both to obedience. He was more successful with the nobles than with the Church. He believed his chance had come when he appointed St. Thomas Becket, his own chancellor, a man who had hitherto been entirely dependent on his favor, as Archbishop of Canterbury. Thomas, Henry thought, would help him with a matter that was of increasing consequence to him, the attempt to make a uniform English law code, and the establishment of the king's justice over feudal and ecclesiastical law.

But Thomas understood very well the nature of his own power as archbishop, that it was conferred upon him by the pope, even though the king had chosen him in the first place and prevailed upon the pope to accept him. And he no longer felt himself the king's servant, but the servant of the Church. When Henry in 1164 issued the Constitutions of Clarendon, declaring that in future all clerks in holy orders accused of secular

*The murder of Thomas Becket by the knights of King Henry II of England. From the* Ramsey Abbey Psalter *(English), 1285–1300.* (COURTESY THE PIERPONT MORGAN LIBRARY. Ms. 302, folio 4)

crimes were to be tried in the king's courts, Thomas protested; he then went abroad and for several years waged a verbal war with his monarch. Finally in 1170, returning with a bull of excommunication in his pocket ready to be used if necessary, he was murdered at the altar of his cathedral in Canterbury by a party of Henry's knights who had taken a wrathful outburst of the king's to be an order.[2] Public opinion was outraged, Henry had to do penance and allow the monks of Canterbury to scourge him, and was forced to withdraw his Constitutions. The Church had won, though not on this occasion at the initiative of the pope. It was, however, the backing that St. Thomas Becket received from the Papacy that enabled him to stand up against his master who had appointed him.

[2] T. S. Eliot's famous play, *Murder in the Cathedral,* concerns this incident.

## Quarrel between John and Innocent III— England a fief of the papacy

Henry's younger son John, as we have seen, embroiled himself with Innocent III; and again the struggle was over the appointment of the Archbishop of Canterbury. John, in desperate need of funds to sustain his unpopular war with Philip Augustus of France over the French possessions of his house, seems to have thought he could lay his hands on the possessions of the Church with impunity. At all events, his challenge of Innocent III seems to have been deliberate, since the appointment itself was of little real consequence, not at all proportionate to the stubbornness with which John tried to get his way. On the death of the previous archbishop there had been a difference of opinion between John and the clergy of Canterbury, who had the right to select a candidate for the king's approval. The king's friends at Canterbury chose one candidate, and his opponents another. Both sides appealed to the pope, who decided to appoint neither, preferring an English cardinal, Stephen Langton, with better qualifications than either of the two suggested candidates. The clergy of Canterbury were converted to the papal viewpoint, and all that was needed was John's assent. This he refused; and Innocent, again using first his bludgeon weapon against the whole people, laid an interdict upon England, later also excommunicating John himself. John then proceeded to confiscate Church property, paying no attention to the interdict or his excommunication. But the country, suffering from the interdict which lasted five years, from John's futile wars in defense of his possessions, and from the refusal of the clergy to assist even in the burial of the dead, was in the utmost misery; and the feudal lords, who had no interest in John's wars in France, and objected strenuously to his illegal collection of taxes, were only looking for a chance to overthrow him.

Finally Innocent used his last weapon, made possible only by the willingness of Philip Augustus of France to cooperate. He deposed John and offered the kingdom to the French monarch, who began to make preparations for an invasion. The English nobles thought it a good opportunity to desert John, and made ready to welcome Philip and his son. At this point John submitted to Innocent, giving him the whole country as a fief, doing him homage, and agreeing to pay him heavy feudal dues as his vassal.

But this was the limit of Innocent's success. Now anxious to protect his vassal, he found that he had encouraged the nobles to revolt, and they were no longer willing to acquiesce in John's arbitrary rule. When John joined the Holy Roman Emperor in an alliance against Philip Augustus and both were defeated at the battle of Bouvines in 1214, the barons were able to bring John to the point of renouncing his arbitrary rule, and signing Magna Carta, dealt with in more detail in a later chapter. This infuriated Innocent, who had by this time called off Philip Augustus, was not at all interested in the grievances of his vassal's nobles, and naturally wished to control them himself through John. He forbade John to observe the Charter (in any case John had no intention of doing so if he could help it). Innocent also forbade the nobles to insist on its enforcement on pain of excommunication. But the nobles were beyond Innocent's reach; they were not afraid of his spiritual weapons, and even Innocent's own appointee to Canterbury joined them. They were all duly excommunicated. The nobles then personally asked Philip Augustus to come over and take the throne. Louis, his son, had already arrived in England when John and the pope both died in the same year, and the invasion was abandoned, while the nobles hastened to try to obtain control over John's young son, who was not yet of age.

Like Innocent's other victories, this long quarrel showed to the world the real weakness of papal power underneath the apparent glittering success. He had not been able to control the English nobles, and had helped to break the power of the English monarchy only to hand it over to a far less easily controlled nobility. By using the interdict he had aroused an enmity in the English people which was never to be overcome. Both nobles and people resented bitterly the aids which the king had to pay as a vassal under feudal law; even a monk like Matthew Paris complained throughout the next reign of the rapacity of papal tax collectors. And within half a century, as a direct result of pious Henry III's efforts to fulfill faithfully his duties as a vassal, the English people had their first Parliament, an instrument of government that was quite beyond the understanding or control of an autocratic papacy. This Parliament, in a later century, was to create a new English Church under the direction of a monarch who was no longer frightened of papal displeasure.

▶ ## Unification of Christendom against the Muslims—The Crusades

THE BACKGROUND FOR THE FIRST CRUSADE

### Papal interest

We must now return to the close of

the eleventh century and take up the history of a movement that first added power to the papacy and then, like the struggle with the secular powers, escaped its control and helped aid those forces working against all religious authority. It will be understood that the Crusades could be described under any of a number of possible headings, and that they have been inserted in this chapter because they will be dealt with here especially from the point of view of their consequences for the growth of papal power.

In 1095, while the reformed Cluniac papacy was still in power and the investiture struggle was not yet settled, Pope Urban II called for the First Crusade in a masterly and impassioned speech. The Seljuk Turks, a warlike and semicivilized group of Muslims, had taken control of the decaying Abbasid dynasty of Bagdad and had gradually encroached on the territories still officially under Abbasid control. Unlike, however, the enlightened caliphs of Bagdad, they showed no respect for Christians, no understanding of the value of the pilgrimage trade to Jerusalem, and still less for the venerable empire of Constantinople. The Byzantines were also threatened by further invasions of Asiatic barbarians from the northeast.

Ordinarily the papacy would have had little sympathy for Alexius Comnenus, the emperor of Constantinople. For forty years the Eastern Empire had been altogether cut off from the papacy, and had set up its own Greek Orthodox Church, which held, among other things, as we have seen, a different opinion from the Western Church on the matter of the procession of the Holy Spirit. But Western Christians did revere Jerusalem, and pilgrimages to the Holy City were a recognized form of penance as well as a means of acquiring merit. So when the Turks started to rob and harass the pilgrims, even refusing them entry to the Holy City, this action was a serious matter for the Church, and tended to make the papacy more ready than usual to listen to the request sent by Alexius for help.

A crusade was not a new thing. For years, under the auspices of the Church, the nobility of Europe had been nibbling away at Muslim domination of Spain, but the sporadic expeditions had never become a mass movement; they did not hold the religious appeal that an all-out war with infidels would provide. The papacy had just been able to assert its spiritual supremacy by bringing the emperor to Canossa. But it could use still more prestige in its struggle with the secular powers; there could be no more glorious way of gaining it than by preaching and supplying the spiritual leadership for an expansion of Christendom into the East and capturing the very center of the religion, the Holy City where Christ had died and been resurrected.

It was also true that there was, from the papal point of view, too much feudal warfare in Europe. The Truce of God could never be fully enforced. The nobles loved fighting; it was their chief business in life. Could some of this excess vigor be used in a holy cause? It might be that some would not return, and that churchmen, as noncombatants, would look after their possessions while they were away. If Jerusalem and Syria were indeed conquered, then who should be the new overlord but the papacy who inspired the conquest? And perhaps Alexius, in exchange for suitable help, would consent to bring his Church once more under papal authority and back to doctrinal orthodoxy.

All these things must have passed through Urban's mind while he played upon the religious feelings of the people, upon the martial feelings of the nobility, and while he promised a plenary or full indulgence for all their sins to those who died for the cause, and when he gave permission to Peter the Hermit to preach a crusade throughout Christendom.

### Interest in crusade of other classes in society—Cities, nobility, kings, peasants

The maritime cities, especially Genoa and Venice, had been going ahead rapidly since the Muslims had been driven from the Mediterranean; but the Byzantines kept a tight hold on the Aegean. Timely aid or pressure from the West might persuade them to be less monopolistic with their trade. New trade with Muslims was, of course, reprehensible, but surely possible. And crusaders would not care perhaps to march through Europe when ships could be put at their disposal, for a price. The Venetians and Genoese welcomed the crusade and began to build ships, which they would be delighted to provide in such a noble cause. If the crusaders were successful they could take the Muslim luxuries without payment—a considerable boon to trade which had always been kept to small proportions for the lack of suitable Western goods to export. And if they failed, they still had to pay for transportation, in advance. So how could they lose?

The feudal lords looked first at their own lands, and then thought of Syria and Jerusalem. Europe was getting a little small and overcrowded, and it was very poor. Travelers' tales said the East was rich. The great lords thought it would be a fine thing if the smaller lords went and did not come back; the smaller lords dreamed of fiefs without overlords, and wondered whether they could raise funds for the expedition, and if so from whom. The Normans remembered their Viking ancestry; it had been a long time since they had been permitted a good looting, except those few who had been allowed to sack Rome a few years ago. Europe was becoming a very tame place; perhaps they should not have settled down so quickly. Their cousins had taken Sicily from the Muslims and built themselves a kingdom. Why not a larger and more glorious kingdom in the even more wealthy East? And they all thought what a pleasure it would be to be allowed to fight a holy war, sanctified by the Church, killing infidels and being forgiven one's own sins into the bargain.

The kings thought what a blessing it would be if there were fewer feudal lords in the country. A wide-awake monarch ought to be able to pick up a few lands here and there. He would be glad to act as trustee and protect his theoretical vassals and perhaps even make them into real ones. At all events it was wiser to stay at home where there was much work to be done. Let the

crusaders have their glory; and if they won some fiefs in Palestine, so much the better. Perhaps they would stay there.

But beyond and above all these private considerations the religious zeal was unmistakable. Many in the full flood of enthusiasm went against their material interests. With scarcely the vaguest idea even of where Jerusalem was, still less of what they would find there, never having seen an infidel, they received absolution from the Church, donned the sacred emblems which showed they were crusaders, and set out by land determined to recover the Holy Sepulcher, without thought of the lands they had mortgaged and left behind them or the dangers which lay in front of them. Afterward it became necessary for the popes to use coercion, and leadership fell into the hands of kings who went because it was expected of them. But no one was coerced for the First Crusade; and it was the only crusade that was successful.

### THE FIRST CRUSADE

An army of peasants was the first to be ready. Unable, even if it had occurred to them, to afford the expense of a sea passage, they marched in a disorderly rabble through Europe, led by Peter the Hermit himself. Unable to take along any food for themselves, they lived off the country they passed through, to the great annoyance of the owners who were forced to defend their territories, at high cost to the peasant army. Many died of starvation and exposure. The remnant reached Constantinople in advance of the nobility and was given hasty passage across the Bosporus. In Asia Minor the Turks quickly took care of them; few escaped, though Peter the Hermit was one who did.

Slightly less disorderly were the armies of the feudal nobles and their vassals who followed, also by land, for the few ships available could not transport so many, nor could the nobility afford the cost of sea transport in an economy which contained so little money. But these lords could defend themselves going through Europe, and they were not quite so numerous as the earlier

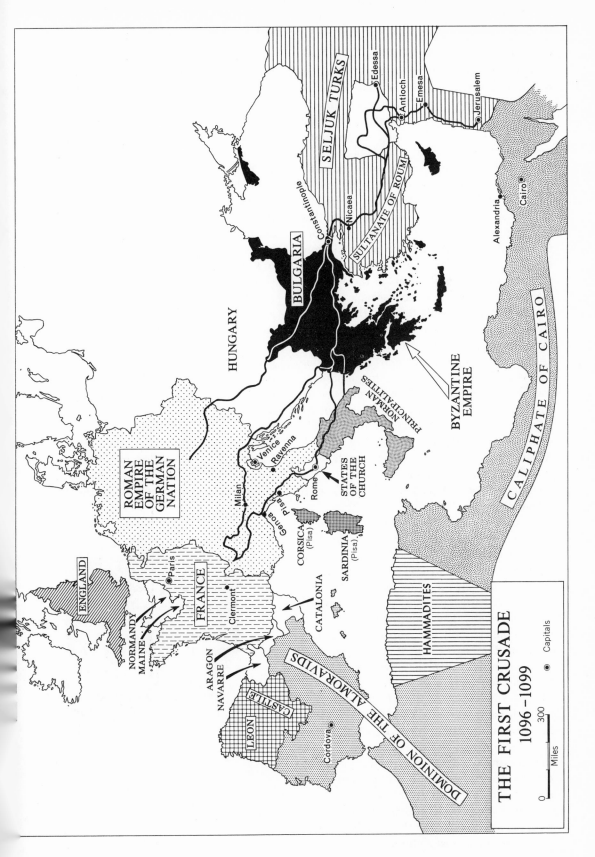

THE FIRST CRUSADE
1096–1099

SELJUK TURKS

Edessa
Antioch
Emesa
Jerusalem

SULTANATE OF ROUM

Nicaea

Constantinople

BULGARIA

HUNGARY

BYZANTINE EMPIRE

NORMAN PRINCIPALITIES

Alexandria

Cairo

CALIPHATE OF CAIRO

ROMAN EMPIRE OF THE GERMAN NATION

Venice
Ravenna

Milan

Genoa

Pisa

Rome

STATES OF THE CHURCH

CORSICA (Pisa)

SARDINIA (Pisa)

HAMMADITES

ENGLAND

FRANCE

Paris

Clermont

NORMANDY
MAINE

CATALONIA

ARAGON
NAVARRE

LEON
CASTILE

Cordova

DOMINION OF THE ALMORAVIDS

● Capitals

0    300
Miles

575

peasantry. Yet their passage was described by contemporaries as worse than a plague. Reaching Constantinople, they shocked Emperor Alexius by their barbarous manners. But, knowing himself powerless to resist them, and realizing that they might easily turn against his own city, he kept them as satisfied and peaceful as he could, courteously putting up with extreme indignities until he could get rid of them. But he did succeed in extracting an oath from them that they would return to him all his possessions in Asia Minor that they reconquered from the Turks, which he may have promised to give them back again as fiefs in the Western manner, though this is not certain.

At last he was able to move them across the Bosporus, and they captured Nicaea for him. Moving further into Asia Minor, the crusaders began to complain that Alexius was unfairly forbidding them to plunder as was their right, even though the cities were Greek and had been only temporarily occupied by the Turks. Finding it increasingly difficult to keep them in any kind of control, Alexius at last left them, content with what they had reconquered for him and free for a while from any danger of further Turkish inroads.

The crusaders, ignorant of the route to Palestine, and having no central leadership, began to split into small bands. One lord was invited into Edessa by its Christian ruler. He accepted and left the expedition. But at last, after many hardships, most of them reached Antioch, where they found a Genoese fleet with supplies, with the help of which they captured the city, giving it to another crusader for a fief. Then they proceeded down the coast and with only a minor battle captured Jerusalem from the Muslim garrison. They did not know that the Seljuk Empire had broken up some three years before the crusade, and that the reason they had been so successful was that the cities were manned only by Turkish governors without any prospect of reinforcement from Asia.

On capturing Jerusalem the crusaders went berserk, massacring the infidels, a harmless group of almost defenseless Egyptians, until they were up to the waists in corpses, and in Solomon's temple they rode up to their knees in blood, chanting praises to God at the same time for delivering the Holy Sepulcher into their hands. Such of Palestine as was conquered was organized into fiefs on the feudal model, owing allegiance to the papacy, with a Latin Kingdom of Jerusalem being organized soon afterward to take in all territory south of Edessa. For permanent defense various crusading orders of fighting monks were established, and castles were erected throughout the country to keep away the Muslims should their power show signs of reviving.

Every year the fleets of Venice, Genoa, and Pisa brought out reinforcements and supplies, taking back superior Oriental goods in return, which began to move into European markets. Lacking religious zeal, these merchants encouraged fraternization and peaceful relations with the infidels; and in due course the crusaders began to relax their severity, adopt Muslim customs and dress, and lord it over their realms like Oriental princelings, leaving defense to the new crusading orders and to mercenary armies locally recruited from the Oriental population.

*A Knight Templar, a member of one of the orders organized to guard the Holy Land after the first crusade. In the particular manuscript from which this minature is taken, various occupations are shown, and a representative of each is seen being taken away by Death. From* Hours of the Virgin, *ca. 1450.* (COURTESY THE PIERPONT MORGAN LIBRARY. Ms. 359, folio 128)

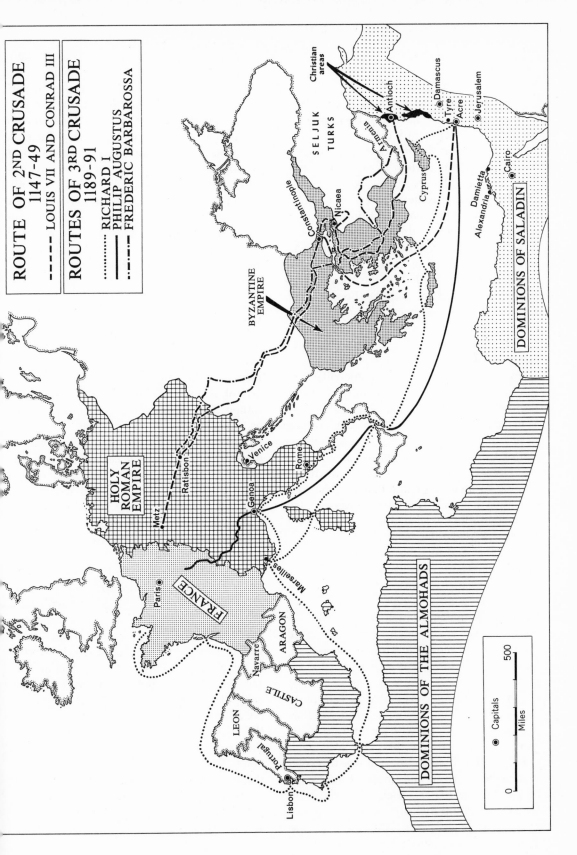

ROUTE OF 2ND CRUSADE
1147-49
— — — LOUIS VII AND CONRAD III

ROUTES OF 3RD CRUSADE
1189-91
· · · · · · · · RICHARD I
———— PHILIP AUGUSTUS
—·—·— FREDERIC BARBAROSSA

Christian areas

SELJUK TURKS

Armenia

Damascus
Antioch
Tyre
Acre
Jerusalem

Cairo

DOMINIONS OF SALADIN

Cyprus

Damietta
Alexandria

BYZANTINE EMPIRE

Constantinople
Nicaea

HOLY ROMAN EMPIRE

Metz
Ratisbon

Venice

Genoa

Rome

FRANCE

Paris

Marseilles

ARAGON

Navarre

CASTILE

LEON

Portugal

Lisbon

DOMINIONS OF THE ALMOHADS

Capitals

Miles
0          500

### RECOVERY OF MUSLIM POWER—SECOND AND THIRD CRUSADES

The conquest by such an ill-organized and disunited army had only been possible because of the temporary collapse of Muslim power due to invasions that the Muslims themselves had to sustain from Asiatic Mongols. As soon, however, as Muslim power recovered, the crusaders, so far from home and utterly dependent on European reinforcements, were unable to survive. When Edessa, the independent fief to the northeast of the kingdom, fell in 1144 another crusade was called. This was led by the Holy Roman Emperor, Conrad III, and the French king, Louis VII, who had been shamed into the effort by the preaching of St. Bernard. Again the expedition went by land, and again thousands of lives were lost before Palestine was reached. The Muslims waged guerrilla warfare against the crusaders; finally the kings decided their presence was needed nearer home, and proceeded to return. The crusade never approached close to Edessa, and the rest of Palestine was not yet threatened.

However, the Muslims were already beginning to recover their initiative. The Syrian cities that remained to them were united under one rule, and Saladin, the nephew of the new Syrian ruler, was sent to Egypt to hasten the end of the tottering Fatimid dynasty in Cairo, and if possible take the crown himself. He was successful in this mission, reorganized Egypt, and in 1187 recaptured Jerusalem, which he treated in a conspicuously gentle manner, permitting all those who had money to ransom themselves, and letting those who were too poor to pay ransom go free.

A new crusade was called in Europe to recover Jerusalem. Emperor Frederic Barbarossa agreed to go with an army of Germans. The expedition this time was well organized, but Frederic himself was drowned in crossing a river and most of his army returned home (1190). Richard I (the Lion Heart) and Philip Augustus of France, sworn enemies at home, were both coerced into going, especially Philip, who was no warrior, and had pressing interests in France where he was trying to take possession of Richard's lands. The armies had little success, in part because of the quarreling of the leaders. When Philip thought he had done enough for honor, he went home, leaving Richard, who was a warrior and liked fighting, to bear the brunt alone. The city of Acre was captured from the Muslims, but otherwise nothing of importance was accomplished. After making a truce with Saladin, which left Jerusalem in the latter's hands, Richard returned home to be captured and held for ransom by the new emperor, Henry VI.

### PAPAL PERSISTENCE IN CALLING CRUSADES—THE FOURTH "CRUSADE" TO CONSTANTINOPLE

Pope Innocent III could not view these disasters with equanimity. He refused to recognize the obvious reality that the interests of Europe had turned away from crusading. The feudal nobility were now almost as much interested in obtaining luxuries as in fighting, and their religious zeal was at a low ebb. The upper classes of Europe had begun to know prosperity for the first time since the Roman Empire, and commercial interests were increasing in influence. But Innocent, not to be outdone by his predecessors, used all his authority to get a new crusade started.

No king was willing to leave his territories at the time. Philip Augustus and John of England were engaged in war with each other and turned a deaf ear to his pleas; Innocent himself had seen to it that there was also no Holy Roman Emperor worthy of the name at the moment. The feudal lords pleaded poverty; but Innocent was inexorable. Finally a number of lords agreed to go, after making financial arrangements with the Venetians. But when it was time to go they still had not raised the price. At this point the Venetians graciously permitted them transportation expenses to be paid out of the proceeds of the expedition, and Dandolo, the aged and blind Doge of Venice, added that the city would even provide fifty ships of its own.

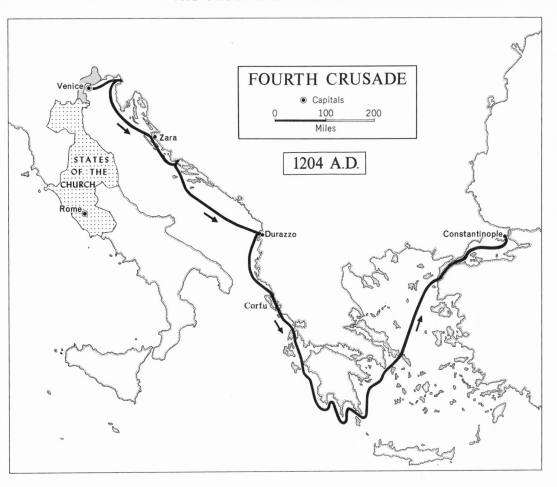

**FOURTH CRUSADE**

⊙ Capitals

0    100    200

Miles

1204 A.D.

As they started down the Adriatic Dandolo suggested to the crusaders that it would be to the benefit of all if they captured a city for him which had once belonged to Venice, but had been recently lost to the Hungarian king. Obligingly the crusaders turned aside and took Zara on the Dalmatian coast. After looting and sacking the city, they then destroyed it. Innocent, horrified at this crime against a perfectly good Christian city, excommunicated the whole body of crusaders; then, suddenly thinking better of it, he released them from the ban, and allowed them to proceed.

The ships started off again. But now a further temptation assailed them. A Byzantine pretender to the throne of Constantinople who had some real claim to it asked them to lend him some aid. If they succeeded in restoring him, he would pay off all the debts owed by the crusaders to Venice. Seeing no opportunity for similar rewards in Palestine, which by now was no longer so wealthy as in earlier days and offered few opportunities for loot, the fleet proceeded to Constantinople, restored the pretender to his throne, and awaited payment. No serious resistance was offered to the Crusaders save by the imperial guard of Swedes.

The new emperor was slow in paying, but at last he gave the bulk of the promised sum. But the Venetians cornered most of it, leaving the crusaders only a pittance for all their trouble. So when a rebellion broke out against the newly installed monarch, they regarded themselves as freed from all obligations to the Byzantines, and proceeded to besiege the city. Unable to withstand both a fleet and an army, the city soon fell, and was looted by the crusaders and the Venetians for three days. Completely ignorant of the value of anything in the city except precious metals, they broke up priceless works of art simply for their metal content; they destroyed mosaics for their jewels. They wantonly violated the church of Santa Sophia, breaking up the altar and carrying away everything they could lay hands on. The looting of Constantinople in 1204 lost forever most of the precious manuscripts of the ancient world. With the manuscripts went the unique works of classical Hellenic art pillaged from Greece by Constantine. The loss is irreparable, since the other great repository of manuscripts, the Library at Alexandria, had already been pillaged many centuries before during a fourth-century theological riot and by the invading Muslims.

The bulk of the crusaders then returned home laden with booty, while the Venetians busied themselves founding a colonial empire which included all the choicest seaports. And on the ruins of the Eastern Empire a new Latin Empire was organized under the rulership of the Count of Flanders, who held it as a fief of the papacy. It passed an unmeritorious existence till in 1261 the Greeks reconquered it. But the power of the Byzantine Empire was never fully restored after 1204, and it fell a victim to the Ottoman Turks two centuries later without being able to put up much resistance.

Innocent III did penance for the crusaders' victory, but thanked God that the Eastern and Western Churches had at last been united again. And, nothing daunted, he proclaimed another crusade at the Lateran Council of 1215. The king of Hungary agreed to go, but thought the best procedure was to go by way of Egypt. He captured Damietta, but promptly lost it and returned home. A crusade called in 1212 for the reconquest of Spain from the Muslims had better success. By 1236 the Muslims were driven out of Cordova, their capital, and the greater part of the country was in Christian hands.

Before his death Innocent had also forced his youthful protégé, Frederic of Sicily, to take the vow as a crusader. The crusade on which he finally went, after delaying as long as possible, will be described in the next chapter since it is symptomatic of the decline of the Church and belongs to the period after Innocent.

## CONSEQUENCES OF THE CRUSADES FOR THE PAPACY

The economic results of the Crusades will be dealt with separately in a later chapter. Here we are concerned with their effect on the power of the Church and the papacy.

There is no doubt that the success of the First Crusade redounded to the prestige of the papacy, which had called it, as the failure of the others to some extent discredited it. The overlordship exercised by the popes over the Latin Kingdom of Jerusalem was never more than nominal. The papacy was unable to prevent the crusaders from tolerating and fraternizing with Muslims, once the early fanaticism was over. And very little attempt was made to convert the Muslims themselves to Christianity. Many crusaders married Muslims and took over many of their customs. They were far more influenced by the superior Muslim civilization even in its decay than they themselves influenced the Muslims. It has also been suggested that contact with the Greek Orthodox Church and with the various heretical groups that had been living peaceably in Palestine for centuries under Muslim rule made them realize that Western Catholicism was not as universally accepted as they had been led to believe, but actual evidence is necessarily missing for this assumption. There can be no doubt that the inability of Innocent to control the crusaders who sacked Constantinople was a blow to his prestige for which even the temporary forced union between Greek and Roman Churches was but a slight compensation, though the failure did not prevent his subsequent success in dictating to the kings of Europe.

The times had changed. The true crusading spirit had disappeared from all but a few remaining knights-errant such as St. Louis IX of France. The commercial spirit symbolized by the Fourth Crusade showed that men now had other interests than salvation. Indulgences had been cheapened by indiscriminate gifts of them to crusaders, the purity of whose deeds and motives was questionable. The political activities and worldliness of the Church were not escaping the notice of the more earnest Christians. And, as we shall see in the next section, the faith of the people, which was ultimately the only basis upon which all papal claims must rest, a truth which had been recognized by Gregory VII but forgotten by Innocent, had been put to a severe test by the actions of the papacy. Within the Church and outside it a movement had been growing since the eleventh century which called for a return to an earlier and more ideal Christianity.

▶ **Reaction to the worldliness of the Church**

REFORM OF MONASTERIES—ST. BERNARD

The Cluny movement, as we have seen, started as a reform of the monasteries and a return to the strictness of the Benedictine Rule. But the peculiar nature of the political framework of the Cluniac system, which fitted it for use as a means for increasing papal power, militated against its persistence as a thoroughgoing reform movement. Monks ambitious for power in the Church joined it, as well as sincere Christians who wished for a life of strict purity and religious observance; and before the end of the eleventh century the need was already becoming apparent for yet another monastic reform to take care of those Christians who still sought a purely religious life separated altogether from worldly concerns. The chief leader, though not the earliest, in the demand for reform was a man who had started life as a Burgundian noble, known to posterity as St. Bernard of Clairvaux (*ca.* 1090–1153).

There had already been an increase in the number of hermits living alone in small communities, and one order of extreme austerity had been founded, with its center in a forbidding district of southern France. The Carthusian Order, named for the district of La Grande Chartreuse, really preserved its original purity, and claims today that it is the only order that has never been reformed since it never has needed reformation. But St. Bernard's work was within the regular monastic system itself.

A little before his time the Cistercian Order had been founded by an abbot of a Benedictine monastery who had been unable to reform his own house. But it received a new impulse when Bernard entered it and became abbot of a daughter monastery of the Cistercians at Clairvaux. An ascetic and a mystic, St. Bernard believed that the only truly Christian life was to be found in communion with God. With a profound contempt for this world, its luxuries, and its knowledge, which, in his view, drew man away from his true task and delivered him into the hands of the Devil, he opposed with his matchless eloquence the whole trend of his age toward the secularization of Christianity and toward an increasing interest in earthly life. St. Bernard carried to an extreme the tendency of the early Western Christian Church to despise earthly power, possessions, and wisdom. The only purpose of life on earth was to prepare for salvation. Bernard attacked the secular clergy as grasping and interested only in power and display, to the neglect of its religious duties; he attacked the monks for laxity, loose living, and gluttony. He even attacked the Church builders for the excessive decoration of their churches, and he attacked Abélard for his pride in believing that the unaided human mind was capable of understanding and contributing to the knowledge of religious truth.

Such a man could have been dangerous to the Church, for his eloquence spared no man. In a later century, indeed, he might, like Savonarola, have used it against the Church itself. But in his own time the zeal for reform was widespread, and the papal chair was still occupied by men who had not yet become wholly politicians and diplomats. Christians in high places and low submitted to the lash of his tongue because in his day they still believed that what he said was true. And for forty years he was the most influential man in Christendom, the acknowledged keeper of the conscience of medieval Christianity.

For a time his Cistercian Order maintained its austerity; but, as with all the other successful orders which did not keep themselves altogether separated from the world, the wealth that flowed into it from the faithful undermined its discipline. Many of the Cistercian abbeys pioneered in good farming, and, as wool producers, entered industry; but by the fourteenth century their reputation as holy men and the tradition of St. Bernard had long been swallowed up by the commercial and secular interests of the age.

THE GROWTH OF HERESY

### The nature of twelfth-century heresy

As early as the eleventh century attacks on the worldliness of the Church and the failure of the Church to heed them had driven occasional reformers into an uncompromising position which could only mean actual separation from organized religion. There were no other Churches to join; only one great Church, authoritarian and dogmatic, which had to be accepted or rejected. And the penalty for rejection, or heresy, was death if the heretic refused to change his views. Many such heretics no doubt found their way into the reformed monasteries where they could spend their lives in personal worship and outward conformity. If no such monastery appealed to them, then there was no other recourse than heresy.

When we have had occasion to deal with heresy in earlier chapters, the heresies, in the main, concerned questions of theology; at a time when Christian theology had not yet crystallized into dogma, or beliefs necessary for salvation promulgated by authority, such heresy was to be expected until the authority was universally accepted. Twelfth-century heresy is of a different kind. With a few minor exceptions it was anticlerical in origin, it was above everything against the established Church; and though in some cases a different doctrine was preached, the doctrine was subsidiary to the

anticlericalism, and usually grew out of it. The common element in all twelfth-century heresy was the belief that true Christianity consisted in leading a life more consistent with the life of Christ as it had been portrayed in the Gospels. It was, then, a reaction against the apparently non-Christian life of the Church and its clergy.

If this Church and its sacraments were really necessary for salvation, then there could be no escape from it, however irreligious it appeared to be. The difference between the heretic and the reformer was the simple fact that the heretic was willing to "throw out the baby with the bathwater"; he was forced into the position of denying the power of the Church to save souls, and into claiming that a Christian life on earth was the principal requirement for salvation rather than sacraments and rituals. As we have seen, even among the ancient Hebrews this question had arisen, and it could never be settled; it was the chief difference between the priestly and prophetic traditions— as it was to be later the core of the Protestant divergence from Catholicism. The twelfth-century heretic could find clear Scriptural justification for his view; the Church, by careful interpretation of the Scriptures, could also find justification. But the tradition of most of the Christian Fathers leaned far more heavily in favor of the view of the Church. So the heretics threw over the Christian Fathers and their interpretation, and were thus driven into heretical statements in doctrine which could be used in evidence against them. Certain key beliefs of the Catholic Church they could not accept in good conscience; and by their insistent denials of these it was possible for the secular clergy, and later the Inquisition, to condemn them.

### The Cathari or Albigensians—Revived Manichaeism

The only important early medieval heresy that had any serious pretensions to being a separate religion, with an intellectual ancestry stretching back into the past, was of Oriental origin. The Cathari or, as they were called from the area where their successes were greatest, the Albigensians, believed, like the Persian Manichaeans, that there were two great forces in the world, good and evil, light and darkness, of equal power. Darkness was equated with matter and light with spirit. The true believer should devote his life to the attempt to purify himself from everything that partook of the nature of darkness, including a rather arbitrarily determined list of foods, and he should avoid sexual union. The possession of private property and all forms of authority, spiritual and secular alike, were repudiated, and the Cathari refused to go to war for any purpose whatever. The Church, with its wealth and materialism, was an instrument of the powers of darkness, as was also the God of the Old Testament, in contrast to the God of the New Testament, and to Christ, whom they accepted as the emissary of the power of the light. They rejected Hell, saying that the soul of the unbeliever was simply punished by entering the body of an impure animal, until it learned by the experience of impurity to appreciate the necessity of being purified. They did not believe in capital punishment and they refused to take oaths; and as they naturally preached celibacy and continence, it is hardly surprising that they were detested by Church, State, and the general public equally, the latter looking upon them with a frenzied superstitious hate that was later to be of the greatest assistance to the Inquisition.

Such an austerity of practice, however, was not required of all Cathari equally. There was a lower class of "believers," and an upper class of ascetics, known as the *perfecti*. But all were expected to purify themselves as they felt death approaching, and to receive the sacred laying on of hands, called the *consolamentum*. This ceremony could be performed only once, and if it was performed while the believer was still in good health, he was thus transformed into one of the *perfecti*, and was expected thereafter to undergo the full austerities of the religion. If he received it when dying he was expected to undergo the extreme initiation rite of the *endura*, a ritual suicide through complete abstention from nourishment.

The surprising thing about this apparently unattractive religion is its popularity, and the way it spread throughout southern France and northern Italy. Indeed, in Languedoc—Albi is one of its leading cities—by the end of the twelfth century with its own ministers drawn from the *perfecti*, its own ceremonies, and its own church organization, it had almost entirely ousted Catholic Christianity, and it was protected by the local feudal lord. And this in the area in France which in its day was also the most civilized, with a flourishing literary and musical culture, the land of the troubadours.

It seems unlikely that the nobles were entirely convinced of the truth of the Catharist doctrine, but they went along with the Cathari in their dislike for the Church. And for the lower grades of the believers it was probably enough to be able to worship in their own communities, to follow a simple life with rewards in prestige or in the next life for any austerities they might wish to practice in this, without inquiring any more than did ordinary Christians into the more esoteric beliefs they were supposed to hold.

### The "Poor Men of Lyons"—Waldensians

Another important heretical group was composed of the Waldensians, or "poor men of Lyons," called after their founder, one Peter Waldo, who had discovered in the Gospels that Christ had owned no property but given all his goods to the poor. Waldo followed his example; then, gathering around him a number of disciples, began to preach poverty. This was precisely the same initial impulse that started St. Francis of Assisi on his mission; and at the beginning Waldo, who was obviously a Christian, met with a kindly reception from Pope Alexander III, who allowed the "poor men" to teach and take vows of poverty, provided they obtained permission from the local clergy. This, however, they neglected to do, since their opinion of the local clergy was a low one, and they did not attempt to conceal it. When they were condemned by a Church council they became more outspoken; and it was an easy step to say that there need be no clergy at all, that the only true Christian life was one of renunciation and poverty, and that all the Church customs and ceremonies not specifically mentioned in the Bible did not have to be observed.

In the growing towns, whose spiritual needs were seriously neglected till the thirteenth century, there had always been loose, semi-organized groups of the poorer classes who had had to find their Christianity for themselves; and for lack of more authoritative instruction in the matter had simply taken the Gospels and the life of Christ and his disciples as suitable examples for daily living. These medieval prototypes of modern dissident groups in society had always been regarded as dangerous by Church and secular authorities alike, and had been visited with varying degrees of persecution. The Waldensians, with their missionary fervor, naturally drew members of such groups to them, and the movement began to become really dangerous to the Church, especially when those in northern Italy started to form their own churches with simple ceremonies, and to appoint their own clergy and organize their own schools. In spite of continuous persecution, the Waldensians were never suppressed altogether in Italy; and though in time they became part of the Protestant movement a Church of Waldensians still exists today as a separate Protestant sect.

▶ **Reaction of the Church to the rise of heresy, and the issue of apostolic poverty**

FAILURE OF THE MONASTIC ORDERS

The issue of poverty was a very real one to an organized Church. Although at one time a pope was forced into the position of declaring that it was a heresy to teach that the apostles possessed no common property but lived in absolute poverty, it was not an opinion easily quelled by authority when the Gospels were the heart of Christian teaching, and were available to anyone who could read Latin, and soon to any who could read

at all. The time-honored answer had been to permit all those who sought for a life of poverty and religious devotion to go into a monastery apart from the world. But by the early thirteenth century there was hardly a monastic order that could fulfill the requirements of so many sincere seekers. Moreover, why must the choice be so narrow? That a Christian wished to worship his God simply, with a minimum of ritual, freely, without being forced to believe what he did not believe, trying to follow the example of Christ and his apostles as far as he could, did not necessarily mean that he wanted to quit the world and go into a monastery.

Yet the Church, if it were to exist at all, could not do without money and property; within the feudal system it could not maintain itself without feudal dues. Was it to refuse money genuinely bequeathed to it? If the Church did not supply an expensive organization, what organization would there be? Who would administer the sacraments which it had declared were necessary for salvation? Either it had to abdicate what it believed to be its responsibility to satisfy the objections of a small number of dissidents, or it had to devise a policy for dealing with the dissidents. For it is clear that it could never reform itself enough to satisfy them and still remain an organized Church.

SUPPRESSION OF HERETICS

### The Albigensian Crusade

To Innocent III it must have seemed that the only policy that held any hope of success against the Albigensians was repression. The vast majority lived in a limited area under the overlordship of the Count of Toulouse, who was reputed to be sympathetic to them and in any case made no effort to suppress them. The secular clergy in the diocese had tried to convert them back to orthodox Catholicism for years without success, but their weapons were feeble since they lacked the support of the local nobility; even public opinion was not on their side. Their arguments, based on the authority of the Church, fell on deaf ears, for the Cathari accepted no such authority. The Cistercian monks did not take easily to missionary work. A Spanish bishop, assisted by a group of Cistercians and a young and ardent missionary named Dominic who was in the retinue of the bishop, obtained permission from Innocent in 1205 to attempt the reconversion of the territory. It was clear to these missionaries that much of the heresy was due to simple ignorance of Christianity, an ignorance that they tried to relieve. They met, however, with but indifferent success. The Cistercians did not like the work, and the bishop could not spend too much time away from his diocese. Yet, if they had been given time, and the effort had been better organized they might have made some impression on the Cathari. Perhaps Innocent did not know enough of the work to give it proper support, or perhaps he did not have enough missionaries available with the right kind of enthusiasm, and he did not recognize St. Dominic's outstanding talents. At all events he lost patience with the Albigensians, and in 1208 proclaimed a "crusade" against them.

Philip Augustus, king of France, refused his approval to the project; he thought that any proceeding against heretics should be dignified and orderly. The Count of Toulouse should be convicted of heresy if guilty, and he, the king, should then be allowed to sequestrate his fiefs, although it was not certain that he was in fact the count's overlord. Philip did not seem to be convinced of the extreme danger of the beliefs of the Albigensians. But neither he nor anyone else was able to prevent the pope from proclaiming the crusade and promising the territories of the heretics to the faithful crusaders.

So Innocent went ahead with the second "Crusade" of his eventful pontificate (the first, of course, went to Constantinople), this time against heretics in Europe; and noble lords bent on the plunder of the fairest area in France answered his call, no better organized than usual until a number of small bands united under the leadership of their most capable general, Simon de Montfort. However, generalship in the highest degree was not necessary, for the majority of the Cathari,

not given a chance, like other heretics, to recant and thus save their lives, and mindful, no doubt, of their belief in nonresistance and fortified by the thought that this was the *endura,* the last test of their faith and purity, received the *consolamentum* and prepared to die. The nobility who had protected them, and who now found themselves menaced by covetous nobles in quest of their fiefs, resisted stoutly, aided by some of the less stoical heretics; but the bulk of the Cathari was simply massacred in one of the easiest and most horrible campaigns in history. Innocent, as usual, repented too late of what he had initiated, and tried to call off the crusaders. But they paid no attention to him, and the war which started as a crusade ended as a war of conquest. Raymond, the Count of Toulouse, protector of the heretics, received assistance from his feudal overlord, the good Catholic Peter II of Aragon, who was killed in a battle which followed (1213). Simon de Montfort and his crew finally defeated the heretics and their protectors, he himself became overlord of the territory, and did homage to Philip Augustus for it.

But Raymond's son was able to collect an army. Joined by his father he found the crusaders bickering over the spoils, and was able to defeat and kill Simon de Montfort and recover the fiefs of his family. At this point the French king intervened, and in 1229 a compromise was patched up. Raymond's son, the victor over Simon de Montfort, who had become Count of Toulouse on the death of his father, undertook to help in eradicating the last of the heretics, and the newly organized papal Inquisition, under the successors of the same St. Dominic who had earlier tried to convert them, was able to complete the work to the satisfaction of the orthodox. The most advanced civilization in France had been destroyed, the entire land was desolate, a desolation from which it has never fully recovered to this day; but the heresy had been extirpated. It continued to influence northern Italy, where it joined forces with other anticlerical groups. But on the whole the crusade must be considered a success, since its original purpose had been achieved. A university was founded under the auspices of Pope Gregory IX at Toulouse to instruct the surviving inhabitants in the truths that had hitherto been neglected in that area.

RECONVERSION—THE MENDICANT ORDERS

### Dominicans

Already before the Albigensian Crusade Dominic had approached Innocent III with a request that he be allowed to form a new order. The Pope listened politely but temporized. He was not sure that a new order was desirable, especially not one whose members were vowed to poverty. But he did not forbid Dominic from going ahead, and the young man returned to the scene of his labors, remaining there through the first stages of the crusade, ministering to the wounded and dying, often at serious risk to his life. Returning to Rome he was now able to obtain official recognition for his greatly enlarged group of companions, and a Rule was drawn up, confirmed by Pope Honorius III in 1220. The new order, called the Order of Preachers, but commonly known as Dominicans, with its companion, the Order of Lesser Brothers, or Franciscans, was a radical departure in Christianity; and though both orders derived from the original initiative of the founders, the Church was soon able to see their value, and give them unusual honors and very full support, which brought upon them the envy and enmity of the pillars of medieval conservatism, the secular clergy and the universities.

The towns had been seriously neglected, as we have seen, for centuries. The parish priest had far more difficulty in the towns than on a compact manor in keeping in touch with his flock, and the higher clergy had too many other duties to give the townspeople much attention. The monasteries were, as a rule, founded in country districts, and had no influence in the cities. But these new orders of friars (brothers), as they were called, went out preaching to the people directly in the market place or in the local church. The Dominicans early became noted for their

learning, and were able to give instruction in a manner hitherto unknown. As missionaries, first within Christianity and then to heathen countries, their influence and activity were enormous. Convents were founded throughout Europe where the friars could live, and which they could use as their headquarters for missionary activity. But unlike the monasteries, the convents were modest institutions. Very little land was required nor was regular income needed from feudal dues, since they lived at the beginning entirely from begging (hence they were called mendicant orders). And from the first they were directly subject to the papacy through their chief officer, called a Minister General, who ruled authoritatively through Provincial Ministers in each country.

### The Franciscans

*The personality and teaching of St. Francis*—The Franciscan Order was founded by St. Francis of Assisi, the son of a merchant in good circumstances who was able to provide Francis with a life of modest luxury. But Francis was suddenly converted from this life of ease by reading the Gospels. At once he gave all his possessions away save the coarsest and simplest of clothing, took, in his own words, Lady Poverty for his bride, and began to preach.

If there has ever been a true Christian saint since the founding of Christianity, then St. Francis was he. By his example and utter sincerity and by the simplicity of his life, he won the hearts of all those who listened to him, and quickly a band of disciples grew up around him. It was not only that he was kind to everyone, even the outcasts of society, the sick and the maimed and the lepers whom no one would touch; the quality of love seemed to shine out from him in a way that no one could resist or wished to resist. But behind this genuine simplicity there was also a rare intuitive understanding of the life around him. He knew that it was impossible for the Church ever fully to accept him, he knew what dangers and temptations his order would have to meet, he knew to how few it is given really to lead such a life of absolute poverty as his. He did not want to organize his order formally, he did not want it to have rules and regulations which would inhibit the spontaneous outpouring of love in which lay his own special genius. He did, however, see Innocent; but it was only natural that the pope should be hesitant, his shrewd diplomatic mind grasping the dangers that such a movement held for his Church, dangerous enough with Dominic, but a hundred times more so with a leader like Francis. It is said that Innocent had a dream in which he saw the Church supported by only these two orders, a dream later enshrined in a famous fresco of Giotto. Whether he heeded the dream or not, he temporized again, and it was his successor who drew up the Franciscan Rule and confirmed the order. Francis himself refused to be Minister General, and insisted on appointing the most worldly of his band to the position, because, as he said, it was right for himself also to be subject to discipline as a Christian duty.

Francis disapproved of learning as unnecessary in a pure gospel of love, and the preaching of his order in his lifetime corresponded to his own. The task of Franciscans was rather to help and heal, to teach by example and not by precept, to go about among the poor bearing the Gospel and praising God for his blessings, and encouraging them to do likewise.

*The struggle within the Franciscan Order on the question of poverty*—It was inevitable that after the death of Francis there should be a schism within his order. No organized body, but only rare individuals, could live up to such an ideal. Money poured in upon the order, which was not permitted by its Rule to keep it. The appointment of a papal procurator to handle the funds of the order did not solve the problem, and in the eyes of the uncompromising followers of St. Francis, this subterfuge was a betrayal. With the resounding success of both the Dominican and Franciscan Orders and the support given them by the papacy, privileges showered in upon them, and ever more and more recruits to the Franciscan Order. The life of primitive

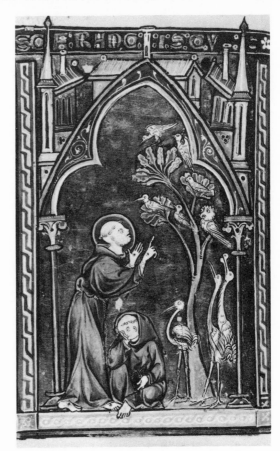

*An almost contemporary (ca. 1265) miniature of St. Francis of Assisi preaching to the birds. From a* Psalter *(Franco-Flemish).* (COURTESY THE PIERPONT MORGAN LIBRARY. Ms. 72, folio 139)

simplicity had to be abandoned; and the begging of the friars before long became a scandal to those who knew of the order's wealth. Friars of both orders began to seek learning, and the influence of the papacy was able to gain them chairs in theology even at Paris, to the fury of the secular professors who, resenting this unfair competition, unleashed a torrent of scurrilous pamphlets on their way of life and their hypocrisy, replied to in kind by the leading friars. In the convents of both orders learning was approved, and preaching to the people ceased to be universal; friars were permitted to hear confessions, and before the end of the century a friar was pope.

The Dominicans, to whom in any case poverty had never been such an essential part of their movement, accepted the inevitable; the Franciscans split into two. For a while most of the Ministers General were men who had known St. Francis and knew what poverty had meant to him; and those dissident Franciscans who objected to the ownership of property whether by brothers or by the order itself were protected by them. But by the end of the thirteenth century it was clear that the order was doomed if it could not heal the schism. The path that was probably inevitable from the first was chosen. The Conventuals, who accepted the compromise on absolute poverty and who were in a majority within the order, expelled the Spirituals, who wished to retain strict poverty and were ultimately treated as heretics by the Conventuals. By the early fourteenth century the Spirituals had been formally declared heretical,[3] and some were handed over to the Inquisition, while many more languished in Franciscan prisons. Their movement persisted for a long time, being used by secular powers against the Avignon papacy when they wished to castigate its pride and luxury. Ultimately the remnants found refuge in Protestantism.

The friars, however, left an indelible mark upon later medieval Christianity. Much of the art of the early Italian Renaissance was influenced by them, especially by the Franciscans. The human side of Christianity, already visible in the veneration of the Virgin Mary, and the late medieval cult of the Mother and Child, was now emphasized in both art and literature more than ever before. There can be no doubt that there was a real renewal of religious life in all ranks of society in the thirteenth century which can be in large measure put to the credit of the friars who first brought religion to the mass of the people. And the missionary enterprises which multiplied from the thirteenth century onward, reaching to China and throughout the known world, were a result of this spirit.

### PERMANENT COURT FOR DISCOVERY AND SUPPRESSION OF HERETICS—THE INQUISITION

Great though the influence of this last pre-Reformation reform was, it was not sufficient to extirpate heresy altogether. In the early thirteenth century Pope Gregory IX established a regular Inquisition into the beliefs of supposed heretics, which was entrusted first to the Dominicans, and later to both orders. The purpose of the Inquisition was to fix a procedure for this detection and punishment of heretics. The inquisitor, a papal appointee, paid periodical visits to the various cities within his jurisdiction and called on heretics to declare themselves, and upon the faithful to denounce those suspected of heresy. If a heretic confessed and recanted, he was usually let off with a comparatively light penance imposed by the Church. If he refused to recant, then torture was permitted, as in Roman times with slaves, and as in the medieval secular state, to compel the confession. Testimony was taken, but the defendant was not allowed a lawyer nor was he permitted to know the names of his accusers and the nature of the evidence. If two witnesses of good character agreed, then he could be condemned.

The purpose, however, was always to obtain a confession and to persuade the heretic to recant, in which case, if he had been a long time making up his mind to confess, he might receive a severe, but not a capital, punishment. Except when in later years the Inquisition became a tool of the secular powers who used it to confiscate the property of heretics, this provision was usually carried out, and there were far fewer death sentences imposed than penances. If the heretic refused to recant, he was handed over to the secular authorities to be put to death, customarily by burning. If a heretic recanted and then relapsed into heresy he was regarded as incorrigible, and likewise handed over to the secular authorities.

The Inquisition has gained its evil reputation largely from the later so-called Span-

---

[3] By this time, indeed, they had accepted certain prophetic teachings which could be considered formally heretical, although the Spirituals themselves denied that they were.

ish Inquisition, used by the Spanish rulers as a political weapon. The medieval Inquisition never claimed so many victims, and on the whole it seems to have preferred not to impose the death penalty. Its secret procedure laid it open to many abuses, and it does not accord with modern Western ideas of justice. The crime against which it was exclusively used lent itself especially to inquisitorial methods, as has been rediscovered in the present century. Heresy was regarded in a way not unlike political crimes of modern times, as treason to Christendom; now such crimes are treason to a totalitarian state.

The Church, however, was not all-powerful in the medieval period; it could not impose the death penalty itself, and monarchs could and did refuse to have the Inquisition within their dominions. It was never introduced into England or Scandinavia, though Queen Mary I of England burned some three hundred Protestants for heresy and treason without the benefit of the Inquisition. Only when the secular authorities agreed could the death penalty be exacted. They must therefore share the opprobrium for the Inquistion in this case with the Church. That they backed it up as much as they did is because they too regarded heresy as treason, and heretics as rebels against the established order.

► ## Summary: The papacy at the height of its apparent power—Innocent III

THE ELEMENT OF GOOD FORTUNE DURING THE PERIOD OF HIS PONTIFICATE

In the last section we have, for the sake of convenience, included events after the death of Innocent III which could equally well have been dealt with as part of the decline of the Church and not of its growth to power, which was the central study of this chapter.

When Innocent called the fourth Lateran Council in 1215, and all the potentates of Christendom came or were represented, while he gave instructions and promulgated dogma, it might have been thought by a contemporary that Christendom was close to becoming a true theocracy, ruled by the representative of God upon earth. It has been the purpose of this chapter to trace the growth of the Papacy to this commanding position, while revealing the cracks in the imposing edifice, and the hollow nature of most of the papal pretensions.

On the surface Innocent had been extraordinarily successful, using to the full the power accumulated in his office by his predecessors. He had reduced the kings of England and France to obedience; not only England but half the smaller countries of Europe were his feudal vassals. He had curbed the power of the Empire, he was on the way to extirpating the Albigensian heretics, and in his time, though not by his efforts, the Eastern and Western Churches had been reunited.

But not one of these triumphs was really significant. The two kings were not in fact properly controlled. They had given way when it suited them, and another time they could resist the same weapons. The quarrel between England and France had been the pope's opportunity, as the premature death of Emperor Henry VI had been his opportunity in Central Europe. He had crushed the Albigensians because he offered land to the nobles; not because they were the obedient Christian executors of his wishes. He had been unable to prevent the Venetians and crusaders from sacking Constantinople, though he had been willing enough to take advantage of their victory. In short, whatever the appearances, the secular powers held all the sources of power in their hands, and they only needed a more favorable moment to throw off the illusory yoke of the pretended theocracy.

SHORTCOMINGS OF INNOCENT'S METHODS AND UNDERSTANDINGS

Innocent III betrayed no real understanding of this state of affairs; though if he had, there was still little that he could do about it save the last thought that would have occurred to him—to become a spiritual power alone, the moral arbiter of Europe

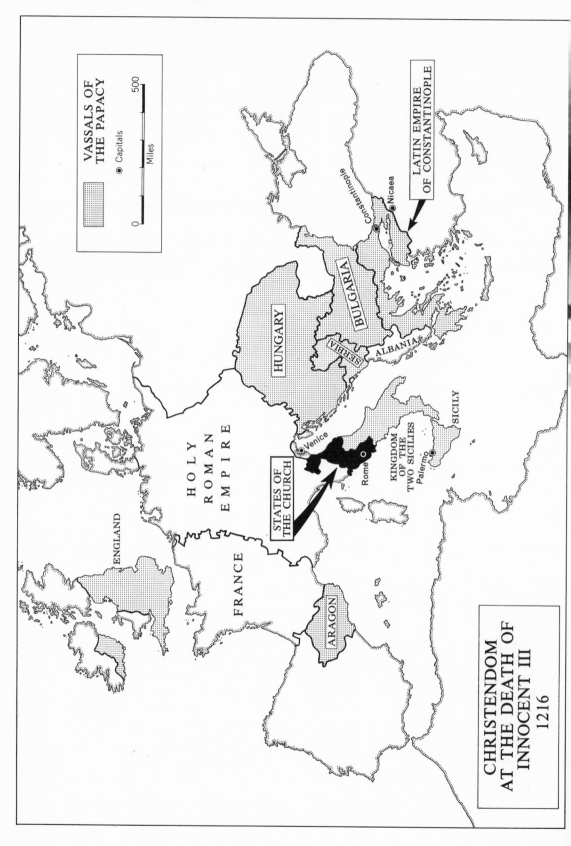

VASSALS OF
THE PAPACY

● Capitals

Miles

0          500

LATIN EMPIRE
OF CONSTANTINOPLE

Constantinople

Nicaea

BULGARIA

HUNGARY

SERBIA

ALBANIA

SICILY

HOLY
ROMAN
EMPIRE

STATES OF
THE CHURCH

Venice

Rome

KINGDOM
OF THE
TWO SICILIES

Palermo

ENGLAND

FRANCE

ARAGON

CHRISTENDOM
AT THE DEATH OF
INNOCENT III
1216

and not its dictator. When a hint of this other way was revealed to him by St. Francis, he looked hastily in the other direction.

He had no understanding of the growth of commercialism in the century before his day; his eyes were on the past glories of the crusades, and not upon the present reality that the crusading spirit had disappeared from Europe. His political interferences without exception led in the longer run to exactly those results most dangerous to his office and authority, as when he made the English king his vassal; he failed to understand the basis of heresy in a justified anti-clericalism, and preferred to wipe heretics out with the sword.

The heritage he left to his successors was a long struggle with the secular powers which could never be won, a universal Church with ambitions beyond its power to achieve, and a tradition of authoritarian dictation which made an ultimate schism inevitable.

By not understanding the nature of the City of God he helped to make it forever impossible.

▶ Suggestions for further reading

A fine study of the position of the Church in the life of medieval man is to be found in the first article by F. M. Powicke in C. G. Crump and E. F. Jacob, eds., *The Legacy of the Middle Ages* (Oxford: The Clarendon Press, 1926), in which the necessary conflict between Christian ideals and the organized Christian Church is lucidly explained. Good histories of this period in English are very scarce, and most of them are rather old. In recent times most of the published works have dealt with special subjects and are unsuitable for the beginning student. Perhaps not too specialized is Lucy M. Smith, *The Early History of the Monastery of Cluny* (Oxford: The Clarendon Press, 1920). J. A. Foakes-Jackson, *Introduction to the History of Christianity, A.D. 590–1314* (London: Macmillan & Co., 1921), has a fairly good section on the Middle Ages, while A. Lagarde, *The Latin Church in the Middle Ages* (New York: Charles Scribner's Sons, 1915), is a clear, competent, and fair-minded account of the things the student most

needs to know about the medieval church. There is, however, an excellent short survey which overlaps the material of this Chapter 18, and Chapter 19: S. Packard, *Europe and the Church under Innocent III* (Berkshire Studies in European History; New York: Henry Holt & Co., Inc., 1927). Much material will also be found in the classic J. Bryce, *The Holy Roman Empire* (new ed., rev. and enlarged; New York: The Macmillan Company, 1926). This book, originally written before the end of the nineteenth century, cannot be too highly recommended for its important insights into the nature of the Holy Roman Empire as an attempt to revive the long-defunct Roman Empire during times unsuitable for any such attempt; and the remarks on the Church as an alternative institution, with aspirations toward a universal spiritual dominion, should also be studied with care, though the viewpoint of Bryce may be one-sided. A standard history, not yet outmoded, giving a clear enough record of the facts, is T. F. Tout, *The Empire and the Papacy, 918–1273* (8th ed.; London: Rivingtons, 1941).

Finally, another of Toynbee's brilliant studies, in which the distinguished historian studies the medieval papacy as an example of what he calls "the nemesis of creativity," or an institution that was so successful that it moved beyond its competence and thus met its own destruction, is to be found in his *A Study of History* (London: Oxford University Press, 1939), IV, 512–584.

The best short history of the Crusades is another Berkshire Study, R. A. Newhall, *The Crusades* (New York: Henry Holt & Co., Inc., 1927), in which the Crusades are kept in the proper perspective and not made responsible for all the changes in medieval life that occurred in the twelfth and later centuries. Newhall, however, manages to encompass a great many topics within his allotted space, and though of course none of them is dealt with at all fully, there are quite enough facts for the needs of the beginning student. A fuller account of the Crusades is S. Runciman, *A History of the Crusades* (2 vols.; Cambridge: Cambridge University Press, 1951–1952).

On the heresies the standard book is still the old H. C. Lea, *A History of the Inquisition in the Middle Ages* (3 vols.; New York: The Macmillan Company, 1908–1911), which, although in some respects outmoded by later scholarship and perhaps unduly anticlerical, has many fine passages and gives a full account of this aspect of the work of the Church. One passage in J. B. Ross and M. M. McLaughlin, *The Portable Medieval Reader* (New York: The Viking Press, Inc., 1949), will be found specially useful for the study of heresy, since it comes straight from the manual of inquisitorial procedure drawn up by an inquisitor himself (pp. 202–216). The standard life of St. Francis is P. Sabatier, *The Life of St. Francis of Assisi* (New York: Charles Scribner's Sons, 1901), many times reprinted, but it suffers from a little too much piety toward the founder of the Franciscan Order, though generally reliable as to fact. Another shorter account is to be found in a very eloquent chapter of H. O. Taylor, *The Medieval Mind* (4th ed., 2 vols.; Cambridge, Mass.: Harvard University Press, 1949). The life of St. Dominic is studied in a work by a Dominican scholar, P. Mandonnet: *St. Dominic and His Work* (St. Louis, Mo.: B. Herder Book Company, 1944).

# 19

# The Decline of the Church
# as a World Power

*Internal efficiency of the ecclesiastical system under Innocent III • Resumption of the struggle with the Empire • The papacy and the national states • The papacy at Avignon and the Great Schism • The papacy at the close of the Middle Ages*

---

▶ ## Internal efficiency of the ecclesiastical system under Innocent III

THE PAPAL COURT (CURIA)

At the conclusion of the preceding chapter an attempt was made to show in what way Innocent III misjudged the temper of his times, as well as the flaws in understanding which underlay his policy toward the secular powers. It should, however, be emphasized that the internal structure of the ecclesiastical system was far from weak. Though the papacy was not to be able to force a theocracy upon Western Europe, the struggles of the eleventh and twelfth centuries had succeeded in giving it an efficient bureaucracy far ahead of any administrative system in the secular world of the time. Though the clergy might be chosen by the secular powers with papal approval, nevertheless after their appointment they were by various means kept under the control of the papacy, which had indeed become a true international state within the various state structures of Europe.

At the head was the pope himself. Immediately subject to him was the papal court or Curia, made up of clerks, secretaries, lawyers, and other officials, several of whom held the honorary title of Cardinal. The Curia itself was divided into departments concerned with such matters as the administration of justice and revenue. The popes had striven long and hard to establish their court as the supreme appeal court for all cases tried under canon law, and in this effort they had been largely successful. Canon law had been codified by the middle of the twelfth century, and was generally accepted throughout Europe; the pope and his court were indeed continually appealed to for decisions in numerous cases covering contracts, wills, and such other matters that the still primitive royal and feudal courts could not handle satisfactorily. The popes and clergy constantly fought for the right to judge all clerics, whatever their crimes; and as a rule the kings did not trouble to argue with Church officials, but let them have their own way. Only with the increasing use of the civil law, based, like canon law, on the ancient Roman codes, and the growth of the legal profession within the national states, did the kings begin seriously to resent clerical interference.

### REVENUE SYSTEM

The tax-collecting system of the papacy had gradually been systematized. The Church was constantly receiving legacies, it had its regular income from the Papal States, it collected feudal dues from kings and nobles who held land as vassals from the pope, and it subjected the clergy to general taxes for the crusades, even when there were no crusades actually in progress. The popes could also require aids from the clergy similar to those demanded by feudal lords in time of emergency, and there were regular charges for indulgences and other penances. The higher clergy, when appointed to positions in the Church, usually had to pay a percentage of the first year's dues (annates) for the privilege of confirmation by the pope. The custom also arose in the thirteenth century of appointing prelates to benefices which involved no duties for themselves, the duties being farmed out to lesser clergy at a fraction of the salary. Many prelates held several benefices of this kind which they used simply as sources of income and which were shared, at least to some degree, with the pope. Moreover, as the papacy gradually took into its hands ever more and more appointments, the sums derived from patronage became one of the most important sources of income available to it. It was, of course, pointed out by opponents of the papacy that such practices amounted to simony, but the accusation made little noticeable difference in their prevalence.

### ATTITUDE OF THE CLERGY TO PAPAL EXACTIONS

To collect all these varied sums the popes had to use skilled administrators; and it was no accident that throughout the thirteenth and fourteenth centuries the majority of the popes, including Innocent III himself, were thoroughly conversant with both civil and canon law. Even when the influence of the popes in external affairs declined and when they could no longer force secular powers to obey them, they continued to administer their estates effectively; indeed, control reached its height when they left Rome in the fourteenth century and took up their residence at Avignon. And as they put ever greater pressure on their clergy for ever more money, the clergy had no way of protecting themselves except by recourse to the kings. There are many instances of kings supporting the clergy against papal exactions and claims, while the clergy in return backed the kings in their policy. But the process continued until the Protestant Reformation, the success of which in several countries was primarily due to the desire on the part of kings and princes to tax the Church themselves, rather than let all the funds go to support the foreign potentate at Rome.

From the thirteenth century on, this domination of the papacy by lawyers and the ever-increasing concern for money go far toward explaining the failure of the papacy to make its moral influence felt, demonstrating at the same time how changed was the whole spirit of the age, and to what an extent commercial interests had usurped the place of religious.

## ▶ Resumption of the struggle with the Empire

### INNOCENT III'S EFFORTS TO DIVIDE AND RULE IN GERMANY

When Emperor Henry VI of the Hohenstaufen family died so opportunely in 1197, the way lay open, as we have seen, for papal interference with the new election of an emperor. Henry's son Frederic, a child of three, could be ignored, and Innocent took the child under his protection while supporting in Germany the Welf candidate, Otto of Brunswick. The Hohenstaufen family, however, would not permit the throne to escape from its hands without a fight, and chose a king of their own, Philip of Swabia, the brother of Henry VI. The result was a destructive civil war which lasted for fourteen years. Innocent proceeded to enlarge the Papal States by conquest until they reached the Adriatic, and forced recognition of his conquests from Otto of Brunswick in exchange for papal support. Otto also had to give up any control over the

# ► chronological chart

## Resumption of struggle between Empire and papacy

| | |
|---|---|
| Pontificate of Innocent III | 1198–1216 |
| Civil War in Germany | 1197–1212 |
| Murder of Philip of Swabia | 1208 |
| Otto of Brunswick crowned emperor | 1209 |
| Frederic II becomes king of the Romans | 1212 |
| Frederic II crowned emperor by Honorius III | 1220 |
| Sixth (Frederic's) Crusade | 1227–1229 |
| Excommunication of Frederic by Gregory IX | 1227 |
| Papal mercenaries (Soldiers of the Keys) wage war against Frederic's territories in Italy | 1228–1229 |
| Frederic negotiates ten-year truce with Muslims | 1229 |
| Peace of San Germano between Frederic and Gregory IX | 1230 |
| Defeat of Lombard League by Frederic at Cortenuova | 1237 |
| Second excommunication of Frederic by Gregory IX | 1239 |
| Capture of prelates on way to Rome by Frederic | 1241 |
| Death of Gregory IX | 1241 |
| Two-year interregnum in papacy | 1241–1243 |
| Innocent IV elected pope | 1243 |
| Innocent escapes to France | 1244 |
| Synod of Lyons—Deposition of Frederic by Innocent IV | 1245 |
| Lombard cities defeat Frederic at Parma | 1248 |
| Death of Frederic II | 1250 |
| Conrad IV emperor | 1250–1254 |
| Manfred regent, later king, of Sicily | 1250–1266 |
| Interregnum in Empire | 1254–1273 |
| Charles of Anjou invades Italy | 1266 |
| Battle of Benevento—Defeat and death of Manfred | 1266 |
| Conradin, last Hohenstaufen prince, executed | 1268 |
| Rudolf of Hapsburg elected emperor | 1273 |
| Sicilian Vespers | 1282 |
| Peter III of Aragon conquers Sicily and becomes king | 1282 |

## The pontificate of Boniface VIII

| | |
|---|---|
| Abdication of Pope Celestine V | 1294 |
| Pontificate of Boniface VIII | 1294–1303 |
| Wars between Philip IV of France and Edward I of England | 1294–1298 |
| Philip IV assesses French Church for a war levy | 1294 |
| Boniface issues bull *Clericis laicos* | 1296 |
| Philip forbids export of precious metals from France | 1297 |
| Papal jubilee | 1300 |
| Philip summons States-General | 1302 |
| "Battle of the Spurs"—Defeat of Philip by Flemish | 1302 |
| Boniface issues bull *Unam sanctam* | 1302 |
| Death of Boniface VIII (Anagni) | 1303 |
| Clement V elected Pope | 1305 |

## The papacy at Avignon and the Great Schism

| | |
|---|---|
| "Babylonian Captivity" of papacy | 1305–1376 |
| Philip IV confiscates property of Knights Templars | 1307 |
| *Defensor Pacis* of Marsiglio of Padua | 1324 |
| William of Occam at court of Emperor Ludwig IV | 1328–1346 |
| Golden Bull | 1356 |
| The Great Schism | 1378–1417 |
| Wyclif translates Bible into English | ca. 1378 |
| Wyclif denies transubstantiation | 1380 |
| Foundation of the Brethren of the Common Life | ca. 1380 |
| Council of Pisa | 1409 |
| Pope John XXIII | 1410–1415 |
| Sigismund emperor (king of Bohemia 1419–1437) | 1410–1437 |
| Council of Constance | 1414–1418 |
| Deposition of Pope John XXIII | 1415 |
| John Hus burned at Constance | 1415 |
| Pope Martin V returns to Rome | 1417 |
| Hussite Wars | 1420–1433 |
| Council of Basel | 1431–1449 |
| Taborites defeated by Utraquists in Bohemia | 1434 |
| Pontificate of Nicholas V (humanist) | 1447–1455 |
| Pontificate of Alexander VI (Borgia) | 1492–1503 |
| Savonarola master of Florence | 1494–1498 |
| Pontificate of Leo X | 1513–1521 |
| Ninety-five theses of Martin Luther | 1517 |

appointment of the higher clergy of the German Church.

Unfortunately for himself, Innocent could not control the course of the civil war; and when it appeared that the Hohenstaufens would win, he suddenly changed sides, accepting Philip of Swabia as his preferred candidate until Philip was suddenly murdered in 1208. Then Innocent had to return to Otto, whom he crowned emperor. Otto, however, seems to have lost the respect he owed to the head of Christendom, for no sooner had the new emperor been crowned than he withdrew his recognition of Innocent's conquests in central Italy and began a campaign to recover them, even seizing part of the kingdom of Sicily that had been reserved for Frederic of Hohenstaufen.

Innocent, at last realizing that he would be used by Otto in accordance with his own needs, played his trump card. He brought forth Frederic, who was now seventeen years old and a typical Hohenstaufen in appearance, and supported his claim to the throne of Germany. Frederic made a triumphal procession to Aachen, supported by Innocent's obedient if bewildered clergy and conquering all hearts by his charm (they called him the Boy of Apulia), and was duly elected king of the Romans.[1] Otto returning to Germany had first to face the army of Philip Augustus of France, which thoroughly defeated him at the battle of Bouvines in 1214. This finished Otto, who was solemnly excommunicated and deposed at the Lateran Council held next year by Innocent. In due course Frederic was elected emperor and crowned at Rome in 1220 by Innocent's successor.

### BANKRUPTCY OF INNOCENT'S GERMAN POLICY

Innocent providentially died before he was able to see the disastrous effects of his

[1] This was a title given to the elected German king before he was crowned emperor. Occasionally the emperors had the title bestowed upon their sons during their own lifetime in the attempt to ensure the succession for them. Theoretically, it is clear that the two titles were considered divisible, and not necessarily embodied in the same person.

policy. For Frederic was king of the Romans, and he had a clear title to the throne of Sicily, though at this moment it still needed to be reconquered. But beyond a promise he had made to Innocent there was nothing whatever to prevent Frederic from reuniting Germany with Sicily, and there was no other claimant who had any legitimate title at all. Thus the original purpose of the prolonged civil war in Germany fostered by Innocent had been frustrated. The only change effected by Innocent's efforts had been the destruction of the house of Welf at Bouvines. Frederic therefore came into a heritage which was in fact more secure than it would otherwise have been, allowing him to concentrate on his Italian and Sicilian possessions, without fear, for a long time, of any trouble in Germany. On the death of Innocent he proceeded at once to take possession of Sicily and reorganize it into a compact kingdom with a government entirely subservient to himself and unequaled in efficiency in the Western world.

### THE REIGN OF FREDERIC II

#### Character and policy of Frederic

Frederic himself was a remarkable man. Half German, half Norman, in ancestry, brought up in Sicily, after the death of his mother, by various protectors who left him largely to himself, he became probably the best-educated man in the entire Western world, with a fluent knowledge of German, Latin, Greek, and Arabic. A freethinker, he seems to have been little influenced by traditional Christian thought, and was indeed far closer to the less dogmatic Islam of his day than to Christianity. He took nothing on trust; he had a considerable respect, for instance, for Aristotle, but condemned the philosopher's occasional remarks on subjects, such as falconry, with which he was imperfectly acquainted. Frederic questioned the immortality of the soul, which he claimed had not been proven; and indeed he was credited with an experiment in this direction himself. He had an enormous interest not only in birds, on which he wrote

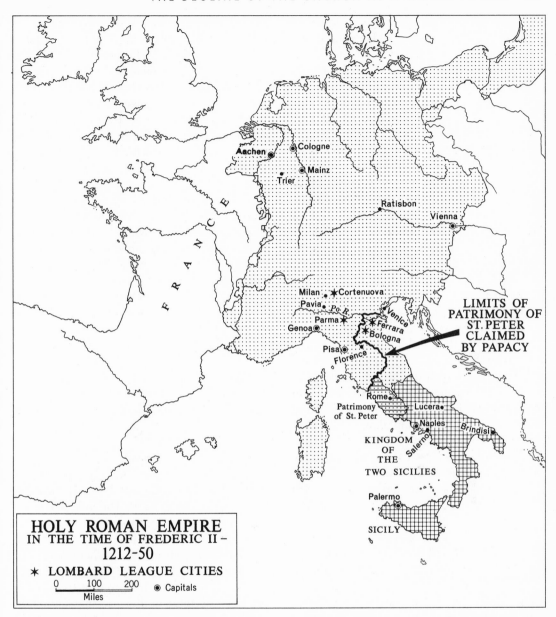

**HOLY ROMAN EMPIRE**
IN THE TIME OF FREDERIC II –
1212-50
★ **LOMBARD LEAGUE CITIES**
0    100    200    ◉ Capitals
Miles

a valuable treatise, but in animals, and he traveled through Europe with a private menagerie, to the astonishment of his contemporaries, who were not at all sure that he was not in league with the Devil. It is not difficult to see what excellent openings he afforded Christian propagandists when they were instructed to discredit him.

As a monarch he believed in complete absolutism. While he admitted the superiority of spiritual over temporal power, saying that on moral questions he would submit to rebuke even from the humblest priest, he denied the right of the papacy to dictate to him in his own secular realm, believing that he had received his rights as an emperor from God and not from the pope. As an administrator he was surpassed by no ruler in medieval times, and approached only by his own Norman predecessors in Sicily. He understood the importance of trade and industry for his Sicilian kingdom; like the early modern mercantilist kings, he encouraged his merchants, worked hard for their prosperity, and then taxed them in exchange for his assistance. He established monopolies in the Byzantine manner when private enterprise failed to fulfill his demands. He built a fleet to protect his trade which was the equal of the fleet of any Italian city of his day. He understood very well the power of money, and how necessary it was to secure a regular income if he were going to keep and extend his empire. He was able to keep armies in the field all his life with the aid of his Sicilian revenues; and the core of his army was a band of Muslims from Sicily, immune from influence by his great enemy the papacy. He established his Muslims, to the great offense of his enemies, in a special town of their own in southern Italy, from which Christians were excluded. It was not surprising that in his own day he was called "stupor mundi," the wonder of the world, by earnest Christians who had never seen such a strange combination of qualities in one man.

It seems to have been his fixed intention to extend his effective rule over all Italy and unite it to his southern kingdom, while leaving Germany, of which he was the titular ruler, largely to its own devices. His policy in Germany was always conciliatory to the great nobles, whom he left, together with the German Church, virtually independent of him. As early as he could he had his eldest son crowned king of the Romans, a title which gave him effective rule in Germany. But the son intrigued against him and finally joined his enemies, the Lombard towns in Italy. Frederic defeated and imprisoned this son, giving the crown to a younger son who cooperated with the nobles according to his father's policy, and never made any serious attempt to control them.

But Frederic's efforts to make the Italian towns submit to him met with resistance not only from them but also from the papacy. All his life he tried to come to a working agreement with the popes, but was never successful except for brief periods when his power was too great to resist. Even when a former friend of his was chosen pope, under his influence, the new pope at once

ceased to be his friend, driving Frederic to the observation, "It is impossible for a pope to be a Ghibelline." The papal treasury was as extensive as his own, and the popes used it to hire mercenary troops and pay subsidies to the Italian towns who did not wish to submit to the emperor. For almost the whole of his reign Frederic fought against both papacy and towns, to the accompaniment, for the first time in medieval history, of a torrent of pamphlets addressed both to public opinion and to the other rulers in Europe. The papacy insisted on its right to discipline monarchs, while Frederic declared that the popes were endangering the tranquillity of Europe, sowing dissension for no purpose. The popes constituted as great a danger to the other monarchs as to himself, Frederic told his fellow rulers; indeed he was fighting their battle for them. On the whole, except for the pious English king, who was also a vassal of the papacy but lacked authority in his own country, the monarchs stayed benevolently neutral toward the emperor but gave him no active support.

### Frederic's "Crusade"

Even before Frederic had shown the direction his policy would take, the papacy initiated the struggle which was to last till Frederic's death in 1250. The mild successor of Innocent, Pope Honorius III, had crowned Frederic emperor and had not attempted to prevent him from taking his Sicilian throne; but Honorius had gently though firmly reminded him also of his promise to go on a crusade. Because of the pressing nature of his Sicilian interests, Frederic had continually postponed this enterprise, a promise for which had been exacted from him by Innocent. But he made Honorius a firm promise that he would go at the latest by 1227; if he failed to do so, then he would submit to excommunication. However, in 1227 Honorius died, to be succeeded by stern old Gregory IX, then about eighty years of age, but vigorous and stubborn, and apparently determined that his principal mission as pope was to destroy the Hohenstaufens and break their power forever. At all events, his policy was constantly provocative, he never accepted sincerely any of Frederic's olive branches, which were offered frequently in earlier years, and his propaganda against the emperor, with its Biblical imagery, was scarcely if ever equaled even in an age noted for its invective.

Frederic duly started on his crusade in 1227, but at once fell ill and returned. Gregory, choosing to regard this illness as a piece of diplomatic hypochondria, promptly excommunicated him. On his recovery, in spite of the ban, Frederic sailed for Palestine, where he invited the overlord of the country, the sultan of Egypt, to negotiate with him. The sultan was very affable to this enlightened Westerner, who spoke Arabic so fluently; and he was careful not to offend the presumed susceptibilities of a man whom he regarded as a representative of Christianity, even giving instructions to the local muezzins in Jerusalem to refrain from calling the faithful to prayer while he was there. Frederic, however, told the sultan that he was anxious to observe Muslim customs in their own land, and he made a number of jokes about Christians which astounded the Muslim chroniclers of his visit. The business part of the crusade was quickly settled. Frederic could have Jerusalem except for the area around the sacred Mosque of Omar, and he could have Nazareth, Bethlehem, and a valuable strip of coast. Frederic had recently married the heiress to the old Latin Kingdom of Jerusalem, so that he was entitled to be its king. Unable to persuade the Christian patriarch in Jerusalem to crown an excommunicated emperor, he had to crown himself. Then after arranging for a ten-year truce he returned home, having accomplished by a skillful piece of negotiation and goodwill what fifty years of military crusades had failed to win.

It might be added here that Frederic's settlement lasted for fifteen years, after which the Muslims again captured the city. Two more crusades went from the West led by St. Louis IX, king of France. But on the first occasion Louis was captured in Egypt and had to ransom himself; on the second

he died and his army returned home. This was the end of the attempts to recapture the Holy City, though crusades were still called against the Turks in later centuries to stem their advances into Europe.

Gregory IX in Rome and all the faithful were scandalized by Frederic's achievement. First of all, the emperor was excommunicate, so the crusade was not sanctioned by the papacy. Furthermore, Frederic's behavior was not the traditional way to treat infidels, who were fit only for the treatment accorded them on the glorious First Crusade. That he had succeeded where Christian armies had failed added insult to injury. The pope therefore had raised an army of mercenaries in the emperor's absence, and it was ravaging Frederic's southern Italian territories, which no longer belonged to him as an excommunicated emperor and thus were forfeited to his papal overlord.

Frederic, however, made short work of the papal armies and proceeded to threaten the Papal States themselves. The pope was forced to negotiate and lift the excommunication. Frederic now became for a short time Gregory's "beloved son," and returned to Sicily, which at last he had time to organize, founding also the University of Naples for the primary purpose of training officials for his court.

### Frederic's attempted conquest of Italy—Papal resistance

Then the emperor began to reveal his plans for Italy. Ever since the Peace of Constance in 1183 the Lombard towns had enjoyed virtual independence. The emperor was still their overlord, and they owed him certain duties. But these had not been offered in the time of Innocent, and they refused to give them now to Frederic. The emperor wanted, moreover, to have the substance of power in northern Italy that had been claimed by his grandfather, Frederic Barbarossa, before his defeat by the Lombard League. When Frederic tried to assert his claim, the towns revived the league but were disastrously defeated by the emperor. He then announced his full plan to revive a

Roman Empire in Italy with its center at Rome, as in the old days, and with every town ruled by a Ghibelline government subservient to him. This plan Gregory could hardly submit to, for it meant the probable extinction of the Papal States, and the cutting off of his important revenue from them. He encouraged the towns to resist and again excommunicated Frederic, accompanying that act with a barrage of propaganda, replied to in kind by the emperor, who suggested a league of monarchs against the papacy. While the tide was still with him, Frederic organized the now prostrate towns into his kingdom and began to make inroads into the Papal States.

Gregory replied by summoning a council of prelates from all Christendom to come to Rome for the solemn deposition of the emperor. Frederic retaliated by sending his fleet to the northern Mediterranean and capturing a boatload of high dignitaries of the Church, who were then imprisoned by the emperor in one of his castles. At this moment Gregory could stand no more and gave up the ghost, being already well over ninety and with his dignity shocked beyond repair. Frederic, now having the bulk of the electors to the papacy under his personal protection, naturally insisted that their new choice be a pope favorable to himself. The good cardinals, hoping to be freed, hit on the idea of choosing a man who was apparently on the point of death. But the Grim Reaper was first on the scene and the cardinals were left again to make a choice. This time they made no mistake, and elected an old friend of Frederic's, a Genoese jurist who assumed the ominous title of Innocent IV (1243–1254).

### The papacy of Innocent IV—Deposition and death of Frederic

No sooner had Innocent escaped the imperial clutches than he began to show himself as anti-Hohenstaufen as his predecessors. While appearing to negotiate with Frederic he shrewdly played for time, then suddenly escaped to France where he called a council which solemnly deposed the emperor, in spite of a remarkable defense by an imperial secretary. Carefully staying out of Italy, Innocent proclaimed a crusade against Frederic; sent legates throughout Europe to stir up tumult, and especially to raise rebellion in Germany, where they gained some support from anti-Hohenstaufen nobles; and encouraged the friars to preach against the emperor in unmeasured terms. A conspiracy against Frederic's life was fomented, and of course the Italian towns were subsidized and resumed their warfare. Frederic's delight in the chase was to prove his ruin. While besieging a town in northern Italy, he carelessly left his army and baggage for a while to go hunting, and the citizens made a sortie and cut the army to pieces. Though this defeat was not fatal to him, it was a severe blow to his prestige, and other towns, hitherto neutral, turned out their Ghibelline governments and joined the fight against him. Nevertheless, Frederic continued to receive support from Ghibelline parties, and would probably have recovered his position if he had not suddenly died the next year at the age of fifty-six.

### THE END OF THE HOHENSTAUFENS AND THE COLLAPSE OF THE EMPIRE

The struggle was not yet over. The Empire went to Conrad IV, already king of Germany, while Sicily went to an illegitimate son of Frederic as regent for his half brother. But Conrad died soon afterward, and Manfred, his half brother, could not inherit the Empire. However, it was not possible to take Italy from him without reinforcements; he had secured complete control of Sicily and recovered most of his father's strength throughout the peninsula. At this point, Pope Clement IV, a Frenchman, called in Charles of Anjou, a soldier of fortune, feudal lord of a large part of France, and the brother of Louis IX, and gave him the Sicilian kingdom. Charles gathered an army and invaded Italy, Manfred was killed in battle, and Conrad's thirteen-year-old son, the last of the Hohenstaufens, took over the inheritance. But he too was defeated by Charles, and beheaded at Naples with the approval of the pope. Thus was the male line of the Hohenstaufens extinguished; but Manfred's daughter Constance married the king of Aragon in Spain, who was ultimately to take over the Sicilian heritage.

Charles conquered much of Italy and Sicily. But his armies desolated both countries, discrediting his whole enterprise and the papacy which had sponsored it. The anti-French feeling in Sicily was so strong that one night in 1282 every Frenchman in the entire island was massacred (Sicilian Vespers). Charles and his successors never recovered the country, which passed to Peter of Aragon, who maintained his kingdom even when the unrelenting popes called a crusade against him. Sicily remained in Spanish hands for several centuries in spite of claims by the descendants of Charles of Anjou, and in the fiftheenth century southern Italy was joined to it to make the kingdom of the Two Sicilies, which survived until modern times.

In Germany the extinction of the Hohenstaufen family was followed by an interregnum until 1273. The nobles were anxious to bestow the throne only upon minor princes in order to prevent any future ascendancy of any one family like the Hohenstaufens or Welfs. In 1273 they chose Count Rudolf of Hapsburg, a noble of Swiss origin; but even he was able to use the prestige of his position and the right to take possession of vacant fiefs, which traditionally belonged to the monarchy, to add considerably to his power and territory. The electors then turned to a minor prince from the Rhineland of the Luxembourg family. But he was even more successful in turning the monarchy to his advantage, retaining the throne within his family with a few breaks until it too died out, leaving the Hapsburgs the leading family in the country, and without a serious rival. Thereafter the title became a perquisite of the Hapsburgs (except for three years from 1742 to 1745) until the Empire was formally ended by Napoleon.

The Empire never presented any further threat to Italy, and only a few emperors even troubled to go to Rome to be crowned.

Occasionally an emperor crossed the Alps intending to add Italy to his possessions, but invariably he had to return with little accomplished. High hopes were held of Henry VII of Luxembourg, especially by the passionately Ghibelline poet Dante, who thought even the rule of a German emperor was preferable to the eternal quarrels of the petty governments of the cities. But the hopes were never realized, and Italy did not know unity till the nineteenth century. Germany also became a country of semi-independent principalities, ruled by local lords, until the Hohenzollern family of Brandenburg came to prominence in the eighteenth century and united Germany, with the exception of Hapsburg Austria, in the nineteenth century.

## ▶ The papacy and the national states

### EUROPEAN REACTION TO PAPAL POLITICS

The papal policy in the thirteenth century was clearly based upon little but considerations of power and the secular interests of the Papal States. The popes were, of course, secular rulers, and as such the interests of the Papal States were the equivalent of national interests to be maintained with all the power available to their rulers. But the papacy claimed to be so much more than this; and only by virtue of its position as spiritual leader of Europe did it have at its disposal the services of the ecclesiastical bureaucracy, the clergy, and the religious orders. These latter groups were dragged along behind the papal chariot to their own irreparable damage. The Empire had been destroyed, for what the victory was worth; but it had not been destroyed by the united forces of an outraged Christendom, nor even by the authority of the pope, entitled as God's vicegerent on earth to see that the monarchies of the world were in worthy hands, but by the naked swords of Charles of Anjou and his feudal vassals and by papal mercenaries whose wages were paid out of the gifts and tithes of faithful Christians.

Naturally in an age of dawning self-consciousness when the Church no longer had the monopoly of learning, when the peoples of the West were beginning to criticize their rulers on legal as well as on moral grounds, sincere Christians were deeply distressed by the wars and desolation for which many did not hesitate to blame the Church. While some looked for a new reform, and left-wing Franciscans criticized the papacy openly for its neglect of the teachings of Christ, others began to prophesy doom. It was a century of prophecy and of looking for some redeemer who would sit on the papal throne and usher in a new golden age of righteousness. When Gregory x, after a short interregnum that followed the death of Clement iv, was elected pope, it was hoped by the would-be reformers and evangelists that he was the chosen one, for a prophecy of "Merlin," a magician of Celtic legend, seemed to refer specifically to him, and he was known to have read the prophecies. But though Gregory ended the interregnum in the Empire, he did nothing else of note, and his successors returned to the old policy, continuing to support Charles of Anjou and making no reforms at all. At last the situation was so serious that an aged hermit with a reputation for sanctity was brought out of his retreat and forced onto the papal throne under the title of Celestine v. But the cardinals only intended him to be a venerable figurehead under whom they could continue to neglect reform. The leading cardinal, Benedetto Gaetani, a noble from a lesser Italian family, a skilled jurist with a very great knowledge of the canon law, made things so difficult for the elderly pope that he resigned the papacy, an unheard-of act, commemorated for all time by Dante as the "Great Refusal." Though Celestine was later canonized as a saint, all chance of reform was gone, and Gaetani succeeded to the papacy under the title of Boniface viii. His tenure of the office was to be epochal.

## THE PAPACY OF BONIFACE VIII

### Controversy with English and French monarchies over taxation of clergy

It was not long before Boniface embroiled himself with the kings of England and France, both of whom were in extremely strong positions in comparison with the papacy, which had been steadily losing prestige for half a century; even the clergy of Europe who had been appointed by the papacy resented bitterly the heavy taxation laid upon them for papal wars in which they had no interest, and disliked intensely the strict authoritarian control imposed upon them. Since they could no longer be relied upon for unconditional support, the pope was left with little but his pretensions and his bureaucracy.

Philip iv, the Fair, of France (1285–1314) was not slow to take advantage of the situation. His interests were exclusively national, he was not afraid of excommunication or any other penalties the pope might impose, regarding them only as a minor nuisance; and he was quite sure that he held a sufficiently powerful weapon to bring any pope to terms. Philip, engaged in war with Edward i of England (1272–1307) and in need of funds for the mercenary armies which he now employed exclusively for the expansion and consolidation of his kingdom, decided that the best place to turn was to the Church. Under canon law it was forbidden to tax the Church; it could be asked for feudal aids in time of emergency, but did not have to submit to regular taxation. Any taxation beyond these aids and voluntary gifts had to receive the approval of the pope.

Philip and Edward both decided to lay ordinary taxes upon the clergy for state expenses. The French clergy, who were already hard enough hit by papal taxes, appealed to Boniface to help against this double taxation. Boniface then issued a bull known as the *Clericis laicos* (1296), in which he reiterated the long-established principle that the state had no right to tax the clergy without the consent of the pope, adding that kings who did so would be automatically excommunicated.

Edward gave an answer to be expected of the greatest lawmaker in English history. He withdrew the protection of his law from the clergy, who came to terms at once, with the exception of the Archbishop of Canterbury, who could safely be ignored since his only protector could be the pope, whom Edward was prepared to antagonize. In addition Edward prohibited proceeds of certain papal taxes from leaving the country.

Philip took the war right into the enemy's camp, hitting him where it was bound to hurt most. He laid an embargo upon all gold, silver, and bills of exchange leaving France, an embargo which in a national state as well consolidated as France was in Philip's reign, could be effectively enforced. Boniface, at the urgent plea of his bankers, was forced to reverse his position, permitting the French king to tax the clergy in case of emergency, then, under further pressure, agreeing that the king himself could decide when such an emergency existed. Since Philip could ask no more complete submission than this, he withdrew the embargo.

### Renewed controversy with Philip— Immunity of clergy from prosecution

But the quarrel was not yet over. In the year 1300 Boniface proclaimed a jubilee, and invited pilgrims to Rome, offering special indulgences to any who might come. The jubilee was a resounding success. Collections were beyond all expectation, and Boniface, now well on in his seventies, was so pleased with the loyalty to Rome shown by the good Christians of Europe that his always latent delusions of grandeur got the better of him, and he felt competent once more to withstand the worst that the French king could do.

A bishop in southern France was accused of treason by Philip, who collected evidence against him and proposed to try him in the king's court. The French clergy pointed out that an appeal to Rome should be allowed. Philip agreed, thinking his evidence was sufficiently damning to convince even Boniface. But the pope, objecting bitterly to the whole procedure and the indignities the bishop had already suffered, countered with the withdrawal of his concessions on the taxation of the clergy, reminded Philip that even a king was subject to discipline from the Holy See, and added

that he was calling a council for the following year in which the clergy of Christendom, including the French, would sit in judgment upon the king's crimes, and make suggestions as to how the government of France was to be reformed.

Naturally this was too much for Philip, and the bull was probably never published in France. Instead of replying personally, Philip summoned to a special assembly representatives of the three estates of the realm, all of whom were in theory his vassals, the real innovation being that for the first time the burgesses of the towns were recognized as his vassals, subject to feudal duties.[2] This assembly—the prototype of the later States-General, with its three estates of clergy, nobility, and the remainder, including towns —voted, under Philip's direction, to protest to the pope; and each estate sent its own message, thus demonstrating to the pope that even his own clergy were against him in France. At the same time Philip unleashed a propaganda warfare against Boniface, including an edited copy of the recent bull.

But in the same year Philip was heavily defeated in battle by the Flemish burghers at the so-called "Battle of the Spurs" (or Courtrai, 1302), and Boniface, misjudging the importance of one battle to a king whose country was so well organized, thought the time had come to make an example of Philip. He therefore issued the bull *Unam sanctam* (1302), in which he reiterated his claim that both the spiritual and temporal powers were in the hands of the pope, and followed this up with the startling declaration that "we state, define, and pronounce that it is altogether necessary for salvation for every human being to be subject to the Roman pontiff." He then demanded complete submission from Philip under the threat of excommunication.

Philip's patience was exhausted. Boniface's claim to the papacy was in some doubt owing to the resignation of his predecessor, and the most was made of this fact in Philip's propaganda. Moreover, the pope was accused of heresy and other crimes, for which

[2] In theory, of course, it was the town itself that was the vassal, not its inhabitants.

Philip proposed to bring him to trial, after calling a council for the purpose. Meanwhile he sent one of his jurists, a man named Nogaret, to Italy to take possession of the person of the pope and bring him to France, where he was to stand trial. Nogaret, allying himself with some Italian opponents of the pope, forced his way into Boniface's presence as he was resting in a palace in his own birthplace of Anagni. Meanwhile Boniface had prepared a last bull, excommunicating the king, releasing Philip's subjects from obedience to him, and forbidding him to make any further Church appointments. The bull, however, was never published, for Nogaret and his accomplices arrived first. The aged pope, dressed in his robes of office, remained adamant, refused to abdicate, and invited them to murder him if that was what they wished. As a murder would spoil all their plans, they were uncertain what to do next, and in their dilemma they were suddenly set upon by the townsmen of Anagni and driven from the city. The pope, however, survived only a month, dying at Rome, whither he had been taken by the solicitous citizens (1303).

THE PAPACY FALLS INTO FRENCH CONTROL

After this violent end to the struggle between France and the papacy, it was clear that no pope's life would be safe without protection. The Italian nobles who had taken a leading part in the affair, having tasted an easy victory for which no punishment was to be inflicted, might endanger the life of any other pope who went contrary to their wishes, and no real protection was possible any longer in Rome. Moreover, the French were now determined to have a pope who was favorable to their interests. With some difficulty, and after one brief effort to escape the choice, the cardinals finally accepted the inevitable and elected a Frenchman, the Archbishop of Bordeaux, technically a vassal of the English king, as pope under the title of Clement v. As pope, however, Clement had no further need to rely on any English support, but delivered himself completely into French hands, after a few unsuccessful attempts to preserve his dignity and integrity by refusing his consent to some of Philip's more outrageous demands.

But ultimately Philip gained all that he could have desired. He was absolved of all complicity in the death of Boniface, and Nogaret also was absolved after a decent interval; Boniface's famous bulls were withdrawn, and the king's claim that a national state was of divine origin was accepted. Clement also gave permission to Philip to dissolve and confiscate the property of the Knights Templars, a crusading order which had become wealthy and owned too much property in France to please the avaricious king. The Templars were accused of horrible crimes, and many of them were tortured and forced to confess, whereupon they were put to death. Theoretically their property was bestowed by the pope on another order, the Knights Hospitalers; but in fact Philip saw that the Hospitalers received but a small portion of the original Templar property.

Engaged in this work on behalf of Philip for much of his reign, Clement v never found the opportunity to go to Rome, and the papacy took up residence in a city which was within the territorial borders of France, though not actually the property of the French king. Here, at Avignon, under the protection of the French monarch, the popes built a huge papal palace still extant, and gradually concentrated in their hands all the power that had been theirs at Rome, with the additional advantage that they no longer had to fear physical violence. Indeed, Avignon was nothing but a papal city, devoted entirely to papal business, unlike Rome, which had been a world capital and had importance entirely apart from the papal Curia. During the period spent by the popes at Avignon (1309–1376), ecclesiastic centralization was completed, and the power of the popes over the churches throughout Europe through the control of appointments and collection of revenue through the bureaucracy was never greater, in spite of the prestige lost by the papacy as a whole, the envy of other nations over the preponderance of French clergy in high positions, and the very general feeling throughout Europe that the proper place for the See of Peter was in Peter's city of Rome.

### ▶ The papacy at Avignon and the Great Schism

THE PERFECTION OF THE BUREAUCRACY—THE CHURCH AS A FINANCIAL INSTITUTION

The period which follows was called by contemporaries the "Babylonian Captivity of the Church." If one considers only the fact that the papacy was under the protection of the French king, and followed consistently pro-French policies, the term is accurate enough. But, as has been suggested, such was not the whole story. For the power of the papacy over its own clergy was at its height, and, in spite of the loss of much revenue from the abandoned Papal States, new sources were tapped which more than compensated. Papal revenue was higher than the revenue of any king in Europe except

the French, and sometimes, as during the Hundred Years' War between England and France, it was undoubtedly higher. By the close of the Avignon period the popes had in their hands the right of appointment to every clerical office in Europe that was worth any income of importance. They did not insist on the appointment also of parish priests only because the income would scarcely repay the cost of collection. It became established that the first year's revenue from any clerical appointment went to the papacy (annates), and the popes even insisted on collecting fees paid to bishops for visitations in the regular course of their duties. Wherever the clergy turned, a papal tax collector was at hand, and they had no protection against him, except such as kings might give for their own purposes, which were hardly disinterested. Edward III of England legislated against papal appointment of foreign clergy to English benefices, since such appointments resulted in money

*The Palace of the Popes at Avignon, used during the "Babylonian Captivity" and the Great Schism.*

leaving the country, and for the same reason he refused to allow cases under canon law to be appealed to the pope. But the result was a compromise under which the king was able to share in the proceeds, giving no relief to the clergy themselves. Since no one prevented the pope from exercising his prerogatives, the clergy had to submit on pain of losing their offices; but they ceased to perform duties the proceeds of which went to the pope, with further consequences for the prestige of the Church as a spiritual institution. Graft and simony of all kinds were rife, tax collectors kept their share before handing on the remainder to their masters at Avignon, and few offices of the Church would now be performed without appropriate financial recognition. In short, under the highly efficient and by no means captive lawyers who administered the papacy from Avignon, the Church became almost wholly captive to the commercial interests of the time, developing an absolutism which no secular state approached for many centuries to come, taking care of the needs of its own clergy and bureaucrats, but ceasing to perform those essential services for which the money was paid. It was therefore only a matter of time before monarchs would arise who would sequestrate the wealth of the Church and appropriate it to their own secular uses.

THE SUPREMACY OF THE POPE

### Unabated claims of the papacy in secular affairs

Over the last few centuries the popes had elaborated the doctrines of the *plenitudo potestatis,* or fullness of power, of the papacy to justify whatever action they might take, either against their own clergy or against the state. We have seen how Boniface VIII asserted the doctrine and with what effects. But his experience did not prevent the Avignon popes from continuing to assert it, continuing to excommunicate monarchs (not, however, including the French), and even attempting to depose them. One such comedy was staged against Emperor Louis

IV, who replied with a deposition of the pope. Neither was, of course, able to make good his claims. But the emperor could suffer inconvenience from an excommunication, while the pope could suffer nothing whatever from an emperor, even though the latter went so far as to proclaim a nominee of his own as pope (such nominees are usually called antipopes). The whole trouble arose from a claim that the election of the emperor had to be approved by the pope, and the successful candidate crowned by him. Louis's successor, Charles, was willing to make a few minor concessions to gain papal approval, but the same emperor also issued a bull of his own, known as the Golden Bull of 1356, which stated clearly how the emperor was in future to be elected (by three archbishops and four designated German princes). The pope was altogether omitted from the document. Emperors were, in fact, elected according to the regulations of the Golden Bull until the end of the Empire in 1806.

### Opposition by theorists to doctrine of papal supremacy

As we shall see in the next chapter, all the known works of Aristotle had been now translated into Latin, and were studied at the universities; the great Greek had been partly responsible for a truly revolutionary change in the medieval attitude toward human and earthly activities. For two centuries the proponents of the rights of reason had been gaining ground at the expense of those who, like St. Bernard, had despised reason and exalted faith. The rationalists had not hesitated to turn their weapons against the Church itself, which was, after all, an edifice erected on faith. Reason did not necessarily dictate the supremacy of the spiritual over the temporal unless it was believed, on faith, that the whole purpose of man on earth was to seek salvation in another world. Aristotle had regarded man as competent to decide himself what was the best form of earthly government, and that this should be decided on other grounds than that God willed it. Aristotle's *Politics* was a mine of suggestions as to the nature, purpose, and possible forms of government, and it was difficult indeed for a rational political thinker steeped in the *Politics* to think of earthly society in the stereotypes propounded so long by the Church without opposition. It should be possible to discuss human society without such preconceptions, and medieval students of Aristotle saw no reason why they should not make the attempt.

A Franciscan, who naturally had a distaste for the Church as a secular organization, was one of the earliest critics of the absolutism of the pope. William of Occam denied the papal claims to temporal authority altogether, and thought the papacy should not be so supreme as it was, even in spiritual matters. Protected by Emperor Louis IV, who was glad of any ammunition against the Avignon papacy, William in his later years at the emperor's court argued subtly and effectively against papal claims, and especially attacked the right of pope and clergy to interpret the Bible in any manner they saw fit. William thought that all believing Christians had a similar competence, and that there could be no supreme authority in this field. For this reason a Church council would obviously be a better instrument than the pope in the realm of dogma.

But far more radical was Marsiglio of Padua, who with the aid of a Parisian master, John of Jandun, produced a remarkable work called the *Defender of the Peace (Defensor Pacis)*. Fully conversant with the politics of his day and protected also by Louis, Marsiglio made a sweeping attack on all the pretensions of the Church, including the Petrine supremacy, treating the Church as clearly inferior to the secular monarchy, with certain special and useful duties assigned to it in the sphere of religion, but incompetent outside that field. Marsiglio wished the monarchy itself to be under the control of the people, and kings were subject even to deposition in certain circumstances. The monarch was to be the servant of the people and act in accordance with the advice of the best people in his country. The clergy,

according to Marsiglio, only had the task of administering the sacraments and preaching. However important such work might be, it did not confer upon them any special authority, especially not in secular affairs. The pope was merely the servant of the people, as indeed the pope always officially claimed to be. As for the Church, which, according to Marsiglio, was composed of the whole body of the faithful, neither clergy nor laity should govern it but a combination of both clergy and laity in the form of a council, whose wishes should be respected by all, the laity, the clergy, and the pope himself. Marsiglio therefore called for the appointment of a representative council, which should strive to reform the pope and clergy and alter the institutions of the Church in conformity with their true function.

Other thinkers, such as the Frenchman Pierre Dubois, attacked the wealth of the Church and denied its right to possess it. He suggested that it would be to the advantage of all if the French king simply confiscated the wealth of the Church and used it for establishing his overlordship over Europe, after which he could perhaps recover the Holy Land.

## THE GREAT SCHISM (1378–1417)

### The two papacies—Reasons

The papacy at Avignon had been able to maintain its position in part thanks to the electoral procedure. The first French pope to rule from Avignon had taken care to pack the electoral college with French cardinals, who continued to choose Frenchmen as popes. The Italians, however, who had been accustomed for so many centuries to Italian popes, did not take the change quietly, but continued to agitate for the return to Rome; and in due course the cry was taken up by all those who felt that the Eternal City was the only suitable seat for a pope. At length one of the French popes, persuaded thereto by a saintly nun, St. Catherine of Siena, did decide he would return, though the College of Cardinals was still crowded with French prelates, without whose vote no Italian cardinal could hope to be elected. Gregory XI ruled as pope in Rome for one year, from 1377 to 1378, and then died, leaving a vacancy which had to be filled by someone whom the French cardinals would approve. The people and nobles of Rome were clamorous for an Italian after all these years, and the cardinals, who were holding their election in Rome, feared for their lives if they failed to obey. They therefore chose an Italian archbishop, Urban VI, who had no sympathy whatever, as it turned out, with the Avignon papacy, and wished to make sweeping reforms of the whole system. Thereupon the French cardinals retired to a safe post, declared the Italian's election had been carried out by intimidation, and proceeded to elect a Frenchman who went to Avignon with his cardinals and resumed work where it had been left off a year before.

So now there were two popes, and no one knew which was the true one; for it was clear that the cardinals had indeed been intimidated, though certainly not for the first time, and the action of the Italians seemed to many to have been the only way of breaking the French monopoly. Europe divided in its recognition. Germany was split between the emperor, who favored the Italian, and many of the princes and cities, which supported the Frenchman. France naturally supported Avignon, while England, constantly at war with France, equally naturally took the other side. The only thing that was certain was that the situation was a great scandal to every Christian, and that it must be put to an end as soon as possible.

### The rise of the conciliar movement

*Effort by the cardinals—Council of Pisa* —The University of Paris and other more or less disinterested parties tried all means available to them for reaching a compromise. There were now two Colleges of Cardinals as well as two popes; attempts were made to amalgamate the colleges and to extract promises from individual cardinals that if they were elected pope next time they would heal the schism. Conciliators tried to bring the popes together for an interview, and they

tried to get each pope to abdicate in favor of a third. The University of Paris then put forward the claim, already advanced, as we have seen, by theorists, that a council should be called with full authority over both parties, not only to heal the schism, but to put in hand a radical reform of the whole Church. A majority of the cardinals of each pope, heedless of the fact that they had been excommunicated and anathematized by the other, finally left their respective masters and called a general council at Pisa which met in 1409 and assumed the full direction of the Church. Needless to say, the two popes refused to recognize the authority of the council, which, however, ignored them. At the second attempt, the first choice having died, the council chose a third pope, a highly unsuitable candidate, and deposed the other two. The new pope, John XXIII, an Italian ex-pirate, was unable to establish himself in full authority in spite of the backing of the council, and distinguished himself chiefly by sending out indulgence sellers to support his position. So now there were three popes, and the schism was no nearer to being healed than before.

*Theory of the supremacy of the council over the Church*—The Council of Pisa had been called by cardinals in the exercise of their obvious duty. But it had failed, and the secular rulers began to play a more important part. It was at this time that every publicist of importance seems to have written on the subject of whether a council had the right to overrule the papacy, and many were the explanations as to how the council could have acquired this right. Using theories that had originally been intended to apply to the state, defenders of the council claimed that the papacy was a limited monarchy, subject to regular control by a body representing all Christians, and that this body received its authority from Christ. Such theories, however, were hardly likely to appeal to kings and emperors, who were only interested temporarily in councils as a means of ending the schism. Once the schism was ended, as we shall see, the monarchs deserted the conciliar movement, and made little effort to

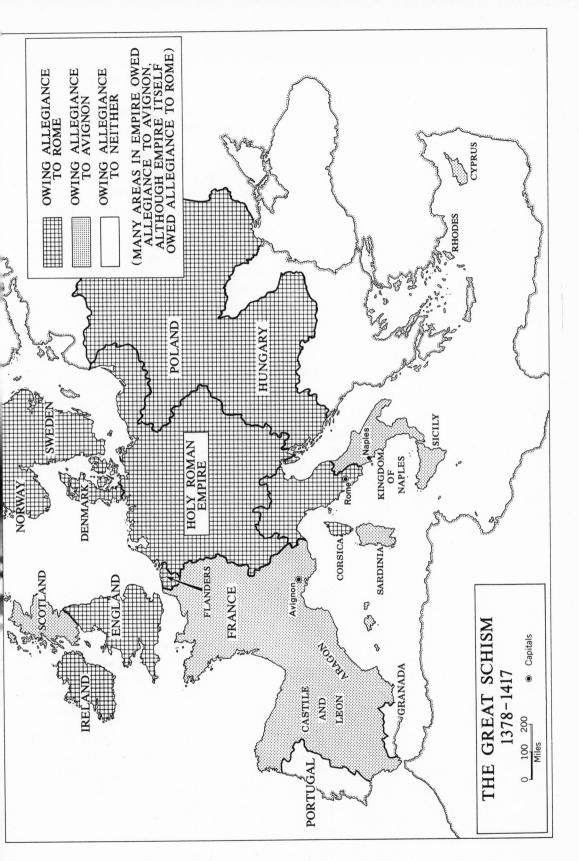

THE GREAT SCHISM
1378–1417

0  100  200
Miles

● Capitals

OWING ALLEGIANCE
TO ROME

OWING ALLEGIANCE
TO AVIGNON

OWING ALLEGIANCE
TO NEITHER

(MANY AREAS IN EMPIRE OWED
ALLEGIANCE TO AVIGNON,
ALTHOUGH EMPIRE ITSELF
OWED ALLEGIANCE TO ROME)

NORWAY

SWEDEN

DENMARK

SCOTLAND

IRELAND

ENGLAND

FLANDERS

FRANCE

POLAND

HUNGARY

HOLY ROMAN
EMPIRE

Avignon

PORTUGAL

CASTILE
AND
LEON

ARAGON

GRANADA

CORSICA

SARDINIA

Rome

Naples

KINGDOM
OF
NAPLES

SICILY

RHODES

CYPRUS

prevent the popes from resuming their old authority, from which the rulers personally had little to fear, much less to fear, in fact, than from the revolutionary doctrine that absolutism should be curbed by the voice of the people in council.

*The Council of Constance*—Emperor Sigismund, the last member of the Luxembourg family to wear the imperial crown, took the initiative in calling the next council, having forced the Pisan pope, John XXIII, to issue the necessary proclamation. An enormous assembly of prelates and laity, learned doctors, and princes assembled in 1414 at Constance under the general direction of the emperor. But each country had its own problems to be settled with the papacy, and the rulers were as much interested in preventing a monopoly of the papacy by Italians or Frenchmen, and in making private arrangements for improvement of papal practices in their own territories, as they were in the thoroughgoing reform of the Church proposed by the radicals. The clergy were interested in reforming all but those practices which benefited themselves. Agreement was therefore found to be extremely difficult, and the system of voting by nations allowed new national interests to be fully represented and gave much opportunity for political maneuvering. John XXIII realized at once that the council was likely to depose him as well as the other two schismatic popes, and that he did not have enough influence in the council to save himself. He therefore escaped, but was recaptured, put on trial for an assortment of sins, and deposed. The Italian pope, seeing further struggle useless, exchanged his now empty title for a lucrative appointment, while the French pope alone remained obdurate, retiring to a castle in Spain where, as Gibbon asserts, he spent his leisure "excommunicating his enemies three times a day." The schism over,[3] the next thing to do was to fill the vacant see.

[3] It should be added that the Church today recognizes the Roman popes of this period of schism as the true canonically elected successors of Peter, since the dissident cardinals had no authority to depose Urban VI, the first of these Roman popes.

The council's intention was to ensure that a new pope would reform the Church and would submit to the authority of regular councils. The problem was how to be certain that any pope after election would submit either to reform or to the conciliar authority. Furthermore there was no unanimity upon what kinds of reforms were needed. The council, however, did agree on its choice of pope, unanimously electing an Italian noble, who took the name of Martin V. Then it proceeded to try to persuade him to agree to reforms. But by this time the meeting had been going on for three years, and many of the most distinguished participants had gone home. Martin V believed that arrangements could be made which would not detract greatly from his authority, and that once he had taken possession of Rome he could abandon his commitments to the council without fear of reprisals. After satisfying the nations individually by giving up some of his income, he was permitted to dissolve the now thoroughly weary Council and return to Rome (1418). The only promise which the pope could not escape was an agreement to call a council at regular intervals, the first to be held five years after Constance.

## RETURN OF THE PAPACY TO ROME

### Re-establishment of papal control

The schism was over and there was once more a single pope, ruling from Rome. The papacy under Martin V was apparently only interested in reasserting control over the neglected Papal States and securing revenue from them, and in asserting papal prerogatives as in the days before the councils. Martin at once issued new regulations for the collection of the papal income, and tightened the administration, which had naturally become lax during the schism. He did not, however, dare to refuse to call the council after five years; but few were present, as interest in the conciliar movement seemed to have lapsed with the settlement of the schism. Martin was able to dismiss the council without difficulty, on the promise to call a new one in 1431.

## Council of Basel—Collapse of conciliar movement

Contrary to expectations, the Council of Basel was well attended, and the issues between pope and council over the control of the Church were bitterly fought. Before deliberations were completed, the new pope, Eugenius iv, dissolved the council, a dismissal which it refused to accept; and the council chose an antipope who lasted for some years. The Hussite Wars, described in the next section, were raging, and a further question which required the pope's attention was the matter of how to negotiate with the Greek Church, which had offered to unite with Rome in exchange for protection against the advancing Turks. The pope by skillful diplomacy split the council on the latter issue, enabling him to follow the policy of his predecessor, Martin v, in making private agreements with the secular powers over the scope of papal taxation. The French, in the person of Charles vii, asserted full authority over the French Church, prohibiting many taxes and judicial appeals to Rome except in extreme circumstances, while the emperor was content with the handing over to his patronage of a number of important Church benefices. Deprived of the support of the monarchs, the Council, which had dragged on for eighteen years, finally dissolved itself in 1449.

The conciliar movement had failed largely because no one of sufficient power was interested in seeing it succeed. The monarchs were interested in gaining financial concessions from the papacy, and in sharing in the proceeds of papal taxation. They were not interested in seeing a council supreme over the pope, though they were quite glad to use the councils as a tool for extracting concessions. The papacy naturally did not wish to lose or share its supreme control over the Church, which it considered had been entrusted to it by Christ. In the event, the papacy had lost some of its income, and some of its power over clerical appointments, which now had to be shared with the kings. But it had recovered the Papal States, and, though its supposed supremacy over secular powers was shown to be unenforceable, this was a small loss in comparison with its accepted supremacy over the Church.

On the whole the outcome of the councils was a triumph for the monarchs, though the papacy had emerged, if not with prestige, at least with its position intact and its revenues substantially unimpaired. But the conciliar movement had probably made the Protestant Reformation inevitable; the Church had shown itself unwilling to undertake reform of its own accord. The next great council was to be a serious one, and seriously devoted to reform. But it would not be held for another century, and it was the Protestants who, by their successes, forced it upon the papacy. It could hardly be considered as a spontaneous initiative on the part of a papacy earnestly devoted to a reform which it considered necessary.

## Violent anticlericalism among all classes

There can be no doubt from the unanimity of the literary evidence that the failure of the clergy to perform their proper spiritual offices and their ostentatious luxury made them a favorite target for ridicule and contempt. As early as the end of the thirteenth century, *The Romance of the Rose* of John de Meun was accusing the clergy of avarice, pride, and laziness. In the fourteenth century Chaucer ridiculed with more gentleness the monk and the pardoner; Boccaccio's stories carry their sharpest sting when directed at the clergy and monks. When the peasants revolted in England at the end of the fourteenth century, many of their grievances were concerned with the exactions of the clergy. It was a common saying that no peasant's daughter was safe while priests lived in celibacy, and, especially in the period after the Black Death in the middle of the fourteenth century, there were violent outbursts against the way in which the clergy (with certain honorable exceptions, especially among the Franciscans) had escaped the plague and had done nothing to help the stricken. Clergy were accused of blasphemy and of selling themselves to the Devil in addition to their more obvious and usual sins, which were visible to all. It was not surprising that in many parts of Europe there was a widespread attempt to come to a simpler and purer religion outside the jurisdiction of the Church altogether, though relatively few of the seekers after righteousness actually broke with the Church and ventured into heresy.

### The rise of mysticism

There has always been a mystic element in Christianity, and among many believers there has been a profound desire to enter into a more personal relationship with God than the mere adherence to formal beliefs and participation in the ritual of the Church. In earlier centuries this tendency found its expression in monasticism, especially of the Oriental kind, which sought for inner experience through mortification of the flesh. But in most monasteries of the fourteenth and fifteenth centuries there was no longer a place for such practices. The theory of mysticism—that it is possible for the soul to find union with God though still in the body—had been expressed in a very complete form in the Neoplatonic philosophy of Plotinus, a late pagan philosopher. It was now revived, though unquestionably through a desire to explain his own personal experiences, by the Dominican Meister Eckhart, who lived in the second half of the thirteenth and into the fourteenth century. His disciples, John Tauler and Henry Suso, also from the German Rhineland, wrote in the same vein. The distinctive feature of Christian mysticism was the effort to imagine as a deep inner personal experience the sufferings of Christ and to identify one's self with them. This interest belongs to the whole temper of the fourteenth and fifteenth centuries, an age when the Black Death decimated the population of Europe, when the Great Schism to some portended the final collapse of Christianity, when France was visited with the desolation of the Hundred Years' War. It was no accident that so much of the painting of the period depicts the *Pietà*, the death of Christ upon the Cross, with his mourning mother and with the gaping wounds realistically portrayed, and that some of the

more ascetic mystics should have come to believe that purification through suffering was the true path to perfection (e.g. St. Catherine of Siena).

But the mystics were not content only to seek mystic perfection for themselves. They founded schools where the inner life was cultivated and where the initiation ceremonies of esoteric Christianity were taught. Such a school was the Friends of God in the Rhineland. In the Netherlands, John Ruysbroeck described the mystics' exercises and their trials and the states of consciousness through which they pass. Such men naturally could not be expected to think of salvation in some future life as the sole aim of mankind, and thus they gave less importance to the sacraments than did the Church as a whole. The Church therefore was doubtful whether it should approve or condemn; but in the end it decided at least not to disapprove, and Eckhart, though not canonized, received the title of Blessed, and other mystics later actually became saints.

The most practical and popular mysticism was to be found in the Brethren of the Common Life, founded by Gerard Groote at Deventer in the Netherlands. The members of this group did not organize themselves into a monastery nor did they take vows; but they lived together in a community, and meditated, prayed, and taught the people. They were especially noted for their schools, which for a time were unquestionably the best in Europe, and they published many books on the devotional life, the most famous being the *Imitation of Christ*, a simple personal imagination of the true Christian life, based upon the life and teachings of Christ as found in the Gospels. This work, attributed to Thomas à Kempis, has remained since its writing the second bestseller in the Christian world and has never been out of print since its first publication. The work of the mystics had a direct effect upon the early Protestant thinkers, especially Luther, and Erasmus received his early education with the Brethren of the Common Life. Luther's own struggle with the Devil and his earnest desire to submit himself totally to Christ betray the mysticism of his nature, and he admitted the effect especially of Suso upon his own life.

### ▶ The heretics

WYCLIF AND THE LOLLARDS

John Wyclif may properly be put among the heretics in part because of the work of the last six years of his life, when he wrote most of his attacks upon the teachings of the Church, and in part because heretics undoubtedly made use of his writings. But he was known for most of his life as an ardent anticlerical, and a critic of the Church as an institution. He is first met with as an influential master at Oxford, protected by the English king with whose views on the Church he was, of course, in sympathy. But though Wyclif supported the theory that the Church had no right to own any property at all but should live on voluntary offerings, which would be given in accordance with the services it performed, and though he attacked papal collection of taxes in England, his views were firmly based not upon the reasonings of Aristotle, but upon the teachings of the Scriptures, as he interpreted them. His most notable work of all perhaps was his first translation of the Bible into English, which already has some of the majestic cadences later incorporated into the famous King James version. Like the Spiritual Franciscans, his contemporaries, he castigated the worldliness of the Church, and thought that the only true Christianity was to be found in the system of the early Christian Church, and in imitation of the life of Christ.

In his later years he became ever more radical, so much so that the University of Oxford found his presence altogether too compromising; whereupon he retired to his parish at Lutterworth and continued to write. Now he denied that the Catholic Church was a true Church at all, and the Church became, for him as for the later John Calvin, the body of all those predestined to be saved; and each man could be his own priest, as in the teachings of Luther. The Church could not ordain true priests, for only Christ could choose these, and they made known their priesthood by the manner of their life. Since above all the Church and priesthood were not necessary as an intermediary between man and God, he was led to reject all the sacraments except marriage, and to deny that any miracle took place in the Mass; and he attacked the whole pomp and glory of the Church as likely to lead man away from God, not toward him. He trained a company of preachers called Lollards who were to go out and spread his doctrines, and these indeed went through Europe preaching, and creating a profound impression, especially, as we shall see, in Bohemia.

Wyclif, though lacking the personality and the organizing ability of the Protestants Luther and Calvin, was undoubtedly in his last years a full Protestant of the later age, and there is hardly a teaching of either Luther or Calvin which is not to be found in his writings, though he did not carry them to their full conclusions in the same degree as these successors. But the time was not yet ripe for such teaching in England. Many of his Lollards seems to have taken part in the famous Peasants' Revolt of 1381, three years before Wyclif's death, and in any case his teachings were blamed in part for the uprising. Such an uprising was bound to bring down upon it all the forces of law and order; and though Wyclif himself died peacefully, still protected by the crown, many of his Lollards were put to death on the order of a later monarch in England, and the papacy was sufficiently influential to have his remains disinterred and buried in unconsecrated ground, after the bulk of his teachings had been condemned at the Council of Constance.

JOHN HUS AND THE BOHEMIAN WARS

It is difficult to disentangle the actual heresy in Bohemia from the manifestations of Czech patriotism which undoubtedly made use of religious unrest; but it is certain that the whole of Bohemia in the fourteenth and fifteenth centuries seethed with hatred of the Church, and that all heresies of the day found refuge there. Among the peasants the Waldensian teachings had taken root, elements of the persecuted Cathari found a home there, and there were considerable numbers of people of all classes who expected an immediate end of the world; for it had been prophesied in the Bible that there would be trials and tribulations before the last day and that the Antichrist would appear. To these earnest souls it seemed that the degradation of the Great Schism and the terrors of the Black Death heralded the end of the world, and many were the suggestions made as to who the Antichrist was.

The Bohemian Church was itself an offshoot of the German Church, and German clerics had always held a preferred position in Bohemia in spite of the fact that they were a minority in the country. Moreover, Bohemia was also generally under the rule of Germans, who were detested by the Slavic Czech population. But Emperor Charles IV, king also of Bohemia, chose, for reasons connected with his feudal interests, to support Czech nationalism; and he gave Prague, the Bohemian capital, an archbishop and a university which was to become the center of Czech nationalism. The Bohemian Church, under its new archbishop, was very strongly opposed to papal exactions, which were for the first time forced upon this rather isolated church by the papacy at Avignon. Supported by the new Bohemian king, Wenceslas IV (1378–1419), who was also emperor until he was deposed in 1400, a young theologian named John Hus came to prominence as an antipapal preacher.

But Hus was also a follower of Wyclif in all except his most radical teachings. He insisted that the Bible was an authority superior to the teachings of the Church, he condemned ecclesiastical simony and wealth, and he advocated the confiscation of Church property. And with such teachings even the Bohemian Church could hardly be expected to agree. It wished to be free from papal exactions, but it was far from prepared to live on nothing but voluntary donations. So

Hus had to rely solely on royal support, which was withdrawn from him when King Wenceslas was deposed from his position as emperor and was succeeded by his brother Sigismund, whom we have seen as the organizer of the Council of Constance, and who was also the king of Germany and Hungary. Such a monarch naturally was disturbed by Czech nationalism, for which Hus was the spokesman. Though without royal support Hus continued to preach, and was excommunicated by the Pisan pope, John XXIII, for attacking the theory and practice of indulgences. When the indulgence sellers, sent by the notorious pirate-turned-pope, arrived in Prague there was such a commotion that Hus retired for a while from the university.

Two years later the Council of Constance met, with the avowed intention of ending the Great Schism, and at the same time checking the spread of heresy. Hus did not consider himself in any way heretical, in spite of his interest in the work of Wyclif, and had no objection to defending himself before the council, provided his person was protected by the secular powers who controlled the conference. He and his disciple Jerome of Prague asked for and received a safe-conduct to and from Constance from Emperor Sigismund. But the council, determined to check the spread of heresy and in particular of the Lollards—one of the few items on the agenda on which all parties were agreed—explained to the emperor that if Hus were convicted of heresy his safe-conduct did not hold good, as heretics were not entitled to such consideration. The emperor cravenly gave way and Hus was brought to trial. A list of supposed errors from his teachings was drawn up, many of them held by Wyclif and not by himself, and he was told he must recant them all, whether he had held them or not. Hus refused to recant all the errors the council chose to impute to him; but he did go so far as to admit some of the teachings, though denying they were errors. On what authority, he asked, did the council presume to treat them as errors? He could accept no

HUSSITE WARS
(1420-1436)

EXPANSION OF
HUSSITES INTO
NEIGHBORING LANDS

⊙  Capital

0          100          200
              Miles

teaching as an error unless it could be shown to be so by the authority of Scripture. This position, of course, was heresy, so at last the council had the evidence. In spite of the safe-conduct, Hus was condemned to death and burned in 1415 outside the city of Constance. Jerome of Prague, after recanting, withdrew his recantation and was also burned as a relapsed heretic.

Hus martyred was more powerful than he had ever been in his lifetime. He became at once what he has remained ever since, a Czech national hero, condemned to death for having stood up for the rights of Czechs against a German dominated council. The council, Sigismund, and the new pope all proclaimed the followers of Hus in Bohemia as heretics, and crusades were called against them. If they had not been heretics before, they soon became heretics, even the more conservative among them. Sigismund was driven from Bohemia for violating the safe-conduct, national armies were formed, and Bohemia became entirely independent within the next few years, carrying the offensive over into Germany. The Council of Basel, frightened by the passions let loose, withdrew from the position taken at Constance, and offered to negotiate the differences. The original program contained provisions for the confiscation of the property of the clergy, freedom of speech in preaching, and an important change in the practice of giving the Communion. The conservatives (Utraquists) were willing to compromise on all except the last, and thus made their peace with the Catholics, while the more radical group composed of the peasants and lower classes had a full program of social reform which gained them no sympathy with the more powerful Utraquists. These radicals were called Taborites.

The Taborites and Utraquists then engaged in a ruinous civil war, which was suppressed by a coalition between Catholics and Utraquists. The remnants of the Taborites survived only as individuals until the opportunities offered by the Lutheran movement brought them into prominence again as Anabaptists and other radical reformers. The Utraquists, however, did not keep to their alliance with the Catholics; and after several attempts at compromise formed an independent Hussite Church which rejected altogether the Petrine supremacy. The papacy was never able to suppress the several branches of the Hussite Church, which were in due course absorbed into the Protestant Reformation.

▶ **The papacy at the close of the Middle Ages**

Before the end of the Council of Basel a new secular movement had come into being in Italy, which soon claimed the interest of a succession of popes. This movement, commonly called the Renaissance, or the revival of classical humanism and secularism, falls outside the scope of this volume, and is generally studied under modern history, since in many respects it represents a trend distinctively modern and not medieval. It is sufficient to say here that start-

ing with the papacy of Nicholas v, who ascended the papal throne before the end of the Council of Basel, the majority of the popes found a new interest in life in the patronage of humanists, searchers for ancient manuscripts, and artists who succeeded in escaping from the medieval style into one more naturalistic and less stiffly symbolic at least than those painters prior to Giotto.

The popes thus began to pay even less attention to ecclesiastical matters than before. They were not so much interested in asserting their authority as seeing to it that they had enough funds for their vast building projects and other hobbies. The tax system was maintained as before; but as long as it was kept adequately supplied with money, the papacy did not try much interference with secular affairs. When Savonarola, a Dominican friar, purged the city of Florence and preached violent sermons against the luxury of the papacy, Alexander vi, the notorious Borgia, at first merely yawned, and took no action until he was forced to. The disgruntled and exiled nobles took care of Savonarola with the assistance of a bull of excommunication, and the papacy was not greatly disturbed.

When the art-loving Medici, Leo x, took the papal throne in the early sixteenth century, he is said to have remarked: "Let us enjoy the papacy since God has given it to us." Leo was nevertheless forced to bestir himself against Martin Luther, but not too much. It was left to his successors under Spanish influence to bring about the Catholic Reformation, so long overdue, and for the Council of Trent (1545–1563) to set the Catholic Church firmly upon the foundations on which it has rested till the present day.

▶ **Suggestions for further reading**

For this chapter, unlike the preceding one, there are several excellent books, embodying the latest scholarship. An excellent introduction, which gives all the information necessary to understand both the decline of the medieval Church and the decay of medieval society and its transition to the modern era, is to be found in E. P. Cheyney, *The Dawn of a New Era, 1250–1453* (4th ed.; New York: Harper & Brothers, 1936). There are several chapters in this book which deal specifically with the decline of the Church and the rise of the later heresies, but the whole is well worth reading for the background, and it is written in an easy style which the student will find agreeable. Another work, not as formidable as its bulk would indicate, is A. C. Flick, *The Decline of the Medieval Church* (2 vols.; New York: Alfred A. Knopf, Inc., 1930). Although the official subject of this book is specifically the Church, like Cheyney's, it has a tremendous amount of useful information regarding all phases of life at this time, which is organized in a masterful manner around the decline of the Church as the key medieval institution. There is a third extremely useful book, by J. Huizinga, *The Waning of the Middle Ages* (New York: Doubleday Anchor Books, 1954), which is already something of a classic; it should be read by students who are especially interested in cultural history. The author, while ostensibly studying culture, especially in the Low Countries, nevertheless manages to paint a remarkable picture of the gradual decay of the whole medieval spirit, which he connects with the new cult of death (itself in part the result of the Black Death), and which will serve as a partial comment on the two pictures in the text which portray the Knight Templar and the money-changer being carried away by death (Chapters 18 and 21). While few would accept Huizinga's entire thesis, the book cannot be neglected by serious students of the period.

There is an excellent biography of Frederic II by a renowned scholar: E. Kantorowicz, *Frederic II* (New York: Richard R. Smith, Inc., 1931), which, for its picture of the last stages of the struggle between the Empire and the papacy, is greatly superior to the many popular biographies of this remarkable personage. The student is also referred to Packard's study of Innocent III and the Church, and to Toynbee's study of the growth and decline of the medieval church referred to at the close of the previous chapter. These books deal also in part with the period covered by the present chapter.

Finally, there is a useful Pelican book by A. R. Myers, *England in the Late Middle Ages* (London: Penguin Books, 1952), which has a valuable chapter on religious and educational movements in England, presenting an important sidelight on the decline of the Church as it affected England; and there are several good chapters (Chaps. 13–16) on the conflict between Church and State during this period, in Sabine's book, already referred to several times in these notes, *A History of Political Theory* (New York: Henry Holt & Co., Inc., 1937). Here will be found a fuller discussion on Marsiglio and William of Occam than that given in the text above.

# 20

# Medieval Culture

*General characteristics of medieval culture • Learning and education in the Dark Ages • The triumph of reason in theology • Medieval science • Education in the Middle Ages • Medieval art: architecture, music • Medieval literature*

---

▶ General characteristics of medieval culture

THE MIDDLE AGES AS THE FORMATIVE PERIOD OF MODERN WESTERN CIVILIZATION

In the plan of this book separate chapters were devoted to the culture of the Greeks and the culture of the Romans, and separate sections to the cultures of the other peoples considered. This procedure could be justified when it was possible to perceive in the perspective of history the total achievement of a particular civilization in the realm of culture. These earlier civilizations have all come to an end, and their legacy has been absorbed by their successors. But medieval civilization is merely the earlier period of our own Western civilization. There is no pronounced break between medieval and modern times, and historians in general have simply agreed to accept the quite arbitrary date of around 1500 as the end of the Middle Ages, while the beginning may be placed about the time of the fall of the Roman Empire.

The achievements of medieval people are the achievements of our own immediate ancestors. Most of our institutions date back to medieval times; the modern university

is in the direct line of descent from the medieval university. The gowns still worn for graduation at our universities are now only decorative, but served to keep the medieval student warm; in the older English universities they are used to distinguish the student from the townsman, and must be worn every evening and for all academic activities in the daytime. The English Parliament and English law have evolved since medieval times; but they have never been destroyed and replaced by something else, as happened to the institutions of Greece and Rome.

The history of our own particular civilization should therefore start with the invasions of the barbarians, should continue with their gradual absorption of the legacy of their predecessors, and should then give their characteristic original achievements. And if we stop short at the year 1500, or even 1955, this is bound to be an arbitrary procedure, dictated by convenience, or the fortuitous fact that we happen to have reached the latter year. Since, however, this volume ends with the year 1500, we shall try to show the beginnings of Western culture and to impose upon medieval culture a finiteness which it does not possess, since it did not come to a recognizable end.

A generation ago this procedure would not have seemed as arbitrary as it does now; for a curious phenomenon was then believed in, called a "Renaissance," or rebirth, which was supposed to have taken place in Italy and then been diffused over the rest of Europe, marking a radical change from everything medieval. Everything post-Renaissance, according to this view, could be clearly marked as "modern," or different in kind from what was labeled "medieval." Descriptions of this phenomenon were primarily distinguished by an ignorance of exactly what the medieval peoples did accomplish, an ignorance which is only gradually, even today, being dispelled by the efforts of many devoted medievalists; and the "Renaissance" can now be seen more clearly in perspective as a partly reactionary movement, especially in its insistence on a return to Greek and Roman antiquity and in its neglect of science, and partly as a releasing from medieval inhibitions, especially in the field of art. But a secular attitude to life, usually cited as the distinctive feature of the Renaissance, was far from being a Renaissance phenomenon; the development of this attitude was a long process, with its roots back in time at least as early as the Crusades.

The curious feature of the Renaissance thinkers was that they reacted more violently against their immediate past than is customary. Believing themselves to be heralds of an altogether new era, they consistently derided the achievements of their immediate ancestors, labeling their new and distinctive architecture—perhaps the single great original artistic achievement of our civilization, and certainly the greatest architectural innovation until the twentieth century—as "Gothic" (barbarian), and their philosophy as mere playing with words. Men of the Renaissance pictured their forebears as living in total bondage to an authoritarian Church, unable and unwilling to think for themselves, with every slightest deviation from orthodoxy punishable with a horrible death at the hands of the Inquisition.

This stereotype of the Middle Ages was accepted for so many centuries, and is, even now, dying so hard, that we do not regard medieval times frequently enough as the formative period of our own age, nor examine closely enough the immense obstacles that had to be overcome by the barbarians in a society that had collapsed as completely as the old Greco-Roman civilization. It was centuries before the static manorial feudal society was undermined deeply enough for an urban society to develop, and, as we have seen, civilized arts have hitherto never appeared in a rural society. But the medieval people did finally develop an urban civilization and an urban culture, and the cities which they founded have continued into our own times without serious breaks, excepting a few affected by external causes such as the Black Death.

What should be studied therefore in medieval culture is the struggle of the people to absorb what was left of the heritage of older civilizations, and the new creative effort to strike out on a line of their own afterward, to emancipate themselves from the static conception of life natural to a rural existence, to discover the power of reason and free themselves from the bondage to authority, and to see how in doing this they made possible the enormous scientific and political advances which have been the main glory of Western civilization as a whole. We shall understand their achievement better if we emancipate ourselves from the outworn stereotype that medieval civilization was a thing in itself that began with the barbarian invasions and ended with the Renaissance, that it was an age of faith and acceptance of authority, and that reason did not begin until at least the seventeenth century, that the all-embracing Church stifled the efforts of men to improve their lot on earth by assuring them that the next life alone was of importance. It is true enough that the last was the official teaching of the Church, but it is not true that the teaching stifled initiative and freedom of thought, nor that it succeeded in turning men exclusively to preparation for the hereafter.

The story of medieval culture is, in a sense, extraordinarily dramatic if viewed sympathetically, with a realization of the enormous obstacles to freedom of thought which were progressively overcome; if we try to see the objectives of medieval thinkers and scientists and writers, and realize how consistently they were striving to relate their actual experience to the picture of life on earth and in the hereafter presented to them by the conservative elements in their society; and how the human mind showed itself unable to tolerate restrictions which it ultimately recognized to be artificial. Progress in the Middle Ages was slow, and perhaps the total of its achievements was small in comparison with achievement in the centuries since. But preparatory and formative periods must necessarily last longer and show less spectacular results than the later flowering. It was many centuries after the Dorian invasions that the Greeks came to the height of their powers. There is no flower until the roots have taken hold; and the roots of Western civilization lie far back in the Middle Ages when the struggle was being fought between reason and faith, between freedom and authority, between the miracle and the natural law, between the pull of the past and the urge toward the future.

CONTRAST BETWEEN EARLY AND LATER
PERIODS OF MIDDLE AGES

Medieval culture falls into two periods. The period that has already been characterized as the Dark Ages is really entitled to the adjective. Outside the fold of the Church there was almost no education at all; and even within the Church only a very small percentage of men and women were even literate. In some of the monasteries manuscripts from the ancient world were diligently copied; but, as we know from the errors in copying, too often the contents were not understood. Charlemagne never learned to read or write; and when he

wished to make a modest beginning toward a revival of learning in his empire, the scholars that he found, though the best in Europe in his day, would never have been considered anything but mediocre in any more enlightened age. Outside Ireland, Greek had been forgotten. There is but one creative European thinker known in more than three centuries, and he was an Irishman; yet this dark time was also the period of the flowering of the Muslim civilization. When, in the late tenth century, Gerbert became known as the most learned man in the West, and was finally elected pope as Sylvester II, we are told that he had studied every branch of knowledge available in his day. But the sum total is pitiful indeed. Except for those few who could understand Arabic and had access to Muslim works, the only reading available was the Bible, some of the works of the Christian Fathers, a few inaccurate and highly simplified encyclopedias, and some elementary textbooks.

Then, almost suddenly, the Western mind seemed to awake and ask questions, and the Dark Ages were over. On the one side, it began to learn to reason, and to apply reason to what it had hitherto received as dogma, bestowed by authority; and, on the other side, certain individuals began to become aware of the wider world of Muslim culture and become interested, and at once began to contrast this knowledge with the abysmal ignorance of the West. Bringing back knowledge to their homelands, they stimulated others to the same quest. Then, as the Western mind began to sharpen its tools for reasoning, it began also to demand more sustenance. And to satisfy this hunger, one after another the works of Aristotle were translated, an enormous fund of knowledge, gradually assimilated over a period of centuries. Bewildered and impressed by this knowledge, the Westerners in their humility at first thought him almost superhuman, and with the attitude of faith and reverence customary to them they thought he had known everything, and all they had to do was to recover for themselves what he had known, and elaborate on it. Then came the realization that Aristotle too had made mistakes; he was a master mind, but not omniscient. So they understood that it was Aristotle's task to train them in method, but not to give them the finished answers. Not many men had understood this, perhaps, by the close of the Middle Ages; but it was nevertheless the work done by Aristotelians at the Universities of Paris and Padua that, as is now known, prepared the way for Galileo, modern mechanics, and all modern science which is based on it—as it was the thorough reworking of Aristotle by St. Thomas Aquinas that was able to make the teachings of Christianity conform to the requirements of natural reason.

### THE LATIN LANGUAGE AND THE VERNACULARS

Through both periods the language of learning was Latin, preserved from the wreckage of the Roman Empire by the Church, but predominant also among the laity in those countries which had been civilized by Rome and adopted her language. This Latin was not, however, the language of the Classical Age, but one that was both more flexible and more simple, lacking the formal elegance of the classical tongue but compensating for this by supplementing it with many new constructions unknown to Cicero. This medieval Latin had developed from the language spoken in the late centuries of the empire. Severe classicists naturally call it a degenerate form; but at least it was a living language, as shown by the very considerable medieval literature in Latin which can in no sense be considered as the work of secluded monks or clerics. From this Latin came the Romance languages, the vernaculars of France, Spain, Italy, and Portugal. It lived side by side with the vernaculars for centuries, but increasingly came to be an official language which was learned at school, a means of communication among learned men of every country. Latin remains, of course, today the language of the Roman Catholic Church, understood by priests throughout the world,

whatever their country of origin. The educated class of the Renaissance, however, in their dislike of their predecessors, despised medieval Latin as barbarous, preferring themselves to return to a style and diction nearly fifteen hundred years out of date. The influence of these so-called humanists in the world of the fifteenth and sixteenth centuries was such that it became fashionable for all educated men to deride the medieval Latin, and they successfully killed it; while the style of Latin they favored, cut off from common speech, was unable to take its place as a living language. Latin became, like classical Greek, a dead language, to be studied at school as a discipline, but separated forever from the common man, and no longer possible as the universal European language it had been in the Middle Ages.

Medieval literature, then, is partly in Latin and partly in the vernaculars, either those of Germanic origin or the Romance languages. Medieval philosophy and science, intended to appeal to educated men in every country, continued to be written only in Latin during the Middle Ages, and much was written in Latin in subsequent centuries even by masters of the vernacular such as Francis Bacon and René Descartes. Newton wrote his epoch-making *Principia* in Latin. But poetry and stories, intended for a more mixed audience, were written increasingly in the vernacular throughout the Middle Ages. The masterpieces of Dante and Chaucer, the tales of Boccaccio and the love lyrics of Petrarch, the great Icelandic, Norse, and German sagas, the French *chansons de geste* are all written in the languages of their countries, and indeed helped to form those languages. Especially is this true of the *Divine Comedy* of Dante, which made the old Tuscan dialect the real literary language of Italy to this day.

### THE VARIETY OF MEDIEVAL CULTURE AND OUR DEBT TO IT

From what has been said above it will be seen that it is impossible to characterize medieval culture as being of such or such a kind, for it lacked uniformity. If we say the medievals lacked intellectual curiosity, as we said of the Romans, exceptions at once spring to the mind, and we can see that acceptance of the given world without questioning it was a passing phase. If we say that they were not interested in new knowledge so much as in pondering the old, reading new meanings into it without adding to it, then this attitude too disappeared as reason began to supplant blind faith. If we say they wanted to reconcile all knowledge with the teachings of Christianity, the suggestion of intellectual dishonesty implied in this statement is unfair. Thomas Aquinas undoubtedly believed in Christianity, but he knew that if it was true it *could* not conflict with what reason told him. He did not dishonestly shirk the difficulties, and he honestly tried to resolve them. He was not trying to explain away the findings of his reason in order to bolster an unsound theology. Indeed, he was extremely scrupulous in avoiding the temptation of trying to prove by reason things which he did not think could be proved by it. Naturally as a medieval Christian he believed in the creation of the world out of nothing by God; but he was careful to show that Aristotle had not believed in it, and that his reasoning was justified. The story of the creation was one of the matters which could not be proved, and so must remain in the realm of faith.

Medieval thought, like all thought, was concerned with the problems of the time, and it reflects an honest and not unsuccessful attempt to deal with them within the framework of its presuppositions and assumptions. But, more important, as these assumptions ceased to appear valid, new thinkers arose who grappled with new assumptions and new knowledge. This eagerness for new knowledge is the mark of a living culture, which, in this case, has continued to live and move forward, even into our own time. If the medieval answers no longer seem valid, this is because the compass of our knowledge has been so greatly extended. But it was the medievals

who first in our civilization fought for the rights of reason, the medievals who trained us in logic and analysis and gave us our tools of inquiry, and the medievals who formed the very language in which we continue to express ourselves and who gave the world the first great masterpieces in every Western European tongue. And since it was also the medievals who taught the world to use representative assemblies to limit the powers of monarchs, it is perhaps time that the word "medieval" cease to be used as a term of abuse for all that we like to think of as reactionary.

## ► Learning and education in the Dark Ages

### READING MATERIAL OF THE DARK AGES

It has already been noted that when the Western world relapsed into the Dark Ages with the disintegration of the Roman Empire one man in Italy foresaw the complete loss of Greek learning and tried to remedy it insofar as it was possible for one man to do so. This was Boethius, who was executed by the Ostrogothic king in the early sixth century. It was his intention to translate from Greek into Latin as many of the indispensable Greek works of learning as he could. He translated two elementary logical works of Aristotle, the *Categories* and *Concerning Interpretation,* together with an important introduction to the *Categories* by a Neoplatonist. But either he tired of his huge project or circumstances made him realize that it was impossible. For instead of continuing his translation he proceeded to write textbooks on arithmetic, geometry, and music. These works were considered authoritative, and were standard at all schools and universities until translations were again available from the Greek. Contemporary with Boethius was the learned abbot Cassiodorus, who directed his monks to collect and copy all the manuscripts of Latin and Greek they could lay hands on. Undertaking leadership in this work himself, he made his monastery an outstanding center for study. Although such work had not originally been prescribed by the Benedictine Rule, many monasteries followed his example, and it became a regular Benedictine activity to copy manuscripts, although in later centuries it is clear that the monks knew very little of what they were translating. Nevertheless, very many manuscripts are only known to us from these monasteries, and as a work of preservation of the past, these translations proved of the greatest value for future generations.

As has already been mentioned, the chief sources of sustenance for a would-be scholar in the Dark Ages were the encyclopedias, scrapbooks compiled from earlier learning by earnest teachers. The best known and most successful of these was a work called *Etymologies,* by St. Isidore, Bishop of Seville in the early seventh century. The book is full of misinformation and even contradictory statements, culled from various sources. It purports to explain the origin of different words in use; but most of the etymologies are fantastic and completely unreliable. Isidore was aware of the growing decadence of all learning, and tried very nobly to remedy the almost universal ignorance. He discourses on almost all the subjects he can think of, sacred and profane, very occasionally with some accuracy. But since much of his work was taken from Pliny's *Natural History,* itself a book of much pretension but feeble in accurate information, he could hardly be expected to have done much better. Such as it was, the *Etymologies* served as a manual of universal knowledge for many centuries.

Later in the same century an English scholar, the Venerable Bede, a Benedictine monk, devoted the whole of a long life to trying to improve the standard of Christian education by his writings. Most of his work, though well written for his age, showing a good knowledge of Latin and some, even, of Greek (probably under Irish influence), repeats earlier writers on such subjects as the work of God in creating the world in six days, and shows little originality, but greater accuracy and understanding than Isidore. But Bede also wrote one truly original work, the *Ecclesiastical History of England,* in which he showed himself as a first-rate historian, especially remarkable in his age, carefully checking his statements and explaining the nature of his sources. Bede also wrote a book on chronology which had an important influence in that from it was later taken the method of dating years before and after the birth of Christ (B.C. and A.D.); though modern scholars believe he made an error in his calculations by which Jesus was held to be born four years after he really was.

## THE CAROLINGIAN RENAISSANCE

### Royal support for learning

It has already been noted in an earlier chapter that Charlemagne made a serious effort to revive learning in his empire, especially by the founding of his palace school at Aachen. Scouring the Western world for scholars, he succeeded in finding a few, led by Alcuin of York, whom he made superintendent of the school. Alcuin himself wrote many textbooks for the use of his students, and commentaries on the Scriptures, none of which is of very high standard. But the school itself was a notable initiative, and its influence spread to the rest of the kingdom of the Franks and stimulated learning in the monasteries. One product of the palace school was Einhard, the biographer of Charlemagne, whose work is certainly the most interesting of its time, though unfortunately he chose to copy in too many respects the Roman biographer Suetonius, whose lives of the Caesars have been criticized earlier. Einhard was almost the only man among all the teachers uncovered by Charlemagne who was not himself a churchman.

Two important consequences stemmed from the educational work of Charlemagne. One was the improvement of the handwriting of the scribes, and the development of a script known as Carolingian minuscule, a very neat script, highly legible, though small, from which came the "Roman" letters

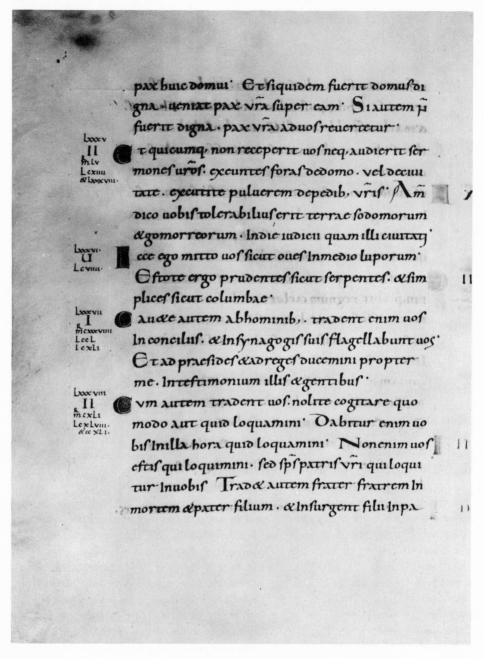

*Example of the new manuscript writing which came into vogue during the Carolingian Renaissance and which is the precursor of our ordinary cursive writing. Previously all writing had been done in capital letters. From a late ninth-century manuscript, Evangelia IV (Switzerland ?). (COURTESY THE PIERPONT MORGAN LIBRARY. Ms. 1, folio 29)*

used in most European writing thereafter, replacing, except in Germany, the "Gothic" script. From this script came ultimately those letters which are commonly used

today, and which were adopted by printers when printing was finally brought into use in Europe. The other consequence was the gradual development of schools attached to monasteries and cathedrals, where clergy and public officials could obtain such education as was available.

## Curriculum of the Carolingian schools

From an early date it was accepted that education should consist of the so-called seven liberal arts. Boethius had subdivided this into the *trivium* and the *quadrivium* (the triple and quadruple paths to knowledge). These were as follows: *Trivium*, grammar (including literature), rhetoric, and logic; *Quadrivium*, arithmetic, geometry, astronomy, and music. This curriculum was now made standard in the Carolingian schools, and many were the learned disquisitions written for centuries to come on the mystical significance of the fact that there were seven and only seven liberal arts. When these had been mastered, the way lay open for study of the supreme knowledge of Theology.

It is clear that an education could be good or indifferent according to what was available in these fields. And unfortunately in the Carolingian age this was precious little. When we reach the high Middle Ages we shall find that really serious progress could be made within this framework of the seven liberal arts, especially with a little juggling, as, for instance, when Aristotle's *Ethics* was classed as rhetoric, for no better reason than that it did not fit in anywhere else.

Under grammar, which of course meant Latin grammar, were studied first of all the grammarians, Donatus and Priscian, elementary but adequate when supplemented by literature, extracts from which were given in the texts themselves. The student could progress to other Latin literature if he wished, but not much was available in the Carolingian age. Under rhetoric, the student could use a textbook of Alcuin, and he could study the sermons and homilies of the Fathers, especially Gregory the Great. He would not be able to understand any of the great Latin classical orators, as their language would be foreign to him and the subjects of no practical importance in

the Carolingian age. Under logic or dialectic, he could read the works translated by Boethius referred to above. But we have no evidence that anyone in the Carolingian age mastered the principles of logic and was able to make use of it for argument. This art came much later in the Middle Ages. Until the Western mind was capable of handling logical problems, even the best textbooks would be as useful as a book on calculus to students without mathematical training.

Under the quadrivium, there were three textbooks of Boethius in the fields of arithmetic, geometry, and music. The first was very feeble because of the difficulty experienced by Greeks and Romans alike from the absence of a positional notation and from the use of letters as numbers. Euclid seems to have disappeared from the curriculum, presumably as being too difficult, and Boethius' geometry was extremely elementary. Music had been treated by the Greeks as a branch of mathematics, and it was the mathematical ratios between the notes of the scale that should have been taught under the quadrivium. But there is little evidence that the subject was seriously taught at all. In astronomy nothing was available at all, as far as we know, and the subject was included in the curriculum only because it traditionally belonged there. Astronomy became a real subject only at the beginning of the thirteenth century, when Ptolemy's *Almagest* was translated from the Arabic and reached the universities.

Carolingian education therefore became what it primarily was, and was no doubt intended to be—a training in language and literacy. Without the indispensable tools of reading and writing, there could have been no progress; and the establishment of schools was at least a beginning.

### ALFRED THE GREAT IN ENGLAND

Alfred the Great, who reigned over England for thirty years at the end of the ninth century (871–899) has already been mentioned as the defender of his country against the Danes. Alfred himself was also no mean scholar, and in the intervals of his public activities he translated several important Latin works into Anglo-Saxon, including Boethius' *Consolations of Philosophy* and the *Pastoral Rules* of Pope Gregory the Great. He was also responsible for the beginning of the *Anglo-Saxon Chronicle,* a most important source for early English history, which was maintained by his successors until well after the Norman Conquest. Alfred, too, founded a court school, gathered scholars about him, and tried to revive learning, especially among the clergy, after the manner of Charlemagne. Other Anglo-Saxon literature, especially heroic poetry, had already been flourishing for a long time before Alfred, notably the oldest English epic, *Beowulf.*

RESUMPTION OF THE DARK AGES AFTER THE
DEATH OF CHARLEMAGNE

The chaotic conditions in Europe after the death of Charlemagne were not conducive to the spread of learning and education. Some of the monastery and cathedral schools continued to spread a little light in a dark world. But, curiously enough, in the century after Charles's death appeared the one great creative thinker of the whole period, John Scotus Erigena, an Irishman who for a time lived at the court of Charles the Bald in France. Thoroughly familiar with Greek, and especially with Neoplatonist philosophy, he translated the work of one Dionysius (usually called Pseudo-Dionysius), supposed to have been St. Dionysius the Areopagite mentioned in the Acts of the Apostles, a disciple of Paul, but who clearly lived many centuries later than the time of Paul. In this work was introduced to the West a knowledge of the activities of higher beings above man but lower than God, called Intelligences or Hierarchies, who were God's assistants in the task of creation and continued to play a most important part in the created universe afterward. This book had a remarkable success in the later Middle Ages, being commented on both by Albertus Magnus

and by Thomas Aquinas. John Scotus Erigena, familiar, of course, with the Pseudo-Dionysius, developed a complete metaphysical system, patterned after that of the Neoplatonists, in which he shows how all created beings emanate from the Absolute or God through various stages of being. Man's task, therefore, is to return to the Absolute through mystical contemplation, as also recommended by the Neoplatonists. Erigena has a few words also to say on authority, which he says is weak if not approved by reason, an attitude which foreshadows the later discussions on the subject which will be the heart of the struggle between the Church and the philosophers to be dealt with in the next section. Erigena was far ahead of his time, and few in his day could have understood what he was trying to express. But his book was known and read widely in the later medieval period of the twelfth and thirteenth centuries, and was for a time banned as unfit for Christian use.

At the end of the tenth century another remarkable man appeared who again seems to have had no rivals in his own day and few for a long time afterward. This was Gerbert of Aurillac, who later became Pope Sylvester II (999–1003). As scholar and teacher he was outstanding, introducing new material into the curriculum from his studies in Barcelona and elsewhere in Spain, where he apparently picked up the Arabic numerals, though without the zero. As a mathematician he not only enlarged the understanding of the mathematical basis of music, but was able to demonstrate his teachings by the use of special inventions of his own. He taught some serious astronomy, and constructed spheres to show the planets and constellations. He was also most proficient with the abacus. Furthermore, into the grammatical field he introduced more Latin authors than had ever been used before, and he seriously studied such of Aristotle's logic as was then known through Boethius.

The work of Gerbert was not lost, however; and for this reason he perhaps belongs

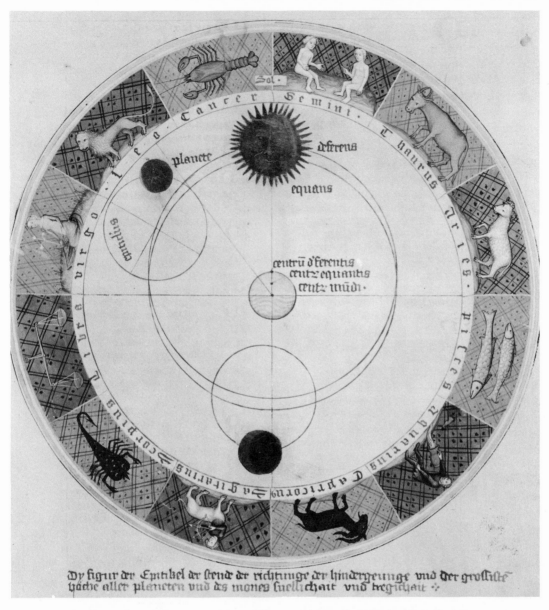

*A sphere depicting the signs of the zodiac, the earth, the deferent and equant circles in which the sun and moon's epicyles move, and the epicycles of the planets. In the original, which is an illustration from the famous medieval textbook* The Sphere, *by John of Sacrobosco, the signs of the zodiac are upon alternating green and rose-red grounds in the outer circle. The sun and planets are shown in gold, and the moon in silver.* (COURTESY THE PIERPONT MORGAN LIBRARY. Ms. 722, folio 18)

at the beginning of the next section as the pioneer in the real revival of learning of the Middle Ages. Pupils taught by him continued to be interested in Muslim science, and others, especially at the Cathedral School of Chartres, undertook a close study of the classical Latin authors, while still others profited by his teaching of logic to apply it to some fundamental philosophic questions. Yet the sum total of knowledge acquired by Gerbert—for which he gained such great renown in his lifetime that he was accused of selling his soul to the Devil in exchange for it—was small indeed; but by contrast with his contemporaries as the Dark Ages drew to their close, he was indeed a giant. However, he was the only one of his century. And though he was a learned scholar, and a practical and inventive man with a claim to be considered a scientist, he does not seem to have been a great creative thinker, nor to have put forward any of the profound problems which were to be discussed throughout the later Middle Ages.

## ▶ The triumph of reason in theology

THE EARLY PHASE

### Berengar of Tours—Logic and authority

As has been suggested earlier, perhaps the most outstanding contribution of medieval thinkers to civilization was the reversal of the position taken by the African Fathers of the Church, and especially by Tertullian, that it was morally superior, and more meritorious in the eyes of God, to believe something that to the ordinary mind seemed inherently improbable than to believe something that seemed reasonable. In other words, faith was a moral virtue; and one should not try to lessen the opportunity for exercising it by trying to prove by reason what should be accepted by faith. Tertullian even went so far himself as to make the famous remark that he believed a thing *because* it was absurd. The Scriptural authority for this predominance given to faith was the saying of Christ to the apostle Thomas, "Blessed are they who have not seen and yet have believed." Even as late as the thirteenth century we find Pope Gregory ix telling students in theology that there was no merit in believing what could be shown to be true by natural reason, and urging them to eschew natural reason accordingly.

Moreover, there was also a danger that a Christian would forget that man could not really know of himself; only grace freely bestowed by God enabled man to know.

He might thus fall into the sin of pride, intoxication with his own powers of reasoning, of which St. Bernard accused Abélard, and fall into all kinds of error. The human mind was a weak and imperfect instrument, created for man's undoing, as evidenced by the story of the Tree of Knowledge and the Fall of Man; the attempt to gain earthly knowledge unaided was one of the wiles of the Devil. To the medieval Christian the sins of the mind, and especially intellectual pride, were far more deadly than any sins of the flesh.

Thus there was a formidable barrier of theological opinion to be overcome by medieval thinkers if they were to free themselves for a true pursuit of knowledge. Reason had to be given at least equal rights with faith, and the powerlessness of the human mind to find truth had to be denied before medieval man could be freed. Because of the fundamental importance of this struggle a whole extended section will be devoted to it; and since the struggle was naturally strongest in the realm of theology, we shall try to show how rationalism invaded and took over theology, a strategic position which, in spite of appearances, it still holds today in the theology of the Roman Catholic Church.

One of the first to announce boldly the rights of reason was Berengar of Tours in the eleventh century, who had studied logic[1] at Chartres and thus come to the conclusion that it could not be ignored, even in theological discussion. Logic, he said, is nothing but the power of reasoning, and it was by virtue of his reason that man could be said to be made in the image of God. When authority and reason conflict, he added, then it is reason that must be followed. Armed with his new tool, he brashly attacked the doctrine of transubstantiation. There is no apparent difference to any of the senses in the bread and wine after the sacrament of the Eucharist, he said, and therefore no miracle has taken place. This

[1] The medievals used the word "dialectic," but the more familiar synonym will be used here, since it has substantially the same meaning.

was a remarkable use of logic, which incicentally begs all the questions involved in the difference between spiritual and physical substance and the adequacy of the senses to distinguish between them, and it was unlikely that Berengar would be permitted to announce such doctrines. He was commanded to recant or be declared a heretic. He recanted, but it was hardly a notable defeat for reason itself, for Berengar's use of it was scarcely convincing even to would-be skeptics.

## St. Anselm of Bec and Canterbury (1034?–1109)—Proofs for the existence of God

Toward the end of the eleventh century it occurred to St. Anselm not to question the existence of God, but to see whether it was possible by logical demonstration to *prove* this existence, and so confound all atheists and unbelievers. He made his position quite clear by explaining that no Christian should doubt any revealed truth of his religion, but that this truth should be capable of being made intelligible to man. Some truths were above reason and should be accepted unconditionally; but without losing his faith a Christian might nevertheless seek to understand as far as his fallible reason could take him. Anselm and all medieval Christians believed that there could be no contradiction between reason and the truths of revelation; but the opening of the whole subject to discussion was a dangerous path, as was realized by some thinkers even in the eleventh century. For the time might come when an irreconcilable conflict might occur. What, then, was to be done? Abandon what reason seemed to demonstrate, or what the Christian revelation had taught for centuries? For Anselm faith came first ("I do not seek to understand in order that I may believe, but I believe in order that I may understand"); but this position was soon to be reversed by other Christians, as faithful and sincere as himself.

Using his logic, Anselm tried to prove the existence of God. His argument that every mind can conceive of the greatest possible being, and that this Being, to be really greatest, must also have existence, which is known as the "ontological" argument for the existence of God, need not detain us. But it is of the utmost significance that at this moment in the eleventh century a Christian saint and archbishop should have thought it either possible or valuable to be able to prove the existence of God, and it shows that the era was passing in which it was morally superior to believe without seeking for proof. Anselm also undertook to prove why it was necessary for Christ to become a man (*Cur Deus homo?*) and gave a clear systematic theory of the atonement of the Son of God for the sins of mankind, which had hitherto been missing from Christian theology.

But Anselm also played his part in a controversy which split the schools of his time and was the first great problem to be thrashed out thoroughly by the new logicians. The controversy concerned the nature of abstract ideas, or what the medievals called "universals" as distinct from "particulars," and the issue resolved itself into the differences between "realists" and "nominalists."[2] According to Plato and Platonists, the universal idea had permanent reality, and all earthly phenomena were only relative and inferior copies of this heavenly reality. Goodness, for instance, was a heavenly archetype, which must be sought for but could never be attained by human

[2] It has been pointed out by historians of medieval philosophy that the nominalism of this period may better be described as "antirealism," and that real nominalism, recognizable as similar to modern nominalism, does not exist before William of Occam in the fourteenth century. The author has not considered the problem of sufficient importance to give an extended and adequate explanation in this text, preferring to give a fuller treatment to the other great problem of medieval thinkers, the relation between faith and reason, which, in his view, is more valuable for the student as well as more comprehensible to the reader not versed in technical philosophy. If the reader requires a more comprehensive treatment, a textbook on philosophy may be consulted, as, for instance, the short but lucid account in W. T. Jones, *A History of Western Philosophy* (New York: Harcourt, Brace & Company, 1952), pp. 422–430, 519–520.

beings. On earth there may be relatively good men who had approached the perfect idea of goodness but had not attained it nor could they. The "realists" of medieval times claimed that only the universal ideas were real. The Church, as a whole, for instance, really existed as a perfect idea; individual churches were only part of this great whole and gained whatever sanctity they had from being part of the universal ideal Church. The nominalists retorted that the universal ideas were only names given for the sake of convenience, but that they had no real existence. By examining plants we came to the understanding of what a plant was, as such. But this did not mean that the ideal plant which all earthly plants approximated had any actual existence.

Clearly the subject has theological implications. If universal man, or "humanity" exists, then God might have justification in punishing all men for the sin of Adam, who was a part of humanity. If, on the other hand, only individual men exist, then each should be judged on his own merits and all men do not have a share in the sin of Adam. The Holy Trinity, according to strict nominalists, must consist of three Gods; and the Trinity itself was only a convenient term for describing the three. This view of the Trinity was indeed a position taken by the most eminent nominalist of the eleventh century, Roscellinus, who was severely taken to task for heresy by Anselm, who insisted that all men are in species one man, and likewise the three members of the Trinity are each perfect God and one God, partaking of the universal Godhead.

### Abélard—"I seek to understand in order that I may believe."

With the great teacher and critic Peter Abélard (1079–1142), the first phase of the struggle for the rights of reason was completed. A man of clear incisive thinking, potentially a skeptic though remaining formally true to his Christian faith, he made a contribution of the utmost significance to medieval thought. Few men in the whole history of thought have been so influential as he, in spite of the fact that he was in no way a creative thinker. But his penetrating logic and clear exposition attracted thousands of students to his lectures, and started them working in a direction from which there was never to be any return.

A brief mention may first be made of his contribution to the controversy on universals. Universals are not true realities, he declared; but they are more than mere names. The common element in things is discovered by the mind, and this element has its own reality, though a mental one, called by Abélard a concept. Humanity is a perfectly legitimate concept, derived from our perception of the common elements between human beings; but it is not more real than the individual human beings, and human beings are not real merely because they partake in the universal idea of humanity. This position, called conceptualism, is very similar to the position taken by Aristotle, which was not known to Abélard. Aristotle's position, however, was known to Thomas Aquinas a century later when he stated a similar point of view as "moderate realism." According to the latter view, the ideas are abstracted from the phenomena by the active intellect, a spiritual faculty of man which can only perceive the ideal or spiritual element in things. This, for St. Thomas Aquinas, is the immortal part of man, and man's ability to abstract the universal ideas is the central element in the Thomistic proof of human immortality. The active intellect, being spiritual, can never die.

Abélard studied for a period with Anselm of Laon and with William of Champeaux, both confirmed realists in the controversy, but did not think very highly of either of them, since they were not his equal in logical prowess. Then he began to teach, and from the first he was followed by hordes of infatuated pupils. Driven out of Paris after an unfortunate love affair with Héloïse followed by tragedy, he escaped to a monastery for a while, then returned to teaching but got into trouble with the Church because of his divergent views on the Trinity. Even in a desolate rural retreat students followed him. The significance of this extraordinary popularity was that he was teaching them to think, and to doubt. His most famous book, called *Sic et Non* (*Yes or No?*), is typical of his method, and permits us to understand what his students found so fascinating. He thought it was the duty of a Christian to use his reason even on the substance of theology. He was the first to point out clearly that the Fathers of the Church who were accepted as authorities had themselves been in doubt, and that there were contradictory opinions on theological subjects even among these authorities. Abélard did not conclude that the Fathers did not know what they were talking about, but rather that there were reasonable grounds for doubting where the truth lay. What he proceeded to do, therefore, was to list a number of important theological questions, and then draw up the various opinions that the Fathers had held about them. Sometimes the contradictions could be reconciled, but more often the only thing to do was to accept the best authority. But, above all, the student must work out the answer for himself, for only by doubting could there be any inquiry, and only by inquiry could one come to truth.

This was already a reversal of the position taken by St. Anselm. Abélard wished to arrive at belief through the process of doubting and trying to understand. Faith no longer was primary, and indeed, implicitly, was an enemy to understanding. Abélard had firmly planted the seed of honest and disinterested inquiry, and suggested that the way to resolve a problem was to think about it, not to see what some great man in the past had thought about it whose opinion had afterward been accepted as authoritative by the Church. Only after one had tried to reason it out for one's self should one have recourse to some predecessor, whose other work had entitled him to be considered as an authority in theology.

## REACTION OF THE CHURCH TO THE METHOD OF ABÉLARD

Abélard was unfortunate in that in his own generation he was opposed by so severe a critic and such a sworn foe of human reason as the mystic St. Bernard, of whom we have already spoken in an earlier chapter. Bernard at once saw the danger and pursued Abélard bitterly all his life. If human reason were to triumph, there would be no mystery left. "He thinks himself able by human reason to understand God, completely," Bernard charged. He accused Abélard of pride and arrogance in thinking that man with his puny mind could ever comprehend the mysteries of faith, and he did not hesitate to accuse him of heresy in questioning authority, and arriving at conclusions contrary to those held by the Church. By his influence he was able to have Abélard condemned to silence, but it is doubtful if he could have sustained the conviction at Rome whither Abélard was going to defend himself when he died.

But Bernard was already behind the times, and the victory lay with his opponent. One of Abélard's own pupils, Peter Lombard, Bishop of Paris, using his master's method, became the teacher of generations of churchmen; his book of the *Sentences* became the standard text for theology for centuries and is still not altogether outmoded today. The great Pope Alexander III was also one of Abélard's pupils. Fundamentally any opponent of Abélard must take the untenable position that Christianity is contrary to reason. For if it is not contrary, then reason can only serve to support faith, and help to convert the doubting or the unbelievers.

Nevertheless, for centuries there was opposition to the use of even Peter Lombard's book of the *Sentences*. In the process of discussing theological questions by the use of reason, there was a natural tendency to escape from essential Christianity as it was revealed in the Gospels. Well on into the thirteenth century we find complaints that theological students were wasting their time studying logic and learning to resolve knotty points of doctrine, rather than learning to preach the way of salvation and the teachings of Christ. We find Roger Bacon, with his fundamentally mystical outlook, praising Robert Grosseteste, Bishop of Lincoln, for neglecting the *Sentences* in favor of Scriptural exegesis; we find, as already mentioned, Pope Gregory IX telling the theological students at Paris to refrain from studying philosophy on the grounds that it cramped their style as preachers, and reproducing the hoary old argument that it is better to believe what cannot be proved than try to prove what should be accepted on faith. It is not, however, recorded that the students paid him any attention, and the *Book of the Sentences* continued to be used in the schools, nor, indeed, did Gregory suggest that it should be given up.

## THE DEVELOPED SCHOLASTIC METHOD OF PETER LOMBARD

Systematic theology in the hands of Peter Lombard became, following his master Abélard, a discussion of important theological questions. The teacher would propound a question, as, for instance, whether God created the world out of nothing himself or through "intelligences." The discussion therefore always starts with *Utrum*—Whether. The following step is to take the authorities who have spoken in favor of the proposition—*Quod sic videtur*, For it seems so. The arguments will be listed clearly, and perhaps disposed of, at once, if there is an inherent contradiction. Then the arguments on the other side will be taken. *Sed contra*—But, on the other hand. Finally the master will try to reconcile the difficulties in his own *Solutio*, which carries no authority beyond the weight of the particular master's name. These solutions are the master's *Sententiae* or Opinions (hence, the title of Peter's book, the *Sentences*). It became the custom at the universities where theology was taught for every student to dispute publicly on these questions, and to

give his opinions. Thus from many masters of theology in the thirteenth century we possess *Commentaries on the Sentences*, which are usually a publication of their opinions given on disputed questions during their period of study, and thus represent something close to the doctoral dissertations of our own day.

The method is intellectually of the utmost honesty, for no one was allowed to propound opinions in this public manner which relied on anything except the best that reason could offer. Though authorities were used, the master's solution had to be his own or at least one that appealed to reason and itself reconciled the conflicting opinions. It was not, in the last analysis, the weight of authority that decided the question for the successors of Peter Lombard, but the best opinion available at the time; and this is how all questions are decided in a free world.

One of the most interesting and symptomatic discussions which was carried on for nearly a century was on the subject whether theology is a science. By science was meant something which could be known by natural reason, whether theology, in fact, was different from other branches of knowledge, whether it had axioms from which could be deduced further knowledge, and if so what was the origin of these axioms. Alexander of Hales preferred to call it a *sapientia*, or wisdom, rather than science, while others claimed that the data of Biblical revelation were the axioms, and were implanted in the human mind in the same way as geometrical truths. God implanted geometrical axioms in the human mind at birth, while he revealed theological truths to the apostles, the prophets and evangelists, and the Fathers of the Church.

The discussion is not interesting so much for itself as for the evident need on the part of theologians to feel that they were being "scientific" and reasonable, rather than blindly believing; and it suggests parallels in our own day of theologians who still wish to prove that their teachings are in accordance with "science" as represented by modern psychology or the doctrine of biological evolution.

## GRADUAL RECOVERY OF ARISTOTLE AND MUSLIM SCIENCE

### Effects on theology

In the early twelfth century, medieval thinkers were already becoming aware of the superiority of Muslim knowledge to the very scanty materials of knowledge available in the West. After the conquest of Sicily there were many contacts made with Muslim scholars by Western inquirers, and at the medical school of Salerno in Italy several important Muslim treatises were in use as well as some of the scientific work of Aristotle translated from the Arabic. But with the gradual conquest of Spain, and in particular the capture of Toledo in 1085, a new phase in the assimilation of Muslim learning began. In the middle of the twelfth century, Raymond, Archbishop of Toledo, fascinated by the wealth of Muslim and Greek works of learning available in his archdiocese, began to authorize translations of the more important works. It was difficult at first to find translators who knew both Latin and Arabic; hence the services of many Jews were bespoken, and a number of Latins painfully acquired sufficient familiarity with Arabic to be able to make translations, not all of high quality, but serving until something better was possible. Among the first works to be translated, especially by Gerard of Cremona, dean of the translators (died 1187), who in his lifetime is said to have translated no fewer than seventy-three works from the Arabic, was Aristotle, who thus entered the West via Syriac, Arabic, and sometimes Hebrew. Translations of a few works were available directly from the Greek, but, on the whole, this first phase of translating was mostly from the Arabic. Translating became the rage for a while, and books were poured forth into the eager Latin world, starved for material for half a century.

It was more than a century before the whole corpus of the immense work of Aristotle was available, and such a huge body of work could only be gradually assimilated by Western scholars. But they were assisted by the commentaries, first of Avicenna, who was more acceptable to Christians in part because of his Neoplatonist tendencies already familiar in the West; and then by those of Averroës from about 1230. Often enough, it would appear, the Western scholars did not trouble to read Aristotle himself, but preferred the commentaries which explained to them more simply what the difficult Aristotle had said, as we may be more inclined to read commentaries on Karl Marx rather than the formidable *Das Capital*, or commentaries on Kant rather than the *Critique of Pure Reason* of the master himself.

The Church at first took little official notice of the influx of Aristotelian thought, perhaps because it was sponsored by such an eminent churchman as the Archbishop of Toledo. But then suddenly very strange teachings began to be heard at the newly founded University of Paris in the first decade of the thirteenth century, apparently deriving from Aristotle. And it was remembered that Aristotle was a pagan and knew nothing of Christianity, and, what was worse, he had been commented on by Muslims, actual unbelievers and opponents of Christianity. The first two heresies heard of at Paris in the early thirteenth century in reality had no connection with the teachings of the Greek philosopher; and it was difficult indeed to show that the materialism of Amaury of Bénes or of David of Dinant could have derived from him. Nevertheless when a number of professors were condemned for teaching the heresy of Amaury, and David of Dinant's books were likewise condemned to be burned, Aristotle was caught up in the same holocaust, and the reactionary and stubborn Archbishop of Sens, within whose archdiocese the University of Paris was situated, formally forbade the teaching of the natural scientific work of Aristotle at the university, together with his *Metaphysics*.

This was a serious blow to the scholars,

from whom was withheld the very work which they most wanted to study; for after the long famine in intellectual fodder there was now for the first time a surfeit. They were not, however, formally forbidden to read the works for themselves, though reading was a poor substitute for hearing a master discourse on Aristotle and explain him. It is almost certain that nothing had yet been found in Aristotle which actually conflicted with Christian teaching, and there is no specific complaint of any portion of his work. But this was soon to come. Aristotle's views on creation were clearly not those of the Church, and he was rather ambiguous on the immortality of the soul. And, of course, as a good Greek pagan, he was, in general, extremely secular in his views, and naturally Divine Providence did not appear in his scheme, although his teleological view of the universe was not hostile to it.

When Pope Gregory ix in 1231 confirmed the ban on the same works forbidden in 1209 by the Archbishop of Sens, he set up a commission of three to expurgate them for Christian consumption. Until this was done there must still be no public lecturing on him. It would seem that the pope had not read Aristotle himself or he would have seen the futility of the task. For Aristotle's method could be used by anyone, and similar conclusions would be drawn from the same premises. The true difficulty lay in the naturalistic, secular attitude of the Greek master, which was so contrary to Christian habits of thought. Specific teachings were of minor importance in comparison with this fundamental danger. At all events one member of the committee died soon after his appointment, and the others seem never to have tackled their task.

For some time the ban seems to have been observed fairly strictly in spite of the certainty that the students were bitter against it; and they were made to content themselves with a far more intensive study of logic, made possible by the translation of the advanced work of Aristotle, and a more intensive study of grammar. Then came the long struggle between Pope Innocent iv and Emperor Frederic ii, and discipline at the university seems to have been relaxed. At all events, suddenly, in spite of the ban, we find Aristotle being taught in all his completeness and without any action being taken against the faculty. But now there was a really grave danger. For Michael Scotus had been rash enough to translate the Commentaries of Averroës from the Arabic, and these contained the real stuff of heresy. For Averroës thought that Aristotle had disbelieved in personal immortality, and that the active intellect of individual men was merged with the active intellect of all humanity at death; there was thus no personal immortality but only a collective immortality as part of the one great world mind. In 1250 the pope took cognizance of this teaching. But now, instead of simply banning it, he asked the greatest theological authority of the day, Albertus Magnus, to defend the Christian teaching against those who were proclaiming the doctrine of Averroës. Albert, in fact, was not much of a theologian, but he did his best. The teaching, however, continued, causing a serious schism in the Faculty of Arts at the university twenty years later, when a far more formidable theologian, Thomas Aquinas, with devastating logic tore the arguments of Averroës apart, insisting at the same time that Aristotle had never held such a pernicious doctrine. It was actually difficult to see what Aristotle had in fact taught, for he seems to make different points in two of his works. It was certainly possible to deduce from his remarks the conclusions that Averroës had drawn. But when Siger of Brabant and others at the university persisted in supporting the Averroistic conclusions it was not unnatural for the Church to think of Siger as a heretic. But, even so, he was only banished from his teaching position, and otherwise seems to have gone unpunished save for a mild exile in Italy. From the burning of 1209 right through the century there is no case of the use by the Church of its Inquisition against academic heresies or potential heresies.

## The work of Albertus Magnus and Thomas Aquinas in reconciling Aristotle and Christianity

With the rise of the Averroists, it was already clear by the middle of the thirteenth century that Aristotle and his kind of thinking were potential dynamite to Christianity. It had begun to seem that what could be discovered by pure natural reason was not in conformity with Christianity in several important respects; and a horrible formula attributed to Averroës began to find currency in academic circles, that there was a double truth—the truth of Christian revelation and the truth of natural philosophy. If this notion were ever accepted, then it must mean that faith would be subjected to a severe strain, and might come ultimately to be rejected by many.

There was one possible answer to this crisis, but it could be given only by a man of great learning and industry, competent in science and theology, fully aware of the teachings of Christianity while at the same time able to understand and, if necessary, criticize Aristotle. For the work that required to be done was an intensive study of everything that Aristotle wrote that was available in the West, followed by the demonstration, chapter by chapter, either that Aristotle was making statements which could be shown to be untrue or unproved, or that what he said in no way contradicted the teachings of Christianity. This huge enterprise was carried through to completion by the German scholar Albertus Magnus, Albert the Great (1206–1280), the only man in history who received the title of "the Great" for his scholarship.

Albert, in his introduction to his commentaries on Aristotle's *Physics*, explained that he had undertaken his task because in his order, the Dominican, many brothers had been criticizing both Aristotle and philosophy in general while remaining entirely in ignorance of what they consisted. Philosophy, in Albert's view, was of the greatest aid to the study of theology and Christianity, because it showed how reasonable were all Christian beliefs if rightly understood. Aristotle was by no means infallible, and he was not to be regarded as a supreme authority, beyond questioning; and there were many things of which he was ignorant, even in the field of natural science. Nevertheless, in science he was a great master whose views should always be treated with respect; he simply was unfortunate in that he was born too soon to have the benefit of Christian revelation. Aristotle could not therefore be blamed for not understanding that a Divine Providence ruled over the world, but at the same time there was nothing in his biology which disproved such an idea; on the contrary, rightly understood, Aristotle's observations in themselves tended to suggest precisely this.

Albert planned, both as a scientist and reconciler of Aristotle and Christianity, to write a commentary on every subject that Aristotle himself had treated, and supplement it from his own observations. In addition he would write other books on subjects such as mineralogy which Aristotle had neglected, but which he himself had studied. The commentaries that Albert wrote are not detailed verbal commentaries of the kind made by his successor and pupil Thomas Aquinas, but rather digressions on the general subject treated by the master. They are thus not strictly philosophical, but far closer to what we call science. Albert, indeed, was a self-taught man, and had never studied either philosophy or theology very thoroughly; he was always too busy organizing schools within the Dominican Order, engaging in public activity on behalf of the Church, and even for a while serving as Bishop of Ratisbon. He was thus inclined to gloss over some of the philosophical difficulties, and to assume that Aristotle had agreed with the Christian position when a more careful examination would have revealed that he did not, as with the question of the creation of the world out of nothing by God—which Albert, certainly incorrectly, attributed to Aristotle. His work therefore was in no sense definitive, and in itself would not have been completely convincing to a better-trained philosopher. But it was a magnificent pioneer work in what has since come to be called scholasticism, or the reconciliation of philosophy and Christianity.

St. Thomas Aquinas, a much younger contemporary of Albert, had his early education at the University of Naples, and then went to Paris to study theology. There he met Albertus Magnus, and apparently became fascinated with the work he was doing. Instead of finishing his courses at Paris, he chose to accompany Albert to Cologne, whither Albert was called on business for his order, and continued his studies there with his master. Evidently he recognized that this work of reconciliation was of supreme importance for the whole future of philosophical studies and of Christianity; being better trained than Albert, and having a more acute philosophical mind, he was able to bring his master's work to fruition in such a way that, for those who accepted his main premise that there was no contradiction possible between true philosophy and equally true Christianity, and that reason could and should be applied to the understanding of the Christian religion, his work really was definitive and never had to be performed again. For this reason the Catholic Church today regards the work of Thomas Aquinas as supreme, and requires its study by all theologians; since Pope Leo XIII in the nineteenth century it has been accepted as the official teaching of the Church.

Thomas's procedure differed from that of his master in that he wrote a careful and complete textual commentary on every book of Aristotle, from a philosophical point of view, neglecting those works which were not concerned with philosophy. His purpose is to explain exactly what Aristotle said, the consequences that could be deduced

from it, and why every statement should be accepted or rejected. In one of his masterpieces, the *Summa contra Gentiles,* Thomas builds up with subtle logic that is hardly refutable, provided the premises be accepted, an entire structure of natural theology, or theodicy, endeavoring to show how much of theology can be determined by natural reason alone. Using Aristotle's *Physics* and the master's theory of motion he essays to prove by metaphysical arguments the existence of God, on the grounds that everything that is moved requires a mover, leaving a necessary First Mover, which is God. Using Aristotle's *Metaphysics,* he tries to show that everything on earth requires a cause; tracing these causes back he arrives at a First Cause, which must be God. Again using the *Metaphysics,* with much elaboration from his own thinking, he declares that everything on earth and in the universe was not *necessarily* there; it might have not been there. In other words, everything created is contingent, an accident, as distinct from a necessity. The presence of all these contingent things requires the presence also of one Necessary Being, and this is God. He therefore goes on to define God as the Self-subsistent Being.

Having reached this conclusion, he then proceeds to deduce those attributes of God which it cannot be doubted he must possess, building a tremendous logical structure, perhaps the supreme achievement in the history of human thought of a purely rational nature, without reference to observable facts in the world but entirely spun out of the unaided human reason. This was natural theology, and it only needed to be supplemented by knowledge which the human reason could not reach unaided. This God had supplied to man by revelation, the inspired words of the Scriptures. It was impossible, for instance, for man to arrive at the mystery of the Holy Trinity for himself; such knowledge had to be revealed by God. But Thomas wished to grant as much as possible to the reason, and reason should also be used to try to make intelligible those things which had been revealed.

Man could not, according to St. Thomas, arrive for certain by natural reason at the conclusion that the world was created out of nothing by God; but once this had been revealed to him by the Scriptures, then it was possible and proper for man to try to understand for himself the means of creation, and to see that it was reasonable. So the triumph of reason was complete. Revelation was necessary as a supplement, and this required faith from man, which faith was at once to be supplemented by reason. Medieval thought had moved a very long way indeed from St. Bernard in not much more than a century.

### Opposition to Thomism—Duns Scotus and William of Occam

Thomas Aquinas in his own day never attained quite the reputation acquired by his master Albertus Magnus, who outlived his pupil by several years. And during the period of Thomas's greatest production, the period of the *Summa Theologica* which undertook to explain the whole drama of salvation and the part played in it by the Church, the University of Paris was no quiet place, full of students anxious for knowledge, but a center of the most violent polemics, first between the regulars and seculars (those clergy who belonged to an order and those who did not), and then within the Faculty of Arts on the doctrine of the double truth and collective or individual immortality (Averroism). Thomas rarely visited Paris during those years, though he defended his Dominican Order against the attacks of the seculars, and he wrote a strongly worded attack on Averroism. It is very probable that his greatest works were not known to the university at this time in any detail, though their general tendency was understood. Finally the squabbles at the university became so severe that the Bishop of Paris, Stephen Tempier, took a hand and drew up a huge list of errors being apparently publicly taught or discussed, including not only those which could be attributed to the Averroists but a considerable number which emanated un-

doubtedly from St. Thomas himself. And though Thomas had himself died three years earlier and could therefore undertake no defense, his aged master, Albertus Magnus, hurried to Paris to see what could be done. The whole rational movement was clearly under fire from the irate bishop, who must have acted under orders from Rome. And when the University of Oxford a few months later followed the example of Paris and condemned a similar series of errors, the danger of a collapse of the whole work of the century was imminent; for the Church had officially taken no action up to this time ever since the original condemnation of Aristotle, and the weight of its authority, backed by many Franciscans and probably the bulk of the secular clergy, could have been decisive.

But Thomas, Albert, and the movement they represented fortunately were not unrepresented at Rome. Devoted Dominicans, determined that the two great lights of their order should not be suppressed, kept the ear of successive popes, evidently impressing upon them how great an aid to faith the work of their masters could be. Gradually they swung the papacy in their direction, and in 1328 they succeeded in having Thomas Aquinas canonized as a saint, and his works from that time on became authoritative (every article is a miracle, declared the pope in his bull authorizing the canonization).

But the Franciscans, especially those at Oxford, who, as we shall see, early took an interest in science, were far from content; and two considerable theologians and philosophers, at the end of the thirteenth century and during the next, denied the whole possibility of attaining truth by the means advocated by St. Thomas Aquinas. Like most Franciscans, they believed in divine illumination of the human mind, and, following St. Augustine, insisted on the mind's incompetence, especially in the field of religion. Duns Scotus (died 1308) denied categorically that it was possible to prove the existence of God, the immortality of the soul, and such truths of religion by reason. The only possible approach to the truths of religion was by faith and meditation. William of Occam (died 1349) took substantially the same line, denying the ability of human reason in heavenly matters but emphasizing it in earthly things. William revived the old doctrine of nominalism in a new form, insisting that the great universal ideas and abstractions of Thomas had no real validity, and that the ideas were only names which described objects of experience in a convenient way. Ideas therefore are applicable only to things of the sense world revealed by experience, and it is only in this realm that reason and its logic are competent. William's influence in his own century was considerable, and those nominalists who followed him, especially at the University of Paris, for a time became interested in a number of scientific questions, for which they hoped to find answers by reason, and to some degree neglected theology.

But it will be noted that these men only denied the competence of logic and reason in religion; they did not deny its competence altogether as St. Bernard would have done, nor did they suggest that its use was likely to lead to the deadly sin of pride. The form of their criticism therefore is the surest sign that reason had at last emerged as the greatest of human faculties, limited indeed, but powerful as an instrument for discovering the truth about the created world. The way lay open for the scientific achievements of Western civilization.

▶ **Medieval science**

GENERAL CHARACTERISTICS OF ARISTOTELIAN SCIENCE, AS INTERPRETED BY THE MEDIEVALS

It may be safely said that there was really no medieval science of any importance before the recovery of Aristotle, and that the theory of medieval science was always Aristotelian, as interpreted by Muslim Neoplatonists, within a framework of Christian ideology. Modern science is distinguished from medieval, indeed, by its very lack of a comprehensive general theory. We have minor limited theories in the special sciences, but none to cover the whole field of science. Vaguely we believe that science ought to be useful to mankind in rather obvious ways, such as prolonging life, minimizing pain, increasing pleasure; and we believe, equally vaguely, that it is a good thing to have more knowledge and understanding about the world we live in.

The medievals started from the opposite standpoint. They believed they knew why we are on earth in the first place, the relationship of the soul to the body, the relationship of man to the universe, the purposes served by the animals and plants; they had all the answers to those questions which we think it illegitimate to ask because science is incompetent to deal with them. So-called laws of nature, discovered by induction, were not interesting to them because nature itself as a conception was unacceptable. God was the lawgiver, and laws of nature were God's laws, which were entirely under his control, and he could interfere as often as he wished. At any moment a miracle might happen which would invalidate a law. A relic of a saint, or a suitable prayer offered in the right quarters, might be able to cure a dangerous disease in a moment, or rain could appear out of a cloudless sky. What was the use of trying to discover the mundane causes of a disease or of studying the science of meteorology?

Every medieval scientist had to struggle with these commonly accepted assumptions of his age; hence it was a great step forward when Albertus Magnus proclaimed that God works through natural causes which can be investigated, implying that in the ordinary course of affairs God does not interfere, but allowing him freedom to do so if he wishes. Adopting such an attitude, and performing serious investigation, it would not be too long before a scientist noticed the extreme rarity of miracles, and went ahead without paying too much attention to their possibility.

But it was not so easy to escape from

the leading strings imposed by the more respectable philosophy and science of the Greeks and the Muslims. Astrology was not to the medievals an unscientific aberration as it is to modern scientists, if not to the layman. It was based on the understanding (derived from Plato via Avicenna) that the relationship of man to the universe is as the microcosm (or little world) to the macrocosm (the great world). Man, in Plato's phrase, is a lesser world. Everything in the heavens is reflected in man. A planet seen in the heavens is also present in concentrated form in the organs of man—Saturn, for instance, in his spleen, and Venus in his kidneys. The plant also is directly connected with the planets, the blue-colored flower with Saturn, the yellow with Jupiter, the red with Mars. Thus a knowledge of the heavens is essential for a true understanding of man himself, and is not just a separate science to be studied for its own sake. Astronomy might be a branch of mathematics, but it was also a part of psychology and medicine. A knowledge of the movements of the planets, and their position in the heavens, would therefore be of the utmost importance for man since, in the medieval phrase, superiors (in the heavens) ruled inferiors (on earth); and not only man but all his doings were subject to the decrees of the heavens, which themselves, according to those who remembered their Christianity, expressed the will of God (Neoplatonists and Avicenna had indeed speculated as to whether the stars were not, in fact, gods).

Moreover, every man at birth was an exact image of the cosmos at the moment of his birth; and if the cosmos could be read at that moment, then the physiology and psychology of the man could be exactly determined. Hence the importance of ascertaining the exact hour of birth and casting a horoscope. Up to this point medieval thinkers were in agreement. But there was considerable dispute on how all this affected the free will of man, and whether what was called judicial astrology was equally true and permissible. For it might also be possible to determine the path of life for man; and, as the heavens were perfect and unchangeable, this looked as if the path of man's life was likewise unchangeable and determined from his birth. After the great age of rationalism in the thirteenth century was over, judicial astrology, appealing to the superstitions of mankind then as now, became ever more popular. Philosophers produced a theory that the movements of the planets paralleled the life of man but did not determine it, thus saving free will; and horoscopes continued to be cast for centuries with only sporadic opposition, at one time being the major interest of the majority of scientists of the day, who found, like Paracelsus, that at the least the casting of horoscopes provided them with a living, allowing them leisure to engage in other and more worth-while pursuits.

Biology was dominated throughout the medieval period by Aristotle, whose biological theories could be made to conform to the Christian idea of Divine Providence. Aristotle had produced a very comprehensive set of observations, most of them extremely accurate. But he had not been content with this; he had also tied them together with a remarkable theory whose central observation was that "nature does nothing in vain." Nothing in the living world exists which does not have a purpose that can be understood by the unaided human mind. The phenomena themselves needed to be investigated for the purpose of adding to human knowledge (Aristotle had begun his *Metaphysics* with the dictum that "all men by nature desire to know"), but once they had been investigated, they could be understood in terms of purposes. If it were seen that a mistletoe grows on an oak tree, then the *how* of this phenomenon did not need to be investigated, though of course it could be if desired. Aristotle himself might very well have also investigated how it is nourished and maintains itself, and what effect it has on the tree. But for purposes of understanding the mistletoe, one must only ask why it is there. And the answer might be, in natural terms, that it relieves the tree of some of its evil humors, or alternatively, and more probably, that it sucks the life out of the tree; or, in human terms, it might exist as an example for man of the evils of parasitism, and thus a moral example for man. Or it might exist because mistletoe is necessary for man and the tree was as convienient a place as any for nature to put it. But of one thing the medieval man could be certain: it must serve some real purpose in the total economy of nature which included man. Roger Bacon was once called upon to answer the question whether plants feel. In Aristotelian terms the answer, to us insoluble, was not difficult. The purpose served by feeling, he replied, is to enable one to move either toward or away from an object exciting it (sympathy and antipathy). A plant is stationary and cannot move. Therefore feeling would be unnecessary to a plant, and nature would have given feeling to it in vain. But nature does nothing in vain. Therefore the plant cannot feel. Q.E.D.

It is clear that the supposed understanding of purposes in nature would conduce to reverence for the Divine Providence which had ordered all things in this beneficent way; but it would not tend to encourage investigation of how they actually worked, and it would certainly inhibit our modern practice of manipulating natural things for human ends. As long as this attitude remained, there could be no practical and applied science.

But medieval practice in time became much better than its theory. We do not find any thinker in medieval times urging the usefulness of knowledge and encouraging scientists to investigate for the purpose of alleviating man's lot on earth, though Roger Bacon does emphasize its usefulness for theology and for helping kings to defeat their enemies. It was a later Bacon, Francis, who in the seventeenth century really for the first time sounded the clarion call for scientific investigation for the improvement of man's ordinary life. But we do find medieval scientists encouraging experiments, if only in the hopes of proving theories which

they could never have proved since they were demonstrably false. We do find a number of experiments being made, though as a rule in an unplanned manner. We find the spirit of criticism growing, and serious efforts to escape from the authority of Aristotle, and we find it gradually becoming natural not to take things for granted without testing by experience. We find, in short, the native curiosity of man escaping from the fetters imposed upon it by a premature belief that everything that was worth knowing was already known. It can hardly be claimed that the Middle Ages were among the great ages of science, but, as in other fields, they were preparing quietly and diligently for the future.

### THIRTEENTH-CENTURY SCIENCE—ALBERTUS MAGNUS (1206–1280), ROGER BACON (1214–1292?)

It is impossible in a book of this scope to discuss the work of the several hundred scientists in medieval times whose names, and some of whose work, are known to us. For the most part these men were engaged in assimilating some aspect of Muslim science to which they added little that was original; or they were compilers of other people's work, presenting it in a form likely to interest their contemporaries. In the twelfth century such works were already appearing, giving accounts of what their authors had been able to glean from Muslim material, a few making attempts to be selective and reasonably critical, while the majority merely seem to have inserted what was likely to be interesting and fascinating. The most complete and in many respects the best, and certainly for us the most useful of these encyclopedias, was the *Speculum Majus* of Vincent of Beauvais (1190?–1264?), a Dominican friar, which contains the bulk of what was known of scientific information in the thirteenth century and makes extensive use of the Muslim material. But the two really great names in the thirteenth-century science deserve rather more attention, since in their different ways they represent what was best in science of their time. Moreover, Bacon in himself so often combines at the same time the best and the worst that a more extended study of his work will reveal the scientific shortcomings of the period as well as those tendencies which in later centuries were to create our modern science.

We have already dealt with the purpose of Albert's work—the reconciliation of science and the Christian religion. But it was also remarked that the scientist reveals himself throughout his work, because in fact Albert was a better scientist than he was philosopher or theologian. Though Albert's many volumes are mostly in the form of commentaries on Aristotle, it is the digressions that constitute the value of the work, for in them he adds information that he has personally acquired. He shows in several places that he understands the value of experiment, even though his experiments were not very advanced. He wished to check old wives' tales as well as remarks he had found in Aristotle, as for instance, when he tried to tempt an ostrich with iron but was unable to persuade him to touch it, contrary to a current superstition that the ostrich will eat iron. He is severely critical of many of the statements he has found in other books, once going so far as to say that philosophers are full of lies. And he explains that the method which the student of science must follow is this: he should be critical of everything he is told, and he must try to find the natural causes behind all phenomena. Albert himself was most skilled as a botanist, having been described as the best botanist between the Greeks and the moderns. He has left us many accurate descriptions of flowers and plants, and he does not discourse to the same degree as his contemporaries on the pleasing moral lessons to be obtained from them. He was greatly interested in alchemy, and had studied what he could of the Muslim work in this field, and he has given us his own observations on the properties of rocks and metals—a field neglected by Aristotle. But knowing neither Greek nor Arabic, he was dependent entirely upon what had been translated up to that

time, and this included the more fascinating rather than necessarily the more informative of Aristotle's works. But, like most medieval thinkers, Albertus Magnus touched on the majority of fields of study, trying to gain a comprehensive picture of the totality of science, even though, as Bacon observes, he was quite ignorant of both mathematics and optics and therefore could not come to any real understanding of science for want of perceiving how each is dependent on the other.

For this was the heart of Roger Bacon's own efforts. He wanted to have a complete knowledge of all the sciences and was prepared to go to endless trouble in trying to obtain it. He was obsessed with the idea that it was the duty of a Christian, with all the advantages that he had that were denied to infidels and pagans, to become a fully equipped scientist, with up-to-date knowledge in every field; only thus could a man appreciate the way each science contributes to another. He was not the man to be content with a few fragments, or even an intensive knowledge of one or two fields, but he must have a knowledge of them all. It would then be perfect and complete, and a man could contemplate the imposing edifice with aesthetic satisfaction.

Roger Bacon (1214–1292?) reveals himself very clearly in his writings as a man with an insatiable drive toward knowledge, for which he was willing to sacrifice everything and work with single-hearted devotion. But at the same time there was scarcely a single one of his contemporaries whom he did not criticize and profess to despise. When his private means ran out, he became a Franciscan friar, but deeply resented the fact that he was made to do menial tasks instead of writing and carrying out his experiments. But he was determined, whatever the rules of his order, that he would bring his work to the attention of those in authority because he was so certain that he had a message which everyone else was neglecting, a message of supreme importance which justified an appeal directly to the head of Christendom. So he approached one of the leading cardinals through an intermediary, and was rewarded by a mandate to send him his work. But, unable to do so, because of conditions within his order, he delayed, until suddenly the cardinal became Pope Clement IV. Bacon sent another message, asking if His Holiness was still interested, and was rewarded by yet another request. In spite of extreme difficulties due to his own perfectionism and the haste with which he had to work, as well as due to the opposition of his order, he finally dispatched what he called a *persuasio* to the pope, a work intended to persuade him of the urgency of patronizing Bacon's work, and making a number of suggestions for the advancement of science which are of the deepest interest.

This *Opus Majus,* accompanied by a short digest containing some extra information on alchemy, is one of the masterpieces of the Middle Ages—in spite of its great imperfections, perhaps its only scientific masterpiece. From this and from other work Bacon carried out more thoroughly and with more detachment both before and after the *Opus Majus,* it is possible to discover a coherent philosophy of science which is a very strange compound indeed of reactionary and superstitious thinking and brilliant and suggestive observations. Bacon was not primarily an experimenter, though it is clear he was working in conjunction with a number of people who were actually making serious experiments, especially one Peter de Maricourt, who produced an original work on the magnet of evident scientific value. Bacon speaks of the possibility of flying machines and complicated machines for lifting huge weights, and he speaks of gunpowder at some length and other "secret works of nature." But these marvels were merely observed experiments among his contemporaries, and Bacon says nothing of having performed them himself. This is not to say that he performed none; but the only ones he describes of his own are extremely primitive, of the same stature as Albert's efforts to feed iron to an ostrich. But he undoubtedly carried out many observations in astronomy and optics, in which sciences he had probably been interested by Robert Grosseteste, Bishop of Lincoln, a teacher of the Franciscans at Oxford. Grosseteste had studied the work of the Muslims in optics, especially the great Al-Hazen, and in the intervals of a very busy life wrote several books on light which show insight of a high order. Bacon added to what his predecessor had done, and he has much to say that is of interest, especially on the phenomenon of the rainbow, of which he had made repeated observations.

But Bacon was not a great scientist because of his experiments and his observations; his title to fame rests in the thought he gave to scientific problems and the serious attempt he made both to perceive the purpose science should serve and to work out the relationships between the sciences and their relationship as a whole to moral philosophy or ethics; and in his correct understanding of the place experiments should fill in the study of science.

Unfortunately it is difficult to overlook the manifest contradictions in his work, and his thoroughly reactionary attitude toward authority, which was already outmoded in the scholarly world of the thirteenth century. For Bacon did not believe that man finds out knowledge for himself. Over and over again he repeats that science is revealed by God. It was revealed fully to the "sons of Seth" (Seth was the son of Adam) by God, and then again to Solomon. It was not simply some parts of science that were revealed; the whole had been revealed, that universal science which Bacon was himself seeking so ardently. The Greeks had been able to touch some of this wisdom by their contacts with the ancient Hebrews by whom it had been preserved. Plato had access to it, and also Aristotle. Aristotle, by virtue of his character and his saintly life, had had universal science revealed in part to him, and in part he had gained it from the descendants of Solomon. Avicenna, among the Muslims, had received some of it. Bacon therefore considered that the proper task for a scientist in his age was to find out exactly what

Aristotle had said; but what made him really furious with disappointment was that no one now knew just what Aristotle had said. The translations were execrable. The men who had translated him either did not know Greek properly, or did not know Arabic, or did not know Latin. So there was only one thing to do and Bacon did it. He studied Greek and Hebrew (even writing grammars in these languages) to get at the truth of what Aristotle and the ancient writers of the Old Testament had said. There is one passage in Albert which almost certainly refers to Bacon, where he speaks of the fact that even poor translations will give the sense of what Aristotle had said, unless, of course, we think Aristotle was a god and could not make mistakes. But we, for our part, Albert concludes, think Aristotle was a man and could make mistakes as easily as you or I. Because of Bacon's obsession, much of his writing, even when addressed to the pope, is concerned with the errors in translations of Aristotle, urging his patron to subsidize new and better ones; but all for the sad reason that Aristotle had known much revealed truth, and his precious words had been lost or mangled.

Much of Bacon's work is propaganda on behalf of Muslim scientists, who, according to him, are seriously neglected, and could be used by Christians to great advantage if anyone were competent to read them, and if they had been better translated. He urges especially that mathematics should be studied more, as the key to so many other sciences. Astrology, he thinks, is the most practical of sciences, and hardly understood, according to Bacon, at all in the West. It is necessary for medicine, and it would be helpful to kings. But—and here is where Bacon's good scientific sense escapes from his theories—none of what has been given by revelation to Solomon, Aristotle, and the rest, should be taken simply on trust. Nor should anyone believe in astrology from a sole desire to believe. These sciences should be tested thoroughly by planned experiments. In his *Opus Majus* he devotes a whole book to what he calls the science of experi-

ence (*scientia experimentalis*), a term he appears to have picked up from Ptolemy. This, the supreme science (he regards it as a separate science of its own), must be used for proving the theories which derive from the theoretical sciences including the data of revelation, and, of course, mathematics in all its branches. The combination of theory and experience can alone give certitude, and allow the mind to rest in the assurance that it has found truth. And, in turn, the experience itself serves also to confirm the original hypothesis.

It was this last feature that was of especial interest to Bacon. He was a thoroughly religious man, steeped in the Scriptures (and disliking intensely theological studies based on Peter Lombard), and anxious to do all he could to save souls. He believed that successful experiments which went far to prove the truths of Christian revelation might convince even Muslims and heathen, as successful experiments based on astrology or alchemy would serve to show that these sciences were trustworthy and accurate. But above all he insisted, and this is something of which in our atomic age we are sometimes in need of being reminded, that all science must serve a moral purpose. The sciences are indeed related in a kind of hierarchy, with moral philosophy at the summit. The mathematical and observational sciences, according to Bacon, must supply data for the engineer and technologist; but they in turn must consult the moral philosopher to discover if the purpose they are to serve is ethical. Moreover, the special separate sciences must also supply information to each other, making necessary the services of synthesists, who will coordinate the work in these different fields—undoubtedly a desirable plan today, even though extremely difficult in our era of specialization to put into practice.

Bacon, it is clear, had originally thought of himself as occupying the position of chief synthesist; but even he, as he completed his work for the pope and composed his prefatory letter, realized that his ambition was an impossible dream. He would never know enough, and no one ever could know enough again. So he suggests that the pope gather together specialists in every field and encourage them to work with each other. And he outlines the specialties which must be represented, and explains the kind of cooperative outline of scientific knowledge they should try to produce to direct men's attention to the possibilities of science.

Unfortunately, though Bacon's work certainly reached the pope, there is no evidence that Clement ever read it, and he died the following year. Bacon only once briefly referred to his dispatch of these works, but he said nothing of their reception, and it is certain that nothing came of his suggestions. If he was not as consistently scientific in spirit as Albert, if his criticism ran to personalities rather than taking its proper place in the field of ideas, and if he was too anxious to believe to be adequately skeptical where skepticism would have been a virtue, yet for his outstanding insights he deserves an honored place in the history of science, and an especially honored place when one considers the mediocrity in scientific understanding shown by almost all his contemporaries.

A third figure requires more than a passing mention, the great emperor, Frederic II (1197–1250), who has already been dealt with in some detail in an earlier chapter. He is worthy of consideration in this chapter more for his attitude than for his actual accomplishments. Although nearly all the material we have about him comes from his enemies, they frequently referred to his love of experiment and his desire to discover the truth of matters which were usually taken on trust by his contemporaries. He is said to have weighed a dying man before and after his death, to see if there was any change in weight and therefore whether the escaping soul had any material basis; he repeated an experiment attributed by the Greek Herodotus to the king of Egypt, who wanted to find out what was the first human language, and for the purpose shut up newborn babies away from all sound of human speech to see what words they would first utter. The chronicler tells us that the chil-

dren all died, so the experiment was worthless. Another horrible experiment ascribed to him was the killing of two men, one after exercise and one after rest; their intestines were then examined to see which had digested his food more thoroughly. Moreover, Frederic several times sent out questionnaires to distinguished Muslim philosophers asking them their opinions on many different subjects of philosophical interest; further, he asked his court scientist and astrologer, Michael Scot, to give him detailed information about the planets and whether they possessed any inhabitants, where God lived, and what the saints did in heaven. But, in addition to all this inquiry, Frederic also wrote a book on falconry which is our main source for our knowledge of this sport of which medieval nobles were so passionately fond. The book is far more than a description. Frederic was deeply interested in birds, and he had taken the trouble to bring them at great expense from all parts of the world to compare them and to study both their habits and their bodies. He dissected many, and he takes Aristotle to task for several false observations, ridiculing also Aristotle's love of inserting moral rather than physical truths into his work. Aristotle, for instance, according to Frederic, stated that all birds that fly well walk badly and vice versa, this being a pleasantly moral compensation. But Frederic dryly remarks that a crane both flies and walks badly. Elsewhere he makes the equally dry observation that he has not followed Aristotle when he deals with falcons, for "Aristotle seldom or never hunted with birds." Anything more incongruous than the idea of the severe scientist and philosopher Aristotle hunting with falcons, even "seldom," can hardly be imagined!

FOURTEENTH-CENTURY SCIENTISTS—
JEAN BURIDAN, NICHOLAS OF ORESME

There are more scientific names in the fourteenth century even than in the thirteenth, though few of outstanding importance. But at the University of Paris, perhaps under the influence of the nominalists, prolonged attention was paid to a serious problem which arose out of the new use of gunpowder and projectiles. Aristotle's theory of motion was soon seen to be unsatisfactory, and could not adequately explain why a projectile fired from a gun should move at a higher speed when fired than after a few seconds, nor why it should describe a parabola when falling to the earth. A scientist named Jean Buridan suggested the idea of "impetus," a step in the right direction, though the problem was not solved till Galileo solved it by a combination of theory and experiment with inclined planes. Nicholas of Oresme, a bishop, began to question the theory of the movement of the sun around the earth, accepted by nearly all medievals on the authority of the Hellenistic scientist Ptolemy. But, more important, Nicholas liked to use diagrams for the illustration of theological problems. In the process he hit upon the idea of coordinates and curves to show the relation between two variables, thus anticipating by centuries the invention of analytical geometry. At the University of Padua the Averroists, driven forth from Paris at the end of the thirteenth century after the condemnation of their philosophical findings, found a refuge under the protection of Venice. There among much speculation on the immortality of the soul and similar dogmas, they devoted themselves to mathematics, being interested, like the Parisians, especially in the study of acceleration. It was probably at Padua that the first serious work was done in the use of the Arabic numerals, which had been introduced to the West as early as 1202 by Leonardo of Pisa, but had not at first attracted much attention. It was the work done at Padua over several centuries that prepared the ground for the great advances of Galileo which ushered in the age of modern science.

## ► Education in the Middle Ages

### THE UNIVERSITY OF PARIS

#### Organization

We have already dealt with elementary education as it existed under the Carolingians, and we have seen how a great teacher like Abélard might attract thousands of students to his lectures, in spite of the fact that there was no organized instruction and there were no facilities for lectures beyond those rather simple ones offered by the cathedral schools. In Paris, where Abélard had taught, the cathedral school was an important center of learning, and a considerable number of students attended for varying periods during the twelfth century according to the fare offered by the masters. Many of these students were very young, and required some discipline, but there was no effective centrally organized administrative body capable of managing the considerable numbers of students who wished to receive instruction. They spilled over into the city far beyond the immediate confines of the cathedral school of Notre Dame, and had many altercations with the townsmen, who resented the presence of so many foreigners, most of whom, in their view, were unruly, yet who claimed protection by their clerical status from secular interference. After a more serious fracas than usual, the French king, Philip Augustus, in 1200 gave formal recognition to the school as a *studium generale* or university, with certain specified rights of self-government, and official clerical status immune from all but ecclesiastical courts for the entire student body.

The university offered courses in theology, medicine, and civil law at the advanced level, and at the more elementary level, courses in the trivium and the quadrivium, or the seven liberal arts. There was now a recognized faculty for each of these groups of studies. The Faculty of Arts was by far the largest, since many students never progressed beyond the degree of master of arts, which was a prerequisite for all higher degrees. The masters in this faculty were divided according to the country from which they hailed, resulting in four "nations," the French (including Italians and Spanish), the Normans, the Picards (from Flanders and the Netherlands), and the English, (including Germans and other Germanic peoples). These nations united in electing a Rector of the Faculty of Arts who was the virtual governor of the university, although the title officially belonged to the Bishop of Paris, who rarely troubled to exercise his authority. The teaching masters were in general responsible for the organization and discipline of the university.

### Curriculum

It has already been explained that medieval education was always formally concerned with only the seven liberal arts, although in earlier times the instruction in the quadrivium was extremely sketchy. This changed with the gradual progress of the study of logic in the twelfth century, and with the recovery of the works of Aristotle and the Muslims. So many new subjects now became available that it was difficult to fit them into the famous and immutable seven, and there was a demand for almost all the new subjects, which the Faculty of Arts was anxious to fulfill. The textbooks were greatly improved, especially in the field of logic, where the advanced works of Aristotle made up a very respectable collection. There was a considerable effort also to study language at a profounder level, and especially one John of Garland in the early thirteenth century wrote several important textbooks on the subject. Aristotle's *Ethics* was squeezed into rhetoric, completing the trivium. Euclid was recovered from the Muslims, greatly improving the study of geometry, which to the trained logical mind of the medieval student presented no further difficulties. Muslim works on trigonometry were soon added. Ptolemy's *Almagest,* in which the great astronomer expounded his geocentric views of the universe, found a natural place under astronomy, together with Muslim works in the same field and Aristotle's discussion of the heavens. But arithmetic still seems to have been neglected, and for centuries little use was made of the Arabic numerals. This still left the vast bulk of the natural scientific work of Aristotle with no official place in the curriculum, even after the ban had ceased to be observed. Yet the works of Aristotle on *Physics,* on *Metaphysics,* and *On the Soul* and his work on coming into being and decaying ( *De generatione et corruptione* ) were undoubtedly lectured

on, as was also a work on plants by one of his pupils. It is still not known how this bulging curriculum was classified and how it managed to fit into the seven liberal arts, but at all events lectures were given on all these subjects. As will be noticed, the emphasis is still strongly on mental training, and indeed the works of Aristotle are all discussed by the masters in a logical manner, and seldom is there any reference to actual experience by any of them whose work we possess.

The student might go to the university as early as the age of thirteen; if he went at this age he would probably have to study for eight years in the Faculty of Arts, obtaining at the end a master's degree and the right to teach in Paris or in a similar Faculty of Arts. About halfway through his career in this faculty he would receive a bachelor's degree, but this was of little value, and conferred no privileges. At Paris the study which offered the greatest prestige was the study of theology, but the period required for study was extremely long and the courses were arduous. Though there was a minimum of eight years, this was in fact seldom permitted and it became customary to insist on fourteen. And no master of theology could in any case teach theology before the age of thirty-five. As explained earlier, much of a student's theological study consisted in mastering the *Book of Sentences* and in learning how to handle theological problems in the same manner as Peter Lombard. Public disputes were frequent, especially when the student had become a Bachelor of Sentences part way through his career. He would probably have gained a reputation as a disputer long before he came to his final examination in defence of his dissertation. Naturally such a long grind took its toll of casualties. There were never very many masters of theology, and the names of most of them for the thirteenth and fourteenth centuries are known to us.

The other faculties were not held in such high esteem, though in the late medieval period it was probably more profitable, from a worldly point of view, to graduate in civil law, which required only three or four years. Medicine also took about the same time. But Paris was not especially famous for either of these subjects—Bologna was the real center of legal studies, and Montpellier or Salerno for medicine—and as theology was the queen of sciences for the medieval student, and Parisian masters were incomparably greater than those to be found elsewhere, the university in the thirteenth and fourteenth centuries always found enough students, and always maintained its position as the real center of education in Europe.

## Student life

The medieval student was not a meek citizen, in spite of his tonsure and his clerical status. He was quarrelsome and did not submit to discipline readily, at least according to contemporary preachers; he was drunken, violent, and decidedly unchaste. He frequented taverns, sang songs of a lewd variety, and composed and recited poems, usually on immoral themes. But preachers do not perhaps offer the best evidence about the lives of the ordinary students, for then, as now, they could make better sermons when there was some sin to be castigated. Perhaps it would be better to listen to Chaucer, whose Clerk of Oxenford was a good student, living quietly, poor, but spending any money he could obtain on books. Probably, then, as now, the student body was mixed. The noisy ones drew attention to themselves and were more noticeable, while the quiet ones stuck to their textbooks, prepared their work, and passed all their exams, and no one but their friends knew them.

In early times there were no buildings to house the students, and few facilities even for lectures. The professors used whatever buildings were available, usually bare church buildings; and sometimes they had to hire halls themselves at their own expense. With luck they might have a desk or a podium; the students had none, and customarily sat on the floor. Books were scarce before the invention of printing and few students possessed them. The master, however, read from his own text slowly, and then commented on it. Paper was also not available in the thirteenth century, and parchment was very expensive. The students as a rule took down what they could on wax tablets, and compared notes afterward with their fellows. They disputed incessantly on the meaning of what the master had said and frequently violently disagreed with him. But the time would come, in all probability, when the master would be expected to give a public disputation, and the opportunity for questioning him directly would not be missed. In some of the extant books of *Questions* published by the various masters, it seems likely that actual students were participating in the discussion, since the objections are such as have always been made by students. It is possible that the masters thought all the objections up themselves, but to the modern reader the masters certainly appear to have had considerable "cooperation" from their students.

UNIVERSITY OF BOLOGNA

## Purpose of the university—The study of Roman law

In the late eleventh century, soon after the conquest of Sicily by the Normans, the law code of Justinian was recovered and brought out of the oblivion in which it had rested since the Muslim conquest of the island. This code, which has been described in an earlier chapter, came into the hands of one Irnerius, apparently already a student of law but ignorant of any of the details of the Roman codes. In the Italy of his day there were only the Lombard Code and remnants of the earlier Roman practice; but there could be no systematic study of law until its logical basis had been grasped. Until that time there were only laws, not law. It is clear that Roman law, as applicable to the late Roman or Byzantine Empires, could have little relevance to conditions in Italy in the eleventh century; indeed, even the canon law of the Church, originally Roman, had necessarily been modified over the centuries. However, the fact that Roman law was not at once relevant to eleventh-century conditions did not mean that its ancient logical principles no longer applied. To be sure, these principles must be modified to fit the actual circumstances of the day, but there would always remain the permanent and unchanging principles of jurisprudence, which had been discovered by the Romans and written down in accordance with the best thinking of which a whole line of distinguished jurists and philosophers were capable. Indeed this law, if used widely in Europe, would have a noticeably civilizing effect on the German barbarians, and perhaps be able to wean them from their barbarous methods of determining and executing justice and disposing of property.

### Organization of the university— Control by students

Some such thoughts must have been in the mind of Irnerius when he undertook his epoch-making work. The procedure used by him and his successors was to write notes and commentaries on the text of the code, called glosses, suggestions as to how to modify the Roman laws to fit the new circumstances. He began to teach law in the northern Italian city of Bologna, and quickly gathered around him an earnest and enthusiastic group of students, the best of whom became in their turn teachers and writers of glosses. From the beginning it seems that the students were the real controllers of this school at Bologna, hiring and paying the teachers, fining them if they were late, insisting on full value for their money. The students, however, were not young boys as at Paris, but mature men who needed instruction, and were prepared to pay for it, but not willing to tolerate any laxity on the part of their professors. The latter, to protect themselves from their overzealous students, likewise organized themselves into a kind of guild of masters, and, merging with the guild of students who had drawn up their rules for the proper behavior of professors, formed a regular university in the early twelfth century. Both canon and

civil law were studied, and the same method was used for each. In the middle of the twelfth century a monk named Gratian codified the canon law, and about a century later several glossators codified the glosses from the greatest of the legal masters since the time of Irnerius, under the leadership of one Accursius. But new glosses in the civil law continued to be made whenever especially gifted teachers appeared.

### Diffusion of Roman law

From Bologna masters went throughout Europe organizing Faculties of Civil Law in most of the universities, and as the demand for trained lawyers grew, so ever more students began to study, for the most part not clerics at the time of their study though many later attained high office in the Church. Few popes in the thirteenth or fourteenth centuries had failed to study at least canon law, and the majority of them, at least in the thirteenth century, at Bologna. We have seen how Philip IV of France used a corps of trained lawyers as a means of aiding in his establishment of absolute government and the complete unification of his country. Most kings chose their officials from among trained lawyers, and, with some exceptions, used the logical and equitable Roman law as a means of breaking down the old feudal courts and the feudal system which they upheld. Roman law presupposed an absolute ruler, and the famous Roman dictum that "what pleases the emperor has the force of law" was entirely acceptable to monarchs trying to establish their right to legislate. It was no accident that of the European countries only in England was there serious opposition to it, and the kings who tried to introduce it were forced to abandon the attempt. For, excellent though Roman law might be for absolute kings, it remained the greatest obstacle to parliamentary institutions. The papacy, however, did not approve of its use by monarchs, since it was implicit in Roman law that the ruler owed obedience to no one on earth; indeed, on several occasions the papacy forbade its study. It was no answer to say

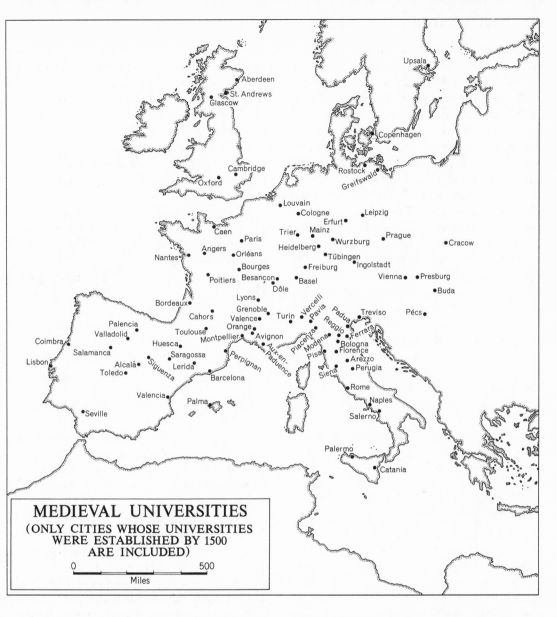

## MEDIEVAL UNIVERSITIES
### (ONLY CITIES WHOSE UNIVERSITIES WERE ESTABLISHED BY 1500 ARE INCLUDED)

0            500
Miles

that the Church itself used it, for the pope did not regard himself as a monarch, and was, in his own view, really supreme on earth. So Roman law continued to flourish, even while earnest theologians were trying to claim, with the English Parliament, that sovereignty resided in the people and not in the monarch.

Although detailed attention has been given here only to the universities of Paris and Bologna, the founding of new universities was continued during the entire medieval period and into modern times. Some idea of the extent of medieval foundations will be gained from a study of the map above. The majority of these universities were organized according to the Parisian model, including the ancient English universities of Oxford and Cambridge.

## ▶ Medieval art

ARCHITECTURE

### Church building, characteristic art of the Middle Ages

Until the late medieval period there was no secular art at all, and all the very considerable artistic achievements of medieval people were in some way connected with their religion. This does not mean that the medieval artist was prevented from exercising his natural gifts freely because the building of churches was almost the sole opportunity for their exercise; on the contrary, the building of churches supplied him with almost unlimited opportunity, especially in sculpture, which was not forbidden by the Christians as it had been by Jews and Muslims. The figures of saints had to follow an approved and customary style, but within this convention it was possible to give life and character to the figures. It was possible to decorate capitals and pillars with scenes from nature, closely observed and accurately rendered, as in the famous "vintage" capitals of the cathedral of Rheims, and in the Romanesque capitals of St. Trophime of Arles shown in the illustration. But in general it must be admitted that the art par excellence of the medievals was church building, and that architecture overshadows all other medieval artistic achievements, although the development of church music runs it a close second.

### The development of Romanesque from Roman antecedents

In the Dark Ages there was very little building beyond the mere provision of places of worship. The Germanic peoples had had no experience in building such edifices as churches, and skill and materials were lacking. Such building as there was consisted for the most part of wooden churches, easily destroyed by fire, and later churches built of stone, but with wooden roofs, also easily destroyed by fire, as the Vikings proved. The plan of all medieval churches in early times was derived from the Roman basilica or meeting place, modified to meet the needs of worshipers in a Christian church. The general plan was to have three aisles, the center aisle called the nave, separated from each other by arcades of arches, capitals, and columns. The walls were solid, and light was provided only by small windows set in a clerestory above the nave. At the end of the nave, where the Romans had usually built a semicircular apse in which the presiding officer had his seat, the Christians placed their altar. The apse by religious custom faced the East. In time it became necessary to enlarge this apse in order to contain the choir, and transepts were added by the side of the aisles, bringing the whole church into the form of a Latin cross.

The great difficulty to be overcome, as has been suggested, was the danger of fire on account of the wooden roof. The Romans, however, had not been content with wooden roofs but built them of stone and concrete. The early medievals knew that the Romans had used vaults of different kinds for their roofs, but for many centuries the Christians were unable to build vaults in such a way that the walls were strong enough to hold them. The thrust and weight of the Roman vaults necessitated very strong walls, and if the walls were very massive then it was dangerous to pierce them for windows. We know of many early medieval buildings which indeed did collapse while the architects experimented with different kinds of vaults. Cross vaults were used for the smaller areas to be roofed, while the nave itself had to be roofed, as a rule, with a massive barrel vault. But this doomed the church to shortage of light and only the smallest of windows, owing to the great weight of the roof. In some of the earlier Romanesque churches which had wooden roofs this problem did not arise in such an acute form, and the characteristic gloom of the Romanesque, which some find impressive, was avoided. Moreover, the height of the church was severely limited again by the weight to be supported.

This Romanesque style was capable of modification, therefore, but only within certain well-defined limits. Many of the problems were indeed solved, especially by the Norman builders of the eleventh century, but certain fundamental changes were necessary if a church was to be able to soar to heaven, and be filled with light, as the builders themselves would have wished. It should be emphasized that such changes as

ABOVE

*Very early sculptured figure of Christ at Santillana del Mar (Spain).*

UPPER RIGHT

*Sculptured stone image of St. James the apostle in the cathedral at Santiago de Compostela (Spain, twelfth century), where St. James's bones are said to have been brought after his martyrdom at the hands of Herod Antipas. The city is now a place of pilgrimage, especially in the years when the feast of St. James (July 25) falls on a Sunday.*

LOWER RIGHT

*Details from the Portico de la Gloria in the cathedral of St. James at Compostela. Note the rounded Romanesque style arch.*

UPPER LEFT

*The Virgin of Notre Dame de Paris (thirteenth-century Gothic).*

ABOVE

*Detail of the portal of Notre Dame de Paris.*

LEFT

*Figures of saints from the Royal Portal of the Cathedral of Chartres (thirteenth-century Gothic).*

*Early Romanesque interior at Santillana del Mar (Spain), with decorated Romanesque capitals.*

*The cathedral and the leaning tower of Pisa. The church is built in the style of the old Roman basilica.*

*Exterior of the Romanesque cathedral of St. Sernin at Toulouse. Note the heavy construction of the Romanesque used before the Gothic pointed arch had been invented to take the stress of the masonry.*

*Interior of Toulouse cathedral. Note the relative absence of light, and the rounded Romanesque arches.*

*Decorated sculptured capitals of Romanesque arches at St. Trophime of Arles.*

*This picture shows the transition between the Romanesque and the Gothic. On the right are Gothic pointed arches, on the left Romanesque (cloister of St. Trophime, Arles).*

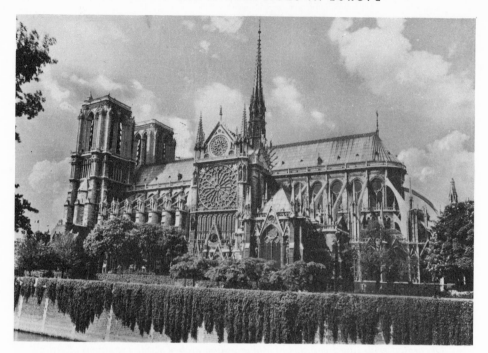

*Exterior of the Gothic cathedral of Notre Dame de Paris. Note the flying buttresses which distribute the weight of the roof, enabling the building to have many windows. The Gothic framework is little but a stone skeleton.*

*Interior of Notre Dame de Paris. Note the pointed arches and the abundance of light in contrast with St. Sernin at Toulouse.*

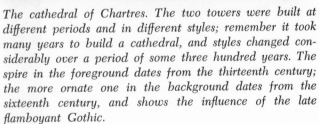

*The cathedral of Chartres. The two towers were built at different periods and in different styles; remember it took many years to build a cathedral, and styles changed considerably over a period of some three hundred years. The spire in the foreground dates from the thirteenth century; the more ornate one in the background dates from the sixteenth century, and shows the influence of the late flamboyant Gothic.*

*The Virgin of Chartres.*

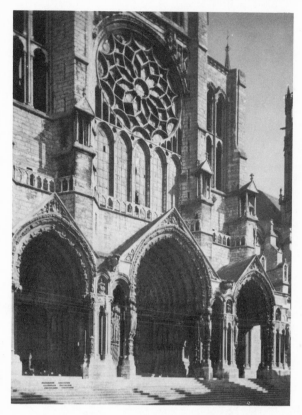

*North façade of Chartres cathedral. The famous rose window is above this portal.*

was the same religious enthusiasm that was responsible for the success of the First Crusade.

### The Gothic style—Pointed arches and flying buttresses

The Gothic style, which solved the outstanding problems of the Romanesque, was developed almost entirely in northern France, though spreading into Germany and elsewhere afterward. The use of the pointed arch, which distributes the weight differently from the rounded arch and the vault, was the key to the new style. It was soon discovered that an entirely different sys-

*The north rose window of Chartres cathedral. Many of the Chartres windows were contributed by the various guilds of the city, and some of them depict the mundane occupations of the contributors. A black-and-white picture does not do justice to these windows; imagine sunlight shining through them, bringing out all the brilliant coloring of the glass. Unfortunately, the secret of the medieval processing of the glass has been lost.*

took place were figured out by the architects and craftsmen actually on the job. It was impossible in medieval times to work out in advance, as do modern architects, the theoretical stresses to which the various parts of the building would be submitted, and there was much trial and error before the immense difficulties were overcome.

But there was an enormous demand for churches. Every bishop desired to have a great church in his diocese, and an enthusiasm and local patriotism amounting almost to a mania set in during the eleventh and twelfth centuries. The buildings were nearly always raised by cooperative labor, in which every person in the area joined, some yoking themselves to the cart which carried the materials needed for the church and pulling it, while priests chanted and prayed. Throughout the day psalms and canticles were sung, relics of the saints were brought along, and miracles were hourly expected. It

*Gothic cathedral of Rheims, before the World War I bombardment destroyed much of the building.* (COURTESY FRENCH GOVERNMENT TOURIST OFFICE)

tem of ribbing and support was possible with the pointed arch, which took the weight off the walls and gave the builder freedom to alter the shape of his church as required. The developed Gothic church is nothing but a gigantic skeleton of wall buttresses within the church, flying buttresses outside it, piers and ribbing, all in perfect equilibrium; the walls themselves now cease to be of importance and can be made even of glass. And the best Gothic churches are indeed full of glass, stained glass colored and painted to show whatever scenes the artist wished. And usually over the portal was the great rose window, which was so designed that it lighted the church in a different way at the different hours of the day. Early stained glass was always in solid colors, set into lead frames as a kind of mosaic, with figures suggested by these frames and small, lightly penciled touches. Medieval stained glass was one of the age's greatest achievements, and has never been equaled, even in modern times, with all the advantages of modern technical inventions.

The Gothic church, with its soaring arches aspiring toward heaven, has often been compared with the logical structure of the great medieval *Summae*, those works in which medieval theologians attempted to set forth the whole plan of salvation, tied together by the Aristotelian syllogism; and the comparison is not inept, for the Gothic structures are faultlessly worked out, with perfect balance, each part dependent upon the other, and, in the best examples, free of any unnecessary decoration or striving for effect. The façades of the cathedrals could be and were decorated, and it was here that the sculptor was given a chance to display his mastery, especially in and over the portals, where saints, devils, plants, and animals real and mythological could be shown, and even the Last Judgment. Inside the cathedrals, especially in the wonderful Cathedral of Chartres, the artist was free to fill the windows with scenes from the Old and New Testaments and stories from the lives of saints, with delicate pencil work touching up the solid-colored panes of glass. Even scenes of everyday life are depicted in these windows, scenes often provided by the particular guild represented. The last details of the work, whether inside and visible, or high

*Gothic cathedral of Amiens, which gives a good impression of the way in which a medieval cathedral—even if it commanded no outstanding physical site—stood out above all the buildings around it.* (COURTESY FRENCH GOVERNMENT TOURIST OFFICE)

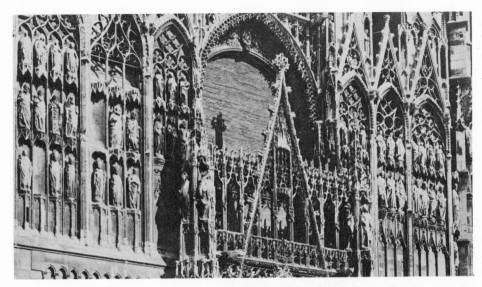

*West façade of Rouen Cathedral (fifteenth century). Note the tendency to overelaborate characteristics of the flamboyant Gothic of this period.*

*Fan vaulting in the King Henry VII chapel at Westminster (1503).*

up on the towers where no man could see them once they had been set in position, were almost invariably beautifully and honestly wrought. The medieval craftsman, like the Greek craftsman of the time of Phidias, would not have tolerated anything less than the best he could give in the service of his religion and art.

In a book of this kind it is not worth while to attempt the description of these Gothic masterpieces, since the bare words will do no justice to them, and mean little to those who have not viewed them. The accompanying pictures are inadequate, but they may suggest what the written word cannot, and the special features of the style can be picked out with the aid of the brief remarks printed under each picture. There is no perfect cathedral. Some cathedrals have features that seem to approach perfection, as the fan vaulting in Westminster Abbey, the façade and *chevet* of Notre Dame of Paris, the structural design of Amiens, the incomparable majesty of the site of Rheims, and the interior of Chartres. But in every cathedral there are some dissident elements, the necessary consequence of the long time consumed in the building. The building of a cathedral might take fifty years. Yet the style was living, always growing and evolving, so that the builders who completed the edifice would be working in a different manner from their predecessors when the work was first put in hand. The most familiar of these discords is the pair of spires at Chartres, constructed nearly four centuries apart in time. The twelfth-century spire is simple and chaste, while the sixteenth-century one, a few feet higher, is elaborate and ornate, constructed at a time when Gothic was past its best, and structural simplicity had to some degree been sacrificed to exuberance of decoration—a tendency we have already noted in contrasting Hellenic and Hellenistic art in an earlier chapter.

The Gothic style continues to be a matter of delight and wonder to the modern architect who marvels at the authority which the medieval architect was able to wield over his whole building, subordinating all decoration to the needs of the architecture itself, and who is constantly astonished at what his medieval forebears were able to accomplish with primitive tools, working in stone and with none of the aids he now considers essential, to say nothing of the new materials available in the twentieth century. The artist appreciates the absolute integrity of his medieval ancestor, the truth that he built into his works of stone, and the consummate skill with which he used what was available to him to create beauty, especially in the use of the natural light of the day to shed color and light over the whole interior of the cathedral through the medium of his stained glass windows. Even the modern religious skeptic is made to pause before this revelation in form of a faith that was as fully experienced by the medieval artist as it is alien to himself.

For medieval Gothic really is an expression, caught once and for all time, of a compelling vision whose essence is religious. The purpose of man's life on earth was to aspire toward Heaven. For a brief period medieval man really believed this. Man was a child of God, placed on earth in a particular position of honor or servitude which was none of his fault but merely God's will. He was taught not to envy the great man but to accept his lot, whatever it might be, knowing that after death he and the great man would be equal in the eyes of God and man. Only in the house of God on earth could he know himself as an equal. In the cathedral there was a place for him as there was a place, though a different one, for the noble and the bishop. Together they made up humanity as God had ordained it, and together their souls were lifted up toward the unseen God above. This was the symbolism of the Gothic, the ribs and the vaults and the pointed arches that gave the illusion of height and aspiration toward the great world above where saints and sinners, nobles and serfs, were together before the judgment seat of God, saved through the blood of Christ.

When for the first time in the twelfth and thirteenth centuries it was possible for the medieval man to gain a tiny surplus over and above his daily needs, a surplus of either goods or leisure, the first task, the very first task, that he set himself was the building of a church or cathedral. As the Egyptians in the early part of their civilization built pyramids for the ascent of their king-god to heaven, as the Greeks in the halcyon early days of Pericles built their temples for the gods to live in and protect them by their presence, so the men of the Middle Ages in the springtime of their religious fervor built a cathedral, not for their God to live in, for he was in Heaven, but for a place of assembly for themselves, the congregation of the faithful to worship their God and soar upward in their souls toward him.

It was no wonder that the ages of skeptical "enlightenment" that followed the great age of church building termed the architecture of medieval man Gothic, or barbarian. The vision was too great for them to comprehend. They pretended to feel at home with the classic and the simple, the art forms of this world, not the aspiration toward Heaven and the striving toward infinity that had been the glory of their rude ancestors. Not until the nineteenth century was the supreme achievement of medieval man appreciated; and now we can only visit and wonder, trying to encompass in our imagination what it was that this strange semibarbarian felt in his inner world that could drive him to such a frenzy of creation, to so many hundreds, even thousands, of magnificent buildings, while he lived his ordinary life in unrelieved squalor. The bishop who commanded the task was moved by rivalry with his fellow bishops, the bourgeois who paid out the small profits of his business was moved perhaps by civic pride. But what of the poor unnamed worker, he who dragged the cart, who climbed the scaffolding, who had nothing but his labor to give, for him did the task only represent a day's wage on a public works project? It is hard to think so. And it is certain that there will be no more Gothic cathedrals, that our poor imitations are at once seen as frauds—for even the ignoramus in all matters of art feels no doubt when he comes to distinguish the genuine Gothic from the spurious.

The church we build today is the expression of ourselves. It may have admirable qualities, but it is not an expression of that compelling religious emotion, disciplined by a clear and logical mind, that came to maturity in the twelfth and thirteenth centuries of our era and found its architectural expression in the Gothic cathedral and its literary masterpiece in the *Divine Comedy* of Dante. As the Egyptians after the Old Kingdom built no more pyramids, save a few shoddy efforts by imperial imitators, so shall we build no more cathedrals. But for a few more years we may still hope to see those built by our ancestors, and, seeing them, pause for a few moments in respect for a vision we have lost.

## MUSIC

As the great medieval cathedral is not truly itself without the throng of worshipers within, as it is filled with light of many colors streaming through the incomparable stained glass, so also is it only to be recognized truly when filled with song. And of course it is no accident that medieval music, which spread from the cathedral and church into the outer world and ultimately gave birth to the secular instrumental music of our own day, was developed to its fullest within these cathedrals, especially in Notre Dame of Paris, which was famed in medieval times for the excellence of its music. And it is also no accident that the music thus developed fitted in perfectly with the architecture of the buildings themselves.

The voice is the first great musical instrument, and it was the use of the human voice in medieval services of worship that gave birth to the great advance of music in all its forms during the medieval age. Very early in the Middle Ages the voice was used to chant the words of the Latin Liturgy in unison, or what was called *plain song*. In plain song all the voices followed the melody without variation except according to the pitch of the voice, at intervals of a full octave. This Gregorian chant, so called after Pope Gregory I the Great, is still used in church worship, and never died out in spite of the many other forms of song that now supplement it. But by the ninth century other intervals than the octave were used, and the enormous possibilities inherent in these variations were increasingly realized in subsequent centuries. While one voice held the melody, another sang the same melody but at an interval of one fifth (beginnings of polyphony or many sounds). Then other intervals were also found to add beauty and fullness to the total sound, and other altogether different melodies were made to interweave with the whole (the interweaving, note by note, of separate melodies with the basic one was called *counterpoint*). Finally, with the motet, even different words were sung at the same time as the basic melody, which was carried by one of the parts (hence the word "tenor," the "holder" of the melody). Naturally during the process of development, which occupied several centuries, a musical notation had to be adopted which was conventionalized into substantially the same notation that we use today.

The organ, which had originally been invented by the Greeks, and had been developed in the Byzantine Empire, was still rather a primitive instrument when introduced into the West in the ninth century, but it was continually developed into the complex instrument that it was by the end of the fourteenth century. The late medieval organ was able to perform the same kind of interweaving of sound that the human voices had already been trained to make; and ultimately in later centuries of the modern era the various instruments likewise interweave to make the whole which we call the symphony (literally, "coordinated" sound as distinct from merely many sounds, *poly*phony).

In the later days of the medieval period, as the severe Gothic became the overdecorated Gothic, with the decoration in part obscuring the basic design, so did the variations in the musical composition tend to hide the basic melody, thus obscuring the original purpose of setting the words of the Liturgy themselves to music. Cleverness and dexterity became ends in themselves to such an extent that at the time of the Catholic Reformation in the sixteenth century efforts were made to return altogether to the original simple plain song. Here the work, especially of Palestrina, whose period lies outside the scope of this book, was crucial. He was a church composer of such excellence that his partial reform was acceptable even to the conservatives. Without returning to the simple plain song of earlier centuries he was nevertheless able in his work to set the Liturgy in its true place by restoring some much-needed simplicity, firmly placing

church music on the path which it has followed in all essentials since his time.

Secular music was greatly affected by music of the church, although other influences from the Muslim world also contributed to it. Wandering musicians, the troubadours, trouvères (northern France), and jongleurs accompanied their poetry with music, played on the harp, viol, lute, guitar, and similar instruments. Minnesingers in Germany sang their love poems to the accompaniment of their instruments. Probably these singers were little affected by the music of the churches. But popular music such as part songs and rounds were clearly influenced by the development of polyphony in the churches. Each voice took a different part, sometimes different words, sometimes the same words at different times as in such well-known rounds as Three Blind Mice and Frère Jacques. Perhaps the most complex development of part singing was the madrigal, an Italian innovation of the fourteenth century which needed the cooperation of the poets, who made the complex words fit in with each other, and the musician, who set it polyphonically in accordance with the rules of counterpoint. In Germany the artisans formed what today would be called glee clubs, which were often organized by the members of a craft guild. These glee clubs had their own guild laws and rules of organization, and their own degrees of excellence, the master being called a "Master Singer." *The Mastersingers of Nuremberg* of Richard Wagner is a faithful reproduction of the atmosphere and workings of one such guild.

► **Medieval literature**

LATIN LITERATURE—HYMNS, POEMS

Such an abundance of medieval literature of all kinds is extant that it is impossible here to do more than merely indicate the types, and to devote a little more space to the few acknowledged masterpieces. As has already been explained in the early part of this chapter, the Latin language as used in medieval times was a living tongue, and its use was not confined to works of erudition, though, because it had to be learned, a modicum of education was needed before it could be used as a suitable vehicle for expression. Medieval Latin went easily into poetry, and rhyming was usual. We have the stately hymns of the medieval church, many of which are still in use, either in Latin or in the vernacular. But we also have great quantities of lighthearted verse, much of it composed by students at the universities, singing cheerfully of love and the springtime and similar subjects. There is also much satire, especially on the manners and customs of the clergy. A whole series of these poems are given the name of Goliardic poems probably from the frequent references to a certain Bishop Golias, a mythical character who was supposed to be the poets' patron.

As the Middle Ages drew on, Latin Literature became more confined to the clergy and educated classes, and was the official medium of communication for those who had to appeal to a wider audience than the inhabitants of any single area in Europe. History, memoirs, philosophy, and religious and scientific work continued to be written, for the most part, in Latin, while each area began to develop literature in the vernacular tongues, the medium of expression in everyday life.

VERNACULAR LITERATURE

### Heroic epic

Most of the great civilizations known to us produced their first literature in the form of heroic epics, sung and recited perhaps for centuries before they were written down. Western civilization was no exception. All the Germanic peoples had their sagas, dating from very ancient times, long before the advent of Christianity. The content of these is pagan, the deeds of pagan warriors and their gods, though sometimes overlaid with Christian feeling of a later age. *Beowulf,* the great Anglo-Saxon poem, is of the former kind; other examples are the Norse and Icelandic sagas. On the other hand, the *Nibelungenlied,* transformed into an operatic cycle by Richard Wagner in the nineteenth century, retains the pagan background, but even in the early Germanic version the ancient warrior ideals have been partly transformed by Christian tradition and chivalry.

### Poetry of feudalism

*Chansons de geste*—This early folk material was succeeded in the eleventh century by at least three distinct types of poetry composed for the entertainment of the feudal nobility, and on subjects of the greatest appeal for them.

The first type is the *chanson de geste,* or tale of heroic deeds, for the most part of northern French origin and headed by a masterpiece, the *Song of Roland,* which concerns the heroic death of Count Roland, one of Charlemagne's knights, at the battle of Roncesvalles against the Muslims. Around the figure of Roland a whole cycle of songs sprang up, even in countries quite unconnected with the hero. The songs also tell of the marvelous deeds of Charlemagne himself, and his other knights. No attempt is made to relate the poems to the actual time of Charlemagne, but all describe the feudal world of the era when they were written and recited.

*The troubadours and the poetry of chivalry and courtesy*—In southern France, probably under Muslim influence, grew up a school of lyric poetry recited and sung by troubadour minstrels in the noble houses and castles of this area. The troubadours introduced the element of love into their songs, rather than simply a recital of heroic deeds. It was under their influence that the cult of romantic love, still with us, first entered the Western world, since the troubadour by convention addressed his songs to the great lady of the castle, whose charms he extolled endlessly, and for whose smile he was willing to endure any torture. The influence of the troubadours spread into Germany, where they were called *minnesingers* (*minne*—love). In the hands especially of Walther von der Vogelweide (1170?–1230?) the romantic theme is handled with great freshness and delicacy as well as with greater depth than is usual in poetry of this type.

*Christian influence—The Arthurian and Grail legends*—The third type of poetry is a combination of the *chanson de geste* with the chivalric romance. Instead of the ordinary feudal world of the warrior, we now find portrayed idealized kings and knights, as in the legends of King Arthur, originally of Celtic origin. These knights often perform deeds of heroism for the sake of fair ladies, rescuing them from enchanted castles and such. This world of perfect chivalry is best described in the poetry of Chrétien de Troyes (last half of the twelfth century).

As time went on, the Arthurian legends became suffused with Christian thought and feeling. The culmination of this process is to be found in the legendary search for the Holy Grail, the vessel in which the blood of Christ was caught, or in another version, the vessel used for the Last Supper, or a magic stone. All were equally a symbol of Christian aspiration. The hero who alone can find the Grail is a Christian, not merely a feudal or chivalric hero, whose purity and chastity rather than his deeds as a warrior bring him to his goal. The *Parzival* of Wolfram von Eschenbach (1170?–1220?) is the most fully Christian account of the wanderings of the hero in search of the Grail, while the culmination of the Arthurian legend is to be found in the prose *Morte d'Arthur* of the Englishman Sir Thomas Malory in the fifteenth century.

It has only been possible to touch upon the varieties of medieval poetry as sung and recited among the nobility, in part for reasons of space limitation, and in part on account of the difficulty of making any adequate generalizations when the total bulk is so large and of such varying quality. At their best the heroic sagas are almost, if not quite, the equal of the sagas of the heroic ages of earlier peoples dealt with in earlier chapters; medieval epic at its worst is feeble and derivative, using stock stories from the decadent periods of Greek and Alexandrine literature. On the other hand, the Arthurian legends are ancient Celtic tales which have certainly been transformed out of all recognition by sophisticated poets of a later age, writing for an aristocratic audience for whom they were quite consciously extolling the cult of chivalry.

The fantastic world they depict was no doubt a welcome escape for their audience from the anarchic feudal world of their day. Yet it bears also a direct relationship to it; it is a less harsh world, a world softened by the application in life of Christian ethical teachings. The poets have a secondary purpose beyond mere entertainment; their poems are truly didactic, not spontaneous and descriptive. The virtues they extol are not the heroic and martial virtues of an Achilles; courtesy and gentleness may be rewarded better than mere valor. In the Grail legends and especially in the poem *Parzival*, this tendency comes to full fruition and is entirely explicit. It is instructive to compare such a poem as *Parzival* with the earlier "wandering" epics of Gilgamesh (see Chapter 4) and the *Odyssey*, and to see revealed one aspect of the medieval mind, and the medieval attitude to life. All these poems reflect the preoccupations of their time, as such poems always must. The Sumerian hero Gilgamesh searches for the plant of immortality, but having found it, he loses it again; the gods are arbitrary and unjust, they cheat mankind, and the hero has no recourse but to plunge himself back into life and build a city. Odysseus is stripped of his possessions and loses his companions in a shipwreck. He learns humility by hard experience, and through this experience he regains his lost rights as a king and vanquishes his enemies.

But Parzival in the poem of Wolfram begins as a fool and an ingrate; he leaves his mother without a thought, and she dies of grief. He kills a knight who turns out to be his kinsman, and is so unskilled he cannot even strip the dead knight of his armor. He reaches early the Grail Castle which he is destined some day to rule, but he does not ask the crucial question which would heal the wounded guardian of the Castle. In his subsequent loneliness and suffering he seems to deny even God. Yet this folly is also simplicity; it is culpable, but it can be redeemed and changed through the growth of wisdom. The poem is the story of how through the help of suffering he at last learns wisdom, and is permitted first to meet and become reconciled to his brother, the Oriental pagan prince Feirefiz, then finally to find again the Grail Castle with the help of sages who give him advice and warning. This time he asks the right question and achieves the Grail.

The poem does not seem to be allegorical in essence; it is not a *summa* of salvation like the *Divine Comedy* of Dante, to be described later. The Church plays almost no part in it. It seems to be the pursuit of the Christian ideal through life experience rather than through the mediation of the Church, and in this aspect it is significant. Parzival as a Christian prince is pursuing a Christian ideal. It is not his valor that triumphs. His first victory is not gained through valor, but through foolhardiness and good fortune, and he is defeated in combat by the heathen Feirefiz, who spares his life after Parzival's magical sword has broken. It is the sword of his kinsman whom he killed so wantonly in his youth. In the end it is the purity and simplicity of his human heart and his ability to learn wisdom that make him worthy of the Grail. The wisdom he has learned and the reconciliation with, and ultimate conversion of, his heathen brother lead him to his goal. Thus this German poem already looks forward to a later age of religious thought than Dante's masterpiece, although it was written almost a century earlier; and it was no doubt this element in the poem that made such an appeal to Richard Wagner. Though medieval in setting, *Parzival* transcends the medieval thought of the age when it was written. In the homelessness and loneliness and individual suffering of its hero it seems to picture in advance the modern man, a prototype of Faust rather than of the medieval man who

was led by Vergil and Beatrice on a spiritual journey to the contemplation of God.

## Literature of the towns

*The fabliaux and their successors—* When we enter the world of the growing towns, the life of chivalry and courtesy is left behind, for these qualities are conspicuously missing in popular urban literature. The townsman preferred raw, earthy stories which were concerned with his own experience. He liked, in particular, animal stories and fables, above all the adventures of the cunning Reynard the Fox. The *fabliaux,* especially designed for the taste of townsmen, were undistinguished by literary graces of any kind, and their sense of humor appears to us as extremely primitive. The unfaithfulness, laziness, and untidiness of housewives were pilloried, as were similar sins on the part of monks, friars, and secular clergy. Women and the clergy were the principal butts of the satire of the fabliaux, and the plots hold no surprise. In the same vein as the fabliaux, but at a far higher stage of literary accomplishment, were the fourteenth-century stories of the Italian Boccaccio (1313?–1375) in his *Decameron.* The English popular poet Chaucer (1343–1400), however, stands in a class by himself. The characters in the *Canterbury Tales* are no longer mere types; each is sharply differentiated with wit, humor, and sometimes profound insight. Most of Chaucer's plots, however, are closely related to those of the fabliaux.

It is useless to try to describe Chaucer intelligibly in a few sentences. Always when writing of him, one drops into quotations, the only way to convey his flavor. The *Canterbury Tales,* his masterpiece, though by no means his only poem—he was skilled also as a translator—tells of a pilgrimage made by a group of assorted characters to the tomb of St. Thomas Becket. Each of the characters is introduced to us; then his or her character is hit off with exquisite precision in a series of rhymed couplets, sometimes sympathetic, sometimes malicious. Then Chaucer allows each of them to tell a tale to while away the time on the journey. No other work gives us so full a picture of the ordinary medieval man and woman. When we have taken the journey with them and listened to their tales, we feel that we have indeed met and talked for a time with fourteenth-century human beings; we feel we should recognize them if we met them in life. Though the Middle English of Chaucer is no longer comprehensible to most of us, it slips easily into modern English; and though he has not always been admired as much for his poetical and especially metrical skill as he is today, there has never been a time since his death in 1400 when he has not been read for his narrative ability, his unerring character painting, and the vitality and freshness of his picture of medieval man as he really was in the fourteenth century.

*Poetry of social criticism*—An earlier contemporary of Chaucer gives us the first piece of serious social criticism of Western civilization, the *Vision of Piers Plowman*, by one William Langland, of whom nothing else is known. In this poem the poor peasant finds his voice. The poem, though couched in the form of an allegory, is a realistic description of the hard lot of the English poor in the fourteenth century, hardships which were later to lead to prolonged revolts, perhaps in part the result of this very poem.

*The Romance of the Rose*—Perhaps the most popular of all medieval poems was a composite work known as the *Romance of the Rose*. The first part was an allegory, written by William de Lorris (early thirteenth century). It is an ingenious love poem in the conventional style of courteous poetry, but no longer directed only to the noble classes, and clearly influenced by Christian tradition. It tells the story of a youth who is pierced by an arrow sped from the bow of the God of Love, whose heart leaves his own breast to be embodied in the Rose, which is surrounded by thorns and presents a difficult obstacle to be overcome. Jealousy, Reason, Danger, and other abstractions play their part in his efforts to reach the Rose, and after over four thousand lines, when

William's poem breaks off, the unfortunate lover has still not attained his goal. It is at this point that a later writer, John de Meun (second half of the thirteenth century) takes up, and the poem ceases at once to be an idyllic dream and becomes a cynical satire on all contemporary institutions. Hypocrisy (the friars) is given a chance to speak, Reason and the other characters from the earlier poem flay superstition, Nature gives a discourse on medieval science and current history. In short, the poet is able to grasp the opportunity of the unfinished poem to give an invaluable account of medieval life. With the aid of Venus the youth is able to gain his Rose; but this is only incidental to the satire, which has been called a "guidebook to the Middle Ages." But it was a guidebook in an entirely different sense from the greatest of medieval masterpieces which sums up the knowledge and aspiration equally, welding the whole into a perfect synthesis, unique in history, entirely inimitable, and almost untranslatable, the *Divine Comedy* of Dante.

*The Divine Comedy*—The *Divine Comedy* was not the name Dante Alighieri (1265–1321) gave to his own poem. He himself simply called it the *Comedy*, because it begins in sadness and ends in supreme happiness. But it was early given the epithet "Divine" which has now been incorporated in the title. No poem has ever deserved it more, both for its beauty and for the sublimity of the theme.

It is impossible to do any justice to the poem in a short space; in fact, it cannot properly be described at all. It must be read and experienced, preferably in the original Italian, a language full of vowels and music which Dante himself helped to fix. The Tuscan dialect of the poet indeed became, through his work, the literary language of Italy, and it has in essentials changed very little to this day.

One aspect of the *Comedy* cannot be understood without knowledge of the poet's first work, the *Vita Nuova*, in which he tells how at the age of nine he saw Beatrice, who was herself only eight, and thereafter she remained his ideal though he never knew her well in this earthly life, and she married without being aware of his unspoken feelings. He tells us that he had determined to express one day his love for Beatrice in poetry. It is this human and yet unearthly love that in manhood has transformed the poet's whole inner being, giving especially to the *Paradiso,* the third part of the *Comedy,* an extraordinary intensity of thought and emotion which is recognizably medieval and closely akin to the work of the medieval church builders. It is impossible to separate the poet's sublimated love for Beatrice from the Christian love which has made it possible.

Beatrice is a guide to the poet in his journey through the realm of the spirit to the vision of God, a realm in which the planetary spheres are not only seen but experienced, in which thought is not only apprehended but actually perceived. Yet Beatrice is also a woman before whom Dante is tongue-tied so that at one moment he is unable even to pronounce her name. And she represents also revelation in the sense in which Thomas Aquinas understood it, the visitor from the world of the spirit who adds to what he cannot find for himself. Vergil, the Roman poet, takes Dante as far as the summit of the Mount of Purgatory, but the pagan can go no farther. Reason must be supplemented by Revelation. Vergil was first sent to Dante by Beatrice as he faced the gates of Hell and feared to enter—Divine Grace must aid the natural reason which then, with the help of Revelation, can ascend to the full contemplation of God.

So the poem is profoundly allegorical; and yet at the same time it is real. The journey may have been the ascent of a soul to salvation, but the poet feels and perceives as a human being. The sufferings of the damned are portrayed with gruesome realism, and Dante experiences all the shock and revulsion of a healthy mortal. When Vergil leaves, Dante grieves and wishes him back; he suffers the pangs of loneliness in a deserted Garden of Eden until he recognizes Beatrice, who comes riding to him in her

chariot drawn by a gryphon. If the chariot is the Church and the gryphon is the animal symbol of Christ, this symbolism does not intrude. The symbolic or the allegorical and the real are so wonderfully fused that the reader is caught up with his imagination into the experience, and need know nothing of the symbolism until he feels the need of it.

Finally it may be added that the poem has certain important political meanings. Dante was through and through a political man; he played an important part in the affairs of his native Florence, and for a time he was a leading figure in the city's government before being forced into exile by his political enemies. He was a partisan of the Empire in the struggle between the Empire and the papacy. In his work *De Monarchia* (*On the Monarchy*) he makes clear the reasons for this partisanship. He believed that the spheres of Church and State should be separate, but that the State should be a true World State, such as had been known in the early centuries of the Christian Era under the aegis of Rome. The political condition of man is a consequence of sin, and leads to ever more deadly sins. Dante's choice of characters for the dwellers in his three realms of Hell, Purgatory, and Paradise is undoubtedly to some degree determined by his political views. It is significant that the Byzantine emperor, Justinian, noted by historians for his universal law code and for his reconquest of Italy, is greatly exalted in Dante's Paradise, and is seen by the poet as having been permitted by God "the glory of avenging his wrath by the living justice that inspires me"—surely a line hardly equaled for concentrated thought in all literature.

The poem begins on the night preceding Good Friday; during that night the moon is to be at the full. Throughout the next day and night the poet will make his horrifying journey through Hell (the *Inferno*). For twenty-four hours more he struggles to the foot of the Mount of Purgatory (the *Purgatorio*). Then for three days he is on the Mount and at last ascends to Paradise (the *Paradiso*), where there ceases to be any time. It remains the same day (Thursday) as Dante circles the earth in company with the heavenly planets until he is over Italy and the sun is setting in Jerusalem. The journey has taken exactly a week.

In Hell, accompanied by Vergil, he passes by all the various grades of sinners undergoing punishment, till he comes to Satan himself; then he is pulled past the center of gravity by his guide. The worst is over. Those whom he will meet hereafter are souls who are saved but are not yet ready for Heaven. On the Mount of Purgatory there are many terraces, each with its different sinners, and before he even reaches the terraces the poet sees others who have for some reason not yet begun to make the ascent, though in time they will be able to undertake it. In the *Purgatorio* the whole atmosphere is different from that of Hell, where all hope has been abandoned for eternity. Here in Purgatory one first comes to the realization that though the way be long, salvation is ahead. There is hope, indeed certainty, for the sinner in Purgatory. Then at last the Garden of Eden is reached, Vergil leaves the poet, and Beatrice comes for him as his new guide.

Light, music, joy, and love are the glories of Paradise, marvelously conveyed in the liquid Italian, with its many beautiful images; the planets dance and sing as they wheel in the Ptolemaic universe, so deeply experienced by Dante that it seems impossible to doubt that this is the way the universe is in the world of imagination, and Copernicus was wrong. ("Like the clock that calls us to prayer, in which one part draws and impels the other, chiming 'tin tin' so sweetly that the well-disposed spirit swells with love"—"Tin tin sonando con si dolce nota Che il ben disposto spirto d'amor turge.") Here are the great saints, Bernard and Thomas Aquinas, Peter and, at last, the Virgin Mary and a momentary vision of God, which, as soon as it is experienced, cannot be remembered save as an afterglow of something indescribable. But among the blessed this vision is always there. When Dante looks into the eyes of Beatrice, the Light is reflected there, and though he turns about to discover the source of the Light, it eludes him.

In all the great medieval thinkers there is nothing abstract or arid. The Latin of Thomas Aquinas, crystal-clear and sharp, bears the reader along with him, sharing his enthusiasm for the adventures of the mind, the logical thrust and counterthrust corresponding to the thrust and counterthrust of the piers and buttresses of the cathedral, pulled onward toward the summit of the vision, the "intellectual contemplation of God" in which there is nothing cold as Thomas experiences it—the love of the heart leading to the understanding of the Divine (as, also, in Plato's *Symposium*), the love that leads to this ascent having been implanted in man as grace, the gift of God. So also in Dante. "Luce intellettual pien d'amore, Amore del vero pien di letizia, Letizia che trascende ogni dolzore—Light of the mind, full of love, Love of the truth, full of joy, Joy that transcends every sorrow," this is Dante's description of that love which draws mankind to the contemplation of God. Every word in the great poem is full of the profoundest thought, often untranslatable into languages other than Italian, in which feeling and thought are fused as in no other. It lacks the extreme clarity of the cold intellect which is the genius of the French language, and the Italian itself was never again used as it was by Dante, who found in it the perfect vehicle for his experience. The whole knowledge of the world of the senses and the world of the spirit as known to medieval man is in the *Divine Comedy*—the deadliness of sin and the eternal punishment that it entails, the great hope held out to man by God and the means for its attainment, and at last a vision of eternal blessedness with the saints and heavenly hosts in the spaceless, timeless kingdom of heaven.

### The medieval drama

A few words should be said of medieval drama, which was in no sense one of the great dramas of the world, but was original and owed nothing to the great drama of the earlier peoples we have discussed. In early medieval times the drama consisted of the re-enacting of Biblical scenes in the churches at times of festival. These re-enactments developed into the mystery play, which also used Biblical subjects, but combined them with legends and tales from the lives of the saints. Mystery plays, too, were performed in church, but quite early were presented in the vernacular since the purpose was to instruct the people. The performers were usually the clergy, though lay actors were also used. An outgrowth of the mystery play is the Passion play, which represented with deep sincerity the crucifixion of Christ. Some of the Passion plays still survive, played by village actors, and joined in by the whole village community. The Oberammergau Passion play, performed in the Bavarian village of that name every ten years, is the outstanding surviving example.

The miracle plays, which became popular by the twelfth century, usually represented some exceptional intervention of a saint or the Virgin Mary in the ordinary lives of men. Finally, with the growth of the towns, came the play we most associate with the Middle Ages, the morality play, originally of a religious nature. By far the best known of these morality plays is the famous *Everyman*, a very free adaptation of which is still played every year in the open air at the Salzburg festival.

As the title of this play implies, the hero is a type rather than an individual. But he is not a type of a particular man; he is a representative of mankind. One of the paradoxes of the Middle Ages, which it has not been possible to stress in this book, is the contrast between the medieval political and religious institutions, which were hierarchical and authoritarian, and the universal belief, implicit, of course, in Christianity, that all human beings are equal in the hour of death. Each man is judged for his sins and saved or condemned as an individual man. The great emperor Frederic ii, so arrogant and exalted in his lifetime, put on the garments of a penitent to cross the threshold of death. So the play *Everyman* is concerned with the rich young man who cares nothing for his soul until death appears to warn him of the

few hours he has still to live. When Everyman's bribe to Death is refused, he tries first to persuade his kindred, his friends, and then his Worldly Goods to go with him, but all refuse. Only Good Deeds can help, and Everyman's Good Deeds are so feeble that "she" cannot rise from the ground. But Knowledge takes him to Confession, where he receives absolution and undergoes penance. This revives Good Deeds, but in turn Beauty, Five Wits, Strength, and Discretion leave him. He is accompanied to the edge of the grave by Knowledge; but he must descend into the grave with only Good Deeds, who helps him to ultimate salvation.

The play in its modern adaptation is more dramatically presented, with Death appearing at a feast, which shocks Everyman into a kind of stupor. His companions, failing to understand, then desert him. At the last Everyman is saved by Repentance and Faith. In spite of the simplicity of the theme, it is still possible in the great square in front of the Salzburg cathedral to sense something of the loneliness of the soul in the moment of death which the unknown medieval writer strove to dramatize. And it is seen that there is not, after all, such a great distance from Everyman to Marlowe and Shakespeare, and the tremendous individuals of Elizabethan drama.

The medieval view of man was too simple for Shakespeare. He was not content to say only that man sinned on earth and could be redeemed by repentance and faith. He wished to show how man sins on earth, what was the nature of his sins, and how they bring about their own penalty and judgment on earth. *King Lear, Macbeth, Othello,* all the great tragedies, are as truly morality plays as *Everyman.* But henceforth there is to be no simple answer, no one fate for all mankind, and salvation after death ceases to be the preoccupation of the dramatist. The character, deeds, and motives of man on earth, his relations with other human beings, his actions in the face of his destiny—these were to become the stuff of the drama of Shakespeare, as they are the stuff of life itself as it is known to man.

With the fading of the medieval conviction that all the answers were known, the adolescence of the human being was over.

▶ **Suggestions for further reading**

If the student is interested in reading primary sources, including the works of any of the writers referred to in this chapter, he should consult an extremely useful book which lists every medieval writer whose works had been translated into English prior to 1946: C. P. Farrar and A. P. Evans, *Bibliography of English Translations from Medieval Sources* (New York: Columbia University Press, 1946).

Of the several hundred books available on different subjects discussed in this chapter the author believes that E. Gilson, *The Spirit of Medieval Philosophy* (New York: Charles Scribner's Sons, 1940), is probably the one that he should choose for an understanding of the subjects considered important by medieval thinkers. The book is extremely well written, and the writer is sympathetic to the medieval viewpoint; also, his work is free from the plethora of names which will confuse most beginning students who attempt the more formal histories of philosophy. Another book that should not be missed is H. O. Taylor, *The Medieval Mind* (4th ed., 2 vols.; Cambridge, Mass.: Harvard University Press, 1949), which devotes a chapter to each of a considerable number of medieval thinkers. The book is slightly uneven, as it is hardly possible for any writer to be completely familiar with all these men and women; but for the most part Taylor's judgments are based on his own readings, and the whole is eloquently written, especially in chapters devoted to writers with whom Taylor feels a special sympathy. A recent historical survey containing a great deal of material on the Byzantine and Muslim civilizations, in addition to strictly medieval thought and culture, is F. B. Artz, *The Mind of the Middle Ages* (New York: Alfred A. Knopf, Inc., 1953). This book also contains the best medieval bibliography easily accessible to a student. In general, the book may be safely used to find additional information on almost everything discussed in this text in the medieval chapters.

On medieval science the writer's own work: S. C. Easton, *Roger Bacon and His Search for a Universal Science* (New York: Columbia University Press, 1952), may be consulted, especially Chapter 9, on the general nature of medieval science. Lynn Thorndike, *A History of Magic and Experimental Science* (6 vols.; New York: The Macmillan Company and Columbia University Press, 1923–1941), may be consulted for reference. Thorndike makes no attempt at a synthesis in these monumental volumes but devotes each chapter to a different scientist. His long chapter on Albertus Magnus is one of the best in the book. An interesting study of several problems handled by medieval scientists is to be found in the early chapters of Herbert Butterfield, *The Origins of Modern Science, 1300–1800* (New York: The Macmillan Company, 1951).

A fine reconstruction of the life of Peter Abélard has been couched in the form of a novel: Helen Waddell, *Peter Abélard* (New York: Henry Holt & Co., Inc., 1933). The author is a fine medieval scholar, and her book captures the medieval spirit probably better than any other.

Two books by Sartell Prentice give a great deal of technical information about the cathedrals in a reasonably simple manner: *The Voice of the Cathedrals* (New York: William Morrow & Co., Inc., 1938) and *The Heritage of the Cathedrals* (New York: William Morrow & Co., Inc., 1939). But a wonderful work of evocation of the spirit that informed the building of the cathedrals, which is still unequaled in its field and is true literature, is Henry Adams, *Mont St. Michel and Chartres* (Boston: Houghton Mifflin Company, 1905), many times reprinted.

A useful recent source book which gives a number of well-chosen selections from medieval literature is C. W. Jones, *Medieval Literature in Translation* (New York: Longmans, Green & Co., Inc., 1950). Among many translations of the *Divine Comedy* this author prefers a very recent inexpensive edition; the poem is simply but accurately translated, in prose, but it is printed in stanzas as if it were poetry: Dante, *The Divine Comedy* (tr. H. R. Huse; New York: Rinehart & Company, Inc., 1954). An excellent book on the wandering poets is H. Waddell, *Wandering Scholars* (New York: Henry Holt & Co., Inc., 1950). Finally, the reader is referred to C. G. Crump and E. F. Jacob, eds., *The Legacy of the Middle Ages* (Oxford: The Clarendon Press, 1926), for a number of excellent articles, not too technical, on medieval art and craftsmanship and other fields of culture, some of which have evidently been written by men with a real enthusiasm for things medieval. The book has also a number of valuable illustrations which make it one of the best in a distinguished series.

# 21

## Commerce and Industry
## in the Middle Ages

*Revival of trade • The rise of the towns • Organization of trade and industry • Medieval economic concepts • Merchant and craft guilds • The rise of medieval capitalism • Breakdown of control over profit seeking • The accumulation of capital • Improvement of business techniques*

---

### ▶ Revival of trade

TRADE CONDITIONS IN THE DARK AGES

The economic conditions of Europe in the Dark Ages have been touched on briefly in an earlier chapter. During the ninth and tenth centuries the Mediterranean Sea was virtually a Muslim lake, and the ports, such as Marseilles, which had retained some prosperity even after the fall of Rome, now declined into small towns. The great city with which the West wished to trade, by far the greatest city in Europe, was, of course, Constantinople, but only the smallest trickle of trade could get through directly by sea. Such trade as there was had to be carried on, at least in part, by land, by the hazardous route through Eastern Europe, which was itself constantly being invaded by waves of nomads from Asia. Not until Hungary was settled as a country and the Magyars had accepted Christianity was there any reasonable assurance that merchants could reach Constantinople.

There were, however, two exceptions to this general condition. The chief European trade with Constantinople was carried on by the Swedes, who had settled first at

Novgorod, then at Kiev in Russia, as described in Chapter 15. These Russians, or Varangians (they were known by both names), traveled down the great Russian rivers into the Black Sea. The first groups often started out without any trade goods at all, but pillaged some small communities and then used their loot for trade, selling it in Constantinople and the Black Sea cities in the Byzantine Empire. Later they also used the booty taken in the Viking raids in Europe, which was assembled on the Baltic island of Gothland before being distributed through Russia, and even back into the Western cities again. Here they also brought native products from the north, lumber, furs, hides, and similar articles. By the ninth century they had regularized their position in Constantinople, by treaty, and were allotted a special quarter in the imperial capital. But the total of goods that reached Constantinople must have been small enough, and smaller still the Byzantine luxuries that reached the West up the rivers via Gothland. And while the Vikings were still raiding Europe, naturally they did not supply their victims with luxuries from the East. Later, as has been seen, this trade was regu-

*An old corner of modern Venice.*

*The Rialto at Venice (late medieval, early renaissance).* (COURTESY ITALIAN STATE TOURIST OFFICE)

*The Palace of the Doge (Duke) of Venice. Note the Byzantine influence.* (COURTESY ITALIAN STATE TOURIST OFFICE)

larized, and Kiev became an industrial and commercial center of the first importance. The other exception was the city of Venice, on the Adriatic Sea, which was immune to the Muslim ravages as long as it kept to its northern section of the sea. The city, which was built almost on the sea itself, with its thoroughfares in the form of canals and lagoons, had been founded in the sixth century as a refuge for fugitives from the nomad invasions. It was held for a brief period by Charlemagne, though not long enough for him to exercise effective sovereignty over it. So when the emperor in the year 810 was negotiating for the recognition of his title by the Byzantines, he gave up, among other possessions, the city of Venice. Though the Byzantines likewise exercised little effective sovereignty over the city, the connection was valuable for the Venetians, as it permitted them a certain amount of trade with the capital; and, even though the sea voyage to Constantinople was to be impossible for two more centuries, goods could be transported across the Adriatic by sea, whence

the land routes were comparatively short, and passed through territory which was usually under some kind of control by the Byzantines. From the ninth to the eleventh century Venice grew rapidly, and was in fact a republic, self-governed, independent in all but name from Constantinople. When during the eleventh century she aided the Byzantines in a war against the Normans, she was rewarded by being permitted full free trade throughout the Byzantine Empire, a very important advantage over all her competitors in view of the restrictive trade policies adopted by the empire. It amounted to a virtual monopoly for Venice of all trade between Constantinople and the West. Thereafter she was to lead the Western world in sea trade, and rapidly developed overland routes to circulate the Byzantine and Oriental products within Europe.

Aside from these two exceptions, during the whole period of anarchy and desolation in Europe which followed the breakdown of the Carolingian Empire and the Viking raids, trade was on a very small scale in-

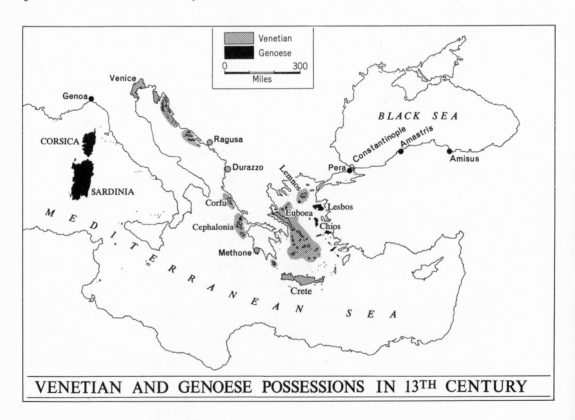

## VENETIAN AND GENOESE POSSESSIONS IN 13TH CENTURY

# ► chronological chart

<table>
<tr><td colspan="2">The Great Trading Cities</td><td colspan="2">The Leagues of Towns</td></tr>
<tr><td>Foundation of Venice</td><td>ca. 568</td><td>Diet of Roncaglia—Frederic I asserts<br>imperial rights over Italian towns</td><td>1158</td></tr>
<tr><td>Election of first Doge of Venice</td><td>587</td><td></td><td></td></tr>
<tr><td>Venice recognized as Byzantine<br>territory</td><td>810</td><td>Formation of Lombard League</td><td>1159</td></tr>
<tr><td>Foundation of Novgorod, traditionally<br>by Rurik</td><td>862</td><td>Battle of Legnano—Defeat of<br>Frederic I by Lombard League</td><td>1176</td></tr>
<tr><td>Foundation of Kiev</td><td>882</td><td></td><td></td></tr>
<tr><td>Trading rights granted in<br>Constantinople to Varangians</td><td>907</td><td>Peace of Constance between Frederic I<br>and Lombard League</td><td>1183</td></tr>
<tr><td>Venetian war with Constantinople—<br>extensive maritime trading rights<br>granted to Venetians</td><td>1063</td><td>Wars between Frederic II and<br>Lombard League</td><td>1237–1250</td></tr>
<tr><td>Institution of Great Council of Venice<br>(Venetian oligarchy)</td><td>1063</td><td>Alliance of Lübeck and Hamburg to<br>protect Baltic trade routes</td><td>1244</td></tr>
<tr><td>Norman conquest of Sicily</td><td>1072–1091</td><td></td><td></td></tr>
<tr><td>Genoese and Pisans clear western<br>Mediterranean of Muslims</td><td>1087</td><td>Privileges granted to German towns in<br>London</td><td>1282</td></tr>
<tr><td>Pisans granted trade privileges by<br>Byzantine Empire</td><td>1111</td><td>Confederation of Cologne—League of<br>Hansa towns against Denmark</td><td>1370</td></tr>
<tr><td>Fourth Crusade—Sack of<br>Constantinople, led by Venetians</td><td>1204</td><td>Richard II of England renews Hansa<br>privileges</td><td>1377</td></tr>
<tr><td>War between Venice and Genoa</td><td>1253–1299</td><td></td><td></td></tr>
<tr><td>Battle of Meloria—Defeat of Pisans<br>by Genoese</td><td>1284</td><td>Last assembly of Hanseatic League</td><td>1669</td></tr>
</table>

deed, and amounted to little more than the exchange of local products, varied by the occasional presence of some courageous small trader who had braved the hazardous overland journey to the East and had been successful.

RISE OF THE ITALIAN SEAPORTS

### Rivalry among Genoa, Pisa, and Venice

Meanwhile other Italian cities had been making headway, notably Genoa and Pisa. The Genoese and Pisans, after capturing and keeping for themselves Corsica and Sardinia, aided the Normans in the capture of Sicily (1091), and were given special privileges and quarters in Sicily itself. Before the end of the eleventh century they had also established trading colonies in Northern Africa, and thereafter traded with the Muslims, not allowing religious differences to affect their search for profitable business, even during the Crusades themselves. The western Mediterranean now belonged to these western Italian seaports as much as the Adriatic belonged to the Venetians. The Crusades gave the three cities a command of the whole Mediterranean, although by now they had become rivals poaching upon each other's territory. The Genoese succeeded in eliminating the Pisans by war, but they competed with the Venetians for several centuries afterward. As we have seen, the notorious Fourth Crusade and the subsequent Latin Kingdom of Constantinople gave great advantages to the Venetians, whose project it was. But the Genoese retaliated in 1261 when they helped

*Though this minature shows an incident in the life of Sir Galahad, and the persons on the boat are not typical, the ship itself is medieval. From* Roman de Tristan *(French)*, ca. 1450. (COURTESY THE PIERPONT MORGAN LIBRARY. Ms. 41, folio 259)

restore the Greek emperor to his throne. There was, however, enough trade for both after the Crusades, and the Genoese, in general, continued to exploit the western Mediterranean, retaining valuable footholds in the East, while the Venetians did a greater share of the Oriental trade. The Genoese traded constantly with North Africa, even passing through the Pillars of Hercules (the Strait of Gibraltar) into the Atlantic and sailing a short distance down the Moroccan coast. Both Genoa and Venice were aristocratic merchant republics of which we shall have more to say later.

### The nature of sea trade in the Middle Ages

Travel by sea in early medieval times was still far from safe, and wrecks, sometimes assisted by robbers on shore who guided ships onto the rocks by the use of false lights, were very frequent. The ships hugged the coast, as in ancient times, at least until the general use of the mariner's

compass toward the end of the thirteenth century; on the other hand, sea traders could transport several hundred tons of cargo in each vessel and were free from the nuisance and expense of having to pay heavy tolls in order to pass through territory belonging to feudal lords, as did overland travelers. Seafarers still had to contend with pirates, even when the Muslims had been driven from the sea, for the maritime cities did not hesitate to engage in piracy against ships belonging to their rivals. But the same cities that profited so heavily from the voyages of their citizens through customs and excise taxes thought it worth while both to sweep the seas of pirates when possible and to supply armed fleets to protect the merchant vessels. Many medieval fleets sailed in convoy, and their strength was usually too great for any except well-organized pirates.

Both sails and oars were used for propulsion, since medieval sailors learned late how to sail into the wind, and the tiller for steering was not effective till the end of the

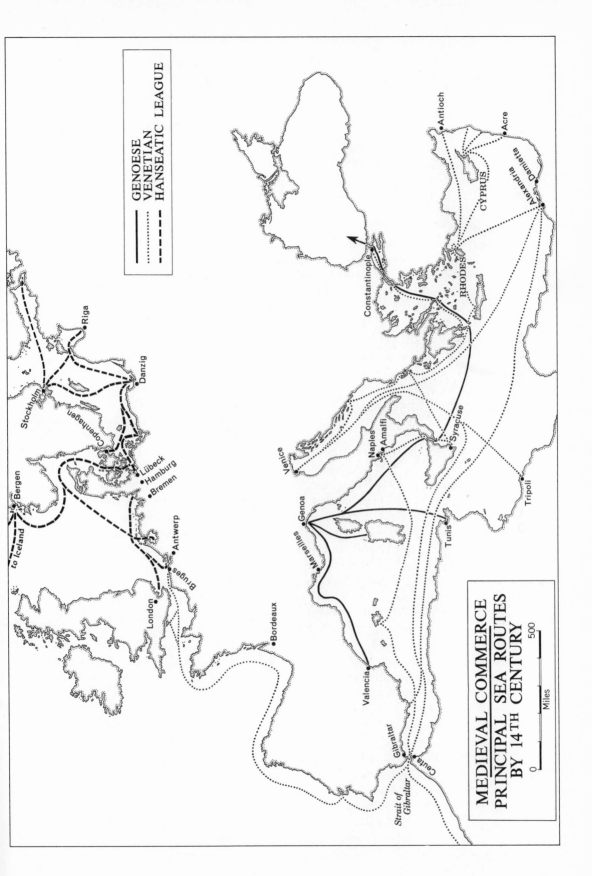

MEDIEVAL COMMERCE
PRINCIPAL SEA ROUTES
BY 14TH CENTURY

GENOESE
VENETIAN
HANSEATIC LEAGUE

0    500
Miles

Riga

Stockholm

Danzig

Copenhagen

Bergen

Lübeck
Hamburg
Bremen

to Iceland

Antwerp

Bruges

London

Bordeaux

Valencia

Gibraltar
Ceuta
Strait of
Gibraltar

Marseilles

Genoa

Tunis

Venice

Naples
Amalfi

Syracuse

Tripoli

Constantinople

RHODES

CYPRUS

Antioch

Acre

Damietta

Alexandria

medieval period. The sails were used only for relieving the oarsmen when the wind was behind them. Voyages were made only during the spring and summer, for the hazards of storms and the extreme cold on the overcrowded, cramped ships prevented year-round sailing except on rare occasions when it could not be avoided. Commercial shipping out of Italian ports was confined to the Mediterranean itself until the early fourteenth century, when at last the Venetians inaugurated a service direct to Flanders and the north through the dangerous Bay of Biscay. The northern peoples, however, used the Baltic for trade between the Scandinavian countries, Germany, Flanders, France, and England. Goods imported from the East therefore had to be transferred in the Italian ports for overland transportation, and were stored in warehouses in the ports until such transportation was available.

OVERLAND TRANSPORTATION—ROADS
AND RIVERS

It is difficult for us in these days of speedy freight by train, truck, and airplane to imagine the hardships to which a medieval trader had to submit. The invention in the early medieval period of an improved harness, which enabled a horse or mule to pull heavier loads, made vehicular transport possible; but it was still limited by the terrible roads, so that transportation by cart was used, as a rule, only for short hauls between towns in Europe, and not for long-distance haulage from the coast. The roads were full of holes, dusty or muddy according to the season, and had to go over high mountain passes from Italy into Europe. The tolls demanded by the lords through whose territory the roads passed were supposed to be spent on the upkeep of the roads; but the always penurious nobles usually had better uses for the money, and little of it probably found its way into road improvement. A conscientious lord was in no better position to collect tolls than a neglectful one if both were on a main route, since the territory had to be crossed whether the roads were in good or bad condition. The Cistercian

Brothers formed an honorable exception to the general rule, as the building of roads was considered by them and by the Church as an act of piety.

Since vehicular traffic was so difficult, by far the commonest form of transport was the pack train of mules and horses; but as each animal could carry only a very limited amount, it was natural that the chief goods transported would be luxuries, and equally natural that the journey by road should be confined to as short distances as possible. So the goods would be transshipped to the navigable rivers whenever there were any. In barges a far greater quantity could be carried with comparative ease, and for the flat-bottomed medieval boats, even for seagoing boats, rivers were navigable for very much greater distances than now. The navigable waterways were the real heart of European trade, as they are to some extent even today, since water transport remains so much cheaper than transport by land. Towns situated on rivers sprang into existence as trade grew; and it was to the interest of these towns to provide facilities for the traders in exchange for the tolls they collected, and to ensure protection for the traders insofar as it was in their power. As a rule, the towns made themselves responsible for the upkeep of the towpaths along which animals pulled the barges. But the lords through whose territory the rivers ran continued to exact tolls for their use without doing any service in return, and no authority was in a position to prevent this practice, though sometimes the lord took advantage of his position in a constructive manner by encouraging the growth of a town on his property, from which he could draw a more stable and regular income.

Many of the great French rivers, such as the Loire, Seine, and Garonne, became important waterways, fed by roads which left them at certain strategic places and dotted with towns, especially at transshipment points. Other towns grew up where there were important fords or bridges on the overland routes. The greatest concentration of towns was perhaps to be found at the mouth of the Rhine, the longest and most important waterway in Western Europe. These towns in Flanders, and later the Netherlands, were also seaports with a maritime trade with England and the Baltic, so that by the twelfth century they had become extremely important and already prosperous as import and export centers, as well as manufacturing centers, the headquarters of the cloth industry, as we shall see. The great German rivers also provided the Holy Roman Empire with a network of waterways, of which the towns were in later times to take full advantage.

## THE NATURE OF OVERSEAS TRADE—THE BALANCE OF TRADE

With all the difficulty and expense of transportation it was to be expected that the goods transported through Europe from the East should be confined to luxuries whose weight and bulk were small in relation to the price obtained. Especially desired were the spices from the East—ginger, cloves, nutmegs, and, above all, pepper. These were used in far greater quantities than now by all who could afford them, to disguise, no doubt, the taste of the meat in the days before refrigeration, and to give some flavor other than salt to meat preserved by the only method known to medieval people. Other small and precious items were medicines, incense, dyestuffs, perfumes, and jewels. Larger items were the Oriental textile specialties such as satin, damask, muslin, gauze, and Oriental carpets, and luxury fruits such as the apricot, orange, and lemon. In late medieval times the West was first introduced to sugar cane, which could supplement honey, the only sweetening hitherto known. Papyrus was still imported from Egypt, since paper appeared only at the end of the medieval period and parchment was probably even more expensive than imported papyrus in spite of the cost of transportation.

In the early Middle Ages, Western Europeans had little enough to give in exchange for all these imports, and raw materials and primary products, which could ill be spared

in Europe itself, were the major export items, together with silver, new sources of which were discovered and exploited during this period. European wine, however, early became an important item of export, though more in European trade than abroad. But in the high Middle Ages the products of medieval craftsmen became known for their quality and were more than the equal of the best that the Orient could offer, especially in its declining days. Textiles of all kinds, but especially woolen and silken materials, tapestries, linen, and exquisite brocades were manufactured and exported, together with armor from central France and glass from Venice, as well as the staple raw materials from the north—lumber, hides, and furs. By the fourteenth century it is certain that the balance of trade was heavily in favor of the West, and gold and silver were shipped with ever greater frequency into Europe, helping the economy immeasurably even before the discovery of new sources in the New World.

## OBSTACLES TO A MONEY ECONOMY

Coined money, however, for a long time remained extremely scarce, and very difficult to use for commerce until the close of the Middle Ages. Gold was hardly available at all until the thirteenth century, the only gold coins in use being Byzantine and Oriental. Silver was the generally accepted precious metal, but its use was hampered by the fact that hundreds of nobles had the right to coin it. They would stamp a value on a coin, but there was no guarantee whatever that the silver content would equal its face value, and there was every temptation for a noble to devalue coins to as low a silver content as he could get away with. Moreover those who received the coins could chip and clip them before handing them on. Wherever there was any large-scale exchange of goods, as at fairs and markets, it was absolutely essential to make use of the services of a money-changer, an expert who, for a consideration, could determine the gold or silver content of coins handed to him for valuation. Without the medieval money-changer there could have been no money economy at all, for it was impossible for any but the expert to know the value of a silver coin struck in the West. In the course of time kings and city governments managed to dispossess the nobles of their right to strike coins, and these larger powers thereafter guaranteed the silver and gold content. The Venetian ducat and the Florentine florin, both gold coins, became generally acceptable at face value, and greatly helped in the exchange of goods. But the kings were by no means above devaluing their own coins when short of cash, and they had difficulty in suppressing counterfeiting and the clipping of coins, which remained a profitable enterprise for centuries in spite of the severe punishments meted out to the counterfeiters by rulers if they were caught.

*A medieval money-changer being carried away by Death, as in the picture of the Knight Templar shown in Chapter 18. From* Hours of the Virgin, *ca. 1450.* (COURTESY THE PIERPONT MORGAN LIBRARY. Ms. 359, folio 144)

INTRA-EUROPEAN TRADE

### The market

It has been explained in an earlier chapter that the bulk of the goods produced on the manors was consumed at home. The lord of the manor had his own land worked by the peasants, but as he had a large household to feed, the smaller manors had little surplus. But he also required payment in money from his peasants for many of their manorial dues, and the peasants on most

manors had only one place to go for money —the town. Likewise, if the lord had many manors and wanted to convert his surplus into cash for luxuries, he too had to patronize the town. Every town of any size therefore had a market, usually opened once a week, often, in earlier times, on Sundays, where the manors could send their surplus food to be sold in exchange for money. The townsmen also displayed their wares for the countryfolk, and supplied them with the few things they could afford.

The towns and their markets were always under the protection of some lord, or even the king, except in the case of the rare self-governing towns. The lord gave his permission for a regular market to be held in exchange for market dues paid to him. If the market was the center of a flourishing area with many manors, there would probably be enough surplus food, as well as agricultural raw materials such as flax, so that the merchant could buy in quantity for export. The markets therefore to some extent served as feeders for the export trade as well as centers for the exchange of agricultural and urban goods. The market day was always the most important commercial day of the week, as it still is in English and European towns even though the stores may be open every day for regular purchases. It is on market day that the countryfolk come to town to display and sell their produce directly in stalls, and often side by side with them the townsmen set up their stalls with special bargains, and sometimes especially cheap prices, to attract their rural customers.

### The fairs

A market on a much larger scale was the international fair, held in some area where access was easy by either boat or road. Preparations for these fairs might take weeks while the goods were being assembled from all parts of the country, or indeed from many parts of Europe. Transactions were carried out on a considerable scale and needed many special arrangements. Certain lords took a keen interest in these fairs, since they could be made into an excellent source of income if handled honestly and with benefit to all concerned. The greatest European fairs during the twelfth and thirteenth centuries were those held in the plain of Champagne, under the patronage of the counts of Champagne, who were responsible for their management. Safe passage to the fair through the count's territories was guaranteed, and extended as far as possible beyond them. The Church also lent what protection it could. The fairs were under the management of a warden, with a considerable staff under him made up of weighers, measurers, porters, and such, and the fairs were well policed. A special seal of the fair was used to authenticate all purchases made by contract, and, of course, money-changers had to be present to facilitate trade between the participants from various countries with different monies. Moneylenders were also to be found for those who needed quick cash. Storage facilities were provided, and entertainment of all kinds, minstrels, jongleurs, dancers, clowns, and all other amusements which appealed to medieval people. Peasants were usually permitted to make at least one trip to the fairs by their manorial lords; even though they might lack money to make purchases, they could always enjoy themselves at small expense.

At the Champagne fairs different items were sold at different times: textiles, perhaps for two weeks; then leathers and furs for another two weeks; and then domestic animals. The fairs were also held in different seasons of the year at certain fair towns, so that the fair season in Champagne lasted the best part of the year, to the considerable advantage of the worthy count's purse. But the counts of Champagne always kept the dues to a reasonable rate, and their moderation ensured the long-continued success of the fairs in their county. When the king of France interfered at the beginning of the fourteenth century and raised the dues, it was no longer profitable for some of the merchants to display their goods, and the fairs rapidly declined in importance; but by then there were enough large towns where goods could be bought at all times of the

year for the fairs to be no longer the necessity that they had been in earlier times. Nevertheless, many fairs throughout Europe continued, some, such as the famous international fair of Leipzig, to this day. Industry fairs of the twentieth century, such as the British Industries Fair, and occasional large expositions, such as the New York World's Fair of the 1930's, are in the same tradition. The agricultural fairs still held regularly in nearly every state of the United States, by combining amusement and entertainment with business, carry on the medieval tradition.

▶ **The rise of the towns**

THE POSITION OF THE TOWNS IN THE
EARLY MIDDLE AGES

After the fall of Rome and during the decline of the Carolingian Empire there were very few large towns, since the basis for their existence as centers of trade and industry had been lost in the centuries of semibarbarism. The manors were largely self-sufficient, and from most of them there was only a small surplus available for trade, far too little to support the needs of a whole group of specialized workers who would have formed the population of a town. Only a few nobles and higher clergy, with the produce of many manors to draw upon, could guarantee a regular supply of food and at the same time provide a market for the specialized wares of a town; and in those days of poor communications it would be essential to have a surplus regularly moving into a town, or for the townsmen themselves to spend a large part of their time in agriculture. In the earliest medieval towns we find, as a rule, both of these conditions fulfilled. A noble or a bishop with his entourage would live in a town and provide it with its market from the produce of their lands, and the workers themselves who lived there under his protection looked after some of their own food supply, while producing at the same time various specialized wares which could be exchanged for their additional needs. A very few continuously inhabited cities centered in strategic places on trade routes, where communications were relatively good, might be able to make their living from trade and industry alone, exchanging their products for agricultural goods drawn from fairly wide areas; but on the whole the vast majority were of the first kind, the seats of lords or bishops who provided the food and protection needed by the townsmen.

During the period of the invasions such centers of production would naturally attract marauders, for they provided more booty than isolated manors. It was necessary, therefore, that they be protected as efficiently as possible. Almost all medieval towns were to some extent fortified, and surrounded by a wall and moat; and many of them were actually founded during the invasions by great nobles who desired to protect as much of their property as possible, and at the same time to have enough resources within the town to enable it to withstand a siege, the only means of conquest available to the Vikings. Such towns, called burgs, were really enlarged castles, and the artisans were engaged primarily in manufacturing for de-

fense needs. They might be serfs or freemen; but whatever their status they were completely dependent on the lord, whether he was a clergyman or a noble. The fortified nature of the towns and the walls surrounding them made their expansion very difficult. The houses were huddled together and the streets were necessarily narrow to take advantage of all the space available. Only when the invasions were over was it possible to add to them; but such expansion had to be outside the walls. And even when the large-scale invasions were at an end, there was still no secure peace. Thus we find in many medieval cities inner walls surrounding the old town, and then outer walls built in later days to protect the burg itself, and the *faubourg* (outside the burg) or suburbs. By the eleventh century, when the major invasions of the West were over, most European towns were of this kind, either a plain burg, or a burg and *faubourg*. Few of the inhabitants would be engaged full time in trade or manufacture; but the nucleus was there ready for expansion and increased specialization should conditions ever become suitable.

*Óbidos, in Portugal, stands at the top of a hill overlooking a valley. Within the walls, which completely surround the village, live a few hundred people; their houses are only slightly modernized from medieval times. This is one of the two European cities which still possess their medieval walls intact (the other being Carcassonne).*

THE TOWN AS A FREE CORPORATION

## The escape from feudal servitude

The majority of European towns owed their very foundation to feudal lords or to the higher clergy. As they began to grow, and especially as merchants engaged exclusively in trade, men who had been free for generations and had never been personally dependent upon feudal overlords, began to settle there permanently, it was natural that they should resent the disabilities placed upon them because the town itself was subordinate to these lords. They began to think themselves capable of making their own defense without calling upon their lord; and yet within the city the lord had certain traditional rights of collecting tolls and rents which seriously interfered with the merchants' freedom and ability to make profits. Lords, in other words, ceased to be worth their keep, from the townsmen's point of view, and at the same time, as their demands for money and luxuries increased, especially after the Crusades, they tended to try to milk the burghers or townsmen for more, while their actual services to them grew less.

So we find from as early as the end of the eleventh century onward efforts made by towns throughout Europe to escape from the galling restrictions of an earlier age. It was not difficult for the burghers to recognize their strong position against the aristocracy. The lords possessed military power and they had the old feudal law on their side. On the other hand, if they used this military power they would destroy the source of their income. They needed regular income, not one single great looting followed by nothing. If they destroyed a town, they would have to rebuild it afterward or forgo their income. If traders refused to trade because conditions were made too onerous, then likewise no tolls could be collected. Most independent lords in these circumstances found it better to compromise with their towns, and draw up a charter stating exactly what the towns had to do for them, what rents and tolls had to be paid, what

scutage or commutation of military service had to be paid, what hospitality and similar feudal services were owed, thus saving themselves from possible total loss if the town fought for and was able to secure complete independence in spite of the theoretical rights of the nobility.

Very great lords, and kings, not being dependent in the same way upon their income from any particular town, could hold out against the demands of the towns and could even afford to inflict punishment upon them. On the other hand, these great lords could provide them with more efficient protection and were thus worth more of what they cost the burghers than was the smaller lord. So we find that in countries where there was an efficient central government under a king the towns maintained only a limited independence and usually did not have their rights confirmed by charters. This was the case with England, and with France after the thirteenth century, where indeed many towns lost their charters after the king had established his supremacy over the whole country. On the other hand, the Italian and German burghers, living in countries where the official ruler exercised only sporadic and never very efficient control, were able to secure and maintain their independence far more effectively. As we have seen, the northern Italian towns united in a league were able to defeat and force concessions out of even such a powerful ruler as Frederic Barbarossa, the Holy Roman Emperor, and were also able to hold their own against his grandson Frederic II.

It was not only the Lombard League which had to fight for its freedom. Throughout Europe many of the higher clergy and the nobility refused to accept the inevitable peacefully, and resisted the rising power of the bourgeoisie with all the force at their disposal. Perhaps the class of people most difficult to handle, from the point of view of the towns, were the simoniacal clergy who had bought their offices, expecting them to carry the overlordship of at least the town in which the bishop had his seat, a bishop who had possibly gone into debt to buy the office and had to repay it from his revenues. Faced with resistance, he could not afford to wait. He could not pass his office on to his children, and, unlike a feudal lord, he had no real proprietorship. But he could always command ecclesiastical sanctions and excommunicate the townsmen, and he would often be backed by the papacy (though not the reformed papacy of the eleventh century, which used the townsmen against the simoniacal clergy). Though the Church did not approve of townsmen, and in particular distrusted their search for profits instead of sanctity and salvation, and was well aware that the atmosphere of a town was not one in which religion was likely to flourish, nevertheless it often had to make use of them against the nobility. So we know of many instances where the town had to fight hard against the bishop and his hired mercenaries, and cases where a victorious bishop looted his own town are not unknown.

The townsmen were often assisted by the division of jurisdiction between the various lords who claimed rights in it—perhaps a king, a count, a bishop, and a smaller lord who was in possession and owned the castle. Such a town was the northern French city of Amiens. In other cases the town was divided into fiefs belonging to several different nobles. It was possible in these circumstances for the townsmen to play one lord against the other, and throw their effective and probably decisive support to the power which was willing to give them their freedom on the best terms.

In the short run, therefore, it can be seen that everything was in favor of the town as against the nobility; in the long run the rise of central governments and national states was likely to doom their independence. They were too weak to stand against a king with all the resources he could command, even from the other cities in his country, their rivals, who would often enough be glad to see them weakened. But for a time there was a real revival of civilization in Europe, especially in Italy and Germany, based upon the growth of city-states. And Italian experience and inventiveness in these

states were to prepare the groundwork for the whole of Western commercial and industrial supremacy, which ultimately, under monarchical national governments, was to produce our modern commercial and industrial civilization.

### Noble initiative in the foundation of towns—Effect on manorial system

As the feudal lords felt the pressure of an increasing need for money, two methods of increasing their income presented themselves for consideration, both severely disruptive of the old static order, but both promising rich rewards. Here again the Crusades accelerated the process, for the crusading lord needed cash to pay for transportation to the Holy Land, and if he returned safely he had probably acquired a new taste for Oriental luxuries. If, therefore, he possessed a manor which had a suitable strategic position, he could encourage the expansion of the manorial village into a town by establishing a market and allowing his artisans to specialize in some useful and valuable production. From this increased production and from the market he could draw increased revenues at the cost of permitting some measure of freedom to the workers and setting up a center to which his own serfs would hope to go to earn their freedom. He could also bring under cultivation some of his waste swamp or forest land, of which there was an enormous surplus in early medieval times. But to attract workers for this difficult task he could not impose upon them the same disabilities under which his own serfs labored. It was not possible for him to reduce freemen to serfs for the purpose, or nothing would be accomplished. The only method open to him was to give the pioneers a real share in the proceeds of the new territories. Thus came into existence the system of *hôtes*, as the French called them, free peasant proprietors who paid to the lord the equivalent of rent, who were allowed to keep the proceeds of their labor in exchange for the payment of fixed and definite sums of money. The produce of these new lands was naturally sold in the town markets for cash, thus ensuring an increased supply of food for the towns and at the same time contributing to their growth.

Finally, this development also had its effects on the servile system on the old, established manors. There was a constant demand for men and women in the cities. Thus the city authorities tended to extend protection to escaped serfs until they had gained their freedom legally by staying away from their manors for a year and a day. Moreover, as the lords themselves gave privileges to workers on their newly cultivated territories, they found it difficult to enforce the old restrictions on their manors which had been in cultivation for centuries. Over a long period of time in most parts of Europe we find the serf gradually losing his official disabilities, and becoming in effect a small peasant proprietor or tenant or, more probably, a sharecropper, still hampered, it is true, by many restrictions and payments such as the *banalités*, but at least no longer subject to the lord's will in everything, now able to marry and leave the land at will, able to dispose of his own personal property, and able to sell his goods as he wished provided he paid his dues.

Thus the rise of the towns and the decline of the older manorial system reacted upon each other to the general benefit of the lower classes in society, and seriously undermined the primitive feudal system itself.

### The government of a commune

Self-governing towns, with or without a charter, are usually called *communes*. The essential element in a commune was its right to be treated as a whole, a corporation, as distinct from its constituent members. The town as a whole undertook obligations toward the lords, and received privileges in return, thus making a distinct break from feudal traditions, where obligations were always binding upon individual persons and not on groups. In order that the town could fulfill these obligations it had to be self-governing, assessing taxes and duties upon its citizens and paying them in a lump sum to the lord; and though its independence might be limited by the terms of its charter and it thus might not have full control of its foreign relations, within the city itself the governments were substantially autonomous. And when the charter could not be easily enforced, as in the cities of northern Italy, they became for all practical purposes city-states not unlike those of the ancient world. We have seen that when Frederic II (1197–1250), wished to enforce the Peace of Constance (1183), which defined the rights of the Holy Roman Emperor, he had to go to war for the purpose, since the cities had grown accustomed to performing no duties while the imperial throne had been in dispute during the reign of Pope Innocent III (1198–1216).

The towns, as self-governing units, were substantially outside the feudal system, and refused to recognize feudal law or customs as operative within them. The needs of a trading and manufacturing community being entirely different from those of the feudal nobility, the towns developed a much more equitable law which took better account of evidence and was naturally especially concerned with the sanctity and enforcement of contracts. This law, which was close to Roman practice and to some extent influenced by Roman law, was called the *law merchant*.

The government of the towns varied in different parts of Europe; almost the only generalization that can be safely made is that the richer merchants usually had effective control, unless the town was still ruled by its hereditary feudal aristocracy. The commonest early form of government was by a board of elected magistrates, who in time relinquished part of their duties to one or more executive officers, called *consuls* in Italy and southern France, and *aldermen* in England. The Venetian republic remained an oligarchy for centuries, headed by an elected official, the Doge, or Duke. In several Italian towns the violence of party politics within the government resulted in the substitution of government by a manager, a *podesta,* who was appointed, as a rule, from another city, and who was supposed to keep the rival factions in order. Several notable Italians became *podeste* in many different cities during their lifetime, becoming a kind of small professional class of municipal officials. Elsewhere the chief executives of the towns, called *mayors* in England and France and *burgermeisters* in Germany and Flanders, continued to rule with their councils and were eligible for re-election. As early as the twelfth century, efforts were made by the lower classes to take away the monopoly of power from the richer merchants, who were able to use it tyrannically in the interests of their class, and at one time the commune of Milan was ruled briefly by a kind of trade union of workers; but none of these efforts was permanently successful, and it was the individual despot, merchant, or feudal prince, or some adventurer who replaced the city governments with one-man rule, instead of the power of the oligarchy becoming more widely based and democratic.

### Intercity rivalry, and factional strife in the cities

The towns in northern Italy competed against each other and were not hesitant about engaging in war in order to get the better of their rivals. Moreover, within the cities were parties which originally had supported the pretensions of the emperors (Ghibellines) as against those who favored the papacy (Guelphs), but who continued to contend under the same names even when the emperors as such had ceased to play any part in Italian affairs. Only rarely did they unite against a common enemy, as against the two emperors, Frederic I and Frederic II; and even then not all the cities were included in the anti-imperial alliance. In each city also there was a substantial minority always in favor of collaboration. So we see in the independent cities of northern Italy the same disruptive influences, treachery, intercity warfare, and virulent party politics that had existed in ancient Greece and had prevented unification of that country except

by external force. But medieval Italy never found its Philip of Macedon, and submitted instead to smaller despots under whom some of the cities attained remarkable heights of culture, especially Florence under the banker princes the Medici. When trade shifted to the Atlantic seaboard in the sixteenth century the Italian towns sank into a lethargy, and their political system became a network of duchies, in which they remained till stirred from it by Napoleon and nineteenth-century liberal nationalism.

### Physical features of the medieval town

A medieval town, surrounded by its walls, with suburbs huddling close under them, was a crowded, unsanitary place, only rarely separated from its rural origins, with pigs wandering around the streets, performing the functions of garbage disposal units, and cows and horses often kept in sheds adjoining the houses. Refuse was thrown from the upper stories of the houses onto the streets, to be flushed only by the next rain. It is hardly necessary to add that plagues and epidemics were common; and as most of the houses were made of wood, fire hazards were serious. The streets were narrow, and the upper stories of the houses often projected so far that they almost met across the street. Each city had gates which could be shut in case of attack, and where customs duties could be collected. And, like a medieval castle, the typical city was surrounded with a moat which could only be crossed by a drawbridge. To us these medieval towns, of which many still exist without any very great change as the nucleus of the much larger modern town on the same site, look picturesque; and they were certainly bustling, vital centers of activity, as full of humanity as our own slum areas.

In the larger towns, however, several improvements were made, even within the medieval period. A few adopted regular methods of street cleaning, there were some with good public baths and a pure water supply, and by the late Middle Ages many of the cities had started to build sidewalks made of great paving stones embedded in sand. And in every city of importance there were some good buildings other than the church, more attractive areas where the merchant princes lived in their fortress palaces, and some imposing public buildings, especially in Italy and in the prosperous cities of Flanders.

### Population of medieval towns

Estimates of population vary very widely, and there can be no certainty on the figures. By the middle of the thirteenth century, after the destruction of Kiev by the Mongols, there can be no doubt that Palermo, the capital of the Sicilian kingdom, was the largest and most populous city in Europe after Constantinople, with a population estimated as not much short of half a million. Paris was the next, but with considerably less than half the population of Palermo, though it grew tremendously through the century and was perhaps a quarter of a million by its close. Venice probably came third, with a population of not much less than Paris. Probably no other city in Europe reached one hundred thousand, and the average city that could be called large had about fifty thousand. But these figures

*A medieval corner of Nürnberg (Germany).* (COURTESY GERMAN TOURIST INFORMATION OFFICE)

*Medieval section of the imperial city of Nördlingen. Note the similarity of this setting to the houses shown in the medieval miniatures in Chapter 17.* (COURTESY GERMAN TOURIST INFORMATION OFFICE)

are still large when the area occupied by a city is considered, for such a population was only made possible through overcrowding and by building the houses as high as, and often higher than, safety permitted.

### LEAGUES OF TOWNS

#### The Lombard League

We have already had occasion to refer to the Lombard League, which was formed to resist the demands and encroachments of the Holy Roman Empire. This league, however, made up as it was of so many rival and constantly quarreling towns with divergent

interests, never became a permanent institution. As soon as the immediate purpose for its existence had disappeared, the league split up into its component parts. The reason for this was the sporadic nature of imperial efforts to keep Italy in subjection. When the emperor and his troops had disappeared over the Alps, the spirit of independence at once revived, and with it the intercity rivalry. But in Germany, where the emperor lived and exercised a rule which was more frequently effective than in Italy, a league came into being, originally for solely commercial purposes. This league was able to develop a real unity which lasted, in spite of local rivalry, for centuries, and probably exercised at all times a more important influence than the emperor himself. This was the league of Hansa towns, usually known as the Hanseatic League.

### The Hanseatic League

Quite early in the Middle Ages various groups of merchants engaged in the import and export business from various cities used to unite for the purpose of putting pressure upon various political authorities to gain trading and economic privileges for their class, as, for instance, at the Champagne fairs, and in foreign ports. A subsidiary purpose was to restrict the entry of outsiders into their privileged group. These leagues, called *Hansas*, were essentially made up of

*Traces of medieval architecture are still apparent in Lüneburg, which was one of the principal cities in the Hanseatic League.* (COURTESY GERMAN TOURIST INFORMATION OFFICE)

individual merchants, and could not expect adequate protection for their special interests from their own city governments.

From the thirteenth century onward, German merchants belonging to a number of important trading cities banded together seriously to obtain concessions by joint action in foreign countries, especially in England, Flanders, and the Scandinavian countries at a time when Germans were also expanding politically into the Slavic countries to the northeast under the auspices of the Teutonic Knights (see Chapter 15, above). Being financially far more secure than ordinary merchants, able to extend credit even to kings, and in possession of a number of products that could not be obtained easily elsewhere and were in great demand, the Hansa merchants were found extremely useful by European rulers and were given special quarters and monopolies in the trading of many kinds of goods by these rulers, even to the detriment of their own nationals. Groups of merchants (Hansas) used to live in these foreign countries, where they proceeded to organize monopolies, even defending themselves against occasional risings by the local peoples. They had their own laws and their own courts. As time went on, these merchants were able to arrange for governments by their own class in their home cities, which they completely controlled, again against frequent opposition from the craft guilds in these cities which resented their ability to dictate prices and conditions of labor through their political power.

The league of merchant cities thus formed never had any formal rules or constitution as such, though congresses were held when necessary to discuss joint problems. The league even went to war for economic purposes on several occasions, using the militia of the Hansa towns and mercenaries, whom they could well afford to pay. By the middle of the fourteenth century almost two hundred towns and villages were directly associated with the League, and Hansa merchants had almost a monopoly of the rich Baltic trade, including trade into northern Russia, and controlled much

of the important wool trade between England and Flanders. Their great financial power in an age of small concentration of capital was their principal strength, and no European ruler could afford to antagonize them. When the king of Denmark in the fourteenth century tried to break their monopoly in the Baltic and take possession of his own herring trade, the league took to arms, and with the aid of the king of Sweden thoroughly defeated him and dictated a peace on terms extremely favorable to itself.

The league endured for several centuries, but it was on the decline by the middle of the fifteenth. The leadership was always in the hands of the chief city Lübeck, and this was resented by the second greatest city, Cologne, which at one time tried to organize a separatist league of its own. It was impossible to prevent other minor rivalries from growing up between the several cities, and naturally the excluded groups, such as the English and Dutch merchants, struggled against them, especially since the Hansa towns did not even trouble to give reciprocal privileges in their own cities to nationals of the countries where they were installed. The growing realization of the importance of trade to the economy of their countries tempted the monarchs ultimately to try conclusions with the league, and alternative routes for transportation which did not pass through Hansa territories were organized.

It was, of course, impossible in an era of increasing trade for any group permanently to maintain a trade monopoly of this kind over such a wide area, and perhaps it is surprising that the league lasted as long as it did. In any case the discovery of the Americas and so many new sources of trade would have doomed the league even if it had not already been steeply on the decline. Perhaps one continuing result of its success can still be seen in Europe. The Germans to this day are far more fond than any other people of cartels with which they have had a greater success; and the industrial cartel of the nineteenth and twentieth centuries would seem to be a direct descendant of the

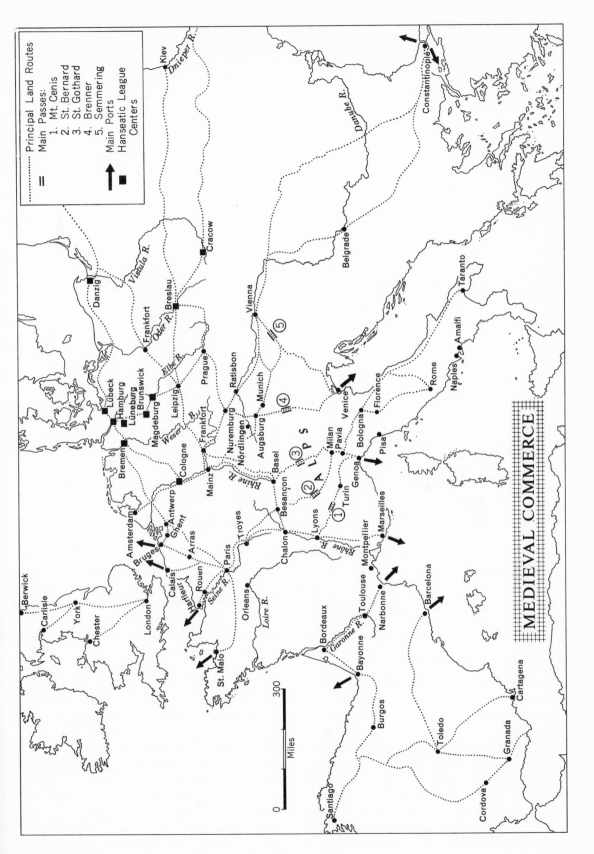

## MEDIEVAL COMMERCE

Principal Land Routes
Main Passes:
1. Mt. Cenis
2. St. Bernard
3. St. Gothard
4. Brenner
5. Semmering
Main Ports
Hanseatic League Centers

Berwick
Carlisle
York
Chester
London
Calais
Bruges
Amsterdam
Antwerp
Ghent
Arras
Rouen
Hatfleur
St. Malo
Paris
Troyes
Orleans
Chalon
Lyons
Bordeaux
Bayonne
Toulouse
Narbonne
Montpellier
Marseilles
Burgos
Santiago
Toledo
Cordova
Granada
Cartagena
Barcelona
Besançon
Basel
Mainz
Cologne
Bremen
Lübeck
Hamburg
Lüneburg
Brunswick
Magdeburg
Leipzig
Frankfort
Danzig
Breslau
Cracow
Kiev
Prague
Ratisbon
Nuremburg
Nördlingen
Augsburg
Munich
Vienna
Belgrade
Constantinople
Turin
Milan
Pavia
Genoa
Bologna
Pisa
Florence
Rome
Naples
Amalfi
Taranto
Venice

Vistula R.
Oder R.
Dnieper R.
Danube R.
Elbe R.
Weser R.
Rhine R.
Loire R.
Seine R.
Rhône R.
Garonne R.

ALPS

Miles
0    300

693

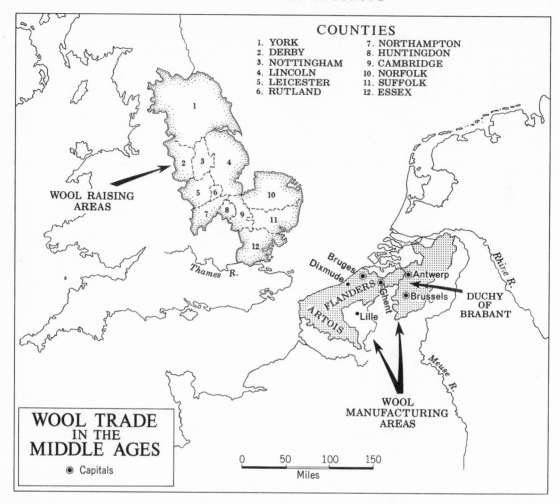

**COUNTIES**

1. YORK        7. NORTHAMPTON
2. DERBY       8. HUNTINGDON
3. NOTTINGHAM  9. CAMBRIDGE
4. LINCOLN     10. NORFOLK
5. LEICESTER   11. SUFFOLK
6. RUTLAND     12. ESSEX

WOOL RAISING AREAS

WOOL MANUFACTURING AREAS

DUCHY OF BRABANT

**WOOL TRADE IN THE MIDDLE AGES**
⊙ Capitals

0    50    100    150
Miles

medieval monopoly of the German Hanseatic merchants.

### ▶ Organization of trade and industry

OBJECTIVES OF MEDIEVAL ORGANIZATION

#### Trade for a static society

We have now examined an attempted monopoly of foreign trade over an extensive area. In this section we shall deal with the efforts at monopolistic control of trade and industry within the cities themselves.

In a static society in which it was generally believed that only a limited quantity of trade and industry was possible, all efforts were directed toward ensuring first that foreigners should have as little share of it as could be managed, and that the workers in the city should all be assured of a reasonable living and secure employment. Competition was frowned upon, especially unfair competition by means of such devices as price cutting, and cooperation was rather the ideal, enforced by strict regulation on the part of the authorities.

#### Church defense of a controlled economy

The theory behind the system was that every man was born to a certain position in society in which he was expected to remain. His economic needs were determined by his status. A noble was naturally entitled to consume more than a peasant, and it was permissible for him to indulge in display and to consume luxuries which would have been out of place in the life of an artisan or a peasant. If the latter had aspirations beyond their station, then it was likely that these were dictated by envy or pride, deadly sins condemned by the Church and society. If the common man had a desire for luxury or display, he must be actuated by some form of sensuality, another sin. If he simply wished to accumulate wealth, then he was motivated by avarice; or if he wished to consume too many of the good things of life, then he was a glutton. Finally, if he wished to save enough money for a comfortable old age, then he was slothful and lazy; he wished to avoid work, and this desire, too, was a deadly sin. In view of such restrictions, it was clear that public and ecclesiastical opinion would condemn any enterprise undertaken by the poor and lowborn man for the sake of profit. It was certainly not considered in the Middle Ages that the appetite for gain was a natural principle of human nature, nor that enlightened self-interest was a virtue. Life on earth, in any case, according to the teachings of the Church, should not be too pleasurable; the proper task of man was to prepare for the hereafter and endure whatever came to him in this life without expecting too much of it. Work was a consequence of the sin of Adam. Before the Fall, Adam and Eve had been permitted to live a lazy life in Paradise, but when they were driven out of the Garden of Eden, the Lord God had told the guilty pair that they would have to live by hard work. But the Middle Ages never regarded work as anything but a curse; it was left for the Protestants to glorify work and even write a hymn, every line of which begins with the word "work," concluding with the deathless line, "Work for the night is coming when man works no more!"

The Church likewise objected to the making of profits by merchants, unless the profits were a payment for work honestly performed such as the legitimate charge made for the transportation of goods. Like Karl Marx, the Church held a labor theory of value. The cost of an article plus a reasonable wage was all that the merchant was entitled to. Thus it was possible to calculate a fair and just price for every piece of merchandise. Any price fixed above this was profiteering. It was particularly reprehensible to engross, or try to corner the market, since the increased price represented no honest labor; the practice was morally evil in that it meant taking advantage of the necessities of poor men and charging them highly because the goods which they needed had been made artificially scarce. Forestalling was a similar crime; this was the practice of buying up goods from the peasant before they reached the market, and for the same purpose of pushing up prices. Even coming between the producer and the consumer unnecessarily and buying and selling at a profit was considered wrong, unless there was an obvious need for a middleman's service. The practice was called *regrating*.

Lending money at interest had always been considered wicked by Christians because money was supposed to be sterile, having no value in itself; and, further, to take money for helping others when such a service should be provided free was contrary to Scripture. It was taking advantage of the poor; and indeed, since loans for consumption purposes—the type of borrowing a poor man usually does—were poorly secured, the interest rates for consumer credit were high then, as now. In the early Middle Ages, since it was impossible to do without some form of consumer credit, this business was in the hands of Jews, who were, of course, not bound by ecclesiastical regulations, and who were prevented by various restrictions from making a living in other fields. All lending of money was called usury, whether for high or low rates of interest, and was considered sinful. Secular and clerical authorities constantly condemned and attempted to regulate it. But in an age of growing capitalism it was found impossible to maintain all the artificial restrictions which were suited to a static society. For several centuries, however, the guilds followed faithfully the rules laid down by the Church, with which, indeed, they were fully in sympathy, since they prevented one man from taking unfair advantage of his fellows with consequent unemployment.

## THE MERCHANT GUILDS

The earliest form of organization within the towns was the merchant guild, or guild merchant. This was originally a union of merchants and traders, including also the upper class of artisans; and its purpose was to prevent foreign competition and to divide up the home trade equitably between the members. In some cases the merchant guild came into existence before a town even had a charter, and, indeed, it was often the guild which succeeded in extracting the charter from the overlord of the town; in many towns the guild became the actual municipal government afterward. The merchant guild, like the later craft guild, was a closed shop; traders who did not belong to the guild would find themselves excluded from trade within the city.

At the same time it was in the nature also of a fraternal society, taking care of the funerals and other sudden expenses of members, and for a long time it worked closely in conjunction with the Church in other matters, making its own penalties against members who forestalled and engrossed and seeing to it that the widows of deceased members were properly treated, and that prayers were said for the souls of the departed.

The monopolies held in trade matters varied from town to town. Reciprocal privileges could be granted to foreign traders when they seemed to be in the interest of the guild, but severe penalties were always enforced against price cutters; and it was possible to enforce penalties because exclusion from a guild in early times would mean that the offending trader lost his business. And cases are known of the assaulting and beating of offenders.

One interesting example of guild activity is the arrangement made for the export of English wool, which was grown in England and sent abroad to Flanders to be made into cloth. An organization came into existence to collect the wool and ship it to France, where it was stored in the city of Calais, which belonged to the English until the sixteenth century. The ships in which the wool was carried were owned jointly by members of the guild, though each man traded for himself in the collection and distribution of the wool. Such organizations were greatly favored by the English kings, who were able to tax the wool far more easily than if hundreds of separate traders had to be assessed or hundreds of shipments examined. The Merchants Staplers flourished for almost three centuries, until the wool trade declined at the end of the fifteenth century.

As has been said, the early merchant guilds included also representatives of the manufacturers, the crafts. But these soon split off and formed their own analogous associations which will be dealt with in the next section. Thereafter the merchant guilds acted as selling agents for the craft guilds. They always remained both more powerful and more prosperous than the much smaller craft guilds, and it was almost always the merchant guilds rather than the craftsmen which were able to control the government of the town. But by the same token, the merchant guilds declined long before the craft guilds, since with the increase in their trade the individual merchants preferred to carry on business for themselves and compete with their former colleagues, and restrictions were far more hampering to trade than to small-scale manufacture.

Merchant guilds today are common in the Far East, especially among Chinese merchants in such cities as Singapore, where the trade is largely in Chinese hands although the government is alien. All major trading in foreign imports is in the hands of rings, or guilds, and interlopers are forced to be content with relatively small sales. In the West, however, with the increase in the importance of manufacturing, associations of traders alone have only rarely any useful function to perform, though some of the activities such as price fixing are still attempted. It is in foreign markets that the guild still survives under various forms.

THE CRAFT GUILDS

### Purpose and function

The craft guild was an organization formed to protect the working conditions in a particular industry and also to protect the public. Not all industries were formed into guilds, and the guild organization was not uniform throughout Europe, being strongest in the German and northern towns and weakest in Italy. The regulations of the craft guild were very rigid and very strictly enforced, but always with the same objectives in mind and logically worked out to attain them.

The product had to be sold at a just price, which included the cost of labor and raw materials. It is clear that if any artisan skimped on his material, used inferior workmanship, or cut wages, then the resulting product would be priced too high in relation to its actual value if the price were the same as for goods of standard quality; and of course price cutting was strictly forbidden. Regulations as to the standard of quality were set up by the guild masters in each guild, since only these experts could determine what was the correct quality in their particular craft.

Hours of labor were prescribed and enforced. Nightwork was, as a rule, entirely forbidden, both because it tended to spoil the quality of the work and because the worker who labored for additional hours would in this way be able to get ahead of his neighbors. If one group of workers did overtime, it was clear to the medievals that others would have to do the same, in the same way that one price cutter would force all others to cut their prices too. Improved methods of manufacture were not regarded kindly if introduced by individual craftsmen; it was therefore usual to insist that any such improvements should be agreed to by the guild, which would have the opportunity of spreading the information among all its members.

Advertising of all kinds was forbidden. No salesman could draw attention to his wares in any manner whatever; even a diplomatic sneeze when a customer passed was considered improper and in one place forbidden. Craftsmen had to do their work in shops which were visible from the street so that their practices were at all times open to inspection. Shops were limited in size so that no master could become a regular employer of labor, and thus drive down his costs and perhaps cut prices; and it was forbidden also to attempt to entice away workers from a rival shop.

In brief, the central ideas of the craft guilds were that there was enough work for all if everyone worked for reasonable hours and produced goods of first-rate quality; that every article had a fair price which customers should be able to pay; that the customer who paid this fixed price should be protected from his probable ignorance of the quality of his purchase; and that there was no need to cut this price, since everyone would suffer, and in a limited market no increased business for all would result.

The guilds died very slowly; indeed, some are still in existence today with comparatively small modifications. Their usefulness was impaired when it was discovered that the market was not so limited as had been once thought, and that more goods could in fact be sold if the price were reduced. The guild system was fitted for a truly static society, and unquestionably prevented the terrible abuses which occurred in the early factory system under the Industrial Revolution. Conditions for the medieval worker were incomparably better than those in the early nineteenth century. His living was secured, he did not have to compete for jobs with his fellow workers, and there was a far closer personal relationship between an apprentice and a journeyman and their master than the simple cash nexus of the pay envelope under the industrial system. He did not have to work long hours, and he did not have to work overtime; nor did his wife and family have to aid in the work in order to secure a living wage for the family unit, as in the early nineteenth century.

Moreover, the guild itself was a fraternal society with many social functions to perform. The guilds produced plays, they organized processions on days of festivals, and on the feast day of the saint of a particular guild the latter usually had a colorful pageant. They had fraternal drinking parties, sometimes held in a building of their own, a guildhall. If a guildsman fell sick or died, his fellow members took care of him or paid the expenses of the funeral and tried to assist his widow and family. When a member got into trouble with the law, the guild was expected to defend him and even visit him in jail, and cases between members were settled by arbitration within the guild rather than in the public court. Insults offered to fellow members were punished with fines assessed by the guild.

The guild was able to protect the in-terests of its members only because of its restraint of competition and the consequence that a price could be fixed which would cover expenses with a sufficient margin. Only when competition can be restrained in this way and when desire or possibility is lacking to increase one's own business at the expense of one's neighbors can a guild of the medieval kind flourish. Unfair practices in later centuries within the guild, refusal to allow qualified journeymen to become masters, and competition between these journeymen and the established masters, with consequent price cutting, helped to break down their organization. But above all the realization that the market was not limited, and the growth of competition and price cutting, undermined them even before the Industrial Revolution which gave most of them the *coup de grâce*. Trade unions to-

*The Cloth Hall of Ypres (Belgium), one of the most perfect examples of a medieval commercial building. The hall was destroyed during World War I.* (COURTESY BELGIUM GOVERNMENT INFORMATION CENTER)

day still use, however, many guild practices, and their use is increasing even in America, where certain commodities can be sold at a fixed price which allows the unions to demand and receive fraternal benefits paid by the corporations that employ them. And the apprentice system, about to be described, is still applicable in many industries which require skills that can only be acquired over an extended period, although the system itself has naturally been modified to meet conditions brought about by the Industrial Revolution.

### Internal organization of the craft guild

The young artisan first entered the guild by becoming apprentice to a master, on payment of a fee. The apprenticeship might last for as long as twelve years according to the nature of the particular craft; the usual period for most crafts was seven years. The boy, however, became an apprentice, when his family signed an indenture. It was the master's task to supervise the boy's morals and behavior as well as his work. He boarded at his master's home, and had to obey his orders in everything. When the apprenticeship was over and the boy was thoroughly trained in his craft, he became a journeyman (dayworker) and was free to leave his master and take work at regular wages wherever he could find it. He could stay on with his master, and perhaps it was the usual custom in early times for him to do so. But in certain trades, especially the building trade, it was of great advantage for the journeyman to work in foreign cities, improving his knowledge of his trade by examining or taking part in the building of churches, cathedrals, and public offices.

In the early Middle Ages, there was no difficulty in the way of a journeyman who wanted to set up himself as a master. While business was gradually increasing there was enough work for all, and the guild had no objections, provided the journeyman had sufficient savings to enable him to purchase the shop and the raw materials and had a wife who could take care of his apprentices. He had to pass an examination before the

guild master (or warden), demonstrating his efficiency and his good character and financial standing. The former, however, would be well known from his work as apprentice or journeyman if he remained in the same town. Foreign journeymen were sometimes admitted as masters in early times, though in later times, when the market had become saturated, this practice was abandoned.

All artisans were theoretically members of the guild, though apprentices could not take part in elections or in the management of the guild until they became journeymen. In later times journeymen were also excluded, leaving the guild a monopoly of the masters. As trade increased, and with the decline of serfdom, it was increasingly difficult to maintain the monopoly, but for a long time the masters attempted to maintain it by every means at their disposal. Probably before the middle of the fourteenth century, members of the guilds, apprentices, and journeymen had not felt the guild as a restriction upon their freedom, since there really was enough work for all at a fair price, and an apprentice could look forward to a secure future and ultimately a mastership in his chosen craft. But from this time the situation changed seriously for the worse, and the monopolies had to be broken down if any freedom and security were to be achieved.

The masters had gradually realized the extensive power that had been put into their hands by the system, and with the growing freedom of enterprise and the larger profits gained by the capitalist merchants, the masters evidently felt they should also be entitled to similar rewards, if not through the exercise of increased initiative. They began to try to limit the entries of masters into their respective industries and to keep apprentices and journeymen as their employees whom they could exploit for profit. An ingenious system was invented under which a journeyman had to produce a masterpiece approved by the guild of masters before he could set up for himself, an excellent opportunity for the use of discrimination.[1] The masters began to hand over their businesses only to their sons, and to wait until they were grown up, whether or not they were as skilled as the available journeymen. The masters also used economic pressure against the journeymen by keeping their wages down so that they would not have enough capital to start their own shops. And as the numbers of journeymen increased, it was possible to use the shortage of jobs for this purpose. The masters also charged substantial fees for the privilege of becoming masters, whereas in the earlier days only the capital required for the business was asked of a newcomer. Even among the masters themselves distinctions began to be drawn between wealthy and less wealthy members, and masters of the lower rank were excluded from some of the guild functions, and sometimes had to work for the richer masters not unlike the ordinary journeymen.

The result was inevitable. The journeymen, who were usually just as skilled as the masters, began to band together into journeymen's societies apart from the guild, and set up shops of their own where they could compete with the masters and cut prices. Though in cities where they possessed it the masters used their control of the government to legislate against the journeymen, they were unable to suppress them everywhere. Strikes by journeymen wage earners also became common. But the richer masters were by this time securely entrenched, and having accumulated capital, many of them entered into associations for the promotion of exports similar to the organizations of the merchant guilds. They bought raw materials and had them worked up into export goods by the lesser masters and journeymen. Thus the manufacturing system gradually became capitalistic in the modern manner, and apprentices and journeymen and masters became merely distinguished by their degrees of skill and the wages they could command

[1] The plot of Wagner's opera *The Mastersingers of Nuremberg* is concerned with the production of a "song-masterpiece" in accordance with guild regulations for song writers, the intricacies of which are unknown to the hero of the opera.

for their skill. The guilds, as such, had lost their original purpose; they served to regulate conditions for the apprenticeship, and to some extent could still ensure standards of workmanship. But with the rise of competition the temptation to cut corners, and to debase the standards of craftsmanship and thus sell at a lower price, became irresistible; and with this the monopolistic structure of the guilds could no longer be maintained. Capitalism in industry caught up with capitalism in trade, and the way was open for the Industrial Revolution.

▶ **The rise of medieval capitalism**

BREAKDOWN OF CONTROL OVER
PROFIT SEEKING

From the above discussion it will be seen that the possibility of making profits, as distinct from commanding a living wage in exchange for one's labor, was present from the early thirteenth century in the merchant guilds, and rather later in the craft guilds. But first the social and religious control over the economy had to be broken, and enough money had to be available, or suitable substitutes for coined money developed, so that it would be worth while for the private enterpriser to go ahead and seek profits and the higher standard of living that resulted from profit making. The individual merchant had to escape from the restrictions of the guild merchant, and the individual master had to escape from the necessity of sharing any advances he made with his fellow guild members.

Severe competition among individual traders led naturally to efforts to avoid the traditional cooperation. But few could individually afford, for instance, the cost of a voyage to the Near East, and survive the long wait for financial returns. It was possible for a few traders to get together and plan a joint voyage by pooling their resources. But even this arrangement was difficult unless credit could be acquired. And credit came up at once against the laws of usury, backed not only by the Church but by the State.

The merchants did not attempt a frontal attack on the laws. They gradually learned to circumvent them. And the Church, which was a large property owner itself and often also needed to borrow on the strength of its expected income from ecclesiastical revenues, began to permit certain disguised forms of lending money at interest. One of the earliest forms of borrowing was on the equivalent of a mortgage. A man who owned a piece of property on which a regular rent was paid could sell the land for a limited number of years for a fixed price paid down at one time. He would thus receive a sum of money equal to, say, ten years' revenue, and the sale would be for eleven years. Thus the creditor would collect income for eleven years, although he had advanced money which would be repaid in ten. The eleventh year's income therefore was the equivalent of interest on the original loan. A similar device was used by cities and by the Church itself when short of ready money. All tax farming is based on the same principle. The difference between this device and a mortgage, which for social reasons was frowned upon, was that the borrower did not himself have to repay the loan at all, and his land could not be foreclosed upon since it already belonged for the limited period to the creditor.

A common device was to promise the return of a loan, officially made without interest, at a date by which it was impossible to repay. Then the debtor paid a fine for not keeping his promise. Shylock's famous loan, in Shakespeare's *Merchant of Venice,* was of this nature. A forfeit had to be made, in this case the pound of flesh, as a penalty for not repaying the loan on the due date. Interest was also concealed on agreements for sale when cash was paid in advance. The price agreed upon would take care of the fact that payment, that is, the loan, had been made so early, and would be rather lower than if it had been paid for at the time of delivery. Even if no goods at all were sold, a bill of sale could be made out on the lines indicated above without much fear of discovery.

The Church did not raise such serious objections to usury when the lender risked his capital as when security was good. Theoretically he could be compensated for not having the use of his own money at a time when he needed it. Partnerships of the kinds used so often to finance voyages could conceal the giving of credit and the payment of interest. A merchant could buy himself a share in an enterprise, and when the voyage was successful the share due him could be calculated on the basis of the capital invested plus a return for the use of the money. The same arrangement could also be made to take care of the losses sustained if a ship were sunk. A substantial bonus could be paid if the voyage were successful, while the lender would not even get his money back if the ship were lost. This was, of course, the equivalent of insurance, reinvented by the medieval Italian capitalists, though known also to the ingenious Greeks of an earlier civilization. By the fifteenth century this insurance had become regularized by underwriting, an arrangement by which a number of merchants and financiers agreed in writing to absorb a share of the risks of a voyage in exchange for a bonus if it was successful.

The Church, and many states, continued to legislate against usury, and in the early fourteenth century the Church even tried to bring it within the reach of the Inquisition by announcing that anyone who denied that usury was a sin was a heretic; but by this time business had largely moved out of the reach of spiritual sanctions, and kings profited too much by the prosperity that came from the use of credit to be willing to enforce the laws too strictly. But loans for consumption purposes remained a serious crime, and as they were made in general by professional moneylenders who did not possess as much political power as ordinary merchants, these men could be brought into court and heavily fined for usury, a useful addition to the coffers of penurious kings. And the feeling was never lost that such credit really was an unproductive use of money and took advantage of the hardships of poor men. In time the Franciscans undertook to take care of consumer credit, setting up *montes pietatis* (hills of piety), where the poor man could borrow at very low rates of interest on the security of some small piece of personal property which he handed over for safekeeping until the loan was repaid. This, of course, was the origin of the pawnbroking establishment which soon spread beyond the Franciscan Order.

In addition to the laws on usury, the law on the just price had to be abrogated or circumvented. This, however, was much easier to get around than the laws on usury, since it was impossible to enforce a just price, as no one knew for certain exactly what did constitute a just price. It was only possible to enforce this law ordinarily by purely commercial sanctions, such as refusing to do business with a profiteer; and such sanctions needed a strong merchant guild. Since offenses against the just price would usually be in the direction of an excessively low price, it was not to the interest of anyone except the merchants to enforce the law, though engrossing and cornering the market could be dealt with by kings if they had the power. Even the Venetian government of merchants could not prevent the lowering of prices through the ordinary working of competition and soon ceased to attempt it.

As the older medieval idea that a man's proper business in life was to seek salvation disappeared in favor of the search for wealth and comfort in this life through accumulating riches, even the Church accommodated itself to the reality, emphasizing that the profits should be used for a moral end, such as philanthropic bequests and, of course, gifts to the Church for the souls of deceased merchants. All Churches, including the later Protestant ones, have continued to insist that wealth has its responsibilities, and most Churches have observed the special dangers to a man's soul inherent in both the possession and the pursuit of riches, which can be more easily misused for sinful purposes than the

few possessions of the poor. But at all events by the fourteenth century the capitalist was a respectable member of society to all but ascetic reformers; and such social and religious control over his activities as had operated in the early medieval period was virtually at an end. Only the techniques necessary for business growth and opportunities for the full expansion of trade and profit seeking remained to be discovered.

### THE ACCUMULATION OF CAPITAL

Europe had always, even in Roman times, been seriously short of the precious metals, and so far no acceptable substitute had been found. There was very little gold in Europe, and even silver mines could not supply enough to finance all the transactions for which silver was needed. As was noticed above, the balance of trade turned in favor of the West before the end of the thirteenth century, and thereafter gold and silver and precious stones began to move into Europe from the better-supplied Oriental world. The conquest of Constantinople by the crusaders must have added no mean amount to the meager supplies of the West as early as 1204. We have seen also that the flow of gold, especially into Italy, enabled both Florence and Venice to institute gold coinages in the thirteenth century, and florins and ducats circulated all through Europe, being accepted at their face value. As a whole, Europe was developing slowly into a money economy, and even in the manorial system payment in money instead of kind became the rule; and money was always to be found in the local markets. Nevertheless, the chronic shortage remained until the discovery of the Americas, which removed all fear of shortage for the foreseeable future; some African gold resulting from the Portuguese expansion at the end of the fifteenth century, and a few new silver mines, would not have sufficed without the Americas. In the later Middle Ages opportunities for using money were so great that little coin was hidden and accumulated without being used. There was no reason to fear any devaluation; on the contrary, there was every incentive to put coin into circulation at once and allow it to make more money for the owner. In Italy it was not unusual for a sleeping partner, providing capital for a man who was energetic and enterprising but lacked capital, to take up to 75 per cent of the profits of a whole voyage in exchange for a purely financial contribution.

The largest accumulators of capital were the Church and those kings who had an effective control of their finances, such as Philip IV of France. Tax payments to the Church and to the State had to be made in cash and could hardly be made in kind. Nobles and peasants alike had to turn their produce into money before they could pay taxes. But often the kings did not look after their money well, leaving its handling to favorites, many of whom built up enormous fortunes through graft, speculation in land, moneylending, and various financial operations. Both Church and kings frequently had to resort to banking houses for ready cash, secured against future revenues; and the Church for centuries made use of the specialized banking services that came to be offered by Italian bankers, who were known as Lombards, whether they hailed from Lombardy or not. These bankers often acted as collectors of papal revenue, transferring deposits from European countries to Rome for the benefit of the papacy, and taking their share in the process so that over a period of time they were able to accumulate very considerable sums. Nevertheless, these bankers, with so much money tied up in loans to the great, were often very insecure financially because of their lack of liquidity. When King Edward III of England defaulted on his debts to the Italian houses in the middle of the fourteenth century, many of them, including the greatest of all, were ruined.

Banks run by Christians existed in Europe from at least the twelfth century, and the thirteenth century saw a great extension of their activities. On the whole they specialized in business credit of the types referred to above. They lent money for profitable enterprises such as voyages, and they opened branches in every country of Europe, whose cities to this day often have their Lombard Streets, which may be still, as in London, in the center of the financial district. Bankers began to accept deposits and lend out as loans the bulk of what was deposited and on which they charged interest. In due course they tried to attract deposits by paying interest in turn. In this way they kept the limited amount of money in circulation, only retaining a small amount in hand for repayment to depositors. One of the early banking groups was the crusading Order of the Templars, whose strong castles in Europe attracted those who wished to keep their money safe. But the Templars themselves also lent out the money deposited with them, and became so rich that in the early fourteenth century Philip IV of France trumped up charges of sorcery and heresy against them and was able, with the assistance of the pope, to dispossess them.

The deposit banks were, for the most part, moneylenders who lent money for comparatively small business transactions and sometimes for consumer credit. The larger merchant banks, however, specialized in financing large transactions and in lending money to kings and to the papacy. By the fifteenth century many cities had set up banks of their own to facilitate municipal transactions; these accepted small deposits, and were the forerunners of modern deposit banking; some of them, notably the Bank of St. George in Genoa, still exist today. But far greater profits were to be gained from participating in trade voyages and other large-scale commercial transactions than from lending to individuals; for this reason it was the great Italian private banking houses which engaged in activities of this sort that made the really startling profits of these early days of capitalism. And it was almost entirely due to the efforts of these great houses that the important late medieval inventions for facilitating trade were introduced to the Western world. So many commercial techniques were invented that not much remained for the ingenuity of modern times except to perfect them.

## IMPROVEMENT OF BUSINESS TECHNIQUES

Perhaps the most important single invention was the *bill of exchange,* which obviated the necessity for the transport of bullion on horseback through Europe, with all the dangers from bandits and robbers entailed, to say nothing of legal regulations against the exporting of gold and silver coins, which almost every ruler tried to enforce. The bill of exchange is simply an agreement to pay in a certain currency at a named date a specified sum of money. The merchant who gave the bill could then make arrangements to suit his own convenience to send the money to the specified place. If he had debtors in the foreign city, he could have them pay the bill, or he could at least shorten the journey for the bullion by sending it from some place where he had a debtor. As a natural evolution of the bill of exchange came the *draft,* which directed the merchant's debtor to pay to some third party a specified sum of money, and the *acceptance,* which made the draft negotiable since the acceptor had agreed to pay. When the Italian merchants developed a world-wide trade with correspondents and customers in all important cities, they seldom needed to send much cash. Transfers of actual bullion were only necessary to settle an unfavorable balance of trade, and before the final transfer was made a vast number of transactions might have taken place. Such devices at least in part compensated for the chronic shortage of gold and silver.

Right at the end of the Middle Ages at the close of the fifteenth century came the most symptomatic invention in the business field, showing clearly that the capitalists had at last understood the goal of their business operations, namely, profit making. This invention, first described by the Italian Pacioli, was double-entry bookkeeping, which divided all business transactions into debits and credits, thus enabling the merchant to learn at any moment the exact condition of his business, and whether or

not he was making a profit. This invention, of course, was hardly possible as long as Roman numerals and the abacus were the only tools available for addition and subtraction. By the end of the fifteenth century, however, the Arabic numerals and the positional and decimal system had been accepted so widely that Pacioli's treatise became the standard work in accountancy, and his method was adopted everywhere throughout Europe by progressive businessmen.

The true joint-stock company was not a medieval invention, but the arrangements for financing the voyages of Italian merchants came close to it. Mention has already been made of simple partnerships, under which one partner was likely to provide the capital while the other made the actual voyage. The second partner was thus enabled to accumulate some capital as a reward for his enterprise, and might be able on the next occasion to share also in the financing. In the Middle Ages accumulation of capital was sufficiently rare for money to breed money with extreme rapidity, and the capitalist was paid excessively for the risk he took, frequently, as already mentioned, receiving as much as 75 per cent of the proceeds of the voyage. But if he put up only two thirds and the active partner put up as much as one third, then the profits would be divided equally. Curiously enough, it is in the early Middle Ages that this arrangement, the nearest thing to a joint-stock company, emerged at a time when capital was so rare that for an extensive voyage the risk and the profits would often be shared among a considerable number of merchants, each of whom received in proportion to the shares he had purchased. In later times this plan was regarded as too cumbersome, except perhaps in the case of very large loans to monarchs to which a number of bankers would subscribe. As soon as enough capital accumulated in the hands of individuals, such men then preferred to assume all the expenses, and to profit accordingly. The joint-stock company was only revived in modern times for the same reasons

*A page from the earliest European printed work, the Gutenberg Bible.* (COURTESY THE PIERPONT MORGAN LIBRARY) that the Genoese used its earlier form in the thirteenth century—when business transactions became too great to be financed by single men or by small partnerships.

OTHER MEDIEVAL INVENTIONS

The improvements in navigation have already been referred to briefly. The mariner's compass, taken over from the Muslims, was improved by having the needle put on a pivot as in the modern compass. The astrolabe, used for determining latitude, was known in the early Middle Ages, but was perfected for nautical use later. Direct water power was in use in mills for grinding grain, the water falling on a wheel and making it revolve. Milling was the earliest use of the water wheel, but in the later Middle Ages it was used for many other purposes, one of the earliest being for the sawing of wood. The windmill was also employed for various purposes, but windmills were not very widespread by the end of the Middle Ages. Gunpowder, mentioned by Roger Bacon in the thirteenth century as an invention of great possibilities, was used for cannon by the fourteenth, and some time during the next century it was used in hand guns, though the crossbow and the longbow, far more accurate weapons, were not outmoded for a considerable time.

One of the most influential inventions, however, was not made by Europeans but was imported from the East. Paper from rags, originally made in China many centuries earlier, was used also by the Muslims during the height of their civilization, and probably came to the Western world from Spain. Before the advent of rag paper, parchment and papyrus had been used; but their excessive cost had a hampering effect upon all forms of written communication. Once paper had come into the West, business quickly seized upon the invention and used it as an aid in keeping accurate accounts. And it was not long before paper was also used in the printing of books.

The story of the Western invention of printing from movable type is still a matter of dispute. There is no doubt that priority in the invention of printing itself belongs to China. The fundamental idea behind printing lies far back in history in ancient Sumer, where seals were used for impressing clay tablets. The Chinese used wooden blocks, and the earliest printing in the West likewise made use of wooden blocks, a separate block having to be made for each page of a book. This process, however, was scarcely less expensive than copying each page by hand. It is not yet certain whether the idea of these wooden blocks actually came to the West from China by the process of diffusion, or whether it was separately invented in, the West. At all events, the crucial invention was the printing from movable metal type, which seems to have originated in Korea, but will forever be associated in the West with the name of John Gutenberg (*ca.* 1398–1468). Almost every European country had a share in the perfecting of printing with movable metal type, but there can be no doubt that the first great center of printing was Mainz, where Gutenberg was the leading craftsman and inventor in the field. Gutenberg's Mazarin Bible (so called because the first copy to attract widespread attention in modern times was in Cardinal Mazarin's library) is the first printed book known (completed 1456), took several years to print, and is still one of the finest examples of the printer's art ever produced.

The earliest printed books, called *incunabula* if printed before 1500,[2] were made with extreme care. Most of them were religious books which remained for many years in great demand. But before the end of the fifteenth century the Venetians and Flemish in particular started to print the classics of Greece and Rome, and other more popular works. Perhaps no invention in the history of mankind has been more influential and has changed more lives than printing.

Medieval inventions in the field of commerce, industry, and technology may not amount to a very impressive total, but it can surely be claimed that they were crucial.

[2] The word means "cradle books," i.e., books printed in the cradle days of printing.

In this, as in so many other fields of activity, our medieval forebears may clearly be seen to have laid the foundations of the modern world.

► ## Suggestions for further reading

There has been a great deal of controversy in recent years among scholars on the question of the origin of the towns of medieval Europe. On the whole, the thesis of H. Pirenne, in *Medieval Cities, Their Origin and the Revival of Trade* (tr. F. D. Halsey; Princeton, N. J.: Princeton University Press, 1925), is now accepted by the majority of scholars, and it is still probably the best book on medieval cities for the student. A great deal of information, based on a lifetime of historical research, is contained within this small book.

Pirenne was also to the fore with a theory, sustained by some evidence, that trade in the Mediterranean area suffered only a short period of decline when the Muslims controlled the sea, and revived quickly as soon as the Christians again took possession of it. Later scholars, though, have been impressed with the amount of trade still carried on by European cities with the Muslims and so have tended to modify Pirenne's thesis. However this may be, there is a great deal of solid material on medieval trade to be found in his brilliant book, *The Economic and Social History of Medieval Europe* (tr. I. E. Clegg; New York: Harcourt, Brace & Co., Inc., 1937), which is an extract from a much larger work not yet translated from the French. A monumental work, which is a little out of date but a mine of information, is J. W. Thompson, *The Economic and Social History of the Middle Ages, 300–1300*, and *The Economic*

*and Social History of Europe in the later Middle Ages, 1300–1530* (New York: Appleton-Century-Crofts, Inc., 1928–1931). However, for the beginning student it is probably best to read the medieval chapters in any of the standard economic histories of Europe. Excellent is H. Heaton, *Economic History of Europe* (rev. ed.; New York: Harper & Brothers, 1948). The medieval chapters in S. B. Clough and C. W. Cole, *Economic History of Europe* (rev. ed.; Boston: D. C. Heath and Company, 1947), also contain a great deal of useful information not to be found in ordinary histories. There is a Berkshire study by S. Baldwin, *Business in the Middle Ages* (New York: Henry Holt & Co., Inc., 1937), which has its uses, but the author is so anxious to confound opponents and change stereotypes which he feels are still too often accepted that his book seems rather too argumentative for such a short study, and his material appears somewhat arbitrarily selected. Though there is a good deal of useful information in the book, it should not be read by itself without supplementary information from other sources.

R. H. Tawney, *Religion and the Rise of Capitalism* (New York: Penguin Books, 1947), is a classic study in English of the relationship between religious ideas and the growth of trade and commerce. Making effective use of a theory of the German sociologist Max Weber, Tawney undoubtedly overstates his case for the influence of Protestant ethics on the growth of modern capitalism, and his view of the medieval economy as the antithesis of this capitalism is equally overstated. But the theoretical views of the Church on the place of business in society are very clearly shown in the early chapters of this work, even though theory in this case was often far removed from practice.

**Nulli vendemus, nulli negabimus, aut differemus, rectum aut justiciam . . .**

*To no one will we sell, to no one will we deny or delay, right or justice . . .*

# VI The Beginnings of the Modern State System

*Facsimile of Magna Carta. The passage quoted is from Section 40.*

# 22

# The Emergence of National
# States in Europe

*The national state: key political institution of Western civilization • The failure of Germany and Italy to attain national statehood • The English national state • The unification of France • The Spanish national state*

---

▶ **The national state as the key political institution of Western civilization**

CONTRAST WITH CITY-STATE AND EMPIRES

Prior to our own Western civilization the key governmental institution which developed the most advanced political forms was the city-state, whose weaknesses were discussed at length in the chapter on Greece. City-states, unable to solve their problems, and especially unable to refrain from fratricidal warfare, were usually replaced by great empires, of which we have seen many examples in this book. But it is difficult to point to many instances in the ancient world of the true national state, whose inhabitants were bound by ties of loyalty to their fellow nationals, who felt that they had some kind of common kinship merely because they inhabited a certain area of land, larger than a city.

Perhaps the nearest to the modern national state was ancient Egypt, which was considerably more than a mere geographic entity. The Pharaoh of Egypt was a king-god who was responsible for the welfare of Egypt and not that of other countries; he commanded loyalty from his people as their protector. The Egyptians, in the manner of some modern states, despised the people of Babylonia, who were unfortunate enough to have a "Nile in the sky," and called them "wretched Asiatics." The ancient Hebrews also had a patriotic feeling beyond that of the city-states, and again they had a national God to lead them. But their loyalty was religious and cultural rather than based on the possession of a particular territory, and northerners soon separated from southerners when political and economic conditions suggested a division.

The national state, therefore, is a relatively modern phenomenon, and is not even necessarily the final political form to be evolved by the human race. But its achievements up to this time have been impressive enough, even though it too has failed to solve the problem of fratricidal interstate warfare; which may yet result in the establishment of new empires recognizably similar to those of the ancient world. The national state, possessing within its borders economic resources far greater than those commanded by city-states, has proved superior to the city-state in that it has been able to support comparatively efficient governments manned by professional officials, free from excessive

# ► chronological chart

| The English National State | | The French National State | |
|---|---|---|---|
| Reign of Edward the Confessor | 1042–1066 | Reign of Hugh Capet | 987–996 |
| Norman Conquest of England | 1066 | Reign of Louis vi, the Fat | 1108–1137 |
| Domesday Book completed | 1086 | Dissolution of marriage between | |
| Oath of Salisbury | 1086 | Louis vii and Eleanor of Aquitaine | 1152 |
| Reign of Henry i | 1100–1135 | Reign of Philip Augustus | 1180–1223 |
| Interregnum in English monarchy (reign of Stephen) | 1135–1154 | Reign of Louis ix | 1226–1270 |
| Marriage of Henry Plantagenet to Eleanor of Aquitaine | 1152 | Reign of Philip iv, the Fair | 1285–1314 |
| Henry ii king of England | 1154–1189 | Summoning of States-General | 1302 |
| Assize of Clarendon (grand jury) | 1166 | End of Capetian monarchy | 1328 |
| Murder of St. Thomas Becket | 1170 | Hundred Years' War with England | 1337–1453 |
| Richard i held to ransom by Emperor Henry vi | 1194 | Battle of Poitiers—Capture of King John ii | 1356 |
| Reign of John | 1199–1216 | The Jacquerie—Murder of Etienne Marcel | 1358 |
| Loss of French lands to Philip | 1202–1204 | | |
| Struggle with Pope Innocent iii | 1205–1213 | Treaty of Brétigny | 1360 |
| Battle of Bouvines | 1214 | Duchy of Burgundy granted by John ii to his son Philip | 1363 |
| Magna Carta | 1215 | | |
| Provisions of Oxford | 1258 | Reconquest of most of territory lost to England | 1369–1380 |
| Battle of Lewes—Henry iii captured by Simon de Montfort | 1264 | John the Fearless becomes Duke of Burgundy | 1404 |
| Simon de Montfort's Parliament | 1265 | | |
| Battle of Evesham—Defeat and death of Simon | 1265 | Intermittent civil war in France between Burgundy and House of Valois (Armagnacs) | 1407–1435 |
| Reign of Edward i | 1272–1307 | | |
| Conquest of Wales | 1276–1284 | Henry v of England invades France | 1415 |
| The Model Parliament | 1295 | Reign of Charles vii | 1422–1461 |
| Battle of Bannockburn—Scottish independence | 1314 | Joan of Arc at siege of Orléans | 1429 |
| Outbreak of the Hundred Years' War | 1337 | Coronation of Charles vii at Rheims | 1429 |
| Battle of Crécy | 1346 | Death of Joan of Arc | 1431 |
| Battle of Poitiers | 1356 | Peace of Arras between Charles and Burgundians | 1435 |
| Treaty of Brétigny | 1360 | | |
| Reign of Richard ii | 1377–1399 | Reform of French army | 1445–1446 |
| Great Peasants' Revolt | 1381 | Expulsion of the English | 1449–1461 |
| Renewal of war with France | 1383 | Reign of Louis xi | 1461–1483 |
| Constitutional rule of Richard ii | 1389–1397 | Charles the Bold, Duke of Burgundy | 1467–1477 |
| Absolute rule of Richard ii | 1397–1399 | Edward iv of England bought off by Louis | 1475 |
| Deposition of Richard ii | 1399 | | |
| Reign of Henry iv | 1399–1413 | Battle of Nancy—Defeat and death of Charles the Bold | 1477 |
| Henry v claims throne of France | 1415 | | |
| Battle of Agincourt | 1415 | Unification of France as a national state | 1480 |
| Treaty of Troyes—Henry v regent of France | 1420 | | |
| Deaths of Henry v and Charles vi of France | 1422 | | |
| Joan of Arc burned at Rouen | 1431 | | |
| Loss of all France except Calais | 1453 | | |
| Wars of the Roses | 1455–1485 | | |
| Henry Tudor, Henry vii of England | 1485 | | |

## Spanish and Portuguese national states

| | |
|---|---|
| Muslim conquest of Spain | 711–719 |
| Christian kingdom of the Asturias reconquered | 718–737 |
| Partial conquest of northeastern Spain by Charlemagne | 778 |
| Expansion of Christian kingdom of Leon | 910–914 |
| Reign of Abdu-r-Rahman III (height of Muslim power) | 912–961 |
| Rise of Castile to independence | 930–966 |
| Breakup of Ommeyad dynasty into small chiefdoms | 1031 |
| Conquest of Leon by Castile | 1037 |
| Capture of Toledo by Alphonso VI of Castile | 1085 |
| Christian advance into Muslim Spain | 1072 onward |
| Berber dynasties based on Africa in central and southern Spain | 1056–1269 |
| Advances by Alphonso VII and Alphonso VIII of Castile | 1126–1214 |
| Union of Catalonia and Aragon | 1137 |
| Earliest Cortes in Castile | ca. 1188 |
| Battle of Las Navas de Tolosa— decisive defeat of Muslims by Alphonso VIII | 1212 |
| Capture of Cordova by Ferdinand III of Castile | 1236 |
| Capture of Seville by Ferdinand | 1248 |
| Conquest of Sicily by Peter III of Aragon | 1282 |
| Portuguese independence secured by decisive victory over Castile | 1385 |
| Marriage of Isabella, heiress of Castile, to Ferdinand, heir of Aragon | 1469 |
| Isabella succeeds to Castilian throne | 1474 |
| Establishment of Spanish Inquisition under royal control | 1478 |
| Ferdinand succeeds to throne of Aragon | 1479 |
| Fall of Granada, last Muslim stronghold in Spain | 1492 |
| Expulsion of Jews from Spain | 1492 |
| Expulsion of Moriscos from Spain | 1609 |

dependence upon foreigners and possible enemies for essential supplies; and it has been able to maintain public security better than the empires. But above all the national state has not proved too large to enable individual citizens to feel they have some share in the government. As a consequence of this added sense of responsibility on the part of the public, the modern national government has been able to enforce certain basic human rights in a way that even Roman law could not, since Roman law was not written in Heaven, as the philosophers claimed, but drawn up and administered by servants of the ultimately irresponsible empire.

While a national state must always have a national government in effective control of the whole territory, a government which must be recognized as such by the people of the state, there are otherwise no acceptable criteria for what constitutes a national state. A common language may be an important aid to the establishment of such a state, but multilingual national states such as Switzerland exist; and, conversely, many different states speak the same language. If culture is taken in the widest sense, a common national culture and common ideals are an even greater aid; and it is perhaps arguable that no state has ever been permanently united without them, though, for instance, present-day Yugoslavia has a partly Catholic and a partly Orthodox religious culture.

If the national state is the dominant institution in the world at any given time, as at present, then it is likely that all countries which feel they have enough in common will desire to organize themselves into separate sovereign states. This process can be observed in operation in the twentieth century, though great difficulties have arisen in the attempt to determine into how small units nations should be split. And even in the great national states founded in the Middle Ages, separatist tendencies have still not disappeared; or, if there is not a demand for altogether separate governments, at least there is often agitation for a substantial measure of self-government for the separate parts.

## THE FAILURE OF GERMANY AND ITALY TO ATTAIN NATIONAL STATEHOOD

Three major national states, whose history as national entities has been continuous to this day, came into existence in the Middle Ages—England, France, and Spain. The more populous and in some ways more advanced countries, Italy and Germany, did not become national states until the second half of the nineteenth century. Germany was bedeviled by the ghost of the Roman Empire. At a time when both France and England were relatively unimportant, the Germans under the Holy Roman Emperors were trying to establish their dominion over territories where geography made permanent union unlikely. After the imperial dream was over, the German feudal nobles had grasped so much substantial power that for centuries it was impossible to dislodge them; and German towns, as was seen in the previous chapter, constituted a league of states beyond the control of German monarchs for two crucial centuries. No one lord was powerful enough to rule the whole. The emperor was elected by the very nobles to whom he presented a threat, and they were therefore careful to elect only those of their peers who seemed to be least dangerous; if a family made gains while it held the imperial throne, an effort would be made to see that none of its members was elected next time. The feudal lords of Germany developed into modern princes, paternally interested in their subjects and governing their states despotically, sticking together when necessary to defend their ancient prerogatives. It took more than half a century of patient work in the nineteenth century by the largest state, masterly diplomacy, a modern army, and three wars, before Germany could be united as a nation.

Italy, at first forced to defend herself against the regular invasions of the emperor, for a while experienced freedom under city-state government, and for two centuries led Europe in commercial development. But the country was divided. Venice always dominated the northeast, the Papal States stretched across the backbone of the country from the Mediterranean to the Adriatic, extremely resistant to any moves looking toward the unity of the country as a whole. The south was under foreign domination, either Spanish or Angevin princes who could usually count on foreign aid to bolster their kingdoms. Several times the possibility of union seemed to open, and Italian writers and publicists from Dante to Machiavelli were well aware that Italy desperately needed unity. But not until Napoleon was the dream almost realized; and with his collapse more than half a century of propaganda, war, and diplomacy was needed to achieve it.

In this chapter, therefore, we shall discuss those states whose development was continuous. In England national unity under a strong monarchy was early achieved, and interest is centered both upon the means by which this early achievement was possible, and upon the efforts made by the nobles to curb the power of the monarchy; in France the central monarchy had difficulty in establishing itself, but once it had done so, the king's power remained intact until the French Revolution in the eighteenth century. Unity in Spain was attained largely through the shared experience of driving out the Muslims, and though partially representative institutions were developed, the kings retained almost absolute power until recent times. The contrast, especially between England and France, will serve to explain much of the modern political history of these countries: the strength of representative government in England based upon so many centuries of tradition, and the weakness of French representative government in a country whose traditions until such recent times were all absolutist and monarchical.

## ▶ The English national state

### THE NATURE OF THE ANGLO-SAXON MONARCHY

#### The king

As we saw in an earlier chapter, the English king Alfred the Great (871–899) united England against the Danes, and thereafter he and his successors ruled over an England that was no longer split into minor kingdoms. Even when England was altogether conquered by Sweyn and Canute from Scandinavia, the monarchy remained united though England was part of a Scandinavian empire, and English laws and customs remained substantially unchanged. The great council (the *Witan*) of thanes or lords, together with other wise men of the kingdom, still officially elected each king, although the custom had gradually developed for the rule to descend from father to son. The Witan theoretically could have bestowed the crown outside the descendants of Alfred, but the Anglo-Saxon people seem to have expected the council to choose a king from that family, and, as in other countries, a certain sanctity attached to the kingship. The Witan also felt competent to depose a king in certain circumstances, for he possessed no divine right to the office. He swore a coronation oath to support the Church and to maintain justice and mercy.

In late Anglo-Saxon times, before the Norman Conquest, something akin to feudalism had been growing in England, although it is wiser not to use the word to describe the Anglo-Saxon system in view of the real feudalism of the Continental type introduced by the Normans. Though there were as yet far more differences than similarities between the English system and Continental feudalism, the power of the king, as in feudal states, was seriously limited by the independence of the nobility. The king had the right to summon the national army or militia in times of danger. But the period of service was limited; after the service had been completed, the lords and their servants were entitled to return home. The conquest by the Normans was largely due to the fact that the king could not prevent his troops from returning home for harvest and had to rely upon special troops known as *housecarls,* who formed his personal retinue and were dependent upon him. The latter were not, however, the king's personal feudal vassals, as they were in France, and later in England.

The king was also the theoretical head of the justiciary, and certain kinds of lawsuits were always referred to him for decision, in spite of the fact that other law courts existed with their own systems of law. In general, however, almost all law was local, and enforced locally, until the Norman and Plantagenet kings were able to make inroads into local and feudal courts and establish the king's justice as the supreme law of the land.

### Anglo-Saxon "feudal" counterparts

The same causes that operated in the direction of increased feudalism on the Continent also operated in Anglo-Saxon England. The old German comitatus, the personal relationship between man and lord, was held to be as sacred in England as elsewhere. The central government was rarely strong enough to control the whole country, and though the king had many rights owed him by villagers in the country, he usually granted these rights to his lords or thanes, and it was the thanes who maintained order and executed justice in their territories. According to an Anglo-Saxon law, every man must either have land which he possessed freehold, or have a lord. This lord must give him the protection that the king, too distant and with too little authority, was unable to provide. Thus the practice of commendation, voluntary elsewhere, was compulsory in England, and in return the lord was entitled to various specified contributions from his men.

On the Continent, commendation, as a whole, usually meant that the land was held by military service. In England, however, there was also a fairly common form of service called a *tenancy in socage,* under which the lord was entitled to various goods and services from his men rather than a specified number of troops. This meant that the lord could not engage so easily in private warfare, since he lacked troops. It also meant that the monarch, when he wished to call out troops, was not hindered by the fact that the men he called had prior obligations toward their feudal overlords. After the Norman Conquest, William I made good use of these ancient English customs to preserve his own position.

By the time of the Conquest, then, there was no fully developed feudal system in England. The relationship between lord and vassal existed, but in primitive form; courts presided over by the lords operated in cases involving themselves and their dependents, while other courts operated for different offenses not concerned with land tenure. The king had certain rights over the common land of England, and these rights had real meaning; but he was not even the theoretical owner of the remainder of the land, as in France. The English thanes owed him military service as a national obligation rather than because they held land from him; they owed it to him as chief warrior who was constantly having to call upon them through the persistence of national danger from the Danes.

The great change made by the Norman Conquest was therefore not the establishment of an entirely different system, but the imposition of order upon a mass of customs which had been gradually growing up, and the speeding up of the feudalization process by a series of able kings, in whose French possessions there was already a well-developed feudal system.

### Local government

One of the greatest achievements of the Anglo-Saxons in England was their system of local government, much of which was maintained by the Normans. The country had already been divided into *shires,* later called counties, which differ little from those of the present day. The shires were administered by the bishop, the earl, or the chief lord, and an appointee of the king known as the *shire-reeve* or sheriff. The latter had the important function of looking after the king's business in the shire, especially the mustering of the national militia, and the collection of such taxes as the Danegeld, originally paid to keep the Northmen away, but which was continued, like so many taxes in modern times, long after the immediate necessity had passed away. There was also

a shire court that tried civil and criminal cases which came under its jurisdiction, presided over by the sheriff with the aid of the bishop and occasionally the earl, when necessary. Minor cases were handled in a subdivision of the shire, called a *hundred.* It was in the hundred that the apportionment of taxes to each person was made by men of local knowledge under the guidance of the sheriff.[1] These administrative divisions had given the kings since early times a means of enforcing their will; and because the sheriff in most cases, and the assessors in all cases, were local men, the germ existed for the combination of decentralized government and responsibility to the central government which made representative government possible later, and provided a vehicle by which consent for taxation could be asked and given.

### THE NORMAN CONQUEST

#### The establishment of Continental feudalism

The English king Edward, known as the Confessor, died in 1066 without leaving any obvious heir to the throne, though there was still one direct descendant of Alfred available. But he was a boy, and the times were so troubled that the Witan was ready to pass him over. They therefore chose Harold, the son of the greatest earl of the realm, and a renowned warrior, and he was proclaimed and anointed king.

But there were also two foreign claimants. One, Harold Hardrada, the king of Norway, a close relative of Edward the Confessor, was supported by a traitorous brother of Harold of England, while the other contender, William, Duke of Normandy, claimed that Edward had bequeathed the crown to him, and that Harold had sworn to support him. The issue could only be decided by force of arms.

[1] It is not certain that taxes were assessed in these local bodies as early as Anglo-Saxon times. But at all events the later kings, when they wished to have tax assessments made, were able to make use of the administrative division of the hundred for the purpose.

Harold summoned the national militia for service on land and on sea, but the navy had been allowed to deteriorate in the time of Edward and was no match for that of either of the competing foreign kings. The Norwegian king gained a favorable wind first and landed in the north of England. Harold of England, whose army had waited for the attack throughout the summer and was now far under full strength, met the Norwegian army and defeated it at Stamford Bridge. But the victorious army then heard that William had landed in the south. Marching quickly to meet him, Harold's army was almost exhausted when it finally met the feudal barons of the Norman duke, whose numbers had been swelled by recruits of nobles from all over France who had hoped to share in the booty. Harold was defeated and killed in the ensuing battle of Hastings (1066). Duke William then forced the English to choose him as king (1066–1087), and he was duly crowned.

Over the next few years all the lands of England were declared forfeited to the Conqueror. Any English lords who wished to retain their land were compelled to swear allegiance to him and do homage as his vassals. The remainder of the lands were given to William's Norman followers in return for the same recognition of himself as their suzerain. Thus the Conquest made what was elsewhere only a theoretical position real in England. William was the actual lord or suzerain of the entire land of England. Under the Norman kings there was no land whatsoever that was free (or alodial); every land had at least one lord, the king.

The king, however, could not administer such a vast estate himself through his nominees or servants. He retained the greater nobles as his direct vassals, or tenants in chief. But these were permitted, indeed encouraged, to let out the land again to subvassals (subinfeudation), who owed service to the king's tenants in chief as vassals. The service was composed of the usual feudal aids, and these subvassals were said to hold their land, as customary in the feudal system, by knight or military service.

POSSESSIONS OF
WILLIAM I OF ENGLAND
1066–1087
* Battles

But, in William's eyes, this did not justify the subvassals' fighting on behalf of their lord in his private quarrels. Though private warfare was not altogether quelled, especially under later kings, it was never legal for a vassal to fight for his lord unless the king himself had authorized the calling out of troops. And this he did only in national wars. A subvassal under this system therefore owed military service only to the king; but he was called upon for military service by his own overlord on behalf of the king. Thus the king had the advantage of indirect control over his subvassals, saving him the labor of administration involved, while at the same time he had all the benefits which accrued to a mighty feudal landowner, able to command the military service not only of his own tenants in chief but of every landowner in the country.

HIC:NVNTIATVM EST: WILLELM ✠ DE HAROLD

*The Bayeux tapestry recounts the deeds of Duke William of Normandy and his conquest of England. Here Harold, King of England, is shown as he receives the news that William had landed in Sussex.*

Through the sheriffs the king likewise exercised the old Anglo-Saxon privilege of direct taxation of the people without the intervention of the vassals and subvassals, and he retained and extended the power of the king's courts, though feudal lords could hold their courts to deal with matters within their own jurisdiction. No lord could erect a castle except with the king's license, and theoretically every castle in the country belonged to him. It will be seen, therefore, that, with customary Norman intelligence, William made full use of everything that could help him in the existing Anglo-Saxon

*Scene of the battle of Hastings, from the Bayeux tapestry. The tide of battle is said to have been turned by a feigned flight on the part of the Normans.*

system, while adding to it elements of Norman-French feudalism which could be used with profit to himself.[2]

[2] It may be added that the same combination of Anglo-Saxon and Norman French is to be found in the developed English language. Norman architecture in England is a modification of continental Romanesque architecture incorporating also some elements taken over from the Anglo-Saxons.

### Contrast between English and continental feudalism

Under William the great nobles of the realm held their land, as has been said, directly from him as tenants in chief, and they owed military service to him in addition to the usual feudal aids. This secured to the king a regular supply of troops and some money. He also had the right to tax directly through the shires and the hundreds. The lands of the Church were sometimes held by military service, which the ecclesiastical lords had to arrange for as best they could. But in addition in certain cases a church or a monastery would be permitted to hold land by *frankalmoign*. This meant that the religious institution still owed service, but it was service of a religious nature. The clergymen had to say Masses, pray, give alms or some other service suitable to their profession. This mode of service was never very common, but it preserved the façade of feudalism—that all land was held in exchange for some kind of service.

A further service sometimes given in exchange for land was *serjeanty*. Under this arrangement the holder would have to give some special specified service, and his duties were limited to this, perhaps the bearing of the king's shield in battle, or providing him with a suit of armor on occasion.

It was also possible, as has been seen, for tenants to hold land by socage, instead of by knight service. This was an Anglo-Saxon arrangement continued and systematized by William. Instead of owing military service, the tenant owed a specified amount of produce, and definite services such as the *corvée* and working the lord's lands for certain days in the year (as described in Chapter 17 above in the sections on feudalism and manorialism).[3] Naturally the king himself was too great a lord to be able to manage such minor services as these, and he did not have many tenants in chief who held from him by socage. But the king's tenants in chief let out much of their land in this way, and thus were enabled to take care of their own living expenses without having to manage their demesnes themselves or through their agents and stewards, as in

France. Thus while the feudal and manorial systems were connected in France by the fact that each feudal lord had to set aside some manors for his own subsistence out of his total estates and had to make direct arrangements for the farming of these manors, in England a manorial owner owed a certain amount of produce to his lord directly and was responsible for its payment as part of his feudal duties. If he held his land in socage he owed, not the feudal aids which were comparatively small and irregular, but food and produce and labor service which was, of course, not performed by himself but by his villeins and serfs. The result, for the suzerain, was that he was spared the labor of farming his own manors, and could rely upon his vassals in socage for his own subsistence. It was natural, therefore, that he was inclined to favor letting out his land on these terms rather than for military service, of which he could take but little advantage since he could not use for his own advancement the troops provided him under knight service. He was, however, limited in the amount he could let out in socage by the necessity he was under to provide troops for the king.

The holding of land in socage tended to increase under the Norman and Plantagenet kings. But it never took the place of the most common form of landholding in England, the holding by villeinage, which had been fully entrenched even in Anglo-Saxon times. English villeinage is complicated by the fact that some villeins were serfs and tied to the land, while others were legally free and could leave the land at will. But whether serfs or free, the villeins (peasants) held land from their lords and were obligated to provide them with certain goods and services of the same kind as those described under manorialism in an earlier chapter. The difference, of course, between English villeinage and the usual manorial system in Europe was that the villein could manage his land without interference from his lord, thus relieving the lord of onerous responsibilities, while at the same

[3] The student is urged at this point to refresh his memory on the details of feudalism as described in Chapter 17, since an understanding of feudalism is basic for an understanding of the rise of national monarchies.

time helping to provide him with an assured income.

## The full establishment of royal authority

The crafty Norman was also quick to take advantage of the system of sheriffs. Bishops and earls were far harder to control than his own appointees. He therefore excluded the former from the government of the shires and hundreds, and made the sheriffs supreme, subject only to dismissal by himself. Hoping to make it entirely clear that the members of the new English nobility were no longer to have the privilege of making private war and that all military service was owed only to himself, in 1086 William summoned to Salisbury all the landowners in the country, whether tenants in chief or only subvassals, and made them swear fealty to himself. They swore that they would be loyal to him even against their direct suzerains. Thereafter every tenant doing homage to his own lord for his fief had to add, "Saving the faith that I owe to my lord the king," which, of course, expressly covered military service, taxation, and legal appeals which were the prerogatives of the crown.

In order to have an exact knowledge of the dues of all kinds owed by every man in the kingdom, whether to himself or to any of his vassals, William sent out clerks into his shire courts where every landholder, whether free or serf, had to appear and under oath answer certain questions about his land, how many people worked on it, how much meadow and forest it contained, how many streams, and who had the various rights involved. All this information was written down in the Domesday Book, a magnificent example of Norman administrative genius altogether unique for that period, and only possible in a country which had developed the necessary local institutions through which the information could be collected. The king now had his hands upon the pulse of the whole realm, but few English kings ever had such power again. The lords, who had been robbed of so much

that belonged to their class elsewhere, did not hesitate to take advantage of any later weakening in the central government, and in so doing ultimately paved the way for the limited monarchy and representative institutions which have been the special glory of the English political genius.

## Machinery of government

The king had so many tenants in chief that the customary feudal council made up of the king's vassals would, in England, have been a most cumbersome body. William did call it on occasion, but preferred to work with a committee of these tenants in chief, which took the place of the Witan. The whole body was entitled to be consulted, but few lords desired the privilege, and it became the custom for this smaller council to give advice to the king when he summoned it for the purpose. The whole assembly at this time is known as the *Curia Regis*, or Court of the King, but in practice the Curia was made up of those tenants in chief whose presence William especially desired, and the majority did not attend. William's younger son, Henry I, made this committee a formal institution. William used a small number of regular officials in a full-time capacity. Chief of these was the justiciar, who ruled England in the king's name when, as fairly often happened, he was forced to look after his ducal interests in Normandy. The justiciar also became head of the departments of finance and justice in William's time, though these were separated by his younger son. The chancellor and chamberlain at this time had duties in the king's household. Whenever the king needed any further help he called upon his higher clergy and members of his Curia, whom he authorized to perform special limited tasks in the country, usually in conjunction with the sheriffs. With the feudal system working so efficiently in his behalf, William did not need a great corps of officials in his employ. All that was really needed was competent supervision of the work carried out for him by his tenants in chief in return for the land they had received from him, and this was provided by the few officials that he had.

## THE REIGN OF HENRY I

### Improved machinery of government

The second son of William the Conqueror succeeded to his throne, leaving Normandy for the eldest. The younger, William Rufus (1087–1100), acquired Normandy from his brother by some sharp tactics, but as king of England he made no innovations beyond tightening his financial hold on the feudal nobility and increasing taxation. When he was killed by an unknown hand while hunting, the youngest son of the Conqueror, Henry Beauclerc, or Henry I (1100–1135) took the throne, and continued to keep his eldest brother from the duchy of Normandy, so that Henry ruled both England and Normandy. Henry, with a thorough understanding of his father's policy and the conditions in England that favored the monarchy, succeeded, in a long reign of thirty-five years, in improving the administration and in strengthening the monarchy still further. Appointing to his personal staff a number of gentlemen who were not of the highest nobility, granting them lands as his direct vassals, and paying careful attention to his ecclesiastical appointments in order to put these into the hands of the best administrators he could find, he created a real council of advisers whose positions were not hereditary and who were thus closely tied to himself. This small council was the governing body of the realm under the king, and the great council of tenants in chief was rarely called together by Henry. Thus was the beginning made in England of the bureaucracy of government officials and heads of departments, which in later times became the king's Privy Council, the executive arm of the English kingdom as long as the king himself was the chief executive. When the king's office became largely honorary, the Privy Council became the Cabinet, still the executive of the country, still containing the heads of the various departments

of state, and still officially responsible to the king—who in theory chooses the chief official, the prime minister.

The considerable secretarial work of the king was entrusted to a special department known as the Chancery, the head of which, an appointee of the monarch, was called the chancellor. As ever, the most important department of government was the Treasury. Henry was both an extremely able and an extremely careful man, especially with his money, as he recognized that much of his power was based on it. It was he who really created the English Treasury, and systematized the collection of the very considerable revenues that accrued to the crown from many different sources, feudal and specifically royal. He was the first English king to make extensive use of scutage (shield money) under which his vassals were excused from military service on payment of a sum of money. Henry thought he could use the money to better advantage than he could the excused man-power, especially since his reign was very peaceful for the times. All his senior officials had care of the Treasury, though the chamberlain was primarily responsible. Twice every year these officials met to scrutinize the accounts, using a table covered by a cloth divided into squares representing the pounds, shillings, and pence received. This cloth gave rise to the word "exchequer," which has ever since been used for the English Treasury.

### Legal reforms of Henry I

The law at the beginning of Henry's reign was in a chaotic state owing to the different kinds of law in use: Anglo-Saxon law in the local courts (shires and hundreds), feudal (Norman) law in the feudal courts, canon (Roman) law in the ecclesiastical courts, even merchant law in the towns; and in addition to these were the courts of the king which held jurisdiction in certain cases. Henry, anxious to improve the position of the king's law in relation to the other systems, conceived the project of enforcing a single law which should cover all cases in the kingdom and gradually oust all competitive forms of law.[4] This would mean a tremendous increase of power for the king if it could be carried out. Henry himself did not achieve much more than the beginnings of the project, which could not be imposed simply by decree but must in time receive public acceptance so that people would wish to have their cases tried by the king's law. This law is what is known as the common law, because it was intended to be common to the whole realm.

Henry, as is evident from the claims made by his officials in his behalf, had no clear idea of just what cases would be permitted to come to his courts by local authorities. He therefore made very large, but not easily defensible claims, without any apparent logical system. Every case that had ever been decided by kings was apparently included, but it was not as yet considered exactly what should, in reason and logic, belong to them. The majority of his claims were concerned with the king's rights to taxation and with crimes involving royal property, suggesting the primary motives behind his zeal. His method of enforcing these claims was to appoint a few officials in important shires whose task was to observe the conduct of sheriffs and to see that they executed justice honestly and efficiently; to send notes to sheriffs instructing them to deal with certain cases in their shires which had been brought to his attention, and calling upon them to hold sworn inquests (the germ of the grand jury) under which neighbors were summoned to give

[4] In saying that Henry "conceived" this project, it should be understood that the development of common law was a result of the efforts of Henry and his successors, and it must be considered doubtful whether he in fact realized what would be the result of his efforts to improve and to some degree centralize the administration of justice. As so often happens in life, a project started for one purpose, or adopted to meet certain well-defined ends, succeeds in accomplishing other ends altogether unforeseen. The procedural changes initiated by Henry succeeded in giving birth in later centuries to what we call common law, but it is only an inference from his acts to say that he had any intention of creating such law.

testimony on oath that a crime had been committed; and, finally, to send out some of the members of his Curia of permanent officials with the right to try cases (with jurisdiction over wider areas than the single shires), to examine the conduct of local officials, including the sheriff, and to listen to complaints, while at the same time they had to keep an eye open to see that no one was cheating the king or usurping any of his prerogatives. It may be imagined that these innovations were more satisfactory to the complainant in search of justice than they were to the local officials, whose conduct was thus opened to scrutiny; but it must have accustomed the people to look toward the king for justice, by-passing if possible the local men, and was thus an important factor in the growth of the king's power.

All this, however, was only pioneered by Henry I, and was never regularized and systematized, since he was evidently still experimenting. The work was brought to fruition by his grandson, Henry II, and from his time became incorporated into English administrative procedure. Henry I's own work was halted by the long interregnum and civil war that followed his death.

## THE REIGN OF STEPHEN (1135–1154)—CIVIL WAR AND DISINTEGRATION OF CENTRALIZED GOVERNMENT OF THE NORMAN MONARCHS

When Henry died he left only a daughter to succeed him, and it had not yet been settled that a woman could come to the English throne; her son was as yet only two years old. Many of the great nobles favored Stephen of Blois, the son of Henry's sister Adela, the daughter of William the Conqueror, and they thought the disputed crown provided an excellent chance to escape from the rigors of the earlier Norman reigns. Stephen had to make many promises and issue a charter relieving the nobles of some of their burdens before they would consent to his election; many nobles, however, would not accept him at all but took up arms on behalf of Matilda, Henry's daughter, who was married to a French prince, Geoffrey of Anjou.

The civil war that followed was utterly ruinous to the newly organized and efficient country. The nobles did almost whatever they wished. They built castles without license, they refused to pay their dues to the crown, they forced the peasants everywhere to build castles for them, and they tortured and imprisoned freemen, peasants, and townsmen for their money. All organized government broke down except unrestrained feudalism, and Stephen did not succeed in establishing his authority until almost at the end of the period described as his reign. Meanwhile Matilda's son Henry was growing up, and acquired his father's county of Anjou in France. When Louis VII of France divorced Eleanor of Aquitaine, Henry (surnamed Plantagenet) was able to capture the heiress and marry her though she was several years older than himself, and he thus inherited her vast lands of Poitou and Aquitaine. From his mother he inherited Normandy, which had not fallen to the English king Stephen with the throne of England. With this immense territory, far larger and richer than England, Henry was able to force Stephen to make a treaty with him recognizing his right to the English succession after Stephen's death. Since Stephen died soon afterward, Henry was the undisputed heir to the English throne, and in 1154 he made a determined effort to gain it.

THE REIGN OF HENRY II

### Re-establishment of centralized government

It was natural that many of the nobles, with their unlicensed castles and their recovered sovereignty in their own domains, should have intensely disliked the prospect of Henry's arrival. They could not hope to resist him, however, in view of his possession of loyal French troops. The townsmen, of course, would welcome any king who was capable of keeping order, and the people in general would greatly prefer royal order to feudal anarchy. Henry, therefore, was able to make a triumphant procession through England; and though he spent most of his life in his French possessions, he was nevertheless one of the greatest, if not the greatest, of all the kings of England. He had a very considerable understanding of public finance, a necessity in his time; he chose competent public officials; and he was one of the best administrators that ever sat on a throne. He regarded England as a domain which, by efficient administration, could supply him with funds adequate to maintain his Continental possessions, as Frederic II, Holy Roman Emperor and king of Sicily, used Sicily to try to establish his imperial claims. But, though much English money was funneled abroad to pay for military expenditures in France, an incidental by-product was the excellent administration in England, and the expense was probably worth it to the English. When, however, Henry's younger son John tried to use the same policy, lost his Continental wars, and by foolish quarrels with the pope ruined his English administration, the result was Magna Carta, and the diminution of the power of the king. The French possessions of the English monarchy were never anything but a source of weakness to all English kings after Henry II, though the dream of a united France and England was many centuries in dying.

In administration Henry restored the system of his grandfather Henry I. He relieved the chancellor of all financial duties, keeping him as the king's chief official, while the Treasury was reorganized with a professional staff of full-time officials. To make his income more secure and larger, it was, of course, necessary at once to reduce the feudal nobility to submission. It was hardly possible for the nobles to resist a king with such additional sources of strength as his French domains, and they made little resistance when he began to pull down all the unlicensed castles and enforce the payment of the same taxes to which they had been subjected by Henry I, with some additions and heavier scutage. He dismissed almost every sheriff in the realm for activities under Stephen or for inefficiency, though he was

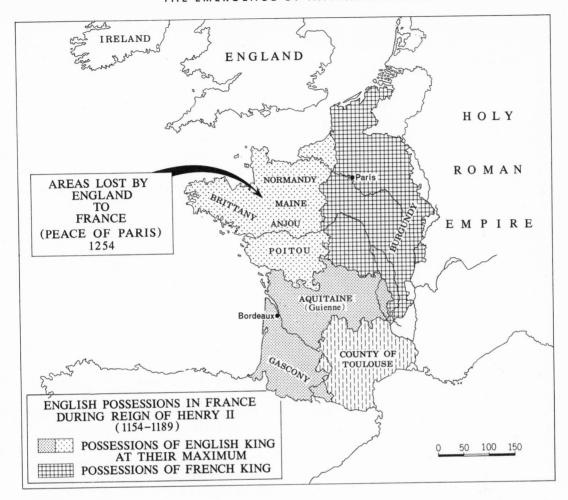

AREAS LOST BY
ENGLAND
TO
FRANCE
(PEACE OF PARIS)
1254

IRELAND

ENGLAND

HOLY

ROMAN

EMPIRE

NORMANDY
Paris
BRITTANY
MAINE
ANJOU
BURGUNDY
POITOU

AQUITAINE
(Guienne)
Bordeaux

GASCONY

COUNTY OF
TOULOUSE

ENGLISH POSSESSIONS IN FRANCE
DURING REIGN OF HENRY II
(1154–1189)
POSSESSIONS OF ENGLISH KING
AT THEIR MAXIMUM
POSSESSIONS OF FRENCH KING

0    50    100    150

careful to have regular sworn inquests testifying to their failings. He instituted the Assize of Arms, which reformed the old militia, ordering all freemen to possess their own arms according to their means, so that they could serve in his army at short notice.

### Legal and judicial reforms

Henry's greatest claim to fame, however, rests on his reform of the judicial system on the lines indicated by his grandfather, and the institution of many new arrangements which laid the foundation for the entire modern legal system of all English-speaking countries. Influenced by Roman law, which was beginning to be studied in England, he neverthless retained the bulk of the English law, thus making the English system in some ways superior to the ancient law of Rome, and capable of very great modification and development. From the beginning Henry seems to have realized that the enforcement of the common law above all earlier systems of law was essential to his power, and this unification was fundamental to all his reforms.

While the sheriff's courts remained, any complainant could apply to the chancery of the king to set a legal case in action within these courts. A writ could be purchased from the chancery for any of a great number of cases, and these at once became cases in which the king was interested, to be settled by the king's law. Writs could even be obtained in which the king directed the sheriff to enforce judgments which were the results of lawsuits, thus giving the king also a hand in legal matters previously under the jurisdiction of local courts and accustoming the people to the idea that the king was the source of all justice.

The grand and the petty or trial jury both have their origin in Henry II's reign, although the grand jury of Henry is much closer to the modern grand jury than was his small jury to the modern counterpart. The origin of the trial jury is to be found in the grand and possessory assizes of Henry II. It had been customary, when there was a dispute over the possession of land, to settle the matter in a feudal court, where the wager of battle decided the outcome. If, under Henry's legislation, the man from whom land was demanded wished to appeal to the king he could do so. Then both parties chose two knights, who would then elect twelve other knights who would state on oath before the king's justices which of the parties had the better right to the land. Henry's justiciar Ranulf de Glanville, in one of the earliest English lawbooks, states that the procedure was granted by the king in order to prevent any freeholder who was really entitled to the land from having to endanger it by the uncertain process of judicial combat. This was the grand assize.

Under the possessory assize, if a freeman had been ejected from his land, he could obtain a writ from the chancery calling upon the sheriff to call together twelve men who would certify whether there had been a wrongful ejection or not. In this case the jury had to state a matter of fact, whereas under the grand assize the twelve men were witnesses as to rights. In both cases evidence was used rather than the older method of trial by ordeal or combat; but the procedure applied only to certain specified cases. It was to be a century before a similar procedure was used for the majority of law cases. A beginning, however, had been made.

It is clear that this procedure interfered with feudal prerogatives and feudal courts, which were supposed to deal with disputed questions concerning the possession of property. The nobles, however, were in no position to protest, not even when the king proceeded to legislate changes in the hold-

ing of such property, as, for instance, in his insistence on primogeniture and prohibition of the bequeathing of land by will. Once the new procedure had become customary, much of the feudal procedure seems to have died out. The king had won another great victory over the feudal system in the direction of centralized monarchy.

The grand jury's primary function was to ascertain what duties were owed to the king and whether they were being fulfilled. This was the sworn inquest of the earlier Norman monarchs in a different form. The sheriff was instructed by the king's writ to call a body of jurors together who were to swear such matters before the royal justices. But under the Assizes of Clarendon and Northampton (1166 and 1176) the sheriffs were now instructed to bring before the king's justices a group of men who were to swear if any of various specified crimes had been committed in their neighborhood, and to say who, in their opinion, had committed them. The accused would then be subjected to the ordeal or trial by combat. But as time went on, perhaps not at all in the reign of Henry, certain pleas could be made by the accused in front of a sworn jury such as that he had been elsewhere at the time (alibi) or that his accuser had been actuated by malice. He was finally allowed to appeal to a jury of his neighbors on the whole question of guilt or innocence; but it should be emphasized that for a long time the accused did not need to submit to the new procedure but could demand the old trial by ordeal or combat. Nevertheless, even if the accused were successful in the ordeal, the king could order him banished from the realm.

Under Henry I, as has been seen, the king's justices paid visits to the shires to see that justice was done. These visits, however, in Henry I's time seem to have been spasmodic and not regular. Henry II sent out justices regularly into each shire to hear criminal cases brought before them by the grand jury, and he sent out members of his own Curia irregularly to check upon officials, again using the device of the grand jury or sworn inquest. These judges even listened to complaints about the quality of beer sold in a shire, and a check was supposed to be kept on every matter of public importance; but, needless to say, this court was popular with few, and in later years its visits became rare, though it remained a salutary reminder to the people that the king's justice was capable of reaching them in any case of offense against the public interest.

It was as a result of his attempts to make a uniform law code for England that Henry quarreled with the Church in the person of his Archbishop of Canterbury, St. Thomas Becket. Becket had been Henry's chancellor, and the king felt sure that he could rely

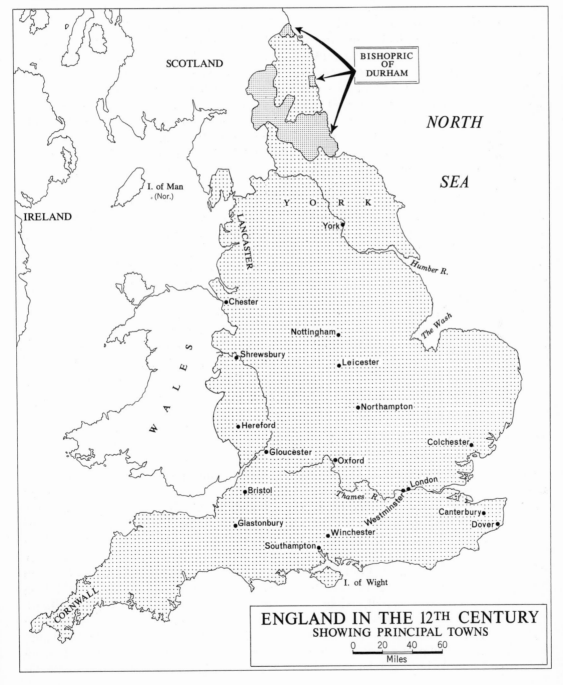

SCOTLAND

BISHOPRIC OF DURHAM

NORTH

SEA

I. of Man (Nor.)

IRELAND

Y O R K

York

LANCASTER

Humber R.

Chester

The Wash

Nottingham

Shrewsbury

W A L E S

Leicester

Northampton

Hereford

Colchester

Gloucester

Oxford

London

Bristol

Thames R.

Westminster

Canterbury

Glastonbury

Dover

Winchester

Southampton

CORNWALL

I. of Wight

ENGLAND IN THE 12TH CENTURY
SHOWING PRINCIPAL TOWNS

0    20    40    60

Miles

upon him as Archbishop to support the royal reforms. But Becket at once upon investiture became a stubborn supporter of all papal claims, and in particular of the right of the Church to try all offenders, whatever their crimes, as long as they were ecclesiastics. Becket refused to accept the Constitutions of Clarendon (1164), the main provisions of which deprived the ecclesiastical courts of the right to try "criminous clerks," or clerics who had committed a crime against the king's law. The recalcitrance of the archbishop ultimately resulted in his murder after the king had in a rage incited some of his knights to the deed. The murder shocked the country. Henry had to do severe penance, and he withdrew part of the Constitutions. The remainder continued in force, allowing the king to make ecclesiastical appointments and preventing the papacy from directly taxing the English Church without the king's consent. In addition, certain important regulations regarding the possession of property by the Church were allowed to stand. The ecclesiastical courts experienced a continuous growth for some time in England after the murder, and Henry was effectively prevented from establishing his jurisdiction in the matters which had customarily been allowed to the Church, as has been discussed in an earlier chapter.

### RECRUDESCENCE OF POWER OF FEUDAL NOBILITY—CHECKS UPON ROYAL POWER

#### Foreign wars of Richard I and John

Richard I, the Lion-Hearted, who was already in possession of many of his father's lands in France while Henry was still alive, was interested in England primarily as a source of revenue, and spent only six months of his reign (1189–1199) in England. But Richard's financial needs were enormous. Philip Augustus was king of France, and was busily engaged in trying to take the English possessions for himself; while he had only indifferent success against Richard when the English king was present to defend his lands, Philip was usually able to win against Richard's brother John, who was

a feeble warrior. Richard, as has been seen in an earlier chapter, spent a large part of his reign on the Third Crusade, an extremely expensive campaign for which his people in England had to pay. Richard's resources thus were squandered all his life on unproductive and unprofitable warfare; and when he was finally captured on his way home from the Crusade, and was forced to pay a huge ransom, the English people found themselves saddled with a debt which it was impossible to pay from regular income.

Nevertheless, his brother John, succeeding to the throne when Richard was killed in 1199, had to carry on the French wars, for which he never possessed adequate funds. Moreover, the English nobles, seeing no profit or likely success under John in this war, were determined to resist the new king's efforts to make the national militia serve in his own personal foreign wars. It was therefore not surprising that John, with no military talent of his own, with a poorly paid mercenary army, and with disgruntled nobles, was unable to make any headway against such an able monarch as Philip Augustus of France, who could not stand up perhaps to Richard in battle but was more than a match for John. Moreover, John fell into most of the traps set for him by Philip, useful legal traps connected with the fact that John, as well as being king of England, was a vassal of the French king for his French lands.

Philip needed to put John in the wrong because as a feudal king himself he could not force his own lords to follow him on lengthy campaigns; under the cover of a legal excuse he could, however, command his lords to execute justice on John and they would be inclined to obey. At all events when John committed a flagrant breach of feudal custom by marrying a wife already promised to one of his French vassals, Philip had no difficulty in having the English king condemned in his feudal court. John, indeed, was so clearly in the wrong under feudal law that he did not bother to attend Philip's court. When, finally, John murdered his own nephew Arthur, who had perhaps a better title to the English throne than had John himself, and who was also a vassal of Philip and supported by him, almost every French noble of importance joined the French king in his attempt to drive John from his French possessions.

It was impossible for John, with his attenuated resources drawn exclusively from England, to defend these possessions. He lost Brittany, Anjou, Maine, Touraine, and even Normandy. Only Poitou, the private possession of John's mother, Eleanor of Aquitaine, remained loyal to the English crown and could not be captured, though under John's successor this too was lost to Louis VIII, who had succeeded Philip Augustus in 1223. Only Aquitaine itself, of all the English possessions in France, remained to Henry III of England (1216–1272), and this really remained in English hands only by courtesy of St. Louis IX of France (1226–1270), who agreed to leave it to Henry in exchange for recognition of French sovereignty over the remainder of the French conquests. Thus England, to her own great advantage, was shorn of most of her French possessions, enabling her kings to concentrate upon English needs until the middle of the fourteenth century, when another series of English kings foolishly renewed the attempt to rule France as well as England.

### Internal consequences of foreign policy of Richard and John

Henry II's bureaucracy was so well organized and it had such a firm hold on the country that for a time the absence of his successors from England made little difference. But the unfortunate English officials were compelled to tighten the screws upon the people for the purpose of extracting enough money for the kings. New taxes were added, much property was confiscated, including the possessions of Jews, who were unable to defend themselves against arbitrary exactions. Offices were sold, especially the office of sheriff. Although the king's Curia appointed new officials to watch the sheriffs and to take over some of their duties, the sheriffs, forced to recuperate their finances by exactions of their own, got into the habit of selling justice. Gradually the efficiency of the governmental machinery was undermined. Perhaps the only gain for the people in the reigns of these two irresponsible monarchs lay in the numerous charters which were granted to the towns in exchange for money and which gave them for a time a considerable degree of autonomy.

John's financial needs were as great as those of Richard. He had to try to complete the payment of Richard's ransom, which had been paid at the time only at the expense of future revenue; he had his own wars in France to pay for; and finally (as has been seen in Chapter 18), he became involved with Pope Innocent III over his appointment of an Archbishop of Canterbury, and England had to suffer the rigors of an interdict, which seriously damaged the revenue-producing abilities of the country. To complete the ruin of the king, his own chancery, after the death of his able chancellor Hubert Walter, was made up of men who were no longer of the caliber of the great officials of the previous reigns. In these circumstances, as we have already seen, the English nobles began to abandon John and even look to the French monarchy for help. The English clergy objected to John's efforts to tax them, and even Innocent's acceptance of John as his vassal did not reconcile them to him. The towns were perhaps the hardest hit of all, since their wealth was visible and could be more easily extracted than that of the nobles. But the nobles objected also to John's efforts to force them to serve in France and to his general ill success.

This royal irresponsibility was the background to Magna Carta, which the nobles forced John to sign at Runnymede in 1215. John's only support at this time came from his mercenaries, whose loyalty was dependent upon his ability to pay them, and a very small minority of his nobles. The aid of Innocent III was entirely useless to him, since Innocent did not command the loyalty of the English Church in the struggle, not even that of the Archbishop of Canterbury, his own nominee for whom he had fought so hard with the king. The Charter therefore was a dictated document, and the nobles were fully aware that it was. They would have been astonished to learn that future generations would come to regard it as the cornerstone of English liberties.

### Magna Carta (1215)

In order to understand the importance of the Great Charter a short review of the position of the English king in 1215 may be helpful. The king was still in theory elected; his title had to be confirmed by the assembly of the great nobles of the realm, his tenants in chief. What the nobles could bestow they also could theoretically take away. They could have elected the nephew of John to the throne, and it is possible that they might have done so if Arthur had been of age, and if John's mother, Eleanor of Aquitaine, had not advised her son on the matter of seizing the reins of government and putting pressure on the nobles for an immediate decision. Though the king was overlord of the whole country and every noble owed him allegiance as suzerain, the king himself was bound by feudal custom and law, and was entitled only to feudal aids, which could be commuted by money payments, or scutage. Nevertheless the amount of money paid in scutage was theoretically subject to negotiation between the king and the lord, and could not be raised by unilateral executive action on the part of the king. When, therefore, the king was made to agree in the Charter that he would not levy scutage without the consent of the great council, the nobles were simply protecting their own legal rights. But they were also trying to put to the fore the old council of all tenants in chief, whose functions had been so largely usurped by the king's bureaucracy. This latter body of officials had retained the title of the Curia Regis but was in fact composed of the king's nominees, who, if they were even tenants in chief at all, had probably been given their position by the reigning king who had endowed them with lands from his own royal territories. Though in later generations the article in the Charter which forced the king to tax only with the consent of the Great Council was interpreted to mean "no taxation without representation," it was in 1215 only the reiteration of a principle which was the existing custom and law of the land.

The nobles made a further effort to prevent the encroachment of the king's legal powers over their own. The king's feudal court was concerned only with matters affecting the king and his relations with his tenants in chief. But all these tenants had their own feudal courts, whose functions had been largely usurped by the monarchy. The nobles did not wish to put the clock back altogether. They recognized the value of some of the king's efforts. But in matters affecting feudal relationships, and a suzerain's rights over his vassal, they would not accept the king's claims. And they especially did not want to abandon their old prerogatives in favor of arbitrary confiscation, buying and selling of justice for the financial benefit of the king and his officials. Thus, when in the Charter the king promised not to imprison or dispossess any free man, nor to outlaw and banish him, except by the legal judgment of his peers, the nobles were trying to reassert the feudal authority of their own courts, and at the same time to prevent the abuses in the king's courts. But again it can be seen how such a promise could later be interpreted to mean that jury trial was to be guaranteed by the monarch.

It cannot be too strongly emphasized that a medieval English king was bound by feudal and local custom and was in no sense absolute, though English monarchs since the Conquest had in fact by administrative action forged much of the machinery of absolutism. In the Great Charter the nobles tried to underline this point, to take away some of the power usurped by the king's small council and give it to the large council of tenants in chief, who held their position by birth as fiefholders in the feudal system, and thus could not be dismissed by the king unless the king were permitted to use his own courts to dispossess them of their land.

When the nobles asserted that the king was below the law, the feudal law, they were only stating what was undoubtedly the legal position of the king in 1215; though parliamentary supporters in later centuries were to enunciate this principle again when they wished to exalt the power of the legislature over the executive, and to insist that the king obey the laws which had been passed by themselves with his approval.

Realizing that the Charter was worth very little without means of enforcement, the nobles inserted one clause which authorized the council of nobles to choose twenty-five of their number who should try first to obtain redress of grievances, and if this failed the clause stated that they should be authorized to organize an armed rebellion against the king. Naturally this was not worth the paper it was written on. It was merely an attempt by the nobles to devise a procedure for taking action against the king, and it did give some color of legality to such action; but no king could be expected to authorize action against himself in the event that he failed to redress grievances. But in the course of the next century there were efforts to force the king to observe the law, and these efforts included armed rebellion. Since the king resisted all such efforts as far as he could, he can hardly be supposed to have felt himself bound by the Charter to authorize them.

THE GROWTH OF PARLIAMENTARY INSTITUTIONS

### The Provisions of Oxford and the "Baron's Parliament"

In 1216 John died and was succeeded by his son, a boy of nine. As we have seen already, John made no attempt to observe the Charter in the last year of his reign, and in this he was supported by his feudal overlord the pope. The English lords, called "barons" in the Charter, who had been intriguing with Philip Augustus and had received his son into England as their nominee for king, were largely disarmed by John's death. In the expectation of improved conditions under his son and the regency, which

was to rule until he was of age, they returned to their allegiance. Philip abandoned the attempt to win the English throne, and the minority of completely recalcitrant barons were defeated by the regents, who renewed the Charter in the name of Henry III. Frequently throughout the next centuries the king was called upon to swear to observe the Charter, with some clauses omitted, a pledge he usually made on the promise of increased voluntary aids from the nobles. This renewal gradually gave it the fundamental position in the evolution of the English monarchy that it has held in modern opinion.

Henry III was still interested in the recovery of his foreign possessions, and was thus constantly in need of money. Nevertheless he and his advisers did not dare to break the Charter quite openly; on several occasions during his reign Henry summoned his barons and prelates to obtain their voluntary acceptance of his proposals for increased taxation of the clergy and nobility. But his futile foreign policy involved the country in wars with France at the behest of the papacy, and he was too partial to foreigners whenever he had to appoint officials and clergy. So at last the barons lost patience with him. In 1258 a number of feudal lords summoned a "parliament," known as the Mad Parliament, to concert measures for keeping the king under control and restraining his taxation. They proceeded to issue the Provisions of Oxford, a series of reforms which the king was forced to accept. Some of their grievances he was compelled to redress, and he was virtually controlled for a while by this self-constituted committee of greater barons.

Two years later the barons evidently felt that they, too, needed a wider basis of support and authority. They therefore summoned to a special assembly three knights from each shire, who would represent the interests of the lesser lords of the realm who were not tenants in chief of the king. The king issued counterinstructions to the knights to come to meet him instead, thus adding to the confusion. It was impossible for the king to accept indefinitely this kind of dictation from his vassals, and it was clear that civil war could not be long delayed.

When it finally came, in 1264, the barons had discovered a capable leader in the person of Simon de Montfort, son of the leader of the Albigensian Crusade, a French nobleman who had originally been brought to England as one of the king's French favorites. But by this time he had quarreled with the king and identified himself with the baronial interests. Putting himself at the head of an army of barons, he gave battle to the king, who was severely defeated at the battle of Lewes (1264) and taken prisoner. Simon was, for the moment, supreme. But there was no intention of harming the monarch; the sole interest of Simon and the barons was in forcing Henry to yield some of his powers to the feudal aristocracy. The king's own son, later to become Edward I, supported the lords against his father for a time. Simon summoned four knights to be elected to meet the king during 1264, but nothing came of the effort. Then he summoned a full parliament, of lords and higher clergy, though he was careful to choose only those who favored his party, and to these he added representatives from the shires (two knights from each to be elected in the presence of the sheriff) and, for the first time, two representatives from each city and borough. This Parliament of Simon de Montfort was the most representative assembly that had been called since the Conquest, but it came to nothing, for Edward deserted him, returning to his father, and Simon was defeated and killed in the battle of Evesham in 1265. But Edward seems to have remembered the salutary lesson, and it was in his reign that Parliament first became an established institution, giving advice to the king, who was expected to legislate only after having taken careful consideration of such advice. As soon as the war was over Henry conceded many of the desired reforms in the Statute of Marlborough (1267), which to a large extent summed up and confirmed concessions extracted from him during the revolutionary period.

These for the most part concerned the crown's claims to jurisdiction over questions of land tenure traditionally handled by the feudal courts.

### The Reign of Edward I (1272–1307)

In 1295 the same Edward, now King Edward I, summoned the most inclusive parliament hitherto called, which was to receive the name of the Model Parliament. But he had already been reigning for twenty-three years (1272–1295) before he found this move necessary, and for years he had been legislating, sometimes with the assent of an advisory body and sometimes not. Indeed, the bulk of his legislation—and he was the first English king who seriously attempted to make statutes which would endure permanently and thus constitute the law of the whole land until repealed—took place before his Model Parliament. To his court the year after his accession came not only the tenants in chief, but knights of the shire and burgesses from the towns, for the primary purpose of swearing fealty to him. Since Edward declared publicly that he had promulgated the great statutes of his reign upon the advice of various great men of the realm, we may presume that he consulted those whose interests were affected before he legislated. But after the Model Parliament it became established as a precedent that statutes would be made only after consultation with a Parliament of this new and comprehensive nature. For more than a century the king continued to draw up the statutes himself with the aid of his council, but the statutes were supposed to be in conformity with what the Parliament had advised him. When members of Parliament complained that the statutes did not in fact conform, it was with a sense of grievance as if the king and council had cheated them; and ultimately they forced him to allow them to make the statutes to which he had only to give his assent.

In this Model Parliament the sheriffs were summoned to cause two knights of each shire, two citizens of each city, and two burgesses of each borough to be elected. The election was to take place in the county court, though it has never been determined for certain what the method of election was at this time and who was eligible to vote. It seems probable that every freeman possessing any property at all in his own right was eligible, though in practice the sheriff regarded the right to vote as belonging to certain properties only. Conjointly with these new additions to the body of the king's advisers, the lords temporal and the lords spiritual were also summoned—the nobility and the clergy; but by no means all the king's tenants in chief were thus honored. To the Parliament of 1296 only forty-eight lords were summoned. The higher clergy, bishops and archbishops, were to attend in force, incidentally considerably outnumbering at this period the nobility in the Parliament; they were supposed to bring with them representatives of the lower clergy, though in practice this procedure was abandoned, as the Church preferred to vote its taxes in ecclesiastical assemblies, and was not interested in the other functions of the Parliament. The higher clergy, however, continued to sit in Parliament by virtue of their positions as barons.

It is important to note that from the beginning the representatives of the Commons (knights of the shire and the townsmen—constituting the third estate) were instructed to receive full powers from their constituents to represent them in all matters. They were not supposed, as in the French States-General, to refer back to their constituencies for further advice and instructions, like ambassadors; and it has remained the theory to this day, and in England largely the practice, that the members of Parliament are national representatives advising the government rather than spokesmen for the local interests which elected them.

It is not known whether the ex officio members of the Parliament and the elected members sat separately from the beginning, but before long they were doing so. The knights of the shire were, of course, landholders and might be presumed to have many interests in common with the larger barons. But they also had divergent interests as subvassals rather than tenants in chief; though they might also be minor tenants in chief of the king, they usually were not. At all events, these knights decided, and it was a decision of supreme importance for the development of constitutional government, that they would throw in their lot with the townsmen, by whom they were outnumbered, but to whom for centuries they supplied leadership in Parliament. These two groups grew into the modern House of Commons, and both were classified as part of the third estate, while the higher clergy (the first estate) and the higher nobility (the second estate) became the House of Lords.

As a member of either House would have considered it in his time, the primary purpose of having a Parliament was to regulate and minimize the power of the king, especially in matters of taxation. The Parliament presented petitions to the king and could ask for justice even in minor complaints, which the king would refer to the suitable court or department of state. In time these petitions became a means of initiating legislation; the petitions would be discussed and recommendations given, and the king was then expected to act upon them. But the king usually only willingly called Parliament when he needed money and thus gave Parliament the opportunity to go into the whole question of his expenditures. It gradually became accepted that the power of taxation was in the hands of Parliament except for those taxes which belonged to the king from ancient times and were his under feudal law. It was this principle, and its acceptance, that led directly to the limited monarchy at the end of the seventeenth century, and also was ultimately to make the House of Commons superior to the House of Lords, since revenue from the former was far more elastic than anything a few lords and bishops could hope to raise. Only two years after the Model Parliament, at a time when Edward i was in great need of money, and was engaged in controversy with Pope Boniface viii over the taxing of the clergy, Edward tried to collect money without the consent of his Parliament and to force his barons to serve in a foreign war. The barons took to arms, supported by the merchants whose commodities the king had claimed to be able to tax, and the king was forced to give way, swearing an oath that he would not make such new taxes in the future without the common consent of the realm. His grandson later had to confirm the promise, and it became generally accepted as the law and custom of the land.

*Foreign wars of Edward I—Addition of Wales to England*—Edward made a serious attempt to unite both Wales and Scotland to his kingdom. After a long and difficult war he was successful in adding Wales, though there were many revolts afterward which were ultimately suppressed. As symbol of the union, he made his son Prince of Wales, a title held by the eldest son of the king to the present time.[5] He intervened in a disputed succession to the crown of Scotland, and was successful in several battles. He was successful largely because, under the Statute of Winchester (1285), he had remodeled the English army, specifying the arms each freeman must bear, and because he relied more upon the bowmen of the English free peasantry and townsmen than upon the feudal nobility, whose fighting was by now seriously out of date. But Edward's son in 1314 lost the battle of Bannockburn to the Scots under Robert I (the Bruce), and thereafter Scotland had full independence until the union of the two crowns under James I (a Scot) in 1603. On the whole Edward I maintained the precarious hold of the English crown on the parts of southern France that remained to it after the defeats of John and Henry III.

### Further growth of parliamentary power to the end of Middle Ages

In a book of this kind it is unnecessary to go in detail into the growth of Parliament once it had been established as a going institution entitled to be called regularly for the purpose of petitioning the king, even if

he had no demands to make upon it. Edward II, a weak king (1302–1327) was taken to task by Parliament for the activities of his council, of which more will be said in the next section, and Parliament made certain demands upon him for more regular sessions, to which he agreed, later revoking his decision. The barons took up arms and forced Edward to abdicate, while stating officially in Parliament that he had been deposed, thus arrogating to themselves the right of deposition. However, as they forced him to abdicate after they had deposed him, they do not appear to have been greatly impressed with the legality of their action. Edward III (1327–1377) was in constant need of money for the Hundred Years' War, which was, for the most part, popular with the soldiers and nobility; it was usually successful and loot was available. But the townsmen were not always so contented with the war, and Edward had to find many new sources of revenue. It is at this time that the customs and excise (tunnage and poundage) became a regular imposition, though granted by Parliament for only limited periods and not intended to be a permanent source of revenue for the king. There were a number of other experimental taxes, including income, personal property, and poll taxes. But, as always in the Middle Ages, the new taxes were only temporary grants for definite needs. A permanent source of revenue beyond the king's regular income from crown resources, and the proceeds of his courts of justice, was never acceptable until comparatively modern times. Edward even resorted to loans from Italian bankers, then found himself unable to repay, in spite of their acceptance of the English crown as security.

The reign of Richard II (1377–1399), short as it was, was of considerable constitutional importance. Coming to the throne as a boy of eleven, Richard was at first dominated by his council, which was constantly opposed by the great lords in Parliament who were not in the council. When he finally came of age, he attempted to rule personally, calling Parliament irregularly or not at all, and

---

[5] The son of the reigning queen of England has, however, not yet been declared Prince of Wales.

trying to use his executive power to collect sufficient money for his needs. But a baronial revolution overthrew him, and the indictment drawn up against him in Parliament declared that he had offended against the laws and customs of the realm by trying to rule and tax without the consent of Parliament, and, again as in the case of Edward II, Parliament deposed him and compelled him to abdicate, choosing as king, under the title of Henry IV (1399–1413), a noble of the House of Lancaster who was clearly not the best heir to the throne. No doubt Parliament was influenced in its choice by the fact that Henry had led the revolt against Richard, who was murdered shortly afterward.

Owing his position to parliamentary support, Henry allowed Parliament to perform all the functions it claimed for itself, and rarely succeeded in imposing his will upon it. He was the only fully constitutional king of the Middle Ages. The House of Commons began to audit the king's accounts, and directed the expenditure of the money it voted to him, and the wording of legislation was now determined by Parliament before a bill reached the king for signature.

Though Henry V (1413–1422) safely succeeded to his father's position, it was not without opposition from another noble house, which had, in its own opinion, a better right to the throne—the House of York. At least in part in order to head off such dynastic opposition, Henry V picked a quarrel with France and plunged his country into a foreign war, in which he was brilliantly successful, winning by the Treaty of Troyes (1420) the consent of the deranged French king to his own succession to the throne of France. Henry, however, died prematurely, and, as we shall see, his son was unable to make good his father's claim to the French crown. As this son, Henry VI (1422–1461) was intermittently insane and never exercised an effective control over it, Parliament in his time was usually supreme.

When Henry VI became permanently insane, the House of York decided to take matters into its own hands. The whole of France except Calais had been lost, mer-

cenaries defeated in France returned to England, where they preyed upon the countryside almost with impunity, while the officials of the government were unable to exercise their functions and were frequently unpaid and corrupt. In these circumstances Richard, Duke of York, claimed that the country required a competent king and that this should be himself, by a hereditary right superior to that of the actual reigning monarch Henry VI. The supporters of the Lancastrian house did not accept his claim and war broke out.[6] Richard was killed. His son and heir Edward (IV) proclaimed himself king in 1461. But his title was not uncontested, and he continued to wage the War of the Roses until his chief opponent, the Earl of Warwick (the Kingmaker), was killed at the battle of Barnet (1471) and Henry's wife and young son were defeated in the same year at the battle of Tewkesbury. Edward's title to the throne was then formally acknowledged by a subservient Parliament.

Edward may be considered as the real founder of the absolute monarchy. Henry VII, the first Tudor king, merely followed Edward's policy, with various improvements. Edward called Parliament rarely, and used various indirect means for gaining money for his rule, especially from the townsmen, who did not mind taxation, even severe taxation including forced loans (called benevolences!), provided the War of the Roses did not break out again and ruin everyone. Edward's monarchy was strong, and it was far from constitutional. He had come to power by violence and he did not mind using some violent means to maintain his throne. He no longer had any wars with France on his hands, and his increased revenue obtained from the towns, plus a merciless use of his judicial powers to extract further income, enabled him to be free of Parliament, as Henry VII was able to be when he wished. When Edward died his sons were children, and they were imprisoned and murdered by their uncle, Richard III, who usurped the

[6] This war is called the "War of the Roses" because the Lancastrian emblem was a red rose, while that of the House of York was a white rose.

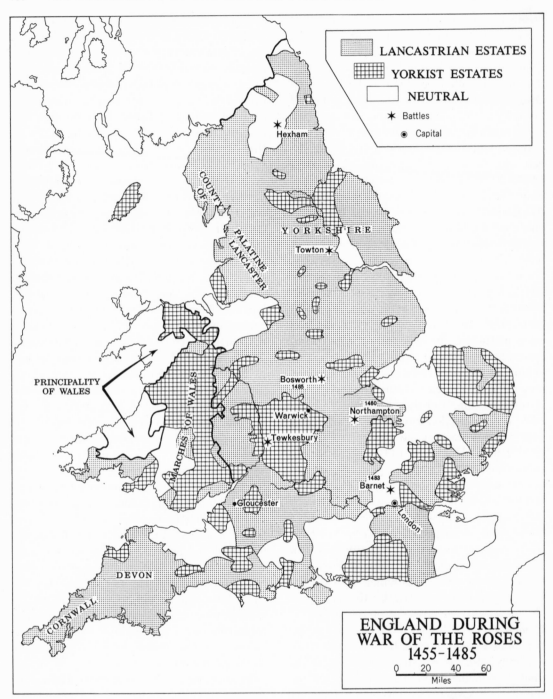

ENGLAND DURING
WAR OF THE ROSES
1455-1485

0    20    40    60
Miles

throne, but reigned for too short a time (1483–1485) and with too little security for any constitutional changes to take place in that period. He called only one Parliament. In 1485 he was killed at the battle of Bosworth, and an outright usurper, with hardly more than a shadow of a claim to the throne through his mother, was accepted as king by Parliament, on the condition, or at least after a promise, that he would marry the heiress of the House of York. Thus began the great Tudor monarchy, and the establishment of an absolutism under which Parliament was clearly an unequal partner in the rule of the country. But the history of the Tudor Henry VII, belongs by convention to modern times; and since his government does indeed mark a very definite new direction away from medieval constitutionalism, the convention is eminently justifiable.

## THE MACHINERY OF GOVERNMENT IN THE LATER MIDDLE AGES

### The king's council

We have already seen how the Curia Regis had gradually become a body of officials who held their position by appointment of the monarch. In Edward I's time the council was very large, and almost half of its members did not belong to the feudal nobility. They were well paid by the king for their services, and in his time were far more important than the fledgling Parliament; they drew up all legislation and altered it in accordance with the king's wishes. The king usually consulted at least his chief barons before legislating, and in several cases he also consulted his full Parliament. The Lords and the Commons were both anxious to curb the power of this council and bring it to some extent under their own control, and by this means use it even as a check upon the king himself. When the medieval kings were strong the council obeyed the monarch; when they were weak the nobles usually managed to put some of their number on the council and thus kept the king under their control. In the time of Henry VI the council itself was rent by faction, some favoring the Lancastrians and some the Yorkists.

The Parliament invented a useful device for getting rid of unpopular members of the council. This was impeachment, under which the Commons drew up a complaint and the Lords, in their judicial capacity, tried the particular minister. The procedure, however, was not used very frequently in the Middle Ages, and all the known cases occurred within a period of seventy-three years. Thereafter there were none until the reign of the Stuarts in the seventeenth century. A bill of attainder could also be passed, a bill which went through both houses of Parliament simply decreeing that such or such a man should be punished, usually with death. This deprived the man of any form of trial, and was only used in the Middle Ages during the Wars of the Roses when the ruling faction disposed of the opposition by this means.

Richard II, in his efforts to establish his personal rule and independence of Parliament, appointed commoners to his council almost exclusively as an instrument for keeping the feudal nobility in subjection. In order to legislate as needed he used the council to make decrees or ordinances, a right which he claimed, but which was of doubtful legality at this time. He claimed also another ancient royal right—to dispense with the laws which were already on the statute books. This right had certainly been exercised by kings in the past, and it was doubtful if Parliament could have insisted that the king could not exempt individuals from certain laws, especially when the laws in question had to be executed by him. But in the bill of indictment against Richard at the time of his deposition his claims to be above the law and to be able to make new law were listed among his many offenses.[7]

Under the Lancastrian monarchy, which, as we have seen, was unusually constitutional, Parliament had a considerable hand in the appointment of the council. The majority of its members belonged to the House of Lords, either lords spiritual or lords temporal. However, it was at this time that the nobles in the council, as partisans of the Lancastrian or Yorkist cause, quarreled incessantly with each other, and majority groups in the council virtually ruled England during the reign of Henry VI, whose incompetence and intermittent insanity necessitated rule by a regency for most of his reign.

The council was also a law court for special cases. For much of the later Middle

[7] The charge that the king had illegally dispensed with the laws was also brought against James II in the seventeenth century, and was the principal ground for declaring that he had forfeited the throne ("Glorious Revolution," 1688–1689).

Ages it claimed to be a court of appeal, entitled to call in question decisions of lower courts. It was also a tool of the monarchy as a court under the direct control of the king which was in a position to try important offenders without any means of appeal. It could be, and was, used against the feudal nobility on occasion, and was necessarily objected to by Parliament, which passed a considerable number of laws trying to take away its power and guarantee elementary liberties and jury trials for all offenders. Only a small minority of the council actually sat in judgment as a law court; its procedure was speedy and lacked the formality of the lower courts, and for this reason even Parliament sometimes approved of its use, as, for instance, against rioters and for offenses against wage-fixing legislation approved of by everyone except those affected by it. This committee of the council was revived by Henry vii as the Court of Star Chamber, and in the time of the Stuarts, Parliament resurrected all the legislation of the Middle Ages against the jurisdiction of the council in the effort to show that the laws of England from ancient times did not approve of it.

### Justices of the Peace

We have seen earlier that Richard i, or his Curia, first began to appoint assistants to the sheriff who were supposed to watch him and see that the king's peace was maintained. Gradually in the later Middle Ages these guardians of the peace began to be given the bulk of the powers of the sheriffs, and from this time on the sheriff's position became a burden which most men preferred to avoid. It carried little power and small chance of recompense and was an annual position. All it had was dignity. But the guardians of the peace, soon to be called justices, took their place as perhaps the most useful and important of all the instruments of government devised by medieval monarchs. They were at first authorized only to receive indictments against offenders and commit them to trial when the king's justices arrived in their neighborhood. But very soon they were given jurisdiction over minor

criminal cases. When Parliament after the Black Death proposed to keep the wages of laborers down to the figure they had commanded before the plague and the shortage of labor that resulted from it, it was to the justices that it turned for enforcement. The kings used them for all minor and even some major cases which affected the king and which were entitled to be tried by royal justice. The justices were empowered first to try minor cases without a jury (summary jurisdiction) and then they were commanded to hold court four times a year (quarter sessions) to try with a jury any offenses except treason, though if the cases were difficult they had to remand to the assizes when the itinerant king's justices visited their area. The justices originally were paid, and the practice continued for several centuries until with the falling value of money their wage was so small, being fixed by statute, that payment was allowed to lapse.

The class from which the justices were drawn was the lower nobility and gentry, only very rarely from the upper nobility. It was a position of great prestige, if little profit. There was for centuries a demand from Parliament that the judges should be elected; but this was never conceded by the kings, not even in modern times. They remained the instrument of the king's rule at the local level. They looked after the king's interest, and had the power of enforcing both his instructions and the statutes made by Parliament, everything from the failure to pay taxes to the suppression of riots. By the sixteenth century all local administration was in their hands. Though in very modern times they have lost some of their power, to this day in England anyone who commits a misdemeanor in any rural area will be haled before a justice of the peace, who may remand him to quarter sessions, where that justice or another will try him in front of a jury and sentence him afterward to his just deserts.

### THE WARS WITH FRANCE

As we have seen, the foreign wars waged by English monarchs gave an opportunity to

Parliament to limit their power by withholding funds unless grievances were redressed. In this section we shall consider the wars themselves in a little more detail. The duchy of Aquitaine, comprising Guienne and Gascony, remained in English hands after the first series of wars which ended in 1259. The French kings, once they had almost completed the unification of the territorial area of France, spared no efforts to finish their work. But the English found these provinces economically valuable, especially the export duties on the wine which was the chief product of the area. Few kings troubled to consider whether these duties compensated for the treasure poured out in trying to retain them, because it was not usual for kings to consider such wars in terms of economic loss or gain, whatever the merchants concerned thought of the matter. The English king, as feudal vassal of the French king for this territory, always objected to the ceremony of homage to him which by custom the English king had to perform, and the French king usually made complaints about the improper way in which the English king performed it. A faulty performance of the ceremony gave the former a chance to declare the latter a faithless vassal and call upon his other vassals to take the English king's land. The nobles of the area also could be induced to take complaints to the French rather than the English courts when it suited their interest, and the French king, nothing loath, would often support them.

Moreover, there were frequent quarrels between English and Flemish towns over fishery rights in the North Sea, and their ships sometimes preyed upon each other. But in most respects England and Flanders were in agreement with each other since the English produced raw wool which the Flemish towns manufactured into cloth. The Flemish towns were officially under the rule of the Count of Flanders, a vassal of the French crown, but they resented his rule as strongly as the Italian towns resented their noble masters, all except the ruling oligarchies in these towns. The Count of Flanders would support the oligarchies in the towns and would invite his overlord the French king to support him, while the smaller merchants, those who were dependent upon the English trade, invited the English king, who was vitally interested in doing business with them, to support them. In the early fourteenth century the Count of Flanders, in obedience to the French crown, arrested all Englishmen in his realm, and the English king retaliated by stopping all trade between England and Flanders. Under this kind of pressure the Flemish burghers overthrew the oligarchic governments in their cities and invited the English king to become their overlord in return for a restoration of the old trade between the countries.

At this moment Edward III, a warrior king, discovered that his claim to the French throne was at least as good as the French king's own, crossed over to Flanders, and at Ghent was proclaimed King of France (1340). The first part of the Hundred Years' War which followed went uniformly in favor of the English, whose army was more than a match for the feudal hosts of the French monarchy, and after they had won the naval battle of Sluys (1340) and the land battles of Crécy and Poitiers (1346, 1356) and had

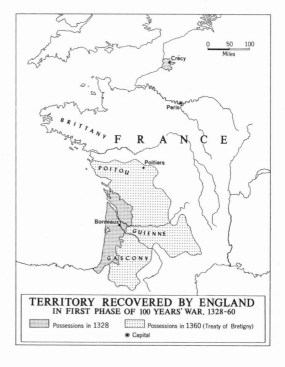

**TERRITORY RECOVERED BY ENGLAND**
IN FIRST PHASE OF 100 YEARS' WAR, 1328-60
Possessions in 1328      Possessions in 1360 (Treaty of Bretigny)
● Capital

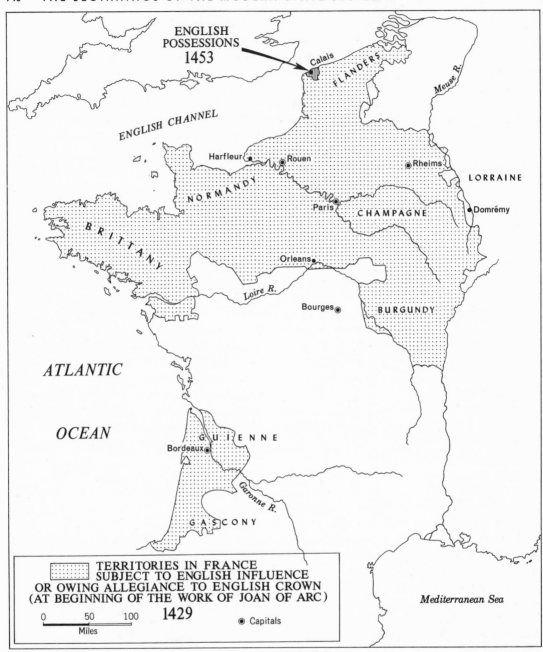

ENGLISH
POSSESSIONS
1453

TERRITORIES IN FRANCE
SUBJECT TO ENGLISH INFLUENCE
OR OWING ALLEGIANCE TO ENGLISH CROWN
(AT BEGINNING OF THE WORK OF JOAN OF ARC)
1429

0    50    100
Miles

⊙ Capitals

taken the French king prisoner, a treaty was signed giving three counties in the north including Calais to the English, recognizing the English king's right to Aquitaine, and adding the important province of Poitou, but relieving him of the obligation of performing feudal homage for them. Much of this gain was lost by a renewal of the war a short time later, but the successors of Edward III were kept too busy at home to renew the war until the time of Henry V. And by this time France itself was rent by civil war and struggles between two factions for the control of an intermittently insane monarch and his extremely sane queen, Isabel of Bavaria.

Henry V in 1415, allied with the Burgundians, one of the French factions whose position will be explained in the next section, won the battle of Agincourt against tremendous odds, though favored by the French insistence on using the armor which was traditional but a deathtrap against the English yeomen archers. This time it was impossible for the French to recover, and the Burgundian duke, aided by Isabel of Bavaria, arranged the Treaty of Troyes (1420) under which Henry was to inherit the throne of France after the death of the mad king, was to become Regent of France, and was to marry the daughter of the French king. This was the nearest the English ever reached to the full throne of France; but at the same time the success of the English claim was dependent upon the continued support of the Burgundians since the treaty could never be enforced against a united France. Henry's claim to the French throne through his wife and the ancient claim of Edward III could never be the equal of that of the king's reigning son, in spite of the fact that for the moment the latter happened to be at odds with the powerful Burgundians.

But in any case the English cause was ruined by the premature death of Henry v in the same year as the death of the mad king Charles VI of France. The heir of Henry was a child, while the heir of the French king possessed only part of the south of France, being excluded from the remainder by the Burgundians and the English. As long as the Burgundians supported the boy Henry VI of England, the English were able to hold northern France and their remaining possessions in the south. Together they pursued the war against the Dauphin[8] Charles (VII) with some vigor, while the latter sank into a despondency from which it needed a miracle to rescue him. Harassed by lack of funds through the inability to collect any taxes of substantial value, cut off from his capital, which was in Burgundian hands, the Dauphin seemed to have little in his favor except that the Duke of Burgundy had no title to the French crown and did not claim it, and the English king who had was only

a boy—while his regents, beset by faction as they were, could not organize the country without far more funds than the English Parliament allowed its Lancastrian monarchs, even though these greatly exceeded the resources of Charles the Dauphin.

But the miracle came in the person of Joan of Arc, who not only succeeded in arousing Charles, who always seems to have believed in her, but in awakening a kind of nascent patriotism and anti-English sentiment which was to prove of great value as an aid to the diplomatic ability shown later by Charles VII. The English and Burgundians were driven from their siege of Orléans, by the personal efforts of the Maid of Orléans, as she was called thereafter. Then, with a sure instinct for the dramatic patriotic gesture, she insisted that Charles go to Rheims to be crowned king as his ancestors had been crowned before him. Thereafter Charles and his counselors concentrated on the attempt to dislodge the Duke of Burgundy from his English alliance, an effort which was ultimately successful, though not till after the capture and death of Joan, as will be seen in the next section. Although the Burgundian dukes had to be paid a high price and played almost no part in the expulsion of the English, Charles VII was able to obtain funds from the States-General and to reorganize his army. In the later years of his reign he was uniformly successful, gaining, very surprisingly, the title of Charles the Victorious —surprisingly for one who had started in such an unpromising manner—and ultimately expelling the English in 1453 from all their possessions in France except Calais. The dream of Joan of Arc and her prophecy for Charles himself had been fulfilled.

▶ **The unification of France as a national state**

THE CAPETIAN MONARCHY TO
PHILIP AUGUSTUS

The rise of the French national state does not require such detail as was needed for the English. France never became a limited monarchy till after the Revolution, and

---

[8] This title, held by the French king's eldest son, corresponds to that of the Prince of Wales in England.

much of the history of the unification is the attempt of the monarchy to rid itself, first of control by French nobles whose possessions were greater than those of the king himself for many centuries, and then of recurrent English invasions in support of English feudal possessions in the country. When we have seen how unification was finally achieved, we must examine the machinery of absolutism, and the few abortive attempts by the States-General and the Parliaments to limit the power of the king, and why they failed to do so.

We have already described the position of the Capetian monarchy in the early Middle Ages. The king was the feudal lord of only a small area in north central France, a compact holding, but greatly inferior to that of many of the other French nobles. But, as feudal king, he was the titular overlord of every noble who had any possessions within an area generally conceded to be that of "France." His position was one not only of prestige, but of some power. As the titular head of the state, he was the natural leader in a crusade, and thus sometimes commanded French contingents made up of men who were not his actual vassals. Lords who died without leaving male heirs often entrusted the wardship of heiresses to the kings. Some kings married their wards thus acquired, but in any case could choose their husbands. If the lords had no heirs at all then their lands escheated to the crown. When lords wished to commend themselves to a superior in exchange for protection the king seemed to many to be a suitable protector. Finally, the Capetian kings had a very fair amount of ecclesiastical patronage in their hands, and the French clergy on the whole favored a monarchy over feudal decentralization. They were continually urging the kings to establish and maintain justice beyond their mere feudal domains, and were willing to give such aid as they could.

The early Capetians, very sensibly in view of their position, rigidly refused foreign adventures in which their vassals were gaining glory and even kingdoms. They stayed at home looking after their affairs;

and they had the very great advantage that, from 987 to 1328, eldest son succeeded eldest son in the monarchy, thus establishing a certain sanctity for the line and making extremely unlikely any disputed succession, since there could be no occasion for dispute. The French kings, unlike the German and the English, thus appeared from the beginning to be marked out by God as rulers. The Archbishop of Rheims consecrated them as kings with sacred oil, but there was no occasion to submit the choice to a body of electors or to a national assembly. Moreover, most of these kings reigned for a considerable number of years; this meant that there would be no minority period under a regency, a situation which frequently caused trouble in England, since it gave various factions the chance to quarrel over the control of the child.

The first thing to do was to establish some kind of administration. The French kings used the old Germanic custom of appointing household officials and giving them charge of various departments connected with the management of their feudal estates. But for a long time they did not even have control over these appointments, which tended to pass from father to son, like the old "mayors of the palace." However, the king also gave appointments to clergymen, who were barred by celibacy from handing down such offices. And as the kings from the twelfth century onward managed to establish some order in their own territories, a task in which some of the earlier kings had had indifferent success, so they were able to obtain control of their official appointments and began to appoint commoners who were more susceptible to royal control.

Louis VI, the Fat (1108–1137) was the first French king who really fully controlled his own poor territories, and he began to extend his jurisdiction beyond them, summoning to his court occasional vassals who only owed him allegiance as king and sometimes succeeding in enforcing his will. His son Louis VII married Eleanor of Aquitaine, adding for a time territories far greater than his own to the kingdom. This marriage was the direct result of his prestige as king, since the lady's father had asked Louis to look after her when he died. But Louis divorced her after the Second Crusade, and she married Henry II of England, who thus became a landholder far more powerful than the French king, possessing not only England but two thirds of France, though he was still supposed to do homage to the French king for his lands.

Louis had little success in dealing with Henry, though he lost nothing. But his successor Philip Augustus was able to use shrewd diplomacy and occasional military campaigns to take almost the whole of Henry's lands from his sons. John, the younger brother of Henry's heir Richard I, as long as he was not king, intrigued with Philip Augustus against his brother. Philip returned from the Holy Land whither he had gone with Richard on the Third Crusade, leaving Richard there. He found that John was quite amenable to a few bribes in the form of Richard's French possessions. When Richard was taken prisoner and held to ransom by the emperor, John continued to enjoy Philip's support; but when Richard at last was freed and rushed back to France to put an end to Philip's depredations, for a few years Philip could barely hold his own. Then, fortunately for him, Richard was killed in France and John came to the English throne (1199). Of course he was no longer willing to play with Philip, but Philip had acquired another card, a better heir to the throne than either Richard or John, though he had been too young to be considered at the time of Richard's accession. This was Prince Arthur of Brittany.

Philip proceeded to espouse this young man's claim, and called John to his French feudal court to defend himself against charges brought by Arthur, who as lord of Brittany was also a vassal of the French king. John refused to come, and we have already seen how Philip was able to gain the support of the French nobility with promises of loot and lands from the English possessions in France, and how with their aid and some useful support from the pope he succeeded in conquering the bulk of John's possessions. Some more were added by his son Louis VIII, and recognition of the conquests in return for the cession of Aquitaine to England was agreed to by Louis IX in 1259. Meanwhile, as we have also seen, much of southern France was given to Philip and his successors through the Albigensian Crusade. Philip also by the battle of Bouvines (1214) defeated not only the English and the Germans but also the Count of Flanders, who now became his vassal.

## THE MACHINERY OF GOVERNMENT IN THE TIME OF PHILIP AUGUSTUS

The French king, unlike the English, had no ancient customary rights to enforce, nor had he hedged his barons with restrictions on their independence like William the Conqueror of England, for his vassals owed a more direct obedience, more easily enforceable, to their own suzerains. So the kings had to concentrate their attention on trying to make their own domains at least subservient to themselves, and within this domain they did provide an administration far superior to those of other ordinary feudal lords, and which was capable of being extended as soon as the domain itself was enlarged. The earliest official was the *prévôt*, who looked after the king's interests in matters of justice and finance. As prévôts were paid by the grant of fiefs, their offices became hereditary, and it was not possible to do much to improve their administration until the king was in a position to pay them in money, and appoint and dismiss them at will. This reform was largely the work of Philip Augustus, who, by the help of his new feudal possessions, was able to find for the first time enough money for royal needs. He appointed *baillis* to watch the *prévôts*. These new officials at once became the chief instruments of royal policy. Their instructions were to support not only the king's feudal prerogatives but also as many of his kingly ones as they could, including within their jurisdiction as much of the king's non-feudal territory as possible, and extending his influence in areas where he was not the feudal suzerain. This was done especially through listening to complaints against the local administrations of justice and trying to substitute an appeal to the king's justice instead of to the feudal court.

The king himself made effective use of his power of summoning his vassals, direct and titular, to his court for advice and assistance, accustoming them to regard themselves as his real vassals, and, as we have seen, he led them against the English possessions in France at a profit to themselves as well as to him. But one of his greatest titles to fame was his recognition of the importance of the towns, which were as prosperous as any in Europe in the thirteenth century. Philip was entirely willing to grant them charters giving them freedom to organize local internal government, in exchange for suitable amounts of money. The towns recognized the value to themselves of having an efficient king rather than an irresponsible feudal nobility as their protector. So they provided him not only with money but with soldiery, and in many cases guaranteed to undertake their own defense. Philip also appointed townsmen to high positions in his government.

But it was, on the whole, the conquests of Philip that made all the other successes possible. He had the nucleus of an administration which took care of very small territories; when the territories were enlarged he increased the number of his officials and maintained the same organs of government, adding only a few new officials, such as seneschals. All the officials had to be watched carefully by each king, as it was not easy to control them.

## CONTINUED GROWTH OF POWER OF CAPETIAN KINGS

### Louis IX and full exploitation of feudal powers

Perhaps as early as Philip Augustus the officials of the king sometimes, in committee, tried cases under feudal law in which the king's interests were involved. This committee of the king's council ultimately developed

*St. Louis IX, King of France. From a* Moralized Bible *(French), 1226–1234.* (COURTESY THE PIERPONT MORGAN LIBRARY. Ms. 240, folio 8)

into the Parlement of Paris, the chief law court of the realm. Another committee looked into the receipts of money that came into the king's treasury to see that the *baillis* and seneschals were doing their duty. But by the time of Louis IX (1226–1270) the king was asserting successfully his prerogative of administering justice for the entire kingdom of France, and not only for his feudal vassals. The king had always in theory been supposed to be the protector of all and the maintainer of peace. He and his lawyers now asserted that many cases tried locally by feudal nobles came within his jurisdiction. By decree Louis forbade feudal warfare, and tried to persuade contenders in disputes that might have led to war to come to his courts, either to himself, for he often gave personal judgments, or to the Parlement of Paris, which was under his control; and he forbade also, following the example of the Church, all recourse to trial by ordeal and combat. He did not trouble, as a rule, to obtain the consent of his vassals to his decrees, as had been the previous custom; but since he was everywhere revered as a saintly person—he was later formally canonized as a saint—this addition to royal authority was generally accepted, and on several occasions he obtained the signatures of a representative selection of vassals. Louis, finding that the communal government of the towns given charters by Philip Augustus too often failed to work well because of internal quarrels between merchants and other burghers, suspended many charters and renewed them only when the towns could show that they deserved them. He made the towns have their public accounts audited by his officers, and introduced officials of his own such as mayors, which for centuries were royal and not local appointees.

### Philip IV (the Fair, 1285–1314)

*Centralization of public finance—importance—*It should be understood that the French kings as yet had no right to tax, and though occasionally they attempted taxes for special purposes, such as crusades, there was always such an outcry that the attempts were abandoned immediately. Philip and the able corps of lawyers who formed his body of advisers recognized the importance of money in any centralized administration, and set themselves determinedly to find new sources of royal income, which was used for the purpose of enlarging the realm and controlling the feudal nobility by an increasing use of mercenary rather than feudal troops. On the towns he laid increased customs duties, forced loans, and sales taxes. He assessed the nobles highly for the privilege of avoiding military service, he expropriated the Templars, hitherto the king's bankers, and, as we have seen, he succeeded in taxing the French clergy. All accounts were carefully scrutinized by a special accounting department staffed by salaried officials.

*The bureaucracy—*Philip reorganized the official organs of state into what will hereafter be called the king's council, which had an inner group consulted on special occasions. The latter remained the chief advisory body to the crown until the Revolution. The Parlement of Paris under the king's direction became a real law court composed of trained lawyers. One branch was given the task of listening to requests that the king rather than any other court render justice. The Parlement of Paris also assumed jurisdiction over local courts, transferring their cases when necessary to itself.

It may be mentioned that this council, made up so largely of lawyers trained in the Roman law, was something new at this early period, and was found to be extremely effective in enhancing the king's authority. Looked at with suspicion by the feudal nobility, which in France throughout history remained an aristocratic military caste and made no effort to control the civil administration or even to cooperate with it, these lawyers had only one duty and one aim— to aid the monarchy which had appointed and could dismiss them. Paid in money and not in lands, they never became part of the aristocracy; even in later times when lawyers and assistants to the king were ennobled, they became a separate nobility, known as the nobility of the robe rather than of the sword. Moreover they were, in the time of Philip IV, laymen and not clergymen, and thus could be independent even in dealing with the Church. As the power of the monarchy grew, so must their own power with it; while if the monarchy's power declined they personally would lose any authority they possessed. They therefore took every opportunity to exalt the power of the monarchy over any competitor that threatened it, and, being thoroughly educated men, took the lead even in appeals to public opinion. It was the king's counselors in particular who dominated the great appeal to national unity presented by the quarrel with Pope Boniface VIII, which has already been discussed from a papal point of view in an earlier chapter.

*The States-General*—For the calling of the States-General in 1302 by Philip IV was essentially an appeal to public opinion, and was intended by the lawyers who dominated it to be precisely this, presenting a complete contrast with the English Parliaments of the same period, which were called by the English kings in response to pressure by the barons and taxpayers, and diminished rather than increased the absolute authority of the monarchy. In later times the States-General was called for the purpose of gaining consent to new taxes, and, since these could be refused, a refusal could have been a step toward limiting the monarchy. But Pierre Flotte, doctor of laws in the University of Montpellier, the royal chancellor, at the assembly of 1302 devoted almost his entire address to the iniquities of the pope who, according to him, was trying to submit the French monarchy to dictation by a foreign power. One pamphleteer, engaged in laying the groundwork of public opinion for the royal defiance of the pope, had even gone so far as to accuse Boniface of having said that he would "rather be a dog than a Frenchman."

The representation in the States-General called by Philip IV was substantially similar to that of the English Parliaments. The first estate, the clergy; the second estate, the nobility; and the third estate, the remainder, especially representatives of the towns, was the same as in England, though there was nothing in France to correspond with the crucial group in England, the knights of the shire who gave leadership to the bourgeoisie without being dominated by their special urban interests. In Philip's assembly his policy had virtually unanimous support because the quarrel was so well calculated to appeal to all. No one was anxious to see France dominated by an authoritarian and grasping papacy. Bishops, monks, and friars were as favorable to the king's position as were lords, bourgeoisie, and university professors. But if the king had called them, as later kings were compelled to call them, for the purpose of extracting funds from them, there would have been no such im-

pressive unanimity. However, the precedent had been set for an assembly of all classes of the realm dominated by the king and his council; and we should note in passing that the sentiment of nationality must have been growing if the well-informed and able lawyers who knew what they wanted found it worth while to couch their appeals in patriotic vein as the sentiment most likely to command the gesture of unanimity which they needed.

### The end of the Capetians

After the death of Philip the Fair in 1314 the feudal lords made a determined effort to regain some of their power lost to the encroachments of the monarchy, so that Philip's successors were forced to make a few concessions, defining limits of the king's power within the feudal system; and one lawyer was dismissed who was particularly hated because he had unduly enriched himself. But Louis X, who reigned only two years, left no son to succeed him. Not since the tenth century had the throne failed to pass from father to son. He was succeeded by each of his brothers in succession, none of whom left any male heir. The last of the Capetian kings designated his cousin Philip of Valois, son of the brother of Philip the Fair, as king and he was accepted by the French nobility and duly assumed the crown. But Edward III, king of England, whose mother was the daughter of Philip the Fair, asserted that the French throne could descend through daughters in default of sons, as had been accepted by this time in England. This was the excuse for the Hundred Years' War, which has been dealt with from the English point of view in the first part of this chapter.

THE HUNDRED YEARS' WAR

### The first phase to the Treaty of Brétigny (1360)

In a very real sense the end of the Capetian monarchy in France marks the close of the consolidation of the French kingdom as much as the reign of Edward I in England marks the greatest power of the later medieval English monarchy. Thereafter both monarchies lost power to the as yet undefeated forces of feudalism, while the two countries fought with each other and with the feudal nobility. But France had developed no constitutional counterbalance to the crown and at the end of the period of medieval disintegration absolutism was re-established in a modern form with relatively few changes from the monarchy of Philip IV, while in England the institution of Parliament had grown throughout the period of disintegration, and remained still potentially strong even during the period of absolutism that followed it. During the Hundred Years' War for a brief period it seemed that the French monarchy would be brought under control by the same forces that limited it in England; but the chance was missed and it never recurred again. Fundamentally it was the failure of the nobility to accept any social responsibilities and its insistence on remaining a privileged and irresponsible group harking back to a long-outmoded military tradition that handed absolute power back to the monarchy; the bourgeoisie found it impossible to cooperate with the lords, and made few attempts at effective action on their own. Preferring an orderly absolute monarchy to a disorderly and irresponsible feudalism, they were willing to pay the price exacted of them right down to the Revolution in 1789. When for a few years in the middle of the seventeenth century the nobles and the bourgeoisie found that it was to their joint interest to control the monarchy, and an opportunity presented itself in the form of the minority of a king under a grasping and detested chancellor, they could agree neither on a program of reform nor on the means for accomplishing it. The *Fronde,* the name of their party of opposition, petered out, and the absolute monarchy was established more firmly than ever under Louis XIV.

The period of the Hundred Years' War therefore presents a picture of gloom relieved only by individual heroism and the appealing figure of the Maid of Orléans.

The consolidation of the national state which followed was carried out by force and diplomacy and did not really become permanent until the end of the sixteenth century with the accession of Henry IV and the Bourbon dynasty. Nothing really new came out of it; the French nobles learned nothing from their disasters, 'and far too much of the monarchs' energies had to be spent in combating them. Throughout the sixteenth century the nobility still pursued its own interests, waging war against the monarchs, intriguing for the succession, or trying to gain the ear of the kings. It was, in the last analysis, the failure to make any political and social gains out of the long period of royal weakness and civil war that made France into the politically backward country which had to submit, too late, to the French Revolution—and this, in spite of the fact that for almost the whole period she was the most culturally advanced of any European nation.

We have seen already how the English brought on the Hundred Years' War in defense of trade interests in Flanders and southern France as well as of the English claim to the French throne. We have seen also how the English kings were forced to obtain from the English Parliament the money for fighting the war and had to make concessions accordingly. At the time when national feeling was still in the process of formation it did not seem impossible, even to the English bourgeoisie, that the French and the English thrones should be united under one monarchy, with all the commercial advantages that this would entail; otherwise it seems unlikely that the English Parliament should have given the crown the subsidies which the feudal nobility had refused to John and Henry III when they wished to defend the personal possessions of their family in France. The English therefore always had an advantage in this war in that England itself was in no danger. The war was fought on French soil, and the French kings were for a long time unable to persuade their feudal vassals that the war was any real concern of theirs as long as it was kept away from their own territories. The territory of France, if it had been recognized as something that needed to be defended as a whole, was far more populous and prosperous than England, and there could have been only one result if all classes in the realm had united to defend it against an army that was so far from home. But the English could almost always count on support not only from the feudal possessions of its kings in southern France but from individual lords of varying power, who were theoretically vassals of the French crown but wished to throw off the allegiance and become independent, even if this meant accepting English overlordship instead. And if they could not count on actual allies, then at least they could count on neutrality, which as often worked in their favor.

The first phase of the war was marked by continuous English successes, even though the actual battles were invariably fought against heavy paper odds. The members of the French nobility who formed the bulk of the French king's armies were useless against the English militia. They fought in the old spirit of chivalry, which could hardly be expected to be observed by the English common soldiers. On one famous occasion the English army under Edward III had been drawn up in a well-chosen position in which it was relatively safe from attack by the French cavalry. Philip VI, the French king, sent to Edward to ask him if he would not be kind enough to move his army into another position where the rules of chivalric warfare could be better observed. When Edward summarily refused the reasonable request, Philip was badly put out, and regarded the English king as false to the traditions of knighthood. The French chronicler Froissart is entirely at one with the nobility in the matter. If war was not fought any longer within the rules of proper knightly behavior, it was the English fault, and not the fault of the French nobility.

When the French King John was taken prisoner at the battle of Poitiers in 1356, and the heir had to try to struggle along with only the authority of a Dauphin, a real opportunity arose to gain concessions from the Dauphin, who was short of money with which to pursue the war. He was forced to call the States-General—this time, unlike Philip IV, as a suppliant. Not only had France been suffering from the ravages of war, which were serious enough because the English troops did not hesitate to try to live off the country, *their* country as Edward III claimed; the Black Death of the years 1347–1350 decimated many of the towns and killed off perhaps as much as 20 per cent of the whole population. The peasants were hardest hit, the nobles and richer bourgeoisie suffering much less. Moreover, after the battle of Poitiers the enormous numbers of ransoms for the knights who had fallen in their heavy armor and been taken prisoner without even much fighting further impoverished the peasantry, who ultimately had to find the sums required.

The States-General, made up of classes who were already heavily enough burdened by either taxation or ransoms, was in no mood to grant the Dauphin any further sums for the pursuit of the war. It made demands on him, insisting that he account for his expenditures and allow his ministers to be supervised, but it did not present a coherent program to him, and he doubted in fact whether it would even be able to find the money he needed. He therefore refused any demands that would have seriously limited his power, and on several occasions went behind its back and by personal requests to provincial notables was able to obtain enough for current needs. Meanwhile Paris, a city which was many times larger than any other in the country, had organized a private revolution of its own under Étienne Marcel, a merchant prince of the city who seems to have hoped for some kind of bourgeois control of the monarchy, perhaps through helping to put a pretender, one Charles the Bad of Navarre, on the throne. Marcel succeeded in rallying bourgeois and workers in Paris to his side, and welcomed assistance elsewhere wherever it could be found, among the Jacquerie, groups of peasants in Normandy and Picardy and Champagne who had broken loose and were burning and pillaging the castles of their lords; from Charles of Navarre, and finally from the English, with whose Flemish allies Marcel hoped an accord could be reached. Faced with this situation, the States-General and the nobles who largely controlled it realized that they needed the king or the Dauphin to restore order. They voted two important taxes which were easily collectible, a sales tax and a tax on hearths, and ceased to press their demands for control of the monarchy. The Dauphin, thus fortified, was able to suppress both the Parisian revolution and the Jacquerie. He then negotiated a peace with the English (Brétigny, 1360) under which the king of England renounced his claim to the French throne in return for a considerable increase in his French lands and a huge ransom for the French King John, who returned to France for a time, leaving a son as hostage for the fulfillment of the treaty. As the hostage escaped, John considered it his duty to return to captivity in England, which was at this time a far more attractive situation than being king in France.

### The failure of the States-General to control the king

It has been contended, probably with some justice, that the decision of the nobles at this time to make common cause with the king against the Jacquerie and some of the bourgeoisie and the granting of important permanent taxes to the king were a crucial failure from which the States-General never recovered. The English barons, working in cooperation with the townsmen and lesser nobility, had presented a united front to the king, and a parliament had resulted, which, though it was sometimes kept in subjection by absolute monarchs, nevertheless did succeed in establishing itself as a regular institution which controlled especially the king's arbitrary power of taxation. The right to wage and declare war remained in the power of the English monarch, but he could not in fact go to war without the consent of the people, since the funds under his personal control were insufficient for the purpose. This meant that he must call his parliament to obtain financial backing.

The French king, as we have seen, was given taxes in perpetuity for which the English king had to ask his parliament; and in a later section of this chapter we shall see how many more taxes were granted to Charles VII, also in perpetuity, in the last phases of the Hundred Years' War. When the French king wanted more he could call the States-General, and if this failed he could call the lesser provincial estates, and hope to obtain enough to carry on temporarily; while the towns, for lack of support from the nobility, were powerless to resist royal exactions. Thus an instrument which in England was found most potent for exercising control over the monarchs was thrown away by the French nobility at a time when it was perhaps within its grasp.

Whatever truth there may be in this contention, there is no doubt that the States-General was never again able to stand up to the king, and of course it never became a parliament. The history of England has shown that wars provide a wonderful opportunity to force the monarch to grant concessions; yet in France the Hundred Years' War resulted in the consolidation of power in the hands of the French monarchy. Probably the answer to the enigma is to be sought in the different kinds of war waged by the two monarchies. The Hundred Years' War was as much a civil conflict as it was war with a foreigner; and the English War of the Roses, a civil conflict, also resulted in the consolidation of power in the hands of an absolute monarch. It is doubtful whether the States-General could have held any gains it had made in the absence of those valuable local institutions which had been inherited by the English from Anglo-Saxon times, the system of sheriffs and justices and the local courts which actually supervised the collection of taxes agreed upon by Parliament. The French monarchy had too much control over the local institutions in France, as we shall see; while the tradition of royal legislation, a feature of the Roman law operative in France, was probably too strong to allow any gradual evolution of self-government. Even the French Revolution at the end of the eighteenth century did not substantially change the centralized government which France inherited from her medieval kings.

### The second phase of the war—Uniting of the French and English crowns

Nevertheless at the Treaty of Brétigny the authority of the French kings was at a low enough ebb. The reigning king himself was a prisoner in England, and more than half of France was in English hands. Though in the later years of the fourteenth century a remarkable soldier, the constable Bertrand du Guesclin, was able to take the initiative in the war and recover much of the land lost to the English, in the second decade of the fifteenth century England was again on the offensive under her young warrior king, Henry v (1413–1422), and after the battle of Agincourt (1415) all northern France fell into his hands. Under the Treaty of Troyes (1420) Henry was recognized as the heir to the French throne, and a marriage was arranged between him and Catherine of Valois, the daughter of the French King Charles vi, who was intermittently insane (as was Henry vi of England, the offspring of this unfortunate marriage). This union was intended to settle forever in favor of England the claims of the English monarchy to the throne of France. The claim of the Dauphin Charles (later Charles vii), whose legitimacy was in doubt, was passed over.

This arrangement was the result of the rise of the House of Burgundy to a position in France equal to or superior to that of the French king himself. It is unnecessary here to go into details concerning the means by which the dukes of this house achieved such a position by war, carefully planned marriages, and the ownership of lands outside the jurisdiction of the French king. But the Burgundian support was crucial to the success of the English, who could not have made much headway against a united France. The dukes of Burgundy had no loyalty to the nation of France, nor, certainly, to her kings. They were looking solely to the advancement of their own house, which for a time seemed best assured by the abasement of the French monarchy.

On the death of the English King Henry v in 1422, the succession of his infant son Henry vi to the thrones of England and France was proclaimed by the English and Burgundians. The allies held northern France, and a considerable portion of the rest of the country. The Dauphin Charles was also proclaimed king by his supporters, but he was lazy and lacked energy, and he was in grave financial difficulties. It is possible that he might never have consolidated his throne against such odds had it not been for the Maid of Orléans, Joan of Arc.

### St. Joan of Arc and the end of the Hundred Years' War

It is often the fashion to minimize the importance of Joan of Arc, since the unification of France came after her death, and the policy which she favored, outright war against Burgundians and English, was not the one that was adopted. The policy of attempting to separate the Burgundians from the English, which Charles vii and his advisers, especially Reginald of Chartres, Archbishop of Rheims, followed, was brilliantly successful after her death. Nevertheless, if it had not been for her, Charles would never have been in a position to negotiate with the Burgundians. He was not yet crowned king, and he had as yet no victories to his name. Joan gave him both his first taste of victory, with the consequent return of many vacillating towns and territories to his cause, and she made his doubtful title clear and acceptable by having him crowned publicly at Rheims by the only man competent to perform the ceremony, his one loyal churchman of note, Reginald of Chartres. But, more than this, she never wavered at any time, even while the king she had crowned appeared to have deserted her; she never wavered in her loyalty to him and her certainty that he would expel the English from France. She evoked the idea of France under a legitimate king, the chosen of God, in a way that was really new in her

*Portrait of Charles VII, King of France (the Dauphin, later king, to whom Joan of Arc was sent with her famous message). Painted by Fouquet.*

time. The great force of patriotism unquestionably brought back many waverers to their allegiance to the throne, and for the first time anti-English feeling became so dominant that even the warring nobles could not altogether neglect it in pursuit of their own private interests. It was Joan who made possible the negotiations with Burgundy that in turn made possible the expulsion of the English, which she had promised to her king, without knowing the means by which it would be accomplished.

St. Joan of Arc was born in a family of fairly well-to-do free farmers in an area that had remained faithful to the king. Her fam-

ily was not, as is sometimes supposed, a family of poor peasants; nor was Joan herself a shepherdess, as was later suggested in order to exalt the miracle of her work, though she did occasionally look after the flocks of her family. She could not read or write and she was not educated. From an early age she heard "voices" telling her she must go to the Dauphin and by her work rescue France from the English, and crown Charles as king. For years she resisted this supernatural advice until the position of the king became so desperate that at last she decided she must obey, and relieve the city of Orléans, which was being besieged by the English and was in danger of falling. Orléans was the strategic key to the whole south of the country; if it fell then it seemed that nothing could save the king and his adherents.

Going to the lord of the local castle she was able by her simple sincerity to persuade him to lend her a horse and attendants, whom she also convinced of her mission. She was led to the presence of the Dauphin, whom she found among his courtiers with no insignia of office by which she could tell that he was the king. She went directly up to him and greeted him as king, saying that she had been sent to his aid. The king was clearly impressed, especially by her recognition of him and of his title, which he had previously had reason to doubt. But he took the precaution of having her examined by a committee of theologians led by Reginald of Chartres, who pronounced that the voices heard by Joan were apparently from heaven and could be trusted. Joan was then fitted out with splendid armor, dressed in male clothes, and a new spirit became visible in the royal forces. The army marched to Orléans, and under Joan's leadership the siege was raised, and the English army retreated. One of the most remarkable consequences of Joan's early campaigns was the superstitious awe engendered in the English troops who began to desert, fearing that they were opposed by a sorceress.

With clear vision Joan saw that what must be done was to establish the Dauphin as king, so that the doubtful and the waverers would return to their allegiance; and this, at the moment, she thought was more valuable even than more military victories. So, against the advice of the military men, she insisted that the Dauphin proceed to Rheims, the city where all the French kings had been crowned, in spite of the fact that much of the territory in between was in the hands of the English or the Burgundians. The venture was successful, the royal party reached Rheims, and Reginald of Chartres performed the ceremony. Joan's work was really done; the great gesture had been made, and it could have been left to the men of politics to complete what she had

begun. But the "voices" continued to urge her on, and she insisted that now more military victories were needed, including the conquest of Paris, which was in the hands of the Burgundians. But here Charles and Reginald would not follow her. They knew that, from a political point of view, there could be no lasting peace unless the Burgundians came over to the support of the French crown and could be persuaded to abandon the English. Joan was now a heroine, the people all clamored for her to be given her way, and many of the troops of the French army wished to follow her. She proceeded, with doubtful or no recognition from the king and the archbishop, to continue to wage war on the English until at last she was captured, sold to the English by her Burgundian captors, who thereupon tried her for heresy under the auspices of the Inquisition.

Charles has often been accused of deserting her. But only two courses were available to him, and he in fact tried them both. He could not match the price the English were prepared to pay for the destruction of her influence, which they feared especially for its effect on their own soldiers. He complained bitterly that she was a prisoner of war and under the rules of war of the time she should be held to ransom; and he tried to raise a sum of money sufficient to tempt the Burgundians who had originally captured her, but could not offer enough. Once she was sold to the English the only thing he could do was to try to rescue her by force; but his forces were insufficient to hope to be able to capture Rouen, where she was ultimately imprisoned, and he was unsuccessful. As soon as the war was over he took steps to see that her good name was restored and her trial declared illegal, though of course this was a political necessity, as he would not wish to owe his crown to the efforts of a sorceress and heretic. It is difficult to see what else he could have done; nor did Joan in her trial think that he had deserted her then. She thought only that he ought to have supported her military efforts before her capture.

The trial was entirely illegal, and always under pressure by the English, who were determined to ensure a verdict of guilty and would not have tolerated any other after they had paid such a high price for the captive. The Bishop of Beauvais, the presiding officer, had few claims to be the proper authority for the purpose. He was personally vindictive against the Maid, having been driven out of his bishopric by troops under her command; he had altogether sold out to the English, and anyone during the trial who suggested that his procedure was in any way irregular and that there was anything to be said on behalf of the defendant was summarily dismissed. Several objectors to the procedure were, in fact, imprisoned by the English. Nevertheless, the authorities wanted a regular conviction, and if possible an admission that her "voices" were inspired by the Devil or had been invented. So the trial lasted for many months while the untutored and illiterate girl gave such astonishing answers that the learned theologians were frequently confounded, and had to fall back upon intimidation. At last, after Joan had been weakened by nearly a year of imprisonment and a long Lenten fast, they showed her the stake to which they had already condemned her, and told her she could be spared it if she would recant. She did so, denying her voices but continuing to insist that the king would expel the English from France all the same; but when she had time to think over what she had done, and had resumed her feminine clothes, she withdrew her recantation, and as a relapsed heretic she was handed over to the English to be burned.[9]

But the policy of Reginald of Chartres, pursued ceaselessly during the trial and afterward, was successful. The Duke of Burgundy was detached from the English alliance, and before his death Charles VII was able indeed to drive out the English, leaving them only Calais out of all the English possessions in France. It was not a spontaneous uprising of French patriotism that worked the miracle. It was patient negotiation, combined with careful attention to the improvement of French finances and of the army, followed by a remarkable series of military victories. But the way had been prepared by the Maid, and it is doubtful whether any of it would have been accomplished without the aid of her "voices."

## LOUIS XI AND THE RECONSTITUTION OF ABSOLUTE MONARCHY

### The destruction of the Burgundian realm

Charles VII had bought off the dukes of Burgundy, but the price had been heavy. There can be no doubt that the last duke of the line, Charles the Bold, desired to become a king, sever his lands from France, and add more to them from territories that had never belonged to France. For a time he was successful in his efforts, adding to his domain some of the fairest lands of Holland and Flanders, and even negotiating for the title of Holy Roman Emperor. But in the end his designs were foiled by the patient persistence of the new French king, Louis XI (1461–1483), and the latter's judicious use of bribes and diplomacy to foment insurrections in Charles's home territories. At last Charles was killed in battle by the Swiss, who resisted his attempts to add the ever-disputed Alsace-Lorraine to his empire (1477). Louis allowed the Burgundian lands held outside France to go to the duke's daughter Mary, who married a Hapsburg, but he took Burgundy itself and the northern French possessions of the Burgundian dukes, and his son married the heiress of Brittany, which had been lost to France for generations. So France was again united within substantially the boundaries that it has today.

### The machinery of absolutism as developed by Charles VII and Louis XI

The secret of French absolutism is to be found in the financial autonomy granted

[9] It may be added that in 1456 the papacy had the case retried, and Joan was declared to have been wrongly convicted. She was canonized as a saint in 1919.

by the States-General to the French kings during the Hundred Years' War, and in the efficient organization of an improved bureaucracy to collect the new permanent taxes, devised in part by Charles VII but perfected by Louis XI and his two Valois successors. Until the rise of modern Germany France was always potentially the richest country in Europe, possessed of the finest resources and the hardest working peasantry. When she has been well governed prosperity has always been quick to return, but she has always needed a strong hand at the helm. In a centrally administered kingdom so many possibilities existed for corruption, so many opportunities presented themselves to unwatched officials for personal enrichment that the kings were often ludicrously short of money in a country where ample funds were really available.

The work of Charles VII consisted in obtaining the authorization from the States-General, or the nobility and bourgeoisie, to collect taxes on a permanent basis beyond the simple receipts from the king's property which were all that a feudal king commanded. Charles was granted this in order that he might be enabled to defeat and expel the English. The taxes thus granted, however, were never abandoned by the monarchy, though the fiction was observed that some revenues were temporary and extraordinary, while others were ordinary and regular. The chief tax granted in 1439 was the *taille,* a tax imposed upon all financial and real property throughout the kingdom. A remarkably complex system was inaugurated to collect this tax, which remained the chief tax in France till the Revolution and even afterward. The total amount needed by the crown for each particular year was assessed. This total was then divided by the officials through each unit of government down to the level of the parish, which was assessed for its portion of the whole. On tax collection day in the parish the bells were tolled and the citizens were informed what their contribution was to be. Then they had to elect assessors who determined what the individual share of each must be. Naturally

every peasant wished to avoid his tax, and tried to conceal his wealth—a French custom which has persisted to this day—and many were the expedients adopted. But the taille could be collected, even though large parts of the collections found their way into the pockets of the officials through whose hands it passed on the way to the treasury. Louis XI was extremely careful to check all corruption, and in general the best French kings have done their utmost, until the later kings defeated their own objectives by granting excessive numbers of immunities from taxes to favorites.

The aids, or sales taxes, and the customs duties, both interior and those collected at the ports, and the proceeds from royal monopolies, especially the infamous *gabelle,* or salt tax, were given into the hands of tax farmers, who established their own collection posts and bought the whole contract for taxes from the king. The latter was therefore able to command the expected income from these taxes without having to go to the trouble of instituting a system for collecting it himself. This task was thus performed by private enterprise, which helped itself to considerably more profit from the collection than was officially permitted by the kings. The difficulty, however, was the control of the tax farmers, and, again, only the most efficient kings were able to keep them in order. And, with such possibilities for living beyond their means many French kings in later times would persuade the tax farmers to give them several years' income in advance, and thus would be short of income in later years when it might be equally needed.

With the money thus newly available, and with the services of a great financial expert to assist him, Charles VII reorganized the French army. It was officially announced in 1439 that only the king could levy and maintain troops. But he then proceeded to enforce this decree by levying an army of professional troops, with a permanent cavalry of twenty companies, of about six hundred men to a company, including bowmen and lancers. Then a further body of bowmen was organized for the infantry, the soldiers being exempted from the taille (free-archers) in time of peace. They were to be chosen by the king's officials, the *baillis*. They were instructed in the use of firearms and artillery, engaged in periodic maneuvers, and were kept together according to the regions from which they hailed—the ancestors of the modern regiments. In addition to these French soldiers, enormous numbers of mercenaries from all the countries of Europe were added when necessary. But it will be seen that the basis for all this military activity was the ability to collect the taxes to pay for it. If the mercenaries were unpaid they preyed upon the country, if the king could not establish his authority firmly the trained troops might just as easily join a pretender or a feudal lord who promised to pay them. For most of a century, or at least until the death of Francis i in 1547, the French kings were the masters of France through possession of an adequate income and well-paid troops able to maintain the king's peace against any feudal lord, and during this period France had a growing prosperity. When the royal government again failed in the middle of the sixteenth century, feudalism, which had only been held in control, burst forth anew.

The new financial regime called forth thousands of new officials, and it is from this time that a bureaucratic career became the position of honor in France that it remained until very recent times. Louis xi, an indefatigable bureaucrat himself, took very great care of all the appointments that he made, and he watched the behavior of his nominees with the most meticulous attention. He would stand no communal nonsense from the towns and insisted on appointing all the superior officials in them. Every official in the country had to be absolutely loyal to Louis on pain of instant dismissal. Each official felt it to be his duty to enhance the authority of the king, his master, and incidentally his own at the same time. He received a good salary, and there were many valuable perquisites to be obtained from office. Thus it came to be the

custom that the positions were actually purchased by the incumbents; and the kings did not usually dismiss them unless they proved exceptionally inefficient or disloyal. The majority of the officials of whom we know died safely in office, after designating a successor who would have to pay an indemnity to the king for confirmation of his appointment as well as to the departing official who had selected him. When a king died, the officials were all required to receive a confirmation of their title to the office, which assisted the new king over what would otherwise have been financially a difficult time.

But the system worked, for the interests of kings and officials were one. The sufferers were the taxpayers who groaned, but for a long time thought that the comparative efficiency of the government was at least far better than the anarchy and civil war that had preceded it. Under feeble kings the officials paid less to the treasury than under the efficient ones, but they still paid something and the country was administered, and a high degree of stability was ensured. The law courts functioned, administering the king's justice as in the earlier medieval period, and the accounts were audited or at least examined by the central bureaus set up in earlier reigns for the purpose. At the top were the great officials of the king's council, appointed directly by him, usually from the ranks of the Church or the upper bourgeoisie.

When the crown failed in the middle of the sixteenth century the system endured for a while until it too collapsed under the recrudescence of feudal anarchy. But as soon as the centralized government was reestablished by Henry iv in 1589 few indeed were the changes that had to be made. The machinery of the late medieval *ancien régime* was the machinery in all essentials that lasted till the French Revolution of 1789; and by no means all its earlier features were changed even by the Revolution. Almost as much as in England can the structure of modern France be traced back to its medieval antecedents.

▶ **The Spanish national state**

SPAIN PREVIOUS TO THE DUAL MONARCHY

Spain was not unified into a national state until the close of the Middle Ages. Details of the process of unification are of little interest in a text of this kind, but a few facts of the consolidation of the kingdoms of Aragon and Castile in the fifteenth century will be summarized, since the whole Iberian peninsula played such an important part in European history in early modern times.

We have already seen how almost the whole of the peninsula fell into Muslim hands, and for centuries Muslim influence and civilization predominated there. Out of the centuries-long warfare for the Christianization of the country and reconquest from the Muslims, by the twelfth century four Christian kingdoms had emerged—Leon, Portugal, Castile, and Aragon. In Granada, the southern tip of the peninsula, a small kingdom of Muslims remained, while in the north there was a Christian kingdom ruled by French feudal princes. This kingdom, called Navarre, occupied the regions immediately north and south of the Pyrenees. During the twelfth century Leon united with Castile, making the new kingdom by far the most powerful in the peninsula, while Aragon in the following century acquired extensive interests in the Mediterranean, especially when Peter III of Aragon married a Hohenstaufen heiress, and in 1282 took Sicily from the French. By the fifteenth century, Aragon had also gained influence in southern Italy, which was ruled by Aragonese princes, and at one time had extensive trade rights as far away as Greece. Meanwhile the kingdom of Portugal remained independent, and turned her attention to the sea, colonizing various islands in the Atlantic and systematically sending out explorers in search of new territories. Castile, at all times the most important land power in the peninsula, acquired with Leon important maritime interests in the Bay of Biscay region and, with the conquest of Seville from the Muslims in the thirteenth century, also gained an outlet to the Mediterranean. In the fifteenth century the Castilian navy was a powerful organization and Castile had an important merchant fleet. Although she is usually regarded as primarily a land power, she was by no means exclusively this, and her navy was in these centuries a force to be reckoned with.

In all the Iberian states there were several important towns remaining over from the Muslim civilization, and representatives of towns, as well as the nobles, exercised some control over royal policies through fairly powerful assemblies known as *Cortes*, organized on the same lines as the French States-General.

FERDINAND AND ISABELLA

In the earlier Middle Ages the Iberian kingdoms constantly warred among themselves, and much energy had to be spent by the rulers in combating the feudal nobility. But in 1469 a decisive change came over the situation when the heirs of Aragon and Castile were secretly married, against the expectations and efforts of many interested parties throughout Europe, especially King Louis XI of France, who would have preferred that Spain remain disunited and never develop into the great power which she potentially was. In due course Ferdinand of Aragon and Isabella of Castile inherited their respective thrones; and though the two countries were not officially amalgamated, and the union was only a personal union of the monarchs, in fact under their joint rule Spain became at last a national entity (1479). When Isabella died before her husband, a number of important Castilians tried to sever their kingdom from Aragon. But the movement quickly collapsed, and the whole kingdom was inherited by the daughter of the two monarchs, who proceeded to marry into the Hapsburg family. The son of Joanna, this first queen of Spain, was Charles V, who was elected Holy Roman Emperor, thus bringing Spain as a great power into the politics of Central Europe.

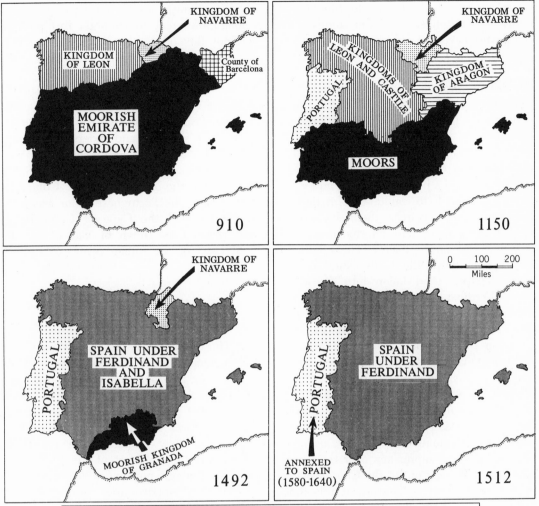

KINGDOM OF NAVARRE

KINGDOM OF LEON

County of Barcelona

MOORISH EMIRATE OF CORDOVA

910

KINGDOM OF NAVARRE

PORTUGAL

KINGDOMS OF LEON AND CASTILE

KINGDOM OF ARAGON

MOORS

1150

KINGDOM OF NAVARRE

PORTUGAL

SPAIN UNDER FERDINAND AND ISABELLA

MOORISH KINGDOM OF GRANADA

1492

0    100    200
Miles

PORTUGAL

SPAIN UNDER FERDINAND

ANNEXED TO SPAIN (1580-1640)

1512

## TERRITORIAL UNIFICATION OF SPAIN

Ferdinand and Isabella brought together the commercial experience of Aragon and the great military tradition of Castile, which had been the leader in the wars against the Muslims. At once they proceeded to consolidate the entire peninsula except for Portugal. They drove the French out of that part of Navarre that was south of the Pyrenees, and they drove the Muslims out of Granada in the south, where they had been harmlessly living for centuries, paying regular tribute to the kings of Castile. For good measure Ferdinand and Isabella then expelled the Jews to an estimated number of two hundred thousand. This was an economic as well as a human disaster for the country, as many of these people, skilled in commerce, industry, and agriculture, could hardly be replaced. However, converted Muslims (Moriscos) were permitted to remain for another century, and it was not till the expulsion of these latter in 1609 that the disastrous policy of persecution had its full effect. It is generally conceded that much of Spanish economic backwardness to this day can be traced back to the systematic destruction or expulsion of those classes which had always borne such a large share of the economic activity of the country.

For the suppression of the feudal nobility the monarchs, especially in Castile, won the support of the towns, which, as usual, preferred absolutism to feudal anarchy, and by enlisting picked troops from the towns they were able to make considerable headway. But perhaps the greatest instrument for enforcing absolutism was the Spanish Inquisition, the adaptation of an established and accepted institution for new ends hardly in conformity with its original purpose.

As a "crusading" people, engaged for centuries in war against the Muslim infidels, the Spanish had a horror of heresy, and were deeply attached to militant Christianity. Moreover, the monarchs themselves were very strict Catholics and detested heresy no less than did their subjects. The relatively mild papal Inquisition, discussed in an earlier chapter, had fallen into disuse in Spain. Ferdinand and Isabella therefore requested the papacy to set up a new and more severe Inquisition, no doubt with the intention of subordinating it to the monarchy and using it for political ends. Pope Sixtus IV was reluctant to permit it, but allowed himself to be persuaded, and in 1478 the so-called Spanish Inquisition was duly established. The monarchs were indeed successful in gaining control of it, using it to establish their supremacy over the Spanish Church, driving out of the Church many of the local clergy, who were at this time rather lax in their discipline and observances, and replacing them with rigid disciplinarians. They also used the Inquisition against dissenters and their own personal enemies, and later, of course, against Protestants. They met little opposition from their own subjects who were, on the whole, very religious and very orthodox. As long as the monarchs presented their persecutions under a religious guise they could rely upon popular support.

The result was a reformed Church in Spain which was able in the following century to give much-needed leadership to the Catholic Reformation, made necessary by the initial successes of the Protestants. Spain was thus enabled to become dominant in Europe for a time by the use of religious as well as political and military means. Even

so, the Spanish would not have possessed enough resources to maintain this position without the aid of the riches of the New World, discovered at the end of the fifteenth century by the Italian sailor Christopher Columbus, who had taken service under the monarchs of Aragon and Castile. A few years previously, the Portuguese, from their separate and independent kingdom, had succeeded in making their way down the coast of Africa, and in 1498, six years after the first voyage of Columbus to the East, the Portuguese sailor Vasco da Gama rounded the Cape of Good Hope, and reached the town of Calicut on the west coast of the Indian peninsula.

▶ **The national state as the key political institution of modern times**

The discovery of the New World, and the opening up of Asia, is as fitting a dividing line as any between the Middle Ages and the early modern era. Europe had been consolidated into several national states, under a form of government sometimes called the "new monarchy," a monarchy which was fully abreast of the times, and was in a strategic position to take advantage of the new opportunities, economic and political, which were opened up by the new discoveries. The old universal state, which had always been the ideal of the Middle Ages, was now gone forever, or at least postponed for an unforeseeable future. There was to be no restoration of the Roman Empire, which had long ago served its purpose and had only been lingering on as a strange ghost in Central Europe, far from its original home.

The great political fact of the centuries since 1500 has been the rise and growth of the national state, an entity larger than the ancient city-states of Greece and Rome, but smaller than medieval Christendom. These national states have shown themselves capable of taking care of tremendous commercial and industrial expansion, and of ensuring certain basic rights, ultimately including self-government, for their particular nationals. In the process they have fought terrible internecine wars with each other, and they have competed by war and diplomacy for the resources not only of each other, but also of the distant lands which they have subjected to their control. Above all, the national state has shown itself capable of inspiring loyalty in its nationals, a kind of substitute religion which has, to a large extent, taken the place of the universal religion which was the norm of the medieval world. Now, in the present century, the Oriental peoples have done the West the compliment of learning from it, purloining Western nationalism and adapting it to their own purposes.

Thus nationalism remains, possibly the single most potent force in the modern world. An institution which grew out of the needs of men in the Middle Ages has been sanctified as the natural form of government among men, as the Roman Empire was once sanctified by Christians who had grown up beneath its shadow. It remains to be seen whether the national state can survive the trials of the present epoch, or whether, as Toynbee has urged, it is already obsolete and will give way to some other equally "natural" form of government. But it cannot be denied that from the sixteenth to the twentieth century A.D., it was the predominant form of governmental organization, and this, too, we owe to our medieval forebears.

▶ **Suggestions for further reading**

Books on the English national state are far more plentiful in English than similar works on the French state. But to set the stage, a remarkable novel which deals with the conquest of Britain by Duke William of Normandy will first be recommended: Hope Muntz, *The Golden Warrior, the Story of Harold and William* (New York: Charles Scribner's Sons, 1949). Few historical novels have surpassed this moving account, based on many years' research by the author into all the available documents of the period. It is a living piece of work, written in a language admirably fitting to the subject, without self-conscious archaism, and yet without a false note, even in the language, in the entire volume.

The standard book on English constitutional history, G. B. Adams and R. L. Schuyler, *Constitutional History of England* (New York: Henry Holt & Co., Inc., 1934), is a fine piece of work, containing almost everything that the beginning student needs to know of English constitutional development in the Middle Ages. This should, however, be supplemented for the historical material, by a book such as G. M. Trevelyan, *History of England* (New York: Doubleday & Co., Inc., 1953), a Doubleday Anchor Book. Volume 1 covers the Middle Ages. Other books which may be profitably used to supplement these works for specially important periods are S. Painter, *The Reign of King John* (Baltimore: Johns Hopkins University Press, 1949), and relevant parts of two books in the Pelican History of England series: D. M. Stenton, *English Society in the Early Middle Ages* (2nd ed.; Harmondsworth, Middlesex: Penguin Books, 1952), and A. R. Myers, *England in the Late Middle Ages* (London: Penguin Books, 1952). Any really interested student should also attempt the pioneer work on which almost all later writers base their own studies in constitutional history, a series of lectures given by the great legal historian, F. W. Maitland, *The Constitutional History of England* (Cambridge, England: Cambridge University Press, 1908). The peculiar organization of this work, which does not at first seem easy to grasp, combined with the easy conversational style, permits the reader to glimpse a great mind at work in a field hitherto hardly touched. This fact alone would make the effort of reading the book well worth while.

Several books cover both the French and English national states, since they deal with a time when the relations between them were of the first importance. An attractive study of the reigns of Henry II and his sons, built around the charming figure of Eleanor of Aquitaine, is Amy Kelly, *Eleanor of Aquitaine and the Four Kings* (Cambridge, Mass.: Harvard University Press, 1950), which presents an accurate picture of the times, based on solid research, although the book was intended primarily for popular consumption. S. Painter, *The Rise of Feudal Monarchies* (Ithaca: Cornell University Press, 1951), gives a good deal of useful and necessary information in a short space. But for France, undoubtedly the best work in English is C. Petit-Dutaillis, *Feudal Monarchy in France and England from the 10th to the 13th Century* (tr. E. D. Hunt; London: Kegan Paul & Co., 1936). The writer of this book was probably the greatest expert in the field; he presents material on the French monarchy and its relations with England that can hardly be found elsewhere in English. A very good recent book on the Hundred Years' War, E. Perroy, *The Hundred Years' War* (tr. W. B. Wells; New York: Oxford University Press, 1951), gives a full political history of the relations between England and France during this period and includes a fair-minded estimate of the work and influence of Joan of Arc. The early history of Spain is best studied in Rafael Altamira y Crevea, *History of Spain: From the Beginnings to the Present Day* (tr. Muna Lee; New York: D. Van Nostrand Company, 1949).

# Index

# ► pronunciation key

This Pronunciation Key is reprinted from *The American College Dictionary*, edited by Clarence L. Barnhart, with the permission of Random House, Inc., publishers. Copyright, 1947, Random House, Inc. Most of the pronunciations given in the Index are taken from *The American College Dictionary*.

The symbol ('), as in **moth·er** (mŭŧh'er), is used to mark primary stress; the syllable preceding it is pronounced with greater prominence than the other syllables in the word. The symbol ('), as in **grand·moth·er** (grănd'mŭŧh'er), is used to mark secondary stress; a syllable marked for secondary stress is pronounced with less prominence than the one marked (') but with more prominence than those bearing no stress mark at all.

| | | | | | |
|---|---|---|---|---|---|
| ă | act, bat | l | low, all | ŭ | up, love |
| ā | able, cape | m | my, him | ū | use, cute |
| â | air, dare | n | now, on | û | urge, burn |
| ä | art, calm | ng | sing, England | | |
| | | | | v | voice, live |
| b | back, rub | ŏ | box, hot | w | west, away |
| ch | chief, beach | ō | over, no | y | yes, young |
| d | do, bed | ô | order, ball | z | zeal, lazy, those |
| | | oi | oil, joy | zh | vision, measure |
| ĕ | ebb, set | o͞o | book, put | | |
| ē | equal, bee | o͞o | ooze, rule | ə | occurs only in un- |
| | | ou | out, loud | | accented sylla- |
| f | fit, puff | | | | bles and indicates |
| g | give, beg | p | page, stop | | the sound of |
| h | hit, heart | r | read, cry | | a *in* alone |
| | | s | see, miss | | e *in* system |
| ĭ | if, big | sh | shoe, push | | i *in* easily |
| ī | ice, bite | t | ten, bit | | o *in* gallop |
| | | th | thin, path | | u *in* circus |
| j | just, edge | ŧh | that, other | | |
| k | kept, make | | | | |

## Foreign Sounds

**à**    as in French *ami* [a vowel intermediate in quality between the ă of *cat* and the ä of *calm*, but closer to the former]

**KH**    as in German *ach*; Scottish *loch* [a consonant made by bringing the tongue into the position for *k*, as in *key, coo*, while pronouncing a strong *h*]

**N**    [a symbol used to indicate nasalized vowels as in *bon*. There are four such vowels in French, found in *un bon vin blanc* (oeN bôN văN bläN)]

**œ**    as in French *feu*; German *schön* [a vowel made with the lips rounded in position for ō as in *over*, while trying to say ā as in *able*]

**Y**    as in French *tu*; German *über* [a vowel made with the lips rounded in position for o͞o as in *ooze*, while trying to ē as in *easy*]

# Index

(NOTE: Page references to illustrations are given in bold face; page references to maps are given in italics.)